Encyclopedia of Recorded Sound in the United States

Garland Reference Library of the Humanities
(Vol. 936)

GUY A. MARCO is a librarian, educator, and bibliographer. He is at present a Senior Fellow in the Graduate School of Library and Information Science, Rosary College, River Forest, Illinois. His earlier books include *Information on Music* (3 vols., 1975–1984) and *Opera: A Research and Information Guide* (1984). He edits the Composer Resource Manuals series for Garland Publishing.

FRANK ANDREWS is a retired diamond tool maker, discographer, and historian of the record industry. He is a member of the City of London Phonograph and Gramophone Society (founded 1919; the present Patron being Oliver Berliner, of California). He has for many years contributed research articles on recorded sound to the Society's journal, *Hillandale News*, and to other periodicals. His monographs include *Columbia Ten-inch Records Issued 1904 to 1930* (1985) and *The Edison Phonograph; The British Connection* (1986).

Encyclopedia of Recorded Sound in the United States

Guy A. Marco
Editor

Frank Andrews
Contributing Editor

Garland Publishing, Inc.
New York & London
1993

ML
102
. S67
E5
1993

Library of Congress Cataloging-in-Publication Data

Encyclopedia of recorded sound in the United States / Guy Marco,
   editor; Frank Andrews, associate editor.
       p.   cm. — (Garland reference library of the humanities; vol.
936)
    Includes bibliographical references and index.
    ISBN 0-8240-4782-6 (acid-free paper)
    1. Sound recordings—United States—Dictionaries. 2. Sound
recording industry—United States—Dictionaries. I. Marco, Guy A.
II. Andrews, Frank. III. Series.
ML102.S67E5 1993
780.26'6'03—dc20
                                                      93-18166
                                                      CIP
                                                      MN

Printed on acid-free, 250-year-life paper
Manufactured in the United States of America

To Howard, Shari, Annie, and Katie

Contents

Preface

Scope and limitations. This is the first edition of the *Encyclopedia of Recorded Sound in the United States* (ERSUS), but I think of it as the third edition. I wrote the original edition in 1984–1985, never completing the text; it was too foolish to present for publication. Those two years of research in the Library of Congress gradually showed me that what I had started to write—a world encyclopedia of recorded sound—could not be written. Sources do not exist, even in that incomparable archive, to permit the narration of this topic on a universal scale. My second "edition" concentrated on the hundred years of recorded sound in the United States and Europe. In that stage I had a much stronger base of documentation, but not enough time to exploit it. (Employment destiny took me away from Washington then, but even had I been able to continue daily study at L.C. I would not have been able to encompass the material.) I thought to make up for the time deficit by asking expert writers from a number of European countries to contribute essays on the sound recording industry of their nations— a sensible idea, perhaps, but one that brought no actual essays. I also confronted, in my imaginary second edition, the mushrooming events of recent years: the innumerable new record labels, musical styles, and greatly successful recording artists in the popular and classical fields.

So I finally came to the third "edition" (this one). Guided by solid counsel from several of my Advisory Board, and pressed by my patient publisher to turn out something, I established the national limitation indicated by the title. And although the title would be too long

to show it, I also established a cutoff date for inclusion of major material, at 1970. Both my limitations have been exceeded frequently. There is quite a lot of coverage in ERSUS to matters British, and some coverage to other countries as well. And there is attention to certain trends, record labels, and artists of the past 20 years. But where I have concentrated my efforts, and where I hope I have been able to offer the most useful information, is in the coverage of sound recording in the United States up to about 1970.

Strict observation of the cutoff date would mean that firms that were founded after 1970 would not be included, performers whose careers were established after 1970 would be omitted, and recent products and events would not be discussed. I have not been so strict as that. Entries were made for compact disc, Michael Jackson, PolyGram International, and serial copy management system— and quite a few similar topics and persons of special interest. Recent industry activity and the latest Grammy winners are given their places. But overall the last two decades are treated in less depth than the hundred years that preceded them, the first century of recorded sound. My justification for this focus on the background rather than the foreground is that the field needs to have its foundations documented as a framework for specialized research into later trends.

There was another change of perspective in the transfer from my imaginary first edition to the actual publication. I think of an encyclopedia as a compilation of verified knowledge, not as an outlet for original research. But as contributions from specialists began to come in, I realized that many of their essays did in fact grow out of examination of primary sources. Much of the historical data on early record companies, for example, is offered here for the first time. With that said, it may also be observed that the preponderance of material in ERSUS is encyclopedia/dictionary information, drawn from secondary sources. The key task of the encyclopedist is to find the right sources and to extract what is most useful from them.

Advisory Board. Without the patience and expertise of a group of scholars—the Advisory Board—ERSUS would not have been completed, nor would it have the quality of original exposition that it has. The members of the Advisory Board are identified on page xiii. Certain persons from that group displayed special enthusiasm and provided valuable essays in addition to general guidance. Many members read carefully every page of several drafts that I belabored them with, and removed innumerable errors and defects. I must single out for particular praise the extensive line-by-line amendatory efforts of Tim Brooks, David Hall, Bill Klinger, Allen Koenigsberg, and Brian Rust. Klinger's close perusal included special attention to the technical entries, a group of articles also examined and improved by Warren Rex Isom. The role of Frank Andrews shifted over the last two years. He was one who took immediate pains to scrutinize every line of every draft I sent him, transmitting handwritten corrections and elaborations. Then he began to type out supplementary material and even new articles. In time we both recognized that his participation had exceeded that of an Advisor, and become that of a partner in authorship. I am pleased that he finally decided to accept the title Contributing Editor.

Contributions by specialists. Although most of the entries in ERSUS were written by me, many articles—including some of the longest ones—were the work of specialist contributors. Such contributors are identified at the end of the entries they wrote. When a substantial portion of the information in an article I wrote was derived from material sent to me by one or more scholars, the names of the donors are listed among the bibliographic citations at the end of the entry, marked with an asterisk.

Arrangement and style. The order of entries is alphabetical, word by word.

> New York Trio
> New Yorkers
> New Zealand
> Newark Tinware and Metal Works

When more than one entry consists of the same word before the first comma or period, the entries are in this sequence: personal name, label name, entity, object.

> Edison, Charles A.
> Edison, Thomas Alva.
> Edison (label)
> Edison (Thomas A.), Inc.
> Edison Bell (label)
> Edison Bell Consolidated Phonograph
>   Co., Ltd.

Personal names with connectives in "de" "del" or "di" are treated as though the entire surname were a single word:

> Delay System
> De Leath, Vaughn
> Deller, Alfred
> Del Monaco, Mario
> De Lussan, Zélie
> Deluxe (label)

Names that begin with numerals are filed in numerical sequence, and all appear before the letter A entries.

Reference citations, in brackets at the end of an entry, are abbreviated to author and publication date; their full imprint data appears in the Bibliography.

When specific recordings are mentioned in the text, the usual fact sequence is manufacturer (label), catalog number, and date. "Victor" is given as the label name for discs from the various Victor firms, and for certain issues from RCA Victor. G & T is the identifier for discs issued by the Gramophone & Typewriter, Ltd. (London, 12 Dec 1900 to 17 Nov 1907); later Gramophone Co. records are cited as "HMV" discs. A slash (/) is used in catalog numbers to show a series of discs, as in #4002/5 (which stands for #4002, 4003, 4004, 4005).

As a rule the full name of a firm is given the first time it is mentioned in an article, including

Co., Corp., Ltd., etc. A few ubiquitous firms are generally presented in brief form: Victor, Columbia, Brunswick, Decca, Pathé, and the like.

Standard arias and vocal ensembles, and the most familiar characters from opera are given without the opera names. These are the arias and vocal ensembles:

"Addio del passato" (Traviata)
"Ah! Fors' è lui" (Traviata)
"Anvil Chorus" (Trovatore)
"Avant de quitter ces lieux" (Faust)
"Ave Maria" (Otello)
"Caro nome" (Rigoletto)
"Casta diva" (Norma)
"Celeste Aida" (Aida)
"Connais tu le pays?" (Mignon)
"Depuis le jour" (Louise)
"Ecco ridente" (Barbiere di Siviglia)
"Elsas Traum" (Lohengrin)
"Di provenza il mar" (Traviata)
"Dio possente" (Faust)
"Eri tu" (Ballo in maschera)
"Evening Star" (Tannhäuser)
"Habanera" (Carmen)
"Il balen" (Trovatore)
"Il lacerato spirito" (Simon Boccanegra)
"Il mio tesoro" (Don Giovanni)
"Je crois entendre encore" (Pecheurs de perles)
"Jewel Song" (Faust)
"La ci darem la mano" (Don Giovanni)
"La donna è mobile" (Rigoletto)
"Le rêve" (Manon)
"Mi chiamano Mimi" (Boheme)
"Miserere" (Trovatore)
"Mon coeur s'ouvre à ta voix" (Samson et Dalila)
"Non piu andrai" (Nozze di Figaro)
"O patria mia" (Aida)
"O don fatale" (Don Carlos)
"O terra, addio" (Aida)
"Pace, pace, mio Dio" (Forza del destino)
"Prize Song" (Meistersinger)
"Queen of the Night Aria" (Zauberflöte)
"Questa o quella" (Rigoletto)
"Ritorna vincitor" (Aida)
"Salce, salce" (Otello)
"Salut! demeure" (Faust)
"Sempre libera" (Traviata)
"Siciliana" (Cavalleria rusticana)

"Tacea la notte" (Trovatore)
"Toreador Song" (Carmen)
"Un bel di" (Madama Butterfly)
"Una furtiva lagrima" (Elisir d'amore)
"Una voce poco fa" (Barbiere di Siviglia)
"Vesti la giubba" (Pagliacci)
"Vision fugitive" (Herodiade)
"Vissi d'arte" (Tosca)
"Voi lo sapete" (Cavalleria rusticana)
"Winterstürme" (Walküre)

These are the operatic characters:

Alcindoro (Boheme)
Alfredo (Traviata)
Almaviva (Barbiere di Siviglia)
Amneris (Aida)
Amonasro (Aida)
Beckmesser (Meistersinger)
Baron Ochs (Rosenkavalier)
Brünnhilde (Ring)
Canio (Pagliacci)
Cavaradossi (Tosca)
Cherubino (Nozze di Figaro)
Cio-cio-san (Madama Butterfly)
Colline (Boheme)
Countess (Nozze di Figaro)
Desdemona (Otello)
Don Ottavio (Don Giovanni)
The Duke (Rigoletto)
Elvira (Don Giovanni)
Escamillo (Carmen)
Germont (Traviata)
Gilda (Rigoletto)
Gurnemanz (Parsifal)
Hans Sachs (Meistersinger)
Isolde (Tristan und Isolde)
Leporello (Don Giovanni)
Lucia (Lucia di Lammermoor)
Manrico (Trovatore)
Marguerite (Faust)
Marschallin (Rosenkavalier)
Mélisande (Pelléas et Mélisande)
Mephistopheles (Faust)
Micaela (Carmen)
Mimi (Boheme)
Nemorino (Elisir d'amore)
Octavian (Rosenkavalier)
Pamina (Zauberflöte)
Pinkerton (Madama Butterfly)
Papageno (Zauberflöte)
Queen of the Night (Zauberflöte)

Radames (Aida)
Rodolfo (Boheme)
Rosina (Barbiere di Siviglia)
Santuzza (Cavalleria rusticana)
Sarastro (Zauberflöte)
Scarpia (Tosca)
Siegfried (Ring)
Sieglinde (Walküre)
Siegmund (Walküre)
Silvio (Pagliacci)
Sophie (Rosenkavalier)
Susanna (Nozze di Figaro)
Tonio (Pagliacci)
Turiddu (Cavalleria rusticana)
Venus (Tannhäuser)
Violetta (Traviata)
Wotan (The Ring)
Zerlina (Don Giovanni)

Abbreviations. Not many abbreviations are used. Record labels are spelled out, and full names of firms and organizations are given. A few journal titles are cited by their initials:

APM—*Antique Phonograph Monthly*
ARSCJ—*Association for Recorded Sound Collections. Journal.*
HN—*Hillandale News*
NAG—*New Amberola Graphic*
RR—*Record Research*
TMN—*Talking Machine News*
TMR—*Talking Machine Review International*
TMW—*Talking Machine World*

Cross references. There are two kinds. The *see* reference takes the reader from a term not used to a term that is used.

Automatic record changer. *See* Record Changer.
BBC. *See* British Broadcasting Corp. (BBC).

The *see also* reference takes the reader to an entry with additional information about the topic being discussed. A boldface word or phrase in the text of an article has the same purpose as *see also*, guiding the reader to an article that gives further information. *See also* or boldface is not used unless the cited entry provides added information about the topic in hand. (Thus the recording artists mentioned in an article about a recording firm are not *see also* references, since the articles about the artists will not give facts about the recording firm.)

Biographies. The extent of biographical information on recording artists is variable, depending on what is generally available in standard reference sources. For individuals well described in such sources, I have confined my presentation to birth/death dates and places, dates and places of debuts, first appearances in the U.S., and other key events. For persons who are not thoroughly treated in the reference literature, such as the early recording artists, I have endeavored to give more data on life and career. Where birth dates are not offered, the reason is lack of availability. *Biography and Genealogy Master Index* was searched, along with *Variety Obituary Index* and the *New York Times Index*. Advisory Board members were asked to provide missing dates. Readers who have any of the dates (or other facts on the more obscure persons) are invited to send them to me. Conflicting information was usually resolved in favor of data in contemporary sources (like obituaries) and reference works of renowned reliability (*e.g., Baker's Biographical Dictionary of Musicians*).

Racial designations are used only to make specific points, such as: Bud Freeman was the first important white jazz saxophonist; Marian Anderson was the first Black female to sing at the Metropolitan Opera. There are entries for prominent deceased discographers and writers on recorded sound, but not for living persons in that field.

Charts. Unless otherwise indicated, all references to "chart records" and "chart albums" point to the *Cash Box* chart data compiled by Frank Hoffmann and George Albert.

Readers are invited to send corrections and comments to the editor. A supplement volume is under consideration, and errata from the present volume can be incorporated into it.

Advisory Board

DAVID MATTISON is a reference archivist, British Columbia Archives and Records Service, Victoria, British Columbia. He was formerly an archivist, Sound and Moving Image Division, Provincial Archives of British Columbia, then librarian of the division. He is the author of *Voices: A Guide to Oral History* (1984).

BRIAN RUST is an independent scholar and collector, Swanage, Dorset, England. He was formerly librarian, BBC Gramophone Library. Publications are listed in the bibliography.

JAMES SMART (retired) was formerly a reference librarian, Music Division, Library of Congress, Washington, D.C. Publications are listed in the bibliography.

Acknowledgments

A number of persons offered initial encouragement and counsel as the idea for this book took shape in 1984. They include Gary Kuris, vice president of Garland Publishing, and Marie Ellen Larcada, senior editor at Garland; and Gerald Gibson, Samuel Brylawski, and Wyn Matthias of the Library of Congress. Subsequently I benefitted from the guidance of the Advisory Board members, listed separately in this volume; Frank Andrews and Bill Klinger deserve special mention for their patient, invaluable advice.

My research support came primarily from the Library of Congress, Music Division and Recorded Sound Reference Section; and Chicago Public Library, Music Information Center (with primary assistance from the head of the center, Richard Schwegel, and fact finding by Elaine Halama and Kathryn Taylor). Many of the reference materials I used came from the University of Chicago, Regenstein Library; Newberry Library; and interlibrary loans arranged by the staff at Rosary College Library (Inez Ringland, director; Kenneth Black, head of reference). Kenneth Nelson of the Municipal Reference Library, Chicago, searched out facts about old Chicago firms. Urzula Kerkhoven located information for me at the John Crerar Library. Norman Horrocks (vice president of Scarecrow Press), Diane Kozelka, and Seena Solomon helped to track down elusive material. Péter Szántó of the Hungarian Central Technical Library, Budapest, provided information about the cylinder by Lajos Kossuth.

Rosary College generously provided material support for the enterprise, through the Graduate School of Library and Information Science (Michael E. D. Koenig, dean). The online searching skills of MaryFrances Watson, assistant to the dean and lecturer in GSLIS, brought me quantities of indispensable documentation. Student assistants who helped at one time or another were Joann Giese, Ellen Herrmann, Sandy Qiu, Felicia Reilly, Jenny Haxia Zhan, and Jian-Zhong Zhou.

Introduction

In 1977 there was universal observation of the centennial of sound recording, marking the invention of the tinfoil phonograph by Thomas A. Edison. A hundred years of technological improvements in that invention have culminated in the near-perfect media of sound reproduction we enjoy today. The relatively simple, hand-operated cylinder machine that was constructed in Menlo Park, New Jersey, in December 1877, has engendered a variety of formats—cylinder, disc, wire, and tape. Those formats have employed mechanical energy, electrical energy, electromagnetism, and digital technology. A rich history of laboratory experimentation, product modifications, market failures and successes, and unexpected innovations could be written about the sound industry (some of it has been written). There is also a business history—partly written—in which thousands of firms were confidently established to make or sell a product thought to be in some way superior to those already in the marketplace; in which patent litigation, agreements, takeovers, and mergers gradually defined the direction of events. Throughout the century of recorded sound there have been enterprising men and women who have shaped the recorded repertoire in its infinite variety, and talented recording artists who have transmitted their interpretations to the future. Biographies of those individuals exist, for the most part, in fragments.

Although the documentation of the recorded sound is still slight, there exists a culminating document. If we want to grasp the panorama of recorded sound we need only pick up a Schwann catalog. The 100,000 records listed in any recent issue are vivid testimony to the accomplishments of today's artists and to the decades of effort that have made their contributions possible. Yet those compact discs, cassettes, and LPs actually represent a small fraction of the total recordings made over the years. Probably there were about 2 million 78 rpm discs on the market at one time or another, and at least a million LPs. Fortunately many are included, as reissues, in the current catalogs. Many more are lost, and many exist only in a few archives. Lists of those titles are being published at a steady pace; in this field (enumerative discography) the publication accomplishments are most impressive.

Writing about the phonograph, and about recordings, began almost simultaneously with the invention. There were articles in music magazines and technical periodicals as early as 1878, and there were trade journals from 1891. Manufacturers published catalogs of products and lists of their cylinders or discs from the 1890s. Artists and industry leaders wrote their life stories. Organizations were formed, statistics were compiled, legal cases were argued, patents were awarded, producing a substantial paper trail.

The growth of scholarship in any field necessarily lags behind practice and events. When it does begin to examine its topic, scholarship is likely to be microcosmic. After a generation or two some attempts at the macrocosmic may emerge. Still later there will be a reference literature: sources of access to information, in the form of bibliographies, dictionaries, indexes and abstracts, etc. Recorded sound as a field of study has followed that generic pattern of development. The microcosmic phase is illustrated in hundreds of label lists and summary histories of individual firms. Possibly the micro-period has been prolonged because the scholars have almost invariably been amateurs (occupied full-time in other work). The field has not had the typical base of scholarly endeavor found in other disciplines, the university department. Nevertheless a considerable literature has accumulated: several hundred useful monographs and several thousand periodical articles. Bibliographic control of that literature has not been attained, nor even attempted until recent years.

Macro-scholarship is beginning. A few commendable attempts have been made to write general histories of recorded sound. Discographies are assuming grander scope, at the same time becoming more complete and accurate. The aims and methods of the field have been considered by numerous scholars, and appear to have reached some consensus.

What is by and large absent is the reference literature. Here is a centenarian discipline without an standard dictionary exclusive to its terms, without a collected biography of its personalities, without a retrospective bibliography of its own scholarly output, without indexing of its current periodical and monographic research publications, without an almanac of basic facts and data, without an annual review of progress. Much reference data is published, but it is scattered among sources in various fields.

It is the modest aspiration of the present work to fill one gap in the reference apparatus, by providing a compendium of the knowledge that has been attained in certain areas. It may be that this encyclopedic endeavor is premature in a field that is yet nebulous in scholarly terms. But the presence of one survey volume, imperfect as it may be, that begins to address the information requirements of recorded sound may stimulate the preparation of a more adequate access literature. The magnificent accomplishments represented by a Schwann catalog deserve a reference library of comparable dimension and quality.

Authors of Articles

Rev. Claude G. Arnold, C.S.B. is an associate professor, Department of English, St. Michael's College, University of Toronto.
"Orchestra Recordings"

William Ashbrook is a distinguished professor emeritus, Indiana State University, Terre Haute, Indiana, and a contributing editor, *Opera Quarterly*.
"Opera Recordings"

Edward R. Bahr is a professor of Music, Delta State University, Cleveland, Mississippi, and record review editor, *International Trombone Association Journal*. Publications are listed in the bibliography.
"Brass Instrument Recordings"

Garrett Bowles is music librarian, University of California at San Diego, La Jolla, California, and a past president, Association for Recorded Sound Collections.
"Sound Recordings and the Library"

E. T. Bryant (deceased) was formerly the city librarian, Widnes, England. Publications are listed in the bibliography.
"Gramophone Societies"/"Organ Recordings"

Richard C. Burns is an audio engineer at Packburn Electronics, Inc., Dewitt, New York. He was formerly an audio engineer, Syracuse University School of Music, and producer of Overtone Records in the 1950s.
"Packburn Audio Noise Suppressor"

John Case is the owner of Priority/Anomaly Records, Fort Worth, Texas.
"Instantaneous Recordings"

Gary Galo is audio engineer, Crane School of Music, State University College, Potsdam, New York, and a contributing editor, *Audio Amateur* and *Speaker Builder*. Publications are listed in the bibliography.
"Loudspeakers"

David Hall is a critic and reviewer, Castine, Maine. He was formerly curator, Rodgers and Hammerstein Archives of Recorded Sound, New York Public Library, a past president, Association for Recorded Sound Collections, and editor of its *Journal*. Publications are listed in the bibliography.
"Mercury (label)"

Val Hicks is an instructor of Music, Santa Rosa College, Santa Rosa, California.
"Male Quartets"

Frank Hoffmann is an associate professor, School of Library Science, Sam Houston State University, Huntsville, Texas. Publications are listed in the bibliography.
"Country and Western Music Recordings"/"Recording Industry Charts"/"Rhythm and Blues Recordings"/"Rock Music Recordings"

Edgar Hutto, Jr., St. George, South Carolina, was formerly principal member, Advanced

Technology Laboratories, Radio Corporation of America (RCA).
"Victor Talking Machine Co." (Part 1).

Warren Rex Isom, Mitchell, Indiana, was formerly chief engineer (1966–1975), RCA Records. Previously (1941–1966) he was with RCA Applied Research. Publications are listed in the bibliography.
"Victor Talking Machine Co." (Part 2).

Paul T. Jackson is an independent scholar and collector, Lapeer, Michigan, a past vice president, Association for Recorded Sound Collections, and a contributing editor to its *Journal*. Publications are listed in the bibliography.
"Collectors and Collecting"

Bill Klinger is an electronics reliability engineer with The Lincoln Electric Co., Cleveland, Ohio. Publications are listed in the bibliography.
"Cleveland Phonograph Record Co."/ "Edison School Records"/"Indestructible Phonographic Record Co."/"Lambert Co."/"U-S Everlasting Record"/"U-S Phonograph Co."

Allen Koenigsberg is the editor and publisher of *Antique Phonograph Monthly*, Brooklyn, New York. Publications are listed in the bibliography.
"Patents"

Michael R. Lane is a recording engineer with Lane Audio and Records, Vista, California. Publications are listed in the bibliography.
"Sonic Restoration of Historical Recordings"

R. Dale McIntosh is an associate professor and chair, Arts in Education, University of Victoria, Victoria, British Columbia. He was formerly director of Performing Arts, Province of Alberta.
"Canada"

William R. Moran is honorary curator at the Archive of Recorded Sound, Stanford University, Stanford, California. Publications are listed in the bibliography.
"Stanford Archive of Recorded Sound"

Susan Nelson. is a librarian, Bemidji State University, Bemidji, Minnesota.
"Woodwind Recordings"

Robert J. O'Brien is a professor of English, West Virginia Wesleyan College, Buckhannon, West Virginia.
"Literary Recordings"

Steven Permut is senior music cataloger, Library of Congress, Washington, D.C. He was formerly a music cataloger and reference librarian, University of Maryland.
"Piano Recordings"/"Reproducing Piano Recordings"

Jeffrey Place is an archivist, Center for Folklife Programs and Cultural Studies, Smithsonian Institution, Washington, D.C
"Folk Music Recordings"

Felicia Reilly is a reference librarian, Niles (Illinois) Public Library.
"Beatles"/"Paul McCartney"/"Rolling Stones"

Robert C. Reinehr is an associate professor of Psychology, Southwestern University, Georgetown, Texas. Publications are listed in the bibliography.
"Radio Programs Recorded" (with Jon D. Swartz)

Gerald Seaman is a professor of Music, University of Auckland, Auckland, New Zealand.
"Australia"/"New Zealand"

Ron Streicher is the proprietor of Pacific Audio-Visual Enterprises, Monrovia, California, secretary, Audio Engineering Society, producer for broadcasts of Los Angeles Philharmonic Orchestra, and recording or audio supervisor for the Philadelphia Orchestra, Metropolitan Opera, and Bolshoi Theatre.
"Recording Practice"

Jon D. Swartz is the chief of Psychological Services, Central Counties Center for MH-MR Services, Temple, Texas. He was formerly associate dean for Libraries and Learning Resources, and professor of Education and

Psychology, Southwestern University, Georgetown, Texas. Publications are listed in the bibliography.
"Radio Programs Recorded" (with Robert C. Reinehr)

Susan Garretson Swartzburg is a preservation specialist and assistant librarian for Collection Management, Rutgers University Libraries, New Brunswick, New Jersey. Publications are in the bibliography.
"Preservation of Sound Recordings"

Sara Velez is a librarian, Rodgers and Hammerstein Archives of Recorded Sound, New York Public Library.
"Sound Recording Periodicals"

Larry Warner is an assistant professor of Theatre, Loyola University of the South, New Orleans, Louisiana. Publications are listed in the bibliography.
"Musical Theatre Recordings"

List of Articles and See References

HAPPINESS BOYS.
HARDING, ROGER, 1858–1901.
HARE, ERNEST, 1883–1939.
HARLAN, BYRON G., 1861–1936.
HARMOGRAPH (label).
HARMONIA MUNDI (label).
HARMONIC.
Harmonic distortion. *See* DISTORTION, VI.
HARMONIZERS QUARTET.
HARMON-KARDON, INC.
HARMONOLA CO.
HARMONY.
HARMONY (label).
HARMONY FOUR.
HARNONCOURT, NIKOLAUS, 1929– .
HARPVOLA TALKING MACHINE CO.
HARRIS, GWIN, 1897–1985.
HARRIS, MARION, 1896–1944.
Harris Everlasting Record. *See* CLEVELAND PHONOGRAPH RECORD CO.
HARRISON, CHARLES WILLIAM, 1890– ?.
HART, CHARLES, 1884– ?.
HARTY, HAMILTON, *Sir*, 1879–1941.
HARVEY, MORTON, 1886–1961.
HAWAIIAN MUSIC RECORDINGS.
HAWKINS, COLEMAN, 1904–1969.
HAWTHORNE & SHEBLE MANUFACTURING CO.
HAY, GEORGE DEWEY, 1895–1968.
HAYDEN LABORATORIES, LTD.
HAYDEN QUARTET.
HAYES, ROLAND, 1887–1977.
Head. *See* ERASE HEAD; PLAYBACK HEAD; RECORD HEAD.
HEAD SHELL.
HEADPHONE.

HEALTH BUILDER RECORDS (label).
HEARING.
HEGAMIN, LUCILLE, 1894–1970.
HEIDT, HORACE, 1901–1986.
HEIFETZ, JASCHA, 1901–1987.
HEINEMANN, OTTO.
HELIODOR (label).
HEMPEL, FRIEDA, 1885–1955.
HEMUS, PERCY, ca.1878–1945.
HENDERSON, FLETCHER, 1897–1952.
HENDRIX, JIMI, 1942–1970.
HERMAN, WOODY, 1913–1987.
HERSCHEL GOLD SEAL (label).
HERTZ (Hz).
HERWIN (label).
HESS, MYRA, *Dame*, 1890–1965.
HEXAPHONE.
Hi Fi. *See* HIGH FIDELITY.
HIGGINBOTHAM, J. C., 1906–1973.
HIGH FIDELITY (HI FI).
HIGH FIDELITY
High pass filter. *See* FILTER.
HIGHAM AMPLIFIER.
HILL, MURRY K., 1865–1942.
HILL, RICHARD S., 1901–1961.
Hill and dale. *See* VERTICAL-CUT RECORDS.
Hillbilly recordings. *See* COUNTRY AND WESTERN RECORDINGS.
HIMMELREICH, FERDINAND M., 1880–1937.
HINDERMYER, HARVEY WILSON.
HINES, EARL "FATHA," 1905–1983.
HIRT, AL, 1922– .
HIS MASTER'S VOICE.
HISS.
HISTORIC MASTERS, LTD.
HISTORIC RECORD SOCIETY (HRS).
HIT (label).
HIT OF THE WEEK (label).

HMV. *See* HIS MASTER'S VOICE.
HODGES, JOHHNY, 1907–1970.
HOFFAY, J.
HOFMANN, JOSEF, 1876–1957.
HOGWOOD, CHRISTOPHER, 1941– .
HOLCOMB & HOKE MANUFACTURING CO.
HOLCOMBE, HERBERT, ca. 1867–1908.
HOLIDAY, BILLIE, 1915–1959.
HOLLAND BROTHERS.
HOLLY, BUDDY, 1938–1959.
HOLLYWOOD (label).
HOME RECORDING.
HOMER, LOUISE, 1871–1947.
HOMESTEAD (label).
HOMESTEAD TRIO.
HOMOCHORD (label).
Homokord (label). *See* HOMOCHORD (label).
HOMOPHON (HOMOPHONE) (label).
HOOLEY, WILLIAM F., 1861–1918.
HOPPER, WILLIAM DE WOLFE, 1858–1935.
HORIZONTAL TRACKING ERROR.
HORN.
HOROWITZ, VLADIMIR, 1904–1989.
HOT AIR MOTOR.
HOT RECORD SOCIETY (HRS) (label).
HOUGH, JAMES EDWARD, 1848–1925.
HOUSTON, DAVID, 1938– .
HOWL.
HOWLIN' WOLF, 1910–1976.
HOXIE, CHARLES A., 1867–1941.
HUDSON (label).
HUGO WOLF SOCIETY.
HUGUET, JOSEFINA, 1871–1944.
HUM.
HUNGAROTON (label).

MAPLESON CYLINDERS.
MARATHON (label).
MARATHON RECORD (label).
MARCONI, FRANCESCO, 1855–1916.
MARCONI VELVET TONE (label).
MARGIN CONTROL.
MARRINER, NEVILLE, *Sir*, 1924– .
MARSALIS, WYNTON, 1961– .
MARSH LABORATORIES, INC.
MARSPEN (label).
MARTIN, FREDDY, 1906–1983.
MARTIN, RICCARDO, 1874–1952.
MARTIN, TONY, 1912– .
MARTINELLI, GIOVANNI, 1885–1969.
MASCOT TALKING MACHINE CO.
MASKING.
MASTER.
MASTER (label).
MASTER TONE (label).
MASTERPHONE CO.
MASTER-PHONE CORP.
MASTERS, FRANKIE, 1904–1990.
MATHIS, JOHHNY, 1935– .
MATLOCK, MATTY, 1909–1978.
MATRIX.
MATRIX NUMBER.
MATZENAUER, MARGARETE, 1881–1963.
MAUREL, VICTOR, 1848–1923.
MAURO, PHILIP.
MAXICUT PROCESS.
MAYFAIR (label).
MCA, INC. (MUSIC CORPORATION OF AMERICA).
McCARTNEY, PAUL, 1942– .
MC CORMACK, JOHN, 1884–1945.
MC GILVRA, J. H.
MC GREAL, LAWRENCE.
MC KENZIE, RED, 1899–1948.
MC KINLEY, RAY, 1910– .

MC KUEN, ROD, 1933– .
MC PARTLAND, JIMMY, 1907–1991.
MC PARTLAND, MARIAN, 1920– .
MECHANICAL ELECTRICAL ANALOGIES.
Mechanical recording. *See* ACOUSTIC RECORDING.
MEDALLION (label).
MEEKER, EDWARD WARREN, 1874–1937.
MEEKLENS, BESSIE.
MEHTA, ZUBIN, 1936– .
MEISSELBACH (A. F.) AND BRO., INC.
MELBA, NELLIE, *Dame*, 1861–1931.
MELCHIOR, LAURITZ, 1890–1973.
MELODISC RECORDS (label).
MELODIYA (label).
MELODOGRAPH CORP.
MELODY (label).
MELODY THREE.
MELOGRAPH (label).
MELOPHONE TALKING MACHINE CO.
MELOTO (label).
MELOTONE (label).
MELTON, JAMES, 1904–1961.
MELVA (label).
MENDELSSOHN MIXED QUARTETTE.
MENGELBERG, WILLEM, 1871–1951.
MENUHIN, YEHUDI, *Sir*, 1916– .
MERCURY (label).
MERITT (label).
MERLI, FRANCESCO, 1887–1976.
MERRIMAN, HORACE OWEN, 1888–1972.
Metaphone. *See* ECHOPHONE.
METEOR (label).
METRO (label).
METRO-GOLDWYN-MAYER (label).
METROPOLE (label).
METROPOLITAN BAND.

METROPOLITAN ENTERTAINERS.
METROPOLITAN MIXED TRIO.
METROPOLITAN OPERA COMPANY.
METROPOLITAN PHONOGRAPH CO.
METROPOLITAN QUARTETTE.
MEYER, JOHN H., 1877–1949.
MGM (label).
MICHIGAN PHONOGRAPH CO.
MICKEL, GEORGE E.
MICROCASSETTE.
Microgroove record. *See* LONG PLAYING RECORD.
MICROPHONE.
MICRO-PHONOGRAPH.
MIDDLE-OF-THE-ROAD (MOR).
MIGNON (label).
MIL.
MILANOV, ZINKA, 1906–1989.
MILITARY BAND RECORDINGS.
MILLER, EDDIE, 1911– .
MILLER, GLENN, 1904–1944.
MILLER, POLK, 1844–1913.
MILLER, REED, 1880–1943.
MILLER, ROGER, 1936–1992.
MILLER, WALTER.
MILLS BROTHERS.
MILLS NOVELTY CO.
MILWAUKEE TALKING MACHINE MANUFACTURING CO.
MIMOSA (label).
MINGUS, CHARLIE, 1922–1979.
MINNESOTA MINING AND MANUFACTURING CO. (3M).
MINNESOTA PHONOGRAPH CO.
MINSTREL RECORDINGS.
MISSOURI PHONOGRAPH CO.
MITCHELL RECORD (label).

MITROPOULOS, DIMITRI, 1896–1960.

MIXDOWN.

MIXER.

MOBLEY, EDWIN H.

MODERN JAZZ QUARTET.

MODULATION.

MONARCH RECORD (label).

MONAURAL.

MONK, THELONIOUS, 1917–1982.

Mono. *See* MONAURAL.

Monophonic. *See* MONAURAL.

MONROE, BILL, 1911– .

MONTANA, PATSY, 1914– .

MONTANA PHONOGRAPH CO.

MONTAUK TRIO.

MONTEUX, PIERRE, 1875–1964.

MONTGOMERY, WES, 1925–1968.

MONTGOMERY WARD AND CO., INC.

MOOGK, EDWARD B., 1914–1979.

MOONLIGHT TRIO.

MORGAN, CORINNE, ca. 1874–1950.

MORRIS, ELIDA, 1886–1977.

MORTON, EDDIE, 1870–1938.

MORTON, JELLY ROLL, 1885–1941.

MOSAIC (label).

MOTEN, BENNIE, 1894–1935.

MOTHER GOOSE BOOK.

MOTHER GOOSE RECORDS.

MOTION PICTURE MUSIC.

MOTION PICTURE SOUND RECORDING.

MOTOWN (label).

MOUTRIE (S.) AND CO., LTD.

MOXIE (label).

MOYSE, MARCEL, 1889–1984.

MOZART TALKING MACHINE CO.

MUCK, KARL, 1859–1940.

MULTINOLA.

MULTIPHONE.

MULTIPLEX GRAND.

MULTIPLEXER.

MULTITRACK RECORDING.

MUNCH, CHARLES, 1891–1968.

MURDOCH (JOHN G.) AND CO., LTD.

MURPHY, LAMBERT, 1885–1954.

MURRAY, BILLY, 1877–1954.

MUSE (label).

Music Corporation of America. *See* MCA, INC.

MUSICAL HERITAGE SOCIETY.

MUSICAL THEATRE RECORDINGS.

MUSICASSETTE.

MUSICRAFT (label).

MUTE.

MUTE (label).

MUTI, RICCARDO, 1941– .

MUTING CIRCUIT.

MUTUAL TALKING MACHINE CO.

MUZAK.

MUZIO, CLAUDIA, 1889–1936.

MYERS, JOHN W., ca. 1864– ?.

NADSCO (label).

NAKAMICHI.

NANES ART FURNITURE CO.

NAPOLEON, PHIL, 1901– .

NARELLE, MARIE, 1874?–1941.

NASSAU (label).

NATIONAL (label).

NATIONAL ACADEMY OF RECORDING ARTS AND SCIENCES (NARAS).

NATIONAL ASSOCIATION OF TALKING MACHINE JOBBERS.

NATIONAL AUTOMATIC MUSIC CO.

NATIONAL BARN DANCE.

NATIONAL GRAMOPHONE CO.

NATIONAL GRAMOPHONE CO., LTD.

NATIONAL GRAMOPHONE CORP.

NATIONAL MALE QUARTET.

NATIONAL MUSIC LOVERS, INC. (label).

NATIONAL PHONOGRAPH ASSOCIATION.

NATIONAL PHONOGRAPH CO.

NATIONAL PHONOGRAPH CO., LTD.

NATIONAL SOUND ARCHIVE (NSA).

NATIONAL TALKING MACHINE CO.

NATIONAL VOICE LIBRARY.

NATION'S FORUM (label).

NATUS, JOE, 1860–1917.

NAXOS (label).

NEBRASKA PHONOGRAPH CO.

NEEDLE CHATTER.

Needle cut. *See* LATERAL RECORDING.

NEEDLE TINS.

NEEDLES.

NEGATIVE FEEDBACK.

NELSON, RICK, 1940–1985.

NELSON, WILLIE, 1933– .

NEOPHONE CO., LTD.

NEVEU, GINETTE, 1919–1949.

NEW CHRISTY MINSTRELS.

NEW COMFORT RECORDS (label).

NEW ENGLAND PHONOGRAPH CO.

NEW FLEXO (label).

NEW GRAMOPHONE.

NEW JERSEY PHONOGRAPH CO.

NEW JERSEY SHEET METAL CO.

NEW MUSIC QUARTERLY RECORDINGS (label).

NEW ORLEANS RHYTHM KINGS (NORK).

NEW PHONIC (label).

NEW WORLD RECORDS (label).

NEW YORK GRAMOPHONE CO.

NEW YORK PHILHARMONIC ORCHESTRA.

NUMERALS

3M. *See* MINNESOTA MINING AND MANU-FACTURING CO.

16 2/3 RPM DISCS. In the 1950s several manufacturers produced discs that rotated at half the speed of the **long-playing record**, to double the amount of content material. Turntables were marketed with the 16 2/3 speed as well as 33 1/3 and 45 rpm. Sound quality did not prove acceptable for music, but the speed was used for **talking books** and other **literary recordings** until the **cassette** became available.

33 1/3 RPM DISCS. *See* LONG-PLAYING RECORD.

45 RPM DISCS. Records revolving at 45 rpm were introduced by RCA Victor in the U.S. in February 1949. They were seven inches in diameter, made first of vinyl and later of polystyrene. Victor intended that the 45 would compete with the Columbia LP in the classical music field; the 45 did have the same groove dimensions and audio quality. Victor made a two-speed turntable (78 rpm and 45 rpm) while Columbia sold a turntable for 78 rpm and 33 1/3 rpm. The Victor player had a 10-disc changing apparatus to atone for the 45's short playing time, which was no more than five minutes 20 seconds. Consumers, forced to choose between the rival turntables and discs, selected the more convenient LP. Victor phased out the 45 and the so-called war of the speeds was won by Columbia. Ironically, each company then began to see the advantages of using the other's new format. Columbia began producing 45 rpm discs of popular songs in late 1950 that carried one song on a side (or two songs, in the EP format) and proved quickly successful with younger buyers. Victor embraced the LP, and also used the 45 rpm for popular recordings. By late 1951 both manufacturers were selling three-speed turntables and discs in all the speeds. By 1954 the sales of 45s in the U.S. reached 200 million, almost entirely in the pop market. [Mawhinney 1983.]

78 RPM DISCS. Records revolving at 78 rpm, also known as standard or coarse groove discs, were the international industry norm from the 1920s until the introduction of the Columbia **long-playing record** (LP) in 1948. Earlier discs had displayed a variety of speeds, from 70 rpm to more than 90 rpm (*see* SPEEDS), although 78–80 was most common after 1900. By 1957 mass commercial manufacture of 78s had ceased. There were a few later releases: 15 are listed in Biel 1982/1, three others in Biel 1982/2. Not mentioned in those two lists was the 1962 Pickwick release in Britain of 36 children's records on seven-inch 78s. Sound effects records for professional use continued to appear in the 78 rpm format.

78s have been the prime focus of record collectors (*see* COLLECTORS AND COLLECTING). While no complete inventory of 78s exists, many useful lists have been published (*see* DISCOGRAPHY). Much attention has been given by audio experts to the best means of playing 78s on modern equipment, to eliminating hiss and scratch noises (*see* NOISE REDUCTION SYSTEMS), and to improving their sound (*see* REPROCESSED STEREO). [Biel 1982/1; Biel 1982/2; Shipway 1984; Tuddenham 1988; Williamson 1971.] *See also* CLEANING; DISC; PRESERVATION OF SOUND RECORDINGS.

1

A

A & B SWITCH. A control in a stereo **amplifier** that is used to channel the signal from a monaural record into both speakers, for greater sound spread. It also removes one cause of **rumble** and noise in the playback by canceling the vertical response of the **cartridge**.

A & M RECORDS. A firm established in 1962 by Herb Alpert, leader and trumpeter of the Tijuana Brass, with promoter Jerry Moss. The first Tijuana Brass release, A & M #703, was "Lonely Bull"; it sold 700,000 copies. The group sold 13 million records in 1966, a total exceeded only by the Beatles. "A Taste of Honey" won the Grammy as (single) record of the year in 1965 (A & M #775). "What Now My Love" won a Grammy for best instrumental other than jazz single of 1966 (A & M #792); an album of the same name was a great chart success. Other highly popular albums included *Going Places* (A & M #LP-112 and #SP-4112; 1965), 104 weeks on the charts; and *Whipped Cream and Other Delights* (A & M #LP-110 and #SP-4110; 1965), 136 weeks on the charts. Another Grammy was awarded for Alpert's 1979 single, "Rise" (#2151).

Sergio Mendes was another prominent A & M artist, beginning in 1966 with the album *Sergio Mendes and Brasil '66* (A & M #LP-116 and #SP-4116). The label remained a **middle-of-the-road** company until the Monterey Jazz Festival (1967), after which the label signed Joe Cocker, The Move, and other rock stars. A & M is located in Hollywood, its domestic distribution and promotion handled by **PolyGram International.** [Denisoff 1986.]

A & R. Artist and repertoire. A major unit in contemporary record companies, reaching greatest significance in the large popular music firms of the 1950s. The A & R director is a talent scout and also the person who determines what will be recorded. Among the notable A & R men, Mitch Miller of Columbia may have been the most successful, discovering and producing Frankie Laine, Johnnie Ray, Tony Bennett, Jill Corey, and Rosemary Clooney; Columbia sold 80 million records by his stars between 1950 and 1956. **John Hammond** was a major force with Columbia, Majestic, and Mercury from the 1930s into the 1950s.

Other prominent A & R directors of modern times have been Gordon Jenkins (Decca), Ken Nelson (Capitol), Art Talmadge (Mercury), and Hugo Winterhalter (RCA). [Denisoff 1986.]

A & R CAMBRIDGE. A British electronics firm established in Cambridge in 1972 by John Dawson, the present managing director. Achieving great success in the 1970s with its A60 integrated amplifier and T21 tuner, the company moved to a larger site in 1979 (Waterbeach, north of Cambridge) and began to produce loudspeakers of international quality (Arcam One, Two, Three). In 1985 A & R began to manufacture CD and DAT products. In 1990 the firm employed 130 staff and posted annual sales above £4 million. [Humphreys 1990.]

A SIDE. The two sides of a double-sided disc are usually identified as A and B, with the A side being the featured selection.

ABBADO, CLAUDIO, 1933– . Italian symphony and opera conductor, born in Milan on 26 June 1933. He studied in Milan and Vienna, and conducted in several Italian cities. In 1965 he conducted the Vienna Philharmonic Orchestra, and became its principal conductor. He was also appointed artistic director at La Scala, and principal conductor of the London Philharmonic Orchestra. On 8 Oct 1989 he succeeded Herbert von Karajan as music director of the Berlin Philharmonic Orchestra. Abbado began to record in 1967. Among his outstanding recordings are the Mahler symphonies with the Chicago Symphony Orchestra and the Vienna Philharmonic.

ABBEY ROAD STUDIOS. An **EMI, Ltd.**, recording complex in London, inaugurated 12 Nov 1931 with Edward Elgar conducting the London Symphony Orchestra in a performance of his *Falstaff*. Although **Fred Gaisberg** was opposed to the construction of the new facility, preferring to remain at the Hayes studios, **Alfred C. Clark** prevailed. That first studio (475 square meters) is still in use for the recording of orchestras and other large groups. It once held a Compton organ that was used by Fats Waller and other distinguished artists. Studio 2 is a smaller hall (200 square meters) used for about 50 performers or fewer (it was here that the Beatles made their 1969 *Abbey Road* album). Studio 3 was for many years the smallest hall (105 square meters), used for chamber music and soloists as well as pop artists. Extensive upgrading of equipment in Studio 3 was completed in 1988, offering state-of-the-art technology for pop music; this studio was also used in 1990 for small-scale classical recordings. A small Penthouse Studio was added to the complex in 1980. [Southall, 1982; technical details for the renovated Studio 3 are in *Gramophone*, May 1989, p. 1817.]

ABC-PARAMOUNT (label). An important pop/rock label of the 1950s and early 1960s, issued by the Am-Par Record Co., 1501 Broadway, New York. The American Broadcasting Co. and Paramount Theaters, Inc., were the parent firms. The earliest releases appeared in late 1955. Pop, jazz, rhythm & blues, children's records, and spoken word discs were issued.

Featured artists included Paul Anka, Lloyd Price, and Ray Charles. The label was also an early producer of stereo discs, with six releases in 1958. There was a subsidiary label named Apt.

ABENDROTH, IRENE, 1872–1932. German soprano, born in Lemberg. Her debut was in Vienna, in 1889. She recorded in Dresden (1902) for G & T (black label), singing arias from *Trovatore*, *Semiramis*, *Mignon*, *Nozze di Figaro*, and *Barbiere di Siviglia* (all in German), as well as Mendelssohn's "Auf Flügeln des Gesanges." The *Trovatore* aria "Tacea la notte" (sung as "Ein unnennbares Sehnen") is a favorite with collectors. [Riemens 1951.]

ABOTT, BESSIE, 1878–1919. American soprano, born Bessie Pickens in Riverside, New York. Her debut was in Paris, in 1901. Her first recordings were three duets with J. Abott made for **Bettini** in 1897, the first of which was "I Want You My Honey." She cut three Edison cylinders, beginning in August 1906 with the "Jewel Song" from *Faust* (#B23), followed by "The Last Rose of Summer" (#B56) and "Caro nome" (#B37). She began recording for Victor in December 1906, with "Qui sola vergin rosa" from *Martha* (#87003), and made a number of important Victor recordings, including the *Rigoletto* Quartet with Enrico Caruso, Louise Homer, and Antonio Scotti (#96000; 1907), and the "Queen of the Night Aria" from *Zauberflöte* (#88051; 1906). She died in New York on 7 Feb 1919.

ABSORPTION. In an acoustic system, the process through which all or part of the signal energy is transferred to an element of the system that comes into contact with the signal. Absorption is measured in "sabins"; one sabin represents one square foot of a perfectly absorptive surface.

ACCORDION RECORDINGS. Early recordings of the instrument were made by **John J. Kimmel** on Edison cylinders in 1906; the initial offering was "American Cakewalk" (#9341; September 1906). Kimmel made another 12 cylinders, all marches, jigs, and other dance numbers. He also recorded as Joseph Kimmel,

John Kimmble, Edward McConnell, and Edward Kelly. Victor recorded Kimmel in August 1907, and later engaged several other accordionists; in Victor's 1917 catalog there were about 70 accordion items, by **Guido Deiro**, **Pietro Deiro** ("Pietro"), **Pietro Frosini**, and **Alexander Prince** (who played the concertina rather than the accordion), as well as Kimmel.

In the later 78 rpm era the accordion was heard primarily in dance orchestras, particularly in tango and polka numbers. It was also a typical member of ensembles playing French popular music. Charles Magnante was a soloist who recorded for Columbia in the 1940s (set #C-53), doing arrangements of pieces like the "Blue Danube Waltz" and "Two Guitars." Anthony Galla-Rini was a Victor artist of the time who performed a similar repertoire.

Dick Contino was a well-known soloist in the 1940s. The limited classical repertoire has been explored by a few artists, such as Yuri Kazakov, Robert Young McMahana, Julia Haines, and William Schimmel. Pauline Oliveros composed and performed several works for accordion. Her composition "The Wanderer" was recorded for the Lovely Music label (#1902) by the Springfield Accordion Orchestra. [Walsh 1971/5.]

ACERBI, GIUSEPPE, 1871– ?. Italian tenor, born in Codogno. He made 30 records for G & T in Milan during 1905 and 1906. They were arias from the popular Italian repertoire of the time.

Acetate disc. *See* LACQUER DISC.

ACKTÉ, AINO, 1876–1944. Finnish soprano, born on 23 Apr 1876 in Helsinki. She studied at the Paris Conservatory, and made her debut with the Paris Opéra as Marguerite on 8 Oct 1897. Her Metropolitan Opera debut was also in *Faust*, on 20 Feb 1904. She had a great success in Covent Garden as Salomé—in the first English performance of the opera (1910)—attracting praise from the composer. Her other major roles were as Gilda, Nedda, and the Wagnerian heroines. Ackté recorded first for Zonophone in Paris in 1902, singing "Le baiser" (Zonophone #1998) and the "Jewel Song" from *Faust* (#1999). A year later she made five discs for G & T, and

in 1904–1905 she did four others for the same label. She also recorded for Fonotipia in 1905, and made an Edison Diamond Disc in London, "Salce, salce" (#83014; 1913, reissued by IRCC), but did not work for any other American labels. Most of her later career was spent in Finland, where she helped to found the national opera company in 1911. On 8 Aug 1944 she died in Nummela, Finland.

ACME CABINET CO. A New York firm, maker of the Eufonola disc player. The address in 1916 was 116 W. 32nd St.

ACO (label). One of the labels issued by the **Vocalion Gramophone Co., Ltd.**, of London, between November 1922 and August 1927. The material was dance, comedy, and popular songs. Many of the early matrices came from the Guardsman label. [Badrock 1965 (label list); Rust 1978.]

ACOUSTIC. The name given to a recording made without electrical technology. As extensive **electrical recording** began in 1925, the period up to that time is usually identified as the acoustic era. *See also* ACOUSTIC RECORDING.

ACOUSTIC COMPENSATOR. A device in a **binaural** sound system that adjusts the signal path lengths so that they are properly matched.

ACOUSTIC FEEDBACK. The effect that occurs when sound from a **loudspeaker** is picked up by a microphone, amplified, and sent again through the speaker: the result is a **howl**. It may also cause vibration in a **cartridge**. Altering the distance between speaker and microphone (or cartridge) may remove the howl.

ACOUSTIC GENERATOR. A **transducer** that converts electrical, mechanical, or other energy into sound.

Acoustic horn. *See* HORN.

ACOUSTIC RECORDING. Also known as mechanical recording. The method of recording in which all energy comes from the sound waves themselves; it was used from the earliest days of Edison and Berliner until the onset of **electrical recording** in 1925. Sounds to be recorded were sung, played, or spoken into a **horn**, which activated a **diaphragm** attached to a **stylus**. The stylus transferred the vibration patterns to the surface of a cylinder or a disc. To concentrate this acoustic energy sufficiently for the stylus to etch a usable pattern it was necessary for singers and performers to direct their vibrations into a large collecting horn; this requirement favored strong sound producers, and worked against inclusion of weaker vessels like string instruments. (*See* STROH VIOLIN.) Great ingenuity was applied in the acoustic recording studio to overcome these inherent obstacles. Horns were varied in diameter for different sound sources; they were wrapped with tapes to counter their own resonance; they might be used in clusters, running to a single tube which moved the diaphragm. For a few recordings, Edison used one brass recording horn 125 feet long with a bell five feet in diameter. Different thicknesses of diaphragm were used depending on the volume of sound being handled—thinner for weak sounds, thicker for heavy sounds.

As there was no **volume control** device to regulate acoustic recording, artists had to be positioned in the studio in ways that would bring their contributions to the diaphragm in proper balance. Brasses were placed at some distance from the recording horns, and French hornists had to play with their backs to the conductor to put their tones on the right track to the horn. Bass drums did not record well, and were usually omitted; tubas typically played the parts written for double basses. (However, the string bass can be heard on early jazz recordings, such as Victors of 1917, and dance band discs.)

A recording orchestra in the acoustic studio had to squeeze into a tight formation around one or more horns, a requirement that mitigated against large ensembles; thus an orchestra of 60 musicians might be reduced to 30 for the recording session. Military bands often recorded with a group of about 15 of their membership. Problems of blend and balance were dealt with by moving the musicians here and there, closer and farther from the sound collector. Cellos were mounted on movable platforms.

For an experienced musical listener, the resulting reproduction of a familiar work could be embellished by memory and imagination—techniques used even in later sophisticated eras of recording to achieve "concert hall realism." For the many persons who listened to orchestras only on cylinder or disc, the impression gained of the symphonic world of music must have been as imprecise as that of Queen Victoria's appearance derived from one of the early postage stamps.

ACOUSTIC RESEARCH, INC. A Boston audio equipment firm established ca. 1954; principals were Edgar Villchur and Henry Kloss. Their first major product was a bookshelf speaker system, AR-1, utilizing an **acoustical suspension** system (also known as air suspension). In 1968 they made the earliest known **quadraphonic recording.** The firm later produced a full line of speakers and other equipment. The air suspension principle was adopted by other manufacturers.

ACOUSTICAL ELEMENTS. Parameters in an acoustical system that are analogous to electrical elements. *See also* MECHANICAL ELECTRICAL ANALOGIES.

ACOUSTICAL LABYRINTH. A kind of **loudspeaker** enclosure in which a maze-like folded passage is added behind the speaker to improve its bass response without promoting unwanted **resonance** of the enclosure.

ACOUSTICAL SUSPENSION. Also known as air suspension. A **loudspeaker** in which the diaphragm is supported at the edge by a flexible material, and allowed to vibrate against a sealed cushion of air. When the speaker cone is responding to a heavy bass note, it compresses the air cushion around it, and the air—acting like a spring—returns the cone with enhanced energy, thus reinforcing the bass frequencies. This type of speaker was developed by **Acoustic Research, Inc.**

ACOUSTICS. The science or physics of sound. Often the term is used in a narrow sense, to describe the sound qualities of a room or auditorium. *See also* ACOUSTIC; AUDIO FREQUENCY; HEARING; PITCH.

ACTUELLE (label). A lateral-cut disc, marketed in Britain and the U.S. from 1921 to 1930, by the **Pathé Frères Compagnie** (London) and the **Pathé Frères Phonograph Co., Inc.** (New York). Material was classical, dance music, race, and jazz. Among the New York recordings were numbers by Red Nichols, Duke Ellington, and the Original Memphis Five. The California Ramblers appeared under the pseudonym of Golden Gate Orchestra. Maurice Chevalier was heard on masters cut in Paris. The disc label itself was hexagonal shaped, brown and tan, with the red Pathé rooster. Much of the Actuelle list was issued also on the **Perfect** label.

ACUFF, ROY, 1903–1992. American country music singer, fiddler, songwriter, and publisher; born in Maynardsville, Tennessee, on 15 Sep 1903. Originally planning to be a professional baseball player, he was obstructed by a tendency to sunstroke, and turned to music. He was fiddler in a touring group during 1932, then in 1933 appeared on Knoxville (Tennessee) radio and in 1936 made his first records, for the Conqueror label: "Weary River" (Conqueror #9434) and his composition "The Precious Jewel" coupled with "Broken Heart" (Conqueror #9741). He then moved to the major labels, Vocalion, Okeh—"Great Speckle Bird" (his composition; Okeh #04252), "Wreck on the Highway" (Okeh #06685), and "Night Train to Memphis" (Okeh #06693)—and Columbia. "Wabash Cannon Ball" was probably his greatest hit. Acuff's total record sales have been estimated at over 30 million discs.

After 1940 he was a regular artist on *Grand Ole Opry*, helping to make that program the principal country music forum. He went into publishing in 1942, with Fred Rose, forming Acuff-Rose, which became one of the largest music publishers in the U.S. Acuff was also part owner of Hickory Records, which issued many of his own performances. Columbia, Capitol, Hilltop, and Hickory issued LP albums of his songs in the 1960s.

Acuff and his group remained a traditional mountain string band until the end of the 1950s, when he began to use some electric instruments, but he kept his country style of singing. In 1962 he was elected to the Country Music Hall of Fame, and in 1991 he was a recipient of the National Medal of Arts. He died in Nashville on 23 Nov 1992.

ADAMI, BICE, 1865– ?. Italian soprano who made records for the Gramophone Co. in 1900–1901, and for G & T in Milan in 1901. Bauer 1947 lists 23 arias from the Italian repertoire.

ADAMINI, ARTURO B. Tenor, one of the first to record operatic material; he made Edison cylinder #4276 in 1898, "La donna è mobile." His other Edisons were Spanish and Italian songs; they are listed in Koenigsberg 1987.

ADAMS, SUZANNE, 1872–1953. American soprano, born in Cambridge, Massachusetts, on 28 Nov 1872. She studied in Paris and made her debut at the Opéra as Juliette on 9 Jan 1895, staying with the company for three seasons. She was Juliette again for her first appearance at Covent Garden in 1898, and also in her Metropolitan Opera debut on 4 Jan 1899. Her other famous roles were Marguerite, Nedda, Gilda, and Micaela. She gave two command performances for King Edward VII. Ill health forced an early retirement in 1904. Her death came in London on 5 Feb 1953.

Adams made five **Bettini** cylinders in 1898, four solos (the first being the "Jewel Song") and a *Traviata* duet with Giuseppe Campanari. She then recorded for G & T Red Label in London, in 1902 (the discs were issued a year later in the U.S. on Victor Red Seal), doing the "Jewel Song" (#3291), the "Waltz" from *Romeo et Juliette* (#3293), and three songs. She performed the same numbers plus two others for Columbia in 1903.

ADD-A-PART RECORDS. A type of recording in which a vocal or instrumental part of the score is omitted, to enable the listener to participate in the ensemble. It seems that the earliest specimens were practice discs issued by the Tilophane Co. in Austria in 1935. Parlophone made aria records without the voice parts in 1938. Columbia issued such records under the name Add-a-Part, covering an extensive repertoire in the mid-1940s. The missing parts were graded as easy, medium, or difficult to play. Add-A-Parts were no longer carried in the 1947 catalog. In the LP era, a label named Music Minus One offered a series of rhythm accompaniments for singers or soloists to complete. There was a similar German series, Spiel Mit (DGG, 1948). Recent practice discs concentrate on the popular music field, providing rhythm backups in various genres.

ADC. *See* ANALOG TO DIGITAL CONVERTER.

ADLER (MAX) PHONOGRAPH CO. A German manufacturer of cylinder and disc players in the early 20th century, located in Berlin. Its cylinders were on the market as early as June 1901. The firm was still active in 1916, after which no information is available. Among the model names were Adler, Baby, Monarch, and Luxus. The **Exhibition soundbox** was used. One portable was in folding box-camera style: the tone arm fit into an opening in the cover, and there was a drawer in the cover that opened out on one side to form a horn; the turntable was composed of three spokes that opened out to hold the record. This odd model was only seven inches by four inches by seven inches in size. *TMR* #27 and #28 (1974) reprinted some of the Adler 1905/06 catalog.

ADT. *See* AUTOMATIC DOUBLE TRACKING.

AEOLIAN CO. A firm established in 1878 in New York by William B. Tremaine, originally known as the Mechanical Orguinette Co. From this company developed the Orchestrelle Co. of Westfield, New Jersey, (also headed by Tremaine) and then the Aeolian Organ and Music Co, in New York, ca. 1888. The company advertised itself at one time as the "largest manufacturer of musical instruments in the world." A London branch opened on Regent Street in 1899. The **Aeolian Co., Ltd.** was registered at 1 Bloomfield Place, New Bond St., in November 1903. The Orchestrelle branch re-

mained viable, however, becoming the **Orchestrelle Co., Ltd.,** on 1 July 1912.

After a period of making automatic organs and piano rolls, the Aeolian Co. moved into the player piano market, specializing in the **Duo-Art** instrument, an **inner player** and **reproducing piano**. Mergers and acquisitions were numerous after 1903, when the Aeolian Weber Piano and Pianola Co. was founded. Among the other firms controlled by Aeolian were Chilton Piano Co., Mason and Hamlin, George Steck and Co., Stroud Piano Co., Technola Piano Co., Votey Organ Co., Weber Piano Co., and Wheelock Piano Co. in the U.S.; in addition, there were the Aeolian Co., Ltd., in Britain and Aeolian Co., Ltd., in Australia. The **Pianola** player was among the most popular of its time, lending its name in generic fashion to other makes of player piano. It was used in the Steinway pianos, as well as the instruments of other makers cited in this article. Piano rolls were sold under the name of Melodee. There were 15,308 selections available on these rolls in 1905.

A gramophone was produced in 1912 under the name of Aeolian-Vocalion; it played both vertical-cut and lateral-cut discs. It had a "tone control" system called the **Graduola** invented by F. J. Empson, an Australian. Discs were made as well, from 1918, under several names: Aeolian, **Aeolian Vocalion, Broadcast,** and **Aco.**

Aeolian Hall, located at 29 W. 42nd St., New York, was a famous concert hall, venue of the premiere (by Paul Whiteman) of "Rhapsody in Blue" on 12 Feb 1924.

There were factories in Worcester, Massachusetts; Meriden, Connecticut; New York; and Garwood, New Jersey. The main office was at 362 Fifth Ave. in New York. In 1932 a merger with **American Piano Co.** resulted in the Aeolian American Corp.; this became the Aeolian Corp. in 1964. [Andrews 1980/10; Cole 1970; Hoover 1980.]

AEOLIAN CO., LTD. The London branch of the Orchestrelle Co., of New Jersey (later the **Aeolian Co.** of New York), registered at 1 Bloomfield Place, New Bond St., in November 1903. Aeolian organs were the principal product offered. Concerts were staged at Aeolian

Hall, 131–137 New Bond Street. Aeolian Co., Ltd. was taken over by the newly registered **Orchestrelle Co., Ltd.** in July 1912, but the Aeolian firm continued to trade under its own name. In October 1915 the Vocalion gramophone with its novel **Graduola** "tone control" was put on the market in six different models, and a special salon was installed in Aeolian Hall to demonstrate it. In 1917 the Aeolian Co., Ltd., absorbed the Orchestrelle Co., Ltd. The **Aeolian Vocalion** record was introduced in Britain in 1920; and the **Guardsman** record, formerly pressed by Aeolian for the Invicta Record Co., Ltd., was acquired from Invicta and marketed in 1922. Another label issued from 1922 was **Aco**, a low-cost record.

With the purchase by **Brunswick-Balke-Collender Co.** of American Vocalion records from the Aeolian Co. in November 1924, the British firm sold its record business to a newly established entity, the **Vocalion Gramophone Co., Ltd.** The new firm continued to sell records—the Vocalion label and Aco label—into 1927. [Andrews 1980/10.]

AEOLIAN VOCALION (label). The name given by the **Aeolian Co.** to its **vertical-cut** discs, first announced in the U.S. in May 1918 and in the U.K. in December 1920. "Aeolian" was dropped from the title in 1920. **Vocalion** was sold to Brunswick in 1924. After March 1920 all production was **lateral cut**. Because Aeolian entered late into the disc field, the firm had difficulty signing classical artists and produced much dance music and popular instrumental items. There were many series, identified by brown-, pink-, red-, green-, and red-colored disc labels. *See also* ACO (label); BROADCAST (label).

AEROPHONE DISQUE (label). A French record, also sold in Britain (50 High Holborn, London) from September 1911. It was a 10-inch double-sided disc, **vertical cut**.

AF. *See* AUDIO FREQUENCY.

Air suspension. *See* ACOUSTICAL SUSPENSION.

Airplane records. *See* AVIATION RECORDS.

AJAX (label). A record produced by the **Compo Co., Ltd.**, a Berliner office in Lachine, Quebec, from about 1923. The headquarters office for Ajax was in Chicago, at 108 W. Lake St. Recording was done in New York. Masters and files of Compo were later in New York, then in Montreal. Material recorded was jazz, country, blues, and race, and the roster included some important artists, such as Mamie Smith, Rosa Henderson, and Fletcher Henderson. Masters from various **Plaza** labels were used for some issues. There was no recording after July 1925. [Kendziora 1966 gives a complete label list; Rust 1978; Rust 1980.]

ALABAMA. American country and western group, established in the early 1970s. The members were Randy Owen, Jeffrey Alan Cook, Teddy Gentry, and Mark Herndon. They began recording for the GRT label in 1977, achieving modest success with a single, "I Want to Be with You." Moving to the MDJ label, the group made two chart singles, "I Wanna Come Over" (MDJ #7906; 1979) and "My Home's in Alabama" (MDJ #1002; 1980). Contracting with RCA, Alabama reached its popular peak with "Tennessee River" (RCA #12018; 1980), and their greatest hit, "Why Lady Why" (RCA #12091; 1980). "Old Flame" was the top country single of 1981 (RCA #12169).

Although the 1980s were a period that favored country soloists, Alabama remained in the public eye through the decade, the only group to to so. There have been a dozen compact discs, including *Just Us* (RCA #6495-1-R8; 1987).

ALABAMA PHONOGRAPH CO. One of the affiliated firms of the **North American Phonograph Co.**, located in Anniston, Alabama, operating in 1890. **Charles A. Cheever** was president.

ALBANESE, LICIA, 1913– . Italian soprano, born in Bari on 22 July 1913. She made her debut as a last-minute substitute in Milan's Teatro Lirico, then made a formal debut in Parma on 10 Dec 1935. In both appearances she sang Cio-Cio-San, a role that she made her own throughout her career at the San Carlo Opera, La Scala, and the Metropolitan Opera (where she sang first on 9 Feb 1940, and remained for 26 years). Her other great roles were Mimi, Violetta, Marguerite, Desdemona, and Tosca. She last appeared at a Town Hall (New York) benefit concert on 5 Feb 1975.

Her Mimi was recorded in Victor's complete *Boheme* (#VM-518–519) with Beniamino Gigli ("O soave fanciulla" receives a particularly brilliant performance, with both singers holding high Cs at the end); Albanese sang another complete *Boheme* with Jan Peerce, under Arturo Toscanini, on LP (Victor #LM6006). "Un bel di" from *Madama Butterfly* was recorded on Victor #11–9254, and on LP she recorded excerpts from the opera with Peerce, but she did not take part in a complete recording of the work. *Tosca* was not recorded complete with Albanese, but her "Vissi d'arte" is on Victor #11–9115. "Ave Maria" and "Salce" from *Otello* represent her Desdemona role (Victor #11–9957). Albanese recorded the complete *Traviata* with Peerce and Toscanini (Victor LP #6003), and the "Sempre libera" aria (Victor #11–9331).

ALBANI, EMMA, *Dame,* **1847–1930.** Canadian soprano, born Marie Louise Cécile Emma Lajeunesse near Montreal on 1 Nov 1847. She studied in Italy and took an Italian stage name, making her debut in Messina in 1870 as Amina in *Sonnambula.* In the same role she had debuts in Covent Garden (1872) and the New York Academy of Music (1874); then she was heard at the Metropolitan Opera on 23 Dec 1891 as Gilda. She sang opera only to 1896, thereafter devoting herself to concertizing. She was named Dame of the British Empire in 1925. Albani died in London on 3 Apr 1930.

Among her special roles were Elsa and Elisabeth, which she was first to sing for London performances, as well as Lucia, Desdemona, and Elvira in *Puritani.* Unfortunately she made only a few recordings. Her first, probably lost, was an attempt by Edison's representative, Colonel Gouraud, to record at the 1888 Handel Festival at the Crystal Palace. (Some white wax cylinders from the Handel Festival survive, at the Edison National Historical Site; they are not yet fully identified.) Her extant material—only seven titles—was made for G & T (1904) and Pathé (1907). "Ombra

mai fu" from *Serse* was the earliest and perhaps the finest of these (G & T #53325; reissued on IRCC #182, 1941; and HRS LP #3008, 1950). [Moran 1977; Ridley 1959.]

ALBUM. Originally the name of the holder for two or more 78s, or by extension for the discs themselves. Later the term was applied to a single 45 or LP in a sleeve, or to a disc with more than one piece on a side. It has not been established when the earliest albums appeared on the market. In April 1909 English Odeon marketed an album with four double-sided records, for 16 shillings. The content was a performance of the *Nutcracker Suite* by the London Palace Orchestra under Hermann Finck. In 1910 Odeon offered another four-disc album, *Midsummer Night's Dream.* The **Bubble Books** (copyrighted 1917) may have been the earliest U.S. albums. Victor issued boxed language sets during World War I. Classical music album sets were sold widely after the war. There were numerous albums on the American market by 1924, nearly all of them European imports. It appears that the *Roycroft Album,* by the English Singers, was the first non-classical multi-disc issue; this was a 12-record set sold in 1928.

ALBUM COVER. A term loosely applied to all packaging for discs, whether singles or parts of **album** sets, with particular reference to the graphic art involved. Most 78 singles were offered in plain wrappers, possibly with advertising of the label's other records; 78 albums often had portraits of the performers or composers, or reproductions of artworks. LP popular and jazz albums began to show livelier scenes, including psychedelic art on rock covers, and eventually there emerged the notion of the cover as an "artistic statement." With the *Sgt. Pepper's Lonely Hearts Club Band* album by the Beatles (1967) the cover was said to be "as important as the recorded material itself. The Beatles extended the theme of the album to the cover, and the 'total-package' idea was born" [Denisoff 1986, p.189]. On popular albums this idea often led to controversy, with nudity or representations of violence bringing organized opposition. In the classical field, album art has remained limited to artist portraits, evocative photographs, pictures of the instruments, and representations of paintings. An exhibition of the album cover as art, said to be the first of its kind, was presented at the Galerie Beaumont, Luxembourg, in 1989. [Denisoff 1986; Garlick 1977; Thorgerson 1977.]

ALBUM NUMBER. The number assigned to an **album** (set) of discs by the manufacturer. In the 78 rpm era individual disc numbers bore no relation to the album numbers (e.g., Decca's 1946 Ink Spots album is #A-477, while the discs themselves are numbered 23632 to 23635). Closer relationship between album and disc numbers can be found in LP issues (e.g., Columbia's *Dave Brubeck Quartet—Jazz Impressions of New York* has album number CS 9075, and the disc within has the same number. (A monophonic version, however, carried the album number CL 2275.) Album numbers can vary with the country of issue: for example, CBS #D2 37852, *Rondine*, was made in Holland and issued in Europe in 1983, but, the U.S.A.-Canadian release has a different prefix, #12M 37852. The single disc carries the same number as the album. Angel's three-disc album of the Mozart string quartets, issued under their Seraphim label, is #SIC 6028, while the discs are numbered consecutively by side: #YRX-X-1405 to #YRX-X-1410. *See also* AUTOMATIC SEQUENCE; MANUAL SEQUENCE.

ALBUM ORIENTED ROCK (AOR). A term applied since the early 1970s to a fairly conservative programming approach that originated on FM radio stations KMPX, KSAN (San Francisco), WPLJ (New York), and KPRI (San Diego). Group sounds were stressed, and a schedule followed that targeted various audiences through the broadcast day. **Disc jockeys** in AOR do not choose the records; however at least one station, KBCO (Denver) initiated in 1988 a practice of allowing announcers some control over selection.

ALC. *See* AUTOMATIC LEVEL CONTROL.

ALDA, FRANCES, 1883–1952. New Zealand soprano, born Frances Davies in Christchurch on 31 May 1883. She played both piano and violin as a child, and in her teens was singing with a light opera company. Taken to England to study, she sang for King Edward VII. Her debut was at the Opéra Comique, Paris, in *Manon* on 15 Apr 1904, under her new stage name, Frances Alda. Jules Massenet, composer of *Manon*, taught her the role. She went on to perform in Brussels and then made her Covent Garden debut with Enrico Caruso in *Rigoletto*. At La Scala in 1908 she sang the premiere of *Louise*. She began with the Metropolitan Opera in the 1908/1909 season, and remained with the company to 1929, missing only one season. Alda married the Metropolitan's director, Giulio Gatti-Casazza, in 1910 (divorced 1929). She died on 18 Sep 1952, in Venice.

Her recording career began in 1910 with Victor; she made all her records for that label. By 1917 there were 35 solo items by Alda in the catalog, plus a notable duet with Enrico Caruso ("Miserere" from *Trovatore*, #89030, #8042), a trio, and four quartets. Among her finest recordings are "O mio babbino caro" from *Gianni Schicchi*; "Ah! dunque ei m'amerà" from *Loreley*; "L'altra notte in fondo al mare" from *Mefistofele*; "Sul fil d'un soffio etesio" from *Falstaff*; and "Un bel di" from *Madama Butterfly*. These were included in an LP transfer issued by Court Opera Classics (CO 383) in 1979. [Favia-Artsay 1951.]

ALDRIDGE, SALMON & CO., LTD. A firm registered in Britain in 1902, but originally established in Bombay, India, in the 1840s as general merchants. The U.K. location was on Fenchurch Ave., London. In July and August 1907 agreements with E. J. Sabine and Thomas Frederick Bragg led to the opening of a record department which they named the Universal Talking Machine Co. It sold Columbia, Pathé, and Favorite labels.

ALEXANDER, GEORGE, 1867–1913. American baritone, born Clifford Alexander Wiley on 9 July 1867 in Baltimore. His repertoire was primarily light opera and concert songs. He is first identified as a recording artist on Columbia #1098, "Three Roses Red," made in 1902. Although he made a few Victor discs in 1903 (all out of the catalog by 1908), he worked almost exclusively for Columbia, making more than 50 cylinders and 75 discs by 1907; some of his records were still being marketed in 1927. Alexander died in New York on 2 Mar 1913.

ALIGNMENT. In a **tape recorder**, the position of the tape head with respect to the tape. If alignment is imprecise there will be distortion and/or reduced output; this is more critical with cassette decks than with reel-to-reel recorders because of the cassette tape's narrow recording tracks. Some cassette decks have built-in alignment equipment. Test tapes are used to check accuracy of alignment.

ALL-AMERICAN MOHAWK CORP. A Chicago manufacturer of radios and phonographs, located in 1929 at 4201 W. Belmont Ave., selling combination radio-phonographs from $245 to $425. The product trade name was Mohawk-American.

ALLEN, WALTER C., 1920–1974. Ceramic engineer, member of the engineering faculty at Rutgers University, New Jersey; also a jazz researcher, discographer, and member of the executive committee of the Rutgers **Institute of Jazz Studies**. He was the author of books on King Joe Oliver (written with Brian Rust) and Fletcher Henderson (*see* the Bibliography). At the time of his death he was preparing a revised edition of the Oliver book. Allen was a tireless advocate of high standards in biographical and discographical research in the jazz field.

ALLGEMEINE ELEKTRIZITÄTS GESELLSCHAFT (AEG). A German firm, responsible for early work on **tape recorders**. In 1931, pursuing an interest in Fritz Pfleumer's tape machine, AEG developed the **Magnetophon**, which solved the old problems of slip-free constant speed tape transport and of recording head design. Researchers at the firm included Erwin Meyer, Emil Mechau, Richard Keller, Theo Volk, and Veronika Oexmann.

ALTHOUSE, PAUL, 1889–1954. American tenor, born in Reading, Pennsylvania, on 2 Dec 1889. He made his debut at the Metropolitan Opera as Dmitri on 19 Mar 1913, and sang there (with some interruptions) until 1940. His roles were from the Italian and Wagnerian reper-

toires, as well as his debut role in *Boris Godunov*. Althouse was a well-known teacher, whose pupils included Eleanor Steber and Richard Tucker.

He made five Edison cylinders in 1913–1914, the first being "All Hail Thou Dwelling" ("Salut demeure") from *Faust* (#28195). That aria, and two other numbers, were also on Edison Diamond Discs. He then recorded for Victor; there were eight arias by him in the 1917 Victor catalog. In 1917–1918 he recorded patriotic and concert numbers for Pathé. Althouse died in New York on 6 Feb 1954.

ALTO SALES CO. A San Francisco firm, located in 1912 in Room 1407, Humboldt Savings Bank Building. It was manufacturing, in 1912, the "Alto Brake," a self-adjusting **automatic-stop** for disc players.

AMATO, PASQUALE, 1878–1942. Italian baritone, born in Naples on 21 Mar 1878. His debut was in Naples in 1900; he sang first at the Metropolitan Opera on 20 Nov 1908 as Germont and remained with the company until 1921. He recorded first for Fonotipia in Italy, making 60 sides in 1907–1910. His first Victor recordings were made in 1911; within five years he had made 16 opera solos, plus duets with Enrico Caruso, Geraldine Farrar, Johanna Gadski, Frieda Hempel, Marcel Journet, and Margarete Matzenhauer. He took part in the *Lucia* Sextette recording (Victor #96201) with Caruso, Luisa Tetrazzini, Journet, Josephine Jacoby, and Angelo Bada; this disc sold for $7, the highest price then in Victor's catalog. Amato's voice was shown at its best in recordings of the "Toreador Song" (Victor #88327), "Di provenza il mar" (Victor #88–474), and "O vecchio cor che batti" from *Due Foscari* (Victor #88438, #V-15–1005; 1913). He recorded for Columbia in 1916.

Although he left the Metropolitan because of ill health in 1921, Amato continued singing in Europe, South America, and in the U.S. In 1924 he was in Berlin, and made records for Homochord; these were also issued by the Italian label Phonotype. All the LP reissue labels carried his acoustic recordings.

In 1928 he appeared in a **Vitaphone** film entitled *A Neapolitan Romance*, singing "Torna a Surriento" and the "Toreador Song"; unfortunately, only the video segment of the film has survived. Amato died in Jackson Heights, New York, on 12 Aug 1942. [Kenyon 1973.]

AMBASSADORS. An American dance band of the 1920s, known by many names on various record labels. Leaders included Louis Katzman and Willie Creager; among the vocalists were Ernest Hare, Irving Kaufman, and Gene Austin. The band began to record with "Tell Me a Story" (Vocalion #14620; 1923). The last known record was "Song of Siberia" (Vocalion #15832; 1929). [Rust 1989.]

AMBEROL. A new cylinder material, and label of the same name, introduced in the U.S. by Thomas Edison in November 1908. With 200 threads per inch instead of 100 per inch, it could play four minutes (the Crystol, a British counterpart manufactured by Edison Bell, was said to play five or six minutes). The material was a wax-like metallic soap compound, fragile and quick to wear. A special sapphire point reproducer was used to play the records; this was incorporated in the **Amberola** phonograph. In 1912 Edison improved on the formula, and offered the much more effective **Blue Amberol.** The name Amberol was selected from several alternatives, despite the lack of amber in the record, because it was thought to suggest the popular amber products of the day notable for their beauty and quality.

"William Tell Overture," played by the Edison Concert Band, was the first Amberol number issued. A total of 1,157 items were released in the popular series through November 1912; there were also 40 concert records and 121 grand opera records. Among the artists represented were Albert Spalding, Riccardo Martin, Anna Case, Blanche Arral, Leo Slezak, Sarah Bernhardt, Maria Galvany, and Lucrezia Bori. [Koenigsberg 1987; Petersen 1975.]

Amberola. *See* EDISON RECORD PLAYERS— AMBEROLA.

AMBIANCE. Also Ambience. In sound recording, the environment in the recording studio or hall, and likewise the acoustic conditions in the playback room. Ambiance, in contrast to **ambient sounds,** may be incorporated (intentionally or not) in the recorded program. *See also* REVERBERATION; SURROUND SOUND.

AMBIENT SOUNDS. Sounds that are external to an audio system. They are not a part of the recorded or broadcast program, but are audible to the listener along with the program. Such sounds are often described as background noise. The audio system itself may produce extraneous sounds, such as **hum.** *See also* AMBIANCE; SIGNAL-TO-NOISE RATIO.

AMBISONICS. A **surround sound** recording technique, developed in U.K. by the Nimbus Co. It endeavors to create the aural effect of reverberation by means of a second pair of speakers and an encoder. In 1991 it was used in making **Nimbus** records and Collins Classics. Licenses were granted by Nimbus to Mitsubishi and Onyko.

AMCO (label). An American label of the mid-1920s, which "derived its meager catalog from **Grey Gull**" (Rust). Examples are rare, but the material was not distinguished. [Rust 1978.]

American (label). *See* AMERICAN RECORD CO.

American Engineering Standards Committee. *See* AMERICAN NATIONAL STANDARDS INSTITUTE (ANSI).

AMERICAN FEDERATION OF MUSICIANS OF THE UNITED STATES AND CANADA (AFM). A trade union founded in 1896 under the name American Federation of Musicians (the current name was adopted in 1965). The address is 1501 Broadway, New York. There are more than 230,000 members in 530 locals. The union engages in collective bargaining with firms in the recording, radio, television, and film industries. Its most historic action in the recording field was a strike called by federation president **James C. Petrillo** in August 1942, effecting a ban on record making by all instrumentalists (except harmonica performers). The dispute, inspired by Petrillo's concern that **juke boxes** were putting live musicians out of work, brought most American record production to a quick halt, so that hit songs from Broadway and Hollywood went unrecorded except for curious arrangements by all-vocal groups trying to sound like orchestras.

In September 1943 Decca reached agreement with Petrillo, attracting artists away from Columbia and Victor; these companies reached agreement with the union in November 1944. As part of the agreement, a percent of the sales of every record sold went to the AFM for the benefit of unemployed musicians.

AMERICAN FOLKLIFE CENTER. In 1928 the Archive of Folk-Song (from 1981 the Archive of Folk Culture) was established in the Library of Congress to collect recordings, printed and manuscript materials on folksong, folk music, folk tales and related materials. With the passage of the American Folklife Preservation Act, Public Law 94–201 (1976), the U.S. Congress established the American Folklife Center, which incorporated the Archive in 1978, into the Library of Congress. Although the center is located in the library and it is under the general supervision of the Librarian of Congress, it is fiscally and administratively a separate institution of the federal government. Alan Jabbour was named the first director—he still held the post in 1991—and Ray Dockstader the deputy director. The combined unit has multiple functions and diverse collections: "preserving and presenting American folklife" is a central goal, met through research, documentation, preservation, exhibitions, publications, and so forth. A reading room in the Library of Congress is the focus of communication with researchers.

John A. Lomax had a long association with the archive, and served as curator from 1934. A recording laboratory was established in the library in 1941, and folk recordings have been issued periodically. Special attention is devoted to the archive of field cylinders, one of the largest of its kind in the world (*see* FEDERAL CYLINDER PROJECT).

Publications of the center include a quarterly newsletter, *Folklife Center News*, and *Folklife Annual*. The Archive of Folk Culture issues a series of *Finding Aids* (descriptions of the collections in the archive's library), and *Reference Aids* (bibliographies, discographies, and directories). An active reference service is maintained, as well as a fieldwork program.

AMERICAN GRAMOPHONE CO. Emile Berliner's early firm, established on 20 Apr 1891, located at 613 New York Ave., Washington, D.C. It engaged only in research and development, with no sales reported. A **coin-op** was one of the devices the firm patented. The company was replaced by the **United States Gramophone Co.** in April 1893.

AMERICAN GRAPHOPHONE CO. (AGC). A firm established in Washington, D.C., on 28 Mar 1887 (incorporated 15 May 1887) through an agreement arranged by **James O. Clephane**, **Andrew Devine**, and John H. White with **Volta Graphophone Co.** AGC made business machines as a licensee for the Volta Co., which was holder of the Bell and Tainter patents. The general manager, and later its president, was **Edward D. Easton**, and the manager of the Bridgeport plant (opened in 1888) was **Thomas Hood Macdonald**. In 1888 **Jesse Lippincott**, who paid $200,000 for AGC stock, became the personal licensee of the company, with rights to sell instruments and supplies, but he had to pay royalties to the company on his sales. A favorable contract with **North American Phonograph Co.** required North American to buy 5,000 cylinder machines per year from AGC, but this arrangement proved to be impractical since by 1891 the graphophone was losing out to the Edison phonograph in the marketplace. North American, forced by American Graphophone to meet its purchase obligation, collapsed in 1894. In the following year a group headed by Easton took control of American Graphophone and merged it with Columbia Phonograph Co., which had been a licensee of North American. Thereafter AGC concentrated on research and manufacturing, while Columbia handled sales and distribution. Showrooms were opened in Boston, Chicago, Philadelphia, and St. Louis.

A long patent litigation with Edison ended in a cross-licensing agreement on 7 Dec 1896. Market success was achieved with the **Graphophone Grand** player, developed by

Macdonald, in 1898. Important industry figure **Frederick M. Prescott** was an officer in the company in 1899–1900. AGC had a legal mastermind, **Philip Mauro**, who brought patent actions against various parties in the recording industry; he won injunctions against **Hawthorne & Sheble** (to stop them from unauthorized conversions of Edison machines into Graphophone Grands), **Frank Seaman**, and Emile Berliner. An early attempt to enter the disc field was stopped (1899) by a Berliner suit, but AGC was able to produce discs in 1902–1906, using the patents of **Joseph Jones**. They also sold (1905) the "Twentieth-Century" graphophone, with a six-inch mandrel. At that time there was a general reorganization of the Easton interests, and AGC was absorbed into the Columbia Graphophone Co. [Klinger*; Wile 1974; Wile 1990/2.] *See also* AMERICAN TALKING MACHINE CO.; COLUMBIA; VITAPHONE.

AMERICAN HOME RECORDER CO. A New York firm, located in 1920 at 49 W. 45th St. It made the first U.S. home disc recorder, marketed in August 1920.

American Multinola Co. *See* MULTINOLA.

AMERICAN NATIONAL STANDARDS INSTITUTE (ANSI). An organization located at 1430 Broadway, New York; it was established in 1918 as the American Engineering Standards Committee. Later it was the American Standards Association (1928) and the United States of America Standards Institute (1966), taking its present name in 1969. ANSI's purpose is to act as a clearinghouse for norms and specifications developed voluntarily by organizations in the safety, engineering, and industrial fields. It represents the U.S. in international standardization work. There were 1,100 members and a staff of 107 in 1988.

AMERICAN ODEON CORP. European **Odeon Record** discs were first sold in the U.S. during 1908–1911, on the Fonotipia label, distributed by Columbia. In 1921 the American Odeon Co., which had been set up after World War I (at 100 W. 21st St., New York) arranged with Okeh to distribute European recordings on the American Odeon Record label, and also to record in New York. There were popular discs and "red label" classics (reissues of recordings made in 1906–1909) by stars like Emmy Destinn and John McCormack. Columbia purchased Odeon in 1926, and used the label name for some issues in 1930–1931. [Andrews*.]

AMERICAN PHONOGRAPH CO. The original name of the **North American Phonograph Co.**, for a short period only: 28 June 1888 to 14 July 1888.

AMERICAN PHONOGRAPH CO. (Detroit). A firm operating in 1908, located at 106 Woodward Ave. It was an Edison distributor with a sales territory of Michigan plus sections of Ohio and Indiana.

AMERICAN PHONOGRAPH CO. (New York City). A firm incorporated in 1910; five years later it announced its **Autophone**, which could play 12 cylinders consecutively.

AMERICAN PHONOGRAPH RECORD CO. A short-lived cylinder maker, operated by several prominent recording artists at the turn of the century. One of the artists was singer Harry Macdonough; others were Steve Porter, William F. Hooley, and S.H. Dudley. They produced a brown wax cylinder named Perfection, and offered to record songs on demand. [Klinger*; Walsh 1943/11.]

AMERICAN PIANO CO. A conglomerate established in June 1908 in New York, bringing together Chickering & Sons, William Knabe, and the various interests of Foster-Armstrong. In 1922 the company also acquired Mason and Hamlin. The address given in a 1926 directory was "Knabe Building," Fifth Ave. and 39th St.; the president at that time was George G. Foster. A player piano department opened in 1909, selling the **Ampico** mechanism, and in 1913 the American Electric player piano, which operated from a mains circuit or storage battery, could transpose, and had expression controls. American Piano was maker of the Rythmodik [sic] music rolls, which included performances by Harold Bauer, Leopold Godowsky, and Ferruccio Busoni. The name was changed to American Piano Corporation in 1930, marking some adjustments in retail operations. In 1932 the firm merged with the **Aeolian Co.** to form the Aeolian American Corp.

American Quartet. *See* PREMIER QUARTET.

AMERICAN RECORD CO. A firm set up in 1904 by Odeon, through Hawthorne & Sheble, with **Frederick Marion Prescott**; the plant was in Springfield, Massachusetts. John Prescott, brother of Frederick Prescott, was manager. In October 1904 the first records were announced, in two sizes: 10 5/8 inches (the same size as the German Odeons) and seven inches. They were double-sided discs.

Reciprocal arrangements were made with the **International Talking Machine Co. mbH**, the Berlin producer of Odeon records, so that each firm could use the other's material. The U.S. discs came to be referred to as "Indian Records" because of the depiction of an American Indian on the label, although the word "Indian" never appeared on the record, which was styled "American Record Co." The discs themselves were made of a blue material. In March 1905 the 10 5/8-inch discs were available both single- and double-faced, selling for $1 and $1.50, respectively. The general offices moved to Springfield in 1905, leaving the recording laboratory and the foreign sales department in New York, managed by John Prescott. A Chicago office opened at 189 La Salle St. in September 1905. A phonograph was marketed by Chicago's Rudolph Wurlitzer Co., a machine named the "American Indian."

The first exports to Europe arrived in Britain in September 1905, styled "American Odeon Record," and the shipments continued until January 1906. The records were all of the 10 5/8-inch size. By October 1905 there were worldwide sales. The 10 5/8-inch size was dropped in favor of a 10-inch size.

Although business was good, the firm was in legal trouble. Columbia claimed infringements of its Jones patents in the recording and manufacturing processes. After a setback in a lower court, Columbia won a decree of injunc-

tion in the U.S. Court of Appeals on 14 Jan 1907, and American Record Co. ceased production of records. The company's recording laboratories at 241 W. 23rd St. were leased to Sonora Phonograph Co. A British entrepreneur purchased the matrices, and pressings therefrom appeared in the U.K. on such diverse labels as Britannic, Burlington, Defiance, The Leader, Pelican, Pioneer, and probably others. John Prescott went on to a career in Japan, and later in Turkey. [Andrews*.]

AMERICAN RECORD CORP. (ARC). A firm established in August 1929 in New York, resulting from a merger of interests. The companies involved, each of which retained its own corporate identity, were **Scranton Button Works**, Regal Record Co. (New York), and **Cameo Record Corp.** A British firm, **Crystalate Gramophone Record Manufacturing Co., Ltd.**, was involved because it held a controlling interest in Cameo. ARC was capitalized at $9 million. Louis G. Silver was the first president, and representatives of Scranton, Crystalate, and Cameo were board members.

Under the agreement, Regal and Cameo undertook recording and sales, while Scranton did the manufacturing and pressing. The main office of ARC was at 1776 Broadway, New York. Its plants were in Scranton; Auburn, New York; Framingham, Massachusetts; and Glendale, California. Its labels were Regal Records, Cameo Records, and Perfect. In 1931 ARC purchased the Brunswick recording enterprise from Warner Brothers, and named it **Brunswick Record Corp.** (Brunswick's interests in Britain were sold to Decca.) ARC thus owned the Brunswick label and Brunswick's associated labels Melotone and Vocalion. During the Depression, ARC also acquired the Banner, Lincoln, Paramount, American Pathé, and Romeo labels. Its principal purchase was the Columbia assets, from Grigsby-Grunow, Inc., in 1933.

ARC maintained market momentum through chain store sales of low-priced discs, by providing a series of intermission music records to theatres, and by supplying **juke box** operators. The firm sold 17 million discs of all types in 1931. In late 1938 the **Columbia Broadcasting System** bought ARC, with some rights going to **EMI, Ltd.** [Andrews*.]

AMERICAN RECORDING LABORATORIES. A firm incorporated in May 1918 in Passaic, New Jersey. It engaged in personal recording services (records made to order). In February 1921 it was acquired by Phonograph Recording Laboratories (address from then was 49 W. 54th St., New York). Hartwick W. Walt was managing director. The firm issued a set of five exercise records in October 1922, sold at $7.50. [Andrews*.]

AMERICAN RECORDING STUDIOS. A firm founded in 1968 by Chips Moman and Tommy Cogbill in Memphis, Tennessee. It rose to prominence as one of the shapers of the "Memphis Sound."

AMERICAN SINGERS. A male quartet, active from ca. 1927 into the 1930s. Charles Harrison organized the group and sang first tenor; other members were Redferne Hollinshead, second tenor (later replaced by Lambert Murphy); Vernon Archibald, baritone; and Frank Croxton, bass. Their earliest recording was an Edison Diamond Disc of January 1928, consisting of "Why Adam Sinned" and "When the Little Ones Say 'Good-Night.'" (#52179). They made three other Edison Diamond Discs, and later recorded for Victor, making a notable disc of "On the Banks of the Wabash," and "Dear Old Girl" (#22387; 1930). The quartet made a Victor record with Rudy Vallee and his orchestra of "To the Legion" and "Songs of the Navy" (#24075; 1930). In the 1930s the group was more active on the radio and on stage than in the studio. [Walsh 1962/10; Walsh 1972/5.]

AMERICAN SOCIETY OF COMPOSERS, AUTHORS AND PUBLISHERS (ASCAP). A performing rights association founded in 1914, gradually assuming strong control over the emerging radio industry with respect to copyrighted works. The society may negotiate and sue in the name of its members, and it makes royalty distributions as well. Agreements are enforced in part through a complex system of program sampling. Licensing terms introduced in 1940, demanding large fees for playing records on the air, led to resistance by the broadcasters, and the formation of the rival **Broadcast Music, Inc. (BMI)**. The ASCAP board of directors, consisting of writers and publishers, votes on the admission of new members.

American Standards Association. *See* AMERICAN NATIONAL STANDARDS INSTITUTE (ANSI).

AMERICAN TALKING MACHINE CO. A firm established in 1898 by Albert T. Armstrong, licensed by the American Graphophone Co. It achieved prominence as maker of the **Vitaphone** disc player and its red discs. Having lost a patent case brought by Berliner, it ceased operations in 1900.

AMERICAN TALKING MACHINE CO. (London). A firm operated by John Nottingham, located in 1903 at 32–34 Glendarvon St., Putney. It was an unlicensed outlet for Edison products, Columbia, and other imports.

AMERICAN TALKING MACHINE CO. (New York City). A firm in operation at 17th St. and Broadway (Hartford Building) in 1896, selling cylinder records. Henry C. Spencer was manager. [Klinger*.]

AMET, EDWARD H., 1860–1948. Inventor of a spring motor for Edison's phonograph (Class M) in 1894; he was the first to receive a patent (U.S. #462,228; filed 28 Jan 1891; granted 3 Nov 1891) for a spring-driven phonograph motor. Later, he introduced double-mainspring models, and portable two- or four-mainspring **coin-ops**. He also developed the Metaphone (later called the **Echophone**) in 1895; it was the first cylinder phonograph with a distinct tone arm. It sold for only $5 (Edison and Columbia machines were then sold for $30–$40). However, Amet had to suspend manufacture of his player after only a few months because of court action taken by American Graphophone Co. He was also a pioneer in early sound motion pictures, using **Lambert** cylinders synchronized with the film. He received 11 U.S. patents in the sound recording field. [Koenigsberg 1990; Paul 1985.]

AMMONS, ALBERT, 1907–1949. Chicago-born jazz pianist, famous for his 1936 recording of Pinetop Smith's "Boogie Woogie" (Salabert #12001; reissued in Columbia set C-44: *Boogie Woogie*); "Shout for Joy" (Columbia #35961; 1939) and "Bass Goin' Crazy" (1942) were later hits. In 1941 he made an important series of duets with **Pete Johnson.**

AMPEX CORP. An American electronics firm, located at 401 Broadway, Redwood City, California. Established in 1948, it pioneered high quality **tape recorders,** tapes, and related equipment in the U.S., and maintained preeminence. The Ampex 300 series was widely found in recording and broadcast studios, and the ATR-102 tape deck became recognized as the state of the art in analog magnetic recording technology. In 1957 Ampex made the first commercially successful video tape recorders.

Amphion Quartet. *See* HARMONIZERS.

AMPICO. An electrically operated **inner-player** that was built into various makes of piano, manufactured by the **American Piano Co.** The Marque-Ampico was foot operated. Sergei Rachmaninoff was an exclusive recording artist on the Ampico **reproducing piano,** which was a major competitor of **Duo-Art** and Welte-Mignon.

AMPLIFICATION. The process or mechanism that increases signal magnitude. The effectiveness of amplification is a dimensionless ratio known as gain. In electrical systems, it is the ratio of the output voltage or power to the input voltage or power. Non-electrical amplification is possible in playback machines. Edison achieved this with a type of mechanical advantage device, using a lever and a floating weight principle in his phonograph reproducers. The idea was to increase the pressure of the stylus on the record and thus to increase diaphragm movement amplitude. [Klinger*.] *See also* AMPLIFIER; HIGHAM AMPLIFIER; OPEN LOOP GAIN.

AMPLIFIER. A device that increases the strength of a signal input, drawing the necessary power from a source other than the signal itself. The signal may be received from a **tuner** (in a radio), a **cartridge** (in a phonograph), a **tape deck,** a **microphone,** or a **preamplifier.** Signal strength may be increased hundreds or thousands of times. Since the amplifier provides the necessary power to operate the **loudspeaker,** it is also called a **power amplifier.** Where there is a separate preamplifier, or voltage amplifier, its function is to magnify the signal voltage from the source and pass it to the amplifier for further enhancement as needed to drive the loudspeaker. The more recent commercial amplifiers incorporate the preamplifier function into one unit, the integrated amplifier. Modern amplifiers are often combined with input devices into receivers.

Lee De Forest invented the electronic amplifier in 1907. His device was a three-electrode vacuum tube which he named the "audion." Later amplifiers used triodes, pentodes, or beam-power tubes; the design effort has been directed toward high efficiency and low distortion. **Distortion** could be practically eliminated by the use of beam-power tubes in a push-pull circuit and the application of **negative feedback.**

The newest amplifiers are tubeless **solid state** devices. When they appeared in the early 1960s, solid state amplifiers quickly demonstrated superiority over tube amplifiers. Solid state amplifiers offered low measured distortion in combination with much higher power output. While tube amplifiers of the time had 20–50 watt output norms, solid state devices of the early 1970s had surpassed 200 watts. Manufacturers such as CM Labs, Dynaco, Kenwood, Marantz, and McIntosh competed in the power race, which peaked around 1971 with the Carver 350 watt/channel Phase Linear Model 700. (In the late 1980s amplifiers with power outputs of more than 100 watts were available in a medium price range.) Another advantage of solid state was in its use of differential circuits—these had been found in tube amplifiers, but they functioned better in the stable thermal environment of solid state. By converting differential output to a single output, with the so-called current mirror, extra gain was achieved and thus more feedback was possible. Concerns over the type of feedback that offered the most pleasing result developed in the 1970s and continued through the 1980s.

Recent systems have operated successfully to reduce distortion further, among them cascoding and Class A. The cascode is a pair of transistors acting together; one provides high voltage gain while shielding the other from voltage changes; the second provides voltage and current gain. Giving high gain, high linearity, and broad bandwidth, the cascode system has found a place in contemporary amplifiers.

Class A operation originated in tube systems, and was carried into transistor systems around 1968. It removes switching distortion in transistors, while keeping the transistors thermally stable; it leads to a strong output power. High cost has kept Class A devices out of the mass market. Less expensive adaptations of Class A, such as the so-called sliding bias circuit, have been produced for the mass market by many Japanese firms.

Pulse-width modulation amplifiers, known also as digital amplifiers or Class D amplifiers, were marketed by Sony and others in the late 1970s, with moderate success. "Current dumping" designs—said to give superior depth imaging—have been more widely accepted; they have been made by Nakamichi, Quad, Technics, and Threshold. In the late 1980s, "high current" amplifier design became a topic of discussion and experiment, beginning with the work of the Finnish audio engineer Matti Otala. It is most useful in connection with electrostatic, rather than dynamic, loudspeakers.

Among so many esoteric innovations it is interesting to observe that a group of audio enthusiasts has endeavored to revive vacuum tube design on the basis of its supposed capability to offer a more realistic sound output.

Controls on an amplifier may include: **balance control**, **filter** switch, **input selector**, loudness compensation, mode selector, monitor, phase reverse control (**phasing switch**), **tone control**, and **volume control**. Amplifiers are compared with respect to their **channel separation**, **frequency response**, **hum**, **distortion**, **bandwidth** power output (in watts), and **signal-to-noise ratio.** Distortion is specified as a percent at given power output (e.g., 1 percent at 20 watts), and comparison must be made at equal power outputs to be meaningful. A 30-watt power output is sufficient for most purposes, but more power is desirable for playback at very high volume or in unusually large rooms, and for playback of **compact discs**. The effect of the amplifier's power output is related to the **impedance** of the loudspeaker(s) attached to it; in general the lower impedance, the more current it draws from the amplifier.

The most dependable measure of output is root-mean-square power, or RMS. This is derived from the amplifiers's capability to enhance a single pure continuous tone. A less meaningful measure is IHF power (named for the Institute of High Fidelity); it identifies peak performance of short duration. The amount of extra power delivered by an amplifier on musical peaks is its dynamic headroom. A frequency response of 10 Hz-25,000 Hz, plus or minus five dB, is expected in a quality amplifier, with channel separation of at least 30 dB, intermodulation distortion of less than 0.5 percent, and a signal-to-noise ratio of at least 65 dB. [Klinger*; Rosenberg 1983; Sweeney 1988 (includes extensive technical data and diagrams of solid state systems).]

AMPLIPHONE. (I) A kind of **Muzak** for homes, advertised in *TMW*, 1906. Subscribers were wired into a central playback point; they could hear continuous music at the touch of a button, apparently with non-musical entertainments interspersed.

AMPLIPHONE. (II) A **coin-op** offering 10 disc selections, marketed in 1932 by the Mid-West Automatic Phonograph Co.

AMPLITUDE. In a vibratory movement, the distance from the equilibrium position to either point of maximum displacement is called the amplitude of the vibration. One cycle includes movements to both displacement points and back. The amplitude determines the intensity of a sound.

Amplitude/Frequency Distortion. *See* DISTORTION, II.

ANALOG RECORDING. The process using an electronic signal whose continuously varying waveform resembles that of the original sound. An analog recording pattern may be the cuts in the **groove** of a disc, or the arrangement of magnetized particles on a **tape**. *See also* DIGITAL RECORDING; DISC, 3; ELECTRICAL RECORDING; MAGNETIC RECORDING; RECORDING PRACTICE.

ANCONA, MARIO, 1860–1931. Italian baritone, born in Livorno on 28 Feb 1860. His debut was in Trieste in 1889. In 1893 he gave his first performances at Covent Garden and at the Metropolitan Opera, singing Tonio in *Pagliacci*. Later he appeared with the Chicago Civic Opera, the Manhattan Opera, and on stages around the world. Ancona made 23 **Bettini** cylinders during 1897–1899, singing the standard baritone parts. In 1904 he made 12 records for G & T, in Milan and London. He then went to Pathé (1905–1906) and Victor, where he made 19 Red Seals in 1906–1909; only three remained in the 1917 Victor catalog. His most popular recording was "A tanto amor" from *Favorita* (Victor #88063; 1907); this was reissued as IRCC #130. He died in Florence on 23 Feb 1931. [Moran 1965/1.]

ANDEM, JAMES L. American record industry executive. He was president of the **Ohio Phonograph Co.** ca. 1890–1896, and general manager of its successor firm, the **Edison Phonograph Co. (Ohio)** from May 1897 to 1899. At the 1891 convention of the **National Phonograph Association** he was elected its treasurer. Andem's Ohio company was active in pursuing the entertainment uses of the new phonograph, particularly through **coin-op** rentals.

ANDERSON, MARIAN, 1902– . American contralto, among the first Black artists to achieve world distinction on the concert stage. She was born to poor parents in Philadelphia on 17 Feb 1902. After singing in church, she won a contest in 1923, which enabled her to compete in another in 1925; victorious in the second contest, she was given an appearance with the New York Philharmonic. In 1929 she made her Carnegie Hall debut, and then made an acclaimed European tour, singing concert numbers and Negro spirituals. When she was refused the use of Constitution Hall in Washington, D.C., by the Daughters of the American Revolution, Eleanor Roosevelt arranged for her to sing at the Lincoln Memorial; Anderson's concert there on Easter Sunday 1939 essentially broke the racial barrier in the U.S. against Black performers. She was the first Black to sing at the Metropolitan Opera (albeit only one time), as Ulrica in *Ballo in maschera* on 7 Jan 1955. Among her Victor recordings, the most durable have been her spirituals, especially "Go Down, Moses" (Victor #1799; 1924), and the Brahms *Alto Rhapsody* with the San Francisco Symphony Orchestra (Victor #11–8983/4; 1945). Victor released a CD of Anderson performances in 1990 (#GD87911). In 1991 Anderson received a Grammy lifetime achievement award.

ANDERSON, (W. R.) CO. A New York firm that initiated distribution of the **Domino** label in 1916; the address was 220 Fifth Ave. (This label had no connection with the Domino produced by **Plaza** in the 1920s.)

ANDREA, INC. A firm located in 1929 at Jackson Ave., Orchard and Queens Streets, in Long Island City, New York. It manufactured radios, phonographs, and audio equipment. A radio-phonograph combination in a hand-carved walnut cabinet in that year sold for $890.

ANDREWS, W. D., ca. 1858–1929. American record industry executive. He was president of the **Eastern Talking Machine Jobbers Association** on its organization in 1906, and reelected in 1907. He was the first vice president of the **Talking Machine Jobbers National Association** when it was formed in 1907, and was elected to that post again in 1909.

ANDREWS SISTERS. Three sisters, born in Minneapolis: LaVerne on 6 July 1915, Maxene on 3 Jan 1918, Patti on 16 Feb 1920. They were the most celebrated popular ensemble of the late 1930s and 1940s, starting in vaudeville and night clubs and then going into radio work in 1937. A hit record, "Bei mir bist du schoen" (Decca #1562; Brunswick #23605; 1937), led a long list of best sellers. Other outstanding discs were "Beer Barrel Polka" (Decca #2462; 1939), "Pennsylvania 6–5000" (Decca #3375; 1940), "Boogie Woogie Bugle Boy" (Decca #3598; 1941), and "Strip Polka" (Decca #18470; 1942). Discs made with Bing Crosby were notably successful; "Ciribiribin" / "Yodelin' Jive" was the first and one of the best (Decca #2800; 1939); the favorite was "Pistol Packin' Mama" (Decca #23277; 1943), coupled with "Victory Polka." The sisters appeared in 17 motion pictures from 1940 to 1948. The team broke up in 1953, got together again briefly in 1956, then went into semi-retirement with occasional appearances until the death of LaVerne in 1967.

ANGEL (label). A name for various series of classical discs offered by Angel Records (New York) since 1954. **Dario Soria** was the first president. Capitol acquired the label in 1957 and remains its distributor.

ANGEL (trademark). An angel writing with a quill on a disc was designed and registered as a trademark in the U.K. in 1898 (and in the U.S. in 1901) by **Theodore B. Birnbaum.** The Gramophone Co., established in 1898, used the Angel trademark until 1909, when **Nipper** replaced it. Angel Records revived it in 1953. It is seen today on EMI advertising, a little angel seated on a gleaming compact disc. Aside from Nipper, it is the best known international trademark, with variants in many countries. [Petts 1973 illustrates 22 angelic manifestations.]

ANGELICA. A German cylinder phonograph marketed in England in 1906. [Chew 1981 (illus.).]

ANGELOPHONE (label). A disc record made by Angelico, a firm with offices in New York and London, ca. 1919. It was seven inches in diameter, and vertical cut. Nothing is known about the items issued. [Rust 1978.]

ANGELUS. A German disc phonograph marketed in England in 1906. [Chew 1981 (illus.).]

ANGLO-ITALIAN COMMERCE CO. An Italian agency for **Frederick Marion Prescott.** It was associated with the International

Zonophone Co. after that firm was acquired by Gramophone & Typewriter, Ltd., in July 1903. In most other countries the Zonophone agents were loyal to Prescott and switched to his Odeon records. The company was located at 6 Via Dante, in Milan. It was for this firm that **Enrico Caruso** made seven Zonophone discs and three cylinders in 1903. [Andrews*.]

ANIMAL IMITATIONS. There was considerable novelty interest in this genre in the early cylinder days, primarily in whistlers doing bird calls. As late as 1917 Victor carried 12 animal numbers in its catalog, including "Barnyard Serenade," by Len Spencer (#4596; 1905—reissued as #16779); "Dog Fight," #16107, and "Morning in Noah's Ark," by Pryor's Band (#4499; 1907—reissued as #16022 and #16955). In "Donkey and Driver" violinist Charles D'Almaine made the appropriate sounds on a **Stroh violin** (#2770; 1904—reissued as #16169). *See also* WHISTLING RECORDINGS; WILDLIFE SOUNDS.

Animal Sounds. *See* WILDLIFE SOUNDS.

ANKER (label). Records issued by a German company, the Anker Phonogram GmbH, from about 1908. Originally the firm was Richter and Co., Berlin; it also traded as the National Phonogram Co. Among its artists were Felix Senius (tenor) and Julia Culp (contralto). The label was successful in Britain, its name anglicized to Anchor. The Anker firm merged with **Kalliope Musikwerke AG** in March 1913. [Andrews 1988/10.]

ANNOUNCEMENTS. Spoken introductions on cylinders or discs, common in the 19th and early 20th century. For example, "The following record taken for the Columbia Phonograph Company of Washington, D.C., entitled 'The National Fencibles March,' as played by the United States Marine Band" (Brooks). Edison's announcers included **Arthur Collins** and **Edward Warren Meeker. Len Spencer** did many announcements for Columbia. The identification function of the announcement was displaced by the arrival of disc labels and molded cylinder markings, and few are found after

1908 (on the earliest Edison Amberols). [Brooks 1978.]

ANSELMI, GIUSEPPE, 1876–1929. Italian tenor, born Antonio Giuseppe Anselmi in Catania on 6 Oct 1876. After his operatic debut in Athens, in 1896, he sang throughout Europe. During 1907–1910 he made 139 records for Fonotipia in Milan, beginning with "Sogno soave e casto" from *Don Pasquale* (#62183; 1907). The outstanding effort was "Quando le sere" from *Louisa Miller* (#62166). In 1913–1915 he sang six numbers for Edison Diamond Discs, the first being "Cielo e mar" (#83004). Anselmi retired in 1917, and died 27 May 1929 in Zoagli, having bequeathed his heart to the Madrid Conservatory in gratitude for the reception given him by Spanish audiences.

ANSERMET, ERNEST, 1883–1969. Swiss conductor, born in Vevey on 11 Nov 1883. While teaching mathematics in Lausanne, in 1906–1910, he studied music and then became a conducting student of Felix Mottl and Artur Nikisch. In 1918 he organized the Orchestre de la Suisse Romande in Geneva, and conducted it for 50 years. He was a guest conductor with most of the major world orchestras, concentrating on works by Russian and French composers. He made recordings as early as 1929, but did not become an important recording artist until 1946, when he contracted with Decca. His acclaimed rendition of *The Fire Bird* was made with the London Philharmonic on 78 rpm (Decca #ED30) and on LP with his own Suisse Romande (London #LL-889). More than 100 of his recordings subsequently appeared on LPs issued by the London label.

ANSI. *See* AMERICAN NATIONAL STANDARDS INSTITUTE (ANSI).

ANSONIA (label). A record made by the Ansonia Phonograph and Record Co., Inc., of New York, in 1920–1921. It appeared to be overpriced compared to Victor and Columbia releases of the day, which may explain its early demise. [Rust 1978.]

ANTHES, GEORG. Tenor, known to record collectors for his appearance on a **Mapleson** cylinder; the performance (*Lohengrin*) from which the extract was recorded took place on 19 Jan 1903. Anthes had made his Metropolitan Opera debut in the role on 28 Nov 1902.

ANTHOLOGIE SONORE (label). An important series initiated in 1933, pressed in Paris by Pathé-Marconi; interrupted by World War II, then resumed and continued into the 1950s. Musicologist Curt Sachs was the first artistic director and author of the program notes. Most of the repertoire recorded was from the Middle Ages and Renaissance. In many cases they were the first recordings of the early dances, chansons, ballades, madrigals, and church music. Works of the 18th century also appeared. A particularly notable issue was the *Mass* of Guillaume de Machaut (records 31 and 32).

ANTHOLOGIES. Early efforts to compile sets of 78 rpm albums on educational and historical themes date from the 1930s. Parlophone issued *2,000 Years of Music*, a set consisting of 12 10-inch records that covered music history to the time of J. S. Bach. Curt Sachs, a distinguished musicologist, was the editor; he also directed the most important of the historical sets, *Anthologie sonore*. The *Columbia History of Music*, edited by Percy Scholes, was issued in Britain on 40 10-inch discs from 1930 to 1939. *The Carnegie Set* was a major venture of the Carnegie Foundation. On LP, the publisher W.W. Norton and the Haydn Society (label) joined to issue sets that accompanied Norton's printed anthologies: *Masterpieces of Music before 1750* (Haydn #9038-39-40) and *A Treasury of Early Music*. Victor's *History of Music in Sound* (18 LPs, issued 1958–1960) was designed to accompany the *New Oxford History of Music*. With the flowering of the LP record, historical anthologies proliferated. Active labels included Telefunken, Deutsche Grammophon, Nonesuch, and L'Oiseau Lyre. [Miller 1972; Rust 1980.]

ANTHONY, HARRY, 1870–1954. American tenor, born John Young in New York City. He specialized in gospel songs, primarily in duets with **Charles William Harrison.** Their first recorded duet was for Edison in May 1905: Longfellow's "Excelsior," set by the composer

Michael Balfe (#8935). They began gospel singing in October 1905 with cylinder #9109, "When the Mists Have Rolled Away." In 1910 they made "See the Pale Moon" for Victor (#5780); they also made Columbia cylinders from December 1906, and U-S Everlasting cylinders in 1910 and 1912. Anthony and Agnes Kimball recorded the "Miserere" in 1912 for Edison Diamond Discs (#80002). After 1912 Anthony and Harrison did little work together, except for some Edison talking pictures that were made in 1913–1914. Anthony made **tone tests** for Edison with the Criterion Quartet, and also sang with other groups. In 1918 he took the place of John Bieling in the American Quartet. Anthony and Harrison were brought together again by Columbia in 1926 to make an electric recording of "Almost Persuaded" and "Softly and Tenderly" (#611D). Anthony died in New York in 1954. [Walsh 1945/7–8–9.]

AOR. *See* ALBUM ORIENTED ROCK.

APEX (label). One of the records issued by the **Compo Co., Ltd.**, Lachine, Montreal; Compo was the Berliner establishment in Canada. The Apex trademark, covering talking machines and records, was in use from 21 June 1921, and the earliest Apex records appeared in 1921 or 1922. Some of the material was original with Compo, such as the series of French language items. Other series came from Gennett masters, from Plaza, Pathé, and Okeh. The label had a long life, until at least 1954. [Kendziora 1962/1.]

APGA (label). A French company whose full name was L'Association Phonique des Grands Artistes, established in Paris in 1906. It made discs of 27 centimeters in diameter, larger than the usual 10-inch size. Artists were French, Belgian, and Italian; several, such as Lucien Muratore and Léon Melchissedec, were prominent. The company went out of business in 1913. [*Record Collector*, March 1954 (label list and other details).]

APOLLO. (I) A line of disc players marketed in London in 1909 by Craies and Stavridi, 101 Bunhill Row. Models included hornless portables (the Dulcephone), advertised as "shut

up entirely and require no carrying case." The Dulcephone was eight inches high, 13 1/4 inches long, and 10 3/8 inches wide. It evolved into the Dwarf model two years later. There were also consoles and table models. Some models used a **hot air motor**.

APOLLO. (II) A push-up player made by **Melville Clark Piano Co.**, capable of handling any size piano roll. It featured a "transposing mouthpiece" that apparently adjusted the speed of the roll to sound in different keys.

APOLLO (label). (I) A British label, actually a stencil of **Edison Bell** discs or **Kalliope Musikwerke** discs.

APOLLO (label). (II) An American label of the early 1920s, issuing material from the Rialto masters.

APOLLO (label). (III) An American label of the late 1920s, releasing Pathé material.

APOLLO (label). (IV) A New York label established in 1943 in Harlem's Rainbow Music Shop (102 W. 125th St.), specializing in race and jazz material. "Rainbow Mist" with Coleman Hawkins was an early hit. By 1946 the firm had expanded nationwide, with several subsidiary labels. Apollo continued well into the LP era, but is not a CD label. [Rust 1978.]

ARANGI-LOMBARDI, GIANNINA, 1891–1951. Italian soprano and mezzo-soprano, born near Naples (Marigliano) on 20 June 1891. She made her debut as Lola in *Cavalleria rusticana* in Rome (1920), then appeared at La Scala from 1924 to 1930 and in other European cities. She sang with Nellie Melba on an Australian tour in 1928, and toured South America, but did not visit the U.S. Singing in an age of dramatic sopranos, Arangi-Lombardi retained an affinity for the bel canto style. Her major roles were the Verdi and Puccini heroines, but she excelled also in *Gioconda* and *Norma*. Retiring from the stage in 1938, she devoted herself to teaching, with posts in Milan and Ankara. Her death came in Milan on 9 July 1951.

Most of her records were made for Columbia in Milan, from 1927 to 1933. "Tacea la notte" from *Trovatore* is perhaps her finest disc (Columbia #18028; 1932), but "Vissi d'arte" (#10508; 1932) is outstanding as well. She participated in the complete La Scala recordings of *Aida, Cavalleria rusticana, Gioconda,* and *Mefistofele.* A CD reissue of her principal Columbia arias appeared in 1990 (Harmonia Mundi #89013); another in 1991 (Preiser #89013).

Arcam. *See* A & R CAMBRIDGE.

ARCHIBALD, VERNON, 1886–1964. American concert baritone and pianist, born in Morocco, Indiana, on 30 June 1886. He began recording in 1910 for Columbia, moved to Edison in 1913, and apparently worked for no other label, except to make one Victor and one Operaphone. His first Columbia was "Juanita" / "The Two Roses" (October 1910), made with his own Archibald Quartet. While with Edison he became one of the most popular recording artists, on both cylinder and Diamond Disc. "Somewhere a Voice is Calling"—a duet with Elizabeth Spencer—was a great success (Diamond Disc #80125; 1914). Many of his later recordings were as the baritone of the American Singers, which recorded until 1930. He died in Los Angeles on 24 May 1964. [Walsh 1972/4–5.]

ARCHIV / ARCHIVE (label). A record issued by **Deutsche Grammophon,** using the "Archiv" spelling in Germany and (from November 1954) the "Archive" spelling for Britain and America. It is now a CD series.

Archive of Folk Culture. *See* AMERICAN FOLKLIFE CENTER.

Archive of Folk Song. *See* AMERICAN FOLKLIFE CENTER.

ARCHIVES OF TRADITIONAL MUSIC. A unit of the College of Arts and Sciences at Indiana University, Bloomington, Indiana; established in 1949. It was formerly known as the Archives of Folk and Primitive Music. The collection, consisting of some 350,000 musical and textual items, covers folk music and folklore of all regions. There are two audio labora-

tories and a video laboratory for dubbing archival materials. Anthony Seeger was director in 1991. A quarterly periodical, *Resound,* and catalogs of the sound recordings are published by the Archives. [Lee 1979; Seeger 1987]

ARETINO CO., INC. A Chicago firm established on 3 June 1907, marketing a disc player made by Hawthorne & Sheble. The machine had a three-inch spindle, requiring a disc with a center hole of comparable diameter: this was provided by the company under the Aretino label. Most of the discs were 10-inch single or double (with a few 12-inch, single faced), relabeled from Columbia or Leeds & Catlin matrices. It may be that the label name was drawn from that of the founder, **Arthur O'Neill,** in some anagramatic fashion, but Fabrizio suggests the name of the renaissance satirist Pietro Aretino as the source. After injunction difficulties with Victor in 1909, Aretino had to switch from Hawthorne & Sheble machines to one made by Columbia. The firm did not recover from the financial loss involved, though it continued to sell machines (later with adapters to accommodate normal discs) and records into 1913. In 1910 it was merged with the **O'Neill-James Co.,** which was succeeded in 1918 by the **Consolidated Talking Machine Co.** [Andrews*; Fabrizio 1973; Fabrizio 1977; Fabrizio 1980; Rust 1978.]

ARGO (label). (I) A specialist company, registered in the U.K. in 1952, with the intention of issuing performances by Britons. In 1954 there was a notable success with the BBC production of *Under Milk Wood.* Decca acquired the firm in 1957 but retained use of the label name. An acclaimed set of 137 LP records, covering the complete works of Shakespeare, was completed in 1964. It is believed to be the largest set of records ever issued. In 1991 the label was revived for Decca compact discs. [Usill 1980.]

ARGO (label).(II) An important pop label of the 1950s in the U.S. and Australia, specializing in rhythm and blues and jazz. It was issued by the Argo Record Co., Chicago, a subsidiary of Chess Records, from 1956. As a CD label, it is distributed by Polygram.

ARIAL (label). A British record of the 1920s, pressed from **Duophone** masters.

ARIEL (label). A group of British labels (Ariel Celebrity Records, Ariel Concert Records, and Ariel Grand Records) issued from about 1910 to 1938 by J.G. Graves, Ltd., of Sheffield. Material was from masters of Beka Grand, Beka Meister, Favorite, Grammavox, Jumbo, Odeon, Parlophone, Polyphon, Popular, Winner, and Zonophone. Graves sold records and gramophones by mail order, primarily to rural areas of England. He had 4,000 selections available in 1912, and was selling some 600,000 discs per year. Among the artists to appear on Ariel were Billy Williams, Peter Dawson, and John McCormack. There were also several major jazz stars, including the Dorsey brothers and Louis Armstrong. But much of the repertoire was band music, comedy turns, and sentimental songs. There were a number of series and number blocks, which are detailed by Badrock. [Badrock 1988; Rust 1978.]

ARIOLA (label). Once a leading American independent company, sharing about 30 percent of the independent market with Arista until 1983, when both labels merged with RCA. BMG distributes the Ariola compact disc.

ARISTA (label). A company founded in New York by Clive Davis, following his removal from Columbia in 1973. Arista acquired Savoy in 1975. As one of the principal American independents, Arista divided a 30 percent share of the independent market with Ariola; then both labels merged with RCA in 1983. BMG distributes the Arista CD label.

ARISTON ACOUSTICS, LTD. A Scottish equipment firm located in Prestwick. It had specialized in turntables, but has diversified into amplifiers and most recently into complete systems priced in midrange for both vinyl discs and CDs.

ARKANSAS TRIO. An Edison recording ensemble of 1924, consisting of Vernon Dalhart, Ed Smalle, and banjoist John Cali. "Boll Weevil Blues" (Diamond Disc #51373; 1924) was in the catalog for three years.

ARMATURE. The movable part in an electronic device; the vibrating element in a magnetic cartridge.

ARMSTRONG, LOUIS, 1901–1971. American jazz trumpeter, singer, and bandleader (nicknamed "Satchmo"), born in a poor section of New Orleans on 8 Aug 1901, brought up fatherless in abject poverty. In a juvenile detention home he learned the cornet and played in the band. From there he went on to perform in local bars and brothels, eventually gaining the sponsorship of cornetist **King Oliver,** who invited him to Chicago in 1922 to play in his Creole Jazz Band at Lincoln Gardens. Oliver's group was focused on the blues, at a time when there was a national craze in progress. In 1923 the band made its first records on the Gennett label (6 Apr 1923 and 5 Oct 1923; issued in the album *King Oliver's Creole Jazz Band*, Rhapsody #6032). Shortly thereafter the group recorded for Okeh (22–23 June 1923; issued in the album *King Oliver's Jazz Band* (Parlophone #7032), Columbia (15–16 Oct 1923) and Paramount (probably 24 Dec 1923; issued in the album *Louis Armstrong and King Oliver*, with all but one of the Gennetts, Milestone #M-47017); Armstrong's noticeable cornet graces these discs.

His first recorded solo was "Chimes Blues"; his first significant jazz solo was "Froggie Moore." Personnel on Okeh #4918, "Dippermouth Blues," included Johnny Dodds, clarinet, and Armstrong's wife Lil Hardin at the piano. He left Oliver in 1924 to join Fletcher Henderson's band in New York (a selection of his work with Henderson was issued as *Fletcher Henderson's Orchestra*, Biograph #BLP-C12; and in *Louis Armstrong 1924–25 with Fletcher Henderson's Orchestra*, Archive of Jazz #BYG 529086). From 1924 to 1929 Armstrong recorded as accompanist for great jazz and blues singers like Bessie Smith ("St. Louis Blues," 1925; available in *The Bessie Smith Story*, Columbia #CL 855, Vol. I) and Ma Rainey (available in the album *Ma Rainey*, Milestone #M-47021).

In late 1925 he established his Hot Five group, and made more than 60 innovative records with them. The members were Kid Ory, trombone; Johnny Dodds, clarinet; Lil (Hardin) Armstrong, piano; Johnny St. Cyr, banjo; and Armstrong, cornet and vocals. He then changed from cornet to trumpet, and also began to sing in the scat style. The Hot Five made 26 recordings in 1925–1926 that display a New Orleans style. In May 1927 the group, with drums and tuba added, became the Hot Seven, and made another set of records in which Armstrong moved away from the New Orleans style to his own rich style of improvisation. In the fall of 1927, the original Hot Five made five records of great brilliance, notably "Hotter than That" (Okeh #8535). Joined by pianist Earl Hines, the group went on to record in 1928, displaying Armstrong in ever more expressive and creative performances. He developed a unique swinging style that was much admired and imitated, and created improvisations that were structured as well as imaginative. Volumes 1–5 of the French Columbia album *Louis Armstrong V.S.O.P,* #88001–4, has all the Hot Five recordings.

During the 1930s and 1940s he performed and recorded with numerous star orchestras and singers (e.g., Decca #15027: "Pennies from Heaven" with Jimmy Dorsey, trumpet and vocal by Armstrong) and he appeared in motion pictures (e.g., *High Society* (1956) with Bing Crosby and Frank Sinatra). He was the first Black artist to have his own radio show and to appear regularly in feature films. His scat style of singing and his ability to blend smoothly with another artist are both exhibited to perfection in his album with Ella Fitzgerald, *Ella and Louis* (MGM #2–V6S-8811).

Armstrong recorded for Decca from 1935, and in 1957 the label issued an LP album, *"Satchmo"—A Musical Autobiography of Louis Armstrong* (#DXM 155), featuring new recordings of Armstrong's classics of the 1920s. All the Armstrong Deccas were issued in the album *Louis Armstrong and His Orchestra* (Swaggie #701–07). A retrospective set of four LPs, *The Louis Armstrong Legend* (World Records, #SH 404–07; 1982), presented many of the great performances. Curiously, Armstrong won only one Grammy, that for his singing of "Hello, Dolly!" (Kapp #573; 1964).

When Louis Armstrong died in New York on 6 July 1971 he was one of the best known and beloved entertainers in the world, credited with shaping the vocabulary of jazz. In 1991

the Louis Armstrong Archive, consisting of 20,000 recordings and memorabilia, was opened at Queens College, New York. [Collier 1983 is the standard biography and guide to the recordings (much of the discographical information above is drawn from it); *Record Changer,* July 1950, is an issue devoted to Armstrong, with a discography by Albert McCarthy.]

ARNHEIM, GUS, 1897–1955. American popular pianist, composer, and bandleader, born in Philadelphia. He played with Abe Lyman's band in Los Angeles during 1921–1923, and composed the hit "I Cried for You" in 1923. Forming his own band, he toured the U.S. and Europe. He began to record in 1928 with "I Can't Do Without You" (Okeh #41057). In 1929–1931 he made records with Russ Columbo, then in 1930–1931 with Bing Crosby. He made a hit record of his composition "Sweet and Lovely" in 1931 (Victor #22770), made radio appearances, and gained national popularity. Among his star players were Woody Herman and Earl Hines. The final recording was made in 1937 for Brunswick, just as Stan Kenton joined the group as pianist and arranger. Arnheim retired in the mid-1940s, then returned to lead a small ensemble on television shows in 1954. He died in Los Angeles in 1955.

ARNOLD, EDDY, 1918– . American country singer and guitarist, born in Henderson, Tennessee, on 15 May 1918. He started out as guitarist in a band in Jackson, Tennessee, then performed on various radio stations from 1936. As vocalist with Pee Wee King's Golden West Cowboys he attracted much attention, and began to record for Victor in 1943. His first hit record was "That's How Much I Love You" (Victor #20–1948; 1946). His "Cattle Call" (Victor #20–2128; 1947) was used as the theme song on his daily radio show in 1947. Soon he dominated the country music field, starring on *Grand Ole Opry* and making a long series of hit records; often he had two or three records on the charts at one time at his peak, 1948–1952. In 1952, as a summer replacement for Perry Como, he was the first country artist to host a television program. Arnold's singing style changed from plain rural to a more mainstream crooning sound; by the 1960s he had become a nightclub and television performer quite removed from his origins. He continued to make the charts, with "Make the World Go Away" (Victor #8879; 1965), "What's He Doing in My World" (Victor #8516; 1965), and "I Want to Go with You" (Victor #8749; 1966). He was elected to the Country Music Hall of Fame in 1966.

ARRAL, BLANCHE, 1864–1945. Belgian soprano, born Clara Lardinois, performer of both lyric and coloratura roles. She began singing at the Paris Opéra Comique at age 15, and became the protegée of Marie van Zandt, the original *Lakmé*; Arral sang that role and much of the other French repertoire. She made 48 cylinders for **Bettini** in 1898–1899, and in 1908 she recorded nine cylinders for Edison, the first being the "Polonaise" from *Mignon* (#B166). Thomas Edison is said to have stated that hers was organically the most perfect voice he knew. She recorded for Victor in May 1909, singing eight numbers; perhaps the finest were "Polonaise" from *Lombardi* (Victor #74146; reissued IRCC 19A), and "The Jewel Song" from *Faust* (Victor #74147). Arral died in a sanatorium near Cliffside Park, New Jersey, on 3 Mar 1945.

ARRAU, CLAUDIO, 1903–1991. Chilean pianist, born on 6 Feb 1903 in Chillán. A child prodigy, he studied in Germany and gave recitals there and in Scandinavia in 1914–1915. His teacher was Martin Krause, a student of Franz Liszt. In 1924 he was heard in the U.S., with the Boston and Chicago orchestras; he eventually settled in New York. Arrau played the complete keyboard works of J. S. Bach in 12 Berlin recitals, in 1935–1936; and the complete Mozart works in five recitals there in 1936. During 1938–1939 he performed the complete Beethoven piano works in various cities. He remained active in concerts and recitals throughout his life. Arrau died on 9 June 1991 in Mürzzuschlag, Austria.

The pianist's virtuoso capabilities were demonstrated in 1927 with "Islamey" by Mili Balakirev (Polydor #95112)—at one time considered to be the most difficult concert piece to play—and in 1928 with the fifth "Elegie" by Ferruccio Busoni (Polydor #90025). In 1928 he

also recorded the *Transcendental Études* of Franz Liszt. On LP he recorded the Beethoven concertos with the Concertgebouw Orchestra (Philips #SC71 AX501; five discs) and the Beethoven sonatas (Philips #6747035; 13 discs).

ARROW (label). A short-lived, lateral-cut record issued by the **Liberty Phonograph Co.** (as of March 1920 the Arrow Phonograph Co.), of Cleveland, Ohio. In 1919 the firm had issued discs under the Liberty label name. Eighteen releases are known, perhaps taken from masters by other companies. Material was primarily jazz and blues, although #512 is Wilfred Glenn's "Rocked in the Cradle of the Deep" (originally done for Victor). [Kendziora 1985/7.]

ARTHUR FIELDS MELODY RECORD (label). A disc issued by the Arthur Fields Record Co., New York, in 1923. Baritone Arthur Fields was featured on the few items issued. The label was one of the Olympic group of records, sharing at least some of its material with the label named Melody. [Kendziora 1961/1.]

ARTIA (label). Discs made in the U.S. (Artia Records, 600 Fifth Ave., New York) from Russian masters. They were released in Britain by Associated Recordings, in the 1960s. The material was classical.

ARTO (label). A record issued by the Arto Co., Inc., a subsidiary of the Standard Music Roll Co. of Orange, New Jersey. Advertising began in April 1919, announcing that G. Howlett Davis was president (he was also president of Standard Music Roll Co.). The new records were to be made at recording laboratories at 233 W. 23rd St., New York, using a new process that would allow them to be played laterally or vertically. In June 1920 the first selection of discs appeared, offering dance, blues, jazz, and popular vocal material. The price was $1 for a 10-inch disc in January 1921; an $.85 disc was marketed in February 1921. In October 1920 the office was at 1604 Broadway, New York, and in May 1921 it moved to 1658 Broadway. Arto also pressed records for the Globe and Bell labels, and some Cleartones, Hy Tones, Ansonias, and Nordskogs. When the company went bankrupt in January 1922, it continued to press Bell and Globe issues for a time but ceased production of Arto records. Plant fittings and masters went up for public sale on 3 May 1923. [Andrews*.]

ARTOFOLA CO. An American firm, located in Springfield, Illinois. It was the manufacturer of the Artofola disc player, advertised in *TMW*, 1916. There were seven models. The company also made vertical-cut discs: a 10-inch sold for $.75, and a 12-inch sold for $1.00.

ARTOPHONE CORP. A firm established in St. Louis in 1915; maker of the Artophone disc players. The address in 1916 was 1113 Olive St. Later the firm issued records under the **Herwin** label. In 1926 it were located in Kansas City, Missouri (203 Kansas City Life Building), distributing Paramount records, and selling both phonographs and radios. Edwin Schiele was president at that time.

ASCH, MOSES, 1905–1986. Polish-born record industry executive, son of the author Sholem Asch. He got into the music business by installing sound equipment in Yiddish theaters in New York. He began to issue records in 1939, under the **Asch** label. His great interest was folk music, and he made the early recordings of Leadbelly, Pete Seeger, Josh White, and Burl Ives. He started the **Folkways** label in 1947, engaging outstanding folk and ethnic artists. Eventually he published more than 2,000 albums, documenting traditional music from around the world.

ASCH (label). A record issued by **Moses Asch** in New York, from 1939 to 1946. The address was 117 W. 46th St. Content was folk music and jazz. The Norman Granz series "Jazz at the Philharmonic" appeared on the Asch label in 1946, leading to the establishment in 1953 of the Granz Clef label. The **Folkways** label took over the folk material of the Asch label in 1947.

ASH, SAM, 1884–1951. American vaudeville performer and singer of popular songs, born 28 Aug 1884 in Kentucky. He made numerous appearances in Broadway musicals from 1915–1931. His first recording was "I'm Not Ashamed of You, Molly," accompanied by Prince's Orchestra, made in December 1914 (Columbia #A-1701). He began recording also for the Little Wonder label in 1914 with "Chinatown, My Chinatown" (Little Wonder #98). His next Columbia was "Goodbye, Virginia" (Columbia #A1697; 1915), made with the Peerless Quartet. He remained with Columbia until 1916, while recording also for Little Wonder, doing solos, duets, and numbers with quartets. From 1917 he worked also for Emerson, Gennett, Okeh, and others. "When I Found You, Poor Little Ritz Girl" was made for Edison Diamond Discs in 1921 (#50721). In the 1930s he gave up recording to go into motion pictures. Ash died in Hollywood on 21 Oct 1951. [Walsh 1971/3.]

ASHLAND MANUFACTURING CO. A Chicago firm, located at 43rd St. and Hermitage Ave. It made the Ashland disc player, advertised in *TMW* in 1916.

ASPIR (label). The name used in the British market in 1909 for Disque Aspir, made by the Compagnie Général d'Électricité. A label of the same name marketed in Britain in 1910 was attributed (in a *TMW* advertisement in March) to Établissements Phonographiques d'Ivry. The records were double sided, vertical cut, 11 1/2-inch and 12 1/3-inch; the repertoire was predominantly French, inclusive of opera, orchestral works, and songs. Epiphone talking machines were sold by the same firm, from an address at 15 Victoria St., London.

Associated Audio Archives. *See* ASSOCIATION FOR RECORDED SOUND COLLECTIONS, INC. (ARSC).

ASSOCIATION FOR RECORDED SOUND COLLECTIONS, INC. (ARSC). An organization of record collectors, librarian/curators, and researchers, established in 1966. The address in 1991 was POB 10162, Silver Spring, Maryland. About 90 percent of the 1,000 members (including institutions and individuals) are American. Aims of the association include enhancement of communication among sound archivists and the encouragement of research. The *ARSC Journal* (two per year) was issued first in 1968; it presents research articles and continuing lists of discographies and writings about recordings. A quarterly *Newsletter* is also published, in addition to occasional monographs. A recent project of great significance is the **Rigler-Deutsch Index**, carried out by the Associated Audio Archives (established 1974; an ad hoc subcommittee of the ARSC Bibliographic Access Committee since 1976).

Grants are awarded annually by ARSC to individuals pursuing research in any field of recording. Annual awards for excellence are given for the best publications on recording artists or recording history. [Brooks*; Brooks 1983; McKee 1989/1.]

ASV GROUP. A British conglomerate, located at 179–181 North End Road, London. It controls these labels: ASV, COE, Gaudeaumus, Living Era, Musicmasters, Novalis, Quicksilver, RPO, **Teldec**, and Transacord.

ATKINS, CHET, 1924– . American guitarist, country singer, composer, and record industry executive, born Chester Burton Atkins in Luttrell, Tennessee, on 20 June 1924. As a child he taught himself to play the guitar, and was playing on local radio in his teens. From there he went on to radio shows in Cincinnati; Raleigh, North Carolina; Richmond, Virginia; and Denver. He began to record for Victor, singing and playing guitar, achieving success in 1949 with "Gallopin' Guitar," "Main St. Breakdown," and "Country Gentleman." In 1946 he appeared for the first time at the Grand Ole Opry. Atkins toured Europe, Asia, and Africa, achieving international status. From 1957 he worked for RCA in Nashville, as production manager and A & R director; he helped to develop the "Nashville sound" and to make that city the center of country music.

Some of his hits in this period were "Boo Boo Stick Beat" (Victor #7589; 1959) and "Teensville" (Victor #7684; 1960). He was invited to play for President John F. Kennedy in 1961, and performed as a soloist with several symphony orchestras. In 1973 he was elected to the Country Music Hall of Fame. Recordings by Atkins have won nine Grammy awards in the country instrumental category: *Chet Atkins Picks the Best* (1967), *Me and Jerry* (1970), *Snowbird* (1971), *Atkins-Travis Traveling Show* (with Merle Travis; 1974), *The Entertainer* (1975), *Chester and Lester* (with Les Paul; 1976), *Country—After All These Years* (1981), "So Soft, Your Goodbye" (1990), and *Neck and Neck* (with Mark Knopfler; 1990).

ATLANTIC (label). A New York label, with offices at 75 Rockefeller Plaza. It was one of the principal independent labels of the post-World War II era, with first issues in the summer of 1947. Founders of Atlantic Records were Ahmet Ertegun and Herb Abramson. Jerry Wexler and Nesuhi Ertegun, brother of Ahmet, joined the firm later. The first recordings were rhythm & blues, gospel, and jazz, many being reissues and leased masters. The company leaped forward after signing Ray Charles in 1952; among other stars on the label were the Bee Gees, Eric Clapton, Ornette Coleman, John Coltrane, Cream, Bobby Darin, Roberta Flack, Aretha Franklin, Lee Konitz, Led Zeppelin, Charles Mingus, the Modern Jazz Quartet, and the Rolling Stones. The company made early stereo records in 1955. In Ruppli's massive Atlantic label discography more than 40,000 masters are listed. In the early 1970s the label was acquired by Warner Communications, and it became part of the Warner Brothers-Elektra-Atlantic conglomerate. Atlantic Jazz, a series of 15 LPs, was issued in the 1980s as a summary of the label's major accomplishments; and digitally remastered versions are being issued on CD. [Ruppli 1979.]

ATLEE, JOHN YORKE, 1842–1910. American whistler, born in Detroit on 28 Jan 1842; made very popular cylinders for Columbia from 1889 to 1897 (there were 21 numbers by him in the November 1890 Columbia catalog). He also made some discs for Berliner and a few cylinders for Edison. The material included "Mocking Bird," "Anvil Chorus," "Annie Laurie," and "Marching through Georgia." "His whistling was loud, clear and piercing" (Brooks) as was required by the early recording equipment, but he lacked the talent to survive in a time of improved taste and technology. The January 1899 *Phonoscope* reported that he was managing the phonograph department of the Duston-Smith Piano Co., in Charleston, South Carolina. He did make a few more records, and was mentioned in the June 1900 *Phonoscope* as a supervisor of language instruction records. AtLee died in Washington on 1 Apr 1910. The spelling of his name is variously offered in the literature: Fred Gaisberg (who was his accompanist on some of the records) spells it "Atlee," and so does an 1893 issue of *Phonogram*. Columbia's record lists spelled it AtLee; his death certificate has "AtLee (At Lee)." [Brooks*; Brooks 1978.]

ATMOSPHERE MICROPHONE. A **microphone** placed at some distance from the performers, in order to include environmental **ambience** in the recording.

ATTENUATION. A reduction of voltage, intensity, amplitude, or loudness; the opposite of **amplification.**

Attenuation distortion. *See* DISTORTION, II.

ATWOOD, HARRIET, 1865–?. American pianist, born Harriet Haddon (or Hadden). She was probably the first pianist to record, having been called on by Thomas Edison to play for his experimental tinfoil phonograph in 1887. Her husband, George Atwood (1864–1933), was an engineer for Edison; when a piano player was needed in the laboratory Atwood sent for his wife. [Walsh 1970/4–5.]

AUDAK CO. A New York firm, located at 565 Fifth Ave. in 1924. It advertised in *TMW* 1924 as a maker of listening stations for record shops, intended to replace enclosed booths. Earphones were used.

Audible frequency range. *See* AUDIO FREQUENCY.

AUDIO. (I) A general term pertaining to hearing or sound, from the Latin *audire*, to hear; often used as a modifier to identify a system designed to record and/or to reproduce sound, or an element of such a system.

AUDIO. (II) The sound portion of a film or television program.

Audio cassette. *See* CASSETTE.

AUDIO ENGINEERING SOCIETY. A prominent professional society, established in 1948. The address (in 1991) was 60 E. 42nd St., New York. Among its 10,000 members are specialists in most branches of recorded sound: designers of equipment, installers and operators, teachers, salespersons, and technicians. The *Journal of the AES* is published 10 times a year. The society holds two conventions each year, in Europe in the spring and in the U.S. in autumn. In 1991 Donald J. Plunkett was its executive director.

AUDIO FIDELITY (label). An American record, issued by Audio Fidelity Records, New York, from May 1955. Classical, jazz, and gospel material was offered. The label was a pioneer in stereo, with first releases in November 1957. "The masters were cut with an automatic Scully Record Lathe mounting a Westrex 45–45 stereo cutter head system with special feedback electronic circuitry driven by custom 200 watt amplifiers. The frequency range . . . exceeded the range of previous high fidelity records. . . ." [Case*, source of the quote.]

AUDIO FREQUENCY. One of the frequencies within the range of sound frequencies audible to humans, from ca. 15 to 20,000 cycles per second (or Hz). **Acoustic recording** achieved coverage of about 1,000 to 2,000 or 3,000 Hz. With the emergence of **electrical recording** in 1925, manufacturers could claim coverage of 100 to 8,000 Hz. The frequency range of notes playable on certain instruments is encompassed by the capabilities of early electrical recording; for example, all the high brasses and winds, the violin, and the viola. Female voices and higher male voices could also be reproduced with all fundamental frequencies. One reason that realistic reproduction did not occur was that a sounding note produces not only a fundamental frequency but also an entire series of overtones, or **harmonics**, and it is these elements that give color and distinctiveness to the sound of an instrument or a voice. Some instruments, especially the percussions, also produce "transient tones," heard on initialization of a tone and then subject to quick fading. The audio experience of record listeners in the 1920s is often suggested today when loudspeakers of limited range are heard—for example, in elevators or in small portable radios. The effect is one of blurred identity for instruments and voices. Outside the audio frequency range humans perceive vibrations as feelings, not sounds: "There is thus a 'threshold of feeling,' and between these two lies the audibility area. At very high and very low frequencies these thresholds intersect: the sensations of hearing and feeling become merged, and it is difficult to distinguish between them" [Wilson 1957, source of the quotation.] *See also* HEARING.

Audio spectrum. *See* AUDIO FREQUENCY.

Audio tape. *See* TAPE.

Audiocassette. *See* CASSETTE.

AUDIOGRAPHIC ROLLS. Player piano rolls marketed by the **Aeolian Co.** in 1927, with a special feature: the printed music was inscribed on the roll, visible to the operator. However, the rolls moved vertically, and it would not have been possible to read the music as it went by, in order to sing along with the piano sound or to try duplicating the performance on the roll with one's own fingers on the keyboard. The concept seems to have originated in 1912 with **Audiscript** rolls.

AUDION. The three-element vacuum tube invented by **Lee De Forest.** *See also* AMPLIFIER.

AUDIOPHILE RECORDING. A technology of the 1950s, using **digital recording, half-speed mastering,** improved vinyl, and **direct-to-disc** methods to reach better instrumental definition, improved channel separation, and greater frequency range. The technique originated in smaller record companies, who were endeavoring to correct the problems that resulted from mass-produced LPs, then moved to the major labels. Sheffield Records was a pioneer of this type of recording.

AUDISCRIPT ROLLS. Player piano rolls patented by Carrol Brent Chilton, of Washington, D.C, in 1912. They had two innovative aspects: they moved right to left, instead of vertically;

and they contained the printed score, visible to the performer. They did not find a market, nor did the later **Audiographic rolls** of 1927.

AURAL EXCITER. A device used by radio stations to improve the broadcast signal, and in record production for the enhancement of clarity and presence.

AURORA (label). A Canadian record issued from 1926 to 1932. Material came from Brunswick, Melotone, and Victor masters. Content was popular songs and dance numbers. Artists included Gene Autry (under pseudonyms), Henry Burr, and the Peerless Quartet. [Robertson, A. 1986 lists the known items.]

AUSTIN, GENE, 1900–1972. American singer and composer, born in Gainesville, Texas, 24 June 1900. After serving with U.S. forces in France as a bugler, he formed a dance band (playing piano), worked in vaudeville, and then became a successful crooner and radio personality. He began recording for Vocalion in 1924, but his first great success did not come until 1927, when he wrote and recorded "My Blue Heaven" (Victor #20964); a copy of which was placed in the Smithsonian Institution as an exemplar of the fine music of the day. A second hit came in the following year, "Voice of the Southland" (Victor #21714). Another best seller was "Ramona," a vocal solo with pipe organ and instrumental backup (Victor #21334; 1928). Austin also composed (with Roy Bergere) the successful songs "How Come You Do Me Like You Do?" and "When My Sugar Walks Down the Street." In 1948 Universal Records acquired the rights to the Austin masters and reissued many of the favorites. "Too Late" (Victor #6880; 1957) was his final chart appearance. He died in Palm Springs, California, on 24 Jan 1972. [Magnusson 1983 is a complete discography; Walsh 1957/2–3.]

AUSTRAL, FLORENCE, 1892–1968. Australian soprano, born Florence Wilson in Richmond, 26 Apr 1892. After study in Melbourne, she went to England for a debut at Covent Garden as Brünnhilde—a role she sang without peers—on 16 May 1922; her later roles there were Isolde and Aida. Her Victor records include "Yo-ho-he!" from *Fliegende Holländer* (#7117), an aria from the Brahms *Requiem* (#9395) and the part of Brünnhilde in the *Götterdämmerung* set (#M-60). For the Gramophone Co. she recorded the church scene from *Faust* with Feodor Chaliapin (#DB899), and "O terra addio" with Miguel Fleta (#DB580). Austral made a total of 102 recordings, encompassing lieder, oratorio, Wagnerian roles, and both dramatic and lyric roles from the Italian/French repertoire. Fred Gaisberg of the Gramophone Co. said that "in the early twenties, Florence Austral was the most important recording soprano we had." [White 1962.]

AUSTRALASIAN PERFORMING RIGHT ASSOCIATION, LTD. An organization established in 1926 to monitor the performing rights of its members, who are from Australia and New Zealand.

AUSTRALIA. During the 19th and early 20th centuries mechanical music played a significant part in Australian musical life. Such music had many forms: the music box, the barrel organ, the symphonion, the orchestrion, and the band organ, among others. Most of these were devices that replicated the sound of instruments by responding to encoded instructions in a perforated paper or cardboard roll. Player pianos and piano rolls were imported from the U.S. prior to 1919. The QRS Co. set up an Australian branch office, which was purchased by G.H. Horton of Sydney, who made rolls under the trade name Mastertouch. Horton's firm continued through the Depression and in the face of competing media, albeit at a lower production level. In 1959 the company was acquired by its present owner, Barclay Wright. It is now the only active piano roll manufacturer in the Southern Hemisphere. Nellie Melba offered a "Complete Singing Course" on a Mastertouch piano roll.

The earliest reference to a phonograph in Australia appeared in the *Sydney Morning Herald* of 7 June 1879, announcing an entertainment that would feature "Edison's World-Renowned Phonograph or Talking Machine." In 1890–1892 an English educator and showman, Douglas Archibald, exhibited the Edison Improved Phonograph in Australia, New Zealand, India, and Ceylon. He also made recordings of such individuals as the Governor-General of Australia, the Earl of Hopetoun; and the actress Nellie Stewart.

By the late 1890s the cylinder phonograph was commercially established in the country, the market being dominated by the Edison, Columbia, and Pathé interests. One notable use of the phonograph was made by the anthropologist Charles Baldwin Spencer, who set out for central Australia on camels in 1901 to record Aboriginal music and dialect.

Disc players, with their single-sided seven-inch flat "plates," appeared at the turn of the century, but they did not have great impact at first; indeed, the Australia Phono Record Co. was established in 1907 in Sydney, to produce cylinder records, and a similar venture existed in Melbourne. However, the Gramophone Co. and Columbia set up offices in Sydney in 1904 for the distribution of disc records, primarily imports from the U.K. and the U.S. Between 1924 and 1926 four manufacturing plants were built—three in Sydney and one in Melbourne—for local disc production. The first, in Darlinghurst, was operated by the music publisher D. Davis and Co.; in 1925 it was pressing Brunswick records from American metal masters. In the same year the Gramophone Co. built a stamping plant at Erskineville, using English and American masters, for release on the HMV and Zonophone labels. Columbia built a factory at Homebush; and the World Record Co. opened one in Melbourne, also setting up a facility at North Brighton, Victoria, for making local recordings (1924). World's pioneer effort at issuing Australian artists was, however, short-lived.

Brunswick was forced to close during the Depression, but Columbia's Homebush plant became the headquarters of the new EMI conglomerate, and it was there that the recording of local performers finally began on a steady footing. Commencing in June 1936, discs were made by Jack Lumsdaine, Gladys Moncrieff, Tex Morton, Smoky Dawson, Dick Bentley, Rex Shaw's orchestra, and others—among them Jacko, the broadcasting kookaburra (a laughing jackass). Radio drama, musicals, and variety shows were also recorded, including 16–

inch transcriptions of programs that were part of the way of life, such as *Dad and Dave of Snake Gully*.

In about 1936 the Australian Record Co. commenced operations, later becoming a subsidiary of the American CBS. An insurance company, Mainguard, started up a record company in the early 1950s, issuing the Manhattan label. In 1952 it became Festival Records, and then finally a subsidiary of News Limited, Australia.

Other major companies opened Australian branches: Philips in 1954; RCA in 1956; and Phonogram in 1968. There are also a number of smaller independent companies active in recording national artists, but only a few have their own studios and all have their records pressed by other firms. Locally pressed Australian labels established from ca. 1928 included Angelus, Broadcast, Kismet, Lyric, Melotone, Polydor, Summit, and Vocalion; none were still active after the Depression. Swaggie was a later label, successful in the jazz field.

Among the best known Australian performers to record were Ada Crossley, Peter Dawson, Florrie Forde, Percy Grainger, Nellie Melba, Albert Whelan, and Billy Williams. Others who were internationally active included Dan Agar, Irene Ainsley, Harry Atkinson, Catherine Aulsebrook, Humphrey Bishop, Eileen Boyd, Doris Carter, Ella Caspers, Amy Castles, Hope Charteris, Violet Elliot, A. H. Gee, Elsie Hall, Hamilton Hill, Alice Hollander, Carrie Lancelley, Marsh Little, Lalla Miranda, Marie Narelle, Lempriere Pringle, Harry Reynolds, Frances Saville, and Harry Taylor. Recent pop artists to gain international recognition include INXS, Midnight Oil, and the Bee Gees.

According to figures in an Industries Assistance Commission report (1978) employment in the record industry was estimated at 2,200 persons in 1976. Record and tape sales in 1980 reached A$225,000,000. Some 22 million LPs were produced in 1979–1980, and nearly 11 million pre-recorded tapes (60 million blank tapes were sold that year). But sales declined after 1980 in Australia, as in other countries.

In 1991 six companies controlled 90 percent of Australian record production: Sony, EMI, Festival, PolyGram, BMG, and Warner—all but Festival being foreign owned.

Of the earliest Australian-made gramophones, the Salonola of Home Recreations, Ltd., Sydney, appears to have been the most successful. Others were the Homophone, the Concordia Gramophone, and the Concertrola—the motor of which was made by the Russell Gear and Machine Co., Ltd., of Toronto.

A special part in the history of sound recording in Australia has been played by the Australian Broadcasting Commission (ABC), which came into being in 1932, though regular broadcasts had been transmitted well before this time. Under terms of the Broadcasting Act, all stations are required to devote 2 1/2 percent of musical programming to Australian works, though in actual fact ABC's percentage far exceeds this minimum. Recording and transcription services have always been prominent among the ABC's activities. Until the introduction of tape recording, acetate discs were used. From its comprehensive collection of native compositions, the ABC has issued a series of 10 discs entitled Australian Composers. Percy Grainger's works have had special attention. Another great native was honored in 1981–1982 with the issue of *Melba—the American Recordings, 1907–1916*. The first digitally mastered symphonic recording by the ABC Permanent Recordings Unit was Eugene Goossens' monumental choral work *The Apocalypse*, made in 1982.

ABC has an Enterprises Unit for the production of commercial recordings by Australian composers. It also produces a series of jazz compact discs and LPs, digitally remastered. The ABC sound libraries hold enormous collections of Australian discs, all registered in an online database. The Canberra School of Music produced a 15-CD set called *Anthology of Australian Music on Disc* in 1989.

The Music Board of the Australia Music Council released an important report in 1987 entitled "The Australian Music Industry; An Economic Evaluation." It covered funding, numbers of musicians and other workers, ethnic musicians, studios, radio broadcasting, and television. The report revealed that in 1986 Australian consumers bought more than 15 million records, 13 million cassettes, and 2 million CDs.

A compact disc plant, Distronics, was established in Melbourne in 1987, with an expected production of 25 million discs per year. Despite some early financial problems, Distronics is now firmly operating and is expected to have sales of around $A20 million per year.

The National Library of Australia has accepted the role of establishing a national sound archive covering the full spectrum of sound history. The Library has gathered more than 300,000 discs and tapes, including many rare and historical items.

Sounds Australian, formerly the Australian Music Center, is an agency in Sydney that promotes Australian music. Its journal publishes varied material on the recording industry. [Australian 1987; Directory 1985; Mulholland 1980; Music Recording 1978.]

Gerald R. Seaman

AUTO PNEUMATIC ACTION CO. A New York firm, located at 629 W. 50th St. It made the Auto Deluxe Reproducing Action (as a Welte-Mignon licensee), used in 64 makes of **reproducing piano.**

AUTOGRAPH (label). (I) A British record of the period before World War I, pressed for issue of material by comedian **Billy Whitlock.**

AUTOGRAPH (label).(II) Records issued by the **Marsh Laboratories** of Chicago, ca. 1923–1925. Marsh is credited with the earliest commercial **electrical recordings,** in 1924; survivors are so scarce that Autograph has been called "second if not on a par with Black Patti as the rarest of recording labels" (Henriksen). The repertoire included jazz and dance music. Jelly Roll Morton and Jesse Crawford were among the artists—they were the first persons to make commercial electric records.

The earliest known matrix numbers of the label are #30 and #35, a pair of test pressings (apparently not released) from ca. 1922; they feature Bennie Moten's Kansas City Orchestra playing "Muscle Shoal Blues" and "Oh Baby Dear." It seems that the first item issued was a piano solo by Clarence M. Jones, "Modula-tion" (matrix #202). Organ music was a specialty; Crawford performed acoustically and electrically on the Chicago Theatre organ, beginning with "Until Tomorrow" (#4004; matrix #581), and Milton Charles recorded electrically on the organ of the Tivoli Theatre (also in Chicago). Morton's jazz material is also of great interest, and rarity. He recorded with various jazz ensembles, beginning with "Fish Tail Blues" (#606; matrix #635) in September 1924. He and King Oliver performed jazz duets in December 1924: "King Porter Stomp" and "Tom Cat Blues" (#617; matrices #685 and 687).

In a departure from the typical repertoire of the label, classical pianist Moissaye Boguslawski played "Dizzy Fingers" and "Prelude in C-Sharp Minor" (presumably Rachmaninoff's) on #500 (matrices #981 and #980). [Bryan 1990; Henriksen 1978 has a label list; Rust 1978; Rust 1980; *TMR* #52–53, p. 1376.]

AUTO-LOCATE. Also known as automatic search. The feature in a **tape recorder** or **tape deck** that allows rapid location of a chosen point on the tape.

Automatic Double Tracking (ADT). *See* DOUBLE TRACKING.

Automatic Entertainer. *See* JOHN GABEL'S AUTOMATIC ENTERTAINER.

AUTOMATIC LEVEL CONTROL (ALC). A circuit used to maintain a recording level despite changes in the amplitude of the signal. In playback, extremes of volume are evened out to a middle ground (e.g., presenting ffff as ff).

AUTOMATIC MACHINE AND TOOL CO. A Chicago firm, established at 43 S. Canal St. in 1898 by John Gabel. A later address, from a 1908 advertisement in *TMW*, was 46 N. Ann St. The company was maker of the popular **John Gabel's Automatic Entertainer** in 1906, an early **juke box.** In 1916 the firm was making a home version, under the name of Gabelola (or Gabel-ola); it handled 24 discs in sequence or could play any one (one side only) selected. **David C. Rockola** acquired the company in 1949.

AUTOMATIC MUSICAL CO. A firm located at 53 Chenango St., Binghamton, New York, making **coin-ops**, including a self-playing xylophone. Bankrupt in 1912, it was revived as the **Link Piano Co.**

AUTOMATIC MUSICAL INSTRUMENT CO. A firm located in Grand Rapids, Michigan, established in 1909 as the National Piano Manufacturing Co. It made a player that allowed automatic selection of player piano rolls from a magazine. A division of the firm, **National Automatic Music Co.**, was independent for some time, but rejoined the parent company in 1925; in 1927 it was making a **juke box** that could play either side of 10 discs. Operation of that juke box was fully electrical, employing the first electrostatic speaker. About 12,000 of those machines were on location by 1930. The company became incorporated in 1946, as AMI, Inc.; its president was John W. Haddock. A 1951 model juke box for 45 rpm discs could handle up to 120 selections, and a 1955 model 200 selections. The firm also made phonographs for home use.

AUTOMATIC PHONOGRAPH EXHIBITION CO. A New York firm established by Felix Gottschalk in February 1890. It made, operated, and leased **coin-op** cylinder players. The machines, in glass-topped cabinets and run by storage batteries, were exhibited at the first convention of the National Phonograph Association in May 1890. Records were changed daily. Selections were comic songs, monologs, whistling, bands, and hymns. In 1891, 16 of the **North American Phonograph Co.** affiliated firms were leasing coin-ops from the Automatic Phonograph Exhibition Co. Contract disputes resulted in abandonment of the lease plan.

Automatic record changer. *See* RECORD CHANGER.

Automatic Reginaphone. *See* REGINA MUSIC BOX CO.

AUTOMATIC REPLAY. A system that allows repeated playbacks of a recorded program without user intervention. It operates on a signal within the recording, or can be activated by a preset mechanical device. *See also* AUTOMATIC REVERSE; TALKING DOLL.

AUTOMATIC REVERSE. In a magnetic **tape recorder**, a system that begins playback of the second tape track upon completion of the first track. The reversal is achieved by a foil sensing tape at the proper point on the magnetic tape, or by means of a signal on the tape. In earlier **cassette** devices there was a mechanism to turn the cassette over for playback of the second track. The foil sensing or signal systems require two playback heads, one for each direction. *See also* AUTOMATIC REPLAY.

AUTOMATIC SEARCH. A system in a **tape recorder** for rapid movement of the tape to a desired point, for playback of selected material.

Automatic sequence. *See* MANUAL SEQUENCE.

AUTOMATIC SHUTOFF. A device that turns off the motor of all or part of an audio system when playback of a recording has concluded.

AUTOMATIC STOP. Beginning around 1911 or earlier many inventions were introduced for the purpose of bringing a **turntable** to a stop at the end of a disc; the reason was to avoid the noise made by the needle as it reached the tail groove. Earliest advertisers in *TMW* were Sonora and **Condon-Autostop Co.** The latter's Autostop device required adjustment for each disc, but in 1912 Condon offered the Altobrake, which was self-adjusting. Simplex was the name of a 1912 device by **Standard Gramophone Appliance Co.**; it could stop the turntable and restart it for a repeat of the record. Edison's Diamond Disc Phonograph had a Duncan Automatic Stop in models offered from April 1917 to mid-1918 (described and illustrated in Paul). Several similar devices appeared in the next few years, and the Columbia Grafonola player of 1920 had one built in. [Paul 1988.]

Automatic turntable. *See* TURNTABLE.

AUTOMOBILE SOUND SYSTEMS. The first generally marketed cars to be radio equipped appeared in the U.S. in 1930. Equipment was rudimentary and the results were poor. No serious attention to the problem of overcoming the auto's hostile environment was given until the hi-fi revolution of the 1950s. Then audio manufacturers began to deal with the need for miniaturization (to fit into the relatively small space available), for amplification to counter road and engine noise, and for physical toughness of components to withstand vibration and extremes of temperature. Those problems notwithstanding, there are favorable factors present in the automobile that are not usually found in a home audio environment. The listeners are located in fixed positions; **reverberation** time is short; and there is greater discrimination against **ambient sounds** because the loudspeaker(s) and the listeners are so close to each other.

FM radio was the first major breakthrough; it became available in American cars in the 1950s. The four-track and eight-track tape **cartridge** appeared in the mid-1960s, gradually giving way to the **cassette** in the late 1970s. **Noise reduction systems** were added, and electronic tuning, followed by computerized controls in certain "high-end" installations like the Blaupunkt TQR-07 Berlin, or the Polk 12–speaker, 160 watt, H700 system; these were selling for around $1,500 in 1990. While these complexities have tended to take more and more of the space in the driver area—at a time when other gadgetry was also crowding into the dashboard—some success has been achieved in space saving. Cassette/receivers with built-in multichannel amplifiers can power all the speakers; and CD changers can be mounted in the trunk.

Compact disc changers for automobiles became available in the U.S. in 1988, made by Alpine, Pioneer, Sony, and Technics. Ten- and 12-disc models by Clarion, Concord, and Kenwood were brought out in 1989. **DAT** players for automobiles were marketed in 1988, by Alpine, Clarion, JVC, and Kenwood. Lincoln Continental and Cadillac Fleetwood offered DAT as a factory-installed option. Single-band parametric **equalizers** came into use in these players, to improve fidelity of the bass frequencies in both front and rear speakers. Optical fiber technology is applied to the elimination of interference by removing the analog signals from long cables.

AUTOPHONE. A cylinder player made by the **American Phonograph Co.**, New York, from about 1913 to 1919. It was also marketed, and perhaps assembled, in Canada by the Dominion Autophone Co., Vancouver. The machine could play 12 cylinders in succession without stopping and without the need to rewind its three-spring motor. Julius Roever filed for the patent in 1907, and received U.S. patent #883,971 on 7 Apr 1908. (Koenigsberg notes also the patent granted to Allison A. Pratt on 27 Aug 1907, #864,686, for a 30-cylinder **coin-op**.) Operation was based on a ferris wheel housing of the cylinders, each of which had its own adjustable mandrel. Adjustment was needed to set the first groove of each cylinder in line with the diamond point **reproducer**. By rotation of the wheel, any cylinder could be brought to the first playing position. A coin-op version was also patented and manufactured. Advertisements and photos appear in *TMR* #14. [Koenigsberg 1990; Stephenson 1983.]

AUTOPIANO CO. Maker of a quality player piano that was purchased by European royal families and by the Vatican. A 1926 directory gave these addresses: general offices 627–629 W. 50th St., New York; 1222 Kimball Bldg., Chicago; 462 Phelan Bldg., San Francisco; 45 Prince of Wales Rd., London NW5; and 36 Boulevard Haussmann, Paris. Its president in 1926 was Corley Gibson. The deluxe Autopiano player action was used in more than 100 Welte-Mignon licensee brands of piano, appearing in grands, uprights, and **reproducing pianos**. The Pianista Player-Piano was another brand name for the product.

Autostop. *See* AUTOMATIC STOP; CONDON-AUTOSTOP CO.

AUTRY, GENE, 1907– . American country singer and guitarist, actor, songwriter, and business executive; born Orvon Autry in Tioga, Texas, on 29 Sep 1907. His style of cowboy song became the mode of a more sophisticated country music, superseding the simpler hillbilly style. He taught himself guitar while working as a telegraph operator in Oklahoma, and was lucky enough to be heard by a customer named Will Rogers. Rogers told him to go into radio, and Autry found a job with an Oklahoma station. By 1929 he was well known in the region. He was the first person to record cowboy songs, one of the first being his own composition "That Silver Haired Daddy of Mine," which was a great best seller in the early 1930s. He wrote more that 250 songs. The singer was highly popular on the Chicago radio show *National Barn Dance* and in 1934 he had a small singing role in a western film, *In Old Santa Fe*; he eventually made more than 100 feature pictures. He had his own radio show, *Melody Ranch*, from 1939 to 1956.

Autry served as a flight officer in World War II, then returned to make dozens of all-time hit records. He left Okeh, which had recorded such chart songs as "Back in the Saddle Again" (his own composition; #05080) and "When the Swallows Come Back to Capistrano" (#05780), for Columbia and had great success with such numbers as "Rudolph the Red-Nosed Reindeer" (Columbia #38610; 1949). His last single to appear on the charts was "Peter Cottontail" (Columbia #38750; 1950). There were various LP reissues, including his *Greatest Hits* (Columbia, 1961).

While continuing to perform in film and on television during the 1950s, Autry went into the business world, establishing his own record label, **Challenge**, and acquiring two others, **Champion** and Republic. He also bought several radio stations, and became part owner of the California Angels major league baseball club. In 1969 he was elected to the Country Music Hall of Fame.

AUXETOPHONE. A disc player with a compressed air device used to amplify the output. The inventor is usually thought to have been **Charles A. Parsons** of London (inventor of the steam turbine), who received for it British patents #10,468 and #10,469 in 1903, plus #20,892 in 1904; and he did exhibit a working model of the Auxetophone to the Royal Society in 1904. However, Horace Short, who had been associated with Thomas Edison in Menlo Park, held

an earlier British patent: #22,768, of 1898. Horace's device was named The Gouraudophone, after its financial backer **George Gouraud**. Following some controversy, Short assigned his patent to Parsons in 1904. Later the patent was acquired by Gramophone and Typewriter, Ltd., for use in Britain; in the U.S. the license was held by Victor. Various demonstrations in London during 1905–1912 proved that great amplification could be achieved. In a concert arranged by the Gramophone Co. in Finsbury Park, London, it was reported (by *TMN*, September 1912) that 3,000 persons were present, and that the music "was distinctly heard at a distance of a quarter of a mile."

The principle was that of a **soundbox** with a modified diaphragm incorporating an air valve mechanism. As compressed air, supplied by a small electrically driven unit, passes the valve and is suddenly expanded—due to the effect of sound waves from the recording or other source—this expansion carries the sound with it. One application of the concept was in the megaphonic Aerophone and the later Stentorphone, both used to amplify outdoor voices. Despite the utility of the Auxetophone for various purposes, just a few were sold; one estimate says only about 500 were manufactured. Cost (ca. $500) was one problem for the salesman, but more serious was the nuisance of the hissing sound created by the air movement. [*TMR* #12 and #19 have photos; Carter 1977/12 has details of operation and a drawing.]

AUXILIARY INPUT. An audio device, usually found on a **tuner** or **amplifier**, that allows receipt of a signal from an outside source. For example, a turntable or a radio tuner may be attached, via a cable, plug, and jack, to an amplifier. Connecting components should be matched in **impedance** and voltage level, for optimum performance.

AVIATION RECORDINGS. The sounds of aircraft have been recorded for diverse reasons, from technical interest (e.g., "Aeroplane: Starting; Steady Flight; Stopping," Columbia #YB-5) to a desire for historical documentation (air battles, the Hindenburg Zeppelin disaster (Romeo #70876; 1937), etc.).

Songs about airships were popular in early days of recording. The first was "My Sweetheart's the Man in the Moon" (Edison cylinder #484; 1892), which tells of a spaceship voyage. The earliest record about an airplane—made just after the Wright Brothers experiments at Kitty Hawk—was "Come Take a Trip in My Airship" (Victor #2986; October 1904), sung by Billy Murray. "Come Josephine in My Flying Machine," sung by Blanche Ring, was the greatest aviation hit (Victor 60032; 1911). Victor made another version of it later in the year, by Ada Jones and the American Quartet, with Billy Murray. Charles Lindbergh's solo crossing of the Atlantic in 1927 produced a number of songs; one hit record was Vernon Dalhart's rendition of "Lucky Lindy" and "Lindbergh, Eagle of the U.S.A." (Columbia #1000–D). During World War II there were songs about the U.S. Air Force and its pilots, of which the best was probably "He Wears a Pair of Silver Wings" (by the Gordon Jenkins band, Capitol #106; 1942). Later airplane songs have been few. "Leaving on a Jet Plane" was a hit record by Peter, Paul & Mary in 1969 (Warner #7340). "Jet" by Wings (Paul and Linda McCartney) was on the charts in 1974 (Apple #1871). [Mason 1984; Walsh 1974/1.]

AVON COMEDY FOUR. An American vaudeville singing comedy team, greatly popular from 1916 to 1924. The original members were Irving Kaufman, Harry Goodwin, Charles Dale, and Joe Smith. Eddie Miller replaced Kaufmann and Frank Corbett replaced Goodwin in 1919; Arthur Fields was a member for a brief period. Their first recording was "Yaaka Hula Hickey Dula (Hawaiian Love Song)" (Victor #18081; 1916). In the 1917 Victor catalog they were represented by 13 discs. The last Avon record was "Clancy's Minstrels" / "The New School Teacher" (Victor #35750; 1924). [Walsh 1962/10.]

AYLSWORTH, JONAS WALTER, ca. 1868–1916. A chemist with Thomas Edison from ca. 1890; after his retirement in 1903 he remained as a consultant in the West Orange laboratories. His inventions included the commercial nickel-iron alkaline storage battery and various cylinder molding processes. He was known particularly for the Edison gold molded cylinder. He also improved the cast solid-wax cylinder that could be shaved and re-used. The brittleness of the 1908 black-wax Amberol led him into research on materials for disc records (see EDISON DIAMOND DISC). Aylsworth held, alone or jointly, 38 patents for audio-related inventions, the last of which was filed in June 1911. [Klinger*.]

AZIMUTH. In a tape recorder, the angle between the gap in the tape head and the longitudinal axis of the tape. It should be 90 degrees. *See also* GAP ALIGNMENT.

B

B & H FIBRE MANUFACTURING CO. A Chicago firm, established in 1907, located (1916) at 33 W. Kinzie St. The initials stood for Barry and Hall. B & H made bamboo **needles**, under a U.S. patent (#870,723) issued to **Frederick Durive Hall** on 12 Nov 1907. Reduced hiss was the selling point of bamboo, quick deterioration its problem. The claim, in *TMW* (September 1916), of "perfect tonal reproduction, reliability, and durability," was typical of the sales presentations for the product. Sometime before 1923 the company took the name of Hall Manufacturing Co., having become associated with the inventor. The president then was Lester C. Wiswell.

B SIDE. The reverse side of a double-sided disc, the side with the less featured material. It is also known as the flip side. *See also* A SIDE.

BABY. A one-minute disc made in Germany, sold in 1905 as Baby-Platten for one mark (two sides) and .75 mark (single side). It was distributed under the Baby name by the Compagnie Française du Gramophone in Paris, selling for one franc. The first repertoire consisted of marches, while later issues included waltzes and other instrumental modes. Baby discs, with a diameter of 12.5 centimeters., could be played on any gramophone without the need for extra gadgetry.

BABY GRAND GRAPHOPHONE. One of the first spring motor cylinder players, marketed in early 1895 by Columbia. It weighed 15 pounds and cost $75, or $100 with all accesso-

ries. [Chew 1981 (illus.).] *See also* GRAPHOPHONE.

BABY ODEON (label). A small disc (six inches in diameter) sold by Carl Lindström in London, in August 1914. It featured patriotic titles, played by the Band of the Grenadier Guards.

BABY TOURNAPHONE. A German disc player introduced in England in 1906. [Chew 1981 (illus.)]

BACCALONI, SALVATORE, 1900–1969. Italian basso, born in Rome on 4 Apr 1900. As a child he sang with the Sistine Chapel choir. In 1922 he made his operatic debut in Rome; he was at La Scala in 1926, and with the Chicago Civic Opera from 1930 to 1931. From 7 Dec 1940 (as Bartolo in *Nozze di Figaro*) to 14 Feb 1962 he sang with the Metropolitan Opera. His repertoire covered 150 roles, most of them basso buffo parts, but including Wotan in *Siegfried*. Among Baccaloni's greatest recordings were those made for Columbia from 1926 to 1932. These included two fine solos and a duet from *Elisir d'amore* (#CQ75; #CQX16451, later #71383D), and the role of Bartolo in the complete recording of *Barbiere di Siviglia* (#D14564–79). In 1936 he was Leporello in the outstanding recording of *Don Giovanni* made at the Glyndebourne Festival (Victor #VM 423–425). Baccaloni was heard as Alcindoro in complete recordings of *Boheme* made at La Scala (Columbia #D14515–14527) and at the Metropolitan (Columbia #OP27). He died in New York on 31 Dec 1969.

BACK COATING. The addition of a conductive material to the back of a **magnetic tape** to eliminate static buildup and improve winding characteristics.

BACK CUEING. A means of starting a disc so that the music begins exactly on cue. The stylus is placed at the point of the first recorded sound, then the disc is backed up slightly with the stylus left in the groove. The idea is for the first note to encounter the stylus as the turntable reaches proper speed. This technique is commonly used by disc jockeys. Experts are divided on the question of damage to cartridge or disc that may result from frequent back cueing, such as would take place at a radio station.

BACK TRACKING. The technique of composite recording in which a new live sound is combined with a previously recorded track (the backing track). In this process the performer listens through headphones to the backing track and adds a new solo part to it. The resulting composite track may be used as the backing track for other new parts.

BACKHAUS, WILHELM, 1884–1969. German pianist, born in Leipzig on 26 Mar 1884. He made his debut at the age of eight, and concertized for 70 years. As a recording artist, he spanned the formats from cylinder to stereo disc. His specialties were the works of Beethoven and Brahms (he had met Brahms and played for him in 1894; and he had heard him conduct the two concertos). He was the earliest famous pianist to make records, for G & T in 1908. Backhaus was the first pianist to record a composition by J.S. Bach, the "Prelude in C-Sharp Major" from *Wohltemperierte Klavier*; it was on an HMV issue of 1909. In January 1910 Backhaus, at age 26, made the earliest concerto recording; it was a part of the Grieg piano concerto, an abbreviated version of the first movement, filling two single-faced HMV discs. The orchestra was the New Symphony Orchestra, formed three years earlier by Thomas Beecham. It was conducted—in its recording debut—by Landon Ronald. Later Backhaus and the same orchestra recorded the entire concerto, under John Barbirolli, on HMV

#DB2074–06. Fred Gaisberg invited Backhaus to record many of the Brahms piano works during the mid-1930s for HMV; a CD reissue of that series appeared in 1990 (Pearl #GEMM CD 9385).

Backhaus died in Villach, Austria, on 5 July 1969.

Backing. *See* BASE.

Badische Anilin und Soda Fabrik. *See* BASF AG.

BAEZ, JOAN, 1941– . American popular and folk singer, born on 9 Jan 1941 in Staten Island, New York. She attracted attention at the Newport Folk Festival of 1959 and was signed to make records for Vanguard. Her first LP album, *Joan Baez* (Vanguard #2077; 1962) was a success, and her second, *Joan Baez in Concert* (Vanguard #VRS 9112; 1962) became her all-time best seller, on the charts 78 weeks. A year later *Joan Baez in Concert, Volume 2* (Vanguard #9113) was a chart album for 44 weeks. She appeared in Boston coffeehouses, then at the Gate of Horn in Chicago, singing protest songs against the Vietnam War as well as Latino material. Baez remained popular through the 1970s, making her last chart album in 1979, *Honest Lullaby* (Epic #JR 35766).

BAFFLE. A **loudspeaker** enclosure, or a rigid surface encircling the loudspeaker rim, or a board on which a speaker is mounted, intended to prevent interference between the sound waves created simultaneously on both sides of the speaker's diaphragm. *See also* BASS REFLEX BAFFLE; INFINITE BAFFLE.

BAGSHAW (W. H.) CO. A Massachusetts firm, established in Lowell in 1870; it became the earliest manufacturer of **needles** for disc talking machines. The firm may have made the needles used by Emile Berliner. In 1911 it claimed to be producing 6 million needles a day. One of the brand names was **Petmecky.**

BAILEY, MILDRED, 1907–1951. American vocalist, born in Tekoa, Washington, on 27 Feb 1907. At an early age she played piano in movie theatres, then performed on the radio in Los

Angeles. Through her brother, Al Rinker (Bing Crosby's first partner), she auditioned for Paul Whiteman and sang with his orchestra from 1929 to 1933. Her popular record of "Rockin' Chair" (Victor #24117; 1932) earned her the nickname of "Rockin' Chair Lady." Then she teamed with Red Norvo (indeed, she was married to him from 1933 to 1945) and did some of her best work with his swing band in 1936–1939. A good example of her style at that time is "I've Got My Love to Keep Me Warm" (Brunswick #7813; 1937). During 1939–1940 she sang with Benny Goodman; one of her best records with his band was "Darn That Dream" (Columbia #3533; 1940). Serious illness in the 1940s kept her mostly inactive until her death on 12 Dec 1951 in Poughkeepsie, New York. Columbia issued a three-disc LP album, *Her Greatest Performances* (#C3L22). *Rockin' Chair*, a VJC label compact disc, includes material made with Goodman, Teddy Wilson, and Roy Eldridge.

BAKER, ELSIE, 1886–1958. American contralto, born in Philadelphia, on 27 Sep 1886. She was "probably the most popular contralto who ever recorded for the Victor black and blue labels" (Walsh). Her "Silent Night" (Victor #19823; 1925) remained in the catalog into the 1940s. She also appeared on Red Seal, one popular number being "He Shall Feed His Flock" from *Messiah* (Victor #4026); and made Edison cylinders in 1913–1914. On U-S Everlasting cylinders she was identified as Elsie West Baker. She was Edna Brown on one Edison Blue Amberol and on one Indestructible cylinder. She died in New York on 28 Apr 1958. [Walsh 1950/10.]

BAKER, GEORGE, 1885– ?. British baritone, born in Birkenhead on 10 Feb 1885; also known as Arthur George. He began recording for Pathé in London, ca. 1910, and made records for one company or another for 50 years, primarily in the light concert and operetta repertoire, including HMV recordings of Gilbert and Sullivan.

BALANCE. The characteristic of a stereo sound system that describes the relative volume of playback signal emanating from the several loudspeakers.

BALANCE CONTROL. A device in a stereo sound system that adjusts the relative loudness of the channels to obtain an accurate reproduction of the input sound.

BALDWIN (label). (I) A record issued by the **Bridgeport Die and Machine Co.**, Bridgeport, Connecticut, ca. 1922, apparently sold in chain stores and/or by mail order; Paramount masters were used. [Rust 1978.]

BALDWIN (label). (II) A label available before 1942 in the U.S., named for the New York recording engineer who manufactured it; one known area of interest was Haitian music. There was a likely connection with the Varsity label. [Blacker 1981/7.]

BALDWIN PIANO CO. A firm established in Cincinnati as D. H. Baldwin & Co. in 1873 by Dwight Hamilton Baldwin (1821–1899) and his partner Lucien Wulsin (1845–1912). It became one of the great international piano makers, winner of numerous prizes at expositions. During the player-piano era, Baldwin was active and successful in the manufacture of players and **reproducing pianos.** Among the brands and models listed in a 1926 directory were the Manualo (winner of the Grand Prize at the London Exposition of 1914 as "the player-piano with the human touch"), which appeared as the Baldwin Manualo, Ellington Manualo, Hamilton Manualo, and Howard Manualo; the Monarch, the St. Regis, and the Modello.

Wulsin and George W. Armstrong, Jr. (1857–1932) bought the company in 1903, and Wulsin was president until his death in 1912. Armstrong was president from 1912 to 1926, succeeded by Lucien Wulsin, Jr., who held office until 1964. His son Lucien (b.1916), grandson of the co-founder, was chief executive after him. General offices were in Cincinnati, with other offices in Chicago, New York, St. Louis, Louisville (Kentucky), Indianapolis, Dallas, Denver, and San Francisco. In its various divisions Baldwin was producing 20,000 pianos and 15,000 player pianos annually in the mid-

1920s. In 1947 the firm introduced its electronic organ, and much diversification followed.

BALLARD, GEORGE WILTON, 1877–1950.

American concert tenor, born in Syracuse, New York, on 24 Nov 1877. He was also known as George Winton, on Indestructible records. He had a sweet, clear voice, well suited to his frequent church work. His first recordings were on U-S Everlasting cylinders between 1910 and 1913, beginning with "A Dream" (#1043). He started his 15-year association with Edison singing "Carissima" (two-minute cylinder #213). His most popular offering was "When the Twilight Comes to Kiss the Rose Goodnight" (Blue Amberol #2150). In December 1914 he went to Victor, singing "You're More than the World to Me" (Victor #17654). Ballard's voice seemed to record best on **vertical-cut discs**, so it was on Edison Diamond Discs that he achieved his greatest successes, during 1915–1922. In addition to his solo work, he was a member of the **Moonlight Trio** on Edison records. When he quit performing and recording he returned to his earlier work as a salesman in a jewelry store. Ballard died in Syracuse, New York, on 6 Apr 1950. [Walsh 1960/4.]

BALLEW, SMITH, 1902–1984.

American popular vocalist, active in 1929–1936, when he made records with numerous groups. He also had his own hotel band, with many distinguished artists among the personnel at one time or another. Ballew had a radio show in the mid-1930s, and appeared in motion pictures.

BAND.

Also known as a cut. The portion of the recorded surface of a disc that is separated from adjacent bands by a marker space or scroll. It usually contains one song, or one movement of a larger work.

Band music. *See* BIG BANDS; MILITARY BAND RECORDINGS.

BAND OF THE COLDSTREAM GUARDS.

One of the early recording military bands, with a series of excellent recordings for HMV from 1904 to 1935, including military music and arrangements like the "Mikado Selections"

(#2602). An LP reissue was marketed in 1986 by the International Military Band Society of Wellingborough, England (#IMMS 104).

BANDA ROSSA.

One of the earliest military bands to record, for Berliner. Among their 1895 offerings was "William Tell Overture" (#7y).

BANDWIDTH.

The characteristic of an **amplifier** or **receiver** that expresses its frequency range; for example, 20 Hz-20,000 Hz. It is stated for given output levels and distortion percentages.

BANJO RECORDINGS.

The five-string "American" banjo was the most popular instrument on early records; its acoustic qualities were well suited to the possibilities of recording equipment, and there were a number of outstanding artists available. The first banjo music to be heard was on Edison North American cylinders in 1889, performed by Will Lyle; "Banjo Jingles" was the earliest noted in the Edison "Musical Cylinder Accounts"—the date was 30 Sep 1889. Lyle performed in a total of nine sessions that year. W.S. Grinsted made Edison cylinders on 22 Oct 1891.

Columbia cylinders initiated their banjo catalog in ca. 1893, with the "Banjo King" **Vess Ossman** and two lesser known players named Cullen and Collins. Steph Clement made a seven-inch Berliner disc, "Mittoam Gallop," on 18 Oct 1896. Ossman made 11 records for **Bettini** in 1898. Ruby Brooks made Edison cylinders from before 1900 (e.g., "Belle of Columbia," #2636) until he died in 1906. **Fred Van Eps** was the star performer later on; he began with Edison in 1901 and recorded until 1922. Van Eps, Ossman, and F.J. Bacon were the artists listed in the Victor 1917 catalog, which carried 40 banjo titles. British banjoists included Alfred Cammeyer, Emile Grimshaw, Joe Morley, **Olly Oakley**, John Pidoux, and Charlie Rogers.

The first women to make banjo records were also British: Bessie and Rose Skinner, in 1903 for Zonophone in London. Helen Sealy was the first woman on HMV ("Kettledrums," #B648). Shirley Spaulding was the first American woman to make a banjo record: it was "Royal Tourist—March Novelette" (Edison

Diamond Disc #80625; 1921). The five-string banjo declined in popularity during the 1930s and 1940s. Jazz and ragtime groups were using a four-string tenor banjo, and only a few artists remained with the five-string instrument, notably Uncle Dave Macon and Grandpa Jones, and **Bill Monroe**'s Bluegrass Boys; **Pete Seeger** also used the banjo in some of his work after World War II.

Bluegrass music had a revival in the 1950s and 1960s, led by **Earl Scruggs** (one of the Bluegrass Boys) and **Lester Flatt**. A popular American television show, *Beverly Hillbillies*, premiered in 1962 with a bluegrass theme song played by Scruggs. Eddie Peabody made several hit LP albums on the Dot label in 1958. The Banjo Kings, John Cali (who had recorded for Grey Gull in the 1920s), Joe Maphis, and Jad Paul were among the other successful artists of the 1950s. Banjo music received another boost with the film *Bonnie and Clyde* (1966); it had a Grammy-winning bluegrass score by Charles Strouse. "Dueling Banjos," from the soundtrack to *Deliverance*, was a popular album in 1973 (Warner #7659).

BANNER (label). A record issued by the **Plaza Music Co.** beginning in 1922 with Paramount and Emerson reissues. Plaza produced its own masters by the end of 1922, and the label survived into the LP era under various corporate arrangements. Dance music and popular vocals were featured in the 1920s. Under parent company **American Record Corp.**, beginning in 1938, famous bands joined the roster (e.g., Vincent Lopez, Duke Ellington) and some notable artists from Brunswick (also taken over by American Record Corp.) appeared on Banner: Bing Crosby, the Mills Brothers, Guy Lombardo, and the Boswell Sisters. [*RR* (full matrix list appears beginning in July 1961); Rust 1978.]

BANTA, FRANK E., 1897–1969. American pianist, son of **Frank P. Banta**, born in New York. He was studio pianist for Victor, participating in all sorts of recordings as soloist, accompanist, and ensemble player. He was one of the **Eight Famous Victor Artists** and he played with the **Van Eps Trio**. Rust has noted two jazz solos by Banta: "Wild Cherry Rag" (Gennett

#4735; 1921), and "Sweet Man" (Victor #19839; 1925). [Rust 1969.]

BANTA, FRANK P., 1870–1903. American pianist, father of **Frank E. Banta**. He was accompanist for many record companies, assisting singers and other instrumentalists. His "Violets" seems to have been his first piano solo record on Edison wax cylinders (#8394; May 1903). A photo of Banta making a record in 1900, with violinist Charles D'Almaine, appears in Moogk 1975, p. 35, and in Hoover 1971, p. 75.

BAR AUTOMATICO. The name given to **phonograph parlors** in Italy, around the turn of the century. Customers could listen to cylinder recordings of opera or popular music for 10 centesimi.

BARBIROLLI, JOHN, *Sir*, **1899–1970.** English conductor and cellist, born Giovanni Battista Barbirolli (of French-Italian parents) in London, on 2 Dec 1899. He made his debut at age 12, playing the cello in Queen's Hall. After army service he toured with a quartet, then conducted the British National Opera (1926–1929) and Covent Garden Opera (1929–1933). In 1933 he became conductor of the Scottish Orchestra (Glasgow) and the Leeds Symphony. From 1937 to 1943 he was conductor of the New York Philharmonic, from 1943 to 1961 of the Hallé Orchestra, and from 1961 to 1968 of the Houston Symphony. He was knighted in 1949. His death came in London on 29 July 1970.

Barbirolli's first records (for Edison Bell) were as a child cellist, accompanied by his sister, and as a string quartet player. His recording career as a conductor, spanning 1911–1970, featured distinguished performances of Brahms, Bruckner, Mahler, Sibelius, and the British composers of his time. He also made a notable early record of the Grieg Piano Concerto with Wilhelm Backhaus and the New Symphony Orchestra (HMV #DB2074/76). [Kennedy 1973.]

BARDINI. A console record player made by **Sonora** Phonograph Co., selling for $5,000 in 1921.

BARENBOIM, DANIEL, 1942– . Pianist and conductor, born in Buenos Aires on 15 Nov 1942. His first public appearance was at age seven. His family moved to Israel in 1952. Barenboim studied at the Academy of Santa Cecilia in Rome, gaining a diploma in 1956. He gave recitals in Paris and London, then made his Carnegie Hall debut in 1957. He conducted many orchestras before being appointed director of the Orchestre de Paris in 1975. In 1989 he was selected to succeed George Solti as conductor of the Chicago Symphony Orchestra.

Barenboim's recording career began at age 13 with Philips. Between 1967 and 1970 he recorded the complete Beethoven piano sonatas for EMI, released on 14 Angel LPs (#S3755) and then all the Mozart piano concertos while conducting the English Chamber Orchestra from the keyboard. Angel LP album #3752 offered all the Beethoven concertos on four LPs with the New Philharmonia Orchestra. The recording of Brahms' three violin sonatas, with Itzhak Perlman, won a Grammy (Sony #SK-45819; 1990). And Barenboim's 1990 recording of the First Symphony by John Corigliano, with the Chicago Symphony (Erato #2292–45601–2), won a Grammy as best classical disc.

BARNET, CHARLIE, 1913–1991. American tenor saxophone player and Big Band leader, born 26 Oct 1913 in New York. After working with various bands across the U.S. he formed his own group in 1933, performing mostly in New York hotels. A second band, organized in 1936, featured the Modernaires, a vocal swing group. Another band, formed in 1938, was his best ensemble. It had fine arrangements by Billy May, one being Barnet's great hit "Cherokee" (Bluebird #10373). Lena Horne and Kay Starr were among his vocalists in the 1940s, when the band was at its peak, appearing in several motion pictures. With the decline of the Big Band era, Barnet became much less active. He died in San Diego, California, on 4 Sep 1991. Victor issued a two-volume LP set of his Bluebird recordings (*Charlie Barnet*, #LPV 551, LPV 567). Six compact disc reissues were available in 1992.

Barnett Samuel. *See* SAMUEL (BARNETT) AND SONS, LTD.

BARRAUD, FRANCIS, 1856–1924. English painter of French descent, famous in recording history for his rendition of **Nipper**, the Victor and Gramophone Co. trademark dog. He went into the Maiden Lane office of the Gramophone Co. in September 1899 to borrow a horn for use as a model, and there met William Barry Owen, managing director of the new firm. Owen asked him to paint a dog listening to a gramophone, similar to Barraud's earlier dog listening to an Edison cylinder phonograph. A month later Barraud returned with a palimpsest: he had erased the phonograph from his first painting and substituted the **Improved Gramophone.** Owen gave him £100 for it. (In the original work, which now hangs in the EMI board room, a ghostly image of the Edison machine can still be seen.) Berliner began to use the painting, and its name "His Master's Voice," in advertising in 1900, despite the fact that Nipper could not be hearing what he might have heard in the first version of the painting: home recording was possible on cylinders from the beginning, but not on discs until 1905. (Allen Koenigsberg has also noted that the machine's brake is in position, so its turntable could not be moving.) In 1924 Barraud painted a miniature of his masterwork for the Queen's doll house. It is curious that no record was made of Barraud's voice. [Koenigsberg*.]

BARRAUD, WILLIAM ANDREW, 1851–1937. Recording industry executive, brother of **Francis Barraud**; the trademark dog **Nipper** was also one of the family. He worked in South Africa as an explorer and miner, then returned to London in 1900. In 1908 he was active in the talking machine business in India and Britain as an agent of **Aldridge, Salmon & Co.** Barraud was the London representative for the German **Dacapo** record in 1910–1912. When Dacapo reorganized in 1912, he became an agent for another German label, **Invicta**, issued by the **Berolina Schallplatten GmbH**, trading under the name W. A. Barraud, Ltd. When disputes with Berolina resulted in the liquidation of his company, Barraud established (1913) the **Invicta Record Co., Ltd.** He went into semi-retirement ca. 1915, but Invicta remained in business until the late 1920s. [Andrews 1990.]

BARRIENTOS, MARIA, 1883–1946. Spanish coloratura soprano, born in Barcelona on 10 Mar 1884. She made her debut at age 15 in Barcelona, and then toured Europe. On 31 Jan 1916 she sang at the Metropolitan Opera, as Lucia, and remained with the company until 1920. Then she returned to Europe, where she made her last stage appearance in 1922. Barrientos was one of the first artists to record for **Fonotipia**, beginning with "Son vergine vezzosa" from *Puritani* (#39010; 1905?), a flawless ""Ah non giunge" from *Sonnambula* (#39011; 1905?), and 21 other numbers through 1906. In the 1906 Fonotipia catalog she had two outstanding renditions from *Fra diavolo*: "Or son sola" (#39538) and "Già per la danza" (#39539), both of which were later issued by IRCC. For Columbia she made 34 discs, the first being the *Lucia* Mad Scene (#48627; 1916) and the last Handel's "Sweet Bird" (49805; 1920). In 1927–1928 she made eight discs for French Columbia, all of them Spanish songs. Her death came in Ciboure, France, on 8 Aug 1946.

BARTÓK, BÉLA, 1881–1945. Hungarian composer and scholar of folksong, born in Nagyszentmiklós on 25 Mar 1881. He began writing down peasant songs in 1904, and two years later issued *Magyar népdalok* in collaboration with Zoltán Kodály, a collection of songs arranged for voice and piano. His work is of interest in the history of sound recording because his later field studies (from 1906) involved an Edison phonograph, which he took to various regions in present-day Hungary, Czechoslovakia, and Romania. This was the earliest use of the phonograph for field recordings on the continent, contemporary with Percy Grainger's work in Britain. Bartók donated about 1,000 cylinders to the Ethnographic Museum in Budapest. As a pianist, Bartók recorded a number of his own works, and also made a notable disc of the Beethoven "Kreutzer" sonata and the Debussy Violin Sonata with Joseph Szigeti (Vanguard #304–05E, 2 LPs). He wrote *Contrasts* on commission from Benny Goodman, and recorded it with Goodman and Joseph Szigeti (1939). *See also* FIELD RECORDINGS.

BASE. Also known as backing. The material of which a **magnetic tape** is made; that is, the carrier of the magnetizable coating that holds the pattern representing the signal. Acetate (lacquer) and polyester bases have predominated, with a thickness of 1/2 mil, 1 mil, or 1 1/2 mil. Tapes of greater thickness are less liable to **print-through**.

BASEBALL RECORDINGS. The rise of the phonograph coincided with the emergence of professional baseball as the American national pastime. Many recordings about the game, in song and story, appeared on early Edison, Columbia, and Victor labels. The earliest known is "Slide, Kelly, Slide" by George J. Gaskin, on a North American brown wax cylinder (#146; 1893). Cal Stewart did some Uncle Josh episodes involving baseball on Edison from 1897, and later many more for Columbia cylinders and Victor discs. Other noted artists were also heard on the two-minute wax Edison cylinders up to 1909 (among them Edward M. Favor; Arthur Collins; and accordionist John J. Kimmel, playing "The Fans' March," #10172).

The perennial hit "Take Me Out to the Ball Game" was recorded first by the Hayden Quartet (Victor #5510; 1908) and Edward Meeker (Edison #9926; 1908). "Casey at the Bat" first appeared in 1906 (Victor #31559), read by William De Wolf Hopper—it remained in the catalog until the late 1920s. "Cubs on Parade" seems to have been the first song with the name of a specific team (Zonophone #1099; 1908). Babe Ruth was the first player to be honored by a phonograph record, and to speak on it: "Babe Ruth's Home Run Story" (Perfect #022443; 1920). But the most catchy of the player tunes was "Joltin' Joe DiMaggio" (recorded by Les Brown on Okeh #6377; 1941).

The Baseball Hall of Fame in Cooperstown, New York, has thousands of taped interviews with baseball players, and many novelty items, including songs by a quartet of professional baseball players. In 1982 a series of records named "Talkin' Baseball" was released on the Lifesong label; it included separate discs about each major league club except two. [Walsh 1971/12; 1972/7.]

BASF AG. A German firm, located in Ludwigshafen. It is one of the world's largest chemical manufacturers, with 136,000 employees and sales of 47 billion marks (1989). Among its many products are audio and video tapes.

The firm was founded in 1861 as the Badische Anilin und Soda Fabrik. It was successful in producing synthetic dyes, and diversified into various petrochemical products. Experiments with **magnetic tape** in the 1930s led to the cellulose acetate tape, coated with ferric oxide, used in the **Magnetophon.** Easy breakage and brittleness with age were its defects. In 1976 the firm introduced the Unisette cassette, with tape a quarter of an inch wide; it was similar to the **Elcaset.**

Basic amplifier. *See* POWER AMPLIFIER.

BASIE, COUNT, 1904–1984. American jazz pianist and Big Band leader, born William Basie in Red Bank, New Jersey, on 21 Aug 1904. His early experience included vaudeville and performing on a theatre organ in Kansas City. He played with Bennie Moten's band from 1932, and made his first records when Moten died in 1935 and Basie took over direction of the group. He came to prominence in Kansas City after forming a band of his own in 1935; it included drummer Jo Jones and tenor saxophonist Lester Young. Basie signed a Decca contract, moving in 1939 to Vocalion and other companies. His international hit records included "One O'Clock Jump" (Decca #1363; 1937), "Jumpin' at the Woodside" (Decca #2212; 1938), and "Taxi War Dance" (Vocalion #4748; 1939). His uncluttered, energetic improvisations influenced the **cool jazz** pianists of the 1950s.

Basie's popularity spanned a half century. He won Grammy awards for records made in 1958 and 1960 for the Roulette label and in 1963 for a Reprise album. He was recognized again in 1976, 1977, 1980, and 1982 with Grammys for solo and band releases on the Pablo label. He and Ella Fitzgerald won a Grammy in 1980 for their Pablo album *A Perfect Match.* A posthumous Grammy was awarded in 1984. In 1960 and 1961 his band won the *Down Beat* polls.

An important LP reissue, *The Complete Count Basie* (CBS #66101; 1981), covered his

Vocalion and Okeh material to September 1941. A pair of CDs from Bellaphon (#625–50–005 / 010; 1991) document performances of 1936–1958.

BASS. A **loudspeaker** of special capability for reproduction of bass sounds, usually in the range of 20 Hz to ca. 500 Hz; a "woofer."

BASS REFLEX BAFFLE. Also known as a ported or vented baffle. A type of **loudspeaker** enclosure (*see* BAFFLE) in which an auxiliary opening or port serves to release the rear sound waves of the speaker so that they are in phase with the front waves. It extends the low-frequency range of the speaker and smooths its **frequency response.**

BASS TRAP. An acoustical device used in **multitrack recording** to minimize the reflection of sound from one instrument to the microphone of an adjacent instrument. It is built into the floor beneath each performer, and by means of its absorbent surface it draws much of the sound down into its interior, which is filled with spaced fiberglass panels. The same principle can be applied to walls and ceilings to avoid reflected signals.

BASTIANINI, ETTORE, 1922–1967. Italian baritone, born 24 Sep 1922 in Siena. His debut was as a bass, in Ravenna, in 1945. He was with the Metropolitan Opera from 15 Dec 1953 (debut as Germont) to 1965. Verdi roles were his special strengths: he was heard in the complete recordings of *Ballo in maschera* (DGG #38680–82), *Forza del destino* (Decca #LXT 5131–34), *Rigoletto* (Mercury #436–38), and *Traviata* (DGG #138832–34). He was also a distinguished Figaro in *Barbiere di Siviglia* (Decca #LXT 5283–85). Bastianini died in Sirmione, Italy, on 25 Jan 1967.

BATCHELOR, CHARLES, 1845–1910. British / American inventor, born in Dalston, near London, on 21 Dec 1845. He went to the U.S. around 1870 as a representative of J.P. Coates, the Manchester thread manufacturer. He decided to remain in America, working for Thomas Edison from 1871 as a machinist and laboratory associate. He and Edison worked closely in telegraphy experiments during 1874–1875, then in developing the "electric pen" (mimeograph machine). The Edison establishment at Menlo Park, New Jersey, was planned by Batchelor and Edison, and he became the "keeper of notes and designer of prototypes" there. In 1877 the first project was the telephone, which was greatly improved beyond the stage reached by Alexander Graham Bell—the Menlo Park work made the modern Bell System possible, and created the mode for long distance calling.

Batchelor's connection with the phonograph began with the first working model; he and **John Kruesi** made it together on Edison's plan in November 1877. Probably Batchelor was responsible for "constructing the phonets [reproducer] and provided the mechanisms for the fine adjustments necessary for successful operation."

Later he and Edison made thousands of experiments with filaments and carbonization methods to perfect the incandescent lamp—succeeding finally in October 1879. Batchelor extended the electrical work to the design of dynamos for the Pearl Street power station in New York, where operations began in May 1882. At the same time he planned the Edison exhibit for the Paris Electrical Exposition of 1881, displaying a complete lighting system that won the highest awards. Remaining most of four years in Europe, he organized electrical installations in France and elsewhere.

The great Edison establishment in Schenectady, New York, was built by Kruesi and Batchelor. In 1889, when the Edison interests were sold and a new firm, Edison General Electric Co., was formed, Batchelor was named to the board of directors. He was able to work on a small scale as well, inventing the **talking doll** in 1888; this was based on a tiny phonograph with an automatic return motion (U.S. patent #400,629; filed 30 Oct 1888, granted 2 Apr 1889). The **Edison Toy Phonograph Co.** was formed, and by February 1889 425 dolls had been shipped to New York City for sale.

Batchelor produced artificial sapphire for use in recording styli, and filed a patent application for it in May 1890. It was this sapphire that was used by Eldridge Johnson in making disc masters and that remained in use through the LP era for cutting lacquer masters. After 1890 he spent little time on the phonograph or other key inventions, having been detoured by Edison into iron ore research, one of the master's less inspired projects. He did develop a "belt-type ore concentrator" in late 1889, but this area of experiment proved unsatisfying and exhausting. The ore business failed, and the effort was converted in time to the production of Portland cement. Batchelor left regular employment with Edison in 1893, and after 1899 he devoted himself to travel with his family. He died on 1 Jan 1910 in New York. He is regarded as "next to Edison . . . the second man in the phonograph development." [Welch 1972, from which the above quotes are taken.]

BATTELLE MEMORIAL INSTITUTE. A research and development firm located in Columbus, Ohio, said to be the world's largest nonprofit scientific institute. Xerography was developed there, and titanium for aerospace applications. In audio history Battelle is noted for participation in wire recorder development during World War II. The organization now employs more than 5,000 staff, and has research establishments in the state of Washington, Geneva, Switzerland, and Frankfurt, Germany.

BATTEN, JOE, 1885–1956. British pianist and record producer, with 50 years of service in at least 30 companies. His first work in recording was as a piano accompanist for Musiphone, a cylinder maker. He was a producer with Edison Bell from 1920 to 1927, then with Columbia Graphophone. As a ragtime pianist he recorded under the name Joe Bolton. His autobiography, *Joe Batten's Book,* carries interesting anecdotes about the pioneer days of the industry in Britain.

BATTISTINI, MATTIA, 1856–1928. "The most wonderful baritone of our Golden Age" (Hurst, p. 115), born in Rome on 27 Feb 1856. His debut was at the Teatro Argentina in Rome on 11 Dec 1878 in *Favorita*. In 1883 he was at Covent Garden, and from 1888 at La Scala; he then sang throughout the world except for North America. In a Covent Garden *Traviata* of 1905, his Germont "was of overwhelming splendour, actually overshadowing Melba and Caruso" (Hurst). Praise for his singing was universal: Richard Wagner said he was the greatest Wolfram; Verdi named him perfect in *Ernani* and *Ballo in maschera*, and wrote the role of Falstaff for him (though Battistini declined the honor, claiming he could not sing clownish parts). He gave up opera in 1924, but concertized to 1927. He died of emphysema on 7 Nov 1928 in Collebaccaro, Italy, just as he was preparing a return to opera.

Between December 1902 and February 1924, Battistini recorded for HMV, making 120 discs; he also made two for Fonografia Nazionale, Zurich. Of the 1902 recordings, made in Warsaw, the most notable is "O tu bel astro" ("Evening Star") from *Tannhäuser* (#52664). Most of these first recordings were below the artist's standard and made with technical carelessness. The 1906 group of discs—issued with an orange label at 15 shillings—are far superior. They were recorded in Milan with the La Scala Orchestra and Chorus. Among the best were "O dei verd'anni" from *Ernani* (HMV #052141), "Il mio Lionel" from *Martha* (#052143), "Perchè tremar" from *Zampa* (#052148), and "Eri tu" from *Ballo in maschera* (#052146). In June 1911, also in Milan, Battistini sang *Traviata* and *Tannhäuser*, as well as the new verismo repertoire. In his later sessions signs of vocal deterioration were evident, but there were gems also, such as "Ai miei rivali cedere" from *Ruy blas* by Marchetti (Victor #88650; 1921). His last records were made in February 1924, when he was already suffering from emphysema. Seraphim issued a set of seven LPs in 1986, remastered at the original speeds. [Dennis 1953/11; Hurst 1963; Moran 1977/7; Phillips 1947; Stroff 1987/1.]

BAUR, FRANKLIN, 1904–1950. Popular American tenor, born in Brooklyn; his first name is sometimes spelled "Franklyn." He was one of the most acclaimed recording artists of the 1920s, recording for Victor from March 1924 to March 1929, with an interval of freelancing. In addition to solo work, he sang many duets with Gladys Rice and was one of the Shannon Four (later the Revelers). Baur sang in the *Ziegfeld Follies* of 1927 and 1928, and was the original "Voice of Firestone" on the radio program of that name from 1929 to 1931. A typical disc was "When Day Is Done" (Victor #38795–3; 1927). Baur died in Brooklyn on 24 Feb 1950.

BAY (H.C.) CO. An American piano manufacturer established in 1909. Maker of the H.C. Bay reproducing grand piano action, and an upright action, used in many brands of inexpensive pianos. The apparatus would slide under the keyboard when not in use. In a 1926 directory the address was given as 832–834 Republic Bldg., Chicago, with a factory in Bluffton, Indiana. The president then was Harry C. Bay. The firm made as many as 4,000 **reproducing pianos**, 8,000 grands, and 18,000 upright and player pianos annually.

BBC. *See* BRITISH BROADCASTING CORP. (BBC).

BEACH BOYS. A rock group formed in California in 1961. The members were Brian Wilson, pianist and bass guitarist; Dennis Wilson, drummer; Carl Wilson, guitarist; Mike Love, drummer; and Alan Jardine, guitarist. All the instrumentalists were vocalists as well. The Wilsons were brothers. There were various other musicians with the group from time to time. "Surf music" was the principal style of the Beach Boys, a genre devoted to celebration of youth, surfing, and California. Brian Wilson (himself a non-swimmer and non-surfer) was the principal songwriter and arranger for the group, which remained popular for 20 years, and returned for new popularity in 1988 with a hit, "Kokomo."

Distinctive singles by the Beach Boys were numerous, beginning with "Surfin'" (Candix #331; 1962) and including "Surfer Girl" (Capitol #5009; 1963), "I Get Around" (Capitol #5174; 1964), "Help Me, Rhonda" (Capitol #5395; 1965), and the complexly orchestrated "Good Vibrations" (Capitol #5676; 1966). There were 47 chart singles. Of 41 albums on the charts, the most enduring was *Endless Summer*, (Capitol #SVBB 11307; 1975), which was listed for 104 weeks. The album *Pet Sounds* (Capitol #T2458; 1966) was said to have inspired some of the techniques used in the Beatles' *Sgt. Pepper's Lonely Hearts Club Band* album. After 12 years without a hit record, the Beach Boys scored with "Kokomo," which reached the top of the charts in November 1988. Total sales of Beach Boy albums are said to have reached 200 million. Capitol has released most of their early output on more than 40 CDs, along with material from the 1980s.

BEATLES. British rock group from Liverpool, England, enormously popular worldwide from 1963 to 1970. George Harrison, lead guitar, John Lennon, rhythm guitar, and **Paul McCartney**, bass guitar, formed the group in 1957 with various other temporary members. Drummer Ringo Starr (real name Richard Starkey) joined in 1962, replacing Peter Best. Early influences on the Beatles included skiffle music, which was popular in Britain in the 1950s, characterized by a strong beat and the use of common, everyday items as makeshift instruments. Other influences included American rhythm & blues, rock and roll, and jazz, particularly music that originated in Chicago. They played in Hamburg, Germany, from 1960 to 1963 at clubs in the Reeperbahn area. It was in Hamburg in 1961 that they made their first recording, credited as "The Beat Brothers." They backed singer Tony Sheridan on the German record label Polydor, recording "My Bonnie" (Polydor #24 673), with "The Saints" on the B side. It was produced by Bert Kaempfert. During this period they also performed in Liverpool at the Cavern, a jazz club turned rock and roll club that was located in a converted underground warehouse.

Brian Epstein, manager of a Liverpool record shop, was prompted to see them perform after a customer requested "My Bonnie" in 1962. He offered to manage them, and arranged an audition for Decca records, which turned them down. They eventually passed an audition for Parlophone. With the assistance of their producer George Martin, they made recordings that were innovative and fresh, often trying techniques never before attempted. In later years, the Beatles produced their own recordings with Martin's assistance. Their music reflected influences from a myriad of genres—classical, country & western, jazz, reggae, blues, and East Indian music. They recorded most of their later material at the Abbey Road Studios in London.

A unique talent of the group was their songwriting ability. Lennon and McCartney wrote most of the group's material, jointly writing 23 number-one songs. Their 1965 song "Yesterday" (Capitol #5498, now #A-6291) featured a string quartet. It has been recorded by many other artists, in at least 1,186 versions. Harrison and Starr also wrote Beatles material.

After the group stopped touring in 1966, they devoted more time to recording and experimenting with new techniques. In 1967, they released the critically acclaimed album *Sgt. Pepper's Lonely Hearts Club Band* (Parlophone #PMC 7027 mono / #PCS 7027 stereo; Capitol #MAS-2653 mono / #SMAS-2653 stereo). It was recorded onto four-track tape with overdubs of sound effects and animal sounds, and experimentation with tape speeds. Brass instruments and an entire orchestra were also employed for some pieces. The Beatles broke up in 1970, but all four pursued successful solo careers that included writing original material and live performances. The Beatles were the most successful recording artists in history, with sales estimated at over a billion discs and tapes. [Castleman 1976; Goddard 1989; McCoy 1990.

Felicia Reilly

BEBOP. Also known as bop. A form of "hot jazz" that was prevalent in the U.S. from the end of World War II to about 1958, as successor to swing. The name was derived from a two-note motive that was typically played to terminate a phrase: a be-bop figure. In contrast to the Big Bands that played swing music, bebop was usually played by small combos—though a few large groups like those of Dizzy Gillespie and Woody Herman did join in later—made up of soloists with rhythm sections. In the standard form, the combo played 12–measure blues or 32–measure popular songs, with the theme announced by the ensemble, followed by a solo, and the return of the group. Improvisations followed chord progressions but often they extended diatonic practice by means of chromatic alterations or substitutions. The rhythmic beat departed from the square swing accompaniment and added its own free patterns.

Among the artists associated with the origin of bebop are pianist **Thelonious Monk**, trumpeter **Dizzy Gillespie**, and alto saxophonist **Charlie Parker**. Because of a ban on all recordings enacted by the **American Federation of Musicians** (AFM), effective 1 Aug 1942, much of the pioneering work in bebop went undocumented. However, some private recordings were made at jam sessions, and a few have been issued commercially: Archive of Folk Music #FS-219 includes Gillespie's "Stardust" and "Kerouac" of 1941; Xanadu #107 has Monk's solo in "Sweet Lorraine"; Onyx #221 and Spotlite #120 have Parker's 1942 version of "Cherokee." With the lifting of the ban on 11 Nov 1944 record companies were free to take on bebop, and eventually they did so. It was the small label Guild that signed Dizzy Gillespie to an exclusive contract. Blue Note and Dial were two other labels that made commitments to bebop. During the 1950s bebop's moderate aspects assumed prominence over its "hot" manner, and it gave rise to **cool jazz**. The other trend of the period saw rhythm & blues turning into rock. [De Veaux 1988.]

BECHET, SIDNEY, 1897–1959. American jazz clarinetist and saxophonist, born in New Orleans on 14 May 1897. At age six he was playing in the honky-tonks of Storyville in New Orleans. He moved to Chicago in 1917, and to New York in 1919; he led his own band and performed also with Noble Sissle, Duke Ellington, and others. After 1919 he spent much of his time playing in Europe, finally settling in France in 1947. He died in Garches, France, on 14 May 1959.

Bechet's first published record dates from 1923, as he and the King Bechet Trio accompanied singer Rosetta Crawford on Okeh #8096. His first-ever records were made in London in the early 1920s for Columbia, with Benny Peyton's Jazz Kings ("High Society" and "Tiger Rag"); they were never issued. Between 1923 and 1925 he made many discs with various groups. On 30 May 1924 he and an unidentified pianist accompanied singer Maureen Englin on "Foolin' Me" (Pathé Actuelle #032056). His first principal recordings were made 15 Sep 1932 for Victor in New York, with his New Orleans Feetwarmers; they included "Maple Leaf Rag" (#23360 and many reissues). Among later popular items were "One O'Clock Jump" (Victor #27204; 1940) and "Nobody Knows the Way I Feel Dis Mornin'" on which he plays both clarinet and soprano saxophone (Victor #26663; 1940); both had several reissues. A remarkable "Sheik of Araby" made on 18 Apr 1941 (Victor #27485, many reissues) had Bechet as a one-man band; he "overdubbed" himself playing clarinet, soprano sax, tenor sax, piano, bass, and drums—the first such effort on a jazz record, and long preceding the overdub technique employing multitrack tape. Another famous record is "Les oignons," done for the Vogue (French) label in 1949. LP and CD reissues cover the 1924–1928 period (BBC CD #700, LP #REB700; 1989), and the 1932–1941 period (RCA LP #AXM2–5516, and RCA CD #ND 86590; 1976).[Mauerer 1970.]

BEECHAM, THOMAS, *Sir*, **1879–1961.** British conductor, born in St. Helens, on 29 Apr 1879, into a wealthy family. At age 20 he conducted the Hallé Orchestra; in 1906 he established the New Symphony Orchestra and led it until 1908. From 1910 to 1913 he was impresario of Covent Garden; in 1916 he conducted concerts of the Royal Philharmonic Society. Beecham's American debut was with the New York Philharmonic in 1928. He organized another orchestra, the London Philharmonic, in 1932. During World War II he took the post of conductor of the Seattle Symphony Orchestra. He founded yet another orchestra, the Royal Philharmonic, in 1946. Among his many honors was a knighthood (1916) and the issue of a commemorative stamp for his (approximate) birth centennial on 1 Sep 1980. He died in London on 8 Mar 1961.

Beecham's conducting was most notable in works of Delius, Handel, Mozart, Schubert, Sibelius, and Richard Strauss; his best recordings are of those composers. He began to make discs for the Gramophone Co. in London in 1910, then for Odeon ca. 1912. Mozart overtures were among his 1915–1917 releases by Columbia, including *Zauberflöte* (#6559–60) and *Nozze di Figaro* (#6908). However, his acoustic records were in general inferior to the later electrics, made for Columbia in Britain, in 1926–1932. Several Delius works were recorded, beginning with *Brigg Fair* in 1928 (#4335–5). He directed the first complete *Messiah* recording from June to October 1927 (discs issued separately and in album DX 630/637). He conducted for the Delius Society during 1934–1938; he made a popular record of his own arrangement from Handel, *The Faithful Shepherd: Suite* (Columbia #LX 915/917; 1940), and other Handel numbers in the 1930s. His Mozart symphonies were issued from 1933 to 1940. The Sibelius Society set included Beecham with Jascha Heifetz in the Violin Concerto (Victor #14016/19, album #M-309; 1935), still regarded as the definitive performance, as well as *Finlandia*, the fourth symphony, and *Kuolema*.

Beecham was one of the Britons who did not develop an early distaste for Nazism; in 1937 he was in Berlin to record the complete *Zauberflöte* for HMV (#DB3465/83 and #8475/93). With Tiana Lemnitz, Erna Berger, and Gerhard Hüsch, it remains one of the outstanding versions of the opera on record. He continued to record, for Columbia and then EMI, after World War II, producing fine releases of his favorite composers, directing "his" London orchestras as well as leading orchestras of the U.S. His final issue was the Prelude to *Meistersinger*, made in a London concert on 4 Nov 1959 (HMV #ALP-2003). CD reissues of Delius works appeared from the Beecham Memorial Trust in 1989; and EMI has transferred to CD most of the Beecham legacy from 78s and LPs. [*Gramophone*, July 1990, p. 195 (CD listing); Beecham Society 1975, Gray 1979, Lewis 1980 (for earlier discographies).]

BÉGUÉ, BERNARD. French baritone, singer of minor roles at the Paris Opéra and later at the Metropolitan Opera. He made 10 cylinders for Columbia in 1898, among the first recordings of operatic arias (from *Carmen, Rigoletto, Huguenots, William Tell*, and *L'africaine*); other early arias on record were recorded for **Bettini** and Edison cylinders (*see* OPERA RECORDINGS). Bégué's Edison records included arias from *Charles VI* (Halévy; #7256), *L'africaine* (#7372) and *William Tell* (#7424) in 1899. Other labels he worked for were Berliner and Zonophone.

BEIDERBECKE, BIX, 1903–1931. American jazz cornetist and pianist, born Leon Bismarck Beiderbecke in Davenport, Iowa, on 10 Mar 1903. He played with various groups in Chicago and St. Louis, then joined the Paul Whiteman band in 1927; he left Whiteman because of ill health in 1929. He died on 6 Aug 1931 in New York. The earliest record by Beiderbecke was "Fidgety Feet" with the Wolverines Orchestra (Gennett #5408; 18 Feb 1924). He began recording with "Bix and His Rhythm Jugglers"—a small group that included Tommy Dorsey—in January 1925, beginning with "Toddlin' Blues" (Gennett #5654). His final recording with his own orchestra—including Bud Freeman, the Dorsey brothers, Benny Goodman, Gene Krupa, and Joe Venuti—was made on 8 Sep 1930 for Victor. Beiderbecke was last heard on disc performing with Hoagy Carmichael's Orchestra, in a Victor session of 15 Sep 1930. Among his other notable recordings: "Singin' the Blues" with the Frankie Trumbauer band (Okeh #40772; 1927), and "In a Mist"—his own composition, which he played on piano (Okeh #40916; 1927). Columbia, Victor, and Riverside issued LP collections of his discs. Columbia has released two CDs of Beiderbecke performances.

BEKA RECORD GmbH. A company formed at 105–106 Alexandrinen Strasse, Berlin, in October 1904. It was founded by the Bumb and König's Institute for Modern Inventions, which had been set up in 1903 by Heinrich Bumb and a partner named König; it is supposed that the firm's name emerged from their initials. Beka made double-sided discs in 1904, among the earliest to be marketed in Europe. Label names were Beka, Beka Grand Record, Beka Ideal, Beka Meister Record, Beka Saphir Record, and Beka Sinfonie Record, in seven-inch, eight-inch, 10-inch, 11-inch, and 12-inch sizes. In 1906 Beka was selling seven-inch discs in Britain for only one shilling, forcing a price war with Zonophone. By 1907 the company was offering an international disc catalog of 224 pages, including items in Arabic and Asian languages. This catholicity resulted from a remarkable voyage made by Bumb in 1905–1906 to record local genres; he visited Eastern Europe, Egypt, India, Burma, Java, China, and Japan. Vocal recordings were dominant, but the singers were not of great distinction; an exception was Zélie de Lussan, who did four items in 1906. Although a special recording ensemble, the Meister Orchester, was established in 1911, the instrumental repertoire was not exploited. Beka records had a grotesque trademark evidently patterned on **Nipper**, showing a flamingo listening to a gramophone horn. There was overlapping in the output of Beka, **Scala**, and **Coliseum** labels; in some cases an identical singer appeared on more than one of them, using different names. The company also made gramophones, with tapered tone arms; a reprint of their 1911/1912 equipment catalog is found in *TMR* #50 (1978). Other addresses noted for the firm, in Berlin, were Heidelberger Strasse 75–76, and Bouché-Strasse 35–36. The name shown in the 1911/1912 equipment catalog was Beka Record Actien-Gesellschaft, which the firm took in 1910. After 1916 the company was acquired by the **Carl Lindström** group. [Andrews*; *TMR* 50 (1978); Want 1976.]

BEL CANTO (label). A disc of the Bel Canto Record GmbH, Berlin, established in August 1909. Some of the material was British and some was from **Dacapo** recordings. The London agent was of **John G. Murdoch and Co., Ltd.**, who also did recording for Bel Canto in studios on Farringdon St. [Andrews 1990.]

BELAFONTE, HARRY, 1927– . American popular and folk singer, born Harold George Belafonte, Jr., in New York on 1 Mar 1927. He lived with his family in Jamaica from 1935 to 1940, absorbing the **calypso** style that he later helped to make famous in the U.S. After U.S. Navy service in World War II he appeared as a pop singer in Broadway clubs and then nationally. Belafonte achieved success as a folksinger, at New York's Village Vanguard and elsewhere. He secured a Victor recording contract in 1952, and appeared on the *Ed Sullivan Show* and other television programs. Belafonte had 20 chart albums. His most important recordings were calypso songs he put to disc in 1956–1957, including "Jamaica Farewell" (Victor #6663; 1956), "Day-O (Banana Boat Song)"

(Victor 6771; 1957), and the 1956 Victor album *Calypso* (#LPM 1248), which was on the charts 58 weeks. Belafonte won Grammys for two RCA Victor albums, *Swing dat Hammer* (# LSP 2194; 1960) and *Belafonte Folk Singers* (1961). *An Evening with Belafonte/Makeba* (Victor #LP)M 3420; 1965), was another Grammy album.

BELL, ALEXANDER GRAHAM, 1847–1922. Scottish/American inventor most famous for his development of the telephone, but one who was also active in early sound recording. He was born in Edinburgh, the son of Alexander Melville Bell, a specialist in vocal physiology. From 1868 to 1870 he worked with his father in London, and studied anatomy and physiology at University College, developing a keen interest in education of the deaf. When his family moved to Canada in 1870, Bell went on to Boston where he taught teachers of the deaf. During 1873–1876 he experimented with the **phonautograph** and the telegraph, developing the theory of the "speaking telegraph" or telephone in 1874. In 1876 he transmitted the first intelligible telephonic message. In 1877 he organized the Bell Telephone Co. to produce and market the telephone, and after considerable patent litigation his rights to the invention were upheld by the U.S. Supreme Court.

Bell married Mabel G. Hubbard in 1877, a woman who had been deaf from childhood, and settled in Washington, D.C., taking U.S. citizenship in 1882. He gave some ideas, as well as financial support, to his cousin **Chichester Bell**, who worked with **Charles Sumner Tainter** on the **graphophone** cylinder player. His own voice was presumably used to make one of the first wax cylinder recordings, in 1881. (Sealed in the Smithsonian in 1881, this recording was supposedly played in public for the first time in 1937, but clear documentation is lacking for the event.) Bell (or, as some have said, Tainter) was then heard to say, "There are more things in heaven and earth, Horatio, than are dreamed of in your philosophy. I am a graphophone, and my mother was a phonograph." Bell also invented the **Photophone** system of recording by light rays, and experimented with **binaural** sound.

He had set up a laboratory in Washington in 1879, with Tainter employed as engineer; in

1881 he established the **Volta Laboratory**.

From 1896 to 1904 Bell was president of the National Geographic Society. After 1897 he turned to aviation research and experimentation. He died in Nova Scotia. [Ford 1962.]

BELL, CHICHESTER A., 1848–1924. Cousin of **Alexander Graham Bell**, and also a prominent inventor. In the **Volta Laboratory** in Washington, D.C., he and **Charles Sumner Tainter** worked in the early 1880s on improvements in cylinder recording and on transmitting sound through light (the **Photophone**). In place of tinfoil coating on cylinders, they used beeswax, and they applied the same surface to cardboard discs. Another area of novel experimentation may have been in **magnetic recording.** They made both **lateral** recordings and **vertical-cut discs,** and they approached the problem of angular versus linear velocity in disc players. The landmark product of their association was the **graphophone**, U.S. patent #341,214, filed 27 June 1885, issued 4 May 1886: a wax-covered cylinder device (though cylinder is not mentioned in the application, nor the word graphophone), for "recording and reproducing speech and other sounds," primarily a dictating machine. This patent was the center of legal controversy in the industry for many years. The Edison Speaking Phonograph Co. refused to buy the patent, so it remained with Volta, and later **American Graphophone Co.,** until the patent expired in 1903. Edison had to be licensed to use the wax-cutting method of recording. Related patents by Bell and Tainter were U.S. #341,288 (filed 4 Dec 1885, granted 4 May 1886), which featured the wax-covered stiff paper cylinder; and U.S. #375,579 (filed 7 July 1887, granted 27 Dec 1887), which presented a foot-treadle operation, and wax-coated cardboard cylinders with finer threading and faster rotation than was found in earlier patents. The mineral wax compound ozocerite was introduced in U.S. patent #374,133 (filed 27 Apr 1887; granted 29 Nov 1887).

Chichester Bell left Volta in 1885 to work in Europe. [Koenigsberg 1990.]

BELL (label). (I) A disc issued by the Standard Music Roll Co., Orange, New Jersey, from ca.

1920 to 1923, and then by the Bell Record Corp., Newark, New Jersey, to July 1928. Records were made for the W. T. Grant department store chain, which sold them at $.10 each. Bell was a subsidiary label to **Arto** until that firm went bankrupt in 1923. After that, W. T. Grant acquired pressings from Emerson, and some from Gennett; Plaza was a later source. Content of the records was primarily dance numbers, with some jazz and blues. Among the artists were Arthur Hall, Franklin Baur, and Charles Harrison. [Barr 1983; Rust 1978.]

BELL (label).(II) A children's record, styled "The Bell," issued by **J. E. Hough** in London during the mid-1920s.

Bell Laboratories. *See* BELL TELEPHONE LABORATORIES.

BELL RECORDING LABORATORIES. A subsidiary of the National Metals Depositing Corp. with offices at 34 E. Sidney Ave., Mount Vernon, New York, and laboratories at 415 Fourth Ave., New York. It advertised monthly in *TMW* from January 1922, offering to make masters, mothers, and stampers from the wax originals supplied by clients. In July 1922 advertising emanated from the Bell Recording Corp. C.R. Johnston, formerly a recording expert in Britain (1888–1889) and then with the Aeolian Co. in New York, was director of recording. While in England Johnston had made the famous recording of Florence Nightingale (the first notable woman to make a record). Louis Young was president of Bell Recording Corp. and also of the National Metals Depositing Corp. In August 1922 Johnston was described as vice president of Bell, which was located at 9 E. 47th St., New York. Johnston was still with the company as late as January 1923. [Andrews*.]

BELL TALKING MACHINE CO. A firm located at 44 W. 37th St., New York. It made records with the **Schubert Record** label, marketed in 1918.

BELL TELEPHONE LABORATORIES. A research organization established in 1925 as a unit of AT&T (American Telephone and Telegraph Corp.), now operating in about 30 centers throughout the U.S. Many discoveries have issued from the Laboratories, including the transistor, solar battery, laser beams, transoceanic radiotelephone, the first communications satellite, and microwave radio relay systems. More than 25,000 patents have been acquired. Bell was the first major organization to conduct research in **electrical recording**, commencing in 1915; Joseph P. Maxfield and Henry C. Harrison were the investigators. An electrical system was developed by 1924.

In 1926 the Laboratories created the **Vitaphone** records for motion picture soundtracks. These were the first 33 1/3 rpm discs. There were a number of projects in the area of recorded sound during the 1930s. In March 1932 a team of scientists led by **Arthur Charles Keller** experimented with **stereophonic sound**, using two microphones to create discs with two parallel tracks. The records, of the Philadelphia Orchestra, were demonstrated at the Chicago Century of Progress Exposition in 1933. In 1933 an extended range **vertical-cut** disc recording system was announced; it covered up to 10,000 Hz in both recording and reproduction, and as high as 15,000 Hz in recording alone. In 1937 the Laboratories patented a precursor to stereo: a vertical-lateral disc system in which one sound channel was carried by motion 45 degrees to the right and the other channel 45 degrees to the left of vertical, producing a balanced effect. Also in 1937, engineer C. N. Hickman demonstrated a steel-tape recorder that operated at the slow speed of 16 inches per second; the tape was made of Vicalloy.

BELLINCIONI, GEMMA, 1864–1950. Italian soprano/mezzo-soprano, born in Monza on 18 Aug 1864. Her debut was at age 15 in Naples; at age 22 she sang at La Scala. Though she toured Europe and appeared in Buenos Aires, she did not sing in the U.S. On 17 Nov 1898 she sang in the premiere of *Fedora*, with Enrico Caruso, in the Teatro Lirico, Milan. Carmen was one of her most acclaimed roles. For most of her last half century she avoided the opera stage, devoting herself to concerts and teaching; in 1933 she was professor of singing at the

Naples Conservatory. Bellincioni made just 14 recordings—all of poor sound quality—among them a fine "Voi lo sapete" (G & T #053018; 1903, and IRCC #3140) and "Ah fors' è lui" (G & T #053019; 1903). Among the Pathé records she made in Milan, in 1905–1906, was her famous "Habanera" (#4395). An LP reissue covered her *Cavalleria, Traviata, Fedora,* and *Mefistofele* roles (Olympus #214). She died in Naples on 25 Apr 1950. [Richards 1966.]

BELMONT, JOE, 1876–1949. American baritone and bird imitator, born Joseph Walter Fulton in Shamokin, Pennsylvania, on 22 July 1876. By 1900 he had become one of the most popular recording artists, in America and Europe (on Favorite, Jumbo, and other labels in Britain). In addition to solo work he sang with the original Columbia Quartet. Belmont is best remembered for his whistling. An early Edison cylinder, "Beautiful Birds, Sing On," made with Byron G. Harlan (#8639; 1904) helped to give him the nickname of "the human bird." A hit for Victor was made with Billy Murray: "Whistle While You Walk" (1915). There was also a highly successful duet with Murray on Edison Diamond Disc #50506 (1919), "Gentle Spring." Belmont died in New York on 28 Aug 1949.

BELTONA (label). A 10–inch and 12–inch record sold in Britain by the Murdoch Trading Co., in 1922–1939, and afterwards by Decca (to 1968). Most of the masters were from Vocalion, Gennett, and Aco; they came through Guardsman (which was acquired by Aeolian Co., Ltd., in 1923), or from Aeolian Co., Ltd., and Vocalion Gramophone Co., Ltd. Edison Bell also supplied Beltona with masters, besides recording directly for the label. The Vocalion Gramophone Co. of Hayes, Middlesex, did the pressings. In 1927 **Edison Bell Consolidated Phonograph Co., Ltd.,** took control of the label; then Decca assumed ownership in 1933. Content included Irish and Scottish numbers, dance music, and some jazz. [Andrews*; Rust 1978.]

BENNETT, CHARLES K. President of the Eclipse Musical Co., Cleveland, Ohio. In 1921 he was elected secretary of the **National Association of Talking Machine Jobbers.**

BENNETT, TONY, 1926– . American popular singer, born Anthony Dominick Benedetto in New York, on 3 Aug 1926. After singing in clubs and with U.S. Army bands during military service, he was discovered by Bob Hope in 1950. Hope suggested a change from Joe Bari—then the singer's stage name—to Bennett; and he arranged for a New York stage engagement. A recording contract with Columbia in 1950 led to a series of hit records, notably "Boulevard of Broken Dreams" (Columbia #38825; 1950), and "Because of You" (#39362; 1951). Bennett's style went out of fashion in the later 1950s, but he returned to favor with his all-time hit in 1962, "I Left My Heart in San Francisco" (Columbia #42332), and followed it with more than a dozen chart songs, including "Fly Me to the Moon" (Columbia #43331; 1965). His earlier singing was in the romantic ballad mode of Frank Sinatra and Vic Damone, but he developed a jazz-oriented style in his maturity.

BENOIST, ANDRÉ, 1879–1954. French/American pianist, born in Paris on 4 Apr 1879. He studied with Raoul Pugno and Camille Saint-Saëns. On recordings he is heard primarily as an accompanist, with Pablo Casals, Jascha Heifetz, Fritz Kreisler, and Albert Spalding. "Rustle of Spring" (Edison Diamond Disc #50309; 1915) was among his solo records. He died in Middletown, New Jersey, on 19 June 1954.

BENSON, ERASTUS A. A director of the **Central Nebraska Phonograph Co.**, and later president of the **Nebraska Phonograph Co.** in 1890, 1892, and 1893. In 1890 he was also a director of the **Chicago Central Phonograph Co.**

BENZLER, ALBERT W., 1867–1934. American pianist and xylophonist, born in Newark, New Jersey, on 13 Nov 1867. He was an early Edison artist, appearing in the 1903 catalog with "Alita (Wild Flower)" on which he played orchestra bells (cylinder #8462). Until 1909 he was one of the Edison studio pianists; then he became musical director of the **U-S Phonograph Co.** in Cleveland, Ohio, and recorded many piano, bell, and xylophone numbers for them. One of those, "Peter Piper March" (#223), may have been the cylinder played more times

than any other; according to *TMW* (November 1910) it achieved 40,444 performances in a juke box with no discernible wear. Benzler played in various bands and groups around Newark after U-S Phonograph Co. folded in 1913; he had his own Benzler's Band for a time. He died in Newark on 19 Feb 1934.

BERGER, ERNA, 1900–1990. German coloratura and lyric soprano, born in Cossebaude on 19 Oct 1900. She made her debut in Dresden in 1925, and in the next few years was heard at Bayreuth and Salzburg. She sang with the Metropolitan Opera from 21 Nov 1949 (debut as Sophie) to 1951, and retired from the opera stage in 1955. Her main roles were Gilda, Rosina, and the Mozart heroines, though she also sang the other standard repertoire. Berger appeared as Queen of the Night in the notable complete recording of *Zauberflöte* conducted by Thomas Beecham (Victor #VM541/542). She recorded from 1932 to 1959. An LP reissue of 1981 included many of her finest arias (EMI Electrola #137/146). Her complete *Don Giovanni*, *Rigoletto*, and *Zauberflöte* have been released on compact disc.

BERIGAN, BUNNY, 1908–1942. American jazz trumpeter, born Rowland Bernard Berigan in Hilbert, Wisconsin, on 2 Nov 1908. He played violin before turning to the trumpet, which he played with several famous bands (Paul Whiteman, Dorsey Brothers, Benny Goodman) as well as in his own band after 1937. His most famous sides were made with Tommy Dorsey in 1937: "Marie" / "Song of India" (Victor #25523). Another hit, "I Can't Get Started" (Decca #790), became his theme song. He died in New York on 2 June 1942. [Danca 1978.]

BERLIN PHILHARMONIC ORCHESTRA. One of the leading symphonic ensembles of the world, established as the Philharmonic Orchestra in 1882; Franz Wüllner was the first director. Hans Joachim conducted in 1884–1887, succeeded by Hans von Bülow (1887–1894), **Arthur Nikisch** (1895–1922), and **Wilhelm Furtwängler** (1922–1945), under whom the orchestra gained its great reputation. After World War II Leo Borchard and Sergiu Celibidache conducted, succeeded by

Furtwängler once more, from 1947 until his death in 1954. **Herbert von Karajan** became conductor in 1954 and remained until he died in 1989. **Claudio Abbado** is the current artistic director.

The orchestra is significant in audio history as the first to make a "complete" recording of a symphonic score. This was a set of eight single-sided HMVs (#040784/91) issued in May-August 1914, offering a version of the Beethoven Fifth Symphony. Nikisch was the conductor of this truncated performance, which departed in many respects from the score (the orchestral forces had to be reduced for the studio, and tubas took the place of basses). The orchestra also recorded music from *Parsifal* in 1914, under Alfred Hertz. Later recordings of the orchestra are noted in the articles on its conductors.

BERLIN PHONOGRAMM-ARCHIV. A significant archive of recorded sound, established in 1905 by **Carl Stumpf**; based on the collection of field recordings in the Berlin University Psychological Institute. Erich Moritz von Hornbostel, a prominent ethno-musicologist, was head of the Archiv from 1905 to 1934. Government support commenced in 1922, and in 1934 the Archiv became part of the Berlin Museum for Folk Culture (Museum für Völkerkunde). By 1906 the collection included about 1,000 Edison cylinders—all of them field recordings—and by 1939 the number of recordings had grown to 11,000. Only about 20 percent of the holdings survived the World War II; they were transferred in 1948 to the Free University (Freie Universität Berlin). In 1950 there was another transfer, back to the Berlin Museum. Among the leading collections are folk materials from Turkey, Lapland, Yugoslavia, Kurdistan, Corsica, Tunisia, New Guinea, and the Ellice Islands. [Reinhard 1961.]

BERLINER, EMILÉ, 1851–1929. Inventor of the gramophone. Born in Hanover, Germany, son of a Talmudic scholar, fourth of 11 children. His given name was Emil, to which he later added the final "e" in the U.S. His formal education, in Wolfenbüttel, ended at age 14, and gave no indication of special talent. After working for a printer and as a salesclerk, he emigrated to America in 1870, settling in Washington, D.C. For three years he clerked in the dry goods store of a friend of the family before moving on to New York. There he taught himself electricity and acoustics while employed in menial occupations. He returned to Washington in 1876, set up a home laboratory for experimenting with electrical communication, and patented a telephone transmitter that utilized a principle basic to the development of the microphone. Bell Telephone purchased the patent from him in 1878, establishing a professional relationship between Bell and Berliner that allowed him to work on the problems of sound recording. In 1881 he married Cora Adler, with whom he had eight children.

Experimenting with sound recording, he tried cylinders first, influenced by the **phonautograph** he had seen in the Smithsonian Institution, then in 1887 invented the lateral (side-to-side) method of recording on a flat zinc disc. Pressings were on glass at first, then on celluloid, then—as mass production began in 1894—on hard rubber. On 16 May 1888 Berliner demonstrated his device at the Franklin Institute in Philadelphia. It consisted of a recording machine and a reproducing machine (both illustrated in Chew 1981). On a visit to Germany in the following year he made another important demonstration, at the Elektrotechnische Verein, and arranged for the first commercialization of his invention: a toy gramophone manufactured by Kämmer und Reinhardt of Waltershausen. (By coincidence, Edison was at the same time marketing his talking doll in America.) He also devised a duplicating system to make records from a master.

In 1890 Berliner returned to the U.S. and set up a structure for his gramophone work. He established the **American Gramophone Co.** in Washington in April 1891, and in the building that housed that firm he made the first seven-inch disc records (June 1892); these were issued beginning in late 1894 by the successor company to American Gramophone, the **United States Gramophone Co.** (established April 1893). That firm also made and sold gramophones. The discs—about 90 of them by the end of 1894—were made of black celluloid at first, then of hard rubber, from zinc masters.

The label was not a paste-on piece of paper, but an actual engraving into the record surface; it read "E. Berliner's Gramophone" and gave the Berliner patent dates of 8 Nov 1887 (U.S. patent #372,786) and 15 May 1888 (U.S. #382,790).

In the following year the **Berliner Gramophone Co.** was formed in Philadelphia, and in 1896 the **National Gramophone Co.** was set up in New York by Frank Seaman to take care of Berliner advertising and sales. Another piece of the Berliner enterprise resided in Camden, New Jersey, across the Delaware River from Philadelphia: there inventor **Eldridge Johnson** contributed numerous improvements to the gramophone, including a spring motor (the first machines were hand cranked). Johnson also replaced the zinc master with a disc of wax. Johnson had powerful entrepreneurial impulses, which were matched by those of Frank Seaman, who headed the National Gramophone Co. Johnson's version of the disc player, named the **Improved Gramophone**, included a new **soundbox** he had developed with the assistance of Alfred Clark; it was this machine that appeared in the famous **Nipper** painting (1899), and that was marketed in 1898 by Seaman under the trade name **Zonophone**. Seaman's firm was sued by American Graphophone Co., with a claim for priority of the Chichester Bell and Charles Sumner Tainter patents, which dealt with recording processes using the method of cutting into wax (whether disc or cylinder). There were years of litigation over patents in the recording industry, but by 1902 Berliner (Victor) and American Graphophone (Columbia) had taken control of the lateral-disc market, and retained it until electrical recording and expiration of patents brought forth new competitors. Berliner himself received 12 U.S. patents in the sound recording field.

In Europe, Berliner worked toward the establishment of the **Deutsche Grammophon Gesellschaft**—headed by his brother **Joseph Berliner**—in Hanover; and the **Gramophone Co.** in London, developed by **William Barry Owen**. Both firms were set up in 1898; pressing was done in Hanover, and recording in London. Berliner himself took a less active part in the gramophone business after the demise of his Philadelphia firm; he retained a financial connection with Victor, and with the Montreal company, acting as a consultant for them. But most of his time was devoted to various other interests after 1900: he was active in an educational campaign about the risks of drinking raw milk (this following the illness of a daughter); he studied aeronautics, and guided his son, Henry, in the development of a successful helicopter (1919). Research in sound waves led to the invention of sonar, used for submarine detection during World War II. He invented a practical acoustic tile for theaters and halls. According to a story in *TMW*, January 1918, he was also inventor of a "flying torpedo." He died 3 Aug 1929 of a cerebral hemorrhage, at home in Washington. A few weeks before his death he received the Benjamin Franklin Medal for scientific achievement. [Andrews*; Burlingame 1944; Chew 1981 (illus.); Koenigsberg*; Smart 1985; Wile 1984; Wile 1990/1.]

BERLINER, JOSEPH, 1858–1938. German engineer, brother of **Emile Berliner** and founder with him of the J. Berliner Telephon-Fabrik in Hanover (Kniestrasse 18) on 3 Aug 1881. The firm had branches in Berlin, Vienna, Budapest, Paris, and London. It was this company that introduced the telephone to Germany. In 1898 he and his brothers Emile and Jacob established **Deutsche Grammophon Gesellschaft** at the same Hanover address, and ran it until the takeover by the Gramophone Co. in 1900; it had several European branches. When Berliner retired in 1930, he donated 70,000 marks to the workers in his factory.

BERLINER (label). **Emile Berliner** used his own name for disc labels, beginning in 1889 with the five-inch, lateral-cut "plates" for the so-called toy gramophones made and sold in Germany and Britain. Contents included monologs in English or German, some of which were delivered by Berliner himself. One disc, apparently recorded in 1890, features a four-trumpet rendition of a "Marsch No. 1." There were also songs, bugle calls, piano solos, and farmyard imitations. The first Berliners not sold as toys were marketed in Washington, D.C., in late 1894 by the **United States Gramophone Co.** Actual recording dates were as early as June 1892, made in the Berliner laboratory housed with his first U.S. firm, the **American Gramophone Co.** The first list of discs for sale was issued 1 Nov 1894; it contained 52 titles, including band music, cornet solos, a drum and fife number, a trombone solo, a piano solo, an instrumental quartet, a clarinet solo, a vocal quartet, children's songs, Indian songs, baritone solos, soprano solos, and a recitation. These were seven-inch discs. A January 1895 "List of Plates" had 85 items.

Over the next six years the repertoire on Berliner's label grew to cover whistling, songs in various languages, instrumental solos and groups, operatic excerpts (described in Taylor 1990), and bands—with Sousa's Band recording in August 1897. The discs were identified with letters etched into the centers, reading "E. Berliner's Gramophone" with the title of the content.

Sales were satisfying: in 1897 248,652 discs were sold; in 1898, the peak year, 713,859 were sold; by April 1900 the total sales had reached about 2 million discs. Typically, Berliners were single-sided, with etched information (no paper labels). They included the angel trademark after late 1898, on discs sold in Europe. (Three double-sided discs bearing the Berliner name were discovered in 1975; they are described in Brooks 1975, where the suggestion is made that they were actually test records pressed by Eldridge Johnson). The playing speed was variable, from 60 rpm to 75 rpm, although it was usually 70 rpm. All Berliner discs are rare collectibles today, but the most valuable are those made by a young Fred Gaisberg of opera singers in Europe. As a result of an injunction instigated by Frank Seaman, and brought by American Graphophone, production of Berliner discs in America ended in May 1900. The last one to be issued was #01304, "Doan You Cry, My Honey" by the Hayden Quartet. As the industry realigned, the Berliner label passed to the **Gramophone Co.** name in Britain and the **Victor Talking Machine Co.** name in the U.S.

In 1988 a CD reissue covered 39 Berliner discs (Symposium #1058; described in Klee and Petts). [Adamson 1973 (illustrating 20 label designs); Andrews*; Bayly 1988; Hoover 1971 (reprints the 1895 sales list); Klee 1990/3; Koenigsberg*; Petts 1988; Rust 1978; Rust 1981 (a label list of seven-inch British issues); Sherman 1990 (reprints the November 1894 sales list); Smart 1985 (with an illustration of the 1895 sales broadside); Taylor 1990 (with comments by Peter Adamson in *HN* #174, p. 36); Wile 1979/2; Wile 1984.]

BERLINER GRAMOPHONE CO. A firm established at 1026 Filbert St., Philadelphia, on 8 Oct 1895, by **Emile Berliner,** to manufacture discs and disc players under patents held by the **United States Gramophone Co.** A retail store was opened nearby, managed by Alfred Clark, to sell the products, and a laboratory was located at 1023 12th St. NW, (later at 1410 Pennsylvania Ave., NW) Washington, D.C. Sales rights were reserved for Washington, D.C., with the rights for the rest of the country contracted to **Frank Seaman** of New York; Seaman set up the National Gramophone Co. in Yonkers, New York, to handle his sales. The first year was unsuccessful. But business improved with the improvement of the product. During the years 1896–1900, the new spring motor machine of **Eldridge R. Johnson** replaced the old hand-cranked models, and shellac pressings created by the **Duranoid Co.** of Newark, New Jersey, provided "plates" with reasonably smooth playback. Sales of $478,740 were listed for the fiscal year ending in 1898. In 1897 the company opened a London office under **William Barry Owen** (to become the **Gramophone Co.** in April 1898), and in 1899 the firm was established in Canada as "E. Berliner, Montreal." There were four record presses in Montreal, at 367–71 Aqueduct St., and a shop on Fortification Lane where machines were assembled (the motors and turntables being imported from Eldridge Johnson). About 43,000 gramophones were sold by April 1900.

However, litigations quickly caused difficulties for the company; *see* BERLINER (label). In 1900 Johnson acquired the patents and even the **Nipper** trademark that Berliner had registered in July of that year. The Berliner Gramophone Co. shut down in September 1900, and the gramophone passed to the **Consolidated Talking Machine Co.**; then in 1901 to its successor firm, the **Victor Talking Machine Co.**. Berliner himself retained a one-third interest in Victor.

The Filbert St. building in Philadelphia was razed for construction of the Gallery II shopping mall in 1983. [Andrews*; Smart 1985; Wile 1979/2; Wile 1984.]

BERNARD, AL, 1888–1949. American popular singer, born in New Orleans on 3 Nov 1888. He was the leading white blues singer of the acoustic period, known also for minstrel songs. His first record for Edison was possibly the earliest authentic blues vocal to be released: "Hesitation Blues" (Diamond Disc #50524 and cylinder #6621; 1919). His next offering, "Nigger Blues," sold well on Diamond Disc (#50542; 1919) and Blue Amberol cylinder. Bernard's blues were rhythmic and humorous in style. Duets with Ernest Hare were especially amusing; one of the best being "I Want to Hold You in My Arms" (Diamond Disc #50558; 1919), which stayed in the catalog for 10 years. Bernard first recorded "St. Louis Blues" in July 1918 on Aeolian-Vocalion #12148, with backup by a group that was at one time thought to be "probably the Original Dixieland Jazz Band" (Walsh); but was in fact a studio band directed by Harry Yerkes. It later came out on Edison and became one of the all-time best sellers on that label (Diamond Disc #50620; 1919), issued also on 19 other labels. He became a popular Columbia artist also, beginning with "I Want My Mammy," a duet with Vernon Dalhart in 1922. Bernard's final record for Edison was made in 1927; then in 1949 he made a last appearance on disc with a double-78 album entitled *Al Bernard's Merry Minstrel Show* (Celebrity #1). Bernard could not read music nor play any instrument. He sang under many pseudonyms, including John Bennett, Dave Sanborn, Al Simpson, and Uncle Joe. He died in New York on 9 Mar 1949. [Rust*; Walsh 1974/3–12; Walsh 1975/1–2.]

BERNHARDT, SARAH, 1844–1923. French actress; of interest to recorded sound because she made a number of early cylinders and discs. In early 1896 she inscribed monologs by Eugene Sylvestre and Victor Hugo for **Bettini** (no copies extant). In 1900, at the Phono-Cinéma-Théatre Exposition in Paris, she did a scene from *Hamlet* and some readings from French authors in the earliest talking motion picture. Later, from 1902 to 1918, she recorded for Pathé, HMV, Zonophone, Edison, and Aeolian-Vocalion. [Marty 1979 has an illustration; Rust 1989.]

BERNSTEIN, LEONARD, 1918–1990. American composer, pianist, and conductor, born Louis Bernstein in Lawrence, Massachusetts, on 25 Aug 1918. He studied composition and conducting with such distinguished musicians as Fritz Reiner, Randall Thompson, Walter Piston, and Serge Koussevitzky. He was engaged as assistant conductor of the New York Philharmonic Orchestra in 1943, and became conductor in 1958. After a decade of international success, he resigned from the orchestra in 1969. Thereafter he composed, appeared as guest conductor in opera and concert around the world, wrote books, and gave acclaimed talks on television. On Christmas morning 1989, Bernstein marked the reunion of East and West Berlin with a televised performance of the Beethoven Ninth Symphony (changing the "Ode to Joy" to an "Ode to Freedom"; Deutsche Grammophon CD #429–861–4.)

Bernstein's records of Haydn and Mahler have been most highly praised, but his discs of the complete Beethoven and Brahms symphonies, of Copland and Gershwin, and many others have been placed among the best interpretations available. His recordings won Grammy awards in 1964, 1967, 1973, 1977, 1989, 1990, and 1992. He was the first American appointed to head a major orchestra, and the first to conduct a regular performance at La Scala. Bernstein died in New York on 15 Oct 1990.

BEROLINA SCHALLPLATTEN GmbH. A recording firm established in Berlin on 31 Oct 1911 by Paul Kuchler and Albert Vogt. They issued two labels in 1912: Berolina for Germany, and **Invicta** for other countries; and they had rights to sell Syrena discs in Germany. There were 358 Invicta titles on sale in Britain by November 1912. After a dispute over trademark, Berolina changed its London outlet from Invicta Record Co., Ltd. to John Abrahams and Co., 54 Redcross St., London (1913). Thus it turned out that the Invicta label was being sold by two London agents. [Andrews 1990.]

BERRY, CHUCK, 1926– . American popular singer, songwriter, and guitarist, born Charles Edward Anderson in St. Louis, on 18 Oct 1926. After nightclub and miscellaneous work in St. Louis with a trio, he began to record for the Chess label in 1955. His first disc, "Maybellene" (Chess #1604; 1955) was one of the earliest hits of the new rock 'n' roll idiom. Most of his popular song records featured pianist Johnnie Johnson. For several years Berry was a leading and critically acclaimed rock star, making movies and records, and establishing much of the rock vocabulary. Top records included "Johnny B. Goode" (Chess #1691; 1958), "Carol" (Chess #1700; 1958), "Sweet Little Rock 'n' Roller" (Chess: 1709; 1958), "Bye Bye Johnny" (Chess #1754; 1960), "Nadine" (Chess #1883; 1964), and "My Ding-A-Ling" (Chess #2131; 1972). His songwriting and innovative guitar playing influenced many of the British rock bands of the 1960s, including the Beatles and the Rolling Stones.

BERTELSMANN AG. An international conglomerate, controlling large publishing and media interests. The firm was established in Gütersloh, Germany, in 1835, by Carl Bertelsmann. It printed hymnals and religious books and consequently was closed by the Nazis. After World War II Richard Mohn rebuilt the company. He initiated a book club, and acquired several publishers, achieving international diversification. Sales in 1989 amounted to 12 billion marks. The BMG (Bertelsmann Music Group) Division acquired RCA Records from General Electric in 1986 after General Electric had acquired RCA. From 1989 the old RCA label was renamed "BMG Classics," with the venerable Red Seal becoming a Gold Seal. Both Gold Seal and Red Seal names were being used for the BMG Classics in 1991. Victor material is being reissued on CD, including one remarkable set initiated in 1990 that will include (on 82 compact discs) all the recordings made by Arturo Toscanini.

BETHEL QUARTET. Also known as the Bethel Jubilee Quartet, a male group that recorded for Victor from 1923 to 1928. Members in 1928 were Norman Chestang and W.W. Coleman, tenors; B. McCants, baritone; and Robert Jo-

seph, bass. Their output was religious and inspirational, for example, "Guiding Angels, Please Guide Me" (their last disc, #47081–2; 21 Sep 1928). [Rust 1970.]

BETTINI, GIANNI, 1860–1938. Italian army officer, born in Novarra. He immigrated to the U.S. in the mid-1880s, marrying an American socialite, Daisy Abbott of Stamford, Connecticut. Although he had no scientific training, he experimented in sound recording, attempting to improve on Thomas Edison's cylinder **reproducer.** On 13 Aug 1889 he received three U.S. patents (#409,003; #409,004; #409,005—described in Koenigsberg 1990) for a "spider," an attachment that connected a mica **diaphragm** to a **stylus** with a view to capturing more vibrations (detail photo in Marty 1979). The actual effect of the spider was to shift the response downward, strengthening the bass and weakening the treble; it improved the rendition of the female singing voice. Eventually (1902) Edison bought the patent from him. Bettini also patented reproducing devices for copying cylinders (U.S. #488,381, described in Koenigsberg 1990, which gives later patents also). He received a total of 14 U.S. patents in the sound recording field.

In 1891 or 1892 he established the Bettini Phonograph Laboratory in the Judge Building, 110 Fifth Ave., New York. The firm was a maker of cylinders. His May 1897 catalog styled those cylinders as Micro-Phonograph "Excelsior" Records. Due to the social position of his wife he met the great singers of the day—Enrico Caruso, Nellie Melba, Victor Maurel, Mario Ancona, Giuseppe Campanari, Pol Plançon, and others, as well as Lily Langtree, Ellen Terry, Sarah Bernhardt, and Mark Twain, and engaged them to record for him. He also personally recorded the voices of Pope Leo XIII and ex-President Benjamin Harrison. His sales were good: in 1897 he was able to produce a 12–page catalog, which grew to 32 pages in the next year. He offered more than 200 items of serious music, copied to order (at relatively high prices, $2–$6 each; competitors were selling at $.50) without mass production. These records are very rare today, since most of the inventory was destroyed in France during World War II. One expert listening to 15 surviving cylinders pronounced them to be badly sung and poorly recorded (Fassett 1976) but the prevailing view is that they were excellent. Bettini also sold his micro-diaphragm. The music reproducer was available in 1899 in models suitable for the Edison Home or Standard phonograph, as well as for the Columbia **graphophone.**

Bettini established his name in France in 1898 by selling French rights to the Compagnie Microphonographes Bettini. In 1901 he moved to Paris, setting up the Société des Microphonographes Bettini, and leaving the New York firm under new management at 80 Chambers St. His successors used the name Bettini Phonograph Co. That firm sold a German disc machine called the **Hymnophone,** the first to have an inside horn (anticipating the **Victrola**).

Five years later he abandoned the record business. In a 1904 advertisement in *TMW*, he was offering to manufacture discs or to teach anyone how to do so; his address then was 32 Avenue de l'Opéra, Paris. Bettini lost most of his fortune in the stock market crash of 1929, but continued to experiment, working on various projects including television and games. He died in San Remo, Italy, on 27 Feb 1938. [Bettini 1898 (reprints the catalogs of 1898, 1900, and 1901); Fassett 1976/7; Favia-Artsay 1955/12 (reprints Bettini catalogs of 1897, 1898, 1899); Feinstein 1985; Klinger*; Koenigsberg*; Koenigsberg 1990; Marty 1979 (color photos of Bettini phonographs, and of the spider); Moran 1965/2 (fullest coverage of the Bettini material); Taylor 1987/4 (on the operatic records).]

BIAMPING. A **loudspeaker** system in which the **woofer** and **tweeter** are driven by separate **amplifiers.** By dividing the audio frequency spectrum between two amplifiers, inter-modulation distortion is evaded. There is also better damping control over cone motion, and avoidance of ring in the **crossover network.** Disadvantages of these systems are the cost and bulk that result from having a second power amplifier and crossover network.

BIANCHI, "PROFESSOR." This is the identification given to the music director of **Columbia Phonograph Co.** in the 1890s. Except that

he was a former bandmaster, biographical data are lacking.

BIAS. In **tape recording,** a high-frequency alternating current, usually between 75 kHz and 100 kHz, applied to the tape **record head** along with the audio signal with the purpose of reducing distortion and enhancing **signal-to-noise ratio.** The reason for applying bias is the nonlinearity of the magnetic recording medium. Various tape types (*see* CASSETTE) require different amounts of bias. There are no absolute standards for bias or **equalization,** which leads to problems of compatibility between tapes and equipment. "Biasing" is also achieved by superimposing a magnetic field on the signal magnetic field during recording.

BIAS TRAP. A low-pass **filter** in a tape relay circuit, intended to reduce any excessive high frequency **bias** present.

Biasing. *See* BIAS.

BIELEFELDER KATALOG. The periodic listings of classical and popular recordings in print in Germany; equivalent to the American **Schwann** set.

BIELING, JOHN, 1869–1948. American tenor, born in New York on 18 Mar 1869. He had an unusual recording career, singing very few solos. Most of his work was in quartets, some in duets. Bieling was a member of the first quartet to make records, the Manhasset Quartet. The Edison Quartet succeeded it, with Bieling as first tenor. He was also first tenor for the American Quartet, Hayden Quartet, and the Premier Quartet. Many of his duets were with Harry MacDonough. Experiencing voice trouble in 1913, he gave up recording and went into the business end of the industry. He was a representative for the New York Talking Machine Co. in 1918, and in 1920 he opened a Victrola shop in Hempstead, Long Island. Bieling retired in 1926, and died in Hempstead on 20 Mar 1948.

Most of the tenor's records were made for Edison and Victor. His earliest Victor was a duet with MacDonough, "The Silver Slipper"

(#B-409; 10 Sep 1903); his first Edison cylinder was also with MacDonough, "Somebody's Waiting 'Neath Southern Skies" (#8628; 1904). By 1912 he had made 25 Victors and 12 Edisons in addition to his quartet material, but none were carried into catalogs of the electric era. [Walsh 1942/7–8, 1948/6, 1950/12, with corrections in 1952/5.]

BIG BAND. The large swing orchestra that dominated popular music from about 1936 to about 1950; representing an international phenomenon most pervasive in the U.S. and in Britain. Some of the Big Bands had started out as smaller jazz groups in the 1920s. The typical ensemble consisted of a four- or five-piece rhythm section (piano, double bass, guitar, and percussion), four or five saxophones, three or four trumpets, and three or four trombones. There was usually a pair of solo singers (a male and a female) and often a vocal group. In America the outstanding Big Bands were those of **Louis Armstrong**, Desi Arnaz, **Charlie Barnet, Count Basie, Bunny Berigan**, Ben Bernie, Will Bradley, Les Brown, **Henry Busse, Benny Carter, Larry Clinton, Coon-Sanders, Bob Crosby, Xavier Cugat, Jimmy Dorsey, Tommy Dorsey, Eddy Duchin, Duke Ellington, Shep Fields, Dizzy Gillespie, Benny Goodman**, Glen Gray and the **Casa Loma Orchestra, Lionel Hampton**, Phil Harris, **Coleman Hawkins**, Erskine Hawkins, **Horace Heidt, Fletcher Henderson, Earl Hines**, Ina Ray Hutton, **Harry James**, Isham Jones, **Spike Jones, Dick Jurgens, Sammy Kaye, Hal Kemp, Stan Kenton, Wayne King, Gene Krupa, Kay Kyser**, Ada Leonard, Ted Lewis, **Guy Lombardo, Jimmie Lunceford, Glenn Miller**, Vaughn Monroe, Russ Morgan. **Ray Noble, Red Norvo**, Jan Savitt, **Artie Shaw, Jack Teagarden, Claude Thornhill, Chick Webb, Ted Weems, Lawrence Welk, Paul Whiteman**, and **Teddy Wilson**.

Britain had its own Big Bands, such as that of Lew Stone, **Jack Hylton**, Ambrose and His Orchestra, and Roy Fox; Ray Noble was British by birth, and had established himself in the U.K. before leaving for the U.S. in September 1934. Many American groups performed in London.

Although a certain sound—based on tightly harmonized brasses, an ensemble swing, and a pervasive dance beat—characterized these bands, there were many subtypes among them. The most sophisticated (as we see them now) were the jazzy groups with complex arrangements and freely improvised solos: Armstrong, Basie, Tommy Dorsey, Ellington, Goodman, Kenton, Miller, and Shaw. Most of the bands fell into a less venturesome category of sweet-swing. Some became so sweet that the swing was lost: Brown, Duchin, Gray, Kaye, and Lombardo. A number were essentially accompanists for great soloists who led them: Hawkins, James, Krupa, Norvo, and Thornhill.

The famous Latin bands were led by Arnaz and Cugat. Two "all-girl" orchestras were headed by Hutton and Leonard. Comic elements were characteristic of a few, like Spike Jones and Kyser.

Most of the great vocalists came from the bands; many remained in that milieu, while others went on to solo careers. Bing Crosby started with Whiteman (but left him before the Big Band era); Frank Sinatra with Tommy Dorsey; Ella Fitzgerald with Webb. Peggy Lee was with Goodman; Doris Day with Brown; Perry Como with Weems. Dinah Shore made her early records with Cugat.

With the end of the Big Band era there came also the end of the time when one style of popular music was appealing to all age groups. The same quintessential image of the period emerged from high school proms as much as from the great adult ballrooms: a vast throng of dancers, moving cheek-to-cheek to a slow foxtrot, while a singer gave forth a romantic ballad, followed by a dreamy instrumental chorus. [Edwards 1965; Fenton 1971; Rust 1972; Simon, 1974.]

BIGARD, BARNEY, 1906–1980. American jazz clarinetist, born in New Orleans on 3 Mar 1906 as Albany Barney Leon Bigard. He started as a saxophone player, working in New Orleans and from 1925 in the Chicago area. He joined King Oliver and began to emphasize clarinet, developing a particularly liquid tone and a vivid low register. In 1927 he entered into a 15-year association with Duke Ellington, and made outstanding records like "Mood Indigo" (Brunswick #4952; 1930)—his own composition—and "Clarinet Lament" (Brunswick #7650; 1936)—a work written for him by Ellington, said to be first jazz concerto for solo instrument and orchestra. Leaving Ellington in 1942, he freelanced, then became one of the Louis Armstrong All-Stars (1947–1952, 1953–1955, 1960–1961) making a world tour and recording notable discs of "Tea for Two" (Decca #9–28099/28100; 1947), "C-Jam Blues" (Decca #9–28102; 1947), and "Just You, Just Me" (Decca #9–28175; 1951). He moved to Los Angeles in 1956, playing with his own ensemble, and from 1969 giving lectures on jazz to university students. He continued performing through the 1970s, in Europe and America. Bigard died in Culver City, California, on 27 June 1980.

BIGGS, E. POWER, 1906–1977. British/American organist, born in Westcliff on 29 Mar 1906. He studied at the Royal Academy of Music, and came to the U.S. in 1930, becoming a citizen in 1937. His concert and recording career did much to establish the organ as a solo instrument outside of the church environment, and to bring baroque music into the repertoire. Beginning on the Technichord label in 1938, then going to Victor, Biggs recorded Bach on an Aeolian-Skinner organ at Harvard University; he also made a series of discs illustrating "Historic Organs of England" and recorded on organs in other European cities. From 1942 to 1958 he gave weekly radio recitals from Harvard, then finally gave up concert work because of arthritis. He never performed on electric organs, but did enjoy the harpsichord; among his odd recordings are some Scott Joplin ragtime pieces on a pedal harpsichord made for him by John Challis. Columbia issued an LP album illustrating the great variety of his interests in 1981 (#M4X 35180).

BIKEL, THEODORE, 1924– . Austrian/American actor and folk singer, born in Vienna on 2 May 1924. He went with his family to Palestine in 1938, becoming a British subject. While working as a farm laborer he began a lifelong study of languages. He was in theatre work in Tel Aviv from 1943–47, and then in London. Bikel appeared in *Streetcar Named Desire* in London,

and in the film *African Queen* (1951) as well as other motion pictures during the 1950s. His major debut as a folksinger took place in Town Hall, New York, on 5 Oct 1958; he recorded this concert for Elektra and commenced an international concert career. His most important stage role was Baron von Trapp in the *Sound of Music* (1959). Be became an American citizen in 1961.

BILL, EDWARD LYMAN, 1862–1916. Founder, editor, and proprietor of the journal *Talking Machine World*, 1905–1916. His son, Raymond, was also an editor of *TMW*.

BINAURAL SOUND. Two-channel sound in which each ear receives only one of the channels. To record binaurally, microphones are mounted on a **dummy head**, possibly with actual models of human ears on it. Ideally, playback is through headphones at the same respective sound levels that were received by the microphones. One of the early experimenters was **Alexander Graham Bell** (in ca. 1881). During World War I a binaural apparatus consisting of two receiving trumpets spaced several feet apart, connected by rubber tubes to the ears of an operator, was used to locate enemy airplanes. The principle was applied in World War II in underwater submarine detection. Radio use of binaural sound began experimentally in Germany in 1925, in broadcasts from the Berlin Opera House. In the same year there were binaural transmissions from New Haven, Connecticut, on station WPAJ. Listeners used two radio sets, tuned to slightly different frequencies, each attached to a tube going to one ear. The need for two radio sets was a deterrent to progress and binaural work was soon abandoned, despite the attractive results that had been achieved.

At the Chicago Century of Progress Exposition in 1933, General Electric engineers demonstrated a binaurally equipped dummy named Oscar (originally displayed in 1932 at the Academy of Music in Philadelphia). Oscar's two microphones picked up sounds from various parts of the room, which could be precisely located by listeners with binaural headphones. With the rise of **stereo** tape recording in the 1950s, the term binaural became confused with stereo, and since stereo did not require special headphones, the binaural systems faded from sight for two decades.

There is a significant difference between the binaural and stereophonic modes:

> In binaural listening the listener wears earphones which critically separate left ear sounds from right ear sounds—*as if he were listening with two ears at the microphone location.* This gives dimension and depth to the music, but . . . [also] a fatiguing reaction caused by the violation of the normal listening position. . . .

> In stereo listening you are transported to the best seat in the concert hall, for the effect is *like listening with two ears at the audience location.* Here we find that all discomfort has vanished, and not only the music, but the beneficial tonal qualities of the concert hall itself are included in the living room reproduction. (Crowhurst)

In the 1970s some experimental discs were made in Japan that provided remarkable environmental realism. But problems inherent in the system remain to be solved; for example a sound source moving perpendicularly across the front of the dummy head will produce in the listener the effect of a source describing an arc rather than a straight line; and a circle around the microphones becomes an oval to the listener. Experiments of the 1980s have included Hugo Zuccarelli's "holophonics"—a digital system based on the way we perceive (rather than receive) sound. A firm called Optimax III has made "total dimensional" sound systems for motion pictures and television, using individual stereo headsets. [Crowhurst 1960; Sunier 1986.] *See also* STEREOPHONIC RECORDING; SURROUND SOUND.

BINDER. A glue used to fasten magnetic particles to the **base** material on a **tape.** Thickness in use for open-reel tape is 0.56 mil; for cassette tape it is 0.24 mil. In preparation of the tape, the **coating** is mixed with the binder—both wet— so that the magnetic particles are evenly dispersed. The binder when dry has to remain flexible, and it must adhere firmly to the base

without attaching itself to adjacent layers when the tape is tightly wound.

BINGHAM, RALPH, 1870–1925. American comedian, born in Richmond, Virginia, on 2 Aug 1870. He was a child prodigy on the violin, but soon became more interested in monologs. He became famous for his Negro and Jewish dialect stories. In 1915 he recorded "Mrs. Rastus at the Telephone" (Victor #17818), and went on to make seven other discs for the label. The final effort was "Mrs. Rastus Johnson's Joy Ride" (Victor #18517; 1919). One of the Mrs. Rastus monologs was in the catalog of 1927, along with "Goldstein behind the Bars" (#18231). Bingham died in Philadelphia on 27 Dec 1925. [Rust 1989; Walsh 1964/4.]

BINGOLA (label). A rare disc issued by the Bing Corp., 33 E. 17th St., New York, between ca. 1927 and ca. 1930. It was related to Grey Gull. Only eight issues have been traced, dance and popular numbers. One is "Last Rose of Summer" sung by Arthur Fields (#2703A). [Barr 1982; Kendziora 1987/3; Rust 1978.]

Bird sounds. *See* ANIMAL IMITATIONS; WHISTLING RECORDINGS; WILDLIFE SOUNDS.

BIRNBAUM, THEODORE B., 1865–1914. British recording industry executive, born in Islington, London, on 27 Feb 1865. He and his brother went into the importing business, and evidently included talking machines among their stock. In 1898 he became associated with William Barry Owen, who was establishing the Berliner interests in London in what was to be the Gramophone Co. When that firm took over the **International Zonophone Co.** of Berlin in 1903, Birnbaum was made director there. Birnbaum became managing director of the Gramophone Co. in April 1904, remaining with the organization until 1910, when he returned to the import business. He died on 19 Mar 1914. He was designer of the Gramophone **angel** trademark. [Martland 1989.]

BISCUIT. The plastic material from which a commercial disc is pressed. (*See* DISC, 3.)

BISPHAM, DAVID SCULL, 1857–1921. American baritone, born in Philadelphia on 5 Jan 1857. He made his operatic debut in London, in 1891; sang first at the Metropolitan Opera in 1896, and remained on the roster there until 1903. His voice is heard on two of the Mapleson cylinders (1903), and on Columbia cylinders beginning in 1906. A favorite recording was Schubert's "Der Wanderer" (Columbia #36476; 1913 [with orchestra; earlier with piano in 1906]). His final records were "Dixie" (Pathé 11526B; 1917) and "The Two Grenadiers" (Pathé #025099A; 1918). Bispham died in New York on 2 Oct 1921. [Hervingham-Root 1970.]

BJÖRLING, JUSSI, 1911–1960. Swedish tenor, born Johan Jonatän Björling on 5 Feb 1911 in Stora Tuna. He began to sing as a child in the family's male quartet, which toured Sweden in 1916–1919 and then came to the U.S. The group spent four years in the east and midwest, singing mostly for Swedish immigrants. They recorded some hymns and traditional songs for Columbia in 1920. When the father died in 1926, young Björling worked at odd jobs in Stockholm until he was able to secure some singing engagements and make radio broadcasts; eventually he got a recording contract with EMI (the first record accepted was "Torna a Sorrento," #HMV X-3376; 1929). On 21 July 1930 he made a debut at the Royal Opera in a small part; in the next month he sang Don Ottavio, and he remained with the company until 1939. EMI (Swedish HMV) recorded him doing film songs and popular items in 1932–1933, under the pseudonym of Erik Odde.

Björling's Metropolitan career began on 24 Nov 1938, as Rodolfo; he remained—with a wartime interruption, and minus the 1954/1955 season—until 1957, gaining recognition as one of the greatest singers of the French/Italian repertoire since Enrico Caruso. He made outstanding recordings of all the major arias, for Victor and HMV, and complete recordings of *Aida* (with Zinka Milanov), *Boheme* (with Victoria de los Angeles), *Cavalleria rusticana* (twice: with Zinka Milanov in 1953 [Victor CD #6510] and with Renata Tebaldi in 1958 [Victor #LSC-6059]) *Madama Butterfly* (with de los Angeles), *Manon Lescaut* (with Licia Albanese), *Rigoletto* (with Roberta Peters), and *Trovatore* (with Milanov). All are available on CD. A 1959 album on the London label, *Björling in Opera*, won a Grammy. EMI issued an LP album of three discs in 1979 covering the recordings of 1919–1936: *The Art of Jussi Björling* (#715). He died in Siarö, Sweden, on 9 Sep 1960. [Henrysson 1984; Stroff 1988/10.]

BLACK PATTI (label). A short-lived label (issued for only six months in 1927), now extremely rare and sought after; recorded by Gennett and produced by the Chicago Record Co. The name of the label came from a legendary Black soprano of the later 19th century, Sissieretta Jones, who had been compared to Adelina Patti. Of the 55 known issues (110 sides), most are jazz, blues, and sacred. Rust (p.8) describes the label itself as "purple, framed and printed in gold and embodying on the entire top half a peacock with tail feathers fully extended." One writer describes the label as the most beautiful in all recording history—"a masterpiece of art" (Henriksen p.9). The first release of Black Patti records, as announced in the *Chicago Defender* (a newspaper for the Black community) on 21 May 1927, consisted of 24 10inch discs, numbered 8001–8024, selling by mail at $.75 each. Artists included Papa Harvey Hull, Mozelle Alderson, Hattie Garland, Eloise Bennett, and Trixie Williams. [Henriksen 1979; Rust 1978.]

BLACK SWAN (label). Records made by the Pace Phonograph Corp., established in 1921 at 257 W. 138th St. (later located at 2289 Seventh Ave.), New York. The "Black Swan" for whom the label was named was the soprano Elizabeth Taylor Greenfield (1809–1876). The intent of the co-founders, Harry Pace and the composer William C. Handy, was to appeal to Black listeners with a roster of Black artists, without the stigmatic tag of race records used by white-owned companies for their Black performers. This approach was in some cases fraudulent, as a number of Black Swan discs were issued with white artists using pseudonyms. Black Swan records were in fact pressed by the Olympic Disc Record Corp. of Long Island, and a number of issues appear under both the Olympic and Black Swan labels, identical except for the names of the performers. (Examples are cited in Kendziora 1955.) Pace and John Fletcher purchased the Olympic Corp. in July 1922 and renamed it Fletcher Record Co., Inc.; the address was 156 Meadow St., Long Island City, New York. The new firm pressed Black Swan discs thereafter. Pace changed the firm's name to Black Swan Phonograph Co. in February 1923, but a few months later ceased producing records. In April 1924 the label was acquired by Paramount, who reissued many of the pressings as a race series. Color scheme of the label was black and gold, with a swan—not always black—at the top. Ethel Waters and Trixie Smith made successful records for the firm. [Andrews*; Kendziora 1955; Kunstadt 1987; Rust 1978.]

BLACKER, GEORGE, 1931–1990. American disc jockey and writer, known for his extensive research and publication in the field of recorded sound; born in Cheshire, Connecticut, on 8 Feb 1931. Blacker wrote primarily for the journal *Record Research*, contributing regularly from 1955 to 1990. His column "Discoing In" was the outlet for much of his investigations. For articles in other periodicals, see the Bibliography. Blacker died in Cheshire, Connecticut, on 6 July 1990.

BLACKMAN, J. NEWCOMB, 1881–1958. American record industry executive, born in New York. After some work in the bicycle business, he formed the **Blackman Talking Machine Co.** in 1902. He was vice president of the Eastern Talking Machine Jobbers Association in 1907, 1909, and 1910; later he was president of the **National Association of Talking Machine Jobbers** (1912 and 1917). He was a friend of Thomas Edison. The record brush was his invention. With the decline of the record business in the 1930s, Blackman diversified his interests: selling electrical appliances, then consulting in the investment field. He died on 3 July 1958 in Brightwaters, New York, a community he had helped to incorporate. [Koenigsberg*.]

BLACKMAN TALKING MACHINE CO. A New York firm established on 1 May 1902 by **J. Newcomb Blackman;** it sold records and play-

ers—Edison products at first, then exclusively wholesale Victor products after April 1919, in addition to Playrite and Melotone steel needles and Cleanrite record brushes. Originally at 97 Chambers St., it moved to 28–30 W. 23rd St. in 1921. The name was changed to Blackman Distributing Co. in 1926 or 1927, marking a diversification of inventory to include various electrical appliances. The firm was liquidated in 1932.

BLAKE, EUBIE, 1883–1983. American ragtime pianist and composer, born 7 Feb 1883 in Baltimore. After various jobs playing piano and organ in hotels and cafes, and some vaudeville work, he joined the Noble Sissle band in 1915, maintaining a sporadic association into the late 1930s. He and Sissle wrote the songs for *Shuffle Along* (1921), which played 504 performances on Broadway; the hit song was "I'm Just Wild about Harry" which Blake recorded on Victor #18791. Another hit song, "Memories of You," was in the Blake/Andy Razaf score for *Blackbirds of 1930*; (recorded by Blake on Columbia #C2S-847). He was still performing in concert and on television at 100 years of age. Blake died in New York, on 12 Feb 1983. [Montgomery 1978 lists his piano rolls; Rose 1979 includes a discography.]

BLAKEY, ART, 1919–1990. American jazz drummer, born 11 Oct 1919 in Pittsburgh. He worked in many idioms—most influentially in bebop—and with many groups from 1939 until his death, offering a hard, loud style that was particularly effective with strong soloists. He began as a pianist, then turned to the percussions, working in New York with Fletcher Henderson (1939), Mary Lou Williams (1941), Billy Eckstine (1944–1947), numerous soloists (notably Thelonious Monk), and most importantly with his own Jazz Messengers (from 1954). The Blue Note label recorded the best of his own group on two LPs: #BLP 1507/08 (1954). Some of Blakey's finest work is in the album *Jazz Messengers with Thelonious Monk* (London #LTZ-K15157). His 1984 album, *New York Scene* (Concord Jazz #CJ-307), won a Grammy. More than 40 compact discs of Blakey performances are available.

BLATTNERPHONE. A magnetic recorder produced by Ludwig Blattner, a licensee of patents registered by the inventor Kurt Stille. Blattner, a filmmaker, intended to synchronize sound with image, but a London demonstration was unsuccessful. The machine used a six-millimeter-wide steel tape, traveling at six feet per second, with a playing time of 20 minutes. A basic problem was the erratic speed drive, powered by a battery-operated DC motor, that required an operator to monitor a tachometer dial and make manual adjustments. Despite this flaw, the BBC saw the promise of the Blattnerphone in broadcasting, and acquired two of them in 1930. An improved model, substituting an AC motor for the original battery or DC motor, using three-millimeter-wide tape, was produced by the British Blattnerphone Co., with a playing time of 30 minutes for each tape. Rights were later assigned to Marconi's Wireless Telegram Co., from which a further improved model emerged in 1934 (U.K. patents #458,255 and #467,105). By the time of World War II, the BBC had eight machines running. They were abandoned with the introduction of plastic tape. *See also* MAGNETIC RECORDING.

BLAUVELT, LILLIAN, 1873–1947. American coloratura soprano, born in Brooklyn on 16 Mar 1873. She studied violin at first, then voice in New York and Paris. Having concertized in Europe, she made her opera debut in Brussels in 1893. In 1899 she performed for Queen Victoria and sang at Covent Garden. Blauvelt recorded for Victor from 1903 to 1906, making a number of discs that have maintained lasting interest with collectors. Among them were her earliest record, "Merci, compagnons" from *Vêpres siciliennes* (Victor #81067; reissued on IRCC #8) and the "Jewel Song" from *Faust* (recorded in 1903, and again in 1906, her final Victor). She made 11 records for Columbia in 1907–1909, notably "Una voce poco fa" from *Barbiere di Siviglia* (#30150). She died in Chicago, on 29 Aug 1947.

BLEND CONTROL. A device in a stereo **amplifier** that mixes small portions of the signals coming from both channels. The purpose is to create a smoother sound front across the two speakers.

BLOOD TONE ARM. A device (named for its inventor) sold by the **Jewel Phonograph Co.**, Chicago, in 1921, compatible for lateral- or vertical-cut discs.

BLU-DISC (label). A short-lived American record sold by the Blu-Disc Record Co., New York, in 1924. Nine items were released in December (Kendziora 1973/6 reproduces the advertising poster). Duke Ellington's piano is heard on three of them, but the two sides credited to his orchestra are really by "a commercial white band of no jazz interest whatever" (Rust). [Kendziora 1973/6; Rust 1978.]

BLUE AMBEROL. The name given by Thomas Edison to his best line of cylinder records, introduced in October 1912. It was an improvement on his 1908 **Amberol**, having a smooth hard celluloid surface over a plaster of Paris core; it was said to be unbreakable and playable for 3,000 or more times with no wear. Its exterior was a rich glossy blue—examples from different periods show various shades of color, ranging into the purple area (a later "celebrity series" was colored reddish purple). Run at 160 rpm, a Blue Amberol cylinder played four minutes or longer. The **Amberola** phonograph was fitted with a diamond point **reproducer** for these new records, and the acoustic results were excellent. Record slips, giving information about the artist, the music, and advertising for other records, were included from 1912 to 1914. Blue Amberols sold for $.50.

Competition from discs was mounting, and after a few years the primary product for Edison had become the **Edison Diamond Disc**. But $2.5 million came in as late as 1920 from Amberola and Blue Amberol sales, most of the customers being in rural areas. In 1913 there were a million cylinder players in use in America. Until 1914, all Blue Amberol cylinders were direct live recordings; but in December of that year transfers were introduced via dubbing from discs. Dubbing became the standard recording process in 1915. Cylinder sales fell drastically after 1922, due to competition from radio, and dealers began to drop their Edison franchises. Figures in Dethlefson show an impressive total sale in the period 1911–1929: 21,400,000 records and 356,000 players; but in the years 1927 and 1928 operating losses were posted. The last Blue Amberol catalog appeared in 1927, the final Amberolas were made in 1928, and cylinder production ceased in 1929 with Edison's abandonment of phonographs and entertainment records in all formats, with the exception of Edison School Records. [Dethlefson 1980; Klinger*; Wile 1990/3.]

BLUE NOTE (label). A premier American jazz label for 30 years, established in 1939 by Alfred Lion and Frank Wolfe. It was located at 767 Lexington Ave., New York. Albert Ammons and Meade Lux Lewis performed boogie-woogie in the first session on 6 Jan 39 ("Boogie Woogie Stomp"; Blue Note #2). Among the star performers to follow were Sidney Bechet, Earl Hines, Bud Powell, Thelonious Monk, and Art Blakey. Quality of recording was high, in part due to the practice of paying artists for rehearsal time, although pressing materials were often poor. Designer Reid Miles was engaged in the early 1950s, and created about 1,000 distinctive album covers.

In 1966 Lion and Wolff sold the label to Liberty Records, which was later acquired by Capitol. Abandoned in 1981, the Blue Note label was revived by Capitol/EMI in 1984, under the guidance of Bruce Lundvall. New releases and digitally remastered reissues have appeared. [Cuscuna 1988 is a complete discography through 1987.]

BLUEBIRD (label). A subsidiary of Victor, issued from 1932 to 1950 and reactivated in 1976. Originally an eight-inch format, it moved to a standard 10-inch size in 1933, selling at $.35. Pricing was competitive with Decca, Columbia's chain store products, and discount labels that came out during the Depression, all of which were cutting into sales of Victor's regular $.75 line. With notable artists and high standards of recording, Bluebird was a quick success. Big Bands like those of Shep Fields, Vincent Lopez, Freddy Martin; vocalists like Dick Todd; and jazzmen like Earl Hines and Fats Waller were major attractions. Artie Shaw and Glenn Miller recorded for Bluebird; Miller's most famous contributions were "Moonlight Serenade" (#10214; 1939) and "Chattanooga Choo Choo" (#11230; 1941).

BLUEBIRD TALKING MACHINE CO. A firm located in Los Angeles. In October 1920 it sold Bluebird record players. Four models were marketed by 1922. The general manager was F. Flybush. [Andrews*.]

BLUES RECORDINGS. Blues refers to a style of music marked by a melancholy mood (and lyrics) and—as it developed—a standard chord pattern typically occupying 12 measures. Blues singing emerged in the Black culture of the southern U.S. during the mid-19th century. The first instrumental blues record was "Memphis Blues" (Victor #17619; 25 Sep 1914). "Memphis Blues" was also the first vocal blues record, sung by Morton Harvey: (Victor #17657; January 1915—with accompaniment by the New York Philharmonic Orchestra). But these were not authentic blues renditions. **Al Bernard's** "Hesitation Blues" (Edison Diamond Disc #50524; Blue Amberol cylinder #6621; 19 Feb 1919) was possibly the first authentic vocal blues number to be released, albeit by a white singer. The earliest Black blues vocal was "That Thing Called Love" / "You Can't Keep a Good Man Down" (Okeh #4113; February 1920, released in July) sung by **Mamie Smith**, accompanied by a group named the Rega Orchestra; Smith had made a rejected test record of "That Thing Called Love" for Victor in January 1920. She went on to make many more Okeh blues discs, achieving great success, the last being "Keep a Song in Your Soul" (Okeh #8864; 19 Feb 1931). Her great hit was "Crazy Blues" (#4169; 10 Aug 1920). Another pioneer Black singer was **Lucille Hegamin**, with "Jazz Me Blues" and "Everybody's Blues" (Arto #9045; November 1920); she sang for many labels until 1932.

Victor was the only major company to hold back from recording blues by Black artists, leaving the market to Columbia—which did not move aggressively either—and new independents like Okeh, Paramount, and Black Swan. Other prominent Black artists of the

1920s were **Alberta Hunter, Ma Rainey, Bessie Smith** ("Empress of the Blues"), Trixie Smith, and **Ethel Waters.**

The term "race records" was generally used in the industry at this time to identify blues and other material performed by Black musicians for a Black audience. By 1923 Columbia had become a major race label, signing Bessie Smith in 1923; she became the best-selling blues singer. Okeh and Paramount prospered as well. Victor did little, and Edison made only a few race records. Gennett made some attempts at blues without great success. Ajax, a Canadian label, was active in blues from 1923 to 1925, offering items by Rosa Henderson and Mamie Smith, among others. Vocalion was able to put out only two dozen race records, by minor performers, but when it was acquired by Brunswick in 1924 the situation changed. Brunswick entered the blues market in 1926, establishing a Race Record Division under **Jack Kapp.** Nearly all the blues vocalists were women, but in 1924 Paramount had several successful discs with Charlie Jackson, and in 1926 with **Blind Lemon Jefferson.** Among white performers, Al Bernard stands out as a leading blues singer of the acoustic period.

Peak years for blues records were 1927–1930, as the various labels issued 10 new items a week. Columbia acquired Okeh and became the major player. Victor made another move into the market during 1927, recording on location in Atlanta, Memphis, and New Orleans. "Sun Brimmer's Blues" and "Stingy Woman Blues" (#20552; 24 Feb 1927) by the Memphis Jug Band was an immediate hit; the group followed it with more than 70 other records until 1934. The Black Patti label had a brief but distinguished career in 1927. Paramount was successful with material by Charley Patton. Leroy Carr began to record for Vocalion in June 1928, with a major hit "How Long How Long Blues" (#1191); Carr became the leading blues artist of the next several years. He was the first notable blues pianist, as well as a singer. Blues was not fully amenable to the piano, since the style relies on pitches that fall between the piano keys; blues offshoots like barrelhouse and **boogie woogie** came in to fill the void.

A 1930s idiom called urban blues developed in the Depression years in Chicago. It is marked by a more aggressive sound and by group performance, e.g., by Tampa Red, a guitarist with a small combo. **Big Bill Broonzy** was a leading figure of this school. But the 1930s were bad years for record makers in any genre. Paramount, Gennett, and Columbia were bankrupt. Brunswick, bought by Warner Brothers and then transferred to Consolidated Film Industries in 1931, survived as a label, and had good market results with discs by Tampa Red and Leroy Carr. Victor made further attempts to get a share of the race market, using its Bluebird label; they scored with Joe Pullem's "Black Gal What Makes Your Head So Hard?" (#B-5459; 1934), and with Washboard Sam, one of the most popular singers of the late 1930s. The new Decca label, 1934, did well with its low-priced discs ($.35, compared to the standard $.75). Among their artists were Sleepy John Estes, Rosetta Howard, Louis Jordan, Ollie Shepard, Johnnie Temple, Peetie Wheatstraw, and the Norfolk Jubilee Quartet. There were other cheap labels, sold in Woolworth's and other dime stores for $.25. One was Melotone, which had **Josh White**'s successful "Crying Blues" (#M12727), issued also by Perfect, Romeo, Oriole, and Banner. An important noncommercial record producer, the Library of Congress Archive of Folk Song (*see* AMERICAN FOLKLIFE CENTER), released important material throughout this period, including songs by **Leadbelly** and **Muddy Waters.** The Archive made more than 4,000 records on location between 1933 and 1942.

After World War II, notable blues singers included Muddy Waters and Jimmy Rushing. A noteworthy new label was Bluesville. The old race record disappeared, and blues was largely directed toward the new rhythm & blues style. [Dixon 1970; Godrich 1969.]

BLUESVILLE (label). A subsidiary record of **Prestige**, issued from the early 1960s to 1965. Rotante gives a list of 91 issues, most of them blues. Big Joe Williams, Tampa Red, and Victoria Spivey were among the artists. Some of the albums were assigned to a lower price Prestige line, Status. [Rotante 1966.]

BLUM & CO., LTD. A British firm established 23 Feb 1911 by Joseph Leonard Blum at 89 Chiswell St., London, E.C. Beginning in August 1911 it advertised a **Diploma** label disc, said to be British made, with 350 titles available. Edison Bell matrices were used. In 1912 the company merged with **Kalliope Musikwerke AG.** of Leipzig, and began to issue a new label named Stella; the establishment moved to 220 Old St., where it occupied a six-story building. Stella's debut with 300 titles was disturbed by the discovery that Pathé was already using that label name; so the record name was changed to **Victory.** Blum also produced a **Famous** label from September 1912, for 10-inch discs (Victory was a 12-inch record). Victory was very successful, but following some legal altercations between Blum and Kalliope in 1913 the name Victory was changed to Diploma. During the industry price war of 1913 Blum introduced the Pelican label at one shilling. Pelican was replaced in early 1914 by Pioneer, selling at 1s. 6d, marked "made in Germany," indicating that old ties were still there. Despite considerable success with all his labels, Blum decided to wind up his firm in May 1914. However, a second company of the same name was founded on 17 June 1914; it continued the release of Diploma and Pioneer records. A final liquidation of the Blum interests took place on 15 Jan 1917; Columbia Graphophone Co., Ltd., took over the Blum trademarks. Blum himself left the record industry until 1927, when he surfaced as managing director of a new firm, Metropole Gramophone Co., Ltd. He left that firm after a dispute among board members in August 1930. [Andrews 1988/10.]

BLUMLEIN, ALAN DOWER, 1903–1942. British electroacoustics engineer; one of the research team at Columbia Graphophone Co., Ltd., in London from 1929. He and H.E. Holman developed a moving coil **microphone**—known as the EMI type HB-1; patenting this device (U.K. #350,998) and also a single-turn, moving coil **cutting head** (U.K. #350,954 and #350,998). However, he is best known for his pioneering research into **stereophonic recording**, having demonstrated stereo discs in the early 1930s that illustrated the same principles employed commercially a quarter century later. He designed and patented a stereo system in 1931, and directed a recording of the London Philharmonic, under Thomas Beecham, partly in stereo, on 19 Jan 1934. He also made a successful stereo motion picture soundtrack (1935). He died in the crash of a Halifax bomber on 7 June 1942.

BMG CLASSICS (label). *See* BERTELSMANN AG.

BOB-O-LINK TALKING BOOK. An imitation of the American **Bubble Books,** offered in Britain from 1922 to 1923. Each book included two seven-inch discs. Ten titles were offered, priced from 1s 6d to 6s. The publisher was A.G. Gilbert and Co., New Haven, Connecticut.

BÖHM, KARL, 1894–1981. Austrian conductor, born in Graz on 28 Aug 1894. His career was shaped in a number of major opera houses, as he moved as director from Munich (1921), to Hamburg (1931–1933), Dresden (1934–1943), and Vienna (1944–1945; 1954–1956). In Dresden he also conducted the Saxon State Orchestra. He appeared first in the U.S. with the Chicago Symphony Orchestra in 1956, then with the Metropolitan Opera in 1957, conducting there intermittently through 1974. He made a notable tour of the U.S. and Japan with the Berlin Philharmonic Orchestra in 1963–1964.

His favored composers were Alban Berg, Mozart, Wagner, and Richard Strauss, and he recorded most of their works. With the Saxon State Orchestra in 1938–1939 he put to disc for HMV many of the outstanding items in their catalog, including a group reissued in four LP albums by EMI/Electrola in 1982 (#1C-137-53500–53519). CDs of eight Mozart operas under his direction were issued in 1990. The recording of *Wozzeck* (DGG #2707023; 1965) won a Grammy. He died in Salzburg on 14 Aug 1981.

BOLET, JORGE, 1914–1990. Cuban pianist, born in Havana on 15 Nov 1914. He went to the U.S. in 1926 to study at the Curtis Institute in Philadelphia, and eventually became head of the piano department there. Among his teachers were Leopold Godowsky, Moriz Rosenthal,

Abram Chasins, and Rudolf Serkin. Bolet became known for his virtuosity, receiving special acclaim for his interpretations of Chopin and Liszt; he recorded those composers on LP for Victor, and then made CDs of the major Liszt works for Decca in 1984–1986.

BONCI, ALESSANDRO, 1870–1940. Italian tenor, born in Cesena on 10 Feb 1870; described by Hurst as "the perfect tenor." His operatic debut was in Parma in 1896; then he was heard at La Scala and at Covent Garden (debut as Rodolfo in 1900, creating a sensation). He continued at Covent Garden, while performing also in America. In 1906–1909 he sang with the Manhattan Opera in New York, and in 1907–1910 with the Metropolitan Opera (debut as the Duke on 22 Nov 1907). Bonci's recordings for Fonotipia in Milan, ca. 1905–1908, are much prized by collectors. His first disc was a splendid "Una furtiva lagrima" (#39083). Perhaps the finest of the early records was "A te, o cara" from *Puritani* (#39084; 1905). His *Rigoletto* arias, recorded for Columbia in 1913, are also noteworthy: "Questa o quella" / "La donna è mobile" (#A-1286); and he made a distinguished "Che gelida manina" as well (#A-5449). Bonci made seven Edison Diamond Discs in 1913–1914, and in 1926—after his prime—his only electrics, for Columbia. He died in Viserba, Italy, on 8 Aug 1940. [Hutchinson 1957.]

BONINSEGNA, CELESTINA, 1877–1947. Italian soprano, born in Reggio Emilia on 26 Feb 1877. She was heard at age 15 in Reggio Emilia, before undertaking formal study. In 1896 she made a formal debut in Fana as Gilda, then toured Italy and South America specializing in the Verdi operas. She sang at Covent Garden in 1904–1905, and made her Metropolitan Opera debut as Aida on 21 Dec 1906, but did not return for the next season. Having retired from the stage in 1920, she devoted herself to teaching. She died in Milan on 14 Feb 1947.

Boninsegna began to record in 1904, for G & T in Milan; her first disc was "In quelle trine morbide" from *Manon Lescaut* (#53372). Between 1904 and 1918 she made more than 30 recordings for that label. In 1905 she recorded in Paris for Pathé, and then made some of her most acclaimed records for Columbia in the

U.S., in 1909–1910. Her arias from *Aida* show her at her best: "Ritorna vincitor" (Columbia #30381) and "O patria mia" (#30382). Later she worked for various labels in Europe and America, and was represented in many LP series of historical reissues. [Williams, C. 1958.]

BOOGIE WOOGIE. A style of popular piano playing that developed from the blues in the 1920s. It is characterized by ostinato bass figures in the left hand, often with eight notes to the bar, harmonized in blues chord progressions. **Clarence "Pinetop" Smith** is credited with the first boogie composition and recording: "Pinetop's Boogie Woogie" (1928). Early performers of the idiom on record included Romeo Nelson, Arthur Taylor, and Charles Avery. Widespread enthusiasm for the style came in the mid-1930s with the performances of **Albert Ammons, Pete Johnson,** and **Meade Lux Lewis.** One of the hit songs of World War II was "Boogie Woogie Bugle Boy" sung by the **Andrews Sisters.** A basic boogie-woogie collection was issued by the Solo Art label on 11 discs in 1941. A compact disc collection, *Best of Boogie Woogie* (EPM #ZET-740; 1991), offers a representation of the major artists.

Bootleg. *See* PIRATED RECORDS.

BORI, LUCREZIA, 1887–1960. Spanish soprano, born Lucrecia Borja y Gonzales de Riancho on 24 Dec 1887 in Valencia. She made her debut as Micaela in Rome in 1908, then appeared in Paris, La Scala, and Buenos Aires. Her Metropolitan Opera debut was in *Manon Lescaut*; she remained with the company until 1935/1936 (missing the seasons 1916–1920), then retired. Her greatest successes came in the roles of Mimi and Manon Lescaut. She recorded "Mi chiamano Mimi" on Edison Blue Amberol, and made 10 Edison Diamond Discs between 1913 and 1923. There were many outstanding Victor records, including the *Rigoletto* Quartet with John McCormack, Josephine Jacoby, and Reinald Werrenrath (#89080) which sold at the premium price of $4. There were 11 solos and two duets as well in the 1917 Victor catalog, and 15 items in the 1927 catalog. They included the notable "In quelle trine morbide" from *Manon Lescaut* (#40032) and a 1910 reissue of "Mi chiamano Mimi" (#40036). Bori died in New York on 14 May 1960. [Richards 1948/10; Richards 1973.]

BOSE CORP. American electronics firm, located in Framingham, Massachusetts, specializing in **loudspeakers.** Amar Bose founded the company in 1964. He emphasized the use of multiple small speakers as alternatives to single large units; and he added special electronics and directional design to his products. The Bose 901 was acclaimed in 1968 as unsurpassed for realistic reproduction. In 1990 the 901 Concerto System was selling for $2,200. [Klinger*.]

BOSS RADIO. A term given to the format for popular music broadcasts that originated in Los Angeles in 1965 at station KHJ; Bill Drake and Ron Jacobs devised the approach. Boss programming was rather automatic, depending heavily on multiple plays of Top 40 records, plus four or five uncharted items. The **disc jockey**—tarnished in the **payola** scandals of the 1950s—became little more than an announcer, with program selections made by the program director. But a competing format, **free-form programming**, emerged quickly and restored initiative to the deejay.

BOSTON SYMPHONY ORCHESTRA. Established in 1881, one of the oldest and most distinguished American orchestras, and the first to make recordings. Conductors have been Georg Henschel, 1881–1883; Wilhelm Gericke, 1884–1888, and 1898–1905; **Arthur Nikisch,** 1889–1892; Emil Paur, 1893–1897; **Karl Muck,** 1917–1918; Henri Rabaud, 1918–1919; **Pierre Monteux,** 1919–1923; **Serge Koussevitzky,** 1924–1949, **Charles Munch,** 1949–1962, **Erich Leinsdorf,** 1963–1967; William Steinberg, 1968–1972; and **Seiji Ozawa,** 1973– . The orchestra's pioneer recording was of the Tchaikovsky Fourth Symphony, made in the Victor Camden studios (#6050; 1917); it remained in the Victor catalog into the electrical era until replaced by the Koussevitzky version. Victor held the exclusive contract for the orchestra until 1969, when Deutsche Grammophon acquired it. Later the ensemble was heard on CBS, Philips, and other labels. Among the outstanding recordings by the orchestra were Debussy pieces

made under Munch, for example, *La mer* (#LM 2111); and contemporary works commissioned for them under Koussevitzky (by Bartók, Bliss, Britten, Ibert, Milhaud, Ravel, Villa-Lobos, Walton, and others). A large collection of noncommercial recordings (acetates) of the Orchestra is at the Library of Congress (described in Young 1990).

The Boston Pops Orchestra, drawn from the Symphony's members, began to give informal concerts modeled on the London Promenade events of the 1920s, and engaged **Arthur Fiedler** as conductor in 1930. The Pops performs the lighter repertoire and has recorded extensively under Fiedler and his successor (in 1979), John Williams. Symphony Hall in Boston, designed by McKim, Mead, and White in 1900, is one of the finest acoustical auditoriums in the United States. [Young, E. 1990.]

BOSTON TALKING MACHINE CO. A record manufacturer located in Boston, issuing the **Phonocut** label from 1910. After two or three years, the label was sold to a Philadelphia business man named Morris Keen, who renamed it **Keen-O-Phone**; later it took the name **Rex.**

BOSWELL SISTERS. American vocal trio (Connie or Connee; Martha; and Helvetia, known as Vet), all born in New Orleans. They were the leading female vocal group of the early 1930s, appearing with major jazz bands; they also had jazz stars as backup for many records. They were radio and movie performers as well. The group broke up in 1936, but Connie continued her career into the 1950s.

The first Boswell Sisters record to be issued was made for Victor in New Orleans on 22 Mar 1925, "I'm Gonna Cry" (#19639). They went on to many other labels, especially Brunswick. "Between the Devil and the Deep Blue Sea" was a notable hit (Brunswick #6291; 1932), with Bunny Berigan and the Dorsey brothers among the musicians heard. Another acclaimed song was "I'm Gonna Sit Right Down and Write Myself a Letter" (Decca #671; 1936), backed up by Russ Case, Artie Shaw, and others. Connie made some notable duets with Bing Crosby in 1937: "Basin Street Blues" / "Bob White" (Decca #1483; 1937). The Silver

Swan label issued many of their hits on LP #1001 in 1976.

BOTTOM. A term for the bass response of a sound system.

Bottom radius. *See* GROOVE.

BOULEZ, PIERRE, 1925– . French composer and conductor, born in Montbrisson on 26 Mar 1925. He studied composition at the Paris Conservatory, graduating in 1945. He became a theatre and ballet conductor, then directed major orchestras and opera companies in Europe and the U.S. In 1971 he was appointed music director of the New York Philharmonic Orchestra, and began a vigorous promotion of 12-tone and avant-garde works. His choice of repertoire brought mixed reactions from the concert subscribers, and his tenure in New York ended in 1978. Thereafter he was active as an opera conductor while also devoting himself to electronic composition.

Boulez made a Grammy-winning *Daphnis et Chloe* with the New York Philharmonic in 1975, and won three Grammys later for operatic work: the *Lulu* album on Deutsche Grammophon took two awards in 1980, and the *Ring* recording for Philips won the opera award for 1982.

BOULT, ADRIAN, *Sir*, **1889–1983.** English conductor, born on 8 Apr 1889 in Chester. He was one of the few major conductors to have a high academic qualification, the doctorate in music from Oxford (1914). In 1918 he conducted in London, and for the Ballets Russes. He became music director for the British Broadcasting Corp. (BBC) in 1928 and organized the BBC Symphony Orchestra, remaining as conductor until 1950. From 1950 to 1967 he was conductor of the London Philharmonic Orchestra. Boult was knighted in 1937 for his service to British music, which he championed vigorously. His principal recordings were from the British 20th-century school, for example, Holst's *The Planets* (HMV #GM387, on seven 12-inch discs), Elgar's Second Symphony (HMV #GM378, on six discs), and Vaughan Williams' "Fantasia on a Theme of Thomas Tallis" (Victor #769, two discs). All these were made with the BBC Orchestra. In 1960 he recorded a stereo accompaniment for a 1953 recital by Kathleen Ferrier (originally with monophonic accompaniment). Boult died in Tunbridge Wells on 22 Feb 1983. [Sanders 1981.]

BOWERS, JAMES F., 1858–1925. American music and record industry executive. He was president of the Music Publishers' Association for 14 years, and president of the National **Association of Talking Machine Jobbers** for 12 years. Most of his career was spent with Lyon & Healy; during 55 years with that music instrument company he was president and finally chairman of the board. He died in Chicago on 11 Nov 1925.

BOWLLY, AL, 1899–1941. Popular singer, born in Natal, South Africa, on 7 Jan 1899. He was self-taught on the piano, banjo, guitar, and ukulele. Having toured South Africa and the Far East with Edgar Adeler's band in 1923, he received world acclaim and moved to Britain in 1928. In 1931 he began a long association with Ray Noble, and he sang also with Lew Stone's band from 1932. In 1934 he transferred to the U.S. Bowlly's recorded output was vast: more than 1,500 discs (most on HMV, Columbia, Decca, Victor and Bluebird) are credited to him (in Rust 1989), made from 1927 to 1941. Among his most elegant renditions is "The Touch of Your Lips" (by Ray Noble; Victor #25277; 1936). Bowlly's rendition of "Midnight, the Stars, and You," with Noble (1934) was used in the motion picture *The Shining*. He was killed in a London air raid on 17 Apr 1941.

BOXING RECORDINGS. The first record of any sporting event was the one made by the first Black firm to issue records. It was the Jack Johnson Record, describing the championship match between Jack Johnson and Jim Jeffries on 4 July 1910. The bout between Jack Dempsey and Gene Tunney, 22 Sep 1927, was recorded on five discs by Paramount. *Great Moments in Boxing* was a 1961 LP released on the Coral label.

BOYD, BILL, 1911–1977. American western singer and guitarist, born in Texas and raised as a cowboy. He should not be confused with the actor of the same name, who played "Hopalong Cassidy." Boyd had a radio show in Dallas from 1932 into the 1960s. In 1934 he began recording with Victor, and eventually made more than 300 records. He was in a number of western movies in the 1930s and 1940s. He retired in the early 1950s, and died in 1977.

Bill Boyd and His Cowboy Ramblers were the group that initiated the Victor series of western discs, with "I'm Gonna Hop off the Train" (#B-5740) and nine other numbers made on 7 Aug 1934 in San Antonio. The group performed 10 more songs on 27 Jan 1935. On 12 Aug 1935 they recorded one of their major hits, "Get Aboard That Southbound Train" (#B-6085).

BRAIN, DENNIS, 1921–1957. British hornist, the first to make significant solo recordings of his instrument. He was born in London on 17 May 1921, son of the eminent horn player Aubrey Brain. Dennis Brain was principal hornist of the Royal Philharmonic and Philharmonia Orchestras. Among his notable discs, which spanned the concert repertoire of the horn, were the four Mozart concertos, made with Herbert Von Karajan and the Philharmonia Orchestra in 1953 (Angel #35092; HMV #ASD-1140); and a composition written for him, the "Serenade for Tenor, Horn and Strings" by Benjamin Britten, recorded with Peter Pears and the Boyd Neel String Orchestra (Decca #D-ED7, on three 12–inch 78s). He was also heard in the Hoffnung Music Festival, playing on a garden hose (Angel #35500; HMV #SLS-5069). Brain died in an automobile accident in Hertfordshire on 1 Sep 1957.

BRASS INSTRUMENT RECORDINGS. Recordings offer a historical perspective of brass music. While the repertoire for brass instruments is not extensive when compared with the number of compositions for voice, violin, or flute, recordings do include works from the pre-baroque period to the present.

Many worthwhile recordings exemplify early music on musical instruments of each period. The sounds of the clarion trumpet, slide trumpet, the 16th- and 17th-century cornetto (cornett), sackbut, serpent, and other instruments of the middle ages, renaissance, and baroque are displayed on discs. Authentic recordings, such as those by English musicologist David Munrow, present the instruments in contemporary settings. Munrow's LP album *Instruments of the Middle Ages and Renaissance* (Angel #SBZ-3810; 1976) includes compositions such as "Der Trumpet" by Herman, Monk of Salzburg (1365–1396), and "Adagio and Allegro" from the Sonata for Trombone by Heinrich Biber (1644–1704).

The band and orchestral repertoire presents solo and ensemble parts for trumpet, cornet, horn, trombone, bass trombone, euphonium, baritone horn, and tuba. Orchestral examples include Leo Janáček's *Sinfonietta* (1926) and Richard Strauss' *Also sprach Zarathustra* (1896), while concert band examples include Percy Grainger's *Lincolnshire Posey* (1937) and William Walton's *Crown Imperial* (1937).

In a different category there are comic or novelty recordings. An early example is "Yellow Dog Blues" by Joseph C. Smith's Orchestra, featuring Harry Rederman and his "laughing trombone" (Victor #18618B; 1919). A similar example was made by **Spike Jones** and His City Slickers, featuring Bruce Hudson on trumpet in Oliver Wallace's "Der Fuehrer's Face" (Bluebird #11586; 1942). Another comic number was Tommy Pederson on trombone doing "Flight of the Bumblebee" on *The Jones Laughing Record* (RCA #LSC 3235; reissued 1971).

In 1956, the Hoffnumg Music Festival in England offered "an extravagant evening of symphonic caricature," with a trumpet fanfare by Francis Baines (played after a drum roll that brought the audience to its feet in expectation of the national anthem) and a tuba quartet arrangement by Daniel Abrams of Chopin's Mazurka in A-Minor (Angel #35500; 1956). While this Mazurka arrangement may have been comical at the 13 Nov 1956 concert, such transcriptions have gained common acceptance by euphonium/tuba ensembles today.

Until the 20th century, brass solo and ensemble literature was limited. Certainly the invention of valves in the early 1800s and the development of the euphonium and tuba in the middle 19th century offered composers and arrangers a completely different scope.

Further improvements of brass instruments and enlargement of the brass repertoire in the 19th century offered players and recording companies new opportunities.

Through recordings one recognizes different styles of playing in the early 1900s in comparison to later styles. For example, vibrato similar to that of operatic vocalists at the turn of the century was quite prominent on early brass recordings.

Important cornet and trombone players who recorded solos on acoustic discs or cylinders, included **Herbert L. Clarke**, Bohumir Kryl (1875–1961), **Jules Levy**, and **Walter Rogers** on cornet; Jaroslav (Jerry) Cimera, **Arthur Pryor**, and Leo Zimmerman (1866–1935) on trombone; and Simone Mantia (1873–1951) on euphonium. These soloists recorded compositions such as "Stars in a Velvety Sky" by Clarke (Brunswick #2367; 1921), "King Carnival" by Kryl (Victor #2596; 1904) and "Blue Bells of Scotland" by Pryor (Victor Monarch #3251; 1901).

Brass ensemble recordings were released from the early 1900s. An early example was the Sextet from *Lucia di Lammermoor*, which included Emil Keneke and Bert Brown, cornets; Arthur Pryor, trombone; and Simone Mantia, euphonium; with Pryor's Band (Victor #31460; 1905). Other examples include Verdi's "Attila Trio" with Kryl on cornet, Cimera on trombone, and Cinconne on euphonium (Victor #35195; 1912); and "The Kerry Dance" with the Boston Symphony Trombone Quartet (Victor #4369; 1908).

Early recordings frequently failed to identify performers. For example, the names of the Edison Brass Quartette members are not known: they made 17 cylinders from before 1900 to 1904.

While the cornet and trombone were most prominent in early recordings, solo and brass ensemble recordings using all instruments have gained considerable momentum since the invention of the LP. Recordings have been made of major classical solo and ensemble works, such as Haydn's *Concerto in E-Flat Major* for trumpet; Hummel's *Concerto in E-Flat Major* for trumpet; Mozart's concertos for horn; Richard Strauss' Concerto No. 1 for horn; Paul Hindemith's *Sonata for Trombone and Piano*; Rimsky-Korsakoff's *Concerto for Trombone and Band*; Thom Ritter George's *Sonatina for Baritone Horn and Piano*; Gordon Jacob's *Fantasia for Euphonium and Band*; Hindemith's *Sonata for Bass Tuba and Piano*; and Ralph Vaughan Williams' *Concerto for Tuba*.

Homogeneous brass ensemble compositions recorded on LP include Verne Reynolds' *Music for 5 Trumpets*, Hindemith's *Sonata for Four French Horns*, Beethoven's *Three Equale for Four Trombones*; and Thom Ritter George's *Tubasonatina* for euphonium/tuba ensemble.

Recorded ensemble compositions with a heterogeneous instrumentation include: David Borden's *Six Dialogues for Trumpet and Trombone*; Francis Poulenc's *Sonata for Horn, Trumpet, and Trombone*; Aaron Copland's *Fanfare for the Common Man* for brass ensemble; and Giovanni Gabrielli's "Sonata pian' e forte" from his *Sacrae symphoniae*. But the most prominent repertoire is for brass quintet, including such works as Daniel Speer's "Sonata" from *Die Bänkelsängerlieder* (ca. 1684); Malcolm Arnold's *Quintet, Op. 73* (1961); Eugene Bozza's *Sonatine for Brass Quintet* (1951); John Cheetham's *Scherzo*; Victor Ewald's *Quintet in B-Flat Minor, Op. 5* (1912); and Johann Christoph Pezel's "Sonata" from *Hora decima* (1685).

With expansion of the repertoire and increasing numbers of performers, there were numerous brass recordings on LP records. Some of the principal players have included: Maurice André, Edward Tarr, and Roger Voisin, trumpet; **Dennis Brain**, Philip Farkas, and Barry Tuckwell, horn; Ralph Sauer, Branimir Slokar, and Denis Wick, trombone; Edward Kleinhammer, bass trombone; Brian Bowman, euphonium; William Bell, Roger Bobo, and Arnold Jacobs, tuba. Brass ensembles include the American Brass Quintet, the Annapolis Brass Quintet, the Canadian Brass, the Edward Tarr and Philip Jones Brass Ensembles, and the New York Brass Quintet.

Some artists who recorded the less common instruments included: *Horn*: Willie Ruff (b. 1931); *Euphonium*: Rich Mattesson (b. 1929); *Tuba*: Don Butterfield (b. 1923), and Howard Johnson (b. 1941). Trumpet players often recorded the cornet as well, or the flugelhorn. (For jazz and swing recordings involving brass players, see TRUMPET RECORDINGS and

TROMBONE RECORDINGS.) [Bahr 1988; Bridges 1968; Hernon 1986; Little 1977; Lowrey 1990; Whitaker 1966. Periodicals of interest include: *Brass Bulletin, Cadence, International Horn Society Horn Call, International Trombone Association Journal, International Trumpet Guild Journal, T.U.B.A. Journal.*]

See also CORNET RECORDINGS; MILITARY BAND RECORDINGS; TROMBONE RECORDINGS; TRUMPET RECORDINGS; TUBA RECORDINGS.

Edward R. Bahr

BRIDGEPORT DIE AND MACHINE CO. A firm located at 174 Elm St. in Bridgeport, Connecticut, which produced phonograph records in addition to its manufacturing activity. These were released under various label names: **Broadway, Carnival, Hudson, Master Tone, Mitchell Record, National, Pennington, Puretone, Puritan, Resona, Ross,** and **Triangle.** Recording work took place from ca. 1922 to 1925, when the firm went bankrupt.

BRIDGING. The process of connecting two channels in a stereo **amplifier** to play back a monophonic signal; also called strapping.

BRILLIANT QUARTETTE. An early recording group for Columbia, first listed in their September 1891 catalog, and carried through the 1895 catalog. Although they were the first vocal group widely featured by Columbia, the members were never identified. They sang Negro songs and popular numbers of the day. Another group of the same name, or perhaps the same singers, recorded for Berliner in the late 1890s.

BRILLIANTONE STEEL NEEDLE CO. A New York firm established in 1918, located at Sixth Ave. and Broadway. It produced phonograph needles.

BRISTOPHONE. The first electrically amplified **cartridge**, designed and patented in 1924, and marketed in 1926, by the Bristol Co. of Waterbury, Connecticut. It consisted of "a tone arm and reproducer designed to be set inside the phonograph cabinet (next to the old tone arm) and connected to a separate amplifier and

speaker system" (Barnes). It operated through the speaker, or both the speaker and amplifier, of a radio. Its price was $45 in 1926. [Barnes, K. 1975.]

BRITISH BROADCASTING CORP. (BBC). A firm established in London, in November 1922, as the British Broadcasting Co., with six major companies as founder members: Marconi's Wireless Telegraph Co., Ltd.; Metropolitan Vickers Electrical Co., Ltd.; British Thomson Houston Co., Ltd.; General Electric Co., Ltd.; Western Electric Co., Ltd.; and Radio Communication Co., Ltd. John Reith was the general manager. The BBC began broadcasting on 14 Nov 1922 (following some experimental transmissions in the previous year). Peter P. Eckersley was the first chief engineer. At first the company held a monopoly on sales of radio sets in Britain (1922–1925), and it kept exclusive rights to broadcast on radio and television until 1955. In 1927 the company became a corporation.

Research and development activities were prominent from the early days, and in 1990 were the responsibility of 215 workers. Over the years important research has been done in loudspeaker design, microphones, diaphragms, and studio design. The BBC pioneered in magnetic recording, having initiated use of the **Blattnerphone** in 1930.

One of the world's principal libraries of sound recordings (dating from 1933) has been assembled in Broadcasting House, the BBC's main building since 1932. The archival collection was stored in a coal mine during World War II; other records were moved out of London. There are more than a million discs, cylinders, and tapes in the collection.

Christopher Stone was radio's first "disk jockey," playing records on a regularly scheduled series of broadcasts. The BBC Symphony Orchestra was created in 1928, and under conductor **Adrian Boult** it became one of the leading symphonic ensembles of its time.

BRITISH BRUNSWICK, LTD. A firm established 20 Sep 1926, at George St., Hanover Square, London, with W. Sinkler Darby as managing director and Count Anthony Herbert de Bosdari as general manager. The firm made discs and **Panatrope** players, beginning with pressings from the **Brunswick-Balke-Collender Co.** (of the U.S.), and issuing their first British made records in July 1927. A 10–year exclusive contract was arranged to sell American **Brunswick** records; exchange of matrices and mutual sales agreements continued with Deutsche Grammophon. A series of **tone tests** was held, using the Panatrope. In April 1928 British Brunswick became affiliated with **Duophone**, through a merger of manufacturing and sales functions, and soon Duophone was in full control of the enterprise.

With the establishment of the **Decca Record Co., Ltd.,** in February 1929, Duophone/Brunswick pressed discs for that firm, and the Brunswick name appeared on record labels. But resources were overextended, and liquidation proceedings began. British Brunswick closed down in September 1929. However, the label name reappeared in December 1930 with the formation of the **Brunswick Radio Corp.** in America, and the establishment of a new British partner company, **Warner Brunswick, Ltd.** Both 10–inch and 12–inch Brunswick records appeared in Britain until 1949. [Andrews*; Andrews 1981/1; Rust*.]

BRITISH COPYRIGHT PROTECTION ASSOCIATION.

An organization devoted to the collection of royalties for members, and for members of certain affiliated non-British associations.

BRITISH HOMOPHONE CO., LTD.

A firm incorporated on 3 Aug 1921, located at 19 City Road, London. It had agreements to use the masters of the Homophon Co. of Berlin, which had been distributing records in Britain on their **Homophon** label since 1906. The label of the new firm was named **Homochord**, also the label name of a record sold in Britain by the Berlin firm, from 1912 to 1916. After World War I some American pressings were issued on Homochord, via Pathé Frères Phonograph Co., Inc., and Pathé Frères Compagnie of London, Vocalion (and others) through the Aeolian and Vocalion companies in Britain.

On 19 May 1928 the firm became a public limited company, acquiring at that time the assets of the Sterno Manufacturing Co.; in April 1929 a label named **Sterno** was introduced. Columbia bought all shares of the Berlin Homophon Co. in 1928, creating business difficulties. There was a considerable loss during the first year of operation and cutbacks followed. Sterno also lost money, but British Homophone carried on and entered the radio field as well in 1932. They produced an early long-playing record, the **Four-in-One** label, in August 1932: with a finer cut spiral it could squeeze two numbers on each side of a 10–inch disc. In the same year the firm trademarked the **Kid-Kord** and Kindakord labels for children's material. Despite these initiatives, the company could not long survive in the Depression years. No records were advertised after April 1935, although the company continued to press discs for other makers. **Crystalate Gramophone Record Manufacturing Co., Ltd.,** took control of the firm by August 1939; but the name of the company has persisted to this day, with an address on Rollins St. in London. It remains in the recording business, but not for public sales. [Andrews*; Andrews 1985/10.]

British Institute of Recorded Sound. *See* NATIONAL SOUND ARCHIVE.

British Library of Wildlife Sounds. *See* NATIONAL SOUND ARCHIVE.

BRITISH OZAPHANE, LTD.

A firm established 9 Mar 1936, located at 72a Carlton Hill, London, licensed by two French companies to use a patent for film soundtracks. W.H. Ogden was managing director. **Duo-Trac** was the name of their product; it had negligible success, and the company ceased functioning in 1946. It was officially struck from register on 10 Oct 1950.

BRITISH PHONOGRAPH INDUSTRIES, LTD.

A maker of "electric cylinders"—not electrically recorded—established in March 1904. It had no advertising after 1905, and was ordered to wind up in March 1906.

BRITISH SONOGRAM CO., LTD.

A firm established in 1907, at 77 City Road, and 23 Christopher St., London. It flourished in 1907, selling 10–inch, double-sided discs in the U.K. and U.S. The label name was **Sovereign**.

BRITISH ZONOPHONE CO. A firm established 1903 as outlet for the British recordings of **International Zonophone Co.**, at 81 City Road, London, with **Louis Sterling** as manager. The firm was actually a somewhat clandestine subsidiary of **Gramophone and Typewriter, Ltd.**, intended to sell cheap discs without compromising the company name. Its records were made by Deutsche Grammophon in Hanover, or made at the Berlin plant of International Zonophone, and the labels at first carried the name International Zonophone. Sterling issued a "Catalogue of Zonophone Disc Records: July 1904" (facsimile reprint, London: City of London Phonograph and Gramophone Society, 1977). With the label name changed to **Zonophone** new recordings were made in several international series, presenting a varied popular repertoire. The firm's playback machine, as advertised in *TMN* 1905, featured a new tone arm. In 1910 the firm incorporated as British Zonophone Co., Ltd.

The company admitted, in a 1920 story in *TMN*, that their records and machines had been made by the Gramophone Co. "for quite a long time," and that henceforth they would use the HMV name on their products. It was, however, the **Nipper** trademark that was used, not the words "His Master's Voice," and in 1924 that logo was abandoned in favor of the earlier "Zonophone Cross" design. In the summer of 1931 British Zonophone moved into a new home on Oxford St., shared with HMV. [Andrews*.]

BRITT, ELTON, 1917–1972. American country singer, born James Britt Baker in Marshall, Arkansas, on 7 July 1917. He was featured on the *Grand Ole Opry, Camel Caravan, Elton Britt Show,* and other radio programs, and was one of the leading stars during the 1940s and 1950s. A Victor artist from 1937, he made 672 singles and 56 albums for the label over 22 years. Later he also worked for Decca, ABC-Paramount, and others. His greatest hit record was the 1943 "There's a Star Spangled Banner Waving Somewhere," on the Bluebird label (#9000; 1942), the first country song to sell a million records. Britt died in McConnellsburg, Pennsylvania, on 23 June 1972.

BROADCAST (label). A **Vocalion** subsidiary record, first issued in Britain in July 1927. The discs were eight inches in diameter, but with finer than ordinary grooves so that the playing time was that of the standard 10–inch record. Selling at a bargain price of 1s 3d, the new product threatened to upset the market balance of the gramophone industry, and there was an effort to stifle advertising and retailing of it. Vocalion sold the label nevertheless, using chain stores and stationers such as W.H. Smith and Boots. Broadcast was a great success, and the factory was hard put to bring out enough discs to meet demand: around 1.25 million per month.

Beginning in January 1928, the label was sold in Australia; and later that year it was available in China, Italy, and France. But the success faded quickly, and by 1930 Vocalion was losing money on its foreign operations and suffering from domestic competition in Britain. The price of the eight-inch disc was lowered to 1 shilling in March 1931, and the 10–inch Broadcast Twelve was put on the market in July 1928—said to have the playing time of an ordinary 12–inch disc. Then in September 1931 the original eight-inch disc was increased in size to nine inches. These approaches were not fruitful, and in March 1932 Vocalion was acquired by the **Crystalate Gramophone Record Manufacturing Co., Ltd.** Crystalate initiated two new labels: Broadcast International (using U.S. masters from the American Record Corp., in which Crystalate was a partner), and Broadcast Four-Tune, both in January 1933; they were 10–inch records selling at 1s 6d. The fine grooving drew five to six minutes of playing time from the Four-Tune (the tunes were dance music numbers). In 1933 and 1934 the name Crystalate began to replace the Broadcast and Vocalion identification on the discs, so the label disappeared finally in March 1934. [Andrews 1982/12.]

BROADCAST MUSIC, INC. (BMI). A licensing organization established by U.S. broadcasting companies in 1940 as a response to ASCAP (**American Society of Composers, Authors, and Publishers**). When ASCAP demanded a huge increase in rights fees from broadcasters who played songs on the air, BMI endeavored to enlist artists and composers who were not affiliated with ASCAP. In 1941 agreements were reached between ASCAP and the radio networks, although it was said that the radio stations favored BMI works after that. BMI is located at 320 W. 57th St., New York. It has more than 47,000 writer and 29,000 publisher affiliates, for whom it acts as guardian of performing rights and negotiates fees. The board of directors is drawn from the broadcasting industry, and so are the stockholders.

BROADWAY (label). An American bargain label of the 1920s. It used Paramount material at first, then Emerson, Crown, and Banner masters. Pressing was done by the **Bridgeport Die and Machine Co.** until 1925, then by the **New York Recording Laboratories** of Port Washington, Wisconsin. Blues, race records, hillbilly, and dance music provided the repertoire. It ceased operating in 1931. [MacKenzie 1963; Rust 1978.]

BROADWAY QUARTET. The name used on Vocalion records in 1922 by the **Criterion Quartet.**

BROCKMAN, JAMES, 1886–1967. American tenor, dialect comedian, and composer; probably born in Cleveland on 8 Dec 1886. He made only five records, all of them two-minute Edison wax cylinders. He began with his own composition, "Marianna," in Italian dialect (#9712; 1907). His final record was a Jewish dialect song, (#10165; 1911). He wrote or collaborated on "I'm Forever Blowing Bubbles" (1918), "Down Among the Sheltering Palms" (1915), and "I'm Like a Ship Without a Sail" (1920). Brockman died in Santa Monica, California, on 22 May 1967. [Walsh 1967/10.]

BROOKS MANUFACTURING CO. An American firm established in 1903 in Saginaw, Michigan. Advertising in *TMW* (1916) shows the firm as the maker of a coin operated disc player named Brooks.

BROONZY, BIG BILL, 1893–1958. American blues singer and guitarist, born William Lee Conley Broonzy in Scott, Mississippi, on 26 June 1893. He taught himself the fiddle while working as a sharecropper; served in World War I; then went to Chicago in 1920 to work for the Pullman Co. There he took up the guitar, and sang blues songs. In the late 1920s he was performing with leading blues artists, and made some unnoticed records. Then he began to record in 1928 for Paramount and in 1930 (under the name Sammy Sampson) for the American Recording Corp. (ARC). In 1931 ARC recorded him under his own name on its dime store subsidiary labels. For example, "I Wanta See My Baby" / "Hobo Blues," on Romeo #5494, sold for $.25 in the S.H. Kress stores. He was a major exponent of the urban blues style through the 1930s, making a new disc every few weeks, primarily for Vocalion; he had more than 100 issues by 1942. Broonzy made successful European tours in 1951, 1955, and 1957. He died in Chicago on 14 Aug 1958. [McCarthy 1964.]

BROWN, JAMES, 1933– . American blues, gospel, and soul singer; and dancer; born in Augusta, Georgia, on 3 May 1928. He began professional performance as a singer in a vocal quartet, the Famous Flames, with which he continued to work for 10 years. He recorded a rhythm & blues hit, "Please, Please, Please" (Federal #12258; 1958), and another, "Try Me" in the following year (Federal #12337; 1959). Thereafter he worked in many styles, bringing together an acrobatic dance routine with energetic musical idioms drawn from African and Caribbean roots. In the 1960s Brown developed a new style called "funk," but he was also identified as the "godfather of soul." He made about 80 chart singles by the mid-1970s, and around 30 chart albums. His best selling album was recorded live at a Harlem concert with the Famous Flames: *The Apollo Theatre Presents—In Person! The James Brown Show* (King #LP 826; 1963); it was on the charts 33 weeks and sold over a million copies. Brown's last hit album was *People* (Polydor #PD-1–6212; 1980). There were 18 CD reissues available in 1991, notably the retrospective *Star Time*—71 songs on four compact discs (Polydor #849108; 1991). Greg Kot, rock critic of the *Chicago Tribune*, declared in his review of *Star Time* that Brown was "the most influential and innovative figure in Black music in the last 30 years, and every bit as important as more widely revered artists such as Elvis Presley and the Beatles in shaping the sound of the rock era."

BROWNLEE, JOHN, 1900–1969. Australian baritone, born in Geelong on 7 Jan 1900. After study in Europe he made his debut in Paris in 1926 and at Covent Garden in the same year, then joined the Paris Opéra, where he remained until 1933. He sang first at the Metropolitan Opera as Rigoletto on 17 Feb 1937, and stayed with the company until 1956. Settled in New York, he headed the Manhattan School of Music from 1956 until his death on 10 Jan 1969.

Brownlee's appearances at the Glyndebourne Festivals of 1933–1939 brought him great acclaim, and resulted in his outstanding recording of *Don Giovanni* with Salvatore Baccaloni, under Fritz Busch (Victor #423/424/425, 23 12–inch discs). With the same company he was in the complete *Così fan tutte* (Victor #812/813/814, 20 12–inch discs).

BRUBECK, DAVE, 1920– . American jazz pianist, composer, and ensemble leader, born David Warren Brubeck in Concord, California, on 6 Dec 1920. After studying classical music he began to play with jazz groups at age 13. He studied composition with Darius Milhaud, then led a military band during World War II. From 1946 to 1951 he formed and performed with various jazz groups. In 1951 he founded the Dave Brubeck Quartet, with alto saxophonist Paul Desmond; in its final form the group included drummer Joe Morello and bassist Eugene Wright. During the 1950s and 1960s the quartet achieved great popularity for their cool and sophisticated improvisations, particularly in unusual time signatures. "Take Five" in 5/4 meter (a Desmond composition) and Brubeck's own "Blue Rondo à la Turk" in 9/8 meter were outstanding examples (in Columbia album *Time Out* (#CL8192; 1961). Another 1961 hit album was *Time Further Out* (Columbia #CS8490).

BRUCKNER (FRANZ) MANUFACTURING CO. A firm established in New York, at 405 Broadway, in 1912. It was listed in the 1916

TMW directory as maker of the Metro-Phone disc player, offered in seven models.

BRUNSWICK (label). One of the premier labels in North America and Britain, with great international artists in classical and popular music, first issued, in Canada only, by **Brunswick-Balke-Collender Co.** in 1916. The earliest offerings were vertical-cut, with labels in green. Lateral-cut discs, with violet labels, appeared in the U.S. in January 1920; after 1923 the label color was black, and the price was $.75, except for a special double-sided purple series of opera and classics, selling at $1 for 10–inch and $1.50 for 12–inch records. During the acoustic period major dance bands were recorded, such as those of Fletcher Henderson, Ray Miller, and Isham Jones. A hit record by the Mound City Blue Blowers was made in February 1924, "Arkansaw [sic] Blues" / "Blue Blues" (#2581); it was followed by five more by the Blowers, before the group turned to other labels. Operatic celebrities included Mario Chamlee, Sigrid Onegin, Elisabeth Rethberg, Friedrich Schorr, and John Charles Thomas. Access to Polydor matrices was a favorable factor, bringing such artists as Leopold Godowsky, and the Berlin Philharmonic Orchestra under Wilhelm Furtwängler.

The quality of the discs was high, and the parent company also produced excellent playback machines with tapered tone arms. The company pioneered the all-electric phonograph with its **Panatrope** in 1926, and used the electric **Pallatrope** recording method for its discs. The combination was strong enough to be used in **tone tests**. A **race record** division was established, headed by **Jack Kapp**. Difficulties appeared around 1927 as radio began to be a serious competitor for the phonograph. (Brunswick itself entered the radio field in 1928.) New artists were constantly added to the catalog, which before the Wall Street crash of 1929 included Walter Gieseking, the New York Philharmonic, Red Nichols, King Oliver, and Al Jolson (whose "Sonny Boy" required a factory running 24 hours a day to meet buyer demand).

The stock market collapse affected operations in both the U.S. and U.K. Warner Brothers acquired Brunswick-Balke-Collender in April 1930, bringing film stars like Gloria Swanson to the artist list. However, in December 1931 Warner sold the Brunswick interests to the new **American Record Corp.**, which renamed their acquisition the Brunswick Radio Corp. The label flourished in the 1930s, as many popular artists were brought into the fold: Fred Astaire, Mary Martin, Gene Krupa, Jack Teagarden, Artie Shaw, Harry James, Glenn Miller, Teddy Wilson, and Frank Sinatra (making his record debut). Then in December 1939 the American Record Corp. was bought by Columbia Broadcasting System, and the Brunswick label was discontinued in September 1940. Decca acquired and revived it in 1943 with the 80,000 series. As a rock label from the 1950s to the 1970s, it presented such stars as Buddy Holly and the Crickets, Jackie Wilson, and the Chi-Lites. The label finally disappeared in the U.S. in 1977, following a major fraud scandal. It had not been seen on the British market after 1967. [Andrews*; Rust 1978.] *See also* BRITISH BRUNSWICK, LTD.

BRUNSWICK-BALKE-COLLENDER CO. A firm established in 1845, with varied interests (furniture, carriages, equipment for games), that entered the phonograph business in 1916. The address at that time was 623 S. Wabash Ave., Chicago. It seems that the firm entered into an agreement with Pathé to sell only its discs in the U.S. in exchange for Pathé's undertaking to stay out of the American talking machine market; Brunswick did sell Pathé records in 1916–1920. Brunswick records were sold in Canada from 1916. However, this arrangement did not endure beyond 1919, when Brunswick records came to the U.S. and Pathé began to advertise its phonographs in the American national magazines.

The first products were eight models of the Brunswick player. Its Ultona reproducer was adaptable to play vertical-cut Pathé discs as well as standard lateral-cut records. Success was quick to come, and fortunes were greatly enhanced by some favorable court judgments. The tapered tone arm was a contested product at the time, with patents held by Eldridge Johnson (owned by Victor) and John B. Brown-

ing (owned by Brunswick). Victor sued Brunswick; but the suit was dismissed in 1922 with Browning's patent found valid. Another litigation—over the enclosed horn with doors—was also decided in Brunswick's favor. In 1924 the firm acquired **Vocalion** records from Aeolian Co., and a year later announced a technological breakthrough: the **Panatrope** all-electric phonograph and the **Pallotrope** system of electrical recording developed with General Electric. The "light ray" recording process used a microphone (called a "palatrope"), a crystal mirror, a light source, and a photo-electric cell.

Despite these advances, and despite the gathering of an international star roster of artists on the Brunswick label, sales peaked in 1926 and dropped $2 million to $27 million in 1927. Brunswick joined the radio manufacturers in 1928, then in April 1930 sold out both radio and phonograph interests to Warner Brothers.

Today the Brunswick Corp, located in Skokie, Illinois, has more than 25,000 employees, and annual revenue near $2.8 billion (1989). It manufactures sports equipment, paper, marine engines, and pharmaceutical products.

BRUNSWICK QUARTET. Also known as the Brunswick Male Quartet. A group that recorded for Columbia in 1911–1912. Its members were Aubrey A. Hackett, first tenor; Arthur Clough, lead tenor; Harry Wieting, baritone; and A. Duncan Cornwall, bass.

BRUSH DEVELOPMENT CORP. A firm established by Charles Brush to manufacture his piezo-electric **cartridges.** In 1937 the company produced the Soundmirror—a commercially available magnetic recorder using endless loop steel tape. During World War II Brush made wire recorders for the government; one type was a cassette wire recorder. The firm's director was Semi Joseph Begun, a one-time researcher with Lorenz in Germany. In its current manifestation, as Brush Magnetic Heads Division of the Forgflo Corp., Sunbury, Pennsylvania, the company continues to make audio-video components, especially recording heads.

BRYANT, ERIC THOMAS, 1914–1990. British librarian and author, born in London. He had a distinguished career as a public librarian, notably in Widnes, where he established a successful gramophone library. Bryant was an enthusiastic promoter of recordings, giving lecture recitals throughout England. He was a senior lecturer in music librarianship at the Manchester Polytechnic, and was a visiting speaker in library schools in Britain and America. His 1962 book, *Collecting Gramophone Records*, was widely praised for its guidance to librarians and private collectors. He was also author of the standard work, *Music Librarianship* (1959; 2nd ed. 1985), in which the administration of recording collections in libraries was treated with exhaustive detail. He retired in 1979, and died in Devizes, England, on 20 July 1990. Bryant wrote major sections of the articles on Organ Music Recordings and Record Collector Societies in this Encyclopedia. Imprint data on his books is in the Bibliography.

BRYANT, LILLIAN. British pianist and conductor; the first female conductor to make records, with the Pathé Symphony Orchestra and the Pathé Military Band. She was also the first woman to record commercially as a solo pianist, on HMV and Edison Bell, around 1900.

BUBBLE BOOKS. Children's books published by Harper & Brothers in 1919, under the name *Harper-Columbia Book That Sings*, with three single-sided, 5 1/2-inch phonograph records included; they were apparently the first singing books. The British publisher was Hodder and Stoughton; in Britain the title was *Hodder-Columbia Books That Sing*. Fourteen titles were issued by 1923, including *Mother Goose*; *A Child's Garden of Verses*; and *Funny Froggy B.B.* Victor acquired the patents in September 1924. [Andrews 1976/10; Andrews 1988/6.]

BUDAPEST QUARTET. A string quartet originally drawn from the Budapest Opera Orchestra; it first performed in 1917 in Hungary. The original members were Emil Hauser, Imre Poganyi, István Ipolyi, and Harry Son. Joseph Roisman replaced Poganyi in 1927, then moved to first violin; Alexander Schneider replaced Ipolyi and Mischa Schneider replaced Son in the early 1930s. Boris Kroyt was the violist from 1936. With Roisman as the leader, the quartet achieved international recognition. They settled in the U.S. in 1938, and became quartet-in-residence at the Library of Congress in 1962. Their final public concert was in 1967.

From 1932 to 1936 the Budapest Quartet made notable recordings for EMI (on the Victor label in the U.S.), establishing their mastery of the Beethoven works and producing an acclaimed rendition of the "Italian Serenade" by Hugo Wolf. LP reissues cover that period (Columbia-Odyssey #Y34643, four discs; 1979) and both the previous and subsequent periods (Toshiba-EMI Angel #EAC 60055/59, five discs; 1979 and Columbia Odyssey #Y34644, four discs; 1979). Odyssey transferred the complete Beethoven quartets to CD as well, and Novello/BMG released a CD of Schubert, Mendelssohn, Tchaikovsky, Borodin, and Dvořák in 1990; it presented recordings made in 1926–1929. [Smolian 1970.]

BUDDY (label). Six American aluminum manufacturers joined forces to make this record, sold from 1923 to 1926. The discs were intended to boost sales of the Buddy portable phonograph, which was made of aluminum; all the aluminum firms are named on the record label. There is no list of the output, and survivors are rare. Gennett masters were used. [Rust 1978.]

BUEHN, LOUIS, 1877–1936. American phonograph dealer, active at the national level in the trade. His posts included treasurer, Eastern Talking Machine Jobbers Association (1907), and its successor, the **Talking Machine Jobbers National Association**. With the **National Association of Talking Machine Jobbers** (NATMJ) he was treasurer in 1909 and 1910, secretary in 1912, vice president in 1920, and president in 1921. His own business was incorporated October 1912 as the Buehn Phonograph Co., 713 Penn Ave., Pittsburgh. In 1915 he opened Louis Buehn, Inc., at 825 Arch St., Philadelphia, handling Victor products exclusively. Edison acquired the company in 1926.

BULK ERASER. A device used to erase the signal from a recorded **magnetic tape** (cassette or reel-to-reel). It operates by producing a strong magnetic field; when it is passed over the tape in a circular motion it cancels the extant signal. Metal tapes are difficult to erase in this manner.

BUMP. "To bump" on a tape means to reduce the number of tracks (e.g., four to two) to make space for new material. Also known as jump.

BUREAU INTERNATIONAL DE L'ÉDITION MÉCANIQUE (BIEM). The international association of national organizations and agencies concerned with the rights of artists with respect to sound recordings.

BURKE AND ROUS PHONOGRAPH RECORDS. A Brooklyn firm, located at 336 65th Ave. in 1905. It produced records for use in **phonograph parlors.** [Andrews*.]

Burnishing facet. *See* STYLUS.

BURR, HENRY, 1882–1941. Canadian tenor and ballad singer, born Harry McClaskey in St. Stephen, New Brunswick, on 15 Jan 1882. He started singing at age 13 with a military band; then he was heard by Giuseppe Campanari and urged to go to New York for study. One of his teachers there was Ellen Burr, whose name he took for a pseudonym later.

One of the most prolific of the early recording musicians, he made cylinders and discs from 1902 to 1929, and is said to have made more records than any other singer. (Walsh estimates more than 12,000 items before 1920.) Burr was the pseudonym most used by McClaskey, who was also known as Irving Gillette (on Edison records and some Columbias) and Harry Haley; on Pathé he was identified as Alfred L. Alexander or Robert Bruce. He began to record in 1902 for Columbia, and made the hit "All Through the Night" in 1907 (#3498). His best seller was probably "Good Night, Little Girl, Good Night" for Columbia, said to have sold over 3 million copies, "partly perhaps because it was issued as one side of a sample record distributed for a quarter instead of the usual 65 cent price" (Walsh). In addition to solo work, Burr sang duets and in many ensembles. He sang with the Peerless

Quartet from 1906 or 1907, and became their manager in 1910. Popular duet discs made for Columbia included "I'm Forever Blowing Bubbles" (#78263; 1920) and "Let the Rest of the World Go By" (#78752; 1920), both with Albert Campbell. Among his other duet partners were John Meyer, Frank Croxton, and Helen Clark. His earliest Victor disc was "Daddy" in 1904. His Victor recording of "Just a Baby's Prayer at Twilight" (1918) was especially popular. After 17 years of freelancing, Burr signed an exclusive Victor contract in 1920. He was an original member, then manager, of the Eight Famous Victor Artists. After 1928, when he disbanded the Eight, he made only a few records for various labels, then gave up performing and became program director for the Columbia Broadcasting Co. He did return to singing, on Chicago radio with the *National Barn Dance*, and remained with that show until he died on 6 Apr 1941, in Chicago. [Moogk 1975 has a 20–page discography; Walsh 1943/4–6, with corrections in May 1952.]

BURROWS AND CO. A British firm, located at 107 Market St., Manchester in 1903. It was the exclusive wholesaler for Edison's National Phonograph Co., claiming in one advertisement to have 500 phonographs and 20,000 gold molded cylinders in stock.

BURT, GEORGE HENRY. British record company executive, one of the founders of **Crystalate Gramophone Record Manufacturing Co.** (1901). American born, he had a firm (George Burt Co., of Milburn, New Jersey) that made discs for Berliner and Zonophone. Burt set up the **Globe Record Co.** in 1901. He had supplied Berliner with "a mix for his records" in both the U.S. and at Deutsche Grammophon. In 1903 he was a director of **Nicole Record Co., Ltd.**

BUSCH, ADOLF, 1891–1952. German violinist, conductor, and composer, born in Siegen on 8 Aug 1891; brother of **Fritz Busch.** In 1912 he was conductor of the Konzertverein Orchester in Vienna; he also taught violin at the Berlin Hochschule für Musik. He established the Wiener-Konzertvereins Quartett in 1913, and reorganized it in 1919 as the **Busch**

Quartet. Aside from his performances with that group, he made an important recording of the Brahms Horn Trio with Aubrey Brain and Rudolf Serkin (Victor # 7965/8, album #VM 199). He also recorded with his Busch Chamber Players, helping to bring wide attention to the baroque masters. The 12 Handel Concerti Grossi (opus 6) were recorded for Columbia (album #SL 158) and five of the Bach Brandenburg Concerti were recorded for Angel (album #COLC 13). Yehudi Menuhin was one of his pupils. Busch died in Guildford, Vermont, on 9 June 1952. [Potter 1985 is a discography.]

BUSCH, FRITZ, 1890–1951. German conductor and pianist, born in Siegen on 13 Mar 1890; brother of Adolf Busch. He conducted the Deutsches Theater in Riga, and gave two-piano recitals with Max Reger. In 1912 he was music director in Aachen, and then he went to the Stuttgart Opera. From 1922 to 1933 he directed the Dresden Staatsoper. He was invited to Glyndebourne in 1934, and for five years conducted outstanding performances and made classic recordings of the Mozart operas for HMV/Victor (Cosí fan tutte, #VM 812/813/814, 20 discs; Don Giovanni, #VM423/424/425, 23 discs; Nozze di Figaro, #VM 313/314/315, 17 discs). Then he toured South America in 1940–1945, and had four seasons conducting at the Metropolitan Opera, 1945–1949. Busch died in London on 14 Sep 1951. [Delalande 1984 is a discography.]

BUSCH QUARTET. A string quartet established in 1919 by Adolf Busch, as a continuation of his Wiener-Konzertvereins Quartett. The original members with Busch were Karl Reitz, (replaced by Gösta Andreasson in 1921), Emil Bohnke (replaced by Karl Doktor in 1921), and Paul Grümmer (replaced by Hermann Busch in 1930). The group soon achieved international acclaim; it made world tours and came to the U.S. in 1939. The quartet was active until 1952; there were further member changes in 1948. Recording for HMV/Victor, the group made significant discs of the Beethoven and Schubert quartets.

BUSH & LANE PIANO CO. An American piano manufacturing firm established in 1901 in Chicago, moving after a few years to Holland, Michigan. In addition to its Bush & Lane and its Victor pianos, it offered the Cecilian player piano; plus the Bush & Lane and Duo-Vox phonographs. It was active as late as 1926, at which time the president was Walter Lane.

BUSONI, FERRUCCIO, 1866–1924. Italian pianist and composer, born Dante Michelangelo Benvenuto Busoni in Empoli, on 1 Apr 1866. He was an acclaimed prodigy, and by 1889 was professor of piano in Helsinki (Sibelius was among his pupils); and he taught also in Moscow and at the New England Conservatory of Music. In concert he specialized in the works of Bach and Liszt. Pianists who studied with him included Alexander Brailovsky, Rudolph Ganz, Percy Grainger, and Egon Petri.

In 1905 Busoni made some piano rolls for Welte-Mignon; the recordings have been released on CD by the Recorded Treasures label (#CD-1; 1989). The pieces put on the roll were by Liszt, including the paraphrases of Don Juan and Rigoletto.

Busoni made only four double-sided discs, short numbers for Columbia released in 1919 and 1922. His playing is curious in terms of tempo, added measures, and in the linking of two Chopin works with an improvised bridge (see PIANO RECORDINGS, 4). He died in Berlin on 27 July 1924.

BUSSE, HENRY, 1894–1955. German-born trumpeter and Big Band leader, and composer of "Wang Wang Blues" which he recorded with Paul Whiteman for Victor in 1920 (#18694). He was also co-composer of "Hot Lips," which Whiteman recorded in 1922 (Victor #18920). These two numbers having sold extremely well, Busse recorded them with his own band on one disc in 1935 for Decca (#198). "Hot Lips" became his theme song. In "When Day is Done," recorded with the Whiteman Band (12–inch Victor #35828;1927) Busse played the pioneer example of what became known as sweet jazz. He was the first to use a trumpet mute. Busse was heard for many years on Chicago radio as his band settled in at the Chez Paree nightclub.

He continued performing until he died in Memphis, Tennessee, just before going on stage.

BUSY BEE (label). Cylinders and discs made by Columbia for the **O'Neill-James Co.** of Chicago, from ca. 1904 to ca. 1909. The discs were notable for their extra hole at the edge of the label, notched to fit a nub on the turntable sold by the same company. (This special turntable was not required to play the discs, but only the Busy Bee discs could be played on the special turntable.) Busy Bee cylinders had a large bore diameter; the oversized mandrel on the Busy Bee phonographs would not accept Edison or Columbia cylinders.

The label name seems to have derived from the name of Sherwin Bisbee, one of the partners in the firm. Masters from various companies were used: American (Odeon), Columbia, Star, Leeds & Catlin, and Zonophone. Disc sizes offered were seven-inch, 10–inch, 10 3/4 inch, and probably 12–inch. Sales did not match expectations, and when Victor sued successfully on patent infringement charges in 1909, the company phased out of the disc business. Its most fa-

mous record was one of William Jennings Bryan addressing a crowd. [Fabrizio 1973; Petty 1988.]

BUTT, CLARA, *Dame*, **1872–1936.** English contralto, born on 1 Feb 1872 in Southwick. Her debut was in Arthur Sullivan's *Golden Legend*, in London on 7 Dec 1892, but most of her appearances thereafter were on the concert stage. She made successful world tours, including the U.S., and was designated a Dame of the British Empire in 1920. Her repertoire emphasized religious song and oratorio; but she recorded Stephen Foster, and was identified with Elgar's work (a famous recording was HMV #03239, #03570, "Land of Hope and Glory"). She had four items in the Victor 1917 catalog, but none in 1927. She died on 23 Jan 1936 at North Stoke, Oxfordshire, England.

BUTTERFLY HEAD. In a **tape recorder**, a multitrack head with a flared guard band; it provides protection against **crosstalk.**

BUTTERFLY RECORDS. A British label issued after 1910, proprietor unknown, pressed from Grammavox masters of the **Sound Recording Co., Ltd.,** or overlabeled.

C/S. Cycles per second. It is usually expressed as **Hertz (Hz).**

CADILLAC (label). A "very obscure **vertical-cut** record of the Edison type" (Rust), made in eight-inch size by the Clements Manufacturing Co. of Chicago. [Rust 1978.]

CAEDMON (label). A firm established in New York by Barbara Holdridge and Marianne Mantell in 1952, with the purpose of recording great literature; it was the first company to operate with that intention. Dylan Thomas, Thomas Mann, W.B. Yeats, T.S. Eliot, e.e. cummings, Robert Frost, W.H. Auden, Archibald MacLeish, Marianne Moore, Eudora Welty, Katherine Anne Porter, Colette, Albert Camus, Tennessee Williams, and William Faulkner were in the earliest group to read their own works. "A Child's Christmas in Wales" (#TC 1002; 1952), read by Thomas, along with his readings of "Fern Hill" and "Do Not Go Gentle into that Good Night," has been an enduring success.

Major anthologies of English poetry and drama appeared, and a complete Shakespeare with great actors such as John Gielgud, Claire Bloom, and Richard Burton. Over 900 titles were in the catalog in the late 1980s. In 1987 Harper & Row (now HarperCollins) acquired the firm. Since 1989 the Caedmon material has been issued on audiotapes and compact discs. [Roach 1988.] *See also* LITERARY RECORDINGS.

CAILLE BROTHERS. A Detroit firm, manufacturers of **picturized phonographs** sold under names Cailophone and Scopephone. In 1907 it offered a **coin-op**, the Cailoscope, that showed pictures but had no audio component. There was also a coin-op phonograph.

CALIFORNIA RAMBLERS. The "most prolifically recorded dance orchestra" (Rust), active on discs from 1921 to 1937. Arthur Hand was leader of the group, which included such great artists as **Adrian Rollini, Tommy Dorsey, Jimmy Dorsey,** Stan King, and Ed Kirkeby. About 600 records are listed in Rust 1982 (jazz numbers) and about 700 more in Rust 1975 (dance numbers). "The Sheik" (Vocalion #14275; 1921) was their first disc and first hit. In 1924 they had another top record with "California Here I Come (Columbia #67-D). The orchestra had a variety of pseudonyms, including the Golden Gate Orchestra, and the Palm Beach Players. There were also smaller units drawn from the band that had separate names and recordings. The Ramblers appeared on numerous labels, from Edison Blue Amberol cylinders to Edison Diamond Discs and Bluebird. [Brooks*; Rust 1975; Rust 1982.]

CALLAS, MARIA, 1923–1977. American soprano, born Maria Anna Sofia Cecilia Kologeropoulos to Greek immigrant parents in New York on 3 Dec 1923. When the family returned to Greece in 1937, she studied voice and made a debut in Athens (in a minor role) three years later. Her major debut was as Tosca in July 1942. She appeared in Verona as Gioconda on 3 Aug 1947, and joined La Scala in 1950, singing Aida. She was an immediate success in Cherubini's *Medea,* a role that was identified with her throughout her career. Another acclaimed role was Norma, which she sang at Covent Garden on 8 Nov 1952 and in her American debut, in Chicago, on 1 Nov 1954. For her Metropolitan Opera debut on 29 Oct 1956 she was Norma once more. Callas enjoyed great international success as one of the great operatic stars of her time. Unfortunately, she was involved in numerous disputes with managers, causing interruptions to her career; she did sing in New York until 1965, then gave up the stage after a final appearance at Covent Garden. She died in Paris on 16 Sep 1977.

The recordings of Callas reveal the great versatility of her art; she made outstanding discs of the Verdi/Puccini repertoire, and also of the earlier Italian masters (Bellini, Donizetti); and she sang Isolde, Carmen, Orfeo, and Marguerite, and Rosina. Her first discs were for Cetra in 1950, after which Walter Legge took her to EMI. EMI issued CDs of her major repertoire in 1990 on six discs. [Ardoin 1991; Korenhof 1977.]

CALLOWAY, CAB, 1907– . American Big Band leader, jazz singer, and pianist, born Cabell Calloway on Christmas day 1907, in Rochester, New York. He began working in Chicago clubs, then toured the country. He established a group called the Alabamians which was successful in Chicago and at the Savoy in Harlem. The first Calloway recording was "Market Street Stomp" (Victor #38067; 1929). Several hit records followed: "Minnie the Moocher (Ho De Ho)" (Brunswick #6074; 1931); "St. James Infirmary" (Brunswick #6105; 1930); "Kickin' the Gong Around" (Brunswick #6209; 1931); and "Eadie Was a Lady" (Banner 32647; 1932); these appeared on other labels as well. Calloway's Big Band was a sensation in 1931–1932, especially at the Cotton Club; it included such great artists as Cozy Cole (drums), Dizzy Gillespie (trumpet), Milt Hinton (bass), and Jonah Jones (trumpet). George Gershwin modeled the character Sportin' Life (in Porgy and Bess) on Calloway, who took the role in 1952–1954 in the U.S. and overseas. Three CDs from the Classics label (#516, 526, 554; 1991), the beginning of a series named the Chronological Calloway, offered his material of 1930–1937. [Popa 1987.]

CALORIC SALES CO. A Chicago firm, established in 1916, located at #1381 Continental and Commercial Bank Bldg. It made the Phonola disc player.

CALVÉ, EMMA, 1858–1942. French soprano and mezzo-soprano, born Emma Calvé de Roquer in Décazeville on 15 Aug 1858. Her debut was in Brussels on 23 Sep 1881, as Marguerite; she appeared at La Scala in 1887, Covent Garden in 1892 (creating a sensation as Santuzza, and singing command performances for the Queen), and at the Metropolitan Opera on 29 Nov 1893, also as Santuzza. In Carmen she sang with Jean de Reszke, Nellie Melba, and Pol Plançon. Calvé stayed with the Metropolitan 13 seasons, until 1904, then made world tours. After 1910 she mainly devoted herself to the concert stage. Calvé's most acclaimed role was Carmen, and her recording of "Habanera" is regarded as the finest made of that aria (G & T #3281 and Victor #5000; 1902). She also recorded the "Seguidilla" (G & T #3285 and Victor #5002; 1902), less successfully—with a screech and an "Oh Dieu!" at the end. But earlier, in the 1890s, she had made a group of home cylinders for Jules Massenet, who sent her the numbers from his opera Sappho as he composed them; she sang them and sent him the cylinders. Those records have not survived, nor have the commercial records she made for Bettini. Mapleson recorded her live at the Metropolitan in 1902–1903, singing in Cavalleria and Faust.

Zonophone was the first to record Calvé on disc: "Voi lo sapete" in 1902, made in Paris. Then there were six G & Ts—including the Carmen arias cited above—and seven arias for Victor in 1907–1910. One of the finest in that group is "Charmant oiseau" from Perle du Brésil (Victor #88087). Her final discs were made after World War I for Pathé in Paris. She died in Millau, Aveyron, on 6 Jan 1942. [Moran 1977/1.]

CALYPSO (label). A Decca series of the early 1940s, consisting of music from Trinidad.

Wilmoth Houdini was the principal artist and composer of many of the songs. One of his numbers was a musical tribute to Bing Crosby, with such lines as "His millions of listeners never fail to rejoice / About his golden voice" (Decca #18142). Other performers in the series included The Lion, Mighty Destroyer, Attila the Hun (Raymond Quevedo), King Radio, and The Growler.

CAMDEN (label). A Victor low-priced LP label, issued from 1954, featuring material from Victor matrices; often the artists were not identified. Decca was the first British distributor, then Pickwick International.

CAMEO RECORD CORP. A New York producer of inexpensive discs, established in 1921 at 662 Sixth Ave., New York, with C.F. Siemon as president (he was also president of the Siemon Hard Rubber Co., Bridgeport, Connecticut, the parent firm of Cameo). Henry Waterson was vice president, then became president sometime before 1925. Recording was done in the laboratories of Earle W. Jones, an ex-member of the Columbia Graphophone Co. recording staff. Pressing was done at the Siemon plant in Bridgeport, which could turn out 50,000 discs per day. In February 1922 the first discs were released, offering a repertoire of dance music and other popular items. In a brief effort to bring in classical material as well, Eugene Ormandy—beginning his American career as concertmaster of the Capitol Theatre Orchestra in New York City—was signed for several violin solo discs. Special records were made for individuals, with client labels if desired. Macy's department store was the principal outlet for Cameo records, which sold for $.50 each.

In March 1922 Cameo announced that it had secured a second pressing plant, in Framingham, Massachusetts, to supplement the output of its Bridgeport plant. The new facility had a capacity output of 20,000 discs per day. The office address in January 1924 was 249 W. 34th St., New York.

A subsidiary label, **Lincoln**, was launched in January 1924, and another one, **Romeo**, appeared in July 1926. A line of children's records, Cameo-Kid, was announced in January 1925, with a selling price of only $.15. At that time the Cameo Record Corp. was consolidated with David Grimes, Inc., to form the David Grimes Radio and Cameo Record Corp. Henry Waterson was president. Another 1925 series from Cameo was the Official Boy Scout Records, featuring Jackie Coogan on the label; these records sold for $.20 each. In 1926 electrically recorded discs were released on the Cameo and Lincoln labels. Then Waterson was bankrupt in 1927, and sold Cameo to James E. MacPherson, who controlled the Pathé Phonograph and Record Corp. In the following year Cameo was merged with Pathé. During the Depression Cameo was one of several labels absorbed by the **American Record Corp.**, which discontinued the use of the Cameo name.

In Britain the **Dominion Gramophone Record Co., Ltd.**, was licensed to market Cameos, but not until 1928, when the American firm was approaching its final days. [Andrews*; Rust 1978; label lists in *RR* #92 (1968) and earlier issues.]

CAMERAPHONE. A small, portable disc player manufactured by Lee & Pollack and marketed in Britain by Thorens in 1926; it was also sold in the U.S. The machine looked like a folding box camera. It had a turntable composed of three metal spokes and an odd, egg-shaped loudspeaker. [Andrews*.]

CAMPBELL, ALBERT, 1872–1947. American lyric tenor, born in Brooklyn on 17 Aug 1872; he was among the first to make a career of recording. During the 1880s and 1890s he was on stage in operettas, then he began recording with a group named the **Diamond Comedy Four**. By 1896 he was doing solo discs for Berliner, and he made what were "probably the first recorded advertisements" (Walsh) for Quaker Oats, on Jumbo cylinders issued by the Talking Machine Co. of Chicago in 1899. He was an Edison mainstay by 1899, making notable cylinders of "For All Eternity" (#7296; 1899) and "Mandy Lee" (#7297; 1899). For Columbia he made several popular items, including "School Days" (#3745; 1908)

Campbell began ensemble work with the Columbia Quartet; then went to the Peerless Quartet, and from 1908 on he recorded almost entirely in groups. He belonged to the Sterling Trio from 1916. After 1928, when Peerless disbanded, he did duets with Jack Kaufman for two or three years, and then operated a booking agency in New York. Campbell died in Flushing, New York, on 25 Jan 1947. [Walsh 1942/9–10; corrections in May 1952.]

CAMPBELL, GLEN, 1938– . American pop and country singer and guitarist, born in Delight, Arkansas, on 10 Apr 1938. At age six he was playing the guitar, and soon had a regional reputation through radio appearances. In the 1950s he toured the southwest, then became a sideman for various recording artists. His first hit record was "Turn Around, Look at Me" (Crest #1087; 1961). Under contract with Capitol, he made another hit, "Too Late to Worry" (Capitol #4783; 1962). The year 1967 brought two more chart songs, both Grammy winners: "Gentle on My Mind" (Capitol #5939) and "By the Time I Get to Phoenix" (Capitol #2015). Campbell earned another Grammy for his 1968 album, *By the Time I Get to Phoenix* (Capitol #T-2851); it was on the charts for 62 weeks. He appeared on television (including his own variety show) and made national tours. "Wichita Lineman" (Capitol #2302; 1968) and "Galveston" (Capitol #2428; 1969) were both gold records. There have been 20 chart albums, the last in 1977.

CAMRAS, MARVIN, 1916– . American electronics engineer, born in Chicago on 1 Jan 1916. He is noted for research in magnetic recording. He has been with the Armour Research Foundation since 1940. Among his 500 patents are one for AC bias (1941) and U.S. #2,351,007 (filed 1942) for a recording head. He designed a wire recorder that played 30 minutes, at five feet per second, or 60 minutes at 2.5 feet per second, on 0.004 diameter stainless steel wire. General Electric manufactured it for use by the American and British military during World War II. Camras continued his influential research in video recording technology through the 1980s. [Klinger*.]

CANADA. The recording industry in Canada has always been closely allied to the major American and European recording companies and, indeed, even today most recordings distributed and purchased in Canada are pressed from foreign matrices. There have been, however, many notable, even unique, contributions made by Canada and Canadians to the field which has concerned itself with the preservation of sound.

The first recordings made in Canada were those produced at Rideau Hall in Ottawa by the governor-general, Lord Dufferin, and his guests who gathered on 17 May 1878 to witness a demonstration of Edison's tinfoil talking machine. Several months later, on 19 Oct 1878, Edison was granted Canadian patent #9282 for "improvements in means for recording Sounds and in reproducing such Sounds from such Record." This patent, as well as the demonstration, involved a disc recording device, a system Edison would not further develop for another 35 years. At about this time **Alexander Graham Bell**, then a resident of Brantford, Ontario, together with his cousin, **Chichester Bell** and British-born scientist **Charles Sumner Tainter**, were working on various improvements to Edison's concept, including the use of wax-coated cylinders. The Bell-Tainter group were granted Canadian patent #26703 on 20 Apr 1885 embodying these improvements.

Emile Berliner divested himself of his U.S. patents in 1897 (they were taken over by Eldridge Johnson, who later founded the Victor Talking Machine Company). On 25 Nov 1895 Berliner had been granted Canadian patent #55079 and in 1899 he moved to Montreal where he set up the first Canadian recording and distribution business at 2315-2316 Catherine Street under the name E. Berliner, Montreal. He rented space from the Bell Telephone Company at 367-71 Aqueduct Street (he had previously worked as a consultant to this firm) and installed four record presses. Here he also assembled cabinets for his gramophone, the inner workings of which were imported from Eldridge Johnson in the United States.

On 8 Apr 1904 the Berliner Gramophone Company of Canada, Ltd., was incorporated to "manufacture and deal in gramophones, gramophone records, and accessories, devices and appliances pertaining to or in any way connected with gramophones or talking machines generally. . . ." The new company also became the presser and distributor in Canada of recordings from the Victor Talking Machine Company and other Berliner affiliates throughout the world. Herbert Samuel Berliner (1882–1966), Emile Berliner's oldest son, was a prominent stockholder of this company and was later named vice president and general manager, which put him in a position to have a profound effect upon the Canadian recording industry.

Early in this century, sensing Berliner's attempt to corner the Canadian record market, Edison and Columbia, Berliner-Victor's major competitors, set up distribution companies in Toronto. Berliner, however, appears to have been the only company to have done any mastering there during the first decade of the 20th century. Edison's American-made cylinders (and, from 1913, discs) were simply distributed in Canada and Columbia did not begin pressing records in Canada until 1912. Berliner was taken over entirely by the Victor Talking Machine Company (U.S.) in 1924. Columbia was active under various names (1954–1976 as Columbia Records, now CBS Records Canada, Ltd.) from 1904 with production coming under the control of Sparton of Canada (a subsidiary of Sparks-Worthington of the U.S.) in 1939. Thomas Edison ceased all Canadian activity in 1926.

The first entirely Canadian-made recordings were issued by Berliner in 1900. They were 18 centimeter (seven-inch) discs, followed in 1901 by 25.5 centimeter (10 inch) and in 1903 by his De Luxe 30 centimeter (12-inch) discs. Double-sided discs were first issued in Canada in 1908. These initial recordings were pressed from matrices belonging to affiliated Berliner companies in Britain, Germany, France, and the U.S. The first commercial recording by a Canadian artist was a performance of "La marseillaise" by Joseph Saucier (1869–1941) which was recorded in Montreal. It is not known exactly when this master was made, as it replaced Ferruccio Giannini's earlier release of the same work (Berliner #9).

In addition to Berliner (Victor), Edison, and Columbia, other early Canadian recording and distribution companies included Canadian Vitaphone (Toronto 1913–1916), which pressed imported masters; Pathé Frères (Montreal 1915–ca. 1921), distributor of recordings pressed in France; Brunswick-Balke-Collender (Toronto 1917–1934), a subsidiary of the U.S. firm with processing taken over by the **Compo Co., Ltd.**, in 1932; and Phonola (Pollock Manufacturing Co., Kitchener, Ontario, 1918–ca. 1925), distributor of imported labels and manufacturer of Phonola equipment from 1914.

Despite this early activity Canada depended largely upon recordings imported from the U.S. and other countries in the early decades of the century, although discs were often pressed in Canada from imported masters. Similarly, Canadian artists usually had to travel elsewhere to prepare masters for pressing by local production companies. Canadian artists who made significant contributions to record catalogues at this time included **Emma Albani**, **Henry Burr**, Pauline Donalda, **Harry Macdonough**, and cornetist-conductor **Herbert L. Clarke** (U.S. born, but raised in Canada). The first ensemble recordings produced in Canada were those made in July 1902 by the Gordon Highlanders Regimental Band (the Kilties Band) of Belleville, Ontario, directed by William F. Robinson (Berliner #802-810).

In the first half of the century the demands of the large French-speaking population of Canada created a ready market for recordings indigenous to their unique culture. Thus a large number of early recordings were produced for a market that had no foreign source. French-Canadian artists who recorded in this genre included Joseph Allard (fiddler), La Bolduc (pseudonym of Marie or Mary-Rose-Anne Travers, singer), Conrad Gauthier (folksinger), Henri Lacroix (harmonicist), and Charles Marchand (singer) both as an individual and with his Bytown Troubadours. Canadian artists who developed an international recording career at this time included **Guy Lombardo** and his Royal Canadians, Wilf Carter, **Percy Faith**, and Hank Snow.

The advent of radio broadcasting in the mid-1920s seriously affected record sales in Canada, and the ensuing economic Depression caused all but the most stable firms (most, significantly, tied to U.S. or European concerns) to cease operations—even Columbia folded temporarily. The surviving firms included RCA Victor, Starr Co. of Canada (formerly Canadian Phonograph Supply Co.), and **Compo Co., Ltd.**, all of which featured Canadian performers. Starr (active 1918–ca. 1955) was based in London (Ontario); it distributed the Starr-Gennett label (U.S.) with records pressed at the Compo plant. Compo (active 1918–1964) was founded by Herbert S. Berliner in Lachine, Quebec, fundamentally as a pressing plant for several labels including Decca, Phonola, Sun, and Apex as well as Starr-Gennett. It had several labels of its own (including Compo) that featured Canadian performers. Compo was acquired by the Music Corporation of America (MCA) in 1964.

Sparton of Canada, Ltd. (London, Ontario), established in 1930, was the pressing plant for Columbia from 1939 until 1954, after which date it became independent. Sparton was the first Canadian company to press stereo records. A small company active at this time was Celtic (Antigonish, Nova Scotia), which began operations in 1933 but was taken over by Rodeo of Montreal in 1960. This company specialized in traditional music of the Maritime region.

A new era in Canadian recording began in 1945 when the **Canadian Broadcasting Corporation (CBC)** began to record works by Canadian composers and artists. These recordings were, at first, not available commercially, but were distributed to affiliated radio stations in an attempt to increase Canadian content in broadcasting. In a related development the Radio Canada International (RCI) transcription service was established in 1947 to provide recordings of Canadian performances to foreign audiences. In 1966, as demand grew for distinctly Canadian performances, the CBC recordings began to be issued commercially.

A plethora of Canadian recording companies sprang up across the country in mid-century, urged on by a growing demand, both from the broadcasting industry and the public, for recordings with Canadian content. Capitol Records of Canada, Ltd. (from 1955 Capitol-EMI), was established in 1954, although Capitol records had been pressed in Canada by Regal Records under licence to Musicana (U.S.) since 1946. Tip Top Records of Newmarket, Ontario, was established in 1948 by Max Boag (pseudonym of Harry Glenn) and specialized

in commercial and custom recording. Other companies active in this era included: Aragon (Vancouver, 1945); Rodeo (Montreal, 1949); Beaver (Toronto, 1950); Canadian Music Sales operating under the Dominion label (Toronto, 1950); Quality (Toronto, 1950); Allied (Montreal ca. 1950); Ed Archambault's Alouette label (Montreal, 1952) and Select label (1959); Hallmark (Toronto, 1952); Gordon V. Thompson's Gavotte label (Toronto, 1952); Orfeo (Montreal, 1954); Ross, Court and Co.'s Rococo label (Toronto, 1955); and Arc (Toronto, 1958).

Despite the large number of Canadian record producers active by 1960, the broadcasting industry could not meet the growing demand for material with Canadian content. Thus in 1962 the Canadian Talent Library (CTL), a non-profit trust, was formed to produce recordings by Canadian artists and composers. Initially these discs were provided only to affiliated private radio stations across Canada but in 1966, by which time 80 albums had been produced, CTL masters began to be leased to RCA, Columbia (CBS), Capitol, and other major record producers so that they might be released for public sale. By 1977 a total of 211 albums had been recorded by the trust. A similar project was begun in 1963 by the Composers, Authors and Publishers Association of Canada (CAPAC) in cooperation with the Canadian Association of Broadcasters (CAB) which subsidized Canadian recordings issued commercially by Capitol, Columbia, RCA, Decca, and others. In a related development, Toronto radio station CHUM established the Maple Leaf System in 1969 to promote the broadcasting of Canadian recordings.

Several new recording companies emerged in the 1960s, including Baroque (Montreal, 1962); Gamma (Montreal, 1965); Cantilena (Toronto, 1966); Polydor (Montreal, 1966) which became Polygram in 1978; London, a subsidiary of Decca of London (Montreal, 1967); Aquarius (Montreal, 1968); Sackville (Toronto, 1968); and General Recorded Tape (GRT), a subsidiary of the American Firm which originated in London (Ontario) in 1969 and moved in the same year to Toronto.

The Canadian Radio and Television Commission (CRTC) established new regulations in 1970 increasing to 30 percent the amount of

Canadian content that would be required of Canadian radio broadcasters, greatly increasing the market for the many new record companies that emerged in this decade. These included: A & M (Toronto, 1970); True North (Toronto, 1970); Boot (Toronto, 1979); Astra (Montreal, 1972), a label of the Canadian Association of Broadcasters; Goldfish (Richmond, British Columbia, 1973); Melbourne (Peterborough, Ontario, 1973); Onari (Toronto, 1973); Attic (Toronto, 1975); Kébec-Disk (Montreal, 1974); Masters of the Bow (Toronto, 1974) which reissued historical discs; Aquitaine (Toronto, 1974); Bernadol (Toronto, 1975); Music Gallery (Toronto, 1976) devoted to experimental and native music; Umbrella (Toronto, 1976) a direct-to-disc label introduced by Nimbus 9 and acquired in 1979 by Sine Qua Non of Toronto; Tapestry (Ottawa, 1978); and Magnum (Toronto, 1979) the Canadian label of GRT (see above). The Canadian Independent Record Producers Association (CIRPA) was established in 1974 to coordinate the activities of the many production companies then operating.

By 1970 the largest percentage of recordings sold in Canada were being pressed there, but prior to that time the studio production of recordings by Canadian artists still largely took place elsewhere, principally in the U.S. Before 1970 only six recording studios of international calibre existed in Toronto (RCA, Hallmark, Sound Canada, Bay Music, Eastern Sound, and Toronto Sound), while by 1981 almost 150 recording studios capable of producing quality multitrack master tapes were active across the country. While many of these operations lacked any permanence, some of the most successful and long-lived included: Solar Audio and Recording (Dartmouth, Nova Scotia); Bobinason Sound, Studio Tempo (Montreal); P.S.M. Studio (Quebec City); Le Studio (Morin Heights, Quebec); Marc Studios (Ottawa); Comfort Sound, Eastern Sound, Kinck Sound, Manta Sound, Sound Kitchen, Sounds Interchange, Nimbus 9/Soundstage, Zaza Sound Productions (Toronto); The Waxworks (St. Jacobs, Ontario); Century 21, Wayne Finucan Productions (Winnipeg); Damon Sound (Edmonton); Andromeda Sound, Bullfrog Studios, Little Mountain Studio, Mushroom Studios, Ocean Sound, and Pinewood Productions (Vancouver). By 1971 several of these studios possessed equipment sophisticated enough to attract international recording artists. Le Studio, for example, currently operates a 48-channel production studio with advanced CAD capabilities, which allows mastering of increasingly popular high-tech music videos as well as advanced album-cover design.

The RPM Gold Leaf Awards, established in 1964 by the periodical *RPM* (see references, below) and commonly known after 1970 as the Juno Awards, are presented annually to the most outstanding Canadian recordings artists, based upon record sales tabulated over a 14-month period. Categories and means of selection have varied over the years, but since 1975 the Canadian Academy of Recording Arts and Sciences (CARAS) has administered the awards. In 1974 the Juno awards were supplemented by the Canadian Music Hall of Fame and the Big Country Awards, and in 1976 categories for classical and jazz recordings were included for the first time. In the same year the Canadian Music Industry Awards were instituted. From 1965 until 1960 awards were presented to French-Canadian artists during a week-long exhibition in Montreal known as Festival du Disque and in 1979 the Association du Disque et de l'Industrie du Spectacle Québecois (ADISQ) established similar awards in Quebec.

The problem of disseminating information to record dealers and the broadcasting industry with respect to the availability of Canadian recordings was becoming increasingly difficult by 1982, due to the large amount of material then available. Thus the CIRPA/ADISQ foundation was established for the specific purpose of making available catalogue listings of recordings by Canadian artists. Known as the Canadian Record Catalogue, the data were entirely computerized from the inception of the project and were initially available in hard-copy versions of about 1,000 pages including 43,000 data records indexed on 80 fields and updated about every three months. By 1984 the data were so extensive that the catalogue is now available only in an online version accessible directly from the main computer database in Toronto.

A consortium of broadcasters, record producers and publishers banded together in 1982 to form the Foundation to Assist Canadian Talent on Records (FACTOR) to promote the production and marketing of Canadian records. Principals among the participants in this venture included the Canadian Independent Record Production Association (CIRPA) and the Canadian Music Publishers Association (CMPA). In 1983 the foundation administered almost $400,000 for the promotion of Canadian talent and in 1985 the CTL (see above), then operated by Standard Broadcasting of Toronto, joined forces with FACTOR, creating FACTOR/CTL with a budget of more than $1 million.

Checklist of Canadian record labels, production companies, and distributors:

A & M Records of Canada, Ltd.: established Toronto 1970, a subsidiary of the U.S. firm.

ABC: distributed by GRT.

ABC-Paramount: distributed by Sparton until 1969.

Ace of Clubs: produced by London Records.

Ace of Diamonds: produced by London Records.

Airdale: produced by London Records.

*Allied Record Corp.: active Montreal ca. 1950–ca. 1960, also label of same name.

*Alouette: Label of Ed Archambault, Montreal, established 1952.

*Alvina: pop music label active 1954.

America: jazz label distributed by GRT.

Angel: distributed by Capital Records.

*Apex: pressed by Compo 1921–1971, label revived 1979 by MCA.

*Aquarius: established 1968, distributed by London and from 1978 by Capitol.

*Aquitaine: established Toronto 1975, distributed by Columbia.

*Aragon: established Vancouver 1945.

*Arc Records: established Toronto 1958, pop music label established 1959.

*ASTRA: Canadian Association of Broadcasters label established Montreal 1972.

*Attic: established Toronto 1974, distributed by London until 1978, then by CBS, Quality, and PolyGram (from 1982).

*Audiophile: established 1979, produced and distributed by A & M.

*Axe: distributed by London Records and later by GRT.

*Banff: produced by Rodeo and distributed by London Records.

*Baroque (Canada Baroque Records, Ltd.): active Montreal 1962–ca. 1973, taken over by Everest (U.S.) ca. 1968.

Barclay: distributed by Polydor.

*Beaver Records, Ltd.: established Toronto 1950, pressed by RCA.

*Bernadol Records: established Toronto 1975, a division of Bernadol Music, Ltd.

*Birchmount: label of Quality Records, Toronto.

Bluebird: label of RCA Victor.

*Boot: Country and Western label established Toronto 1971, distributed by London Records.

Broadland: distributed by Quality.

Brunswick: imported 1920–1932, pressed in Canada and distributed by Compo from 1932.

*Canadian Talent Library: established Toronto 1962, broadcast discs.

*Cantilena: established Toronto 1966, historical recordings distributed by Rococo.

*CAPAC-CAB: recording project established Toronto 1963.

Capitol (Capitol Records-EMI of Canada, Ltd.): recordings distributed by Musicana Records (1946–1947) and Regal Records (1947–1954) both of London (Ontario), Capitol-EMI established Toronto 1955.

*Caprice: French-Canadian country label produced by Rodeo, distributed by London Records.

Capricorn: distributed by Polydor.

Caprice: distributed by London.

Casablanca: distributed by Polydor.

*Casino: established 1978, distributed by London.

CBS Records Canada, Ltd: see Columbia, below.

*Celtic: established Antigonish (Nova Scotia) 1933, taken over by Rodeo, distributed by London Records.

*Celebration: label of Quality Records, Toronto.

Chess: blues label distributed by GRT.

Chrysalis: distributed by Capitol Records.

*Club du Disque: label of Jeunesses Musicales of Canada, established Montreal, 1956.

Columbia Records of Canada (CBS): established Toronto 1904, pressed and distributed by Sparton Records 1939–1954, re-established Toronto 1954, from 1979 CBS Records Canada, Ltd.

*Compo Company, Ltd.: established Lachine (Quebec) 1918, basically a pressing plant and distributor of many labels; the company's own labels numbered more than 20, purchased by Decca 1950.

*Corner Store: established 1976.

*Cynda: budget reissues of Boot, distributed by London Records.

*Daffodil: established 1970, distributed by Capitol and later by GRT.

Decca: pressed by Compo 1935–1950, acquired by MCA and became part of PolyGram in 1980.

DGG: distributed by Polydor.

Disneyland: distributed by Sparton until 1969.

*Domino: pressed by Compo.

*Dominion: label of Canadian Music Sales, 1950–ca. 1970.

Dunhill: distributed by GRT.

Edison: Imported and distributed by R. S. Williams (Toronto) ca. 1900–1926.

EMI: distributed by Capitol.

Festival: distributed by GRT.

Festivo: distributed by Polydor.

*Flèche: produced by Kébec-Disk.

Fonotipia: imported and distributed by Phonola (Kitchener, Ontario) from 1914.

*Frog: produced by Kébec-Disk.

*Fundy: established Sackville (New Brunswick) 1971.

*Gamma Records, Ltd.: established Montreal 1965, distributed by London Records until 1978.

*Gatsby: distributed by Kébec-Disk.

*Gavotte: label of G.V. Thompson, Toronto, 1952–1955.

*Giant: established 1967 by Ben McPeek of Toronto.

*Goldfish: established Richmond (British Columbia) 1973, distributed by London.

*Gram-O-Phone: manufactured and distributed by E. Berliner (Montreal) 1899–1924.

GRT of Canada, Ltd.: established London (Ontario) 1969, then Toronto 1969–1979.

*Hallmark Recordings, Ltd.: active Toronto 1952–1959.

*Hawk: established 1970 by Ronnie Hawkins.

Hifirecord: distributed by Sparton until 1969.

Impulse: jazz label distributed by GRT.

Island: distributed by GRT.

*Janus: produced by Baroque.

Jumbo: imported and distributed by Phonola (Kitchener, Ontario) from 1914.

*Kanata: established Toronto 1971, distributed by Quality.

*Kébec-Disk, Inc.: established Montreal 1974.

*Le Nordet: distributed by Kébec-Disk.

London Gramophone Corp. of Canada: established Montreal 1948 as a subsidiary of Decca of London, later London Records of Canada (1967), Ltd., distributed by PolyGram after 1980.

*Lucky Strike: pressed by Compo.

*Magnum: established Toronto 1979 by GRT.

*Masters of the Bow: established Toronto 1974, historical recordings.

*Melotone: pressed by Compo.

*Melbourne: classical music label of Rodeo established Peterborough (Ontario) 1973, distributed by London, acquired by Waterloo Music in 1977.

Mercury: distributed by Polydor.

MGM: distributed by Polydor.

*Microphone: pressed by Compo.

*Much: established by Toronto radio station CHUM in 1970, distributed by London.

Musicana: pressed by Capitol.

Musidisk: jazz label distributed by GRT.

Music World Creations (MWC): distributed by Quality Records.

*Music Gallery Editions: established Toronto 1976.

Odeon: imported and distributed by Phonola (Kitchener, Ontario) from 1914.

*Onari: established Toronto 1973, distributed by Sackville.

*Orfeo: established Montreal 1954.

Otto Heinemann: imported and distributed by Phonola. (Kitchener, Ontario) from 1918.

Pathé: imported and distributed by J. A. Hurteau and Co., Ltd. (Montreal) and M. W. Glendon (Toronto) 1914–1918, then Pathé Frères Phonograph Co. of Canada, Ltd. (Toronto) 1918–1921.

Philips: distributed by Polydor.

Philo: distributed by London Records by 1973.

Phonola: pressed by Compo.

*Pirouette: produced by Baroque.

Polydor, Ltd.: established Montreal 1966, became PolyGram 1980.

Portrait: distributed by CBS.

*Potato: established 1972, distributed by Polydor.

*Quality Records, Ltd.: established Toronto 1950, also label by same name.

RCA Limited (also RCA Victor): originally Victor Talking Machine Co. of Canada, established 1924, see also Berliner, Victor.

Regal: pressed and distributed by Columbia Records, 1947–1954.

Resonance: see Polydor.

*Revolver: established 1968, distributed by Compo.

Richesse Classique: distributed by GRT.

*Rococo: label of Ross, Court & Co., Toronto, established 1955, reissues of historical recordings.

*Rodeo: country and folk label active Montreal 1948–1956, Halifax 1956–1969, Peterborough from 1969, distributed by London Records.

*Sackville: jazz label, established Toronto 1968.

*Select: label of Ed Archambault, established Montreal 1959, distributed by London Records until 1976.

Seraphim: distributed by Capitol.

*Solution: distributed by Kébec-Disk.

*Songs of My People: produced by Hallmark.

Sparton of Canada, Ltd.: established London (Ontario) 1930, subsidiary of Sparks-Worthington (U.S.), also label by this name.

*Spiral: produced by Hallmark.

Starr-Gennett: distributed by Canadian Phonograph Supply Co. (1917–1918) and later Starr Co. of Canada (1918–1930) of London (Ontario), records pressed by Compo (1918–1953) and distributed by that company 1930–1953.

*Sterling: pressed by Compo.

Sun: pressed by Compo.

*Tamarac: established 1963.

*Tapestry: established Ottawa 1978, distributed by RCA.

*Tip Top: founded by Max Boag (Harry Glenn) in Newmarket, Ontario, 1948–1980, commercial recordings.

*Tréma: produced by Kébec-Disk.

*True North: folk music label established Toronto 1970, distributed by CBS.

*Umbrella: label of Nimbus 9, established Toronto 1976.

Victor (His Master's Voice): imported and distributed by E. Berliner (Montreal) 1901–1924, later RCA Victor, then RCA.

Vitaphone (Canadian Vitaphone Co.): recordings pressed in Canada from Columbia masters, 1913–1916.

*WAA: established 1933.

Westminster: distributed by GRT.

* indicates a distinctly Canadian record label

Sources of further information:

Audio Key: The Canadian Record & Tape Guide. Winnipeg: Audio Key, 1985 (annual).

Encyclopedia of Music in Canada. Edited by Helmut Kallmann, Gilles Potvin, and Kenneth Winters. Toronto: University of Toronto Press, 1981. French version: Montreal: Fides, 1982.

Articles in the *Encyclopedia* on the recording industry include: "A & M Records of Canada, Ltd." (p. 1); "Ed Archambault, Inc." (p. 27); "Arc Records" (p. 30); "Beaver Records, Ltd." (p. 70); "Berliner Gramophone Company" (p. 80); "Bernadol Music Limited" (p. 79); "Boot Records, Ltd." (p. 99); "Brunswick" (p. 126); "Canada Baroque Records. Ltd." (p. 137); "Canadian Academy of Recording Arts and Sciences" (p. 140); "Canadian Recording Industry Association" (p. 154); "Canadian Talent Library" (p. 155); "Canadian Vitaphone Company" (p. 155); "CAPAC" (pp. 156–157); "Capitol Records-EMI of Canada, Ltd." (p. 157); "CBC Recordings" (p. 167); "CBS Records Canada, Ltd." (pp. 169–170); "Compo Company, Ltd." (p. 212); "CRTC" (p. 246); "Gamma Records, Ltd." (pp. 364–365); "GRT of Canada, Ltd." (p. 395); "Hallmark Recordings, Ltd." (p. 406); "Juno Awards" (p. 487); "Kébec-Disk, Inc." (p. 492); "London Records of Canada (1967), Ltd." (p. 561); "Pathé Frères" (p. 729); "Polydor, Ltd." (p. 769); "Quality Records, Ltd." (p. 784); "RCA Limited" (p. 795); "Recorded Sound" (pp. 796–800); "Rococo Records" (p. 816); "Rodeo Records, Ltd." (pp. 816–817); "Sparton of Canada, Ltd." (p. 888); "Starr" (p. 891); "Gordon V. Thompson, Ltd." (p. 914); "True North Records" (p. 936); "Waterloo Music Company, Ltd." (p. 988).

The *Encyclopedia* also contains bio-bibliographies of many of the artists listed in this entry.

Litchfield, Jack. *The Canadian Jazz Discography: 1916–1980.* Toronto: University of Toronto Press, 1982.

Moogk, Edward B. *Roll Back the Years: History of Canadian Recorded Sound and its Legacy: Genesis to 1930.* Ottawa: National Library of Canada, 1975. (Includes biographies of important Canadian performers and an extensive discography; volume II (1931–ca. 1955) in preparation.)

Periodicals containing detailed information on the Canadian recording industry include:

Canadian Music and Trades Journal (1900–1933).
Phonograph Journal of Canada (ca. 1923), later *Phonograph Journal and Radio Trades.*
RP (1964–), also *Canadian Music Industry Directory* (1965–) published annually by RPM.
Sound (1970–1976), later *Sound Canada* (1976–).
Sono: Sonorization au Canada (1973–1978).
AudioScene Canada (1974–).
Record Week (1975–1977).
Record Month (1976–1977).
Music Express (1976–).
Music Market Canada (1977–1979).
Music Magazine (1978–).
Canadian Musician (1979–).
Music Directory Canada (1984–).
Professional Musician (1985–).

R. Dale McIntosh

CANADIAN BROADCASTING CORP. (CBC).

A Crown Corporation responsible to Parliament but independent of the government, established by Act of Parliament on 2 Nov 1936; successor to the Canadian Radio Broadcasting Commission (CRBC), a government agency established by Parliament in 1932. The CRBC was intended to broadcast Canadian programs across the country; in carrying out this function the agency also made a number of acetate disc recordings of historic interest (speeches, ceremonies, etc.). A **Blattnerphone** was acquired and utilized to record overseas transmissions. Unfortunately, there was no practice of preserving the ordinary broadcasts of music and entertainment, so most of popular culture of the 1930s was lost. With the arrival of the new CBC the opposite condition prevailed, as vast quantities of program material were recorded—although not carefully indexed or cared for. Much of the potential archive was disposed of in a "willy-nilly policy" of weeding (Woods). Nevertheless a substantial record collection did emerge, enhanced by wartime documentary material and stimulated by the development of tape recording. And in 1959 a Program Archives Department was inaugurated, under the supervision of Robin Woods. Cataloging and preservation developed systematically from that point. [Woods 1970.]

CANS. Another term for **headphones.**

CANTILEVER. In a **cartridge,** the vertically compliant link between **stylus** and armature. It must be unbreakable, yet not resonant. It is usually made of magnesium, boron, or titanium.

CAPACITANCE. The measure, in farads or microfarads, of the energy-storage capability of a **capacitor.**

CAPACITOR. An electrical device—often two metal plates separated by an insulator—that can store electrical charge and will block current flow in a DC circuit. In AC circuits capacitors provide frequency-dependent **impedance,** useful in filtering and tuning applications. *See also* CAPACITANCE.

CAPEHART, HOMER EARL, 1897–1979. American industrialist and statesman, born in Algiers, Indiana, on 6 June 1897. He worked on his father's farm until World War I, then enlisted and served until April 1919. After holding various sales posts—one was general sales manager for Holcomb and Hoke, an early maker of **coin-op** vending machines—he founded the **Capehart Co.** in 1927. His intention was to manufacture **juke boxes** that could play either side of a record; he engaged the inventor of the disc-turning device, a man named Small, to join him in the enterprise. His new device, named the **Orchestrope,** was successfully placed in roadhouses and bars, but the Depression brought him financial crisis. He then shifted his target market to wealthier home buyers, and offered a deluxe phonograph that played both sides of discs. This venture was not sufficiently remunerative to save the business, and Capehart endeavored to sell out to RCA and other firms, eventually merging with Farnsworth Television and Radio Corp.

In 1932 Capehart established the **Packard Manufacturing Co.**, another coin-op maker. In 1933 he became associated with Wurlitzer, serving until 1940 as vice president. He was successful in a bid for the U.S. Senate in 1944, and was re-elected in 1950 and 1956. Capehart died in Indianapolis on 3 Sep 1979.

CAPEHART CO. A firm established by **Homer Earl Capehart** in 1927, in Huntington, Indiana. The name was given as the Capehart Automatic Phonograph Co. in 1928 advertising. The president was J.W. Caswell. An early product was the **Orchestrope**, a **coin-op** that played 56 discs, but did not allow the user to choose among them. Producing a superior record changing player, the firm became recognized in the 1930s as the leader in its field. A unique mechanism that turned records over to play both sides, handling 10-inch and 12-inch discs intermixed, was based on patents acquired from Columbia in 1929; the firm moved to a new factory in Fort Wayne at that time and began to perfect its Capehart Deluxe Automatic Home Phonograph, first offered in 1931. Around 1940 Farnsworth Radio and Television Corp. took over the company.

CAPITOL (label). A very successful pop label established in Los Angeles in 1942. Its founders were Johnny Mercer, Buddy DeSylva, and Glenn Wallichs. Singles were issued in 1942 (the first issues bore the name Liberty, but this was quickly changed to Capitol) with a black-colored label depicting the U.S. Capitol; a purple label appeared in 1949. During the "war of the speeds" both LPs and 45s were issued. Artists included Frank Sinatra (from the early 1950s), Johnny Mercer, Ray McKinley, Gordon Jenkins, Martha Tilton, The King Cole Trio, Jo Stafford, Kay Starr, Peggy Lee, and Stan Kenton; Paul Whiteman's last 78s were Capitols. In 1948 Capitol appeared in Britain, as a Decca affiliate. **EMI, Ltd.**, acquired a controlling interest in Capitol in 1956, and later released EMI's Beatles records in the U.S. Bad times came in the early 1970s, as the company found itself out of the mainstream and with an $8 million deficit, at a time when the record industry was thriving. Capitol recovered, and became the distributor of several prominent labels by 1973: Angel, Melodiya, Seraphim, Harvest, Invictus, Island, Purple, and Shelter. Address in 1991 was 1750 N. Vine, Hollywood, California. The company name is now Capitol Records, Inc.; it is a subsidiary of Capitol Industries-EMI, Inc., which in turn is part of the Thorn-EMI conglomerate. [Bennett, B. 1981 has a matrix list; Bennett, B. 1987 lists the 15,000 series; Rust 1978.]

CAPPS, FRANK L., ca. 1868–1943. American inventor and recording expert. He worked with Emile Berliner, Thomas Edison, and Columbia, and later was production manager for U.S. Pathé. Among his 50 U.S. audio patents were #836,089 (granted 20 Nov 1906) for the Pantograph cylinder duplicating device, and #570,378 (granted 27 Oct 1896) for a spring motor. The motor had three springs; it was used in the 1899 Edison Concert machine. In 1923 Capps produced one of the earliest **electrical recordings**, of a speech by Woodrow Wilson, pressed by the Compo Co. In the 1940s he devised a cutting stylus with a burnishing facet. His work for Columbia included making records of Czar Nicholas in Russia, and of many artists in Vienna and Berlin. He retired in 1942. Capps died in New York on 2 June 1943. [Koenigsberg 1990.]

CAPRICCIO (label). A CD product of Delta Music GmbH, of Königsdorf, Germany; opera and vocal music are the specialties. American distribution is by Delta Music, Inc., Los Angeles; the British agent is Target Records, Croydon, Surrey.

CAPSTAN. The drive spindle of a **tape recorder.** It consists of a motor-driven cylinder that works with a pinch roller (also known as the puck) to advance the tape at a constant speed. Actual tape speed is determined by the rotational velocity and diameter of the capstan.

CARBONA CO. A New Jersey firm, located (1919) at 3 & 5 Burnett St., Newark. Advertising of 1919 identified the company as maker of the disc cleaner Carbona.

CARDINAL (label). A disc made by the Cardinal Phonograph Co., trading at 106 E. 19th St., New York, first offered in December 1920. Factories were at Zanesville, Ohio; Newark, Ohio (home of the firm); and Point Pleasant, New Jersey. Cardinal also sold phonographs. The disc repertoire was pop, standards, and sacred music. Label color was red, with a cardinal bird on it; surfaces were poor. Nothing unusual or distinguished was recorded in the 100 or so issues.

Cardinal moved to Cincinnati in November 1921. A new Cardinal record, of somewhat improved quality, appeared in 1922 or 1923, drawing masters from Gennett. [Andrews*; Rust 1978.]

CARLOS, WALTER [WENDY], 1939– . American organist and composer, born in Pawtucket, Rhode Island, on 14 Nov 1939. He studied music and physics at Brown University and Columbia University. Working with Robert Moog, inventor of the Moog synthesizer, he made an album demonstrating the device. Entitled *Switched on Bach* (Columbia #MS 7194; 1969), it became the first successful record of electronic music, on the charts 31 weeks, and winner of two Grammy awards. Following a sex-change operation in 1979, the artist performed as Wendy Carlos. There were nine CDs by her in the 1991 catalog.

CARNEGIE MUSIC SET. One of the monumental **anthologies** issued in the 78 rpm era, sponsored by the Carnegie Corporation. The intent was to provide material for small colleges, useful in teaching music appreciation. Beginning in 1933, sets of records were distributed—each with a record player and a four-drawer file of catalog cards. The standard repertoire was represented, performed by a variety of artists, along with a number of less familiar modern works. [Miller, P. 1972.]

CARNIVAL (label). A house label for the John Wanamaker department stores (New York and Philadelphia) in 1924–1925. Pressing was done by the Bridgeport Die and Machine Co.; masters were mostly from Emerson and Paramount. The only original take seems to have been "Mr

Jelly Lord" / "Steady Roll" (#11397), played by Jelly Roll Morton. [Rust 1978.]

CARRERAS, JOSÉ MARIA, 1946– . Spanish tenor, born in Barcelona on 5 Dec 1946. He studied in Bacelona and made his debut there in 1970. He sang for the first time in Italy in 1971, performing Rodolfo in Parma. He appeared at the Metropolitan Opera as Cavaradossi on 18 Nov 1974, and in the same year at Covent Garden; his La Scala debut was in 1975. Carreras has been greatly acclaimed for his Italian roles, notably Alfredo, Nemorino, Don José, the Duke, and Don Carlo. Despite an attack of leukemia in 1987, he was on stage again in 1988.

Carreras has recorded a number of complete operas, including *Elisir d'amore* (Philips #412714), *Lucia di Lamermoor* (Philips #6703080), *Pagliacci* and *Cavalleria rusticana* (Angel #SZX-3895), and the principal Puccini and Verdi works. He took the male lead in a complete *West Side Story* recording under Leonard Bernstein's direction (DG #415253; 1986). He was one of the "three tenors" on the greatly popular CD *Carreras, Domingo, Pavarotti in Concert* (London #430433-2; 1990), which has sold some 5,700,000 copies.

CARRYOLA COMPANY OF AMERICA. A firm located at 647 Clinton St., Milwaukee, Wisconsin. It made a portable disc player in 1926–1927, claiming in *TMW* advertising to be the world's largest producer of these. In early 1929, Carryola was acquired by the Allen-Hough Manufacturing Co., of Milwaukee.

CARSON, MARY. American soprano, born in Houston, Texas. She studied in Italy, and made her opera debut there before 1912 in *Sonnambula*, scoring a great success. A noteworthy achievement was the performance of *Barbiere di Siviglia* two times in one night. When she returned to America she began to record for Edison, but the repertoire was one of popular songs and ballads, not opera. The Edison November 1912 catalog included her interpretation of "Oh Dry Those Tears " (#1592); her later work was similar. Carson's best-selling records were "The Simple Melody" on Blue Amberol (#2607; a duet with Walter van Brunt), and "Kiss Waltz" (with chorus; #2665 and Diamond Disc #80061; 1913). She was heard under the name of Kathleen Kingston on Blue Amberol #2253, "You're Here and I'm Here," a duet with Billy Murray. Three of her Diamond Discs were still popular enough for the 1927 Edison catalog, and two—"Kiss Waltz" and "I'll Change the Shadows" (#80122)—were sold until Edison quit the record business in 1929.

CARTER, BENNY, 1907– . American jazz trumpeter, alto saxophonist, Big Band leader, and arranger; born Bennett Lester Carter on 8 Aug 1907 in New York. He played with and made important arrangements for many great jazz ensembles, including those of Duke Ellington, Fletcher Henderson, and Chick Webb. Touring and recording in Europe in 1935–1938, he earned international acclaim. Returning to America in 1938, he led his own groups, which included such stellar performers as drummer Sid Catlett, trombonist J.C. Higginbotham, and pianist Teddy Wilson. Carter's band was featured in the motion picture *As Thousands Cheer* (1943), and Carter did arrangements for films and television.

Among his fine recordings are "Lonesome Nights" (Okeh #41567; 1933) and one made in The Hague: "My Buddy" (Decca #F-42136; 1937). [Berger, M. 1982.]

CARTER FAMILY. A country music ensemble, originally established in Virginia in the 1920s, with Alvin Pleasant ("A.P.") Carter as the lead and bass singer, his wife Sara as singer and guitarist, and her sister Maybelle, also a singer and guitarist. Discovered by a Victor talent scout, they began to record in August 1927, and became famous in the 1930s. By 1941 they had recorded more than 250 songs. Children of Maybelle and of A.P. and Sara joined the group in the 1940s, and the Family was heard on *Grand Ole Opry*. "Wabash Cannonball" was one of their hit numbers; original pieces by A.P. also became country standards. The group broke up in 1943.

CARTRIDGE. (I) An enclosure for a roll of magnetic tape, so designed that it will be ready for use when it is inserted into a mated **tape**

recorder or tape player. The advantage of the cartridge over the **reel-to-reel** tape mechanism is that it is self-contained, and can be inserted without manual threading; it automatically engages the **capstan** and magnetic heads. The term usually refers to the **cassette** format introduced by Philips in 1963. With its great size advantage, the cassette made obsolete all the previous configurations, such as the four-track and eight-track cartridges that had been used in automobiles. This kind of enclosure is also known as the closed-loop cartridge, or continuous-loop cartridge.

CARTRIDGE. (II) A device (also known as a pickup) consisting of a **stylus** or **needle** and a **transducer**, whose function is to convert the groove patterns of a disc into electric signals.

There are four basic varieties: the moving iron, the moving coil or dynamic, the moving magnet, and the crystal or ceramic.

In the *moving iron cartridge*, a piece of metal (the vane) is attached to the stylus; as it vibrates in the record groove it activates a coil of wire that is surrounded by a permanent magnet, producing the audio signal. Those with "variable reluctance"—introduced in the late 1940s—use a minute cantilever of magnetic material to vary the reluctance of a gap between two coils when the stylus is activated by the groove pattern; an example is the British Goldring 500 cartridge, known in the U.S. as the Recoton. Because of its low-voltage output, the variable reluctance pickup required a **preamplifier**. With some modifications it was used successfully on LPs.

In the *moving coil cartridge*, also known as "dynamic," the stylus moves the coil through a constant magnetic field, setting up electrical variations that comprise the signal. For stereophonic playback, there are two coils, each responding to stylus movement against one of the groove walls. A cartridge usable for both monophonic and stereophonic discs, such as the Western Electric Model 9A or Westrex Model 10A, can be set so that the stylus moves vertically for mono or laterally for stereo. Problems encountered with this kind of pickup are the need for amplification, and the need to return the entire assembly to the factory for stylus replacement. Denon, Fairchild, Grado,

Kiseki, and Ortofon are manufacturers associated with this type of pickup. Recent moving coil cartridges by Denon and Ortofon require no extra amplification stage.

In a *moving magnet cartridge* the stylus carries a tiny permanent magnet; as it vibrates with the stylus it induces voltage in the coil. Among the manufacturers: Audio-Technica, Empire, Fairchild, General Electric, Pickering, Shure, Signet, and Stereotwin.

The early *crystal cartridges* were based on the piezo-electric properties of a material known as Rochelle salt: when a piece of this salt is bent or twisted an electrical output results. The original crystal cartridge had two slices of Rochelle about an inch long, pressed together with a metal foil separating them; each slice had a lead connecting it to an external circuit. At the end opposite the lead the slices were held in a "torque jaw" clamp. When the stylus, also attached to the torque jaw, vibrated in the record groove, the motion was carried to the Rochelle slices, twisting them enough to generate a voltage. Such a pickup was inexpensive and simple to construct, and did not require **equalization** as other types do. Certain problems with Rochelle salt—for example its tendency to absorb moisture and deteriorate— were corrected with the introduction of ceramic piezo materials. Ceramic cartridges have been made by Astatic, Electro-Voice, Ronette, and Weathers.

A less common pickup is the capacitive type, modeled on the principle of the capacitive microphone: its stylus is attached to a diaphragm biased with a polarizing voltage.

In the 78 rpm era, with steel needles as the styli, the moving iron pickup was standard; its efficiency was limited by the mass of the armature, and **frequency response** was not above 8,000 Hz. The moving coil cartridge had similar limits based on size of coil. Later designs with smaller moving parts allowed an extension of range to about 16,000 Hz. During the LP period great improvements were made in all aspects of cartridge manufacture. By 1988 quality pickups offered almost perfectly flat responses up to 20,000 Hz. Other measures applied to cartridges include vertical tracking angle (VTA), which should be 20 degrees; **channel separation**; and tracking ability. Newer

products in higher price ranges ($300–$1,300) perform superbly on discs in good condition, but they do nothing to conceal the defects in worn or dirty grooves. [AudioC 1969; Bauer, B. 1945; Bauer, B. 1963; Hirsch 1988; Klinger*.] *See also* STYLUS; TONE ARM.

CARUSO, ENRICO, 1873–1921. Neapolitan tenor, born on 25 Feb 1873, widely regarded as the finest to sing the French-Italian repertoire, whose early discs had great impact on the recording industry. His debut took place in Naples, on 15 March 1895; he performed with variable success for several years thereafter until he acquired stellar rank during the 1900/ 1901 season at La Scala. In 1902 he made his first appearance at Covent Garden and on 23 Nov 1903, in *Rigoletto*, at the Metropolitan Opera. It was the Metropolitan that became his favorite venue, and his final public rendition was there, in *La juive*, on Christmas eve, 1920. He died in Naples on 2 Aug 1921.

While in Milan in 1902, Caruso was approached by the enterprising Fred Gaisberg of Gramophone & Typewriter, Ltd., and for a fee of £100 he recorded 10 numbers on 11 April. They were two arias from Franchetti's *Germania*—"Studenti! Udite" was his first record (matrix #1782)—two from *Mefistofole*, "Questa o quella," "Celeste Aida," "Chiudo gli occhi" from *Manon*, "Una furtiva lagrima," "E lucevan le stelle," and "Apri la tua finestra" from *Iris*. (When Heinrich Conried of the Metropolitan heard one of them, he offered Caruso a contract.)

Caruso made 10 other records for G & T in Milan, in November and December 1902— then another 10 records in 1903 for the International Zonophone Co., under auspices of their Italian agent, the Anglo-Italian Commerce Co. Seven were lateral-cut discs issued by Zonophone, and the other three were cylinders (and later discs) issued by Pathé. A valuable essay by Canon H.J. Drummond presents rich detail about the Zonophone set, which consisted of these works: "Un bacio ancora" (Trimarchi); "Luna fedel" (Zardo); "Una furtiva lagrima"; "E lucevan le stelle"; "No non chiuder gli occhi vaghi" from *Germania* (which was also in his first G & T group); "La donna è mobile"; and "Siciliana" from *Cavalleria rusticana*. In the last-named piece, Caruso's voice impressed Drummond as being "warm and full of ardour so that when I first heard it something of the beauty of that marvellous organ seemed to break through the haze of this early recording and I could almost fancy that the great singer stood again before me."

It should be mentioned also that Caruso apparently made some records for **Bettini** before Victor signed him to an exclusive contract in 1904. There is testimony from Bettini's son that "Caruso . . . often came to his office and sang through his machine. . . . I used to have them in the unfortunately destroyed material stored in France." None of those recordings were listed in the Bettini sale catalogs, and none are known to exist today.

The recordings by Caruso, and those of other major voices in 1903 and 1904—notably Charles Santley, Francesco Tamagno, and Nellie Melba—helped to change public and corporate attitudes toward the function of sound recording. Although the big producers were doing well enough, their output had been sharply tilted toward popular, novelty, and band numbers. A new emphasis on operatic music emerged, and soon after an interest in the symphonic repertoire.

Caruso's labors—exclusively for Victor after 1904—resulted in 245 sides of 78 rpm records, and royalties estimated at $3.5 million. All his records are "in print," in the sense that they are available in one reissue format or another. Many were reissued as enhanced electrics, in the 1930s, and the material from 1906 was offered by RCA in 13 LP albums (*The Complete Caruso*, #ARK1; projected to be 16 LPs, but the first three, which would have contained all the 1902–1904 Milan recordings, as well as the 1904–1905 Victors with piano accompaniment, were never issued) and in various enhanced formats (*see* SOUNDSTREAM).

The first CD issue was *The Legendary Enrico Caruso* (RCA 5911–2RD, 1987), consisting of 21 arias. Fifteen CDs by a German label named Bayer were released as the *Complete Caruso* in 1990, but the set had many shortcomings (see the review by Gary Galo in *ARSCJ* 21–2, Fall 1990). Pearl released a CD of his 1902–1908 recordings in 1990, and of the 1908–1912 re-

cordings in 1991 (#EVC I and EVC II; three CDs each). With volume 3 of the set, #EVC3 (1991), the 1912–1916 records were offered; and with the final volume, #EVC4 (1991), the 1916–1921 records were presented. RCA offered a CD *Complete Caruso* on 12 CDs (#60495–2–RG). Galo's review of these sets points out that RCA inadvertently presented two recordings of an unpublished take, of Tosti's "L'alba separa dalla luce l'ombra," instead of both the published and unpublished versions. Thus the Pearl set is the only CD version to include all the known recordings. Those who listen to any CD transfers should be advised that pitch reference is inconsistent. The pitch problem in Caruso's recordings is discussed in Favia-Artsay 1965 and Galo 1991.

"Vesti la giubba" was the greatest of his market sensations, selling more than a million copies in its various versions. It was among those discs first made in Milan for Gaisberg, with piano only, then recorded with orchestral accompaniment in 1907 for Victor (#88061), and electrically re-recorded (#7720); both the acoustic and electric versions remained in the Victor catalog. [Bolig 1973; Caruso 1990; Drummond 1969; Favia-Artsay 1965; Feinstein 1985; Galo*; Galo 1984; Galo 1990; Galo 1991; Hanna 1978; Klee 1981; Klee 1983; Klee 1987; Scott 1988.]

CARVER CORP. A leading American audio electronics manufacturer, located in Lynnwood, Washington. Founded by Bob Carver in 1979, it was quickly recognized for its M400 power amplifier and C-4000 sonic holography auto correlation preamplifier. Carver developed these products further, and added FM tuners, flat panel loudspeakers, CD players and automobile audio to its line of products.

CASA LOMA ORCHESTRA. One of the outstanding Big Bands of the 1930s, established 1928; it took its name from a hotel in Toronto. Although Henry Biagini was the first director, Glen Gray (1906–1963) was the actual leader from 1929; Gray preferred to sit in the saxophone section, and did not appear in front of the band until 1937. The common designation "Glen Gray and the Casa Loma Orchestra" was in use from 1933. The orchestra had various other stage names, including the Carolina Club Orchestra, Palais de Danse Orchestra, Louisiana Rhythmakers, Blue Racketeers, Sands Point Orchestra, Castle Orchestra, and Supertone Dance Orchestra.

Two brilliant arrangers were associated with the group, and defined its style: Gene Gifford (also the composer of "Smoke Rings," the band's theme song, heard on Decca #1473; 1937) and Larry Clinton. Among the fine Casa Loma vocalists were Kenny Sargent, Mildred Bailey, Connie Boswell, Ray Eberle, Lee Wiley, and Pee Wee Hunt (a trombonist who sang in lighter numbers). The band was featured on the *Camel Caravan* and *Burns and Allen* radio shows. Their earliest recording was "Love is a Dreamer" (Okeh #41329; 1929) with Eberle's vocal. One of Lee Wiley's fine renditions was "A Hundred Years from Today" (Brunswick #6775; 1934). Other hits were "Sunrise Serenade" (Decca #2321; 1939) and "No Name Jive" (Decca #3089; 1940). Hoagy Carmichael made one of his few singing appearances with the orchestra in 1939, doing "Washboard Blues" and "Little Old Lady" (Decca #2394).

CASALS, PABLO, 1876–1973.
Spanish cellist and conductor, born Pau Carlos Salvador Defilló Casals in Vendrell on 29 Dec 1876. A child prodigy, he studied in Barcelona and gave his first solo recital there at age 14. He performed at the palace in Madrid, and also in a music hall in Paris, then joined the music faculty in Barcelona in 1896. He received great acclaim in London in 1899, and was invited to perform for the Queen. Further tours brought him international renown, and an invitation to play at the White House in 1904 (he played there again, for President John F. Kennedy, in 1961). Casals formed an orchestra in Barcelona, and a trio in Paris (with Alfred Cortot and Jacques Thibaud). Finally he settled in San Juan, Puerto Rico, his mother's birthplace. The annual Festival Casals has been held there since 1957. He died in San Juan on 22 Oct 1973. On the centenary of his birth, the Spanish government issued a commemorative postage stamp in his honor.

Among the outstanding recordings by Casals are the Dvořák Cello Concerto, with Georg Szell (HMV #HLM-7013; 1937), the unaccompanied Bach suites (Victor #M611, three discs), and the Beethoven "Archduke Trio" with Cortot and Thibaud (Victor 8196/8200; 1928). These, and other discs he made in that period, were heard also on other labels. After World War II his most famous records were the five-disc rendition of the Schubert Quintet in C-Major, with Isaac Stern, Alexander Schneider, Milton Katims, and Paul Tortelier (Columbia #M5–30069). A CD reissue of the Dvorak and Elgar concertos appeared in 1990 (EMI #CDH7). [Morin 1982 has a complete discography.]

CASE, ANNA, 1888–1984.
American soprano, born in Clinton, New Jersey, on 29 Oct 1888. She has been referred to as "Edison's favorite singer"—certainly she was one of his prolific artists. Case made her debut at the Metropolitan Opera in a minor role on 20 Nov 1909, and stayed with the company until 1919; Aida and Carmen were her best roles. In 1913 she sang Sophie in the American premiere of *Rosenkavalier*. She began to record on Edison wax cylinders with "Believe Me If All Those Endearing Young Charms" (#28108; 21 June 1912) and two other numbers. She then made 98 Diamond Discs, the first on 19 Sep 1913 ("Charmant oiseau" from *Perle du Brésil*; #80120) and the last on 24 June 1926 ("A Night of Love"; #80872). Her recorded repertoire consisted primarily of concert songs, though she included a few arias (Aida's not among them). Two of the experimental Edison long-playing records of 1928 included Case's voice, doing four songs on each disc. She made only one Victor record, taking part in the ensemble of "Du also bist mein" from *Zauberflöte* (#C13131; 16 Apr 1913).

Following some work for **Vitaphone** in 1926, Case moved to Columbia and made 41 discs from 1928 to 1930, again drawing on the concert repertoire. She retired in 1931. She died in New York on 7 Jan 1984. [Wile 1979 is a complete discography.]

CASH, JOHNNY, 1932– .
American country singer, born John R. Cash in Kingsland, Arkansas, on 26 Feb 1932. He escaped from his childhood poverty by joining the U.S. Air Force, serving from 1950 to 1954. When he returned to

civilian life he formed a musical group in Memphis and received a Sun (label) contract in 1955. His first release was a Top 10 record: "Hey Porter" and "Cry, Cry, Cry." In 1956 three of his compositions were on the charts: "So Doggone Lonesome," "There You Go," and "I Walk the Line" (Sun #241). On Columbia from 1958, he made very successful pressings of "Don't Take Your Guns to Town" (Columbia #41313; 1959), "Ring of Fire" (Columbia #42788; 1963), and "Understand Your Man" (Columbia #42964; 1964). His most famous record is "Folsom Prison Blues" (Columbia #44513; 1968), for which he won a Grammy. He also received Grammys for the 1969 single " A Boy Named Sue" (Columbia #44944) and for a duet with his wife, June Carter (of the Carter Family), "If I Were a Carpenter" (Columbia #45064; 1970). In 1986 he left Columbia for Polygram, and made several successful LP albums, including *Boom Chicka Boom* (1990), consisting almost entirely of new material. Cash was elected to the Country Music Hall of Fame in 1980. [Hurd 1990; Smith, 1985.]

CASSETTE. Also known as Audiocassette, or MusiCassette. The medium for **magnetic recording** introduced by **Philips** in 1963, intended to replace the **reel-to-reel** or open-reel format, and the awkward tape **cartridge**. The cassette reduced the size of that cartridge by a factor of five.

A cassette is a twin-hub tape cartridge of the co-planar type, suitable for mono/stereo compatible use. It is symmetrical, its two sides labelled "1" and "2" or "A" and "B" respectively. When recording with side 1 uppermost, and the end of the tape is reached, the cassette is turned over and recording continues with side 2 uppermost.

Dimensions of the cassette are 100 millimeters (3.965 inches) in length; 63 millimeters (2.524 inches) in width, and 12.3 millimeters (0.484 inch) in thickness. The two tape hubs each have 10.4 millimeters (0.4094 inch) diameter center holes to engage the corresponding recorder or player spindles. Those spindles draw the tape from hub to hub during the various operations: record, play, rewind, or fast forward. Three large openings in the front of the case permit guided contact of the tape

with the erase, record/play heads, and between the pressure roller and the **capstan** which protrudes into the cassette from the recorder/player. A pressure pad maintains constant head-to-tape contact.

The tape itself—completely confined within the housing at all times—is 3.81 millimeters (.150 inches) wide, a maximum of 0.20 millimeters (0.0008 inch) thick, and has a speed of 47.6 millimeters (1 7/8 inches) per second. International standards for cassettes are found in Publication 94A of the International Electrotechnical Commission (IEC). Of course, playing time is determined by the length of the tape, usually indicated by a "C" code. A C-0 is empty; C-30 of 46 meters (151 feet) plays 30 minutes. C-60 has 92 meters (302 feet) and plays 60 minutes; C-90 has 138 meters (543 feet) and plays 90 minutes. The longest tape in common use is the C-120, 207 meters (815 feet) in length, with playing time of 120 minutes. There are four tracks (two stereo pairs) recorded linearly on the tape. The bottom pair is always used for stereo, and combined for mono.

Early cassette tapes did not produce high fidelity output, because of the slow playback speed that made flaws more obvious, and because particle density inhibited high frequency response. (Wider tapes moving at 3 3/4 inches per second have been marketed to overcome these disadvantages, but have not been generally accepted.) Ferric oxide was the medium, as with open-reel tapes, until DuPont introduced chrome (chromium dioxide) tape. Other companies produced "chrome-equivalent" tapes; and then a pure metal tape, whose advantages were obscured by the need for special playback equipment. Ferric tapes still represent the industry norm, with technical efforts aimed at reducing particle size and improving binders.

Noise reduction systems have also gained much attention, beginning with the Dolby A device of 1966. Through constant improvements in tape and tape recorder design, the medium achieved a quality of reproduction that rivaled that of LP discs played on fine equipment. In the U.S. the number of prerecorded cassettes produced each year in the 1970s and early 1980s was about the same as the number of LP albums; major record companies frequently issued tape versions of their new discs, and both formats were listed in Schwann and other catalogs of new releases. Sales were enhanced by the introduction of the Walkman (a small portable player), by the Sony Corporation, in 1979. The arrival of the compact disc in 1983 changed the market situation, and digital technology was applied to tapes as well (see DAT). However, the sale of traditional stereo cassettes remained very high: from January to June 1989 more than 211 million were sold in the U.S., compared to 97 million CDs. The introduction of the Cassingle (1987) for the recording of one popular song per side helped to remove the seven-inch vinyl disc from the American market.

Purchase of blank cassette tapes for home recording has become a way of life in many countries, bringing up the problem of illegal copying (see COPYRIGHT); more than 100 million blank tapes are sold annually in the U.S. alone. Many cassette recorders are available with dual mechanisms to facilitate tape duplication.

According to the classification of the International Electrotechnical Commission, cassette tapes are referred to as Type I (ferric, requiring normal **bias** and 120 microsecond playback **equalization** [EQ]); Type II (chrome or chrome-compatible coatings, higher bias, requiring 70 microsecond playback EQ); Type III (dual-layered ferrichromes, also 70 microsecond playback EQ; various biases and recording EQs; this type is no longer manufactured); and Type IV (metal particle or alloy, with highest bias, and 70 microsecond EQ). Type I has the highest MOL (maximum output level) for 3 percent distortion, a small high-frequency boost in equalization. Type II has a lower MOL, but usually a higher **signal-to-noise ratio**. The highest quality Type IV tapes are the best performers, and they have the greatest resistance to erasure. Sony's Music Master tape has a dynamic range at 315 Hz of 64 dB. Type I is vulnerable to erasure of high frequencies by exposure to small magnetic fields.

The shell or housing of the audiocassette has improved over the years. Metal tapes are usually sold in carefully crafted shells that are designed to reduce external vibrations and increase **azimuth** stability through precision in construction.

Among the manufacturers (in 1990) of superior blank tapes are BASF AG, Denon, Fuji, General Electric, JVC, Loran, Maxell, Memorex, Nakamichi, PDMagnetics, Realistic, Recoton, Sony, TDK, That's America, 3M, and Visa. [Isom*.] *See also* CASSETTE DECK; DAT.

Cassette book. *See* TALKING BOOK.

CASSETTE DECK. The transport, recording, and playback device used with **cassettes;** it is part of an audio system, requiring attachment to an **amplifier** or **receiver,** as well as **loudspeakers.** In principle the cassette deck is the same as the reel-to-reel **tape recorder,** but the size and spacing of the drive and rewind components is adjusted to the smaller and self-contained cassette. Decks available in 1990 included both Dolby B and Dolby C **noise reductions systems** (in some cases the dbx also). Several models had three heads, to give a better fidelity and allow instant comparison between the input signal and the recorded output. Many decks have some form of **bias** or sensitivity adjustment. All the better decks have two motors, one to turn the **capstan,** the other to handle fast-forward and rewind operations.

Auto-reverse is a questionable feature that has become standard on good decks. It presents problems of audio quality that can only be overcome with additional expensive mechanisms, and it offers the possibility of confusion regarding which side of the tape is being played. Various convenience features are found in the high-end decks: random access program play, music search, remote controls, remaining time indicators, and linear time counters. Among the principal manufacturers of cassette decks in 1991 were a/d/s, Aiwa, Akai, Kenwood, Luxman, Nakamichi, Onkyo, Pioneer, SAE, Sansui, and Sherwood. Prices ranged from $350 to $1,000 or more.

CASSETTE NUMBER. The manufacturer's number on a **cassette,** equivalent to the **disc number.**

CASWELL, JOHN WALLACE, 1870–1943. American industry executive, born in Fort

Wayne, Indiana, on 6 Oct 1870. After various jobs as a clerk and salesman, in 1906 he and Winifred Runyan organized the Caswell-Runyan Co. in North Manchester, Indiana; the firm manufactured cedar chests. Caswell was president of the company from 1907 to 1935, and thereafter until his death was chairman of the board. Caswell was also the first president of the new **Capehart Automatic Phonograph Co.** in Fort Wayne, and a director of Utah Radio Products Co., Chicago. He died in Huntington, Indiana, on 25 Jan 1943.

CASWELL MANUFACTURING CO. Maker of portable phonographs, first advertised in 1926. Address was St. Paul Ave. and 10th St., Milwaukee, Wisconsin.

Cataloging and Classification. *See* SOUND RECORDINGS AND THE LIBRARY.

Catalogs. *See* DISCOGRAPHY.

CBS. *See* COLUMBIA BROADCASTING SYSTEM (CBS).

CD. *See* COMPACT DISC.

CD DIRECT. An input switch on an integrated **amplifier** that bypasses all circuitry except **volume control** and perhaps **balance control.**

CEDAR. A reprocessor for 78 rpm records, developed at the **National Sound Archive** in London. It was made by Cambridge Electronic Design, and first demonstrated at the Audio Engineering Society conference of March 1990. CEDAR is said to out perform other systems that suppress the clicks and noises in 78s. The acronym stands for Computer Enhanced Digital Audio Restoration. EMI and Columbia have used the system in preparing CD reissues. [Reid 1990.]

CELESTION INTERNATIONAL, LTD. An audio electronic firm located in Ipswich, Suffolk, England. The specialty is **loudspeakers.** In 1990 Celestion's 3000 and 5000 series speakers won the annual award from the Federation of British Audio, and the 7000 model won the Component of the Year award in Japan. [Horn 1988.]

CELLO RECORDINGS. Hans Kronold of the New York College of Music was the first to record on the cello, making cylinders for **Bettini.** The latter's June 1898 catalog includes 12 numbers by Kronold, the first being a "Romance" by Fisher. Kronold also recorded for Edison, from 1905. William Henry Squire recorded for the Gramophone Co. on 19 Oct 1898, performing his own "Serenade" (#7850), and recorded again in November.

Josef Hollman (1862–1927) recorded for G & T in 1906, beginning with an arrangement of Chopin's Nocturne in E-Flat (matrix #C-3025) and doing three other numbers on the same day, 19 January. On 1 Feb 1906 he made three more discs. Rosario Bourdon (1889–1961) recorded for Victor in 1906, on two dates in June. Hollman and Bourdon were still in the Victor catalog in 1917, joined by Victor Herbert and Hans Kindler, but by the issue of the 1927 catalog they had all faded away before the arrival of **Pablo Casals.** In the electric era two more great cellists were recorded: **Emanuel Feuermann** on Columbia, and Gregor Piatigorsky on Columbia and Victor. The LP brought the added artistry of Jacqueline Du Pré (on Angel), Pierre Fournier (Deutsche Grammophon and others), Antonio Janigro (Vanguard), Leonard Rose (Columbia), Mstislav Rostropovich (London and others), and Janos Starker (Angel and others).

CELLOPHONE. A recording system based on the principle of the sound film, marketed for home use in 1937 by **British Ozaphane, Ltd.** The name Duo-trac was used for the device when it first appeared in February; advertising in August refers to the "Duo-trac" Cellophone. (It was the reels that were Duo-tracs, and the machine that was the Cellophone.) "Ozaphane" film—a kind of cellophane—carried two sound tracks that were read by a photoelectric cell. Playing time was either 15 or 30 minutes in each direction, depending on the spool size (seven or nine inch), and an automatic reverse moved from the first to the second track to double the duration of play. Back and forth running time of 90 minutes was achieved with reels that were recorded and played at a slower speed, but this was only suitable for non-musical records.

Cellophones were offered in various models, including a basic "console"; and a "Radio Cellophone" that featured "an all-wave superheterodyne radio set, with triple diode circuit and inverse back-coupling." A deluxe version also had "a special high fidelity amplifier, with 10-watt undistorted output." Prices ranged from about £30 to £60. Since there was no needle scratch, no record wear, and a very long playing time, it is somewhat surprising that market outcome was only fair. One problem was the lack of artists; the company had to find unattached performers and start from nothing to build a catalog. Little of consequence emerged, and the possibility of recording symphonies and operas without troublesome interruptions was left unexploited. Buyers had to choose from dance music, variety numbers, salon orchestras, or band pieces. But the crushing defects of the system were the same ones that kept open reel **tape recording** from overcoming the disc: it was necessary to thread the film onto the take-up reel by hand; and it was a lot of bother to find a given musical number somewhere on the film. On 29 July 1939 the last advertisement for the machine appeared in *Wireless Trader*. Documentation on the Cellophone is incomplete. No catalog or list of the reel records has survived. [Andrews 1984/4.]

CENTER CHANNEL. In **stereophonic** recording, a mix of the left and right channels; intended to spread the sound and improve the sense of aural perspective. The center signal is provided by a matrix decoder; there is no actual signal generated from the position between the left and right inputs. Recent research (1990) shows that the center image is lost in a portion of the **audio frequency range**, and that the inclusion of an actual center-channel speaker may be desirable. Center speakers are found already in motion picture presentations. [Hodges 1990.]

CENTRAL NEBRASKA PHONOGRAPH CO. One of the **North American Phonograph**

Co. group, established in Kearney, Nebraska, in 1890; E.A. Benson was director.

CENTRAL STATES TALKING MACHINE JOBBERS ASSOCIATION. A trade organization established in Columbus, Ohio, in March 1906 (at first lacking the "jobbers" in the title), with George Ilsen as President. Members were all jobbers. It merged with **Eastern Talking Machine Jobbers Association** to form the **Talking Machine Jobbers National Association** in September 1907.

Ceramic pickup. *See* CARTRIDGE (II).

CETRA (label). An Italian independent label established in Turin in 1937, devoted entirely to classical music. Parlophone, Odeon, and HMV issued their materials for a time in Britain. In 1953 Capitol took over the firm, but the label name was continued into the early 1970s.

CHALIA, ROSALIA, 1864–1948. Cuban soprano, born in Havana on 17 Nov 1864, one of the most prolific artists to record before 1900. Educated in Europe, she married a Philadelphian and came to America. Her opera debut was in Washington, D.C., as a substitute Aida; then she sang in Milan in 1895, and for Mapleson in New York (1896–97). Her only Metropolitan Opera appearance was as Santuzza on 17 Dec 1898. Thereafter she concentrated on Latin American performances. Most of her records were for **Bettini**; in his 1897 catalog she had eight numbers, in the 1898 catalog 15, and in the 1899 catalog there were 67 arias and songs, plus 36 duets. Of this 193-cylinder output none have survived.

One of the first opera singers to make discs, she recorded for Zonophone ca. 1900, making seven records. Then she made a fine "Jewel Song" for Eldridge Johnson's new label in 1901 (#3431), and continued on Victor until 1913; her South American records were for Columbia. "Voi lo sapete" (Victor #68400; 1913) is a particularly fine effort. Chalia died in Havana on 16 Nov 1948. [Fassett 1945/9–10; 1956/2.]

CHALIAPIN, FEODOR, 1873–1938. Russian bass, born on 13 Feb 1873 in Kazan. He left his apprenticeship (to a cobbler) to join a traveling opera company at age 14, with the author Maxim Gorky as a fellow chorister. A generous teacher gave him free lessons, and he was able to gain employment in the St. Petersburg summer opera in 1894. From there he went to the Imperial Opera, and to solo concertizing which brought him great acclaim in Moscow and elsewhere. In 1901 he made his La Scala debut in Boito's *Mefistofele*, and sang the same role at the Metropolitan Opera on 20 Nov 1907. His unsurpassed interpretation of Boris Goudonov was heard at the Metropolitan on 9 Dec 1921; he remained with the company until 1929. Chaliapin came to be known as the greatest of singing actors. He died in Paris on 12 Apr 1938.

Chaliapin's earliest discs—apart from some private cylinders in 1898—were made for G & T in Moscow in 1901; they do not reveal a particularly smooth or attractive voice. Of the eight numbers he did then "Le veau d'or" from *Faust* (#22824) may be the most effective. In 1907–1914 he recorded for HMV in St. Petersburg, Riga, Paris, and London; producing about 65 discs; among them were five arias from *Boris Goudonov*, including his famous death scene (#022223; subsequently recorded 12 more times, five being issued).

In 1921 and 1923–1934 Chaliapin sang for HMV in London and Paris. Then he was with Victor in New York, in 1922, 1924, and 1927. His final Victor was made in Tokyo in 1936.

He sang the standard bass repertoire, but his finest work on record was in the Russian operas: *Prince Igor, Sadko, Ruslan and Ludmilla, Life of the Czar,* and *Boris;* he re-recorded material from these works many times on acoustic and electric discs. Excerpts from *Boris* were made in 1928 at a live Covent Garden performance, and issued by HMV on #DB 1181/83; #3464. Altogether his discs carried about 130 different titles, most of which were reissued in 1973 on LP by Melodiya. EMI issued a CD (#CDH 7610092) in 1988, surveying performances from 1926 to 1931, and Pearl offered another in the same year (GEMM #CD 9314) with 15 selections not on the EMI. [Kelly 1988; Semeonoff 1974.]

CHALLENGE (label). (I) A stepchild in the **Plaza** family, given masters from **Gennett** and other companies; it issued discs in the late 1920s. Distribution was through **Sears, Roebuck, and Co.,** whose name appears on the label along with a knight in shining armor. Repertoire was dance and pop, and artists were often presented under pseudonyms.

CHALLENGE (label). (II) A successful pop label of the 1950s, owned by **Gene Autry.**

CHALMERS, THOMAS, 1884–1966. American bass-baritone, born in New York on 20 Oct 1884. He studied in Florence, and made his opera debut in Fossombrone (Italy) as Marcello on 30 Apr 1911. From 1913 he performed in New York, Boston, and other American cities, and on 17 Nov 1917 he appeared at the Metropolitan Opera, singing Valentine. He remained with the Metropolitan through 1922, doing the French/Italian roles. After a tonsillectomy in 1922, his voice deteriorated and he had to withdraw from opera and to some extent from recording. Chalmers was a dramatic actor as well as a singer, with many important stage roles. After he retired from stage appearances, he went into motion picture production. Later he was seen on television, and his voice was heard as the narrator in the classic documentary films *The Plough that Broke the Plains* and *The River.* He died on 17 June 1966 in Greenwich, Connecticut.

On record, Chalmers drew his repertoire from the narrow list of songs that were favorites of Thomas Edison—"Old Man Edison's mother, home and heaven repertoire"—old ballads and hymns. He was successful in portraying these genres on Edison Diamond Discs. Before he became an Edison artist in 1908, Chalmers had made one Columbia disc and a few Zonophone discs. His first Edison cylinder was issued in November 1908, "Evening Star" (#9982). In May 1909 he made his earliest four-minute Amberol cylinder, #127, Valentine's aria (in English) from *Faust.* After his study and performances in Italy, Chalmers returned to Edison and made his acclaimed series of Diamond Discs, and many of the most impressive **tone tests.** One side of the second Diamond Disc to be issued was his "Nearer, My God to Thee" (#50002). Among his best-selling discs were #80055, "Carry Me Back to Old Virginny";

"Abide with Me" with Elizabeth Spencer (#80276; 1915); "My Old Kentucky Home" with chorus (#80321; 1916); and "O That We Two Were Maying" with Spencer (#82510; 1913). His final discs were made in 1925. Chalmers was also heard on Edison Amberol cylinders until 1925. Although he was a member of the American Quartet, Criterion Quartet, Harmony Four, Metropolitan Quartette, and Knickerbocker Quartet, he made only one record in a quartet, "I Surrender All" (#80343; 1916) with the Metropolitan group. [Walsh 1981/5–9; Wile 1977.]

CHAMBERS, W. PARIS, 1854–1913. American cornetist, one of the first to record his instrument. Chambers was heard on Berliner records made in 1895 and 1897: "Last Night" (#215), "Nellie Bly" (#237), and "Narcissus" (#259). He was in the Columbia cylinder catalog of 1897, and performed also for Edison.

CHAMPION (label). A **Gennett** subsidiary, issuing jazz, dance, blues, and pop discs from September 1925 to December 1934. Decca acquired the label and kept using it into 1936. **Riverside** offered reissues in 1953. Champions are rare collectibles because of their scarcity and the high quality of some performances. Among artists found on Champion are Gene Autry, Vernon Dalhart, Jack Kaufman, Clyde McCoy, and Red Norvo. [Blacker 1980/1 is a complete list, 1925–1930; Rust 1978.]

CHANDOS (label). A British label, produced by Chandos Records, Commerce Way, Colchester, since 1979. Music of British composers (e.g., the complete symphonies of Arnold Bax) has been a specialty. Chaconne, a subsidiary label, is devoted to early music.

CHANNEL. The path followed by a signal through a sound system. In a **monaural** system there is just one signal, and one channel. A basic **stereophonic** system has two channels, one for each of the signals, each signal representing the sound from a given segment of the recording studio. Elaborations on this principle result in **multichannel** recording. *See also* CENTER CHANNEL.

CHANNEL BALANCE. The condition of a sound system when equal response is derived from every **channel**.

CHANNEL REVERSAL. An arrangement in which the sound emanations from right and left speakers in a **stereophonic** system are reversed.

CHANNEL SEPARATION. The extent to which the two **channels** of a **stereophonic** system are able to keep their signals isolated from each other. Poor separation produces **crosstalk.**

CHAPPELL PIANO CO., LTD. A firm of piano makers, publishers, and concert agents, established in 1810; located at 50 New Bond St., London W1. It had strong connections to the recording industry in the U.K. An association with **Cliftophone** was followed by one with U.S. **Brunswick** in 1923. The masters from America were pressed under the Brunswick Cliftophone label. In 1926 Chappell marketed discs made under Brunswick's "light-ray method" and in the same year British manufacture of Brunswicks began, with the creation of **British Brunswick, Ltd.** Chappell's name was no longer included in the advertising after August 1927. But when the new **Warner Brunswick, Ltd.** appeared Chappell was again involved, as sole vendor of the records. The company has made many of the recordings used as background music for television programs and motion pictures. Today the firm is a subsidiary of Philips. It ceased manufacture of pianos ca. 1965. [Andrews 1981/1.]

CHAPPELLE AND STINNETTE (label). In March 1922 the Black husband-wife vaudeville team of Thomas Chappelle and Juanita Stinnette produced their own records, making just nine blues discs. The C & S Phonograph Record Co. was cited on the discs as the manufacturer. Clarence Williams "Decatur Street Blues" (#5005) is one of the numbers, and the other eight are by the two producers. All the records are rare today. [Rust 1978.]

CHARLES, RAY, 1930– . American singer, pianist, and composer of popular songs; born Ray

Charles Robinson in Albany, Georgia, on 23 Sep 1930. He began to lose his vision at age six, and eventually became totally blind. Nevertheless he played the piano, and wrote music in the rhythm & blues idiom, later turning to soul music and country/western styles. His greatest record is "Georgia on My Mind" (ABC #10135; 1960), one of his nine Grammy winners. Other discs that topped the charts were "Hit the Road Jack" (ABC #10244; 1961), and "I Can't Stop Loving You" (ABC #10330; 1962), both Grammy winners. He had more than 60 other hit records in the 1960s and 1970s. A 1975 single, "Living for the City" (Crossover #981), took the Grammy for rhythm & blues vocal. A duet with Chaka Khan won a Grammy in 1990: "I'll Be Good to You." There were about 40 compact discs in the 1992 catalog.

CHASSIS. The frame on which working components of an electronic system are mounted.

CHECKER, CHUBBY, 1941– . American rock singer and dancer, born Ernest Evans in Philadelphia on 3 Oct 1941. He learned to play the drums and piano as a youth, and sang novelty pieces. He was successful with "The Class" (Parkway #804; 1959), and then gained international renown for his song and dance number, "The Twist" (Parkway #811; 1960, two versions) which was on the charts for 43 weeks. Checker made many "twist" recordings, feeding a craze for the dance; he had 15 chart albums before his popularity waned around 1964. *Let's Twist Again* (Parkway #P7004) won the rock and roll Grammy award in 1961. The single "Back in the U.S.S.R." (Buddha #100) was recorded during a brief comeback in 1969; and a chart album, *The Change Has Come* (MCA #5291), marked a second return to popular favor in 1982.

CHEEVER, CHARLES A., ca. 1853–1900. Record company executive who held multiple posts in 1890: president of the **Metropolitan Phonograph Co.** and the **Alabama Phonograph Co.**, and director of the **New England Phonograph Co.**

CHENEY TALKING MACHINE CO. A firm located at 24 N. Wabash Ave., Chicago; maker, from 1914, of deluxe and custom-built phonograph cabinets and then the actual phonographs. Litigation with Victor developed over Cheney's brazen use of a tapered **tone arm**, one of the prize patents of Victor; but in 1922 Cheney was successful in convincing the court that their tone arm was not really tapered, but "octagonally stepped." President in 1923 was Alfred C. Harper.

CHEROKEE RANCH. A Hollywood recording studio used by many rock stars (Alice Cooper, David Bowie, Elton John, etc.). By the end of the 1970s, 30 gold albums and about 20 platinum albums had been produced at the studio.

CHESS (label). A record made in Chicago from 1947 to 1971, named for founder-producers Leonard and Philip Chess, specializing in blues, jazz, and popular music. The label was known at first as Aristocrat. Checker, a blues label (1952), and later **Argo**—which became Cadet in 1965—were parts of the same group. Neptune, Thomas, and St. Lawrence were Chess subsidiaries. Artists associated with the labels include Chuck Berry, Bo Diddley, Willie Dixon, Red Holt, Howlin' Wolf, Ahmad Jamal, Ramsey Lewis, Little Walter, Jimmy Rogers, Sunny Stitt, Muddy Waters, and Sonny Boy Williamson. Gene Ammons, Jamal, and Lewis recorded extensively for Argo. Sermons by Rev. C.L. Franklin were of special interest; his daughter, Aretha Franklin, made her debut on the label.

On 10 June and 11 June 1964 the Rolling Stones cut 13 numbers at the Chess Studios, including one named for the firm's address: "2120 S. Michigan Ave." The songs were released on various commercial and bootleg labels, not on Chess.

After the death of Leonard Chess in 1971, the firm was sold to GRT, which continued to use the Chess, Checker, and Cadet labels until 1975. A firm named All Platinum Records acquired the Chess matrices in August 1975, and later sold them to Sugar Hill Records, producers of Roulette. CD reissues are in progress from the French label Vogue, and the German label Teldec. [Ruppli 1983.]

CHEVALIER, MAURICE, 1888–1972. French singer and motion picture actor, born in Paris on 12 Sep 1888. He appeared in the Folies-Bergère and other cabarets in Paris, served in the World War I, performed in musicals in Paris and London, then went to Hollywood in 1929. International fame came with two later movies, *Gigi* (1958) and *Can Can* (1960). He was presented with a special Academy Award in 1958. Chevalier died in Paris on 1 Jan 1972.

He recorded extensively, beginning in March 1919 with one song for HMV, "On the Level You're a Little Devil" (#B-1024). Then he did many French songs on Pathé from 1920–27 and also for Columbia. Turning to Victor in 1929, he made his signature record of "Louise" (Victor #21916). He remained with Victor through the 78 era, then made LPs for various companies. His famous songs from *Gigi*, "Thank Heaven for Little Girls" and "Ah Yes, I Remember It Well," were in the MGM soundtrack album #3641. [Rotante 1975 is a complete discography.]

CHICAGO CENTRAL PHONOGRAPH CO. A Chicago firm located in rooms #801 and #804, Home Insurance Building (1890); one of the **North American Phonograph Company** affiliates. Charles L. Raymond was president in 1892, with Ernest A. Hamill, vice president, and George B. Hoit, general manager. Hoit spoke at the 1890 convention of the **National Phonograph Association**, saying that phonographs were already in use by "every first-class court reporter in the city." The firm had 187 machines on lease to clients. Chicago Central was succeeded in 1892 by the **Chicago Talking Machine Co.**

CHICAGO PUBLIC LIBRARY. One of the world's largest city libraries, established in 1873. In 1990 the main library moved to an imposing new building, the Harold Washington Library Center. The library's collection of musical scores includes more than 110,000 items. There are about 160,000 sound recordings. Music materials are housed in the Music information center, headed by Richard Schwegel.

Among the research collections of recordings are the Chicago Blues Archive, the New Music Chicago Festival tapes, the Made in Chicago collection, the Jazz-Blues-Gospel Hall of Fame Repository, the Jubilee Showcase video collection of gospel music (100 programs), and the Arnold Jacobsen Recorded Sound Collection. The Jacobsen Collection, including classical and popular material, includes 30,000 78s and 10,000 LPs. There are extensive holdings of popular music in all disc formats. Twenty listening stations are available for public use.

CHICAGO RECORD CO. A firm located at 3621 State St., Chicago, established by J. Mayo Williams, a **race record** talent scout for major labels in the 1920s. It distributed **Black Patti** records, recorded by **Gennett**, in 1927. At that time the management team consisted of J. Mayo Williams, general manager, and Robert E. Butler, sales manager.

CHICAGO SYMPHONY ORCHESTRA. One of the world's premier orchestras, founded in 1891 as the Theodore Thomas Orchestra (for its first conductor; renamed in 1912). It performed in the Auditorium Theatre, then in 1904 moved to the new Orchestra Hall which remains its concert home. When Thomas died in 1905 he was succeeded by **Frederick Stock**, who was conductor until 1942. Subsequently the orchestra was directed by Désiré Defauw (1943–1947), Artur Rodzinski (1947–1948), **Rafael Kubelik** (1950–1953), **Fritz Reiner** (1953–1962, and guest conductor 1962–1963), Jean Martinon (1963–1968), **Georg Solti** (1969–1991) and **Daniel Barenboim** (1991–).

The Chicago Symphony was the first major American orchestra to record under its regular conductor, as Stock took the group to Aeolian Hall in New York to record 20 light concert pieces for Victor on the first two days of May 1916. The orchestra made more records in 1925, in Orchestra Hall, and then went on to cover most of the standard symphonic repertoire under its various conductors. "Sabre Dance" from Khatchaturian's *Gayne Ballet Suite* was its first million-selling record.

Important discs were made in 1951 by Mercury, including an acclaimed *Pictures at an Exhibition*. Renovations in Orchestra Hall in summer 1966 made it less satisfactory for recording, and records were made elsewhere, e.g., at the University of Illinois in Urbana, and after 1973 in Chicago's Medinah Temple. Improvements in the acoustic situation made it possible to record again in Orchestra Hall in 1989, under guest conductor Neeme Järvi (for the Chandos label). Victor was the orchestra's principal label until the arrival of Solti, who contracted with London/Decca. EMI, Mercury, and Angel are other labels that have been used. Barenboim's records have been for Erato.

Among the outstanding discs made by the orchestra are the most popular concertos of Beethoven (with Vladimir Ashkenazy), Brahms (with Emil Gilels, Jascha Heifetz), Rachmaninoff (with Artur Rubinstein), and Tchaikovsky (with Gilels, Heifetz); all these under Fritz Reiner. Acclaimed discs by Georg Solti include the Bartók *Concerto for Orchestra*, symphonies of Bruckner and Mahler, and the complete Beethoven symphonies. The orchestra won 20 Grammys under Solti, and has one under Barenboim.

In observance of the orchestra's 100th anniversary, the orchestra issued a monumental set of 12 compact discs, offering 13 hours of historic recordings, many of them previously unpublished.

CHICAGO TALKING MACHINE CO. A cylinder and phonograph sales company established in 1892 by Charles Dickinson, **Leon F. Douglass**, and H.B. Babson, a successor to the **Chicago Central Phonograph Co.** of 1890. The firm was identified later as the Talking Machine Co., or Talking Machine Co. of Chicago. Columbia took control of it in 1897. The address was 107 Madison St. Another firm advertised (in *Phonoscope*) from that address: the Polyphone Co. Both firms sold the **Polyphone**, a double-reproducer phonograph described in the Talking Machine Co. 1899 catalog, sold for $15–$35. A Polyphone Concert Grand, advertised as the "loudest talking machine made," sold for $130. Cylinders by Silas Leachman were featured in the 1899 catalog. There was also a wide array of records by Columbia artists, such as Len Spencer and Cal Stewart.

Victor bought the company in 1905. The name was again Chicago Talking Machine Co. in 1916. The address at that time was 12 N. Michigan Ave. It advertised itself as the largest Victor distributor in the world. **H.D. Geissler** was president in 1920.

CHILD, CALVIN G., ?–1943. Phonograph industry executive, who operated a recording studio in 1897 as part of the **Berliner** structure. He had worked earlier with the **Ohio Phonograph Co.** and the **New England Phonograph Co.** In 1894 he was music director for **Columbia**, then recording director for **Victor**. Although he retired in 1923, he served as a Victor board member as late as 1927.

CHILDREN'S RECORDS. The earliest discs sold commercially (1889), by Berliner in Germany, were probably aimed at children; they were used on his toy gramophone. Records for regular play on turntables were available early in the 20th century, and Victor's 1917 catalog had 70 such items. Included were games, Orphan Annie, nursery rhymes, and **Christmas records**. The genre was gradually subsumed under the heading **Educational Records**. *See also* TALKING DOLL; TOY RECORDS.

Chip. *See* SWARF.

CHR. *See* CONTEMPORARY HITS RADIO.

CHRISTIAN, CHARLIE, 1916–1942. American jazz guitarist, born in Dallas. During the time of his brief career the guitar was established as a solo instrument in modern jazz, and electric amplification of the instrument was accepted. Christian began with trumpet, turned at age 12 to guitar, but also played string bass and piano; he did local work in Oklahoma City and played in his brother Edward's band. He was introduced to Benny Goodman by jazz critic John Hammond in Los Angeles, and became a member of the Benny Goodman Sextet in 1939. Christian was first heard on the *Camel Caravan* radio program, 19 Aug 1939 in "Flying Home," which was recorded for Columbia in October (#35254). The coupling had another outstanding guitar improvisation in "Rose Room." Christian's famous contribution to "Stardust" was recorded then too, but not given a regular issue until CBS #62581 on LP. He performed and recorded also with Lionel Hampton, Louis Armstrong, Ida Cox, Count

Basie, and others. Two Vanguard issues (#8523, 8524), made at the Carnegie Hall concert of the Kansas City Six on 24 Dec 1939, present Christian playing three numbers with Lester Young; his performance was described as "so perfect that it will be remembered as long as a single jazz fan is alive." He died of tuberculosis and pneumonia in New York, on 2 Mar 1942. [Evensmo 1976, source of the quote above, is a complete discography.]

CHRISTMAS RECORDS. The first Christmas record was "Jingle Bells," played on a banjo by Will Lyle (an Edison cylinder of October 1899). Among the famous early renditions of traditional carols were "O Holy Night," by Enrico Caruso, and also by Marcel Journet (Victor #6559), John McCormack's "Adeste Fideles" (Victor #6607), Ernestine Schumann-Heink's "Stille Nacht" (Victor #6723, backed by Engelbert Humperdinck's "Weihnachten"; also on Victrola #88138), and another "Silent Night" by Elisabeth Schumann (Victor #2093, backed by the "Coventry Carol"). In 1908 Victor offered the Irish specialty singer/monologist Steve Porter in "Christmas Morning at Clancy's" (Victor #5604, then #16936), a dramatization of children opening gifts; and in 1918 there was Victor #35679, "Santa Claus Tells About His Toy Shop," a reading by Gilbert Girard. (Texts of the Porter and Girard efforts are in Ault 1987.) Among the novelty records of the acoustic era was "Santa Claus Hides in the Phonograph," on Edison and Brunswick.

Columbia got a late start on Christmas, but had a full list of carols in its catalogs of the 1940s, in addition to Basil Rathbone's version of the Dickens *Christmas Carol* (on six sides, in #MM-521). *Amahl and the Night Visitors*, by Gian-Carlo Menotti, was a Christmas opera produced for television (NBC, 1951); Victor has the original cast on #6485-2.

The best seller among Christmas records is "White Christmas," which has had more than 400 versions on disc; the first and most important is that by Bing Crosby. Crosby also recorded very successful renditions of "Silent Night" and "Adeste Fidelis" for Decca, in 1935. Mel Tormé's 1946 "Christmas Song" and Gene Autry's 1949 "Rudolph the Red-Nosed Reindeer" (Columbia) stand out among later examples of the genre. Autry's "Rudolph" may have been the second highest seller of holiday songs; there were about 450 recordings of it by other artists.

The current scene presents an impressive array of Christmas music. There were more than 400 CDs, tapes, or LP albums listed in the 1990 *Schwann*. Many of the titles cited above appeared in two releases by Rhino (#11E-70636/37) entitled *Billboard's Greatest Christmas Hits*. [Ault 1987.]

CHRISTOFF, BORIS, 1914– . Bulgarian bass, born in Plovdiv on 18 May 1914. He studied in Rome with Riccardo Stracciari, and made a solo debut there in 1946. He appeared at La Scala in the following year, and made his American debut in San Francisco, as Boris, on 25 Sep 1956. His great role is Boris, and he has often been described as the successor to Feodor Chaliapin. Christoff has also sung the regular bass/baritone repertoire. The Boris arias were recorded for HMV in 1949. An LP reissue of favorite numbers was produced in 1976 (EMI Electrola #1C 147003 336/337).

CINCH. A disc player made by **British Zonophone Co., Ltd.,** also known as the Zonophone Cinch. Measurements as given in advertisement July 1907: 14 1/2 x 12 1/2 x 10 1/2 inches. It had a tapered tone arm, 10-inch turntable, and a wood interior horn. The price was £2 12s 6d.

CINCH (label). A British record introduced in 1913 by the Gramophone Co., sold for 1s 1d, as part of the price war in that year.

CINCINNATI SYMPHONY ORCHESTRA. The fourth oldest orchestra in the United States, organized in 1895; it was the first American orchestra to make a world tour (1967) and the third to be recorded. Conductors have been Frank van der Stucken (to 1909), **Leopold Stokowski** (1909–1912), Ernst Kunwald (1912–1917), Eugène Ysaÿe (1918–1922), **Fritz Reiner** (1922–1931), Eugene Goossens (1931–1947), Thor Johnson (1947–1958), Max Rudolf (1958–1970), Thomas Schippers (1970–1977), and Michael Gielen (1980–).

The orchestra recorded first on Columbia #A5966 (July 1917) under Kunwald (Offenbach's "Barcarolle") and made three other records that were released. In 1919 it recorded again for Columbia, under Ysaye, doing the "Navarraise" from Massenet's *Le Cid* (#A6159); in 1921 it added 11 others. A distinguished period of recording took place for Victor, under Goossens, in the city's fine Music Hall from 1941 to 1946. Among the outstanding examples perhaps the most notable is the Walton Violin Concerto with **Jascha Heifetz** (Victor #M-868, three discs; 1941). Other important discs were of the Vaughan Williams Second Symphony ((Victor #M916, five discs; 1941) and Respighi's *Pines of Rome* (Victor #M-1309, two discs; 1946). Under Thor Johnson and Max Rudolf, the Cincinnati Orchestra made another group of acclaimed discs, for London and Remington; many of the composers were contemporary.

Beginning in 1977, there were concerts and recordings by the new Cincinnati Pops Orchestra under Erich Kunzel. This ensemble has taken its place as one of the principals of its type. [Fellers 1978.]

CIRCUIT. A network consisting of one or more closed paths.

CIRELLIGRAPH CO., INC. A Philadelphia firm, maker of a disc player, "The Cirelligraph," which—according to a 1917 advertisement—would play "any make of record without . . . any special extra attachment or apparatus." An elaborate console model, similar to the Victrola, cost $1,500; portables sold for $50.

CITY OF LONDON PHONOGRAPH & GRAMOPHONE SOCIETY. One of the early **gramophone societies**, and probably the oldest one extant, organized in April 1919 by Norman Hillyer. Its original name was the "London Edison Society"; its founding membership consisted of about 40 persons, "a number of whom were ladies." Thomas Edison himself was invited to be president, but he declined, and he also disapproved the use of his name. So the name of the group was changed to "City of London Phonograph Society." In August 1919 Edison became "patron" of the society. At the fifth meeting, in September 1919, Adrian Sykes became the first president. To suit the interests of various radio enthusiasts among the members, another name change took place in 1923, to "City of London Phonograph and Radio Society," but "radio" was quietly dropped from the name in 1925, although it remained in the official title until the outbreak of World War II, when meetings were suspended until 1946. With the resumption of meetings "gramophone" was substituted for "radio." Sykes served as president until he died in 1959. Major H.H. Annand became the second president of the society. George Frow was president in 1991, and Oliver Berliner (grandson of Emile Berliner) the "honorary patron."

In addition to regular meetings, held for the most part in London pubs—but from October 1991 at the National Sound Archive—the society has promoted research and invention related to the cylinder phonograph. Sykes was a significant inventor, who patented a magnetic pickup for playing cylinder recordings. R.H. Clarke, hon. secretary, also produced a pickup, one usable on hill-and-dale discs or cylinders. *Hillandale News* was established as the society's official publication in October 1960. [Andrews*; Lewis, T. 1964.].

CLANCY, A. W. Record industry executive; vice president (1890) of the **Missouri Phonograph Co.**, and president in 1891–1892. In association with Charles Swift, he worked toward unification of all the American phonograph interests, and was elected first president of the **National Phonograph Association** in 1891. He was reelected in 1893.

CLARANCE, EDWARD, 1861–1903. American singer, whose surname also appears as Clarence. He was in the **New Jersey Phonograph Co.** catalog in 1892, worked for Edison from 1892 to the late 1890s, and was in the Columbia catalog in 1896–1897. He performed popular ballads and lyric numbers, such as "The Gallant Emmett Guards" (Columbia #7902; 1896) and "The Day That You'll Forget Me" (Columbia #7903; 1896). [Brooks 1979.]

CLARINET RECORDINGS. The first artist to record the clarinet was Henry Giese, who joined C.A. Joepel (flute) and John Helleberg (bassoon) in trio cylinders for Edison on 29 May 1889. Twelve records resulted from that day's work. Giese then made 12 solo cylinders for Edison on 31 May 1889, a set that began with "Dorscht March" by Wiegand, and included selections from *Carmen, Freischütz,* and *Barbiere di Siviglia* as well as waltzes and songs. Giese was back for six more recording sessions in 1889.

William Tuson was another early clarinetist to record, with popular selections like "Comin' thro' the Rye" for Columbia in 1897. He also worked for Edison until 1903, making 32 solo records and a clarinet duet with George Rubel. Leo Medaer was another pioneer, with 14 **Bettini** cylinders in 1898.

Reginald Kell was the first artist to explore the serious repertoire of the clarinet on record, during the 1930s for Victor. Other classical clarinetists with important recordings have included Gervase De Peyer, Stanley Drucker, and Richard Stoltzman. Jazz performers who performed in the classical repertoire included **Benny Goodman** and **Artie Shaw**.

It is in jazz and Big Band music that the greatest number of clarinet recordings have appeared. Among the important names are **Buddy De Franco, Jimmy Dorsey**, Irving Fazola, Jimmy Giuffre, Benny Goodman, Jimmy Hamilton, Roland Kirk, **Pee Wee Russell**, Tony Scott, and Artie Shaw. Many saxophone players have doubled on the clarinet and have made fine recordings, for example **Lester Young**.

CLARION (label). (I) A British cylinder label, manufactured by the **Premier Manufacturing Co., Ltd.** beginning in 1905. It seems that the firm took the name Clarion Record Company, Ltd., after a reorganization in 1910. The factory was at The Point, Wandsworth, London. A 1907 advertisement describes the product as "long gold moulded." Discs were made as well, first announced in December 1908; the two examples available to one writer were of different types: one needle-cut (lateral), the other vertical cut with an edge start. Around 1907 a cylinder player was made in Britain, and

sold also in America. Clarion seems to have been the longest surviving British cylinder manufacturer, continuing production until at least February 1922; the evidence for this late date is a letter from the company to a customer, printed in the October 1974 *Hillandale News* (however the letter may have referred to old factory stock, rather than to current production). [Carter 1977.]

CLARION (label). (II) A disc produced by the Clarion Record Co., 56 Bleeker St., New York, first advertised in September 1921. J.M. Kohner was general manager of the firm. The repertoire was dance music, with fewer than 150 known releases. There was no advertising after November 1921. [Kendziora 1954/11, reprinted in *RR* 211/212.]

CLARION (label). (III) "A high-water mark in the achievements of the recording industry during the first half-century of its life," according to Rust, this label was a Columbia product, selling at only $.35 but of superior quality both in its acoustic and electrical manifestations. Among the performers were Bing Crosby, the Boswell Sisters, Kate Smith, and Gene Autry. Between August 1930 and June 1932, 477 records were issued. [Rust 1978.]

CLARK, ALFRED C., 1873–1950. American/British inventor and recording industry executive, born in New York on 19 Dec 1873. He was educated at City College of New York and Cooper Union, and became an associate of Thomas Edison in 1889. In 1895 he developed, at the Edison Laboratory in New Jersey, the first motion picture films with continuity; he made Edison's only feature film. Joining the Berliner organization in Camden in 1896, he was co-inventor with **Eldridge Johnson** of a new **soundbox** for the gramophone in 1896; the improved hand drive eliminated much of the old **turntable** waver. This research led to the **Improved Gramophone.** In the summer of 1896 Clark managed a retail store in Philadelphia (1237 Chestnut St.), selling Berliner discs and equipment. Moving to Britain, he was one of the founders and an early executive of the new **Gramophone Co.** (established in April 1898), and opened the Paris branch in 1899. In

1907 he founded the Musée de la Voix in the Archives of the Paris Opéra. He began using **Nipper** as a symbol in 1907, several months before the Gramophone Co. From 1909–1931 he was managing director of the Gramophone Co., becoming a naturalized British subject in 1928. With the formation of **EMI, Ltd.**, in 1931, he became its first chairman; he was also managing director of EMI from 1931–1939. In April 1946 he was appointed president of EMI, then he retired in September of that year. He was also the first president of the Radio Industry Council. Clark died in London on 16 June 1950.

CLARK, DICK, 1929– . One of the most influential American **disc jockeys**, host of television's *American Bandstand* program from 5 Aug 1957; the show had first aired on Philadelphia's WFH in 1952, and grew in a few years to a national network program including more than 100 stations. Clark was a force in bringing rock and roll music to mass audiences, and in legitimizing its image. More than 65,000 records were played on the show over the years. It provided the first national forum for such performers as Chubby Checker, Bill Haley, Johnny Mathis, the Supremes, Fabian, Madonna, Beach Boys, Linda Ronstadt, James Brown, Neil Diamond, Bobby Darin, Tina Turner, and Buddy Holly. Though Clark was a central figure in the **payola** scandals of 1959–1960, he was never indicted and his career did not suffer. He developed extensive interests in music publishing and artist management, as well as in record industry activities. In April 1989 he left *Bandstand*, which continued on the air with David Hirsch as host. Clark remained as host of the *$25,000 Pyramid* and *$100,000 Pyramid* television game shows.

CLARK, TOM, 1854–1943. British-born cornetist and band director, playing in Gilmore's and Sousa's bands and then conducting the Columbia Orchestra. He made cornet cylinders for Edison, **New Jersey Phonograph Co.**, and **New York Phonograph Co.** between 1891 and 1893. In 1898–1899 he worked for Berliner. Later he made arrangements for the publisher G. Schirmer. [Brooks 1979.]

CLARK (MELVILLE) PIANO CO. A Chicago piano making firm, established in 1900 by Melville Clark (1850–1918). The Clark Co. was the first to market (1901) an 88–note player piano roll (Clark's invention). In 1911 another of Clark's inventions was produced: a music roll cutting machine that was said to capture the nuances of the pianist's performance. Clark died in 1918, and the firm was acquired by **Wurlitzer** in the following year. The Clark family was also involved in the formation and management of the QRS Co.

CLARK PHONOGRAPH RECORD CO. A Newark, New Jersey, firm, located at 317 Market St. in 1922–1923. It offered to make records for clients, and produced its own "Wallace Reducing Method" records. [Andrews*.]

CLARKE, HERBERT L., 1867–1945. American cornetist, regarded as the finest of his era, born in Massachusetts. He moved to Toronto with his family in 1880. While a teenager he taught himself the cornet and violin, and played in various groups. He became a band director, and joined the faculty of the Toronto Conservatory. From 1893 to 1917 he was with the Sousa Band as soloist and assistant director. Then he led the Anglo-Canadian Leather Co. Band until 1923, before moving back to the U.S., where he conducted the Municipal Band in Long Beach, California.

Clarke recorded first for Berliner, making seven-inch discs in Montreal during 1899–1903 as conductor and soloist. Most of his work was for Victor from October 1900 to 1908. He also made discs for Columbia in 1917, and Brunswick in 1923; and he made a few Edison cylinders from 1903 to 1906. [Moogk 1975 gives list of his records.]

CLARKE, KENNY, 1914–1985. American jazz drummer, one of the developers of **bebop**, and a founding member of the **Modern Jazz Quartet** (1952). He settled in France in 1956, playing with Bud Powell and then organizing his own band with Francy Boland. His style was highly innovative in its departure from the steady bass drum beat and the introduction of rhythmic counterpoints to the soloists. "Epistrophy," his own composition, was recorded on Swing #224 in 1946.

CLARKSON, J. C. American recording industry executive in the 1890s, identified as the "Superintendent" of both the **Florida Phonograph Co.** and the **Georgia Phonograph Co.** In 1890 he represented those firms at the convention of the **National Phonograph Association.**

CLAXTONOLA (label). An American disc made by the Brenard Manufacturing Co., Iowa City, from 1922 to 1925. The material came from Paramount and Gennett. Some important jazz numbers appeared, with the names of artists changed. [Rust 1978.]

CLEAN FEED. In recording, a version of the program signal that omits one source—for example, the voice part—to allow overdubbing, as in another language.

CLEANING. (I) *Cylinders*—One expert recommends that cylinders be cleaned with "a specially formulated treatment of L.A.S.T. [Liquid Archival Sound Treatment]" (Owen). Alternatively distilled water may be used, with suction drying; the water must not be hot, and the exposed plaster core should not be wet. Water is not advisable on cracked cylinders. "Probably the safest" cleaning implement is an air gun. (Owen).

(II) *78s*—"The best method of cleaning is the Keith Monks Record Cleaning Machine [in which a vacuum removes water and suspended dust from the disc as it is being washed] and a dose of Liquid Archival Sound Treatment" (Owen); Ivory soap and water, freon-based cleaning, and such commercial products as Discwasher are other possibilities. Most discs can be cleaned with water, but laminated shellac must not be (including most Columbia 78s and all **instantaneous recordings**). Distilled water is used, often mixed with ordinary non-ammoniated detergent at one teaspoon per gallon of water. Discs are rubbed with a soft cloth in a circular motion while in the solution, then wiped with a lint-free cloth and dried in a rack away from heat without rinsing. Freon TF or another organic solvent is used on oil-based discs such as acetates and nitrates. Ultrasonic

vibration, favored by some writers, "can lead to structural damage" (Owen). Vinyl discs (78 or LP) are washed like shellacs, but separately; the grit that is removed from shellac surfaces may damage vinyl surfaces. Both 78s and LPs should be wiped before and after playing with a soft bristled brush, followed by a "dust bug"— a carbon fiber brush that releases static.

Something else to watch for in washing discs is the label; if it is printed in water soluble ink, like the Victor Red Seal, it may be damaged by water. One approach is to polish the label with beeswax prior to washing the disc.

(III) *LPs*—The cleaning methods for 78s apply. But static is a major problem with LPs, as it causes dust buildup and may interfere with stylus performance. An effective antistatic pistol, such as the original one by Zerostat, incorporates a quartz element; it releases positive and then negative charged ions. After an LP is cleaned it may be sprayed with Sound Guard to protect its surface; however, Sound Guard cannot be removed, and its long term effects are not known.

(IV) *Compact discs*—"If you must, clean a disc with a soft, moistened cloth. If possible, pat it dry. Otherwise, wipe the disc from the center out. . . . Preventive cleaning is unnecessary and potentially harmful. . . . Do not use solvents . . . . (Pohlmann).

Discwasher Compact Disc Cleaner is a handcranked device that sprays the disc with fluid and wipes it in a radial motion. Oily fingerprints on a CD can actually prevent the player from functioning, and they are hard to remove. Whyte recommends the Nitty Gritty CD-1 Compact Disc Cleaner as an effective print extractor and general cleaner; it is motorized.

(V) *Tapes*—Emphasis falls upon the equipment, rather than the tape itself. A tape player should be cleaned after eight hours of use. Parts needing attention are the magnetic heads, capstan, pinch roller, tape guides and lifters, scrape and flutter filters, and tape tension arms. Isopropyl alcohol, methyl alcohol (methanol), xylene, or Freon TF, applied with a lint-free wiper (or if necessary, in hard to reach places, a cotton Q-tip), will serve the purpose, but a rubber cleaner instead of alcohol should be used on the pinch roller. Aerosol cans of Freon are best avoided, since they have metallic particles that may contaminate the equipment. As for the actual tape, it is cleaned by scraping, not washing, followed by a tissue wipe to remove shreds. This task may be performed with a simple razor blade, or with a commercial device that runs a tape through a cleaning assembly. BOW Industries, Computer-Link Corp., and Recortec, Inc. are among the makers of such cleaning devices. For cassette players there are cleaning tapes that may be played through the machine to do what is needed; of course the cassette tape itself is not subject to direct cleaning. [Barnes, K. 1974; Owen 1983; Pohlmann 1989; Whyte 1986/8.] *See also* PRESERVATION OF SOUND RECORDINGS.

CLEARTONE (label). A product of the Cleartone Phonograph Co., New York, during 1920–1923. The material was from Arto, with some pressings from Pathé. Jazz and blues were featured. [Rust 1978.]

CLEF (label). A record issued during 1953–1957 by Clef Records, 451 N. Canon Drive, Beverly Hills, California. It was founded by Norman Granz as successor to his Jazz at the Philharmonic series that had been released on the Asch and Mercury labels. Granz engaged many leading artists, including Count Basie, Ella Fitzgerald (after 1956), Stan Getz, Dizzy Gillespie, Gene Krupa, Charlie Parker, Oscar Peterson, and Lester Young. He consolidated his several labels (Clef, Down Home, Norgran) under the label name **Verve** in 1956. The final Clef release was in March 1957. [Ruppli 1986.]

CLÉMENT, EDMOND, 1867–1928. French tenor, born in Paris on 28 Mar 1867. His debut was at the Opéra-Comique on 29 Nov 1889, in Gounod's *Mireille*. He then sang across Europe, and at the Metropolitan Opera from 1911 to 1913. His special role was as Des Grieux in *Manon*, and his record of "La rêve" (Odéon #56050; 1905, and Victor #74258; 1912 or 1913) is regarded as one of the best tenor renditions of the acoustic era. Clément recorded also for Pathé (1916–1918). There have been many reissues on LP.

CLEPHANE, JAMES OGILVIE, ca. 1840–1910. American inventor and record industry executive, born in Washington, D.C. As secretary of Samuel Seward, U.S. Secretary of State, he became interested in office machines and contributed to the invention of the typewriter, the first of which was built for the use of his staff. Later he and Ottmar Mergenthaler began the development of the linotype machine, revolutionizing printing technology. Impressed with a demonstration of the Graphophone, he— with Andrew Devine and John H. White— entered into a marketing agreement with **Volta Graphophone Co.** on 28 Mar 1887, in effect establishing the **American Graphophone Co.**

Clephane was a director of the Mergenthaler Linotype Co., and of the American Graphophone Co. From 1890 to 1893 he was secretary of the **Eastern Pennsylvania Phonograph Co.** He died in Englewood, New Jersey, on 30 Nov 1910. [Wile 1990/2.]

CLEVELAND ORCHESTRA. One of the distinguished orchestras of the world, established in 1918. The first conductor was Nikolai Sokoloff (1918–1933), followed by Artur Rodzinski (1933–1943) and **Erich Leinsdorf** (1943–1946). A peak period began with the engagement of **George Szell**, who was musical director from 1946 until his death in 1970. **Lorin Maazel** directed in 1971–1982, and Christoph von Dohnányi has been director since 1984. The orchestra moved into its permanent home, Severance Hall, in 1931.

The first recording was the *1812 Overture*, made for Brunswick (#50047) in January 1924. Another 10 discs were made for Brunswick in October 1924, and 18 more through 1928. There was then a recording gap until Rodzinski led the orchestra in *Finlandia* and the *Khovantchina* Prelude in December 1939 for Columbia. Outstanding records were made by Szell on the Epic label in the 1950s and 1960s, including works by Mozart (piano concertos with Robert Casadeseus), Schumann, and Wagner. The new recordings under von Dohnányi have also been highly praised, especially the Mahler First Symphony (London #425718–4). [Fellers 1978.]

CLEVELAND PHONOGRAPH RECORD CO. A firm incorporated in Ohio, 19 Aug 1908, by a group of businessmen with the intent to manufacture cylinder phonographs and records. Offices were established in Cleveland and Chicago, and crucial patent rights were acquired, but production did not commence until after the new corporate name "United States Phonograph Co." was adopted on 14 July 1909.

Chicago chemist Varian M. Harris was engaged by the Cleveland group to provide the record manufacturing technology he had developed and patented. (Harris had been one of the original founders of the Lambert Co. in 1900—the first firm to mold and market unbreakable cylinder records in the U.S.—but Harris was dissatisfied with the raw celluloid tubing then available.) After the demise of Lambert, Harris continued to work on celluloid cylinders in his own laboratory at home. He believed that thin celluloid in sheet form would permit more faithful molding of the impressions originally recorded in the master record. In the fall of 1909, Harris went to Cleveland to help establish the U-S Phonograph record manufacturing plant.

The Cleveland Phonograph Record Co. had apparently once intended to issue Harris Everlasting Records (as a few surviving [hidden] box labels show). The design of the Harris label was very similar to that used for U-S Everlasting records when they were placed on the market in 1910. It is unlikely that any cylinders were actually shipped in boxes with the Harris label appearing on the outside. [Klinger 1991.] *See also* U-S EVERLASTING RECORD; U-S PHONOGRAPH CO.

Bill Klinger

CLIBURN, VAN, 1930– . American pianist, born Harvey Lavan Cliburn, Jr., in Shreveport, Louisiana, on 12 July 1930. He studied at the Juilliard School, made a debut with the Houston Symphony Orchestra at age 13, and played with the New York Philharmonic at 24. He gained sudden world attention in 1958 by winning the Tchaikovsky competition in Moscow. Cliburn's recording of the Tchaikovsky First Concerto was the first classical LP to sell a million copies (Victor #LSC 2252; 1958); indeed, sales had reached 2.5 million by the end of the 1960s. Cliburn made other important

recordings, all for Victor, including the Liszt concertos with the Philadelphia Orchestra and the Rachmaninoff Second Concerto with the Chicago Symphony Orchestra.

CLICK TRACK. A device used to help conductors and performers to synchronize music with action on a film. The track was at first made up of sprocket holes punched at fixed intervals into a piece of 35 millimeter film that ran concurrently with the image film; the sprockets clicked in the manner of a metronome, audible through headphones. Later the click track was electronically constructed, and allowed for tempo variations as needed.

CLIFTOPHONE. A line of disc players marketed in Britain by **Chappell Piano Co., Ltd.,** in 1925, offering "new musical joy" and the promise of "Great Artistes . . . with you, as in life, vivid, real, just as you heard them in living flesh sing or play upon a platform." Console models sold for £7 10s; there was also a portable, seven inches by 12 inches by 14 inches in size.

CLIMAX (label). (I) Under this name Columbia entered the disc field, in late 1901. The matrixes were made by the **Globe Record Co.,** and pressing was done by the Burt Co., a button manufacturer in Milburn, New Jersey. Label color was black and gold. In January 1902 Victor's **Eldridge Johnson** purchased the firm without the knowledge of **Edward Easton,** Columbia president. When, in the following month, the two companies came to their agreement to share patents (*see* DISC, 6), the Climax matrices went back to Columbia. Some of the records had been embossed with "VTM" in the wax near the edge of the label. Performances by the Climax Band included "The Jolly Coppersmith" (#628) and "Tell Me, Pretty Maiden" (#82). Use of the Climax name ceased in fall 1902 as Columbia inscribed labels with its own name, beginning the so-called black and silver series. [Brooks 1975; Foote 1970.]

CLIMAX (label). (II) A subsidiary label of **Blue Note,** devoted in 1943 to the George Lewis group of New Orleans jazz veteran artists; the records were made on location. [Rust 1978.]

CLINE, PATSY, 1932–1963. American country music singer, born Virginia Hensley in Winchester, Virginia, on 8 Sep 1932. She was known both for her traditional country singing (with yodeling and growling) and for the country-pop style of the 1950s. She recorded first on the Four Star label in 1955, then moved to Decca. Her first big hit was "Walkin' after Midnight" in 1957 (Decca #30221). "I Fall to Pieces" (Decca #31205; reissued as MCA #51038; 1980) and the Willie Nelson song "Crazy" (Decca #31317) were two 1961 records that reached top hit status. She had 14 other chart songs, some of which were released posthumously. Loretta Lynn was a frequent touring partner. After her death in an air crash, Decca issued the *Patsy Cline Story* album (DXSB 7176) which appeared on the *Cash Box* chart for eight weeks. In 1973 she was elected to the Country Music Hall of Fame. Her career was the subject of a 1985 film, *Sweet Dreams* (Jessica Lange in the Cline role; the title coming from another of her songs). Cline was also portrayed (more effectively, by Beverly D'Angelo) in the 1980 film about Lynn's life, *Coal Miner's Daughter*. A stage re-creation by singer Rainie Cole, *Always, Patsy Cline*, was presented in 1991.

CLINTON, LARRY, 1909–1985. American Big Band leader, composer, and arranger, born in Brooklyn on 17 Aug 1909. He was most prolific in his twenties, as a prominent arranger for Isham Jones, the Casa Loma Orchestra, both the Dorsey bands, Bunny Berigan, and others. An example of his distinguished arrangements is "I Dreamt I Dwelt in Marble Halls" and "Martha"—a record made with his own orchestra, which he established in 1937 (Victor #25789; 1938); the vocalist, Bea Wain, was a great asset to his group. She also sang on Clinton's most acclaimed record, "Deep Purple" (Victor #26141; 1939). Clinton's most popular compositions were "Dipsy Doodle" (1937), "My Reverie" (sung by Wain on Victor #26006; 1938), and "Our Love" (1939). Clinton saw military service, and when he returned the dance band style was losing public appeal; he did not regain his pre-war popularity. Later he worked with Kapp Records as **A & R** man. He died in Tucson, Arizona, on 2 May 1985.

Clipping. *See* DISTORTION, III.

CLOONEY, ROSEMARY, 1928– . American popular singer, born 23 May 1928 in Maysville, Kentucky. She and her sister, Betty, sang on radio in the mid-1940s, and later with the Tony Pastor band. She made a great hit in 1951 with "Come on-a My House" (Columbia #39467), and was on the charts again the next year with "Tenderly" (Columbia #39648). She appeared on various television shows and in several motion pictures during the 1950s.

Closed loop cartridge. *See* CARTRIDGE, I.

CLOUGH, ARTHUR C. American tenor and vaudeville artist, active in recording from 1908 to 1915. His first disc was "Somebody That I Know and You Know Too" (Victor #5527; 1908); his best seller was "When I Dream of Old Erin" (Victor #17412; 1913). On Columbia his earliest disc was a great success: "Put on Your Old Gray Bonnet" (#A778; 1909). He was also heard on Edison Amberols, beginning in March 1911 with "Let Me Call You Sweetheart" (#637), and on two Edison Diamond Discs (in 1915 and 1922). Clough was a member of the Brunswick Quartet.

CLOVER (label). An American issue of the mid-1920s, produced by the Nutmeg Record Corp., one of the Emerson-Consolidated group. The repertoire was primarily dance and popular vocal. [Rust 1978.]

CM/S. Centimeters per second; a rate of speed applied to tape velocity in recording or playback.

COARSE GROOVE. A designation of the 78 rpm disc, in contrast to the microgroove LP. *See also* GROOVE.

COAXIAL CABLE. An electrical cable in which a center conductor is surrounded by insulation and a braided shield.

COAXIAL LOUDSPEAKER. A type of **loudspeaker** in which a **tweeter** is mounted concentrically within a **woofer**, each having its own voice coil. A substantial frequency overlap is desirable between them.

COBRA PICKUP. One of the popular **cartridges** of the high fidelity era, marketed by Zenith ca. 1948. It was a moving iron type, lightweight to give three times as many plays per record without loss of frequency response. A round flat vane was attached to the top of the stylus, with a small coil adjacent to the vane; movements of the vane were transmitted to a connected oscillator.

COHEN, PAUL, 1908–1971. American recording industry executive, born in Chicago on 10 Nov 1908. From 1927 to 1933 he worked with Columbia, then moved to Decca as a salesman. He was given direction of the Decca country music operation in the 1940s, and built it into the finest of its kind. Focusing on Nashville, he made the first commercial recordings there in 1945 (Red Foley), and contracted with stars of the *Grand Ole Opry* to join Decca. Bill Monroe and Ernest Tubb were among his artists. Cohen moved to the Decca subsidiary Coral label in 1958, and later set up his own Todd label. In the 1960s he was with Kapp Records and ABC Records. He died in Bryan, Texas, on 1 Apr 1971.

COINCIDENT MICROPHONES. A pair of **microphones** placed next to each other and picking up the same signal; there is no perceptible difference in the times of arrival of the sound.

COIN-OP. The name given to a variety of devices in which playback of one or more recordings is activated by the insertion of a coin into a slot. Also known as coin-slots, or coin-in-the-slots. The final development of the concept was the juke box.

"The earliest known musical coin-operated phonograph was filed for in England on July 5, 1888, by electrician Charles Adams Randall (#9762), who called it a Parlophone. There is some dispute as to whether it was actually built. . . ." (Koenigsberg).

Louis Glass, manager of the **Pacific Phonograph Corp.,** introduced a coin-op on 23 Nov 1889, at the Palais Royal Saloon; for five

cents it played a single Edison cylinder audible through any of four listening tubes. These humble gadgets quickly found a national public, and many firms hastened to manufacture and distribute them: the principal one was the **Automatic Phonograph Exhibition Co.** Before 1900 there were models capable of playing four or five cylinders in sequence—but the customer could not choose among them. The Automatic Reginaphone offered by the **Regina Music Box. Co.** in 1905 played six cylinders consecutively, requiring a coin for each one; its successor was the Hexaphone of 1908, which offered the customer a choice among six two-minute "indestructible" cylinders—it ran on an electric motor and gave good acoustic results from a wooden horn. But the first machine to give ample choice to the patron was the 1905 **Multiphone,** which allowed a selection among 24 cylinders. The 1906 **Concertophone** offered 25 choices; it was sold also in a home model, without the coin slot, becoming the first of its kind. By 1900 there were also disc coin-ops, with the first apparently made for export to Germany by the **Universal Talking Machine Co.;** it played one seven-inch record. The Gramophone Co. advertised a penny-in-the-slot device in 1902. Soon America had various multi-disc and multi-cylinder devices made by **Autophone** and the **Automatic Machine and Tool Co.**—the last-named being the producer of the spectacular **John Gabel's Automatic Entertainer** in 1906.

The coin-slot idea was also applied to music boxes, player pianos, a combination disc player and music box (*see* REGINA MUSIC BOX CO.), and to machines that showed pictures along with music (*see* PICTURIZED PHONOGRAPHS). For later developments *see* JUKE BOX. [Edison 1893; Koenigsberg 1990; Marty 1979, illustration of an Automatic Graphophone; *HN* #149 (April 1986), p. 12 has an illustrated account of the Excelsior concert coin-op; Hoover 1971 has a photo of the Reginaphone.]

COLE, NAT KING, 1917–1965. American jazz pianist and—perhaps in spite of himself—popular singer, born Nathaniel Adams Cole in Montgomery, Alabama, on 17 Mar 1917. A nightclub pianist in the 1930s, he began to sing in response to audience requests. His King Cole Trio (1939–1951) brought him recognition as both pianist and vocalist. "Sweet Lorraine" (Decca #8520; 1940) was an early favorite, and his first as a vocalist. "Nature Boy," recorded for Capitol in 1948—as a singer only, with an orchestral accompaniment—was a surprise hit, remaining 15 weeks on the charts. Other notable recordings were "The Christmas Song" in 1946 (Capitol #311); and "Mona Lisa" in 1950 (Capitol #1010). In 1946 he became the first Black artist to have a sponsored radio show. Cole's records were on the charts for 23 years; he had more than 100 hits. He won a Grammy for the single "Midnight Flyer" (Capitol #4258; 1959) and also received the Grammy lifetime achievement award (1989). His daughter Natalie is also a successful singer. She won a Grammy in 1992 for her overdubbed duet with her father, "Unforgettable" (Elektra CD #61049–2).

During 1959–1961 Cole toured Europe (with a command performance for Queen Elizabeth), South America, and Japan. He died on 15 Feb 1965 in Santa Monica, California.

COLISEUM (label). A British issue of 1912–1927, The offerings were mainly dance records, made from Gennett, Vocalion, and other masters, with the artists adorned by pseudonyms; for example Fletcher Henderson's orchestra, including Louis Armstrong and Coleman Hawkins, appeared as the Maryland Dance Orchestra doing "Words," taken from Vocalion #14925 (1924). [Rust 1978.]

COLLARO, LTD. A British high-fidelity manufacturer, located in Barking, Essex. In the 1950s it made the successful RC 456 **record-changer** that intermixed seven-inch, 10-inch, and 12-inch discs at any of four speeds.

COLLECTORS AND COLLECTING. Collectors of recorded sound were active before the turn of the century. A note in an 1898 issue of *Phonoscope* stated that "old records are now in great demand, by enthusiasts who aim to possess valuable collections" (quoted in Brooks 1979). In 1897, *Phonoscope* reported that Edgar Caypless of Denver had a collection of 1,760

records; and there were numerous other cumulations of cylinders in private hands.

Many libraries and archives of recorded sound were developed around the collections of individuals. Some of the earliest archives were based on field recordings of ethnomusicologists, or the collections of journalists, or of radio and record company personnel. For example, the original collection in the **Berlin Phonogramm-Archiv** (1905) consisted of field recordings deposited there by Carl Stumpf. Parts of that collection later found their way to America via George Herzog, who established the Archives of Folk and Primitive Music at Columbia University 1936 and later moved the collection to Indiana University's **Archives of Traditional Music.** That archive also houses the Laura Boulton Collection of folk music and liturgical music.

The Frances Densmore collection of Native American Indian music recordings became an important part of the Archive of Folk Song in the Library of Congress, which is now the **American Folklife Center.** Other significant private collections have shaped the research holdings of the Library of Congress; for example, the John Secrist collection of recordings by Enrico Caruso.

G. Robert Vincent began recording the voices of important people when he was still a youth, and eventually accumulated several thousand items which are now in the **National Voice Library** of Michigan State University. The outstanding resources of the **Stanford Archive of Recorded Sound** were based on donated private collections, notably that of William R. Moran. Walter C. Allen's collection of jazz materials formed the foundation for the Rutgers University **Institute of Jazz Studies.** The country/western collection of **John Edwards** was the basis for the archive that was originally at the University of California at Los Angeles, and is now at the Middle Tennessee State University.

Considerable impetus was given to collecting of records with the refinement of research and of discographical method, from the 1930s (*see* DISCOGRAPHY). In the 1930s and 1940s the British **record collector societies** flourished. Magazines devoted to records and collecting began to appear in quantity during the same period (*see* SOUND RECORDING PERIODICALS). The **Gramophone Shop** opened in New York in 1928, providing American collectors with access to imported discs. Julius Gabler's **Commodore Music Shop**, opened in 1924, became a haven for jazz collectors. Another New York emporium that featured jazz and popular music was the **Liberty Music Shop** (1927). In the 1930s there were also mail order sales available from such emporia as Arnold's Archive (of Arnold Jacobson) in Grand Rapids, Michigan; and Records Unlimited (of Frank B. Pope) in Carnegie, Pennsylvania.

Compton Mackenzie (an avid collector) and Christopher Stone founded *The Gramophone* magazine in 1923, offering a forum and information source for British enthusiasts. It was through their journal that recognition of the collector was made, via the "Collectors' Corner" column that was featured from June 1928.

It was in *The Gramophone* that the earliest published attempts to list all the known records by certain artists were found; the April 1930 issue included a discography of Emmy Destinn. (*See* DISCOGRAPHY for an account of subsequent developments in that area.) With the increase in the number of journals about records, especially in the U.S. and Britain, collectors benefitted from an improved factual base. The *Phonograph Monthly Review* (1926) was the earliest magazine entirely devoted to commentary on new records; in 1935 it took the name *American Record Guide*. Another journal of importance was *New Records* (1933). *Record Research* (1955) has offered a forum for the publication of label discographies based on private collections. *Antique Phonograph Monthly* (1973) is a periodical emphasizing the cylinder record; the editor, Allen Koenigsberg, has a collection of more than 5,000 cylinders. (*See* SOUND RECORDING PERIODICALS for other collector magazines.)

During the 1930s there emerged the supportive movements of **record clubs** and the issue of **society records**. Guides for collectors began to appear in print in this period, too, beginning with B. H. Haggin's *Music on Records* (1938) (*see* CRITICISM for later titles in this genre).

As private collections gained in strength and organization, a number of them were used by authors of scholarly treatises. For example, the 1970 study and discography of the Sousa Band, by James Smart, grew out of a collaboration with Glenn D. Bridges of Detroit; Bridges had accumulated an exhaustive Sousa march collection.

A devoted collector of recordings by the earliest performers, **Jim Walsh**, began to write in 1942 an invaluable series of articles for *Hobbies* magazine, entitled "Favorite Pioneer Recording Artists"; the series continued under his authorship until 1985. *Hobbies* also published a series of articles on operatic records and artists by Aida Favia-Artsay. James F.E. Dennis, Alfred Frankenstein, William R. Moran, John B. Richards, Leo Riemens, John Stratton, and Laurence C. Witten were among the collectors of vocal recordings who wrote regularly for the U.K. journal *Record Collector*, established by Dennis in 1946.

Important library archives were being shaped and formalized in the 1930s and 1940s, and to a large extent they have replaced private collections as the sites of discographical research. (*See* ARCHIVES OF TRADITIONAL MUSIC; CHICAGO PUBLIC LIBRARY; LIBRARY OF CONGRESS; NATIONAL SOUND ARCHIVE; RODGERS AND HAMMERSTEIN ARCHIVES OF RECORDED SOUND; STANFORD ARCHIVE OF RECORDED SOUND; SYRACUSE AUDIO ARCHIVES; YALE COLLECTION OF HISTORICAL SOUND RECORDINGS.) Communication among collectors—private and institutional—has benefitted from the establishment of active organizations like the **Association for Recorded Sound Collections** (1966), International Association of Music Libraries (1949), **International Association of Sound Archives** (1968), International Folk Music Council (1947), and the International Society for Jazz Research (1969).

Directories of private and library archives began with various specialized listings (for folk music and jazz) in the 1930s and 1940s; these included Herzog (1936), Fry (1942), and Bannister (1948). The *World Wide Record Collectors Directory* first appeared in 1957. The first attempt at a comprehensive inventory of private and library collections was the *Preliminary Directory of Sound Recordings Collections in the United States and Canada*, prepared by the Association for Recorded Sound Collections in 1967. Many specialized directories appeared in the 1970s. An important recent directory is James Heintze's *Scholars' Guide to Washington, D.C. for Audio Resources* (1985).

An early directory of mail order sources for record collectors was edited by Paul T. Jackson in 1973, the *Collector's Contact Guide, 1973–74*. A revised edition appeared in 1975. Later directories of sources were issued as the *Record/Tape Collector's Directory* (1976, 1978), and as the *Kastlemusick Directory for Collectors of Recordings* (1981). Recently the annual membership directory of the Association for Recorded Sound Collections has served to identify the interests and holdings of most private collectors in America. *See also* SOUND RECORDINGS AND THE LIBRARY. For details on titles cited *see* the Bibliography.

Paul T. Jackson

COLLINS, ARTHUR, 1864–1933. American dialect singer, born in Philadelphia on 7 Feb 1864. His recording of "The Preacher and the Bear," made for Victor in May 1905 (#4431) and repeated on numerous labels, sold steadily for 20 years and may have been the all-time best-selling acoustic record. (Its Negro speech required an explanatory leaflet with its British issues.) Collins was one of the greatest performers of **coon songs**, and "one of the half dozen most popular singers on record" (Walsh). As a young man he studied voice in Philadelphia and sang with a touring opera group; then he appeared with the St. Louis Summer Opera. He began recording for Edison cylinders in 1898, and did most of his work for that firm, though he also made Berliner, Victor, Columbia, and Zonophone discs. In addition to a vast solo repertoire, Collins made more than 80 records in duet with **Byron Harlan** after 1900, creating what Walsh calls "the most popular team of comedians in the history of the phonograph."

Collins was one of the Eight Famous Victor Artists and for 10 years he sang with the Peerless Quartet. He and Harlan were among those chosen to do Edison **tone tests**, and during one of them (in 1921) he walked into an open trapdoor on stage as he was slipping away in the dark; even after a two-year recovery he was never the same performer. He did return to the recording horn for Edison with Harlan duets and some solo work in 1923–1924. Collins died in Tice, Florida, on 3 Aug 1933. [Walsh 1942/11–12, 1943/1.]

COLLINS, JUDY, 1939– . American folk and popular singer, born in Seattle on 1 May 1939. A prodigy on the piano, she moved to the guitar at age 16 and began playing in clubs. On 21 Mar 1964 she gave a Town Hall concert which brought her great acclaim; an Elektra LP of it was a best seller. Her major single, a Grammy winner, was "Both Sides Now" (Elektra #45639; 1968). A major participant in the war-protest movement and the folk music revivals of the 1960s, she was highly popular on college campuses as well as in conventional club and concert settings. Her repertoire included hard rock as well as folk music, and she offered a notable interpretation of "Send in the Clowns" in 1975 (Elektra #46253) that was on the charts nine weeks, then another 17 weeks in 1977.

COLONIAL (label). A disc distributed in Britain only, by Lockwood's in the City Road, London, trademark registered November 1910. Matrices were from the **Homophone Co.**

COLONIAL QUARTET. Another name for the **Rambler Minstrel Co.**

COLORADO AND UTAH PHONOGRAPH CO. A Denver firm, in 1890 one of the **North American Phonograph Co.** affiliates. S.W. Cantrill was manager, John Barber was assistant manager.

COLORATION. In a sound system, the change in **frequency response** occasioned by **resonance** peaks; subtle variations of intensity or quality of tone.

COLTRANE, JOHN WILLIAM, 1926–1967. American tenor and soprano jazz saxophonist, born in Hamlet, North Carolina, on 23 Sep 1926. He studied in Philadelphia, then played in a band while serving in the U.S. Navy (1945–1946). After the war he worked with various groups, including those of Dizzy Gillespie, Johnny Hodges, and Thelonious Monk. Upon joining the Miles Davis Quintet in 1955 he became recognized for his innovative artistry. The album *Blue Trane* (Blue Note #1577; 1957) demonstrated his ideas of the late 1950s.

Coltrane formed his own quartet in 1960, and made a notable record, *My Favorite Things* (Atlantic #1361; 1960). During the 1960s he was one of the most influential leaders of avant-garde jazz, incorporating elements of African and Asian traditional music in his performances. "A Love Supreme" (Impulse #77; 1964) marked a peak in his creativity. He was a winner in the *Down Beat* polls of 1961 and 1964–1966. He died in New York on 17 July 1967.

Coltrane won no Grammys while he was alive, but received a posthumous award for the Pablo album of reissues in 1981, *Bye Bye Black-bird*. Most of his work is now available on compact discs. [Jepsen 1969.]

COLUMBIA. The story of Columbia, most recently CBS Records, is a tangle of similar company names. It seems useful to begin this account with a list of those companies, with abbreviations that will be employed in the article:

AGC—American Graphophone Co. (See also separate article.) Established 28 Mar 1887 in Washington, D.C. A merger with Columbia Phonograph Co., ca. 1894, left the two firms with separate corporate identities. AGC and CPC combined to form CPCG in May 1894.

CBS—Columbia Broadcasting System. Established July 1927 by CPC, acting for its parent firm, CGraphCL; originally named the Columbia Phonograph Broadcasting System.

CGraphC—Columbia Graphophone Co. A re-naming, in January 1913, of CPCG. Liquidated 1924. Reorganized as part of the second CPC in February 1924.

CGraphCL—Columbia Graphophone Co., Ltd. Incorporated as a British company in February 1917. Acquired the second CPC on 31 March 1925. Became an EMI subsidiary in 1931.

CGraphMC—Columbia Graphophone Manufacturing Co. Established 1918 as the manufacturing division of CGraphC; in fact it did what AGC had been doing. Yet AGC persisted; in *TMW* of February 1922 H. L. Willson is named as president of both firms. Liquidated in 1924, CGraphMC was reorganized as part of the second CPC in February 1924.

CI—Columbia (International) Ltd. Established 3 Oct 1925 as a holding company, to control the second CPC, ColGraphCL, and all Columbia business throughout the world. It also controlled several European firms (Lindström, Transoceanic Co., Parlophone, and finally the record business of French Pathé). On 13 Apr 1931 CPC became independent of CI. The other CI operations merged with EMI, Ltd. on 20 Apr 1931.

CPC—Columbia Phonograph Co. Established 1888, incorporated as Columbia Phonograph Co., Inc. on 15 Jan 1889 in Washington, D.C., by Edward D. Easton and Roland F. Cromelin. Merged interests with AGC ca. 1894. Combined with AGC to form CPCG in May 1894, but retained its corporate identity. Succeeded by CGraphC in 1913. Name revived in 1924, as a second CPC was established February 1924 by a group of American investors as a reorganization of the assets of CGraphC and CGraphMC. Acquired by CGraphCL (Louis Sterling) on 31 Mar 1925. Became part of CI on 3 Oct 1925, then gained independence from CI on 13 Apr 1931, a week before the formation of EMI, Ltd., which acquired the rest of CI.

Acquired by Warner Brothers, which sold it to Grigsby-Grunow in May 1931. In 1933 Grigsby-Grunow failed, and CPC was acquired by the American Record Corp. When CBS acquired American Record Corp. in 1938, the second CPC became a subsidiary of the firm that had once been a subsidiary of the first CPC.

CPCG—Columbia Phonograph Co., General. Established 14 May 1894 in Bridgeport, Connecticut, as worldwide recording and sales agent of AGC and CPC, except for Washington, D.C., Maryland, and Delaware. (Each of the three firms retained its corporate identity.) President was A.B. Cromelin. In 1913 it became part of the new CGraphC. Public documentation of CPCG often omitted the "General" in its name, leading to confusion with CPC, which continued to exist separately after the merger of interests.

CPCG-L—Columbia Phonograph Co., General—London Branch. Established 1900. In January 1913 it was re-named Columbia Graphophone Co., with the re-naming of the American firm. It was succeeded by CGraphCL in February 1917.

CRC—Columbia Recording Co. New name for CPC in 1938, when it was acquired by CBS from American Record Co.

CRI—Columbia Records, Inc. New name for CRC, when it became the record unit within CBS. Sold to **Sony** in 1988.

The **North American Phonograph Co.**, established 14 July 1888 by Jesse H. Lippincott, included among its 33 regional semi-independent subsidiaries the CPC, which had already been operating in 1888 and was formally incorporated in January 1889. CPC was located earliest at 5th St. and Louisiana Ave., moving that summer to 627 E St., NW, Washington, D.C. (the building is still there), with a territory including Maryland and Delaware as well as the District of Columbia. In 1892 the firm moved to 919 Pennsylvania Ave. Although Columbia was supposed to sell and service **graphophones** (dictating machines, cylinder format) made by AGC and the similar Edison phonograph to government offices—and it was successful enough to turn a profit in its first year—it soon branched out. Under president **Edward D. Easton**, CPC pioneered in the area of entertainment recording. John Yorke AtLee, a whistler, began to make records for CPC in 1889, and Easton then signed John Philip Sousa and his United States Marine Band to an exclusive contract. In 1890 the world saw its first ancestor of the *Schwann Catalog*, in a one-page list of cylinders on sale by CPC—a combination of Edison recordings and Columbia's originals. The price per cylinder was between $1 and $2. The rapid growth of the company is demonstrated by the size of its June 1891 sales list—it was 10 pages long. Among the items available were 27 marches; 13 polkas; 10 waltzes; 34 miscellaneous hymns and anthems; various solos with piano for clarinet, cornet, and voice; "comic," "negro," "irish" and like material; 20 spoken records; and 36 of AtLee's specialties accompanied by one "Prof. Gaisberg"—better known later without his (pseudo) academic

title as one of the great impresarios of the industry (*see* GAISBERG, FRED).

Another CPC list, in November 1891, included the first records by the Brilliant Quartette. The 1893 catalog grew to 32 pages, with such novelties as foreign language instruction and Shakespeare recitations. The first female singer to be identified, Susie Davenport, made her only catalog appearance; and George Diamond, the ever-popular tenor, made his first of many. Other famous names of the time included Pat Brady and Russell Hunting, comic monologists. The company was selling 300–500 cylinders a day, mostly by mail. Sales were essentially confined to commercial **coin-ops** (the early juke boxes), since cylinder machines were still too costly—at $150 or more—for most home buyers. Easton opened a **phonograph parlor** at 919 Pennsylvania Ave., moving his office there. By November 1891 Columbia was operating 140 coin-ops in the Washington-Baltimore area.

Easton was at this time the general manager of another Washington company in the cylinder machine business, AGC. By May 1893 he had acquired enough stock in AGC to assume control. When in 1894 the entire North American group collapsed, Easton arranged to merge his two firms, CPC and AGC; Columbia Phonograph Co., General, was established on 14 May 1894 to consolidate those interests and to handle worldwide operations (outside of Washington, D.C., Maryland, and Delaware). Thereafter AGC confined itself to development and manufacturing, while Columbia was devoted to sales and distribution. Both AGC and CPC retained their legal identities and continued to operate in the Washington, D.C., Maryland, and Delaware region. **Calvin Child** was hired in 1894 to direct the CPCG music department. He was a recording expert with experience in the New England Phonograph Co.

Success of CPCG was demonstrated in 1895 by expansion to other cities: a New York office opened at 1159 Broadway, and another office and phonograph parlor opened on the boardwalk in Atlantic City, New Jersey. Sale price dropped to $.60 per cylinder, for the 575 titles in the 1895 catalog. New artists of 1895 included Sousa's own Grand Concert Band

and the famous trombonist Arthur Pryor. In the next year's catalog "the great and only" Jules Levy appeared with 13 cornet numbers.

Brooks (1978) describes 1897 as "the first true boom year for the recording industry." Economic conditions in the U.S. were improved, and a lower price line of cylinder machines had become available. Disc sales were rising rapidly. A half million cylinder and disc records were produced, a number that tripled the following year and rose to 2.8 million in 1899. Columbia was comfortably ahead of its competition, and reduced its cylinder price to $.50. In 1897 Easton moved the headquarters and studios to Broadway and 27th St., New York. Other offices were opened, between 1896 and 1898, in St. Louis, Philadelphia, Chicago, Buffalo (New York), and San Francisco. The first overseas address was 34 Boulevard des Italiens, Paris (1897); others followed in Berlin (1899) and London (1900). The London Branch was re-named Columbia Phonograph Co. General—London in 1900.

Record companies exploited the short Spanish-American War of 1898, issuing topical and patriotic items. Columbia produced at least two lists of "music of the war"; among the selections there was one by the Rough Riders' bugler, playing all the bugle calls relating to the battle of San Juan Hill. The other novelty of 1898 was ragtime, well covered on Columbia cylinders. And in that year the firm offered its first recording by an opera singer, Bernard Bégué of Paris, doing short excerpts.

Over the next few years the industry began to accept the practical superiority of discs over cylinders. Columbia produced a finger-wound toy disc player in 1899, invented by **Thomas H. Macdonald,** with a stock of nursery rhymes and other pieces. In 1901 Columbia began to issue disc records, made by the **Globe Record Co.,** using the label name Climax. Eldridge Johnson bought Globe on 15 Jan 1902, and used the acquisition as leverage in negotiating a seminal deal between his Victor Talking Machine Co. and Columbia. In that settlement the two firms agreed to share their patents, effectively closing out other competition in the U.S. Columbia retrieved Climax, but dropped the name and issued discs with the Columbia name during late summer or fall of 1902.

Cylinders were still made for the Graphophone Grand and other Columbia players—among them the five-inch Grand that gave a louder playback than the standard size—and were selling at 300–550 per day—but attention focused on the new seven-inch and 10-inch records, and in 1903 a 14-inch disc. All were single-sided, with **announcements.** The cylinder phonograph began fading from the scene (Columbia discontinued cylinder production in 1908). In 1913 the term "phonograph" was dropped from the company name, and the Columbia Graphophone Co. succeeded CPCG. In Britain CGraphC was also established as the new corporate name for the Columbia Phonograph Co., General—London Branch.

Columbia's 1902 catalog displayed a great variety of music: love ballads, sacred songs, comedy discs, wind, brass, and string solos. A red label opera series was offered in 1903 to counter the Victor Red Seal series; stars of the Metropolitan Opera were recorded on discs with their autographs on the labels and their own voices doing announcements. But sales of red labels were unsatisfactory; Victor was doing better both in recruitment of artists (such as Enrico Caruso) and in recording technique. Easton pulled back from opera, and Victor took a lead they never relinquished in the classical repertoire.

Columbia pioneered in 1904 with the two-sided disc—all their discs were double-sided after September 1908—and in 1907 they marketed an "indestructible" **Velvet Tone** record that was developed by the inventor Guglielmo Marconi. The Columbia Indestructible Cylinder was also available in late 1908, CPC having taken over the output of the **Indestructible Phonographic Record Co.** of Albany. In 1909 the cylinders were on the U.K. market as well. As a manufacturer of playback machines, Columbia claimed preeminence: an advertisement for CPCG in *TMW* in 1906 claimed the status of "largest talking machine manufacturers in the world." In 1906 Columbia Phonograph Co., General had offices in London (89 Great Eastern St.), Glasgow (50 Union St.), Manchester (54 Market St.), Cardiff (96 St. Mary St.), and Sydney (Paling's Buildings). There were also a hundred Columbia shops throughout the world, and "dealers everywhere." One product advertised in 1906 was the Home Premier "sound-magnifying" cylinder player, selling in U.K. at £16 16 sh. A 1907 graphophone had an aluminum tone arm "to eliminate all false vibrations"; it sold for $30. For discs, CPCG was making a $50 Grafonola Favorite in 1911—the object of one of the first testimonial advertisements, by Mary Garden, in *Leslie's Weekly*.

Between 1908 and 1910 the company reissued operatic performances made by **Fonotipia** and **Odeon**. None of these initiatives proved to be market sensations, but success was achieved with fine recordings of instrumentalists like Josef Hofmann, Leopold Godowsky, Vladimir de Pachmann, Percy Grainger, Eugen Ysaÿe, and Pablo Casals. And Columbia was very strong on the popular side, with dance music, ragtime, and in 1917 one of the earliest jazz records ever made, by the Original Dixieland Jass Band: "Darktown Strutters' Ball."

The U.K. branch of the firm had been Columbia Phonograph Co., General—London until January 1913, when it was re-named (with the American firm) Columbia Graphophone Co. It had been working under the direction of the American company since its establishment in May 1900. **Louis Sterling** became the chief executive in October 1909. Under his direction, the company began to record symphonic music from 1915, conducted by Thomas Beecham or Henry Wood, and chamber music, by the Lener String Quartet or the London String Quartet. This move to the orchestral repertoire had been as early as 1905 by other labels (*see* Orchestral Recording), but Edward Easton of U.S. Columbia had been reluctant to follow them. With his death in 1915, CGraphC contracted to make recordings of major American orchestras, such as those of Chicago and New York. Several years of prosperity followed. The firm moved to the Woolworth Building in 1913, evidence of its rise in the industry. In February 1917 the British company became Columbia Graphophone Co., Ltd., but remained under U.S. ownership.

Sales boomed into the 1920s, then began to fall as the radio appeared on the scene and won the hearts of American consumers. As an economy move, the studios and offices were moved from the Woolworth Building to 1819 Broadway, on 4 Apr 1921. But American Columbia—like so many record companies at that time—was headed for bankruptcy.

In 1924 both CGraphC and CGraphMC were liquidated. But a group of American investors reorganized the assets under the name Columbia Phonograph Co. There was by that time acceptance of the term "phonograph" as the designation of a disc player. Meanwhile in Britain Louis Sterling had acquired the shares of CGraphL from American stockholders (23 Apr 1923). He wanted to acquire a license from Western Electric for the new **electrical recording** process, and saw his opportunity in late 1924, when Western Electric licensed the reorganized CPC. He sailed for New York on 26 Dec 1924, and he succeeded in purchasing CPC (31 Mar 1925) with the options it already had from Western Electric.

Columbia (International) Ltd. was formed on 3 Oct 1925, embracing all the British and U.S. interests. Thus the pioneer U.S. firm became a subsidiary of its former British subsidiary. But Sterling did preserve the venerable name, Columbia Phonograph Co. A new trademark and label design was introduced by Sterling, who brought in fresh management and equipment, and got ready for the electrical age. (Columbia in the U.K. had already been involved with electrical recording as early as 11 Nov 1920, by processing the recording made in Westminster Abbey by two Canadians—in a project undertaken for themselves and for the Abbey—setting down a memorial service quite unsuccessfully.)

Electrical recording made a discreet entrance, with Columbia and Victor (which also had a license to use the Western Electric process) agreeing not to publicize the method. They feared that the enormous stocks of acoustic records would be considered obsolete, and economic disaster (already presaged by the radio) would swiftly follow. The strategy was a good one. The public noted the improved quality of records, and had begun to be aware of the advantages that discs provided over radio; and economic conditions in the mid- to late-1920s favored wider purchasing of entertainment products. Acoustic recordings were gradually replaced in the catalogs by electrics. The famous Columbia Masterworks label was introduced, and great energy was poured into the recording of complete symphonies and other large works. American Columbia was also vigorous in the popular field: Bing Crosby's first record was theirs (1926) and Paul Whiteman was stolen from Victor in 1928. (He went back to Victor in two years, but first gave Columbia a few more Bing Crosby items, and Roy Bargy playing the Gershwin *Concerto in F*.) In September 1925 CPC offered a new low-price label ($.50 instead of the $.75 for regular Columbias): **Harmony**. These were acoustics, featuring dance and popular material. John S. Macdonald became new manager of the recording department in November 1925.

Up to the beginning of the Depression sales were remarkably good in both the U.K. and U.S. During the month of December 1925, 1,750,000 Columbia discs were sold in Britain alone. **Okeh** records was acquired by CI in 1926, Nipponophone (Japan) in May 1927, Homophon Gmbh (Germany) in May 1928, and Pathé (France) ca. October 1928. There were factories in Turkey and Greece. **CBS** was incorporated as a subsidiary in 1927, with 16 stations across America. CPC profits in 1926 were $270,000 net; for 1927, $760,000. An exclusive contract to record performances at Bayreuth was announced in March 1928; selections were recorded from *Parsifal*, *Siegfried*, *Rheingold*, and *Walküre*. Columbia's answer to the Victor **Orthophonic** phonograph was its Viva-Tonal, introduced in 1925, heavily promoted from 1927. Intended for playback of the new electrical recordings, it was however a windup and fully acoustic in its technology. It did not match Victor's model in the market.

With the Wall Street collapse of 1929 the phonograph industry was nearly destroyed. Consolidation of interests was inevitable as a survival move. In April 1931 the conglomerate **EMI, Ltd.** (Electric and Musical Industries, Ltd.) was built up from the assets of Columbia (which already owned Parlophone), and the **Gramophone Co.** (which owned **Marconiphone Co., Ltd.**). EMI acquired 50 factories in 19 countries. It did not acquire CPC, however, since the American firm had gained independence from CI on 13 Apr 1931, a week before EMI was formed. Control of CPC passed to **Warner Brothers**, the motion picture giant,

who then sold it to the radio manufacturer **Grigsby-Grunow**.

With the collapse of Grigsby-Grunow in 1933, U.S. Columbia was taken over by the **American Record Corp.** at a sale price of $70,000. The Columbia label survived these sad maneuvers, and discs under that name continued to appear. (**Brunswick** was the key label of American Record Corp.) **John Hammond**, as recording director from 1933 to 1948, brought many great jazz stars to the label.

A final bizarre turn occurred in 1938–1939, as CBS, once a subsidiary of CPC, acquired the American Record Corp. and CPC along with it. On the initiative of **Edward Wallerstein** of RCA, CBS president **William S. Paley** made the purchase with a view toward reviving the glory of the Columbia label. Wallerstein moved over to become Columbia's new general manager, and the renaissance began. More new company names emerged: Columbia Recording Co. (for manufacture) and Columbia Phonograph Corp. (for sales)—the latter then changing to Columbia Records, Inc.

So the two veteran giants of the industry, Victor and Columbia, faced off once again. Columbia signed up great names in the classical field, making up for lost time: The All-American [Youth] Orchestra under Leopold Stokowski; Salvatore Baccaloni; John Barbirolli; Thomas Beecham, the Budapest Quartet, the Busch Quartet, the Chicago Symphony, the Cleveland Orchestra, the Concertgebouw Orchestra, the Don Cossack Chorus, Nelson Eddy, Walter Gieseking, Roland Hayes, Myra Hess, Jan Kiepura, Andre Kostelanetz, Lotte Lehmann, the London Philharmonic, Lauritz Melchior, Nathan Milstein, Dimitri Mitropoulos, Claudia Muzio, Guiomar Novaes, Egon Petri, the Philharmonic-Symphony Orchestra of New York, Gregor Piatigorsky, Lily Pons, Fritz Reiner, Paul Robeson, Artur Rodzinski, Bidú Sayão, La Scala, Albert Schweitzer, Rudolf Serkin, Risë Stevens, Joseph Szigeti, Astrid Varnay, the Vienna Philharmonic, Bruno Walter, and Felix Weingartner—all these appeared in the catalogs of the next few years. Among the popular stars were harmonicist Larry Adler, Louis Armstrong, Mildred Bailey, Count Basie, Frankie Carle, Eddy Duchin, Duke Ellington,

Benny Goodman, Horace Heidt, Fletcher Henderson, Harry James, Gene Krupa, Kay Kyser, Ted Lewis, Ray Noble, Kate Smith, Jack Teagarden, Claude Thornhill, Orrin Tucker, and Teddy Wilson. Twenty-six complete grand operas were available in 1943, along with the entire standard concert repertoire of the time.

Columbia's last confrontation with Victor took place in 1949–1950, in the "war of the speeds." Both companies had experimented in the early 1930s with discs that rotated 33 1/3 rpm, for cinema, sound effects, and other uses. Both had encountered technical problems. Research and development work was hampered first by the Depression and then by the World War II. Even so, in 1948 Columbia Records introduced its long-playing record (LP), revolutionizing the industry. Victor's first response was the 45 in 1949; it was not as useful as the LP for classical music, and served to delay the advent of Victor's 33 1/3 rpm record until 1950. By that time Columbia and several other LP labels had taken over the classical music area. Columbia stood for the first time as the dominant rival in the half-century struggle with Victor.

Starting in 1951, Columbia made 45s as well as LPs, using the small format for popular singles. Victor used the LP for classical recordings. Columbia rode the crest of an ever-growing wave of disc sales in the U.S., joining (if late) in the rock music craze and taking a larger share of that market than any of the major labels. The 1960s were equally strong. *West Side Story* with the original cast was a great multi-million seller; the soundtrack album was even more popular, on the charts for three years. In the mid-1960s Columbia was one of the five giants of the industry, a place that it held through the 1970s.

A curious decision in 1979 led to the dropping of the venerable label name Columbia, in favor of "CBS." The late 1970s marked the peak of the record market in America, followed by a sharp decline in the 1980s. In 1986 Laurence A. Tisch was named chief executive of CBS Inc. He sold the magazine and recording divisions of the firm; CBS Records went to Sony Corp. in January 1988 for $2 billion. Sales had been $1.5 billion for CBS records in 1986, with a large share of the growing CD market. [Andrews*; Andrews 1985/1; Ault 1986; Brooks*; Brooks 1978; Bryan 1982; Isom*; Klinger*; Lorenz 1981.] *See also* COLUMBIA RECORD PLAYERS.

COLUMBIA BAND. One of the names given to the house band for Columbia; heard on the earliest 1904 double-sided discs (matrix 946 was their *Faust* Ballet Music). In 1906 the band performed on one of the first records to commemorate a disaster: "The Destruction of San Francisco." There were few listings for the band after 1909, as later house recordings were identified with the Charles A. Prince Orchestra.

COLUMBIA BROADCASTING SYSTEM (CBS). A firm incorporated in 1927, originally the Columbia Phonograph Broadcasting System, a subsidiary of the Columbia Phonograph Co., Inc. William S. Paley acquired control in 1928. In addition to great broadcasting innovations and successes, Paley wished to return the firm to recording activities, and purchased the Columbia Phonograph Co., which had become a subsidiary of the American Record Corp., in 1938. He renamed it the Columbia Recording Co. (for manufacture) and Columbia Phonograph Corp. (for sales)—the latter then named Columbia Records, Inc.—and engaged Edward Wallerstein to manage it and revive the old quality of the label. (*See* COLUMBIA.)

CBS Inc., as it is currently identified, became the leading entertainment firm of the 1950s and 1960s, and diversified widely. In 1989 CBS had about 7,000 employees and sales of nearly $3 billion. It owned five television stations and had 212 affiliated stations. The firm also provided radio programming to 574 independent stations and owned 19 radio stations. CBS has extensive interests in film production, but has sold its educational and professional publishing division and its magazine division. Laurence Tisch gradually became the largest stockholder, and was elected chief executive officer in 1986. In 1988 Columbia Records, Inc., was sold to Sony.

COLUMBIA DOUBLE QUARTET. An octet that recorded for Columbia in 1915. The members were not identified, but Walsh surmises that they were the Columbia Stellar Quartet and the **Peerless Quartet**. [Walsh 1962/10.]

Columbia Indestructible Records. *See* INDESTRUCTIBLE PHONOGRAPHIC RECORD CO.

COLUMBIA LADIES QUARTET. A group that made Columbia records in 1913. It consisted of Grace Kerns, Louise MacMahon, Mildred Potter, and Clara Moister. [Walsh 1962/10.]

COLUMBIA MALE QUARTET. A group active from the 1890s to 1912. Although it was renamed as the **Peerless Quartet** in 1906, it kept the old name for Columbia records until 1912. [Walsh 1962/10.]

COLUMBIA MANTEL CO. A Brooklyn firm, established in 1914; in 1916 it was located at Leonard and Devoe Streets. It manufactured and sold the Recordion disc player, in eight models.

COLUMBIA MIXED QUARTET. A group active in 1913, consisting of Grace Kerns, Mildred Potter, **Charles Harrison**, and **Frank Croxton**.

Columbia Octette. *See* COLUMBIA DOUBLE QUARTET.

COLUMBIA ORCHESTRA. A house orchestra for Columbia in 1896–1909, replacing Issler's Orchestra in that capacity. Directors were **Charles Adam Prince** (to 1905) and **Tom Clark**. The first disc record issued with a Columbia label, in 1902, was made by this group; they played "In a Clock Store." Waltz recordings were among their favorites. After 1905 the name favored by the ensemble was Prince's Orchestra.

COLUMBIA RECORD PLAYERS. The various Columbia firms manufactured a great many models of cylinder and disc players. Cylinder machines, known as Graphophones, are taken up first. All types that have been reported in the literature are listed here.

Chichester A. Bell and **Charles Sumner Tainter** invented the Graphophone in 1885 (patent issued 1886) while at work in the **Volta Laboratory** in Washington, D.C. It was primarily a dictation machine, differing from the Edison tinfoil phonograph by incising the sound signal on the wax-coated surface of a cardboard cylinder. The cylinder was stationary, and the reproducer moved along it. (This first Graphophone is illustrated in Chew 1981, p. 10, and in Jewell 1977, p. 11. Materials and manufacture are described in CYLINDER, 2, 3.) Power to the machine was provided by hand cranking, a foot treadle (illustrated in Ault 1987), a battery, or a spring motor—the last-named being the most common and successful in the later models. Clarity was improved in comparison with the Edison player, but the wax surface gave a lower volume and necessitated the use of ear tubes at first.

In 1887 the foot treadle machine (U.S. patent #375,579 granted 27 Dec 1887) was put into production, using Howe Sewing Machine bases; six-inch long cylinders turned at a speed of 200 rpm. Although 2,817 were made by July 1890, with several improved versions in that period, the early Graphophone was not a market success. Battery and spring-motor models took its place in 1894.

The Graphophone was marketed in 1894 by the Columbia Phonograph Co. General., sales agents for the **American Graphophone Co.** Production of the machines, in numerous types, continued to 1908, and distribution ceased after 1910 as the disc player took over the market. The table lists the machines marketed from 1894 to 1908, in chronological order (a list by model designators follows the chronological list).

Year / Model/Type / Trademark/ Comments

1894   F   Spring Motor Graphophone
  Played wax-coated cardboard cylinders, six inches long. Sold for $110.
1894   G   Baby Grand
  First one designed for home entertainment. Played solid wax Edison or Columbia cylinders, powered by Thomas Macdonald's spring motor. Sold for $75, or for $100 with a com-

plete kit of records, horn, and hearing tubes. Illustration in Hazelcorn 1976, p. 2.

1895   F   Perfected Graphophone
Modification of the 1894 version to allow play of solid wax cylinder.

1895   K   Standard
Powered with a spring motor or a 2 1/2 volt battery; played Edison or Columbia cylinders. Illustration in Hazelcorn 1976, p. 4.

1895   N   Bijou
Invented by Thomas H. Macdonald, it was the first model with a fixed mandrel, front-mounted feedscrew, upright reproducer, and left-to-right tracking. Power was supplied by a spring motor or a 2 1/2 volt battery. About 6,000 were sold at $40. A **coin-op** version was available in 1896. Illustrations in Hazelcorn 1976, p. 6; Marty 1979, p. 3031; Paul 1986, pp. 12–13.

1896-97   A   Columbia name on early models
Sold in Washington, D.C. (with a local decal) in 1896; in New York (also with a local decal) in 1897. Price was $25. The machine had the garland trademark on the front of the case; it ran on a one- or two-spring clockwork motor. Illustrations in Hazelcorn 1976, p. 6; Jewell 1977, pp. 38, 64; and Marty 1979, p. 32.

1897   AN   Bijou
A type A with a type N motor.

1897   AS
A coin-op version of A; sold for $35 with spring motor. Illustration in Hazelcorn 1976, p. 10.

1897   B   Eagle or (in Britain) "Domestic"
The American name came from the price, $10, one U.S. gold eagle coin of the time. It had a double-spring motor. About 149,000 were produced. Illustrations in Chew 1981, p. 52; Hazelcorn 1976, p. 8; Marty 1979, p. 24.

1897   C   Universal
For office use and home entertainment. It played six-inch solid wax cylinders with a triple spring motor, turn speed of 120 rpm. Price was $50. Illustration in Marty 1979, p. 29.

1898   BS   Eagle
A coin-op, encased in glass or wood. Illustration in Marty 1979, p. 27.

ca. 1898   BX   Eagle
A $12 version, with oak cabinet, spring motor, and a 10-inch horn. Illustrations in Jewell 1977, p. 65; Read 1976, plate XI.

1898   AT
The first Graphophone with an ornate case; it had a double-spring motor. Some 90,000 were produced. Illustrations in Hazelcorn 1976, p. 10; Jewell 1977, pp. 45, 65; *TMR* 41 (1976), p. 765.

1898   Q
The lowest price model ($5.00), designed by Macdonald. Single-spring motor. Illustrations in Chew 1981, p. 52; Jewell 1977, p. 47; Read 1976, plate XI.

1898   QQ
An elaborate version of Q, with a wood cabinet and clockwork motor; sold for $10. Illustration in Read 1976, plate XI.

1898   GG   Graphophone Grand
Designed by Macdonald to play the new 5-inch diameter "grand" cylinders; it was comparable to the Edison Concert Phonograph. Mandrel was 4 1/2 inches long, and the horn was 56 inches. Despite the much greater volume achieved by the machine, and improvements in the higher frequency response, the Grand was not successful. The original price was $300, soon reduced to $150. Illustrations in Hazelcorn 1976, p. 12; *NAG* 53 (1985), pp. 10, 12.

1899   HG   Home Grand
A compact version of the GG, selling for $100. Edison's Concert machine was selling at $125, and Columbia was trying to stay in competition. Illustration in *NAG* 53 (1985), p. 10.

1899   AG   Columbia Grand
Said to be of "less expensive construction" than the GG and HG, "but embodying the same principles" (an advertisement of Sept 1900, reproduced in Paul 1985), this model was offered in reply to Edison's further price drop on the Concert machine, down to $100. Price of the AG was $75, then reduced to $50. Illustrations in Marty 1979, p. 27; Paul 1985, pp. 10, 12.

1899   SG   Slot Grand
A coin-op version of the Grand, selling for $100.

1900   MG   Multiplex Grand
A Macdonald design, shown at the Paris Exposition of 1900. It was a massive machine, run by a six-spring motor, having three tracks and three reproducers. Each track could handle one part of a trio performance, thus providing the elements of a stereophonic system. Price

was $1000, suitable for the Shah of Iran, who bought one. Illustrations in Chew 1981, p. 62; Jewell 1977, p. 19.

1901   AA

The smallest size cabinet Graphophone, measuring only 10.4 by 7.4 by 9.4 inches, selling for $18. It was crank wound. Illustrations in Hazelcorn 1976, p. 16; Jewell 1977, p. 64; Marty 1979, p. 33.

1901   AB   Double Eagle (in Europe)

A MacDonald machine in an ornate oak cabinet, with a five-inch telescoping mandrel. The motor was weak. It sold for $25. Illustrations in Hazelcorn 1976, p. 18; Marty 1979, p. 31.

1901   AD

Like the AB, a machine with telescoping mandrel; it had a six-spring motor. Price was $75. Illustration in Hazelcorn 1976, p. 14.

1901   AF

A combination of the AD type with an AG cabinet; two-spring motor.

1902   AO

A $30 model in an ornate cabinet, with a three-spring motor. Illustration in Hazelcorn 1976, p. 20.

1903   AP   Lyrophone (in Europe)

A cast-iron machine, based on the Lyrophone prototype of 1897. Illustration in *TMR* 41 (1976), p. 765.

1903   AQ

An inexpensive ($3.00) version of the AP, having an aluminum diaphragm. Playing head movement was controlled by a fork resting on an endless screw. In the Sears catalog this was sold as the Oxford Junior. Illustrations in Hazelcorn 1976, p. 22; Marty 1979, p. 30; *TMR* 41 (1976), p. 765.

1903   AT

Same as the 1898 AT, but designed for the reproducer to be horizontal when playing. Illustrations in Chew 1981, p. 52; Jewell 1977, p. 45.

1903   Q   Languagephone or Mignon (in Europe)   Equivalent to the 1898 Q except for trim. The Languagephone version was used for Rosenthal instructional cylinders. Price was $7.50. Illustration in Jewell 1977, p. 79.

1904   AW

Same as the AO but with a simpler cabinet and a new reproducer.

1904   AZ

Same as the AT, except had the new Lyric reproducer which pressed the stylus against the cylinder by spring pressure. It was popular at $25, with some 20,000 produced. Illustrations in Chew 1981, p. 52; Hazelcorn 1976, p. 24; Jewell 1977, p. 45.

1905   BC   Twentieth Century Premier

A very large machine with a six-inch mandrel and a large (4.3 inch diameter) diaphragm, meant to play the Twentieth Century three-minute cylinder. The **Higham Amplifier** was offered. Price was $100. Illustrations in Chew 1981, p. 66; Hazelcorn 1976, p. 26; Marty 1979, p. 29; Read 1976, pp. 99, 159, and plate XI.

1906   BE   Leader

A triple-spring machine in a dark oak case, with the Lyric reproducer; it sold for $30. Illustration in Read 1976, plate XI.

1906   BF   Peerless

Similar to the BE, but with a four-spring motor that could be wound while playing. It handled six-inch cylinders. Price was $40, with an aluminum horn. Illustration in Read 1976, p. 163 and plate XII.

1906   BG   Sovereign

Same as the BF except for trim; price $50.

1906   BCG   Twentieth Century Grand

A type BC redesigned to play the five-inch Grand cylinder; never advertised.

1906   BK   Jewel

Similar to the AZ, with an aluminum horn and support crane, double spring-motor, and Lyric reproducer. It sold for $20. Illustrations in Jewell 1977, p. 148; Marty 1979, p. 31; and Read 1976, plate XII.

1906   BM   Home Premier or Home (in Britain)   A smaller version of the BC, selling for $75.

1907   BO   Invincible

The first cylinder player to have a rear mounted tone arm assembly, similar to those on disc players. It had a six-inch mandrel, triple-spring motor, and a price of $45. Illustration in Hazelcorn 1976, p 28.

1907   BQ   Crown in Britain

Similar to BK, but with tone arm and the BO type horizontal reproducer; sold for $30. Illustrations in Chew 1981, p. 52; Jewell 1977, p. 46.

1907   BV   Home Queen (by mail order) A single-spring motor model in a small oak cabinet, selling for $15.95. Illustration in Hazelcorn 1976, p. 32.

1907   BET   New Invincible
Similar to BE, but with the rear mounted bracket. The heavy duty motor played two-minute or four-minute cylinders. Illustration in Read 1976, plate XII.

1907   BFT   New Peerless
A $55 machine, similar to the BF but with a rear-mounted assembly. Illustration in Hazelcorn 1976, p. 30.

1907   BGT   New Sovereign
Same as the BG except for the rear mounted assembly; sold for $70.

1907   BKT   New Leader
Same as the BK, except for the rear-mounted bracket and the aluminum tone arm; it played two-minute or four-minute cylinders. Price was $35–40. Illustration in Read 1976, plate XII.

1908   BVT   Oxford Talking Machine
A rear-mounted BV, sold by Sears in its 1908 catalog under the Oxford name at $14.95.

These same machines are listed now by type name (first) and then by type letter.

As consumer preference turned from cylinders to discs, Columbia began to produce disc players. In fact it had made a Toy model disc player, using vertical-cut wax discs, in 1899, sold for only $1.50 including the horn (illustrated in Read 1976, plate XI). In 1901 the firm began production of standard disc players, which it named "disc graphophones." These machines resembled the Victor models, but there were some interesting departures. The AU model could be folded up and carried with an attached handle (illustrated in Marty 1979, p. 34). The 1907 Symphony Grand was the first concealed horn model; in fact it concealed its very nature, being made to look like an upright piano (illustrated in Chew 1981, p. 53). Chew 1981, Jewell 1977, and Marty 1979 illustrate some of the other types sold before 1908. One of them, the open horn machine of ca. 1907, represented a high point of technology for 10 years; but the change to internal horn design did not improve the sonic results. The internal horn did allow designer fancy to roam wildly: one of Columbia's players was made to look like a desk (the Regent) and another to look like a round table (the Colonial); both are illustrated in Jewell 1977, pp. 41 and 44.

Columbia's 1907 disc player, the Grafonola, was the firm's answer to the Victrola, selling at the same price, $200.00. It was audibly inferior to the Victor machine. In 1909 a concealed horn Elite model was introduced at $100. An electric motor version was available in 1915, and in 1920 the "only non-set automatic stop" was advertised. Elaborate cases brought the cost of certain Grafonolas up to $1000. Illustrations of the 1915 windup console Grafonola are in Hoover 1971, pp. 58–59. [Hazelcorn 1976 is the source for most of the information in this entry.]

COLUMBIA SEXTET. A group active in 1902 on Columbia cylinders; they did not carry over to discs. Members were Byron Harlan, Joe Belmont, Frank Stanley, and three unnamed females. [Walsh 1962/10.]

COLUMBIA STELLAR QUARTETTE. A group active on Columbia discs in 1914–1917. Members were Charles Harrison, John Barnes Wells (replaced later by Henry Burr, then by Reed Miller), Andrea Sarto, and Frank Croxton, They were also known as the Broadway Quartet (on Columbia) and as the Stellar Quartet (on Aeolian-Vocalion in the 1920s).

Columbia-Rena (label). *See* RENA (label).

COLUMBO, RUSS, 1908–1934. Popular singer, first heard as a violinist and vocalist with Gus Arnheim in 1928–1930. He recorded for Okeh and Victor, and formed his own band in 1932. "Prisoner of Love," his own composition, brought him great fame (Victor #22867; 1931). Columbo continued with Victor to 1932, then went to other labels. He died in a gun accident in Los Angeles on 2 Sep 1934.

COMBINATION PHONOGRAPH. With the 1908 introduction of four-minute cylinders, the Edison **Amberols**, gearing of new phonographs (by Edison and others) was modified so that either the new records or the older two-minute cylinders could be played. The ma-

Type /Name	Letter	Year		Letter	Year	Name
				A	1896, 1897	Columbia
Baby Grand	G	1894		AA	1901	
Bijou	N	1895		AB	1901	Double Eagle
Bijou	AN	1897		AD	1901	
Columbia	A	1896, 1897		AF	1901	
Columbia Grand	AG	1899		AG	1899	Columbia Grand
Crown	BQ	1907		AN	1897	Bijou
Domestic	B	1897		AO	1902	
Double Eagle	AB	1901		AP	1903	Lyrophone
Eagle	BX	ca. 1898		AQ	1903	Oxford Junior
Eagle	B	1897		AS	1897	
Eagle	BS	1898		AT	1903	
Grand	GG	1898		AT	1898	
Grand	SG	1899		AW	1904	
Grand	AG	1899		AZ	1904	
Grand	BCG	1906		B	1897	Eagle; Domestic
Grand	MG	1900		BC	1905	Twentieth Century Premier
Graphophone Grand	GG	1898		BCG	1906	Twentieth Century Grand
Home	BM	1906		BE	1906	Leader
Home Grand	HG	1899		BET	1907	New Invincible
Home Premier	BM	1906		BF	1906	Peerless
Home Queen	BV	1907		BFT	1907	New Peerless
Invincible	BO	1907		BG	1906	Sovereign
Jewel	BK	1906		BGT	1907	New Sovereign
Languagephone	Q	1903		BK	1906	Jewel
Leader	BE	1906		BKT	1907	New Leader
Lyrophone	AP	1903		BM	1906	Home Premier; Home
Mignon	Q	1903		BO	1907	Invincible
Mignon	QQ	1898		BQ	1907	Crown
Multiplex Grand	MG	1900		BS	1898	Eagle in wood cabinet
New Invincible	BET	1907		BV	1907	Home Queen
New Leader	BKT	1907		BVT	1908	Oxford Talking Machine
New Peerless	BFT	1907		BX	ca. 1898	Eagle in oak cabinet
New Sovereign	BGT	1907		C	1897	Universal
Oxford Junior	AQ	1903		F	1895	Perfected Graphophone
Oxford Talking Machine	BVT	1908		F	1894	Spring Motor Graphophone
Peerless	BF	1906		G	1894	Baby Grand
Perfected Graphophone	F	1895		GG	1898	Graphophone Grand
Premier	BC	1905		HG	1899	Home Grand
Premier	BM	1906		K	1895	Standard
Slot Grand	SG	1899		MG	1900	Multiplex Grand
Sovereign	BG	1906		N	1895	Bijou
Spring Motor Graphophone	F	1894		Q	1903	Languagephone; Mignon
Standard	K	1895		Q	1898	
Twentieth Century Premier	BC	1905		QQ	1898	Mignon
Universal	C	1897		SG	1899	Slot Grand

chines thus designed were the Combination Phonographs. Owners of the older type players were given the opportunity to upgrade their equipment with the purchase of Combination Attachments. [Frow 1978.]

COMEDY RECORDINGS. The sound recording industry emerged at a time when vaudeville (in the U.S.) and the music hall (in the U.K.) were at their height of popularity. So it was natural that the vaudeville genres—sentimental songs and "comic turns"—should become staples of the recorded repertoire. As early as 1892, Edison's North American Phonograph Co. made cylinder records of Ben R. Cook, baritone, in comic songs like "When Hogan Pays His Rent" and "Get Your Whiskers Cut." **Cal Stewart** was a greatly popular comic monologist, recording from ca. 1897 for Edison and Berliner, then many other labels. He made numerous records of his "Uncle Josh" character (there were 57 of them in the 1912 Edison catalog). Negro dialect material, thought to be extremely humorous, was a popular genre; it was highly developed by **Arthur Collins**, whose record of "The Preacher and the Bear" (1905) may have been the all time best-selling acoustic disc. Collins also teamed with **Byron Harlan**, making about 80 comic dialogs; they were perhaps the most popular comic team ever to record. **Harry Lauder** recorded his routines from 1902 to 1940, making some of the most popular acoustic discs; Lauder was the only comedian to appear on Victor Red Seal records. Other early comedians on record included **Florrie Forde, Billy Golden, Murry K. Hill, Ada Jones, Billy Murray, Joe Natus, Dan Quinn, Josie Sadler, Burt Shepard, Len Spencer, Billy Williams** (the American), **Billy Williams** (the Australian), and **Nat Wills** ("The Happy Tramp"). **Minstrel recordings** were primarily comical in intent.

During the late acoustic period, popular comedians included the **Avon Comedy Four, Gallagher and Shean,** and **Monroe Silver.** Silver was one of the many dialect comedians, whose humor was based on ethnic speech and on the supposed ethnic characteristics of various immigrant groups. But the end of vaudeville also marked the decline of comedy recording.

Gracie Fields was one of the few outstanding humorists on record in the 1930s, presenting comic songs. Radio was the medium for comedy before and during World War II (see RADIO PROGRAM RECORDINGS). Radio stars like Jack Benny, Eddie Cantor, Bob Hope, and Red Skelton did not make records of their skits and monologs. Indeed, the category of comedy records does not appear at all in the catalogs of Columbia, Decca, and Victor during the 1940s. There were Big Band novelty numbers that provided some comic relief from love ballads; **Spike Jones** was a popular practitioner of novelty songs.

Comic recording revived after World War II, primarily in the form of solo monologs. Shelley Berman and Bob Newhart made popular albums in the late 1950s and early 1960s. Vaughn Meader's *First Family*, a spoof of President John F. Kennedy and his wife, was on the charts 19 weeks in 1962. Myron Cohen carried the tradition of Jewish dialect humor to sophisticated heights. Bill Cosby initiated a series of 15 chart albums with *I Started Out as a Child* in 1964. His greatest hit was *Why is There Air?* in 1965, 77 weeks on the charts. Anna Russell made albums in the 1950s that spoofed opera and sopranos. Pianist Victor Borge recorded comic monologs and humorous musical performances.

Comedy teams flourished again in the 1960s. Mike Nichols and Elaine May recorded timely dialogs beginning in 1961. Mel Brooks and Carl Reiner made a series of successes on the concept of the "2,000 year old man," in 1961. Bob Elliott and Ray Goulding ("Bob and Ray") created gentle parodies of radio and television. Post-war British humor was represented by Flanders and Swann, whose wit was expressed in music. Allan Sherman sang parodies of popular songs with a Jewish ethnic twist. Tom Lehrer wrote and performed satiric songs with great effect, highlighting political and social material. Almost all of Mort Sahl's comedy was politically oriented. Lenny Bruce was known for "sick humor." Jo Stafford and Paul Weston, recording as Jonathan Edwards and Darlene Paul, made brilliant parodies of pop music performances in the 1970s.

Stan Freberg presented large-cast parodies of radio and television shows. The

Hoffnung Music Festival made fun of composers and concerts.

In addition to Cosby, a number of distinctive Black comedians recorded in the 1960s and 1970s: Red Foxx, Dick Gregory, and Richard Pryor. Eddie Murphy's *Comedian* album (Columbia FC 39005; 1983) was on the charts 42 weeks.

Compact disc reissues have covered most of the comedians who appeared on LP. [Debenham 1988.]

COMMODORE (label). Issues of the **Commodore Music Shop**, New York. Beginning in 1938, the shop released 10-inch and 12-inch discs of jazz artists, featuring Dixieland; it became the first jazz **independent** label with any longevity, a model for Blue Note, Keynote, and similar pre-war competitors of the major firms. Milt Gabler, son of the shop owner, produced the discs. He was the first to list performers and recording dates on record labels. A principal early performer was Eddie Condon, guitarist; the roster eventually included such giants as Billie Holiday, Lester Young, Coleman Hawkins, and Fats Waller. Recording ceased in 1954. Many items were reissued on the Mainstream label (in "phony stereo" as Gabler once described it) in the 1960s; then by **Atlantic** and **Columbia**; and in the U.K. on Decca LPs. "The Complete Commodore Jazz Recordings" began to appear in 1988, a digitally remastered product of **Mosaic Records**. Volume I of the projected three-volume set consisted of 23 LP records. [Fox 1988; Rust 1978.]

COMMODORE MUSIC SHOP. A radio and record store located at 146 E. 42nd St., New York, specializing in jazz material, opened in 1924 by Julius Gabler. The shop became a gathering place for the jazz community, due to the energy and enthusiasm of Gabler's son, Milt. He sponsored Sunday afternoon jam sessions beginning in 1933–1934, apparently the first informal jazz concerts in New York; these took place in various locations, finally at Jimmy Ryan's Club, 53 W. 52nd St. Milt Gabler became interested in the reissue of unavailable records (he was the first to reissue jazz discs) and eventually established the **United Hot Clubs of America** collectors series. In 1938 the

shop began to market its distinguished label, **Commodore**. A significant reference publication originated there too: the first American edition of *Hot Jazz Discography* by **Charles Delaunay**. (1948). The shop closed in 1958, unable to compete with large mass market LP dealers like Sam Goody, who opened nearby. [Fox 1988.]

COMO, PERRY, 1913– . American popular singer and television star, born Pierino Como in Canonsburg, Pennsylvania, on 18 May 1913. While operating a barber shop in his home town he auditioned successfully with Freddie Carlone's band and went on the road with them. He was vocalist with Ted Weems from 1937 to 1942, then sang in clubs, theaters, and films. While with Weems he made records for Decca, starting with "Lazy Weather" (#822; 1936). On his own he signed with Victor in 1942, and initiated a series of million-selling discs: "Till the End of Time" (Victor #20–1709; 1945), "If I Loved You" (Victor # 20-1676; 1945), "A Hubba-hubba-hubba" (1945), "Temptation" (1945; Victor #20-1919; 1945), "Prisoner of Love" (Victor #20-1814; 1946), "I'm Always Chasing Rainbows" (1946), "When You Were Sweet Sixteen" (1947), and "Because" (Victor #20-2653). By 1969 he had sold 50 million discs. His last great hit record was "It's Impossible" (1970). He won the Emmy for male singer of 1954 and 1955; and a Grammy in 1958 for best male vocal, "Catch a Falling Star" (Victor #7128). Como's voice was distinctive and immediately recognizable, having a markedly casual character; though classed as a crooner, he did not indulge in the mannerisms associated with that group.

COMPACT DISC. Commonly known as the CD. A recording made with digital technology instead of the **analog recording** method that was employed from Edison's time through the LP era. The disc and the machine required to play it were offered first by **Philips** and **Sony** in 1983, producing a general sense in the industry that a true revolution had occurred—comparable to the introduction of **electrical recording** in 1924–1925.

In making a CD, the signal is taped first, just as in analog recording. Then it is sampled electronically: measured 44,100 times a second. The measurements are expressed as strings of digits (zeroes and ones), that is, in binary code. These binary strings are interpreted by a laser beam that cuts billions of corresponding pits into a **master** disc; from the master a **stamper** is made; and from the stamper the final CD is pressed. The disc itself is of molded plastic—a tough, scratch-resistant polycarbonate. It has a coating of aluminum film and a thin plastic covering; the signal pits are under the aluminum. There is an aluminum mirror as backing (only one side is used for the signal). During playback, a laser beam follows the spiral signal path—from center to edge—as the disc spins; the pits alternately reflect and scatter the light beam. Pulses of light reflect off the mirror to an optical sensor, which reads the pits in binary code into a microprocessor. At that stage the digital signal is reconverted to analog—and it can be perceived as sound once again.

A standard CD is 4 3/4 inches (11.9 centimeters) in diameter. "Mini CDs" of three-inch diameter came into production in the late 1980s as 20-minute counterparts to **45s**, but did not gain lasting success.

CD technology offers a number of advantages over its predecessors: (1) A standard CD holds a specification-defined maximum of 74 minutes on its single side, but variations can increase the playing time to about 80 minutes; (2) Playback is without added **noise**—nothing is heard but the original signal, with any noise it may have; (3) An ideal, flat **frequency response** is achieved across the entire **audio frequency range**; and (4) Since the surface of the disc is never touched by a stylus or other mechanical part, it does not wear with use. All CD players on the market in the early 1990s produced flawless playback, so the only differences to be noted in the output signal came from characteristics of the **amplifier** and **loudspeakers**, and to some extent from qualities of the disc (discs might occasionally be defective because of uneven coating, or scratches, or warp).

A system of codes has emerged to indicate how a CD was recorded: DDD means that digital equipment was used in the original tape recording, and in the mixing, editing, and mastering of the music. ADD indicates that the signal was tape recorded on analog equipment, but mixed and mastered digitally. AAD indicates that only the final master was digitally produced. CD remastering of records made before CD technology also uses AAD. While DDD is generally thought to give the best results, there are skeptics: some critics and musicians believe that digital recording is "cold," or that it lacks "fuzziness" or nuance. One critic noted in 1987 that "the highest quality sound I've heard on a record was from a **Direct-disc** LP, not a CD" (Ault 1987). But the latest word on the LP/CD question is that "the very best CDs, replayed on first-rate players through high quality replay equipment, do convey almost all that one could ask for, and have an authority of pitch, rhythm and perspective which as previously been unavailable beyond the engineer's mixing desk" (Humphreys).

A lingering doubt about CDs pertains to their longevity. Many people remember unfortunate experiences with acetate **tape** in the 1950s (which seemed to self-destruct in a few years, often with music copied from 78s that had been discarded after the dubbing). Later tape materials have proved more durable, but they are subject to **print-through** and frequently to squeals as well. And the fact must be faced that there is no long-term research to determine what may happen to the CD signals over time, or under adverse conditions of storage. However, there is no evidence that a rumored condition called "CD rot" is real; and the state of knowledge in 1992 suggests that compact discs may well last indefinitely with their signals intact. (*See* PRESERVATION OF SOUND RECORDINGS.)

The making of LPs has virtually ceased in the U.S. and U.K., and sales have fallen steadily (*see* DISC, 6). Many shops no longer carry LPs. Manufacturers are busily transferring LP material to CD. The venerable *Schwann Catalog* actually changed the name of its monthly listing of the American market to *Schwann Compact Disc Catalog*; but this move proved premature, and LPs are still included. (*Schwann* did change its name again; *see* the Bibliography.) CD players are available for automobiles (*see* AUTOMOBILE SOUND SYSTEMS) and there are portable models for joggers. Changers that could handle up to 10 CDs were on the market in 1992.

Interactive compact discs (CD-I) were introduced in 1987, opening yet another technological door. CD-I is an application of the CD-ROM format. It allows simultaneous storage of audio, video, graphics, text, and data—displayed on a screen and played through CD audio systems. This combination of media is possible because the standard for CDs allows only 95 percent of a disc to be utilized for audio information, with the other 5 percent saved for visual data. JVC offered the first adapters for the format, which they term CD+Graphics, or CD+G, in July 1989. Finally, there is CD-R, the blank compact disc on which the user may record (once only: the so-called WORM principle, "write-once-read-many times). These contrast with the CD-E disc, which is erasable and reusable. There are obvious **copyright** considerations connected with these two formats, especially when the possibility of a twin-deck CD-R machine comes forward—a machine that would inspire home copying of CDs. CD-V is a combination of CD and laser-vision technology, offering video with the audio programming.

A by-product of the CD revolution has been the rise of compact disc clubs, primarily the CBS Compact Disc Club, and the BMG Disc Club; they provide mail order service on new discs. Another by-product has been in print media: In addition to *Schwann* there is now the *CD Guide* twice a year (*see* the Bibliography), and a cluster of CD selection aids. [Ault 1987; Borwick 1987/3; 1989; Klinger*; Pohlmann 1989.]

COMPAGNIE AMERICAINE DU PHONO-GRAPH EDISON. Also referred to as the Compagnie du Phonograph Edison. The French branch of Thomas Edison's **National Phonograph Co.,** located in Paris, organized to manufacture and distribute his cylinders. It opened around 1898.

COMPAGNIE FRANÇAISE DU GRAMOPHONE. A branch of the Gramophone Co., established in Paris by **Alfred Clark** in 1899. It sold **Zonophone** records, among them the one-minute **Baby**.

COMPAGNIE GÉNÉRALE DES PHONOGRAPHES. A firm noted for its involvement in landmark litigation in Brussels, Belgium, during 1906. The court supported the right of talking machine companies to make records without paying royalties to the composers, based on a strict interpretation of the Bern Convention. *See also* COPYRIGHT.

COMPANDING. A term derived from the phrase "compressing and expanding," indicating an action upon the signal in a sound system that alternately reduces and increases its **amplitude.**

COMPATIBLE. (I) In relation to sound recordings, a term that refers to the **stereophonic** discs or **cassettes** that can be played without damage on **monophonic** playback equipment, or to **quadraphonic** discs playable on stereo equipment.

COMPATIBLE. (II) A term applied to elements of a sound system that can be used efficiently together. For practical purposes all parts of a modern analog sound system, regardless of manufacturer, will have enough compatibility (e.g., in voltage levels and impedance) to avoid **distortion.** Problems of non-compatibility may arise in digital systems, if an element departs from the original Sony/Philips digital-interface standard. [Hirsch 1988.]

COMPENSATION. An adjustment of responses in a sound system to rectify deficiencies in balance of **frequencies** (*see* EQUALIZATION) or loudness (*see* LOUDNESS CONTROL).

COMPENSATOR. An electronic circuit in a sound system that modifies the **frequency response** in a predetermined manner.

COMPLIANCE. (I) The capability of a **loudspeaker** diaphragm to yield or flex in accord with the power of the incoming signal.

COMPLIANCE. (II) In a **cartridge**, the capability to respond freely to the groove undulations. High compliance, combined with low tip mass in the **stylus**, is the preferred condition for reducing groove wear. However, excessive compliance can introduce **distortion**. The electrical property that corresponds to compliance is **capacitance.** *See also* MECHANICAL-ELECTRICAL ANALOGIES.

COMPO COMPANY, LTD. A Canadian firm, established in the Montreal suburb of Lachine by Herbert S. Berliner on 2 Nov 1921. Berliner (son of Emile Berliner) had been president of Berliner Gramophone Co. of Montreal, the Canadian Victor affiliate, but he resigned in April 1921 in a policy dispute with Victor. The Compo label, **Apex**, provided steady competition for Canadian Victor; it was among the earliest to issue electrical recordings (in late 1925, identified first as "New Process" records, then as "Electrophonic"), and was instrumental in driving down prices of the major firms by lowering its own. From 1923 to 1925 Compo issued **race records** in the U.S., under the label name **Ajax. MCA, Inc.** acquired Compo in 1964. [Robertson 1983; Tennyson 1987.]

COMPOSER RECORDINGS. In 1889 Johannes Brahms became the first major composer to perform his music on record; he played (in Vienna) his "Hungarian Dance Number 1" for an Edison cylinder, using the Perfected Phonograph. Jules Massenet recorded a scene from his *Sappho* in 1903, with soprano Georgette Leblanc Maeterlinck. Camille Saint-Saens was recorded in 1904 and 1919, doing original piano works and transcriptions.

Welte-Mignon's reproducing piano rolls included performances by numerous composer-pianists (*see* REPRODUCING PIANO RECORDINGS).

Composers of later generations appear frequently in the catalogs, performing on disc and tape. Moore 1964 has a useful list of composers, grouped by country, with records (excluding rolls) of their own music. The list gives only material in the Yale Historical Collection. [Griffiths 1976.]

COMPOSER RECORDINGS, INC. A record company established in 1954 by Otto Luening, Douglas Moore, and Oliver Daniel to concentrate on contemporary music. Support was given by the American Composers Alliance, the Martha Baird Rockefeller Fund for Music, Inc., and other foundations. The company was able to release one or two records per month, and had issued more than 200 albums by 1974. All formats have been marketed, LP, cassette, and CD. The company is located at 170 W. 74th St., New York. [Harman 1974.]

COMPOSERS, AUTHORS AND PUBLISHERS ASSOCIATION OF CANADA, LTD. (CAPAC). Also known by its French name, Association des Compositeurs, Auteurs et Éditeurs du Canada. The **performance rights** society for the country, with official jurisdiction over copyright fee collection. Its original name was the Canadian Performing Right Society (1925). The main office is in Toronto.

COMPRESSION MOLDING. The process of forming a disc by compressing a quantity of suitable plastic in a cavity. *See also* DISC, 3.

COMPTON-PRICE CO. A firm located in Coshocton, Ohio. It made the Stradivara disc player in 1916–1918.

CONCENTRIC GROOVE. The closed circular groove on a disc that follows the **lead-out groove**; it is also called the finishing groove.

CONCERT. A term applied to wide (five-inch) diameter cylinders produced by various manufacturers beginning in late 1898, and to the machines used to play them. *See also* CYLINDER, 4.

CONCERT (label). (I) A disc sold by **Leeds & Catlin** in 1906, a sister to their **Imperial** label.

CONCERT (label). (II) A product of the Concert Record Manufacturing Co., 145 W. 45th St., New York. Only one series of 69 discs has been located, all issued in 1920. Henry Burr and the Peerless Quartet were among the artists, but the overall offering was not distinguished. Some of the material was taken from

Lyric records. Priced higher than Victor and Columbia records, and having no special features, the label was not successful, and surviving examples are very rare. [Rust 1978.]

CONCERT HALL (label). One of the early LP labels, listed in the first Schwann Catalog, issued by the Concert Hall Society (250 W. 57th St., New York) from 1949 to 1958. The first issues, sold by subscription, were of violinist Louis Kaufman performing Vivaldi and Khachaturian. Later the records were sold in shops. Popular and international material was also recorded.

Concertgebouw Orchestra. *See* ROYAL CONCERTGEBOUW ORCHESTRA OF AMSTERDAM.

Concertophone. *See* SKELLY MANUFACTURING CO.

CONDENSITE. A plastic coating material for discs, developed by **Jonas Aylsworth** and his associates in the Edison laboratories around 1910. It was a thermosetting pheno resin, virtually the same as Bakelite, which was being developed by Leo Baekeland at the General Bakelite Co. These inventions marked the beginnings of the modern plastics industry.

CONDON-AUTOSTOP CO. A firm located at 26 Front St., New York. It was maker and distributor of the Autostop—a device that stopped rotation of the turntable when a disc had played its final groove. The first advertising appeared in 1911. The Autostop worked by means of a circular weight placed on the center of the record, with a steel pointer extending from it; the pointer had to be adjusted to coincide with the last groove. A tripper attached to the side of the machine would catch the pointer. In 1913 the company announced its Noset device, referred to in the advertising as an "autostartstop."

Cone. *See* LOUDSPEAKER.

CONFÉDÉRATION INTERNATIONALE DE SOCIÉTÉS D'AUTEURS ET COMPOSITEURS (CISAC). An international association of collecting societies, located in Paris. Member associations are those in each country that are concerned with **copyright** protection and collection of royalties in the area of **performance rights.**

CONFREY, ZEZ, 1895–1971. American composer and ragtime pianist, born Edward Elezear Confrey in Peru, Illinois, on 3 Apr 1895; noted for his virtuoso novelty numbers. He recorded on piano rolls, and made highly popular discs of his own "Kitten on the Keys" (Emerson 10486; Victor 18900; Brunswick 2082; 1921), "Dizzy Fingers" (Victor 20777; 1927), and many others. He began as a student of classical piano at the Chicago Musical College; and he appeared in the "Experiment in Modern Music," the Paul Whiteman concert of 1924 in which Gershwin's *Rhapsody in Blue* had its premiere. Confrey died on 22 Nov 1971 in Lakewood, New Jersey. [Jasen 1971.]

CONNOLLY, DOLLY, 1886?-1965?. American popular singer, born in Chicago. She teamed with her husband, composer Percy Wenrich, to make several successful records for Columbia, beginning with "Hula Hula Love" and "Red Rose Rag" (#A1028; 1911). Her big hit was in Wenrich's song "Moonlight Bay" (Columbia #A1128; 1912). Her last Columbia was made in 1916, after which she was heard on Emerson. She made no records after 1920, but continued to perfrom on stage. [Walsh 1973/6.]

CONNORIZED MUSIC CO. A firm located at 144th St. and Austin Place, New York. It was the maker of the "Connorized music rolls," and in 1921–1922 a series of 10-inch lateral-cut discs bearing the Connorized label. About a hundred discs were issued, popular song and dance material, some from Gennett masters, others from Invicta Record Company's Guardsman Record masters. [Andrews*.]

CONQUEROR (label). Originally one of the **Plaza Music Co.** subsidiaries, offering popular selections from 1926 to 1942. For a time it was distributed by **Sears, Roebuck, and Co.** Eventually it became a **CBS** line. [Rust 1978.]

CONSOLIDATED RECORD CORP. A firm located in Newark, New Jersey, incorporated to make records in July 1926. [Andrews*.]

CONSOLIDATED RECORDS, INC. A New York firm whose General Records Division produced the **General** label in the 1930s and 1940s. It was located at 1600 Broadway, then at 415 Lexington Ave. (1947), and at 289 Nepperhan Ave., Yonkers, New York (1949). Popular and jazz material was offered. The catalog was acquired by **Commodore.**

CONSOLIDATED TALKING MACHINE CO. (I) A firm established by **Eldridge Johnson** in 1900 to make disc records and players for them. The **Nipper** trademark was used on company products. On 3 Oct 1901 this organization became the **Victor Talking Machine Co.** [Fagan 1983 includes a label list.]

CONSOLIDATED TALKING MACHINE CO. (II) A Chicago firm, established in January 1916. It was located (1923) at 227 W. Washington St. Consolidated sold 10-inch, double-sided discs under the labels Consolidated, **Harmony, Standard,** and **United.** It also handled record players and supplies. In September 1918 it advertised that it was the successor to the businesses of the **Standard Talking Machine Co., United Talking Machine Co., Harmony Talking Machine Co., O'Neill James Co.,** and the **Aretino Co.** The final report from the firm appeared in 1930. [Andrews*; Fabrizio 1972; Fabrizio 1973.]

CONSOLIDATED TALKING MACHINE CO. (III) A Detroit firm, located at 2957 Gratiot.

CONSOLIDATED TALKING MACHINE CO. (IV) A Minneapolis company, located at 1427 Washington Ave. South.

CONSTANT AMPLITUDE. In disc recording, a characteristic of the **stylus** swing. There is no change in the amplitude of the swing regardless of frequency changes, and groove displacement is proportional to signal amplitude.

CONSTANT VELOCITY. In disc recording, a characteristic of the lateral movement of the **stylus.** Velocity is unchanged despite changes in frequency. Groove displacement is inversely proportional to the signal frequency.

CONTEMPORARY HITS RADIO (CHR). A popular music broadcasting format on FM radio, comparable to **Album Oriented Rock (AOR).** The dominant **disc jockey** style of the 1980s and 1990s, it is basically Top 40 programming, with the greatest number of repetitions given to songs highest on the charts. The intended audience is the 18–34 age group. In contrast to AOR, the CHR format typically rejects material older than one year.

CONTEMPORARY RECORDS (label). A record issued by Contemporary Records, 8481 Melrose, Los Angeles, from 1953. The firm was among the pioneers in stereo. Jazz and classical material was offered. Grammy winning jazz albums by **André Previn** appeared in 1960 and 1961.

Content announcements. *See* ANNOUNCEMENTS.

CONTOUR PULSE. In **magnetic recording,** a secondary pulse that occurs when a recorded tape passes over a gap in the **read head.** This gap results from edges in the core material.

Control amplifier. *See* PREAMPLIFIER.

CONTROL UNIT. The part of an **amplifier** that contains the **controls;** it is usually combined with a **preamplifier.**

CONTROLS. Devices in a playback system that allow the user to modify or direct the signal. Early players were without controls; in order to have a loud or quiet performance of a turn-of-the-century disc, for example, it was necessary to use a **needle** designed for one result or the other. Later the problem of volume was approached through size of **loudspeaker** or by opening doors or louvers that affected the output of **enclosed horns.** The first **volume controls** appear to have been the so-called tone-controls of the 1916 **Pathéphone,** or the **Sonora** "tone modifier."

The need for measurement of and control over **playing speed** of discs was recognized early, since there was wide variation in recording speeds and consequently in the **pitch** of the signal in playback. A speed meter for disc machines was advertised in 1907 by the **Phonographic Music Co.** Phonographs with levers to adjust **turntable** speed were common into the 1940s. Although there had been an attempt by the U.S. sound industry to stabilize recording speed with the advent of **electrical recording,** 78s were in fact made at speeds between 75 rpm and 80 rpm, by major labels, until the end of the 78 era. With the rise of LPs and 45s after 1949, disc players usually had a selector switch to move the turntable at either of those speeds, and also at 78 rpm. But intermediate speeds were no longer under control, until the hi-fi period brought refined concern for pitch, and variable speed turntables.

In the late 1950s, with hi-fi enthusiasm at its peak, the **control unit** of a sound system could have an **input selector** (to bring in a signal from radio, tape player, microphone, or turntable); an output switch (to direct the signal to the tape recorder, or to auxiliary speakers), **equalization** switches to suit the **recording curves** of various labels, or to emphasize certain frequency areas; treble and **rumble** filters; an **A & B switch;** treble and bass lifts; treble and bass attenuators; a gain compensator; and of course a volume control. That kind of array was reserved for expensive equipment. On systems of modest cost the only dials were for volume and "tone," which at that time referred to a bass or treble emphasis.

The controls on a medium-price **receiver** (the Mitsubishi DA-R25) in 1982 included: output switches for the two speakers, allowing either to be turned off; low and high filters; calibrated bass and treble emphasis dials; a tone toggle switch; a **balance control** dial to set the stereo output properly between left and right; and a loudness dial (to "contour the low and high frequency ranges at low volumes for much richer tonal balance").

By 1989 controls had reached extremes of complexity. The Revox B-250 **integrated am-**plifier, made to handle any signal source (standard phonograph, CD, radio, either of two tape decks, video—with an optional B-200 "controller"—or auxiliary input), had a volume control calibrated in 20 decibel increments; adjustments for maximum volume levels of each output; sensitivity adjustments for each input; treble and bass controls; tone-control defeat; a loudness compensation button; channel-balance dials; a button to separate preamp and amp; and a button to turn the pre-cut connections on and off. Like other high-cost models of the time (this Revox sold for $2000), it was digitally engineered.

COOL JAZZ. An idiom popular in the 1950s and 1960s, said to be an outgrowth of **bebop.** Terms applied to the sound include crisp, unemotional, dry, relaxed, light, clean, lyrical, and soft. It was practiced by solo pianists and small combos, among them **George Shearing, Dave Brubeck,** the **Modern Jazz Quartet, Gerry Mulligan, Miles Davis,** and **Stan Getz.** Cool jazz is sometimes identified with "Coast Jazz" or "West Coast Jazz"; definitions are a bit cloudy within this group.

COOMBS, FRANK, 1871–1941. American counter-tenor, heard in vaudeville and on Broadway. He began recording in 1910, with Columbia #A835, "Silver Threads among the Gold" and "Nellie Was a Lady." This initial issue remained his most popular disc. By 1913 he had 20 solos in the Columbia catalog, plus five duets with William H. Thompson and two songs with quartets. In 1914 he made another famous disc: "Caroline." From 1910 to 1913 he also recorded for U-S Everlasting Records. Coombs died in Seattle on 31 Oct 1941. [Walsh 1951/5.]

COON SONGS. It is by this unfortunate designation that the record companies of the first generation referred to comic songs in Negro dialect. Many of the singers were in fact white men and women. The Victor 1917 catalog states that "the humor of many of these songs cannot be called refined, and for that reason we have distinguished them from old-fashioned darky humor, those songs being listed under 'Negro

Songs'. . . ." Artists listed in that catalog as coon singers were the **American Quartet, Arthur Collins, Byron G. Harlan, Billy Golden, May Irwin, Ada Jones, Billy Murray, Len Spencer, Peerless Quartet,** and **Clarice Vance.** The 1927 catalog had no listing under this heading, and nothing under "darky."

COON-SANDERS ORCHESTRA. One of the earliest American Big Bands, organized in Kansas City around 1920, named for Carlton A. Coon (1894–1932) and Joe Sanders (1894–1965). The band was the first to broadcast on commercial radio, on WOAF in Kansas City, 5 Dec 1922. They had already begun to make records—in 1921 for Columbia—and in 1924 they started an association with Victor. Two of their hit records were "Here Comes My Ball and Chain" (Victor 21812; 1928) and "Slue Foot" (Victor 21305; 1927). [Schwartz 1984.]

COPY MASTER. (I) An identical copy of a **master** tape.

COPY MASTER. (II) A metal negative disc produced from the positive, for use as a replacement **master.**

COPYCODE. A system developed by CBS in 1987 to filter out a narrow band ("notch") of musical frequencies in a master recording. The purpose was to give a cue to a decoder device installed by manufacturers of **DAT** recorders; the decoder's response to the notch was to shut down the recorder. Thus unauthorized copying of a CD onto a DAT blank tape would be prevented. The notch itself was taken from the upper-middle range at 3.838 kHz; it was 112 Hz wide at the 3dB point and 90dB deep. Removing this tiny slice of the frequency band did not, according to CBS, affect the quality of the music, but certain specialists claimed to notice differences when the notch was activated. Controversy over the use of Copycode was crystallized in a London conference of the **International Federation of Producers of Phonograms and Videograms (IFPI)** in May 1987; the producers supported legislation by the European Economic Community and the U.S. Congress to require the Copycode device on all machines imported from Japan; but the Electronic Industry Association of Japan, representing the principal DAT manufacturers, opposed such regulation. Congress asked for an assessment from the National Bureau of Standards (NBS), which reported that "there are some selections for which the subjects detected differences between notched and unnotched material." The NBS conclusion was that the Copycode system "audibly degrades music, and can easily be bypassed." No action was taken by Congress to prohibit import of DAT, or to require Copycode protection.

A pair of anti-copying devices have since been developed by Philips to prevent making more than one DAT copy of a CD; but these pose problems. One system, Solo, has met with disfavor by the record companies because it permits multiple copying of analog material. The other, Solo Plus, is unacceptable to audio users because it permits no copying of analog material at all. Finally, a system was created that appeared to find favor among all parties concerned: **Serial Copy Management System (SCMS).** The acquisition of Columbia Records by Sony also tended to mute the controversy.

COPYRIGHT. Intellectual and creative productions are given legal protection in most countries; this protection insuring that the exclusive rights to distribution, reproduction, display, performance, or any commercial use of a work rests with its author, composer, or artist. Copyright is the equivalent, for intangible property, of the **patent.**

Problems in the interpretation of copyright issues, particularly when more than one nation is involved, are substantial. The Bern Convention of 1886 has formed a basis for international cooperation; the effectiveness of that agreement was enhanced in 1988 when the U.S. finally signed into it. The most recent international effort to deal with these matters resulted in the Universal Copyright Convention (UCC) of 1955, signed by all major countries except the Peoples Republic of China. UCC has for a basic principle the acceptance of each country's copyright legalities by all other countries. In most countries this protection extends 50 years after the death of the author. Types of works protected include literary and musical compositions, all forms of graphic art, motion pictures, sound recordings, and other kinds of audiovisual production.

In the U.K. a record company retains copyright for 50 years; legislation passed in 1925 protects artists against unauthorized reproduction of their performances.

In the U.S. the Copyright Act of 1976 (superseding one dating from 1909) became effective 1 Jan 1976. In 1988 Congress passed the Bern Convention Implementation Act, as an amendment of the 1976 legislation, to account for principles in the Bern agreement. The life-plus-50 years term of protection applies to works created after 1977, but for earlier works there is a complex system of terms and renewals. Indeed there are numerous complexities, e.g., in the area of transfers and licenses, which are not appropriate for discussion here. But one aspect of U.S. law is of special interest to those who are involved with recorded sound: the "fair use" principle. Essentially, fair use means that all or part of a copyrighted work may be copied legally without permission of the copyright holder if the use to be made of the copy is non-commercial and does not interfere with the author's own profits or exploitation of the work. Thus a teacher may photocopy a periodical article or section of a book for class distribution (not for sale), and anyone may copy a broadcast program for personal use. Libraries have certain privileges in the making of archival copies.

It is also permitted, under the 1976 Act, to copy commercial discs, audiotapes, and videotapes—always for private non-commercial purposes only—and this element of the law has caused great concern among producers of those media. While one may question the magnitude of financial loss to a record company when someone makes a cassette tape copy of a disc borrowed from the public library—the copy, as often as not, standing in place of non-ownership rather than in place of a personally purchased record—there seems little basis for disputing the claim of great losses to record companies that result from making copies for sale. The making of counterfeit records and tapes, an act usually called "pirating" or "bootlegging," is illegal when the copies are sold, but the practice has been carried on in a brazen manner. Some bootleg records have appeared

with distinctive labels, such as Rubber Dubber, and gained legitimacy by being listed among authorized labels in discographies and lists of new releases.

A special problem exists in the case of so-called parallel imports, imported versions of works copyrighted by U.S. firms. When the American firm holding the copyright does not actually release the material on record, or does release it but allows the record to go out of print, imports of the material are still prohibited under section 602(a) of the 1976 Copyright Act. Record dealers, supported by buyer groups, have held that what is not available in the U.S. should be exempt from import restrictions.

With the advent of **digital recording** it became possible for manufacturers to prevent or limit copying by means of protective codes imbedded in the disc or tape. [Stover 1990; Wallman 1989.] *See also* COPYCODE; PERFORMING RIGHTS ORGANIZATIONS; PIRATED RECORDS; RECORDING INDUSTRY ASSOCIATION OF AMERICA; SERIAL COPY MANAGEMENT SYSTEM.

CORAL (label). An American record issued from 1948, by Coral Records, Inc., 48 W. 57th St., New York, a Decca subsidiary. It was also sold in the U.K. Milt Gabler was one of the A & R men. The label's output covered popular, country, rhythm & blues, jazz, gospel, and spoken material. Coral merged with the new MCA label in 1973.

CORNER HORN. A **loudspeaker** enclosure that utilizes a corner of the room as part of the horn.

CORNET RECORDINGS. The cornet recorded well with early equipment, and music for the instrument was in all the label catalogs around the turn of the century. John Mittauer recorded 11 pieces for Edison on 28 May 1889; the first was the "Amusement Polka." On 8 June 1889 Theodore Hoch made his first five records; Mittauer returned for nine more sessions and Hoch for four more. Other cornetists heard on Edison cylinders during 1889–1892 were **Tom Clark**, D.B. Dana (who was also in the 1893 catalog of the New Jersey Phonograph

Co.), "Mr. Henke," Alvin Jaeger, J. Schmitt, and Frederico Sonty. Later Edison artists were John Hazel, M. Schlossberg, and W. Bartow. **W. Paris Chambers** was the earliest artist to record the cornet on disc, for Berliner in 1895–1897. Frank Martin performed 10 numbers for **Bettini** in 1898. **Herbert L. Clarke** was heard on Berliner seven-inch discs of 1899–1900, on Victor records in 1900–1906, and on Columbia and Brunswick discs; he also made cylinders for Edison. **Jules Levy** was the most famous concert cornetist of the 1890s. [Koenigsberg 1987.] *See also* TRUMPET RECORDINGS.

CORT (label). An American issue of the 1910–1920 period, of which only one specimen has surfaced. Cort Sales Co. was the producer, located at 330 Sixth Ave., New York. It appears that Columbia masters were used. The extant item is a male quartet rendition of "Oh, You Million Dollar Doll," backed by baritone Ed Morton singing "What Do You Mean, You Lost Your Dog?" [Brooks*; Kendziora 1952/11 (reprinted in *RR* 211/212, July 1985).]

CORTINA ACADEMY OF LANGUAGES. A New York firm, established to give language instruction by Rafael Diaz de la Cortina in the 1880s. The firm was the first to record language instruction courses, beginning in 1889 with *Spanish in Twenty Lessons*, on Edison cylinders. Later records appeared on Columbia Graphophone records and U-S Phonograph Co. cylinders, as well as Edison cylinders. Discs were used instead of cylinders after 1913.

CORTOT, ALFRED, 1877–1962. Swiss pianist and conductor, born in Nyon on 26 Sep 1877. He studied with one of Chopin's pupils, and became known as an interpreter of that master's works. He was also a conductor in Paris and Lille, specializing in Wagner. And he was part of the famous Casals-Thibaud-Cortot trio from 1905. Cortot wrote a number of books, edited a Chopin edition, and was director of the École Normale de Musique in Paris.

Cortot's recordings span 50 years. He was heard on the first Victor Red Seal electrical recording, playing the Chopin "Impromptu No. 2" (#6502; recorded 21 Mar 1925, released June 1925). Many of his finest interpretations have been reissued by EMI/Pathé-Marconi: #153–03090/96 includes seven discs of his Chopin performances recorded in 1933–1949; and #153–03490/92 has three discs of Schumann works. Cortot died in Lausanne on 15 June 1962.

COSMO (label). A product of Cosmopolitan Records, Inc., 745 Fifth Ave., New York, organized in 1945 by Harry W. Bank. The first album issued, *Tubby the Tuba*, became the first best seller on vinyl. Among Cosmo's artists were Tony Pastor and Larry Clinton. The final releases were in 1947.

COUNTRY AND WESTERN MUSIC RECORDINGS. Country and western music developed out of the folk traditions brought to North America by Anglo-Celtic immigrants and gradually absorbed influences from other musical sources until it emerged as a force strong enough to survive—and ultimately thrive—in an urban-industrial-oriented society. However, to explain the genre solely in terms of its British background would be a limited and incomplete approach. Settlers of pre-revolutionary America, throughout the 13 colonies, came out of essentially the same ethnic and social backgrounds. Malone points out that southern history must be studied in order to explain how the area east of the Mississippi River and below the Mason-Dixon line produced a diversity of musical styles—both Black and white—which later would coalesce into viable commercial entities. Historical study reveals that because of a complex variety of influences, involving geographical and climatological determinism and cultural preconditioning, southerners became committed very early to an agricultural economy and the rural way of life. Traditions which had once been the common property of Americans therefore endured in the South long after they had ceased to be important elsewhere. Although British ballads and folksongs were perpetuated in all areas of early America, only in the South did they contribute to the creation of a lasting regional music. (Malone 1968, p. 4.)

Two forces which have played a prominent role in shaping modern country music—cultural pride and the cross-fertilization of musical styles—can be traced back to the earliest days of colonization in the deep South. The extreme pride typifying the region was in large part a result of a cultural inferiority complex which, in turn, arose out of the censure of the civilized world with respect to the institution of slavery and the lagging pace of urbanization and industrialization. This situation undoubtedly heightened the cultural isolationism already based on geographical and climatological factors. However, reference to the cultural isolationism of the South is perhaps should not be overemphasized. The South provided the setting for the melding of many cultures—particularly British, French, Spanish, and African elements—as well as the impetus for the settlement of much of the West. The steadfastly conservative stance adopted by southerners to ward off potentially disruptive external influences was concentrated largely within the socio-economic sphere (particularly with respect to the influx of influences from the North); in the face of the region's prejudices relatively few barriers existed to impede the exchange of musical ideas between cultures. While this musical cross-fertilization changed all of the genres concerned, country music continued to maintain its own sense of identity. Malone succinctly outlines the development of this phenomenon:

> Not only are certain songs transmitted from generation to generation, but the manner of performing them, both vocally and instrumentally, is also passed on through the years. A folk style, created by the interchange of musical ideas and techniques among folk musicians and singers, proves to be a very tenacious factor. A folk style will persist long after the folk songs are forgotten. With the coming of urbanization the old rustic-based songs are discarded and the new ones become largely devoid of rural settings; however, in the style of its performance and in its basic construction the song is, in point of origin, rural in nature. A rural inhabitant or an urban dweller who has formerly lived in the country will likely render a song in a country manner even though the words of the song describe an urban

scene or event. This is significant in view of the fact that migration from southern rural areas to southern and northern urban centers has been a steady factor in southern life. Southern cities have been populated largely by individuals of rural origin who carry with them their musical appreciation and tastes. These cities, then, to a great extent continue to be affected by rural attitudes and values. This in great measure explains why country music has endured in an urbanizing south, and why its lyric content has changed to fit the needs of a rural people who no longer live in rural surroundings. That music which thrives in a honky-tonk atmosphere or depicts the problems inherent in an urban existence can accurately be termed country music since it sprang from a rural origin. (Malone 1968, p. 10.)

The spread of country music in an era devoid of mass media outlets such as radio and television was rendered possible by territorial mobility, cultural exchange, and other forces set into motion by the socio-economic climate of the late 19th and early 20th centuries. The process involved the slow but steady evolution of the country genre via the assimilation of minor traits and styles.

> When southern people moved into new areas, their music acquired new characteristics from the cultures with which they came in contact. Still, a distinct southern backwoods style predominated and provided the basis for other styles that ultimately arose. It is for this reason that such urban-oriented styles as "western swing" and "honky-tonk" music developed when rural people adapted their older music to new environments. Western swing, specifically, is the product of the change that took place when southerners moved to Texas and Oklahoma and adapted the rural- or mountain-based music to new developments and surroundings. (Malone 1968, p. 11.)

The rise of radio and the record industry were of inestimable importance in broadening the audience for country music. Long before country headliners began criss-crossing the nation in customized buses, these media brought the performers into the living rooms of fans in the large northern cities. However, the genre was long known by the somewhat derogatory term "hillbilly music." The cultural pride of the antebellum South was updated in the campaign of leading apologists for the genre to have the more dignified heading "country and western" employed (see 1949 below). Others sought mainstream acceptance via the aesthetically misguided strategy of diluting country recordings with pop orchestral arrangements.

A Country Chronology:

June 30, 1922. "Uncle" Eck Robertson and Henry Gilliand record two fiddle tunes—"Sallie Goodin" and "The Arkansas Traveller" for Victor in New York. Scholars are largely in agreement that these were the first country recordings.

August 14, 1922. The Jankins Family, a gospel group from Georgia, become the first "old time" performers to be heard on the radio (WSB, Atlanta).

January 4, 1923. WBAP, Forth Worth, broadcast the first radio "barn dance" program.

June 14, 1923. Ralph Peer records Fiddlin' John Carson's "Little Old Log Cabin in the Lane," considered to be country's earliest hit. The Carson recording proved that country records could sell.

April 19, 1924. The debut of the *Chicago Barn Dance* (WLS), which went on to become the highly successful *National Barn Dance*. The program, which ran continuously until 1970, and launched such stars as **Gene Autry, Red Foley**, George Gobel, Grandpa and Ramona Jones, and Bradley Kincaid.

August 13, 1924. **Vernon Dalhart** records "The Prisoner's Song," backed with "The Wreck of the Old 97," the first country record to sell a million copies. Technically, Dalhart was the first singer to change from pop to country, having specialized in light opera and parlor songs prior to recording "The Prisoner's Song."

November 28, 1925. The *WSM Barn Dance*, later renamed the *Grand Ole Opry*, first broadcast from WSM's Studio A in Nashville. Uncle

Dave Macon, credited with being the *Opry's* initial star, began appearing during the first year.

August 1927. The **Carter Family** and **Jimmie Rodgers** cut their first records for Ralph Peer of Victor, in Bristol, Tennessee/Virginia. These sessions mark the beginning of commercial country music.

September 28, 1928. Technically, the first record ever made in Nashville is a Victor field recording of early *Opry* string bands. The real start of regular recording in Nashville did not begin until 1945.

October 9, 1929. Gene Autry, who would become America's most popular "Singing Cowboy," makes his first record. His first movie role was a cameo in Ken Maynard's *In Old Santa Fe*. Later that same year Autry starred in *The Phantom Empire*.

1929. *The Singing Brakeman*, a 15-minute short starring Jimmie Rodgers, is made; it is probably the earliest country music movie.

1930. Ken Maynard, starring in *Song of the Saddle*, becomes Hollywood's first singing cowboy.

1930. Dr. J.R. Brinkley, the infamous "goat gland doctor," begins broadcasting country music from radio station XERA in Villa Acuna, Mexico, just across the border from Del Rio, Texas. XERA was instrumental in establishing country music on the West Coast via the migrants who left Oklahoma's dust bowl for California.

1933. **Bob Wills** forms his Texas Playboys, the definitive Western swing band in America.

1933. WLS's *National Barn Dance* joins NBC's Blue Network, the first country barn dance show to be aired nationally.

August 16, 1935. **Patsy Montana** records "I Want To Be A Cowboy's Sweetheart," the earliest country release by a female singer to sell a million copies.

1935. **Juke boxes** are introduced to truck stops and restaurants in the South. The juke box had a profound effect on the kinds of music that country performers recorded, and helped influence the development of the honky-tonk style.

May 1939. Red River Dave sings his composition "The Ballad of Amelia Earhart" on television, from the RCA Pavilion at the 1939 World's Fair in New York, and proclaims himself to be "the world's first television star."

October 1939. **Bill Monroe** makes his initial appearance on the Opry stage, singing "Muleskinner Blues," thereby giving birth to bluegrass music.

1940. Clell Summey, of **Pee Wee King**'s Golden West Cowboys, plays the electric guitar on the Opry stage, claiming to be the first musician to do so; however, the priority is also claimed by Sam McGee and Paul Howard.

1941. **Bing Crosby** records "You Are My Sunshine" and "New San Antonio Rose." These were probably the first country "crossover" hits—that is, they were popular with a national, not merely country, audience.

1941. An electric guitar is used for the first time on a country music record. According to the story, juke box operators complained to **Ernest Tubb** that his records could not be heard over the din of their noisy honky tonks. Tubb proceeded to employ Fay (Smitty) Smith, staff guitarist for KGKO in Fort Worth, to play electric guitar on one of his recording sessions.

1943. **Elton Britt**'s "There's A Star-Spangled Banner Waving Somewhere," a song about a crippled boy who wants to help with the war effort, becomes country music's first gold record (awarded by his label).

1943. Fred Rose and **Roy Acuff** form Acuff-Rose, the first song publishing firm located in Nashville. Acuff-Rose became an outlet for country songwriters like **Hank Williams**, who probably could not have obtained songwriting contracts in Northern urban centers.

1944. *Billboard*, the music industry's leading trade publication, introduces the first country music popularity charts, under the heading "Most Played Juke Box Folk Records," thereby further legitimizing the country music business.

March/April 1945. **Red Foley** records at WSM's Studio B; he is considered to be the first performer to record officially in Nashville, aside from the 1928 Victor field recordings.

September 11, 1945. Ernest Tubb makes "It Just Don't Matter Now" and "When Love Turns to Hate," under the direction of Decca's **Paul Cohen**, Nashville's first major producer; many date the real start of commercial recording in Nashville to this session. By 1960, less than 15 years after the first recording studio had been

built, most of the major recording companies were doing all of their country recording in Nashville, and by 1963 Nashville had 10 studios, 10 talent agencies, four recording-pressing plants, 26 record companies, and nearly 2,000 musicians and writers.

September 18/19, 1947. Ernest Tubb and Ray Acuff headline New York's Carnegie Hall, the first country music show ever presented in that venue; people had to be turned away from the doors.

1947. Harold "Sticks" McDonald, of Pee Wee King's Golden West Cowboys, plays drums on the stage of the *Grand Ole Opry*. His claim to have been the first to do so is disputed by Smokey Dacus, of Bob Wills and his Texas Playboys, who says that he played drums at the Opry in 1946—behind the curtains. Even today, nothing more than a simple set of snare drums is allowed on the Opry stage.

January 13, 1948. *Midwestern Hayride*, the first country music show to be broadcast regularly on television, debuts on WLW, Cincinnati.

1949. *Billboard* changes the name of its country music charts from "Most Played Juke Box Folk Records" to "Country and Western," thereby legitimizing the term in the business.

September 30, 1950. The *Opry* is broadcast by television for the first time.

1951. **Patti Page** and **Tony Bennett** record "Tennessee Waltz" and "Cold, Cold Heart," respectively, and achieve mass popularity for country songs for the first time since 1941. The Bennett recording is Hank Williams' first crossover hit and does much to make the latter's name known nationally.

1952. **Eddy Arnold** becomes the first country star to host a network television show when he is chosen to be Perry Como's summer replacement on NBC-TV.

1954. The pedal steel guitar is first used on record, played by Bud Isaacs on **Webb Pierce**'s "Slowly."

1955. George Jones has his first hit, "Why Baby Why?" **Johnny Cash** makes his earliest recordings (on the Sun label).

1957. The **Country Music Association**, the oldest country music trade organization, is formed.

1958. The **Kingston Trio**'s "Tom Dooley" wins the initial country music Grammy award. The group's growing popularity was an early signal that rockabilly was already entering a decline; "Tom Dooley" helped spark the folk music revival of the early 1960s.

July 19, 1960. **Loretta Lynn's** first hit, "Honky Tonk Girl," enters the *Cash Box* country music charts.

November 3, 1961. Fred Rose, Hank Williams, and Jimmie Rodgers are installed as the first members of the Country Music Hall of Fame.

December 13, 1961. Jimmy Dean's album, *Big Bad John*, becomes the first country music record to receive the gold certification (signifying sales of a million dollars) from the Recording Industry Association of America.

1964. Johnny Cash records "It Ain't Me, Babe," becoming the first country singer to cut a **Bob Dylan** song.

1966. Bob Dylan becomes the first of the new generation of rock singers to make a major album in Nashville, *Blonde on Blonde*.

October 1967. The first Country Music Association Awards show is held.

1967. The first country rock album—*Safe At Home* by the International Submarine Band, featuring Gram Parsons—is released. One year later, Parsons joins the Byrds and the group produces *Sweetheart of the Rodeo*, a milestone in that genre.

1969. *Hee Haw*, the highly popular syndicated country television show, makes its debut.

1971. The first annual Fan Fair is held in Nashville's Municipal Auditorium.

March 1972. The first Dripping Springs, Texas, "Picnic" is held; the three-day redneck-meets-hippie festival includes **Willie Nelson**, who began sponsoring the event the following year. Thus begins outlaw music's dominance of the genre.

1972. Loretta Lynn is elected the Country Music Association's "Entertainer of the Year," the first woman to be so honored.

1973. The Opryland amusement park opens for business.

March 19, 1974. The *Grand Ole Opry*'s first show at the new Opry House, on the grounds of Opryland, U.S.A., takes place.

1974. George Hamilton IV becomes the first country performer to tour the U.S.S.R.

1976. *Wanted: The Outlaws* (RCA), featuring **Waylon Jennings,** Willie Nelson, Jessi Colter, and Tompall Glaser, becomes the first country

music record to be awarded the platinum designation (signifying sales of 1,000,000 copies of an album) by the RIAA.

1980. The Mandrell sisters—Barbara, Louise, and Irlene—become the first female country singers to host a regularly scheduled network television show.

1980. Paramount releases the film, *Urban Cowboy*, starring John Travolta. The movie is largely responsible for making country music a bankable commodity with middle America in the early 1980s. Prime growth areas include honky tonks (particularly Gilley's, a bar in Pasadena, Texas, where part of *Urban Cowboy* was filmed), country dress fashions and crossover hits, most notably by Mickey Gilley, Juice Newton, Dolly Parton, **Kenny Rogers,** Ronnie Milsap, and Eddie Rabbitt.

The drive within the country field for respectability in the eyes of the music business establishment as well as the population at large has been the overriding theme in the genre's development during the 20th century. The major record labels were content to allow the independents to dominate the field until after World War II. Radio was somewhat more responsive; however, the modest rise of barn dances and other live country music performances represented a relatively small dent in an overall picture dominated by big-time network programming. Much has been made of the appearance of WSM's *Grand Ole Opry* broadcasts in 1925. In reality the event's short-term impact was largely symbolic in nature; many other clear-channel radio stations (e.g., WLS, Chicago; WBAP, Ft. Worth; WWVA, Wheeling) had successful barn dance programs. In the long-term, though, the Opry acted as a magnet for the country music industry, providing a central focus for recording, promotional, recreational and archival activities (see "September 11, 1945" above). The "Nashville Sound," under the leadership of Chet Atkins, projected the aura of urban sophistication combined with a proper respect for stylistic roots needed to render country music a powerful commercial force within the entertainment business beginning in the mid-1960s. Despite recent challenges to its hegemony, Nashville remains the commercial center and artistic soul of country music, thereby endowing the field with a solidarity and unified posture missing in all other spheres of American popular music. Still, underneath this seemingly homogenous exterior can be found the diversified array of styles that have endowed country music with its present day character. An awareness of these styles is central to an understanding of the broader entity. The leading subgenres (derived from Hume 1982, Malone 1968, and Stambler 1969) include:

1. *The Bakersfield Sound.* Music performed by musicians centered in Bakersfield, California, in the late 1950s and early 1960s; for example, Buck Owens, **Merle Haggard**, and Wynn Stewart. The style is rawer and more rhythmic than the Nashville Sound. The first time country music produced in California achieved popularity on a national level, marking the beginning of the end of Nashville's domination of country music recording.

2. *Bluegrass.* A comparatively modern style; the chief difference between bluegrass and the string band music of the Appalachian region that preceded it is the emphasis the former places on rhythm and on instrumental virtuosity. Two major schools exist: the instrumental style, often compared to jazz, most frequently associated with Bill Monroe, the father of bluegrass music, and "the high lonesome sound" (vocal music), best exemplified by the Stanley Brothers' output. **Flatt & Scruggs**, via the *Beverly Hillbillies* and the college concert circuit, stimulated a revival of the style in the 1960s; many rock artists (e.g. the Grateful Dead, Gram Parsons) incorporated it into their work.

3. *Cajun.* Music made by French colonials who eventually settled in southern Louisiana. It incorporates many elements of the French culture of the region: (a) it is usually sung in the local patois, which is a corrupt form of the French language; (b) many bands include both an accordion player and a fiddler; and (c) most songs are played in three-quarter waltz time. No performer adhering to a pure Cajun style has ever been commercially successful in the country field; however, many Cajun-influenced musicians such as Moon Mullican, Jimmy C. Newman, and Doug and Rusty Kershaw have had country hits.

4. *Conjunto.* A style of music popular along the border between Mexico and the U.S., incorporating elements of both Cajun and German music. Conjunto bands usually employ an accordion player, while the music is played in either waltz or polka time. Doug Sahm, Augie Meyer, and Freddy Fender have all been heavily influenced by the sound.

5. *Country Blues.* Often used as a code phrase to refer to music made by white singers who have incorporated Black elements into their style; for example, Jimmie Rodgers, Hank Williams, Bill Monroe, and Ronnie Milsap.

6. *Country Rock.* Amorphous genre including anything from country songs sung with rock instrumentation to rock songs sung by country singers, to country songs sung by rock singers, to country music sung by anyone who is not from the country. Classic country is generally acknowledged to have been the creation of Gram Parsons; he brought country to the attention of many rock artists, helped stimulate the singer/songwriter movement beginning in the early 1970 and, in the South, encouraged country-based performers to fuse that genre with rock.

7. *Folk Music.* Refers to two major strains: (a) country folk, which includes songs that have been passed down orally from generation to generation, usually originating with European material. Noteworthy exponents have been Bradley Kincaid and the Carter Family. (b) Urban folk differs in that the music is generally employed to achieve a political end. Chief practitioners have included **Woody Guthrie, Pete Seeger, Joan Baez,** and Bob Dylan.

8. *Gospel Music.* Also divided into two styles: while Black gospel is the more energetic and rhythmic of the two, white gospel has exerted a greater influence on country music. Because the genre features a more emotional, exhortative singing style than is the case with country, gospel-influenced singers like Roy Acuff, Wilma Lee, and Stoney Cooper have changed country vocalizing completely and helped to place the solo singer in the foreground, thereby leading to the creation of a star system.

9. *Hard Country*. Generally means making no concessions to fad or fashion, using classic country instruments (usually amplified) and featuring the singer rather than the accompaniment or the song. Sometimes used as a synonym for "classic country"; that is, music not adulterated by rock or blues styles.

10. *Honky Tonk Music*. Originally referred to any music played in a honky tonk. Later, it meant music amplified to be heard over crowd noise and addressing the patrons' real concerns—adultery, divorce, rootlessness, and drinking. A subgenre of hard country; leading practitioners have included Ernest Tubb, Lefty Frizzell, Hank Williams, **George Jones, Hank Thompson,** and Gary Stewart.

11. *The Nashville Sound*. Technically the style played by a certain group of musicians working in Nashville in the late 1950s and early 1960s. Because record companies did not allow individual performers to use their own bands and producers while making a record, and because Chet Atkins, who headed the A & R division for RCA in Nashville, had such a large roster of talent to produce, the instrumental arrangements—which utilized the same group of session musicians—became both predictable and standardized. Compared to the country music that preceded it, the Nashville Sound is slick and sophisticated. Prime exponents include Jim Reeves, Webb Pierce, and Floyd Cramer.

12. *Old Time Music*. Refers to either pre-commercial country music or the work of modern musicians who play in the old styles. Sometimes used interchangeably with the term "country folk music."

13. *Outlaw Country*. Originally designated a loose-knit group of musicians—Waylon Jennings, Willie Nelson, Tompall Glaser, Billy Joe Shaver, **Kris Kristofferson,** for example—who objected to the common Nashville practice of awarding creative control of recording sessions to the record company's staff producers rather than to the artists themselves. These artists chose to work outside the existing system by pressuring the record labels to give them control over their own work. As a result, the outlaws produced some of the best work of their respective careers and sold equally well to the non-country market and the traditional

country core audience. This success undermined the dominance of the Nashville Sound, thereby rendering the movement passé.

14. *Progressive Country*. A term coined in Texas during the early 1970s, when young, rock-influenced musicians began mixing with mainstream country musicians at places like the Armadillo World Headquarters in Austin. Ironically, the genre is often traditional in approach; for example, Asleep at the Wheel's revival of the classic western swing of the late 1930s. Frequently used interchangeably with "redneck rock."

15. *Rockabilly*. A hybrid formed out of the intermingling of rhythm & blues and country. The best-known practitioners began their careers with Sun Records in Memphis, including **Elvis Presley,** Jerry Lee Lewis, Carl Perkins, Johnny Cash, and Charlie Rich. Others such as the **Everly Brothers,** Eddie Cochran, Little Jimmy Dickens, and the Johnny Burnette Trio helped elevate rockabilly to a preeminent position in the 1950s.

16. *Singing Cowboy Music*. Refers to the film output of Gene Autry, **Tex Ritter,** the **Sons of the Pioneers,** and others in the 1930s and 1940s. Because many country performers adopted the dress of a movie cowboy, the "western" designation was added to "country" in the late 1940s.

17. *The Texas Sound*. This term is practically synonymous with progressive country and redneck rock. It has been used to mean any band from Texas; a futile categorization considering that the state has a variety of musical styles.

18. *Tex-Mex Country*. Nationally, the style is represented solely by Freddy Fender. On a local level, the sound thrives in cities like Austin and San Antonio, where bands employ accordions and six-string basses to produce a hybrid conjunto sound.

19. *Western Swing*. While the genre draws from country music for much of its instrumentation and lyrics, it differs with respect to its rhythms (derived mainly from New Orleans jazz of the 1920s and 1930s) and sophisticated dance orchestra arrangements. Chief exponents included Bob Wills and his Texas Playboys, Milton Brown and his Musical Brownies, and Spade Cooley. After a sharp decline in popu-

larity in the 1950s and 1960s, western swing was revived by rock-influenced artists such as Asleep at the Wheel in the 1970s.

Although country music sales were not damaged in the industry declines of 1979 (*see* DISC, 6), and indeed the category increased its market share to around 20 percent in the next few years, in 1985 country record sales began a dramatic fall, with star performers selling only near break-even points (about 80,000 sales). Exceptions, still in the gold-record group in 1991, are Alabama, Willie Nelson, Dolly Parton, the Statler Brothers, and Hank Williams, Jr. [Albert 1984; Hemphill 1970; Hume 1982; Malone 1968.] *See also* FOLK MUSIC RECORDINGS.

Frank Hoffmann

Country Harmonizers. *See* HARMONIZERS QUARTET.

COUNTRY MUSIC ASSOCIATION. An organization established in Nashville in 1958 to promote the playing of country music on radio and television, achieving considerable success in this effort during the 1960s and 1970s. It administers the Country Music Association Awards, and DJ awards for disc jockeys.

COUNTRY MUSIC FOUNDATION. An organization established in 1964, in Nashville. The address (1990) is 4 Music Square East. The purpose of the foundation is to promote interest in country music and the study of it. It has a press, a scholarly periodical (*Journal of Country Music*), a lecture-demonstration program, and a library open to scholars. The Country Music Hall of Fame and Museum, founded in 1961, is a major activity of the foundation.

COURT, HUGH PETER, 1920–1972. Industry executive, born in Britain, founder (with his brothers) of the **Rococo** label in Toronto. He was instrumental in reissuing on LP many treasured recordings of the past. He and his brothers also produced *Record News* from 1957 to 1961.

Cowboy songs. *See* COUNTRY AND WESTERN MUSIC RECORDINGS.

COVERING. A term in the popular record industry for the practice of having one performer record another performer's hit material. It was straightforward in the 1940s; for example, Frank Sinatra did a Columbia issue of "Sunday, Monday, or Always"—a Bing Crosby movie hit, originally on Decca—and record buyers had a choice of renditions. There were more than 400 versions of "White Christmas," following Bing Crosby's. Then in the 1950s some singers began to cover songs from other genres; for example, Tony Bennett offered "Cold, Cold Heart" in a bland style quite removed from the Hank Williams country original. Some rock numbers with racy lyrics were covered in middle-of-the-road idiom with modified texts. Certain white singers like Pat Boone covered material by Black artists in the 1950s and 1960s. *See also* CROSSOVER.

COX, HENRY C., 1891–1954. American motion picture and recording industry executive. An officer with the Columbia Phonograph Co. in the 1920s, he was vice president and treasurer, then (1925) president. In 1927 he was president of the Columbia Broadcasting System. Cox was an associate of Charles P. Skouras in the operation of the latter's theater chain, and was vice president and board member of National Theatres, Inc. He died in New York on 1 Apr 1954.

CRAWFORD, JESSE, 1895–1962. American theatre and radio organist, the first performer to record the instrument extensively. In 1924 he was one of the artists to make the world's first commercial electric recordings, on the **Autograph** label of **Marsh Laboratories**. Most of his discs were made for Victor, but he also appeared on Decca and Bluebird. Probably his most popular record was "At Dawning" / "Roses of Picardy" (Victor #20110; 1927). All his recordings were in the popular vein.

CREAM. British rock group formed in 1966, comprised of Eric Clapton, lead guitar; Jack Bruce, bass; and Ginger Baker, drums. Widely considered to be the finest instrumental rock ensemble, they combined jazz, blues, and rock genres in a texture that was often contrapuntal.

Cream broke up after a sensational 1968 performance in London's Royal Albert Hall.

Each of their nine albums sold at least a million copies. The most notable were *Fresh Cream* (Atco #33–206; 1967), 34 weeks on the charts; *Disraeli Gears* (Atco #33–232; 1967), 65 weeks; and *Wheels of Fire* (Atco #SD-2–700; 1968), 43 weeks.

CREEDENCE CLEARWATER REVIVAL.

American rock group, established in 1959 (originally known as the Blue Velvets, later as the Golliwogs) by guitarist Tom Fogerty. The other members were Tom Fogerty's brother John (singer, lead guitarist, and keyboard player), Stu Cook (bass guitarist), and Doug Clifford (drummer). In 1967 the group took their final name, and made their first successful recordings, for the Fantasy label. *Creedence Clearwater Revival* (Fantasy #8382; 1968) and *Green River* (Fantasy #8393; 1969) presented them at their best. The biggest hit albums were *Bayou Country* (Fantasy #8387; 1969) and *Cosmo's Factory* (Fantasy #8402; 1970). There were acclaimed performances at the Woodstock festival, and on a European tour, before the group broke up in 1972. John Fogerty followed a solo career thereafter, and scored a success with *Centerfield* (Warner #9–25203–1; 1985), 44 weeks on the charts.

CRESCENT TALKING MACHINE CO. A

New York firm, located at 89 Chambers St. (1916), and 109 Reade St. (1917). It was established in 1914 to make discs and players. The Crescent Sales Co., Providence, Rhode Island, was distributing agent. The discs, eight-inch and 10 1/2 inch vertical cut, were mainly taken from Pathé masters, but—apparently through a misunderstanding—were not playable on the Crescent phonographs, which were designed to play lateral-cut records. This was one factor (the other was probably a lack of novel material) that contributed to the quick demise of the company; only 60 records were offered. The disc players were trade-named "Silvertone" and came in 14 different models. [Andrews*; Blacker 1969; Blacker 1970/7; Rust 1978.]

CRESCENT TRIO. A group that recorded for Edison Diamond Discs in 1920–1922. The members were **Elliott Shaw, Charles Hart,** and **Lewis James.** The same singers were also known as the Apollo Trio and Orpheus Trio when they worked for Pathé. [Walsh 1962/10.]

CRITERION QUARTET. A group established in 1905, and popular from 1916 to 1930. The original members were Robert R. Rainey, William A. Washburn, **Reinald Werrenrath,** and Walter A. Downie. There were many changes in the membership later. Their first record was for Edison: "Little Tommy Went A-Fishing" (#8866; 1905). They worked for Edison until 1928, their final Diamond Disc being "Shall I Crucify Him?" (#52254). The quartet also recorded for Columbia, Leeds & Catlin, Talk-O-Phone, and Zonophone. Other names used by the group were Aeolian Male Quartet and Broadway Quartet (for Vocalion), and Strand Quartet (for Brunswick). In the late 1920s they were regular performers at the Roxy Theatre in New York under the name Roxy Quartet.

CRITERION RECORDS, INC. A New York firm, located at 1227 Broadway in 1920–1922. Arthur H. Cushman was vice president and general manager. Criterion Records were issued in May 1921, 10-inch, single- and double-sided; they included arias by Metropolitan Opera and Chicago Opera singers. The firm went into bankruptcy in February 1922. [Andrews*.]

CRITICISM. It was the *Phonographische Zeitschrift* (Berlin) that carried, in 1906, the first serious criticism of sound recordings. *National Magazine* and *World of Today* both began to publish record reviews in 1909. In the 1920s the *New York Times* began weekly record reviews. Criticism of a high standard, examining both performance and technical aspects of new records, began in the U.K. with the establishment of the *Gramophone* in 1923. The first magazine devoted entirely to commentary on new records was the *Phonograph Monthly Review* (1926), which became (1935) the *American Record Guide*.

B. H. Haggin's *Music on Records* (1938) was the first booklength (albeit slim) survey of available discs with commentary. David Hall's *Record Book* (1940) was the earliest substantial collection of evaluations; it had several supplements and revised editions through 1950. Hall confronted virtually the entire classical repertoire on 78s (and LPs in the 1950 edition), offering comparisons and sensible critiques of performance. *A Guide to Recorded Music* by Irving Kolodin (1941) was a worthy rival to Hall's books, also running to three editions before abandoning the cause in the LP avalanche of 1950. Britain produced its own *Record Guide*, by Edward Sackville-West and Desmond Shawe-Taylor, in 1951, plus an annual summary of reviews by the same authors. There was also a multi-volume *Stereo Record Guide* (1960) by Edward Greenfield, et al.

The LP era brought forth numerous journals in which expert reviewing was a principal feature: *High Fidelity* (1951) and *Stereo Review* (1958) were especially noteworthy. *Records in Review, 1955–1981* was a yearly collection of reviews from *High Fidelity*. To assist their readers in coping with the mushrooming review scene, *Notes* began in 1948 to cite the reviews of new classical and folk records that appeared in a group of journals. This "Index to Record Reviews," edited by Kurtz Myers, has had three cumulations.

In 1977 a new journal, *Fanfare*, entered the field and soon became the prime American source for serious reviewing; it now stands with *Gramophone* in offering the most thorough and intelligent evaluations of new classical recordings.

A useful genre of monographic publication is the selective collector's guide, in which an author lists preferred versions of compositions in certain categories. *A Basic Classical and Operatic Recordings Collection on Compact Discs* (1990), by Kenyon C. Rosenberg, is a valuable general guide.

In jazz, pop, and rock, reviewing has been concentrated in the leading journals of those fields; and all major newspapers have coverage of new releases by competent critics. Periodicals with important reviews of popular music include *Jazz Journal International* (1947), *Rolling Stone* (1967), *Cadence* (1976), *Joslin's Jazz*

Journal (1982), and *Discoveries* (1988). The first major "record book" for popular music was the *Rolling Stone Record Guide* (1979), covering "almost 10,000 currently available rock, pop, soul, country, blues, jazz, and gospel albums" with ratings from Worthless to Indispensable.

CRITONA (label). About 100 discs, now extremely rare, were issued in 1920–1921 by Criterion Records, Inc., 1227 Broadway, New York. The first advertisement in *TMW*, May 1921, included opera, light classics, and standards, at a price of $.50. A huntsman design identified the label. Arthur H. Cushman was general manager of Criterion. The firm was bankrupt in 1922. [Andrews*; Kendziora 1967/9.]

CROMELIN, PAUL H., 1870–1929. American recording industry executive, born in Washington, D.C., on 4 Feb 1870. He moved in 1904 to Hackensack, New Jersey, where he remained until his death on 22 Feb 1929. He graduated from the George Washington University Law School in 1891, and worked for the Lincoln Bank in Washington to 1896. Then he became secretary of the **American Graphophone Co.** From 1897 to 1899 he managed branches and stores of Columbia Phonograph Co. in Washington and St. Louis. In 1900 he went to Berlin to establish the Columbia business in Germany and manage the new company there. He was responsible also for the Columbia interests in Russia and Austria-Hungary.

Returning to New York in 1903 he became a vice president of Columbia Phonograph Co., General, directing the legal and recording departments. He also organized the Columbia office in Mexico. Cromelin resigned from Columbia in 1911 to become Thomas Edison's representative in the U.K., managing the **National Phonograph Co., Ltd.**, and remained in Britain until 1914.

When he came back to the U.S. he turned to the motion picture field, organizing Cosmofotofilm Co., Inc. He was a recognized authority on copyright questions, serving as president of the American Musical Copyright League, and representing the mechanical reproducer industry at the Bern Convention of 1908 in Berlin. His testimony at U.S. Congressional hearings helped to shape the U.S. Copyright law of 1909. He was also influential in the design of the British Copyright Act of 1911.

Cromelin remained active in various motion picture ventures and associations, but did not return to the sound recording field. *See also* R. F. CROMELIN and the editor's note at the end of it.

CROMELIN, R. F., 1857–?. U.S. Supreme Court reporter, and later a record company executive, born in New York on 1 Apr 1857. He served with the new **Columbia** Phonograph Co. from its establishment in 1889, being secretary and later vice president. He was elected secretary of the **National Phonograph Association** at its first meeting in May 1890. With his Columbia associate Edward Easton, Cromelin was a major force in shaping the industry: they perceived that phonographs were not going to succeed on a grand scale as stenographic aides, but there was an unlimited potential for the devices as entertainment media. He became general manager of Columbia Graphophone in 1914. He also served for a time as secretary to the governor of Pennsylvania. *See also* PAUL H. CROMELIN. (Editor's note: the similarity between the industry activities of the two Cromelins is striking, and so is the fact that there is no indication of a family relationship between them. Information on Paul H. Cromelin comes from his obituaries in the *New York Times*, 23 Feb 1929, and the Hackensack (New Jersey) *Evening Record*, 23 Feb 1929, provided through the courtesy of Norman Horrocks and Seena Solomon. Information on R. F. Cromelin is almost non-existent. The facts above came from *Phonogram*, vol. 1, no. 4 (April 1891), Proceedings 1974, and Read 1976. The possibility remains that there was only one Cromelin—Paul H.—and that his first name was somehow garbled in the references cited.)

CROONING. A vocal style devised by American male popular singers in the 1920s and carried into the 1950s. It was suited to light voices ("Whispering Jack" Smith, **Rudy Vallee**) which were in turn suited to the microphones in use for early radio. Features of the style included pitch slides and turns on accented notes (short trills with the note above). Quint-

essential crooners include **Russ Columbo, Bing Crosby, Perry Como,** and **Frank Sinatra.**

CROS, CHARLES, 1842–1888. French poet (his poem "L'archet" was set to music by Claude Debussy in 1883) and amateur scientist. He experimented with sound recording and produced a seminal paper on 18 Apr 1877 which described a disc machine; sound waves were to be traced on lampblacked glass, then photoengraved into reliefs. Lacking the means to make a model, he did not immediately seek a patent, but merely deposited his paper with the Académie des Sciences. (He did obtain a French patent, #124.313, in May 1878.) A popularizer of science, Abbé Lenoir, described the Cros machine—naming it "phonograph"—in an article of his own, published 10 Oct 1877. Although the Cros concept was similar to that of Thomas Edison (and even more similar to that of Emile Berliner), and Edison's working model was not completed before 6 Dec 1877 (the first sketch dates from 29 Nov 1877), it is clear that the American knew nothing of Cros. Edison's claim to the invention is firmly based on two points: he was first to demonstrate his idea with a working model, and first to patent it.

CROSBY, BING, 1903–1977. American popular singer, born Harry Lillis Crosby in Tacoma, Washington. The date of birth is 2 May 1901 in Slonimsky, and 2 May 1904 in *New Grove Dictionary of American Music*, but "according to his birth certificate, he was born on May 2, 1903" (Rust). On the other hand, "his date of birth was conclusively established as May 3, 1903, by researchers from the British Bing Crosby Society in 1978" (Brooks). Crosby was a master of the **crooning** style, and one of the most successful recording artists of all time—with record sales possibly as high as 400 million copies. After nightclub engagements in California, singing and drumming to the piano of Al Rinker, he and Rinker were signed in 1926 by **Paul Whiteman** and performed with his orchestra on a midwest tour. He was heard on disc for the first time in "I've Got the Girl" (Columbia #824–D; 18 Oct 1926), singing with Rinker, not with Whiteman, but with Don Clark and his orchestra. (Crosby's name was not on the label, nor on any label until 1929.) Listeners who find Crosby's voice unrecognizable on this disc are advised to play it back at 70 rpm instead of 78 rpm (Ault). He and Rinker were also the vocalists on "Wistful and Blue" (Victor #20418; 22 Dec 1926) with Whiteman. "Muddy Water" was his first solo vocal, also with Whiteman (Victor #20508; 7 Mar 1927).

After 1930 he left Whiteman for a spectacular radio career with CBS, using "When the Blue of the Night" (Brunswick #6226; 1931) as a theme song in a twice-weekly program. He had begun to record for Brunswick in 1931—"Just One More Chance" (Brunswick #6120) exhibiting his developed crooning style to perfection—and remained with that company until 1934. "Temptation" (Brunswick #6695; 1934) was the most memorable issue. In 1932 he appeared in the motion picture *Big Broadcast*, his first starring film.

Moving to Decca in 1934, his famous loose and casual style emerged, and he began to produce million-selling records, the first of which was "Sweet Leilani" with Lani McIntire and His Hawaiians (Decca #1175; 1938). Altogether Crosby had 22 golden discs. "White Christmas" (Decca #18429; 29 May 1942) became the largest selling single record in history, reaching 170 million sales (in all countries) by 1978. Another Christmas record, "Silent Night" / "Adeste Fidelis" (Decca #621; 1935) may have sold almost as many copies. (This was recorded earlier on a private record for a charity benefit; it was so successful that the commercial disc followed.) Meanwhile Crosby was pursuing his radio career, starring on the *Kraft Music Hall* from the fall of 1937.

He made numerous records with other top performers. The **Andrews Sisters** were his collaborators on "Pistol Packin' Mama" (Decca #23277; 1943), a novelty song which became another golden disc. On the same day, Crosby and the Andrews Sisters recorded a second hit—destined to reach 6 million sales—"Jingle Bells" (Decca #23281). In 1944 they made million-selling "Don't Fence Me In" (Decca #23364); and there was another golden disc two years later: "South America, Take It Away." "A Fine Romance" (Decca #907; 1936), with his first wife, Dixie Lee Crosby, had an easy charm. Various duets with Bob Hope had a fresh, improvised character; "Road to Morocco"

(Decca #40000; 1942) is the best example. He teamed with his son Gary to make "Play a Simple Melody" (Decca #27112), and with Grace Kelly for "True Love" (1956).

Other outstanding discs include "Too Romantic," sung to Dorothy Lamour in the film *Road to Singapore*, "Moonlight Becomes You" (Decca #18513; 1942); "Sunday, Monday, or Always" (Decca #18651; 1943), a golden disc; and "I'll Be Home for Christmas" (Decca #18570; 1943), also a golden disc. Three songs from the film *Going My Way*, for which he won the Academy Award for acting, were greatly successful: the title song backed by "Swinging on a Star" (Decca #18597; 1944), and "Too-Ra-Loo-Ra-Loo-Ral" (Decca #18621; 1945).

In his career Crosby made more than 2,600 records, and his voice seemed to retain its quality and luster even in the 1970s. He died on 14 Oct 1977, on a golf course near Madrid.

MCA has reissued many of his hits on compact disc: *Christmas Songs* (MCAD-5765) and *Bing Crosby Sings Again* (MCAD-5764). [Ault 1987; Brooks*; Rust*; Slonimsky 1984.]

CROSBY, BOB, 1913– . American Big Band leader and vocalist, born George Robert Crosby in Spokane, Washington, on 25 Aug 1913; younger brother of **Bing Crosby.** He sang with the Anson Weeks orchestra in 1933–1934, and with The Dorsey Brothers band in 1934–1935. He had his own group from 1935, bringing in over the years star sidemen like Billy Butterfield, Eddie Miller, Matty Matlock, Muggsy Spanier, Charlie Spivak, and Jess Stacy. Crosby developed an updated Dixieland style that set him apart from the other bands of the late 1930s; he exercised the same style in his smaller combo, the Bob Cats. There was great success on radio, in motion pictures, and also on early television shows.

The orchestra recorded first for Decca in June 1935, and remained with the label. Among their finest discs were two with Crosby vocals: "Guess Who" (#836; 1936), and "Loveliness of You" (#1370; 1937). The Bob Cats made acclaimed records like "South Rampart Street Parade" (#15038; 1937), and "March of the Bob Cats" (#1865; 1938). The Andrews Sisters did an outstanding "Begin the Beguine" with the Bob Cats (#2290; 1939). Jess Stacy offered a version of his Commodore 1939 hit, "Ec-Stacy," with the Crosby orchestra in 1942, on Decca #15064.

CROSSFADE. In recording, "to crossfade" means to increase the prominence of one channel while fading out another.

CROSSLEY, ADA JESSICA, 1874–1929. Australian mezzo-soprano, born in Tarraville on 3 Mar 1874. She made her debut in Melbourne, then went to London for study and gave a successful debut there on 18 May 1895; she was invited to give command performances before Queen Victoria. Crossley sang in festivals and made world tours, but she is best known to record collectors as the first artist to appear in Victor's American Red Seal series. Her first and best Red Seal was "Caro mio ben" (#81001; 30 Apr 1903; remastered in 1953); it was a 10-inch Monarch. On the same date she made five more discs, but then did not record again for Victor. She made a few records for Pathé in London in 1904. Crossley died in London on 17 Oct 1919.

CROSSOVER. (I) In popular music, the term given to a record made for one market that becomes successful in another market as well. Performers involved may then be referred to as "crossovers." Early crossover artists were the **Ink Spots**, the **Mills Brothers**, and other Blacks whose appeal reached beyond the intended racial market and were appreciated by white record buyers. Classical artists may also crossover with successful recordings of popular songs, for example, **Placido Domingo** and Elly Ameling. *See also* COVERING.

CROSSOVER. (II) In recording characteristics, the crossover point is that where amplitude adjustment by frequency ceases. It is also known as the crossover frequency, or the turnover. For example, in electrical recording up to about 1935 frequencies above 250 Hz had a pure constant velocity characteristic, with amplitude frequency equalling constant; below 250 Hz—the crossover point—the cut was constant amplitude, with all frequencies being limited to the same amplitude, instead of the amplitude increasing with a decrease in frequency. The rationale for this adjustment was that it allowed a higher recording level at higher frequencies and produced advantageous signal-to-noise ratios. Around 1935 the crossover point was moved up to 500 Hz or 600 Hz in the U.S. and U.K., to extend the dynamic range. Neither cylinders nor acoustic recordings had this characteristic. [Owen 1983.]

CROSSOVER NETWORK. Also known as a dividing network. In a sound reproducing system, the device that divides **amplifier** output into two or more frequency ranges, most commonly bass and treble, and feeds them to separate loudspeakers. The advantage to this separation is smoother frequency response and less distortion. In classical music playback the crossover frequency is around 400 Hz, with perhaps 40 percent of the total signal below that point and directed to the bass speaker.

CROSSTALK. In a sound reproducing system of two or more channels, the signal leakage from one channel to another. **Channel separation** is the absence of crosstalk.

CROWN (label). (I) A British issue, made from Polyphon masters before World War I. [Andrews*.]

CROWN (label). (II) An American label of short life, being a subsidiary of the **Arto** company in 1921. [Kendziora 1963].

CROWN (label). (III) A six-inch electrically recorded disc issued in the U.K. by **Edison Bell** in the late 1920s. [Andrews*.]

CROWN (label). (IV) An American label of 1930–1933, affiliated with Victor, offering about 1,200 releases of dance and popular music.

CROWN (label). (V) A British product of 1935–1937, sold at Woolworth stores for 6d. The manufacturer was **Crystalate Gramophone Record Manufacturing Co., Ltd.** Good quality British dance music and pop vocals were offered, with some items taken from American Vocalion pressings. [Rust 1978.]

CROXTON, FRANK, 1877–1949. American bass, born in Paris, Kentucky, on 7 Oct 1877. He began as a church and concert singer in New York, and began to record for U-S Everlasting Records in 1910 or 1911 with "In the Garden of My Heart" (#239), a duet with Henry Burr. In October 1911 he began working with Edison, singing "Lost, Proscribed" from *Martha*, a duet with Reed Miller (#799). He headed the Frank Croxton Quartet on Edison Amberols, and sang for Columbia and Victor in 1912. He formed his **Croxton Quartet** in 1912. Croxton's repertoire was concert and opera, with no popular songs. By 1914 he had 17 solos in the Columbia catalog, plus many duets and parts in quartet renditions. In 1914 he was one of the Stellar Quartet, then he joined the Peerless Quartet in 1919 and the Eight Famous Victor Artists in 1919. In 1918 he formed the **Croxton Trio**. His best-selling Victor was "Weeping Willow Lane" (#18609; 1919), a duet with Burr. In 1925 he left the Peerless and joined another group, but gave up recording during the Depression. He remained active as a teacher and church singer. He died in New York on 4 Sep 1949.

CROXTON QUARTET. A group formed by **Frank Croxton** in 1912, consisting of himself with Agnes Kimball, Nevada Van der Veer, and **Reed Miller**. Recording for Gennett ca. 1918, Inez Barbour and **Henry Burr** took the place of Kimball and Miller.

CROXTON TRIO. A group formed by **Frank Croxton** in 1918 to record for Okeh; the other singers were Inez Barbour and **Henry Burr**.

CRUMIT, FRANK, 1889–1943. American tenor, noted for successes in Broadway shows. In 1919 he was with Paul Biese's orchestra in Chicago, then went to New York. His first record was "My Gal" (Columbia #A-2884; 1919). Singing in the hit show *Tangerine* in 1921, he recorded its song "Sweet Lady" with Julia Sanderson, who was to become his principal duet partner (Decca #18154; 1921). Subsequently he made more than 500 records, the last in 1941. He died in Springfield, Massachusetts, on 9 Sep 1943.

CRYSTALATE GRAMOPHONE RECORD MANUFACTURING CO., LTD. A British firm, having several names over its 36-year history. It was established on 2 Aug 1901 as the Crystalate Manufacturing Co., Ltd. Originally the products were billiard balls, bottle stoppers, and similar items made of a patented hard plastic material, in addition to disc records. Holder of the patent was **George Henry Burt**, an American inventor of notable business acumen: he contracted to make discs for Berliner, and Zonophone; and he also set up a firm, **Globe Record Co.** (It was Globe that made the first matrices for Columbia, which were released on the **Climax** label.) Whether or not Crystalate was the first British presser of disc records—as it claimed in advertising—remains unproved, but the firm was apparently the earliest to make experimental pressings in the U.K. It may have supplied materials to **Nicole**, which made seven-inch, brown-colored records beginning in 1903 (Burt was associated with that firm too).

In 1906 Crystalate was engaged to make Fonotipia and Odeon records in Britain. Matrix manufacture extended to many other companies, including Champion, Standard Record, Olympic Record, Beacon, Butterfly, Criterion, Popular, Stavophone, Guardsman, Imperial, Rex, Swing, Celebrity, Continental, Broadcast, Crown, Coronet, Neptune, Grammavox, Citizen and Vocalion.

A close affiliate to Crystalate was the **Sound Recording Co., Ltd.**, of Swallow St., Piccadilly, London, founded in March 1910. Around 1915 Sound Recording appeared to own the Crystalate factories; but in 1922 "it was evident that the Crystalate company had taken over the Sound Recording Company and kept it as a going concern" (Andrews). By this time the firm, which did not have a disc label of its own, began to concentrate on the manufacture of Imperials, and made a success of this third introduction of the label. In the mid-1920s depots were opened in Manchester, Dublin, Leeds, Liverpool, Glasgow, and Sheffield. Jewish, Dutch, and French specialty series were issued.

On 30 Jan 1928 a new incorporation was announced, with the name at the head of this article, located at Golden Green, Kent. A period of great prosperity ensued, with international affiliates in France and Germany, the purchase of **Regal** from Plaza, and contracts to provide discs for Woolworth and Marks & Spencer. A new corporate home, Crystalate House, was located at 60/62 City Road. A one-third interest was gained in the huge new conglomerate formed in 1929 under the name of the **American Record Corporation**. That ambitious undertaking was hit by the Depression, and Crystalate's own future was troubled. The formation of **EMI, Ltd.**, in Britain presented a formidable rival—there were also 21 other labels on sale in U.K. in the bleak mid-1930s—and there were reduced profits in 1933. A price war with **British Homophone Co., Ltd.**—who marketed a one-shilling Homochord in October 1933—resulted in Crystalate's one-shilling **Rex**, plus **Broadcasts** and **Imperials** at ls. 6d. for the 10-inch size. Economic conditions were intractable, however, and various gyrations and new labels could not save Crystalate. In March 1937 **Decca Record Co., Ltd.**, acquired the record interests for £150,000 and 400,000 of its own shares held by Crystalate. Yet the firm did persist, without its recordings arm: on 31 Jan 1938 it re-incorporated as Crystalate, Ltd. Successors survive to this day in the electronic component industry. [Andrews*; Andrews 1983/1984.]

Crystol (label). *See* AMBEROL.

CUGAT, XAVIER, 1900–1991. Spanish violinist and Big Band leader, born in Barcelona on 1 Jan 1900. As a youth he moved to the U.S., where he played the violin and worked as a cartoonist for the *Los Angeles Times*. In 1928 he formed his dance band, and was engaged by the Waldorf-Astoria Hotel in New York in 1933. He began recording in that year, for Victor, with whom he stayed until 1940. He moved to Columbia in October 1940. Cugat's style was Latin, but he performed typical dance music as well. He was fortunate to have some outstanding vocalists, most notably **Dinah Shore**. She recorded elegant versions of "When the Swallows Come Back to Capistrano" and

"The Breeze and I" (Victor #26641; 1940). His band was featured in many motion pictures in 1940s, and he was often on television into the 1970s.

CULP, JULIA, 1880–1970. Dutch contralto, born in Groningen on 6 Oct 1880. She made her debut in Magdeburg in 1901, and toured Europe. German Lieder was her specialty; she was one of the early female singers to record that repertoire. She performed the art songs "with full, even, wonderfully modulated tones" (Moses). She did not sing opera. In 1913 she appeared in the U.S. Culp made records for Anker in Germany; she recorded more than 30 concert songs and Lieder for Victor Red Seal in 1914–1918, and made one more record in 1924. She died in Amsterdam on 13 Oct 1970. [Moses 1949; Riemens 1947.]

CULSHAW, JOHN ROYDS, 1924–1980. British recording producer, musician, and author, born in Southport on 28 May 1924. In 1942 he entered naval service as an airman and navigator, emerging as a lieutenant in 1946. He joined English Decca in 1946 as an assistant classical recording producer, remaining until 1953. At that time he took a post with Capitol Records, which intended to launch a European venture; that plan dissolved when Capitol was acquired by EMI in 1955. Decca rehired Culshaw, as classical recording director, and he stayed until 1967. He became the outstanding producer of recorded opera, achieving international recognition for his Vienna studio recording of the Wagner *Ring* under Georg Solti in 1958–1965—described by David Hall as the "first complete and integral commercial recording" of the cycle (London #414100–2; 15 LPs). Culshaw's approach, coming at the beginning of the stereo age, was to exploit the new sonic technology and to make the recording itself a work of art, on equal footing with the music itself.

He was fortunate to have great singers in the studio, including Kirsten Flagstad, Birgit Nilsson, Hans Hotter, and Wolfgang Windgassen. Culshaw was awarded the American Grammy in 1967 for his production of *Walküre*. He had won earlier Grammys in 1963 for the *War Requiem* (classical album of the year) and in 1964 for *Carmen*. He wrote a book about the Wagner recording, *Ring Resounding* (1967).

From 1967 to 1975 Culshaw was head of music for BBC television and a freelance record producer. He was heard frequently as a commentator for Metropolitan Opera broadcasts. In 1975 he became a freelance author and television producer, and lecturer at the Universities of London and Oxford. He died in London on 27 Apr 1980. (*See* the Bibliography for the titles of his books.)

CURRY'S (label). There were four British records with the name Curry's, issued in the 1920s. One was a disc entitled Curry's Cycle Co., from **J. E. Hough**, Ltd., matrices. There was also a Curry's label from **Guardsman** matrices, pressed by Crystalate Gramophone Record Manufacturing Co., Ltd. Another Curry's label was from **Imperial** matrices, pressed by Crystalate. Curry's Electric was a label made from matrices by **Piccadilly** Records, Ltd. [Andrews*.]

CUT. Either a **band** or a **groove** on a disc. By extension, the song or selection that occupies a band. "To cut" means to record. *See also* LATERAL RECORDING; VERTICAL CUT.

CUTOUT. A record withdrawn from normal distribution by the manufacturer and removed from the company's catalog. In publishing terms, a cutout is "out-of-print." The number of cutouts in the pop/rock field may be as much as 85 percent of a company's issues. Records that fail to break even, so-called stiffs, are quickly withdrawn and usually sent to a **rack jobber** for disposal. Like remaindered books, those stiff records are found in bargain sections of the shops, often selling at greatly reduced prices. Retailers have generally denounced this practice as one that undermines their sales of standard material, and requires excessive paperwork. Objections come also from the artists represented on cutout discs, whose royalties are reduced and whose reputations are thought to be injured. Record companies, on the other hand, justify cutouts because they claim that royalty fees are so inflated that only major hit records are profitable.

CUTTING HEAD. Also known as a cutterhead. An electromagnetic device used in disc recording. It includes a **moving coil** and a cutting **stylus**; the latter is activated by amplifier signals and transcribes them into the record **groove**. The "feedback cutting head" was developed at Bell Telephone Laboratories in 1924: it canceled resonances in the cutting head by feeding back a signal from it to the recording amplifier.

CYCLE. In a periodic vibration pattern, a cycle is one complete excursion from a given point through two extremes and back to the given point. The unit of **frequency** is cycles per second (c/s), now generally superseded by **Hertz** (Hz). The number of a Hz in a sound wave determines its **pitch**.

CYLINDER. This article, complementary to **disc**, has eight sections: 1. History of the format; 2 Materials; 3. Manufacturing and copying; 4. Dimensions; 5. Speeds; 6. The industry; 7. Repertoire; and 8. Contemporary playback of cylinders.

1. *History of the format.* The tinfoil cylinder was the first medium to record and replay sounds, in the **phonograph** of **Thomas Alva Edison** (1877). In the language of Edison's U.S. patent application (#200,521, filed 24 Dec 1877, granted 19 Feb 1878) the phonograph was based on "a cylinder having a helical indenting-groove cut from end to end—say, ten grooves to the inch. Upon this is placed the material to be indented, preferably metallic foil. This drum or cylinder is secured to a shaft . . . having at one end a thread cut with ten threads to the inch. . . ." Edison's first demonstration machines had hollow brass cylinders with a continuous spiral groove, tightly wrapped in tinfoil.

The earliest practical thinking about the possibility of recording sound was centered on a flat medium as carrier of the signal: the **phonautograph** invented in 1857 by Léon Scott de Martinville. In 1859 he made a second model, utilizing a cylinder medium. Scott's instrument, which looked quite a bit like Edison's phonograph of two decades later, was designed to trace the fluctuation of sound waves on a sheet of lampblacked paper wrapped around a cylinder on a threaded shaft. Apparently its inventor failed to consider that his machine, with some elaborations, could have been used for playing back the signal as well as storing it. There is no evidence that Edison knew of Scott's work as he was developing the first model of the cylinder phonograph in November 1877, but Emile Berliner had seen the phonautograph at the Smithsonian Institution while he was living in Washington, D.C., and devising his approach to sound recording. Berliner took the step that Scott had missed, and made a version of the phonautograph in 1887 that could reproduce the signal. But he soon gave up on the cylinder and developed the disc **gramophone**, just as Edison had decided to use the cylinder instead of the flat medium that he had also described in his first patent. Through the subsequent competition between cylinder and disc, Edison championed the former while Berliner and his successors held to the latter. In the end it was the disc that triumphed, outselling cylinders after about 1910. Most firms gave up cylinder making at about that time (Columbia in May 1909); the last to be produced were **Blue Amberols** in July 1929. From 1914 most Blue Amberol cylinders were dubbed from disc recordings. **Ediphone School Records** were produced, via electrical dubbing, until 1960. (*See* section 6, below.) [*APM* II-6; Dethlefson 1983; Klinger*; Koenigsberg*.] *See also* OLDEST RECORDS; PATENTS.

2. *Materials.* "Mary Had a Little Lamb," the first words to be recorded and played back, were spoken by Thomas Edison to a sheet of tinfoil wrapped around a brass drum. (One could make a case for something like "Hello" as the first word recorded, since Edison had shouted it at a strip of paper pulled along under a diaphragm in an experiment on 18 July 1877, and then "ran the paper back over the steel point and heard a faint Halloo! Halloo! in return." The *New York Times* of 5 Mar 1992, p. C1+, carried an account of Edison's use of "Hello," based on research by Allen Koenigsberg.) The drum, being solid, differed from the hollow type used later. It was four inches in diameter and four inches long, with a helical groove of 0.1 inch pitch (ten grooves per inch) inscribed on its surface. The number of grooves per inch varied on the pioneer tinfoil

machines; a photo in *TMR* #49b shows one with 16 threads per inch. Edison and his contemporary inventors searched vigorously for materials to replace the tinfoil, which produced various distortions. Sheets of copper and of soft iron were among the substances tested. **Chichester Bell** and **Charles Tainter** filled the grooves of an Edison cylinder with beeswax. Edison turned to wax also, but he made his entire cylinder of it, thus allowing reuse by shaving the surface.

The brass drum of the original phonograph did not satisfy Edison; he and his chemist, **Jonas W. Aylsworth**, experimented with cores of asphaltum and plaster of Paris. During the period when Edison neglected sound recording in favor of perfecting the incandescent lamp, Bell and Tainter developed their cardboard cylinder core, six inches long, 1 5/16 inches in diameter, coated with a .05 inch thickness of beeswax and paraffin, later with ozocerite wax. When Edison returned to his phonograph, he entered into new experiments to improve the core: he tried thin brass shells to fit onto the **mandrel**, the shells having wax cylinders around them to receive the sound signals. To prevent expansion of the shell in high temperature, he proposed also the use of hard rubber shells, and some of these were made for use in **coin-ops**. Glass cylinders with paraffin surfaces were also tried by Edison, and in 1889 he made white-wax cylinders and brown-wax cylinders with a core of string in a helical pattern. Other materials were also tried out. Both Edison and rival **American Graphophone Co.**—under engineer **Thomas H. Macdonald**—began to make cast cylinders in hard wax around 1900 for laboratory use.

Thickness of the wax surface had become about one half inch on the Graphophone cylinders of 1893. Those cylinders were six inches long, 2 1/4 inches in diameter.

In 1900 the **Lambert Co.** of Chicago produced cylinders made of celluloid, their "Indestructible" line. (**Henri Jules Lioret** of Paris had pioneered with celluloid cylinders in 1893.) These were made through a "molding" process, (*see* section 3, below) quickly taken up by Edison, who marketed his first molded cylinders in late 1901. However, there was patent litigation, and a decision favoring Lambert, so that Edison had to use a metallic soap composition instead of celluloid until he acquired the rights to Lambert's patent in 1912 and began producing Blue Amberols of celluloid. [Burt 1977; Klinger*.] *See also* PATENTS.

3. *Manufacturing and copying.* Probably the industry's first significant problem of process, as opposed to materials, related to making copies of recorded cylinders. Without such a method, it was necessary for artists to record each cylinder separately. A first solution to this problem involved putting the artist before several recording machines at once. Next a mechanical pantographic system was developed, through which the grooves on a recorded cylinder were traced by a stylus that was attached to a second stylus which would reproduce the undulations on a second cylinder. Clearly these techniques could not lead to mass production. (One 19th-century producer, **Gianni Bettini**, made copies only to order, pantographically.)

As early as 1889 the Edison laboratory had molded cylinders. They electroplated an original recording and thus produced a **master** cylinder mold, with the groove pattern reversed. To make copies from this master, it could be dipped into a tank of hot wax, or hot wax could be deposited into it. A new cylinder was thereby formed inside the mold, with the original recorded signal on it. There remained the difficulty of getting the copy out of the mold, since it would have to shrink sufficiently on cooling to slide out—and this difficulty persisted for a decade with waxes. (The mold itself could not be split, or the ridges would imprint on the wax copy.) Then in 1893 Lioret devised his method of duplicating recorded cylinders by making the copies of celluloid, which softens when hot and hardens and shrinks as it cools. This was the basis for the method used by Lambert, and patented by him in 1900—causing a setback to Edison and Columbia. Celluloid had its defects too, as it tended to wear under pressure and to deform.

The American laboratories continued to work with wax, since they could not infringe the Lambert patents for celluloid, and attained good results with compounds containing metallic soaps; lead soaps hardened easily, and sodium soaps provided smooth surfaces. Edison's method of producing the requisite

electrically conductive surface on the original cylinder was a "gold sputtering" process, and the records became known as "gold moulded." These records were introduced commercially in January 1902, with the new higher speed of 160 rpm. In April 1902 Columbia marketed its first molded cylinders—not "gold sputtered" but simply gold plated on the interior of the copper matrix. Columbia was then using graphite (plumbago) on the wax master for conductivity. Edison changed to celluloid in 1912.

Blue Amberols were usually dubbed, or copied, from **Edison Diamond Discs**, using a horn-to-horn process. Commercial dubbing began on 23 Sep 1914 with the transfer of Helen Clark's "Firelight Faces." The first such copy to be released was "By the Setting of the Sun," by Walter Van Brunt (Edison #2488; December 1914). Electrical dubbing began on 5 Feb 1929, with "Happy Days and Lonely Nights" by Al Friedman's Orchestra (Blue Amberol #5650). [Dethlefson 1983 describes the dubbing process; Klinger*.] *See also* ACOUSTIC RECORDING.

4. *Dimensions.* Standardization of cylinder size among manufacturers was never fully attained, but the vast majority of records produced from the early 1890s on were 2 1/8 inches in diameter and 4 3/16 inches long, with 100 threads per inch; these were the dimensions of Edison's brown-wax cylinder of 1892. Edison's first tinfoil machine used one of four-inch diameter and four-inch length, with 0.1 pitch (10 threads per inch). Other tinfoil phonographs had cylinders of seven-inch diameter, two inches long. The Edison talking doll of 1890 had a three-inch diameter cylinder, 5/8-inches long, with 100 threads per inch. In 1895 Edison experimented with an early long-playing record, the 400-thread-per-inch cylinder that ran for eight minutes; it was 2 3/4-inches in diameter and 6 1/2-inches long. Concert Cylinders were five inches in diameter and 4 1/4 inches long, 100 threads per inch; those were to be played on the Concert Phonograph introduced in December 1898. Columbia sold those five-inch cylinders too, for its **Graphophone Grand** player that went on sale in December 1898. Five-inch cylinders were also sold in Britain, under the name Grand Concert, by Edison Bell.

Pathé in Paris made 5 1/4 inch diameter Grand Concert cylinders during 1900–1905, to play on their version of Columbia Graphophones. The same firm made extra long cylinders (8 1/2 inches, or 21 centimeters) known as Celeste, which could play four or five minutes. Pathé also made 3 1/2 inch diameter (nine centimeters) cylinders, named Intermédiare; in Britain these were sold as Intermediate Salon records. [Klinger*.]

5. *Speeds.* Rotational speeds were increased gradually from 1889 to 1902, in the attempt to achieve greater fidelity. Edison's first cylinders revolved 100/120 rpm; most two-inch, brown-wax cylinders turned roughly 120 times a minute. Concert records played at 100 or 120 rpm. Edison's late brown-wax record ran at 144 rpm. The gold molded records introduced in 1902 established a standard speed of 160 rpm that was maintained for wax Amberols and celluloid Blue Amberols. Most other cylinder manufacturers adopted the 160 rpm speed. The obscure Jumbo brand cylinder was to be played at 185 rpm—the highest known cylinder speed. But this was not much faster than the designated speed of an 1893 Edison Bell "postal" (small) cylinder: 175 rpm. Edison dictation records used a slower speed than entertainment records. Slowest of all were the various language and instructional records, designed to play at 90 rpm or even 80 rpm. [Klinger*; Koenigsberg*.]

6. *The industry.* If a definite date is to be ascribed to the birth of the sound recording industry, it should be 24 Apr 1878, when the **Edison Speaking Phonograph Co.** was established at 203 Broadway in New York. In the same year the **London Stereoscope Co.**, sole British licensee of the phonograph, began to sell—as Edison was doing—machines to record and playback tinfoil records. Sales were good, for the novelty of hearing a voice emerge from a machine had wide appeal. Edison's principal early rivals were Bell and Tainter, who set up the **Volta Graphophone Co.** in Alexandria, Virginia, in 1886 to sell their variety of cylinder and player; the name of that firm was changed to **American Graphophone Co.** in 1887. Through the financial support of **Jesse H. Lippincott**, the Edison and Volta interests (i.e. the phonograph and the graphophone) were

successfully brought together to share a single sales agency under Lippincott's direction: the **North American Phonograph Co.** (NAPC). Into the cross-country network of regional corporations that comprised NAPC there happened to be certain destructive elements. For Lippincott to bring the American Graphophone people into the fold he had to accept the responsibility of purchasing a minimum of 5,000 graphophones a year from them. The agreement gave him personal liability for meeting this contract, and his downfall came from an inability to do so. Another provision in the arrangements for NAPC was that the **Columbia** Phonograph Co. (incorporated January 1889) would retain sales rights for the graphophone in the District of Columbia, Virginia, Maryland, and Delaware—indeed, the prime sales territory for the device as a dictating machine, which was the envisioned purpose of the phonograph and graphophone at the time.

Following the organizational structure of the American Bell Telephone Co., Lippincott leased sales rights for the phonograph to regional and local companies around the U.S. The individual firms then leased the instruments to customers, and sold them cylinders. Soon there were 33 separate companies in the NAPC. They held a national conference in 1890, dealing with topics like uniform pricing and standardization of equipment. Entertainment cylinders were at the time four inches long, but for dictating machines a six-inch record was introduced. Edison's were 2 1/4 inches in diameter, while graphophone records were only 1 5/16 inches. These differences in size remained, so that customers could not shift from one type to another without having both a phonograph and a graphophone. In fact the market preference was strongly for the phonograph, since the graphophone was showing itself to be unacceptable for dictation or entertainment. Thus came Lippincott's insoluble problem: how to live up to his agreement to buy 5,000 graphophones a year, when they were not marketable. He was forced into bankruptcy.

In any case, the original notion of the cylinder player as a business device was fading. Edison began to supply musical cylinders to

NAPC firms in 1891, to be sold at retail. He also offered to make copies of records in high demand—utilizing the new mold process (*see* section 3, above). But local companies, and even customers, found they could make their own copies by re-recording, or by pantographic methods, albeit with loss of quality. "One of the important factors that was responsible for the almost total collapse of the musical entertainment field was inherent in the lack of quality control of the records, as every machine could also be used to record" (Read 1976). NAPC member companies began to drop out; in 1893 there were just 22 at the national convention, and a year later the organization was liquidated. Meanwhile, American Graphophone was in such poor condition that Columbia, the most successful firm in the industry, was able to absorb it in 1894.

The growth of **coin-op** markets, improvements in the machines, and some progress in standardization (Columbia cylinders were made to be compatible with Edison phonographs) helped to bring about a national rise in business. In 1896 there were additional firms to compete with Columbia and Edison (who established in that year his **National Phonograph Co.**): Bettini, **Chicago Talking Machine Co.**, **New England Phonograph Co.**, **Ohio Phonograph Co.**, and **U.S. Phonograph Co.** (of New Jersey). Walcutt & Leeds was established in 1897, and the **American Talking Machine Co.** was founded in 1898. In addition, singers J.W. Myers and Russell Hunting were selling their own records direct to buyers. But Columbia led the field, claiming to sell more records than all other companies combined; its prices were $.50 per cylinder, or $5 a dozen. The industry's first boom year was 1897, with a half million records produced (including discs). By 1899 sales had reached 2.8 million cylinders and discs per year.

In Europe the industry pioneers were London Stereophonic (1878–1882), **J.E. Hough's** London Phonograph Co., **Edisonia** (founded 1897), and **Pathé Frères** of Paris, which began to make and sell both phonographs and cylinders in 1895. Outside of France and Britain the cylinder never got a dependable foothold in Europe; the gramophone came along too quickly, and it had the powerful support of William Barry Owen, founder of the Gramophone Co. Columbia had moved into London in 1900 with a sales office, then relocated its European headquarters there, from a Paris office that had opened in 1897. Columbia had already been selling its products in Britain, and had met with legal attacks by Edisonia. **Edison Bell,** licensed in 1892 to import and sell phonographic products, was reorganized in London in 1898, and took over Edisonia; there was also an agreement with Columbia at that time, based on Edison Bell's acquisition of the Bell-Tainter patent rights for Britain, Australia, South America, China, and Japan. By 1904 Edison Bell was one of the three major producers of cylinder records in Britain, along with **National Phonograph Co., Ltd.,** and **Sterling Record Co., Ltd.** (which was renamed in March 1905 to **Russell Hunting Record Co., Ltd.**).

Edison Bell's early record labels were the first to bear the name **London Records;** later it offered cylinders under the names of **Standard,** Popular, Concert Grand, Indestructible, and Ebony Indestructible. It began to make gold-molded records as well as phonographs in a Peckham plant in 1904. The firm had no overpowering competition in the cylinder field, but there were many other entertainment labels on sale: Britannia, British Phonogram (later called Brent), Columbia, Electric, Empress, Excelsior, Imperial, International Indestructible, Lambert, New Falcon, Nobles, Pathé, Perfection, Pioneer, and **Star.** The active British companies in 1907 were Columbia, **Clarion,** Edison Bell, Russell Hunting Record Co., Ltd., and White. After various price wars and patent fights, the Russell Hunting firm folded in 1908.

Pathé gave up cylinders for discs in Britain in 1906 (though it continued to sell old stock through dealers) followed by Columbia in 1907 and Edison Bell in 1914. Clarion cylinders remained on the market until at least February 1922—the last cylinder maker in the U.K.

In the U.S., Columbia continued to make cylinders and discs, until 1909. It distributed Indestructibles until 1912, when it abandoned the cylinder field to Edison. The high quality of the Blue Amberol cylinder, introduced in 1912, and the fact that Edison had nurtured a loyal multitude of customers—mainly in rural areas (though Sears, Roebuck was selling Columbia graphophones through its catalogs)—who kept Edison in business. He had produced more than 10,000 different cylinders by 1912. His price for two-minute standard records was $.35; for the four-minute Amberols it was $.50. Grand Opera records sold for $.75–$2. Edison phonographs with sapphire reproducers were marketed at all prices from $15 to $200. The fine **Amberola** phonograph was continually improved from its introduction in 1912 through the late 1920s.

Recently one American company made cylinders on a small scale: Electrophone Cylinder Record Co., Davenport Center, New York. The records were of polypropylene, which was promised to last indefinitely. Repertoire included contemporary material and dubs of old Edison originals. The venture was short-lived. In Britain, Williams' Fox Record was available in 1988, from 21 Park Road, Burntwood, Wallsall. Another British cylinder firm is Miller, Morris and Co., of Exeter. Descriptions of these new cylinders were given in *HN* 170 (October 1989), p. 281. [Andrews*; Andrews 1972; Andrews 1974/4; Andrews 1976/6; Andrews 1985/4; Andrews 1987/1; Klinger*; Koenigsberg*.]

7. *Repertoire.* First conceived and marketed as a device to record and play back the speaking voice, the cylinder's early repertoire was shaped accordingly. When Edison renewed his attention to the instrument in 1887, he perceived that voice recordings would best serve to promote it. His British representative, Colonel George E. Gouraud, set up an exhibit at the London Crystal Palace and recorded there (or elsewhere in London) Robert Browning, William Gladstone, Cardinal Manning, and Alfred Tennyson. He also made records of Florence Nightingale, H.M. Stanley, and P.T. Barnum. Even Queen Victoria made a record, on a Pathé machine, for Edison Bell. In Germany, Prince Otto Bismarck made an Edison record. Other famous voices were preserved, at least for a time: Leo Tolstoy, Henry Irving, Arthur Sullivan, and Emperor Franz Josef of Austria; unfortunately many of these relics were lost or have deteriorated beyond usefulness.

Edison retained his attachment to the spoken voice throughout the cylinder era, notably through comic recitations like those of Cal Stewart. However, his first commercial sales lists were in fact all musical—in the widest sense of the word. The 24 May 1889 list—the initial entries in the *First Book of Phonograph Records* of the Edison Laboratory—consists of 14 titles played by flutist F. Goede: bird imitation pieces, college songs, polkas, waltzes, and marches. The next group of records featured Alfred Amrhein, violinist, and the third was given over to cornet numbers by John Mittauer. One of Amrhein's selections, the overture to *Fra Diavolo*, appears to be the first operatic recording.

From 1889 to 1892 the most recorded artists at Edison were Duffy and Imgrund's Fifth Regiment Band, Henry Giese (clarinet), H. Giesemann (piano), Edward Issler (piano), the Issler Parlor Orchestra, Will Lyle (banjo), John Mittauer (cornet), George F. Schweinfest (flute, piano, piccolo, violin), William Tuson (clarinet), and A.T. Van Winkle (xylophone, metalophone, violin). Works recorded were mostly arrangements of popular songs, well-known classical items, marches, polkas, waltzes, and so forth. "Jingle Bells" on Will Lyle's banjo was the first Christmas record (October 1889). These were all on two-minute cylinders, so the medium itself limited the repertoire to short numbers. And recording technology limited it to certain instruments and combinations that worked best in the studio.

Recordings of the singing voice became numerous in the late 1890s and early 1900s. Ventures into the operatic vocal repertoire were soon common, with international artists interpreting two-minute versions of popular arias. Among the opera stars on Edison cylinders, between 1896 and 1912, were Mario Ancona, Giuseppe Campanari, Andreas Dippel, Antonio Scotti, and Anton Van Rooy. (However, most of the arias done for Edison were rendered by performers of less distinction.) The cylinders of **Gianni Bettini** included more than 200 items, mainly from the operatic repertoire and featuring star singers; these were made in the mid- to late 1890s. Columbia's first recording by an opera singer came out in 1898; the artist was Bernard Bégué.

Edison's repertoire between 1900 and 1912, the period of the two-minute brown wax and gold molded records, was highly varied. Orchestra records appeared in large numbers, by such ensembles as the American Symphony Orchestra, the Edison Symphony Orchestra, Victor Herbert and his orchestra, and the Peerless Orchestra; they played waltzes, marches, and medleys. Military band music was performed by the Edison (Grand) Concert Band, the Edison Military Band, His Majesty's Irish Guards Band, the National Military Band of London, the New York Military Band, Sousa's Band, and the U.S. Marine Band. Probably the most beloved solo vocalist was Arthur Collins; others were Harry Anthony, Albert C. Campbell, Will F. Denny, S.H. Dudley, Edward M. Favor, George J. Gaskin, Irving Gillette, Roger Harding, Byron G. Harlan, Ada Jones, Harry Macdonough, Edward Meeker, Billy Murray, Joseph Natus, Dan Quinn, Bob Roberts, Manuel Romain, Frank C. Stanley, and William H. Thompson. Sophie Tucker and Walter Van Brunt began their long recording careers on Edison cylinders in 1910 and 1912 respectively. Titles chosen by all these singers were ballads of the day, patriotic numbers, Irish songs, and **coon songs**.

In some ways the early repertoire was more diverse than what we see in a modern CD catalog. There were solo pieces featuring the cornet, the euphonium, the ocarina, and various orchestral instruments; there were whistlers, dialect comics, vaudeville groups, and male quartets in abundance. But the piano could not yet be recorded well (the Edison cylinder output included just four piano items between 1903 and 1908), and of the organ just one early example appeared: "Abide with Me," made in August 1909. Educational recording began with **language instruction records**, via courses given on Edison cylinders in 1889.

Although Edison made constant improvements in his products, they lost ground quickly to the disc. His **Amberol** cylinder of 1908 and the **Blue Amberol** of 1912 did not prove competitive against discs of inferior acoustic qual-

ity, and in 1912 Edison offered his own Diamond Disc to the public. Thereafter the cylinder repertoire was second-hand, being dubbed from the Diamond Discs. [Dethlefson 1980; Frow 1978; Klinger*; Koenigsberg*; Koenigsberg 1987; Wile 1982.] *See also* ACCORDION RECORDINGS; BRASS INSTRUMENT RECORDINGS; CELLO RECORDINGS; COMEDY RECORDINGS; HYMN RECORDINGS; LITERARY RECORDINGS; MALE QUARTETS; MILITARY BAND RECORDINGS; OPERA RECORDINGS; ORCHESTRA RECORDINGS; ORGAN RECORDINGS; PIANO RECORDINGS; VIOLIN RECORDINGS; WHISTLING RECORDINGS; WOODWIND RECORDINGS; and names of individual artists.

8. *Contemporary playback of cylinders.* Playing tinfoil recordings is hazardous to them, and most of the extant cylinders of that type are doomed to silence. A laser system for reading the signals in the tinfoil was described by Tom Hedberg in 1978. In separate articles written in 1975, Tim Brooks and George Blacker explained how to play wax and amberol cylinders electrically, using a modern turntable tone arm. If the tone arm is long enough, and if it swivels 180 degrees away from the turntable, it can be placed on a cylinder—which is turned by its own player—and the stylus will track the grooves. It must be borne in mind that special styli are needed to play cylinders because of the variability in groove dimensions. "A far more convenient method is now available with the Owl Audio Kit. This is a modern cartridge and stylus assembly which mounts easily in an original cylinder player's reproducer carriage; the original machine is thus used only as a transport. Alternatively there are some very expensive archival machines, such as those built by Art Shifrin, which provide both a modern transport and cartridge/stylus assembly" (Brooks*)

While playback on authentic cylinder machines may seem appropriate, and it is probably no harder on the records than use of modern equipment, there is no advantage in sound quality. [Blacker 1975/8; Blacker 1980/9; Brooks*; Brooks 1975; Hedberg 1978; Owen, T. 1982.] *See also* SONIC RESTORATION OF HISTORICAL RECORDINGS.

CYLINDROGRAPHY. The study of cylinder records; an equivalent term to **discography.** It was coined by George Blacker. Apparently the first serious research in the field was carried out by Duane Deakins, who published an extensive list of early cylinders in 1956–1961. In Britain H.H. Annand was at work at the same time, listing "indestructibles." Sydney H. Carter compiled Edison cylinder lists, as well as lists of Clarion, Ebonoid, and Sterling. Victor Girard and Harold M. Barnes published their important catalog of cylinders, by artist, in London, in 1964. Much of the British research was superseded by the definitive work of Koenigsberg on Edison cylinders. The Blue Amberols were listed by Ron Dethlefson in 1980–1981. Further research by the persons named above, and by later scholars, has appeared primarily in the collectors' journals, such as *Antique Phonograph Monthly.* [Blacker 1981/2.] (*See* the Bibliography for details on the works cited.)

D & R (label). A product of the D & R Record Co., Chicago, which was probably related to the **Standard Talking Machine Co.** of that city. D & Rs, on sale via mail order around 1910, were made from Columbia masters. The label name stands for "Double and Reversible." [Fabrizio 1980; Rust 1978.]

D/A. *See* DAC.

DA CAPO (label). A Swedish label that offered 94 issues in 1937–1941; it seems to have belonged to a department store. Most of the releases were made from **Silverton** matrices. [Liliedahl 1971; Nationalfonotekets 1969.] *See also* DACAPO (label).

DAC. Also known as D/A converter, or digital-to-analog converter. A circuit for converting digital signals to corresponding analog signals. Twin or dual DACs specialize the process for left and right channels. Super-linear converters are hand-tuned for better performance.

DACAPO (label). A German-made record issued in Germany from 1907, and available in Britain from 1910 to 1912. At least 250 titles were on sale by September 1910, including 40 British recordings. The repertoire was mainly popular, with some opera. **William Andrew Barraud** was the British agent for the firm, setting up the headquarters at No. 1 New Inn Yard, Great Eastern St., London EC, in November 1911. On 12 Jan 1912 the company name was changed to W.A. Barraud, Ltd. A price war in late 1912 in Britain forced the Dacapo import

to reduce its price to 1s 6d, but it was unable to sustain competition; there was no Dacapo advertising after September 1912. Barraud left the organization when there was a new incorporation on 2 Oct 1912. The firm was renamed Dacapo Record Co., Ltd, and directed by **E.F.G. Hale.** [Andrews 1990.] *See also* DA CAPO (label).

DAILY MAIL MYSTERY RECORD (label). A 10-inch record sold by the *Daily Mail*, London, in 1932. Artists were not identified and a prize of £1,950 was offered to the person who could guess who they were. The disc label was the earliest to carry the names of all the new **EMI, Ltd.,** firms: HMV, Columbia, Parlophone, and Regal Zonophone. In January 1933 the artists and numbers were published in the newspaper. The performers were Ambrose and His Orchestra, Leslie Hutchinson, Derickson & Brown, Binnie Hale, Doris Hare, Howard Jacobs, Robert Naylor, Billy Mayerl, Raie da Costa, Debroy Somers and his band, Geraldo Gaucho Tango Band, Peter Dawson, Harold Williams, Albert Sandler, George Baker, Raymond Newell, Jack Mackintosh, Bobby Howes, Francis Day, Melville Gideon, De Groot, John Morel, Albert Sammons, Heddle Nash, Cedric Sharp, Patricia Rossborough, and Sam Browne. [*TMR* #12 (Oct 1971) published this revelation, contributed by Frank Andrews.]

DALHART, VERNON, 1883–1948. American tenor and country singer, born Marion Try Slaughter in Jefferson, Texas (he took his stage name from two towns near there) on 6 Apr 1883. After several years on stage in New York, he began to record for Columbia (1916), Edison (1917), Victor (1918), and many other companies. Under at least 70 pseudonyms, he made thousands of records between 1925 and 1930, perhaps more than any other artist. His repertoire included ballads, patriotic songs, comic numbers, light opera, hillbilly songs, and—most distinctively—disaster songs.

Dalhart's first record for a major label was "Just a Word of Sympathy" (Columbia #2108; December 1916). He then made seven discs in 1917 for Emerson, but did not achieve notable status until his earliest Edison records were issued in 1917. His first Edison, and one of his finest efforts, was "Can't Yo' Heah Me Callin' Caroline?" (Diamond Disc #80334; also on Blue Amberol #3185; 1917); it was in Negro dialect, one of his special styles. He went on **tone test** tours for Edison, and made a great hit with "Wreck of the Old 97" (Diamond Disc #51361; 1924). At the same time he was working for Victor, doing "darky serenades," one of which, "Tuck Me to Sleep in My Old 'Tucky Home," was a best seller (Victor #18807; 1921). His greatest success came with "The Prisoner's Song" (Victor #19427; 1924), said to have been Victor's highest-selling acoustic issue, with more than a million sales. The same song was recorded also on about 30 other labels. During the last years of the cylinder, 1925–1929, Dalhart virtually kept the format alive with more than 137 releases. Many were duets with **Carson Robison**. But there was a quick reversal in his popularity, as public taste shifted to the new **crooning** style, and he was passé by 1930. Furthermore he was financially ruined in the Wall Street crash of 1929. Except for a brief, unsuccessful, comeback with Bluebird in 1939, Dalhart remained outside the record industry. He worked in a war plant, taught voice in Bridgeport, Connecticut, and was a hotel clerk there when he died (15 Sep 1948). [Walsh 1960/5–12.]

D'ALMAINE, CHARLES, 1871–1943. English violinist, born in Hull on 13 June 1971. He was one of the earliest violinists to record, beginning with "Miserere" (Edison cylinder #7324; 1899) and two other numbers. He was concertmaster of the Edison house orchestra, and of the Victor Orchestra when it was established in

1906. D'Almaine had 18 cylinders in the 1902 Edison catalog, and 18 in the 1901 Columbia catalog (presumably it was he; the artist was not named)—the two lists were virtually identical. He worked for Victor from 1901, and made his final discs for Pathé. His repertoire included concert pieces, operatic arrangements, reels, and dances. "Because" (Edison #7420; 1900) and "Oh Come All Ye Faithful" (Edison #7732; 1901) were among his popular releases. On Columbia he was sometimes identified as Charles Gordon. D'Almaine gave up recording in 1914 and worked as a chiropractor. His death came in Newark, New Jersey, on 17 June 1943. [Walsh 19578/11–12; 1958/1; 1959/11.]

DAL MONTE, TOTI, 1893–1975. Italian coloratura soprano, born Antonietta Meneghelli in Mogliano on 27 June 1893. She made her debut at La Scala in 1916, and sang elsewhere in Italy in roles for various soprano types. With a performance of Gilda in Torino, 1918, she became a secure coloratura, singing that repertoire for 10 years at La Scala under Arturo Toscanini. She sang at the Metropolitan Opera on 5 Dec 1924, as Lucia; in Chicago from 1924 to 1928, and at Covent Garden in 1926. Dal Monte recorded for HMV in 1924–1925, doing the *Lucia* Mad Scene, (#DB 712), "Una voce poco fa," "Caro nome" (#DB830), and two other arias; all are outstanding interpretations. During 1927–1935 she made electrical discs for HMV, a number of which have been reissued by Harmonia Mundi on CD #89001. Perhaps her finest record was "Un bel di," recorded in 1935 and reissued in 1989 (EMI CD #CHS7 69990–2). [Renton 1949.]

DALMORÈS, CHARLES, 1871–1939. French dramatic tenor, born in Nancy on 1 Jan 1871. He was a notable horn player, winning the Paris Conservatory prize at age 19, and serving as an orchestral hornist for several years; then he was professor of horn in Lyons. He made his debut as a tenor in 1899 in Rouen, then was heard in Brussels, and for seven seasons at Covent Garden. He was at the Manhattan Opera from 1906 to 1910, and in Chicago from 1910 to 1918 (singing in that city's first *Parsifal*). His repertoire was both French/Italian and Wagnerian. On Victor Red Seal during 1907–

1908 and 1912–1913, Dalmorès produced many fine discs. A favorite among collectors is "Ah si ben mio" from *Trovatore* (Victor #85123). He died in Hollywood on 6 Dec 1939.

DAMONE, VIC, 1928– . American popular singer, born Vito Farinola in Brooklyn on 12 June 1928. His entrance into show business was as an usher at the Paramount Theatre in New York; but not long after that humble beginning he appeared there as a featured performer. In the 1940s he gained quick fame. He had his own radio show in 1947–1948; and he was a sensation at the Mocambo Club in Hollywood. Many films and records followed, including *Kismet* (1955; soundtrack on MGM #E-3281) and *Hit the Deck* (soundtrack on MGM #E-3163). Damone had a light baritone voice of the Frank Sinatra type, best heard on his greatest hit singles: "I Have But One Heart" (Mercury #5053; 1947), "You're Breaking My Heart" (Mercury #5271; 1949), "My Truly, Truly Fair" (Mercury #5646; 1951), "On the Street Where You Live" (Columbia #40654; 1956), and "An Affair to Remember" (Columbia #40945; 1957). He also made successful LP albums for Mercury, Columbia, and Warner.

DAMPING. The action of dissipating part of the oscillating energy in a sound system, usually by the use of non-resonant material. Tone arm or stylus **resonance** is often intentionally damped to prevent frequency distortion. Unwanted **cone** movement in a **loudspeaker** may be damped. [Klinger*.]

DAMPING FACTOR (DF). In a **power amplifier**, the ratio of the load **impedance** to the amplifier output impedance. An amplifier with an 8 ohm load impedance (the EIA standard) and an output impedance of 0.08 ohm would have a DF of 100. With an output impedance of 0.04 ohm, the damping factor would be 200. DFs range from under 20 to about 1,000, and the higher factors are desirable, as they indicate a strong ability of the amplifier to reduce unwanted **cone** movement in the **loudspeaker**. However, other resistances in the system, between the amplifier and the speaker, can easily nullify the benefit of a high DF; and one writer has stated that "high or low damping factors don't do much to alter the performance of today's conventional speakers. . . . Heavy feedback is used in most output circuits to stabilize and enhance performance. That feedback also causes a lowering of the amplifier's output impedance, which means a high DF." (Klein) [Klein, L. 1989; Klinger*.]

DANCE MASTER. A selective **coin-op** machine, with 12 discs on individual turntables in a ferris wheel configuration, marketed by the **Mills Novelty Co.** in 1929. It was similar to the cylinder **Multiphone**.

DANCE MUSIC. Music intended to accompany social dancing, usually associated with ballroom dances like the fox-trot. It became a staple of record producers worldwide beginning with the dance craze in America just before World War I, and exhibited a continuous tradition through the **Big Band** era. The Victor 1917 catalog listed these varieties: barn dances, buck dances, cakewalks, Castle dances, clog dances, fox-trots, furlena, globe trot, half & half, jigs, London taps, one-steps, polkas, reels, schottisches, tango and maxixe, three-steps, two-steps, and waltzes. One-steps, fox-trots, and waltzes were the most recorded types in that catalog, accounting for about 500 discs. By 1927, the Victor catalog was dominated by fox-trots and waltzes, the prime forms of ballroom dancing; but there also records suitable for novelty dances like the Charleston. The Big Bands of the 1930s and 1940s emphasized the fox-trot in various tempos, but they also gave dancers the opportunity to do Latin American dances like the tango, the rumba, and the samba. In the late 1930s and in the 1940s the jitterbug and boogie-woogie styles were favored, in which couples were sometimes separated— each partner improvising—and sometimes together for energetic gyrations.

During the 1950s rock and roll music marked the general demise of close couple dancing among young people. Solo and group movements predominated in that era, and have continued to hold the preference of dancers except in formal social events. The twist and the shake were variant forms, popular in the early 1960s. With the rise of rock music, dance music was largely replaced by **disco**.

From time to time a Latin dance has shared the stage, such as the bossa nova of the early 1960s. Ballroom dancing has remained interesting to older persons, who may return to surviving ballrooms for nostalgic fox-trots and waltzes.

DANDY (label). An obscure American issue of ca. 1924–1926, carrying dance music from Emerson-Consolidated. [Rust 1978.]

DANN TRIO. A group of three women who recorded for Edison in 1919–1923; they were M. Felice Dann (cornetist), Blanche L. Dann (pianist), and Rosalynd Davis (violinist). They recorded for Edison in December 1919, as a trio and with solos for the cornet and violin. The Dann repertoire was composed of ballads of the day. The group was effective enough to be assigned to **tone test** tours from coast to coast, often with tenor Harvey Hindermyer. [Walsh 1977/7–9.]

DARRELL, ROBERT DONALDSON, 1903–1988. Editor and discographer, born in Newton, Massachusetts, on 13 Dec 1903. He attended Harvard College and the New England Conservatory. Darrell edited the *Phonographic Monthly Review* from 1930, and was contributing editor of *High Fidelity* from 1956 to 1984. He wrote the seminal *Gramophone Shop Encyclopedia* in 1936 (*see* DISCOGRAPHY). Darrell was one of the first American critics to focus on recordings, primarily of classical music. He also reviewed discs for *Saturday Review, High Fidelity* (1954–1987), and *Opus*. Darrell died on 1 May 1988 in Kingston, New York.

DAT (DIGITAL AUDIO TAPE). Using a new technology introduced in 1986, Sony made possible a transfer of material from CDs to cassette tapes with no loss of quality. Technics, Luxman, and Mitsubishi were other companies that were making DAT equipment by 1987. DATs are not digital-to-digital clones of the CDs they copy, because the recording systems use different sampling rates. Copies are made using the analog inputs of the DAT recorders. Consumer access to this technology was obstructed by the concerns of CD manufacturers, who introduced a device to prevent

the copying that DAT machines were made to do (*see* COPYCODE). Whether or not such preventive gadgets were to be required on DAT machines imported in the U.S. was a question before the U.S. Congress, never resolved. With the acquisition of CBS Records by Sony in 1988, the issue lost some of its edge. Meanwhile, the first pre-recorded DATs were issued by Delta Music Co. of Los Angeles; the Fall 1988 Schwann listed 44 titles. By 1991 DATs had been integrated with other formats in Schwann catalogs. A new protective technology, **Serial Copy Management System**, emerged that allowed restricted copying, and gained approval from record manufacturers and equipment firms.

DATING. In record collector parlance, establishing the exact date of an issue or of a recording session. Unlike books, recorded media do not typically carry publication or copyright dates, so the discovery of relative dates requires research. Since the files of most defunct recording firms have been lost, and since the files of major extant companies are often incomplete, in awkward arrangements, or closed to investigators, the problem can be a formidable one. Diaries, appointment books, and recollections of performers are sometimes useful in determining session dates. There are also stories about the performers in newspapers and magazines, telling what cities they were playing in; such information serves to limit the possibilities of recording for specific labels in specific places, although major labels have had studios in many cities. Release dates are sometimes found in contemporary periodicals like *Talking Machine World*, and in new record announcements sent by companies to record shops.

The recorded material on a disc or tape may be traced through copyright catalogs to establish an earliest possible date for the record—assuming that music was copyrighted before it was put on record. It is also a fair assumption that a hit tune is recorded by several companies at about the same time, so that if the date of one release is known there is a clue to the timeframe of the others.

What might seem like the most promising clue to dating, the **matrix number**, is occasionally misleading; the matrices were not always chronological. Blocks of matrix numbers might be assigned (as Victor did) to certain studios, or to types of material. Another problem with matrix numbers is that some companies kept the same number for a remake of an earlier record. The physical appearance of a disc is often an indicator of its time period, as label color and designs tend to be constant for a particular series over a period of time.

Students of the various labels have published helpful results of their dating endeavors (examples are found in the bibliographies following the articles on the individual labels in this volume). Likewise, biographers of musicians in recent years have often included detailed dated discographies in their books. [Bryant 1962, makes suggestions for dating British LP issues; Daniels 1985; Gart 1989; Kendziora 1971, a useful introduction to the dating problem; Kinkle 1974; Rust 1978; Walsh 1968/10–12; Walsh 1969/2–4; Warren 1979. Daniels, Gart, Kinkle, and Rust are important guides to dating the issues of a large number of American labels. Both Walsh articles are guides to dating Victor records.]

DAVEGA (label). A record produced for sale in the Davega chain of sporting good stores in New York City from the summer of 1922 to ca. March 1923. One series consisted of dance and popular vocals, while another series had some operatic items. Most of the masters came from **Pathé**, but a few were from **Paramount**, via Plaza, and others were from **Banner**. Among the artists represented were the Synco Jazz Band, California Ramblers (as the Golden Gate Orchestra), and the Original Memphis Five. [Kendziora 1962/3–4; Rust 1978.]

DAVENPORT, EDGAR LONGFELLOW, 1862–1918. American actor, born in Boston on 7 Feb 1862. He recorded poems and recitations, beginning with "Jim Bludsoe" (Edison cylinder #9053; 1905). His second record was also his biggest hit: "Lasca" (Edison #9087; 1905); it appeared also on Columbia, Victor, and other labels. Davenport did not record after 1913. He died in Boston on 25 July 1918. [Brooks 1990; Walsh 1967/8–9, 12.]

DAVIS, MILES DEWEY, III, 1926–1991. American jazz trumpeter and bandleader, born in Alton, Illinois, on 25 May 1926. At age 15 he was already a professional trumpet player. He moved to New York in 1944, ostensibly to study at the Juilliard School, but primarily to work with Charlie Parker, whose quintet he joined in 1945. He also worked with the Benny Carter and Billy Eckstine bands. He led various **bebop** groups in the late 1940s, and recorded with many bebop artists. With the collaboration of arranger Gil Evans, Davis created a calmer and more melodic variant of bebop, and became one of the pioneers of **cool jazz**.

After a highly successful appearance at the Newport Jazz Festival of 1955, Davis formed a quintet and other groups, and made records featuring novel arrangements, playing flugelhorn as well as trumpet. Among his sidemen over the years were saxophonists Cannonball Adderley and John Coltrane; and pianists Chick Corea, Bill Evans, and Keith Jarrett. In the late 1960s he led the development of the fusion style of jazz, mixing improvisations with rock formulas. He experimented with modal sounds, departing from standard harmonies. In the late 1960s and in the late 1970s Davis developed a preference for the loud rock idiom. He was active through the 1980s, despite frequent illnesses. He died on 28 Sep 1991 in Santa Monica, California.

The basic Davis style was crisp, relaxed, and melodic in its improvisations; his ensembles were smoothly blended and restrained. His albums of the 1950s illustrate his best work, among them *Kind of Blue* (Columbia #CL 1355: 1959) and *Porgy and Bess* (Columbia #1275; 1959). "Concierto de Aranjuez" and other numbers in *Sketches of Spain*, with Gil Evans (Columbia #CS 8271 1960), offered an inspired incursion into Spanish music; it was the first Grammy winner for Davis. *Quiet Nights* was a successful album of 1964 (Columbia #CL 2106). The rock-laden texture of *Bitches Brew* (Columbia #GP 26; 1970) created controversy, but also spawned imitations; it was on the charts 17 weeks. Davis had two later Grammy albums: *We Want Miles* (1982) and *Tutu* (1986). He was honored with a lifetime achievement award at the 1989 Grammy presentations.

DAVIS, SAMMY, JR., 1925–1990. American popular singer, dancer, and actor, born in New York on 8 Dec 1925. He was born into a vaudeville family and was on stage at the age of four. At age six he appeared in a motion picture. During the Depression he was part of a group called the Will Mastin Trio that played in various venues across the U.S. Davis saw military service during World War II, and then gained sudden acclaim in a Hollywood engagement at Ciro's nightclub. He appeared as a soloist at the Copacabana in New York in April 1954, creating a sensation. Signed by Decca, he made a quick success with his first album, *Starring Sammy Davis, Jr.* (#DL 8118; 1955), in which he offered impersonations of Bing Crosby and other luminaries. A second album of 1955, *Just for Lovers* (Decca #DL 8170), was also on the charts. In the Broadway show *Mr. Wonderful* he sang several songs that became associated with him, including "Mr. Wonderful." His most popular singles were "What Kind of Fool Am I?" (Reprise #20048; 1962), "The Shelter of Your Arms" (Reprise #20216; 1963), and "I've Gotta Be Me" (Reprise #0779; 1968).

Davis spent most of his later career as a nightclub entertainer. He was the first Black artist to be featured in Las Vegas, and is credited with integrating the hotels there and in Miami. He was active in the Civil Rights movement, marching with Martin Luther King, Jr., in Montgomery, Alabama, but gathered mixed reactions from the Black community for his two marriages to white women and his association with President Richard Nixon. His career was beset with various personal miseries, including the loss of an eye and a long final struggle with cancer.

DAWSON, PETER, 1882–1961. Australian baritone, born in Adelaide on 31 Jan 1882, "grandest of the concert singers of any period of recording" (Rust). He was a choirboy; then won a singing contest at age 19 and gave concerts. In 1902 he was sent to London to study with Charles Santley, who arranged a concert tour in the west of England. Dawson then gave recitals throughout the Empire. An audition for Edison Bell led to his first cylinder records, under the stage name Leonard Dawson; he also made discs for G & T in London, and for

Nicole, then went to other labels as well. His first Edison cylinder was the Scottish comic song "Foo the Noo" (#13396; 1906) under the name of Hector Grant; in that and other records (and in the music hall) he impersonated **Harry Lauder.** Dawson's repertoire was vast and diverse: concert arias, comic songs, patriotic numbers, and ballads, all under pseudonyms.

Dawson's busiest year in the recording studio was 1907, as he worked for a half-dozen companies. In 1909–1910 he made a 20-week Australian tour, and in 1913–1914 another. He sang a concert for Maori tribesmen, in their language. He joined the Australian Army in 1918. With electrical recording Dawson's popularity increased. He made a noteworthy *Pagliacci* "Prologo" in 1926, and won great praise for his "Erlkönig" of 1927. Thomas Beecham regarded him as the ideal Handel singer. During the 1930s he found new audiences, singing children's records and popular tunes. The cowboy song "Empty Saddles" (HMV #B8475) also sold well. But his most appreciated and best remembered disc was "Waltzing Matilda," the only Dawson number to have wide appeal in the U.S., where it appeared on Victor Red Seal (#10-1025; 1938). Another highly popular record was "Mandalay Scena" / "Clancy of the Overflow" (HMV #7EG8159; 1956).

Altogether Dawson made about 3,500 records, with a total sale of more than 13 million. An LP reissue of 1958 covered many of his hits in different genres (HMV #DLP 1180). Pearl and EMI have issued CDs. [Walsh 1962/1–6.]

DAY, DORIS, 1922– . American popular singer and actress, born Doris Kappelhoff in Cincinnati on 3 Apr 1922. As a child she performed as a dancer, but turned to singing after a leg injury. During the 1940s she became a band vocalist and Hollywood actress, beginning with Les Brown's orchestra in 1940–1941 and 1943–1945. With Brown she recorded her greatest single, "Sentimental Journey" (Columbia #36769; 1944). She had a dozen chart singles in the 1950s, notably "Que será, será" (Columbia #40704; 1956). Day took the role of Ruth Etting in the 1955 motion picture *Love Me or Leave Me* (soundtrack record Columbia #CL-710). She was a star on television in the 1960s and 1970s, and had many successful non-singing roles in films.

dB. *See* DECIBEL (dB).

dbx. A **noise reduction system** developed in the early 1970s by David E. Blackmer, using more sophisticated circuitry than the **Dolby Noise Reduction System**. It completely eliminates tape hiss by means of a wide-range 2:1 compressor-expander voltage-controlled amplifier. For reasons unknown, lower-case characters are used in writing the name of the system, which is the same as that of the firm that produces it (and the BX1 power amplifier), in Newton, Massachusetts. [Blackmer 1972.]

DEAD STUDIO. In the strict sense, a studio in which there is no reflection of sound waves and no entrance of sound from outside the room; more generally, a studio with relatively little **reverberation**.

DE BASSINI, ALBERTO, 1847–19 ?. Italian baritone, born in Florence. He was a member of the Lisbon Royal Opera. He is known for his many **Bettini** cylinders, on which he recorded virtually the entire baritone opera repertoire in 1897–1899: 101 solos plus 16 duets with Rosalia Chalia. On disc he recorded for Zonophone in 1903 (eight arias and songs), and Columbia in 1903–1905 (26 numbers). He used the pseudonym "A. del Campo" on some of his records. Nothing is known of his life after 1905.

DECCA GRAMOPHONE CO., LTD. The name taken by the firm of Barnett Samuel & Sons (*see* SAMUEL [BARNETT] AND SONS, LTD.) as they changed from a musical instrument maker to a manufacturer of gramophones. The Decca Dulcephone portable, first marketed in 1914, was the most successful of its products, advertised under Barnett Samuel's name as late as 1926. The portable, which closed into a cubic-foot-size carrying case, was very popular among British military personnel during World War I. In 1929 the company was acquired by the new **Decca Record Co., Ltd.** [Bayly 1974 has illustrations and details; *TMR* #63/64 has advertisements, p. 1770.]

DECCA RECORD CO. One of the major firms in the disc industry of the U.S., established as the American branch of **Decca Record Co., Ltd.** on 4 Aug 1934 at 799 7th Ave., New York, with factory and offices a 619 W. 54th St. Founders were **Jack Kapp**, who became president, **Edward Robert Lewis** (head of the British company; he became chairman of the U.S. board), and E.F. Stevens. Kapp had been a Brunswick executive, and when he left that company to form Decca he used Brunswick series numbers as the basis for Decca's numbering system. (Brunswick was affiliated: English Decca had rights to the label, from an agreement with its owner, the **American Record Corp.**) Thus the first Decca matrix, New York series, was #38290 (13 Aug 1934): Guy Lombardo's "Down by the Old Mill Stream," issued as Decca #102. It was from the Decca studio in Los Angeles that the earliest dated matrix was made, on 8 Aug 1934: "Poor Unlucky Cowboy," by Scott Hamblin and his Covered Wagon Jubilee.

Decca was in financial trouble immediately, with rising debts and some unmet payrolls. Lewis wrote that "at the office in New York we had a pleasant enough waiting room. There the unfortunate creditors used to wait." The year 1934 ended with the U.S. and U.K. companies just surviving bankruptcy. Yet American Decca soon made its place in the market, by means of a low sale price for its product: $.35 per disc, compared to $.75 for competing labels. Decca also attracted highly popular artists such as Bing Crosby, Jimmy Dorsey, Tommy Dorsey, the Mills Brothers, Skitch Henderson, and Arthur Tracey. A successful country music series was offered from 1934 to 1945, consisting of 1,113 releases. By 1936 the company was showing a profit. Reflecting the taste of Jack Kapp, almost all the company's releases until his death in 1949 were of popular music. Great sales success was achieved by many Crosby songs, above all "White Christmas" in 1942. Other acclaimed Decca artists included the Andrews Sisters, Count Basie, Louis Armstrong, and Woody Herman. In 1942 American Decca revived the Brunswick label, defunct since 1939, and reissued many outstanding Brunswick discs, by such performers as Cab Calloway, Crosby,

Duke Ellington, Benny Goodman, Red Nichols, and Pine Top Smith.

A major technological improvement was introduced in 1946: **full frequency range recordings (ffrr)**. It was the outcome of research by Arthur Charles Haddy, who had worked on submarine detection devices. Used in conjunction with the Decca Piccadilly player, this shellac 78 rpm disc achieved a range of 50–14,000 Hz, the best in the industry. It was marketed first by American Decca, then by London. In 1949 the earliest Decca LP appeared, in time to be included with 10 other labels in the first *Long Playing Record Catalog* issued by W. Schwann in October. The firm was among the pioneer stereo labels. An affiliation with **Deutsche Grammophon Gesellschaft (DGG)** was negotiated in 1956. In 1962 **MCA, Inc.** acquired the company, continuing the Decca label name into the 1970s.

Decca's label design began with a blue and gold sunburst pattern, then had many variants. Its most familiar manifestation was the blue color with either shaded or plain block letters for the company name. A Personality series, initiated in 1939, was crimson color with gold letters. [Ginell 1989 (the country music series); Hayes 1971; Rust 1978.]

DECCA RECORD CO., LTD. A British firm, established on 14 Feb 1929 in London, taking over the **Decca Gramophone Co., Ltd.** The founder was **Edward Robert Lewis**, a stockbroker. Entering the record market—with the acquisition of the **Duophone Record Co.**—during a period of worldwide depression in the industry, Decca thrived. Lewis took the approach of acquiring rights to American labels like Brunswick and Melotone, while at the same time underselling the British competition. The trademark was registered in Sweden in 1929, and by 1930 there were distributors in Stockholm and Gothenberg; Swedish artists were recorded in London. Decca acquired British rights to the Polydor label in 1930, gaining a much-needed classical repertoire and a group of classical artists.

In 1931 Lewis persuaded the directors to offer discs at 1s 6d, while other leading labels were selling at 2s 6d or 3s, and only a few bargain labels like Broadcast and Imperial cost

1s 6d. Jack Hylton's orchestra was signed to an exclusive contract, with the quick reward of a hit record, "Rhymes," that sold 300,000 copies. A number of British classical performers were added to the catalog by the mid-1930s, including Henry Wood, Clifford Curzon, Hamilton Harty, and Boyd Neel. Decca's classical records were priced below those of HMV Red Label.

However, the times were bad, and the firm appeared to overextend its resources. It bought **Edison Bell** in 1933. While attempting to acquire **British Brunswick, Ltd.**, a cashflow crisis developed. Lewis wrote that "we were extended generous credit by our suppliers. . . . One day the phones were cut off. . . . Salary cuts were accepted by the loyal and enthusiastic staff. . . ." **Louis Sterling** at **EMI, Ltd.**, was anticipating a takeover of Decca, and so was the **Crystalate Gramophone Record Manufacturing Co.** (Sterling's firm was not that secure either; according to Lewis, Sterling remarked that Decca was such an unconscionable time in dying that by the time the end came EMI themselves would be so weak they would probably fall into the same grave.) But Decca held on, and ironically it acquired a debilitated Crystalate in March 1937. Before that, Lewis moved boldly to acquire American **Columbia** from **Grigsby-Grunow**, but while he was sailing to New York to arrange that transcaction Columbia was sold to the **American Record Corp.** Yet Lewis was insistent on having an American affiliate, and "decided then and there to form a new record company"—it was the new U.S. **Decca Record Co.** Another acquisition took place in May 1935, as Decca and EMI jointly purchased **British Homophone Co., Ltd.**

During the 1930s, the labels sold by Decca were Brunswick 10-inch and 12-inch (through its British Brunswick, Ltd., subsidiary), Decca 10-inch and 12-inch, Decca Polydor 10-inch and 12-inch, Panachord (sometimes from U.S. Melotone masters), Rex 10-inch, Vocalion 10-inch, and some Edison Bell Winners.

World War II brought little economic benefit to Great Britain, but the record industry got some of it. With other entertainment unavailable because of the blackout and threat of bombing, demand for records was stimulated. Some bombing damage to the Decca production plant was sustained. Great prosperity for Decca came in the post-war years, in large measure due to the invention of **full frequency range recording (ffrr)**, which marked the birth of the high-fidelity market. The lightweight Decola pickup, with its diamond or sapphire stylus, turned consumer interest away from the metal needle and its fiber/cactus relatives.

Decca brought the LP record to Europe in June 1950, and in 1958 was among the first to market stereo records in Britain, as ffss (full frequency stereophonic sound) discs.

As many as 80 percent of the Top Twenty pop discs in Britain were Deccas in the late 1950s. The firm's classical output also flourished, with recordings made all over Europe. From Decca in 1958–1966 came what David Hall refers to as "perhaps the grandest achievement of the recording art up to that time"—the complete *Ring* produced by **John Culshaw.** Thus did the early low-price pop label join the great names of classical music recording. Another success of the period was the takeover, from EMI, of RCA Victor distribution in Britain. The new Decca House, on the Albert Embankment, London, was opened on 10 Mar 1958.

Then problems developed: an old, slow production plant was one, a shift of focus to classical repertoire was another. The American situation had become troubling too, as U.K. Decca lost rights to the Decca trademark in the U.S., and had to ship to America under the **London** label. Finally in 1980 the Decca companies were broken up, and the record label was acquired by **PolyGram International**—which still operates the company as a separate firm and makes limited use of the Decca label name. The rest of the Decca interests, including the old Duophone factory at New Malden, were bought by Racal Electronics, just at the time of Lewis's death. [Culshaw 1979; Hall 1980; Lambert 1983; Rust 1978.]

DECIBEL (dB). A logarithmic measure of the relative **intensity** of sound. It represents a ratio between two acoustical or electrical quantities. One dB expresses a ratio of approximately 1.1:1, between the first and second levels. Human hearing is logarithmic with respect to the perception of loudness: the intensity of a signal

must show a certain increase before the human ear perceives change, and the change that is noted is arithmetically smaller than the actual rise in signal intensity. Signal A will be perceived as minimally louder than signal B if it is one dB higher in intensity than B, and it will seem about twice as loud as signal B if their intensities differ by three dB. Signal A will seem four times as loud if there is a six dB increase, and eight times as loud if there is a nine dB increase in the difference between A and B. Twenty dB are 100 times greater than 10 dB, rather than twice as great.

The value of a dB was chosen to match the smallest increment of loudness that the human ear can distinguish in the mid-frequency range. Human hearing has a range from zero dB, the threshold of hearing, to 120 dB, the threshold of pain. (Sustained exposure to sound levels above 120 dB is not only painful, but may lead to temporary or even permanent hearing loss. The noise at rock concerts has been measured as high as 130 dB.) In musical language, the range is from ppp to fff; that 120 dB range actually encompasses a million variations in sound intensity (10^6). A listener 20 feet from a symphony orchestra playing fff would experience about 110 dB. [Backus 1969; Rosenberg 1983.] *See also* HEARING.]

DECK. In open-reel or cassette **tape recording,** the name of the unit containing much of the apparatus: it may include the tape **transport, amplifier, preamplifier, controls,** meters, and a built-in **microphone.** It may or may not be a recording deck as well as a playback deck. Decks do not have **loudspeakers** or **output amplifiers,** so they need to be connected to those components in order to function. The tape deck is often found as an element in a **high-fidelity** system or rack system. Recently, many decks have been made with two tape transports, permitting the user to copy a recorded tape onto a blank.

DECODER. A device that assigns each signal in a multichannel system to its proper **channel.**

DE-EMPHASIS. A change of **frequency response** in a reproducing system. *See also* PRE-EMPHASIS.

DE FOREST, LEE, 1873–1961. American inventor, born in Council Bluffs, Iowa, on 26 Aug 1873. His childhood was spent in Talladega, Alabama, where his father was president of Talladega College. As a boy he was fascinated with machinery, and in time went on to the Sheffield Scientific School at Yale University, where he specialized in electricity and mathematical physics; he took a Ph.D. in 1899. De Forest moved to Chicago, held various jobs and carried out his own research. His invention of the responder provided an improvement in radio reception, and led him to concentrate in the radio field. In 1907 he formed the De Forest Radio Telephone Co. The triode **audion** circuit he developed was patented in U.K. (#1427; 1908), and his single stage **amplifier** received U.S. patent #841,387 in 1907. These inventions introduced the new age of electronics.

On 2 Jan 1910 De Forest used his equipment to broadcast from the stage of the Metropolitan Opera House, transmitting the voice of Enrico Caruso. His laboratory produced the first efficient multi-stage amplifier in 1912. He formed a new company, De Forest Radio, Telephone and Telegraph Co.

Acquiring patent rights to several inventions, including the Tellafide photo-electric cell, he was able to work successfully on **soundtrack** systems. On 12 Apr 1923 he presented the first commercial talking picture, at the Rivoli Theater in New York. By 1925 he had made a number of "phonofilms"—short subjects with synchronized sound—featuring Al Jolson and other popular performers. He set up another firm, Phonovision Co., to exploit the motion picture area.

His firm began to have financial setbacks in the early 1920s, and there was a reorganization in 1923. Bankruptcy came in the summer of 1926, and the company was acquired by Powel Crosley, who became president. De Forest remained with his old company as a consulting engineer. He went on to experiment for another 30 years, working in diathermy and color television. He had more than 300 patents, the last issued when he was 83 years old. His nickname, "Father of Radio," was the name he gave to his autobiography (1950). He died on 30 June 1961.

DE FRANCO, BUDDY, 1923– . American jazz clarinetist, born Boniface Ferdinand Leonardo De Franco in Camden, New Jersey, on 17 Feb 1923. He played with the Big Bands of Gene Krupa, Charlie Barnet, Tommy Dorsey, and Count Basie; then had his own band from 1951 and a quartet from 1952. De Franco led the Glenn Miller orchestra in 1966–1974. He won the *Down Beat* poll as favorite clarinetist every year from 1945 to 1955, again from 1960 to 1963, and also from 1965 to 1967. "Opus No. 1" was one of his finest records with Tommy Dorsey (Victor #20–1608; 1944). "Golden Bullet" / "Bluebeard Blues" was a major disc with Count Basie (Columbia #38888; 1950). Among the popular sides De Franco made with his own combo were "Get Happy" (MGM #11250; 1951) and "Oh Lady Be Good" (MGM #11453; 1953).

DE GOGORZA, EMILIO, 1874–1949. American baritone, born in Brooklyn on 29 May 1874; his name is also seen as Gorgoza. He was first known on record as "Signor Francisco," "E. Francisco," or "Carlos Francisco." The spelling "Francesco" was also used. Under these names he appeared on the Berliner label, singing the *Pagliacci* "Prologo" in 1898 or 1899 (#1120), and on Zonophone in 1900–1901, doing 22 numbers. He recorded for Eldridge R. Johnson's Improved Record in 1900–1902, doing 76 numbers—"La paloma" (#171) was notable in the group. In 1903 he was on Victor's black Monarch label, singing seven pieces, and he continued with Victor to 1906. In all these records he used the Francisco (Francesco) name.

He sang as Edward Franklin for Zonophone in 1900–1901 and for Climax in the same years. He was M. Fernand for Johnson in 1902 and many later Victors. Herbert Goddard was another early stage name, used for Johnson and on black Monarch from 1900 to 1905.

De Gogorza used his own name on black Monarchs in 1903–1909, singing 57 items, some of which came out later on Red Seal. Perhaps his outstanding recordings were "Largo al factotum," "Dio possente," from *Faust*, the "Prologo," "Vison fugitive," and "Il balen" from *Trovatore*. He was also recognized as supreme in Spanish songs and French art songs. The Victor 1917 catalog retained 55 numbers by him. He retired in 1928, headed the vocal department of the Curtis Institute in Philadelphia, then taught in New York, where he died on 10 May 1949. [Walsh 1945/1–2.]

DEIRO, GUIDO, 1886–1950. Italian accordionist, born in Turin on 10 June 1886; brother of **Pietro Deiro.** For most of his recording career he was a Columbia artist, beginning with "Sharpshooter's March" and "Ciribiribin" in May 1911. He made Columbias until 1924, and remained in the catalog into the 1930s. One of the most prolific and popular artists on the accordion, Deiro also made Edison cylinders, beginning with "My Sweetheart Waltz" (#743; August 1911), and continuing with operatic excerpts and ragtime. He was heard on Cameo discs as Carlo Pampini. He died in California on 26 July 1950.

DEIRO, PIETRO, 1888–1954. Italian accordionist, born in Turin on 28 Aug 1888; brother of **Guido Deiro.** He moved to the U.S. in 1907, settling in Seattle. In 1909 he began his long vaudeville career in San Francisco, going on to the New York Palace Theatre and other major venues. He was identified in the 1917 Victor catalog as the "greatest accordionist in the world" and represented there by more than 50 titles. His first records were for Columbia in July 1913: "Row, Row, Row" and "When the Midnight Choo Choo Leaves for Alabam'" (#A1323). Then he went to Victor, starting with "Broadway Medley" and "Great White Way" (#17486; January 1914). Much of his repertoire consisted of operatic excerpts and waltzes. One waltz record remained in the Victor catalog until 1942 ("Kiss Waltz" / "Broadway Waltz"; #21163; 1928). Deiro left Victor in 1919, was less active for a time, then made some Deccas ca. 1936. One of his finest discs was Decca #1276, "Ciribiribin" / "O sole mio." Deiro died in New York on 3 Nov 1954.

DELAUNAY, CHARLES, 1911–1988. French critic, author of the first extensive **discography** in 1934 (*see* the Bibliography) as well as an important jazz discography published in 1948. (He was long credited with coining the term "discographie," but recent research attributes this creation to Compton MacKenzie.) Delaunay established the Hot Club of France,

and with Hugues Panassié started *Le jazz hot,* the earliest jazz magazine (1934). He organized recordings in France by such jazz artists as Django Reinhardt, Stéphane Grappelli, and Benny Carter. Delaunay died near Paris on 16 Feb 1988.

DELAY SYSTEM. A mechanism that holds back in time all or part of an audio signal passing through a sound system. The usual purpose is to introduce special effects such as echoes (achieved with a delay of about 30 milliseconds) or the impression of an increased number of performers (a chorus effect emerges with a delay of about 10–30 milliseconds). In live radio interviewing, delays may be used to give the controller time to remove potentially offensive material. In tape recording, the delay requires a long tape loop, an **erase head**, a **recording head**, and several **playback heads**; as the signal is heard through the first playback head, it can be erased in time to prevent broadcast from a later playhead, or recording. In **digital recording systems,** the delay mechanism involves a low-pass **filter**, a high-frequency sampling switch, a shift register to hold the sampled signal, and connections that move each element of the signal slowly from one stage to the next. The controller can sample the signal before the output stage, and can prescribe the delay interval.

DE LEATH, VAUGHN, 1896–1943. American popular singer, also a whistler and pianist, born in Mt. Pulaski, Illinois, on 26 Sep 1896. She sang in public as a teenager, and was one of the first women to appear regularly on radio. Her singing was of the **crooning** type. De Leath was seen in vaudeville, and on Broadway; she was a great success in *Laugh, Clown, Laugh* (1936). She was one of the early television artists, in 1939.

De Leath began to record in 1920, with "I Love the Land of Old Black Joe" (Edison Blue Amberol cylinder #4097), then made hundreds of records for many labels to 1940. She recorded 44 Edison Diamond Discs, including the final one from that label, in November 1929. Much of her work was with Sam Lanin's orchestra, and she made many duets with Irving Kaufman, but most of her discs were with studio orchestras. Her best known record is "The Man I Love" with the Paul Whiteman band (Columbia #50068–D; 1928).

DELLER, ALFRED, 1912–1979. English countertenor, born in Margate on 31 May 1912. He sang as a child in the Canterbury Cathedral choir and then at St. Paul's in London. In 1950 he formed the Deller Consort which helped to revive interest in British renaissance music. By 1976 he had 16 LP albums in print, including the Bach Society, RCA, and Vanguard labels. He died in Bologna on 16 July 1979.

DEL MONACO, MARIO, 1915–1982. Italian dramatic tenor, born in Florence on 27 July 1915. He taught himself by listening to operatic records, and in 1935 won a vocal contest in Rome. His debut was as Pinkerton in Milan in 1941; then he served in the Italian army to the end of World War II. After the war he appeared in many world opera houses, and made his Metropolitan Opera debut as Des Grieux in *Manon Lescaut* on 27 Nov 1950 and stayed with the company to 1959, singing 102 performances. Otello was his greatest role; he made a complete recording of the opera under Herbert Von Karajan for Decca. He also starred in a dozen other LP recordings of complete operas. Del Monaco died in Mestre, near Venice, on 16 Oct 1982.

DEL PAPA, DANTE, ?–1923. Italian tenor, one of the early operatic recording artists. He made his debut in Milan in 1887, then sang throughout Italy. He first appeared at the Metropolitan Opera in 1898. Del Papa made cylinders for **Bettini** in New York: in the 1897 Bettini catalog Del Papa has 22 numbers; in 1898 he has 23 solos and three duets; and in 1899 there were 61 solo arias and songs, plus duets with Rosalia Chalia. After retiring from the stage, Del Papa directed a vocal school in New York. He died in New York in February 1923.

DELPHEON CO. A firm established in 1916 in Bay City, Michigan. It was maker of the Delpheon line of disc players.

DE LUCA, GIUSEPPE, 1876–1950. Italian baritone, born in Rome on Christmas day, 1876. He

sang in Piacenza in 1897, then at La Scala in 1903. His Metropolitan Opera debut was in *Barbiere di Siviglia* on 25 Nov 1915; he stayed with the company until 1935. He made his first commercial records for G & T in 1903–1904, after which he was primarily a U.S. Victor artist. From 1917 to 1925 he made 36 Red Seals, including a famous version of the *Rigoletto* Quartet with Amelita Galli-Curci and Enrico Caruso (#10000) which sold for a premium price. The reverse side offered a great recording of the *Lucia* Sextette, with Galli-Curci, Caruso, De Luca, and Marcel Journet. Later he re-recorded both ensembles, with Beniamino Gigli, Louise Homer, and Ezio Pinza (#10012).

Other favorite records are "Ah per sempre" from *Puritani* (Victor #74787), "A tanto amor" from *Favorita* (Victor #74591), "Sei vindicata assai" from *Dinorah* (Victor #74872), "Largo al factotum" (Victor #74514), and his final disc: "Quand' ero paggio" from *Falstaff*. The last-named record was made at his farewell concert at Town Hall in New York, on 7 Nov 1947, when he was 71 years old. He died in New York on 26 Aug 1950. [Favia-Artsay 1955/2 gives the playing speeds required to get correct pitches on various records; Williams, C. 1957.]

DE LUCIA, FERNANDO, 1860–1925. Italian lyric tenor, then also dramatic tenor, born in Naples on 11 Oct 1860. His debut was in Naples in 1885; he appeared first at the Metropolitan Opera in 1894. He was unmatched in his interpretations and recordings of Rossini and Donizetti. "Ecco ridente" from *Barbiere di Siviglia* is one of his outstanding discs (G & T #052078; 1904; Victor #76000); another is "Prendi l'anel" from *Sonnambula*, with Maria Galvany (G & T #054217; 1908). He recorded first for G & T, in Milan, in 1903–1904, then again in 1906–1908, covering most of the Italian/French tenor repertoire. During 1910–1912 he recorded for Fonotipia in Milan. The 1917 Victor catalog lists arias from *Carmen, Lohengrin* (in Italian), and *Manon*. De Lucia made over 100 sides for Phonotype in Naples, from around 1915 to 1920. Two of them, arias from *Pagliacci*, were reissued on IRCC #210. In 1918 Phonotype recorded a complete *Rigoletto* and a complete *Barbiere* with him in the leading roles. De Lucia retired in 1917, then sang again—for the last time in public—at Enrico Caruso's funeral in 1921. He died in Naples on 21 Feb 1925. [Henstock 1991.]

DE LUSSAN, ZÉLIE, 1862–1949. American soprano, born in Brooklyn on 21 Dec 1862. She made her debut at age 16, in the Academy of Music in Brooklyn. In 1885 she sang with the Boston Opera Co. She went to London in 1888, earning great acclaim for her magnetic Carmen. She sang at Windsor Castle and at other command performances, and at Covent Garden, mastering 31 roles. She performed with the Metropolitan Opera in 1894–1895, 1898, and 1899–1900. De Lussan's "Habanera" was the first aria to be recorded on Victor (#2198; 17 May 1903). This session was only the second of Red Seal recording (the first was 30 Apr 1903). On the same day she did four songs and another aria, "Connais-tu le pays" from *Mignon*. In 1906 she made four discs for Beka Records GmbH. She died in London on 18 Dec 1949. [Potterton 1967.]

DELUXE (label). An American record established in 1943 by the Jules Braun family, with offices at 20–28 E. Elizabeth Ave., Linden, New Jersey. The specializations were country and western, race records, and Latin-American music. In 1945 the label had more than 120 items available. Deluxe was taken over by the **King** label in 1947, but issues under the Deluxe name continued until ca. 1961. [Rotante 1973 includes a label list of the 5000 and 6000 series.]

DELUXE RECORD (label). A Victor Talking Machine Co. record of ca. 1903–1904. It was a 12-inch disc at first; then from March 1903 it was 14 inches, styled Deluxe Special Record. About 150 of the 12-inch Deluxe Records were made. Although they gave three or four minutes of playing time, their content was basically the same as that of the seven- and 10-inch records that had preceded them, except that the performances went on a little longer. Takes of varying lengths were made in the same session, and releases were available in some cases for all three sizes. For example, "Love Thoughts" by Sousa's Band was recorded on 8 May 1902 in a 10-inch and 12-inch version. Cal Stewart's "Uncle Josh Weatherby in a Depart-

ment Store" was recorded for all three sizes on 21 July 1902. The 14-inch record, which sold for $2, was made to play at 60 rpm. It thus carried between five and six minutes of material, and may be considered the first attempt to produce a long-playing record. The extra playing time was not well exploited, however, since the repertoire consisted primarily of "selections" and arrangements, rather than of complete versions of longer works. Fewer than 50 titles were offered. The innovation was technically acceptable, but proved to be a commercial failure, and the series was dropped from the catalog by 1904. [Fagan 1983.]

DEMAGNETIZATION. A procedure in **tape recorder** player maintenance, used to counteract the buildup of residual magnetism in the tape heads and in the player's metal parts. The device employed produces an alternate magnetic field that neutralizes polarities on the metal parts, creating a random alignment of the polarities instead of a dominant charge. This procedure, followed after every 40 hours or so of operation, will prevent unintentional signal erasure as tapes are played. Demagnetizer cassettes are available for use with cassette tape equipment. [Klinger*.]

DEMO. A record made for demonstration purposes or as a kind of audition by a performer seeking a label contract.

DENNY, WILL F., 1860–1908. American tenor and vaudeville performer, born in Boston. He began to record for the New England Phonograph Company ca. 1891, then went to many labels. He did 10 numbers for Victor, all of which were dropped from the catalog by 1904, and two for Zonophone. Edison had 34 of his cylinders by 1899, including his biggest hit: "A Widow's Plea" (Edison #6602). Most of his records were Columbias; he had 59 items in the 1899 catalog. Denny died in Seattle on 2 Oct 1908.

DENVER, JOHN, 1942– . American popular singer and songwriter, born Henry John Deutschendorf, Jr., in Roswell, New Mexico, on 31 Dec 1942. His family moved to Waco, Texas, while he was in high school, and he began to perform there as a church singer and as a guitarist for local events. He moved to California and achieved some success in a vocal group, then auditioned for the Chad Mitchell Trio. He took Chad Mitchell's place in the trio, which was then renamed the Mitchell Trio, and toured with it from 1965 to 1968, when it disbanded. In 1966 Denver wrote the song "Leaving on Jet Plane" and performed it with the trio; it became a top hit in 1969, having been recorded by Peter, Paul and Mary. Denver's solo career brought him fame as a writer-performer of music with folk, rock, and country aspects. His most popular albums were *Poems, Prayers and Promises* (RCA #LSP 4499; 1971, 1974), which included the hit song "Take Me Home, Country Roads," and *Rocky Mountain High* (RCA #LSP 4731; 1972), which included the hit title song. Another outstanding single, "Annie's Song," helped to carry the album *Back Home Again* into the gold category (RCA #CPL 1–0548; 1974). "Sunshine on My Shoulders" was a song Denver wrote for a television score; it was a number one hit in 1974 (RCA #0213).

Denver was named Entertainer of the Year by the Country Music Association in 1975. His album of that year, *John Denver's Greatest Hits* (RCA #CPL1–0374), was on the charts for two years, selling more than 5 million copies. Although he did not sustain the popularity he attained in the mid-1970s, Denver continued to perform and record successfully in the 1980s. His 23rd RCA album, *Dreamland Express* (#AFL1–5458), was on the charts in 1985.

DENZITE PRODUCTS MANUFACTURING CO. A Brooklyn firm, located (in 1921) at 31 Ellery St. Denzite is known to have been operating in 1920, pressing discs for others. It did not have its own label, so far as is known. [Andrews*]

DE PACHMANN, VLADIMIR, 1848–1933. Russian pianist, born in Odessa on 27 July 1848. He studied in Vienna, then toured Russia in 1869. His American performances of 1891 brought much attention, in part because of his eccentric behavior and additions to the scores he played. He was particularly emotional in performing Chopin, the composer he recorded most frequently. He did 15 numbers for Victor

Red Seal in 1911–1913, and three more in 1924–1925. A reissue of English Columbia discs made in 1915–1916 appeared in 1981; it revealed the pianist to be at times impressively dazzling, at other times given to foolish distortions. He died in Rome on 6 Jan 1933.

DEPARTMENT STORE LABELS. In the U.S. and U.K., record sales sections in department stores became common in the 1920s and 1930s. A number of stores issued discs under house labels, such as—in Britain—Curry's, Ltd. (**Curry's** label, **Portland**, and **Westport**), A.W. Gamage, Ltd. (**Gamage**), Woolworth (**Victory, Eclipse, Crown**), Lewis's, Ltd. (Lewis's Long Life), Marks & Spencer (**Marspen**), Metropolitan Chain Stores, Ltd. (**Empire**), Peacock Stores (**Peacock**), and Selfridge, Ltd. (**Key, Silvertone**). The Selfridge Silvertone was made by British Homophone Co., Ltd., and was not related to the most well known store label, the Silvertone of **Sears, Roebuck, & Co.** Sears, the largest U.S. retailer, also sold **Oxford** discs. Other American department stores with recordings included the W.T. Grant chain, which marketed the **Diva** label. Philadelphia's John Wanamaker issued discs under the **Carnival** label in 1924–1925. J.R. Hudson of Detroit offered its **Hudson** label in 1924. A **Montgomery Ward** label was available from that Chicago store and mail-order house in the 1930s. Another Chicago mail-order firm, Strauss and Schram, Inc., sold **Puritone** records in 1928–1929, and **Supertone**. McCrory's sold its **Oriole** label from 1921 to 1938. Bamberger's, of Newark, New Jersey, had the **Pennington** disc from 1924 to 1925. **Resona** was the label produced for the Charles William Stores, Inc., of New York for a few years, ending in 1925. Buffalo's Larkin Co. had the **Symphonola** label briefly before 1920.

DE RESZKE, EDOUARD, 1853–1917. Polish baritone, born in Warsaw on 3 Dec 1853. He studied in Italy, and made his debut as Amonasro in Paris, under Verdi's direction, on 22 Apr 1876. Then he went to La Scala, London, Chicago, and the Metropolitan Opera—his debut there being on 14 Dec 1891 (on the same evening as his brother Jean's debut) in *Roméo et Juliette*. He stayed with the Metropolitan until 1903, achieving recognition as the leading

Wagnerian and French/Italian baritone of his time, then retired. His greatest role was Mephistopheles in *Faust*. He recorded three items for Columbia in 1903: "Infelice" from *Ernani* (#1221), the Porter's Song from *Martha* (#1222), and the "Don Juan Serenade" by Tchaikovsky (#1223). He made no other records. He died in Garnek, Poland, on 25 May 1917. [Dennis 1951.]

DE RESZKE, JEAN, 1850–1925. Polish tenor, born Jan Mieczislaw De Reszke on 14 Jan 1850 in Warsaw. He started as a baritone, singing in Italy and France. By 1879 he had changed to tenor, and sang in Madrid. He created the title role in *Le Cid* in Paris on 30 Nov 1885, and became a favorite there. Then he sang in London, and made a Metropolitan Opera debut on 14 Dec 1891 as Roméo (his brother Edouard's debut was in the same performance). He remained at the Metropolitan for 11 seasons, and was greatly acclaimed for his French/Italian roles, and also for Tristan (performed 27 Nov 1895). He left the Metropolitan in 1901, recognized as the greatest tenor of his era, and transferred to Paris. He died in Nice on 3 Apr 1925.

Only two commercial recordings by the tenor exist: Fonotipia #69000, the Tomb Scene from *Roméo et Juliette*, and Fonotipia #69001, "O souverain" from *Le Cid*; both were made in 1905. The voice is faint and poorly recorded. There are also some dubbings available from **Mapleson cylinders** made during Metropolitan performances in January and March 1901. These give segments from *Le Cid*, *L'africaine*, *Huguenots*, *Siegfried*, and *Lohengrin*—the last being from his final Metropolitan appearance. Another cylinder, of De Reszke with Milka Ternina in *Tristan* was recorded with so much background noises that David Hall pronounced it "a monumental disaster." [Dennis 1950/1; Hall 1981/1; Stratton 1967; Taylor, G. 1988.]

DE SABATA, VICTOR, 1892–1967. Italian conductor, born in Trieste on 10 Apr 1892. He began as a pianist and violinist, then followed Arturo Toscanini's advice and turned to conducting. He led the Monte Carlo Opera from 1918 to 1930, then conducted and became artistic director at La Scala (1929–1957), conducting also in Bayreuth, London, Chicago, New York, and elsewhere. In 1957 he made his last public appearance, conducting at Toscanini's funeral. He died in Santa Margherita Ligure on 4 Dec 1967.

De Sabata recorded for Cetra, Polydor, HMV, and Decca, producing many outstanding discs. His 1953 *Tosca*, with Maria Callas, Giuseppe Di Stefano, and Tito Gobbi, is one of the great operatic recordings (Angel #3508, reissued on EMI CD #S7 47175). His famous *Tristan* is represented on disc by the *Prelude* and *Liebestod* (with the Berlin Philharmonic Orchestra, Polydor #67498).

DESMOND, PAUL, 1924–1977. American alto saxophonist, born Paul Emil Breitenfeld on 25 Nov 1924 in San Francisco. He was the outstanding performer on his instrument during the **cool jazz** period, noted especially for his participation in the Dave Brubeck Quartet (1951–1967). Earlier he had worked with Jack Fina, Alvino Rey, and others. With Brubeck his most famous recording was his own composition "Take Five" (in Columbia album #CL1397; 1959). Desmond won the *Down Beat* poll for favorite alto saxophonist each year from 1955 to 1959, and from 1962 to 1967. He died on 30 May 1977 in New York.

DESTINN, EMMY, 1878–1930. Bohemian dramatic soprano, born Emmy Kittl in Prague on 26 Feb 1878. She made her debut as Santuzza in Berlin on 19 July 1898, and remained with the Berlin Opera until 1908. Wagner was her specialty, and also *Salome*; she starred in the latter's Berlin and Paris premieres. From 1904 to 1914 she was in Britain, after making her debut at Covent Garden as Donna Anna. She began at the Metropolitan Opera on 16 Nov 1908, singing Aida under Arturo Toscanini, and stayed to 1914. Destinn retired in 1920, and died on 28 Jan 1930, in Budejovice, Bohemia.

She was poorly recorded in her first effort, one side made in Berlin for G & T in 1901, and fared no better recording for Fonotipia in Berlin in 1905. She was heard to better advantage on four Columbias made in Berlin in 1904. The "Habanera" was the earliest of the Columbias (#40483). Destinn recorded for Odeon in 1905–1906, repeating some of her Fonotipia material and offering her first Wagner discs. G & T recorded some her most important material from 1906 to 1909, including the outstanding "Dich teure Halle" (#043133; reissued on IRCC #184 with "Wär es wahr?" (#043138) from Smetana's *Dalibor*. She sang in the 36-disc complete *Carmen* and the 34-disc complete *Faust* of 1908. In 1911 Destinn made three records for Edison Diamond Discs. She was with Columbia again in 1912–1913, presenting brilliant interpretations of "Wie nahte mir" from *Freischütz* (#30974), and "Vissi d'arte" (#30998). The 1917 Victor catalog had 20 items by Destinn, including the remarkable "Miserere" with Giovanni Martinelli (#88530). Her total career output was 218 sides. IRCC reissued seven of her arias, and there were many LP reissues on various labels. On some recordings she is identified as Destinova. Destinn was the subject of the earliest published discography about a singer, in *Gramophone*. April, 1930. [Rektorys 1971.]

DETROIT TALKING MACHINE. A disc player produced by the Detroit Brass and Iron Works Co., Detroit. It was introduced in 1899 at the modest sale price of $1.98 by mail order. The player was similar to the one sold by the **United States Talking Machine Co.** in 1897, both being intended for use with Berliner's discs. [Fabrizio 1976.]

DEUTSCHE GRAMMOPHON GESELL-SCHAFT (DGG). A firm established in Hanover, Germany, by Emile and Joseph Berliner on 6 Dec 1898, to press discs for the European market. The original name of the firm was Deutsche Grammophon GmbH; this was changed to Deutsche Grammophon AG, then reverted to the first form after World War I.

Masters were drawn from Victor and the Gramophone Co. There was quick growth for the firm, which sold both records and players, but the Berliner family did not have the resources to expand. DGG became a joint-stock company on 27 June 1900, owned by three companies, then passed entirely into the hands of the Gramophone Co., and the office was moved to Berlin—headed by **Theodore B. Birnbaum**—with the factory remaining in

Hanover under Joseph Berliner. Within a year the Hanover factory was advertising that it had made more than 5,000 recordings in all languages; a second factory was leased, and purchased in 1908, to handle the demand; it became the "Werk 1" of DGG, located on what is now Podbielskistrasse.

Both seven-inch and 10-inch Grammophon discs were made, sold at 2.5 marks and five marks respectively. With the takeover by the Gramophone Co. of **International Zonophone Co.** in 1903, discs bearing the Zonophon label were also pressed in Hanover, and sold at two marks for seven-inch and four marks for 10-inch sizes. Prices were lowered in 1906. The first double-sided discs (12-inch) appeared in 1907, and the seven-inch size was phased out.

Birnbaum was replaced in 1904 by N.M. Rodkinson, who left in favor of Leo B. Cohn in 1907. At that time daily production was 36,000 discs, coming from about 200 presses. The year 1908 brought 6.2 million records out of Hanover.

The recording **angel** trademark, associated with the Gramophone Co. and DGG since 1898, was dropped in 1909, and **Nipper** came onto the scene; at this time the label name was changed to "Die Stimme seines Herrn," to match the British His Master's Voice. Sales rooms were by then operating in many large German cities.

A famous first in recording history occurred in 1913: a complete symphony was inscribed in wax by DGG. With Arthur Nikisch conducting the Berlin Philharmonic Orchestra, Beethoven's Fifth Symphony (truncated and somewhat rearranged) was issued on four 12-inch discs. Excerpts from *Parsifal* were also done. But this great advance was halted by the World War I, which brought DGG near to a complete shutdown. In 1917 only 400,000 discs were made, and only through the requirement that buyers trade in an old record when buying a new one, to replenish the supply of materials at the factory. Finally the German government took over DGG, along with other British holdings in the country, and sold it to **Polyphon Musikwerke AG** of Leipzig on 24 Apr 1917.

Subsequent reorganizations were nullified by the war's end, at which time the old British parent firm prevented Polyphon from using the Nipper trademark, and from exporting records that had not been made in Germany. Nevertheless, the company prospered in Germany and through affiliated firms established in Austria, Denmark, Norway, and Sweden. The trademark dispute was settled in 1924, as the Anglo-German Arbitration Tribunal gave DGG the right to use both Grammophon and Die Stimme seines Herrn in Germany. But for exports the Polydor label had to be used.

After the war the roster of artists was rapidly built. It included Wilhelm Kempff, Wilhelm Backhaus, Carl Flesch, Richard Strauss, Leo Blech, and Hermann Abendroth. Despite the great inflation of the early 1920s, the company was able to produce 2.1 million discs as well as Polyphon gramophones. With the introduction of **electrical recording** new performers were added to the catalog, among them Wilhelm Furtwängler, whose first release was the Beethoven Fifth with the Berlin Philharmonic Orchestra.

An arrangement with **Brunswick** in 1927 allowed DGG to sell discs in the U.S. on the Brunswick label, and American jazz masters were pressed in Hanover for issue in Germany on the British Brunswick label. In 1928 the company pressed its first million-selling disc, a Christmas item entitled "Erzengel Gabriel verkündet den Hirten Christi Geburt." During that year the Japanese affiliate Nippon Polydor Chikuonki was opened in Tokyo. DGG's prosperity peaked in 1929, with an output of 10 million discs. But in the economic crisis that began in 1929 it was necessary to form a holding company, Polyphon-Holding AG (later renamed Polydor-Holding AG) comprised of Austrian, Danish, Swedish and French interests. Even this move failed, and in 1933 Polydor-Holding was sold. Disc production never entirely ceased, though it was down to 1.4 million per year in the 1934–1936 period, and a restructured directorship negotiated a consortium of the German national bank, and **Telefunken**, to create a new Deutsche Grammophon GmbH. The two labels, Deutsche Grammophon and Telefunken, were able to sell 4.6 million discs in 1938. Progress was shattered in the World War II, and in the turmoil the conglomerate Siemens and Halske acquired control of DGG. At the same time the Telefunken operation was

separated, and sold to **Allgemeine Elektrizitäts Gesellschaft (AEG)**.

Somehow recording continued, and on an important level. The outstanding production during the World War II was the St. Matthew Passion, issued on 18 12-inch discs. At that time the Siemens name was used on labels: Siemens Spezial for classical records, and Siemens Polydor for popular music. A new manufacturing process developed in the Siemens laboratories reduced surface noise. Again the company was surviving under stressful conditions—and again there was disaster. Air raids destroyed the enterprise in 1944–1945.

In June 1946 DGG was permitted to start fresh, and already in 1948 the firm was producing 1.8 million discs; in 1949 the output climbed to 3.2 million. Four different labels were in use after 1949: a yellow one styled Deutsche Grammophon Gesellschaft for classical music (issued in America by Decca); a red Polydor for popular music; a black Brunswick for foreign popular music; and a silver Archiv Produktion for classical music. The firm introduced the LP to the German market.

In 1954 the **Archiv** label appeared in Britain (as Archive), and the DGG and Polydor labels followed in 1955. DGG and Philips merged in 1962, with each company retaining autonomy. With the formation of **PolyGram International** in 1972, DGG was absorbed, but the label independence remained. In 1980 DGG merged with **London Records**. DGG, Philips, and Decca introduced the compact disc to Europe in 1983.

Deutscher Industrie Normenausschus (DIN). *See* DIN DEUTSCHES INSTITUT FÜR NORMUNG.

DEUXPHONE. An English record player, made by the Deuxphone Manufacturing Co., Ltd., Wolborough St., Newton Abbot; notable for its capability of playing either disc or cylinder records. It was first advertised in *Talking Machine News* in October 1906, as the only player to handle both formats, and remained on the market a short time. A **mandrel** was fitted in the center of a **turntable**, and the whole machine had to be set on its side to put a cylinder in horizontal (playing) position.

DEVINE, ANDREW, 1832–1909. American record industry executive. He was one of the founders of the **American Graphophone Co.,** and—according to his obituary in *TMW*—"Father of the talking machine business." He had an early career as a court stenographer, then as a war correspondent during the U.S. Civil War, also covering courts martial and trials. Working for the Associated Press in the U.S. Senate, he was assisted by James G. Blaine, and when Blaine campaigned for president he took Devine along as official reporter. Later, as a U.S. Supreme Court reporter, he became interested in the dictation/shorthand use of the phonograph after seeing a demonstration. He visualized the commercial possibilities of recorded sound, thinking in terms of its business use. With James O. Clephane and John H. White, he entered into a marketing agreement with the Volta Graphophone Co. on 28 Mar 1887, marking the beginning of the **American Graphophone Co.** In addition to his concerns with the graphophone, Devine supported Mergenthaler, the inventor of the typesetting machine, and established with him and Frederick Warburton the Mergenthaler Linotype Co. He was a director of that firm, and of the Columbia Graphophone Co., at the time of his death, in Brooklyn, on 4 May 1909. [Wile 1990/2.]

DEVINEAU BIOPHONE CO. A Cleveland firm, located at 2095 E. 36th St. It made the Biophone, an attachment by which disc records could be played on a cylinder machine. The aggregate device had a ludicrous appearance, with the disc player mounted on top of the cylinder player (illustration in *TMW*, 15 Oct 1907). Marketed first in 1907, at $15, it was not advertised after 1909, when company founder Louis Devineau left Cleveland to reside abroad.

DF. *See* DAMPING FACTOR.

DGG. *See* DEUTSCHE GRAMMOPHON GESELLSCHAFT (DGG).

DIAMOND (label). (I) A disc record produced by the Diamond Record Co., of Chicago, from about 1902 to about 1906. The discs had various spindle hole sizes, including the standard 9/32

inch, and 9/16 inch. Masters came from Columbia. The same company made a player with a half-inch spindle, resembling those of the **Standard Talking Machine Co.** [Rust 1978.]

DIAMOND (label). (II) A disc issued in England during 1915–1918, custom pressed by **Pathé Frères,** who absorbed the business later. It was not an imitation of the Edison Diamond Disc, and looked nothing like it. The name was later changed to Pathé Diamond Record. [Andrews*.]

DIAMOND (label). (III) A record made in the 1930s in England by Diamond Universal Gramophone Records, Ltd. [Rust 1978.]

DIAMOND (label). (IV) An American independent label established in 1944, issuing popular material, spirituals, and light classics. "Miserlou," by pianist Jan August, was an early best seller. I.R. Gwirtz was the first president of the firm. *See also* EDISON DIAMOND DISC.

DIAMOND COMEDY FOUR. Also known as the Diamond Four. An early recording group, heard on Berliner discs ca. 1896. Members were Albert Campbell, Steve Porter, James K. Reynard, and Will C. (Bill) Jones. They made cylinders for Edward B. Marks and Joe Stern, New York music publishers, in the 1890s. Their material was humorous and novelty numbers, including a cat fight and a steamboat imitation.

DIAMOND STYLUS CO., LTD. A firm established in 1950 in Colwyn Bay, Wales, said to be the world's largest producer of diamond-tipped styli. The output was 50,000 per day in 1975. About 70 percent of the goods are exported. A specialty is the low priced stylus with diamond used only for the tip, which is bonded to a metal shaft. [Borwick 1975.]

DIAPASON CATALOGUE. The trade list of classical recordings currently available in France.

DIAPHRAGM. A membrane, in one of the components of a sound system, that vibrates in response to the incoming signal. In the cylinder phonograph this membrane was part of the **recorder** or of the **reproducer**; in the disc gramophone it was part of the counterpart **soundbox**. When a record was being made, the vibration of the diaphragm resulted from sound waves produced by the voice or instrument directed at it. When the record was played back, it was the stylus that created the vibration impulses. In early recording the preferred material for a diaphragm was glass, with various thicknesses used for different situations: a thin membrane was suitable for recording a violinist, while a thick one was needed for a band. As the vibrating membrane does not produce a sound of great volume, it was soon attached to a recording **horn**. By 1909 Victor and Columbia were using mica, imported from India, for their membranes; copper and aluminum were other common materials. Instruments often had adjustable gaskets to hold the diaphragm in place, and to vary the quality of output signal. Playback machines might have detachable soundboxes, each with a different diaphragm, such as one of mica for singing and violin music, and one of a larger diameter—made of alloy—for band music. The "Zora diaphragm" advertised by H. Lange's Successors of London (*TMN*, April 1908), was adaptable for playback with either a needle or a sapphire stylus. Modern diaphragms are made of mylar or other tough plastics.

In addition to the components cited above, both **microphones** and **headphones** utilize these membranes. [Copeland 1990; Waltrip 1990.]

DICKSON, WILLIAM KENNEDY, 1860–1935. British inventor. He came to the U.S. and in 1882 began working for Thomas Edison; he became laboratory chief and assisted in electrical research. In 1888–1889 he developed Edison's idea for combining the phonograph with motion pictures. Dickson wrote in his 1895 *History of the Kinetograph* (the first textbook on cinematography) that "the establishment of harmonious relations between Kinetograph [the camera] and Phonograph was a harrowing task, and would have broken the spirit of inventors less inured to hardship and discouragement than Edison's veterans." On 6 Oct 1889, Dickson showed the first motion pictures with any kind of sound added to them. They ran about 12 seconds, and included Dickson's voice speaking to Edison.

While the combination was still in the experimental stage, the camera alone was being demonstrated under the name Kinetoscope. By 1895 Dickson apparently solved the synchronization problem of sound and image, for he wrote in his *History* that "the inconceivable swiftness of the photographic succession, and the exquisite synchronism of the phonographic attachment have removed the last trace of automatic action, and the illusion is complete."

Although Edison did not vigorously pursue the commercialization of the device, he did produce about 50 machines (Kinetoscopes) and made successful short films (*see* KINETOPHONE). Dickson left Edison in 1897 to market his own Mutoscope. [Brown, A. 1976.] *See also* MOTION PICTURE SOUND RECORDING.

DICTATING MACHINES. The original commercial use of the phonograph was to take down office dictation and courtroom proceedings. Edison's early machine used a cylinder four inches long and 2 1/4 inches in diameter for both entertainment and dictation (with space for about 1,000 words of speech). From 1890 the Edison machine used a cylinder six inches long and 2 1/4 inches in diameter for dictation. That became the standard size of records for business machines of all makes until acetate discs replaced cylinders in the 1940s. Graphophone cylinders, however, were six inches long, 1 5/16 inches in diameter. *See also* EDISON SCHOOL RECORDS; VOICEWRITER.

DIDDLEY, BO, 1928– . American popular singer, guitarist, and songwriter, born Elias McDaniel in McComb, Mississippi, on 30 Dec 1928. His family moved to Chicago where, by the age of 10, he was playing guitar in streetcorner bands. In 1951 he got a nightclub job, and then played with various rhythm & blues groups. His stage name came from the African instrument, Diddley Bow. Leonard Chess auditioned him in 1954 and signed him for the Checker label. His first single, "Bo Diddley" (Checker #814; 1955), was well received. Diddley developed a style of blues with an African-like ostinato figure, a raw sound with a strident electric guitar. Several rock groups were influenced by him and performed his songs. He had a number of chart singles in the late 1950s and early 1960s, notably "Say Man" (Chess #931; 1959). There were also several chart albums, including *Go Bo Diddley* (Checker #LP 1436; 1959, reissued 1986). He was less prominent in the 1970s, but continued to perform and record. Diddley was among the earliest artists named to the Rock and Roll Hall of Fame. Ten compact disc titles were on the market in 1991, including *The Chess Box* two-disc set, with 45 Diddley songs of 1955–1969.

DIFFERENTIAL AMPLIFIER. An electronic device that increases the difference between two input signals.

DIFFRACTION. The characteristic of a sound system that permits longer wavelengths to curve around obstacles.

DIFFUSOR. A **diaphragm** in the form of a shallow paper cone, used in Pathé phonographs. It resembled Auguste Lumière's pleated paper diaphragm used by the French Gramophone Co. (made by the Gramophone Co., Ltd., for Britain and export). Although the Lumière device was not really a cone, the mechanics of the two diaphragms were similar. [Andrews*.]

DIGITAL COUNTER. A device in a **tape deck** that displays, usually in three digits, the location on the tape reel that is being recorded or played back. To find a specific spot on a tape, the user engages fast forward or reverse and stops when the desired point is indicated in the digital counter window. In this context the term "digital" is not drawn from computer digital electronic technology, but from the arithmetic "digit."

DIGITAL RECORDING. A method of recording, introduced in the late 1970s, in which the signal to be recorded is converted to digital form. In that form the signal is computer-readable. The computer examines the signal thou-

sands of times per second (the sampling process) and generates chains of pulses, each related to a segment of the analog signal. In the reproduce mode, the computer converts those pulses back to the instantaneous signal values originally sampled, and then a special filter forms analog curves of them—thus the initial audio signal is recreated. This process preserves all the audio characteristics of the signal, while excluding any extraneous sounds or distortions such as hiss. Current output formats include the compact disc, DAT, and the video disc, but digital LPs were also made before the CD arrived. Decca was the first to issue digitally made LPs, beginning with the live recording of the Vienna Philharmonic New Year's Day Concert (April 1979). *See also* COMPACT DISC; DAT; VIDEO RECORDING.

Digital to analog converter. *See* DAC.

DIN DEUTSCHES INSTITUT FÜR NORMUNG. A German standards organization, founded in Berlin in 1917. It was formerly called Deutscher Industrie Normenausschuss (DIN).

DIPLOMA (label). A record sold in London by **Blum & Co., Ltd.,** from 1911 to 1917. An August 1911 advertisement promised "over 350 well-known titles by well-known artistes." Diploma material was from Edison Bell matrices, pressed by the Edisonia Works. Litigation with the **Kalliope Musikwerke AG,** following an agreement of May 1912, led to the issuance of Diploma records by both Blum and Kalliope, and a dispute that was not resolved until the beginning of the World War II, when Kalliope ceased operating in Britain. Columbia Graphophone Co., Ltd., founded in February 1917, acquired the Blum trademarks and premises. Perhaps the most famous of the Diplomas was an account of the **Robert Falcon Scott** expedition to the South Pole (May 1913). [Andrews 1988/10.]

DIPPEL, ANDREAS, 1866–1932. German tenor, born in Kassel on 30 Nov 1866. He was with the Bremen Stadttheater from 1887 to 1892, then had his Metropolitan Opera debut on 26 Nov 1890. He sang 150 roles, specializing in Wagner, in the major world opera houses. In 1908 he was administrative manager of the Metropolitan Opera. He directed the Chicago Opera from 1910 to 1913. Dippel was heard on Mapleson cylinders; then he made cylinders for Edison's Grand Opera Series of 1906, including the major tenor arias (all in German) from *Martha* (#B2), *Huguenots* (#B15), *Queen of Sheba* (#B24), and *Lohengrin* (#B36). He died in Hollywood on 12 May 1932.

Direct cut. *See* DIRECT TO DISC.

Direct disc recording. *See* DIRECT TO DISC.

DIRECT INJECTION. A process of recording an electronic instrument by wiring it directly to the tape recorder. The signal is sent directly to the tape without the use of a microphone.

DIRECT TO DISC. Also known as direct cut, direct disc recording, or direct recording. The original method of disc recording, in which the signal is inscribed directly on a **master**. In this process the disc itself is termed a direct disc if it is the actual record to be played back, rather than a master to be pressed. With the availability of **tape recording** as an intermediary between signal and master, great advantages were gained over direct to disc: editing became possible, and also enhanced control over groove **modulation.** Commercial recording accepted the tape intermediary for almost all purposes, but some direct to disc recording has continued; its advantages being a certain spontaneity in the performance, greater dynamic range, and omission of tape hiss and other distortions. *See also* INSTANTANEOUS RECORDINGS.

DISC. This article, complementary to CYLINDER, consists of seven sections: 1. Terminology; 2. History of the format; 3. Materials and manufacture; 4. Sizes, sides, speeds; 5. Grooves; 6. The industry; and 7. The repertoire.

　　1. *Terminology.* Disc is frequently spelled "disk," most often in the area of digital technology, but sometimes in reference to phonograph records as well. In the present work "disc" is used for the formats of sound recording. The earliest term for a flat circular object employed to receive and retain sound signals was phonautogram, from the **Phonautograph** invented by Léon Scott de Martinville in 1857. Scott's device—which preserved a visual image of the sound waves only, without audio playback capability—actually used a cylinder rather than a disc. It was **Emile Berliner** who applied the term to his own invention of 1887, the **gramophone.** Berliner's first patent specification refers to the phonautographic recording. Later he called the disc a plate. In **Thomas Edison**'s sketches of 1878 a disc was illustrated as a recording format, also named plate. Edison's working format was the cylinder, known also as a phonogram, but usually identified as a record. Both phonogram and record were later used as synonyms for disc.

　　Modifiers are sometimes needed to specify the particular use of record as part of a sound system. A gramophone record is unambiguously a disc in such a system; but a phonograph record may be either a cylinder (the original usage) or a disc (usage after the end of cylinder manufacture). When patent complications forced **Eldridge Johnson** to avoid the term gramophone as a name for his new product of 1899, he named it simply the Eldridge R. Johnson Record, and then Victor Record. Phonorecord is a term that encompasses the disc, cylinder, and tape formats. CD is a common abbreviation for the digital **compact disc.**

　　Even within the realm of disc recording, the word itself changes meaning in context. The original disc is the one that receives the initial analog impression of the signal or the taped version of the signal (*see* section 4, below). Berliner's original discs were made of glass at first, then of zinc. If the original disc is used for signal playback without further processing, it is an **instantaneous disc** or an acetate. In commercial recording the original disc does not have an standard name, though it is often identified as a lacquer disc—because it is an aluminum blank with a lacquer coating (or just a lacquer)—a blank, a wax, an acetate, a **master,** or a master lacquer. In stricter terminology, the master is the copper or nickel shell that is electroplated from the original disc, with the groove patterns in reverse. Thus the original disc is a positive and the master is a negative—having ridges instead of grooves.

The master may be named a metal master, or a matrix. (Two plural forms of matrix are in use: matrixes and matrices.)

Through a second electrolytic process the master produces another positive, a copy of the original disc known as the mother. In further electrolysis the mother is coated with a copper shell, which is then removed—this is the matrix or stamper—a negative that is actually used to press copies of the original. The very last disc, the one put on sale, is called the pressing. This is a complex tangle, in which expert writers may use the terms differently; see for example the article "Matrix number" in the *New Harvard Dictionary of Music*, or Bachman 1962, where the confusing term master-matrix is introduced. Further refinements of these terms are found in the separate articles about them. [Bachman 1962; Borwick 1987/1; Guy 1964.]

2. *History of the format.* Disc recording began with the **phonautograph** of 1857: Scott de Martinville's invention that preserved analog tracings of sound waves. Although the familiar version of the phonautograph is a cylinder machine, Scott used either a flat sheet (1857) or a cylinder (1859) to hold the lampblacked paper that preserved the lateral lines emerging from the diaphragm. The possibility of reproducing the original sound from the tracings may have occurred to Scott, but he did not give the idea practical form, so the earliest gramophone or phonograph remained mute. Twenty years later **Charles Cros** proposed in a famous paper that with some adjustments the phonautograph—disc version—could play back sound as well as preserve it.

Thomas Edison's work on sound recording appears to have been independent of these French experiments. His 1877 endeavors—focused at first on amplifying mechanical energy in telephony—utilized paper discs, moving tapes, and eventually cylinders. When he finally requested his American patent for the **tinfoil phonograph** (24 Dec 1877) he described both cylinder and disc machines, and he did make experimental discs in 1878. But he was not satisfied with the variations in **groove speed** in disc rotation, and his next experiments—a decade later—concentrated on the cylinder format.

Another French inventor, **Saint-Loup**, went forward with the Cros idea and developed a production model of the disc player; it was described in an 1879 article (quoted in Chew 1982) and put on sale by the instrument maker **Ducretet et Cie.** for 300 francs. Ducretet also offered a hand-driven tinfoil cylinder machine, at 100 francs. It is not known whether Ducretet was producing these sound machines legally or by ignoring the Edison patent and the Cros French patent of 1878.

The work of **Chichester Bell** and **Charles Sumner Tainter** was, like Edison's, multi-media in nature. They were also concerned about groove speed variations in the disc, and in 1887 Tainter applied for a patent on a device that would hold surface movement beneath the stylus at a constant speed. But the road Bell and Tainter finally took was cylindrical, so they do not appear again in the history of the gramophone.

Meanwhile Berliner had been studying the phonautograph in the collection of the Smithsonian Institution in Washington, D.C., without the benefit of knowing Cros' paper or the Ducretet instruments. He discarded the cylinder in favor of a glass disc 125 millimeters (five inches) in diameter, and from this inspiration the gramophone was born (*see* section 3, below.) Although it took Berliner until 1894 to produce commercial records and playback machines, he was the first to do so. His discs grew to seven inches in diameter, stamped from electrotyped matrices. They gave two minutes of playing time.

Within a decade commercial discs had increased further in size, up to 14 inches (even 20 inches on occasion), and in playing time, up to five minutes. The 10-inch and 12-inch size prevailed, and in those manifestations the gramophone record persisted up to the long-playing era. Improvements were made constantly in noise suppression, though surface hiss was never entirely eliminated on pre-LP discs. And the introduction of **electrical recording** in 1925 allowed vast gains in fidelity of reproduction. The advent of the microgroove **long playing record** in 1948 seemed to mark the ultimate development of the format; but **stereophonic recording** offered a further advance. And finally—or so we suppose today—

the **compact disc** stepped out of the computer industry to give still another aspect to the recording "plate." [Chew 1981; Chew 1982; Cros 1877; Ford 1962; Koenigsberg*; Lenoir 1877.]

3. *Materials and manufacture.* "By 1895, Berliner had developed a system utilizing many ideas of his own and others. . . . The system stood up as the industry standard for half a century, thus Berliner deserves a mantle as the father of disk recording and reproduction" (Bachman 1962). In essence Berliner's system translated an audio signal into an analog groove pattern on a disc surface via a recording **horn**, a **diaphragm**, and a **needle** (later called a **stylus**). His method was **lateral recording**, meaning that the groove pattern was lateral (side-to-side; sometimes called needle-cut). That method contrasted with the **vertical-cut** method (up-and-down; also known as phono-cut or hill-and-dale) employed on cylinders. In choosing to cut his grooves laterally, Berliner followed the practice of Scott (the phonautograph) and Cros. It is interesting that Bell and Tainter experimented with lateral recording in wax during 1881–1885, but their patent specifications of 1886 utilized the vertical-cut process only.

Although lateral-cut became the industry standard, there was a considerable manufacture of vertical-cut records in the early years. One reason was simply the preference held by certain industry leaders such as Edison, who carried the idea from cylinders to his Diamond Disc of 1912, though he had tried out lateral-cut and described that method in his first American patent. Another reason was the legal grip on lateral recording achieved by Columbia and Victor in their patent sharing agreement of 1902; this maneuver effectively compelled other producers to follow the hill-and-dale approach. As a consequence, vertical-cut discs were made widely for 20 years, beginning with the Columbia toy graphophone wax discs issued in the U.S. in 1899 and in Britain in 1900. **Stollwerk's** curious chocolate record was vertical-cut (1903) and so were the 1904 records of the **Neophone Co., Ltd. Pathé** made 11-inch vertical-cuts from 1906. In Britain in 1908 there appeared the vertical-cut **Edison Bell, Clarion** (of which some were lateral-cut), **Musogram**, and **Phono**

Disc. The year 1911 saw the **Aerophone** and **Marathon**; 1912 the **Edison Diamond Disc**; 1915 the **Diamond-Double** and **Okeh. Vocalion** (1917) and Pathé's edge-start disc (1918) complete the list of hill-and-dale discs. A switch from vertical to lateral occurred after the expiration of Victor/Columbia patents in 1919. Okeh, Pathé, and Vocalion had all changed over by 1920. A vestige of vertical-cut recording remains with certain toy dolls and other novelties, and in **stereophonic** discs, which consist of two vertical tracks at right angles to one another, each angled 45 degrees in respect to the record's surface.

In the beginning Berliner traced the audio pattern on a coating of lampblack that he had applied to a glass disc. He then etched the pattern so that it could be transferred to copper or nickel, creating a master and leading to the chain of transfers, positive and negative, which resulted in a stamper (*see* section 1, above). In fact Berliner had first coated his glass with printer's ink. The needle was positioned beneath the disc, allowing the particles it made to fall away instead of clogging the groove. From glass Berliner moved to zinc as the base for the recording disc, coated with a fatty film. The stylus itself was of phosphor-bronze. Zinc had a greater noise level than the **wax** being used in cylinder recording, and Berliner was aware of this. However, he was concerned about patent litigation if he took the wax idea from Edison. His collaborator Eldridge Johnson was not deterred by this nicety, and went ahead with wax originals; he made the earliest disc recorded in wax on 2 Feb 1899 (a pressing is in the Gramophone Co. museum).

Wax was quickly established in the disc industry and remained throughout the 78 rpm era the material used for cutting. This substance was either made of carnauba wax, derived from the Brazilian palm *corphera cerifera*, brittle with a high melting point; or a mineral wax made from brown coal by distillation and high pressure. A fresh recording blank was about two inches thick, and would be shaved for reuse after each cut, down to a half-inch thickness. A later alternative method involved flowed wax on glass or metal discs. Lacquer-coated metallic, glass, or fiber discs (hence the name "lacquer" that is sometimes applied to the original disc) were also used. The development of the flowed-wax process resulted from research at the **Bell Telephone Laboratories** in the 1930s, research aimed at overcoming pre-echo distortion in vertical-cut transcription discs. The flow-coat was a thin layer of wax on the backing plate.

In the pre-electric period, the signal (music, speech, etc.) was brought into the system by means of mechanical energy alone (*see* ACOUSTIC RECORDING). The recording needle was made of bronze, and then later of sapphire. When a zinc base was used, the needle cutting the filmy coating exposed a wavy line on the zinc. The zinc was then etched with chromic acid, producing a groove, and a record that could be played back. However it was not played back, but was used to produce a number of transfers (described in section 1, above), ending with a matrix (stamper). A rich procedure ensued, to create the final pressings. It is vividly described in a 1918 book, which is worth quoting for its detail:

> The first operation in pressing is to knead the composition on the warm bed plates (steam heated) and divide it into lumps like patties, approximately in size which experience has shown to be sufficient, and not more than sufficient to produce a full record when pressed flat. About half a pound of ordinary material is sufficient for a ten-inch disc of average thickness. The *modus operandi* is as follows: the dies, with the matrices fitted therein, are well warmed on the bed-plate at the same time as the material. In double sided record pressing, there is a pair of steel dies each fitted with a matrix, the under die having a pin projecting through the matrix to engage in a corresponding recess in the upper die. The paper label, which serves to indicate the title and number of the particular record, has also a hole in its centre, and it is placed face downward against the matrix in each case. The pin serves to keep the label central. This done, a lump of composition is next placed in the centre of the matrix and covering the back of one of the labels. The second half of the die is then brought

into contact with the material, the whole being boxed in, as it were, ready for the press. The dies, of course, are furnished with stops to ensure the desired thickness in the record. By the application of the power the ram is slowly set in motion, upwards, to effect a squeeze between the dies, which, however takes but a few seconds to effect. . . . The circulation of the cold water through the press soon chills the impression, and the waiting time is usually occupied in preparing the next record for similar treatment. . . . After this operation is finished, the record is transferred to a trimming machine. . . . A workman pressing, say, an average of 250 records per day is considered a good man (Seymour 1918; reprinted in *APM* 1973).

The composition referred to, also known as the **biscuit**, had **shellac** as a major ingredient: 22 percent, according to one description; with 2 percent copal, 35 percent silica, 35 percent pyrites, and 6 percent carbon black for coloring (Ford). Shellac could also contain such fillers as limestone or slate, pigment lubricants (e.g., zinc stearate), plus binders and modifiers (e.g., ongo gum and vinsol). Other materials included in biscuits were "china clay or Fuller's earth, with cotton flock . . . for binding. Sometimes desiccated asbestos . . . in place of cotton. Another method, however, consists in utilising waste material between two thin sheets of rice paper coated with pure shellac" (Seymour). Lamination is the name of the process, in use since 1906 for record manufacture (by Columbia first, with the idea credited to **Guglielmo Marconi**). In the lamination process two or more layers of material are compressed under heat to make a single fused product. Heavy kraft paper was the core layer in the early laminations, with shellac as the coating layer.

This discussion has dealt with manufacture of acoustic 78 rpm discs. With the invention of **electrical recording** the signal input stage of the process changed, but from the point where the original disc had been cut the remaining steps were substantially the same, with some automation introduced over the years to speed it all up. New techniques were needed to handle long-playing records, stereophonic recording, and compact discs; these are taken up in the respective articles. [Bachman 1962; Borwick 1987/1; Ford 1961; McWilliams 1979; Seymour 1918; Watts 1979; Writing 1977.] *See also* RECORDING PRACTICE.

4. *Sizes, sides, speeds.* Berliner's earliest discs, for the 1889 toy gramophone, were five inches in diameter; they were recorded on one side only, and turned at about 70 rpm. The first commercial discs, Berliner's of 1894, were seven inches in diameter, and this was the size employed in Europe and America until 1902. A seven-inch disc rotating at 70 rpm would play two minutes; a slow speed cylinder of the time would last three minutes; thus a larger disc was called for. In 1901 the International Zonophone Co. was producing nine-inch discs, and in September 1901 Zonophone began to offer 10-inch records. Victor's first 10-inch records also appeared in 1901, on their Monarch label; Victor continued with seven-inch discs too, keeping the Victor label for them. Columbia offered 10-inch discs in 1902, for a dollar, while marketing seven-inch discs as well, for $.50. A year later Victor dropped the seven-inch size altogether, moving on to eight inches ($.35), 10 inches ($1), and 12 inches ($1.50). Some 12-inch Victors were issued earlier: "it would seem that perhaps as many as 150 twelve-inch recordings were made between 30 December 1901 and 30 December 1902. We have no way of knowing how many of these were published" (Fagan 1983). In Britain the Gramophone Co. sold 12-inch records in 1903.

During the period 1900–1925 disc speed by most manufacturers varied from 70 rpm to 82 rpm. Some early Berliners and G & T discs played at around 60 rpm. Most Berliners played at 75 rpm or slower. But the Neophone Co., Ltd., and Pathé Frères issued records in Britain and France between 1905 and 1920 that played at 78, 80, 90, 100, 120, and 130 rpm; their sizes were 10, 12, 14, 16, and 19 1/2 inches.

Eldridge Johnson experimented with double-sided records as early as 1900. International Zonophone released the industry's first double-sided discs in 1902, for sale in Brazil. Columbia made a commercial effort in America with 10-inch double-sides in 1904, priced at $1.50. In the same year Odeon issued double-sides in Europe, and within four years most firms were pressing both sides of their discs.

Size standardization arrived gradually, amidst various failed innovations such as Victor's 14-inch record of 1904, which ran at 60 rpm and played up to six minutes. Columbia had one like it, and Fonotipia offered a similar product in 1905. These items weighed a pound each, and had only short numbers on them, somewhat negating the rationale of the longer playing time; after a year they were all withdrawn. The eight-inch size was dropped by Victor around 1908 as the major American companies settled on 10-inch and 12-inch records for their releases. That was the situation of the mass market until 1949. Along the way, there were 16-inch, 33 1/3 rpm discs—the first LPs—made by the **Vitaphone Co.** for use as motion picture sound components (1926). Edison announced his 12-inch LP in the same year, one that played 20 minutes per side; it was not successful because the grooves were too thin for the heavy tone arms of the day. Victor failed with a 1931 LP (not a microgroove) for like reasons. Then there were numerous specimens of small records issued throughout the acoustic period, with diameters of six inches or less, many for children or as advertising promotions.

The "war of the speeds" between Columbia and Victor in 1949 was also a contest of diameters. Columbia's LP was a 33 1/3 rpm disc available in 10-inch and 12-inch sizes. Victor offered a seven-inch disc at 45 rpm. LPs and 45s were **vinyl**, and both had the same groove dimension. As those two formats became established as the industry norms—the 78 rpm record was not mass produced after 1957—no changes were forthcoming in the size or playing speed of discs until the whole technology changed with the **compact disc.** [Bayly 1974; Bayly 1976; Corenthal 1986; Fagan 1983; Gelatt 1977; Haines 1973; Koenigsberg*.]

5. *Grooves.* The wonder of the disc record groove is usually described simplistically. To say that sound waves are cut into analog patterns on a disc surface, or that a groove is the track inscribed by the cutting stylus, is correct; but it suggests an image of compression that is quite misleading. A bundle of sound, like a

spoken syllable or an orchestral chord, is not transcribed in a single spot on the record surface, but in a cluster of spots. This cluster is a link in the chain that is the record **groove**. On a 12-inch 78 rpm disc, the groove is approximately 244 yards long, or would be in a pristine state. As recording takes place the spiral path is undulated to account for the pitch, loudness, duration, and timbre of each sound; thus the final groove length is more like 480 yards. Average speed of the stylus over the groove is about 32 inches per second, if the turntable is revolving at 78 rpm.

The appearance of a groove when a single note is recorded in it is defined by many factors. A sound wave generated by the sounding of a musical note, or tone, is possessed of four basic attributes: **pitch, amplitude, timbre**, and duration. Pitch is shown in the groove by the periodic repetition of cyclic patterns: the number of cycles (or Hz) determining the place of the tone in the **audio frequency range**. The patterns themselves, the vibrations, have a size that depends on the intensity of the sound signal; the size, or amplitude, varies with the intensity of the sound, while the cyclic frequency is constant as long as the pitch remains the same. Timbre—sometimes referred to as tone quality—results from the characteristics of the instruments or voices that produce tones. In the sound wave, and its analog in the groove shape, the timbre results in distinctive shaping of the cyclic curves. Duration is not exactly a quality of the tone, but it does affect the groove appearance by determining its length. A tone lasting one-fourth of a second takes up eight inches of groove space, and shows a regular pattern of curves diminishing in size as the tone fades.

At this point it should be restated that the groove in a record (disc or cylinder) may be vertical or lateral (*see* section 3, above). Its shape in either case will be the same in terms of movement on and away from its center line.

Groove shape is complicated by the sounding of complex tones: the kind usually produced by singers and instrumentalists, as opposed to the pure tones produced by tuning forks. Complex tones have perceptible patterns of **harmonics**, often called overtones or partials. With the presence of harmonics the

wave shape is much elaborated. Yet up to this point it is imaginable that the groove shape might be "read" and analyzed to determine by inspection what the sound source could have been. (One can expect certain patterns of harmonics from certain instruments, regardless of the pitches they play.) But groove shape becomes vastly more intricate when it carries the impulses produced by more than one instrument or voice simultaneously. Each source contributes its own frequency, amplitude, and timbre characteristics to the composite shape of the line. The idea of reading or analyzing such a shape to determine exactly what instruments were involved is forbidding, though one always assumes a computer can be taught to do anything. It is even more stunning to realize that the human ear is able to do just this: read and analyze the squiggles on a groove and make correct judgments about the nature of the sound source, and to do this instantly without apparent effort. (*See* HEARING.)

Few attempts were made to standardize the shape of the groove in discs until the arrival of electrical recording in the mid-1920s. By 1935 consensus in the industry produced grooves of a V-shape, with an included angle of 80–85 degrees and a bottom radius of 0.002 to 0.003 inches At the top of the groove, the width was 0.004–0.006 inches The actual depth of the groove was about 21 mils in the mid-1930s, as compared with four mils in 1908, and 25 mils in the standard British disc of 1962.

Although there is obviously only one groove on a record side, the number of turns or spirals it makes are often named "grooves." The number of turns on a standard 78 varied from 90 to 120 per inch (38–48 per centimeters). The ridge between turns was about 0.004 inch across.

Microgroove discs—usually termed long-playing records, or LPs—are aptly named, since the grooves are much smaller than the 78 grooves. LPs have a bottom radius of less than 0.00025 inch (0.0064 millimeters) and a top width of no less than 0.0022 inch; depth is about 0.00125 inch. The included angle is about 90 degrees. There are about 200–300 turns per inch.

The groove of a stereo disc has to carry two channels of signal information. It does so by inscribing each signal on one side of the groove, one arm of the V, with the axis of operation at 45/45 degrees.

6. *The industry.* Commercial production and sale of disc records, today a multi-billion dollar international operation, began modestly in 1894 in the **Berliner Gramophone Co.** of Philadelphia. In America the new industry was soon dominated by Berliner himself and his early associates **Eldridge Johnson** and **Frank Seaman**; both of those men split with Berliner to set up their own firms. In Europe the Berliner interests were represented by the **Gramophone Co.** in Britain and **Deutsche Grammophon Gesellschaft (DGG)** in the inventor's native Hanover. All those pillars of the disc enterprise were functioning before 1900, delineating the American competitive situation which—with the addition of **Columbia** in 1901—would remain operative for many years to come.

Major challenges to the new entrepreneurs were the presence and public acceptance of the cylinder record (in America more than in Europe, where the cylinder had not taken a strong hold), manufacturing difficulties with the discs themselves (*see* section 4, above), and the primitive state of the disc playing machine. The change from rubber to a shellac material made by the **Duranoid Co.** for the final pressings brought good results, and remained the basis of disc composition through the 78 era.

A key invention that made the disc player saleable was the spring-wound motor. Electric motors were in use, but they did not yet provide a steady motive power. The first Berliner players had to be hand-cranked as the turntable revolved. Levi H. Montross patented a **spring motor record player** (application filed 1896) that was used by Eldridge Johnson. Johnson invented an improved governor for it, using it in his Improved Gramophone. That machine was successfully promoted by Seaman, who had exclusive sales rights for Berliner. In 1898 Seaman was selling 600 machines a week at $15–25 each, for a total year's sales of $1 million. Machine parts made in Johnson's shop were sent to London for assembly and sale by the Gramophone Co. (established 1898). The British firm made its own recordings, in a studio set up by **Fred Gaisberg**; actual press-ing of the records was done in Hanover. Gaisberg developed a substantial catalog through energetic recruitment of popular artists, and the Gramophone Co. was offering 5,000 selections by 1900.

Legal contests over patent rights were pervasive, especially on the American side. Berliner brought a successful suit against **American Talking Machine Co.**, for infringement—by its **Vitaphone Co.**—of his patents. Then a bizarre scenario emerged from the opportunistic mind of Seaman. He had organized two firms: the **National Gramophone Co.** (1896), a sales agency for Berliner products, and the **Universal Talking Machine Co.** (1898). The latter brazenly entered into competition with the former, by producing a clone of the Improved Gramophone under the name **Zonophone.** The Berliner Gramophone Co. then broke with Seaman, refusing to send him any more products to distribute, unilaterally abrogating their contract. Seaman protested this action in court, and eventually there came a curious court decision, in which Berliner Gramophone Co. and Eldridge Johnson were denied the right to the tradename "gramophone." Seaman was sued by the graphophone (cylinder) interests for infringement of the Bell-Tainter patents, bringing about a consent agreement in which **Columbia** gained the assets of the Universal Talking Machine Co. and was able to market disc players with the Zonophone name.

Berliner decided to concentrate on the Canadian market, where the prohibition against use of "gramophone" did not apply. But Johnson took another way around the barrier, by creating his own **Consolidated Talking Machine Co.** (July 1900) to make machines, plus discs under the label name "Eldridge R. Johnson Record"; then in December 1900 he registered the trademark "Victor Record." In October 1901 his firm became the **Victor Talking Machine Co.** Johnson and Victor had strong interests in Europe, with a large stake in Gramophone & Typewriter, Ltd. (established as the **Gramophone Co.** in April 1898; original name restored November 1907). Seaman apparently took no further active part in the industry after the demise of his third firm, **National Gramophone Corp.**, in 1901. He accepted an out-of-court settlement, for his suits against Johnson and Berliner, of $25,000 from Victor in 1903, and was heard from no more. **Frederick Marion Prescott** established **International Zonophone Co.** in Berlin in 1901, and sold Zonophone products. The Gramophone Co. took over that firm in 1903.

A new participant in the disc industry was introduced in late 1901: Columbia Phonograph Co., until then a cylinder firm. The **Globe Record Co.**, a subsidiary of the Burt Co., pressed discs for Columbia in October 1901, with the label name **Climax.** Eldridge Johnson purchased Globe in January 1902 from Burt, and transferred it to Columbia as part of a pivotal agreement between Victor and Columbia interests to achieve patent peace. (Climax was sold in Britain as well, beginning in 1902.) Other elements of that agreement included the licensing of Vitaphone discs, and the pooling of patents concerning wax-cutting methods and floating soundboxes. Those agreements left Victor and Columbia with exclusive American rights to make lateral-cut records. This monopoly on the prime manufacturing method gave the two firms the basis for their decades of rivalry—undisturbed by serious competition until the relevant patents expired.

Meanwhile in Europe the Gramophone Co. was prospering. It showed profits of £79,348 in 1901; £137,268 in 1902; and £252,285 (approximately $1 million) in 1903. The 1902 Red Label catalog of classical works was highly popular (*see* section 8, below). Disc prices were 2s 6d for seven-inch discs in 1903; 5s for 10-inch Concertdiscs; and 10s for Red Labels. Specialty labels for great stars, such as Nellie Melba, were issued under their names at premium prices. The company spread across two continents: by 1910 it had factories in Riga (for the Russian market), France, Austria, Spain, and India. There were sales shops in major cities everywhere. From 12 Dec 1900 to 17 Nov 1907 the firm had the name Gramophone & Typewriter, Ltd., following a misguided effort at diversification.

Some competition for the Gramophone Co. appeared in 1904, as Prescott (from Zonophone) went to Berlin and founded the **International Talking Machine Co. mbH**, marketing **Odeon** products, while in Milan the **Società Italiana di Fonotipia** firm got started. Victor borrowed from Gramophone the idea of a Red Label series for major operatic and classical artists, and began to issue its famous Red Seal series of great music; it soon outdistanced Columbia in the race for the American market, posting $12 million in sales during 1905.

Johnson's promotional concept for Victor was that it should become indelibly associated in the minds of the public as the source of highest quality products. He did not hesitate to ask for amazing prices: his first **Victrola** machine, with enclosed horn and mahogany finish, was sold as a fine musical instrument—for $200, or about $2,000 in today's equivalent. Victor records sold for different prices depending in part on the repute of the artists and how many were represented on a disc; a solo by Enrico Caruso was $3, the Quartet from *Rigoletto* was $6; in today's prices those records were selling for $30 and $60 each, for three minutes of scratchy, wavering sound. But the Victor catalog also held many lower priced discs ($1.50) featuring lesser-known performers.

Columbia did well with its black and silver discs, but their much-promoted **Marconi Velvet Tone** record (1907) was not successful. A copy of the Victrola player, the **Grafonola**, was designed to look like a piece of furniture, rather than a unique musical instrument; the public did not fully accept it. Columbia was handicapped further by its unimaginative classical repertoire. While Victor—through superior promotion and a disc of better technical quality—was becoming a national institution in the U.S., as Gramophone Co. was in Britain, Columbia was slow in finding a key to meaningful competition. It re-entered the operatic repertoire in 1908 (having made a false start in 1903) by acquiring rights to press Odeon and Fonotipia masters in the U.S.—dissolving the arrangement after two years—and scored some gain by converting all production to double-sided discs. Odeon had been the first label in Europe to appear in double-side format, in 1904. The Odeon, 27 centimeters in diameter (about 10 3/4 inches), sold for 4s in the U.K. Odeon produced other sizes, offering 30 centimeters (12 inches) in 1908 and 25 centimeters (10 inches) in 1912, while continuing the early 2-centimeter size.

The situation of the industry in 1910 was one of clear domination by Victor and the Gramophone Co. Both firms were pre-eminent in advertising as well as production and repertoire: the famous **Nipper** symbol had become known around the world. But the next few years before the World War I saw a number of newcomers. **Carl Lindström AG** in Germany acquired the stock of Odeon, Beka, Dacapo, Lyrophon, Jumbo, Jumbola, Favorite, and Fonotipia, and became a worthy rival to the Gramophone Co. **Pathé Frères** remained a factor, although the firm lost ground steadily until it switched from **vertical-cut** discs to **lateral recording** in 1919. In America a superior new product, the **Edison Diamond Disc**, went on sale in 1912. Although it was vertical-cut, sound quality was excellent. Edison managed to sign up some great singers (Claudia Muzio, Maggie Teyte, and Giovanni Martinelli among them) but his catalog was not designed to take advantage of their gifts. Edison's unsophisticated musical taste dictated the creation of a minor repertoire, and prevented him from taking an appropriate share of the market, despite masterly promotion, for example through **tone tests**.

Significant improvements in recording techniques were made constantly by many manufacturers. In playback equipment there was also steady progress. Eldridge Johnson's invention of the tapered **tone arm** (U.S. patent application filed 12 Feb 1903) was widely imitated, often illegally. Steel **needles** were improved and offered in varied shapes to give degrees of loudness as early as 1906; and fiber needles were available before 1910 to diminish **surface noise**. Edison's Diamond Disc required a diamond **stylus** which was advertised as producing "no perceptible scratch." "Multiplaying jewel needles" were advertised by the **Sonora Phonograph Co.** in 1916. Although electric motors drawing on alternating ("mains") current were still not perfected, there were electric attachments for disc players that would wind up the machines automatically (advertised first in 1913). The **spring motor phonographs** could play as many as eight 10-inch discs with a single winding. Battery-powered motors were in use as well; indeed, Edison had demonstrated one as early as 1888. Devices to achieve an **automatic stop** after a record was played were available around 1911 or earlier. Record players abandoned their characteristic external **horns** in favor of internal folded horns, even in table models; the **Victrola** (1906) was the prominent example of the new style. **Volume control** knobs appeared on many gramophones, such as the 1916 Sonora.

It became possible to record a full symphony orchestra and play it back with reasonable fidelity, and various symphonic movements were available around 1910, beginning with the first large-scale orchestral recording: Odeon's *Nutcracker Suite* of 1909. European companies were several years ahead of the Americans in building symphonic repertoire (*see* ORCHESTRAL RECORDINGS). But the American producers took quick advantage of the dance craze that began in America in 1913 and swept into Europe (*see* DANCE MUSIC). Columbia took the lead in this area, and also in the recording of **jazz** and original cast **musicals**. Under the guidance of **Louis Sterling**, the London branch of Columbia began to improve its profit picture after 1910. That branch became the Columbia Graphophone Co., Ltd., in 1917.

Victor, Columbia, and Edison dominated the American industry in 1914, with Victor and Columbia dividing the major sales of lateral-cut records and keeping the prices high: $.75 for 10-inch discs, and more for 12-inch and special releases. Columbia also pressed records for other companies, "but always in such a way that the records could not compete directly with Columbia's own" (Brooks 1979), for example, the **Standard, Harmony, United,** and **Aretino** labels with large spindle holes, the single-sided **Oxford** sold by Sears, Roebuck, and the Lakeside label of Montgomery Ward. Even those were not great bargains ($.30 for an Oxford). The public was ready for a truly low-priced record, and it came in 1914 under the name **Little Wonder**. Those were 5 1/2 inch records, masters and pressings by Columbia, selling for $.10 each. A reported 20 million were sold in two years, and the firm continued until 1919.

In 1919 the Victor/Columbia grip on lateral-cut disc production was loosened as the relevant patents expired. New manufacturers entered the field, among them **Brunswick, Gennett, Paramount,** and **Vocalion.** A boom period ensued, lasting until the economic recession of 1921 and the rise of radio broadcasting after 1922. The industry was hard hit by radio: in the U.S. sales of all talking machine products reached $158 million in 1921, but fell to $98 million in 1921. Columbia was actually insolvent in 1923, but was reorganized as Columbia Phonograph Co., Inc. in 1924. It was acquired by Sterling for Columbia Graphophone Co., Ltd. in 1925.

Victor's sales started to slip in 1921 ($51 million), falling to $37 million in 1924. Still there were 7 million talking machines in use in America in 1922, and popular music was a thriving element in the repertoire despite the enticing competition of radio. The first million-selling record, by **Paul Whiteman,** came from Victor in 1920.

To counter the influx of radio into their sales, gramophone makers began to make machines with radios included, or with room to insert a radio. Prices of records were cut. But there seemed to be no way to stop the fall in record sales; in the U.S. the annual figures were $105.6 million in 1921; $92.4 million in 1922; $79.2 million in 1923; $68.2 million in 1924; $59.4 million in 1924. Then a turnaround came, based on the dramatic introduction of **electrical recording** and the **orthophonic-**type gramophones to play the records made by the new technique.

Electrical recording, using **microphones** in place of the acoustic recording horns, allowed the recording studio to become a concert hall. It also expanded the **audio frequency** range of records, taking the upper limit from about 3,000 Hz to about 8,000 Hz. Following the first commercial issues on the **Autograph** label, Victor and Columbia began to release electrics in April 1925; but in order to retain some sales value for their acoustic record stockpiles both companies refrained from announcing their new process. June 1925 saw the earliest HMV (Gramophone Co.) electrical release, two fox-trots on a pressing from American Victor. Then on 2 Nov 1925, so-called Victor Day, the electric records were demonstrated to the public on the orthophonic player. In the same year Brunswick brought forth the first

all-electric phonograph, the **Panatrope,** and the industry was able to depart from the acoustic era. The Panatrope replaced the old acoustic soundbox with a **cartridge** (pickup) containing a small electrical generator. Side-to-side motion of the **stylus** in the cartridge generated a matching electrical current, which passed through an **amplifier** into the **loudspeaker**—fundamentally the same process in use today. It is true that the new systems were vulnerable to **distortions** in the wider frequency range; and it was concern about those distortions that kept Edison out of the electrical parade. So the great inventor ironically fell behind in his own area of expertise, failing to produce an electric record until 1927.

From 1926 to 1929 a financial revival occurred in the U.S. and European industries. In America record sales were again growing each year: $70.4 million in 1926 and the same in 1927; $72.6 million in 1927; $74.8 million in 1929. Seven different labels in the U.S. and Britain had electrical recordings on sale by 1926: Victor, Columbia, Gramophone Co., **Parlophone, Regal,** Zonophone, and Brunswick. Not long after there were also **Vocalions** and **Crystalates.** Pathé's electrically recorded **Actuelle** label appeared in spring 1927.

Victor and Columbia each acquired radio interests: the National Broadcasting Co. (NBC) went to Victor in 1926, and the **Columbia Broadcasting System (CBS)** went to Columbia in 1927. It seemed that the record industry might be able to control parts of the radio industry. Victor began to record major orchestras in their resident concert halls. HMV and British Columbia recorded complete operas in profusion. And **Deutsche Grammophon Gesellschaft** (DGG) in Germany, which had achieved independence from the Gramophone Co. after World War I, came into prominence with uncut orchestral works by the Berlin Philharmonic Orchestra and others. The future seemed unlimited.

However, with the Wall Street crash of October 1929, and its universal aftershock, chaos replaced burgeoning prosperity in the record industry. American disc sales fell to $46.2 million in 1930, to $17.6 million in 1931, $11 million in 1932, and $5.5 million in 1933.

What had been the world's largest corporation became a subsidiary, as **RCA (Radio Corporation of America)** acquired the Victor Talking Machine Co. in January 1929. Edison ceased production of entertainment records and players (he continued making radios, and dictating machines). The Gramophone Co. made a belated, desperate entry into the radio business in 1929 by acquiring Marconiphone, Ltd., a division of the Marconi complex of companies. Brunswick sold its record/phonograph division to Warner Brothers, who passed it on a year later to the **American Record Corp.** American Columbia was acquired by radio manufacturer **Grigsby-Grunow**, from which it also passed into the hands of the American Record Corp.

A brilliant strategy saved the British industry from demise: the merger in March 1931 of the ancient rivals, Columbia (International), Ltd. and the Gramophone Co. They became elements in the new **EMI, Ltd.** Since Columbia (International) already controlled **Carl Lindström**, the record business of French **Pathé Frères, Parlophone,** and some other interests, nearly all the major firms in Europe were combined. (U.S. Columbia was not included in the merger.) EMI began to provide matrices for the enfeebled American firms. It also led the way into a new market by starting to issue **society records.**

Victor demonstrated a **long-playing record** (not a microgroove) in 1931. It was a 10-inch or 12-inch disc running at 33 1/3 rpm, just like the later Columbia microgroove. But it was poorly timed in market terms: requiring a $247.50 player to reproduce it. Critical reception was favorable, but the public had no funds to invest in it. Columbia in Britain produced, at this time, a 33 1/3 rpm center-start disc for use in theatres and motion picture houses. These were used to present the national anthem at the close of each evening, and to provide intermission entertainment—not to accompany the performances.

Only 6 million discs were sold in the U.S. in 1932 (as opposed to 104 million in 1927); and only 40,000 phonographs (987,000 in 1927). But some economic improvements in the U.S. were noted in 1933, and record sales began to rise slightly. Victor was under control of RCA, but the executives at the radio firm had the acumen to recognize the potential of the phonograph even in depressed times. **Edward Wallerstein** left Brunswick in 1932 to take over the RCA record branch, and became one of the rejuvenators of the industry in America. He produced the first cheap turntable that could play through a radio—it sold well at $16.50. He also moved with determination to recreate the old Victor prestige by signing up great classical artists. Victor had special success with Arturo Toscanini. Another man who deserves credit for pulling the industry out of despond is **Jack Kapp,** who founded **Decca Record Co.** in 1934 on the premise that cutting record prices in half would bring them within reach of the financially pressed consumer. Kapp, another former Brunswick executive, set a $.35 price on his records, competing with the Victor $.75 standard price of the time. **Bluebird** and **Okeh** were also selling at $.35, but Kapp assembled a roster of popular artists they could not match, such as Bing Crosby, Jimmy Dorsey, and Louis Armstrong. In 1935 American disc sales climbed to $8.8 million, and in 1936 to $11 million.

Radio, the old rival, began to help the record companies in the mid-1930s. Broadcasts of concerts sparked the consumer appetite for classics, and the Texaco Co. broadcasts of the Metropolitan Opera—still on the air, the longest running radio program—built interest in operatic recordings. On the pop side, the rise of the **juke box** created a new market in the U.S. (not much in Britain). By 1940 there were 350,000 juke boxes in operation. Sales of over 100,000 copies of a pop disc became common. CBS, under president **William Paley**, was encouraged by these signs to revive its nearly defunct parent, Columbia Records. Paley bought it from American Record Corp. and brought Wallerstein from RCA to head it. U.S. record sales in 1937 moved up to $13.2 million, and 1938 brought in $26.4 million. A year later there was $44 million in sales. Decca made 19 million records that year, standing second only to RCA. The American situation was at its strongest point since 1930.

However, for the recording artists there were substantial problems, as many musicians were being replaced by juke boxes, and live performers were no longer employed in moving picture houses; furthermore, the rights of musicians in recordings played on the radio were not clearly established. The major licensing organization, the **American Society of Composers, Authors, and Publishers (ASCAP)**, introduced a schedule of fees to be paid to musicians whose records were played on the air. Broadcasters set up a rival and more compatible organization, **Broadcast Music, Inc. (BMI)** in 1940. Unrest culminated in the strike of 1942 (see below).

The outbreak of World War II in Europe disrupted the industry there, but in the U.S. profits continued to rise. Both Victor and Columbia cut prices on their best 12-inch records from $2 to $1, with satisfying public response. All major American orchestras were contracted to record for Victor's Red Seal or Columbia's Masterworks series. Decca continued to reign in the pop field, but other companies had good market shares there. This was the peak of the **Big Band** era, and there were outstanding ensembles in profusion. Sales of $48.4 million were posted for 1940, and a rise to $50.6 million in 1941. Then wartime restrictions on **shellac** began to make problems. Used records had to be recycled, via dealer scrap drives and trade-in programs. Disc surfaces got noisier. And in July 1942 a ban on recordings by members of the **American Federation of Musicians** created havoc for two years, holding down the sales curve. The year 1942 saw $55 million in sales, and 1943 and 1944 each brought $66 million.

British recording had enjoyed technical superiority through the 1930s, but World War II obstructed developments there. The rationing of shellac (imported from India) led to a highly restricted production; the total output from British companies was a mere trickle (Cooper notes that in one issue of *Gramophone* there were just five new issues listed for the month). Then in 1944–1945 Decca in Britain introduced its **full frequency range recording (ffrr)** system, an outgrowth of military research. That system initiated—with its rendition of *Petrouchka* by Ernst Ansermet—the age of **high fidelity**. With the war's end the shellac shortage disappeared, and consumer spending climbed quickly. The industry in Britain was virtually monopolized by Decca and EMI in

1945, but there was a sudden rise of **independents**—among them Tempo, Esquire, **Oriole**, London Jazz, Delta, Tailgate, and Jazz Collector.

American sales in 1945 rose 65 percent, to $109 million, then doubled the next year to $218 million. While disc sales continued to rise (275 million were sold in the U.S. in 1946; 400 million in 1947) there was a new competitor in **magnetic recording. Tape** came into use for pre-recording radio shows (beginning with Bing Crosby's in October 1946), replacing **transcription discs**, and then moved into the home market. The new medium made higher frequencies available and eliminated surface noise considerations. At the same time **Ampex Corp.** produced the first tape recording machine with quality standards suitable for recording studios; within a few years original recordings were all being recorded to tape rather than to disc, with disc transfer later in the process.

Magnetic tape might have had a serious impact on the disc industry if there had been time to develop an extensive pre-recorded repertoire and to produce a gadget to thread the tapes. But before those advances could transpire, Columbia held a lavish demonstration in June 1948 at the Waldorf-Astoria Hotel of its **long-playing record** (LP). The LP microgroove records were made of polyvinyl chloride rather than shellac, and produced negligible surface noise. **Vinyl**, as the material was called, was also cheaper than shellac, and in the U.S. it was more readily available, since it was derived from petroleum. The slower playing speed of LPs permitted up to 25 minutes of uninterrupted music per side. Coupled with inexpensive turntable attachments—$29.95 at first, then down to $9.95—the LP record was an instant sensation. Yet market results were disappointing, because of an economic recession and because the public was put off by the "war of the speeds" in which Victor's **45 rpm disc** was offered as a rival to the LP. Columbia had generously made rights to the LP available to all other firms, and many were quick to accept. Only Victor refused, since they had invested heavily in the 45. Consumer uncertainty brought the American record sales figure down to $189 million in 1948, and to $173 million in 1949.

The war of the speeds ended in February 1950, as Victor marketed its first LP. But it held onto the 45 as well, ingeniously focusing the format on pop music; and the industry followed, using LP for classics and 45 for pop. A blossoming of new companies occurred in the U.S. and Europe. In the initial LP catalog of 1949—progenitor of the **Schwann catalogs**—there were eleven labels listed, including a number of new ones: Allegro, Artist, **Capitol, Cetra-Soria,** Columbia, **Concert Hall,** Decca, London, **Mercury, Polydor,** and **Vox.** British Decca took up the LP in 1950, but EMI held out with 78s until October 1952, for reasons difficult to appreciate from today's perspective. The greater frequency range of LPs, 20 to 20,000 Hz, achieved with the use of tape in recording studios for capturing the original signal, led to peaks of enthusiasm for high-fidelity. Heathkits and other do-it-yourself packages enabled amateurs to construct their own amplifiers, tuners, and turntables. Audio fairs appeared, celebrating the latest manufactured advances. U.S. disc sales climbed back up to $189 million in 1950. The next five years were marked by the proliferation of labels, the enormous growth of recorded repertoire (*see* section 7, below), and technical improvements. Mail-order buying became highly popular, exploiting the fact that LPs could be mailed without being broken in transit; one of the leading exponents was the **Musical Heritage Society,** which concentrated on the baroque repertoire and lesser known works of other periods. U.S. sales of LPs grew to $277 million in 1955, and $377 million in 1956. The standard 78 rpm disc disappeared from commercial production by 1957.

Another revolution in the industry was occasioned by the introduction of **stereophonic recording** (stereo). It began with tape, as EMI introduced domestic stereo tapes in 1955. Stereo discs went on sale in the U.S. in 1958, after a demonstration by Westrex in late 1957. In fact, the history of stereo shows various earlier "introductions" in both disc and tape format, but always with commercial obstacles. One such obstacle, the need for consumers to buy new playback equipment to handle stereo discs, was eliminated with the compatible stereo disc, which could be played without damage on standard monophonic equipment. Thus the record buyer could acquire stereo records and defer the purchase of stereo equipment. Sales of stereo and monophonic discs reached $511 million in the U.S. in 1958, then $603 million in 1959. The *Schwann Long Playing Record Catalog* listed 25,000 records on 425 monophonic labels and 154 stereo labels in 1960. At $4.98, the typical stereo disc was selling for a dollar more than the monophonic version of the same recording.

America in the 1950s was the setting for a tidal change in popular musical taste—a change that shifted the balance of the record industry. Until the end of the Big Band era listeners of all age groups tended to prefer the same pop singers and instrumental groups. The rise of **rhythm & blues** (r & b) in the middle of the decade created some age-related divisions; r & b was considered to be **"race music,"** thought by many white adults to be unsuitable for their children—who were drawn to it. At first the major labels—notably Columbia—kept a distance from the new sounds, even as the style became rock, and stars like Bill Haley, the Crew Cuts, and Elvis Presley took hold among young people. Teenagers did not immediately give up the old idols, however; in a 1958 survey of high school students it was found that the favored singers were Pat Boone, Perry Como, and then Presley. But the charts reflected a gradual acceptance by younger Americans—and soon by their peers around the world—of rock music as their shared language. It was a language spoken by relatively few adults. But the big record labels learned it well. They developed aggressive **A & R** departments, and went after the performers of star quality. New independents, headed by **Atlantic, Chess,** Imperial, and VeeJay, gathered 45 percent of the market in 1956. Columbia took about half the remaining market share.

Technologically, the novelty of the period was **multitrack recording,** permitting a vast increase in the engineer's capability to control the sound of the final product.

With the arrival of the 1960s the musical scene and the industry that both followed and shaped it remained eclectic in character. In counterpoint to the rise of **rock music recordings,** mostly on 45s, there was great interest in **comedy recordings** like Vaughn Meader's album *First Family* (4 million sold), in **folk music recordings**, and **country and western music recordings**. There was also continued demand for classical music, encouraged by the richer quality of stereo. Aggregate sales rose each year: $600 million in 1960; $640 million in 1961; $687 million in 1962. In 1962 the Philadelphia Orchestra became the first symphonic ensemble to sell a million records in a year. Another thriving area was the Broadway musical: Columbia's release of *West Side Story* was the top album of 1962, selling more than 2.5 million in original cast and soundtrack versions (*see* MUSICAL THEATRE RECORDINGS). The early 1960s also saw the leap to fame of many pop/folk groups, such as the Kingston Trio and the Limelighters, as well as soloists like Joan Baez and Harry Belafonte.

Fanzines emerged, following *Crawdaddy* (1964), and also "prozines" (*Rolling Stone*, 1967) to give jazz/rock fans another dimension in their experience. (*See also* SOUND RECORDING PERIODICALS.)

The recording industry in the U.S. was dominated by Columbia, RCA Victor, Capitol, and Decca; they held about half the $698 million market in 1963. **MGM**, Dot, London, **ABC-Paramount**, and Mercury took another 15 percent; and the remaining sales were shared by some 3,000 other labels. The market was dominated by popular music: in 1963 the pop genres (including jazz, musicals, soundtracks, and folk) accounted for almost all the 45s sold, and for three-fourths of the LPs. New York was the center of the music business, with Nashville rising to second place as the country music capital of the nation. Los Angeles and Chicago were the other major locales for the industry.

All the record producers found it difficult to keep up with trends, and with a new fact of life in the pop field: hits did not last. Turnover on the **recording industry charts** was accelerating. In the 1950s a winning song might ride the charts for six months; by 1963 the average visit to the Top-40 list was down to 10 weeks. The firms were forced into a shotgun approach, issuing thousands of discs each year and profiting from only a small percent of them. Hardly any discs made the break-even sales point of around 35,000 copies sold. **Rack jobbers** created a sub-industry from unsold discs. Famil-

iar **record shops**, unable to handle the pace, began to fade from the arena, and new outlets emerged in supermarkets, discount stores, drug stores, and so forth—more than 80,000 of them in the U.S.—to take in a third of sales.

The year 1964 brought the end of American domination over the popular song, as the "British invasion" spread from Liverpool to world supremacy. American record firms did not suffer from the incursion, since they had rights to American releases. During 1964 there were $758 million in sales, with 90 percent of the market falling to pop/rock categories. On the classical side there was interest in charismatic opera sopranos Maria Callas and Leontyne Price.

Manufacturers of playback equipment got the benefit of the **transistor**; phonograph sales were between 5 million and 7 million items a year through the 1960s.

Record sales were growing in most countries. U.S. sales claimed half the world total, with Britain next and Japan third; during the mid-1960s Japan moved into second place. The American trend toward multiple outlets and low-cost close-outs was established in Europe. And the American practice of making illegal copies (**pirated records**) for sale also took root in other lands. U.S. sales moved up to $862 million in 1965, and $959 million in 1966. The Beatles remained the principal international performers; they made personal appearances in Germany, Japan, and Italy, enlisting fresh armies of young record buyers. English and American songs were translated into other languages and became world hits; primarily these were rock numbers, but one was Frank Sinatra's "Strangers in the Night" of 1966, which made the charts in 20 countries.

American record sales passed the billion-dollar mark in 1967, and went to $1.12 billion in 1968. Every kind of pop music was thriving, even the sentimental ballad (e.g., by Engelbert Humperdinck) and its war-protest sibling, the flower-power song. In 1968, 6,540 pop singles and 4,057 albums were released in the U.S. Country and western music prospered greatly, and gave signs of becoming the dominant popular style. But the most significant pop album of the decade was the Beatles' *Sgt. Pepper's Lonely Hearts Club Band*—a set of brilliant compositions that blended classical, rock, and electronic genres.

Rock festivals became sensational mass events in the late 1960s. A crowd of 300,000 attended at the Woodstock festival in August 1969, near Bethel, New York. Joan Baez, Ravi Shankar, and the Jefferson Airplane were among the performers. But rock music itself had so many splinter divisions as to be scarcely identifiable with the way it sounded in the beginning of the decade. Original cast musical records, notably the 1969 *Hair*, remained a strong category. American sales reached $1.17 billion in 1969. Sales of LP albums rose rapidly, while 45 singles began to slide; this change reflected a new price structure that favored the LP.

American manufacturers of **tape recorders** finally saw their product gain in acceptance, essentially through introduction of the Philips **cassette** in 1963. Sales of tape players rose from 6.9 million in 1969 to 10.2 million in 1972; and sales of the pre-recorded cassettes climbed quickly just as **reel to reel tape** sales collapsed. The little tape format became a formidable rival to the disc in the early 1970s, profiting especially from the development of **noise reduction systems**.

Jazz music did not have a huge market share during the 1960s, but important styles were established and major artists were recognized. In the early 1970s jazz and rock fused in the work of certain groups, such as Chicago and Blood, Sweat, and Tears.

The year 1970 marked the final dissolution of the Beatles, and the beginning of a general decline in the power of rock music. "Punk rock"—symbolized by the Sex Pistols band—emphasized visual orgiastics at the expense of musical depth, and brought much negative response. Pop festivals had begun to arouse strong public opposition because of their disruptive impact on local communities and because of the uninhibited behavior of audiences. Meanwhile **soul music** moved ahead in the charts, aided by the worldwide success of the **Motown** labels and their artists, such as the Supremes. Standard pop songs were in demand again, and country music thrived. And nostalgia held an important place: it reached as far back as Scott Joplin's **ragtime** piano, but

also touched more recent decades like the 1950s. Through all this skirmishing sales rose each year. In the U.S., LP albums accounted for $1.203 billion, and 45s for 180 million in 1972. Figures for 1973 were $1.246 billion for LPs and $190 million for singles; for 1974 it was $1.356 billion for albums and $194 million for singles. Monthly Schwann catalogs were listing about 40,000 available records in each issue during 1974. Competition from pre-recorded cassettes began to slip, as that medium experienced a 25 percent decline in sales in 1973.

In America the next few years brought the record industry to its zenith. Sales hit $1.697 billion in 1975; $1.908 billion in 1976; and $2.44 billion in 1977. There were 77.6 million phonographs in American homes, with 4.3 million sold in 1977.

The 1978 film *Saturday Night Fever* energized the **disco** music style and helped to produce a national passion for **discotheques**; its soundtrack album became the biggest seller of all time. Along with the soundtrack of *Grease*—another film with disco music—sales of 27 million were achieved. "Categories are shattered and sales and attendance zoom across all demographic lines as the audience for recorded and live music expands beyond the industry's expectations" (Davis 1979). There were 295 gold and platinum albums, and 71 equivalent singles in 1978 (*see* GOLD DISCS), the year in which American sales reached $4.1 billion. Among the leading mainstream pop artists of the mid-1970s were Bob Dylan, Bruce Springsteen, Linda Ronstadt, Olivia Newton-John, Stevie Wonder, Barbra Streisand, and Rod Stewart. Principal country stars included Waylon Jennings, Crystal Gayle, Dolly Parton, Willie Nelson, and Kenny Rogers. The Bee Gees, who made a successful national tour in 1978 and whose songs were heard on the *Saturday Night Fever* soundtrack, dominated the groups. On the classical side Luciano Pavarotti emerged as the hero of operatic fans, with two of the top 10 classical albums in 1977.

Considerable analysis has been attached to the sudden fall in American record sales that occurred in 1979 (Denisoff 1986). Diminishing quality of pop music, growing competition from cassettes and from video, great losses to the industry from pirating—all these factors had a role. Sales fell to $3.67 billion; the drop was only about 9 percent from the previous year, but it was the first decline in sales since 1960, and caused widespread consternation. Two labels were absorbed by larger ones: ABC-Dunhill by MCA, and United Artists by EMI.

One business failure of the 1970s was the attempt to find a public for **quadraphonic sound**. Although the technology was solid, and equipment was standardized, the companies did not agree among themselves on recording standards, and a promising advance was allowed to dissolve. Consumers proved unwilling to invest in an unsettled product.

A slight recovery in U.S. sales was seen in 1980 ($3.9 billion) and 1981 ($4 billion), but 1982 brought another fall, to $3.6 billion. The **compact disc** was introduced in 1983, leading to a climb in annual dollar sales throughout the industry—a climb that continued to the end of the decade. Sales in 1983 moved up to $3.8 billion. In both 1984 and 1985 the sales total was $4.5 billion, with CDs taking an ever-greater share of the market ($930 million in 1986). Because the early cost of a CD—$12 to $20—was 50 percent to 100 percent higher than that of an LP or cassette, dollar volume grew even though item sales did not. (Sales of units declined from 1985 to 1986 by 5 percent, to 618 million.) In 1986 for the first time the sales of CD players surpassed sales of turntables, and the sense of the industry was that LP production was in a terminal phase. CBS converted its Pitman, New Jersey, plant from LP to CD manufacture, producing 20 million CDs per year. Record sales of 1986 (all formats) in the U.S. came to $4.7 billion. By 1989 the total sales were $6.46 billion.

Stunning acquisitions marked the late 1980s. Both of the great American pioneer companies passed to foreign ownership: RCA Records was bought by **Bertelsmann AG** in 1986, and CBS Records was bought by **Sony Corp.** in 1988. In November 1990 Matsushita announced the acquisition of MCA, Inc. for $6.5 billion; the largest purchase of an American firm by a Japanese company. The third-largest American label, **PolyGram**, is owned by the Dutch conglomerate Philips; and Capitol-EMI is British owned. The principal U.S. firms are under foreign control. **WCI**, a major

conglomerate, had taken over several leading labels by 1983 (Reprise, Atlantic, **Elektra**, Nonesuch) and controlled one-fourth of the American record market. Although the end-of-decade boom was fairly pervasive in the American industry, some firms were not able to participate in it; one old name that dissolved in bankruptcy was **JEM**, in 1988.

Variety announced the triumph of the CD, saying that it "finally outpaced sales of the vinyl record in '88, making the digital revolution a success." In 1988 the three-inch CD was launched; and sales of CD players leaped by 45 percent over 1987. In 1989 CD sales accounted for 55 percent of the American market, and LPs for less than 5 percent. A threat to the CD prosperity was seen in the introduction of **DAT**, whose perfect copies of CD material were thought to encourage commercial bootlegging.

Independent labels did not fare happily with the arrival of the CD. Their share of the American market dwindled to 7 percent by 1990, down from about 26 percent in 1978. The high cost of producing CDs was the decisive factor in the deteriorating situation of the independents.

The leading performers in terms of sales at the beginning of the 1990s were Michael Jackson—who sold 36 million copies of his album *Thriller*—Bruce Springsteen, the group U2, Aretha Franklin, Paul Simon, Madonna, Barbra Streisand, and Pink Floyd. CBS and **Warner** headed the list of profitable labels. [Sources for U.S. data: RIAA figures as reported in *Statistical Abstract*, *World Almanac*, *Information Please Almanac*, and *Variety*. Other principal sources: Andrews*; Brooks*; Brooks 1978; Brooks 1979; Cooper 1980; Davis 1979; Denisoff 1986; Fabrizio 1977; Fabrizio 1980; Fagan 1983; Gelatt 1977; Koenigsberg*; Lambert 1983; Read 1976; Rust*; Rust 1978.]

7. *Repertoire*. As with the rival format (*see* CYLINDER, 7) the content of early discs emphasized the voice and brass instruments. Before 1893 the Berliner five-inch "plates" on sale in Europe were presenting songs in three languages, recitations, poems, comic monologs, and solo or ensemble piece by cornets, trombones, and bugles. Berliner's first commercial seven-inch discs, made and marketed in the U.S., appeared in 1894 with a repertoire of

sparkling variety. The tenor Ferruccio Giannini (father of soprano Dusolina Giannini) made records for Fred Gaisberg in Philadelphia, including condensed arias from *Rigoletto, Traviata, Trovatore*, and *Cavalleria rusticana*, plus some songs. (On Berliner #930 he was heard in the "Miserere" in a duet version with a cornet!) Other American Berliners from before 1898 featured whistling, popular songs, banjo, vocal quartets, xylophone, saxophone, and pioneer attempts at orchestral recordings. In April 1899 the Sousa Band began to record for Berliner.

When Gaisberg went to London in July 1898 he initiated a remarkable series of recordings, for Berliner at first, then for the Gramophone Co. By the end of 1898 he had put to wax more than 1,000 sides, including orchestral marches, overtures, waltzes, polkas, and transcriptions from opera; every kind of song, and hits from the musical theatre—including Gilbert and Sullivan operas as well as London West End successes like *Florodora* (staged 1899; hit songs recorded Oct 1900). He also recorded the ever-popular instrumental solos and duets, with string recordings added to the brass recordings late in the year. Gramophone artists were often the same people who were making cylinders. Not many of their names are known today, aside from their contributions to early recordings. Among the most prolific Berliner performers were Albert Hawthorne (monologist), Will Bates (cornetist), Frank Lawton (whistler), Tom Bryce (singer), Burt Shepard (comedian/singer), the Trocadero Orchestra, Russell Hunting (comic monologist), Charles Foster (singer), Vess L. Ossman (banjoist), and George J. Gaskin (singer). Among those recording for G & T (Gramophone & Typewriter, Ltd., the name used by the Gramophone Co. from 11 Dec 1900 to 17 Nov 1907) were the Band of the Coldstream Guards, Olly Oakley (banjoist), and Stanley Kirkby (baritone). A few discs were made by Harry Lauder, and some by the United States Marine Band.

Eldridge Johnson, heading the Consolidated Talking Machine Co. in 1900, and then the Victor Talking Machine Co. from October 1901, had a catalog of recordings similar in character to those being done by Gaisberg. Among the star performers were soprano Bessie Abott, tenor Jesus Abrego, baritone Mario Ancona, the Mexican Banda de Policia, tenor Henry Burr, soprano Emma Calvé, baritone Giuseppe Campanari, tenor Enrico Caruso, tenor Arthur Collins, baritone Emilio De Gogorza, baritone Samuel H. Dudley, soprano Emma Eames, soprano Johanna Gadski, the same Ferruccio Giannini who sang for Berliner, baritone Byron George Harlan, the Haydn (also Hayden) Quartet, contralto Louise Homer, soprano Ada Jones, bass Marcel Journet, tenor Edouard Le Bel, flutist/cornetist Jules Levy, tenor Harry Macdonough, soprano Nellie Melba, contralto Corinne Morgan, tenor Billy Murray, banjoist Vess Ossman, baritone Leopold Picazo, bass Pol Plançon, Pryor's Band and Pryor's Orchestra, contralto Ernestine Schumann-Heink, baritone Antonio Scotti, soprano Marcella Sembrich, Sousa's Band, baritone/comedian Len Spencer, baritone Frank C. Stanley, monologist Cal Stewart (doing Uncle Josh), United States Marine Band, various Victor ensembles (especially the Victor Orchestra), tenor Evan T. Williams, and bass Herbert Witherspoon. All of these were cutting discs before 1908, many of them using pseudonyms. Obviously the Victor cast had more great names than Gaisberg was able to assemble at first; but by 1902 the Gramophone Co. had begun to issue its Red Label discs, with such artists as Calvé, Caruso, Victor Maurel, Plançon, Charles Santley, Scotti, and tenor Francesco Tamagno. Personality labels from the Gramophone Co. were named for Melba (1904) and Adelina Patti (1906).

Opera was the genre of excitement and competition in the first decade of the century (although the popular modes remained strong). All major arias and ensembles of the standard repertoire operas were available, most of them in many versions. Complete operas (with numerous omissions) began to appear in 1907–1908, with the Gramophone Co. issues of *Fledermaus* and *Faust*; the American companies offered no competition for these ambitious efforts. Columbia, a late starter, signed some Metropolitan Opera singers in 1903 (Campanari, Edouard de Reszke, Schumann-Heink, Scotti, Sembrich). Victor Red Seal records, at first pressed from Gramophone Co. Red Labels, then (1903) made in New York studios, helped make the company a national institution.

Recordings of piano music were not numerous in the early period, because of the difficulty in getting any sort of fidelity in reproduction. HMV (Gramophone Co.) issues from 1910 to 1914 included performances by the eccentric Vladimir de Pachmann, as well as Wilhelm Backhaus and Ignace Paderewski. Eugène d'Albert recorded some short pieces for Odeon. None of the extended works in the piano repertoire was addressed in these recordings, aside from a cut version of the "Moonlight Sonata" in 1910 by Mark Hambourg.

A few renowned violinists were recorded by HMV before World War I: Mischa Elman, Josef Joachim (in his 70s), Fritz Kreisler, Jan Kubelik, Maud Powell, Pablo de Sarasate, and Josef Szigeti. Many other violinists made disc records as well, beginning with Charles D'Almaine on Victor from 1900 to 1907.

"The orchestra came last" is the title of a chapter in Gelatt 1977; for technical reasons it took some time before a sizeable group of symphonic players could perform at once for the recording horn. The orchestral repertoire was not seriously explored by the major companies until the five years before the World War I. It was the British and continental producers who led the way: the first large scale symphonic recording was the 1909 *Nutcracker* by Odeon (on four double-sides), followed by the Odeon four-record *Midsummer Night's Dream* in 1910. In 1911–1912 HMV offered *Finlandia*, another *Midsummer Night's Dream, Marriage of Figaro Overture, Leonora Overture No. 3, Peer Gynt Suite*, and a drastically cut version of the Schubert "Unfinished Symphony." These discs were made by conductors and orchestras of minor rank, some of them formed specifically for record making. One of the latter, the Grosses Odeon Streichorchester, produced an eight-sided Beethoven Fifth Symphony and a 10-sided Beethoven Sixth Symphony in 1913 (conductor not identified). These were uncut, and the original instrumentation was used except for the occasional substitution of bassoons for string basses.

Nineteen-fourteen was a landmark year: in February HMV issued (in Germany) a complete Beethoven Fifth Symphony on four double-sides, played by the Berlin Philharmonic Orchestra under Arthur Nikisch, one of the most celebrated conductors of his time. The event—a recording by a great orchestra and great conductor—was itself the landmark; the actual recording, which was made with reduced forces (six violins, two violas, no tympani, no basses!) has received heavy criticism. All this symphonic fervor passed over the heads of the American companies. As late as 1913 the Columbia and Victor catalogs had only scattered symphony movements, usually abridged.

During World War I the record companies kept up their output of cut and distorted serious music; but they were also caught in the new popular music crazes: dance music (from 1913) and jazz (from 1917). The musical stage received growing attention by the record companies in the early 1900s, especially in London. Victor combined this trend with the discovery of Hawaiian music (first recorded by the American Record Co. in 1905) by recording a musical show set in Hawaii (1912). Al Jolson began his career as a star on both stage and records. World class orchestras and conductors began to make recordings regularly after the Armistice. HMV contracted Thomas Beecham for a few discs, plus Landon Ronald, Albert Coates, and Edward Elgar; Columbia signed Henry Wood and Felix Weingartner, along with Beecham. DGG started to offer uncut symphonic work by the Berlin Philharmonic Orchestra; Victor acquired Leopold Stokowski and the Philadelphia Orchestra, and then Arturo Toscanini. The mid-1920s brought a flood of complete symphonies, and also complete recordings of chamber music. **Electrical recording** brought increased acceptance by the public of symphonic masterworks, and also improved the capabilities of on-site recording—in such acoustically renowned halls as the Festspielhaus in Bayreuth and the Academy of Music in Philadelphia. And so by 1928 the repertoire on disc included most of the principal orchestral, chamber, solo, and operatic compositions that were familiar to concert goers. Those were at last available uncut and in their original instrumentation.

Economic setbacks in the 1930s were felt the hardest in U.S., where serious record making came to a near halt. In the U.K., however, the astute merger of firms into the EMI, Ltd., conglomerate provided a firmer base. Great solo discs were made, such as the landmark harpsichord performances of Wanda Landowska, the Beethoven sonatas played by Artur Schnabel, and the incomparable Chopin of Arthur Rubinstein. There was also a move away from the standard repertoire into rich fields like the J.S. Bach organ works (Albert Schweitzer)—although the organ was still an elusive catch for disc producers—Delius (by Beecham), the Haydn quartets, and cello works by Pablo Casals. With the creation of **society records** (sets offered on subscription for a small group of enthusiasts), relatively obscure works found their way into the catalogs. In 1933 a seminal effort to record "old music"—the **Anthologie Sonore**—opened the ears of listeners to the sounds of the middle ages and renaissance.

A review of Victor's 1940/1941 sales catalog shows how well the company had managed to catch up after the Depression, but also how much was left to be done in the classical repertoire. The catalog has about 250 art songs, and about 50 tone poems; there are three Beethoven symphonies, four by Dvorak, 11 by Haydn, two by Mahler, one by Mendelssohn, eight by Mozart, four each by Schubert and Schumann, seven (!) by Sibelius, two by Shostakovich. The baroque was not yet discovered: Telemann and Schütz are absent, and Vivaldi has only seven pieces; *Messiah* appears only in abridged form. J.S. Bach is rather well represented, but only two of the cantatas are there, one French suite, and none of the cello sonatas. The Red Seal artist list had become an impressive array, including the world's leading names in all categories.

Columbia had made a good recovery from the Depression, as indicated in its 1943 sales catalog. All the Beethoven symphonies were listed, along with a symphony of Dvořák, nine by Haydn, one by Mahler, three by Mendelssohn, 10 by Mozart, four by Schubert, three by Schumann, one by Shostakovich, three by Sibelius, and three by Tchaikovsky. Vivaldi is represented by one sonata in a Respighi arrangement. Beecham's *Messiah* was "nearly complete" on 36 sides, but there were no complete Bach cantatas. As for artists, Columbia was never able to keep pace with Victor. But some outstanding performers appeared on the label, either through direct contract or through agreements with EMI: John Barbirolli, Beecham, Budapest String Quartet, Chicago Symphony Orchestra, Cleveland Orchestra, the Concertgebouw of Amsterdam, Emmanuel Feuermann, Walter Gieseking, Lotte Lehmann, the London Philharmonic Orchestra, Lauritz Melchior, the New York Philharmonic Orchestra, Rudolf Serkin, and Joseph Szigeti. Various artists were also "shared" with Victor, as they refused exclusive contracts.

Such was the repertoire and artist situation for classical music in the 1940s. The next tidal change came with the **long-playing record** at the end of the decade, which liberated the baroque and earlier music from obscurity, and brought thousands of new names before the public.

Popular music of the 1920s in the U.S. was comprised primarily of jazz and dance music. In a fusion of those elements, the Big Band Era of the 1930s and 1940s saw the prominence of the swing style. All the American record labels participated in these movements. Many labels also produced material in the country field, which became important in the 1930s and has held a place through all the changes of taste. As the swing era faded after World War II, new popular styles replaced the Big Band sound: rhythm & blues, then rock and roll, bebop, disco, and varieties of rock. With the enormous appeal of rock stars like the Beatles, Elvis Presley, and the Rolling Stones, the 1960s and 1970s were decades in which the record labels depended on sales of rock material, especially to younger buyers. A few non-rock performers, such as Frank Sinatra and Barbra Streisand, did continue to hold the interest of the public through the 1970s. The 1980s were dominated by rock music. Multi-million sales of albums by such artists as Michael Jackson and Bruce Springsteen became common.

Opera recording reached a zenith in the 1970s and 1980s, with much of the credit due to new stars like Maria Callas, Luciano Pavarotti, and Leontyne Price. Complete opera recordings on compact disc (beginning in the mid-1980s) abound. There are, for example, 18 complete *Tosca* versions, and 11 *Tristan* versions. The standard instrumental repertoire is also represented fully, in multiple versions. Contemporary composers are numerous in the catalogs, but only the most prominent have all their major works on record.

The craze for early music that began with the LP record has continued into the compact disc period. Performance on authentic instruments of the composer's time has become an entire sub-industry, covering all periods through the 19th century. But the great world orchestras have continued to use modern instruments and have resisted the movement toward historical performance practice. The vast popularity on record of such orchestras may be in part attributed to the new wave of conductor superstars, like Leonard Bernstein and Georg Solti.

Reissues of classical and popular material from earlier eras has been another hallmark of the compact disc period. Many of these releases have been carefully produced to bring out sound qualities that were not perceptible in the originals (*see* SONIC RESTORATION OF HISTORICAL RECORDINGS).

The future of recorded repertoire seems to belong to the charismatic rock performers of today and to those who follow them. It does not appear that the classical realm has much new to offer, except a deeper exploration of the output of modern composers and further reinterpretations of standard works in so-called authentic performances. *See also* BIG BAND; BLUES RECORDINGS; CHRISTMAS RECORDS; COMEDY RECORDINGS; COUNTRY AND WESTERN MUSIC RECORDINGS; DANCE MUSIC; FOLK MUSIC RECORDINGS; JAZZ RECORDINGS; LITERARY RECORDINGS; MILITARY BAND RECORDINGS; MUSICAL THEATRE RECORDINGS; OPERA RECORDINGS; ORCHESTRA RECORDINGS; RHYTHM & BLUES RECORDINGS; ROCK MUSIC RECORDINGS; entries for individual instruments (e.g., PIANO RECORDINGS) and groups of instruments (e.g., WOODWIND RECORDINGS), and entries for individual artists.

DISC JOCKEY. Also DJ or deejay. A person who selects and plays records in a systematic program, either in a **discotheque** or on the radio, usually adding personal comments on the music. Although the contemporary connotation relates the term to popular music, the earliest radio disc jockeys aired classical music. Christopher Stone was the first, in regular phonograph concerts on British Broadcasting Corp. programs in 1927; he referred to himself as a "presenter."

In the U.S. the first radio programs of recorded music were simply announced like any other fare, and the personality of the announcer was not emphasized. (In fact, early radio announcers were anonymous, and their names were not given to listeners who asked for them.) The first structured presentations of popular music records on American radio were in the *Make Believe Ballroom* programs, hosted by Al Jarvis at KFWB in Los Angeles. Jarvis interjected his personality into the proceedings, and used the clever device of simulating a real ballroom atmosphere—with one band performing all the pieces on each program. The program moved to WNEW in New York, and led to various imitations. Radio announcers who played records, with or without stressing their personalities, were soon recognized as powerful figures in the market. By the 1950s there was such a concentration of power that a few disc jockeys in major markets could create a hit record or doom another to oblivion.

Performers began early on to pay bonuses to those announcers in order to have their discs spun. Not far down the road was **payola**, or outright bribery. The payola scandals of the late 1950s did lead to reforms. One was the development of Top 40 programming (*see* RECORDING INDUSTRY CHARTS), in which the best-selling discs of the week were played (WTIX in New Orleans had the first of these). The announcer in that format, known as **boss radio**, did not have the power to select the material for the show. Deejays were relegated to giving continuity and "color" to the total program. Then the announcer regained some lost ground with the introduction of **free-form programming**, a format that gave the deejay some latitude in choosing material. A wide range of content is typical of this format, including blues, jazz, spoken records, local talent, and folksong as well as material from the charts. Boss remains the dominant mode of popular music broadcasting on AM radio in the U.S., while free-form is prominent on FM radio. Larry Miller of Detroit's KMPX-FM is credited with the invention of free-form. There were about 400 free-form stations in the U.S. during the 1970s; one was Mike Harrison's KPRI-FM in San Diego, where the content was identified as **album oriented rock (AOR)**.

DISC NUMBER. Also known as the catalog number. The manufacturer's number that appears on the label of a disc recording. *See also* ALBUM NUMBER; MATRIX NUMBER.

Dischi Fonotipia. *See* FONOTIPIA, LTD.; SOCIETÀ ITALIANA DI FONOTIPIA.

DISCO. (I) Abbreviated form of discotheque, a dance hall with recorded music—usually very loud rock—and often with kaleidoscopic and laser lighting effects. Apparently the first such dance halls opened in France in the 1960s, as cabaret owners attempted to save money by replacing live acts with disc jockeys. As the idea moved to the U.S. in the late 1960s and early 1970s it was at first a small movement kept alive by a few special patron groups. But the film *Saturday Night Fever* (1978) and its soundtrack record brought discotheques to enormous popularity. By the end of the 1970s there were about 10,000 discotheques in North America, with some 200 in New York City.

DISCO. (II) The term given to dance-oriented rock music, the genre of the discotheque, in a style patterned after the 1978 hit film *Saturday Night Fever*. It was very popular in the late 1970s, then fell out of favor. The Bee Gees were perhaps the most successful disco stars, but hit disco albums were made by other groups too, for example, *Miss You* by the Rolling Stones. The sudden decline of the disco craze in 1979 has been attributed to "single hits, poor lyrics, a subcultural audience and just plain bad records" (Denisoff 1986).

DISCOGRAPHY. The study of sound recordings, more particularly of disc recordings; it is equivalent to bibliography and like that science it has several subdivisions. Descriptive

bibliography is the study of books as objects: how they are printed, bound, illustrated, and so on. In discography this approach is concerned with the physical aspects of a recording, including the sound signals it carries. A comprehensive description of a disc recording, for example, would include attention to its dimensions, weight, color, label, manufacturer, matrix number, manufacturer's number, other numbers and dates that are present, groove structure, spindle hole, defects, other aspects of condition, and materials from which the disc is produced. These characteristics are discernible by inspection of a disc, without the need to play it. When the disc is played, a whole range of new factors become operative, from rotation speed to elements of performance practice. Of course the reason records exist is for their content, and this may be described at numerous levels of depth. The basic information (title, name of composer or author, and name of performer) is often printed on the label—although in some cases incorrectly, as with the pseudonyms used by early recording artists. Detailed information is usually sought elsewhere: a record jacket may present some data not on the label; and there is a vast array of primary and secondary literature to consult for facts about performers, recording dates, take numbers, reissues, and recording techniques. Part of the description may be subjective, involving a value judgment about performance and/or quality of audio fidelity (*see* CRITICISM). The end product of descriptive discography may turn on any one of the aspects mentioned, or on more than one. Perhaps the most comprehensive descriptions of individual recordings are found in catalogs of specialized archives. There are also fine monographs that provide rich detail about a group of recordings, for example, from one company during a limited period of production (such as Fagan 1983 and Koenigsberg 1987). Generally the work done in descriptive discography is carried over into enumerative or historical discography, as a contribution to a listing of some kind or the account of a record company's activities.

While the term "enumerative discography" is not really in use, the kind of work it names—the enumerating or listing of records—

is the predominant mode of research and publication in the field. The earliest lists of records appear to have been the account books kept in the Edison Laboratory from May 1889 (reprinted in Koenigsberg 1987). Public lists were included in the trade magazine *Phonoscope* (*see* the Bibliography or SOUND RECORDING PERIODICALS for imprint data on this and other works cited). *Phonoscope* (1896–1900), *Phonogram* (1891–1893), and a later *Phonogram* (1900–1902) carried advertisements and notices that mentioned new releases. Edison's first annual printed catalog dates from August 1897; an 1898 catalog listed about 750 titles. The *Edison Phonograph Monthly* (1903–1916) carried various lists, including "best sellers." As new cylinder and disc producers emerged, they compiled their own lists, at least for internal control purposes; one specialist says, of the U.K., that he "would now be prepared to gamble on the fact that all companies did issue lists" (Andrews 1971). The earliest printed catalog of the North American Phonograph Co. was issued in 1890; Columbia's first catalog came out later in the same year. In Britain the Gramophone Co. offered a comprehensive catalog in 1900, with more than 5,000 entries. That firm had produced, from 1898, catalogs of limited scope, including lists of records in languages other than English (*see Voices of the Past* in the Bibliography). Victor's initial catalog dates from 1900.

In the 1920s piano rolls were still significant rivals to the disc; and several manufacturers issued catalogs. It seems the first of these "rollographies" was published in 1924 by Welte-Mignon. In that inventory, and in similar ones by Aeolian, the reproducing piano rolls of great pianists were listed, in performer order.

Ethnomusicologists had turned quickly to the newly invented phonograph, and had begun as early as 1889 to make field recordings, which they listed in their subsequent publications; among these scholars were Walter Fewkes, Carl Stumpf, Béla Bartók, and Percy Grainger.

While a number of public, research, and academic libraries took an early interest in collecting records (from 1909; *see* SOUND RECORDINGS AND THE LIBRARY), they did not participate systematically in the production of discographies, which would have been lists of their own holdings. It seems that those holdings were noted only in card catalogs. Among the great national libraries of the world, the presence of recordings has been largely ignored in published catalogs. The U.S. Library of Congress did not begin until 1953 to include a section on "phonorecords" in its periodic catalogs.

National bibliographies have been slow to consider sound recordings worthy of coverage, so the aggregate output of records from all countries is not available in any centralized list. It was Yugoslavia, in 1945, that first introduced a national bibliography with sound recordings included (actually it was a regional list, for Slovenian materials); Hungary was next, in 1947. (The situation for other countries was described in Marco 1989, from which this summary is taken). Lists of recordings are included in the current national bibliographies of these countries, beginning with the dates given: Bulgaria, 1972; Canada, 1970; Cuba, 1970; Denmark, 1969; Federal Republic of Germany, 1974; Hungary 1946; Iceland, 1974; Jamaica, 1975; Japan, 1948; Kenya (selectively), 1980; Malta, 1983; New Zealand, 1966; Papua New Guinea, 1981; Romania, 1952; and Yugoslavia, 1945. The absence of Britain and the U.S. from that inventory is particularly unfortunate, since they are the countries with the longest history of record production. Great Britain announced the preparation of a national discography, but there is nothing comparable planned for the U.S., which has no official national bibliography either (*American Book Publishing Record* [1960–] approximates a national bibliography, but it is a commercial publication based on information supplied voluntarily by publishers). Probably the most comprehensive American listing, from 1978 only, appears as part of the *Catalog of Copyright Entries* of the U.S. Copyright Office. As a semi-annual, uncumulated list it offers the basic facts without organizational features that would make it a useful reference tool. Other principal nations of the record industry are without national discographical listings: India, Italy, Japan, U.S.S.R., and all of Latin America.

Although various trade magazines had been listing new recordings, there was not until 1923 a journal for listeners outside the industry: this was *The Gramophone*. Between its covers have appeared lists of new issues and critical reviews of them. There were also some artist discographies, the earliest being of Emmy Destinn. Similar treatment was offered later by *Disques* (1930–) and *American Music Lover* (1935–) in the U.S. and by a French *Disques* (1934–).

All of these approaches to enumerative discography were of value for limited purposes. But they did not satisfy the need for "bibliographical control" of record production: a means of identifying any record that had been issued anywhere, and of obtaining fundamental descriptive information about it. The manufacturers' catalogs were the most useful publications, but they invariably listed only records "in print"—currently available. No systematic lists of deleted, out of print items have been published.

It was from a jazz enthusiast in France that discography took a new direction. Charles Delaunay's *Hot discographie* (1936) attempted to list the records by major jazz artists, wherever and by whomever they had been produced. In the same year R.D. Darrell issued *The Gramophone Shop Encyclopedia of Recorded Music* in New York, a compilation of "all listings of serious music currently to be found in the catalogues of the world's record manufacturers. . . ." In other words it was an in-print list, but it had the benefit of showing the available discs from various firms clustered by composer, with some topical groupings, and with a performer index. Through its three editions, the last in 1948, this work dealt with 66 labels from Europe (including the U.S.S.R.) and America. It marked the belated establishment of discography as a systematic field of investigation, comparable to bibliography.

Basing their work on that of Darrell, two British writers, Francis F. Clough and G.J. Cuming, published the *World's Encyclopaedia of Recorded Music* (WERM) in 1952, with supplements in 1952 and 1957. The main volume displayed some 40,000 items on more than 300 labels, all of them issues from period of electrical recording (1925–1951). Descriptive data for

each item included artist, label and label number, speed, and some information about reissues. But release dates were not given, and there was no performer index. All recordings were of "permanent music"; in other words, jazz and pop recordings were excluded.

In 1937 there appeared the first retrospective discography of classical music arranged by performer: the *New Catalogue of Historical Records, 1898–1908/09*, by Robert Bauer. Covering all the lateral-cut disc labels that were active in that period, this landmark discography exhibited the work of 1,920 artists, nearly all of them singers. Unfortunately, the descriptive information about each record was minimal and the listings were incomplete. Bauer did a second edition in 1947; then Rodolfo Celletti, in 1964, produced an update of the recordings by about 250 leading singers.

The amazing growth of the record industry after the introduction of the long-playing record in 1948 is marked by the appearance of the first unified in-print list, covering more than one label, to be published on a periodic basis. It was the *Long Playing Record Catalog*, by William Schwann, predecessor to his *Schwann Catalog* series. Eleven American firms had their output noted in the initial issue, which identified 674 LPs. Similar trade catalogs came along presently in Britain (*Gramophone Classical Catalogue*, 1953–) and Germany (*Bielefelder Katalog*, 1953–). Prerecorded tapes, significant rivals to the LP, have had their own listing, the *Harrison Tape Catalog* (1953–1976), but cassette tapes also came to be listed in Schwann.

Enumerative discographies began to proliferate in the 1950s, prompting the earliest attempt to keep track of them: C.L. Bruun and J. Gray's "Bibliography of Discographies" in the first issue of *Recorded Sound*, in 1961. The compilers presented about 450 entries, each a discography (no cylinder lists) of classical records by a certain artist or of a certain type. This work was extended by David Cooper's *International Bibliography of Discographies* (1975), which listed 1,908 discographies of classical music, jazz, and blues, all published from 1962 to 1972. Clearly the writing of discographies had entered a boom period.

As the number of such publications mushroomed, several scholars began to consider the nature of discography: its objects and proper methodology. (Such concerns were not entirely new: William Moran had written an eloquent plea for discographical standards in a letter to *The Record Collector* in 1958.) Gordon Stevenson, in a 1972 article, sought "solid theoretical underpinnings" for the emerging science. Similar efforts were undertaken by Louis Foreman in 1974, and by J. F. Weber a year later. A 1980 volume, *Brian Rust's Guide to Discography*, offered the most thorough treatment of discography as a science.

By 1976 the approach to discography had climbed to a level that called for "Standards for the Review of Discographical Works" (the title of an article in the *ARSC Journal* by Steven Smolian). Another proposal of 1976, by George Blacker, called for a "clearinghouse of discographical data." A data sheet prepared by Blacker was suitable for international use in entering all relevant facts about a recording in a consistent manner. It is unfortunate that Blacker's data sheet has not had wide acceptance, and that most published discographies present incomplete and often misleading information about the records they cover.

In step with the growth of discography came the march of new specialist magazines, many of them the principal publishing outlets for discographical scholarship. Journals with strong discographies have included *ARSC Journal* (1967–), *Goldmine* (1974–), *Hillandale News* (1960–), *Paul's Record Magazine* (for rock discographies; 1975?-), *Record Collector* (1946–), *Record Research* (1955–), *Recorded Sound* (1961–1984), and *Talking Machine Review International* (1969–).

Among the recent book-length and multivolume discographies of jazz and pop music are Bruyninckx 1980, Jepsen 1963, Kinkle 1974, Rust 1970, and Rust 1974. Hartel 1980 is a chronological list of record releases by various labels, covering jazz, blues, and gospel music. In the classical area, Creighton 1974 is a useful list of violin recordings.

Monographic coverage of individual performers has reached an elegant stage, notably in the publications of Greenwood Press and Scarecrow Press. For example, the Benny Goodman discography from Scarecrow (Connor 1988) is a model of its kind.

Discographic output in all formats and for all kinds of music is kept under control by the continuing bibliography of discography series written by Michael Gray and Gerald Gibson (*see* Gray 1985 in the Bibliography).

While all discographies contribute to knowledge of the recording industry, one type is designed especially to do so: historical discography. Like its parent, historical bibliography, this discipline is focused on the activities of key individuals and firms. Those who examine the record industry usually begin with a single company, or label, and do archival research that leads to a narrative history. Recordings are the basic artifacts that are studied, less for themselves than as pieces of the historical mosaic. Thus part of that history, and as part of the material needed for it, is the list of recordings produced under a label name. Compiling of "label lists" has become a major interest among record specialists like Frank Andrews, Arthur Badrock, John R. Bennett, George Blacker, Tim Brooks, Sydney Carter, Ron Dethlefson, Bjorn Englund, Ted Fagan, Pekka Gronow, Alan Kelly, Carl Kendziora, Karleric Liliedahl, William R. Moran, Anthony Rotante, Michel Ruppli, Brian Rust, and Raymond Wile. Historical discographers try to assemble complete lists, usually with the assistance of the collector community. This drive for completeness is fueled by the fact that record makers, unlike publishers, have invariably given serial numbers to their products; hence it is a reasonable starting point to find one record for each number in a series (although there are complications with the systems used by various manufacturers), and it is in that form—label list by series—that much of the research is published.

Discographical control over 78 rpm records has probably reached its zenith with the **Rigler and Deutsch Index**, a joint effort of five American archives to list and describe their holdings. Will there ever be complete listings of LP records, either of current world production or of retrospective output? It seems doubtful; too much documentation has been missing or lost in these 40 years. The largest compilation of LPs is in the OCLC database, an online union catalog of major libraries. Recently the compact disc has swept over the scene, with no sign of a better control system than the LP has had.

[Andrews 1971/2; Blacker 1976/5; Brooks 1979/2; Directory 1989; Fagan 1983; Foreman 1974; Koenigsberg 1987; Marco 1989; Rust 1980; Smolian 1976; Stevenson 1972; Weber 1975. *See also* entries in the Bibliography for all discographers and discographies cited.]

Discophone. *See* PICTURIZED PHONO-GRAPHS.

DISCOTECA DI STATO. The Italian national sound archive, established in 1928 in Rome. A large collection of ethnic field recordings has been assembled. An extensive catalog of holdings appeared in 1967, with a revision in 1970 and a supplement with index in 1973.

Discotheque. *See* DISCO (I).

Discrete circuit. *See* INTEGRATED CIRCUIT.

DISKO CO. A British firm, established in 1913 at 76–78–80 High St., Shirley, Southampton. It produced a disc cleaner that promised to "make the worst worn record play as well as if it had just left the presses."

DISPERSION. A characteristic of a **loudspeaker**, referring to its ability to distribute sound widely and evenly throughout the listening area.

DI STEFANO, GIUSEPPE, 1921– . Italian lyric tenor, born near Catania on 24 July 1921. His debut was in 1946 at Reggio Emilia; then he sang in Rome and at La Scala. He made his Metropolitan Opera debut as the Duke on 25 Feb 1948, and was with the company until 1952, returning in 1955/1956 and 1964/1965. He sang also in San Francisco and Chicago, and in Europe and South America, widely regarded as the world's leading tenor. Di Stefano made an acclaimed concert tour with Maria Callas in 1973–1974.

His best recordings were 78s made for HMV from 1947 to 1953, for example, "E lucevan le stelle" (#DB 6580) and "Che gelida manina" (#DB 21518). He is heard in nine complete opera LP recordings, many with Callas. An LP of Di Stefano's earliest recordings, some of which appeared under the name of

Nino Florio, was released in 1977 (O.A.S.I. #500). Much of his output is available on compact discs.

DISTORTION. Any alteration to the input **signal** as it passes through a sound system. Various types of distortion are listed here:

(I) *Amplitude distortion*. Also known as non-linear distortion. The name given to any change in the ratio of output **amplitude** to input amplitude for any value of the latter. Both harmonic and intermodulation distortion are outcomes.

(II) *Amplitude/frequency distortion*. Also named attenuation distortion. A change in **amplification** produced by shifts in signal **frequency**.

(III) *Clipping distortion*. A result of **overload**.

(IV) *End of side distortion*. In a disc reproducing systems, the result from the fact that the speed of the disc under the stylus is faster at the edge than at the center. On a 12-inch 33 1/3 rpm LP, the speed at the outside edge is 20.9 inches per second; while at the center, with the radius reduced to about 2 1/2 inches, the speed is only 8.7 inches per second (*see* DISC, 5). In practice this means that the amplitude must be less at the center than at the edge, or amplitude distortion will result, particularly at higher frequencies. It was this problem that led Thomas Edison to prefer the cylinder, where **surface speed** is constant.

(V) *Flutter*. *See* FLUTTER.

(VI) *Harmonic distortion*. A result of amplitude distortion: it refers to overemphasis or underemphasis on certain overtones. The first overtone, or second **harmonic** (the octave above the fundamental), is not a major problem when it is distorted, but the higher harmonics—fifth, seventh, and ninth—are disturbing if reproduced out of balance. A common reason for this effect is that the volume is turned up to a point where the amplifier is overloaded.

(VII) *Intermodulation distortion*. A result (like harmonic distortion) of amplitude distortion: it refers to the production of alien frequencies corresponding to the sums and differences of the fundamentals and harmonics of two or more signal frequencies.

(VIII) *Linear distortion*. A type of amplitude distortion in which the input and output signals are not proportionate, but without the introduction of alien frequencies. It is relatively easy to eliminate in an audio system, with the **volume control** and **balance control.**

(IX) *Non-linear distortion*. The type of distortion that is most troublesome in an audio system, because it stems from the transmission properties of the system, that is, the dependency of the system upon the instantaneous magnitude of the transmitted signal. Non-linear distortion produces flutter, intermodulation distortion, and wow.

(X) *Phase distortion*. Also called phase-frequency distortion. The type of distortion that results when **phase shift** is not in direct proportion to the frequency across the entire transmission range. It is often responsible for "low fidelity" in a sound system, a vague and unpleasant listening experience.

(XI) *Rumble*. The sound produced by vibrations in the recording or playback **turntable** of a disc system.

(XII) *Scale distortion*. The result of widely different dimensions between input and output locations. For example, it may occur when a signal originating in a concert hall is reproduced in a small room.

(XIII) *Tracing distortion*. The result of a misfit between the record **groove** and the playback **stylus**, usually caused by the swing of the **tone arm** from the start to the end of the record. The misfit can be diminished by linear tone arm travel, constant groove-to-stylus angle devices, stylus size, and stylus shape.

(XIV) *Wow. See* WOW.
[Isom*; Klinger*.]

DIVA (label). A subsidiary of Columbia, made for the W.T. Grant department store chain from 1925 to 1932. At first the material was drawn from Harmony, but later it was original, featuring blues. [Rust 1978.]

DIXI (label). A Swedish product introduced in 1932 by the department store chain Ahlen & Holm. The disc was about eight inches in diameter at first; then in 1934 it grew to 10 inches and took the name Silverton. Most of the records were of Swedish dance orchestras. The final year of issue was 1944. [Liliedahl 1973.]

DIXIELAND JAZZ. An early jazz style practiced in New Orleans, primarily associated with white musicians. The first recording of this sound was by the **Original Dixieland Jazz Band** in 1917. *See also* JAZZ RECORDINGS.

DODDS, JOHNNY, 1892–1940. American jazz clarinetist, born in New Orleans on 12 Apr 1892. He played locally as a teenager, then went to Chicago and played with King Oliver during 1920–1924. He freelanced, had his own band, and performed with Louis Armstrong. Dodds died in Chicago on 8 Aug 1940.

Probably his biggest hit record was "Wild Man Blues" (Brunswick #3567; 1927) with his Black Bottom Stompers, a group that included Armstrong, Barney Bigard, and Earl Hines. The Oliver material is on Epic LP #3208; Armstrong material is on Riverside LP #1029.

DODGE, PHILIP T., 1851–1931. American record industry executive. In 1915, with the death of Edward Easton, Dodge became president of **American Graphophone Co.** In April 1917 he became chairman of the board.

DOLBY NOISE REDUCTION SYSTEM. A device invented by Raymond M. Dolby in 1966 for increasing the **signal-to-noise ratio** of a tape recording; it removes most recording noise and hiss. Essentially, the Dolby method is to code the audio signal during recording and then decode during playback, thus circumventing hiss production.

Dolby A is used in professional tape mastering; Dolby B, Dolby C, and Dolby S are simpler systems for domestic cassette machines. Dolby B reduces noise about 10 dB, Dolby C reduces noise about 20 dB. Dolby C has a treble boost curve in recording to diminish tape saturation and treble loss. Dolby S, a new system announced in 1990, achieves comparable noise reduction to Dolby C, but without side effects; it lowers high-frequency hiss more than Dolby C, and improves noise reduction in the low- to middle-frequency range. Dolby S is derived from Dolby SR (or Dolby Spectral), introduced in 1986, a system that analyzes the spectral composition of the input signal and protects it against loss at the audible thresholds of the recording medium.

Decca Record Co., Ltd., of U.K., was the first label to market pre-recorded cassettes using the Dolby system (October 1970). [Stark 1990.] *See also* dbx; NOISE REDUCTION SYSTEMS.

DOMAINS. The small regions of uniform magnetization (typically magnetized iron oxide particles) that store the sound signals in **tape recording.** As the domains move past the receptor head, the varying magnetic field induces changing electrical signals that can be converted back to the original sound. [Klinger*.]

DOMESTIC TALKING MACHINE CORP. A Philadelphia firm, established in 1916 at 33rd and Arch Streets, to make disc players. "Domestic" was the brand name. **Horace Sheble** was president until he retired in February 1918; George Anderson replaced him. **George W. Lyle** was sales agent. In March 1916 the firm offered two vertical-cut discs at $.35. Ten-inch discs of blue material (like the Hawthorne & Sheble "Indian" Records of the American Record Co. in the early 1900s) appeared in September 1917 for $.70. In October 1917 there were also 12-inch records, at $1.25. The repertoire was popular songs and dance music. Domestic moved to Latrobe, Pennsylvania, in April 1919. [Andrews*.]

DOMINGO, PLACIDO, 1941– . Spanish tenor, born in Madrid on 21 Jan 1941. His family moved to Mexico when he was nine years old, and he learned to play the piano there; he also sang in zarzuela performances with his parents, taking baritone roles at first. He sang opera in Israel for two years, then made his American debut at the New York City Opera on 17 Oct 1965 as Pinkerton. He joined the Metropolitan Opera in 1966, singing Turridu at a concert performance on 9 Aug 1966, and stayed 10 years with the company, singing 74 roles. He has been heard in the principal world theaters.

Domingo has recorded extensively on Deutsche Grammophon compact discs. Complete operas include *Nabucco, Luisa Miller, Manon Lescaut, Turandot, Fanciulla del West, Trovatore, Carmen, Rigoletto, Macbeth, Traviata, Ballo in maschera, Tannhäuser, Contes d'Hoffmann,* and *Meistersinger.* He also sings popular love songs, and has had such chart albums as *Perhaps Love* (1981) and *My Life for a Song* (1983), both for Columbia. His 1984 "Siempre en mi corazón" won the Grammy in the Latin category.

DOMINION GRAMOPHONE RECORD CO., LTD. A British firm established on 21 Mar 1928, selling records with a Dominion label at 1s 3d. The address was 55–57 Great Marlborough St., London. Masters from American labels Cameo and Perfect were used, as well as original material. Dominion repertoire included dance music, some opera, and authors reading their own works. One release, "My Man o' War" sung by Elsie Carlisle, was reportedly denounced as pornographic; and it supposedly led to a fine that helped put the company into liquidation in July 1930. [Badrock 1976; Rust 1978.]

DOMINO, FATS, 1928– . American pianist and bandleader, born Antoine Domino, Jr., in New Orleans on 26 Feb 1928. Self taught on the piano, he mixed blues elements into the rock and roll idiom, achieving great success in the 1950s and 1960s with more than 50 chart records. His first hit was "Ain't It a Shame" (Imperial #5348; 1955), followed by "Blueberry Hill" (Imperial #5407; 1956) and "I'm Walkin'" (Imperial #5428; 1957). He continued performing until the mid-1960s, then was less active.

DOMINO (label). (I) A double-sided, vertical-cut,. seven-inch disc first marketed in June 1916 by the Domino Phonograph Co. of New York. Despite their small size, the records had a playing time of 2 1/2 minutes. The sale price was $ .33, the repertoire was pop and standard. A 10-inch disc, glossy red in color, appeared in February 1917, at $.35. W.R. Anderson, 220 Fifth Ave., did the distribution, which seems to have ceased around 1917. [Andrews*.]

DOMINO (label). (II) A subsidiary label of the **Plaza Music Co.,** issued from 1924 to 1933 by the Domino Record Co. of New York. Certain jazz releases were important, several of them by the New Orleans Jazz Band. But most of the repertoire was dance music and popular song. [Rust 1978.]

DORATI, ANTAL, 1906–. Hungarian/American conductor, born in Budapest on 9 Apr 1906; "one of the most prolific conductors on record, his total output of records exceeding 500" (Holmes). His debut came at age 18 in Budapest, after which he was on the staff of the Budapest Opera (1924–1928). Then he conducted the Dresden and Münster operas. After world tours he moved to the U.S. and became a citizen in 1947. He has held many posts: Dallas Symphony Orchestra, 1945–1949; Minneapolis Symphony Orchestra, 1949–1960; BBC Symphony Orchestra, 1963–1966; Stockholm Philharmonic Orchestra, 1966–1970; National Symphony Orchestra (Washington, D.C.), 1970–1977; Detroit Symphony Orchestra, 1977–1981; and the Royal Philharmonic Orchestra, 1975–1979.

On record Dorati's crowning achievement was to do the complete Haydn symphonies with the Philharmonia Hungarica for Decca, in 1971–1974, on 48 LP discs. He has also recorded the complete Beethoven symphonies, for DGG, with the Royal Philharmonic. In 1956 he made a spectacular recording of the *1812 Overture* with the Minneapolis Symphony, using a real cannon in the finale. [Holmes 1988.]

DORFMANN, ANIA, 1899–1984. Russian pianist, born in Odessa on 9 July 1899. She studied with Leschetitzky and Isidor Philipp, and became a specialist in the romantic school. She had world tours, and made an American debut in 1936. She was the only female pianist to appear as soloist with a symphony orchestra conducted by Arturo Toscanini. After 1939 she was less active on stage, concentrating on teaching. She was on the Juilliard School faculty from 1966 to 1983. Her death came in New York on 21 Apr 1984.

Dorfmann recorded in 1930 and 1931 for Columbia, in Britain, doing some lighter pieces by Schubert and Johann Strauss (#DX 91 and DX 328). Among her finest records are the Mendelssohn *Songs without Words* (Victor LM-6128) and the Mendelssohn Piano Concerto,

with the London Symphony Orchestra (Columbia #X-124; 1938).

DORIAN (label). An American record established in 1988, devoted to classical music. Dorian Recordings is the parent firm, located in Troy, New York; Craig Dory is president. Among the first releases were four CDs of Jean Guillou, performing on the new organ of the Tonhalle, Zürich.

DORSEY, JIMMY, 1904–1957. American saxophone and clarinet player, and Big Band leader, born in Shenandoah, Pennsylvania, on 29 Feb 1904. He was a brother of **Tommy Dorsey** with whom he shared the successful Dorsey Brothers Orchestra from 1934 to 1935, based on a less formal joint band that had started in 1928. They recorded for Decca, one of the numbers being "I'm Getting Sentimental Over You," later to be Tommy Dorsey's theme song. Following a dispute in 1935, the brothers went separate ways. Jimmy Dorsey's band was enormously popular, in large part because of the outstanding vocalists he engaged: Kay Weber, Bob Eberly, and Helen O'Connell. Among the band's finest records were its theme song "Contrasts" (Decca #3198), "Green Eyes" / "Maria Elena" (Decca #3698), "Yours" (Decca #3657), "Amapola" (Decca #3629), and "Tangerine" (Decca #4123). The Latin-American style was prominent in those and other favorites of the group. The Dorsey brothers reunited in 1947 to make a biographical film about themselves, *The Fabulous Dorseys*, and were together in the Tommy Dorsey band in 1953. Jimmy Dorsey died in New York on 12 June 1957.

DORSEY, TOMMY, 1905–1956. American trombonist and Big Band leader, born in Mahoney Plains, Pennsylvania, on 19 Nov 1905. He was younger brother to Jimmy Dorsey, with whom he shared the successful Dorsey Brothers Orchestra and other activities (*see* JIMMY DORSEY). His most remarkable achievement was the development of "a virtuoso technique using a unique method of convex breathing that enabled him to maintain miraculously long passages legato" (Slonimsky 1984). The result was a tone of astonishing sweetness that appeared to ignore the limitations of the instrument. But Tommy Dorsey's band had other strengths, including such instrumentalists as trumpeters Bunny Berigan, Ziggy Elman, and Pee Wee Erwin; clarinetist Buddy De Franco; and drummers Buddy Rich and Dave Tough. Connie Haines, Dick Haymes, Frank Sinatra, Jo Stafford, and the Pied Pipers provided outstanding vocals. Arrangers included Sy Oliver, Paul Weston, and Axel Stordahl. One clever type of arrangement had the band members sing a chorus as background to a solo vocal; it produced such hit records as "Marie" (Victor #25523; 1937) and "Who" (Victor #25693; 1937). Some of the best records with Sinatra were "I'll Be Seeing You" (Victor #26539; 1940), "I'll Never Smile Again" (Victor #26628; 1940), and "This Love of Mine" (Victor #27508; 1941). "Boogie-Woogie" was an all-time instrumental hit (Victor #26054; 1937). "Song of India"—a powerful instrumental arrangement by Dorsey and Red Bone, featuring Dorsey's trombone and Bunny Berigan's trumpet—is perhaps the finest recording of the orchestra (Victor #25523; 1937). Dorsey died in Greenwich, Connecticut, on 26 Nov 1956.

DOUBLE TRACKING. A technique in which the same musical material is recorded twice, with one signal superimposed on the other. The effect is to give the listener an impression of multiple performers.

DOUGLASS, LEON F., 1869–1940. American inventor and recording industry executive. He worked for the Nebraska Phonograph Co., Omaha, then moved to Chicago, establishing the **Chicago Talking Machine Co.** (sold to Columbia in 1897). A promoter for Eldridge Johnson's **Consolidated Talking Machine Co.** in 1900, he produced national magazine advertising in the U.S., touting the company's new wax disc and offering free samples to gramophone owners. It was once thought that the name of his wife, Victoria, was the inspiration for the name of the Victor Talking Machine Company that succeeded Consolidated.

Douglass was a successful inventor in several fields: he developed the magnetic torpedo used in World War I, demonstrated color motion pictures in 1918, constructed a periscope

camera for underwater photography, and at his death was researching the problem of communication between planets. He held 13 U.S. patents in the sound recording area, filed between 1890 and 1909, among them a **coin-op** (#431,883; filed 14 Feb 1890), a cylinder record duplicating method (#475,490; filed 17 Mar 1892, granted 24 May 1892), and the Polyphone record player (#613,670; filed 14 Feb 1898, granted 8 Nov 1898). The Polyphone featured two sapphire stylus reproducers, each tracking the same cylinder groove, but 3/8 to 1/2 inch apart, each stylus leading to its own horn. Douglass died in San Francisco on 7 Sep 1940.

Drama recordings. *See* LITERARY RECORDINGS.

DROP-IN. The insertion of a new signal on a recorded track of magnetic tape by playing the tape to a desired point and switching to the record mode.

DROPOUT. A very brief reduction in reproduced signal level on a magnetic tape, resulting from dust or some fault in the tape coating. Its magnitude is expressed in terms of decibel loss and length of time. "Dropout count" refers to the number of dropouts on a given length of tape. [Klinger*.]

DRUG LYRICS. A 1970 speech by U.S. Vice President Spiro Agnew called attention to lyrics of popular songs that appeared to encourage the use of alcohol and illegal drugs. The Federal Communications Commission (FCC) issued a warning to broadcasters, and a number of records were removed from air time. There was considerable opposition to this governmental intrusion, culminating in a protest by the **RIAA**, and in April 1971 the FCC issued a clarification that seemed to recognize the right of the broadcaster to determine what should be played. But the U.S. Supreme Court in 1973, by refusing to review the FCC's original notice, did not take away the FCC's authority to approve or disapprove song lyrics. Nevertheless, the FCC was not aggressive in seeking out drug lyrics, and the whole matter seems to have faded away.

DRUGOLA. A term given to a variety of **payola** in which the bribes to disc jockeys were said to be in the form of drugs, especially marijuana and cocaine. Accusations about this activity in the record industry, made by columnist Jack Anderson in 1972, were followed by a federal investigation. No indictments resulted, and there was no further public concern about the matter.

DUAL GEBRÜDER STEIDINGER. A firm established in 1900 in St. Georgen, Germany, by Christian Steidinger. Originally devoted to clock making, the company turned to gramophone motors in 1906. Its successful spring motors were modified in 1927, resulting in a combination electrical-mechanical drive system. By 1976 the firm was employing 3,500 persons in 12 factories, making turntables, amplifiers, tuners, cassette decks, and complete audio systems. About half of its production is exported. [Borwick 1976.]

Dual track. *See* TRACK.

DUBBING. (I) Copying or re-recording; as a noun, the recording thus obtained.

DUBBING. (II) Re-voicing the dialogue of a film track into another language, or by a different artist in the original language.

DUBBING. (III) Recording additional parts on previously taped material (known also as overdubbing).

DUBBING. (IV) Making a test pressing, known as a dub.

DUCHIN, EDDY, 1910–1951. American Big Band leader and pianist, born in Cambridge, Massachusetts, on 10 Apr 1910. At age 21 he was directing his own band and playing solo parts, employing a simple melodic delivery, often with one finger on the tune. He had a significant engagement at the Congress Hotel, Chicago, in 1934, and went on to radio (including the *Kraft Music Hall*) and motion pictures. Duchin became one of the most popular performers of the period 1934–1940. "My Twilight Dream" (Columbia #35314; 1939) was among his many acclaimed records. He died in New York on 9 Feb 1951. The *Eddy Duchin Story* was a film made of his career, featuring Carmen Cavallaro's piano on the soundtrack (1956). His son is the pianist Peter Duchin.

DUCKING. In recording, the technique of adding one signal to another without increasing total dynamic level, as when a voiceover is dubbed onto music. *See also* DUBBING, III.

DUCRETET ET CIE. A French firm of instrument makers, which produced a "plate phonograph" (i.e., a tinfoil disc player) in 1879. The company also marketed a **tinfoil phonograph** for cylinders. The disc player was ingeniously designed to account for the change in **groove speed** from edge to center of the record. Little is known of these products or their commercial success. The machines were sold for 100 francs (a hand-driven Model) or 550 francs (a spring-driven model). [Chew 1982.]

DUCRETET-THOMSON (label). A French record, issued by Decca in Britain from October 1954. The repertoire focused on world music, including Unesco recordings. In 1958 the label made its final appearance in the English catalog. [Bryant 1962.]

DUDLEY, S.H., ca. 1865–1947. American operatic and popular singer, born Samuel Holland Rous in Greencastle, Indiana. He sang in 72 operas for 34 different companies, accumulating 3,742 performances as a utility buffo. Dudley was heard on Berliner's seven-inch record #01021, "In Old Ben Franklin's Day" (26 Feb 1900), and on Eldridge Johnson's first 10-inch Monarch record, #3001 of 1901: "When Reuben Comes to Town." He made other Berliners in 1902, then recorded for Edison, doing solo and quartet work, making as many as 85 cylinders in one day. The first Edison was "Dreaming, Dreaming" (#1150). In London, in 1902, he recorded with his **Hayden Quartet** for the Gramophone Co. Back in America he was engaged by Calvin Child as assistant director of recording for Victor. One of his tasks was to edit the annual Victor catalog and the *Victor Book of the Opera* (first edition 1912). He retired in 1919.

Most of Dudley's solo recordings were comic numbers, many with whistling. A notable example was the "Whistling Coon," a duet with Billy Murray. He sang ballad duets with Harry Macdonough, such as "Red Wing," a song in the style of an American Indian melody, that became one of the best-selling discs of its time. That number was coupled with the Hayden Quartet rendering of "Rainbow," an authentic Indian melody. Dudley used the pseudonym Frank Kernell on some Victor discs.

Dulcephone. *See* APOLLO (I).

DUMMY HEAD STEREO. Also known by the German name "Kunstkopf." A process of recording in which microphones are placed in the ears of a model head. The earliest reference to the technique was in a 1927 U.S. patent application by Bartlett Jones of Chicago. *See also* BINAURAL RECORDING.

DUMPING. The sales practice of remaindering records at a discount. *See also* RACK JOBBER.

DUNCAN, TODD, 1903– . American baritone, born Robert Todd Duncan in Danville, Kentucky, on 12 Feb 1903. He graduated from Butler University, Indianapolis, and taught music in public schools. In 1930 he received a master's degree from Columbia University, and became a professor of music at Howard University in Washington, D.C. He sang in New York with the Aeolian Negro Opera Co., and attracted the attention of Olin Downes, who recommended him to George Gershwin. As a result Duncan was selected to sing the lead in *Porgy and Bess* (1936). Duncan did other Broadway work, and appeared with the New York City Opera; he retired from the stage in 1965 after singing at President Lyndon Johnson's inaugural ceremony. His principal recording is the complete *Porgy and Bess* (Decca #A145, four 78s). He also recorded for British Columbia in the 1930s, and for Philips in the 1940s.

DUNCAN SISTERS. American singing actresses and vaudeville duo, consisting of Rosetta and Vivian Duncan, both born in Los Angeles around 1900. Their sister Evelyn performed with them at first. Rosetta and Vivian appeared at the Fifth Avenue Theatre in New York in 1917, and in New York plays through 1922; they were also in London in 1921. Their greatest success was in the play *Topsy and Eva*, for which they wrote the music and lyrics; it opened in San Francisco on 9 July 1923, and then broke the box office record at Chicago's Selwyn Theatre. In New York the play ran for 159 performances, starting on 23 Dec 1924. A (silent) movie based on it premiered in June 1927 at Hollywood's Egyptian Theatre.

The sisters made records for HMV in 1922, Victor in 1926–1927 and 1930, Columbia in 1928 and 1931, Parlophone in 1937, and for their own Duncan Disc Co. in 1947. There were also some 1928–1929 Vitaphone talkies, no longer extant. Their outstanding hits were from *Topsy and Eva*: "Rememb'ring" / "I Never Had a Mammy" (Victor #19206; 1923), and "The Music Lesson" (Victor #19050; 1922).

DUO-ART. A reproducing piano made by Aeolian Co.

DUOPHONE. A line of gramophones produced in Britain by C.L. Newland, beginning in March 1922, then by the Duophone Syndicate from July 1922. The firm was at 63 Queen Victoria St., London. "Duo" refers to the special feature of the machines, which was their double **soundbox**. Success of the gramophones, and of Duophone unbreakable discs—mostly of dance music—sold at 1s 6d, was temporary. In 1928 Duophone and Brunswick, both failing, shared offices—two separate companies operating as one. In June 1929 the company went into receivership, heading toward eventual liquidation in June 1930. [Andrews*]

DUO-TRAC. A soundtrack recorded on reels of tape (not a motion picture film), made by **British Ozaphane, Ltd.,** based on certain French patents, demonstrated 15 Feb 1937 in London. It was made of cellophane, 4 millimeters wide, and played 30 minutes on a seven-inch reel, or 60 minutes on a nine-inch reel. For home use, there were audio-only versions of pre-recorded classical and dance music; those "reel records" were playable on the **Cellophone**. [Andrews 1984/4.]

DUPLEX. (I) A table model Pathéphone with two turntables, marketed in 1912. *See* PATHÉ FRÈRES COMPAGNIE.

DUPLEX. (II) A **soundbox** sold by **Favorite** in summer 1912; it played with a needle for lateral-cut discs or sapphire for vertical-cut discs.

DUPLEX PHONOGRAPH CO. A Kalamazoo, Michigan, firm active from 1906 to ca. 1911. It made a double-horned, double-reproducer disc machine and disc records. The machine, incorporating devices patented by Charles E. Hill, was named Duplexophone. (Hill's patent application was filed 20 Mar 1903; patent #773,740 was granted 1 Nov 1904.) Duplexophones were first made in 1905 in Lincoln, Nebraska, then by the **Kalamazoo Novelty Co.**, and finally by the Duplex Phonograph Co., which was located initially at 106 Patterson St., Kalamazoo.

Street addresses for the firm were probably more numerous than actual locations. The firm erected a large building on a vacant Patterson St. site. Four different numbers on Patterson St. are found in advertisements, perhaps reflecting adjustments in the mailing address of the office. An August 1906 advertisement gave one location as 106 Patterson St., and another at 1206 Powers Building, Chicago. In ca. 1907 the advertised address was 716 River St. Col. F. D. Eager was general manager.

Although promotion of the Duplexophone tended to distort reality—claiming, for example, that its double-diaphragm prevented half the sound waves from being wasted as they were on single diaphragm phonographs—the claim of "double volume of sound" was perhaps closer to the mark. Certainly the twin horns, each 30 inches long with a 17-inch brass bell, had a high volume capacity. The horns were attached directly to the reproducer, without a tone arm, a potential weakness that was cleverly exploited in advertising as a favorable feature: "no swing arm to cause harsh, discordant, mechanical sounds." But the best selling point may have been the $29.95 sales price, less than the Edison Home (cylinder) phonograph

or the Victor disc models of the day. (Victor's table model Victrola did not appear until 1911.) Customers were also attracted by the money-back guarantee of satisfaction.

An extensive catalog of recordings was issued by Duplex. One issue of ca. July 1906, described in Petty, listed about 2,000 discs. Most of them were Columbia and Victor records, selling at their regular prices. Others were pressed by Columbia, International Record Co., or American Record Co., and issued with a Kalamazoo Record label. The material was primarily popular vocal and popular band repertoire, but Victor Red Seals and Columbia Grand Opera discs were also available.

After moderate success, Duplex encountered a court challenge from the Victor Talking Machine Co. (5 Feb 1907) over violations of the basic Berliner gramophone patent, U.S. #534,543. On 2 Apr 1907 the Duplex plant was closed, following an injunction issued in favor of the Victor Co. A second suit by Victor, filed in January 1908, alleged violation of patent #624,301 (which covered a double-horned graphophone made by Charles G. Conn). It appears that Duplex remained in business after the shutdown of 1907, at the River St. address, but it was finally forced to close down permanently by 1911. C.Q. De France was the last owner of the firm. [Paul 1984; Petty 1984.]

DUPLEXTONE NEEDLE. A **needle** marketed in 1912, with the capability of playing either loudly or softly; loud play resulted when the needle was positioned flat, soft play from a perpendicular position relative to the disc surface.

DUPRÉ, MARCEL, 1886–1971. French organist, born in Rouen on 3 May 1886. He studied with his father, then with Felix-Alexandre Guilmant, Louis Vierne, and Charles Widor. In 1920 he played 10 recitals from memory, covering all the works of J. S. Bach. After a New York debut in November 1921 he made American and world tours. Dupré was professor of organ at the Paris Conservatory in 1926, and organist at Saint Sulpice, Paris, from 1934 to 1971. From 1954 to 1956 he was director of the Paris Conservatory. He was also a prolific composer.

Dupré recorded 78s for Victor, mostly of J.S. Bach; there were eight titles in the 1940 catalog. On LP he made discs for Mercury (Bach, Franck, and Saint-Saens) and Westminster (Widor).

DUPREZ, FRED, 1864–1938. American comedian, born Frederick August Duprez (pronounced by him as Du-pree) on 6 Sep 1884 in Detroit. He did theater work in Brooklyn, after some youthful years as a cabin boy, coal passer, and sailor; and was finally successful on stage as a substitute for a canceled act. By 1907 he was an established touring comic. He appeared in London in 1908; in France (performing in French) and Germany (performing in German).

His first disc was Columbia #A633 (1909): "A Vaudeville Rehearsal." Other labels he worked for were Indestructible and U-S Everlasting. "Happy Tho' Married" (Edison Blue Amberol #2373; 1914) was a great success, selling in the millions. It appeared on Edison Diamond Disc #50254 and also on Columbia #A1516. Duprez moved to Britain and continued his career, recording there for Columbia and World Record, Ltd. He died during a transatlantic crossing in 1938. [Walsh 1950/6–7.]

DURANOID CO. A Newark, New Jersey, firm that made the new **shellac** composition disc for Emile Berliner in 1897. Duranoid as a trade name was still applied to 78 rpm records into the 1950s. Its composition was shellac, lampblack, pyrites, and a binder of cotton flock.

DURA-TONE RECORD (label). In December 1922 the Dura-Tone Record Co. was formed by the president of Standard Music Roll Co. of Orange, New Jersey. Dura-Tone was at 15 Park Place, Newark, New Jersey. Discs were announced to be laminations of flexible fibrous material coated with shellac; but there is no further information about the product or the firm. [Andrews*.]

DURIUM (label). An inexpensive line of celluloid or cardboard discs marketed by Durium Products (G.B.), Ltd., Slough, from 1932 to 1936. Similar in concept to the American **Hit of the Week** label, Durium produced one new issue each week, sold on newsstands (until

1933). Repertoire was primarily dance music, but there were also language records and children's records; price was as low as "3 records for 6d." The dance material was primarily by Lew Stone's orchestra, with vocals by Al Bowlly. Durium and its successor firm, Dubrico, Ltd., also made some advertising records, both for their own products and for others. Those included a spoken commercial (with a musical segment) for the North Eastern Electric Supply Co. in Newcastle-upon-Tyne, and one for Ford automobiles. [Rust 1978.]

DURIUM PRODUCTS CORPORATION. A New York firm, with offices at 460 W. 34th St. and recording studios in the McGraw-Hill Building on West 42nd St. On 23 Sep 1930 Durium's request for two trademark registrations was granted by the U.S. Patent Office: "Durium" (for phonograph records) and "Hit-of-the-week" (for phonograph needles). In practice the record issued by the firm had the name Hit of the Week, and the steel needles sold were called Durium. But the name "durium" (not trademarked) was also the name given to the material of which the Hit of the Week discs were made: a fiber paper with a synthetic resin lamination. The composition of the disc—which offered tensile strength in an unbreakable, flexible product—resulted from an invention by Hal T. Beans, a Columbia University chemistry professor.

Durium marketed 10-inch Hit of the Week records from February 1930 (after a false start with a seven-inch label titled Broadway) to June 1932. Early prosperity gave way to receivership in 1931, as the Irving Trust Co. and Arthur S. Jones were appointed by the New York Supreme Court to "continue the manufacture of records and attempt to liquidate the claims of creditors." At that time Durium claimed to own patents in 57 countries and to have book assets of $500,000 with liabilities of between $350,000 and $400,000. Weekly distribution of the discs continued, with some of the publishers responding favorably to a request from Irving Trust to reduce the royalty charged to Durium.

Then in May 1931 it was announced that the Irwin-Wasey Advertising Agency had bought the record company, apparently "for a group of preferred stockholders in Chicago." Hit of the Week continued to appear on the newsstands, from August 1931 in a new longer-playing (five-minute) format. Phil Spitalny was placed in charge of recordings for Durium in November 1931, and a strenuous effort was made to recruit top name artists for the discs. But sales of Hit of the Week, at first about 500,000 per week, fell steadily, and reached a low of about 60,000 per week in 1932. Concerns about the impact to be made on Durium sales by the new RCA Victor low cost label (Elektradisc) helped in the decision to discontinue Hit of the Week.

The firm also engaged in the manufacture of custom recordings as promotional and advertising material. A four-inch disc was produced to advertise *College Humor* magazine, and similar items were made for *Redbook* and Chevrolet. [Waters 1960.]

DYER, FRANK LEWIS, 1870–1941. American record company executive, born in Washington, D.C., on 2 Aug 1870. He studied law and was admitted to the bar in 1892, practicing in Washington until 1897, then in New York. Thomas Edison invited him to take charge of legal aspects of his enterprises in 1903. When William E. Gilmore retired in 1908 as manager of the Edison companies, Dyer succeeded him. He then became president of the **National Phonograph Co.** in 1909; and president of **Thomas A. Edison, Inc.** in September 1912, but resigned in December to head the General Film Co., a major distributor of motion pictures throughout the U.S. In 1914 he left that firm to free-lance in New York as a mechanical and electrical expert, and remained in that situation until he retired in 1929. Dyer ahd more than 100 inventions, including the talking book for the blind, a record running about 2 1/2 hours, with 30,000 words per disc. He wrote, with co-author T. Comerford Martin, a two-volume life of Edison (1910; revised 1929). He died in Ventnor, New Jersey, on 4 June 1941.

DYER-BENNET, RICHARD, 1913– . English/American folk singer, born in Leicester, England, on 16 Oct 1913. He became an American citizen in 1935, after study at the University of California at Berkeley. He was popular on U.S. college campuses in the 1930s, accompanying himself on the lute, and later on the Spanish guitar, presenting authentic minstrelsy. He made records for Harvard University, then for commercial labels (including his own, in the mid-1950s). He gave annual concerts at Town Hall in New York, from 1944.

The Dyer-Bennet record label included collections of his best work: *Gems of Minstrelsy* (1960), *Dyer-Bennet* (1962), *Songs in the Spirit of 1601* (1963), and *Of Ships and Seafaring Men* (1965).

DYLAN, BOB, 1941– . American folk and popular singer, born Robert Zimmerman in Duluth, Minnesota, on 24 May 1941. He played the guitar as a child. He went to the University of Minnesota and sang in nearby coffee houses, influenced by Woody Guthrie. In New York he found hardship until he was discovered by **John Hammond** of Columbia Records, who arranged for Dylan's first recording sessions. A successful album was released in 1961, *Bob Dylan*. A half dozen chart albums followed within five years, notably *The Freewheelin' Bob Dylan* (Columbia #CL 1896; 1963) and *The Times They Are A-Changin'* (Columbia #CL 2105; 1964). By 1974 Dylan had posted 17 chart albums. His early style had been a folk idiom, but he moved gradually toward folk-rock and country rock, using intricate lyrics that addressed social problems.

Dylan performed in concert and on television, and gave acclaimed performances at the Newport Jazz Festivals (1962–1965) and the Monterey Jazz Festival. Dylan's first hit single was "Subterranean Homesick Blues" (Columbia #43242; 1965), followed by his most famous disc, "Like a Rolling Stone" (Columbia #43346; 1965). Other top songs of the 1960s were "Rainy Day Women #12 & 35" (Columbia #43592; 1966) and "Lay Lady Lay" (Columbia #44926; 1969). His composition "Blowin' in the Wind" became a hit record for Peter, Paul and Mary, and for Stevie Wonder.

With the expiration of his Columbia contract in 1973, Dylan moved to the Asylum label. Asylum recorded live programs from his greatly successful 1974 national tour, in *Before the Flood* (#AB 201; 1974), a chart album for 18 weeks. He returned to the Columbia label to make further noteworthy albums, in a more pronounced rock style, such as *Desire* (Columbia #PC 33893; 1976). Dylan wrote most of the music he performed and many of the lyrics.

In the 1980s, Dylan appeared with other leading stars in the album *We are the World*, to raise funds for African famine relief. He released a remarkable five-record album, *Biograph* (Columbia #C5X-38830; 1985). He won a Grammy in 1979 for the best rock vocal by a male singer, and in 1990 was presented with the Grammy Lifetime Achievement award. CD reissues by Columbia have covered most of his repertoire. [Hoggard 1978.]

DYNAGROOVE. The RCA trademark for its microgroove record, issued in 1950 as a response to the Columbia long-playing record. [Olson, H. 1964.]

DYNAMIC. (I) Having a moving part; in sound recording the reference is to a moving element related to an electromagnetic field, as in a moving coil or ribbon **cartridge**; or to a **loudspeaker** that uses magnetic fields and electric currents to produce sound vibrations. The same principle is found in the dynamic **microphone**.

DYNAMIC. (II) The force or intensity of sound (also in plural, dynamics), or volume.

DYNAMIC RANGE. In an audio system, the difference (expressed in **decibels**) between the overload level and the minimum acceptable signal level; that is, the difference between the loudest and softest passages reproduced without **distortion**.

DYNE. The force that produces an acceleration of one centimeter per second per second on the free mass of one gram. In acoustics the unit of sound pressure is the dyne per square centimeter. *See also* INTENSITY.

E

E. M. G. HANDMADE GRAMOPHONES, LTD. A London firm that offered, in the 1920s, to "obtain or make anything any gramophone may require." Complete table and console models were sold at prices ranging from £14 to more than £30, and components were available separately, "made to measure." The address was 267 High Holborn; president was E. M. Ginn. In the 1950s the firm was located at 6 Newman St., London, specializing in "modern reconstructions." [*TMR* #46 (1977) reprints some advertisements.]

EAGLE. A very popular cylinder player with a double-spring motor, introduced in 1897 by the Columbia Phonograph Co. The name came from the $10 selling price, equivalent to one U.S. gold eagle coin. About 149,000 were produced. In Britain this model was known as the Domestic. [Hoover 1971 has an illustration, p. 45, but the date is given as 1899.]

EAMES, EMMA, 1865–1952. American lyric soprano, born on 13 Aug 1865 in Shanghai, of American parents. Her opera debut was in Paris as Juliette on 13 Mar 1889. On 14 Dec 1891 she appeared in the same role at the Metropolitan Opera, and remained with the company until 1909. Eames was recorded on **Mapleson cylinders** while singing Tosca on 3 Jan 1903. She sang commercially for Victor from February 1905, beginning with "Still wie die Nacht" by Karl Bohm (Victor #85052) and nine other works, one record being the "Star Spangled Banner" and "Dixie." In 1906–1907 she made 15 more Victors, and by 1911 another 16. She sang duets with Emilio Di Gogorza, Louise

Homer, and Marcella Sembrich. The Victor 1917 catalog carried seven of her solos and four of the duets.

Francesco Tosti's song "Dopo" is one of the finest Eames records (Victor #88344; 1911). "Gretchen am Spinnrade" is another masterful performance (Victor #88361; 1911). Her favored role, Juliette, is represented by the "Valse" on Victor #88011 (1906), reissued on IRCC #43—she sang the part "as Gounod taught it to me" (Migliorini). She died in New York on 13 June 1952. [Lawrence 1962; Moran 1977; Migliorini 1953.]

EASTERN PENNSYLVANIA PHONOGRAPH CO. A Philadelphia firm located at 180 S. 4th St., in operation from 1890 to 1893. It was one of the 33 regional companies that made up the **North American Phonograph Co.** Officers included E. P. Wallace, president and member of the board of directors, 1892–1893; and **James O. Clephane**, secretary in 1890–1893 and member of the board in 1890–1891.

EASTERN TALKING MACHINE CO. A Boston firm located at 177 Tremont St., selling cylinder and disc products beginning in March 1894, and continuing until at least 1923. Officers included E. F. Taft (July 1914) and H. Shoemaker (general manager, January 1923).

EASTERN TALKING MACHINE JOBBERS ASSOCIATION. An organization established 10 Apr 1906 in New York to provide a forum for people in the trade. The first president was **W.D. Andrews**; he was re-elected at the July conference in 1907. Other officers of 1907 were **Louis Buehn,** treasurer; **J. Newcomb Blackman,** vice president, and A.H. Jacot, secretary. The association merged in September 1907 with the **Central States Talking Machine Jobbers Association** to form the **Talking Machine Jobbers National Association.**

EASTON, EDWARD DENISON, 1856–1915. American record industry executive, born in Gloucester, Massachusetts. He went to Washington, D.C., to study law, and received a degree from Georgetown University in 1889. He worked as a court reporter in Washington, becoming interested in the phonograph as a dictating device. Easton was the first general manager of **American Graphophone Co.** (1887), which sold its cylinder machine for court and business use. In 1888 he was one of the founders of the **Columbia Phonograph Co.,** which became the recording and sales agency for American Graphophone. Easton opened a **phonograph parlor** in Washington, and operated **coin-ops** in the Washington-Baltimore area. In 1894 he arranged a merger of the Columbia interests into the Columbia Phonograph Co., General. In 1913 the firm became the Columbia Graphophone Co., which Easton headed until his death.

Easton was instrumental in arranging the first national convention of the phonograph industry in May 1890. He pioneered in the area of entertainment recording, and engaged many famous artists. Columbia was the only affiliate of the **North American Phonograph Co.** to emerge unscathed when North American collapsed in 1894. Columbia disc records appeared in 1902, and double-sided records were offered in 1904. Easton's firm was a world leader in production of cylinder and disc players. He has been criticized for allowing the rival Victor Co. to achieve a near monopoly in operatic recording and in much of the classical repertoire, but Columbia did issue important recordings by such luminaries as Percy Grainger and Pablo Casals.

EASTON, FLORENCE, 1882–1955. English dramatic soprano, born in South Bank, Yorkshire, on 25 Oct 1882. She made her debut at Covent Garden in 1903, then sang with the Berlin Opera in 1907–1913 and the Hamburg Opera from 1912 to 1915. Easton was heard in Chicago during 1915–1917 and at the Metropolitan Opera from 1917 to 1929. She then toured in Europe, returning to the Metropolitan as Brünnhilde in *Walküre* on 29 Feb 1936. Although she was remarkably versatile, Wagnerian roles were her best, and she made several outstanding recordings of them. Her "Liebestod" (in English, IRCC #3004) and her *Siegfried* Act Three with Lauritz Melchior (Victor #7762–65; 1932) are favorites with collectors. Her earliest records were made for Odeon around 1912, after which she recorded for Aeolian-Vocalion. Then she was with Brunswick from 1921 to 1928, and joined Edison in 1928. Altogether she recorded about 100 sides. Cantilena #6245 is an LP reissue that covers all these periods and includes the Melchior duets. Eames died in New York on 13 Aug 1955. [Stratton 1974.]

EBERLE, RAY, 1919–1979. American popular singer, born in Hoosick Falls, New York, on 19 Jan 1919. His family name was spelled Eberle, although his brother Bob changed the spelling of his own name to Eberly. Eberle was a featured vocalist with the Glenn Miller band from 1938 until World War II; then went into military service. Later he was less active. Eberle, regarded as one of the premier vocalists of the Big Band era, was heard on outstanding Miller discs such as "At Last" (Victor #27934; 1942), "Moonlight Cocktail" (Bluebird #11401; 1941), and especially "Serenade in Blue" (Victor #27935; 1942).

EBERLY, BOB, 1916–1981. American popular singer, born in Mechanicsville, New York, on 24 July 1916. He changed the spelling of his family name from Eberle, serving at least to distinguish him from his brother Ray, also a prominent vocalist. Eberly sang with Jimmy Dorsey's band, and was recognized as one of the outstanding popular singers of the period 1938–1942. His great solo records include three made in 1941: "Blue Champagne" (Decca #3775), "The Things I Love" (Decca #3737), and "Maria Elena" (Decca #3698). In the same year he also recorded three remarkable duets with Helen O'Connell: "Green Eyes" (Decca

#3698), "Amapola" (Decca #3629), and "Tangerine" (Decca #4123). He had the principal singing role in the motion picture *The Fabulous Dorseys* (1947).

EBONOID (label). (I) A short-lived, 200 turns-per-inch, five-minute wax cylinder made by the **Premier Manufacturing Co., Ltd.**, of London, in April 1909, and later by **Clarion Record Co., Ltd.** [Klinger*.]

EBONOID (label). (II) A vertical-cut, double-sided, 10-inch disc first issued in December 1909 by the **Premier Manufacturing Co., Ltd.**, London. It was claimed to have a playing time of five minutes.

ECHO. A reflected sound signal, having sufficient magnitude to be audible and reaching the listener long enough after the original signal to be distinguishable from it. *See also* ECHO CHAMBER; FLUTTER ECHO; REVERBERATION.

ECHO CHAMBER. In sound recording, a room used to add an **echo** effect to a signal. The engineer can control the degree of echo, or **reverberation**, by combining the program source with the signal as it passes through the microphone and loudspeaker of the echo chamber.

ECHOPHONE. A cylinder phonograph invented in 1896 by **Edward H. Amet**, marketed around 1898; it appeared first under the name "Metaphone." Apparently it was the earliest phonograph with a distinct **tone arm**—which was a thin shaft of glass with a rounded and tipped end that served as a stylus, with a bellows at the other end. Air vibration in this bellows reproduced the sound; operation was by spring motor. A wooden **mandrel** was the other unique feature of the Echophone, which had no special sound quality. W. Hill & Co., 96 S. State St., Chicago, sold the machine for $5. [Fabrizio 1976; Koenigsberg 1990.]

ECLIPSE (label). A British issue of 1931–1935, produced by **Crystalate Gramophone Record Manufacturing Co., Ltd.**, and sold through Woolworth's for sixpence. A nursery series was included.

EDDY, NELSON, 1901–1967. American baritone, born in Providence, Rhode Island, on 29 June 1901. He studied in New York, Dresden, and Paris; made his debut in 1922; and sang four years with the Philadelphia Opera Co. He also appeared on radio, and in Gilbert and Sullivan productions. His film debut was in 1933, after which he and Jeanette Macdonald began their greatly successful series of musical movies: *Naughty Marietta* (1935), *Rose Marie* (1936), *Blossom Time* (1936), *Maytime* (1937), *Sweethearts* (1938), *Girl of the Golden West* (1938), and *New Moon* (1940). His co-star in *Rosalie* (1938) was Eleanor Powell. Among Eddy's hit records were "I'm Falling in Love with Someone" / "Tramp, Tramp, Tramp Along the Highway" (Victor #4280; 1935); "Rose Marie" (Victor #4305; 1936); and "Will You Remember?" (Victor #4329; 1936)—all from the films. A later film produced the highly popular "At the Balalaika" (Columbia #17173; 1939). But his all-time best seller was a novelty song, "Short'nin' Bread" (Columbia #17329; 1942). Eddy died in Miami Beach, Florida, on 6 Mar 1967.

EDIBEL SOUND FILM APPARATUS, LTD. A British firm associated with Edison Bell, established 5 July 1929. It ceased operations in July 1931.

Ediphone Standard Practice Records. *See* EDISON SCHOOL RECORDS.

EDISON, CHARLES A., 1890–1969. American industrialist and statesman, son of Thomas A. Edison, born in Orange, New Jersey, on 3 Aug 1890. He served as chairman of the board of McGraw-Edison, and as president of **Thomas A. Edison, Inc.**, succeeding his father in August 1926. From 1939 to 1940 he was U.S. Secretary of the Navy, and from 1941 to 1944 he was governor of New Jersey. He died in New York in August 1969.

EDISON, THOMAS ALVA, 1847–1931. Eminent American inventor, born in Milan, Ohio, on 11 Feb 1847. Edison is usually credited with the invention of the cylinder phonograph (*see* CYLINDER 1, 2). His earliest patent application for the device was dated 24 Dec 1877. In July of that year Edison had through serendipity discovered that paper tape he was using for telegraph relay experiments could retain and play back sound signals. He applied the concept in a sketch for a **tinfoil phonograph** on 29 Nov 1877, and conveyed the idea to his assistants Charles Batchelor and John Kruesi. Those men produced a prototype machine and gave it to Edison on 6 Dec 1877; that phonograph was covered by U.S. patent #200,251, granted on 10 Feb 1878. (The wooden model submitted to the Patent Office went to the Science Museum, London, thence to the Henry Ford Museum, in Dearborn, Michigan.)

Although he remained interested in the phonograph, Edison did little work on it for 10 years—during that decade he concentrated on the electric light and the electric power industry. In 1887 he resumed experimentation with recorded sound, and developed the New Phonograph in which solid wax cylinders replaced the tinfoil of the original invention. He followed this with the Improved Phonograph, and then on 16 June 1888 with the Perfected Phonograph (exhibited at the Crystal Palace, London, in August 1888). A long series of ever-improved models emerged from the Edison workshops over the next three decades. (*See* EDISON RECORD PLAYERS.)

With central electric power systems at an unreliable stage, and storage batteries still too bulky to be widely accepted, Edison gave his attention to the spring motor—which he had in fact described in his British patent application (#1644) of 1878; and it was the spring motor that operated most of the cylinder machines to come.

The phonograph had been invented in Edison's first laboratory, located in Menlo Park, New Jersey. However, all subsequent phonographic work was carried out in the new **Edison Phonograph Works**, in West Orange, New Jersey. The parent organization in control of the Works and other Edison interests was the **Edison Phonograph Co.** (1887); but that firm sold its stock to **Jesse H. Lippincott** in 1888, who formed the **North American Phonograph**

Co. to hold the patents. North American licensed 33 semi-independent subsidiaries, one of which was destined to emerge as a rival to Edison and Victor: the **Columbia Phonograph Co.** Edison reacquired control of his patents in 1894, but then liquidated North American (*see* CYLINDER, 6). He set up another firm, the **National Phonograph Co.**, in January 1896, to manufacture and distribute the spring-motor machines, and within three years had established branches in Europe. There were 12,000 affiliated dealers by 1907.

A final name change occurred in 1910, as the earlier companies were reorganized into **Thomas A. Edison, Inc.** Edison was president from December 1912 until August 1926, when he became chairman of the board, and his son Charles succeeded him as president. It was this firm that produced the finest Edison sound media, the **Blue Amberol** cylinder and the **Edison Diamond Disc**. With much reluctance, Edison conceded that discs were winning the market from cylinders, and he did create an outstanding version in the Diamond Disc. A series of **tone tests** demonstrated the remarkable fidelity achieved by it, despite the limitations of **acoustic recording**.

Although the **Edison label** and the machines made to play them were widely perceived to be of the highest quality, the firm was unable to hold a strong place in the burgeoning sound recording market. Many of the difficulties have been traced to Edison's own strongly held views: for example, his conviction that cylinders were inherently superior to discs because they did not encounter end-of-side distortion (*see* DISTORTION, IV). His narrow musical taste tended to hold back the repertoire that his company offered, so that he never seriously competed with Victor and Columbia for the classical and operatic market. His preferred audience was rural, and of simple musical requirements (*see* CYLINDER, 7; DISC, 7). Edison's long-playing record of 1926 failed, for one reason because he did not exploit the repertoire possibilities it presented for uninterrupted renditions of longer compositions. Curiously, the inventor so prominent in the world of electricity was late to enter the field of electrical recording (1927); and he was also behind the competition in combining record players and radios (1928). Cylinder production continued until 1929, though market demand had nearly vanished. Edison ceased making discs, cylinders, and machines on 1 Nov 1929, except for Ediphone dictation records.

While this article has dealt with the Edison contributions to sound recording, it would be incomplete without mention of his other achievements. His first patented invention was a vote recorder in 1869, forerunner of the modern voting machine. In 1870 he developed a successful stock market printer ("ticker"). His automatic repeating telegraph of 1872–1877 allowed the storage and playback of telegraph messages—and led the inventor to the idea of storing and playing back voice signals. The quadraplex telegraph of 1874 expanded the capacity of the national wire system. While he did not originate the electric light bulb, he labored to produce one that would burn long enough to be useful: the incandescent lamp with a carbonized filament (1879). From that beginning he went on to develop the dynamos, conduits, mains, relay circuits, and so forth that went into a total electric power distribution system; and he did this despite opposition from the reigning gaslight interests. Edison improved Alexander Graham Bell's telephone transmitter in 1877, and advanced the march of electronics in 1883 by discovering the so-called Edison Effect in lamps—a basis for the vacuum tube, radio, and television. He did important pioneer work in motion pictures, beginning in 1889; Menlo Park had the first motion picture studio, and produced the earliest action films (most early movie production took place in and around New York City). The classic *Great Train Robbery* of 1903 was an Edison work, filmed in part at Menlo Park. On 6 Oct 1889 Edison and **William A. Kennedy** had synchronized cylinder records with motion picture film to bring sound films into the world. In 1913 he offered a combination of a celluloid cylinder (similar to the Blue Amberol) with film in the **Kinetophone**. He made 19 talking pictures before 1915, when he abandoned the format.

Thomas Edison's life story is a recitation of the American dream. He was born in a "humble cottage" in a small town in Ohio, lived after age seven with his family in another small town, Port Huron, Michigan. He had little formal schooling, but acquired a wide general and technical education through self study. He would later suffer from deafness, due to a childhood mishap. At age 12 he began to work on the railroad that ran from Port Huron to Detroit, selling newspapers and candy; he soon built this modest post into a fruit and vegetable business. He learned telegraphy from a station agent whose son he had saved from death, and by the age of 17 he had become a railway telegrapher. Boston was his home for a period, then New York City—where he arrived impecuniously in 1869. Good fortune came at last when his first commercially successful invention—the stock printer—brought in $40,000.

Edison set up a factory and laboratory in Newark in 1870, then the Menlo Park laboratory in 1876. He began to receive patents for electrical developments, and a stream of inventions followed.

During World War I the genius of Edison (which he described as 2 percent inspiration and 98 percent perspiration) was applied to practical problems. He headed the U.S. Navy research effort that developed submarine detection devices, underwater searchlights, improved torpedoes, and range finders. He was awarded the Congressional Medal of Honor in 1928. At the age of 80 he was still active in experiments, and developed a form of synthetic rubber just before his death in West Orange on 18 Oct 1931.

An early marriage, to 16 year old Mary Stillwell, ended in 1884 with the lady's untimely death. Edison then met and courted Mina Miller, of Akron, Ohio, and eventually proposed to her—via a Morse code message tapped on her palm, as the story goes—in September 1885. The couple, with Edison's three children, settled in Glenmont, a mansion in West Orange. Another three children were born, including Charles (1890), who was to assist in administering his father's enterprises.

His widow outlived Edison by 16 years, and devoted much energy to preserving her husband's workplaces. This interest culminated in the establishment of the **Edison National Historic Site.**

Edison lived a simple life, considering his fame and wealth. Despite his consuming interest in science, he was not a cultural blank. His reputed ignorance about music, for instance, must be ascribed to his preferences rather than to lack of familiarity with the masters. (A conversation with John Philip Sousa, printed in the October 1923 issue of *Etude* magazine, revealed an acute musical ear—despite his poor hearing—and his considered views on Mozart, Chopin, and Wagner.) He did not credit himself with genius, yet "his genius was the spark of history—making advances in the world's social, economic and political life. Imagination, dynamically related to a persistent soul, never discouraged by defeat, comprised the sinew of his fame" (Sarnoff 1948).

An LP presenting all the surviving recordings of Edison speaking was issued in 1986: *Voice Recordings of Thomas Alva Edison* (Mark 56 Records). The disc includes Edison's Morse code message to the Old Time Telegraphers and Historical Association in 1919. [Klinger*; *NAG* #30 (1979) reprints the *Etude* interview; Sarnoff 1948; Wachhorst 1981.]

EDISON (label). The name given to the cylinder records sold by Edison's **North American Phonograph Co.** (1890–1894), the **National Phonograph Co.** (1896–1910), and **Thomas A. Edison, Inc.** (1910–1929). (*See also* CYLINDER; EDISON DIAMOND DISC.)

EDISON (THOMAS A.), INC. A firm incorporated in 1910 in a reorganization of the earlier Edison companies; it was under this name that Thomas Edison carried on his business activities until his death. He himself was president from December 1912, when **Frank L. Dyer** resigned the post, until August 1926, when Edison turned the job over to his son Charles and became chairman of the board. In 1912 C.H. Wilson, general manager, became vice president as well. The firm included various units for particular products: Phonograph Division, Ediphone Division, and divisions to handle non-audio items like storage batteries. **Blue Amberol** cylinders were among the first products offered by the company, along with the Amberola player for them, followed by the **Edison Diamond Disc.** West Orange, New

Jersey, was the center of research activity. In fact the first of the famous **tone tests** took place there, in 1915, when soprano Anna Case and contralto Christine Miller demonstrated that their recorded voices on Diamond Discs were indistinguishable from their live ones.

After a remarkable first decade of invention and advanced products, the company fell behind its competitors. **Electrical recording** of Diamond Discs was put off until 1927. A **long-playing record**, marketed in 1926, was unsuccessful. Acquisition of **Splitdorf Radio Corp.** in 1928 marked a belated move into the radio market. Edison was never able to gather the recording stars of Victor and Columbia, nor to handle the sophisticated repertoires of his rivals.

Both discs and cylinders were manufactured by the firm until 1 Nov 1929, when Edison ordered an end of production except for dictation records. That product was made by the Voicewriter Division, which merged with McGraw Electric Co. in 1956. [Wile 1985/2.]

EDISON BELL (label). Discs marketed by **Edison Bell Consolidated Phonograph Co., Ltd.**, of London, from May 1908 (as Bell Discs) to April 1933. The first records entitled Edison Bell were actually Edison cylinders, marketed in Britain from ca. 1901 until 1914. Although the firm referred to the discs as "Discaphone Records," that name did not appear on the labels. Bells were 10 1/2 inches in diameter, double-sided; they sold for 2s 6d. A few months later a new line of 8 3/4 inch, double-sided vertical-cut discs named "Phonadisc" appeared, selling at 1s 6d. There was also to be an 11-inch or 12-inch Marvel to be sold at 4s, but it seems not to have appeared. A total of 62 Phonadiscs were issued. They had paper labels, and carried spoken **announcements**.

With the formal demise of the Edison Bell Company in 1909, the label name passed to the new firm of **J.E. Hough, Ltd.** Hough had been general manager of Edison Bell. He re-launched the Bell discs in 1910, and the new nine-inch, vertical-cut **Little Champion** label.

Edison Bell Winner was a new label name, the discs being produced by a syndicate named The Winner Record Co., with J.E. Hough, Ltd., providing matrices. Later The Winner Record Co. was incorporated as The Winner Co., Ltd. Winners were sold until January 1935—after November 1932 they came from **Decca Record Co., Ltd.**, which had bought Edison Bell.

Repertoire included worthwhile classical works, and popular items taken from American masters, such as jazz numbers from Gennett (1920–1925), and material from Emerson, Federal, and Paramount. Edison Bell Radio was a an eight-inch label sold from April 1928 to April 1932. [Adrian 1989; Andrews*; Rust 1978.]

EDISON BELL CONSOLIDATED PHONO-GRAPH CO., LTD. A firm located at 39 Charing Cross Rd., London; it held the Thomas Edison and Bell-Tainter British patents, and was the primary owner and purchaser of any phonographic goods from any country. There were two companies of the name, one successor to the other, both preceded by the **Edison Bell Phonograph Corp., Ltd.**, of 1892. All three firms licensed others as long as their patents were alive. **Edisonia, Ltd.,** founded in 1897 by **J.E. Hough** as a reformation of his London Phonograph Co., co-existed with it for a year as a supplier of records and machines; it was found guilty of patent infringement and stopped by the courts. Then in 1898 the Edison Bell interests were brought together into the Edison Bell Consolidated Phonograph Co., Ltd., under Hough's direction. (Edisonia remained as its manufacturing unit.) By 1904 the firm was one of the three major producers of cylinders in Britain, the others being the **National Phonograph Co., Ltd.** and **Pathé.** In 1908, following a few years of price wars and patent litigation, Edison Bell acquired **Sterling and Hunting, Ltd.,** makers of the competitive Sterling record. Success of Edison Bell was further indicated by the extension of patent rights to Australia, China, Japan, and South America.

Cylinders had the label names **London,** Grand Concert, Indestructible, Indestructible Ebony, Popular, and **Standard.** In 1903 a factory in Peckham was built to make phonographs and gold-molded records. Disc records were offered simultaneously with cylinders, from June 1908 (see EDISON BELL [label]).

Competition from formidable disc firms, for example the **Gramophone Co., Jumbo,** and

Rena, took its toll on Edison Bell, and it went into receivership in 1909, dissolving in May 1910. This was evidently a technical bankruptcy only, for business continued and Hough remained in control. Under the name **J.E. Hough, Ltd.,** the Edison Bell Velvet Face disc was released in September 1910, the **Little Champion** in December 1910, the **Velvet Face Edison Bell Celebrity Record** in June 1911, and then the successful **Winner** label in February 1912. Winners, priced at 2s 6d, were sold by a new subsidiary firm, Winner Record Co., Ltd., which was registered on 10 Apr 1912. The **Westport** label was sold from 1922 to 1924. **Beltona** was acquired in 1927. **Decca Record Co., Ltd.,** acquired the Edison Bell interests in 1932. [Andrews*.] See also EDISON BELL INTERNATIONAL, LTD.

EDISON BELL ELECTRON (label). An English issue, released from July 1927 to November 1930. About 370 records were marketed.

EDISON BELL INTERNATIONAL, LTD. A company established in October 1928 in London to manage the foreign business of **Edison Bell.** The new firm took over all overseas rights except for North America. Recordings were made in Budapest and Zagreb. An ensemble from the Dutch East Indies was recorded on a visit to London.

EDISON BELL PHONOGRAPH CORP., LTD. The predecessor firm to the two companies named **Edison Bell Consolidated Phonograph Co., Ltd.,** owner of the Edison and Bell-Tainter patent rights.

Edison Bell Radio (label). See EDISON BELL (label).

Edison Bell Winner (label). See EDISON BELL (label).

EDISON DIAMOND DISC. As early as 1910 there had been experiments in the Edison laboratory directed at the production of a flat disc record. It was put on the market in 1913, as the Diamond Disc, to be played with a diamond stylus in the new Diamond Disc Phonograph (see EDISON RECORD PLAYERS). The disc with the earliest recording date was "Dir che ci sono al mondo" from *Zaza*, performed by Carmen Melis. It came from a session of January or February 1910, but was not issued until 1913 (#83001). The machine had a heavier reproducer than the one used on cylinders, so a hard surface disc was needed; this was achieved with a plastic named Condensite. The records weighed one pound each, and measured a quarter-inch thick. There were 150 turns (grooves) per inch. At 80 rpm, the 12-inch Diamond Disc played 7 1/2 minutes, and the 10-inch record played five minutes. There was no warping, and no perceptible wearing of the surface, even after hundreds of plays. Outstanding audio fidelity for its time brought the Diamond Disc great acclaim; it was the medium of the remarkable **tone tests** that Edison used to demonstrate the quality of his product. Considering the longer playing time of the Diamond Discs, their price was competitive with standard discs: $1 for 10-inch records, while standard records were selling for $.60.

What prevented the Diamond Disc from gaining a greater market share was its excessive surface noise (gradually improved, but a reasonably quiet surface did not emerge until 1924), and the tendency of the earlier discs to separate their layers and to curl or crack. Another difficulty was the need to have an Edison disc player, since the Diamond Discs were not compatible with Victors, Columbias, and other machines. Finally, there was the artist and repertoire problem that always dogged Edison; he did not contract the finest artists and have them perform the quality music that was found on competing labels.

Edison did not begin recording electrically until June 1927, two years after the process had been adopted by other firms. He did pioneer in the manufacture of **long-playing records**, from 1926, but those were not well received. Just before Edison dropped out of the record business, he offered a lateral-cut electrically recorded disc (summer 1929), but it was without outstanding qualities. The final Diamond Disc was cut on 18 Sep 1929. [Wile 1978; Wile 1985/2; Wile 1990/4.]

Edison dictation records. *See* EDISON SCHOOL RECORDS.

EDISON HORNS. The earliest phonographs and gramophones made use of listening tubes to increase audibility during playback. On the first tinfoil phonographs, the cone-shaped mouth pieces also functioned as volume enhancers. A **graphophone** of 1886 had a small horn, and so did the Edison New Phonograph of 1887. In a photograph taken at the Paris 1889 Exposition, an Edison Perfected model was shown next to "what could be the first horn of any size for a phonograph, probably spun from brass or copper . . . but there is no indication of how it fixed to the machine" (Frow, p. 153). Around 1895 14-inch brass horns were first marketed with Edison domestic machines and **coin-ops.**

Horns got larger and larger; by the turn of the century some manufacturers were selling models up to 56 inches in length, collapsible into sections, and held up by cranes or stands. Edison was more restrained, preferring to develop efficient design in place of greater dimension. His products were of curved metal, or later of wood, not more than 19 inches long; they gave superior acoustic results compared to the massive conical shapes of other makers. Music Master was the name given to the wood horns—oak, mahogany, spruce—and also to some British versions in hard cardboard or whale skin. *See also* HORNS. [Frow 1978.]

EDISON NATIONAL HISTORIC SITE. An entity located at Main St. and Lakeside Ave., West Orange, New Jersey. Thomas Edison opened a new laboratory and manufacturing complex in West Orange on 24 Nov 1887, 10 years almost to the day after he had invented the phonograph in Menlo Park. His early work in West Orange resulted in the Improved Phonograph, the Perfected Phonograph, and the **kinetophone**, as well as a successful storage battery; all his later enhancements in recording were developed there. After the inventor's death, activity at the lab began to phase out, and it closed completely by 1935. Manufacturing of phonographs for business use and of electric storage batteries did continue until 1972. The laboratories were preserved by Edison's widow, Mina. After she died in 1947 the firm opened some of the research areas to the public on guided tours. In 1955 the laboratories were turned over to the National Park Service, which administers the facility as an educational museum. President John F. Kennedy signed legislation giving the site—which combines the labs and the Edison home, Glenmont—its present name.

EDISON PHONOGRAPH CO.

A firm established in 1887 for research and development; Edison's current and future patents (extending to October 1892) were assigned to it. The plant was located in West Orange, New Jersey; its general agent was **Ezra T. Gilliland.** Actual manufacturing was carried out at the **Edison Phonograph Works.** On 28 June 1888 the stock was sold to **Jesse H. Lippincott** for $500,000, and his **North Americana Phonograph Co.** became sole U.S. proprietor of the Edison patents, though certain manufacturing rights were retained by the Edison Phonograph Works.

EDISON PHONOGRAPH CO. (OHIO).

The successor to the **Ohio Phonograph Co.,** commencing business in May 1897. There were offices in Cincinnati, Chicago, Cleveland, and Indianapolis. **James L. Andem** was general manager.

EDISON PHONOGRAPH TOY MANUFACTURING CO.

The firm established in October 1887 for the promotion of Edison's **talking dolls.** Legal and manufacturing problems held up production, which finally began in 1890. The doll was featured in *Scientific American* (26 Apr 1890) and distributed to stores. According to claims by the firm, up to 500 dolls a day were manufactured. There were still mechanical faults in the doll, however, leading to returns by many buyers. The doll was withdrawn and further research was undertaken in the fall of 1890. Response from the stock market was negative: the price of doll stock fell from a high of $10 to $3.50 in mid-1890. Thomas Edison, confronted simultaneously with the financial difficulties of his North American Phonograph Co., decided to terminate the contract with the Edison Phonograph Toy Manufacturing Co. as of 23 Mar 1891. The company officially ceased operating on 6 Aug 1901. [Wile 1987.]

EDISON PHONOGRAPH WORKS.

The manufacturer of Edison products, established at West Orange, New Jersey, on 30 Apr 1888. Its manager, **Alfred O. Tate,** entered into a secret agreement on 7 Dec 1896 with the American Graphophone Co. to cross license each other's key patents. In 1910 the facility was part of the reorganization that resulted in **Thomas A. Edison, Inc.**

EDISON RECORD PLAYERS.

Listed here in alphabetical order are the named models of Edison cylinder phonographs. Disc players are identified following the names of the cylinder machines.

—**Alva.** An electric (mains) version of the **Triumph,** available in 1907 in both America and Britain, supplied with a cygnet horn. It sold at $85, or up to $100 with the Model C **reproducer.** In 1908 a Model H reproducer was added, for playing the **Amberol.** A Model O reproducer was available in 1910. The machine was discontinued in 1912 (U.S.) and 1911 or 1912 (Britain). Illustrations in Frow 1978, pp. 23–24.

—**Amberola.** Edison's premier phonograph, produced from 1909 to 1929 to play both the two-minute and four-minute **Amberol** and the four-minute **Blue Amberol** cylinders. The machine appeared in various modifications with different model designators:

Amberola I. Marketed in the U.S. and Britain, 1909–1912, for the two- and four-minute Amberol records. It came in A and B styles, both of them floor models with internal horns; A was belt driven, B had the same motor as the **Opera** player. Selling at $200 (mahogany, oak) or $250 (Circassian walnut), it was aimed at the high end of the market, in competition with the **Victrola** and **Grafonola** gramophones. Reproducers used included Models A, L, and M. Illustrations in Chew 1981, p. 94; and Frow 1978, pp. 89–92.

Amberola III. (Note: there was no Amberola II.) On sale from 1912 to 1915 in U.S. and Britain, to accommodate the four minute Blue Amberols. It came in an open stand instead of a closed console cabinet, using the same motors and reproducers as the I. Price was $125. Illustration in Frow 1978, p. 93.

Amberola IV. On sale from 1913 to 1915 in America and Britain, for the four-minute records. It used the Model B reproducer, with Model N as an optional extra. The motor was a modification of the Home motor, belt driven. The stand had a modern look, with an open shelf in place of the closed cabinet. The appearance was evidently a hindrance to sales, as fewer than 71 were ever sold at the $100 price. Illustration in Frow 1978, p. 94.

Amberola V. Despite its number, this model went on sale before Amberola IV; it was on the market in 1912, the first table model Amberola. Price was $80; sales were brisk. It had a single-spring motor, using a Diamond B reproducer. Illustration in Frow 1978, p. 95.

Amberola VI. Three VI models of this table phonograph have been identified by Frow, offered in 1913–1914 in the U.S. and Britain. The nomenclature was confusing: Amberola VI (later called the A-VI), B-VI, and C-VI. Principal differences were in the motor, which gave trouble from the first. A modified **Fireside** type motor was finally used. All versions sold for $60, but those remaining after the Edison fire of December 1914 were released at $50; they had been fitted with Amberola 50 mechanisms. Reproducer was Diamond B. Illustrations in Frow 1978, p. 97–98.

Amberola VIII. (Note: there was no Amberola VII.) A simple, inexpensive ($45) table model, introduced October 1913 and marketed until 1915. It had the Fireside or **Standard** motor, with Diamond B reproducer (Model N optional extra). Two cabinet styles were available. Illustrations in Frow 1978, pp. 99–100.

Amberola X. (Note: there was no Amberola IX.) Sold from 1913 to 1914, in the U.S. and Britain, in four table models having some mechanical differences. It used the **Gem** type motors at first, then the Fireside type. At $30, it was the cheapest of all Amberolas; and also the smallest. The reproducers were Diamond B, or sapphire Model N as an optional extra. Illustrations in Frow 1978, pp. 100–101.

Amberola 30. In 1915 Edison decided to consolidate the numerous Amberolas into three lines, to be known by the number of dollars required to buy them: 30, 50, and 75. Table model 30 was the sales leader (selling 18,000 in one six-month period of 1916). It was available in the U.S. and Britain. A single-spring motor was supplied, with a Diamond C reproducer. Production ceased in October 1929. Illustrations in Frow 1978, pp. 105, 130.

Amberola 50. Introduced in 1915, in the U.S. and Britain. A table model, with double-spring motor, and Diamond C reproducer. It was modified and sold around December 1928 in Britain as the Amberola 60. Production ceased in October 1929. Illustrations in Frow 1978, pp. 106, 108, 109.

Amberola 60. The British version of Amberola 50.

Amberola 75. Sold in U.S. and Britain from 1915, it was a floor model version of the 50. It seems to have been sold in Britain and Australia, with modifications, as the Amberola 80, from around December 1928. Production ceased in October 1929. Illustrations in Frow 1978, pp. 107–108.

Amberola 80. The British/Australian version of Amberola 75.

—**Balmoral**. The name given in 1906 to the Class M.

—**Business**. A table model machine intended for taking dictation; supplied with a speaking horn and playback horn. It was available with 110–120 volt electric motor, or double-spring motor. The **spectacle** reproducer was used. Illustration in *TMR* 49b (1977), p. 1184.

—**Class E**. An early modification of the Perfected Phonograph, sold ca. 1893–1909 (U.S.) and 1893–1910 (Britain); named the Conqueror in 1901. It operated on DC mains current, 110–120 volts. The first price was $170, but this fell to $90 in 1898 and $75 in 1900; then rose to $80 in 1906. Until October 1908 only the two-minute version was made, while later models played either two- or four-minute records. Reproducers began with the Model A Speaker, followed by the Standard Speaker and the Automatic Speaker. The Model C reproducer was used in 1902, and the Model H in 1908. Listening tubes and 14-inch horns were the first accessories; a 20-inch horn was among those offered later. A modification of the Class E, to play the larger **Concert** cylinders, was available in 1899–1906; it was known as the Class E Concert, and in 1901 as the Oratorio. Price was $100. Illustration in Frow 1978, p. 20.

—**Class M.** A version of the Class E which operated on a DC battery, sold from 1893. Its later names were the Victor (1901) and Balmoral (1906). Prices were $150 including battery in 1893; $75 without battery in 1898; $60 without battery in 1900; $65 without battery in 1910. A Class M Concert model, for the larger cylinders, was sold in 1899–1906; this was renamed the Opera model in 1901. Price was $85. Illustrations in Frow 1978, pp. 16–19; Jewell 1977, p. 51.

—**Coin-Slots.** Also known as coin-ops. By 1898 some Edison players were being adapted for coin use with spring motors; they could play only one record. Various mechanisms and cabinets were found, with model names including Edison H, Bijou, Climax, and Excelsior. All went out of production by 1908. Other coin-slots were run by electric (battery or mains) motors. Names included Class E, Class H, Class M, Ajax, Alva, Climax, Eclipse, Imperial, Majestic, Regal, and Windsor. The Blue Amberol was not used in coin-ops. Production ceased by 1909. Illustrations in Frow 1978, pp. 114, 115, 117, 119, 120, 122, 124–26.

—**Commercial.** A model sold in 1893 by **Edison Bell Phonograph Corp., Ltd.**, London. It was intended for dictation, and had a speaking tube as well as a listening tube. Illustrations in Frow 1978, p. 173; *TMR* 43 (1976), p. 841.

—**Concert.** This name had various applications. It usually referred to the machines that played cylinders of five-inch diameter, the so-called Concert records. The commercial prototype seems to have been the Graphophone Grand. A model with the name Edison Concert Phonograph was marketed in 1899–1906 in the U.S., and from 1899 or 1900 in Britain. Some early versions of the Concert were called Edison Grand Concert Phonograph; the Opera was renamed Concert, and the Amberola I was also the Concert Amberola. The Concert machine had a spring motor that played six to eight cylinders on a single winding; and a 24-inch horn. It sold for $125, reduced quickly to $100. Although concert records gave good volume, they were fragile, bulky, and expensive. Edison reduced production in a few years. Illustrations in Chew 1981, pp. 42–43; Frow 1978, pp. 63–66, 167; Jewell 1977, pp. 51–52; Marty 1979, p. 60.

—**Domestic.** An Edison Bell phonograph, also known as the Drawing Room model, marketed in Britain in December 1893. It was a battery-driven machine with eight hearing tubes to permit group listening. Except for the smaller number of hearing tubes, it was the same as the Exhibition model. Domestics were leased for £10 per year, instead of sold. Illustration (advertisement) in *TMR* 43 (1976), p. 840.

—**Drawing Room.** *See* Domestic, above.

—**Duplex.** A model that played standard cylinders and concert cylinders by means of a slip-on concert mandrel.

—**Exhibition.** An Edison Bell model "let out to showmen and others who desire to exhibit the machine throughout the country for a money payment," as it was advertised in December 1893. It was battery operated, with 14 hearing tubes to allow group demonstrations. *See also* the home version, Domestic, above.

—**Fireside.** One of the most successful cylinder phonographs, introduced in July 1909 (U.S. and Britain). Operated by a single-spring motor, it played both standard records and Amberols. At first (*Model A*) it came with a straight horn, 19 inches long, in two sections; a cygnet horn was available in 1910. Price varied from $32 to $44, depending on the cabinet and horn chosen. The reproducer was Model K, with a Diamond B for the Blue Amberol records. A *Model B* phonograph was released in 1912 (U.S.) and 1913 (Britain). Some 250 machines a week were sold, and although production ended in 1913 sales continued for another two years. Illustration and story in Glastris 1990; illustrations in Frow 1978, pp. 83, 84, 86; Jewell 1977, p. 56; Marty 1979, p. 62.

—**Gem.** The smallest and one of the most popular machines produced by Edison. It measured 7 3/4 by 5 7/8 inches in the base, and weighed only 7 1/2 pounds. *Model A* was introduced in U.S. and Britain in February 1899, selling at $7.50. With a key-wound spring motor it could play two of the two-minute cylinders at one winding. The horn was a 10-inch conical, the reproducer was the Automatic. A crank replaced the key on the 1905 *Model B*, and the reproducer was Model C; the machine weight grew to 13 pounds. When Gem *Model C* came out, basically unchanged from *Model B* (1908 in U.S., 1909 in Britain), the price had climbed to

$12.50. *Model D* (1909) accommodated both standard two-minute records and the new four-minute Amberols; various reproducers were available for it, and a number of cabinets and horns. Price was up to $15. The last version, *Model E* of 1912, played only the four-minute cylinders. It was otherwise essentially the same as the previous model, and sold at the same price. Gem manufacture was discontinued in 1914. Edison Bell revived the name Gem for its radio receiver of 1925. Illustrations in Chew 1981, p. 56; Frow 1978, pp. 68–76; Hoover 1971, p. 44 (the date is given incorrectly there), Jewell 1977, pp. 51, 57; Marty 1979, p. 59.

—**Home.** The history of this very successful machine began in 1895, with the introduction of the "clockwork" model; it had an intricate spring motor made by the **United States Phonograph Co.** of Newark, New Jersey. After a few months this device was replaced by a regular Edison motor, and the name *Model A* was assigned to the phonograph (1896–1905). It sold for $40, later $30, and included a choice of brass horns as long as 36 inches. In 1901 the Automatic Reproducer was offered, and in 1902 the Model C reproducer. Several cabinet styles appeared. *Model B* became available in the U.S. and Britain in late 1905, with some motor refinements and a choice of horns; price was $30. Except for a change in mandrel support, the 1908 *Model C* (1909 in Britain) was the same as the previous version, although more expensive at $35. Both two-minute and four-minute records were playable on the *Model D* (1908 U.S., 1909 Britain); alternatively an attachment could be purchased to play the Amberols on the earlier models. Cost was $40 for the new model, or up to $58 with cygnet horn and mahogany case. *Model E* (1911) had the new Model O reproducer, and a new price tag of $45. The Model R reproducer was introduced later as an option. In the *Model F* (1912 U.S., 1913 Britain) there was yet another reproducer, the Diamond B. This machine played Blue Amberols; cost was $50. Production of the Home ceased in October 1913. Illustrations in Frow 1978, pp. 40–45, 47–50; Hoover 1971, pp. 54–55, Jewell 1977, pp. 67–68; Marty 1979, pp. 58, 61.

—**Household.** The model exhibited by Edison at the **World's Columbian Exposition** of 1893.

—**Idelia.** From 1907 to 1911 this was Edison's luxury model, selling at $125 and featuring oxidized bronze finish on the metal parts. The original spelling, Ideal, was dropped after three months. A spring motor of the Triumph type was used, with a 33 inch horn and a Model C reproducer. *Model D1* (1908 U.S., 1909 U.K.) played both two- and four-minute cylinders. *Model D2* (1909 U.S., 1910 Britain) introduced the new cygnet horn. *Model E*, sold in U.S. in 1910, had a Model O reproducer. Production of the Idelia ended in 1911 in U.S. and 1912 in Britain. Illustrations in Frow 1978, pp. 77–81; Jewell 1977, p. 70.

—**Improved.** This name was given to one result of Edison's renewed attention to the phonograph in 1887. It succeeded the New Phonograph, and preceded the Perfected Phonograph. Heavy-duty batteries provided the power and a steady recording speed. Illustration in Chew 1981, p. 10.

—**Military.** A small machine on display at the Paris Exhibition of 1889. It was an electric portable, with half-size cylinders. Illustration in Frow 1978, p. 12.

—**New.** The first machine made by Edison when he resumed work on the phonograph in 1887, using wax cylinders in place of tinfoil. Its poor quality of reproduction required the inventor to make the improvements that led to the Improved model. Illustrations in Chew 1981, p. 10; Frow 1978, pp. 181–82.

—**New Duplex.** A model offered in Britain in 1902–1903, with two mandrels (for standard and five-inch cylinders) and the Home motor. The horn was a self-supported Herald type. It was sold by Edison Bell for £15. In 1905 Edison Bell offered the Concert Duplex modification, which was basically the Concert phonograph, for £17 5s. Illustration in Frow 1978, p. 172.

—**Opera.** Acclaimed as the greatest of Edison's phonographs, the Opera was introduced in U.S. in 1911 and Britain in 1912. It played only the four-minute Amberols, using a double-spring motor with a Model L reproducer. A Music Master horn was included, and the cabinet was mahogany. Price was $90. The diamond Model A reproducer was offered for the Blue Amberols in 1912 (Britain 1913) and the model's name was changed to Concert. Production ceased in 1913. Illustrations in Chew

1981, p. 43; Frow 1978, pp. 21, 111; Jewell 1977, p. 84; Marty 1979, p. 63.

—**Perfected.** Possibly the most famous photograph of Edison shows him with the Perfected Phonograph, which he had created in June 1888 after a 72-hour marathon effort in the laboratory. The power came from 2.5 volt batteries. Pianist Josef Hofmann made a cylinder in the laboratory, the earliest record by a recognized concert artist. It was to be Edison's first commercial instrument, intended for business use; but in 1889 some music and novelty records were already being made. Edison's British agent, **Colonel Gouraud**, demonstrated the Perfected model in Bath on 6 Sep 1888, in competition with the **graphophone**, and made records of William Gladstone, Alfred Tennyson, Robert Browning, and Florence Nightingale. Gouraud exhibited the machine at the Crystal Palace, London. Brahms performed a piano solo for the machine in 1889, in Vienna. The oldest recording in the BBC library, by naturalist **Ludwig Koch**, was made on a Perfected Phonograph. Illustration in Frow 1978, p. 4.

—**School.** This model was intended for use with the 54 Blue Amberol School Records. It was introduced in 1912 (U.S.) and 1913 (Britain), selling at $75. Mechanically it was identical to the Opera model; it had a diamond Model A reproducer and a cygnet horn. Instead of occupying a wooden cabinet, the School Phonograph stood on plain steel case with four shelves to hold cylinder boxes. Production ceased in 1914. Illustration in Frow 1978, p. 113.

—**Spring motor.** Also identified as the Class SM, and later (1901) as the Triumph; in Britain it was named the Class M Spring Motor Phonograph. This machine was marketed from 1896 to 1900. Using a heavy three-spring motor, it could play up to 14 records on a single winding. The Edison Standard Speaker was on the early models, while later versions had the Edison Automatic Reproducer and Edison Recorder. Listening tubes or a 14-inch brass horn were available. It was originally priced at $100, then reduced to $50. Illustrations in Frow 1978, pp. 25–28, 164; Jewell 1977, p. 97.

—**Standard, Class S.** "By far the most commonly found of the Edison phonographs in Great Britain" (Frow) and highly successful in the U.S. as well, the Standard was sold from 1898 to 1913. *Model A*, with a single-spring motor, played two or three two-minute cylinders at one winding, using the Edison Standard Speaker and Edison Recorder and a 14-inch brass horn; in 1899 the Automatic Reproducer replaced the Standard Speaker. Price was $20. *Model B*, 1905, had a slightly stronger spring motor and could play four records without rewinding; it had the Model C reproducer. Price was $25 with a 30-inch horn. *Model C*, 1908, had only minor changes from the previous model. Both two- and four-minute records were playable on the *Model D*, introduced in 1908 (U.S.) and 1909 (Britain). *Model E* (1911, U.S. only) was for the Amberols only; it had a Model N reproducer and a flower horn; price $30. *Model F* (1911 U.S., 1912 Britain) took either two- or four-minute records. It had a cygnet horn, with a Model S, Model C, or Model H reproducer; it sold for $35. The arrival of the Blue Amberol cylinder required a diamond reproducer on *Model G* (1912), which was otherwise the same as the previous versions. Production ended in October 1913. Illustrations in Frow 1978, pp. 51–55, 57–62, 128–29; Jewell 1977, p. 97; Marty 1979, pp. 59–60.

—**Triumph.** A phonograph that was developed in 1901 from the Spring Motor model; it remained in production until 1913, passing through several versions. *Model A* was a recasing of the Spring Motor model. It handled two-minute cylinders, using the Model C reproducer after 1902 in America and 1903 in Britain. A 14-inch horn, brass and later black japanned, was supplied. Price was $50. In 1906 *Model B* appeared, featuring some mechanical improvements and, from 1907, a 33-inch black horn. *Model C* (1908 U.S., 1909 Britain) had a few mechanical changes, one being a central bearing support for the mandrel. With the arrival of the four-minute record in 1908, *Model D* was introduced to play it (1909 in Britain). It also handled the older two-minute cylinder. A Model C reproducer was used for the two-minute record, and Model H for the new Amberols. After 1909 a 33-inch cygnet horn was supplied. Cost was $65–$85, depending on horn finish and cabinetry. Model O and Model R reproducers were provided for the *Model E*, sold in 1910; various horns were offered. In 1912 U.S., 1913 Britain, *Model F* was introduced; it was for two-minute or four-minute records, with a Model O reproducer and an oak Music Master horn. Price was $75. The series ended with *Model G* in 1912 in the U.S., in 1913 in Britain; it had the Diamond B reproducer, and played only the four-minute Blue Amberol. Equipped with an oak Music Master horn, it was priced at $75. Illustrations in Frow 1978, pp. 29, 32–34, 36–39; Jewell 1977, p. 101.

The Edison phonographs cited above are listed below by the year in which they were first marketed:

1887	New
1887	Improved
1888	Perfected
1893	Class E
1893	Class M
1893	Commercial
1893	Domestic
1893	Drawing Room
1893	Exhibition
1893	Household
1896	Home
1896	Spring Motor
1898	Coin-slots
1898	Standard
1899	Concert
1899	Gem
1901	Triumph
1901	Victor
1906	Balmoral
1907	Idelia
1909	Amberola I
1909	Fireside
1911	Opera
1912	Amberola III
1912	Amberola V
1912	School
1913	Amberola IV
1913	Amberola VI
1913	Amberola VIII
1913	Amberola X
1915	Amberola 30
1915	Amberola 50
1915	Amberola 75
1928	Amberola 60
1928	Amberola 80

[Copeland 1991; Edison 1893/1; Frow 1978 (source of nearly all the above information); Klinger*; Waltrip 1991.]

Edison's first disc phonograph acknowledged the public's preference for flat records. However, his disc machine was more than a late entry into the market, it was superior to all that had preceded it. The Diamond Disc phonograph, marketed in 1912, was designed to play the new Diamond Disc records, and the effect was remarkable. *TMW* reported in July 1912 that there was "no perceptible scratch" made on the discs by the new diamond stylus of the reproducer, and indeed it was claimed that no record wear resulted after a thousand plays. The target audience for the new machine was a more affluent one than had been served by the cylinder phonograph. While cylinder machines were still sold for as little as $15, the lowest price for a disc player was $60, and luxury models were on sale for $1,000. A 1920 Gothic model sold for $6,000, the most expensive acoustic player ever marketed. **Tone tests** demonstrated the astonishing fidelity that the Diamond Disc and Diamond Disc Phonograph could achieve. An auto-stop was installed; attachments were available to play standard (lateral-cut) discs from other manufacturers. More than 800,000 machines were sold by 1929.

Only one substantial model change occurred in the disc player line, when the Edisonic was introduced in 1927 as a challenge to the Victor Orthophonic. This was an acoustic phonograph made by Edison in the electrical recording era, with an improved reproducer and a larger horn. It advertised "close-up" music, so that "in that chuckling jazz the hot sax seems at your shoulder" and "each instrument, each tone, stands out with cameo-like precision." A small console model, the Schubert, sold for $135, and a larger Beethoven model sold for $225. Some models were equipped to play Edison's long-playing records of 1926. Illustrations of various models can be found in Chew 1981, p. 57; Jewell 1977, p. 52; Marty 1979, p. 62. [Odell 1974.] *See also* EDISON DIAMOND DISC.

EDISON RECORDERS. The **recorder** of the acoustic phonograph was the device that carried the audio signal to the record surface. It was basically a **diaphragm** with a **stylus** embedded in it, the whole fitted with a speaking tube or **recording horn**. In the pioneer days, the recorder was set into a **spectacle** carrier, which also held the **reproducer**. Such was the form seen in the New Phonograph produced by Edison in 1887. Nomenclature was less than lucid: the recorder was identified in some advertising as a "speaker for recording" while the reproducer was also called a speaker. As the emphasis within the sound industry shifted from home or business recording to home listening, attention was concentrated on the reproducer. Edison made many versions of the reproducer, but he produced only minor variations on his basic recorder, which had a mica diaphragm and a sapphire cutting stylus. Nevertheless, he continued to offer the opportunity for phonograph owners to make their own records, even with the **Amberola** line of four-minute machines, and at reasonable prices (less than $10 would buy a recorder, a recorder fitting, and a special recording horn). [Frow 1978.]

EDISON REPEATING ATTACHMENTS. Beginning in 1888 Edison produced devices for his phonographs that allowed repeated playing of the cylinder. This repeating attachment was intended for commercial rather than domestic use. It was a forerunner of the **coin-op**. Several mechanical principles were tried (cord and windlass, chain drive and pulley, etc.), but they were not successful, and none were offered after 1912. However, the mechanism was important in language instruction. [Frow 1978.]

EDISON REPRODUCERS. The **diaphragm-and-stylus** device used to play back cylinders was first known as a speaker, or sometimes as a repeater. By use of a **spectacle** carrier, those **reproducers** were mounted in tandem with **recorders**; the one employed to play what the other had inscribed on the cylinder. By 1889 Edison had found a way to meld those functions into a single device (British patent #19153) which he named the Standard Speaker; it had tracking problems and was replaced in 1893 by the Automatic Speaker, also designated as Model A. It must be remembered that the

model numbers of the reproducers had no relation to the model numbers of the phonographs. In 1901 there was a special Gem reproducer for the phonograph of that name; this was replaced in a year by the Model B. This complex scenario was simplified in 1902 with the arrival of the Model C reproducer, which was used on most Edison machines until 1913. Glass diaphragms of earlier reproducers were replaced by mica and then copper alloy. Model C was intended for the new hard molded records. The Model D was similar, but adapted for the large concert cylinder. For the four-minute cylinder of 1908, a Model H was introduced. A reproducer to permit playing of Amberol records on five-inch concert machines—the Model J—came out in 1909.

The first reproducer for both two-minute and four-minute records appeared in the 1909 Model K. The required stylus was brought into playing position by turning a swivel. Model L and Model M (1909) were similar devices, intended for Amberola and Opera phonographs. Model N (1911 U.S., 1912 Britain) played four-minute Amberol records with a sapphire. Model O (1910) was used on players with large carrier arms. Models R and S (1911) were the final sapphire stylus devices from Edison, offering a large diaphragm usable on a small carrier arm. As for the missing model letters in this summary, Frow states that the Model P "has not been accounted for, but is thought to have been a modification of an earlier model"; "Model I was doubtless omitted as liable to cause confusion"; and "further research is needed to trace what happened to Models E, F, and G."

The advent of the Blue Amberol record called for a new series, the diamond reproducers. They were issued from 1912, and bore no model-letter marks; however, researchers refer to them as Diamond A, B, C, and D. They remained on the market until 1929. Lacquered paper and cork were the diaphragm materials. Illustrations in Frow 1978, pp. 134–52 [Frow 1978; Klinger*.]

EDISON SCHOOL RECORDS. Over a period of 50 years, the Edison companies issued a variety of educational material on cylinder records for use in schools. Some of those diverse products are rather obscure today. Each type shares the standard 2 1/8 inch outside diameter of Edison entertainment cylinders and dictation blanks, but they differ in axial length, groove pitch, material, color, and content.

First to be marketed were the Edison Dictation Records, black-wax cylinders similar to the 100–TPI (threads per inch), 160-rpm Edison "Gold Moulded" entertainment records. They were announced in Sales Department Bulletin No. 50 of 10 May 1910. The series of 25 two-minute records of dictation exercises for short-hand instruction was prepared by "Stenographic Expert" J.N. Kimball for use on standard Edison phonographs (not the 150–TPI Edison Business Phonographs). They sold through Edison jobbers and dealers at a U.S. list price of $.50 each.

A 200–TPI, black-wax Amberol Dictation Record was reported by John Dales in 1980. Dales listed a series of 12 "four-minute" titles, also recorded by J.N. Kimball, and described Blue Amberol versions of both the 2M and 4M dictation records.

Another four-minute series soon emerged in celluloid as the Blue Amberol School Record. Physically identical to standard Blue Amberol records (200 TPI; 160 rpm), and numbered among the regular popular entertainment series, they were instead intended for instructional use. They were announced to the trade in December 1912, coincident with the introduction of the Edison School Phonograph. The series totaled 54 records, numbered 1657 through 1710. Material included lessons in dictation and spelling, math drills, and various business practices for secretaries. A separate group of six records numbered 1651 through 1656 offered recitations of "world-famous" speeches and poems by elocutionist Harry E. Humphrey, such as Lincoln's Gettysburg Address, Patrick Henry's speech, and Francis Finch's poem "The Blue and the Gray." These School Records were distributed through Edison jobbers and sold by retail dealers for $.50 each, the same price as regular Blue Amberols.

A second series of standard-size (four-inch-long) blue celluloid cylinders appeared as Blue Amberol School Test Records. They differ in their coarser groove pitch and smooth (non-ribbed) plaster bore, for use on Ediphones in secretarial schools. (The word "Test" in the name may have been used to distinguish these 150–TPI, 80-rpm records from the 200–TPI "Blue Amberol School Records.") Some matching box lids state a price of $1.50 for School Test Records, suggesting that production continued decades later than the 1920s. Record #18 in this series contains an address written by President Calvin Coolidge, but it is uncertain whether the recording was actually made by him. Similar cylinders marked "Dictation Record, 100 RPM, J.N. Kimball" on the bevelled end rim have also turned up.

Ediphone Standard Practice Records were manufactured from 1917 through at least 1929. These celluloid records are the same size as regular Blue Amberols, but have a smooth-bore plaster core, are grooved at 150 TPI, and are colored black. They were shipped in over-size felt-lined boxes with the common blue-and-orange Blue Amberol label of the period. At 80 rpm, they provided durations to six minutes. The name "Ediphone Standard Practice Record" was probably replaced later by "Ediphone School Record." Both four- and six-inch-long examples have been cited. At 80 rpm, they could play up to six minutes and nine minutes, respectively. This series offered dictation exercises at various rates of oral delivery (e.g.: "80 Words per Minute" or "150 WPM") for shorthand practice and typewriter transcription work. They may also have been used for elocution lessons. Some later felt-lined boxes tout the Voice Writing methods associated with the Edison Voicewriter dictating machines. This series of cylinder records was manufactured as late as 1960. [Dales 1980.]

Bill Klinger

EDISON SHAVERS. One of the advantages held by wax cylinders over other recording media was their capability of reuse. From 1887 Edison's home and commercial phonographs had devices for shaving the surface of a used cylinder. Operation was by treadle power at first, then by electric drive. Interest in these gadgets peaked by 1904—when Edison stopped putting shavers on the Home and Standard models. After 1908 he ceased providing them except for the Home Recording Outfit sold in 1912. [Frow 1978.]

EDISON SPEAKING PHONOGRAPH CO.
A firm established on 24 Jan 1878 at 203 Broadway, New York, and incorporated 24 Apr 1878 in Norwalk, Connecticut. It was formed to make phonographs, based on Thomas Edison's **tinfoil phonograph** patent (U.S. #200,521, granted 19 Feb 1878), the rights having been acquired through a syndicate that had purchased them from the inventor. Edison received $10,000 in cash for the manufacturing and sales rights, plus a 20 percent royalty on prospective sales. His instinct in selling out was not misguided, for sales were poor in spite of considerable interest in the invention. S. Bergmann, 104 Wooster St., New York, made the first models to be sold (at $95.50); one Charles H. Sewall was the first purchaser. Smaller models were made by Brenmer Brothers at $10.00, and by Alexander Poole. In Europe E. Hardy and Max Kohl manufactured the machines.

All in all there were only about 2,000 phonographs sold by the end of 1879, with an income of $4,453.97 in 1878, and $1,581.98 in 1879. In 1880 the sales amounted to $478.50. The company was no longer listed in the New York telephone directory after 1879, and was finally sold to **Jesse H. Lippincott** in 1888 or 1889. [Frow 1978; Koenigsberg 1990; Proceedings 1974; Wile 1976.]

EDISON UNITED PHONOGRAPH CO.
An entity established on 24 Feb 1890 to handle Thomas Edison's patents outside of North America. Location was the Mills Building, New York. G.N. Morison was secretary. Edison United acquired British Edison patents and sold them to Edison Bell Phonograph Corp., Ltd.—a firm it set up for the purpose. Activities ceased in 1902 or 1903.

EDISON VENETIAN TRIO.
An instrumental group, also known as the Venetian Instrumental Trio, that recorded for Edison in 1908–1909. The members were Eugene Jaudas, violin; Eugene Rose, flute; and Charles Scheutze, harp. Records listed in Koenigsberg 1987 are "Song of the Mermaids" (#10027; 1908) and "Moszkowski's Serenade" (#10152; 1909).

EDISONIA CO.
A firm incorporated in 1898 by Albert O. Petit, Ademor N. Petit, and Arthur Petit. It was located, in 1909, at 57 Halsey St., Newark, New Jersey. Edisonia bought the Newark branch of the Douglas Phonograph Co. and arranged with the **National Phonograph Co.** to be its sole Newark distributor.

EDISONIA, LTD.
A firm established in 1897 by the redoubtable **J.E. Hough**, located at the 3 Broad St. Buildings, Liverpool St., London. Hough had been engaged in illicit sales of Edison products, but the new company gave his occupation legitimacy through agreements with **Edison Bell Consolidated Phonograph Co., Ltd.** Edisonia's letterhead presented itself as "incorporating the **London Phonograph Co.**" (Hough's previous firm). Edisonia was an independent supplier of records and players for about a year, and then became a subsidiary of Edison Bell, devoted to manufacture of cylinders and phonographs as well as sales. Labels offered were **London, Standard,** Popular, Indestructible, and Indestructible Ebony. In 1903 a factory—Edisonia Works—was set up in Peckham, and gold molded records were made there. There was also a show room at 20 Cheapside, London, and a business office at 25–27–29 Banner St., London.

In addition to sound recording items, Edisonia distributed X-ray machines, "materials for producing animated photographs," and "other scientific apparatus."

Problems developed in the early 1900s, with slowing sales and a serious fire at the Peckham Works leading to a crisis in 1909. Both Edison Bell and Edisonia went into receivership, and Edisonia was put up for auction on 24 Mar 1909. It was bought by Hough himself, for £10,400 (as against a valuation of £50,000) with all its stock, and reborn as **J. E. Hough, Ltd.** in April. [Andrews 1984; Chew 1981; *TMR* #10 reproduces an 1898 letter by Hough.]

EDMUNDS, HENRY.
British engineer who observed Edison's **tinfoil phonograph** while in the U.S. in late 1877 or January 1878. On

returning to England he wrote about the phonograph to the *Times*. It was through this notice, which appeared in the newspaper on 17
Jan 1878, that the British public learned about
the invention. Edmunds demonstrated the
graphophone in Bath on 6 Sep 1888, after Colonel George Gouraud had exhibited Edison's
Perfected Phonograph there.

EDUCATIONAL RECORDINGS. The earliest recordings of an educational character were
language instruction records dating from 1891.
Columbia's "Phono Vocal Method" (1910) offered lessons by means of recorded examples
keyed to textbooks. Later Columbia efforts in
the educational arena included children's
songs, the Columbia History of Music, dramatic re-enactments of landmark events, poetry readings, and add-a-part discs for use by
musicians. In 1928 Columbia issued lectures
on physics and astronomy. During World War
II it made Morse Code training discs.

After early production of **children's
records**, Victor expanded that area into "education." The 1917 catalog had 28 pages of titles
listed in that category, though nearly all were
regular issues thought to have some appropri-
ateness in schools. Some are listed as children's
records. The general aim of these recordings
was "to help in the uplift of the ideals and tastes
of children." Adult education was also touched
on by Victor, with the "Oscar Saenger Course
in Vocal Training" for each voice type, selling
at $25 for a set of 10 discs and a textbook. By the
time of the 1927 catalog, Victor had made
records with specific classroom connections,
explicated through printed manuals such as
"The Victrola in Physical Education," "Music
Manual for Rural Schools," "Music Appreciation with the Victrola for Children," among
others.

In the LP era there were hundreds of instruction discs, many in the self-help category,
like "Improve Your Fishing" and "Look Your
Loveliest" on the Carlton label in 1961. Folkways had records that taught the dulcimer
(1964) and the country fiddle (1965). The BBC
Study Records (1969) presented school programs in diverse subjects. In 1975 PolyGram
cassettes were produced in music appreciation, literature study, bridge playing, etc.

Museums have introduced cassettes timed
to advise the strolling viewer about works on
exhibit. Exercise tapes have become commonplace, the most famous being *Jane Fonda's Work-
out Record* (CBS #8858) and its successors. *See
also* TALKING BOOK.

EDWARDS, CLIFF, 1895–1972. American
popular singer and ukulele player, born in
Hannibal, Missouri, in 1895. He sang in saloons in St. Louis, then at the Palace Theater
there. Edwards was a narrator in movie houses
showing silent films. In Chicago he became a
regular performer, and earned his nickname,
"Ukulele Ike," as he sang and accompanied
himself on the ukulele. Edwards appeared in
several motion pictures in 1929 and the 1930s,
and was on Rudy Vallee's radio show. He also
went to Britain and sang in London music
halls. He had a false start at recording in 1919–
1920, making some discs that were rejected by
Columbia. Then he was successful with
Gennett, beginning in 1922 with "Virginia
Blues" (#4853) in which he did "vocal effects"
for an ensemble. He sang with his ukulele for
Pathé Actuelle in 1923, doing "Old Fashioned
Love" (#021097), then worked for other labels
to 1927. He was with Columbia in 1928–1930,
making a famous record of "Singing in the
Rain" (Columbia 31869–D; 1929). Then he recorded for Brunswick, Vocalion, and others.
Edwards was the voice of Jiminy Cricket in the
film *Pinocchio* (1938), and made a chart record
of "When You Wish upon a Star" from the
soundtrack (Victor #26477; 1939). He died in
Hollywood on 18 July 1972. [Kiner 1987.]

EDWARDS, JOAN, 1919–1981. American
popular singer, born in New York on 13 Feb
1919; niece of Gus Edwards. She was a radio
and hotel vocalist, and was with Paul Whiteman
from 1938 to 1940. She was the featured female
singer on the radio program *Your Hit Parade*,
co-starring with Barry Wood. She and Wood
had a hit record in "Ti-Pi-Tin" (Victor #27865;
1942); and her solo rendition of "All the Things
You Are" was one of the finest made of that
masterpiece (Victor #27866; 1942). She died on
28 Aug 1981.

EDWARDS, JOHN, 1932–1960. Australian authority on American country and western music, and collector of more than 2,000 records of the period 1923–1941. He died in an automobile accident on 24 Dec 1960. His will directed that those recordings be sent to the U.S. for research purposes, and the material was eventually housed at the University of California at Los Angeles. The John Edwards Memorial Foundation was established in 1962 to administer the archive, which grew to more than 12,000 records and included sheet music and instruments of the famous performers. The archive was later transferred to the Middle Tennessee State University. A periodical, the *JEMF Quarterly*, (originally *Newsletter*) was issued from 1965 to 1989; then a new journal replaced it: *American Vernacular Music.*

EFFICIENCY. The ratio of output power (or energy) to input. In an electronic power **amplifier**, the ratio of the output power to the power drawn from the mains (alternating current source). [Klinger*.]

EIA. *See* ELECTRONIC INDUSTRIES ASSOCIATION (EIA).

EIGENTON. A German term (Eigentone in English) identifying the resonance set up in a room or enclosure at frequencies determined by the physical dimensions of the space. The lowest frequency will be at a wavelength corresponding to twice the longest length of the space, and others will be at double and three times that frequency, and so on. *See also* ROOM ACOUSTICS.

EIGHT FAMOUS VICTOR ARTISTS. An ensemble established ca. 1917, named at first "The Record Maker Troupe," originally consisting of Billy Murray, Henry Burr, Albert Campbell, John Meyer, Arthur Collins, Teddy Morse, Byron Harlan, and Vess Ossman. The group toured and made records. Burr was manager in 1917, and made a number of personnel changes: Frank Croxton replaced Collins; Frank E. Banta replaced Morse, Fred Van Eps replaced Ossman, and Monroe Silver replaced Byron Harlan. Later Rudy Wiedoeft took the place of Van Eps, and Sammy Hermann

then replaced Wiedoeft. The group disbanded in 1928, after another change of name to "Eight Popular Victor Artists." Their last record in the catalog was "Miniature Concert" (#35753; 1925). It was the first electric recording made by Victor.

Eight-track tape. *See* TAPE.

ELBOW. The part of a disc player that connects the **horn** to the end of the **tone arm.**

ELCASET. A modification of the standard **cassette** introduced by several Japanese firms in the mid-1970s. It used quarter-inch wide tape, instead of the standard 1/8 inch, and ran at a faster speed. Sony was the only company to promote the Elcaset actively. The format failed in the market because the improvements it offered over the standard cassette did not outweigh the considerable cost difference and the fact that it was incompatible with the millions of cassette players already owned by prospective customers. A European version was named Unisette.

ELDRIDGE, ROY, 1911–1989. American trumpeter, born in Pittsburgh on 30 June 1911. He began playing professionally at age 16, and was performing in Harlem by 1930. In 1935 he joined Fletcher Henderson; a year later he formed his own band in Chicago. "Heckler's Hop" was an important early record with that group (Vocalion #3577; 1937), which made eight other discs for Vocalion and Varsity by the end of 1939. As a member of the Gene Krupa band in 1941 Eldridge was one of the first Black musicians to appear in a Big Band brass section. With Krupa he made a hit record, "Rockin' Chair" (Okeh #6352; 1941), followed by another, with Anita O'Day doing the vocal: "Let Me Off Uptown" (Okeh #6210; 1941). His most modern jazz style is heard in "The Gasser" (Brunswick #80117; 1943). He was with Artie Shaw in 1944–1945. Eldridge performed in Paris in 1950, creating a sensation. He also did remarkable work with the Coleman Hawkins Quintet, and in duets with singer Ella Fitzgerald during 1963–1965. He is regarded as a link between Louis Armstrong and Dizzy Gillespie.

ELECTRADISK (label). An eight-inch record, later 10-inch, made by RCA for distribution by Woolworth stores in 1932–1934. They sold for $.10, offering mostly material that also appeared on Bluebird. [Rust 1978.]

ELECTRIC (label). A record that offered dance and popular material ca. 1925 in the U.S. Despite its name, all known examples are acoustically recorded. [Rust 1978.]

ELECTRIC PHONOGRAPH. A record player driven by an electric motor, with either alternating current or direct current (mains) or direct current (battery) as its power source. Thomas Edison's Perfected Phonograph, which he demonstrated in 1888, had a 2.5 volt battery with a life expectancy of about 15 hours. Certain Edisons had battery power (Class M, certain coin-slots, Domestic, Exhibition, Improved) and/or mains power (Alva, Class E, certain coin-slots). But the principal Edisons (Amberola, Home, Opera, Standard, Triumph, etc.) operated with spring motors. The 1915 Columbia Grafonola was available with an electric motor. And in 1921 Victor was advertising two electric console Victrolas, numbers XVI and XVII. A few disc players had, from 1916, electric attachments that wound up spring-operated machines automatically. Brunswick was the first to offer an all-electric record player, the 1925 **Panatrope**. *See also* TURNTABLE.

ELECTRIC PHONOGRAPH CO. (I) A New York firm, located in 1916 at 29 W. 34th St. It sold the Phonolamp line of disc players, which combined a phonograph with a lamp.

ELECTRIC PHONOGRAPH CO. (II) A New York recording laboratory, located (April 1919) at 235–37–39 W. 23rd St., later (May 1922) at 236 W. 116th St. A petition for bankruptcy was filed in March 1922. [Andrews*.]

ELECTRIC RECORDING LABORATORIES, INC. A New York firm, with recording laboratories located in April 1921 at 210 Fifth Ave. There was a pressing plant at 225 Murray St., Newark, New Jersey. Customers were supplied with the firm's recordings under the buyer's own labels, if requested. A.G. Bryan was manager. Advertising continued to July 1921. [Andrews*.]

Electrical and Musical Industries. *See* EMI, LTD.

ELECTRICAL RECORDING. Also known as electromechanical recording. A number of experiments in several countries during World War I developed the components that were to make up an electrical recording system. The earliest effort that resulted in an actual marketed recording was that of **Lionel Guest** and **Horace O. Merriman** in London. They produced a moving-coil recording head (British patent #141,790) and set up equipment in a truck outside Westminster Abbey. On 11 Nov 1920 they recorded part of the service for the burial of the Unknown Warrior, using four carbon telephone microphones placed in the Abbey. The Columbia Graphophone Co. sold the resulting 12-inch double-faced disc for the benefit of the Abbey restoration fund; it contained the "Recessional" by Rudyard Kipling and "Abide with Me." However, the work of Guest and Merriman, as well as that of Adrian Francis Sykes, Frank B. Dyer, W.S Purser, and others, was eclipsed by the accomplishments of engineers at **Bell Telephone Laboratories** in America.

Research at Bell Laboratories, directed by J.P. Maxfield, had produced experiments in electrical recording as early as 1919. The Bell electrical apparatus consisted of **microphones** (principally the type 394 capacitor), **amplifiers** (two-stage), **recording heads** (balanced armature, moving-iron type), and **loudspeakers** (also balanced armature, moving-iron type, with response from 300–7,000 Hz). Essentially, what the new system did was to substitute electrical energy for mechanical energy, so that the signal to be recorded no longer had to provide its own (acoustic) power. The microphone replaced the venerable recording horn. There was also an appreciable increase in the amount of the **audio frequency** range that could be captured; as much as 2 1/2 octaves were added, giving audibility for the first time to higher frequencies (ultimately extended to 9,000 Hz) and to bass notes (down to 200 Hz).

Western Electric Co., the manufacturing division of American Telegraph and Telephone (parent company of Bell Laboratories), became the licensed owner of the process. An offer was made to extend the licensing to Victor, which refused. Columbia Phonograph Co., Inc., which had been reorganized in 1924 by a group of American investors, gained a Western Electric license. When Western Electric sent their master waxes to Pathé's office in New York to be processed, Russell Hunting and Frank Capps—Pathé executives—decided to let Louis Sterling (an old colleague of Hunting) in on the invention. They sent some duplicate pressings to Sterling, managing director of Columbia Graphophone Co., Ltd., in London. Sterling was sufficiently inspired by them to sail at once for New York. There he contrived to acquire the American Columbia firm, making it a part of the British one, thus acquiring the license to the Western Electric process. Victor thereupon consented to a contract also, an agreement inclusive of the Gramophone Co., so that the industry giants had legal control of the electrical recording system. This system remained in use, with modifications, by Victor until after World War II.

Nevertheless it was an independent company, Chicago's **Marsh Laboratories, Inc.**, that first marketed electrically recorded discs, under the **Autograph** label, in 1924. Columbia and HMV discs appeared first in the summer of 1925. For Columbia, records #3695–140545/140546 were the earliest to come out: they were made by W.C. Polla's Orchestra (under the pseudonym of Denza's Dance Band) and sold in July 1925. A vast choral ensemble was then recorded in the Metropolitan Opera House on 31 Mar 1925, singing "John Peel" and "Adeste Fidelis" (Columbia #9048; September 1925), creating a sensation.

Victor's first electric recording was "A Miniature Concert" by the Eight Famous Victor Artists (#35753; June 1925). "Joan of Arkansas," by the Mask and Wig Club, was made later—according to the matrix numbers—but released earlier (#19626; April 1925). HMV's earliest electricals to be marketed were dance numbers by Ramon Newton, Jack Hylton, and the Mayfair Orchestra, recorded on 24–25 June and sold in August 1925. By the end of the first year of electric recording there were eight labels using the system. Brunswick had not licensed with Western Electric, but instead utilized their own "Palatrope" or "Light-Ray" process, developed by General Electric. The others—Parlophone, Zonophone, Homochord, Sterno, Vocalion—worked with alternative systems that did not infringe on the patent rights of the majors. Crystalate and Pathé joined the electrics in May 1927. Edison, after holding out because he was concerned about distortions endemic in any electrical system, also began to make electrics in 1927. There was a general reticence by the labels to advertise the nature of their new products, for fear that existing stocks of acoustic records would no longer be salable.

While Victor held to the Western Electric system, Columbia moved from it to a new process developed by **Alan Dower Blumlein** in 1929. Blumlein sought to overcome some of the technical problems in the Western Electric apparatus, such as high sensitivity to background noise, the tendency for distortion to be more obvious in the extended frequency range, and certain maintenance requirements. Of course there was also the need to pay royalties to Western Electric. Vocalion's system was developed by an engineer from the Marconi Wireless Telegraph Co.; it was used from 1926 to 1931.

Many refinements were made in electrical recording through the 1930s, primarily in higher quality microphones (including a notable one by Georg Neumann) which began to resemble those of our own time. Other innovations have included disc cutting with the burnishing facet on the stylus (invented by Frank L. Capps), and the "hot stylus" developed in the CBS laboratories while work was going on there to produce the modern long-playing record. Different types of **equalization** came into use, and modern recording was established. *See also* CARTRIDGE; MICROPHONE; RECORDING PRACTICE; STYLUS. [Andrews 1985/6; Brooks*; Ford 1962; Klinger*.]

ELECTROFORMING. The technique, originated by Emile Berliner, of producing positive discs from negatives, and vice versa. It permitted the manufacture of positive mothers from negative metal masters, and then the manufacture of negative stampers from the mothers. *See also* DISC 1, 3.

ELECTROLA (label). A German classical music record, issued by a firm in Cologne that was the reorganized **International Zonophone Co.**, dormant since the end of World War I. It was owned by the Gramophone Co., and its discs (from 1926) were parallels of the Gramophone Co. HMV label. [Andrews*.]

Electromechanical recording. *See* ELECTRICAL RECORDING.

ELECTRONE CO. A firm incorporated in Delaware, in January 1918 to make records. Nothing more is known about it. [Andrews*.]

Electronic crossover. *See* CROSSOVER NETWORK.

ELECTRONIC INDUSTRIES ASSOCIATION (EIA). A trade organization established in 1924 to represent radio manufacturers. It now encompasses the entire audio and video industry. The EIA has headquarters at 1722 I St., NW, in Washington, D.C.. In 1990 Peter F. McCloskey was president; there were 1,200 members. The association absorbed the Magnetic Recording Industry Association in 1965, and the Institute of High Fidelity in 1979.

Electronic stereo. *See* REPROCESSED STEREO.

Electronically reprocessed stereo. *See* REPROCESSED STEREO.

ELECTRO-VOICE, INC. A manufacturer of loudspeakers and other audio components, located in 1990 in Buchanan, Michigan. In 1958 the firm promoted a ceramic stereo cartridge. Its bookshelf loudspeaker was the basis of a 1962 patent infringement action brought by **Acoustic Research, Inc.** The court ruling was in favor of Electro-Voice.

ELEKTRA/ASYLUM/NONESUCH RECORDS. A firm located at 962 N. La Cienega, Los Angeles, distributor of several labels:

Elektra, Elektra/Curb, Full Moon, and Asylum (1990). **WCI** is the parent organization.

Elephone (label). *See* UNIVERSAL TALKING MACHINE CO., LTD.

ELGEPHONE. A disc player manufactured in 1906 by the firm of Léon Gaumont, a French company better known for its activity in the motion picture field. The machine was of interest because it included a natural gas container and a device to allow that gas to flow and burn. The heated gas acted upon the vibrating air in the machine to achieve an increase in the perceived volume of the sound signal. [*TMR* #42 (1976) has a drawing and a 1906 explanation.]

ELLINGTON, DUKE, 1899–1974. American jazz pianist, composer, and bandleader, born Edward Kennedy Ellington in Washington, D.C., on 29 Apr 1899, son of a butler. He began at the piano at age seven, and performed professionally at 17. In 1922 he was in New York, playing with various groups, and leading several of them. He achieved great success in 1927–1932 at the Cotton Club in Harlem with his 12-piece band. Ellington's most acclaimed period followed: he composed extensively, made films, and toured Europe; he and Louis Armstrong were seen as the twin leaders of the jazz universe. He had the advantage of an outstanding arranger in Billy Strayhorn, and star instrumentalists like Barney Bigard, Sonny Greer, Johnny Hodges, Rex Stewart, and Cootie Williams. Ivie (Ivy) Anderson was the principal vocalist. His band offered a new jazz idiom, mixing complex written-out scores with improvised solo playing.

Ellington recorded for the Blu-Disc label in November 1924, "Choo Choo" with "Rainy Nights" (#T-1002). Then he went to Pathé Actuelle in 1925–1926, and Gennett and Vocalion in 1926. He appeared on Okeh, Brunswick, Columbia, and others before settling with Victor in 1940.

Many of his own great compositions became hit records, including "Mood Indigo" (Brunswick #4952; 1930), "Sophisticated Lady" (Columbia #DB-625; 1933), "Prelude to a Kiss" (Brunswick #8204; 1938), "Take the A Train"

(Victor #27380; 1941), "I'm Beginning to See the Light" (Victor #20–1618; 1944), and "Satin Doll" (Capitol #2458; 1953). Ellington penned more than 2,000 works, including serious concert music as well as popular songs. His musical *Jump for Joy* ran for 101 performances in Hollywood in 1941; it was the first all-Black show to offer a Black viewpoint.

From 1943 to 1952 Ellington appeared in annual concerts at Carnegie Hall. In 1959 he composed the score for the film *Anatomy of a Murder*. He received the Presidential Medal of Honor in 1969, and honorary doctorates from Howard University and Yale University. He died in New York, on 24 May 1974.

His great ability as a pianist was somewhat overshadowed by the unique timbre and tonal subtleties of his orchestra, but he was one of the finest soloists of his time. The recording "Clothed Woman" (Columbia #38236; 1947) exhibits his virtuosity.

The discovery of a unique Ellington recording was reported in 1985. As part of RCA Victor's early effort at making **long playing records**, the Ellington orchestra cut a disc in 1932 that was made with two microphones, each directed to a separate wax original disc. This was the basis of a stereophonic record, although it would have required perfect synchronization of two turntables to achieve stereo playback. The company did not follow through with the stereo possibilities; indeed it is not certain whether the engineers were aware of what they had produced. In any case the stereo effect was achieved by Steve Lasker and Brad Kay a half-century later, and a record named "Reflections in Ellington" was released by Everybody's Records, c/o Marlor Productions, Hicksville, New York, in 1985. "No other recording made in 1932 . . . could approach the brilliance, the vivid quality, of this innovative recording" (Feather 1985).

Ellington received nine Grammys. In 1959 his composition and soundtrack for the film *Anatomy of a Murder* was honored. He won the awards for jazz performances and compositions of 1965, 1966, 1967, 1968, 1971, 1972, 1976, and 1979. The 1979 (posthumous) award was for a recording made in 1940 at Fargo, North Dakota (VJC #1019–/20–2).

An important LP reissue appeared in 1979: the Time-Life *Giants of Jazz* (#STL-J02 P3–14729; it offered highlights of Ellington's 1926–1956 career. *Jump for Joy* was reissued by the Smithsonian (#R-037) in 1987. A great many compact disc reissues have appeared. There were four columns of listings in the Winter 1991–1992 issue of *Spectrum*.

The Ellington archives were acquired by the Smithsonian in 1980; they include 200,000 pages of documents, plus scores and tapes. [Feather 1985; Timner 1988.]

ELMAN, MISCHA, 1891–1967. Ukrainian/American violinist, born in Talnoye on 20 Jan 1891. He studied with Leopold Auer in St. Petersburg, and made his debut there in 1904. European tours followed, and a New York debut in 1908; he then played with the major world orchestras. Romantic works were his specialty, but he excelled also in Mozart and Beethoven. In 1911 he settled in the U.S., and took citizenship in 1923. He died in New York on 5 Apr 1967.

Elman was a popular Victor artist, making Red Seals from 1908 to 1925, with total sales of around 2 million records. He had 40 items in the 1917 Victor catalog, all arrangements (no sonatas) except for some obbligatos he played for Enrico Caruso and Frances Alda. He also recorded with his own quartet, with members drawn from the Boston Symphony Orchestra. One of his great records was of the Tchaikovsky Concerto with John Barbirolli and the London Symphony Orchestra (HMV #DB 1405/8). That concerto had been written for Auer, Elman's teacher, who had refused to deal with it, calling it unplayable. BBC Enterprises reissued the recording in 1990 (#LP REH 717). *The Complete Musician* was a collection of his performances from 1910 to 1930, released by BBC Records on CD #753 in 1990.

ELMAN, ZIGGY, 1914–1968. American jazz trumpeter, born Harry Finkelman in Philadelphia, on 26 May 1914. He grew up in Atlantic City, New Jersey, where he played trombone and trumpet, then joined the Benny Goodman band in 1936, staying to 1940. His most famous record was "And the Angels Sing" (Victor

#26170; 1939). Then he went to Tommy Dorsey for the years 1940–1943, and—after military service—again for 1946–1947. Elman won the *Down Beat* poll in 1941, 1943–1945, and 1947. He was seen on television in the 1950s, and performed locally in California, where he died in Van Nuys on 26 June 1968.

ELSHUCO TRIO. An ensemble that recorded for Brunswick in 1920. The members were Elias Breeskin, violin; Willem Willeke, cello; and Aurelio Giorni, piano.

EMBASSY (label). (I) A **Parmount** subsidiary, with releases in 1923–1924.

EMBASSY (label). (II) A British 10-inch record produced for F.W. Woolworth in 1954 by Oriole, Ltd. The label was taken over by CBS in England and used for LP discs there and in Australia. [Andrews*.]

EMBOSSED GROOVE RECORDING. The use of a blunt stylus in disc recording, in order to push aside the groove material without removing it. Masters can therefore be reused, a factor of value in dictating machines.

EMERALD (GREEN) RECORDS (label). A disc advertised in March 1922 by the Union of Irish Industries, Inc., of 236–238 W. 116th St., New York. The firm was incorporated with $1 million by C. Henry, A.E. Claffey, and P.D. Benson. [Andrews*.]

EMERSON, VICTOR HUGO, 1866–1926. American recording engineer and executive. He was employed by Edison and then by the U.S. Phonograph Co., and was manager of the record department for Columbia from 1897 to 1914. In 1915 he established the **Emerson Phonograph Co.** In 1922 he resigned from the presidency of the firm and organized another, the Kodisk Manufacturing Co. But he had to retire because of ill health, and he died in Downey, California, on 22 June 1926. Emerson received 14 U.S. patents.

EMERSON (label). A record produced by the Emerson Phonograph Co. of New York from 1916 (first advertised in May); it was a seven-inch disc selling for $.25. There was also a 5 1/2-inch disc for $.10. A predecessor firm, Emerson Universal Cut Records, had been offering 5 1/2-inch and seven-inch records from October 1915; the discs were obtainable from the Plaza Music Co., 16 W. 20th St., New York. In 1918 there was also a nine-inch record, selling at $.75, and in 1919 a 10-inch disc selling at $.85. Prices rose in the post-war inflation, but quality was good and was maintained. In June 1919 the nine-inch discs were sold as "Hits of the Day." Important artists were signed, including Eddie Cantor in 1920. But the firm was overextended, and in 1920 the label virtually ceased. However, the company reorganized in 1922 and resumed issues. In 1924 the label passed to the **Scranton Button Works**, which continued to release records until 1927. The Emerson material was dance, popular vocal, and some jazz. Eubie Blake, Fletcher Henderson, and Rosa Henderson were among the performers.

During its peak years, Emerson produced a number of subsidiary labels: **Amco, Clover, Medallion, Symphonola,** and **Wise.** [Andrews*; Blacker 1989; Rust 1978.]

EMERSON PHONOGRAPH CO. A firm established in 1915 by Victor Hugo Emerson, who became its president, at 120 Broadway, New York. Richard D. Wychoff was treasurer and Robert Miles Bracewell was secretary. A deal with Pathé Frères enabled Emerson to produce six-inch discs from Pathé's recorded repertoire. The company also contracted to have its phonographs made, under the tradenames Electrola and Ford.

In October 1915 there was advertising for 5 1/2 inch discs at $.10 and seven-inch discs at $.25, with the promise of future recordings by Enrico Caruso, John McCormack, Mischa Elman, and Titta Ruffo. Those future discs—made by Emerson—were described as Emerson Universal Cut Records, capable of being played laterally or vertically. Ten-inch discs appeared in May 1916, at which time the firm's address was 3 W. 35th St., New York. Discs of six-inch diameter were issued in November 1916. Sales were good, although there were also problems for the company. Emerson was sued by Columbia Graphophone Co. in 1916 for infringement of the Jones patents (Emerson was eventually cleared of the charge, by the U.S. District Court, in December 1919). There were indications that the firm was too heavily invested.

A new line of foreign language records appeared in December 1917, selling for $.35. In January 1918 new recording laboratories were opened at 362 Fifth Ave., directed by Arthur Bergh. New series continued to appear, to handle hits of the day, religious, operatic, and folk repertoires. Gold Seal records were offered in September 1919, and Premier Records in October (for bands, opera, and classical instrumental works). New factories opened in 1920, in Framingham, on Long Island, and in Chicago. The firm described itself as the third-largest record manufacturer in the world.

Nevertheless, in December 1920 it was reported that the two Emerson Phonograph Corporations—one registered in New York and one in Delaware—had been put into the hands of receivers. A reorganization developed, and was made final in May 1922. The new company was owned by B. Abrams and Rudolph Kanarak, with an office at 206 Fifth Ave., New York. The only break in record releases was from May 1922 through August 1922; production and sales resumed in September. There was another move, reported in October 1922, to 105–111 W. 20th St., New York. A new subsidiary was chartered in January 1924, Emerson Recording Laboratories, Inc., to make phonographs and records for others. "Race records" were advertised in April 1924. Worldwide distribution was reported for Emerson discs.

The incursion of radio dimmed the bright prospects for Emerson records, but a new firm was created in October 1924 to confront the situation: Emerson Radio and Phonograph Corp. The record interests were subsequently sold to the **Scranton Button Works**, Scranton, Pennsylvania. Emerson has remained in the radio business to the present time, most recently under the name Emerson Radio Corp. It is located in North Bergen, New Jersey. [Andrews*.]

EMI, LTD. A firm incorporated in Britain on 20 Apr 1931 through a merger of the Gramophone Co. (encompassing HMV and Zonophone records), the Columbia Graphophone Co., Ltd. (encompassing Columbia, Parlophone, and Regal records), and the Marconiphone Co., Ltd. This amalgamation resulted in the world's largest recording organization, Electrical and Musical Industries, having capital assets in excess of £6.5 million and control of 50 factories in 19 countries. The U.S. Columbia Phonograph Co. was not included. Earlier agreements between the Gramophone Co. and Victor remained in force, allowing each to issue discs from the other's matrices. The founding directors of EMI, Ltd., were Alfred Clark, Louis Sterling, John Broad, George Croydon (Lord Marks), Edward De Stein, Michael George Herbert, David Sarnoff, and Edmund Trevor Lloyd Williams. Clark was the first chairman of the board, and he was also managing director from 1931 to 1939, and president in 1946.

EMI was created in response to the worldwide Depression and its devastating impact on the record industry (*see* DISC, 6). By virtually eliminating real competition, the firm was able to sail through the economic storms of the 1930s. Much initiative was demonstrated in several areas: the **Abbey Road Studios** were opened in 1931, and in the same year EMI's **Alan Dower Blumlein** took out a patent for stereophonic recording. Research in television started in 1934, and a station was established in London in 1935. In 1936 EMI TV sets were on the market.

After World War II, which brought severe air raid damage to EMI installations in London, Hayes, and Liverpool, the firm returned quickly to expansion. It commenced distribution of the American MGM label in Britain in 1948, and continued important research and development (e.g., the BTR 1 tape recorder of the later 1940s, based on the **Magnetophon**; redesigned in 1950 as the BTR 2). Curiously the firm lagged behind American labels in acceptance of the long-playing record, and did not release an LP until October 1951 (in France, by Pathé-Marconi). In October 1952 EMI offered its first British LP releases, and 45s as well. The HMV label was slow to convert entirely, and continued to issue 78s until February 1960.

A loosening of the EMI monopoly took place in 1952–1953, as reciprocal agreements with American Columbia and with Victor were terminated. But in 1955 EMI acquired control of Capitol Records, and in 1958 began to distribute Mercury label discs in Britain.

Research in stereophony led to a demonstration in April 1955, and a release of "stereosonic" tapes in October. Professional quality stereo tape recorders were produced for the use of BBC and others, and a smaller stereo machine was put on the general market in 1957.

EMI issued its first Beatles record in October 1962, thus asserting a dominant position in the popular field. An agreement with Melodiya in 1968 allowed selections from the Russian catalog to be issued in Britain on the HMV label.

In 1979 **Thorn-EMI** was formed, and EMI Music Worldwide became its subsidiary, under the chairmanship of Bhaskar Menon. That new conglomerate entered into an agreement with **Japanese Victor Co. (JVC)** in 1980 for cooperative marketing and manufacture. Compact disc releases began in 1984. By September 1989, 20 million CDs a year were coming from the U.K. plant at Swindon, another 20 million from the American plant in Jacksonville, Illinois, and up to 35 million units from Gotemba, Japan (a joint venture with Toshiba). At Uden, Netherlands, the needs of the European market were met with the manufacture of about 30 million CDs per year.

Outstanding reissues on CD of the magnificent 78 and LP repertoire controlled by EMI has been coming forth at a rapid rate. One remarkable LP series, the Record of Singing, was issued from 1977 to 1989. It covered—on 47 LP discs—the history of recorded singing from the 1890s to the 1950s, including some 730 voices.

EMPIRE (label). (I) A British label issued by **Nicole** on subcontract, ca. 1906. [Andrews 1988.]

EMPIRE (label). (II) A record pressed from **Dacapo** masters in 1911–1912, not advertised in trade periodicals. It seems that specific discs chosen by the Empire proprietors were offered to customers who would agree to buy a certain number each year. The firm that produced them was named the Empire Record Co. [Andrews 1990.]

EMPIRE (label). (III) A British disc, its label reading "New Empire Record," drawn from **Edison Bell** masters, issued sometime before 1914. [Andrews*.]

EMPIRE (label). (IV) An issue of the Empire Talking Machine Co. of Chicago, available from May 1917. There were 300 selections in a 48-page catalog of August 1917. A 64-page catalog appeared in January 1918. J.H. Steinmetz was president of the firm, which was located in 1920 at 429 S. Wabash Ave., Chicago. A "universal cut" Empire record went on sale in July 1919, but it was "nevertheless vertical cut and in fact [could] play only on phonographs adapted to play Pathé records" (Rust 1978). From January 1920 Empire releases duplicated those of **Operaphone**, with identical catalog numbers; both Empire and Operaphone were using **Pathé** masters. [Andrews*; Rust 1978.]

EMPIRE (label). (V) A British label produced by the **Globe Record Co., Ltd.**, London, in 1931. The record was a 10-inch "unbreakable, non-inflammable" flexible celluloid product selling for only 1s 6d. Most of the material was dance music from American Paramount, but there were also items from the German Phonycord (including three sides by Marian Anderson). [Rust 1978.]

EMPIRE (label). (VI) A British record produced after 1928 for the Metropolitan chain stores, made from **Piccadilly** masters. [Andrews*.]

ENCLOSURE. A housing, usually of wood, for a **loudspeaker.** *See also* specific types: ACOUSTICAL LABYRINTH; BASS REFLEX BAFFLE; FOLDED HORN; INFINITE BAFFLE.

ENCORE (label). (I) A record made from **Beka** Grand Records masters, sold in Britain before World War I. It had two numbers per 10-inch side. They were really Veni-Vidi-Vici masters, from Beka; and Veni-Vidi-Vici was also seen on labels of British Empire issues. [Andrews*.]

ENCORE (label). (II) An EMI low-cost series of the 1960s, offering reissues from HMV and Columbia.

ENGLISH RECORD CO., LTD. A firm incorporated in London in November 1909, having apparently been in business for some two years previous. The address was 128 High Holborn, then 44 Bedford Row. John Bull records (made mostly from Beka matrices) were the discs issued; there was also a player sold under the name of Erco, made by Carl Lindström GmbH. Business was good in 1911, leading to the establishment of branches throughout Britain and in France. An associated firm, the South East Record Co., Ltd., was registered on 26 Feb 1910, and another associated company, the Irolite Manufacturing Co., Ltd., was incorporated on 7 May 1910. Although nothing illegitimate was done by the company, it acquired a reputation for shady business practices. Its method of sale was to require a contract of agreement to purchase a large number of discs in conjunction with the offer of a free gramophone. Some customers committed themselves to expenditures they could not afford.

The company wound itself up voluntarily in April 1911, reorganized in May 1911 (taking new premises at 209–212 Tottenham Court Road and at Alfred Place), then liquidated in July 1913. [Andrews 1988/2.]

Enhanced recordings. See REPROCESSED STEREO; SONIC RESTORATION OF HISTORICAL RECORDINGS.

Enhanced stereo. See REPROCESSED STEREO; SONIC RESTORATION OF HISTORICAL RECORDINGS.

ENIGMA (label). A leading U.S. independent label, produced by Enigma Entertainment Corp., Culver City, California. The firm also makes the Restless label. In 1988 Enigma acquired Mute, the largest British independent. Capitol is the distributor for all these discs, which offer classical and popular material.

ENVELOPE. (I) A graphic representation of a sound wave, showing changes in amplitude.

ENVELOPE. (II) In Britain, another name for a record sleeve during the 78 rpm era.

EPIC (label). A record marketed since 1953 in America under an agreement between Philips and Columbia. The offerings are both classical and popular. One release of special interest was The Four Seasons by Darius Milhaud, conducted by the composer (#BC 1069; 1960). Thriller, an album by Michael Jackson, has posted more sales than any other LP. The compact disc Epic is one of the Sony Corp. labels.

EQUALIZATION (EQ). The attempt to compensate in record playback for alterations made during the recording process. Such alterations are made in the recording studio to add emphasis or reduce emphasis in certain parts of the audio frequency spectrum (to achieve flat overall characteristics), to minimize distortion, and to limit surface noise. A plot of the relative emphasis given to the various frequencies is known as the recording curve or recording characteristic. The reduction is accomplished by lowering or raising the signal level in the appropriate segment(s) of the spectrum. Discs in the electric era, from 1925, were made with treble emphasis, the bass range being restricted to save groove space. Thus the compensation intended by the equalization circuits is to restore the original characteristics of the signal, eliminating the artificial boost in the treble and enhancing the low frequencies that had been attenuated.

Standard playback equalization circuits exist for discs, established by the Recording Industry Association of America (RIAA), and for tapes, established by the National Association of Broadcasters (NAB). Customized sound characteristics may be attained with a device known as a variable equalizer, which allows the operator to increase or decrease the volume level of selected portions of the spectrum. A simple form of equalizer is the tone control device that appears on most radios and disc or tape players; it simply blocks high frequencies to enhance the bass effect. A more refined control, found on high-fidelity receivers, allows the separate increase or decrease of treble and bass ranges. In sophisticated equipment, the multichannel graphic equalizer is typical.

A 10-channel equalizer, with each switch controlling an octave of the spectrum, provides what "may be the best compromise between flexibility in results and complexity in use" (Lane). But devices with controls over narrower bands are useful in professional installations and for sonic restoration. The most complex devices are the **parametric equalizers** allowing three separately adjustable variables in each channel: level, frequency, and shape.

In tape recording the treble and bass are both reduced, and equalization requires boosting both segments of the range. This is usually accomplished by standard circuits in the playback recorder, but there are problems when the recording equalization pattern does not correspond to that of the player. The ideal situation is one in which the tape is recorded and played back on the same machine. High quality playback recorders have equalization controls, based on NAB standards, to compensate for differences between the recording curve and the **playback curve.**

The term "pre-equalization" is used to describe the alterations made during recording, and "post-equalization" is used to describe the compensatory devices in the playback equipment. Record manufacturers did not follow a uniform pattern of pre-equalization until the 1950s, when the RIAA introduced standards (1953) for turnover and rolloff. "Turnover" refers to the frequency in the bass range below which playback boost is necessary (500 Hz; 0 dB reference = 1 KHz). "Rolloff" refers to the rate of treble attenuation needed in playback; it is given in dB at 10 KHz. Modern receivers and amplifiers have a single control to compensate for RIAA normal turnover and rolloff. Research has established the correct playback equalizer settings for records made by many 78 and LP labels that did not conform to RIAA standards. A table of recommended turnover and rolloff settings by label is given in SONIC RESTORATION OF HISTORICAL RECORDINGS; another appears in Powell 1989. [Klinger*; Lane 1982; McWilliams 1979; Powell 1989.] See also DE-EMPHASIS; PRE-EMPHASIS; RECORDING PRACTICE; SONIC RESTORATION OF HISTORICAL RECORDINGS.

ERASE HEAD. The device in a **tape deck** that removes any previous pattern on a recorded tape. When the recorded tape has passed the erase head, the sum of the particles' local magnetic fields is zero at any point, and the tape is said to be neutralized or demagnetized. This neutralization is more difficult with metallic tapes than with ferric-oxide tapes, requiring additional field strength in the erase mechanism. [Klinger*.]

ERATO (label). One of the **WCI** labels, located at 46 Kensington Court, London. Among the artists heard on Erato are Daniel Barenboim, Mstislav Rostropovich, and John Eliot Gardner.

ERWIN, PEE WEE, 1913–1981. American jazz trumpeter, born in Falls City, Nebraska on 30 May 1913. He grew up in Kansas City, where he won many amateur contests when he was eight years old, and appeared on a radio program. Then he played locally in Falls City, and toured in vaudeville. He worked with various bands, including Joe Haymes, Isham Jones, and Freddy Martin. In 1935–1936 he was with Benny Goodman and Ray Noble, in 1937–1939 with Tommy Dorsey. In the 1940s Erwin had his own group and also worked with many others, becoming one of the most acclaimed Dixieland performers. He was seen on several television shows in the 1960s, and continued playing in public into the 1970s. He died on 20 June 1981.

Erwin's first records were with the Joe Haymes band, in 1932. *Joe Haymes and His Orchestra: 1932–35* (Bluebird #AXM2–5552) offers a good selection of Erwin's work. He did some fine solos in August 1934 for Decca, while with Isham Jones, notably "Tiger Rag" (#262) and "Dallas Blues" (#569). He appeared on many of the LP reissues of Benny Goodman. Jazzology and Qualtro issued albums of his performances in 1980–1981. [Vaché 1978.]

ETTING, RUTH, 1903–1978. American popular singer, born in David City, Nebraska, on 23 Nov 1903. She made her debut in Chicago in 1925, then moved to New York. Her first record was "Nothing Else to Do" (Columbia #580–D; 1926). Etting became renowned in *Ziegfeld Follies of 1927*, and made a successful recording of

"Shakin' the Blues Away" from that show (Columbia #1113). She was also in the *Ziegfeld Follies of 1931*, and recorded its "Shine On Harvest Moon" (Banner #32229). "Love Me or Leave Me" was a popular release of 1929 (Columbia #1680–D). Etting was popular on radio, and made a number of motion pictures. She was also acclaimed in London appearances. She remained active through the 1940s.

An LP reissue, *The Original Recordings of Ruth Etting* was released by Columbia (#ML-5050). A film based on Etting's life, *Love Me or Leave Me*, starred Doris Day (1955).

EUFON. A hornless portable gramophone, advertised in *TMN* in April 1909. It weighed only 17 pounds, and operated with single-spring or double-spring motor.

EVANS, BILL, 1929–1980. American jazz pianist, born William John Evans in Plainfield, New Jersey, on 16 Aug 1929. He played violin and flute as well as piano as a child, and at age 16 had formed a band with his brother. He played with various ensembles in the 1950s. In 1956 he made his first recording, with Tony Scott's band. Evans signed with the Riverside label in 1957, and recorded with Charlie Mingus; in 1958 he teamed with Miles Davis. Evans helped to develop the sophisticated post-bebop jazz idiom.

His most acclaimed recordings were *Conversations with Myself* (Verve #68526; 1963, in which he overdubbed his own original performance twice, giving a trio effect), and *Further Conversations with Myself* (Verve #68727; 1967). Other outstanding discs were "Peri's Scope" (Riverside #315; 1959), and the albums *Explorations* (Riverside CD reissue #VDJ-1527; 1961), *How My Heart Sings* (Riverside #463; 1962), and *Paris Concert* (Elektra; 1979, his final recording). There have been numerous CD reissues. He died in New York on 15 Sep 1980.

EVEREADY MIXED QUARTET. A vocal group that recorded in the late 1920s, consisting of Beulah Gaylord Young, Rose Bryant, **Charles Harrison**, and **Wilfred Glenn**.

EVERLY BROTHERS. An American rock duo, consisting of brothers Don Everly and Phil Everly. Both were born in Brownie, Kentucky; Don Everly on 1 Feb 1937, and Phil Everly on 19 Jan 1939. Each sings and plays the guitar. After finishing high school, they moved to Nashville and played in clubs, finally gaining enough attention to begin recording in 1957. They had an early hit with "Bye Bye Love" (Cadence #1315; 1957), on the charts for 20 weeks, presenting a style that blended the high-pitched close harmony of country singing with rhythm & blues. "Wake up Little Susie" was another 1957 single on the charts (Cadence #1337). Between 1957 and 1965 the Everlys made 39 chart singles and seven chart albums for Cadence and Warner Brothers. In 1973 they gave a farewell concert, but returned to the stage 10 years later and have continued to perform. *The Fabulous Style of the Everly Brothers* (Cadence #CLP 3040; 1980) was on the charts for 11 months. *Born Yesterday* was an acclaimed Mercury/PolyGram album of 1986, featuring the title track song by Don Everly. Arista, Ace, RCA, and other labels have issued most of the Everly output in about 25 compact discs.

EVERYBODYS (label). A New York record from Everybodys (*sic*) Record, Inc., with about 85 releases in 1925. Most of the material—dance and popular music—was from **Emerson** and **Paramount**. A firm named Bristol and Barber and Co., Inc., of 3 East 11th St., New York, handled promotion and sales. [Andrews*; Rust 1978.]

EXCELSIOR PHONOGRAPH CO. A New York firm founded in November 1897. It sold the Excelsior cylinder player and brown-wax cylinders. In 1897 it acquired the plant operated by Roger Harding at 18 E. 22nd St., retaining Harding as manager. William F. Hooley replaced him in August 1898. In advertising of June 1898, the firm's name was Excelsior and Musical Phonograph Co., with the address 57 W. 24th St. By January 1899 the firm had relocated to 5 East 14th St. At that time the artists on Excelsior included W. Paris Chambers, S. H. Dudley, William F. Hooley, and Cal Stewart. There were also songs in German and Italian, and there was material for banjo, bells, and cello. The Excelsior Band and Orchestra was a featured ensemble. [Martel 1988.]

EXHIBITION SOUNDBOX. The assembly used by the Gramophone & Typewriter Co. from 1901, based on the Jones soundbox of 1899. It was identifiable by the tension-nut at the top. The device had many imitators in several countries. [*TMR* 33 (1975) gives 11 illustrations of authentic and spurious Exhibitions.]

Exponential horn. *See* HORN.

Extended play discs. *See* LONG PLAYING RECORDS.

EXTERNAL PROCESSOR LOOP. A control found in **amplifiers**; it connects other components, such as equalizers, sound decoders, and so forth.

FAITH, PERCY, 1908–1976. Canadian conductor, born in Toronto on 7 Apr 1908. He played violin and piano, accompanied silent movies, and then arranged for bands and for the Canadian Broadcasting Corp. Faith appeared on many radio programs with his orchestra, a large group that emphasized strings. In 1950 he became a conductor and arranger for Columbia Records, and later went to Hollywood to work in various studios. Faith won Grammys for his single "Theme from A Summer Place" (Columbia #41490; 1960), and for the album *Romeo and Juliet* (Columbia #CD 31004; 1969). *Themes for Young Lovers* was on the charts for 35 weeks (Columbia #CL 2023; 1963). Among his other popular recordings were "Song from Moulin Rouge" (Columbia 39944; 1953) and the soundtrack album from *Love Me or Leave Me*, the Doris Day film about the life of Ruth Etting (Columbia #CL-710; 1955). He continued recording through the 1960s, with a total of 19 chart albums.

FAMOUS (label). (I) A 10-inch record issued by Lugton & Co. in London, from 1912 or 1913 to 1914. **Blum & Co., Ltd.,** registered the trademark (September 1912), transferring it, with other Blum trademarks, to Columbia Graphophone Co., Ltd., in September 1916. More than 400 items were released. [Andrews 1988/10.]

FAMOUS (label). (II) An American label issued by the **New York Recording Laboratories,** Port Washington, Wisconsin, from 1921 to 1924. Material was blues and jazz, derived from **Paramount.** Riverside acquired the rights to reissue Famous records in 1953. [Rust 1978.]

FAMOUS SINGERS RECORDS, INC. A New York firm, located at 269 W. 36th St. It issued 10-inch double-sided discs at $.85 in 1921. A novelty dance series of records by Charles K. Davis and his orchestra included four waltzes and eight other dance pieces. Davis was music director for the firm, and John Stoge was in charge of recording. [Andrews*; Rust 1978.]

FANTASIA. An animated motion picture produced by Walt Disney in 1940, using **multitrack recording** for the soundtrack. The Philadelphia Orchestra, conducted by Leopold Stokowski, was recorded at the center of a cluster of polygonal enclosures with rear walls of sound absorbent material. Each enclosure had a separate microphone, so that instrumental groupings were individually recorded. There were also distant microphones to catch the entire orchestra. Engineers manipulated the separate tracks to create the first stereo soundtrack. In the theater the loudspeakers were placed at all sides of the audience, giving an early "surround sound" effect.

FANZINE. The term given to a periodical issued by a "fan" of pop/rock music, informally produced, and circulated to a small group with similar interests. The first of the genre was *Crawdaddy*, founded in 1964 by Paul Williams and distributed at first around Cambridge, Massachusetts. It soon became a professionally produced nationwide journal, selling over

20,000 copies per issue. *Mojo Navigator Rock and Roll News* began publication in 1966, owned by Greg Shaw and David Harris. It was issued for only two years, circulating primarily in the San Francisco area. Greg Shaw then produced *Who Put the Bomp*, which was successful from 1969 to 1979, achieving a circulation of 30,000. Of the 500 or so fanzines that have entered the marketplace, only a few have gained serious recognition: *Crawdaddy*, *Who Put the Bomp*, and *Transoceanic Trouser Press* (1974–1984; emphasizing punk rock). [Denisoff 1986.] *See also* SOUND RECORDING PERIODICALS.

FARRAR, GERALDINE, 1882–1967. American soprano, born on 28 Feb 1882 in Melrose, Massachusetts. At age 17 she went to study in Europe, and in 1901 she made her debut as Marguerite with the Berlin Opera. Then she had three seasons with the Monte Carlo Opera, 1903–1906. Her Metropolitan Opera debut, as Juliette, was on 26 Nov 1906. She remained with the company for 16 years. Her last public appearance was a Carnegie Hall recital in 1931. She died in Ridgefield, Connecticut, on 11 Mar 1967.

Farrar's greatest roles were Cio Cio San, which she sang opposite Enrico Caruso in the American premiere of *Madama Butterfly* (11 Feb 1907) and about a hundred more times, and Carmen. She began to record for G & T in Berlin in 1904, singing "Aime-moi" by Bemberg (#33457), the *Manon* Gavotte (#43568), and other arias in French, German, and Italian. Her first *Butterfly* numbers were for Victor in 1907–1909, and her first Carmen arias were also for Victor, in 1914–1915 (she had done Micaela's aria earlier). Other fine discs, among the 80 or so she did for Victor, were "La ci darem la mano" with Antonio Scotti (#89015; 1908) and the *Boheme* Quartet with Enrico Caruso, Scotti, and Gina Viafora (#054204; 1908). [Moran 1960.]

FARRELL, EILEEN, 1920–   . American opera and concert singer, known also for her renditions of popular songs; born in Willimantic, Connecticut, on 13 Feb 1920. She made radio and concert appearances in the 1940s, touring the U.S. and Latin America. She was heard in the Decca album of Sigmund Romberg's *Up in Central Park* (#A-395; 1945). Following a great success in her New York recital of 1950, she was chosen by Arturo Toscanini to sing in his performance of the Beethoven Ninth Symphony. She was with the Metropolitan Opera from 1960 to 1966, and was a professor of music at Indiana University from 1971 to 1980. She won a Grammy for her recording of the Wagner "Wesendonck Songs" in 1962.

Farrell's affinity for popular love songs was demonstrated in Columbia LP albums #CL 1653 (*Here I Go Again*) and #CL-1739 (*This Fling Called Love*). In 1990 she came out of retirement to produce two remarkable compact discs: *Eileen Farrell Sings Harold Arlen* (Reference #RR-30CD) and *Eileen Farrell Sings Rodgers and Hart* (Reference #RR-32CD). She was one of the earliest and finest of the operatic divas to create a musically convincing **crossover** style.

FARRELL, MARGUERITE E., 1888–1951. American soprano and vaudeville artist, born on 16 Sep 1888 in Providence, Rhode Island. She performed Shakespeare and also did musical shows, and appeared in 28 operas in a single season for Oscar Hammerstein's company. She turned to operetta and starred in *Step This Way* (1916). Farrell made records for three labels: Columbia and Victor, 1916–1917, and Edison, 1921–1922. Her first disc was "Out of a City of Six Million People" (Columbia #A-1870; 1915). A popular one came soon after: "Along the Rocky Road to Dublin" (Columbia #A1920; 1916). Later that year she made her best-selling record, "If I Knock the 'L' out of Kelly" from *Step This Way* (Columbia #A2040; 1916). "To the Strains of That Wedding March" was her first Edison Diamond Disc (#50769; 1921). One of her finest renditions was "I Certainly Must Be in Love" (Edison Diamond Disc #51006; 1922). Her last records date from 1923. She died in Buffalo, New York, on 26 Jan 1951. [Rust 1989; Walsh 1960/3.]

FAVOR, EDWARD M., ca. 1857–1936. American tenor, one of the first professional artists to make records. His "high, piping, typically Irish voice" (Walsh) suited his preferred repertoire of Irish ditties. He recorded comic songs and show tunes in the early 1890s to about 1914, with the major output on Edison cylinders beginning in 1898 with "I.O.U." (#6101). Koenigsberg lists 85 cylinders to 1912, including such enduring favorites as "Who Threw the Overalls in Mrs. Murphy's Chowder" (#7697; 1901) and "I Love My Wife, But Oh, You Kid!" (#1020; 1909). His most popular record was "Fol-The-Rol-Lol" (Edison #9142; 1905). Favor also recorded four songs for Victor in 1906. He continued singing on Broadway until 1934, when he was 78 years old. [Koenigsberg 1987; Walsh 1942/3 (with corrections in Walsh 1952/5).]

FAVORITA. A German cylinder phonograph marketed in England in 1906. [Illustration in Chew 1981.]

FAVORITE (label). A lateral-cut German record, widely distributed in Europe. It was issued by Schallplatten Fabrik-Favorite GmbH in Hanover from 1906 to 1913, and then was absorbed by Carl Lindström. The repertoire was highly varied, covering all popular formats and instruments, from bagpipers to coon songs. Seven-inch, 10-inch, and 12-inch discs were produced. A Favorite record player was also marketed. [Kinnear 1985.]

FAVORITE TALKING MACHINE CO. A New York firm, established in 1916 at 438 Broadway. It made the Favorite line of disc players, in seven models.

FAY HOME RECORDERS, LTD. A British firm established on 15 Mar 1931, with offices at 121 Victoria St., London. Incorporating in November 1932, it was re-named the Fay Radio & Recorders, Ltd. The company was formed to manufacture devices to permit the making of home recordings on existing gramophones, pursuant to a patent application of Hugh Patrick Fay. A workable product resulted, using an acoustic horn or a microphone, with the sound reproduced on a thin disc. However, there was insufficient capital behind the venture, and Fay closed the business in 1933. [Andrews 1974/5.]

FCC. See FEDERAL COMMUNICATIONS COMMISSION (FCC).

FEDERAL (label). An American record, affiliated with the King label, issued in 1950–1963. It offered rhythm & blues, jazz, and popular vocal groups. [Rotante 1971.]

FEDERAL COMMUNICATIONS COMMISSION (FCC). A U.S. federal agency established in 1934, with authority to regulate radio and television, insuring that broadcasts are in the public interest. While the FCC has no direct control over recordings, it has been able to exert some slight influence on popular song lyrics, endeavoring to expunge more sexual themes and vocabulary. Most of the commission's efforts in this area were concentrated in the 1960s. See also DRUG LYRICS; SEXUALLY ORIENTED LYRICS.

FEDERAL CYLINDER PROJECT. A major program of the Archive of Folk Culture in the Library of Congress, which owns one of the largest collections of field cylinder recordings in the world. In 1979 the Library of Congress inaugurated the project, intending to preserve and duplicate wax cylinder recordings, document and preserve cylinder collections, and disseminate the results to the public. Engineers Robert Carneal and John Howell supervised the delicate task of making tapes from the cylinders. Publication of the inventory began in 1984 (see the Bibliography).

FEDERAL PHONOGRAPH CO. A firm incorporated in Albany, New York, in June 1922 with $100,000 capitalization, originally named Federal Record Corp. It succeeded the Indestructible Phonographic Record Co. of Albany. Some Indestructible cylinders appeared as "Federal" during 1917–1922. Records of dance and popular music were issued on the Federal label. J. P. O'Brien was manager in November 1922. The last reference to the company was in March 1924. [Andrews*.]

FEEDBACK. In a sound system, the return of a fraction of the output signal to the input circuit. It may be positive (increasing the output) or negative (decreasing the output). In most cases feedback is an undesirable distortion, but some rock performers have made deliberate use of it, for example, Jimi Hendrix. *See also* ACOUSTIC FEEDBACK; NEGATIVE FEEDBACK.

FEEDFORWARD. The process of mixing a fraction of the input signal in an **amplifier** with a small amount of the output signal, inverted in phase. This mixing cancels both portions, leaving only the **distortions**, which can then be amplified and subtracted from the final output. *See also* NEGATIVE FEEDBACK.

FEUERMANN, EMANUEL, 1902–1942. Austrian cellist, born in Kolomea, Galicia, on 22 Nov 1902. He made his debut at the age of 11 in Vienna, and when he was 16 years old became a faculty member in the Conservatory at Cologne. He was appointed professor at the Hochschule für Musik, Berlin, in 1929. Fleeing from the Nazis, he made a world tour in 1934–1935, making an American debut with the Chicago Symphony Orchestra on 6 Dec 1934. He remained in the U.S. until his death on 25 May 1942, residing in New York.

Feuermann's commercial recordings were made between December 1921 and September 1941. He worked for Parlophon and Telefunken in Germany during 1921–1932, then recorded in London for Columbia beginning in 1934. During 1934 and 1936 he also recorded in Tokyo for Nipponophone. His first American recordings were for Victor in 1939. Among his important discs are the earliest recording of the Dvořák Concerto, made with members of the Berlin State Opera Orchestra under Michael Taube (Parlophone #10856–58; 1928 and #11071; 1929); the Brahms Double Concerto, with Jascha Heifetz and the Philadelphia Orchestra under Eugene Ormandy (Victor #18132–35; 1939); *Schelomo* with Leopold Stokowski and the Philadelphia Orchestra (Victor #17336–38; 1949); and a brilliant series of trio works by Brahms and Beethoven performed with Heifetz and Artur Rubinstein in 1941. [Samuels 1980.]

FEWKES, JESSE WALTER, 1850–1930. American ethnologist, born in Newton, Massachusetts, on 14 Nov 1850. After earning a Ph.D. from Harvard University in 1877, he studied in Germany. He taught at Harvard, then became chief of the Bureau of American Ethnology. Fewkes carried out extensive field work, notably among North American Indian tribes. Working among the Zuni and Passamaquoddy Indians in 1890, he made the first phonograph records for ethnological purposes. He died on 31 May 1930. [Fewkes 1890/1; Fewkes 1890/2.] *See also* FIELD RECORDINGS.

ffrr. *See* FULL FREQUENCY RANGE RECORDING.

FIEDLER, ARTHUR, 1894–1979. American conductor and violinist, born in Boston on 17 Dec 1894. His father and uncle played the violin in the Boston Symphony Orchestra. He studied in Berlin, then returned to join the Boston Symphony himself, playing violin, viola, and keyboard instruments. In 1929 he began to conduct free open-air summer concerts in Boston, featuring a light classical and popular music repertoire. In 1930 he became conductor of the Boston Pops Orchestra, and remained at its helm until his death, in Brookline, Massachusetts, on 10 July 1979. He was awarded the Presidential Medal of Freedom in 1977.

Fiedler made more than 150 Victor 78 rpm records with the Pops Orchestra (waltzes, marches, overtures, and other light fare), helping to bring the symphonic sound into the lives of persons who were uncomfortable with the standard classical repertoire. His recordings continued on LP, where he compiled a list of more than 75 discs.

FIELD RECORDINGS. Recordings of orally-transmitted music made on site, that is, in the "field" where it naturally occurs. The earliest such recordings were made by **Jesse Walter Fewkes**, an anthropologist who studied the songs of the Zuni and Passamaquoddy American Indians in 1890. His cylinders—made, like most early field cylinders, on the Edison Perfected Phonograph—were the basis for research (by B.I. Gilman and others) into the native melodies. His associate Frances Densmore made numerous recordings and carried out most of the definitive studies of the North American Indian repertoire. Early field recordings in Europe were made by Béla Vikár, of Hungarian folksingers, in 1892. He was followed by composer-ethnologists **Béla Bartók** and Zoltan Kodály, who recorded and analyzed a wide range of folk music in Hungary and (present-day) Romania. By 1912 Bartók had made more than 1,000 cylinders, which he gave to the Budapest Ethnographic Museum.

The Phonogramm-Archiv in Vienna (1899) and its counterpart, the **Berlin Phonogramm-Archiv** (1905), became major depositories of these recordings. The Berlin institution had the benefit of connection with distinguished research scholars **Carl Stumpf** and Erich von Hornbostel (director from 1905), who led the project of organizing, analyzing, and copying the folk materials that accumulated. Stumpf made the first records of Asian music in 1901, when the Siamese court orchestra performed in Berlin. Other non-Western music was inscribed in Australia, as Charles Baldwin Spencer recorded aboriginal songs, a project pursued later by **Percy Grainger**.

Musik des Orients, a set of 12 78 rpm records, was issued by Odeon and Parlophone in 1931; it consisted of material edited by von Hornbostel from the Berlin Archiv. Excerpts from this demonstration collection were issued by Ethnic Folkways in 1963 on two LPs.

Among the major American collections of field recordings are those at the **Archives of Traditional Music**, Indiana University, and the **American Folklife Center**.

FIELDS, ARTHUR, 1888–1953. American baritone, born in Philadelphia on 6 Aug 1888. He began singing at age 15 at Coney Island (New York City), traveled with a minstrel show, and appeared in vaudeville. The first of his thousands of recordings (many under pseudonyms) was "Along Came Ruth" (Victor #17637; Columbia #A1612; 1914). He worked for Edison from 1917 to 1928, and made some of his best recordings on that label: "Ja-Da" and a stuttering song, "Oh Helen." Fields took part in a number of the Edison **tone tests**. During World War I he was in uniform as an Army recruiter, and recorded to great effect songs associated with the conflict: "Oh! How I Hate to Get Up in the Morning" (Victor #18489; 1918) and "How

Ya Gonna Keep 'em Down on the Farm?". In the 1920s Fields recorded on numerous labels, among them Grey Gull, Radiex, Madison, National Music Lover, Phantasie, Harmony, Romeo, and Melva. Later he turned to radio, and to writing songs and hymns. He died in Largo, Florida, on 29 Mar 1953. [Walsh 1953/6–8.]

FIELDS, GRACIE, 1898–1979. English singer, actress, and comedienne, born Gracie Stansfield in Rochdale, Lancashire, on 9 Jan 1898. She began appearing on stage as a child, and was in a London revue at age 17. Fame arrived with a starring role in *Mr. Tower of London*, in which she did more than 4,000 performances from 1918 to 1925. After many successful revues she turned to film, and was seen in the successful *Sally in Our Alley* (1931). Her later career included stage, screen, and worldwide entertainment of troops during World War I. She was designated Commander of the British Empire in 1935.

Fields' first recordings to be issued were on HMV in 1928, beginning with "Because I Love You" (#B-2733). Her records illustrate her comic side: "What Can You Give a Nudist on His Birthday?" (HMV #B8232; 1934) and her way with ballads: "Will You Remember?" (Rex #9117; 1937). One of her popular hits during World War II was "The Biggest Aspidistra in the World," recorded in 1938 (Regal Zonophone #MR-3001). More than 700 songs are listed in Rust. Fields died on 27 Sep 1979. [Rust 1989.]

FIELDS, SHEP, 1910–1981. American Big Band leader, born in Brooklyn on 12 Sep 1910. He began professional work in the early 1930s, in Miami and New York, then directed the touring Veloz & Yolanda Dance Orchestra. In the late 1930s he became established at the Empire Room of the Palmer House hotel in Chicago,, featuring his trademark "rippling rhythm," an introduction to each number accomplished by blowing through a straw into a glass of water at the microphone. Later he had a new style, in which the orchestra had no brass section, but then returned to rippling rhythm. Fields made more than 300 Bluebird records, of which his theme song, "Rippling Rhythm," was one of the most popular (Bluebird #6759; 1936). He died in Los Angeles in February 1981.

FIFTH AVENUE PRESBYTERIAN CHOIR. An ensemble that recorded for Edison ca. 1910, one of the earliest choral groups on record. Featured were Mary Hissem de Moss, Cornelia Marvin, Edward Strong, and Frederic Martin.

FIGNER, FREDERICO. An early promoter of the Edison phonograph in Brazil. He gave demonstrations in Belém in 1891, and in Rio de Janeiro in 1892, using the machine he called the Máquina Figner (it was the Perfected Phonograph). Figner was a pioneer producer of recordings in Brazil (1897). He was an agent for International Zonophone and Casa Edison. In 1909 he acquired Brazilian patent #3465, for double-sided discs, from Odeon, and took legal actions against all other double-sided labels. He also attempted to register this patent in other countries, and was in some cases successful, but the production of double-sided discs had already gone too far for him to have much impact on it.

FIGNER, NIKOLAI, 1857–1918. Russian tenor, born in Kazan on 21 Feb 1857. He was a naval officer when his "voice was discovered" (Slonimsky 1984), and he changed careers. His debut was in Naples in 1882. As a member of the St. Petersburg company he sang in the premiere of *Queen of Spades,* and became famous as Lenski in *Eugene Onegin.* Figner was the most acclaimed Russian tenor of the 19th century. His few discs, made for G & T in St. Petersburg, in 1900–1903, presented him only in Russian songs, French/Italian operas, and duets with his wife, Medea Mey Figner. The records exhibited a voice that was already declining. The best one was "Bianca al par" from *Huguenots* (#022000). [Yankovsky 1990.]

Film music. *See* MOTION PICTURE MUSIC.

FILM SPEED. The rate of film travel in a motion picture, typically 24 frames per second. If the speed is for whatever reason increased, as it is for television in some European countries (to 25 frames per second) the pitch of musical signals is raised significantly, almost a half-tone for each additional frame per second.

FILMOPHONE (label). A British record made by Filmophone Flexible Records, Ltd., London, from ca. 1930 to 1932. The discs were 10 inch, celluloid, light and unbreakable, advertised as particularly suitable for portable phonographs. Repertoire was dance and popular songs. The venture was not successful, because the records tended to warp and the stylus—which had to be a special one—did not ride well in the slim grooves. [Rust 1978; *HN* #32 printed a 1932 label list]

FILTER. An electronic device that removes unwanted frequencies from a sound signal. There are three basic types: (1) a low-pass filter screens all but the lower frequencies; (2) a high-pass filter screens all but the higher frequencies; (3) a band-pass filter allows only a certain range of the **audio frequency** spectrum to pass, screening the lower and higher components. Audio filters are used in **equalization** and to combat **rumble** and **hum** on early discs. [Klinger*.]

FIO RITO, TED, 1900–1971. American Big Band leader and songwriter, born in Newark, New Jersey, on 20 Dec 1900. He began as a pianist, and was with the Ross Gorman band in 1918. In the 1920s he formed his own band, and became established at the Edgewater Beach Hotel in Atlantic City, New Jersey. His sound was sweet if not especially distinctive. Future movie stars Betty Grable and June Haver were vocalists in their younger days. Fio Rito was successful on radio and in several films through the 1930s and 1940s, and became the house leader at Chicago's Chez Paree night club in 1956. In 1970 he led small combos in California and Las Vegas. He died in Scottsdale, Arizona, on 22 July 1971.

Fio Rito recorded primarily for Brunswick, Decca, and Bluebird, beginning with his Atlantic City group in 1929; he made more than 250 records in the next 12 years. His own composition, "Roll Along, Prairie Moon," was one of the favorites (Brunswick #7507; 1935). Another was his theme song, "Rio Rita" (Decca #4258; 1942). His band was innovative in recording dance versions of classical music in 1938, including tunes by Wagner, Offenbach, Saint-Saëns, and Chopin.

FISCHER, EDWIN, 1886–1960. Swiss pianist and conductor, born on 6 Oct 1886 in Basel. He taught piano in Berlin from 1905 to 1914, and from 1931 at the Hochcschule für Musik there. He also conducted in Berlin and in other German cities. In 1942 he returned to Switzerland. He wrote books on Bach and Beethoven, and made important recordings in the 1940s and 1950s. He died on 24 Jan 1960 in Zürich.

Fischer is known for having revived the 18th-century custom of conducting from the keyboard, and for bringing the Bach and Mozart repertoires to the attention of a wide public. He was also acclaimed for his interpretations of Brahms and Beethoven. His first recordings were Duo Art piano rolls, made between 1916 and 1925, including the Brahms Sonata No. 3. On Welte piano rolls he recorded, before 1927, Beethoven, Mozart, and Bach. In October 1931 Fischer made his first commercial discs, a Handel *Chaconne* (HMV #DA4401), the Bach *Chromatic Fantasy and Fugue* (HMV #4403–04), and a Prelude and Fugue from *Wohltemperiertes Klavier*.

From 1933 to 1936 he concentrated on the *Wohltemperiertes Klavier*, completing all 48 preludes and fugues on HMV. He also performed the Bach Concerto No. 1, directing his own chamber orchestra from the keyboard, for HMV (#DB 4420–22; 1933). A notable recording of the Brahms Second Concerto was made with Wilhelm Furtwängler and the Berlin Philharmonic Orchestra for the Russian label Mezhdanarodnya Kniga (#D09883–84; 1942). He collaborated with Elisabeth Schwarzkopf for an LP of Schubert songs in 1952 (Columbia #33CX-1040). On 10 Dec 1954 he made his final recording, the Mozart Concerto No. 20, with Eugen Jochum conducting (Angel #35593).

FISCHER-DIESKAU, DIETRICH, 1925– . German baritone and conductor, born on 28 May 1925 in Zehlendorf, a Berlin suburb. He studied at the Hochschule für Musik until 1942, then was conscripted into military service. A prisoner of war, he was not released until 1947, at which time he resumed his studies at the Hochschule. His opera debut was in 1948 with the Berlin State Opera; he then sang in many European opera houses and gave song recitals. Fischer-Dieskau became a renowned Lieder singer, perhaps the greatest of his generation. A New York recital of Schubert on 2 May 1955 brought critical acclaim. But he continued to sing in opera, doing all the major works in Italian, French, and German, and covering contemporary as well as standard repertoire. He took up conducting in the 1970s, and was heard with the Los Angeles Philharmonic Orchestra, the New Philharmonia Orchestra, and other major ensembles.

Fischer-Dieskau's recordings have been mostly for DG and Angel. They include complete recordings of the principal Mozart, Verdi, and Wagner operas, plus *Lulu* and *Wozzeck*, as well as the B-Minor Mass and the Passions of J.S. Bach. He has made definitive versions of the entire Lieder repertoire. Albums made of Schubert songs (1970) and Brahms songs (1972) won Grammys.

FISH, ROYAL. A popular tenor in opera, oratorio, and concert, and an Edison artist from 1913. His Blue Amberol cylinder "In the Shadow of the Pines" (#2073, a duet with Vernon Archibald) was a favorite; and "On Yonder Rock Reclining" from *Fra diavolo* was a steady seller. He made 15 solo and duet recordings for Edison Diamond Discs, the last in 1929. Fish sang in Edison talking films during 1912–1915, one of which presented a version of the Sextette from *Lucia*. [Walsh 1970/12.]

FISHER, EDDIE, 1928– . American popular vocalist, born in Philadelphia on 10 Aug 1928. He was with several bands in the 1940s, then sang at Grossinger's resort in New York State, leading to an engagement on the Eddie Cantor radio show in 1949. He achieved renown as a singer of ballads and musicals, and though his career was interrupted by military service, he resumed in 1953 and gained stardom on television and in several motion pictures. His major hits included "Oh, My Papa" (Victor #20–5552) and "The Games Lovers Play" (Victor LPM #3726).

FISK UNIVERSITY JUBILEE QUARTET. A group that recorded for Victor from 1910, and for Edison from 1912. On their two Diamond Discs they were identified as the Southern Four. All the singers were connected with Fisk University in Nashville, a traditionally Black institution. Members were John Wesley Work (organizer and leader), Noah Walker Ryder, James A. Myers, and Alfred G. King (later replaced by L.P. O'Hara). There were many later changes in the membership, until the group dissolved ca. 1947.

The quartet was famous for its authentic renditions of Negro spirituals. Victor #16448A, the first 1910 recording, offered "Little David Play on Yo' Harp" and "Shout All Over God's Heaven." There was great success for "Swing Low, Sweet Chariot" (#16453A) and "Golden Slippers" (#16453B). On Edison cylinders they began with "All Over This World" (#4045; 1913) and ended with "Band of Gideon" (#5442; 1927). For Columbia they made two discs as the Fisk University Male Quartette. [Turner 1990; Walsh 1962/10.]

FITZGERALD, ELLA, 1918–. American popular singer, born in Newport News, Virginia, on 25 Apr 1918. In 1934 she attracted attention as a teenager on an "amateur night" at the Apollo Theatre in New York, and was engaged in 1935 by Chick Webb. She made her first records with him: "I'll Chase the Blues Away" (Brunswick #02602; 1935), and "Love and Kisses" (Decca #494; 1936). She and Webb had a great success with "A Tisket, A Tasket" (Decca #1840; 1938) and "Undecided" (Decca #2323; 1939). When Webb died in 1939 she led the band for three years. Having begun as a rather typical pop vocalist, she evolved into a scat singer and jazz artist, while retaining her command of the dulcet ballad repertoire.

Her scat style developed in the 1940s, and her finest work came in the 1950s, especially after she joined the new Verve label. Her series of "songbooks" on individual composers established her in the highest place among American female vocalists. First of those was the *Cole Porter Songbook* (Verve #4001; 1956). Others were devoted to Rodgers and Hart (Verve #4002; 1956), Duke Ellington (Verve #4008/09;

1956), George Gershwin (Verve #4024/29; 1958–1959), Irving Berlin (Verve #4019/20), Harold Arlen (Verve #4057/58; 1960), Jerome Kern (Verve #4060; 1960), and Johnny Mercer (Verve #4067; 1960).

Other remarkable interpretations are found in *Porgy and Bess* (Verve #4011/12; 1958) with Louis Armstrong singing Porgy and Fitzgerald delivering a definitive "Summertime"; and another album with Armstrong, *Ella and Louis* (Verve #4003; 1956), which includes her impeccable renditions of "Nearness of You," and "April in Paris."

Fitzgerald has received 12 Grammys, the first for the *Duke Ellington Songbook*. The 1990 album *All That Jazz* (Pablo #2310–938) is her most recent Grammy winner.

FLAGSTAD, KIRSTEN, 1895–1962. Norwegian dramatic soprano, born in Hamar on 12 July 1895. She made her debut in Oslo on 12 Dec 1913, then sang in Oslo and throughout Scandinavia for 20 years. Her early repertoire was Verdi, Puccini, Weber, and operetta. Substituting in Oslo for an indisposed colleague, she performed Isolde (in German) in 1932; Alexander Kipnis, the King Mark of that evening, was impressed enough to recommend her to Bayreuth, where she sang in 1933 and 1934, establishing herself as a prominent interpreter of Wagnerian roles. On 2 Feb 1935 she sang first at the Metropolitan Opera, as Sieglinde, and went on to great success in the *Ring* operas and as Isolde. Flagstad sang also at Covent Garden and elsewhere in Europe, Chicago, and San Francisco. Lauritz Melchior was the tenor in many of her finest duets, on stage and on disc. Her final appearances were in concert, in New York and at La Scala, in 1955. She then directed the Norwegian Opera from 1958 to 1960. She died in Oslo on 7 Dec 1962.

After making some records in the 1920s for minor Norwegian labels, she worked with Norwegian HMV in 1923. But it was when she began recording for Victor in 1935 that her eminence as a Wagnerian heroine was made apparent. In "Ho-jo-to-ho" (Victor #1726) and "Du bist der Lenz" (Victor #1901) she presented definitive interpretations. Her duets with Melchior, from *Tristan* (Victor #16238–

39;) and *Götterdämmerung* (Victor #17729), brought this music to a wide audience. After semi-retirement during World War II, she returned with a voice of even greater luster and power, and made her greatest recordings for EMI. Those included her Immolation Scene, with Wilhelm Furtwängler conducting (#DB6792–94; 1948), and the 1948 "Liebestod" (#EX291227–30). She sang with Ludwig Suthaus, Furtwängler conducting, in a complete *Tristan* (HMV #RLS 684; 1953). Unfortunately she did not record any of the *Ring* operas in complete form. EMI reissues cover many of the 1930s records (CD #GD87915; 1990) and post-war material (CD #H7–63030–2; 1989). [Dennis 1952.]

FLAMEPHONE. A disc player advertised in Britain in 1923, in which amplification was produced by the "sympathetic pulsation of the fine gas jets" supplied "by ordinary town gas."

FLANGING. In tape recording, a kind of **phasing** effect achieved by slowing the tape movement.

FLAT RESPONSE. The ability of an audio system or audio component to produce a constant dynamic level throughout the **audio frequency** range. In a superior system there is no difference in excess of 4 dB between any one frequency (pitch) and any other. A perfect response, truly flat, shows 0 dB difference from 30 to 20,000 Hz.

FLATT, LESTER RAYMOND, 1914–1979. American country singer and guitarist, born in Overton County, Tennessee, on 28 June 1914. As a mill worker in the 1930s he taught himself to play, and made radio appearances in 1939. He was at the Grand Ole Opry in 1944, with Bill Monroe's Bluegrass Boys. In 1948 he teamed with banjoist Earl Scruggs, formed the Foggy Mountain Boys, and began to make best-selling records for Mercury (to 1951) and then Columbia (1951–1969). "Foggy Mountain Breakdown" (Mercury #6230; 1949) was heard on the soundtrack of the motion picture *Bonnie and Clyde* (1968). The Foggy Mountain Boys

were recognized as the leading country instrumental group of the late 1950s. "Cabin in the Hills" (Columbia #41389; 1959) was one chart disc, followed by "Ballad of Jed Clampett," theme song of the *Beverly Hillbillies* television show (Columbia #42606; 1962), "California Up Tight Band" (Columbia #44294; 1967), and "Nashville Cats" (Columbia #44040; 1967). They toured Europe and Asia before breaking up the act in 1969; Flatt made no best-selling records after that, although he continued to perform with a bluegrass band called Nashville Grass to 1979. He died in Nashville on 11 May 1979.

FLEMING, AMBROSE, *Sir,* **1849–1940.** A British engineer who worked as a consultant for Guglielmo Marconi when the Italian inventor succeeded in transatlantic broadcasting. In 1899 he conducted experiments on the "Edison-effect" and in 1904 he patented the Diode (British #24,850; 1904, and U.S. #803684). Fleming's work was followed by that of **Lee De Forest,** who transformed the Diode into the Audion.

FLEMISH-LYNN PHONOGRAPH CO. A Brooklyn firm established in 1916 at 269 37th St. It manufactured and sold a line of disc players, in nine models, under the name Flemish-Lynn.

FLETCHER-MUNSON EFFECT. A characteristic of human **hearing** that gives the ear variable sensitivity to frequencies, with the result that low frequencies—and less noticeably high frequencies—are perceived to be less loud than they really are. An audio system may endeavor to compensate for this factor by enhancing the projection of those frequencies that are not received naturally at their correct intensity. This is accomplished through **loudness controls** in the amplifiers or receivers. The concept is similar to that of **equalization**, except that it deals with a human imbalance rather than one stemming from the recording/playback process. Fletcher-Munson Curves are graphic representations of frequencies showing which ones are susceptible, and to what degree, to the Fletcher-Munson Effect.

FLETCHER RECORD CO., INC. A New York firm, established by John Fletcher in late 1921 or early 1922 at Creek and Meadow Streets in Queens. Fletcher was vice president of **Operaphone**. He acquired some of the assets of **Remington Phonograph Corp.** in December 1921 and revived its **Olympic** label, which used Operaphone matrices. The firm went bankrupt in December 1923.

FLEXO (label). A San Francisco label produced by the Pacific Coast Record Corp., 1040 Geary St., from December 1929. The discs were flexible and unbreakable, light enough to carry with a portable player; diameters varied from three inches to 16 inches. Flexo repertoire was typical dance music and popular vocals, with some jazz, but it offered nothing sufficiently exceptional to counter the depressed economic conditions of the U.S. when it appeared on the market. The corporation filed for bankruptcy on 8 May 1934. [Cotter 1972; Rust 1978.]

FLONZALEY QUARTET. An ensemble formed and sponsored by Swiss banker Edward J. de Coppet, comprised of Adolfo Betti, first violin; Alfred Pochon, second violin; Ugo Ara, viola; and Iwan d'Archambeau, cello. The quartet first performed publicly in Vienna in 1903, toured Europe, and played in New York in 1905. Until 17 Mar 1929, the date of its last public appearance (Town Hall, New York), the group gave more than 3,000 performances. There were various changes in membership over that 27-year span. The Flonzaley was the first quartet to record extensively.

The quartet recorded exclusively for Victor, beginning on 22 Dec 1913 with the Beethoven Quartet Opus 18 No. 4. It recorded much of the classical and romantic standards, and a number of modern works. Ossip Gabrilowitsch and Harold Bauer were pianists who joined the group in performing quintet literature. A pair of novelty numbers were the last pieces to be recorded, on 3 May 1929: "Turkey in the Straw" and "Sally in Our Alley" (#1569). [Samuels 1987.]

FLORIDA PHONOGRAPH CO. A Jacksonville, Florida, firm established 1890, one of the 33 affiliates of the **North American Phono-**graph Co. J.C. Clarkson represented the company at the **National Phonograph Association** convention of 1890; he was identified as its superintendent.

FLOWER HORN. A type of horn used on gramophones and phonographs, introduced in 1905 by Charles Eichhorn. The name derives from the shape of the horn, but many of those horns also had flower paintings on them.

FLUTTER. A waver in pitch produced by playback equipment. The immediate cause may be fluctuation in **turntable** speed or tape transport speed in a **tape deck**. It may also result from up-and-down movement of the turntable. Flutter is most evident on notes of long duration, especially at upper frequencies, so it is particularly annoying in soprano or flute records. The National Association of Broadcasters (NAB) has a standard for cassette decks, requiring that flutter shall not exceed 0.2 percent. For open-reel recorders the NAB standard varies, with tape speed, from .05 percent to 0.10 percent. *See also* WOW.

FLUTTER ECHO. A multiple **echo** with quick fluctuations.

FM. *See* FREQUENCY MODULATION.

FOLDBACK. A method of cueing performers as they record, by sending signals through their headphones.

FOLDED HORN. A **loudspeaker** designed to channel the signal through a folded path, in order to save cabinet space. While the design may preserve the acoustic characteristics of the straight horn, cross vibrations occur at the bend points. The cross vibrations draw energy from the current flow, thus dimming certain signal frequencies.

FOLEY, RED, 1910–1968. American country singer, born Clyde Julian Foley in Blue Lick, Kentucky, on 17 June 1910. He appeared on the *National Barn Dance* radio program in 1930, and toured with various groups. From 1937 he was heard at the Grand Ole Opry in Nashville, and in 1939 he became the first country artist to have his own network radio program, *Avalon Time*. During the 1940s he was recognized as a preeminent talent, and he had a significant part in creating a wide audience for country music. From 1954 to 1961 he hosted a television program, *Ozark Mountain Jubilee*.

Foley recorded almost entirely for Decca, from 1941. In 1950 he made two chart records: "Chattanooga Shoe Shine Boy" (Decca #46205) and, with Ernest Tubb, "Goodnight, Irene" (Decca #46255). Foley also excelled in the gospel song repertoire, exemplified by his best-selling "Peace in the Valley" (Decca #14573; 1951). His last hit was "The End of the World" (Decca #31194; 1961). Foley died in Ft. Wayne, Indiana, on 19 Sep 1968, while on tour with Grand Ole Opry. He was elected to the Country Music Hall of Fame in 1967.

FOLK MUSIC RECORDINGS. Folk songs of the world were studied primarily as texts prior to 1890. The extra-musical approach began to change when ethnologist **Jesse Walter Fewkes** took an Edison Perfected (cylinder) Phonograph to Maine in 1890 and recorded songs of the Passamaquoddy Indians. Later in the same year Fewkes recorded music of the Zuni and Pueblo Indians of New Mexico. Ethnomusicologists and folklorists began recording tribal groups on cylinder. Many of those cylinder recordings have been transferred to tape and are available in research collections, such as those of the **American Folklife Center** at the Library of Congress and of the **Archives of Traditional Music** at the Indiana University. The Library of Congress administers the **Federal Cylinder Project**, an effort to duplicate cylinders for preservation before they become unplayable. Copies of the recordings are provided to tribal leaders, so that tribal groups are able to hear the music of their ancestors.

Regular use of cylinder machines to collect American folk songs began in the 1920s, when scholars like Robert Winslow Gordon, Martha Beckwith, James Carpenter and Phillips Barry recorded in New England, the South, California, and Jamaica.

From around the turn of the century, record companies like Edison, Columbia, Victor, and the Gramophone Co. began to issue ethnic records of popular and traditional music from all over the world. This genre became an increasing source of record sales. Between 1908 and 1923 Columbia released about 5,000 disc records in their domestic A series and 6,000 records in their foreign E series. For many American immigrants those recordings were links to their home cultures. Ethnic performers were recorded on disc from the 1920s for specialized markets. For example, Cajun musician Joe Falcon was recorded in 1928 by Columbia, with fiddler Dennis McGee and accordionist Amédée Ardoin recorded shortly thereafter. Most labels had a large number of ethnic releases available for different communities.

Among the earlier folk performers who were recorded for the growing "hillbilly" record market were Texas fiddler Alexander Campbell "Eck" Robertson (in 1922; thought to be the earliest country artist on disc), Henry Whittier, George B. Grayson, "Fiddlin John" Carson, Riley Puckett, Buell Kazee, and Charlie Poole. The designation "hillbilly" music came from the name of the group Al Hopkins and the Hillbillies. In the eyes of many, the term "hillbilly" had pejorative connotations, and it has been replaced by the term "old time." (*See* COUNTRY AND WESTERN MUSIC.) A comparable interest was developed by the record labels in **blues music recordings**, which they originally marketed in the 1920s as **race records**.

The folk musicians who were recorded had repertoires consisting of Anglo-American folk songs, minstrel songs, and 19th-century sentimental songs. Often the performers did not know the sources of their material. Two artists of the 1920s rate special mention. They are Uncle Dave Macon and Bradley Kincaid. Macon was the first star of the *Grand Ole Opry* show, and a recording artist for Vocalion from 1924. His material consisted of Anglo-American ballads, minstrel songs, and vaudeville songs. Bradley Kincaid was an early folk singer and folklorist; he recorded for Gennett, Silvertone and Supertone.

In August 1927, Victor talent scout Ralph Peer made a notable recording trip to Bristol, Tennessee. He discovered **Jimmie Rodgers**, the "father of country music," and the highly influential **Carter Family**. The Carter Family went on to record over 300 sides for Victor, the American Record Corp., Decca, and Columbia over the next 13 years. Their material consisted of old time mountain and religious songs, such as "Wildwood Flower," "Keep on the Sunnyside," and "Will the Circle Be Unbroken."

During the 1930s, with commercial record sales in decline, most of the recording of traditional music was non-commercial, done by folklorists in the field. Starting in 1925, Robert Winslow Gordon, later head of the Library of Congress Archive of Folk Song, began to record American folk songs and narratives. **John A. Lomax** and his son **Alan Lomax**, who were later heads of the Archive of Folk Song, collected and created what was probably the largest and most diverse collection of traditional American music. They made over 3,000 recordings of ballads, worksongs, religious songs, blues, cowboys songs, and others They are also credited with making the first recordings of folk titan **Leadbelly**. Alan Lomax has continued to collect materials into the 1990s. His material has been released by the Library of Congress, Prestige International, Columbia, Atlantic, and Caedmon, among others. His collections provide insights into all kinds of traditional music both in the United States and abroad. The holdings of the Library of Congress **Archive of Folk Culture** (the former Archive of Folk Song) include almost 35,000 hours of recordings. More than 80 commercial recordings were made from the material in the archive. The archive's collection contains fieldwork recordings by important ethnomusicologists, collectors, and folklorists. Collections of music recorded by Sidney Robertson Cowell and Herbert Halpert reside there.

The popularity of traditional folk music surged during the 1940s. One important category of performers was the new minstrel, appearing in a refined concert environment, exemplified by **John Jacob Niles**, **Richard Dyer-Bennet**, and **Burl Ives**. Niles collected actively in the South and authored a number of song collections. He wrote the classic folk-like songs "I Wonder as I Wander" and "Black is the Color of My True Love's Hair." Niles recorded for Asch, Tradition, Folkways, and other labels.

Billing himself as the "Twentieth-Century Minstrel," Richard Dyer-Bennet combined his rich voice with a large repertoire of Anglo-American ballads. His recordings can be found on Asch, Decca, Disc, Mercury, Stinson, and Vox, as well as his own label.

The name Burl Ives was almost synonymous with folk singer for many Americans in the 1940s and 1950s. His songs, including titles like "The Blue-Tailed Fly" and "The Erie Canal," came from a multitude of sources. Many were published in popular songbooks during the folk music revival of the 1950s. Actor-singer **Paul Robeson** recorded everything from folk music to opera. His music often addressed labor problems and social causes. He recorded for a number of labels including Vanguard.

Throughout the 20th century, folk music has been universally associated with political, labor, and social causes. One of many American groups to emphasize the social issues of the day was the Almanac Singers. Almanac membership varied, including at times Pete Seeger, Lee Hays, Millard Lampell, Woody Guthrie, Sis Cunningham, Bess Lomax, Butch Hawes, and Arthur Stern. The Almanac Singers recorded for Asch records, leading to a Folkways LP, *Talking Union*.

One of the most important folk composers in American history was **Woody Guthrie**. Alan Lomax recorded Guthrie for the Library of Congress Archive; those recordings were later commercially released by Elektra, and then by Rounder Records. It was Guthrie's association with **Moses Asch** of **Folkways Records** that yielded the bulk of Guthrie's recorded legacy. Another seminal figure who emerged during the 1940s was Huddie "Leadbelly" Ledbetter, who was discovered in a prison in Louisiana by John and Alan Lomax during one of their recording trips. The Lomaxes managed to secure Leadbelly's release from incarceration and he traveled with them. His repertoire included a number of styles of African-American music, from work songs and ring chants to straight blues.

Since the 1920s, record companies had tended to segregate their folk and traditional records into separate numerical series that were designed for specific audiences. The 1940s saw the emergence of a number of record companies whose entire output was folk material. Moses Asch, founder of the Folkways label in 1947, made obscure music more accessible. In addition to American folk material, Asch's catalog included speeches, literature, and music from around the world. Asch was in business early in his career with Herbert Harris. When Asch and Harris parted ways they divided many of the original masters. Harris went on to form Stinson Records. Stinson shares many of the same artists as Folkways, such as Guthrie and Leadbelly. Stinson has kept all its folk recordings of the 1940s available.

Decca recorded both **Bill Monroe** and the **Weavers**, successors to the Almanac Singers.

No one has done more for folk music in the 20th century than **Pete Seeger**. He recorded folk songs from all over the world, for Columbia, Tradition, and Flying Fish records, among others, and made more than 60 records for Folkways. Riverside released the Folklore series, which consisted primarily of Anglo and Anglo-American material. A large number of those records were edited by Kenneth Goldstein, later a professor of folklore at the University of Pennsylvania. Many of the performers were urban folk singers who were important during the folk revival of the 1950s. They included Ed McCurdy, Milt Okun, Paul Clayton, Bob Gibson, Ewan MacColl, John Greenway, Oscar Brand, and A.L. Lloyd. Lloyd was an eminent British scholar who edited numerous records and sang on others. He recorded for many labels, including Topic and Tradition, sometimes with Ewan MacColl, another renowned collector of folksongs. MacColl's material ranged from classic Scottish and British ballads to English work songs. For many years he recorded with his wife, Peggy Seeger, for whom he composed his most famous piece "First Time Ever I Saw Your Face." Peggy Seeger is also an important figure. Having grown up in the Charles and Ruth Seeger household, she was exposed to folk music from an early age. She has recorded more than three dozen solo LPs, in addition to two dozen with Ewan MacColl, for Argo, Folkways, Prestige International, Rounder, and Tradition.

Kentucky-born **Jean Ritchie** played a large role during the folk revival of the 1950s with a repertoire consisting of mountain songs, party songs, and British ballads. Her family had been recorded by the Lomaxes during one of their field collecting trips. She is responsible more than any other for the popularization of the Appalachian dulcimer. She began recording for Elektra in 1950 and continued recording for other labels over the years. Ritchie and George Pickow made field recordings in the British Isles, released by Folkways.

Big Bill Broonzy was a powerful singer who recorded country blues for a number of labels beginning in the 1920s. Some of his classic recordings were "This Train" and the pre-civil rights protest song "When am I Ever Going to Be Called a Man," both on Folkways.

Folk-blues guitarist **Josh White** also protested against racism. Some of his strongest songs were "Jim Crow," "Silicosis is Killing Me," and "Strange Fruit." He recorded for a number of labels.

Important record labels of the 1950s included Elektra, Tradition, Everest, Caedmon, Prestige International, and Vanguard. Early Elektra releases included songs by **Theodore Bikel**, Oscar Brand, Ed McCurdy, and Josh White. There also were records by song collector Frank Warner. One classic Elektra release was *The Folk Box*, made in collaboration with Moses Asch and Folkways Records; it contained four discs, with over 80 songs by various artists, and a 48-page booklet. Elektra continued to be a force during the later folk revival with a roster of such performers as **Judy Collins**, Tom Paxton, Paul Butterfield, Tom Rush, and Phil Ochs.

Tradition Records was formed by the Irish singing group the Clancy Brothers. The label presented folk songs from the U.S. and the British Isles. In addition to music by the Clancy Brothers, Tradition's roster included Carolyn Hester, The Kossoy Sisters, **Odetta**, and Sam "Lightnin'" Hopkins. Prestige International also had a significant folk series, including many of the artists who were on Riverside. One of their interesting series, Southern Journey, stemmed from field work by Alan Lomax in the late 1950s. Other Lomax recordings came out on Atlantic in their Southern Folk Heritage series.

Caedmon Records, which is best known for its spoken word recordings, also issued collections of traditional folk music. One important Caedmon series was Folksongs of Britain, using the material of Lomax and Peter Kennedy.

Vanguard was another important label for folk music in the 1950s and 1960s. The Weavers, Martha Schlamme, Paul Robeson, Joan Baez, The Country Gentlemen, Ian and Sylvia, Buffy Ste. Marie, and Odetta were among their artists. Vanguard recorded performances at the Newport Folk Festival.

An influential series of the 1950s was Harry Smith's Anthology of American Folk Music. It consisted of reissues from the 1920s.

Mike Seeger, John Cohen, and Tom Paley formed a revival string band called the New Lost City Ramblers in 1958. Whereas the interest among urban folk musicians had primarily been towards the ballad tradition, there was then a renewed interest in hillbilly and string band music. The New Lost City Ramblers recorded for Folkways, and in 1983 for the Flying Fish label. Bluegrass music was also popular with urban audiences of the 1950s. A group of New York musicians including Bob Yellin, John Herald, and Frank Wakefield (later replaced by Ralph Rinzler) formed the notable bluegrass group called the Greenbriar Boys. They played in coffee houses and at festivals, and recorded for Vanguard. Rinzler, Mike Seeger, and others began recording older rural musicians on trips to the South. Among the artists they discovered were Arthel "Doc" Watson, Clarence Ashley, Roscoe Holcomb, Dock Boggs, "Mississippi" John Hurt, Son House, Fred McDowell, and the Balfa Brothers. The 2000 series on Folkways is peppered with recordings of those men from 1959 to 1964.

In 1958 the Kingston Trio, named for the capital of Jamaica, hit the top of the charts with a North Carolina murder ballad, "Tom Dooley," on the Capitol label. Other record companies scurried to find their own versions of the Kingston Trio. The Chad Mitchell Trio, The Brothers Four, and the New Christy Minstrels were among the new groups, all of them projecting a collegiate look and performing a mixture of popular songs, satirical songs, and folk songs from around the world. Marketing of folk music was centered on campuses and the coffee house circuit.

Groups modeled after the Weavers began to appear also, making records and playing the coffee houses. The Gateway Singers (on Decca), the Rooftop Singers (Vanguard), and the Limelighters (RCA) were associated with the hungry i, a San Francisco nightclub. The Rooftop Singers had a hit with their 1962 record of the 1920s Gus Cannon jug band song, "Walk Right In."

There were more folk songs in the Billboard Top Ten from 1958 to 1965 than at any other time in the history of the charts. Some of the leading records were "Greenfields" by the Brothers Four; "Michael" by the Highwaymen; "Don't Let the Rain Come Down" by the Serendipity Singers; and "Blowin' in the Wind" and "Puff, the Magic Dragon" by Peter, Paul and Mary.

The popularity of folk music created a star system. Certain artists were guaranteed to sell out large concert halls and to make hit records. Brought to the public eye by performance at the 1960 Newport Folk Festival, Joan Baez was one who captivated the public. Her first albums (for Vanguard) contained mainly traditional folk material, but later she introduced material on social themes. Judy Collins recorded traditional songs, and then included material by contemporary composers. One of the most influential performers was Bob Dylan. Others who were popular in the 1960s included Elektra's Tom Paxton, Phil Ochs, Tom Rush, and Fred Neil; Vanguard's Odetta, Richard and Mimi Farina, Ian and Sylvia, Eric Andersen, and Buffy Ste. Marie; and United Artists' Gordon Lightfoot.

Folk music continued to involve political protest. Singer and songwriter Phil Ochs recorded some of the most powerful material during the 1960s with songs like "I Ain't Marching Anymore" and "The Power and the Glory." The editors of Broadside magazine recorded folk protest singers like Ochs, Bob Dylan (as Blind Boy Grunt), and Janis Ian (Blind Girl Grunt). The Broadside recordings were later released by Folkways. Janis Ian also had a 1967 hit song—about a young woman's battle with her parents over an interracial romance—in "Society's Child" on Verve/Forecast. Folk music was prominent in the civil rights movement. Spirituals were sung, with the words altered, by marchers in the South. This continued the tradition of using folk material with the words changed to fit the current situation in union and political struggles. One of the important groups aligned with the movement was the Freedom Singers, made up of Bernice Johnson, Cordell Reagon, Rutha Harris, Betty Mae Fikes, and Charles Neblett. Folksinger Guy Carawan was also heavily involved with the movement and brought his own compositions to it. Recordings of the Freedom Singers were released by both Folkways and Vanguard.

Aside from protest, another characteristic of the folksong revival was interest in jug and skiffle band traditions, mostly in the coffee houses. Calypso and Irish folk songs also had an important role in the period.

The band that most symbolized folk-rock for many was a Los Angeles group, the Byrds. They added jangly electric guitars and drums to Dylan's "Mr. Tambourine Man" for a Columbia hit in 1965, and had a second chart song in the same year, Pete Seeger's "Turn! Turn! Turn!," also for Columbia. Other groups with folk-rock hits included the **Lovin' Spoonful** (a folk-rock jug band), the **Mamas and the Papas**, **Simon and Garfunkel**, Buffalo Springfield, and **Jefferson Airplane.**

As the 1960s progressed, more and more artists began to write their own material in folk style. This phenomenon peaked in the 1970s with the great popularity of the singer-songwriter. Folk music fans bought the record albums and songbooks of performers like **Kris Kristofferson,** John Prine, Steve Goodman, Joni Mitchell, Melanie Safka, James Taylor, Jimmie Buffett, Cat Stevens, Mickey Newbury, Arlo Guthrie (son of Woody Guthrie), and Carly Simon. Some of their songs have become standards and have gone into the repertoires of revival folk performers. Examples include Kristofferson's "Me and Bobbie McGee," Prine's "Paradise," Goodman's "City of New Orleans," and Mitchell's "Both Sides Now." These artists were marketed to the rock audience, and were well received.

By 1970, most of the record companies that had specialized in folk music had either closed or had gone into other styles of music. Elektra turned to rock, and Prestige to jazz.

Riverside ceased to exist. Folkways continued to issue folk material but not at its former level. A new generation of record companies sprang up to take their place, among them Rounder, Flying Fish, Shanachie, Green Linnet, Alligator, and Arhoolie. Rounder Records had a repertoire of traditional folk, old time, bluegrass, and blues. Over the years they have moved to singer-songwriters, urban blues, and world music. Flying Fish has been consistent with traditional folk music and bluegrass, and remains the label most likely to release politically conscious material. Shanachie built a catalog of British folk music, followed by reggae music, and most recently African material. Green Linnet specializes in folk music from Britain, especially Ireland. Alligator Records of Chicago features urban blues bands. Arhoolie records and its subsidiaries have a full catalog of records and films on country blues, cajun and zydeco, western swing, and norteño music. By the end of the 1980s, the very traditional old time folk music was left to labels like June Appal and Traditional. After the death of Moses Asch in 1986 the ownership of Folkways Records was transferred to the **Smithsonian Institution**. The new label Smithsonian/Folkways continues to reissue old material as well as issue new material within the vision of the original label.

In the late 1980s, the music industry saw the reemergence of folk music as a tool for social struggle. New artists began to write socially conscious songs, and perform them with acoustic guitars. Such artists rediscovered folk music of their forefathers. This group included Tracy Chapman, England's Billy Bragg, Lucinda Williams, Michelle Shocked, and Suzanne Vega. Many rock groups have also begun to turn back to the folk-rock sound.

Cajun music and zydeco, the African-American creole music of Louisiana, were popular in the 1980s. Small Louisiana labels like Swallow, La Louisianne, Maison de Soul, and Jin found their records in demand among urban listeners. The king of zydeco was Clifton

Chenier and his Red Hot Louisiana Band. At the same time companies like Folklyric and Arhoolie were recording the Texas-Mexican border music known as norteño.

The great success of Garrison Keillor's radio program, *Prairie Home Companion*, further increased the national audience for folk music, mostly country music. The lines between folk and country were blurred, and artists who were among the singer-songwriters of the 1960s and 1970s appeared on country radio in the 1980s—among them **Emmylou Harris**, Nanci Griffith, Hugh Moffatt, Rodney Crowell, Roseanne Cash, and Mary Chapin Carpenter.

A spread of interest in world traditional music has brought forward Bulgarian women's choirs, Tuvan overtone throat singing, and various Brazilian styles. Labels like Global Village, Globe Style, Shanachie, and Smithsonian/Folkways have released important international material. [Dixon 1982; Lee 1979; Malone 1985; McCulloh 1982; Spottswood 1991.] *See also* COUNTRY AND WESTERN MUSIC; ROCK MUSIC.

Jeffrey Place

FOLKWAYS RECORDS (label). An American record, established by **Moses Asch** in 1947, distinguished for its coverage of American folk singers, notably Leadbelly and Woody Guthrie. When Asch died in 1986, the **Smithsonian Institution** arranged to buy the label, and did so with the assistance of royalties from a commemorative album (*Folkways, A Vision Shared* on CBS), generously contributed by the artists in it.

FONOTIPIA (label). *See* FONOTIPIA, LTD.; SOCIETÀ ITALIANA DI FONOTIPIA.

FONOTIPIA, LTD. A firm incorporated in London on 24 Apr 1906, located at 20 Bishopsgate Street. Directors were Harry V. Higgins, Baron F.D. d'Erlanger, Duke Uberto Visconti di Modrone, Tito Ricordi, and Francesco R. Queirazza. Alfred Michaelis was general manager until 30 Jan 1907, when Emil Rink replaced him. Two agreements formed the basis of the firm. In one, Fonotipia bought virtually every asset of the **Società Italiana di Fonotipia** of Milan, which had been issuing

discs since early 1905. The second agreement reconstituted the Italian company as the Società Italiana di Fonotipia, Società Anonima, headquartered in Milan and completely controlled by the English Fonotipia, Ltd. After various changes in stock ownership over the years, the Italian firm was incorporated into EMI's Italian branch in June 1947.

The first records offered by Fonotipia, Ltd., were of the Italian Marine Band and Emmy Destinn, in November 1905. **Sterling and Hunting, Ltd.**, operated by Louis Sterling and Russell Hunting, were distributors for the discs, which were first double-sided, of 10 3/4 inch diameter; then from 1906 single-sided, 13 1/2 inches. In 1907 there were operatic offerings, including Giovanni Zenatello's "Vesti la giubba." The new low-priced **Jumbo Record** label was introduced in February 1908. In that year **Barnett Samuel and Sons** took over the distribution of Fonotipia records from Sterling & Hunting.

Fonotipia had a number of affiliations. The **International Talking Machine Co. mbH** of Berlin was licensed to sell Fonotipia material in all countries except the U.K., U.S., and Canada. Columbia Phonograph Company, General, became exclusive manufacturers and sales agents for the U.S. and Canada from March 1908. Odeon, the label of the International Talking Machine Co., was distributed in Italy by the Società Italiana di Fonotipia, and in Britain by Barnett Samuel and Sons, Ltd., from 1906 (Fonotipia, Ltd., was the holding company).

A double-sided record by Alessandro Bonci (#62300–01) was announced with much fanfare in July 1908: "Mai piu Zazà" from Leoncavallo's *Zazà*, and "Vieni amore mio," a song by Leoncavallo; the composer accompanied the tenor on the piano. Other great artists featured on the Fonotipia-Odeon labels included Mario Sammarco, John McCormack, Leo Slezak, and violinist Jan Kubelik. The recording studio that made these Fonotipias was in Milan.

By the end of 1909 the British sales were double those of the previous year. The firm moved to new quarters in November 1909, at 8 Crosby Square. It was successful in a legal cases brought by the Gramophone Co., involving use of the word "gramophone" (declared by the High Court of Justice to be a generic term in common usage) and the tapered tone arm.

Then in July 1911, Fonotipia, Ltd., was acquired by **Carl Lindström**, for about £150,000. Lindstrom emphasized his various other labels, and the Fonotipia record was scarcely noticeable in Britain thereafter. Barnett Samuel continued selling Odeon (until the outbreak of World War I) and Jumbo. War conditions led to the order by the British Board of Trade, in August 1916, that both Fonotipia, Ltd. and its parent company, Lindström, be wound up. In November 1917 a newly created firm, the Hertford Record Co., Ltd., acquired all Fonotipia, Ltd., British assets, and announced it would continue the manufacture of records. However, in April 1919, the Jumbo Record, the only remaining label of the original Fonotipia, Ltd., was taken out of circulation; Hertford kept its repertoire going on a new label named Venus Record until February 1920.

On 3 Nov 1920 Otto Ruhl, former managing director for Carl Lindström (London), Ltd., was appointed agent in England for the Fonotipia records of the Società Italiana di Fonotipia of Milan. Thus two separate enterprises had rights to the Fonotipia record: Ruhl and Hertford—which had been since June 1919 a Columbia Graphophone Co., Ltd., subsidiary. Columbia decided to draw on the stock of matrices held by Hertford, and issued material by Billy Williams on the 10-inch **Regal** label. Further Regals came in late 1921, and other Odeon matrices of Fonotipia, Ltd.—eight sides by John McCormack—were used on the Columbia Record label. Meanwhile Hertford began legal action against Ruhl over the Fonotipia rights, but the court eventually found Ruhl not guilty and free to carry on as agent for Lindström and its affiliates. The Fonotipia trademark was removed from Hertford's domain in August 1921.

In February 1921 "new" Fonotipia records were again advertised, by the Gramophone Exchange. Later that year newly pressed Fonotipias, carrying orchestral pieces by Italian composers, were on sale. Fonotipias were marketed into 1922 by the Gramophone Exchange, and (from November 1922) by Davis's Music Stores of Liverpool. The **Parlophone** Co., Ltd., incorporated in August 1923, became the British agent for Fonotipia records in November of that year, but did little to promote the label. Then advertising of September 1925 indicated the Music Salon, in Edinburgh, was selling Fonotipias; apparently it continued to do so until some time in 1927.

In June 1927 an advertisement announced the "the cream of the world famous Odeon & Fonotipia Celebrity Recordings [are] now available on Parlophone Records—Odeon Series." Fonotipia electric recordings were included among the Parlophone-Odeon Series in Britain into 1928, and in July 1928 the trademark was formally transferred to the Parlophone Co., Ltd., of London (a subsidiary of the Columbia Graphophone Co., Ltd.). Finally in 1931 the label and the Società Italiana di Fonotipia passed to the hands of the new **EMI, Ltd.** Recording continued sporadically on the Fonotipia label under EMI until 1936. Thereafter reissues of acoustic material were made until World War II. In 1948 the final closing down of the Milan firm took place, after some 43 years of operation.

The British Institute of Recorded Sound made the final pressings of Fonotipia recordings in August 1971, with a series of 20 discs entitled the Historic Masters Series. [Andrews*; Andrews 1976/5.]

FOONG, YUEN SING. The Victor agent in "every city and town" of China, operating from the offices of S. Moutrie & Co., Ltd, Shanghai. He was the first Chinese record jobber to be mentioned in the trade literature (*TMW* 1906).

FORD, TENNESSEE ERNIE, 1919–1991. American country and gospel singer, and radio announcer, born Ernest Jennings Ford in Bristol, Tennessee, on 13 Feb 1919. He announced for Atlanta and Knoxville radio stations in 1937–1941, then served as an airman in World War II. He became a disc jockey in San Bernadino, California, and also gained a Capitol contract as a singer. In 1949 he made a chart song, "Mule Train" (Capitol #40258), and a year later another hit with his composition "Shotgun Boogie" (Capitol #1295; 1950). His greatest success was "Sixteen Tons" (Capitol #3262; 1955), 15 weeks on the charts. He had 11 country chart songs before 1956, after which he turned to gospel songs. His *Great Gospel Songs* album won a Grammy Award in 1964. The last of his chart songs was "Sweet Feelings" (Capitol #4333; 1976). Ford had his own television shows from 1955 to 1965, and continued to make concert appearances into the 1980s. He died in Reston, Virginia, on 17 Oct 1991.

FORDE, FLORRIE, 1876–1940. Australian comedienne, born Florence Flanagan in Sydney. She appeared in London from August 1897, and made hundreds of popular recordings in Britain during the early years of the century, such as "Is Everybody Happy?" (HMV #120124) and "Meet Me Down at the Corner" (HMV #120135). "I've Got Rings on My Fingers" was one of her great successes, "Down at the Old Bull and Bush" was another. Still in demand when electrical recording arrived, she re-recorded many of her earlier favorites.

FORESMAN EDUCATIONAL MUSIC RECORDS (label). A disc produced by the Educational Record Co. of Chicago in September 1917. Sets of 26 double-sided records were offered for teaching music in schools. [Andrews*.]

FORREST, HELEN, 1918–. American popular singer, born in Atlantic City, New Jersey, on 12 Apr 1918. She was one of the most successful vocalists of the Big Band era, singing with Artie Shaw (1938), Benny Goodman (1939–41), and Harry James (1941–1943). With James she made her greatest hits, "I Don't Want to Walk without You" (Columbia #36478; 1941), "I Had the Craziest Dream" (Columbia #36659; 1942), "I've Heard that Song Before" (Columbia #36668; 1942), and "I Heard You Cried Last Night" (Columbia #36677; 1942). Later she teamed with Dick Haymes on radio and records, and continued to appear into the 1970s.

FOUNTAIN, PETE, 1930–. American jazz clarinetist, born Peter Dewey Fountain, Jr., in New Orleans on 3 July 1930. At age 19 he was a member of the Dukes of Dixieland. After five years with that group, Fountain freelanced, joined the Lawrence Welk orchestra (1957–1960), and then formed his own band. He was notably successful in recordings of the 1960s made for the Coral label, including *New Orleans* (Coral #CRL 57282; 1960), which was on the charts for over a year; and *Licorice Stick* (Coral #CRL 57460; 1964).

FOUR ARISTOCRATS. A male quartet that recorded for Victor and Edison in 1926–1927. "Don't Sing Aloha When I Go" (Edison Diamond Disc #51858; Victor #20314) was one of their popular records. The singers were Fred Weber, Bert Bennet, Ed Lewis, and Tom Miller.

Four channel stereo. *See* QUADRAPHONIC SOUND.

FOUR-IN-ONE (label). A British record issued from August 1932 to August 1933 by **British Homophone Co., Ltd.** Each 10-inch disc had four dance numbers, thus the label name; it was an early version of **long-playing record**, although at 78 rpm. There were 50 different issues.

FRAAD TALKING MACHINE CO. A New York firm, established in 1915 at 224 W. 26th St. An advertisement of 1916 offered 10 models of disc players under the names Symphony, Fraad Jr., and Symphony Jr., as well as 10-inch and 12-inch discs with a Fraad label. The firm went bankrupt in August 1918. [Andrews*.]

FRANCIS, CONNIE, 1938–. American popular singer, born Concetta Franconero in Newark, New Jersey, on 12 Dec 1938. At age 11 she appeared on the Arthur Godfrey television show, and in high school she sang in cocktail lounges. In 1955 Francis began to record for the MGM label, and in 1958 she had five chart singles beginning with "Who's Sorry Now?" (MGM #12588). She had 58 chart songs by the end of the 1960s, when her ballad style went out of favor. "Where the Boys Are," the title song from one of her films, was one of her most successful discs (MGM #12971; 1961). She also had 19 chart albums, notably *Italian Favorites* (MGM #E 3791; 1959) and *Never on Sunday* (MGM #E 3965; 1961).

Francisco, Signor. *See* DE GOGORZA, EMILIO.

FRANKLIN, ARETHA, 1942– . American soul and gospel singer, born in Memphis, Tennessee, on 25 March 1942. Her father was C. L. Franklin, a minister noted for his recordings of sermons. She sang in churches as a child, was heard by **John Hammond,** and signed by him for Columbia records in 1960. She had only one chart album with Columbia, *Running Out of Fools* (#CL2281; 1964), not having established an individual style. She moved to the Atlantic label in 1966, and developed a powerful gospel repertoire that led to 16 hit albums within seven years, including the acclaimed *I Never Loved a Man* (Atlantic #8139; 1967), and *Aretha Now* (Atlantic #SD 8186; 1968). She was known for highly emotional performances as well as for a well controlled virtuoso voice. The soul classic "Respect," which she sang to great effect in the motion picture *The Blues Brothers,* was a notable single of 1967 (Atlantic #2403). Franklin has received 15 Grammys. Since 1980 she has recorded for Arista. *Through the Storm,* an album made with James Brown, Elton John, Whitney Houston, and the Four Tops, was an important release of 1985 (Arista #ARCD-8572). Her most popular solo work of the 1980s was in *Who's Zoomin' Who* (Arista #ARCD-8286; 1989). In 1991 she was honored with a commemorative postage stamp in a series devoted to distinguished Black Americans.

FREED, ALAN, 1922–1965. American disc jockey, born in Johnstown, Pennsylvania, on 15 Dec 1922. After military service in World War II, he took a master's degree in engineering from The Ohio State University; then went into radio work in Ohio and Pennsylvania. As a disc jockey in Cleveland in the 1950s he attracted interest, and controversy, by playing rhythm & blues records by Black artists and sponsoring integrated concerts. In 1954 he went to station WINS in New York. He may have been the first to use the term "rock and roll," and he diligently promoted the new idiom. Freed became the most successful rock disc jockey, and appeared in rock films. But in 1962 he was found guilty of accepting payola, and received a suspended sentence, effectively ending his career. He died in Palm Springs, California, on 20 Jan 1965.

FREEMAN, BUD, 1906–1991. American tenor saxophonist, born Lawrence Freeman in Chicago on 13 Apr 1906. He was one of the Austin High School Gang, a group of white boys who developed the Chicago jazz style. In 1927 he went to New York and joined Ben Pollack's band; in 1929 he moved to Red Nichols. During the 1930s he played with many orchestras, including those of Paul Whiteman, Tommy Dorsey, and Benny Goodman; then he toured with various smaller groups in the 1940s. Freeman won the *Down Beat* poll in 1938. He led his own groups in the 1950s and 1960s, moved to London, and finally returned to Chicago, where he died on 15 Mar 1991.

Among his distinctive records are "Rose of Washington Square" with Red Nichols (Brunswick #4778; 1929), "The Eel" (Brunswick #6743; 1933), and "At the Codfish Ball" with Tommy Dorsey (Victor #25314; 1936). He also made important discs with his Summa Cum Laude orchestra (featuring Pee Wee Russell and Eddie Condon) in a Bluebird session of 1939, and in three Decca sessions of 1939 and 1940.

FREEMANTLE, FREDERIC C., 1873–1949. English tenor, born in London on 20 Apr 1873. He was a choir boy, then learned to play brass instruments. From 1896 to 1890 he appeared in concert and oratorio in Canada and the U.S., and sang opera in Philadelphia. On stage he was most appreciated for his Beethoven song recitals. He began recording in 1907 for Victor, doing mostly religious material like "Ave Maria" by Franz Abt (#31691); but he also sang "La donna è mobile" (#5068). Freemantle made one two-minute cylinder for Edison, "Ah So Pure" from *Martha* (#9962; 1908). Later he made a 12-record set about public speaking for Victor. He died on 21 Nov 1949. [Walsh 1948/7.]

FREE-FORM PROGRAMMING. An alternative to the prevailing radio **disc jockey** programming format, **boss radio,** of 1965; devised by Russ "The Moose" Syracuse at San Francisco's KYA. In free-form, top chart discs are played but interspersed with folk songs, new work of local performers, and other music ignored by the boss stations. The disc jockey has a greater voice in selection of material than in boss.

FREMSTAD, OLIVE, 1871–1951. Swedish dramatic soprano, born in Stockholm on 14 Mar 1871. As a child she was adopted by a Swedish-American couple who took her to Minnesota. She studied piano and voice, and had worked as a church soloist in New York. Then in 1893 she went to study with Lilli Lehmann in Berlin, and made her operatic debut as a contralto in Cologne, as Azucena (1895). She continued to sing contralto roles in Bayreuth in 1896, and throughout Europe, but began a changeover to the soprano repertoire. Her Metropolitan Opera debut was as Sieglinde on 25 Nov 1903. Among the highlights of her 11-year Metropolitan career were appearances in *Carmen* with Enrico Caruso and as Isolde with Gustav Mahler conducting. She sang Wagner with special distinction, but was also popular in works of Verdi, Puccini, and Richard Strauss. After leaving the Metropolitan she sang with other American companies, then gave a final recital in New York on 19 Jan 1920. She died in Irvington-on-Hudson, New York, on 21 Apr 1951. Willa Cather's novel, *Song of the Lark*, was based on Fremstad's life.

Fremstad's first recording, "Dich, teure Halle" (Columbia #30635; 1911), remains a favorite among collectors. It was reissued by IRCC in 1935. Other fine interpretations include "Oh don fatal" from *Don Carlo* (Columbia # 36807; 1912) and "Elsas Traum" (Columbia #A5281). [Migliorini 1952; Moran 1977/3.]

FRENOPHONE. A radio marketed in 1922–1923 by S.G. Brown that had a physical resemblance to a phonograph. It had a "polished oblong oak box, complete with a winding handle and a cygnet horn." [*TMR* #9 (1971), p. 8, source of the quote, has illustrations.]

FREQUENCY. The rate of vibration of a sound wave; the characteristic that determines the **pitch** of the signal. *See also* AUDIO FREQUENCY.

Frequency distortion. *See* DISTORTION, II.

FREQUENCY MODULATION (FM). The method of radio transmission in which an audio wave is impressed on a so-called carrier wave (of higher **frequency**). The carrier wave undergoes modification of frequency, but not of **amplitude**. The modulation process, and the demodulation process of the FM receiver, give a signal transmission that is much less affected by background noise and static than AM radio.

FREQUENCY RESPONSE. The ability of an audio system or component to reproduce the input signals at their original frequencies. In an **amplifier,** a uniform response is desired, one that does not favor or degrade any segment of the audio spectrum (*see* FLAT RESPONSE). When an amplifier emphasizes particular frequencies, the output signal is distorted (*see* DISTORTION, I.) In specifications for an audio device, frequency response is often stated in **decibels** (dB) for a specified segment of the audio spectrum, for example, plus or minus 3 dB from 20 Hz to 20 kHz.

FRIEDMAN, IGNAZ, 1882–1948. Polish pianist, born on 14 Feb 1882 near Cracow. After study with Theodor Leschetizky in Vienna, he began to concertize in 1904, giving some 2,800 performances in Europe, America, Australia, China, Japan, and South Africa. In 1941 he settled in Sydney. Friedman's special interest was in Chopin, whose works he published in an important edition. Recordings made from 1923 to 1936, mostly for Columbia, were reissued on four CDs in 1990 by Pearl (#IF2000). They display a rich tone and great virtuosity, with a finely controlled pianissimo.

FROLICKERS. A trio that made three Edison Diamond Discs in 1926. The members were Arthur Hall, John Ryan, and Ed Smalle.

FROSINI, PIETRO, 1885–1957. Italian accordionist, born Pietro Giuffrida in Catania on 9 Aug 1885. His eyesight was severely limited after a case of childhood measles, but he went to America and began a 40-year career on stage and recordings. In 1911 he gave a command performance for King George V. Frosini's first record was an Edison Amberol, #103, made in April 1909: "Wedding of the Winds." He also recorded for Edison Diamond Discs from 1915 to 1924. His best seller was Diamond Disc #51030, "Carnival of Venice—Variations." Other labels he worked with included Gennett, Master, Harmonia, Pathé Actuelle, and Decca. Frosini played the button accordion, not the keyboard instrument.

FULL FREQUENCY RANGE RECORDINGS (ffrr). A recording system developed by **Arthur Charles Haddy**, based on submarine detection devices. It was marketed in the U.S. by Decca Record Co. in 1946, with great success. A long-coil, moving-coil recording **cutting head** was used, later modified into a feedback recorder. When discs thus made were played on Decca's new Piccadilly portable, which had a light magnetic **cartridge** with sapphire stylus, and a three-tube amplifier, the spectrum covered was 50–14,000 Hz, outperforming all competing machines of the time.

FULLER'S FAMOUS JAZZ BAND. The second jazz ensemble to make records, for Victor on 4 June 1917. The disc made that day was "Slippery Hank" and "Yah-De-Dah" (#18321). The group, led by Earl Fuller, made two more (issued) Victors in 1917–1918; and recorded the earliest jazz for Edison, on Diamond Disc in 1918–1919. Fuller continued recording with various groups and for several labels until 1921.

FUNDAMENTAL FREQUENCY. The first **harmonic** (lowest **frequency**) of a musical sound; the basic identifying vibration that determines the pitch of the sound. Fundamentals of very low frequency, like the lowest C on a piano keyboard, are not reproducible in certain recording systems. However, the pitch of a sound may be supplied by the human hearing mechanism even when the fundamental is inaudible. This is done by perception of the second harmonic (i.e., the first overtone), which has twice the frequency of the fundamental

and sounds one octave higher. Unless the fundamental and/or the second harmonic is audible, the pitch cannot be recognized. During the acoustic recording era (before 1924), the lower range fundamentals were often missing. *See also* AUDIO FREQUENCY.

FURTWÄNGLER, WILHELM, 1886–1954. German conductor, born in Berlin on 25 Jan 1886. He began conducting at the Strasbourg Opera in 1910, going on to concerts in Lübeck from 1911–1915. He became conductor of the Mannheim orchestra (1915–1918) and then of the Vienna Tonkünstler Orchester (1919–1924). While in Vienna he also directed the Gesellschaft für Musikfreunde. Furtwängler was appointed to the directorship of the Berlin Philharmonic Orchestra in 1922. He held concurrent posts with the Vienna Philharmonic Orchestra from 1927, and with the Berlin State Opera from 1933. He had problems with the Nazi government, but remained in Germany until the final months of World War II; then he emigrated to Switzerland. After the war he resumed relatively normal duties, despite growing deafness. He died in Ebersteinburg on 30 Nov 1954.

Furtwängler was given to an improvisatory approach, and tended to take slower tempi than most of his contemporaries. Thus many of his recordings are less than satisfactory, although the concerts may have gained from the conductor's spirit of the moment. He was a specialist in the German romantics, and made an outstanding recording of *Tristan* in 1947 (EMI #CDS7–47322–28) and another of the *Ring*. It is of interest that some of his wartime concerts in Berlin were taped on the **Magnetophon**, providing remarkable fidelity for its period; these have been released on 10 CDs (DG #427773–2GD010; 1989). [Hunt 1985.]

FUZZ. A form of distortion, deliberately induced to give a special effect with electronic instruments, for example, guitars. A harsh timbre can be achieved by means of a frequency multiplier that adds complex **harmonics** to the **fundamental** tones.

Gabel Entertainer. *See* JOHN GABEL'S AUTO-MATIC ENTERTAINER.

GADSKI, JOHANNA, 1872–1932. German dramatic soprano, born in Anklam on 15 June 1872. She began singing as a child, and made her debut at age 17 in Berlin, going on to perform elsewhere in Germany. Her American debut was as Elsa with the Damrosch Opera Co., New York, on 1 Mar 1895. She sang for the first time at the Metropolitan Opera on 28 Dec 1899, and remained with the company to 1917 except for a three-year hiatus. She was acclaimed for her interpretations of Isolde and Brünnhilde. During World War I Gadski was in Germany; then she returned to the U.S. in 1929–1931, and went back again to Germany, where she died on 23 Feb 1932.

She was recorded by Lionel Mapleson at the Metropolitan Opera in 1903, in fragments from *Huguenots, Lohengrin, Walküre, Meister-singer, Aida,* and *Ero e Leandro* (by Luigi Mancinelli, who conducted the performance); IRCC reissued these on four records.

Gadski recorded for Victor in 1903–1904, in 1906–1910, and 1912–1917, the first discs being "Dich teure Halle" (#85013) and "Ho-yo-to-ho" (#81018). Aside from her favored Wagnerian roles she had recorded by 1910 several arias from *Aida,* two duets from that opera with Enrico Caruso and two other duets with Louise Homer, all kept in the catalog as late as 1917 (where she had 40 solo items listed, in addition to duets). She also inscribed Lieder and other songs. After 1917 her material was deleted, and she was no longer found among the Red Seal artists during the electrical recording period. [Migliorini 1957.]

GAELIC PHONOGRAPH CO. A New York firm, organized in 1921 by Hugh P. Fay, Earle W. Jones, and H.G. Suikert. The first address was 637 Madison Ave. In February 1922 the firm, then located at 40 W. 57th St., was advertising that it was the only company to be exclusively recording Gaelic and Irish records. Thomas F. Dwyer, treasurer at that time, succeeded Fay as director in March 1922. In October 1922 it was reported that the firm was placed in the hands of a creditors committee. [Andrews*.]

Gain. *See* AMPLIFICATION.

GAISBERG, FREDERICK WILLIAM, 1873–1951. American pianist, and for 60 years a record industry executive. He was born in Washington, D.C., of German parents on 1 Jan 1873. A precocious musician, he sang as a schoolboy with a choir directed by John Philip Sousa, and became known around Washington as a pianist and accompanist. In 1889 he took the post of studio pianist for the new Columbia Phonograph Co., then worked for Chichester Bell and Charles Sumner Tainter, developers of the **graphophone.** He found musicians to perform for the paper cylinders, and accompanied them on the piano. Gaisberg was responsible for much of the material available in the array of graphophone **coin-ops** at the World's Columbian Exposition in 1893. He was a pianist and talent scout for Columbia, as that firm was initiating large-scale musical recording. Gaisberg accompanied such famous artists as Goerge Gaskin, Len Spencer, and Billy Golden, and made 36 records with whistler John York AtLee.

The 1894 demise of Columbia's parent firm, the North American Phonograph Co., led to feelings of insecurity among Columbia employees. Gaisberg was taken by Billy Golden to meet Emile Berliner (then in Washington), and he soon became Berliner's studio accompanist. He also worked at promotion of the gramophone, seeking financial backers, and at finding talent, such as the opera singer Ferruccio Giannini. With his brother Will, he opened the first disc recording studio in early 1897, on 12th St., Philadelphia. Alfred Clark managed Berliner's retail shop there.

In May 1898 William Barry Owen and Trevor Williams established the Gramophone Co. in London, using Berliner's British patents; and at once requested Berliner to send a recording expert. Fred Gaisberg was chosen, and he went to London to manage the new studio, in modest quarters at 31 Maiden Lane. He and his brother Will were instrumental in finding a wide European audience for the gramophone. The first recording made in London, on 2 Aug 1898, included Fred Gaisberg's piano accompaniment to Syria Lamonte's singing of "Comin' through the Rye."

Gaisberg assumed A & R responsibilities, and over the years recruited many great artists to the recording horn: Enrico Caruso first and foremost, Mattia Battistini, Emma Calvé, Feodor Chaliapin, Edward Elgar, Beniamino Gigli, Adelina Patti, Arthur Schnabel, Luisa Tetrazzini, and others. He formed an important partnership with Landon Ronald, who became an advisor and talent scout for the Gramophone Co. for nearly 40 years.

In 1902 Gaisberg undertook the first of many recording trips to Russia, where he recorded balalaika players, opera singers, peasant accordionists, the comedian and concertina artist Peter Nevsky, and the composer Alexander Taneiev. He took a recording team to the Far East, and in a year on location he made records of native music in China, India, and Japan. Gaisberg's diaries of those journeys form rich documentation of the early recording industry. He traveled also in southern and western Europe. The last two years of World War I he spent in Italy, scouting the promising singers he would record when peace returned (Gigli among them). He remained with the Gramophone Co., as it grew to be the European giant of the industry, and when it was assimilated by EMI, Ltd., in the 1931 merger he became international artists manager for the new firm. He gathered and maintained the incomparable group of classical artists who performed on the HMV label. Later he was a consultant for the organization. Gaisberg died in London on 2 Sep 1951. His autobiography, *The Music Goes Round*, is one of the prime documents of the early recording years (*see* the Bibliography). [Moore 1976.]

GAISBERG, WILLIAM, 1878–1918. Recording engineer and executive, usually known as Will, younger brother of **Fred Gaisberg**. He worked with his brother in Washington, D.C., then moved to Philadelphia with him and opened the first disc recording studio in 1897, for Emile Berliner. He went to London in 1898 to assist his brother in managing the recording department of the new Berliner firm, the Gramophone Co. While Fred Gaisberg was on his trip to the Far East in 1903, Will brought the temperamental opera star Francesco Tamagno in to record, paying him the first royalties of the record industry. A victim of wartime gassing, which occurred as he was making the first on-site documentary battle recording (of a gas shell bombardment near Lille), he died in England on 5 Nov 1918. The record was sold to the public to raise funds for the war effort.

GALLAGHER AND SHEAN. American vaudeville team of 1910–1925, consisting of Ed Gallagher (1872–1929) and Al Shean (1868–1949), makers of the highly popular disc "Mr. Gallagher and Mr. Shean" (Victor #18941; 1922) from the *Ziegfeld Follies of 1922*. The record was thought by some to have certain offensive lyrics, which were deleted in certain reissues, for example, Veritas #VM-107. In its original version the record sold nearly a million copies.

GALLI-CURCI, AMELITA, 1882–1963. Italian coloratura soprano, born in Milan on 18 Nov 82. A piano student at first, she graduated with a first prize in that instrument from the Milan Conservatory in 1903. She taught herself to sing, in part by listening to herself on cylinder records. On 26 Dec 1906 she made her opera debut as Gilda in Trani, then sang throughout Italy, South America, and Europe. When World War I started she moved to the U.S., making a sensational debut with the Chicago Opera on 18 Nov 1916 as Gilda, and then at the Metropolitan Opera on 14 Nov 1921 as Violetta; she remained with the Metropolitan until 1930, singing the Italian/French repertoire. Galli-Curci retired to La Jolla, California, where she died on 26 Nov 1963.

After a rejected test recording for Edison in 1912 or 1913, she worked for Victor, doing 14 arias in 1916–1917, another eight in 1918–1919, four more in 1920–1921, and about 25 between 1922 and 1924. During the electric era she did another 25 Victor discs. Her first Victor was "Caro nome" (#74499; 1916), which remained one of her most popular renditions (reissued on HRS #2011). Another great success was "Sempre libera," from the 1918–1919 group (#64820; also reissued on HRS #2011). The 1927 Victor catalog had 33 items by her; there were 26 in the 1940 catalog. Many LP reissues appeared, on Victor, HMV, and Camden labels. Nimbus released a CD (#N17806) of many favorites in 1990. [Favia-Artsay 1949.]

GALVANY, MARIA, 1874–1949. Spanish soprano, born in Granada. She studied at the Conservatory in Madrid, and made her debut in Cartagena as Lucia in 1897. She was engaged by the Real in Madrid for two seasons, doing Lucia, other Donizetti and Bellini roles, plus Ines in L'Africaine and the Queen in Huguenots. In 1901 she was heard in Italy and Russia, and the next year in Buenos Aires. Her career took her through Europe, but she did not appear in the U.S. She died in Rio de Janeiro on 2 Nov 1949.

Galvany's earliest recordings were for G & T in Milan, 1903; she sang "Caro nome" (#53293, with HRS reissue #2011) and three other arias. She made Pathé cylinders in 1905. In 1907–1908 she made discs for the Gramophone Co. Among the finest recordings were "Prendi l'anel," from Sonnambula, a duet with Fernando De Lucia (#054217; 1908, reis-

sued on IRCC #64); and the Dinorah "Ombra leggera" (#53307; 1903 and Victor #82222, with an HRS reissue #1010). A non-operatic song, "L'incantatrice" by Luigi Arditi (#053165; 1908), and the Lucia Mad Scene (#053181; 1908, with IRCC reissue) are two other remarkable interpretations.

GAMAGE (label). A department store record issued by A.W. Gamage, Ltd., of London in 1924. Material was from Aco-Homochord and Vocalion; it was mostly dance music by British and American ensembles. The store had offered two earlier labels: Champion Gamage Record, and A.W. Gamage Record, both from about 1911. [Andrews*; Rust 1978.]

GAP. In tape recording, the space cut in the magnetic material of the record head. In open-reel recording the normal gap is between 100 and 500 microinches. In cassettes the normal gap is 50 microinches. See also GAP ALIGNMENT.

GAP ALIGNMENT. The adjustment of the magnetic **gap** orientation in tape recording. Adjustment in relation to the direction of tape motion is called azimuth alignment; the desired angle is exactly 90 degrees, and even a slight deviation results in loss of high frequency response. Lateral alignment refers to adjustment of the gap parallel to the plane of the tape. Pole face alignment refers to the rotation of the contact surface in a plane, at right angles to the direction of tape motion.

GARBER, JAN, 1897–1977. American violinist and Big Band leader, born in Morristown, Pennsylvania, on 5 Nov 1897. He played violin in the Philadelphia Orchestra, then directed a military band during World War I. He and pianist Milton Davis formed the Garber-Davis Orchestra in 1921, and recorded for Columbia and Victor until 1924; the first item was "O sole mio" (Columbia #A-3792; 1921). The style of this band was on the "hot" side, resulting in a few jazzy records, like "Steamboat Sal" (Victor # 19175; 1923). Then Garber formed his own orchestra in 1924, which gradually became a sweet band, and he achieved great popularity on radio in the 1930s as the "Idol of the Air

Lanes." Garber recorded prolifically for Victor, Decca, Vocalion, Okeh, and Brunswick; Lee Bennett was the featured vocalist. The band appeared in two Hollywood films, *Here Comes Elmer* (1943), and *Make Believe Ballroom* (1949). Garber was active through the 1950s.

GARDE RÉPUBLICAINE BAND. A French military band, formed in 1852 and directed first by Monsieur Paulus. Its full title was La Musique du Garde Républicaine de France. The musicians were civilian employees of the government. Winner of international competitions, and successful on world tours, the band held a high place among ensembles that made early recordings. Victor recorded the band in 1904, making 19 discs; the first was "La rentrée à Paris" (#4113). Other pieces were marches, waltzes, and operatic excerpts. A popular record was "La Marsellaise" (#4120), which remained in the catalog along with three other numbers into the 1940s. The group was also in the Pathé catalog of 1904, under director Gabriel Pares.

GARDEN, MARY, 1874–1967. Scottish soprano, born in Aberdeen on 20 Feb 1874. She was brought to the Chicago as a child, and studied violin and piano as well as voice. She went on to study in Paris, and made her debut as Louise at the Opéra Comique on 10 Apr 1900. Debussy chose her, over Maeterlinck's objections, to sing in the premiere of *Pélleas et Mélisande* (1902). Back in America, she sang Thais at the Manhattan Opera Co. on 25 Nov 1907, and was the first U.S. Mélisande on 19 Feb 1908, gaining acclaim as a superb singing actress. Garden returned to Chicago in 1910 to begin a long association with the opera there (her last appearance being 24 Jan 1931). During 1921–1922 she was impresario of the company. After her semi-retirement in 1930, she taught at the Chicago Musical College; then she moved back to Scotland in 1939. She died in Inverurie on 3 Jan 1967.

Garden made her first recordings for Pathé in London in 1903, beginning with "Comin' through the Rye" (cylinder #50088) and five other Scottish songs. Then she worked for G & T in Paris, in 1904, recording first the aria "Mes longs cheveux" of Mélisande, accompanied by

Debussy at the piano (#33447). Three Edison two-minute cylinders were made in Paris in 1905. From 1926 to 1935 she made records for Victor, one of the most popular being "Depuis le jour" (#6623); however, none were carried to the 1938 catalog. She also made successful discs for Columbia, from 1911 to 1914, for example, "Liberté" from *Jongleur de Notre Dame* and "Il est doux, il est bon" from *Hérodiade* (#A5289); these remained in the catalogs through the 1930s. Altogether she made 30 record sides and three cylinders. IRCC reissued several French arias, and many LP releases appeared.

GARDNER, SAMUEL, 1892–1984. Russian/American violinist, brought to the U.S. as an infant. He studied in Boston, and became a member of the Kneisel String Quartet in 1914. When that group dissolved in 1917, Gardner formed the **Elshuco Trio** (with Richard Epstein, piano, and Willem Willeke, cello). He was a conductor also; and as a composer he won the Pulitzer Prize in 1918. Gardner made only a few records. For Victor he played "Long, Long Ago" (#17888) and other songs and arrangements, none of which remained long in the catalog. He was heard also on four Edison cylinders, two of which had works by Fritz Kreisler, and on two Edison Diamond Discs of 1914–1915. [Lewis, J. 1985.]

GARLAND, JUDY, 1922–1969. American popular singer and actress, born Frances Ethel Gumm in Grand Rapids, Michigan, on 10 Jan 1922. At the age of two she was appearing in vaudeville acts with her parents, and she went on to become a juvenile star in Hollywood. Between 1935 and 1950 she made about 30 motion pictures for MGM, notably musicals with Mickey Rooney, and *Wizard of Oz* (1939). Her recording of "Over the Rainbow" from the *Wizard* was her greatest success on disc (Decca #2672; 1939). "I'm Nobody's Baby" (Decca #3174; 1940), and "For Me and My Gal" with Gene Kelly (Decca #18480; 1942) were other outstanding interpretations. Garland was primarily a concert and cabaret entertainer after 1950. She was awarded two Grammys for her album *Judy at Carnegie Hall* (Capitol #BO 1569; 1961), which was on the charts 57 weeks. She died in London on 22 Jan 1969. Her daughter, Liza Minnelli, also became an internationally famous actress and singer.

GARNER, ERROLL, 1921–1977. American jazz pianist and composer, born in Pittsburgh on 15 June 1921. He had no formal training in music, but began playing on radio at age seven, then in clubs and on riverboats in the Pittsburgh area. In 1944 he went to New York to perform with various groups, forming his own trio in 1946. The first of many European tours was in 1948. In the 1950s and 1960s he was a featured artist on television.

Garner's inimitable style of playing included subtle syncopations and complex chord structures. He composed about 200 songs, notably "Misty," which became his hit record (Mercury #70442; 1954). Other great Garner discs include "Laura" (Columbia #39273; 1951) and "Lullaby of Birdland" (Columbia #39996; 1953). He died in Los Angeles on 2 Jan 1977. [Doran 1985.]

GASKIN, GEORGE J., 1863–1920. Irish/American tenor, born in Belfast. Arriving at an early age in the U.S., he sang in churches and in vaudeville, and was a member of the Manhasset Quartet. He began recording in 1892, for the New Jersey Phonograph Co., and went on to inscribe his "strident, piercing voice" (Walsh) for all the major labels. He had 41 records in the 1896 Columbia cylinder catalog. In the late 1890s Gaskin was a prolific Edison artist, with about 100 cylinders; he sang popular items like "Annie Laurie" (#1503), "Sally in Our Alley" (#1540), and "Sweet Rosie O'Grady" (#1551). Gaskin made the first Berliner record in Montreal, "God Save the Queen," before February 1899. An earlier U.S. Berliner was "I'se Gwine Back to Dixie" (#192; 1895). He was said to have earned $25,000 a year for his appearances and recordings, but his career died out after 1900. He made a final disc for Pathé in 1916. [Brooks 1979; Moogk 1975; Walsh 1944/10 with corrections in 1952/5.]

GAUMONT, LÉON, 1864–1946. French inventor, photographer, and motion picture producer, born in Paris on 10 May 1864. He has a place in the history of sound recording as the first person to speak publicly on film, in an address to the Société Française de la Photographie, in November 1902. Gaumont founded a company bearing his name to make and sell photographic equipment in 1885. He financed and collaborated with inventor Georges Demeny in the production of the film apparatus called the Bioscope in 1895. Gaumont made feature films in the early 1900s, both in London and Paris, and established branches in Germany and America. He developed a usable sound system for films, linking a projector and phonograph electrically, and he improved upon the faint sound of early efforts with a compressed air amplifier. His firm used the air-jet principle to make the **Elgephone** disc record player (operated with a gas jet) in 1906. He also made two-minute wax cylinders.

GAY, MARIA, 1879–1943. Spanish mezzo-soprano, born Maria Pitchot in Barcelona on 13 June 1879. She studied in Paris, and made her debut in Brussels as Carmen in 1902; then sang the same role in Covent Garden, La Scala, and at the Metropolitan Opera (3 Dec 1908). She stayed only the one season in New York, then joined the Boston Opera (1909–1917), singing Verdi, Carmen, and Santuzza, while appearing also in Chicago. She retired in 1927, taught in New York with her husband, Giovanni Zenatello, and died there on 29 July 1943.

Gay began recording in 1904 for G & T in Paris, with a song by Saint-Saens, "La brise" (#33384), "Les tringles des sistres" from *Carmen* (#33385), and Fuentes' "La feria" (#33412). In 1905 she made one more G & T, then in 1907 she sang two Carmen arias and two Spanish songs for the Favorite label. She returned to Gramophone Co. in 1908–1910, doing 13 arias. Columbia (U.S.) recorded her in 1913–1914 and 1920–1921; Victor inscribed two *Carmen* pieces with Zenatello in 1930. LP reissues included four arias, three from her great role as Carmen, on Top Artists Platters in 1959–1960.

GAYE, MARVIN, 1939–1984. American popular singer, pianist, drummer, and songwriter, born in Washington, D.C., on 2 Apr 1939. A minister's son, he was involved in church singing from childhood. He taught himself piano and drums, and after high school joined a vocal group, the Moonglows. Gaye's style was the rhythm & blues of the time. Motown's Berry Gordy heard him sing in Detroit, and signed him; there was a quick success with "Stubborn Kind of Fellow" (Tamla #54068; 1962). Many hits followed; Gaye had 48 chart songs by 1977. Among the greatest successes were "Let's Get It On" (Tamla #54234; 1973) and "Got to Give It Up" (Tamla #54280; 1977). His material became overtly sexual as well as political. Tammi Terrell and Diana Ross were among his vocal partners. He also recorded 21 chart albums, most notably the comeback *Midnight Love* (Columbia #FC 38197; 1982), arriving after several years of fading popularity. "Sexual Healing," a cut from that album, won a Grammy. He was riding a new wave of acclaim when his father shot him during a family dispute on 2 Apr 1984.

GEDDA, NICOLAI, 1925– . Swedish tenor, born Nicolai Ustinov in Stockholm on 11 July 1925. He took his mother's surname as a *nom de plume*; his father was a Russian who had sung in the Don Cossack Choir. When the boy was three years old, his family moved to Leipzig, where his father directed the choir of a Russian Orthodox church. In 1934 they returned to Sweden.

After study in Stockholm, Gedda made his debut there on 8 Apr 1952, and went on to La Scala in the following year. Engagements followed at the Paris Opéra, Covent Garden, Vienna, and the Metropolitan Opera (as Faust, 1 Nov 1957). He created the role of Anatol in Samuel Barber's *Vanessa* (1958). Gedda's repertoire has covered the tenor roles of the Russian operas as well as the German, French, and Italian works.

Among his early records were the Cavatina from *Prince Igor* and the Portrait Aria from *Zauberflöte* (Odeon #SD6080; both in Swedish). He made two important discs for Columbia later, "Je crois d'entendre encore" and "Le rêve" (#1614), and arias from *Rigoletto* and *Martha* (#1617). Gedda recorded also on LP, for Columbia and HMV, in 1954–1962. Walter Legge, EMI recording executive, heard Gedda in Stockholm in 1952 and signed him for the HMV recording of *Boris Godunov* with Boris

Christoff. Gedda made an acclaimed recording of the Bach *B Minor Mass* for Angel, under Herbert Von Karajan. He is also heard on complete recordings of *Faust*, *Madama Butterfly*, *Carmen*, *Così fan tutte*, and the *Damnation de Faust*, all available on HMV compact discs.

GEISSLER, H.D. American recording industry executive. In 1920 he was president of both the New York Talking Machine Co. and the Chicago Talking Machine Co.

GEISSLER, LOUIS FREDERICK, 1861–1936. Recording industry executive, born in Evansville, Indiana, on 8 Oct 1861. He went into the musical instrument business in Nashville, remaining there until 1883. Then he moved to San Francisco, and became associated with Sherman Clay & Co., a major dealer in musical products. Geissler was invited by Eldridge Johnson to be general manager of the Victor Talking Machine Co. in 1906, a post he held until 1922. He remained as a director of the company until his retirement in 1923. Under his guidance the firm became one of the great commercial institutions of the world, recognized for quality and a high artistic standard. He died in Fort Salonga, New York, on 14 Nov 1936.

GELATT, ROLAND, 1920–1986. American music critic and writer on recorded sound, born in Kansas City on 24 July 1920. He graduated from Swarthmore College and served in the U.S. Navy during World War II. Then he joined the *Musical Digest* as an associate editor, and moved to the *Saturday Review* in 1947, becoming features editor in 1948. In 1954 he became music editor of *High Fidelity*, and he was editor-in-chief of that journal from 1958 to 1968. From 1969 to 1971 he was managing editor of *Saturday Review*. Gelatt edited several years of the *Records in Review* annual published by *High Fidelity*, and wrote many periodical articles on music and the arts. He is best known for his book *The Fabulous Phonograph*, a survey history of the invention and the industry, first published in 1954, and revised twice (*see* the Bibliography). He died in Philadelphia on 3 Dec 1986.

GEM (label). An American record of the 1930s, pressed by Victor for the Crown Record Co. of New York, to some extent duplicating issues of the Crown label. [Rust 1978.]

GENERAL (label). An American disc produced by General Records Division of Consolidated Records, Inc., of New York. The list included some fine jazz offerings, several of them by Jelly Roll Morton. [Rust 1978.]

GENERAL ELECTRIC CO. An American firm established in 1892, the result of a merger between the Edison General Electric Co. and the Thomson-Houston Co. Thomas Edison was one of the original directors, but he left the firm in 1894. Various electric products were produced successfully. General Electric (GE) was one of the companies that participated in the establishment of RCA, then sold its RCA holdings in 1930 because of an antitrust ruling. The company was involved in development of the **Panatrope,** Brunswick's all-electric phonograph of 1926. It also perfected the **Photophone** sound film method. GE research led to one of the prototype magnetic stereo cartridges in 1958. The British affiliate, General Electric Co., Ltd., was a notable high-fidelity equipment manufacturer in the 1950s.

GE bought RCA in 1986, including the National Broadcasting Co. and RCA Victor Records (which GE then sold to Bertelsmann). In 1990 General Electric's sales of $53.9 billion ranked fifth among U.S. companies and seventh in the world. Consumer audio products include radios, televisions, and VCRs.

GENERAL PHONOGRAPH CO. A New York firm established by **Otto Heinemann** in 1919, succeeding the Heinemann Phonograph Supply Co. The main products were **Okeh** records and a line of record players. Victor brought an unsuccessful suit in 1922 over the tapered tone arm used on the General phonographs. General went into the radio business in 1922, through a subsidiary named the General Wireless Co. In 1926 Heinemann sold the Okeh label to Columbia, while renaming his firm the General Phonograph Manufacturing Co.

GENERAL PHONOGRAPH CO., LTD. A London firm established in 1906, with addresses at 26 Euston Buildings on Euston Road, and at 1 Worship St., Finsbury Square. General took over the business of the Lambert Co., Ltd. In mid-1906 the White cylinders and vertical-cut discs were introduced. There was also a White disc player, which could play both vertical-cut and lateral-cut records. Neophone records were handled by General for a few months, as the firm of Neophone (1905), Ltd., the former Neophone Co., Ltd., was acquired in July 1907. But in 1908 the firm began to wind up, and sold no more discs thereafter. [Andrews*.]

GENNETT (label). A record issued by Gennett Records, 9 E. 37th St., New York, a division of the **Starr Piano Co.**, Richmond, Indiana, named for the Gennett family that owned the business, from October 1917 to December 1930. For the first year and a half the releases were vertical-cut discs, then in March 1919 lateral-cut discs were introduced. The records were cut with extra fine grooves, 150 turns to the inch, allowing for longer playing time than the typical discs of the day: up to five minutes on a 10-inch side. Regular prices ranged from $.65 to $1.25; there was also a $4 disc. In November 1921 the price was $.75. A suit was brought by Victor, alleging infringement of the Eldridge Johnson patent #896,059; the suit was dismissed in March 1921, and Victor's subsequent appeal was denied. (The patent in question was finally ruled invalid in 1922.) Gennett prospered, producing 30,000 discs per day by December 1922. A recording laboratory was opened in Cincinnati in February 1925. In June 1925 a $.50 disc was introduced. A branch factory opened in 1926 at 114 W. 5th St., New York.

Gennetts are significant primarily because of the pioneer jazz material they offered. Masters were licensed to various other labels— Aco, Bell, Beltona, Black Patti, Black Swan, Challenge, Champion, Coliseum, Conqueror, Edison Bell Winner, Guardsman, Herwin, Homochord, Okeh, Paramount, QRS, Scala, Sterno, Superior, Tower, and Vocalion. Sears Roebuck used Gennett masters for its Supertone and Silvertone labels.

Important artists were recorded on the lateral-cut discs of 1919 and thereafter: Louis Armstrong, Gene Autry (discovered by the firm's Fred Wiggins), Bix Beiderbecke, Hoagy Carmichael, Vernon Dalhart, Johnny Dodds, Duke Ellington, Wendell Hall ("The Red Headed Music Maker"), Charles Harrison, Earl Hines, Burl Ives, Lewis James, Sam Lanin, Guy Lombardo (his first records), Wingy Manone, The Mills Brothers, Jelly Roll Morton, The New Orleans Rhythm Kings, Red Nichols, King Oliver, The Original Dixieland Jazz Band, Muggsy Spanier, and the Wolverines.

Jazz recording began with the New Orleans Rhythm Kings (then known as The Friars Society Orchestra) on 29 Aug 1922, as those eight musicians drove from Chicago to perform "Eccentric" (#5009), their first disc. They stayed two days, making five sides, and returned in a memorable spring of 1923, to make eight more sides. A week later King Oliver was in the studio with his Creole Band, recording "Just Gone" (#5133; 6 Apr 1923) and eight more numbers. It was the fate of Gennett, however, to lose its star performers to other labels; Wendell Hall was with them one day only; Oliver left for Okeh in June 1923, returned for another Gennett session in October, then moved among various labels. Jelly Roll Morton and the New Orleans Rhythm Kings recorded in July 1923, then Morton went over to Okeh, Paramount, and others; and the Kings went to Okeh, Decca, and others.

Poor studio conditions in Richmond and some unfortunate recording practices led to a low quality disc during the acoustic period. With electrical recording, from 1925, Gennetts improved in reproduction and had less surface noise. "Electrobeam" was the name given to the electric records, which were recorded in New York, Chicago, Birmingham (Alabama) and St. Paul (Minnesota) as well as Richmond. Records named Starr-Gennett were produced in London, Ontario; they included Guy Lombardo's first recordings in 1924.

Gennetts are scarce today, and some are extremely rare. "Zulu's Ball" by King Oliver (#5275; 5 Oct 1923) is described by Stroff as "the rarest jazz record of all time." Hoagy Carmichael playing his "Stardust" (#6311; 31 Oct 1927) is in great demand; as is his cornet

playing on "Friday Night" (#6295; 31 Oct 1927). The Wolverines' "I Need Some Pettin'" is their rarest record (#20062; 20 June 1924). A non-jazz issue of interest was the documentary set of seven sides, presenting speeches by William Jennings Bryan. It appeared in August 1925, at a price of $.75 per disc.

With the termination of Gennett label records in 1930, because of poor sales and the national economic situation, Decca acquired rights to some of the masters and shipped them overseas for reissue. In 1944 there was an unsuccessful attempt to revive the label in America, by Joe Davis, but the new jazz material released was of poor quality. Finally Riverside purchased the entire Gennett catalog, in 1953, and eventually some LP reissues appeared in the 1970s on the Milestone label with which Riverside had merged. [Andrews*; Henriksen 1968, listing the 6000–7000 series issued from late 1926; Kay 1953; Rust 1978; *Record Changer* December 1950/February 1951 reprinted the 1926 cumulative catalog, and listed releases in December 1953/January 1954; Robertson, A. 1983; Stroff 1989.]

GEORGIA PHONOGRAPH CO. One of the 33 affiliated companies that constituted the **North American Phonograph Co.** It was in operation in 1890–1892, at 43 Walton St., Atlanta, Georgia. J.C. Clarkson was superintendent in 1890; F. Wohlgemuth was general manager in 1891–1892.

GERVILLE-RÉACHE, JEANNE, 1882–1915. French contralto, born in Orthez on 26 March 1882. She grew up in Guadaloupe, West Indies, where her father was governor. In 1898 she began studies in Paris, and a year later made her debut at the Opéra Comique, remaining until 1903. Her American debut was in New York, with Hammerstein's Manhattan Company, in 1907; she remained with that organization until 1910, then sang in Chicago, Boston, Philadelphia, and Montreal. She quickly became one of the most admired opera singers of the time, and has been referred to as the "contralto of the century." She made Victor records from 1909 to 1911, notably "O ma lyre immortelle" from Gounod's *Sapho* (Victor #88166; 1909), "Plus grand dans son obscurité" from

Reine de Saba (#88205; 1909, and IRCC reissue #73), and "Chanson du tigre" from *Paul et Virginie* (#88317; 1911, also on IRCC #73), and. She made two Columbia records in 1913, before her untimely death in New York on 5 Jan 1915. [McPherson 1973.]

GESELLSCHAFT FÜR MUSIKALISCHE AUFFÜHRUNGS- UND MECHANISCHE VERVIELFÄLTIGUNGSRECHTE (GEMA).
A German performing rights organization, operating (under various names) from 1903.

GETZ, STAN, 1927–1991. Jazz tenor saxophonist, born Stanley Getz in Philadelphia on 2 Feb 1927. He left school at age 15 and joined the Dick Rodgers orchestra; a year later he was with Jack Teagarden, and in 1944 he joined Stan Kenton. Getz then played with the Jimmy Dorsey and Benny Goodman bands, and formed his own trio in California. He achieved wide fame from 1947 with Woody Herman, making a hit record of "Early Autumn" (Capitol #57–615; 1948). He formed a quartet in 1949, which became a quintet in 1953. Getz was in Denmark from 1958 to 1961. He returned to the U.S. and earned renewed popularity with his bossa nova albums. Latin American material remained high among his specialties; he recorded with such artists as Laurindo Almeida, Joao Gilberto, and Antonio Carlos Jobim. Getz had a light tone with little vibrato, and though he flourished in the bebop era he did not partake of its rough style, preferring to stay with his own easy and elegant manner. He continued performing and recording into the 1990s. Getz died on 6 June 1991.

LP albums that illustrate Getz at his best include *Captain Marvel* (Columbia #KC32706; 1972); *Stan Getz with the Oscar Peterson Trio* (1957; available on Verve CD #827826–2; including the remarkable "Three Little Words"; and *Stan Getz with European Friends* (made in Stockholm, 1983; available on Vogue CD #651–600034; including the fine interpretation of "They All Fall in Love"). Getz was awarded Grammys for his 1962 single "Desafinado" (Verve #10260), and the 1964 album *Getz/Gilberto* (Verve #V-8545). His "Girl from Ipanema" (Verve #10322; 1964) was the Grammy record of the year.

More than 30 CD releases were available in summer 1991. One particularly notable set is Mosaic's *Stan Getz Quintet with Jimmy Raney* (#131154; 1990), three discs containing material recorded in 1951–1953.

GIALDINI, GUIDO, ca. 1883– ?. German/American whistler. He was heard on record as early as 1907, when Odeon advertised in Britain his rendition of "The Whistling Bowery Boy" and "La Mattchiche" (#34514). Transferring to America, he achieved great success on national tours and on records with Victor, Columbia, and Edison. An early hit disc, recorded in Europe, was "Tout Passe Waltz" (Victor #52007; 1908). He made his first record in a U.S. studio in January 1911 for Columbia ("Señora" and "Song of the Wood Bird"; #A934), but made only eight records for that firm before moving to Victor. Gialdini's repertoire for the American labels was classical and light classical, without popular songs. Sixteen of his performances were issued by Victor, the last in 1913: "Love's Smile Waltz" (#17369). After falling from the catalog in 1925, Gialdini's Victors were restored in 1927. He made two Edison Amberol records, "Birds of the Forest Gavotte" (#701; 1911) and "Spring Voices" (#902; 1912). On Blue Amberols he was represented by four items, the last being "Parla Waltz" (#2742; 1915). Other American labels he worked for included Indestructible, U.S. Everlasting, the American branch of Pathé, and one disc for Okeh. In Europe he recorded widely for many labels, into the 1930s.

GIANNINI, FERRUCCIO, 1869–1948. Italian tenor, one of the earliest to record operatic arias. He made his debut in Boston in 1891, toured the U.S. with the Mapleson Company until 1894, then settled in Philadelphia. He was heard by Fred Gaisberg in Atlantic City, New Jersey, and brought to Emile Berliner's Philadelphia studio. Giannini recorded "La donna è mobile" on 21 Jan 1896 (#967), and made at least 21 other discs by 1899. Later he worked for Columbia, in 1903–1904, and for Victor and Zonophone. Two of his children became famous: Dusolina as an opera singer, and Vittorio as a composer. He died in Upper Darby, Pennsylvania, on 17 Sep 1948.

GIBSON, DON, 1928– . American country singer and guitarist, born in Shelby, North Carolina, on 3 Apr 1928. He was singing professionally at age 14, appearing throughout the South and on many radio stations. From the late 1940s he was based in Knoxville, Tennessee. Gibson wrote and performed hit country songs like "I Can't Stop Loving You" (RCA #7153; 1958) and "Sweet Dreams" (RCA #7805; 1960). His most popular singles, both written by him, were "Oh Lonesome Me" (RCA #7133; 1958), on the charts 20 weeks, and ""Blue Blue Day" (RCA #7010; 1958), with 17 chart weeks. He had 70 singles on the country charts by the end of the 1970s, and also made successful records with Sue Thompson and Dottie West.

GIESEKING, WALTER, 1895–1956. French/German pianist, born in Lyons on 5 Nov 1895. He began his concert career after service in the German army during World War I, playing across Europe. Following his American debut in New York, on 22 Feb 1926, he was soon recognized as "one of the supreme colourists of the instrument" (*Gramophone*, Nov. 1990, p. 1072, review of CD cited below) and for his "profound and intimate interpretations" (Slonimsky). His finest performances were of Debussy, Ravel, Bach, Beethoven, Mozart, and Scarlatti. Gieseking recorded for Columbia, most notably the *Préludes* (Albums #M-352 and 382) and several single works by Debussy; Ravel's *Gaspard de la nuit* (Album #X-141); and the Beethoven "Waldstein" Sonata (#M-358). Angel, Odyssey, Turnabout, and Seraphim issued LP albums. A CD by Music & Arts/Harmonia Mundi (#612; 1990) included radio performances of 1944, 1945, and 1949. Gieseking died in London on 26 Oct 1956.

GIGLI, BENIAMINO, 1890–1957. Italian tenor, born in Recanati on 20 Mar 1920, the son of a poor shoemaker. He went to Rome in 1907 for singing lessons, and won a scholarship to the Academy of Santa Cecilia. In 1914 he won an international competition in Parma, and made his debut in Rovigo in 1914, as Enzo Grimaldo in *Gioconda*. After singing to great acclaim throughout Italy for four years, he made his La Scala debut under Arturo Toscanini on 19 Nov 1918, and his Metropolitan Opera debut (to 34 curtain calls) on 26 Nov 1920, both times as Boito's Faust. He remained with the Metropolitan to 1932—leaving after a salary dispute—and again in 1938/39, singing 29 roles there (from the 60 he knew) in 375 performances. He appeared in six operatic Vitaphone motion pictures beginning in 1927. Later he made 16 full-length films, in Hollywood, Italy, and Germany, and his voice was heard in several others. During the 1930s he won great popularity in London. Gigli spent World War II in Italy, then gave a series of farewell concerts around the world (the last in Washington, D.C.) and retired in 1956. He died in Rome on 30 Nov 1957.

Gigli was widely regarded as the proper successor to Enrico Caruso. He had an emotional involvement with his roles, a factor that tended to produce sobs and breaks that somewhat diminished the impact of his extraordinary voice. He began to record in Milan for HMV during October and November 1918 and again in December 1919. From 1921 to 1930 his discs were made for Victor in the U.S.: 31 acoustics and 60 electrics. Between 1931 and 1954 Gigli recorded in Europe for HMV. Perhaps his finest recorded work is in complete operas and in ensembles, although the "Improviso" from *Andrea Chenier* is one of the acoustics most prized by collectors (Victor #6139; 1922), and "Una furtiva lagrima" (Victor #7194; 1929) is another favorite single. Complete operas made for EMI in Italy, with their original recording years, were *Pagliacci* (1934), *Boheme* (1938), *Tosca* (1938), *Madama Butterfly* (1939), *Cavalleria rusticana* (1940; with Mascagni conducting), *Andrea Chenier* (1942), *Ballo in maschera* (1943), *Aida* (1946), and *Carmen* (a film soundtrack, 1949). Felicitous casting of these sets has made many of them definitive recordings; for example, the *Boheme* with Licia Albanese, and other Puccini works with Maria Caniglia. All have been reissued on EMI compact discs. There are also numerous CD releases of his early Victors, on Pearl and EMI; and various recitals on Conifer, Legato, Suite, Joker, and other labels. [Tesoriero 1990 includes lists of the LP and CD reissues; Peel 1990 is a discography.]

GILBERT AND SULLIVAN OPERAS. This group of works—often referred to as the Savoy operas—by William Schwenck Gilbert (1836–1911) and Arthur Sullivan (1842–1900) has a separate entry here because of its exceptional recording history. From 1907 to 1950 there were 29 complete recordings of 10 operettas; no other stage composer has received such intensive attention (Verdi is second, with 24 complete recordings of eight operas). Most of the 78 rpm recordings have had LP and CD reissues. *Mikado* was recorded first, in 1906 in London for G & T (#3–2476, 3–2491, 3–2493, 3663, 4407/14); Peter Dawson sang the title role, and appeared in many later recordings. Odeon issued a *Mikado* (12 double-sided discs) and a *Pinafore* (10 double-sided discs) in December 1908, featuring Elsa Sinclair, Willie Rouse, and Harry Dearth—all distinguished interpreters of the repertoire.

Among the other singers who became identified with the Gilbert and Sullivan works on stage and record were Ernest Pike. Derek, Oldham, Violet Essex, George Baker, Muriel Harding, Darrell Fancourt, and (most famous of all) Martyn Green. Malcolm Sargent directed some of the finest recordings, in 1928–1932. The D'Oyly Carte Opera Co., directed by Isidore Godfrey, made outstanding recordings beginning in 1949. Decca has reissued the D'Oyly Carte interpretations on CD, and EMI has released CDs of the Malcolm Sargent discs. [Francis 1989 lists the 78 rpm complete recordings.]

GILLESPIE, DIZZY, 1917–1993. Jazz trumpeter, born John Birks Gillespie in Cheraw, South Carolina, on 21 Oct 1917. At age 18 he moved to Philadelphia and played with local groups, then joined Cab Calloway in 1939. In 1941 he teamed with Ella Fitzgerald, Benny Carter, Charlie Barnet, Earl Hines, and Billy Eckstine; then led a successful Big Band from 1946 to 1952. Gillespie played with various ensembles through the 1960s, 1970s, and 1980s. An album made with Oscar Peterson was awarded a Grammy in 1975. In 1990 he attended ceremonies at the Kennedy Center in Washington, D.C., and received that institution's merit award. He is one of the most influential of jazz trumpeters, having been—with Charlie Parker—a prime innovator in the bebop movement.

Gillespie's first record was "San Anton" (Bluebird #36988; 1937), with Teddy Hill's orchestra. In 1939, with Calloway, he recorded four pieces for Vocalion. "Billie's Bounce," with the Charlie Parker Beboppers, typifies his work of mid-1940s (Savoy #MG 12079; 1945). Other outstanding discs of that period were "Woody 'n' You" (Apollo #751; 1944) and "Salt Peanuts" (Manor #5000; 1945). A 1946 record of Jazz at the Philharmonic, "Crazy Rhythm," teamed Gillespie with tenor saxophonists Charlie Ventura and Lester Young, and pianist Mel Powell (Disc #2003). He assembled a star ensemble for his Sextet in 1951 and recorded for Dee Gee label, for example, "Lady Be Good" (#3602), then for the Vogue label in 1952; among the Sextet members were Art Blakey, John Coltrane, and Milt Jackson. Gillespie recorded for 48 labels. The Vogue CD *Dizzy in Paris* (#600047) chronicles his European appearances of 1953. Verve made important records of Gillespie in 1954. Savoy has released a CD of the *Savoy Sessions*. [Jepsen 1969 has the issues of 1937–1952; Koster 1985 has the 1937–1953 discography.]

GILLHAM, ART, 1895–1961. American popular pianist and composer, born in Fulton County, Georgia, on 1 Jan 1895. He was nicknamed "The Whispering Pianist" because he sang along in a whisper as he played. An early radio artist, he played on the election night program for President Calvin Coolidge (4 Nov 1924) with Will Rogers officiating. He was heard on WBBM, Chicago, from 1932 to 1937. Gillham was a Columbia recording artist from 1924 to 1931, beginning with "How Do You Do" (#238D; 1924). His best sellers were "You May Be Lonesome" (#328D; 1925) and "So Tired" (#1282D; 1925). He recorded more than 40 of his own compositions. On 24 July 1930 he made four sides with Benny Goodman, the most interesting being "Confessin' That I Love You" (Columbia #2265). He left the music field in the 1930s and settled in Atlanta. [Walsh 1957/9.]

GILLILAND, EZRA TORRANCE, 1848–1903. American inventor and record industry executive, born in Adrian, Michigan. He was a telegraph operator during the U.S. Civil War, and then became interested in the telephone. Among his inventions were the telephone switchboard, and the exchange. Gilliland was for many years in charge of the Bell Telephone Company's laboratory in Boston, and he was one of the organizers of the Western Electric Co. He became an associate of Thomas A. Edison and general agent for the Edison Phonograph Co. in 1887. He made the first working model of the new type of Edison phonograph, based on the 1878 British patent, and developed other Edison ideas. As payment for his work, Edison gave Gilliland exclusive sales rights in the U.S. on Edison products. The Gilliland (Edison) Sales Co. was established to handle those transactions in June 1888. Gilliland patented a modification of Edison's **Spectacle** device, which permitted an easy switch from record to playback mode on the phonograph; it was used until after 1900 on Edison business machines. A financial imbroglio led to a break with Edison, and to a sale of the Gilliland stock to Jesse H. Lippincott in June 1888 for $250,000. He became associated with the Automatic Phonograph Exhibition Co., and secured a patent on a coin-op for them (#443,254) in 1890. Gilliland died in Pelham Manor, New York, on 13 May 1903. [Koenigsberg 1990.]

GILMORE, PATRICK S., 1829–1892. Irish/American bandmaster, born in County Galway on 25 Dec 1829. He moved first to Canada, then to Salem, Massachusetts. In 1859 he organized Gilmore's Band, and brought it to international fame. He was with the Union Army in the U.S. Civil War, and composed the classic "When Johnny Comes Marching Home" under the pseudonym of Louis Lambert. He gained acclaim for directing huge forces at the Peace Jubilees of 1869 and 1872, the latter with a chorus of 20,000 and an orchestra of 2,000. His band toured Canada, the U.S., and Europe. After he died, in St. Louis on 24 Sep 1892, Victor Herbert directed the band and made recordings with it. Gilmore began recording in 1891 for Edison. His band was heard on brown wax cylinder #2, doing the "Coronation March" from *Prophète*, and on other marches as well as a medley of college songs (#35).

GIRARD, GILBERT, ca. 1868–1910. Animal imitator, storyteller, singer, clown, comedian, and trapeze performer, born in San Francisco. This versatile entertainer recorded for many labels in 1901–1902, most notably with Len Spencer in "A Scene at a Dog Fight" and "Imitation Chinese Song," both for Columbia, where he worked until 1921. Girard also teamed with Russell Hunting, Steve Porter, and the American Quartet. His later Victor and Columbia records include material for children about Santa Claus (1920–1922). He also recorded in Britain for various firms. His last recording was "Duck's Quack" with Kaplan's Melodists, an Edison Diamond Disc (#51189; 1923). [Walsh 1948/2.]

GIRARDI, VITTORIO. Italian basso, heard in the opera houses of Moscow, St. Petersburg, and Buenos Aires. He recorded virtually the entire bass repertoire for Bettini cylinders: 32 items are listed in the 1899 catalog.

GIULINI, CARLO MARIA, 1914– . Italian conductor, born in Barletta on 9 May 1914. He studied violin as a boy, then viola and composition; played viola in the Augusteo Orchestra in Rome and after World War II became its conductor. He was chief conductor of the RAI Orchestra in Rome in 1946 and principal conductor at La Scala in 1954. Giulini gathered critical praise at the Edinburgh Festival in 1955 and for his appearances with the Chicago Symphony Orchestra in that year. He was named associate conductor of the Chicago Symphony in 1971, conductor of the Vienna Symphony Orchestra in 1973, and conductor of the Los Angeles Philharmonic Orchestra in 1978.

Giulini recordings received Grammy awards in 1971 and 1977 (Mahler's First and Ninth symphonies, with the Chicago Symphony) and in 1980 (the Mozart *Requiem* with the Philharmonia Orchestra). Among his other distinguished recordings are the Tchaikovsky Sixth Symphony (Japanese EMI #EAC 30296; 1959), the Brahms First Symphony (Japanese EMI #EAC 30297; 1961), and the Dvorak Eighth Symphony (Japanese EMI #EAC 30298; 1962), all with the Philharmonia Orchestra.

GLASS, LOUIS, 1845–1924. Record company executive, a native of Maryland. He went to California in 1868 as a telegraph operator. He became general manager of the Pacific Phonograph Co. and the West Coast Phonograph Co., as well as one of the directors of the Spokane Phonograph Co. He developed the **coin-op** cylinder player (U.S. patent # 428,750; filed 18 Dec 1889; granted 27 May 1890) and installed the first of those devices in San Francisco. There were hundreds on location by 1890. Glass was also active in the telephone industry, serving as vice president and general manager of the Pacific States Telephone and Telegraph Co., and later was the organizer and president of the telephone system in the Philippine Islands. He died in San Francisco on 12 Nov 1924.

GLENN, WILFRED, 1881–1970. American bass, born on a ranch in the San Joaquin Valley, California, on 20 Apr 1881. He did concert and church work, and became renowned both for the sonority of his voice and for its range, two and a half octaves, beginning at C below the bass clef. Glenn began recording, with choral groups, for Columbia around 1909. He appeared on Victor records from 1913, beginning with "Song of Steel" (#17182). His best known disc was "Asleep in the Deep" and "Rocked in the Cradle of the Deep" (Victor #17309). There were nine other titles in the 1917 Victor catalog. Glenn organized the **Shannon Four** in 1917, and the **Revelers** in 1925. In the late 1920s he made records as Charles Aubrey for Vocalion, with Al Bernard, then was less active. He died on 26 June 1970 in Charlottesville, Virginia.

GLOBE (label). An American record, a subsidiary of Arto until 1922; then an independent until ca. 1930, drawing on material from Grey Gull. The repertoire was dance and popular vocal for the most part, designed for sale in chain stores. [Rust 1978.]

GLOBE RECORD CO. A firm established by the Burt Co. on 1 Aug 1901 as a disc presser for the **Climax** label. The venture may have been backed by Edward Easton, of the Columbia Phonograph Co. Columbia lost its early supplier of (Zonophone) disc records when the National Gramophone Corporation failed in September 1901. The first Climax records were without labels, and showed no connection with Columbia. Only the paper-labelled records that followed indicated a contractual arrangement with Columbia. Eldridge R. Johnson and Leon Douglass bought Globe on 15 Jan 1902. American Graphophone brought suit against Globe, under the Jones patent #688,739 of 1901, leading to a settlement in which Johnson (Victor) and Columbia shared their patents. Globe Record Co. was acquired by Columbia in this arrangement. However, no further issues of the Climax record were made after 1902; Columbia then began to use its own name for its disc label. [Andrews*; Koenigsberg*.]

GLOBE RECORD CO., LTD. A British firm that sold the "New Empire Record," a flexible, 10-inch disc, in 1931. Lido was another of the company labels.

GLOBE RECORD DISTRIBUTING CORP. A New York firm of 1922–1923, located at 30 Church St. In October 1922 the firm, identified then as the Globe Distributing Corp., advertised Globe Records at $.65. each, describing them as "practically free from surface sounds." The records, of popular song and dance material, were also said to "play twice as long as any other." M.E. Schechter was president of the firm, which did not advertise after March 1923. [Andrews*.]

GLORY (label). A King subsidiary of the 1950s that presented gospel songs and other religious material.

GLUCK, ALMA, 1884–1938. Romanian/American soprano, born Reba Fiersohn in Bucharest on 11 May 1884. She was taken to the U.S. as a child, and studied voice in New York. Her debut was in *Werther* on 16 Nov 1909. She sang with the Metropolitan Opera on 23 Dec 1909, in *Orfeo*, under Arturo Toscanini. A Victor artist from ca. 1911 to ca. 1914, she had about 75 numbers in the 1917 catalog; among the most popular were duets with Enrico Caruso (from *Traviata*, #3031) and Louise Homer ("Barcarolle," #87202) and many other ensemble pieces. Her best seller was not operatic, but "Carry Me Back to Old Virginny," (#6141); she also recorded Stephen Foster songs, and even "Aloha Oe" with the Orpheus Quartet (#6143). Gluck married violinist Efrem Zimbalist in 1914. Her daughter Abigail, under the pen name Marcia Davenport, wrote a fictional biography of her mother entitled *Of Lena Geyer* (1936). Gluck died in New York on 27 Oct 1938. [Eke 1946.]

GOBBI, TITO, 1913–1984. Italian baritone, born in Bassano del Grappa on 24 Oct 1913. A man of diverse abilities, he was an athlete and alpinist, then studied law in Padua before taking up singing. His first operatic appearance was in 1935, near Perugia; then he was heard in Rome (1937) and La Scala (1942). Gobbi's American debut was in San Francisco in 1954, after which he joined the Chicago Lyric Opera. His Metropolitan Opera debut was in his most acclaimed role, Scarpia (13 Jan 1956). Among his hundred roles the others best appreciated were Rigoletto, Iago, Figaro, Falstaff, Macbeth, and Don Giovanni. He retired in 1979, and died in Rome on 5 Mar 1984.

Gobbi appeared in numerous complete opera recordings, including the major Puccini and Verdi works, and *Barbiere di Siviglia. Tosca, Nabucco,* and *Rigoletto* are available on CD. [Steane 1979.]

GODOWSKY, LEOPOLD, 1870–1938. Lithuanian/American pianist, born near Vilnius on 13 Feb 1870. At age 14 he was a student in the Berlin Hochschule für Musik; then he moved to the U.S. and made his Boston debut in 1884, going on to perform in Canada and Europe. Returning to the U.S., he became a U.S. citizen, and taught in New York, Philadelphia, and Chicago, while making world concert tours. He retired following a stroke sustained during a recording session (1930), and died in New York on 21 Nov 1938. Godowsky recorded for Brunswick and U.S. Columbia from 1913 to 1926, and for British Columbia from 1928 to 1930. Modern critics regard Godowsky's playing as uneven, with the best results in Chopin and Debussy. Appian released a CD of his major recordings in 1989 (#7010).

GOLD DISCS. The name given to records with sales above a million copies. RCA sprayed a gold surface on Glenn Miller's "Chattanooga Choo Choo" (Bluebird #11230; 1941) to put a name on this award. Van Cliburn's interpretation of the Tchaikovsky Piano Concerto (Victor LSC-2251) was the first classical gold disc. The **Recording Industry Association of America** now certifies which records are entitled to the designation.

GOLDEN, BILLY, 1858–1926. American vaudeville singer and comedian, born in Cincinnati, Ohio. He started doing a blackface act in 1874, and in 1878 teamed with John Merritt. Golden's first records were Columbia cylinders of ca. 1893, beginning a 30-year recording career for many labels. He may have been the first artist to record for Berliner. His best selling recording was "Turkey in the Straw," cited by Walsh as "an infectuous masterpiece"; Golden inscribed it for many labels, beginning with Berliner #726x (9 Dec 1896) and sold millions of copies. Victor's 1927 catalog still carried it (#17256), the only survivor from the 40 Golden titles in the catalog of a decade earlier. Other important work was in duets with Joe Hughes, such as "Clamy Green," and "Bears' Oil," which had enormous sales. Golden's last records were for Edison and Columbia in 1922. [Brooks 1979; Walsh 1944/6.]

GOLDEN (label). One of the earliest records issued from the U.S. Pacific Coast, by the Golden Record Co., 1044 So. Hope St., Los Angeles, from 1922. Material was dance and popular; pressing was done by the Starr Piano Co. Constance Balfour and a Mme. Aldrich were among the artists. [Andrews*; Rust 1978.]

GOLDMARK, PETER CARL, 1906–1977. Engineer and inventor, born in Budapest on 2 Dec 1906. He was a grandnephew of the composer Carl Goldmark, and son of a chemist and inventor. His interests combined music and science; he played piano and cello, and also set up a laboratory at home. He studied in Berlin and took a doctorate in physics in Vienna, beginning the study of television which occupied much of his life. He worked as an engineer in

Britain, then in 1933 moved to the U.S., becoming associated with CBS in 1936. His greatest achievements with Columbia were the development of color television transmitters and receivers, and the creation of the vinyl microgroove **long playing record.** Goldmark and his staff also developed improvements in record turntables, a lightweight tone arm, and a sapphire needle. He was director of engineering research and development at CBS from 1944 to 1950 (interrupted for wartime research on radar), then vice president for engineering research and development (1950–1954) and president of the CBS Laboratories from 1954 until his retirement in 1971. He held about 160 patents of his own, in addition to proprietary developments at CBS. Goldmark was also a faculty member at Yale University and the University of Pennsylvania. He died in Harrison, New York, on 8 Dec 1977.

GOLDRING MANUFACTURING CO., LTD.
An British audio firm, known in the 1950s for its quality four-speed transcription turntables and cartridges, including the Goldring 500 cartridge. (*See* RECORDON.) Recently Goldring has made an acclaimed cartridge named Excel.

GOODMAN, BENNY, 1909–1986.
American clarinetist and Big Band leader, born Benjamin David Goodman in Chicago on 30 May 1909. He had some instruction at Hull House, and was playing professionally at age 12. In 1922 he was with the Austin High School Gang, a year later with Bix Beiderbecke. He joined the Ben Pollack band and went with him to New York, remaining with the group until 1929. Thereafter he played in various bands, mostly Pollack's again, and Ben Selvin's, before forming his own band in 1934. Fortunate in having Fletcher Henderson as his arranger, the band achieved great renown in a short time, especially with the month of concerts they gave in Los Angeles during the summer of 1935 (regarded by many critics as the beginning of the "swing era") and on his radio program *Let's Dance* (1934–1935). Among the famous artists he engaged for the band over the years were Louis Belson, Bunny Berigan, Ruby Braff, Billy Butterfield, Sid Catlett, Charles Christian, Pee Wee Erwin, Ziggy Elman, Bud Freeman, Lionel Hampton,

Harry James, Gene Krupa, Mel Powell, Jess Stacy, Dave Tough and Cootie Williams. Eddie Sauter was another of his outstanding arrangers.

In 1935 Goodman, already the "King of Swing," formed his great Trio, with Teddy Wilson and Gene Krupa; later he created other chamber-size groups with brilliant partners: his Quartet, Quintet, and Sextet. During the later 1930s Goodman brought jazz and swing to a new distinction by performing at Carnegie Hall (16 Jan 1938) and also became the first jazz instrumentalist to excel in the classical repertoire (having studied with Franz Schoepp and Reginald Kell). Bartók's *Contrasts* was his commission, and he premiered it in Carnegie Hall (1939); he also played and recorded the Mozart Clarinet Quintet with the Budapest Quartet. At the same time Goodman was busy in radio and motion pictures. But he was not in harmony with the bebop era, and when the Big Bands began to falter after World War II his prominence was diminished, although he did make his first million-sales disc in 1947, "On a Slow Boat to China" (Capitol #2347). The band was dispersed in 1948, and he was thereafter an independent artist, playing for U.S. State Department world tours through the 1960s, and performing on television and in clubs. He died in New York on 13 June 1986. The motion picture *Benny Goodman Story* appeared in 1956. Goodman was presented with the lifetime achievement award at the 1985 Grammy ceremonies (he never won a Grammy for a specific record).

Goodman's earliest recording session, for Victor in Chicago on 14 Sep 1926, brought no issues. "Deed I Do" (9 Dec 1926) was the first record released to feature Goodman, and his first solo was a week later: "He's the Last Word" (Victor #20425; 17 Dec 1926) with Ben Pollack's band. His series of great hit records began with "After You've Gone," a Trio performance with Krupa and Wilson (Victor #25115; 1935). Among other outstanding discs were "King Porter Stomp" (Victor #25090; 1935), "Lady Be Good" (Victor #25333; 1936); and "Moonglow" (Victor #25398; 1936), by the Quartet, which added Lionel Hampton to the Trio; "Bach Goes to Town" (Victor #26130; 1938), "Why Don't You Do Right" with Peggy

Lee's vocal (V-Disc #233; 1942), and "Sheik of Araby" (V-Disc #366A; 1944) by the Quintet. Martha Tilton was the band's vocalist in splendid recordings like "This Can't Be Love" (Victor #26099; 1938) and "And the Angels Sing" (Victor #26170; 1939).

Reissues on LP included the *Complete B.G.* on Bluebird, and *Giants of Jazz* by Time-Life. Yale University, recipient of Goodman's master tapes through his bequest, began in 1989 to issue CDs in a series named The Yale Library. [Connor 1988.]

GOODSON (label). A British record issued from 1928 to 1931, one of the earliest flexible, unbreakable discs. They came from the Goodson Record Co., Ltd., 12 Old Burlington St., London. An unusual feature was the lack of a paper label; title and performer data were printed on the playing surface. Content was mostly jazz and dance music, drawn from masters of Grey Gull, Emerson, QRS, and others. There was a children's series in 1930. [Rust 1978.]

GOOSSENS, LEON, 1897–1988. British oboist, born on 12 June 1897 in Liverpool; brother of conductor Eugene Goossens. He played with the Queen's Hall Orchestra in 1914–1924, and others in London; joined the London Philharmonic Orchestra and remained from 1932 to 1939. Goossens became the first oboist to gain an international reputation. He recorded for Edison Bell, London, in the early 1920s, and soon covered the entire significant repertoire of the instrument. In 1933 he made an important recording of the Mozart Oboe/String Quartet with the Lener Quartet (World #SH-318). He died in Tunbridge Wells, England, on 12 February 1988.

GORDY, BERRY, JR., 1929– . American record industry executive, born in Detroit on 28 Nov 1929. He worked as a boxer, soldier, songwriter, and on the Ford assembly line; then established Motown Records in 1959. Tamla was the first label of the firm, followed by Motown label. Gordy recruited such artists as Smokey Robinson and the Miracles, the Supremes, Diana Ross, the Temptations, Marvin Gaye, and Stevie Wonder, who developed the new soul style. Michael Jackson was a star of the Motown label in the 1970s. But in the 1980s many of the early Motown artists were going to other labels and replacements were not found. In 1988 the company was sold to MCA and a Boston investment company. Slonimsky notes that Gordy "contributed to the final desegregation of the so-called race music and its integration into the main stream of American popular music."

GOULD, GLENN, 1932–1982. Canadian pianist, born on 25 Sept 1932 in Toronto. At age 10 he entered the Royal Conservatory in Toronto, graduating at age 14. A specialist in J.S. Bach and other contrapuntal composers, he also admired late Beethoven and the atonalists, but eschewed the romantic school. Gould was known as a perfectionist, for whom every note and nuance had to be exactly placed. From that position he found public performance increasingly unsatisfactory, and after a highly successful stage career he determined in 1964 to play only for recordings. He did not hesitate over the editing of his recorded performances; indeed, he believed that this device could bring his work to the highest level of which he was capable. Among the remarkable discs that resulted from his isolated partnership with the recording engineers were the complete Bach works (*Goldberg Variations* won a 1982 Grammy), the three Hindemith sonatas, and the complete Schoenberg piano music; all were on Columbia LPs. Several CDs have been released. Gould died in Toronto on 4 Oct 1982. [Cott 1984.]

GOULET, ROBERT, 1933– . American baritone, born in Lawrence, Massachusetts, on 26 Nov 1933. His family moved to Canada in 1947, where he went to high school and then to the Royal Conservatory of Music, Toronto. He had several roles on Canadian radio and television. In 1960 he tried out successfully for the role of Lancelot in *Camelot*, and was acclaimed for his performance at the New York opening. Goulet became a national favorite on television and began a major recording career. The original cast *Camelot* album (Columbia #KOL 5620; 1960) was on the charts for 99 weeks. At the 1962 Grammy ceremonies Goulet was designated new artist of the year. From 1962 to 1967 he had 14 chart albums, of which the most popular were *Sincerely Yours* (Columbia #CL 1931; 1962), *Two of Us* (Columbia #CL1826; 1962), *My Love Forgive Me* (Columbia #CL 2296; 1964), and *Without You* (Columbia #CL 2200; 1964).

GOURAUD, GEORGE E., *Colonel,* **1842?-1912.** American military officer, later a recording industry executive. He was the agent sent by Thomas Edison to the U.K. in 1888 to promote the "improved phonograph." He brought a model to London in June 1888 and quickly got the attention of the press, then offered a demonstration for journalists at his home on 15 August 1888.

At this and other public demonstrations prominent persons recorded their voices for the ages; among them were Robert Browning, William Gladstone, Henry Irving, Cardinal Manning, Florence Nightingale, Arthur Sullivan, and Alfred, Lord Tennyson. Gouraud also sent out traveling agents to the provinces. Publicity was highly favorable, but the mechanics of recording still held innumerable hazards, and actual sales of the phonograph were modest. [Martland 1988.]

GRADUOLA. An **Aeolian Co.** disc player, or also an attachment for one, which permitted "tone control" via a wire cable, a system resembling modern remote control. It did not control tone in the sense of balancing bass and treble but operated a valve that affected loudness. F.J. Empson, an Australian, was the inventor of the device, which he tried to market in London in 1912. Aeolian acquired it and sent it to New York, where eight years passed before the initial Graduola advertising in 1920.

GRAFTON HIGH GRADE RECORD (label). A British record, issued as a subsidiary of Scala Record Co., Ltd., of London, from ca. September 1923 to ca. December 1927. About 300 discs appeared, mostly of dance and popular music. Matrices used were from Vocalion, Emerson, Federal, and Pathé. [Andrews*; Rust 1978.]

GRAINGER, PERCY ALDRIDGE, 1882–1961. Australian pianist, composer, and folk music specialist, born in Melbourne on 8 July 1882.

He was concertizing by age 10, and in 1894 was sent to Germany for study. In 1901 he toured Britain, South Africa, and Australia. He settled in the U.S. in 1914, teaching in New York and Chicago, and performing in many cities. Grainger met Edvard Grieg, and became known for his definitive interpretation of that composer's concerto. He recorded a part of the first movement as early as 1908 for HMV, then played some of it on a Duo-Art piano roll. He rendered the concerto best in a 1945 performance with the Hollywood Bowl Symphony under Leopold Stokowski (released by the International Piano Archives, on an LP that included the 1908 fragment). But primarily Grainger's fame rests with his own clever compositions as recorded by himself or in orchestral arrangements: "Molly on the Shore," "Country Gardens," and "One More Day, My John," all on Decca #A586; "Handel in the Strand," and "Shepherd's Hey." An LP (Gem #143) reissue presented Grainger playing most of his solo works. British Decca's first classical release in 1929 included one of his compositions, "Jutish Medley."

Grainger's interest in folk music had a great influence on the melodic and rhythmic aspects of his compositions, and it also led him to make early field recordings of aboriginal songs in Australia. He died in White Plains, New York, on 20 Feb 1961. [Grainger 1908.]

GRAMMY. The name of a series of awards given to recording artists since 1958, by the (U.S.) National Academy of Recording Arts and Sciences (NARAS). Awards—in the form of miniature gramophones—are made in about 75 categories, for both popular and classical performances. Categories have varied over the years. They have recently included record of the year, album of the year, song of the year, best new artist, best popular male and female vocal performances, best pop instrumental performance, best male and female rock vocals, best rock group performance, best rock instrumental performance, best hard rock/metal performance, best male and female rhythm and blues vocals, best r & b group and instrumental, and best r & b song. Best rap, new age, and jazz fusion performances are newer categories. Jazz performance awards are presented for vocal and instrumental records, by men, women, and groups. Country vocals and instrumentals have several awards. There are six gospel awards, three Latin, two blues, two folk, a polka, and a reggae. A record for children is singled out. The best comedy and the best spoken recording are honored. There are awards for the best musical cast album, best instrumental pop composition, for motion picture and television scores, and for various arrangements. Album packaging and liner notes have awards. The best historical album and the best engineered pop recording, and the pop producer of the year are selected.

In comparison to the 65 or so pop awards, the classical list is small. There are awards for best classical album, best orchestral recording, best opera and best choral work, best instrumental soloists, best chamber performances, best vocalist, best composition, best engineered record, and classical producer of the year.

Winners were chosen at first by all voting members of NARAS. Since membership is open to recording musicians, the possibility of members voting for their own records was always present. A problem developed in the 1980s when the Atlanta Symphony Orchestra—an ensemble not generally accorded world class status—began to win a large share of the classical Grammys. The orchestra took five of the 11 classical awards in 1989. Nothing illegal occurred, but there was much concern in the classical community and steps were taken to discourage block voting. In the current voting process, NARAS members, plus the record companies, offer candidates, which are then screened by a panel of about 100 experts. The expert panel sends an eligible list to NARAS member, for balloting in four general categories and in no more than nine of 17 other fields. Five nominees are selected in each category, for another round of voting by secret ballot.

Frequent winners over the years have included (in rough chronological order of their first awards) Ella Fitzgerald, Leonard Bernstein, Aretha Franklin, Georg Solti, Henry Mancini, the Boston Symphony Orchestra, Vladimir Horowitz, Erich Leinsdorf, Barbra Streisand, Robert Shaw, Frank Sinatra, Duke Ellington, Bill Cosby, Pierre Boulez, Bill Evans, the Chicago Symphony Orchestra, Leontyne Price, Colin Davis, the Philadelphia Orchestra, Roberta Flack, Chet Atkins, the New York Philharmonic Orchestra, the Cleveland Orchestra, James Levine, Wynton Marsalis, Itzhak Perlman, Chick Corea, Willie Nelson, the Atlanta Symphony Orchestra and Chorus, and Daniel Barenboim.

In 1991 Quincy Jones took six awards, and surpassed Mancini as the winner of the largest number of prizes (25) in the popular field. Georg Solti is the conductor with the greatest number of prizes (24), followed by Leonard Bernstein (12). Leontyne Price has 11 classical vocal awards. Vladimir Horowitz won 20 Grammys.

Other winners in their fields include Chet Atkins with 11 country awards; Ray Charles with 10 pop vocal awards, and Ella Fitzgerald and Aretha Franklin with 12 awards each.

Curiously, some of the most popular artists have received little recognition by NARAS. No Rolling Stones record has won a Grammy, but the group was given a lifetime achievement award in 1985. Two Beatles recordings won awards. John Coltrane won once, Bob Dylan once (and a lifetime achievement award in 1990). Elvis Presley was recognized only for three gospel records. Lester Young did not win a Grammy, nor did Maria Callas. [Variety 1985 lists all the nominees and winners from 1958 to 1983; World Almanac lists winners in major categories every year.]

GRAMOPHONE. The name given by Emile Berliner to his 1887 talking machine, which was the first to use discs as the recording medium. In the 19th century the term remained exclusive to disc machines, indeed to the lateral-cut disc machine; a cylinder player was known as a phonograph. This terminological distinction faded in the U.S. (Thomas Edison referred to his Diamond Disc Phonograph, Columbia to its Disc Graphophone), and the word gramophone was not much used after the early 1900s. In Britain it has remained in use, although phonograph has become its synonym.

The first patent on a disc gramophone was actually held by Edison, and he made experimental disc records in 1878. In 1879 Ducretet marketed a tinfoil disc player in France. (See *also* DISC; and articles on individual manufacturers.)

GRAMOPHONE. One of the principal journals in the recording field, first issued April 1923 in London, published monthly. Compton Mackenzie was the first editor; James Jolly is its current editor. The periodical is distinguished for its perceptive criticism of new recordings.

GRAMOPHONE CO. A British firm, established April 1898 in London, with offices at 31 Maiden Lane. The founders were **William Barry Owen**, on behalf of Emile Berliner, and Trevor Lloyd Williams; the firm had exclusive rights Berliner's British patents and was authorized to distribute Berliner merchandise in Europe. At first the product of the company was limited to spring-motor disc machines and seven-inch discs imported from the U.S. In July 1898 **Fred Gaisberg** came from Berliner's Philadelphia studio to initiate local recording in Britain. Pressing was done by Joesph Berliner's Telephonfabrik in Germany. By 16 Nov 1898 it was possible to issue a stock list of English recordings as well as one of American pressings. In November 1898 a system of matrix numbering was established.

The stock list or record catalog of 22 Feb 1899 included all material available, English and American issues again separated. (*See* BERLINER [label] for artists and works recorded in the U.S. And FRED GAISBERG for material recorded in Europe.) By December 1899 the Gramophone Co. had advanced to a 100-page catalog, with photographs of 41 artists. Recordings made by Gaisberg in Russia, the Middle East, and the Orient were included. On 23 Aug 1899 the firm reorganized as the Gramophone Co., Ltd., and settled out of court some patent litigation with Edison Bell. Beginning with the January 1900 catalog supplement, the famous "His Master's Voice" logo was used, a replacement of the recording **angel (trademark)** symbol that had been devised by Theodore Birnbaum and used since 1898. The angel remained in use, with the **Nipper** illustration, until 1909, and then was relegated to certain celebrity discs (on the blank side, while discs were still recorded on one side only). Gramophone Co. offices were operating in France, Italy, Russia, Spain, Austria, and Hungary by the turn of the century.

In a curious misreading of the future market, which may be credited to Owen, the firm—despite its quick successes—decided to diversify, and reorganized again as the Gramophone & Typewriter, Ltd., on 12 December 1900. It took up production of the "Lambert spin wheel" typewriter, but gave it up in 1904. Owen took responsibility for the failure of the typewriter and resigned in 1905. On 18 Nov 1907 the firm's orginal name, sans typewriter, was restored.

At the end of 1901 10-inch records were introduced, with the recording angel trademark, employing—for the first time—paper labels, these being black with gold printing. In January 1902 the practice began of producing two monthly catalogs, one for seven-inch discs and the other for its 10-inch "concert" discs. As Berliner's American interests passed to Eldridge Johnson, and the new Victor Talking Machine Co. emerged, masters from Victor began to be used by the Gramophone Co. These 1902 records were known as Victor Monarchs in America.

In June 1903 the 12-inch record was announced, but seven- and 10-inch discs were still produced. The company was exceedingly prosperous, with new offices at 31 City Road, London, and branch and factories in India, Persia, and various European locales. A rival firm, **International Zonophone Co.**, was acquired in 1903. The first combined, indexed catalog appeared in November 1904.

Primarily because of Fred Gaisberg's initiatives, great opera singers were joining the Gramophone ranks: Enrico Caruso in 1901, Francesco Tamagno in 1903, Nellie Melba in 1904, and Adelina Patti in 1905. However, the bulk of the catalog remained in the popular domain, with band music, and every imaginable instrumental soloist. There were 10,000 records to choose from, according to an advertisement of 1905.

A major agreement was signed on 25 June 1907 with Victor, formalizing their trading position and dividing the world market between the two firms. Expansion required a new factory, in Hayes; the cornerstone was laid 13 May 1907 by Melba herself, and pressing began a year later. Double-sided 10-inch and

12-inch discs were offered in 1911. The April 1913 catalog ran to 236 pages. More great names were appearing: Feodor Chaliapin, Ignaz Paderewski, and John McCormack, among others.

During World War I the Hayes factory was converted to military manufacture. And the German branch of the Gramophone Co., **Deutsche Grammophon Gesellschaft (DGG)**, was severed from the parent firm. DGG remained independent after the war, but it continued to use the HMV trademark. In Britain records were still made in limited quantities during the war; one field explored successfully was original cast recordings of London shows. In 1918 there was a dramatic attempt to record action at the front, by **Will Gaisberg**; he was gassed, and died some time later.

In June 1920 American Victor acquired a controlling interest in the Gramophone Co., without affecting the flow of business. A record shop was opened, with great fanfare, on 20 July 1921, with Edward Elgar officiating. The 1924 catalog reached 523 pages, including seven-inch discs for children, packaged in albums. A supplement in July 1925 offered, without saying so, the first electrical discs. Emphasis moved to orchestral recordings in the 1920s, first on acoustics, then on electrical recordings. The microphone made it feasible to record on location, and this was done at Covent Garden. But the need for a proper studio was felt as well, and led to the construction of the **Abbey Road studios** beginning in 1929, with its opening on 12 Nov 1931. In the same year Gramophone acquired Marconiphone, Ltd., and went into the radio business. For the year ended 30 June 1928 there was a substantial profit of £1,104,098.

With the arrival of the economic depression after 1929, the American record industry nearly collapsed, and the British firms were in dire condition. Columbia, long the Gramophone Co. arch-rival, agreed to join forces, and on 20 Mar 1931 the two merged to create **EMI, Ltd.** (Electrical and Musical Industries). To some extent both labels retained independence of action and trade. The story of EMI is nonetheless treated in a separate article.

While the above account has stressed the production of discs, the firm was simulta-neously engaged in making record players. Many of the models were the equivalent of American Victor machines. In the tables on pages 297 to 299, Gramophone Co. record players specifically discussed and/or illustrated in a number of standard sources are identified. [Andrews 1987/10 has a detailed account of the record catalogs; Catalogue 1904; Dennis 1946 has dating information; Hanna 1990; *HN* August 1983, gives a matrix dating chart for 1905–1920; Rust 1978; Rust 1980; Taylor, G. 1983 has further dating information.]

GRAMOPHONE QUARTET. A British male group, active around 1906; also known as the Minster Singers, and probably they were also the Meister Singers. Members were Ernest Pike, Wilfred Virgo, Stanley Kirkby, and Peter Dawson.

GRAMOPHONE RECORD. A disc recording, in present-day terminology synonymous with phonograph record; but the latter term originally applied only to cylinder recordings. British usage has favored retention of the word gramophone for record players and gramophone records for the discs, while American usage has moved to phonograph in both instances.

GRAMOPHONE RECORDS, LTD. A British firm of brief duration, established 16 July 1928, wound up 23 Nov of the same year. Its assets were acquired by British Homophone.

GRAMOPHONE SHOP. A New York City record store opened in 1928 by W.H. Tyler and J.F. Brogan, specializing in the sale of European import discs that were unavailable in the U.S. The stock was of classical music. In 1936 the firm issued a major discographical work, *The Gramophone Shop Encyclopedia of Recorded Music*, ed. by R.D. Darrell (*see* the Bibliography).

GRAMOPHONE SOCIETIES. Gramophone societies (most of them now known as "Recorded Music Societies") are groups of people who join together to listen to recorded music concerts presented by one of their own mem-

Gramophone Co. Record Players—By Year

Note: Nomenclature is not always clear between models and types. They are given first in chronological order by date of introduction. All are table models unless otherwise noted.

1898 #2
For seven-inch discs; winding handle in horizontal plane; exposed motor; price £2. 2sh; Clark-Johnson soundbox; soon withdrawn in favor of #5. Illustrations in Chew 1981, p. 46; Jewell 1977, p. 63; Marty 1979, p. 40.

1898 #5
For seven-inch discs; "Trademark" model, first with Nipper logo; winding handle in horizontal plane; enclosed motor; price £5. 10sh; Clark-Johnson soundbox; numbered 3 in France; known as Model B among the U.S. products of Eldridge Johnson; in Canada the Berliner Standard Gram-o-phone, Type A; later evolved into the Junior Monarch. Illustrations in Chew 1981, p. 46; Jewell 1977, p. 63; Marty 1979, p. 41.

1900 #3, #4, #6, #7, Deluxe
Minor modifications of the previous model.

1901 Monarch
For seven- and 10-inch discs (all Monarchs played both sizes); most models priced from £8 to £16, but 1904 Deluxe was £25.

1902 Junior Monarch
Winding handle in horizontal plane.

1903 Monarch #7
Winding handle at side. Illustrations in Chew 1981, p. 48; HN #148 (1986), cover; Marty 1979, p. 43

1904
Monarch with "sound arm" (first version of tone arm), available for first time except for some expensive models offered in September 1903 with the sound arm. Illustration in Chew 1981, p. 48.

1904
Monarch with tapered tone arm; available in a Deluxe model with elaborate cabinet for £25. Illustrations in Chew 1981, p. 48; TMR #45, p. 987; Marty 1979, p. 49.

1905 Monarch #13
With tapered tone arm (in all models hereafter) and flower horn. Illustrations in Chew 1981, p. 48; Marty 1979, p. 44; TMR #72 (1987), cover.

1905 Senior Monarch
Exhibition soundbox; price £11. Illustration: TMR #70 (1985), cover.

1905
Victor; later Victor Monarch.

1906 Auxeto-Gramophone
Cabinet model, with volume amplified by air stream (see AUXETOPHONE). Illustrations in TMR #12 (1971), p. 119 and back cover.

1907 Gramophone Grand (=Victor Victrola)
A console model, the first with a concealed horn; lid over the turntable; front doors to control volume; seven styles sold by 1909, including Sheraton, Chippendale, and Queen Anne; price as high as 50 guineas. Illustrations in Chew 1981, p. 49; Jewell 1977, p. 59; TMR #62 (1980), cover, p. 1661.

1908 Intermediate Monarch
External morning glory horn, no lid over the turntable price £4. 10sh. A 1910 or 1911 example is illustrated on inside front cover and (with interior shown) on inside back cover of HN #151 (1986); another illustration (advertisement) in TMR #70 (1985), p. 2002.

1909 Pigmy Grand   A portable, the first with concealed horn, but not boxed for easy transport; copied by the Dulcephone of 1909. Illustrations in Chew 1981, p. 49; TMR #9, back cover (advertisement); TMR #41, pp. 770–71.

1909 Library Bijou Grand
Table model on its own stand, with lid over the turntable; later renamed as #10. Illustration in Jewell 1977, p. 60.

1910 Model #1
Hornless model, without lid; it was produced to 1924 as a replacement for the 1909 Pigmy Grand; portable, but not boxed for easy transport.

1910–13 Model #7
With external brass horn. Illustration in Jewell 1977, p. 60.

1910   Model #8
Table Grand, with lid, and internal horn; front doors to control volume. Illustrations in Chew 1981, p. 49; Jewell 1977, p. 61.

1910–12 Model #12
With lid and external horn; export name: CZ; Exhibition soundbox. Illustration in Jewell 1977, p. 61

1913–17 Model #3
No lid, internal horn; Exhibition soundbox. Illustration in Jewell 1977, p. 60.

1919   School Model
Cabinet model with external horn; horn could be detached and stored beneath the mechanism, allowing lid to close over turntable. Price £25. Illustration (advertisement) in TMR 60/61 (1979), p. 1655.

1920–24
Interior horn, no lid. Illustration in Jewell 1977, p. 60.

1922–24 Model #265
A wide-body console with lid, and front doors to control volume. Illustration in Jewell 1977, p. 62.

1922–24 Model #125
Interior horn, lid, front doors to control volume. Illustration in Jewell 1977, p. 62.

1923   Model #180
Cabinet Grand. Cabinet model, interior horn, lid. Illustration in Jewell 1977, p. 59.

1924?   Lumiere
A table gramophone-radio combination, incorporating a crystal set; detachable horn allowed lid to close. Illustration in Jewell 1977, p. 60.

1925–31 Model #101
A portable with internal horn and #4 soundbox; played 10- or 12-inch records, and carried six discs in the lid. It closed up completely and had a carrying handle. Price £7. Early versions had winding handle in front. After 1930 an automatic stop was provided. Illustration (advertisement) and discussion in HN #172 (1990), pp 328–30.

1925   Model #109
Internal horn, #4 soundbox, lid. Illustration in Jewell 1977, p. 62.

1926?   Model #501
A table model radio/gramophone, with electric pickup and automatic stop. Price 29 guineas. Illustration (advertisment) in HN #160 (1988), back cover.

1926–28 Model #461
A compact table model with lid, with #4 soundbox. Illustration in Jewell 1977, p. 63.

1927   #202 Upright Grand
Console, lid, front doors, #5A soundbox; used the Western Electric matched impedance system. Illustration in Jewell 1977, p. 63.

ca. 1927 #157
Console, with front doors and lid; "smallest of the re-entrant models"; with #5A soundbox. Illustration in Jewell 1977, p. 62.

1927   #163
Large console, with lid and front doors, and #5A soundbox; a re-entrant model. Illustration in Jewell 1977, p. 62.

1929–31 #130
Similar to #125 (of 1922–1924); without front doors; #5A soundbox. Illustration in Jewell 1977, p. 62.

1930   Model #12
"Automatic gramophone with valve amplification"; an all electric console, mains-driven by alternating current, with DC adaptor available. Included #7B electric soundbox, and model #4 loudspeaker. Plug-in jack for radio, and changeover switch for phonograph/radio operation. Record changer handled 10 discs, with 10- and 12-inch sizes intermixed.

1930   Model #15
Similar to #12, preceding, but changer could handle 20 discs. A "distant control pedwastal" provided some remote operation. Price £215

1930   Model #520
Console radio/phonograph; price £75.

1930   Model #551
Walnut cabinet console; price £105.

Gramophone Co. Record Players—By Number and/or Name

Note: The machines in the tables on pages 297–298 are now listed by number (model or type) and / or name; the date follows as a reference to the chronological array in the previous table.

1	1910	Auxeto-Gramophone	1906
2	1898	Gramophone Grand	1907
3	1900	Intermediate Monarch	1908
3	1913–1917	Junior Monarch	1902
4	1900	Library Bijou Grand	1909
5	1898	Liminere	1924 ?
6	1900	Monarch	1901
7	1900	Monarch (sound arm)	1904
7	1910–1913	Monarch (tapered tone arm)	1904
8	1910	Monarch 7	1903
12	1930	Monarch 13	1905
12	1910–1912	Pigmy Grand	1909
15	1930	School Model	1919
101	1925–1931	Senior Monarch	1905
109	1925	Upright Grand	1927
125	1922–1924	Victor	1905
130	1929–1931	Victor Monarch	1905
157	ca. 1927	Victor Victrola	1907
163	1927		
180	1923		
202	1927		
265	1922–1924		
461	1926–1928		
501	1926?		
520	1930		
551	1930		

bers or by a visitor invited for the purpose. It is felt that listening in a sympathetic group is more enjoyable than listening alone. And while a church hall or schoolroom may be less comfortable than one's home, the acoustics are frequently better. In addition, one can discuss the program during the interval or at the end of the evening, and one does not need to own either playing equipment or recordings to become a member.

The earliest society traced was formed by members of the Prudential Insurance Co. in Holborn, London—an organization that, unlike the society, still flourishes. Members met in a public house in Chancery Lane, bringing both their own machines and some records. Competitions were held for the "best" records, but contemporary reports give no indication of the criteria used. The oldest society that is still active is the **City of London Phonograph and Gramophone Society.**

At the beginning of World War I there were about a dozen such phonograph societies or phonograph and gramophone societies up and down the country. Import of phonograph records (cylinders) from the Edison factory in the U.S. was banned during the war, since those items were classed as non-vital; thus the phonographic side of the societies ceased and did not revive until the end of the war. Some societies lent machines and gave discs to military hospitals. Hundreds of people were able to hear certain society concerts outdoors, thanks to the **Auxetophone** compressed air reproducer; but interest in those events was mainly mechanical rather than musical (aside from operatic selections, music was generally of inferior quality and limited to excerpts of four minutes or less).

With the introduction of electric recording in the mid-1920s the situation was transformed. More orchestral and chamber music recordings were made, and societies departed from an emphasis on equipment to give more attention to the actual music. This new perspective may have led to the increase in membership among women.

After two unsuccessful attempts to link the various societies, W.W. Johnson (a teacher and regular contributor to the magazine *Gramophone*) arranged for the inaugural meeting in 1936 of what would become the National Federation of Gramophone Societies (NFGS). The meeting, at EMI's London studios, was attended by 37 persons representing 14 societies. World War II proved advantageous to the society movement. Since radio broadcasting was restricted to one single national channel, music lovers—including many in the armed forces—turned to the societies. The movement peaked, with some 350 organizations active throughout Britain. Public libraries were frequently chosen as meeting places.

With an increasing number of adverse factors after the war, the society movement might well have foundered, but in fact it keeps afloat today with nearly 300 affiliated groups. NFGS officers and committees (unpaid volunteers) publish a semi-annual magazine with news of their activities. Old societies manage to survive, and new ones are still being formed from time to time. Outside of Britain, there have been occasional societies established in New Zealand and the U.S., but generally with short life spans.

E. T. Bryant

GRAND (label). A Swedish record of 1935–1939 made by Swedish Odeon, pressed by Carl Lindström, distributed in the Grand department store chain. The material was dance music and swing, some of it original, some from British Rex and Parlophone masters. Artists were presented under pseudonyms. [Englund 1970.]

GRAND OLE OPRY. A weekly American radio-television program (televised since the late 1950s), established in 1925 (as *WSM Barn Dance* and given its present name in 1927); the show with the longest continuous broadcast history in the U.S. It is the principal national arena for country-western music performers, located (since 1974) in a 4,000 seat theater outside Nashville, Tennessee. In the early years it featured instrumentalists, but vocalists became prominent in the 1930s with the arrival of star singers like Roy Acuff, Eddy Arnold, and Ernest Tubb.

The first artist to appear on the program, 28 Nov 1925, was Uncle Jimmy Thompson, a fiddler. Uncle Dave Macon, who appeared from 1926, was the first to gain national attention through the program. Among the regulars on the program, Lester Flatt and Earl Scruggs have been most ubiquitous, having held forth from 1955 to 1969.

GRAND RAPIDS PHONOGRAPH CO. A firm located in Grand Rapids, Michigan, maker of L'Artiste, a disc player advertised heavily in 1920.

GRAPHIC EQUALIZER. A device that divides the audio spectrum into segments, usually from 12 to 36 parts, and adjusts the amount of energy that passes through each of them. The results are **equalization** patterns, used to establish the original recording characteristics.

GRAPHOPHONE. A device for recording and reproducing sounds, patented in the U.S. on 4 May 1886 (#341,214) by **Chichester A. Bell** and **Charles Sumner Tainter**, resulting from their research in the **Volta Laboratory**. The unit depicted in the patent application was disc-based; the later commercial model was cylinder-based. The graphophone that appeared on the market was a wax-cylinder machine, and like Edison's phonograph, it was primarily intended to accept and replay business dictation. Production was handled by the **American Graphophone Co.**, and marketing by the Columbia Phonograph Co. General. [Chew 1981, p. 10, and Jewell 1977, p. 11, have illustrations of the first graphophone; Field 1988.] *See* also COLUMBIA; COLUMBIA RECORD PLAYERS.

GRAPPELLI, STÉPHANE, 1908–. French violinist, born 26 Jan 1908 in Paris; surname also seen as Grappelly and Grappely. He played classical music until around 1927, then switched to jazz. In 1934 he organized the **Quintette du Hot Club de France,** and won great acclaim for his work in the ensemble, which featured **Django Reinhardt.** He settled in Britain in 1940–1948, then returned to Paris and made world tours through the 1960s. Among his fine records were "St. Louis Blues" (Decca #F-5824; 1935) and "Tiger Rag" (Decca #F7787; 1941), the former with his Hot Four (including Reinhardt), the latter with a group that included George Shearing at the piano.

Gray, Glen. *See* CASA LOMA ORCHESTRA.

GRAYSON, JAMES, 1897–1980. English recording industry executive who relocated to the U.S. in the 1940s. With Michael Naida and Henry Gage, he established Westminster Records, one of the first LP labels. Most of the masters were made in Vienna, and pressing by Columbia in America. A distinguished catalog of more than 1,000 classical items, including many that contributed to the baroque revival, was assembled by the 1960s. Grayson was responsible for most of the A & R work for the label.

GREAT NORTHERN MANUFACTURING CO. A Chicago firm established on 24 Apr 1907, succeeding the East Liverpool China Co. (founded 11 Oct 1901). Location was 147–153 Fifth Ave. Great Northern introduced a line of record players with 3/4-inch spindles and discs with corresponding center holes under the name of Harmony. The earliest Harmony model to be widely distributed was Model D No. 4, in 1906–1907; it had a long morning glory horn, with no tone arm. Another popular model was No. 12, with internal horn. Matrices came from Columbia and from Star. In 1911 the **United Talking Machine Co.** was created as a division. By 1911 the Harmony products were emanating from a new firm, the Harmony Talking Machine Co. Patent litigation led to a merger, in 1913, with the **Standard Talking Machine Co.**

GREATER NEW YORK PHONOGRAPH CO. A firm located in 1899 at 61 W. 11th St. It sold "original Casey records" and "chemically prepared linen fibre diaphragms for phonographs or graphophones" as well as other accessories.

GREATER NEW YORK QUARTETTE. A male singing group who recorded for Columbia from 1898 to ca. 1901. Members in November 1897 were Roger Harding, Stephen Porter, Len Spencer, and a Mr. Depew. Later members included Albert Campbell and a Mr. Hargrave.

GREEN, THOMAS H., 1876–1924. American recording industry executive. He was twice elected vice president of the National Association of Music Jobbers (in 1919 and 1922).

GREENBERG, NOAH, 1919–1966. American conductor, born in New York on 9 Apr 1919. He directed choral groups in New York, and in 1952 established the **New York Pro Musica Antiqua** to perform medieval and renaissance music on authentic instruments. Greenberg's group brought the early vocal idioms (later including baroque works) to a wide audience. Among his outstanding recordings were the *Play of Daniel* (MCA #2504) and the *Play of Herod* (MCA #2-10008). He died in New York on 9 Jan 1966.

GREENE, GENE, 1878–1930. American singer, vaudeville comedian, and recording artist. His first record was also his biggest hit: "Cancel that Wedding March" and "King of the Bungaloos" (Columbia #A994; 1911). It was also released by several other labels. He worked for Pathé in Britain in 1912–1913, following a successful tour of the U.K., and later made Victors and Columbias. Greene died in Chicago on 5 Apr 1930. [Walsh 1957/6–7.]

GREENE, JACK, 1930–. American country singer, guitarist, and drummer, born in Maryville, Tennessee, on 7 Jan 1930. In the early 1940s he was already playing regularly on local radio. While in his late teens he was in Atlanta, in a group named the Cherokee Trio, then his career was interrupted by military service. He continued performing after World War II, joining Ernest Tubb in 1962 as drummer and guitarist, also doing vocals. Greene appeared on *Grand Ole Opry* and reached stardom in the late 1960s with a series of hit discs. Of the 25 singles he had on the charts over the years, the most popular were "All the Time" (Decca #32123; 1967), 21 weeks; "There Goes My Everything" (Decca #32023; 1966), 20 weeks; and "What Locks the Door" (Decca #32190; 1967), 20 weeks. Although less prominent after the early 1970s, Greene had three singles on the charts in 1980.

GREENHILL, J. E. British inventor and "lecturer on scientific matters" (Chew). He devised the first satisfactory spring motor for the cylinder phonograph, and put it into production in 1893. The machine was made by William Fitch, of Clerkenwell, and sold by J. Lewis Young. Greenhill Mechanical Phonograph Motor Co. was the name of his firm, located at 69 Fore St., London. The motor is illustrated in Frow 1978, p. 164. [Chew 1981.]

GREER, SONNY, 1903–1982. American jazz drummer, born William Alexander Greer in Long Branch, New Jersey, on 13 Dec 1903. He played with various groups, but for most of his career he was with Duke Ellington (1920 to 1951). "Beggar's Blues" (Columbia #1868–D; 1929) was an early success. Greer also did some vocals for Ellington (e.g., in "I'm So in Love with You," Clarion #5391; 1930) and he sometimes played the chimes (e.g., in "Ring dem Bells," Okeh # 41468; 1930).

GREGORIAN CHANT. The plainsong of the Roman Catholic Church, dating from the Middle Ages. It consists of unaccompanied monophonic melodies set to the Latin text of the liturgy. The first recording of the chant took place in the Vatican, after a Solemn High Mass celebrated by Pope Pius X on 11 Apr 1904. Don Antonio Rella directed the recording, which encompassed all the music that had been sung at the Mass; other chants were recorded under

different conductors. G & T issued eight 12-inch discs and four 10-inch discs containing this material. An LP reissue appeared in 1982 (Discant Recordings #1–2). The 1917 Victor catalog carried seven Gregorian items by the Sistine Chapel Choir, plus four by other groups, but attached a warning label to them: "It cannot be denied that these Gregorian Chant records are somewhat monotonous, except to those especially interested." Monotonous or not, there was a fair amount of chant recording during the 78 rpm era, most importantly by the Monks Choir of St. Pierre de Solesmes Abbey, where the most authentic interpretations were made (e.g., HMV #W1115–26, and extensive selection). The chant was represented in the major historical anthologies as well. [Weber 1990 lists about 800 chant recordings from 1904.]

GRENADIER GUARDS BAND. British military band, whose full title is Regimental Band of H.M. Grenadier Guards. It was recorded on seven-inch Berliner and Gramophone Co. discs in 1899–1903, then by Odeon in 1904–1914, and by Pathé in Britain. The band was under Columbia contract from 1926 to the end of the 78 rpm era. The first Columbia issue was made up of selections from *Tales of Hoffman*, conducted by Captain G. Miller (#WA2946–47). Most of the records were directed by Miller, but a number were led by Lieutenant A. Williams. In 1926 the band accompanied 4,000 child violinists in a record made at the Crystal Palace, London. An LP reissue of material recorded under Miller between 1926 and 1932 appeared in 1985, from the International Military Music Society. The band is still making records. [Andrews*.]

GREY GULL (label). An American issue produced by Grey Gull Records, 693 Tremont St. (later 295 Huntington Ave.) in Boston from 1919 to 1930. Matrices of Grey Gull were used by many other labels, including Madison, Radiex, Sunrise, Supreme, and Van Dyke in the U.S.; and Dominion, Goodson, Metropole, and Piccadily in Britain. The material was jazz and dance music. Discs were vertical cut until December 1920, when a lateral-cut record was introduced. The price was $.85. A vertical-cut "Two-in-One" 10-inch record played 5 1/2 minutes per side. When the longer play disc was discontinued, Grey Gull carried the promotional concept to its standard-play record, advertising that they had twice the playing time of the other because they *lasted* twice as long (*TMW*, February 1921). Offices moved to Huntington Ave. in 1921, and the factory was moved from Wareham St. to Macallen St., Boston.

Grey Gull produced confusion with its numbering and use of pseudonyms, rendering a proper documentation of its output extremely difficult. Vincent Lopez led the only well established Big Band on Grey Gull, but Clarence Williams' band offered a fine rendition of "Baby, Won't You Please Come Home?" (#1724). Frank E. Banta, Charlies Butterfield, and Tommy Dorsey are heard on some sides. But most of the dance recording was done by house bands. The Stellar Quartette made a number of records in the 4000 series of standard numbers; Steve Porter, Billy Jones, Charles Harrison, Henry Burr, Arthur Hall, Al Bernard, Ernest Hare, Arthur Fields, and Frank Luther were among the singers and comedians in the 4000s. [Andrews*; Barr 1982; Olson 1986 (label list of 4000 series); *RR* has label lists in various issues from 1967 on; Rust 1978; Rust 1980.]

GRIGSBY-GRUNOW, INC. American radio manufacturer, organized in November 1921 as the Grigsby-Grunow-Hinds Co. by B.J. Grigsby and William C. Grunow; the name was changed in April 1928, and the first radios were sold in June 1928. The address in 1929 was 580 Dickens St., Chicago. The Majestic Radio was its main product until 1932, when it bought the Columbia Phonograph Co. from Warner Brothers. However, the firm went out of business in 1933, and Columbia assets passed to the American Record Co.

GRINDERINO, SIGNOR. "Supposedly the Signor was an anonymous street organ grinder, pulled in off the sidewalk to make a record" (Brooks). "Harrigan Medley" (Victor #5478; 1908) was the result; it remained in the catalog until 1923. [Brooks 1990.]

GROOVE. The track inscribed in a cylinder or disc by the cutting stylus. Originally grooves were incised vertically into the recording medium; this "hill and dale" process was mentioned in U.S. patent #341,214 (granted 4 May 1886) by Chichester Bell and Charles Sumner Tainter for both cylinders and discs. Emile Berliner's U.S. patent #372,786 (granted 8 Nov 1887) depicted a lateral groove. In either method, there is just one continuous groove on a cylinder or disc, although common parlance may describe "grooves." the 78 rpm records were said to have "coarse grooves" or "standard grooves." There were 90–120 grooves per inch of disc surface. [Copeland 1990 has nontechnical descriptions; Frederick 1932 gives technical data on vertical- and lateral-cut grooves.] (*See also* DISC, 5; GROOVE SPEED.)

GROOVE SPEED. The rate of movement of the disc groove beneath the stylus. It varies with the position of the groove track on the disc surface, even though the turntable maintains a constant rate of revolutions per minute. On a 10-inch disc, for example, groove speed is about twice as fast on the outermost turn of the spiral as it is on the innermost point. (*See also* DISC, 5; GROOVE.)

GRUNDIG, MAX, 1909–1990. German electronics industry executive, successful in radio marketing after World War II with models known as Heinzelmanns or Goblins. A British branch manufactured the popular Grundig tape recorders. Philips acquired the firm in 1984.

GUARDBAND. The space between tracks on a magnetic tape.

GUARDSMAN (label). A British label, issued by Invicta from 1914 to 1922, then by Aeolian Co., Ltd. Lugton & Co. were the London agents. There were 700 titles in the July 1915 catalog, a large number of them patriotic numbers. Much of the later material was taken from American Vocalion masters. The label was exported to Canada in 1915 and to the U.S. a year later. Guardsman records of the greatest interest appeared in 1922–1925, in the 7000 "race" series. Of the 38 sides in that series, 13 are by Fletcher Henderson's orchestra, identified as the Original Black Band, and four are by the Mound City Blue Blowers. Louis Armstrong is heard with Henderson. Rosa Henderson and the Carolina Jug Band were included in the series, and Coleman Hawkins' first important solo record, "Dicty Blues," was presented (originally Vocalion #14654; 1923). [Rust 1978.]

GUEST, LIONEL, 1880–1935. British engineer, co-inventor (with H.O. Merriman) of the moving-coil recording head for electric disc recording, British patent #141,790 (1920).

GUINIPHONE. A portable record player produced in 1929 in Britain, said to be the smallest such machine ever made. Dimensions were 10 inches x 10 inches x 3 inches when closed; it had a folding paper cone for a horn, and could play 10-inch discs. The design was similar to the U.S. Polly Portable. Possibly the manufacturer was Guinea Gramophone Co., an English firm that was established in February 1929. The name may have come from the selling price, one guinea. [Andrews 1974/5.]

GUITAR RECORDINGS. The guitar was not one of the instruments popular on the earliest records, and except for Hawaiian music there were only a few items (mandolin-guitar duets) in the Victor 1917 catalog. Interest in jazz guitar playing developed in the 1920s, when Carl Kress, **Eddie Lang**, and George Van Eps were famous on stage and disc. Jazz artists of the 1930s and 1940s included **Charlie Christian** and **Django Reinhardt**. **Les Paul** was a popular performer of the 1940s.

Flamenco guitar playing has been recorded by many artists, among them Pepe Romero and the Romeros.

Andres Segovia brought the Spanish classical guitar to world attention through concerts and Victor records in the 1930s; he had 12 numbers in the the 1940 catalog. Julian Bream, Christopher Parkening, and John Williams are among recent classical artists to record the guitar.

Guitar accompaniment is a feature in many folk music ensembles. All the major groups of the folk music revival in the 1950s had prominent guitars, often played by singers in self-accompaniment.

A problem faced by guitarists is the faint volume of the instrument, making it ill-suited for performance outdoors or in relatively noisy environments. Attempts to increase the volume of the instrument were made in the 1920s, leading to the Gibson L5 (1923–1924) with steel strings, and arched top, and two f-holes. Reinhardt used a Selmer instrument with a double sound chamber. Gibson introduced electrically amplified guitars in the 1920s, and by the mid-1930s the Gibson ES150 "electric-acoustic" instrument was the most popular jazz guitar.

The first commercial solid bodied electric guitar was produced by the Fender Co. in 1948, and was enhanced in 1954 with vibrato effects. Gibson made semi-solid instuments in the late 1950s, designed to counteract feedback. But feedback was used for special effects by rock artists, first by **Jimi Hendrix**. The guitar became the lead instrument in most rock groups. Important performers include John McLaughlin and Larry Coryell. Pat Methany and Kazumi Watanabe are performers on the guitar synthesizer, introduced in the 1980s.

GUN MICROPHONE. A microphone with a long narrow tube along the axis, thus resembling a rifle, leading also to the name "rifle microphone."

GUTHRIE, ARLO, 1947– . American folk and popular singer, son of **Woody Guthrie**, born in Brooklyn on 10 July 1947. He played in New York coffee houses in 1965–1966, gained attention at the Newport Folk Festival of 1967 with his song "Alice's Restaurant" and recorded it successfully (Reprise #6267; 1967); a film of the same name featured Guthrie in 1969. He adopted a counterculture lifestyle, and appeared at Woodstock in 1969. He had a chart song in 1970: "Valley to Pray" (Reprise #0951) and a great hit in 1972: "City of New Orleans" (Reprise #1103). "Comin' into Los Angeles" (on the album *Best of Arlo Guthrie*, WB #3117; 1977) was another success.

GUTHRIE, WOODY, 1912–1967. American folk and popular singer, born Woodrow Wilson Guthrie in Okemah, Oklahoma, on 14 July 1912. He was self-taught on the guitar, and became a street singer and saloon performer during the Depression. Singing socially oriented songs, he appeared at labor meetings and became associated with the class struggle. In 1937 he found success on the radio in Los Angeles, and in 1940 he began singing with Pete Seeger. After World War II he achieved great fame, and attained legendary status in the 1950s and 1960s. Of more than 1,000 songs written or arranged by Guthrie, the most popular was "This Land is Your Land." His career was cut short by illness after 1957; he died in New York on 3 Oct 1967. His son, **Arlo Guthrie**, is also a notable performer. [Kweskin 1979.]

HACKETT, CHARLES, 1889–1942. American tenor, born in Worcester, Massachusetts, on 4 Nov 1889. He studied in Boston and Florence, and made his debut in Genoa; then appeared at La Scala, and toured South America and Europe. Hackett sang at the Metropolitan Opera on 31 Jan 1919 in *Barbiere di Siviglia*, and remained with the company through 1922, returning in 1934–1940. In 1923–1933 he was with the Chicago Opera. He died in New York on 1 Jan 1942.

Hackett was heard on Edison Blue Amberols, singing "Let Me Like a Soldier Fall" from Wallace's *Maritana* (#1724), "Then You'll Remember Me" from *Bohemian Girl* (#1801), and "Lost, Proscribed" from *Martha* with baritone Thomas Chalmers (#28155). The *Bohemian Girl* aria appeared on Edison Diamond Disc #80079 in 1913. Hackett also made Diamond Discs of "For All Eternity" (#50039; 1913) and "Sweet Genevieve" (with chorus, #80007; 1913).

His Columbia (U.S.) recordings of 1919–1930 exhibit his repertoire of Italian/French lyric roles. "Ecco ridente" (#49604; 1919) is a fine rendition, as is "Il mio tesoro" (#98047). He was known also for popular songs, such as "Mother Machree" (#80097) and Irving Berlin's "All Alone" (#140366). He made duets from *Rigoletto* and *Traviata* with Maria Barrientos, and was part of the Columbia recordings of the *Rigoletto* Quartet and the *Lucia* Sextet. Four of his numbers remained in the Columbia catalogs to the end of the 78 rpm era. He was also on the Columbia label in Britain (Columbia Graphophone Co., Ltd.) from 1924 to 1926. Sometime in 1929, Hackett sang five operatic arias for Vitaphone films. [Holdridge 1975.]

HADDY, ARTHUR CHARLES, 1906–1989. British audio engineer, born in Newbury, Berkshire, on 16 May 1906. He was an apprentice for a radio firm, then worked for Western Electric in the late 1920s. He joined Crystalate Gramophone Record Manufacturing Co., Ltd., and remained with the company until 1937, developing improvements in studio equipment. His moving-iron cutting stylus made it possible to raise the upper limit on the recordable spectrum, from 8,000 Hz to 12,000 Hz. Haddy worked with Decca Record Co., Ltd., when the firm acquired Crystalate in 1937, and supervised research on various wartime devices. The most important of these for the history of sound recording was his work on the detection of sonic differences between German and British submarine propellers. Since the differences lay in the upper frequency range, Haddy managed to raise the response of his cutter head to 15,000 Hz. After the war, his innovation was applied to Decca's **Full Frequency Range Recording (fffr)** system, marking the beginning of high fidelity recording. Later he conducted major research in stereo, and in videodisc technology. In 1970 he received the Audio Engineering Society's Emile Berliner Award "for pioneering development of wide-range recording and playback heads and for his significant part in the international adoption of the 45/45 stereo disc recording." Haddy died on 18 Dec 1989.

HAGER, FRED, 1874–1958. American violinist, the first to make a commercial recording of the instrument, born in Susquehanna County, Pennsylvania. He was a band and orchestra conductor for most of the pioneer labels, and recording director for Rex, Okeh, and Keen-O-Phone. The first disc record made by Columbia was conducted by him. In 1898 he made a number of violin solos for Edison cylinders: "Annie Laurie" (#6700), the Gounod "Ave Maria" (#6701), "Ragtime Medley" (#6706), and "Träumerei" (#6707), the earliest recordings of the violin. He died on 3 Mar 1958 in Dunedin, Florida. [Creighton 1974, but users should note that while the list of recordings given there is correct, Hager's birth and death dates are wrong and his name is mistakenly said to be a pseudonym.]

HAGGARD, MERLE, 1937– . American country singer, born on 6 Apr 1937 in Checotah, Oklahoma. His family moved to Bakersfield, California, where they lived in a railroad box car; later he was in prison, where he began to write songs on the themes of crime and despair. On release from incarceration he began to concertize, play on the radio in Bakersfield, and record. He was one of the originators of the raw and rhythmic "Bakersfield Sound." His biggest hit single records were "If We Make It Through December" (Capitol #3746; 1973), and "From Graceland to the Promised Land" (MCA #40804; 1977). He also made a number of chart albums in the 1960s, including *I'm a Lonesome Fugitive* for Capitol in 1967. On 11 Mar 1977 he was seen on the cover of *Time* magazine.

HAITINK, BERNARD, 1929– . Dutch conductor, born on 4 Mar 1929 in Amsterdam. Originally a violinist, he played in the Radio Philharmonic Orchestra, Hilversum, then became its conductor in 1957. In 1961 he was named co-principal conductor (with Eugen Jochum) of the Concertgebouw Orchestra. He was its chief conductor in 1964–1988. From 1967 he also conducted the London Philharmonic Orchestra and the Glyndebourne Festival. Haitink is especially renowned for his interpretations of Mahler and Bruckner (he has recorded all their symphonies), and the classical school.

HALE, E. F. G. British recording industry executive, known as "Alphabet Hale." He was for eight years a sales manager and traveller with the London branch of the Columbia Pho-

nograph Co., General. Then for three years (from February 1910) Hale was with the Andres Brothers, London agents for the German Homophone and Homochord labels. He managed the Dacapo Record Co., Ltd. (for the Dacapo GmbH of Germany) from 2 Oct 1912, succeeding William Andrew Barraud. [Andrews*.]

HALEY, BILL, 1925–1981. American popular singer and guitarist, also a disc jockey, born William John Clifton Haley, Jr., in Highland Park, Michigan, on 6 July 1925. He began performing as a country singer and guitarist with various groups, then turned to the emerging rock and roll style. He had a group called the Saddlemen, which he renamed the Comets in 1952, and achieved great acclaim with them. Several records in the new rock idiom helped to establish that genre in the mainstream of popular sound: "Crazy, Man, Crazy" (Essex #321; 1953), "Shake, Rattle and Roll" (Decca #29204; 1954), and the feature song of the film *Blackboard Jungle*, "Rock around the Clock" (Decca #29124; 1955). Altogether, Haley's albums sold more than 20 million copies. He became a disc jockey after his popularity faded in the 1960s, and died in Harlingen, Texas, on 9 Feb 1981.

HALF-SPEED MASTERING. A technique of cutting a master disc at half the speed of playback time (twice the playback time), permitting the placement of more input into the grooves. The process offers better dynamic range and improved frequency response. *See also* AUDIOPHILE RECORDING.

HALL, ARTHUR, 1888–195_? American concert tenor and vaudeville performer, born Adolph J. Hahl in New York. He recorded for many labels, achieving his highest popularity in 1923–1927. His first Edison Blue Amberol was "Where the Black-Eyed Susans Grow" (#3192); his most popular number was "Here's Love and Success to You." Hall sang with the **Manhattan Quartet**, which made records in German from ca. 1912 to ca. 1929. He also made a record for the Black Swan label—supposedly a label for Black artists—under the name Howard Lewis: "Yes, We Have No Bananas."

(The identical take was released also on the Olympic label, which paralleled many Black Swan issues.) Among the other labels Hall worked for were Banner, Bell, Clarion, Columbia, Domino (as Cliff Stewart), Emerson, Everybodys, Gennett, Globe, Grey Gull, Hy-Tone, Madison, Pathé, Perfect, Playtime, Radiex, and Supreme. Hall and tenor Jack Ryan made a successful series of duets in 1925–1926, beginning with "Hawaiian Nightingale" / "I'm Someone Who's No One to You" (Edison Diamond Disc #51473). In 1925 Hall was a member of the Edison group named The Singing Four, which gave way in 1926 to the **National Male Quartet**. His final Edison Diamond disc was "Sweet Elaine" (#52235; 1928). Hall's date of death is not known, but evidence gathered by Walsh would place it in the early 1950s. [Walsh 1972/12.]

HALL, FREDERICK DURIVE, 1857–1923. American recording industry executive and inventor, born in New Orleans. He set up the **B & H Fibre Manufacturing Co.** in 1907 to make and distribute his bamboo fiber needle; the company name changed sometime before 1923 to the Hall Manufacturing Co.

HALL, WENDELL, 1896–1969. American singer, composer, ukulele player, and vaudeville performer, born in St. George, Kansas, on 23 Aug 1896. He became a stage player after World War I, identified as "The Red Headed Music Maker," and won acclaim in 1923 singing his own composition "It Ain't Gonna Rain No Mo'" (Gennett #5271 and other labels)—this sold over a half million in its Victor manifestation alone (#19171, #19886). It was through Hall that the ukulele became known and popular in America. He directed radio programs in the 1930s, and made many records for Brunswick and other labels through 1933. Later he became an advertising executive. He died on 2 Apr 1969.

Hall acoustics. *See* ROOM ACOUSTICS.

HALLEY, WILLIAM J., 1893–1961. American comedian and popular singer, born William Joseph Hanley in Hoboken, New Jersey, on 17 Jan 1893. He specialized in blackface routines in the manner of Al Jolson, and made records of such numbers from 1913 to 1915. The first was "At Uncle Tom's Cabin Door" (Victor #17316; 1913). He worked also for Columbia in 1914–1915, and for other labels. Halley went on to become a member of the New Jersey State Assembly, and later was a district court judge. He died on 15 Nov 1961. [Walsh 1975/7–8–9.]

HAMMOND, JOHN HENRY, JR., 1910–1987. American music critic and recording industry executive, born in New York on 15 Dec 1910. He attended Yale University, left in 1931 and worked as a disc jockey and radio producer of live jazz programs. In 1933 he became recording director for Columbia Phonograph Co., and spent most of his career with the firm. Known as a talent finder, Hammond discovered such stars as Count Basie, Charlie Christian, Bob Dylan, Aretha Franklin, Billie Holiday, Bruce Springsteen, and Mary Lou Williams. His early recordings included discs by Fletcher Henderson, Coleman Hawkins, Joe Venuti, Chick Webb, Red Norvo, Mildred Bailey, and Jack Teagarden. He befriended the young Benny Goodman, and influenced him to form a swing band in 1933. It was he who recorded the landmark Benny Goodman jazz concert at Carnegie Hall in January 1938.

Hammond became recording director for Majestic Records in 1946, vice president of Mercury Records (1948–1952), and returned to Columbia as an A & R man. He was a critic for *Down Beat* (1934–1941), *Saturday Review*, and various newspapers. He was a strong supporter of equal rights for Black musicians (he was white) and was a significant factor in the eventual success of that civil rights battle; he served as vice president of the National Association for the Advancement of Colored People. His presentation of the Benny Goodman Trio in Carnegie Hall was apparently the first occasion in which a racially integrated musical ensemble had appeared in a major American concert hall. Hammond died in New York on 10 July 1987. [Hammond 1977.]

HAMPTON, LIONEL, 1909– . American jazz vibraphonist, drummer, pianist, singer, and Big Band leader; born in Louisville, Kentucky, on 12 Apr 1909. He began as a drummer in

Chicago clubs, then went to Los Angeles; he drew national attention playing vibraphone—the first jazzman to give identity to the instrument—with Benny Goodman's Quartet in 1936–1940. He had his own bands, and toured Europe. His Jazz Inner Circle sextet was founded in 1965.

Hampton's first solos on record were with Goodman in 1936: "Dinah" (Victor #25398), "Exactly Like You" (Victor #25406) and "Vibraphone Blues" (Victor #25521); he did vocals on the last two. Hampton's band of 1937, featuring at various times Ziggy Elman, Jess Stacy, Cozy Cole, Jonah Jones, Johnny Hodges, Sonny Greer, Benny Carter, Milt Hinton, King Cole, Helen Forrest, and Gene Krupa, recorded for Victor, beginning with "My Last Affair" with Hampton's vocal (#25527) and "Jivin' the Vibes" in which he played his favored instrument (#25535). He stayed with Victor through the 1930s, displaying his own virtuosity and that of his colleagues. "When Lights Are Low" (Victor #26371; 1939) was a notable record in the long list of Hampton hits. He played drums in "Jack the Bellboy" and a piano duet with Nat "King" Cole on the other side of the disc (Victor #26652; 1940). In the LP era Hampton made numerous albums for Columbia, among which the finest may be his set with Gene Krupa and Teddy Wilson, Columbia #CX-10027 (1955).

HAPPINESS BOYS. The name taken by the duo of **Ernest Hare** and **Billy Jones**, one of the most popular radio and recording teams of the 1920s; and "the most accomplished pair of singing comedians ever to be heard on radio" (Walsh). They began recording for Brunswick in 1921, with "All She'd Say Was 'Umh Hum'" (#2063), and went on to make at least 4,000 duet records in addition to hundreds of solos by each man. Many of their records were made with pseudonyms, such as Thomas and West (Banner label); Billy West and Bob Thomas (Harmony label); David Harrow and Thomas Edwards, or Joseph Elliott and Samuel Spencer (National Music Lovers label); Billy Clarke and Bob Thomas (Rex label); Black and White (Champion label); Gale and Fisher (Cameo label). Their finest numbers were "Barney Google" and "Old King Tut," both made for several labels in 1923, together on Columbia

#A-3876 and on Edison Diamond Disc #51155. They made 50 Diamond Discs between 1921 and 1929. "Twisting the Dials" (Victor #35953; 1928) was "one of the funniest records ever issued" (Walsh). On 16 July 1930 they made their final disc, Victor #22491: "The Happiness Boys Going Abroad" / "The Happiness Boys in London." They continued on radio in the 1930s. An LP capturing several of their routines was RCA #LVA-1008. [Rust 1989; Walsh 1959/3–8.]

HARDING, ROGER, 1858–1901. Irish/American tenor who came to the U.S. at an early age and settled in New York City. He sang in light opera and in minstrel shows, and acted as stage manager for some of them. For a short time he advertised his services as a distributor and manufacturer of phonograph cylinders, but he sold this business to Excelsior Phonograph Co. in 1897. Later he had his own music publishing firm, and wrote a number of songs as well.

Harding began to record for Columbia and Edison in 1896 and remained active in the studios until his death. He worked for Victor also, and made some records for Excelsior. The material was Irish, ballads, and popular songs of the day. He was a member of the Spencer Trio and the Greater New York Quartette, plus a group named the Imperial Minstrels. One solo that was successful was "Ah, My Estelle" on the Excelsior label (1898). [Martel 1988.]

HARE, ERNEST, 1883–1939. American singing comedian, born in Norfolk, Virginia, on 16 Mar 1883. He was an understudy to Al Jolson, and "was able to sing all kinds of music from comedy and romantic ballads to sacred songs" (Rust). Hare recorded 31 solo Edison Diamond Discs from 1919 to 1929, but his principal work after 1920 was in the **Happiness Boys** duo with Billy Jones. Hare died in Jamaica, New York, on 9 Mar 1939. [Rust 1989.]

HARLAN, BYRON G., 1861–1936. American tenor and comedian, born in Paris, Kansas, on 29 Aug 1861. He was a versatile performer, described in the Victor 1917 catalog as "one of the cleverest and most amusing of comedians, whether his impersonation be that of a typical

Yankee, a darky wench, or an end man in a minstrel show." Harlan had 12 titles listed in that catalog, and he also worked for Columbia and Edison. His career began with traveling troupes, then as a ballad singer for Edison (appearing also under the name of Cyrus Pippins). In 1902 he began a fruitful partnership with Arthur Collins, recording "First Rehearsal for the Huskin' Bee" (Victor #1723); the two made a successful coon skit, "The Stuttering Coon," in 1904 (Victor #2755). The duo made 42 Edison Diamond Discs, beginning with "Moonlight in Jungleland" (#50001; 1912).

Harlan was a member of the Eight Famous Victor Artists group until 1917. His best-selling solo records were "School Days," which remained 20 years in the Victor catalogs; "Two Little Baby Shoes," and "Where the Sunset Turns the Ocean's Blue to Gold"—the last on Edison cylinder and Columbia disc. After Cal Stewart's death in 1919, Harlan recorded some Uncle Josh monologs. He died in Orange, New Jersey, on 11 Sep 1936. [Walsh 1943/2–3; corrections in March 1943 issue.]

HARMOGRAPH (label). An American record issued from 1922 to 1925 by the Harmograph Talking Machine Co. of St. Louis. The firm, and the Harmograph Record Co., were subsidiaries of the Shapleigh Hardware Co., St. Louis. Matrices came from Cameo, then from Paramount, finally from Pathé. Two examples, vocal blues, came from Plaza. Important jazz and blues material appeared on Harmograph, including numbers by Alberta Hunter, Ethel Waters, and Ma Rainey (all pseudonymously) and Fletcher Henderson, Jelly Roll Morton, and King Oliver under their own names. [Kendziora 1961/10; Rust 1978.]

HARMONIA MUNDI (label). A French label established ca. 1959, with offices in 1991 in the U.K., Germany, Spain, and the U.S. Headquarters is at 3364 S. Robertson Blvd., Los Angeles. Material issued is classical. Both performances and sound quality of the discs have been acclaimed by critics.

HARMONIC. Any frequency in the audio spectrum that is an integral multiple of a fundamental tone. A pure tone is one that contains nothing but the fundamental (such as the pitch of a tuning fork); it is said to have one harmonic, which is equal to the fundamental. Aside from pure tones, all musical sounds are composite tones, consisting of fundamentals and harmonics of higher frequency that they generate. Harmonics above the fundamental are called overtones; thus the first overtone is the second harmonic. The physical cause of the overtones is that vibrating bodies such as strings or pipes of air vibrate simultaneously as a whole and in sections of 1/2, 1/4, 1/3, etc., of their lengths.

Overtones have much smaller amplitudes than their fundamentals (1/5 to 1/50 of the volume) so they do not confuse the pitch frequency of the fundamental. Their effect is to define the timbre of the musical sound. The extent to which a recording or reproduction system can capture overtones is a measure of its success in achieving realistic depiction of vocal and instrumental quality.

Harmonic distortion. *See* DISTORTION, VI.

HARMONIZERS QUARTET. A male group that recorded in the 1920s for Brunswick and Edison. It consisted of Charles Hart, Billy Jones, Steve Porter, and Harry Donaghy. The Harmonizers were also known as the Amphion Quartet, the Country Harmonizers, the Great White Way, and the Premier Quartet.

HARMON-KARDON, INC. An American audio firm, manufacturer of high quality consumer grade equipment for tape and disc playback. Address in 1991 was 240 Crossways Park West, Woodbury, New York.

HARMONOLA CO. A Philadelphia firm, established in 1916, located at 1611 Chestnut St. It relocated to Chicago in 1919, or had a branch there. The Harmonola record player was its main product, offered in various models. Price and Teeple brought litigation against Harmonola in 1919 for use of the name Harmonola.

HARMONY. A disc player made by **Hawthorne & Sheble,** sold by the **Standard**

Talking Machine Co. of Chicago ca. 1908. It is illustrated in *APM* 6–1 (1980), p. 4.

HARMONY (label). (I) A record issued by the **Great Northern Manufacturing Co.** of Chicago, ca. 1907–1913.

HARMONY (label). (II) A product of the Harmony Talking Machine Co., Chicago, having a large spindle hole like the discs of the Standard Talking Machine Co. In March 1918 a 10-inch disc was advertised by a firm that advertised itself as successor to Harmony, the **Consolidated Talking Machine Co.**

HARMONY (label). (III) A low-cost ($.50) line of records offered by Columbia from 1925 to 1931. Major popular and jazz artists were included but disguised by pseudonyms. There was also sacred, band, and novelty material. In 1949 Columbia revived the label for a series reissues of earlier Harmony material. In 1957 the name was again reactivated as a low-cost LP subsidiary of Columbia Records.

HARMONY (label). (IV) A low-cost LP sold in the 1950s and 1960s by Harmony Records, 675 Manhattan Ave., New York. Pop material was offered.

HARMONY FOUR. A mixed quartet that recorded for Edison in 1917. Members were Gladys Rice, John Young, George Wilton Ballard, and Thomas Chalmers.

HARNONCOURT, NIKOLAUS, 1929– . German conductor and cellist, founder in 1952 of the Vienna Concentus Musicus, a group dedicated to authentic performances of baroque music. An extensive list of Bach, Handel, Monteverdi, and Telemann works is available on Teldec CDs. A twenty-fifth anniversary set of 21 volumes was issued by Teldec in 1989. Harnoncourt has also directed and recorded with the Royal Concertgebouw Orchestra, Dresden Staatskapelle, Vienna Symphony Orchestra, Vienna Philharmonic Orchestra, and other major ensembles.

HARPVOLA TALKING MACHINE CO. An American firm located in Harrisburg, Pennsyl-

vania, in 1916. It marketed the Harpvola disc player.

HARRIS, GWIN, 1897–1985. Electrical engineer, an associate of Thomas Edison in 1919–1931. He supervised disc record production, experimented with electrical recording, and became product engineer in the radio division. Later he worked for Western Electric.

HARRIS, MARION, 1896–1944. American vaudeville comedienne, discovered by Vernon Castle, later known as a blues singer. She appeared in New York shows, and began recording in 1916 for Victor. "I Ain't Got Nobody Much" (#18133; 1916) became a popular classic. Her first blues number was "Paradise Blues," in 1917. The best-selling Harris record was "Running Wild" with "You've Got to See Mama Every Night" (Brunswick #2410; 1923).

Her popularity faded in the mid-1920s, but she made a comeback in 1930–1932, and appeared in Britain, making well-received records there for English Columbia, notably "Is I in Love?" (#DB822). She also worked for English Decca. Then she again disappeared from public view. [Walsh 1963/8–9.]

Harris Everlasting Record. *See* CLEVELAND PHONOGRAPH RECORD CO.

HARRISON, CHARLES WILLIAM, 1890– ?. American lyric tenor, born in Jersey City, New Jersey. A prolific recording artist, he once claimed to have made more records than any other singer in the period 1912–1925, sometimes using pseudonyms, such as Billy Burton, Charles Hilton, and Hugo Donivetti. Harrison sang gospel duets with Harry Anthony. He also sang on radio after 1925. Harrison's repertoire included popular ballads and operatic numbers. His first record was for Columbia: "Cujus animam" from Rossini's *Stabat Mater* (#A5275; 1911), then he went to Edison from 1912 to 1915, beginning with cylinder #1003, "Cujus animam" again; and on to Victor for most of his solo work. One of his best sellers was a version of the John McCormack favorite, "I Hear You Calling Me" (Victor #17321; 1913). For Edison Diamond Discs in 1928 Harrison recorded two of his finest interpretations:

"Love's First Kiss" (#18918) and "Sonny Boy" (#18917). He also made some opera records; for example, "Miserere" from *Trovatore*, with Agnes Kimball (#82516). He appeared with Kimball and Mary Jordan, Royal Fish, Frederick J. Wheeler, and Donald Chalmers in an Edison "talking picture" version of the *Lucia* Sextet. Harrison was one of the **tone test** artists.

Harrison sang with the American Singers, the Old Company Singers, Columbia Stellar Quartet, the Metropolitan Entertainers, and with the Revelers. He taught at the Newark Conservatory of Music from 1947. His wife was singer Beulah Gaylord Young. [Ferrara 1991; Walsh 1951/10, corrections in March 1952.]

HART, CHARLES, 1884– ?. American tenor, born in Chicago on 16 May 1884. He lived an impoverished boyhood with his German immigrant parents; attended Chicago Musical College and studied singing. He wandered west and worked as a cowboy, then returned to Chicago and took bit parts in the Studebaker Theatre and in other companies. Hart joined a traveling opera company, then became a member of the Shannon Four in 1917, and was one of the Crescent Trio (1924). He began to record, using various pseudonyms, for Victor, Edison, Vocalion, Columbia, Okeh, HMV (Canada), and others. He sang in churches, and then with the Chicago Opera Co. in 1923. He went to Berlin for radio and recording work (for Electrola) in 1925. On returning to New York he joined the original production of *Student Prince* which had opened in 1924. From 1929 to 1934 he lived in Germany, then returned to America, taking roles with the San Carlo Opera and in many operettas and musicals.

Hart began to record for Victor in 1917, with "Forever is a Long Long Time" (#18283). He made important duet records with Elliott Shaw, beginning with "My Belgian Rose" (1918). His most popular records were "I'm Forever Blowing Bubbles," "Till We Meet Again," and "Let the Rest of the World Go By"—all duets with Elizabeth Spencer. Edison was the only label to carry any of Hart's opera/oratorio repertoire; for example, English versions of "Celeste Aida" / "O paradiso"

(Diamond Disc #80774; 1924). [Walsh 1958/12, 1959/1.]

HARTY, HAMILTON, Sir, 1879–1941. British conductor. composer, and organist, born in County Down, Ireland, on 4 Dec 1879. He was playing the organ professionally at age 14; he went to London in 1901, and began composing and conducting. He directed the Hallé Orchestra in Manchester from 1920 to 1933, and then the London Symphony Orchestra, which he took on world tours. Harty's arrangements of *Water Music* and *Royal Fireworks Music* by Handel were important in popularizing baroque instrumental works; he recorded both compositions for Columbia. He was first heard on records as an accompanist for his wife, Agnes Nicholls. Harty died in Brighton on 19 Feb 1941.

HARVEY, MORTON, 1886–1961. American vaudeville and Broadway singer, born in Omaha, Nebraska. He made the first vocal blues recording, "Memphis Blues," accompanied by members of the New York Philharmonic Orchestra (Victor #17657; January 1915). Among his finer recordings were "In the Hills of Old Kentucky" and "I Didn't Raise My Boy to Be a Soldier" (Edison Diamond Disc #80226; 1915); and "Melody of My Dream" (Victor #18151). "They're Wearing 'Em Higher in Hawaii," his only Columbia record, was a great seller (#A2143; 1917). In 1916–1917 he was with Emerson, using his pseudonym, Gene Rogers. He died in Los Gatos, California, on 15 Aug 1961. [Walsh 1955/11–12.]

HAWAIIAN MUSIC RECORDINGS. This genre was highly popular in the U.S. before World War I. In 1906 the American Record Co. made 27 discs by the royal Hawaiian Troubadours. (Four of the records were issued in Europe on the American Odeon Record label.) Victor had 175 titles in the 1917 catalog. The Hawaiian Quintette—guitars, ukuleles, and vocals—was the outstanding ensemble. There was also a Hawaiian Trio (Helen Louise, Frank Ferrara, and Irene Greenus) active in 1918. Genuine Hawaiian artists, on Victor and Columbia in 1914–1917, included David K. Lua and Pale Kaili of the Irene West Royal Hawaiians.

By 1927 Victor was listing only 16 Hawaiian items; the number had doubled by 1938 and remained at the level into the 1940s. The Hilo Hawaiian Orchestra became one of the leading exponents of the style in the 78 rpm period. Another star in the field was Anthony Franchini. With the arrival of the LP record, the number of groups on disc multiplied quickly. A 1960 Schwann catalog listed (under "Popular Music from Other Countries" although Hawaii had become one of the United States in 1959) about 90 albums; popular artists included Alfred Apaka, Webley Edwards, Arthur Layman, and Danny Stewart.

HAWKINS, COLEMAN, 1904–1969. American jazz tenor saxophonist, born in St. Joseph, Missouri, on 21 Nov 1904. He played piano and cello as a child before taking up the saxophone. In 1921 He was performing in Kansas City, and in 1922 was in New York, where he played duets with singer Mamie Smith, then joined Fletcher Henderson from 1923 to 1934. He developed a full legato tone with a strong vibrato, setting a standard for later saxophonists, and displayed a great gift for melodic improvisation and rhythmic variety. He was much acclaimed in Europe during 1934–1939, in particular for performances with Django Reinhardt and Benny Carter in Paris, 1937. Hawkins toured with various groups, including his own, through the 1940s. During the 1950s he was seen on television and in motion pictures, and he toured Europe again, appearing also with Jazz at the Philharmonic. He was among the first jazzmen to develop the bebop style. His last concert was at Chicago's North Park Hotel, on 20 Apr 1969; he died in New York on 19 May.

The first record with an important Hawkins solo (if not a highly inspired one) was "Dicty Blues" (Vocalion #14614; 1923) with the Fletcher Henderson band. His 1939 "Body and Soul" (Bluebird #10523) is a landmark in jazz, offering a completely shaped melody in flawless counterpoint to the original tune. Another notable example of his art is the unaccompanied "Picasso" (Jazz Scene [no label number]; ca. 1948). [Villetard 1984 lists the 1922–1944 releases; Villetard 1985 covers 1945–1957; Villetard 1987 covers 1958–1969.]

HAWTHORNE & SHEBLE MANUFACTURING CO. A Philadelphia firm, active in the early days of the record industry as manufacturers of audio equipment. It originated in 1894 as the Edison Phonograph Agency, located at 604–606 Chestnut St. Partners were Ellsworth A. Hawthorne and **Horace Sheble**; they gave their name to the firm in 1900. The company made brass and aluminum horns for the Edison phonographs, and claimed to have made patterns for the five-inch Concert cylinder machine. Cabinets were another product, some of them based on a Sheble patent. In another patent, Sheble gained the rights to a tone arm that was intended to rival the tapered tone arm of Eldridge Johnson.

The firm produced record players under the names of Busy Bee, Discophone, Yankee Prince, Harmony, Aretino, and Star, and in 1907 produced a record with the Star label. Its Illustraphone of 1907 showed pictures to accompany music played on **coin-ops**. American Graphophone sued the firm in 1898, for converting without authorization Edison phonographs into Graphophone Grands, and won an injunction. It was Victor that finally forced Hawthorne & Sheble out of business in 1909, through successful litigation over patent infringements.

HAY, GEORGE DEWEY, 1895–1968. American radio announcer and executive, born in Attica, Indiana, on 9 Nov 1895. He was a pioneer promoter of country music, starting the radio *Barn Dance* on station WLS, Chicago, and announcing for it. In 1925 he moved to Nashville to direct a new station, WSM; he initiated the *WSM Barn Dance* show, acting as host. In January 1926 the show was renamed *Grand Ole Opry*. Hay recruited talent and developed the format of *Opry* through the 1940s, then retired in 1951. He was named to the Country Music Hall of Fame in 1966.

HAYDEN LABORATORIES, LTD. A British audio firm established in 1967, known for import and distribution of German products such as the Nagra tape recorder, Dual turntables, and Denon components. The firm has also handled Acoustic Research products, since 1989, and the Korean-made Sherwood line.

HAYDEN QUARTET. A male quartet, the first to make satisfactory quartet recordings, originally consisting of John Bieling, Harry Macdonough, S.H. Dudley, and William Hooley. Tenors on the earliest recording were Fred Rycroft and Charles Belling. Later Reinald Werrenrath sometimes sang in place of Dudley. The group's name was spelled "Haydn" until April 1913. It was known as the Edison Male Quartet on more than 100 Edison cylinders, made over a span of about ten years to 1908. The quartet recorded for G & T in London in 1902. For Victor the group recorded extensively, starting out on 6 May 1903, with "The Tear" and "The Bridge" (#2196); the 1917 catalog listed 120 numbers by them. "Lead Kindly Light" (Victor #16394; 1903) and "In the Sweet By and By" (#16352; 1903) remained in the catalog to 1930. The quartet disbanded in 1914, after making their last (and one of their best) records, "Across the Great Divide I'll Wait for You."

HAYES, ROLAND, 1887–1977. American tenor, born in Curryville, Georgia, on 3 June 1887, the son of former slaves. He studied at Fisk University, Nashville, then in Boston and Europe. His debut was in Boston on 15 Nov 1917, after which he toured the U.S. and Europe, singing a command performance for King George V. He earned great acclaim for his singing of Lieder and French art songs, and above all for Negro spirituals, many of them in his own arrangements. Hayes recorded for Columbia in 1916–1918, notably "Swing Low, Sweet Chariot" (#62050). "Go Down Moses" was made in 1922 for Vocalion (#A21002 in U.S.; #R-6131 in U.K.); "Were You There?" (Columbia #68912–D; 1941) was sung without accompaniment, with great effect. There were several LP reissues of his favorite material, and the HMV *Record of Singing* included his voice (1984). He died in Boston on 1 Jan 1977. [Knight, A. 1955.]

Head. *See* ERASE HEAD; PLAYBACK HEAD; RECORD HEAD.

HEAD SHELL. The housing of a phonograph cartridge.

HEADPHONE. An audio device (sometimes called Earphone, or simply Phone, and often in the plural form) designed to fit over the ears, presenting each with a miniature loudspeaker. The purpose is to allow for individual listening, without disturbance to others nearby, and to focus the listening experience by eliminating much environmental noise. New types of headphone do allow the entrance of external sounds: they are called "open-air," "hear-through," "high velocity," and "dynamic velocity" headphones. Piston speakers are used in less expensive headphones, and electrostatic transducers in more costly types. Low impedance models do not require a separate power amplifier, but the electrostatics and high impedance models do require one. Headphones may transmit monaural signals (both ears receiving the same one) or stereo signals, with the left and right ears receiving the same portions of the signal as full-size loudspeakers do.

HEALTH BUILDER RECORDS (label). American exercise records issued from 1921 to at least 1925, from 334 Fifth Ave., New York. The discs were packaged with 12 charts and 60 illustrations of Walter Camp's exercises. The firm claimed in July 1922 that it was doing a million dollar annual business. It had moved to 254 W. 34th St. by May 1925. Pat Wheelan, president of Health Builders, Inc., was also president of the Wallace Institute, which issued Wallace Reducing Records through mail order on seven-inch discs in March 1923. [Andrews*.]

HEARING. The remarkable organ that is the human ear is a miniature (about a cubic inch) sound system that includes the equivalents of "an impedance matcher, a wide-range mechanical analyzer, a mobile relay-and-amplification unit, a multichannel transducer to convert mechanical energy to electrical energy, a system to maintain a delicate hydraulic balance, and an internal two-way communications system" [Stevens 1965, p. 38]. In the act of hearing, sound waves enter the canal of the outer ear and cause the eardrum to vibrate. Those vibrations are taken up by the ossicles of the middle ear, and transferred to the so-called oval window of the inner ear. This much of the process, complex as it is, no longer offers any puzzle to science. But when vibrations act upon the fluid-filled inner ear, certainty gives way to speculation. It is known that sound vibrations produce rippling waves across the basilar membrane of the cochlea, and it is reasonable to picture these waves as having the same contours as those that are drawn by acoustic instruments; indeed their contours are thought to be the same as the tracings of a **phonautograph** or the cuttings in a record **groove**. As the waves move along the cochlea, thousands of hair tips are bent, producing minute quantities of hydraulic pressure; this pressure is converted to electrical energy by the organ of Corti at the end of the cochlea. And here we cross the border into mystery: for the organ of Corti transmits its electrical impulses through the nervous system to the brain in such a way that the source signal can be decoded into its original composite of frequencies, amplitudes, and timbres. While it is comprehensible that a single pure sound wave—for example, from a tuning fork—may be read and identified by the brain, so that the hearer is able to state what pitch has been struck, it is by no means clear how a signal made up of many pitches, amplitudes, and timbres can at the end of its passage through the ear be again sorted out into its components so that the hearer is able to state (for example) that it is the opening chord of the Eroica Symphony, played by a full orchestra, with one of the horns playing a little flat. Indeed it is not even clear how the ear and brain are able to distinguish among pitches in a simpler signal; a renowned specialist observes that "we must know how the vibrations produced by a sound are distributed along the length of the basilar membrane before we can understand how pitch is discriminated . . . [but] it is hardly possible to observe any vibration in the nearly transparent gelatinous mass in the cochlea of a living organism" (Von Békésy 1960, p. 539). In the resonance theory of Hermann Helmholtz, each of the transverse fibers of the basilar membrane is "tuned" to a different frequency, and is stimulated only by tones of that frequency. Since there are several thousand of those fi-

bers, it may be further theorized that they are clustered in pitch regions, and that certain ones in a given cluster resonate to different patterns of harmonics; if one accepts that view, it is possible to credit the fibers with ability to discern the sources of tones, that is, different musical instruments. And, since each component of a complex sound is carried into the nervous system by distinct fibers, it is also possible to understand how the brain recognizes each bit in the mosaic of an orchestral chord. The trouble with the resonance theory is that the environment of the fibers appears to be hostile to such resonating: they are, after all, buried in a membrane and covered with a fluid.

A variety of theories have been based on the idea of a sound pattern that emerges as sinusoidal movement sets up a series of standing waves along the fibers; each of these waves is perceived by the nervous system as a single tone—but, as Von Békésy comments, "Because the entire task of analysis is relegated to the nervous system, whose activites are completely unknown, it is not possible to draw any further conclusions on the basis of this theory." Von Békésy himself, after a lifetime of imaginative experimentation, was unable to answer the question of tone recognition and the question of how the ear resolves complex sounds.

Lacking any measurable evidence for the theories suggested above, it is probably just as reasonable to approach the act of hearing in another way: "We may concede that one day the whole process, including the chemico-electrical actions in the brain, will be bared. The tone, however, will never be found. It is not an object, to be found in the outer world; and the organ of Corti, the nerves, and the brain are all part of the outer world. One might as well expect to find the soul by dissecting the body" (1965, p. 165).

As we depart from the rigid viewpoint of the physical sciences, we encounter other fascinating questions about "subjective" hearing—recently termed "psychoacoustics." Why, for instance, do we hear music with more pleasure than we hear a screeching noise? Why is a minor chord "sad"? How does our brain allow us to imagine, as we listen to a musical work, what had gone before and what is yet to be heard, and to remember simultaneously other performances of the work? And how does the brain establish, in response to a stereo recording, the source of the signal as somewhere between the loudspeakers? [Backus 1969; Helmholtz 1877; Kohut 1950; Levarie 1965; Levarie 1977; Levarie 1980; Stevens 1965; Von Békésy 1960.]

HEGAMIN, LUCILLE, 1894–1970. American blues singer, born Lucille Nelson in Macon, Georgia, on 29 Nov 1894. She was a church singer, then on stage; she married pianist William Hegamin, who acted as her accompanist. She achieved success on a West Coast tour in 1918–1919, and began recording for Arto. Her earliest record, "Jazz Me Blues" and "Everybody's Blues" (Arto #9045; 1920) "could be considered the first real blues disc" (Dixon). Hegamin had a hit with her next record, "I'll be Good but I'll be Lonesome" / "Arkansas Blues" (Arto #9053; 1921), which was released on ten labels from the Arto masters. She introduced "Pretty Baby" and "Jelly Roll Blues," and she may have been the first to sing the "St. Louis Blues." With a group she named the Blue Flame Syncopaters [sic] she made another dozen popular discs. When Arto went bankrupt in 1923, Hegamin worked mostly for Cameo until 1926. She was heard on more than 20 labels during her career. She quit recording for six years, singing in clubs, then returned briefly with Okeh in 1932. Hegamin retired shortly thereafter, though she made a few more records in 1961–1962 for Prestige, Bluesville, and Victoria Spivey. She died in New York on 1 Mar 1970. [Dixon 1970; Kundstadt 1962.]

HEIDT, HORACE, 1901–1986. American Big Band leader, born in Alameda, California, on 21 May 1901. He was playing piano professionally by 1923, and toured with vaudeville companies. In 1930 he formed an orchestra named the Californians, successful in the New York Palace Theater. He had a long run at the Drake Hotel in Chicago in 1935, and became prominent on the radio. His group was a smooth dance ensemble, with several outstanding musicians in the group: Alvino Rey (electric guitar), Frankie Carle (piano), and Larry Cotton (vocals). The whistler Fred Lowery was featured, and later singer Gordon MacRae and cornetist Bobby Hackett. The orchestra achieved its peak in 1939–1942, renamed Horace Heidt and His Musical Knights. They recorded regularly for Brunswick and then for Columbia. Mary Martin did a series of vocals with the band in 1942, including "That Old Black Magic" (Columbia #36670). Heidt concentrated on radio and television through the mid-1950s, then retired.

HEIFETZ, JASCHA, 1901–1987. Lithuanian/ American violinist, born in Vilnius on 2 Feb 1901. Taught by his father, he played in public at age four. In 1910 he entered the St. Petersburg Conservatory, studying with Leopold Auer, and the next year he gave his debut recital. Young Heifetz performed the Tchaikovsky Concerto with the Berlin Philharmonic Orchestra in 1912, and made world tours. He achieved instant fame in America after his first appearance, at Carnegie Hall on 27 Oct 1917. He became a U.S. citizen in 1925, and continued to perform worldwide until 1970, gaining general recognition as the finest of virtuosos on his instrument. Heifetz made fewer appearances after World War II, and taught at the University of Southern California from 1962.

A Victor artist from 1918, Heifetz at first recorded light recital pieces with piano accompaniment, such as "On Wings of Song" (#6512). In the 1930s he approached the grand repertoire, recording Mozart sonatas (with Emanuel Bay) and the principal concertos. He joined with Thomas Beecham and the London Philharmonic Orchestra in 1935 to produce what may be his finest disc, the Sibelius Concerto (#14016/19). There were 44 items in the 1938 Victor catalog, including his famous arrangement of Dinicu's "Hora staccato" (#1864). He then made an outstanding recording of the Cesar Franck Sonata with Artur Rubinstein (#14895/97). Important chamber music interpretations with Rubinstein, violist William Primrose, and cellist Emmanuel Feuermann appeared in the 1940s. Six albums of four LP discs each, covering the Heifetz releases of 1917 to the 1950s, were issued by RCA on #ARM-0942/47. RCA CD #RD85402 (1985) presented the acclaimed performances of the

Beethoven and Brahms concertos with the Boston Symphony Orchestra.

HEINEMANN, OTTO. German-born recording industry executive, active in Berlin from 1902 and in the U.S. after 1914. He established the Otto Heinemann Phonograph Supply Co. at 45 Broadway, New York, in 1914 (moving to 25 W. 45th St. in the following year), with a factory in Elyria, Ohio. The firm made tone arm rests, needle cups, and other accessories; then began to make the Okeh (spelled "OkeH") disc in May 1918. The success of this record led to the opening of branch offices in Chicago and Toronto. In October 1919 Heinemann renamed his firm the **General Phonograph Co.** When Columbia bought the OkeH label in 1926, he became president of the Okeh Phonograph Co., a Columbia subsidiary. Heinemann was the first vice president of the Phonograph Manufacturers National Association on its establishment in 1925.

HELIODOR (label). A German record, the low-priced series of DGG, issued from June 1959. The name was not carried forward into the CD period.

HEMPEL, FRIEDA, 1885–1955. German coloratura soprano, born in Leipzig on 26 June 1885. She studied at the Leipzig Conservatory from age 15, as a piano student, and then went to Berlin to study voice. She sang in Breslau, then at the Berlin Opera on 22 Aug 1905 and throughout Germany. Hempel made her Metropolitan Opera debut as the Queen in *Huguenots* on 27 Dec 1912, and remained with the company to 1919. She lived in New York most of her life, returning to Berlin just before her death on 7 Oct 1955.

Hempel's repertoire emphasized the Italian/French operas and the lighter German works. She recorded first for Odeon in 1906–1909, then for the Gramophone Co., and for Victor from 1912 to 1917 (25 items in the 1917 catalog). She also made Edison discs and cylinders from 1917 to 1923 (beginning with "Air and Variations" by Heinrich Proch, #5937) and again in 1928. HMV recorded her in 1923–1925. "Infelice sconsolata" from *Zauberflöte* (HMV #DB331) is a favorite among collectors; "Volta

la terra" from *Ballo in maschera* (Victor #87235) is another fine rendition. Hempel sang popular material as well as opera and Lieder, including "My Old Kentucky Home" with the Criterion Quartet (Edison Diamond Disc #82551, Blue Amberol cylinder #5966; 1918) and "Aloha oe" with the Criterion Quartet (Edison Diamond Disc #82551, Blue Amberol #5992; 1918). Her final commercial record was a Diamond Disc of "Songs My Mother Taught Me," in German (#80888; 1928), but she was also recorded on the air during the *Edison Hour* program of 11 Feb 1929, an observation of the inventor's birthday. [Reed 1955; Wile 1971/3.]

HEMUS, PERCY, ca. 1878–1945. New Zealand baritone, born in Auckland. At an early age he moved to the U.S., settling first in Kansas, and then going to New York. He was a soloist at St. Patrick's Cathedral for five years, and sang in operetta; later he performed in minstrel shows. By 1906 he was making records for Columbia and Imperial; and from 1907 to 1916 he was a Victor artist, beginning with "The Sailor's Prayer" (#5348; 1907). Hemus used the pseudonym Charles Gordon at times. He died in New York on 22 Dec 1945.

HENDERSON, FLETCHER, 1897–1952. American Big Band leader and arranger, born in Cuthbert, Georgia, on 18 Dec 1897. He took a chemistry degree in Atlanta before going to New York in 1920, where he worked for a song publisher, became house pianist for Black Swan, and made his first recordings for them in 1921; and toured with Ethel Waters. He formed his first band in 1921 and began to compile a vast list of recordings; his group is considered the earliest major swing band. Star performers in his various groups include Louis Armstrong, Coleman Hawkins (whose first important solo record was made with Henderson in 1923), Rex Stewart, Benny Carter, Roy Eldridge, and J.C. Higginbotham. He began arranging in the 1930s, and was recognized as one of the shapers of the new swing sound. Working with Benny Goodman he wrote the outstanding arrangements of much that Goodman featured during the prime years of his band. He was also pianist in the Benny Goodman Sextet of 1939, recording "Rose Room" (Columbia #35254) and six other numbers. Henderson did arrangements for the Casa Loma Orchestra, the Dorseys, and others.

His bands played under various pseudonyms on myriad labels: High Society Seven, National Music Lovers' Dance Orchestra, Carolinians, Original Black Band, Maryland Dance Orchestra, Eldon's Dance Orchestra, Roseland Dance Orchestra, Club Alabam Orchestra, Sam Hill and His Orchestra, Regent Orchestra, Henri Gendron and His Strand Roof Orchestra, Club Wigwam Orchestra, California Melodie Syncopators, Carolinians, Lenox Dance Orchestra, Southampton Society Orchestra, Missouri Jazz Band, Sid Terry's Collegians, Dixie Stompers, Louisiana Stompers, Earl Randolph's Orchestra, Curry's Dance Orchestra, Savannah Syncopators, and others.

His career ended with a stroke in 1950, and he died in New York on 29 Dec 1952. [Allen 1973 is a bio-discography.]

HENDRIX, JIMI, 1942–1970. Rock singer and guitarist, born James Marshall Hendrix in Seattle, Washington, on 27 Nov 1942. He taught himself to play the guitar and performed with various groups. He toured widely in the 1960s, developing a stage presence that included bizarre costumes, flamboyant guitar techniques, and oftentimes the smashing or burning of his instrument to close a show. He formed a group called the Jimi Hendrix Experience in 1966, and cut a chart single, "Purple Haze" (Reprise #0597; 1967), and a greatly successful album, *Are You Experienced?* (Reprise #R6250; 1967), that was on the charts for 87 weeks. The album featured an extensive repertoire of engineering effects, such as playing some material backwards. In 1967 Hendrix was a hit at the Monterey Pop Festival in California, and he toured the U.S., receiving mixed notices. He opened his own recording studio, Electric Lady, in Greenwich Village and continued to work on new timbres and recording techniques. Hendrix had several important albums in the late 1960s, including *Axis: Bold as Love* (Reprise #RS 6281; 1968) and *Electric Ladyland* (Reprise #2RS 6307; 1968). After his premature death in London, on 18 Sep 1970, there were successful posthumous releases of a half dozen albums by Reprise. The same label has made his output available on CD.

HERMAN, WOODY, 1913–1987. American jazz clarinetist, saxophonist, vocalist, and Big Band leader; born Woodrow Charles Herman in Milwaukee, Wisconsin on 16 May 1913. He studied at Marquette University, and began playing clarinet in bands in 1931. In 1934–1936 he was with Isham Jones, and when that group dissolved he drew on the membership to form his own band in 1936; it soon became known for a progressive jazz style, blended with a blues idiom. In the several bands that he directed—known as "Herds" or "Woodchoppers"—there was a strong ensemble with virtuosic improvisations. Among the great soloists were Herman himself, Dave Tough, Stan Getz, and baritone saxophonist Serge Chaloff. Gordon Jenkins made numerous arrangements. Herman was a skilled performer in the classical idiom as well, and was privileged to have Stravinsky's *Ebony Concerto* written form him; he premiered the work at Carnegie Hall on 25 Mar 1946, and recorded it (Columbia #7479M; 1946). He was active as a leader and soloist with various groups into the 1970s, adjusting to new popular styles as they came along. His band was featured in five motion pictures.

The earliest recording by Herman's orchestra took place on 6 Nov 1936 for Decca: "Wintertime Dreams," with vocal by Herman (#1056). Among his finest records were "At the Woodchopper's Ball" (Decca #2440; 1939); "Blues on Parade" (Decca #3501; 1939); "Blue Prelude" (Decca #3017; 1940); "Caldonia" (Columbia #36789; 1945), and "Lemon Drop" (Capitol #15365; 1948). There were many LP albums and reissues.

HERSCHEL GOLD SEAL (label). An American record issued in 1926–1927 by the Northwest Phonograph and Supply Co., St. Paul/Minneapolis, Minnesota. Masters came from Gennett. Only 21 items were released, mostly dance music. Vaughn De Leath and Vernon Dalhart were among the popular vocalists on the label. [Henriksen 1975; Rust 1978.]

HERTZ (Hz). The name often given to the unit of frequency formerly identified as one cycle per second. This designation, in use since 1967, was derived from the name of Heinrich R. Hertz, German physicist (1857–1894). One kilohertz (kHz) equals 1,000 cycles per second; one megahertz (MHz) equals 1,000,000 cycles per second.

HERWIN (label). An American record issued by the **Artophone Corp.** of St. Louis from 1924 to 1930. The label name was derived from the names of the two chief officers of Artophone, Herbert and Edwin Schiele. Only 18 releases are known, including some interesting jazz material and 11 songs by Vernon Dalhart. Paramount, which had provided some of the masters, bought the firm through its subsidiary, the Wisconsin Chair Co. [*RR* #69 and #71 has lists; Rust 1978.]

HESS, MYRA, *Dame,* **1890–1965.** British pianist, born in London on 25 Feb 1890. She studied at the Royal Academy of Music, and made her London debut at age 17, playing the Beethoven G-Major Concerto under Thomas Beecham. European and American tours followed. During World War II she initiated the National Gallery Concerts as a morale measure, and was awarded the honor Dame of the British Empire in 1941. She died in London on 25 Nov 1965.

Hess recorded for Victor/HMV and Columbia, featuring Mozart, Haydn, Beethoven, Brahms, and Schubert. She assisted in a revival of interest in Schubert through recitals and recordings, including the A-Major Sonata (Columbia #L2119/21; 1928). Early piano roll performances of Bach, Brahms, Rachmaninoff, and others were reissued by HMV in 1974 (#GVC28). Several CD reissues have appeared. [Clough 1966.].

HEXAPHONE. A **coin-op** cylinder phonograph manufactured by **Regina Music Box Co.** in 1906. It allowed a choice among six Indestructible two-minute records, using a spring-driven motor, or in some cases an electric motor, with a wooden horn.

Hi Fi. *See* HIGH FIDELITY.

HIGGINBOTHAM, J.C., 1906–1973. American jazz trombonist, born in Atlanta on 11 May 1906. In the late 1920s he played with Luis Russell, and Chick Webb, then in 1931–1933 with Fletcher Henderson. Later groups were Benny Carter, Louis Armstrong, and Red Allen. He had a strong, bold tone, influential on subsequent artists. Higginbotham led his own band for a time, and remained active into the 1970s. He died 26 May 1973 in New York.

One of his outstanding records was Okeh #8772, of 5 Feb 1930: "Give Me Your Telephone Number" / "Higginbotham Blues." He had prominent solo work in Armstrong's "Once in Awhile" / "On the Sunny Side of the Street" (Decca #1560; 1937) and in Bechet's "Coal Black Shine" / "Baby, Won't You Please Come Home?" (Victor #27386; 1941).

HIGH FIDELITY (HI FI). The term given to realistic reproduction of sound, concerned mainly with its frequency response. It came into use in the mid-1930s in the U.S. record business, although commercial recordings of that time scarcely exceeded 6,000 Hz. During the 1940s, as the capability of 78 rpm discs reached the 30–14,000 Hz audio range, with a 50 dB dynamic spread, a greater credibility was attached to the term. In the 1950s there was a popular appetite for achieving maximum hi fi, expressed through the interest in separate components and in the purchase of audio kits to be constructed at home. Stereo sound in the 1950s enhanced the realistic quality of playback, and the wide public attachment to the concept.

HIGH FIDELITY. The name of a magazine published in the U.S. from 1951 to 1989; *See* SOUND RECORDING PERIODICALS.

High pass filter. *See* FILTER.

HIGHAM AMPLIFIER. A sound amplifying device invented by Daniel Higham of Massachusetts, U.S. patent #678,566 (granted 16 July 1901). "Amplified vibrations were delivered by means of a variable tension device involving a cord running over an amber wheel, augmenting the pull from the stylus bar by force supplied by the motor turning the amber wheel" (Read). In 1904 the inventor formed the Higham-O-Phone Co., and developed the concept continually (six further patents were granted). The device was shown at the St. Louis Exposition of 1904, and was used in the 1905 Columbia Twentieth-Century Premier Graphophone (Model BC) and in the Home Premier (BM). Thomas Edison obtained the rights for use in his **Kinetophone** in 1912. [Koenigsberg 1990; Read 1976.]

HILL, MURRY K., 1865–1942. American vaudeville singer and comedian, born Joseph Tunnicliffe Pope, Jr., in New York on 15 Apr 1865. He had a long stage career, based in Chicago, before making his first Edison cylinder at age 42: "In the Good Old Steamboat Days" (#9619; 1907)—a comic song, in contrast to his later records, which were monologs. Among his hit cylinders were "Grandma's Mustard Plaster" (Edison #291; 1909) and "Seated Around an Oil Stove" (Edison #1019; 1912), both reissued as Blue Amberols. Hill also made at least four U.S. Everlasting cylinders and one Columbia Indestructible. On disc he worked for Columbia in 1911 and Victor from 1910. His most popular disc was "A Bunch of Nonsense" (on cylinder earlier), on Victor #16446 (1910). He died in Chicago on 23 Oct 1942.

HILL, RICHARD S., 1901–1961. American music librarian, born in Chicago on 25 Sep 1901. He took a B.A. from Cornell in 1924, then attended Oxford University. In 1939 he joined the Music Division of the Library of Congress. From 1943 to 1961 he edited *Notes*, the journal of the Music Library Association. Hill was co-editor with Kurtz Myers of *Record Ratings* (1956). He died in Naples, Florida, on 7 Feb 1961.

Hill and dale. *See* VERTICAL-CUT RECORDS.

Hillbilly recordings. *See* COUNTRY AND WESTERN RECORDINGS.

HIMMELREICH, FERDINAND M., 1880–1937. American pianist and organist, born in New York on 15 Nov 1880. Virtually sightless from age five, he was known as "The Blind Pianist." He was organist for nine years at the Wanamaker department stores in New York and Philadelphia. He also played at Gimbel's and Strawbridge and Clothier department stores, and four seasons at Haddon Hall in Atlantic City, New Jersey; and appeared as pianist on the Rudy Vallee radio program. Probably his first recording was a piano roll made for Aeolian in 1905: "Valse brillante" (his own composition; #8094); his first disc was "The Rosary" (Victor #17055; 1912). The latter, his own transcription of the song, was a steady seller for 13 years. He recorded many other arrangements, as well as salon pieces, for Victor (to 1917) and Edison (to 1924), and also worked for Okeh in 1922. Himmelreich died in Laurel Springs, New Jersey, on 11 Dec 1937. [Walsh 1969/11.]

HINDERMYER, HARVEY WILSON. American tenor and ballad singer, born in Easton, Pennsylvania, probably in the 1880s. His name was usually misspelled "Hindermeyer" on record labels. Hindermyer was one of the Shannon Four, and an Edison artist from 1907 until 1929. His first record was "She Was a Grand Old Lady" (Edison #9614; 1907), after which he worked for Victor and Columbia for a time. His "Take Me Out to the Ball Game" was a popular number on Columbia (#A586; 1908). Two favorites were "I Am the Monarch of the Sea" and "Roses, Roses, Everywhere" (Edison cylinder #1554; 1912). One of the most popular of all Edison Diamond Disc records was Hindermyer's "In the Evening by the Moonlight" (#82510; 1914). During the anti-German fervor of World War I in the U.S. Edison issued his discs under the name Harvey Wilson. He participated in Edison **tone tests**, and said that no person had ever been able to distinguish his recorded voice from his real one. Hindermyer was tenor soloist with the **Dann Trio** on all their national tours. He was a church organist and radio performer in the 1920s. [Walsh 1957/8.]

HINES, EARL "FATHA," 1905–1983. American jazz pianist and Big Band leader, born in Duquesne, Pennsylvania, on 28 Dec 1905. He began playing professionally with various groups in Pittsburgh at age 13, then joined Louis Armstrong's Quintet in Chicago in 1927. He formed his own band in 1928 and toured the U.S. with it; the band was among the few Black groups to perform in the South at that time. Hines also performed in Europe, in 1957 and 1966, and in Japan. His band broke up in 1948, after which he was heard as a freelance artist with many partners, continuing through the 1970s. After 1960 he was based in Oakland, California, where he died on 22 Apr 1983.

The first recording by Hines was "Blues in Thirds" backed by "Off-Time Blues" (QRS #R-7036; 1928). He then worked for Okeh in 1928, Victor in 1929, and several labels from 1932 to 1938. In 1939–1942 his band was featured on Bluebird, making many outstanding discs, several of them with vocalist Billy Eckstine. "You Can Depend on Me" (Bluebird #B-10792; 1940), "Jelly Jelly" with Eckstine (Bluebird #B-11065; 1940), and "Stormy Monday Blues" also with Eckstine (Bluebird #B11567; 1942) are among the finest. His biggest hit was "Boogie Woogie on the St. Louis Blues" (Bluebird #B-10674; 1940).

HIRT, AL, 1922– . American jazz trumpeter, born Alois Maxwell Hirt in New Orleans on 7 Nov 1922. After study at the Cincinnati Conservatory of Music from 1940 to 1943, he played in various popular groups, including the bands of Tommy Dorsey and Jimmy Dorsey. In the 1950s he teamed with clarinetist Pete Fountain and was successful on tour and on records with a sophisticated Dixieland idiom. "Java" (RCA #8280) was an acclaimed single; it won a Grammy in 1963. Hirt made 14 chart albums, of which the most popular were *Honey in the Horn* (RCA #LPM 2733; 1963) and *Cotton Candy* (RCA #LPM 2917; 1964). *Pops Goes the Trumpet* was a collection made with the Boston Pops Orchestra (RCA #LPM 2729; 1964).

HIS MASTER'S VOICE. The trademark of the Gramophone Co. and the Victor Talking Machine Co., originally registered in the U.S. Patent Office by Emile Berliner in July 1900. It is the familiar **Nipper** portrait, found in Eldridge Johnson's 1900 catalog of Consolidated Talking Machine Co. products, and used on record

players and (from 1909) on disc labels in Britain. Gramophone Co. records have been customarily identified as "HMV." In other countries, affiliated labels have used translations as their trademarks, for example, La Voce del Padrone (in Italy). From 1931 the trademark was used by EMI, Ltd.

HISS. Random noise of a sibilant character, a byproduct of tape recording for which no antidote existed until the advent of **Noise reduction systems.** High speed recording lowers the amount of hiss, but speed of playback has no effect on it.

HISTORIC MASTERS, LTD. A British firm, located at 10 Yealand Drive, Lancaster, specializing in the reissue of 78 rpm records in cooperation with the National Sound Archive. Beginning in 1972, material by such artists as Nellie Melba, Feodor Chaliapin, Toti Dal Monte and Agnes Nicholls has appeared in four series, the latest dated 1987.

HISTORIC RECORD SOCIETY (HRS). An organization that reissued acoustic vocal records until 1949. It was located at 6613 N. Greenview Ave., Chicago.

HIT (label). An American record issued from 1942 to 1945. Most of the material was by dance bands, including numbers by Abe Lyman, Art Kassel, Ray McKinley, Cootie Williams, and Louis Prima. An interesting item was the only recording by Chico Marx and his short-lived orchestra: "We Must Be Vigilant" and "Johnny Doughboy Found a Rose in Ireland" (#7003; 1942). **Eli Oberstein** was producer of the label, which was an affiliate of his Elite and Majestic labels, all drawing on Varsity and Royale for masters. Some original pressings were also made, in clandestine opposition to the recording ban imposed by the American Federation of Musicians in 1942. The Hit label bore the notice that it was made by the Elite Record Manufacturing Co., or by the Classic Record Co. of New York. [Blacker 1977/10 tells the Oberstein story; the Hit label listing appeared in *RR* #161–62, 163–64, 165–66, 171–72, 173–74, and 181–82.]

HIT OF THE WEEK (label). A 10-inch record issued by the **Durium Products Corp**. of New York from February 1930 to 1932. The disc was a flexible one, made of a paper fiber laminated with a synthetic resin called "durium," recorded on one side, sold on newsstands for only $.15 (while standard labels were selling for $.75). "A ray of sunshine" in the industry—according to *Variety*—the label brought good performers of dance and jazz music to a public that was unable, in the Depression, to buy their work through normal channels. The choice of each week's Hit was made by a committee made up of Florenz Ziegfeld, Eddie Cantor, and Vincent Lopez. Among the artists on the label were the orchestras of Donald Voorhees, Phil Spitalny, Vincent Lopez, Sam Lanin, Dick Robertson, Harry Reser, Erno Rapee, and the Hit of the Week Orchestra directed by Bert Hirsch; with vocalists Morton Downey, Rudy Vallee, Gene Austin, Eddie Cantor, and Smith Ballew. Important jazz/swing instrumentalists like Tommy Dorsey and Duke Ellington were heard on one or two discs. Great success marked the enterprise at first, with weekly releases selling a half million copies.

However, by March 1931, as the economic crisis deepened, sales had dropped sharply, and the corporation went into receivership. A longer-playing Hit of the Week record—the first five-minute 10-inch disc on the American market—appeared in August 1931, offering two songs instead of one. But sales continued to drop, reaching a low point of 60,000 per week at the end of 1931. In June 1932 the final disc went to the newsstands.

Low-cost subsidiary labels by the major companies, issued in the 1930s, probably owe their initiation to the Hit of the Week model. [Englund 1967 is a label list; Rust 1978; Waters 1960 is a history and label list.]

HMV. *See* HIS MASTER'S VOICE.

HODGES, JOHHNY, 1907–1970. American alto and soprano saxophonist, born John Cornelius Hodge on 25 July 1907 in Cambridge, Massachusetts. He is regarded as one of the principal saxophonists of the swing era. As a child Hodges was a pianist and drummer, but he took up the saxophone at age 14. He played in Boston and New York, and in 1928 joined Duke Ellington, remaining 40 years in that partnership. He also led a small group drawn from the Ellington band, and he played with other bands from time to time. He took part in the Benny Goodman Carnegie Hall concert of 1938.

Among the fine discs that feature Hodges are "Passion Rock" (Bluebird #30–0817; 1941), "Castle Rock" (Clef #8944; 1951), and—with Ellington—"I'm Beginning to See the Light" (Victor #20–1618; 1944). He died in New York on 11 May 1970.

HOFFAY, J. A New York firm, with a branch in London, active in 1915. It produced a disc player advertised as one whose sound does not penetrate walls, "no matter how loud it is inside the flat."

HOFMANN, JOSEF, 1876–1957. Polish/ American pianist, born near Cracow on 20 Jan 1876. He first appeared in public at age six, and at age 10 played the first Beethoven concerto with the Berlin Philharmonic Orchestra under Hans von Bülow. His American debut in New York on 29 Nov 1887 "electrified the audience" (Slonimsky), but he determined to resume his studies for several years in Europe before further concertizing. At age 18 he returned to the stage, gaining recognition as one of the greatest artists of the 19th century. Chopin and Liszt were his specialties. When the Curtis Institute was founded in Philadelphia in 1924 Hofmann headed the piano department, and from 1926 to 1938 he directed the Institute. In 1926 he became an American citizen. He retired to California, where he died (in Los Angeles) on 16 Feb 1957.

In the history of sound recording Hofmann holds a significant place, for he was the first recognized artist to make a record. It was an Edison white wax cylinder, made on a Perfected model phonograph in the Edison laboratory while the pianist was 12 years old. He could also be considered the first composer to record, although his composing career (under the name Michel Dvorsky) was not a stellar one. He recorded commercially for Columbia in 1912–1922, beginning with the Mendelssohn "Spring Song" (#1178), and making 13 double-sided discs of Chopin, Liszt, Rachmaninoff, Mendelssohn, etc. He was a Brusnwick performer from 1923 to 1925.

HOGWOOD, CHRISTOPHER, 1941– . English conductor and keyboardist, born in Nottingham on 10 Sept 1941. He studied at Cambridge University, and at Charles University, Prague. In 1967 he and David Munrow established the Early Music Consort to perform medieval music, and in 1973 he founded the Academy of Ancient Music, which has emphasized the baroque period. The Academy has also programmed Mozart and other more recent composers. Hogwood is one of the leaders in the authentic performance movement, using original instruments. He has also been active as an editor, publishing works of J.S. Bach and Purcell.

Among Hogwood's striking recordings there are Beethoven and Haydn symphonies he conducted from the fortepiano, solo discs of the Bach *French Suites* on the harpsichord, and a long list of works with the Academy of Ancient Music (including complete Handel oratorios). Decca, Philharmonia, and L'Oiseau Lyre have been his favored labels.

HOLCOMB & HOKE MANUFACTURING CO. An American firm primarily devoted to popcorn machines and refrigerated display cases; it also made the Electromuse, an early **coin-op** (non-selective) with electrical amplification. Homer Capehart worked for them as a salesman for a time in the 1920s.

HOLCOMBE, HERBERT, ca. 1867–1908. American baritone and vaudeville artist, a partner in the stage team of Sadie Cushman and Holcombe. He recorded for Columbia in 1895–1896, for the Chicago Talking Machine Co., and also for Berliner. [Brooks 1979.]

HOLIDAY, BILLIE, 1915–1959. American blues and jazz singer, known as "Lady Day," born in Baltimore on 15 April 1915. Although facts about her early life are uncertain, it seems her parents were Sadie Fagan and Clarence Holiday, and that her given name was Eleanora. After a troubled childhood that included a reformatory and brothels, she began singing in

Harlem clubs at age 15, was heard by **John Hammond** and brought to the attention of Benny Goodman; she sang with the Goodman band from 1933. She also teamed with Count Basie, Artie Shaw, and Teddy Wilson, and was soon recognized as the foremost female jazz vocalist. Holiday was among the few Black singers to be members of white orchestras in the 1930s. She made European tours, gaining acclaim wherever she appeared. Her voice declined around 1950, leading to a less effective period. Holiday died in New York on 17 July 1959. The motion picture *Lady Sings the Blues* (1972) purported to be her life story.

Her first records were with Benny Goodman in 1933: "Your Mother's Son in Law" (Columbia #2856–D; 27 Nov 1933) and "Riffin' the Scotch" (Columbia #2867–D; 1933). She was next on Brunswick making a landmark series of records with Teddy Wilson's band (including Roy Eldridge), among them "I Wished on the Moon" (Brunswick #7501; 1935), "What a Little Moonlight Can Do" (Brunswick #7498; 1935), "If You Were Mine" (Brunswick #7554; 1935), and "These Foolish Things" (Brunswick #7699; 1936). She led her own group in "Billie's Blues" (Vocalion #3288; 1936), "A Fine Romance" (Vocalion #3333; 1936), "I Can't Get Started" with Lester Young (Vocalion #4457; 1938), "Strange Fruit" (Commodore #526; 1939), and "Lover Man" (Decca #23391; 1944). Most of these were reissued on Time Life STL-J03 P3–14786 (1979), and in the Columbia nine compact disc set (originally on LP) *The Quintessential Billie Holiday* (completed in 1991, with 153 songs recorded up to 1942).

HOLLAND BROTHERS. An Ottawa firm, appointed Edison's sales agent for Canada in 1891. It was one of the affiliated companies of the **North American Phonograph Co.**

HOLLY, BUDDY, 1938–1959. American rock singer, guitarist, and composer, born Charles Hardin Holley in Lubbock, Texas, on 7 Sept 1938. Influenced by Elvis Presley, he combined a country style with rhythm & blues, achieving great success with "Peggy Sue" (Coral #61885; 1957) which stayed 20 weeks on the charts. His group, The Crickets, offered considerable subtlety, and was widely praised for its LP album *The Chirping Crickets* (1957). The single "That'll Be the Day" (Brunswick #55009; 1957) was also on the charts 20 weeks. Other successful singles included "Oh Boy" (Brunswick #55035; 1957), and "It Doesn't Matter Anymore" (Coral #62074; 1959). The Crickets toured America and Australia, but misfortune terminated their triumphs as Holly was killed in a plane crash on 3 Feb 1959 near Clear Lake, Iowa. A motion picture based on his life was released in 1978.

HOLLYWOOD (label). An American record distributed by the Hollywood Record Co., Hollywood, California, in the mid-1920s. Material was dance music and some jazz. [Rust 1978.]

HOME RECORDING. Making records at home (outside a studio) was always a possibility with cylinder phonographs, and remained one of their selling points in competition with disc machines. The earliest home disc maker was offered by the Neophone Co., Ltd. in Britain in around 1905. The earliest U.S. product was marketed by the American Home Recorder Co. in August 1920. An attachment advertised in 1924 permitted direct home recording from radio programming. *See also* INSTANTANEOUS RECORDING.

HOMER, LOUISE, 1871–1947. American soprano and mezzo-soprano, born Louise Dilworth Beatty near Pittsburgh on 28 Apr 1871. She studied in Philadelphia, Boston, and Paris, and married one of her teachers, Sidney Homer, in 1895. Her opera debut was as Leonora in *Favorita* in Vichy, France, on 15 June 1898. She was a great success in Covent Garden, singing Wagner, in the next year, and gave a command performance for the Queen. With a range of three octaves, she was able to select from a wide repertoire, finally settling for roles in the lower register; she made her Metropolitan Opera debut as Amneris on 22 Dec 1900 (also the occasion of Marcel Journet's debut), and remained with the company until 1919, save for one season. She was also heard in Chicago (1920–1925), San Francisco, and Los Angeles. Homer was greatly acclaimed for her Eurydice of 1909 in Paris, and in New York

under Arturo Toscanini. Delilah, opposite Enrico Caruso, was perhaps her highest triumph. Her last appearance was in 1929. She died in Winter Park, Florida, on 6 May 1947.

Homer began recording in 1903, and was a Victor exclusive artist for 25 years. She was known best for her ensemble work, including important duets with Caruso, Geraldine Farrar, Johanna Gadski, Alma Gluck, and Giovanni Martinelli; the *Rigoletto* Quartet, first with Caruso, Antonio Scotti and Bessie Abott (Victor #96000, 1907, selling at a premium price of $6.00), then with Beniamino Gigli, Amelita Galli-Curci, and Giuseppe De Luca, coupled with the *Lucia* Sextet with the same artists plus Ezio Pinza and Angelo Bada (Victor #10012). Her most famous solo discs were from *Samson et Delilah*: "Amour, viens aider" (Victor #6165) and "Mon coeur s'ouvre à ta voix" (Victor #1422); both remained in the catalog into the 1940s. Other distinguished interpretations were "O toi, qui m'abandonne" from *Prophète* (Victor #85004, reissued on IRCC #103–A), and "Fatal divinità" from *Alceste* (Victor #88286, reissued on IRCC #153). [Poole 1947.]

HOMESTEAD (label). A rare American issue, affiliated with Plaza and perhaps with Crown, distributed by the Chicago Mail Order Co. (2611 Indiana Ave.) during the mid-1920s. Material was popular vocals and dance music. [Kendziora 1989/4; Rust 1978.]

HOMESTEAD TRIO. A female vocal trio formed to make Edison Diamond Discs. They recorded from 1917 to 1923, making 24 sides. Members were Gladys Rice, Betsy Lane Shepherd, and Amy Ellerman. Elizabeth Spencer replaced Rice in 1921. Their first record was "Indiana" (Edison Diamond Disc #80334; 1917); it became one of Edison's best sellers. Another popular item was "Keep the Home Fires Burning" (#82149; 1918). [Walsh 1973/2.]

HOMOCHORD (label). A British (originally German) record distributed in the years before World War I, made from European matrices. Discs with the Homochord label and the Homophone label were both issued until 1914, when Homophone ceased. The first issues were sold in 1913 by agents Bernhard Andres & Co., brightened by the registered trademark of a nude harpist on the label. Limited distribution resulted from the War, but the Andres Brothers remained in business until March 1917, when they were interned as enemy aliens. The label was sustained by Carl Lindström (London), Ltd., using British pressings.

In August 1920 a new "Homokord" record was announced in Britain, from the Berlin firm Homophon. Then in October 1921 **British Homophone Co., Ltd.** began to issue a locally produced series, using matrices from pre-war British and European recordings, new recordings from Europe and America, and U.S. matrices owned by the Aeolian Co., Ltd. At first the pressing was done by the Universal Music Co., Ltd., at Hayes, Middlesex. Later, British and American Pathé recordings became available, as well as Zonophone recordings. The spelling of the label was again Homochord. In 1922 actual recording began in London, during 1926–1928 in studios of the Gramophone Co. Material was dance music and popular vocals, some of it by stars like Fletcher Henderson or the California Ramblers, disguised by pseudonyms. There were 10-inch and 12-inch discs, with standard labels, and a series of 10-inch and 12-inch discs with plum and gold labels. Homochords were sold in the U.S. by the Sterno Manufacturing Co. from February 1924 to December 1925. Production stopped in Britain in 1930, then resumed in 1933; a 10-inch disc selling at 1 shilling was advertised in October. However production finally ceased in 1935. [Andrews 1985/12; Andrews*; Rust 1978.] *See also* HOMOPHONE (label).

Homokord (label). *See* HOMOCHORD (label).

HOMOPHON (HOMOPHONE) (label). A German record, issued by the Homophone Co. GmbH of 92 Klosterstrasse, Berlin, from 1905. In the first catalog, September 1905, there were single-sided and double-sided 10-inch discs, and six-inch "Liliput" [*sic*] discs. The record was available in Britain from June 1906, through mail order at first, then through Bernhard Andres & Co. as agent. In the U.K. advertising the spelling "Homophone" was used. Artists on the label included La Garde Republicaine Band, the Johann Strauss Orchestra of Vienna,

and many opera singers (none particularly well known today) from various European houses. From October 1908 Andres began to trade under the name Homophone Disc Record Co. The label trademark (registered in Germany June 1906 and in Britain August 1907) showed a nude harpist with a recording horn in the bushes behind her. Following legal action by International Zonophone Co., claiming too much similarity between the names Homophone and Zonophone, the Homophon Co. obligingly changed its label name to Homokord, with the British spelling Homochord. The change took effect in August 1911. Columbia bought all shares of the German firm in 1928. [Andrews 1985/12; Andrews*.] *See also* BRITISH HOMOPHONE CO., LTD.; HOMOCHORD (label).

HOOLEY, WILLIAM F., 1861–1918. Irish bass, born in Cork on 16 Apr 1861. He sang comic songs, Irish ballads, opera, and the standard bass repertoire, achieving his greatest success in ensemble work, where he earned the name "King of the Quartet Bassos." Hooley was an original member of the Haydn Quartet, and belonged to numerous trios and quartets in the 1890s and 1900s, including the American Quartet and the Lyric Trio (with whom he made early cylinder records for Babson Brothers, Chicago, in 1899). He made discs for Berliner, then went to Victor, which carried four solos in the 1917 catalog, "Asleep in the Deep" (#16949) and "Wearing of the Green" (#17348) among them. Hooley made records in Britain, too, for G & T. He also sang in the Victor Light Opera Co., and was for a time president of the **American Phonograph Record Co.** He died in New York on 12 Oct 1918. [Walsh 1944/3; corrections in May 1952.]

HOPPER, WILLIAM DE WOLFE, 1858–1935. American actor and monologist, born in New York on 30 Mar 1858. His greatest Broadway success was in *El Capitan* (1896), with music by John Philip Sousa. Hopper appeared in many other Broadway shows and Gilbert and Sullivan operettas. His final notable appearance was in *Everything* (1918), with music by Sousa and Irving Berlin.

Hopper is remembered principally for his rendition of "Casey at the Bat," which he first performed in 1888. His recording of that poignant tale (Victor #31559; 1906) was a sensation, remaining in the catalog to 1927 (backed by "O'Toole's Touchdown" on #35783). It was his only successful recording. [Bayly 1985; Brooks 1990.]

HORIZONTAL TRACKING ERROR. The difference between the angle formed by the cutting stylus in disc recording (90 degrees) and the angle formed by the playback cartridge to the disc surface. It results from the pivoting of the tone arm, and the consequent inward slant of the headshell. Distortion in the playback is proportional to the difference between the recording and playback angles. A tangential tone arm eliminates the problem.

HORN. (I) The device used in acoustic recording to capture the sound signal and transmit the vibrations to the cutting stylus.

HORN. (II) The device used in playback of records to amplify the vibrations taken from the disc or cylinder surface by the cartridge. Early recording and playback horns were in simple conical shape, giving poor efficiency and poor tonal quality. As results improved with the length of the horn, manufacturers made them longer and longer; by 1900 a playback horn of 56 inches was marketed, requiring a crane to hold it up.

Experiments led to the exponential horn, in which the cross-sectional area doubles with each increase of x inches in distance along the axis. By 1920 the exponential horn was universally accepted, and in 1925 the orthophonic horn formalized the design and increased the length. Horns were external at first, then (from the Victrola of 1906) were concealed inside the phonograph's cabinet; the concealment was achieved by folding the horn. Internal horns did not improve the sonic quality of the system, and in fact worsened it, but had cosmetic appeal; the term "hornless player" was used in advertising internal horn machines.

The first horns were of spun brass or copper, and brass remained a favored material. Wood horns were introduced in the Regina

Hexaphone of 1908, and were in general use by 1911, and later there were folding cardboard horns on portable machines. With the introduction of electrical recording, the horn was replaced by the **loudspeaker**. *See also* ACOUSTIC RECORDING; EDISON HORNS; FOLDED HORN; MUSIC MASTER HORNS. For the type of horn used on a specific record player, see the player model under the manufacturer's name; for example, EDISON RECORD PLAYERS—TRIUMPH.

HOROWITZ, VLADIMIR, 1904–1989. Russian/American pianist, born in Berdichev on 1 Oct 1904. He made his debut in Kiev on 30 May 1920, and began touring Europe in 1926. His American debut in 1928 was at the concert in which Thomas Beecham was also heard the first time in the U.S.: they collaborated on the Tchaikovsky First Concerto, creating a sensation. Horowitz was recognized, while still in his twenties, as one of the great virtuosos of all time. He specialized in the romantic composers, Scriabin, and Scarlatti. From 1953 to 1965 and from 1969 to 1974, he was absent from the concert stage, but continued to make recordings. In 1986 he made a triumphant return to Russia after a 60-year absence. He died in New York on 5 Nov 1989.

A CD set from HMV (#CHS7 63538–2; 1990) offers a group of recordings from 1930 to 1951: Bach, Chopin, Beethoven, Debussy, Haydn, Schumann (the remarkable "Arabesque" recording of 1935), Liszt, Rachmaninoff, the Prokofieff "Toccata" of 1930, among others. *Horowitz Encores* is a CD from RCA (#GD87755; 1990) that gives performances for the 1940s and 1950s, including the pianist's famed transcription of the Sousa "Stars and Stripes Forever" and his "Variations on a Theme from Bizet's Carmen"—two exuberant showpieces. *Horowitz Plays Chopin* (RCA CD #GD87752; 1990) presents the brilliant "Andante Spianato and Grand Polonaise in E–Flat Major" of 1945 (originally album #VM 1034), played as nobody else at the time could play it, plus Etudes, Ballades, and smaller works. *A Tribute to Vladimir Horowitz* (CBS CD #45829; 1990) is a reissue of a Carnegie Hall recital of 1965, featuring Scarlatti and Scriabin.

One of the immortal Horowitz performances, the Tchaikovsky First Concerto with Arturo Toscanini, recorded 25 Apr 1943 in Carnegie Hall, was reissued in 1990 on RCA CD #87992; it is coupled with another definitive interpretation, of the Beethoven "Emperor" Concerto under Fritz Reiner, made in Carnegie Hall on 26 Apr 1952. Horowitz recordings received 20 Grammy awards (more than any other classical instrumentalist) from 1962 to 1988, and he was also recognized at the 1989 ceremony with a Lifetime Achievement award.

HOT AIR MOTOR. A drive mechanism used in certain gramophones from about 1909 to 1914, based on the Stirling Cycle Engine patented in 1816 by Robert Stirling and James Stirling. It was an external combustion engine, fired by a methylated spirit burner; the fatal flaw in the design was that a flame was present, one that was difficult to stabilize. This feature, plus the cost—eight times the cost of a spring motor—and overall complexity of its mechanism, prevented the device from gaining wide acceptance. It did have quiet operation and maintained constant turntable speed. The motor was used in the Apollo and Maestrophone gramophones. [Evans, H. 1989.]

HOT RECORD SOCIETY (HRS) (label). A record issued from 1937 to 1939 by the Hot Record Society, 827 Seventh Ave., New York. Using masters from American Record Corp. and Decca, the society marketed high quality material, and also made original records of Muggsy Spanier and Sidney Bechet. [Rust 1978.]

HOUGH, JAMES EDWARD, 1848–1925. British recording industry executive. He began as an exhibitor in London, with members of his family, in December 1893. He used equipment of the Edison Bell Phonograph Corp., Ltd., without authorization, making records of songs and speeches. Hough's business was carried on under the name of the **London Phonograph Co.** From 1894 he sold imported cylinders and his own London Records. Edison Bell's suit against Hough required three years of litigation, at the end of which he was enjoined by the court. However, he did obtain sales rights from Edison Bell for their entertainment phono-graphs (not for leased office machines), and set up **Edisonia, Ltd.,** in 1897 to succeed the London Phonograph Co. He continued to sell London Records. Under pressure from Edison Bell, he sold out to them in 1898; and the **Edison Bell Consolidated Phonograph Co.** was created to handle sales and leases of phonographs, with Hough as general sales manager. Hough acquired both Edison Bell Consolidated and Edisonia in 1909, and formed J.E. Hough, Ltd. He introduced the popular **Winner** record in February 1913. [Andrews*.]

HOUSTON, DAVID, 1938–. American country singer and guitarist, born in Shreveport, Louisiana, on 9 Dec 1938. Encouraged by Gene Austin, a friend of his father, Houston learned guitar and piano, and was singing with the *Louisiana Hayride* show at age 12. In the late 1950s he was established on television and on national tours. He signed with Epic records in 1963 and made a great success with his first disc, "Mountain of Love" (#9625); it was on the charts for 15 weeks. Hit records followed regularly thereafter: Houston had 50 chart records by 1980. "Livin' in a House Full of Love" (Epic #9831; 1965) and "Almost Persuaded" (Epic #10025; 1966) were among the most notable singles. An album entitled *Almost Persuaded* (Epic #LN 24213; 1966) was extremely popular, on the charts for 13 weeks.

HOWL. Also known as Howlaround, Howlback. A shrieking animal-like noise that results from excessive buildup of feedback in a sound system. *See also* ACOUSTIC FEED-BACK.

HOWLIN' WOLF, 1910–1976. American blues singer, harmonica player, and guitarist, born Chester Arthur Burnett in West Point, Mississippi, on 10 June 1910. He taught himself guitar as a child, then learned to play the harmonica. His deep voice was shaped in the likeness of the blues singing he heard, notably that of Charley Patton. He began playing in public around 1928, and formed a group that performed in Memphis. Brought to the attention of Leonard Chess, he made a hit record of "Moanin' at Midnight" (Chess #1479; 1957). Burnett earned his stage name Howlin' Wolf with the wolf-like baying he brought to his interpretations. His influence was important in the development of electric Chicago blues. Other notable records included "Smokestack Lightning" (Chess #1618; 1956) and "My Country Sugar Mama" (Chess #1911; 1964). His most popular album was *The London Howlin' Wolf Sessions* (Chess #CH 60008; 1971), 15 weeks on the charts. After several years of ill health, he died in Hines, Illinois, on 10 Jan 1976.

HOXIE, CHARLES A., 1867–1941. American electrical engineer, born in Constable, New York, on 26 Feb 1867. He made an early career in photography, then in 1895 began to study electrical engineering by correspondence, and two years later was an electrician in Detroit. Hoxie moved to Brockton, Massachusetts, in 1899 to work for the Southern Massachusetts Telephone Co., and in 1901 became wire chief for the New England Telephone Co. He built in his home one of the first wireless transmitting and receiving sets. In 1902 he moved to Schenectady, New York, working first for the Hudson River Telephone Co., then in 1912 as an engineer for General Electric. He worked in the areas of telephony, as well as broader fields of electricity. During World War I Hoxie was called on to improve radio communications, and developed the pallophotophone, which recorded sound on film for transmission. That invention was followed by the photophone, which converted the photographed film back into sound. The method was to project the exposed film in front of a photoelectric cell (U.S. patent #1,598,377); this was basically the **Pallatrope** system used by Brunswick discs in the later 1920s. It also was used in the synchronization of sound on talking film, with the film carrying both the audio and visual signals, demonstrated by General Electric in the 1922 motion picture *Wings*. This method eventually replaced the disc/film method used in *The Jazz Singer* (1927). Hoxie retired in 1932, and died in Alplaus, New York, on 13 Oct 1941.

HUDSON (label). (I) An American record issued by the Detroit department store J.. Hudson in 1924. Masters were from Emerson, and pressing was done at the Bridgeport Die and Machine Co. Most of the output consisted of dance and popular vocal numbers.

HUDSON (label). (II) A British label issued during the 1930s by the publishing company of M. de Wolfe. Matrices came from Edison Bell, Filmophone, Tono, and perhaps other companies. The repertoire was classical, including operatic and concert vocals, light orchestral pieces, and several organ works. None of the artists were especially well known.

HUGO WOLF SOCIETY. The first organization to offer a subscription set of lesser known music. Walter Legge and critic Ernest Newman worked out the plan, which gained the support of *Gramophone* editor Compton Mackenzie, and eventually the desired 500 subscribers were acquired, each paying $6 for the first album. Seven 78 rpm albums appeared, between 1931 and 1938, presenting the whole Wolf output of Lieder, sung by Alexander Kipnis, Elena Gerhardt, Herbert Janssen, Gerhard Hüsch, Alexandra Trianti, Friedrich Schorr, John McCormack, Helge Roswaenge, and Karl Erb. Accompanists were Conrad Bos, Michael Raucheisen, Ernst Victor Wolff, and Gerald Moore. All seven albums have been reissued as seven LP records, EMI RLS #759 (1981).

HUGUET, JOSEFINA, 1871–1944. Spanish soprano, born in Barcelona. She sang at La Scala, using the first name Giuseppina. She recorded extensively for G & T in 1903–1908, singing the lyric and coloratura repertoires. A favorite among collectors is "O luce di quest'anima" from *Linda di Chamounix* (G & T #53513; 1907). She also made distinguished duets with tenor Fernando de Lucia: "Parigi o cara" from *Traviata* (G & T #054081; 1906), "Tardi si fa, addio" from *Faust* (G & T #05473; 1907), and several others. She was killed in an air raid in Italy during World War II.

HUM. A low droning sound originating in the alternating current power of an electrical device. In the U.S. the hum frequency is 60 Hz (approximately B natural), but it may be the first or second overtone of 60 Hz, that is 120 Hz (also B natural) or (approximately F sharp). In

Europe the hum frequency is 50 Hz. Various reasons may be given for a hum in an audio system: multiple grounding, placement of components near a magnetic field, inadequate insulation, or faulty valves. Reversal of the plugs in the outlet, or plugs within the system, may alleviate a hum problem.

HUNGAROTON (label). A record issued in Hungary, with worldwide distribution. The U.K. agent is Conifer, Ltd., of Middlesex. The American distribution is handled by Qualiton Imports, of Long Island City, New York.

HUNTER, ALBERTA, 1895–1984. American blues singer, born in Memphis, Tennessee, on 1 Apr 1895. She began her career at age 11 in Chicago night clubs; at one of these, the Dreamland Cafe, she sang with the house orchestra (which included Fletcher Henderson) and made her first records: "He's a Darned Good Man" (Black Swan #2019; 1921) and "How Long, Sweet Daddy, How Long" (Black Swan #2008; 1921), the second being listed with Henderson's Novelty Orchestra, "probably the same group" (Rust). Hunter made a group of blues records for Paramount in 1922, with a pickup group, and sang with Eubie Blake accompanying on three Paramount discs. She became famous in the 1920s, singing and recording with many groups in New York, Chicago, and London. Her labels included Gennett in 1924, Okeh in 1925–1926, Victor in 1927, and Columbia in 1929. In 1939 she worked for Decca, and in 1940 for Bluebird. She wrote the song "Down-hearted Blues," a best-selling record of Bessie Smith (1923) and recorded it herself for Decca in 1939 (#7727).

Hunter left the stage and became a scrub nurse in a New York hospital for 20 years, endeavoring to help humanity. When she was forced to retire from that job, she returned to singing (at age 82) and was a sensation in Greenwich Village. She continued performing until the year of her death (in New York on 19 Oct 1984) at age 89.

HUNTING. The result of a defect in an audio system that causes alternating speeds in the transport mechanism.

HUNTING, RUSSELL, 1864–1943. American monologist and recording industry executive, born in West Roxbury, Massachusetts, on 8 May 1864. He established a reputation for his Irish monologs; he recorded them for the New England Phonograph Co., Columbia, and Edison, becoming "the most popular pre-1900 recording artist" (Gelatt). The Casey series was his favorite: "Casey as Judge" (Columbia #9615; 1898; also on Edison #3810), "Casey's Visit to the Hospital" (Columbia #9653; 1898; also on Edison #3814), and about 20 others. "Casey at the Bat" was one of his originals (Edison #3802, before 1900), but it was taken over by William De Wolfe Hopper. (Walsh has raised the possibility that the Edison titles were in fact made by Jim White rather than by Hunting.) Hunting also recorded Casey numbers in Britain, for Sterling records and for Odeon. Aside from comic numbers, Hunting recorded more serious items like the Lincoln's Gettysburg Address (Edison #3821) and a speech from *Richard III* (Edison #3822).

Hunting took an early interest in the business side of recording. He founded and edited the first independent magazine in the field, *Phonoscope* (1896–1900); and he had a phonograph shop at 45 Clinton Place, New York, in 1896 (in partnership with Charles M. Carlson). In an interesting event of censorship history, he was accused by Anthony Comstock of selling obscene records, and brought to trial; the outcome is not known, but it is clear that Hunting remained active.

Hunting went to Britain in 1898 and worked for James Hough as recording director of Edison Bell. In December 1904 he joined with **Louis Sterling** in founding the Sterling Record Co., Ltd. The firm name was changed on 17 Dec 1904 to **Russell Hunting Record Co., Ltd.** Hunting was recording director. Products of the firm were Sterling cylinder records and Linguaphone language instruction records.

On 27 Aug 1906 **Sterling and Hunting, Ltd.**, was formed by the Russell Hunting Record Co., Ltd., to be the British sales agency for the Odeon and Fonotipia discs of Fonotipia, Ltd. It was also the sales agency for Sterling cylinders and the Linguaphone language course records, the products of the Russell Hunting Record

Co., Ltd. Imaginative promotional methods brought early success to the new agency, but in the poor economic climate of 1908 the Sterling business could not meet the competition of Edison Bell's records, which were selling at 25 percent less than Sterling, and of the new Clarion cylinder records. Sterling left the two firms in the spring of 1908 to set up the new Rena Manufacturing Co., Ltd. The Russell Hunting Record Co., Ltd., was out of business 10 Dec 1908; but Hunting himself continued trading for two more months under the name of Russell Hunting and Co. Then Sterling and Hunting Co., Ltd., dissolved on 6 Aug 1909.

With the demise of his companies, Hunting moved to Pathé as their recording director, and traveled the world for them. He set up the U.S. branch, then from 1922 (as U.S. Pathé came under Columbia control) he worked out of Paris, heading the Pathé European activities. It was not until 1940 that he returned permanently to America, and retired in New York.

Hunting's business life did not prevent him from appearing before the recording horn. He made discs for Zonophone in Britain (ca. 1904), and re-recorded some Casey material after 1914 in the U.S. "Departure of the First U.S. Troops for France" was an interesting topical record of September 1917, complete with bands and crowd noises. During the 1920s he recorded for the Regal label of Sterling's Columbia Graphophone Co., Ltd.

Hunting died on 20 Feb 1943. His son, Russell Jr., was also in the industry; he was reported in January 1921 to be the head of the Nipponophone Co. [Andrews*; Brooks 1979; Walsh 1944/11–12; 1945/1–2; corrections in 1952/5.]

HUNTING (RUSSELL) RECORD CO., LTD.

A London firm established on 17 Dec 1904 by **Russell Hunting** and **Louis Sterling**, being in fact their Sterling Record Co., Ltd., (founded a short time earlier) with a new name. It was located in (1907) at 13–15–17 City Road. Products of the company were **Sterling (label)** cylinders and Linguaphone language instruction cylinders. The firm claimed to sell a million records in the first 22 weeks of issue. On 27 Aug 1906 the company formed **Sterling and Hunting, Ltd.**, to be its sales agency for Sterling and

Linguaphone records, and to handle sales for Odeon and Fonotipia, Ltd., products. Unable to meet the competition of lower-priced Edison Bell records, and the new Clarion records, the Russell Hunting Record Co., Ltd., went out of business on 10 Dec 1908. Hunting acquired some of the stock and matrices and remained active for two more months, trading under the name of Russell Hunting and Co. J. E. Hough, Ltd., bought the manufacturing assets. (Sterling had already left in spring of 1908, to set up the new Rena Manufacturing Co.) Sterling and Hunting, Ltd., dissolved on 6 Aug 1909. [Andrews*.]

HUPFELD SELF-PLAYING PIANO.

A very early player piano, the first of the genre to be seen in the U.S., at the World's Columbian Exposition in 1893. Ludwig Hupfeld, a maker of outstanding orchestrions and band organs, was producer of the instrument. It was referred to by a commentator at the Exposition as "a revelation to thousands of musical visitors to whom the idea had previously come only as a hint of future possibilities." The mechanism was attached under the piano keyboard, with the roll moved either electrically or by a hand crank; there was no pedalling. American rights were held by Blasius, whose name appeared on the instrument at the Exposition.

HÜSCH, GERHARD, 1901–1984.

German baritone, born in Hannover on 2 Feb 1901. He sang with the opera companies in Cologne, Berlin, and Bayreuth, but gained greatest fame as a Lieder singer. His recordings of *Winterreise* (1933) and *Schöne Müllerin* (1935) were important in the promotion of Lieder to a wide audience.

He was one of the performers in the Hugo Wolf Society albums (1931–1938). A CD from Preiser (#89017) in 1990 offered a good selection of Hüsch singing Schubert from Electrola and HMV recordings of 1934–1938.

HUSKY, FERLIN, 1927– .

American country singer, guitarist, and songwriter, born in Flat River, Missouri, on 3 Dec 1927. He was self-taught on the guitar, while pursuing an interest in radio announcing. He held a number of disc jockey jobs, achieving success in Bakersfield, California. For variety, he introduced a comic character—played by himself—named Simon Crum, and made some records for Capitol in that guise. He used the name Terry Preston for country songs. In the 1950s he gained national acclaim as a singer on radio and television, and made a motion picture, *Country Music Holiday* (1958). Husky had a long list of chart records, 50 singles between 1957 and 1980. "Gone" (Capitol #3628; 1957) was the first, 20 weeks on the charts. His greatest hit was "Wings of a Dove" (Capitol #4406; 1960), which was charted for 37 weeks.

HYLTON, JACK, 1892–1965. British Big Band leader, born in Lancashire on 2 July 1892. He became "Britain's most famous—and most widely travelled—bandleader during the years between 1921 and 1940" (Rust). His orchestra was compared to that of Paul Whiteman. It was the first non-American Big Band to tour the U.S. Hylton recorded a vast number of dance items in the U.K., Europe, and America. His players were mostly British (one was Ray Noble), but they included American artists at times; for example, Coleman Hawkins is heard in "Darktown Strutter's Ball" / "Melancholy Baby" (HMV #BD-5550; 1936). Some of Hylton's discs appeared on the American Decca label, including a "Gilbert and Sullivan Medley" (#15029), but most were on Victor (16 discs in the 1938 catalog). In the 1940s Hylton became an impresario. He died 23 Jan 1965. [Rust 1989.]

HYMN RECORDINGS. "Certain to have a powerful influence for good" is the promise Victor made in its 1917 catalog for the 200 plus titles of this category. Fewer than half that number appeared in the 1927 catalog, under the heading Sacred Songs—and the category by then included such non-hymn material as the "Hallelujah Chorus" and "Swing Low Sweet Chariot." By 1938 the number of Sacred Music items was again close to 200, with cross references to Christmas Records, Liturgical Music, Oratorios, Negro Spirituals, and others. Among the enduring hymn discs were Reinald Werrenrath's "Abide with Me" / "Lead Kindly Light" (#1279) and another "Abide with Me" by Olive Kline and Elsie Baker (#19873; 1925),

coupled with their popular "Whispering Hope."

Edison recorded the first hymn cylinder, "Rock of Ages," with an unidentified quartet, in August 1890. The next hymns were performed by the Manhasset Quartette on 27 Sep 1891: "Hail Jerusalem" and "Glory Hallelujah." There were several sacred songs on Pathé cylinders made ca. 1897, including a group of nine "Ave Marias" by different composers, in series #0811–0823. Bettini's 1899 catalog included cylinders by baritone Aristide Franceschetti, who set out to present the evolution of music "from the remotest to the present time," and began with "Vegnareba" and "Edrosh," two Hebrew evening prayers; but Bettini did not otherwise interest himself in the sacred repertoire.

The earliest hymn disc was by Harry Macdonough, singing "The Holy City" (Victor Matrix #A-94; 14 June 1900), which he had done earlier on a cylinder for Edison (#B120). In the following month the Haydn Quartet performed "Lead Kindly Light" for the first time in the studio (Matrix #A-97; 10 July 1900); it was popular enough to be rerecorded in 1903. The Haydn added a few other sacred pieces later on. The Lyric Trio (as the Lyric Choir) made the earliest substantial series of sacred songs on 11 Mar 1901 beginning with "Holy, Holy, Holy" (Victor Matrix #A-716) and including "Rock of Ages," "Come Ye Disconsolate," "Just As I Am," "Blest Be the Tie that Binds," "Beulah Land," "Jesus, Lover of My Soul," and "Stand Up! Stand Up for Jesus!"

The first choral hymns were by the Sistine Chapel Choir, singing in Latin for G & T in Rome, in 1902–1905; the pieces included "Tui sunt coeli" (#54765; 1902) and Mozart's "Ave verum" (#54767; 1902). Victor's first choral hymn was "Onward Christian Soldiers" by the Trinity Choir (#2373; 27 May 1903), a group that returned in the following years to do a few other religious songs, followed by Ferruccio Giannini's "Holy City" (Matrix #A-169; 30 June 1903). The Lyric Quartet began its Victor career with a group of records that included "Rock of Ages" (#717; 1906, re-recorded in 1907); this ensemble (which included Olive Kline) had overlapping membership with the Trinity Choir.

On Columbia 10-inch discs there appeared "O Holy Night" by George Alexander (#3269), and "Ring the Bells of Heaven" by a male quartet (#3511), both recorded in November 1907. In December Columbia added a "Lead Kindly Light" by the Columbia Male Quartet (#510) as well as "Star of Bethlehem" by Henry Burr (#1890) and "Nazareth" by George Alexander (#3152).

In the later 78 rpm period hymns were not a focus of attention. Columbia's 1943 catalog, for example, lists about 100 records under Sacred Music, but Christmas carols, Bach cantata excerpts, and oratorio selections are among them. Decca was offering in 1944 about the same number as Columbia, also inclusive of carols. With the LP the sacred repertoire expanded rapidly. By 1960 there were about 350 sacred albums listed in Schwann. Compact disc catalogs present a wide selection of material in the category Gospel/Religious. A 1991 Schwann *Spectrum* had 10 pages of listings, mostly in the Gospel genre. *See also* CHRIST-MAS RECORDS.

HYMNOPHONE. A disc player manufactured by Holzweissig of Leipzig, and sold by Bettini in New York, in 1907. It was also sold in Eu-rope, with Hymnophone discs. The machine had "a tone arm carrying the reproducer, with a swivel joint connecting the tone arm to a horn which emerged from the front under the turn-table" (Read). It may have suggested the idea of the Victrola to Eldridge Johnson.

HYPERION (label). A London-based British independent record issued from 1980. It now offers more than 450 classical selections. The label has won more *Gramophone* record awards than any other independent. Edward Perry, the founder, has held to the idea of exploring lesser known repertoire, but he has also pre-sented the classic masters (e.g., the complete Schubert songs, in a set to be completed in 1997). One of the fine recordings using authen-tic instruments is Handel's *Fireworks*, with the King's Consort. "A Feather on the Breath of God" (#A66039) by Hildegard of Bingen, was the label's first award winner, and remains one of the most acclaimed of its output.

HY-TONE (label). An American record, affili-ated with Arto, released from 1920 to ca. 1922. The **Indestructible Phonograph Record Co.** was named on the printed label as the pro-ducer. Material was blues and dance music.

Ideal (label). *See* SCALA IDEAL (label).

ILLUSTRAPHONE. A 1907 **coin-op** made by **Hawthorne & Sheble.** It offered a picture to look at through an eye-slot in the top of the cabinet, and records to listen to through earphones ("auditrumpets"). The experience cost $.01. *See also* PICTURIZED PHONOGRAPHS.

Illustrated song machine. *See* PICTURIZED PHONOGRAPHS.

IMAGE ENHANCER. A stereo component that adds the impression of **imaging** to the sounds reproduced by the system. A potentiometer and two extra speakers are needed. The method is that of adjusting the delay time for signals as they reach the left and right ear of the listener.

IMAGING. A characteristic of advanced audio systems that duplicates for the listener the placement of the input signals relative to each other. Thus an orchestral recording will convey a sense of the sound space occupied by each instrument within the larger perceived "stage" of the orchestra itself. Imaging may also be used by the recording engineer to create artificial effects, manipulating the virtual locations of certain signals in departure from their actual placement. *See also* IMAGE ENHANCER.

IMPEDANCE. The total opposition (reactance and resistance) to the flow of current in an electric circuit; it is measured in ohms. In an audio system, matching of the impedance value among components will minimize distortion and maximize energy transfer. For loudspeakers wired in series, the total impedance is the sum of their individual impedances. But for speakers wired in parallel, the total impedance is the sum of the reciprocals of the individual impedances, with the result inverted. For example, two 8-ohm speakers in parallel wiring have a total impedance of four ohms; calculated $1/8 + 1/8 = 1/4$, inverted to $4/1$, or 4. *See also* MECHANICAL-ELECTRICAL ANALOGIES.

IMPERIAL (label). (I) An American lateral-cut, single-sided disc issued by **Leeds & Catlin Co.,** New York, from ca. 1900 to 1909. Imperial was sold in Britain also, for 2 shillings, from April 1906, by Cook's Athletic Co., London. Through agreements between Leeds & Catlin and the German Favorite Schallplatten Fabrik, masters from the Favorite catalog appeared with Imperial labels. The Leeds & Catlin factory in Middletown, Connecticut, was pressing 100,000 records a day in early 1907. Gilbert, Kimpton and Co. assumed the role of European agents for Leeds & Catlin, claiming to be the sole authorized distributors; John G. Murdoch of London and Trevor Jones of Birmingham were licensed factors in the U.K. Success of the label, which carried operatic and popular music, was indicated by the international sales pattern that included South Africa, India, and South America. There were 500 titles in the catalog issued in October 1907.

Gilbert, Kimpton and Co. acquired the label in 1907 and set up a division to handle it, the Imperial Disc Record Co. Remarkable promotion efforts brought great profits to the firm.

However, long litigation in the U.S. finally ended with a ruling by the U.S. Supreme Court in May 1909 that Leeds & Catlin had infringed the Berliner patent #534543 (19 Feb 1895), and would be forbidden to engage in the selling of records; the company filed for bankruptcy in June. Advertising of Imperial continued in Britain for some time, until the stock was sold at auction and made available by Gamage's department stores in London at 10 pence per disc.

Among the artists heard on Imperial were Harry Anthony, Henry Burr, Albert Campbell, Arthur Collins, Byron Harlan, violinist Charles d'Almaine, the Garde Republicaine Band, Billy Murray, the Peerless Quartet, Frank Stanley, Alan Turner, Billy Golden, Ada Jones, Steve Porter, Elise Stevenson, Len Spencer, Edward Favor, George Gaskin, George W. Johnson, John W. Myers, Leo Medaer (clarinet), Vess Ossman, and Cal Stewart. [Andrews*.]

IMPERIAL (label). (II) A British cylinder record sold by the Imperial Phono Exchange, Camden Town, before 1907. The firm was convicted of illegal duplication of records in January 1907 and ceased production.

IMPERIAL (label). (III) A British double-sided record issued before World War I by Sound Recording Co., Ltd. The wording on the label was New Double Sided Imperial Record. [Andrews 1972.]

IMPERIAL (label). (IV) A British record manufactured by Crystalate Gramophone Record Manufacturing Co., Ltd., from 1920 to 1934. Material was primarily dance music, light classical music, and popular songs. Some Wurlitzer organ records were imported from the U.S. Important jazz numbers heard for the first time in Britain on this label included items by Fletcher Henderson and Louis Armstrong. There was also folk music, Hebrew religious and secular music, Irish, Swedish, Scottish, French, and Italian numbers, and operatic music. [Rust 1978.]

IMPERIAL (label). (V) An American record established in January 1946 by the Imperial Record Co., 137–139 N. Western Ave., Los Angeles. Latin American popular music was the specialty, with other national folk music also offered. In addition there were some discs by so-called Boogie-Woogie Stars (Tommy Ridgely, Walter Henry, etc.) and by jazz/pop luminaries (Errol Garner, Fats Domino, etc.). Catalina, Knight, and Post were subsidiary labels. Imperials appeared through the LP era, but are not among current compact disc labels. [Rotante 1985 and Hayes, C. 1988 have matrix listings.]

IMPERIAL QUARTET OF CHICAGO. A male group who recorded for Victor in 1916; they had 11 titles in the 1917 catalog. Members were Wallace Moody, C. R. Wood, Ben Q. Tufts, and Oliver Johnson.

IMPROVED GRAMOPHONE. The Berliner product of mid-1897, developed by Eldridge Johnson and Alfred Clark. It was a disc player with spring motor and a new sound box. In 1898 Frank Seaman marketed the player as the Zonophone. This is the machine that appears in the Nipper painting and trademark.

INDEPENDENT LABELS. In the pop/rock industry, these are often referred to as "indies." They are small companies without the full range of facilities to make and distribute records; therefore, they arrange for other firms—usually the large record corporations, or "majors"—to press discs, and usually to handle marketing. (Historically in the U.S. it could be said that all labels began as independents except Columbia and Victor, who monopolized the manufacturing and distribution of records during the early years of the industry.) A number of pop/rock independents have had highly successful products; a good example being RSO, whose soundtrack albums from Saturday Night Fever (1977) and Grease (1978) were each on the charts more than 100 weeks. Both the Beatles and Elvis Presley recorded first for indies. The smaller firms usually specialize in one type of music and engage only a half-dozen artists as their regular performers. While a few indies, like Warner Brothers and MCA, have been successful enough to become majors, most of them either fail or are taken over by one of the giant companies.

There are also important independent labels in the classical music field, such as Conifer, Gimell, Hyperion, LDR, Pavilion, and Priory. Classical independents proliferated with the arrival of the LP record, the earliest including Allegro, Artist, Concert Hall, Westminster, and Vox. [Cooper, R. 1980; *Goldmine* 4 Nov 1988 has a directory of about 200 current labels.]

INDESTRUCTIBLE PHONOGRAPH RECORD CO. Chicago chemist and electrician Varian Harris, in association with businessman Edmund A. Balm, developed a collapsible celluloid cylinder record that was reportedly used as a premium in breakfast cereals and in connection with the *Chicago Tribune*. (This unbreakable cylinder may predate the first commercial **Lambert Co.** cylinders of May 1900.) No surviving examples of these flexible thin-walled records are known, but a crudely-made record mounted on a brown-wax core (stamped "Indestructible Phono. Record Co. Chicago" at the title-end rim) has been found.

By 1903, Harris had left his employment with the Lambert Co. and he and Balm incorporated in Illinois as the Indestructile Phonograph Record Co. On 4 Aug 1903, at their offices at 224 E. Kinzie St., they unwittingly sold some of their collapsible records and a supporting mandrel for them to an agent of Thomas Edison's National Phonograph Co. With this evidence at hand, Edison's attorneys filed suit for patent infringement in September 1903. After considerable haggling over the validity of several patents, the Edison Patent Department discontinued the suit on 27 Sep 1905.

Little more is known about the Balm and Harris venture or their recordings, but Harris's work continued later for the **Cleveland Phonograph Record Co.** and the **U-S Phonograph Co.**

Bill Klinger

INDESTRUCTIVE PHONOGRAPHIC RECORD CO. (I) A firm organized in Augusta, Maine, 15 June 1906. The five shareholders were James H. Snowden of Indianapolis; P.M. Snowden of Oil City, Pennsylvania; and Lewis A. Burleigh, I. L. Fairbanks, and J. Berry, all of Augusta. Burleigh was a local attorney who filed the incorporation papers from his office; Fairbanks acted as president and treasurer. The Snowdens had built their fortunes in the oil industry.

Angus Joss wrote that Brian F. Philpot interested "Eastern capitalists" (probably the Snowdens and their partners) in the rights to the Lambert patents and that the rights were sold to "Indestructible" in August 1906. The firm was sued by the New Jersey Patent Co. in connection with patented Edison cylinder molding processes. The Maine-based entity ceased to function by 19 June 1907, probably without producing any records.

INDESTRUCTIBLE PHONOGRAPHIC RECORD CO. (II) The second incarnation of this firm was incorporated under the laws of West Virginia in 1907. It again involved the Snowden brothers, this time with Henry McSweeney, an attorney with the Standard Oil Company. Headquarters were at Oil City, Pennsylvania.

INDESTRUCTIBLE PHONOGRAPHIC RECORD CO. (III) The most well-known and successful "Indestructible" venture was based in Albany, New York. George and James Snowden and Henry McSweeney filed as a partnership in Albany County, 20 May 1908. (They had already acquired the deed to a factory building at 226 Hamilton Street on 16 May 1906.) Though IPRCo (II) had been incorporated in West Virginia, the Albany operation was run as an unincorporated partnership financed by the Snowden group until its assets were "turned over" to IPRCo (II), late in 1908.

Finally, "the business carried on at 352 Livingston Street, Brooklyn, N.Y. [record master facility] and 226 Hamilton Street, Albany, N.Y. [factory] was taken over and reincorporated in New York on 31 Oct 1910." Among the directors were Brian F. Philpot and Frederick W. Matthews.

Brian Philpot served as general manager for two years; he had been a founder of the Lambert Co. in 1900. William F. Messer, also formerly with Lambert, was factory superintendent until March 1909 (he claimed that the construction details of the Albany Indestructibles were his own improvements).

Frederick Matthews also contributed record molding technology in two assigned patents.

The Albany firm manufactured cylinder records having a characteristic cardboard-tube core with metal end rings. The very first ones (advertised during the Summer of 1907 and first released November 1907) still had raised-letter title markings like those on the end rims of late Lambert records and they were probably pressed using Lambert Co. equipment at 110–112 S. Jefferson Street, Chicago. Albany Indestructible end rims also bear the 29 July 1902 date of the Messer patent that was a legacy from the Lambert Co.

The records were initially marketed directly by the Albany firm as "Indestructible Records." Edison soon pursued Indestructible in the trade papers and the courts, warning his dealers not to handle any competing cylinder products alongside Edison goods. The Indestructible people approached the management of the Columbia Phonograph Co., General to strike a deal for Columbia to distribute "the whole output" of Indestructible (Columbia having discontinued the manufacture of their own cylinders on 5 May 1909). Under the terms of a contract dated 25 Sep 1908, Columbia marketed the Albany products as "Columbia Indestructible Records." Indestructible stopped selling their records directly. This arrangement continued until 13 May 1912, when Columbia announced "the finish of the cylinder record" (or at least the end of their distribution of the Albany Indestructible records).

Only two-minute Indestructible records were sold until the first four-minute selections were released in January 1910. (A few sample 4M records were made as early as March 1909.) By 1913 Indestructible was again advertising their "Original" Indestructible Records, sold directly and at reduced prices.

The masters for domestic Indestructibles were recorded in the Brooklyn studio under the supervision of musical director John J. Lacalle. He imbued the Indestructible catalogs with some unusual pieces outside of the mainstream of music most often recorded at that time, including drum solos, organ solos, and the new dance orchestras of the late World War I era.

British titles were recorded at John G. Murdoch and Co., Ltd., in London, under the direction of Albert W. Ketelbey. The masters were processed in Albany and the resulting records were issued in specially numbered British series (all 2M: May 1910; 4M: beginning September 1910) and occasionally also in the regular U.S. series. Murdoch acted as the sole authorized distributor for Indestructibles in England, starting in July 1909 and continuing through at least 1913.

About 1,500 Indestructible titles were issued altogether. Beyond the British series, there were no other special series for foreign-language or operatic material. These black celluloid cylinders with "inside" metal rings were sold under various brand names and in a variety of packages. Consequently, there is occasional confusion among modern collectors about these records and their origin. The diverse brand names used include: Indestructible, Columbia Indestructible, Oxford (sold by Sears, Roebuck & Co.), Lakeside (mail-order marketed by Montgomery Ward & Co., after the passing of U-S Phonograph Co.), Everlasting Indestructible, and finally as Federal, from 1 June 1917. All these brands are really the same cylinders, numbered and marked identically, but packaged in containers with different labels.

Indestructible never manufactured phonographs, but did market a spring-tension reproducer designed to play their celluloid records—it was the first (March 1910) commercial reproducer to employ a diamond stylus.

The celluloid cylinders of the Indestructible Phonographic Record Company of Albany, New York, were the first to enjoy truly widespread acceptance and distribution. Their heyday was 1908–1911, with a few additional titles issued through the World War I period. Production ended after a disastrous factory fire on 11 Oct 1922, though the firm apparently limped along into 1925.

Bill Klinger

INDUCTANCE. The extent to which an electric circuit or component is able to store magnetic energy when current is flowing. It is measured in "Henrys." *See also* MECHANICAL-ELECTRICAL ANALOGIES.

INFINITE BAFFLE. A loudspeaker enclosure (*see* BAFFLE) designed to prevent sound waves emanating from the front of the speaker from reaching the back of the speaker. This is accomplished by means of a large open space behind the loudspeaker, causing the rear waves to be completely absorbed.

INFINITY SYSTEMS, INC. A California firm, located in Chatsworth, established in 1968 to make high quality loudspeakers. In 1990 it held a sizeable share of the American market, and was selling models in Britain as well. The Infinitesimal Four is a three-piece speaker system sold in 1991 for about $1,000.

INJECTION MOLDING. The method of making a recording disc by injecting the liquefied plastic **biscuit** into a die cavity of the desired dimensions.

INK SPOTS. Male vocal group, formed in 1934 in New York. The members were Charles Fuqua, tenor and guitar; Jerry Daniels, lead tenor; Ivory Watson, baritone and guitar; and Orville "Hoppy" Jones, bass and string bass. At the peak of their popularity in the 1940s, Bill Kenny was the lead tenor. A distinctive sound was achieved by setting a high tenor against a rumbling—and often speaking—bass, with the middle voices accompanying. Among the first Black groups to achieve wide popularity on disc, the Ink Spots were a great success on radio and jukebox; they were also well received in Britain on several tours.

The group recorded for Victor in 1935, beginning with "Swingin' on the Strings" (#234851). Their outstanding numbers were done for Decca, including "If I Didn't Care" (#2286; 1939), "My Prayer" (#2790; 1939), "Whispering Grass" (#3258; 1940), "We Three" (#3379; 1940), "Do I Worry?" / "Java Jive" (#3432; 1940), and "Until the Real Thing Comes Along" (#3958; 1941).

The group disbanded in 1952, though both Fuqua and Kenny formed new ensembles with the Ink Spots name.

INNER PLAYER. The type of player piano with its integral mechanism built into the piano. It was the opposite of the **push-up player.**

INPUT SELECTOR. The control on a preamplifier that allows the user to choose one signal source from multiple input signals.

INSTANTANEOUS RECORDINGS. Records made for non-retail purposes, mostly in the 1930s and 1940s, by a **direct to disc** process. The material used was typically aluminum, coated with acetate or a nitrate lacquer to make a soft surface. The use of acetate gave the popular name "acetates" to these recordings.

Home recording was a popular use of instantaneous records in the U.S. from 1920. (In Britain, the **Neophone Co., Ltd.,** had offered a home disc recorder ca. 1905.) Radio stations made transcription discs that way, and researchers made field recordings (some of those on zinc, a more durable material than acetate). Diameters were the same as for commercial discs, except for transcriptions and conference/speech records, which were usually 16 inches in diameter. Most ran at 78 rpm.

The earliest instantaneous records sold for home use in the U.S. were pre-grooved zinc blanks, six inches in diameter, sold as Echo Disc and Kodisk. They were offered by the **American Home Recorder Co.** of New York in August 1920. Since the recording method was still acoustic, the recordist had to shout into the horn, and was rewarded with only a faint return. With the arrival of electrical recording in 1925, it was possible to speak at normal volume into the microphone of the player, and to receive an amplified return; the medium was a plain metal disc, the best of them aluminum. The Speak-O-Phone Co. of New York, established in 1926, was a pioneer manufacturer.

Victor introduced a pre-grooved plastic "home record blank" in the early 1930s, to be used on a Victor home disc recorder. As it happened, the audio quality from the pre-grooved record was poorer than that from the ungrooved metal discs, and Victor's apparatus did not gain public acceptance.

An innovation of the early 1930s was the use of lacquer coated discs, first manufactured in France as Pyral records, and marketed in America from 1934 by Presto Recording Corp. of New York. The new surfaces allowed the direct to disc recording of all types of musical ensembles, including orchestras, and gave a clear reproduction. Radio stations embraced the lacquer disc, which could run 33 1/3 rpm on 16-inch blanks, to give uninterrupted programming long enough for broadcast purposes (see RADIO PROGRAM RECORDINGS). Lacquer also replaced wax in the major recording studios as the material used for masters in the production of commercial recordings. The lacquer was applied to an aluminum or glass base, or later to inexpensive fiber or paper bases. Presto solved the problem of freshly cut thread clogging the grooves by means of a blower system introduced in 1940, but a more practical and less expensive solution was provided by Audio Devices, Inc.: a wiper blade that brushed the fresh threads toward the center of the disc. Eventually, a vacuum suction device was developed to draw off the threads.

Early lacquer coated discs usually had three drive-pin holes, equally spaced around the center hole; the purpose was to secure the disc (onto drive pins on the turntable) and prevent slipping during the process. By 1940 there was a flourishing market for domestic disc recorders and their discs. The advent of the LP in 1948 had, in a few years, its application in the instantaneous field. Recordists of the 1950s could select from the 33 1/3, 45, or 78 rpm. Wire recording did not affect the home disc market, but tape recording ultimately obliterated it.

Manufacturers of the home recorders included Recordio (manufactured by Wilcox-Gay), Howard, Federal, Packard-Bell, Phono-Cord, Rek-O-Kut, Universal, and Motorola. Montgomery Ward sold their house brand Airline, and Sears, Roebuck sold Silvertone machines. The most popular models had a built-in radio, allowing direct recording from the air (a feature first available in 1924).

Preservation has been a serious problem with instantaneous discs, since the surfaces permitted only a few playbacks without noticeable wear, and the unstable chemical structure lead to oxidation and brittleness of the entire record. A further problem arose from the breakdown of the bonding between the recording medium and its backing, so that the coating would peel or flake away. Finally, a greasy film often formed on the surfaces, from the castor oil used as an additive, rendering the disc unplayable. Archives seek to re-record an instantaneous disc immediately.

Master blanks of highest grade are still used in commercial record production, as metal masters, mothers, and stampers. (See also DISC, 1; STUDIO PRACTICE.)

John Case

INSTITUTE FOR STUDIES IN AMERICAN MUSIC. An organization established in New York City in 1971 under the direction of H. Wiley Hitchcock. It has published numerous monographs, bibliographies, and discographies, including *American Music Recordings* by Carol J. Oja (1982). The Institute has sponsored important conferences and concerts, one of which was the first international meeting to honor an American composer, the Charles Ives Centennial Festival of 1974. A biennial newsletter is published.

INSTITUTE OF ELECTRICAL AND ELECTRONICS ENGINEERS. An American organization established in 1963, located at 345 E. 47th St., New York. It was formed in a merger of the American Institute of Electrical Engineers (established 1884) and the Institute of Radio Engineers (established 1912). There are more than 275,000 members plus about 47,000 student members, consisting of scientists in in all fields related to electrical and electronic engineering. Support for the Engineering Societies Library in New York is an important activity. The Institute sets standards in areas of impact on audio manufacture. There are ten regional groups, 260 sections, and 44 subsections, plus 700 local groups. A staff of 500 is directed by a general manager (in 1988 this was Eric Herz).

An affiliated group is the IEEE Acoustics, Speech, and Signal Processing Society, with more than 13,000 members; it is directly concerned with sound recording and reproduction, and with related psychological and physiologial factors. It is also located at 345 E. 47th St., New York.

INSTITUTE OF JAZZ STUDIES. A research center established at Rutgers University, New Jersey, in 1952, by Marshall Stearns. The institute operates under its own board of directors, receiving support from the Rutgers, the U.S. government, and industry. An archival collection of 75,000 jazz recordings, sheet music, clippings, photographs, books, and related material is maintained, and rare recordings are being transferred to tape.

Important efforts of 1968–1969 were the organization of conferences on discographical research and on the preservation of the jazz heritage; conference proceedings were published as *Studies in Jazz Discography* (1971). Other publications of the institute have included *Journal of Jazz Studies* (1973–1980)—succeeded by *Annual Review of Jazz Studies*—and a series of 100 recordings: *The Greatest Jazz Recordings of All Time*. Seminars, conferences, and radio programs are sponsored. A recently developed access tool is the IJS Data Base, an index to the record collection that allows searching on all fields of research interest; about 2,000 recordings were in the Data Base in 1991.

INSULATOR. A substance that presents a strong resistance to the flow of electric current, or—in an audio system—to the passage of sound waves. *See also* BAFFLE.

INSULL, SAMUEL, 1859–1938. British/American industrialist and record industry executive, born in London on 11 Nov 1859. He was educated at Reading and Oxford. He was private secretary to Colonel George E. Gouraud, the U.K. representative of Thomas Edison, in 1878. In 1881 Insull moved to the U.S. and became Edison's private secretary, also representing him at meetings of the National Phonograph Association in 1890–1892. In 1889 he became second vice president of the new Edison General Electric Co. He was responsible for building and operating the machine works in Schenectedy, New York, that evolved into the General Electric Co. in 1892, and he was for a short time second vice president of the new firm.

Insull moved to Chicago to become president of the Chicago Edison Co., its successor Commonwealth Electric Co. (1892–1907), and Commonwealth Edison Co. (1907–1930). From 1930 to 1932 he served as chairman of the board of Commonwealth Edison. He took U.S. citizenship in 1896.

In Chicago Insull is remembered especially for his promotion of the new Civic Opera building (1929). He had been president of the Chicago Civic Opera since its organization in 1921, as the replacement of the old Grand Opera Co. Insull died in Chicago on 16 July 1938.

INTEGRATED AMPLIFIER. A device that unifies the functions of a power amplifier and a pre-amplifier. When the integrated amplifier is combined with a tuner, the result is called a receiver. *See also* AMPLIFIER.

INTEGRATED CIRCUIT. A group of electronic components joined into a single package. It is distinguished from a discrete circuit, which consists of individually packaged elements.

INTENSITY. In an audio system, the strength of a sound signal; it is measured in dynes or newtons, or in watts per square meter. The intensity of a sound depends first of all on the amplitude of its vibrations. This value is affected by various factors and components, especially the amplifier. For high fidelity reproduction, peak levels reach 20 dynes per square centimeter (100 dBs) above the threshold of hearing.

What the listener finally perceives to be the relative intensity of the reproduced signal is referred to as loudness. Loudness is a physiological impression of the level of the sound; it has no quantitative measurement. [Isom*.]

Intermodulation distortion. *See* DISTORTION, VII.

INTERNATIONAL ASSOCIATION OF SOUND ARCHIVES (IASA). An organization established in 1963, as Fédération Internationale des Phonothèques. The original base of concern of IASA was the administration, cataloging-classification, and preservation of sound recordings that were housed in large collections. Over the years the scope of the organization has increased to include attention to visual media. Recent discussion has centered on a possible change in aims and structure that would make IASA an international audio-visual association.

Membership of IASA comes from 47 countries. The association has an executive office in Stockholm, and elected officers. In 1991 the president was Gerald D. Gibson. There are various committees, including a technical committee, a copyright committee, a cataloguing committee, a discography committee, and a training committee. Publications include the *Phonographic Bulletin* (1971– ; two per year), a membership directory, *Sound Archives: A Guide to Their Establishment and Development* (1983), and *Selection in Sound Archives* (1984).

INTERNATIONAL ASSOCIATION QUARTET. A male vocal group that recorded for Edison in 1912. Members were Paul J. Gilbert, P.H. Metcalf, C.M. Keeler, and Edward W. Peck.

INTERNATIONAL CORRESPONDENCE SCHOOLS. An American firm, established in 1891 in Scranton, Pennsylvania, originally offering trade-related home study courses for miners in the region. In 1901, when they had enrolled over 350,000 students, they also began giving language study courses (French, German, and Spanish, with Italian added later), aided by Edison cylinders. They were Edison's first molded records, of a surface sufficiently durable to allow for the repetitive playback required in language study; 24 records were included in each of the available languages. In 1902 the firm printed its first catalog entirely devoted to language instruction.

The phonograph first provided to students was the Standard Model A (*see* EDISON RECORD PLAYERS), with a repeat button that skipped back several grooves. In February 1910 a Gem replaced the Standard, and in 1915 the Amberola 30 was used. Blue Amberol I.C.S. records played for about eight minutes at 90 rpm. [Frow 1978; Petersen 1973.]

INTERNATIONAL FEDERATION OF PRODUCERS OF PHONOGRAMS AND VIDEOGRAMS (IFPI). An entity founded in 1933 as the International Federation of the Phonograph Industry, to represent the rights of producers in their interactions with governments and non-governmental organizations. Alfred Clark was the first president, and Louis Sterling one of the earliest vice presidents. In 1959 there were 250 member firms, a number that had grown to 600—in 33 countries—by 1986. Among the affiliated groups are the Recording Industry Association of America (RIAA) and the Australian Record Industry Association. IFPI has consultative status with UNESCO, the Council of Europe, and other international bodies. The Secretariat is located at 54 Regent St., London.

International Indestructible Cylinder Records. *See* INTERNATIONAL PHONOGRAPH AND INDESTRUCTIBLE RECORD CO., LTD.

International Indestructible Record Co. *See* INTERNATIONAL PHONOGRAPH AND INDESTRUCTIBLE RECORD CO., LTD.

INTERNATIONAL JAZZ FEDERATION (IJF). An organization of musicians, composers, record producers, distributors, journalists, collectors, and jazz fans; it is headquartered in London at 13 Fousler Road. It was founded in 1969 as the European Jazz Federation, then took its present name in 1975. IJF is associated with UNESCO, and is a member of the International Music Council.

INTERNATIONAL PHONOGRAPH AND INDESTRUCTIBLE RECORD CO., LTD. A British firm established 16 Apr 1902, at 8 Cook St., Liverpool. Their product was a celluloid unbreakable cylinder record, using for the most part material from Edison recordings. The first three permanent directors were Walter FitzHugh Barry, chairman; Frederick M. Prescott, vice chairman; and Henry T. Cramer Roberts, managing director and secretary. Ademor N. Petit was also a director, and served as works manager. After only two years of operation, the firm's assets were sold on 14 July 1904. However, the making and sale of records continued, by a firm named the International Indestructible Record Co., advertising from 4 Castle Street Arcade, Liverpool. [Andrews 1974/10.]

INTERNATIONAL RECORD COLLECTORS' CLUB (IRCC). An organization established in 1931 by **William H. Seltsam**, at 318

Reservoir Ave., Bridgeport, Connecticut. Its purpose was to offer monthly reisisues of golden age vocal records. Seltsam was able to arrange for special disc pressings from Victor and Columbia vault masters, and from Edison and Pathé. By 1937 he was transferring vertical-cut cylinder records to disc for distribution to the club members. The first discs offered were by Geraldine Farrar, and altogether 16 IRCC discs were Farrar numbers. The club records had exact recording information, and were designed to play back at the correct original speeds. Some of the **Mapleson cylinders** were included in the IRCC offerings.

INTERNATIONAL RECORD CO. An American firm, established ca. 1901, marketing 10-inch discs with the International Record label at $.40. Location was 38 Washington St., Auburn, New York, then 40-46 Washington St. W. P. Bradley was sales manager. The first lists in *TMW* appeared in February 1906. [Andrews*.]

INTERNATIONAL TALKING MACHINE CO. A Chicago firm, established in 1915 at 1719 W. Van Buren St. it manufactured the International and Operola disc players in six models.

INTERNATIONAL TALKING MACHINE CO. mbH. A German firm, established in 1903 in Berlin by **Frederick Marion Prescott** to succeed his **International Zonophone Co.** A double-sided disc, the first to be marketed in Europe, was issued in February 1904 with the label **Odeon Record.** By 1906 there were 14,000 titles in the catalog. Emil Rink was general manager as of February 1908. The firm was out of business in 1932.

INTERNATIONAL ZONOPHONE CO. A firm incorporated in Jersey City, New Jersey (259 Washington St.), on 7 Mar 1901. The directors were Francis T. Sargent, Edward S. Innet, Edward McCarthy, **Frederick Marion Prescott** (managing director), and John Prescott (treasurer). Prescott transferred his rights in the Universal Talking Machine Co. and their Zono-phone trademark in exchange for $20,000 of stock in the new company. An office was set up at 66 Broad St., New York. Prescott went to

Berlin to establish a German company, factory, and recording operation at 71 Ritterstrasse, and by June 1901 that company was advertising the sale of discs and players. The records were both 7-inch and the new 9-inch size. In September 1901 a 10-inch record was introduced, the so-called Concert or Grand record. Discs and machines were on sale in London by November 1901, with Nicole Frères as agent. A sales agent for Germany, Austria, and Hungary was established also, the Zonophone GmbH, at 63 Ritterstrasse.

In April 1902 the firm announced that its stock included records made in Germany, Italy, France, Russia, Britain, and the U.S. Later there were Latin American issues as well. By mid-1902 the firm was pressing double-sided discs (the earliest known in the industry) for the Brazilian agency Casa Edison. Beginning in November 1902 the firm employed a trademark that showed a little girl with her kitten both listening raptly to a Zonophone, in a pose reminiscent of **Nipper** and his "improved gramophone"; Frank Andrews has styled this picture as "Her Master's Voice."

The gramophones sold by the company were priced from £2 to £14 in Britain, and the records were 2 shillings to 4 shillings. A model known as the De Luxe Concert Zonophone No. 110 could play four full 10-inch discs at one winding. There were 3,500 items in the record catalog in November and 2,000 added for Christmas sales.

In early 1903 the firm moved to new quarters at 73 Mühlenstrasse, Berlin. Ullmann's became the London outlet, mangaged by Emil Rink. Another 1,000 records were in the catalog, primarily European and South American pressings. Yet the firm was not to enjoy its success for very long. In June 1903 Gramophone & Typewriter, Ltd., acquired the major share of Zonophone stock, and turned the direction of its new subsidiary over to Theodore Birnbaum. The name of the company was retained, and Zonophone products continued to be advertised. Prescott resigned from the Zonophone board on 11 July 1903 and established the **International Talking Machine Co. mbH.** [Andrews*; Andrews 1980/2*.] *See also* ZONOPHONE (label).

INVICTA (label). A British record sold by W.A. Barraud, Ltd. from November 1912. The label originated with **Berolina Schallplatten GmbH**, which also provided the early material. There were popular vocal and instrumental pieces, some later of British origin. Disputes between Barraud and Berolina resulted in liquidation of Barraud's firm in June 1913, but he was soon back in business as the Invicta Record Co., Ltd., making only British recordings, and keeping the Invicta label name until May 1914. The Invicta label was also carried on by Berolina, which sold them in the U.K. as well as on the continent. Thus there were two distinct Invicta records on sale in Britain for many months, until Berolina won a trademark case in court and Barraud had to cease using the name. [Andrews 1990.]

INVICTA RECORD CO., LTD. A British firm established 4 July 1913 by **William Andrew Barraud**, as a successor to his liquidated company, William A. Barraud, Ltd. The location was Bank Chambers, Kingsland High Road, London; from there the company moved in October 1913 to No. 1, New Inn Yard. Initially the firm used the Invicta label name, but having lost a trademark case to **Berolina Schallplatten GmbH** it dropped Invicta in May 1914 and brought out two new labels, Citizen and **Guardsman**. It also made Invicta gramophones, offering 26 different models in 1915. As Barraud went into semi-retirement, Alfred J. Barton managed the company. He entered military service in 1917, and Athol Conway Simmons became manager. Invicta stayed in business until May 1922, with its labels taken over by others. [Andrews 1990.]

INVINCIBLE FOUR (INVINCIBLE MALE QUARTET). A vocal group that recorded for Edison in 1902. The singers were Byron G. Harlan, George Seymour Lenox, Arthur Collins, and Frank C. Stanley. (The same name, Invincible Four, was used by the Peerless Quartet in some Pathé recordings.) Among the eight records listed in Koenigsberg, the earliest was "On Board the Oregon," (#8042) and the last was "Nigger Stew." (#8537). [Koenigsberg 1987.]

IONOPHONE SPEAKER. A type of **tweeter** that uses a corona discharge to produce a direct acoustic effect through electrical vibration. It operates by application of a high voltage radio frequency oscillation between a Kanthal electrode housed in a small quartz tube and a counter electrode; the result is a glow discharge of the Kanthal. Air pressures in the Kanthal tube vary with the audio modulation. If the open end of the tube is connected to an exponential horn, the horn will be without resonance or amplitude distortion.

IOWA PHONOGRAPH CO. One of the 33 member firms of the **North American Phonograph Co.**, operating from 1890 to 1893 in Sioux City, Iowa. W.P. Manley was president in 1892, with A.C. Brackenbush, vice president.

IRAGEN (label). A rare record issued from Richmond Hill, New York, by the International Records Agency in the mid 1930s. Only seven issues are known, including jazz items, classical piano, and art songs, plus a trombone solo and a cornet solo. [*RR* #87 (December 1967) listed the issues; Rust 1978.]

IRCC. *See* INTERNATIONAL RECORD COLLECTORS' CLUB.

IRISH MUSIC RECORDINGS. Irish songs appeared on record from the earliest days. In November 1899 the Gramophone Co. had an Irish section in its listing of seven-inch discs. Around 1910 major American labels began to identify Irish material in separate series or catalogs. Important labels with Irish series included Decca (to 1937), Vocalion, and Okeh (to ca. 1927, with a few more in ca. 1934).

Columbia had an important early series (33000) of Irish material. Then from 1947 to 1951 Columbia released 563 items in the 33500–F series. Among the popular Columbia tenors were Seamus O'Doherty, Chauncey Olcott, Charles W. Harrison, William A. Kennedy, and Shaun O'Nolan. In addition to vocal material, there were reels, dances, and bagpipe performances. Frank Quinn, who sang, recited, and played the accordion, made one of the most enduring records of the series, "Leg of the Duck" (#33004–F). Sullivan's Shamrock Band (four fiddlers and piano) offered marches, reels, and jigs.

The Victor catalog of 1917 showed 130 titles, including songs and comic numbers, but the total was down to 16 in 1927; there were 30 in the 1938 catalog. The LP did not bring an Irish boom; there were only 11 albums available in 1960. [Carolon 1987; Gronow 1979.]

IRWIN, MARY, 1862–1938. Canadian comedienne, born in Whitby, Ontario, on 27 June 1862. She specialized in Negro dialect songs and "shouts," and held the stage for four decades; once she was called to a White House performance by Woodrow Wilson. Irwin's only recording was done in three sessions for Victor in May 1907. The six titles included her biggest hit, "Mary Irwin's Frog Song" (#5156). She died in New York on 2 Oct 1938. [Walsh 1963/6–7.]

ISSLER, EDWARD. Pianist and orchestra leader, "one of the most familiar names in record catalogs of the 1890s" (Brooks). Issler worked for Edison as early as 1889, then for New Jersey Phonograph Co., Chicago Talking Machine Co., and others. He did not record after 1900. Issler's first Edison session was on 27 Aug 1889, when he and xylophonist A.T. Van Winkle inscribed seven numbers. He had a solo session on 14 Sept 1889, beginning with "Member of Congress March." His final piano cylinder was made on 31 March 1892. Issler's Orchestra (consisting of A.T. Van Winkle, violin; George Schweinfest, flute; D.B. Dana, cornet; and Issler at the piano; with others later) began to record for Edison on 11 Nov 1889, with the "Men of Wall Street March," and remained with Edison to 1891. [Brooks 1979; Koenigsberg 1987.]

ITURBI, JOSÉ, 1895–1980. Spanish/American pianist and conductor, born in Valencia on 28 Nov 1895. He studied in Valencia and Paris, played and taught in Switzerland, and toured widely. Settling in the U.S. in 1929, he performed throughout the country. In 1936–44 he was conductor of the Rochester (New York) Philharmonic Orchestra. Iturbi was not only the most renowned Spanish pianist of the time, but he also developed a large following among film-goers as a result of his playing in the Chopin biography *Song to Remember* (1945). His recording of the "Polonaise No. 6 in A-Flat Major" (Victor #11–8848; 1945) was the first by a classical pianist to exceed sales of a million copies. He died in Hollywood on 28 June 1980.

IVES, BURL, 1909– . American folksinger and actor, born in Jasper County, Illinois, on 14 June 1909. He attended Eastern Illinois State Teachers College in 1927–29, then began touring as a singer and guitarist. He was popular simultaneously as an actor in films—notably in *Cat on a Hot Tin Roof* (1958), and in *The Big Country* (1958), for which he won an Academy Award—and on stage, with a leading role (while in military service) in *This is the Army* (1942). On radio from 1942, he achieved wide recognition, and performed at Town Hall, New York, in 1945. Ives collected and published folksongs, and composed folk-like melodies himself. He was influential in producing the folk music revival of the 1940s and 1950s, and is regarded as one of the major folksingers of the century.

The principal Ives recordings were "Wayfarin' Stranger," "Foggy Foggy Dew," "Blue-Tailed Fly,"—all on the Columbia LP *Wayfarin' Stranger*—and a string of chart discs in the 1960s, including his composition "A Little Bitty Tear" (Decca #31330; 1961), "A Funny Way of Laughin'" (Decca #31373; 1962), and "Mr. In-Between" (Decca #31405; 1962). The Decca album *Versatile Burl Ives* (#DL 4152) was a best seller in 1962. His last great success was the album *Pearly Shells* (Decca #DL 4578; 1965).

IVOGÜN, MARIA, 1891–1987. Austrian soprano, born Maria Kempner in Budapest on 18 Nov 1891. She studied with her mother, Ida von Günther, who had premiered *Merry Widow*, and then at the Musik Akademie in Vienna. Her debut was in Munich, as Mimi, on 1 Apr 1913. She remained with the Munich opera to 1925, working under Bruno Walter. Turning from lyric to coloratura roles, she gained acclaim throughout Europe, notably as Zerbinetta in *Adriane auf Naxos*. In 1922 she made her

American debut in Chicago as Rosina. Later she was a favorite in Covent Garden and Berlin, Vienna, and Scandinavia. From 1925 to 1934 she was with the Berlin Städtische Oper.

Ivogün was recognized for her Mozart interpretations as well as Verdi, Puccini, and Rossini roles. She retired in 1933, and taught in Germany, one of her pupils being Elisabeth Schwarzkopf. She died on 3 Oct 1987.

Her first 25 records were for Odeon, in Berlin, during 1916–1919; the earliest was "Der holle Rache" from *Zauberflöte* (#76970). From 1924 to 1925 she was with DGG in Berlin, for 14 sides, and from 1923 to 1926 she recorded in Chicago for Brunswick (12 items, including some Lieder). There were also six 1932 electrics made for Electrola (HMV), including perhaps her finest record: Zerbinetta's aria from *Ariadne*. Other important discs were a duet with her husband, tenor Karl Erb, from *Don Pasquale* (Odeon # 76972, reissued by IRCC #3081) and "O zittre nicht" from *Zauberflöte* (Polydor #85310; reissued by Club 99—with "Der holle Rache"—as #99-20; 1962). [Frankenstein 1972.]

J

JACKSON, MAHALIA, 1911–1972. American gospel and soul singer, born in New Orleans on 26 Oct 1911. She went to Chicago and was engaged in menial employment while singing in Baptist churches and then for conventions and meetings. Recording for Apollo in the 1940s she earned quick success with her own composition, "Move on up a Little Higher" (#164; 1947). "Silent Night" was another hit disc (Apollo #235; 1950). Jackson went on to international tours, gaining recognition as the world's premier gospel singer. Three of her albums (1961, 1962, 1976) won Grammys. She appeared in the film *St. Louis Blues* in 1958.

In her late career she added popular songs to her repertoire. She died in Evergreen Park, a Chicago suburb, on 27 Jan 1972.

JACKSON, MICHAEL, 1958–. American rock singer, born in Gary, Indiana, on 29 Aug 1958. After a period of singing with his brothers in The Jackson Five, he went into a solo career and rose to world fame with his album *Thriller* (Epic #38112; 1982, also a videocassette), which sold some 30 million copies, the highest sale known of a record album. Jackson won eight Grammys in 1988 for *We are the World,* which he and Lionel Richie wrote to raise funds for African famine relief; 45 top stars were heard on the record. Jackson also won Grammys for his 1979 single "Don't Stop 'till You Get Enough (Epic #50742) and for a 1989 video, *Leave Me Alone.* Epic and Motown have issued CD anthologies of his many hits.

JACKSON, MILT, 1923–. American jazz vibraphonist, born in Detroit on 1 Jan 1923. He played various instruments, and sang in gospel groups, then played vibraphone with Detroit bands in the 1940s. In New York, teaming with Dizzy Gillespie, he helped to shape the **cool jazz** movement. He formed a quartet in 1951, named it the Modern Jazz Quartet a year later, and spent most of he career with it. He did perform also apart from the Quartet, with various bands and soloists, and made such discs as "Anthropology" with Gillespie (Victor #40–0132; 1946) and "Misterioso" with Thelonious Monk (Banner #560; 1948). Atlantic issued LP albums of favorite numbers (#1242, #1294, and #1417), and LPs came from Savoy, Prestige, Apple, United Artists, Riverside, and Impulse.

JACKSON, STONEWALL, 1932–. American country singer, guitarist, and songwriter, born in Tabor City, North Carolina, on 6 Nov 1932. He taught himself guitar, and after leaving naval service in 1954 began to save money for a trip to Nashville; he secured an audition there and was signed by Columbia. He made a quick success with "Life to Go" (#41257; 1958), which was followed by a string of 47 chart singles, most of them for Columbia. His last great hit was on the Little Darlin' label: "My Favorite Sin" (#7806; 1978).

JACKSON, WANDA, 1937–. American country singer, guitarist, pianist, songwriter, born in Maud, Oklahoma, on 20 Oct 1937. Her family moved to California, where she learned guitar and piano; then they settled again in Oklahoma. Jackson won first place in a radio talent contest and was invited to record with

Hank Thompson. "You Can't Have My Love" became a hit on the Decca label. She toured with Elvis Presley, and signed a contract with Capitol Records; Las Vegas became her favored venue. Among her own songs to reach the charts was "Right or Wrong" (Capitol #4553; 1961). She made national and European tours in the 1960s. Jackson had 33 chart singles, and numerous successful LP albums.

JAEGER, HENRY. Flutist with the U.S. Marine Band in the 1890s, the first Columbia recording artist to be identified by name. He made Columbia cylinders from 1890 to 1894. Jaeger is not listed among the Edison artists of the period, nor among the Victor or Columbia disc performers. [Brooks 1979.]

JAMES, HARRY, 1916–1983. American jazz trumpeter and Big Band leader, born in Albany, Georgia, on 15 Mar 1916. He learned to play from his father, a circus bandmaster; and he worked with groups in Texas and New Orleans. His first important affiliation was with Ben Pollack in 1935–1936, after which he joined the Benny Goodman orchestra, and became a principal soloist. In 1938 he formed his own Big Band, one of the most popular of the next 30 years. Although he was a fine improviser, he was most famous as a soloist for virtuoso pieces like "Flight of the Bumble Bee" (Variety #8298; 1940) and for tender ballads like "Sleepy Lagoon" (Columbia #36549; 1942).

The James band, with vocalists Frank Sinatra, Dick Haymes, Kitty Kallen, and Helen Forrest, was at its peak in the 1940s, appearing on radio and in 10 films, then on television from 1952. (See articles on the vocalists mentioned for hit record citations.) Among the artists with James at one time or another were Buck Clayton and Ziggy Elman (trumpet), Jess Stacy (piano), Dave Tough, Jo Jones, and Buddy Rich (drums).

Columbia, which made most of the James records, reissued many on LP; other LP albums came from MGM and Harmony.

JAMES, LEWIS LYMAN, 1892–1959. American tenor, born in Dexter, Michigan, on 29 July 1892. He gave up a naval career, leaving Annapolis to be a professional singer, and became one of the most prolific recording artists. His approximately 3,000 records—about half of them solos—were made for various labels. The first was "I Know I Got More Than My Share" (Columbia #2108; 1916), which happened to be coupled with Vernon Dalhart's debut recording. In May 1918 he made his first Victor: "All Aboard for Home Sweet Home" with the Shannon Four (#18441). On Pathé the first was "Sometime You'll Remember" (#20193). The earliest of his 42 Edison Diamond Discs was "Why Did You Come into My Life?" (#50577; 1919). From these titles it will be noted that the James repertoire was popular songs. James sang with the Knickerbocker Quartet (using the name Robert Lewis), with the Crescent Trio, and with the Revelers. Other pseudonyms included Robert Bruce, Harold Harvey, Bruce Wallace, and—on some children's records— Uncle Lewis. James toured Europe five times and sang for British royalty. He gave up singing for health reasons in 1940, and became program director for WGN radio in Chicago until his retirement in 1957. He died in Chicago in February 1959. [Walsh 1955/10.]

JAMES, SONNY, 1929– . American country singer, guitarist, and songwriter, born Jimmie Loden in Hackleburg, Alabama, on 1 May 1929. He toured with his show business family, then served in the Korean War. On his return from the military he signed a contract with Capitol. In the 1960s he made many hit records, notably "You're the Only World I Know" (Capitol #5280; 1964), 28 weeks on the charts. "Going through the Motions" (Capitol #50887; 1963) and "I'll Never Find Another You" (Capitol #5914; 1967) were among his other great successes. He had 62 chart singles, and made many hit LP albums. James appeared in a number of motion pictures, including *Las Vegas Hillbillies*.

JAPANESE VICTOR CO. (JVC). A firm established in 1927 as a subsidiary of the Victor Talking Machine Co.; it manufactured records and record players. From 1929, when Mitsubishi and Sumitomo acquired substantial shares of the company, it was operated as an American-Japanese venture. In 1989 the company operated 13 factories, plus 23 overseas sales companies, with 14,000 employees. Products were labeled Victor in Japan and JVC elsewhere until 1989, when the single label Victor/JVC was adopted for worldwide use. Matsushita now owns a majority of the stock shares in the firm.

Research at JVC has resulted in the "45–45" stereo phonograph (1957); a color video tape recorder (1958), the VHS ("video home system," 1976), and various other audio devices. A recent product is the K2 Interface, a component designed to eliminate distortions in compact disc recording prior to the analog processing step. Another is the CD+G/M player, which adds still-picture graphics to the basic CD format.

In 1986 JVC America was established as a subsidiary, and in 1989 Nippon Victor (Europe) GmbH, was organized in Germany. [Borwick 1989/10.]

JARVIS, HAROLD, 1865–1924. Canadian church and concert tenor, born in Toronto. At age 14 he went to sea, and eventually became a naval officer, but also took up singing. He left the naval service to study in London, then made concert appearances in Britain and America, settling in Detroit. He died there on 31 Mar 1924. Jarvis recorded Scottish dialect songs and popular ballads for Victor in 1908–1909, for Columbia in 1912, and for Edison in 1914; he also made a Vitaphone of "Beautiful Isle of Somewhere" (#10026; 1914). "Beautiful Isle" was his best-selling number; it appeared on Victor #16008; 1909) and Columbia #A1121; 1912), and remained in the Victor catalog for 15 years. [Moogk 1975; Walsh 1961/5–6–7.]

JAZZ RECORDINGS. Although jazz is a term applied to a variety of related music styles, such as blues, swing, boogie-woogie, and ragtime, this article is concerned only with the idiom that emphasizes improvisation on a fixed series of chords ("changes").

The history of jazz is traceable to the 1890s in the American South, most of the early artists being from New Orleans. Jazz in New Orleans ("Dixieland") style derived from the idiom of the New Orleans dance band—a group typically consisting of violin, cornet, clarinet, trombone, drums, bass, and guitar. Violin and cor-

net were the lead instruments. The jazz band also gave the lead to a cornet, with clarinet and trombone in direct response to it, and other winds doing variations. The performances of these groups displayed fairly standard characteristics: they began with a standard melody and its harmony (usually a familiar song), and then played variants with counterpoints—these being partly improvised, partly "worked out"—supported by a strong 2/4 measure in the bass and percussion. Later the 2/4 measure gave way to the 4/4, with uneven note values and syncopation. The piano became a part of the ensemble, and played the chord progression (often with a guitar or banjo), repeating this as needed, and contributing further melodic decorations. Instruments capable of pitch inflection produced lowered fifths and other slurred tones in the blues manner.

This was the style represented on the first true jazz recordings to be released, by the Original Dixieland Jazz (or Jass) Band (ODJB), "Livery Stable Blues" and "Dixie Jass Band One-Step" (Victor #18255; recorded 26 Feb 1917 and released 7 Mar 1917). Columbia recorded the same group doing "Darktown Strutters' Ball" and "Indiana" (Columbia A-2297; 31 May 1917). RCA LP album #730.703/4, *Original Dixieland Jazz Band*, is a two-disc set covering the ODJB sessions from February 1917 to December 1921, and their five cuts of 10 Nov 1936. Although early jazz was almost exclusively performed by Black musicians, this "Original" group was white; they recorded extensively until 1938. Famous Black musicians from early New Orleans included Louis Armstrong, Sidney Bechet, Johnny Dodds, Kid Ory, and King Oliver.

The great success of the ODJB—a million copies of that first Victor were sold in eight years—was registered with a primarily white audience, marking the move of Black artists into the mainstream of American popular music. Other ensembles came to the fore, such as the Original Memphis Five, which recorded from April 1922 for Arto, and also for Paramount, Pathé, Banner, Vocalion, and others, continuing to 1931. Trumpeter Phil Napoleon led the Five. Folkways #RBF26, *Original Memphis Five*, is an LP of their work from 1922–1924. It should be mentioned that Edison recorded a jazz group in 1917, the Frisco Jazz Band (membership not known); they did "Canary Cottage" and "Johnson 'Jass' Blues" on two Diamond Discs (#50440, #50470; 10 May 1917). An LP by Riverside, *The New York Jazz Scene 1917–20* (#RLP 8801), includes the second number from May 1917, plus material by Earl Fuller's Famous Jazz Band (made for Emerson in 1918), the Louisiana Five (made for Edison in 1919), and [Vincent] Lopez and Hamilton's Kings of Harmony Orchestra (made for Edison in 1920). All these performances are essentially ragtime with jazz patches.

Kid Ory, having gone to Los Angeles, recorded two sides for Nordskog (#3009) with a sextet in June 1922. The group made the earliest jazz record by Black artists: "Ory's Creole Trombone" and "Society Blues" (#3009).

Chicago was a second center of early jazz activity and recording. The Original Dixieland Jazz Band started out there, playing in clubs during 1915–1916, before they took the ODJB name and went on to New York. The Wolverines, a group centered on cornetist Bix Beiderbecke, recorded for Gennett from February 1924, making hits such as "Fidgety Feet" (Gennett #5408; 18 Feb 1924—their first recording) and "Copenhagen" (Gennett #5453; 6 May 1924). A Fountain LP, *The Complete Wolverines* (#FJ114), offers Wolverine material from February 1924 to December 1924. Chicago-style jazz differed from New Orleans in offering a more complex string bass beat, a lighter sound (sometimes without trombones), smoother melodic lines, overlapping solos, shifting accents, and other little variations. It was mainly a province of white musicians. Red McKenzie and Condon's Chicagoans recorded for Okeh in 1927–1928, with an all-star cast consisting of Jimmy McPartland, Frank Teschmacher, Bud Freeman, Joe Sullivan, Eddie Condon, Jim Lannigan, and Gene Krupa, beginning with "Sugar" and "China Boy" (Okeh 41011; 8 Dec 1927). These pieces are on the Parlophone LP #PMC7072, *That Toddling Town: Chicago 1926–28*, along with other Chicago style numbers by Eddie Condon's Quartet and Bud Freeman's Orchestra, made in 1928.

Another Chicago group, the Austin High School Gang, included McPartland, Freeman, and Benny Goodman. Freeman recorded in December 1928 with his "orchestra" for Okeh, making "Craze-O-Logy" and "Can't Help Lovin' Dat Man" (#41168; both on the Parlophone LP just cited); Krupa and McKenzie were in the group.

Red Nichols and Miff Mole performed in Red and Miff's Stompers, making first an Edison Diamond Disc, "Alabama Stomp" (#51854; 13 Oct 1926); Jimmy Dorsey was their clarinetist and alto saxophonist. Nichols then assembled his famous Five Pennies, featuring Pee Wee Russell, and achieved great success in America and Europe. Coral's LP albums #97016/97024, *Red Nichols and His Five Pennies*, present their work from December 1926 to July 1930.

A Black band of importance was playing in Chicago in the early 1920s, the Creole Jazz Band led by King Oliver. When Louis Armstrong joined the group in 1922 they made up the principal Black jazz ensemble of the day. "Canal Street Blues" (Gennett #5133; 6 Apr 1923) and Armstrong's first solo disc, "Chimes Blues" (Gennett #5135; 6 Apr 1923), typify the Dixieland tradition. The Oliver discs, 39 sides made for Gennett, Okeh, and Columbia, were the first significant body of Black jazz on record. In addition to Armstrong, Johnny Dodds and Lil Hardin (Armstrong) were heard in this ensemble. Hardin was the first female jazz performer to record. Two LPs issued by Kings of Jazz, *The Saga of the King Oliver Creole Jazz Band* (#NLJ 18003/4), cover the Oliver sessions of April-December 1923.

Louis Armstrong's Hot Five was the premier jazz group of the decade. It included Kid Ory, Dodds, Lil Hardin (Armstrong) and drummer Johnny St. Cyr. The 60 sides they recorded for Okeh in 1925–1928, beginning with "My Heart" on 12 Nov 1925 (#8320), are landmarks in jazz history. A set of four LPs by World Records, #SM421/4, covers the *Louis Armstrong Legend* of 1925–1929. Columbia has issued the Hot Five material on CD.

Kansas City jazz was another style of the 1920s, a noisy, robust idiom well represented by Bennie Moten's orchestra; that group was first recorded by Okeh in September 1923, doing "Elephant's Wobble" and "Crawdad Blues" (#8100). Moten was with Okeh for two years, then went to Victor in December 1926, staying with that label until 1932. Perhaps his finest record came on 13 Dec 1932, the final

Victor session: "Toby" (#23384), with solos by Count Basie, Hot Lips Page (trumpet), and Ben Webster (tenor saxophone). Moten's work of 1930–1932 is sampled on RCA LP #FXM 17062, *Benny Moten's Great Band of 1930–32*.

Basie carried on with a modified Kansas City style in his own Big Band of 1936. Coral LP #97011LPCM, *The Count Swings Out*, presents the Basie orchestra of 1937–1939. Another selection of Basie in that period is *Swinging the Blues*, Brunswick LP #87036 LPBM. Bellaphon compact discs of 1991 are among those that document Basie's work of 1936 to 1958.

Jazz began to influence dance music, giving it more lilt and spirit, and the two genres often fused; in the Big Bands of the 1930s jazz improvisation was frequently heard over a danceable beat. Paul Whiteman was the first of those large, smooth ensembles to capture the American fancy. He made more than 200 records between 1920 and 1924, including "hot" numbers like "Wang-Wang Blues" (Victor #18694; 9 Aug 1920) and "San" (Victor #19381; 9 June 1924). Whiteman's band was all white; it included performers like Henry Busse and Matty Malneck, and backed up early records of Bing Crosby in 1926. It was really an orchestra, with strings and a symphonic texture; Whiteman himself was a violinist who did not play jazz.

The character of the typical swinging Big Band was established by Fletcher Henderson, whose arranger was Don Redman in 1923–1927; the plan he created was for the winds to play in interacting sections (no strings) and for soloists to improvise above that texture. *Smack*, an LP album by Ace of Hearts (#AH41), presents Henderson/Redman material of 1927–1931. Another album, *Study in Frustration* (CBS #BPG62002), covers 1927–1928.

In the early 1920s the long parade of great solo pianists began its march. Count Basie, Duke Ellington (recording from 1924, famous from 1927 at the New York Cotton Club), Earl Hines (who started with Louis Armstrong in 1927, and recorded from 1928), James P. Johnson (recording from 1921), and Fats Waller (recording from 1922) played sophisticated variations on 32-bar popular songs, locating the jazz mode in a new sphere; while Jelly Roll Morton kept a New Orleans foundation to his complex renditions (recording from 1923; first jazz artist on electrical recordings, 1924). Johnson, one of the seminal "stride" pianists, was earliest of this group to record, making piano rolls in 1918, and "Harlem Strut" on Brunswick #2026 in 1921; he then made a few more discs for Okeh, Arto, Columbia, and Victor by 1923. *Father of Stride Piano* is an LP album by CBS, #BPG62090. The other prototypical stride pianist was Waller, who made two sides for Okeh in 1922: "Muscle Shoals Blues" and "Birmingham Blues" (#4757), then was out of the recording studio until 1926 when he signed with Victor. *Fats Waller Piano Solos* (Bluebird LP AXM2–5518) offers recordings of 1929–1941; material of 1930–1935 is on LP RCA #741.112. A blues-based leaner style was employed by the other men cited.

In the 1930s Art Tatum became recognized as the leading jazz piano virtuoso. His first record was an astonishing "Tea for Two" (Brunswick #6553; 21 Mar 1933). MCA issued *Art Tatum Piano Solos* in an LP series, covering 1934–1940. Teddy Wilson was another prominent pianist, playing with Benny Goodman and on his own, with major recordings from 1935. A CBS LP set, *Teddy Wilson*, gives a variety of Wilson work from 1935–1938.

Benny Goodman brought about the finest merge between jazz and the popular dance idiom, beginning in 1935. His band included trumpeter Bunny Berigan and drummer Gene Krupa, with arrangements by Fletcher Henderson. "King Porter Stomp" was an early triumph (Victor #25090; 1935). Goodman also led various small groups, beginning with a Trio that included Krupa and Teddy Wilson; their series of hit records began with "After You've Gone" (Victor #25115; 1935). Of the many Goodman LP reissues, *Benny Goodman: The Early Years* is of the most interest (Sunbeam #SB139); it goes back to 1933. *Benny Goodman: The Fletcher Henderson Arrangements* (RCA #741.044) presents the band of 1935–1937. A good collection is *Benny Goodman: Solid Gold Instrumental Hits* (CBS #88130), covering 1941–1945. At the end of the 1940s jazz, and the "swing music" that was often identified with it, was the predominant American style. *Down Beat* magazine, established in 1934, began to carry jazz record reviews.

Imaginative orchestrations characterized the bands of the 1930s, with brilliant improvised choruses by pianists or instrumentalists who were often the band leaders. The great jazz orchestras included those of Tommy Dorsey, Ellington, Lionel Hampton, Harry James, Glenn Miller, and Artie Shaw. Vocalists with the bands were mostly smooth ballad singers, but some entered the arena of jazz, notably Ella Fitzgerald, Billie Holiday, and in the late 1940s Sarah Vaughan.

Leading jazz figures on various instruments in the 1930s included Roy Eldridge (trumpet), Benny Carter and Coleman Hawkins (alto saxophone), Charlie Christian (guitar), Gene Krupa (drums), and Lester Young (tenor saxophone).

European tours of major artists—such as those of Armstrong in 1932, Ellington in 1933, and Hawkins 1934–1939 (he stayed five years)—served to engender international interest in jazz, notably in Britain, France, and Scandinavia. A French critic, Charles Delaunay, prepared one of the early jazz discographies in 1936. Europe did not produce many great performers; but Django Reinhardt and Stéphane Grappelli—members of the Quintet of the Hot Club of France—became internationally recognized. An Eclipse LP, *Swing '35–'39* (#ECM2051) presents good examples of the Quintet's exciting performances. Reinhardt's work is well represented on the LP from World Record Club, *The Legendary Django* (#T821). The popular British band leader Jack Hylton made a number of jazz records with small groups, material available on Parlophone LP #PMC7075, *Jazzin Britain: The '20's*. Good local artists contributed significant jazz work in the 1930s, illustrated on the Decca LP set #DDV5013/4, *British Jazz in the '30's*.

Personnel from the Big Bands frequently played in small ensembles in the 1930s and 1940s, in jazz clubs (especially in New York). From such little groups a new style emerged in the 1940s, **bebop.** Its progenitors were Miles Davis, Charlie Parker, Bud Powell, Thelonious Monk, and Dizzy Gillespie. The first great series of bebop records was made by Gillespie and Parker from February 1945. It included "Billie's Bounce" (Savoy #MG 12079) and "Salt Peanuts" (Manor #5000; 1945).

Cool jazz developed in response to bebop in the 1940s, led by Lennie Tristano, Lee Konitz, Miles Davis, Gerry Mulligan, Dave Brubeck, and Paul Desmond. Harmonic and rhythmic subtleties marked the work of Brubeck, as well as the Modern Jazz Quartet, headed by John Lewis (from 1952), and Stan Kenton's band of 1947. Jazz artists with classical training, such as Marian McPartland and George Shearing, gained large followings in the 1940s and 1950s. A blending of Western art music with jazz, so-called third stream music, was popular, and further style mixtures (hard bop, gospel music) were initiated by Charles Mingus, Art Blakey, and others in the late 1950s. By that time the Big Bands had faded from the scene.

Prominent artists in the "free jazz" of the 1960s included pianist Bill Evans and saxophonist John Coltrane, in addition to alto saxophonist Ornette Coleman and trumpeter Don Cherry. Pianist Cecil Taylor went as far as atonal improvisations. Miles Davis and others brought rock music and free jazz together in "fusion" during the 1970s and 1980s. Keyboard players Chick Corea and Keith Jarrett were prominent in the fusion movement. Through these major shifts of direction there remained a potent mainstream jazz style, a mainstream that encompassed the early idioms and later ones. Wynton Marsalis, for example, stayed with the bebop style in the 1980s.

The major American labels were not in the forefront of early jazz recording. Victor and Columbia had strong catalogs of dance music in the years after 1914, but hesitated over the new jazz idiom. Edison virtually ignored jazz after the pioneer records cited above. New labels came to the stage after 1919, such as Brunswick, Gennett, Paramount, and Vocalion, and they embraced jazz music. In 1934 Decca was established, and within ten years had recorded major artists like Louis Armstrong, Count Basie, Bunny Berigan, Benny Carter, Jimmy Dorsey, Ella Fitzgerald, Bud Freeman, Lionel Hampton, Fletcher Henderson, Woody Herman, Billie Holiday, Stan Kenton, Gene Krupa, Jimmie Lunceford, Wingy Manone, Jimmy McPartland, The Quintet of the Hot Club of France, Art Tatum, and Jack Teagarden. Independent labels took a large share of the jazz market, beginning with Commodore in

1938; that company soon had records by Condon, Hawkins, Holiday, Waller, and Young. After World War II several other independent labels had strong positions in the jazz field. Prestige (1950) recorded John Coltrane, and Savoy (1942) had Charlie Parker. Atlantic (1947) recorded Coltrane, Ornette Coleman, Lee Konitz, Charles Mingus, and the Modern Jazz Quartet. Blue Note (1939) featured Sidney Bechet, Earl Hines, Bud Powell, and Thelonious Monk. Riverside (1953) had important catalogs. Verve recorded Charlie Parker (as did Dial) and Art Tatum.

Victor did in time move into jazz, and signed great stars like Fats Waller, Duke Ellington (at first with Columbia), Bix Beiderbecke, Sidney Bechet, Lionel Hampton, and Dizzy Gillespie. Columbia contracted Benny Goodman after he left Victor, plus Woody Herman, Miles Davis, Earl Hines, and Dave Brubeck. Capitol recorded Stan Kenton in his most creative period, 1943–1952, and Miles Davis.

Brunswick's 1944 list included material by Cab Calloway, Duke Ellington, Benny Goodman, Fletcher Henderson, James P. Johnson, Red Nichols, and Jimmie Noone. Brunswick also had an album, *Riverboat Jazz*, featuring numbers by King Oliver and Jelly Roll Morton.

Important LP collections not cited above include *The Smithsonian Collection of Classic Jazz* (#P6–11891; 1973); *A Decade of Jazz* (3 volumes, covering 1939–1969) (Blue Note #LA158–G2, 159–G2, 160–G2; ca. 1970, reissued 1973); *Jazz* (11 albums) (Folkways #FJ 2801–2811; 1950–1953); *Jazz Odyssey* (Columbia #JC3L 30–33 (albums for three periods); 1964) *A Jazz Piano Anthology* (Columbia #KG32355; 1973); *The Jazz Years* (Atlantic #SD2–316; 1973); *Piano Giants* (Prestige #P-24052; 1975); *The Saxophone* (ABC Impulse #ASH 9253–3; 1973); and *25 Years of Prestige* (Prestige P24046; 1974). Most of the important LP releases are available on CD as well. Significant recordings by individual artists are cited in the separate articles about them. [Bruyninckx 1980; Harrison 1984; Jepsen 1963; Rust 1970; Schuller 1968; Schuller 1989.]

JEFFERSON, BLIND LEMON, 1897–1930. American blues singer, born in Couchman, Texas. He lost his sight as a child, and lived by singing in the streets. In 1917 he moved to Dallas, sang with Leadbelly, sang in several southern states, then located in Chicago. There he became famous and influential, singing mostly his own compositions, accompanying himself on the guitar. Around 1925 he signed with Paramount and soon became one of the most popular blues singers on record. Among his biggest hit discs were "Long Lonesome Blues" (Paramount #12354; 1926), "Black Snake Moan" and "Match Box Blues" (Okeh #8455; 1927). He died in Chicago during a snowstorm.

JEFFERSON AIRPLANE. American rock group formed in 1965, originally consisting of Marty Balin, Paul Kantner, Jorma Kaukonen, Bob Harvey (replaced by Jack Casady), and Jerry Pelequin (replaced by Spencer Dryden). The group became successful when vocalist Grace Slick joined it in 1966, and they began performing in what was considered to be psychedelic style. Several acid-rock albums achieved gold status, including *Surrealistic Pillow* (RCA #3766;1967), and *Bark* (Grunt #1001; 1971). There were various membership changes, and then a name change in 1974, to Jefferson Starship. *Red Octopus* (Grunt # 0999; 1975) was a hit album of the new ensemble, with the single "Miracle" (Grunt #10367; 1975). Other chart singles were "With Your Love" (Grunt #10745; 1976) and "Runaway" (Grunt #11274; 1978). Grunt was the group's own label.

JEM (label). An American record of Jem Records Inc., established in 1970 by Marty Scott, Edward J. Grossi, and Jeffrey C. Tenebaum. The firm started out selling British imported discs from a van on college campuses, and went on to great success as an importer/distributor. Jem brought Elton John and Genesis to the American market, and had a hit with the soundtrack of *Rocky Horror Picture Show*. It launched subsidiary labels Passport, Passport Jazz, and Audion. In 1985 Jem encountered legal problems in the form of a suit for copyright infringement, brought by T.B. Harms, an American music publisher. A federal court ruled that importers like Jem would have to pay royalties to publishers. Jem filed for bankruptcy in August 1988.

JENNINGS, WAYLON, 1937– . American country singer, guitarist, and disk jockey, born in Littlefield, Texas, on 15 June 1937. He learned to play guitar as a young child, and was engaged as a disk jockey at age 12 on a local station. Moving to Lubbock, he worked as a deejay and also performed with Buddy Holly. He formed his own group in Phoenix, Arizona, in the early 1960s, was heard by Chet Atkins and signed to a contract with RCA. Soon he was on national tours and *Grand Ole Opry*. "Stop the World" was an early hit (#8652; 1965), followed by "Anita, You're Dreaming" (#8729; 1966). He and Willie Nelson led the so-called outlaw movement among country singers who objected to the commercialized Nashville sound. By 1982 Jennings had posted 45 chart singles. Among his LP albums, *Ramblin' Man* (RCA APL1–0734; 1974) was the most successful.

JESSEL, GEORGE, 1898–1981. American singer and vaudeville artist, born in New York on 3 Apr 1898. At age nine he was already on stage; he appeared in London in 1914. His greatest stage success was in *The Jazz Singer* (1925). Jessel was a film actor from 1927, and after he retired from singing he became a motion picture producer. The record of "My Mother's Eyes" from the film *Lucky Boy* was his biggest hit disc (Victor #21852; 1929).

The first (released) records by Jessel were for Pathé: "Marcelle" (#68587) and "Dolls" (#68588), made in the summer of 1920. He then made "Jing-a-Bula-Jing-Jing-Jing" for Emerson later that year (#10264). His repertoire included Jewish dialect material, humorous monologs, and sentimental songs. He died on 23 May 1981.

JEWEL. A diamond, ruby, or sapphire stylus for pickups, soundboxes, and reproducers on acoustic machines.

JEWEL (label). (I) A record issued in 1920–1923, apparently a Grey Gull subsidiary.

JEWEL (label). (II) One of the Plaza group of labels, released from 1927 to 1932. It had no important material, and sold for a low price, perhaps $.15. [Rust 1978.]

JEWEL PHONOGRAPH CO., INC. A Chicago firm, established in 1916 and incorporated in 1919, located at 670 W. Washington St. A specialty product was the Blood Tone Arm, named for its inventor, first advertised in January 1921. This device was compatible to lateral-cut or vertical-cut discs. It had a tapering design. Three months later the tone arm was renamed the Jewel (but in March 1923 the firm advertised in *TMW* that there were illegal imitators being sold of the Blood Tone Arm). It seems that the name of the company also changed in 1921, to the Jewel Phonoparts Co. The firm moved to 154 Whiting Street in 1921, and moved again in 1923 to 326 River St. There was another move in 1927 to Dearborn and Illinois Streets. The final Chicago directory listing for Jewel was in 1929, when the address was 510 S. Dearborn. At that time William T. Urles was president, and A. H. Davis was vice president.

JEWETT RADIO AND PHONOGRAPH CO. A Detroit firm, the earliest to advertise in *TMW* a radio-phonograph combination (August 1922). In April 1923 a *TMW* story related the acquisition by Jewett of DeForest Radio, Telephone and Telegraph, including the **Audion** patent and 180 other patents. Radio station WJR, in Detroit, belonged to Jewett; it began broadcasting in September 1925.

JOHN BULL (label). A British label, sold by various companies in Britain from 1909 to 1914. The earliest firm to handle the label was the English Record Co., Ltd.; in 1913 the record passed to Schallplatten-Masse-Fabrik, and in December 1913 to Albion Record Co., Ltd. An unusual distribution method was used for these discs: they were sold on contract to individual buyers, requiring an initial purchase of eight discs, and then another 52 of them to qualify for a free gramophone. Matrices came from several labels: Beka, Favorite, Dacapo, and Bel Canto. The material was popular in nature: dances, instrumentals, concert songs, and marches. [Andrews 1973.]

JOHN GABEL'S AUTOMATIC ENTERTAINER.

A disc coin-op produced in 1906 by the **Automatic Machine and Tool Co.** This early juke box held 24 10-inch records, and allowed the user to choose any one by turning a knob. It operated with a hand-wound spring motor, installed in a glass-sided cabinet five feet high that permitted viewing of the mechanism. A needle changing device provided a fresh needle for each playing. The Entertainer even had a magnetic coin detector to defeat the use of slugs in place of official coinage. The machine was shown at the Panama Pacific Exposition of 1915.

JOHNSON, ELDRIDGE REEVES, 1867–1945.

American recording engineer and industry executive, born in Wilmington, Delaware, on 6 Feb 1867. He worked as a machinist in Philadelphia, then managed a small machine shop owned by Andrew Scull in Camden, New Jersey. Johnson became Scull's partner in 1891, and bought the business from him in 1894. He built the spring motor for the Berliner gramophone, and in 1896 got the contract to supply them. In 1897 he and Alfred C. Clark developed the "improved gramophone" with a better motor and sound box; this is the machine immortalized in the **Nipper** painting (U.S. patent #601,198; filed 19 Aug 1897; granted 22 Mar 1898). He also devised the method of recording on wax blanks, which were then covered with gold leaf; this led to a master which produced stampers and finally a pressing of a new, smooth, relatively quiet surface. The records were the seven-inch "Improved Gram-O-Phone Records" that set the industry standard. The first 10-inch disc is also credited to Johnson, who reasoned that with a larger turntable and stronger motor the enhanced record size would be feasible. It sold as the Victor Monarch, following a favorable court decision in litigation brought by Frank Seaman. Johnson sold British rights to the wax

process and the paper label to the Gramophone Co., which became the Victor partner in Europe. (In 1907 an agreement between the firms divided the world market between them.)

Johnson went on to receive 53 other patents, most of them in his own name alone. He developed the famous and frequently litigated tapering tone arm design "which would dominate the industry through the acoustical period" (Koenigsberg) and gained U.S. patent #814,786 (filed 12 Feb 1903; granted 13 March 1906). On 8 August 1900 he filed to patent a disc with a slightly recessed center area to allow placement of a paper label (U.S. #739,318; granted 22 Sept 1903). He developed a cabinet for a table model record player with all movable parts enclosed, for enhanced appearance, although the horn was still exposed during operation (U.S. patent #774,435; filed 19 Nov 1902; granted 8 Nov 1904); it was a step toward the Victrola—the fully enclosed record player, also patented by Johnson (U.S. #856,704; filed 8 Dec 1904; granted 11 June 1907).

Johnson established the **Consolidated Talking Machine Co.** in 1900, and made both discs and players with the Nipper trademark; this firm merged with Berliner to become the Victor Talking Machine Co. (incorporated on 3 Oct 1901), with Johnson as president. Victor acquired the Berliner patents and took the lead in the development of the phonograph industry.

The success of Victor was in large part due to the unprecedented promotional campaign directed by Eldridge Johnson and **Leon Douglass**, Victor vice president. The firm advertised in newspapers and periodicals, presenting the public with an image of quality and sophistication that no rival was able to match. In 1903 Johnson initiated the Red Seal series (based on the Red Label celebrity records of Gramophone & Typewriter in the U.K.) in a special recording studio in Carnegie Hall. The Red Seals presented Metropolitan Opera stars and other great artists, some on 10-inch discs, and others on the new 12-inch discs.

Among Johnson's other contributions to the industry was the exclusive artist contract, which captured Enrico Caruso in 1904 and many other international artists. He continued to experiment with improvements in equipment, and made an experimental model of a record changer in 1920; this was developed into a marketable Victor machine in 1927.

In December 1926 Johnson sold 245,000 shares of Victor stock for $28,175,000 and retired. Control of the firm passed to a pair of New York bankers, Speyer & Co. and J.W. Seligman & Co., and thence to the Radio Corporation of America in 1929. Eldridge Johnson died on 14 Nov 1945, in Moorestown, New Jersey. [Koenigsberg 1989.]

JOHNSON, GEORGE W., ca. 1847–1913. American comedian and whistler, born in slavery; the first Black to become widely known as a recording artist. Johnson had a small repertoire that he performed and recorded extensively in the 1890s. Five pieces were recorded, beginning in 1892 for New Jersey Phonograph Co. "The Whistling Coon" (Edison #4012, etc.), "The Laughing Song" (Edison #4004, etc.), "Laughing Coon" (Edison #4005, etc.) and "Whistling Girl" (Edison #4013, etc.) constituted his principal menu. They were made over and over again, for Berliner, Bettini, Columbia, Kansas City Talking Machine Co., Chicago Talking Machine Co., U.S. Everlasting, Zonophone, Victor, and others. A fifth number, recorded only for Berliner (#403), was "The Mocking Bird." The story that Johnson had been hanged for murdering his wife was disproved by Walsh, who documented that Johnson had been acquitted of that charge. [Brooks 1979; Koenigsberg 1987; Walsh 1944/9 and 1971/1–2.]

JOHNSON, JAMES P., 1894–1955. American jazz pianist, born in New Brunswick, New Jersey, on 1 Feb 1894. In 1908 his family moved to New York, where he studied piano, and had some guidance from Eubie Blake. He played in New York Black clubs, and became known for a driving style and "shout" pieces. As early as 1917 Johnson made some piano rolls, and in 1921 he was on disc in "Harlem Strut" (Black Swan #2026; 1921) and "Keep Off the Grass" with "Carolina Shout" (Okeh #4495; 1921). These were his own compositions, among more than 200 he wrote and performed. He also composed large works, including "Yamecraw"

for piano and orchestra, performed in Carnegie Hall by Fats Waller in 1927.

It was as a jazz pianist that Johnson made his great contributions. He was one of the finest stride pianists, introducing many subtleties to the technique. He was influential in the development of Fats Waller and many later keyboard giants. He also had a fine jazz band, which included J.C. Higginbotham on trombone and Sid Catlett on drums, that recorded notable numbers like "Harlem Woogie" (Vocalion #4768; 1939). His 1921–1939 work is illustrated on Columbia LP #CL1780, his 1943–1945 work on *Original James P. Johnson* (FW #2850). Johnson died in New York on 17 Nov 1955. [Brown, S. 1986.]

JOHNSON, PETE, ca. 1905–1967. American jazz pianist. He was an early specialist in blues piano, making solo records and duets with Albert Ammons in 1938–1939, then with his own group through 1940. In 1941 he teamed with Ammons in a major series of Victor discs that exemplify the boogie-woogie style. "Boogie-Woogie Man" (#27505; 1941) was the first of these; "Movin' the Boogie" was the final issue (#27507; 1941).

JOHNSTON, C. R. British recording expert, known as Johnnie Johnston. He worked with Colonel Gouraud's Edison Phonograph Co. in London, then with Edison Bell, Clarion, Pathé, and Marathon records. He recorded various notable persons for Gouraud, including Alfred, Lord Tennyson, Florence Nightingale, and the explorer Henry M. Stanley. He was with the Orchestrelle Co., Ltd., in London in 1917. During 1918 he was in New York, working in the recording laboratory of the Aeolian Co. Johnston was the recording expert for Chicago's Rodeheaver Record Co. in 1921, and in 1922 he was director of recording and then vice president of Bell Recording Laboratories. [Andrews*.]

JOLSON, AL, 1886–1950. American popular singer, born Asal Yoelson in Srednike, Lithuania, on 26 May 1886. He immigrated to the U.S. with his father in 1890, settling in Washington, D.C., and worked in vaudeville as a boy soprano, whistler, and finally a baritone, achieving great success in blackface roles. After a 1909 success in a New York show he was signed by Victor and soon produced a million-selling record in the new ragtime idiom: "Ragging the Baby to Sleep" (#17081; 1912). The 1917 Victor catalog had nine items, showing him primarily in his comic mode; for example, "Movin' Man, Don't Take My Baby Grand" (#17081; 1912). In 1913 he began to work for Columbia, starting with "Pullman Porters' Parade" and a hit from the film *Honeymoon Express*, "You Made Me Love You" (Columbia #A-1374). Jolson's outstanding discs were his "Rock-a-Bye Your Baby with a Dixie Melody" (Columbia #A-2560; 1918), "April Showers" (Columbia #!-3500; 1921), and "Toot, Toot, Tootsie, Goo'bye" (Columbia #A-3705; 1922). For Brunswick he did "California, Here I Come" (Brunswick #2569, with Isham Jones' orchestra; 1924), the famous blackface rendition of "My Mammy" sung in the film of that name (Brunswick #3912; 1928), and "Sonny Boy" (Brunswick #4033; 1928). After a long absence from the studio, Jolson made V-Discs for the American troops during World War II, including his old favorites and a recording of "Rosie, You Are My Posie" made with the Tommy Dorsey orchestra (V-Disc #306).

Jolson had a notable screen career, beginning with the first feature talking picture, *The Jazz Singer* (1927). A film about his life, *The Jolson Story* (1946) had him singing behind the scenes as Larry Parks acted out the part. He died in San Francisco on 23 Oct 1950. [Kiner 1983.]

JONES, ADA, 1873–1922. Soprano and comic singer, "probably the most popular phonograph singer in the world" around 1906 (Walsh). She began recording around 1894, making two brown wax cylinders: "Sweet Marie" and "The Volunteer Organist." In 1905 she commenced regular recording for Edison, with "My Carolina Lady" (#8948), and made 69 other solo cylinders by 1912, specializing in Negro and other dialect pieces. She was also working for Columbia from 1905, recording the same repertoire. Jones was heard as soloist on six Edison Diamond Discs in 1916–1921, in addition to various duets. Her first Victor disc was "Mandy

Will You Be My Lady Love?" (#4231). She had 17 solos and 50 duets in the Victor 1917 catalog. Jones made many duet records on various labels, including songs with Billy Murray and with Len Spencer. The Murray duets were extremely popular, beginning with "Will You Be My Teddy Bear?" (Edison #9659; 1907). Her studio work tapered off after 1917, and she made her final records in 1921. [Corenthal 1984 lists her dialect records; Walsh 1946/6–12, 1947/1, 1972/6.]

JONES, BILLY, 1889–1940. American tenor and vaudeville artist, born William Reese Jones in New York on 15 March 1889. He made records for Victor in 1920, beginning with "My Sahara Rose" (#18670), then for Edison in 1921 (singing "Casey Jones" on Diamond Disc #50747) and Columbia. His career was transformed when he began to do duets with Ernest Hare in 1920, in a team that became famous as the **Happiness Boys**. They recorded together until 1930, then appeared on radio in the 1930s. Jones died on 23 Nov 1940.

JONES, GEORGE, 1931– . American country singer and guitarist, born in Saratoga, Texas, on 12 Sept 1931. After serving in the U.S. Marines during the Korean War, Jones played and sang at local events, was noticed by a Houston record executive and signed to a contract with the Starday label. After some success with that firm he signed with Mercury and had a national hit in "Treasure of Love" (#71373; 1958). A year later he had another chart number with "White Lightning" (Mercury #71406; 1959), and in 1961 he did "Window Up Above" (Mercury #71700) which rode the charts for 36 weeks. During the 1960s he worked for the United Artists label, making many successful discs, such as "We Must Have Been Out of Our Minds" with Melba Montgomery (#575; 1963). He had 108 chart singles by 1982, including some duets with Montgomery, Johnny Paycheck, and Margie Singleton. Jones also had a long series of popular LP albums. He appeared regularly on *Grand Ole Opry* and on television shows, and toured the U.S. and Europe.

JONES, ISHAM, 1894–1956. American saxophonist, songwriter, and Big Band leader, born in Coalton, Ohio, on 31 Jan 1894. He played in groups in Chicago from 1915, and had his own band there in the 1920s, heard most often at the Hotel Sherman. Gordon Jenkins was one of the arrangers who gave the Jones band a sophisticated sound. Pee Wee Erwin and Woody Herman were among the members. Jones' most successful composition, "It Had to Be You," was recorded, like most of his discs in 1920–1932, for Brunswick (#2614; 1924). "Stardust" (Brunswick #4856; 1931) was one of the most successful later discs. In 1932 he moved to Victor, and made some of the early experimental long-playing records there. When the band broke up in 1936, Woody Herman brought many of the players into his own new one. Jones continued performing with various groups and vocalists into the 1950s. He died in Hollywood on 19 Oct 1956.

JONES, JO, 1911–1985. American jazz drummer, born Jonathan Jones in Chicago on 7 Oct 1911. He played several instruments in various groups, Bennie Moten's band among them, then joined Count Basie as drummer in 1935, remaining intermittently to 1948. Then he played with Lester Young and other bebop artists, and appeared with Jazz at the Philharmonic. In 1957 he toured in Europe with Ella Fitzgerald and Oscar Peterson. He remained freelance, working with groups in various styles. He died in New York on 3 Sep1985.

Jones transformed the jazz drumming style, from the early two-beat on the bass drum to a light four-beat on the hi-hat cymbal, punctuated by irregular accents and sudden "bombs." This technique, coupled with a novel use of brushes, influenced artists like Kenny Clarke and others of the bebop and later schools.

Jones was featured on the Basie records of "One O'Clock Jump" (Decca #1363; 1937), "Swinging the Blues" (Decca #1880; 1938), "Stampede in G Minor" (Okeh #5987; 1940), and many others. He recorded also with the Benny Goodman Sextet, the Goodman orchestra ("I Found a Million Dollar Baby"—Columbia #36136; 1941), Billie Holiday, Lionel Hampton, and Teddy Wilson. LP collections of his work were released by Everest (#5023), Vanguard (#VRS-8503 and #VRS-8525), and Jazztone (#J-1242).

JONES, JONAH, 1909– . American jazz trumpeter, born Robert Elliott Jones in Louisville, Kentucky, on 31 Dec 1909. He played on a Mississippi riverboat, and with various groups, and joined the Stuff Smith combo in 1932. He recorded on Vocalion with Smith, and on Okeh with Cab Calloway, a partner for ten years (e.g., "Jonah Joins the Cab," #6109; 1941). He was a sensation in Europe in 1954, and made a fine recording of "Chinatown" with a group that included Sidney Bechet. Jones gained great success when he formed his own quartet in 1955 and performed at the Embers in New York. "Rose Room" (Capitol #F3747; 1957) was a major hit. His LP release *At the Embers* (Victor #LPM-2004) presents many of his favorites of the period. Jones later had a quintet; he was on television and toured abroad in the 1960s and 1970s.

JONES, JOSEPH W., ca. 1876– ?. American inventor. As a youthful employee of Emile Berliner, he worked a summer at age 17 in the Washington, D.C., laboratory and closely observed the recording process (which employed acid-etched zinc matrices). Jones devised a method of cutting a wax disc with a lateral groove, similar to the method of Eldridge Johnson, and applied for a patent on the process in November 1897, receiving it on 10 Dec 1901 (U.S. #688,739). His success was in part due to the clever adjustments in the application (at first rejected) by Philip Mauro of American Graphophone Co. That firm then bought the patent for $25,000 and hired Jones as a research engineer, gaining an entry into the disc business in 1901. Upheld at first, the Jones patent was finally invalidated after litigation brought by the Victor Company against American Graphophone (1911). Jones had already gone to Europe by then, to make Vitaphone records. And Columbia had taken over American Graphophone and made an agreement with Victor in 1903 for cross-licensing, so the final court decision had no effect on anyone. Jones received ten other patents in the sound recording field. [Koenigsberg 1990.]

JONES, QUINCY DELIGHT, JR., 1933– . American trumpeter, pianist, conductor, composer, and arranger; born in Chicago on 14 Mar

1933. A consistent winner of the Grammy awards, Jones in 1991 took six prizes; this brought his number of winners to 25, the highest total among artists in the popular category.

JONES, SISSIERETTA JOYNER, 1869–1933.

American soprano, one of the first Black artists to gain recognition in opera and concert. She appeared successfully in major cities, and gave a recital in 1893 at the World's Columbian Exposition in Chicago. In 1894–1895 she toured Europe, making a special triumph at Covent Garden. Although the record label Black Patti was named for her, she herself is not known to have made any records. [Henriksen 1979.]

JONES, SPIKE, 1911–1965.

American drummer, Big Band leader, and satirist, born Lindley Armstrong Jones in Long Beach, California, on 14 Dec 1911. After a career as a drummer with radio orchestras, he began to do humorous sound effects, then used them in his own band, The City Slickers (1942), and scored an early success with a novelty record of his composition "Der Fuehrer's Face" (Bluebird #11586; 1942). He then made many popular recordings utilizing bizarre sounds, such as pistols, whistles, and bells, or the hiccups in his greatest hit "Cocktails for Two" (Victor #20–1628; 1944). Jones died on 1 May 1965 in Los Angeles. [Young, J. 1984.]

JOPLIN, JANIS, 1943–1970.

American blues and rock singer, born in Port Arthur, Texas, on 19 Jan 1943. After performing with local bands in Texas and California, she achieved recognition in San Francisco in 1966. Joplin sang in a highly emotional manner, featuring a hoarse growl, howls, and whispers. She and her group, Big Brother and Holding Company, were a success at the Monterey Pop Festival of June 1967 and signed a Columbia contract. Their album *Cheap Thrills* (Columbia #PC-9700) was first on the 1968 charts. Later hit records included *I Got Dem Ol' Kozmic Blues Again Mama!* (an album with a group named Kozmic Blues Band, Columbia #PC-9913; 1969). A posthumous *Joplin in Concert* LP (Columbia #CZX 33160; 1972) was another chart release. Joplin also had five singles on the charts in 1969–1971, the most popular being "Me & Bobby McGee"

(Columbia #45014; 1971). Bette Midler played a role loosely based on Joplin in a 1979 film, *The Rose.*

JOPLIN, SCOTT, 1868–1917.

American pianist and ragtime composer, born in Texarkana, Arkansas, on 24 Nov 1868. He was the son of a former slave. Joplin learned piano and guitar, and sang with a quartet. He traveled as a musician, playing where he could, reaching Chicago in 1893. He led a band at the World's Columbian Exposition, playing cornet, and began to publish songs two years later. Then he settled in Sedalia, Missouri, directed a band and continued composing in the new ragtime style, with which his name has become indelibly associated. (*See* RAGTIME RECORDINGS.) "Maple Leaf Rag" —named for a club in Sedalia—was his first great success (1899); "The Entertainer" was written in 1902. He performed in vaudeville in New York, and continued composing there until his death on 1 Apr 1917.

Joplin made no cylinder or disc recordings but is believed to be the performer on several piano rolls of 1899–1914. Those sounds have been reissued on a Riverside LP (#RLP 8815). A Nonesuch LP (#H 71248) offers modern renditions (1969) of the Joplin rags, by pianist Joshua Rifkin. Many recent CD versions of the Joplin pieces are available, performed by a variety of instruments and groupings; for example, "The Entertainer" by Izthak Perlman and André Previn, and the same work by the Budapest Brass Quartet. The 1974 motion picture *The Sting* featured Joplin rags and brought them fresh popularity.

JORDAN, MARY, 1879–1961.

Welsh/American contralto and dramatic soprano, born in Cardiff on 27 Nov 1879. She lived nearly all her life in the U.S., performing as a church soloist and with major orchestras. Her opera debut was as Amneris with the Boston Opera on 28 Mar 1911. That role and Azucena became associated with her. She sang around the world, and was twice invited to sing in the White House, by Woodrow Wilson and Calvin Coolidge. Jordan was among the first singers on radio, from her home city of San Antonio, Texas.

She recorded first in March 1911, an Edison cylinder with the Metropolitan Quartet: "Barcarolle." Then she made a duet, "Ai nostri monti," with Harry Anthony (Amberol #652) and many more cylinders with other artists. Her first solo record was "My Heart at thy Sweet Voice" ("Mon coeur s'ouvre a ta voix"—#2158; 1910). Jordan sang on two Edison Diamond discs in 1915. She died on 15 May 1961 in San Antonio, Texas.

JOSE, RICHARD JAMES, 1862–1941. English/American ballad singer, born in Cornwall on 5 June. His surname—Cornish, not Spanish—is pronounced as one syllable, to rhyme with rose. When his father died, Jose was sent to America to stay with an uncle in Nevada; he was shipwrecked in the crossing, but eventually arrived in Nevada, only to find there was no uncle there. He apprenticed to a blacksmith, but also studied singing. An opportunity to sing with Reed's Minstrels in San Francisco created a great sensation. He then sang with Lew Dockstader's company, and in the New York play *The Old Homestead* during 1887–1895. Victor signed him in 1903, and he made a best-selling disc in October, "Silver Threads among the Gold" (#2556). Another popular disc, "Abide with Me" (#16660), remained in the catalog until 1923. Soon he was described as the best paid ballad singer in the world. However, after an on-stage accident in 1905 he made no more records. He was seen, not heard, in the film, *Silver Threads among the Gold* in 1915. Jose retired from public performance in 1920 and became a civil servant in California; he then returned to sing on radio from 1931 until his death in San Francisco on 20 Oct 1941. [Walsh 1950/3–4–5.]

JOURNET, MARCEL, 1867–1933. French bass, born in Grasse on 15 July 1867. He studied at the Paris Conservatory, and made his operatic debut at Bezières in *Favorite* in 1891, after which he appeared at Covent Garden during 1893–1900, and Brussels in 1894–1900. Journet made his American debut at the Metropolitan Opera in 1900 and stayed with the company until 1908, when he returned to Europe until 1914. During World War I he was with the Chicago Opera, then he returned to France. He died in Vittel on 5 Sep 1933.

Journet's roles included 100 operas, from the French, Italian, and Wagner repertoires. He was most famous as Leporello, Escamillo, Mephistopheles, and Colline. He was recorded on **Mapleson cylinders** in 1902–1903, doing the *Faust* final trio with Emma Calvé and Andreas Dippel, the *Aida* Nile Scene, and two other numbers. He recorded for Columbia in 1905, beginning with "Infelice" from *Ernani* (#3109), then for Victor in 1905–1922. The 1917 Victor catalog carried 60 solo records and many duets and ensemble contributions. He was heard in the *Lucia* Sextet with Amelita Galli-Curci, Minnie Egener, Enrico Caruso, Giuseppe De Luca, and Angelo Bada (Victor #95212); and he was heard in the outstanding complete *Faust* (HMV #2122–2141). HMV recorded him from 1925 to 1932. Eight of his records were still in the Victor catalog in 1940. Many of Journet's recordings were reissued by the various clubs; IRCC released two numbers from *Faust* and one from *Aida*. There were also numerous LP reissues.

JOYCE, THOMAS F., 1904–1966. American record and television industry executive. A vice president at Victor in the late 1930s, he established the Victor Record Society in 1937. Society members were entitled to buy an inexpensive ($14.95) record player, developed by Joyce, that would play through a radio. It was said that 150,000 of these machines were sold within a year. After World War II Joyce became recognized for his enthusiastic promotion of television, and in 1952 he left RCA to become president of the Raymond Rosen & Co., a leading distributor of television sets and other appliances. He died in Philadelphia on 8 Sep 1966.

JUKE BOX. A coin-operated record player, originating with the **coin-op** of 1889. The name "juke" is probably related to an old southern U.S. word of African origins, "jook," meaning to dance. When coin-ops went out of favor around 1910, as a result of the thriving home-phonograph industry and the competition in public places of the player piano and nickel-odeon, the concept was dormant for many years. With the development of electric amplification after 1925, there was a revival of interest in the record machines. In 1927 a model made by the **Automatic Musical Instrument Co.** of Grand Rapids, Michigan, was able to play either side of 10 discs; about 12,000 of them were on location by 1930. Other manufacturers taking part in the juke box golden age of the 1930s and 1940s included the J.P. Seeburg Co., **Capehart Co.**, Rock-Ola, AMI, and most prominently the **Wurlitzer Co.** It is estimated that there were 25,000 juke boxes in operation in America by 1934; 225,000 by 1938; 300,000 by 1939 (making use of 30 million 78 rpm discs per year). Indeed, the juke box sales were significant in keeping the record industry afloat during the Depression.

An important contribution of the juke box to American musical culture was the exposure it gave, from around 1935, to country and western music. It should be noted that all juke boxes were devoted to pop music, suitable to the preferences of patrons in the places where they were installed: saloons, pool halls, drug stores, ice cream parlors, inexpensive restaurants, and roadhouses. The juke box era came to a close in the late 1970s, following the passage of a new copyright law in the U.S. that required licensing and compensation to the record labels. There had also been a decline in the production of single 45 rpm records as opposed to LP albums. And, of course, television had become the source of background noise in drinking places, while **Muzak** or radio music seemed to serve the needs of restaurants. [Hoover 1971 provides good illustrations, pp. 107–113; Kirvine 1977.]

JUMBO RECORD (label). A German disc made by the Jumbo-Record Fabrik—a subsidiary of International Talking Machine Co. mbH, which was owned by **Fonotipia, Ltd.** The office was located at Ritterstrasse 47, Berlin, from 1908; the factory was in Frankfurt-am-Oder. The British records were controlled in the U.K. by Fonotipia, Ltd., and pressed in both Britain and Germany, with British and European artists. They were marketed in Britain by Barnett Samuel and Sons, Ltd., from September 1908 to January 1914 or later. One Jumbo had a reading

of Queen Alexandra's speech marking the death of King Edward VII (1910); another had the Queen's speech in observation of the accession of George V. The speeches were read by an actress, not by Queen Alexandra (who made no records herself). In August 1910 the cheaper Jumbola record was sold in Germany and elsewhere, but not in Britain.

Jumbo Records became part of **Carl Lindström** in Europe in 1911, but Fonotipia, Ltd., continued to control British issues. Up to the outbreak of World War I in 1914 an Odeon/ Fonotipia matrix system was in use, then the matrices used in Britain were those recorded by Carl Lindström (London), Ltd., at its Beka Records studios, and used by all Lindström labels in Britain: Beka, Coliseum, Favorite, and Scala, as well as their cheaper counterparts Albion, Arrow, Lyceum, and Silvertone.

During the war the British Board of Trade ordered a closing down of Lindström, and the Jumbo label passed in 1917 to a new firm, Hertford Record Co., Ltd., which business went to the Columbia Graphophone Co., Ltd., in June 1919—the Jumbo Record having become "Venus Record" about a month earlier. Venus was a Columbia trademark, and under Columbia's control. [Andrews*; Andrews 1971/1.]

Jump. *See* BUMP.

JUNO PHONOGRAPH MANUFACTURING CO. A British firm, located at 27 Pilgrim St., London, in 1900. It produced the Juno cylinder player, based on British Patent #7594, accepted 23 June 1900. The reproducer was a tubular piece of glass, with a leather cushion between the stylus and the celluloid horn. It was a very inexpensive machine, with no frills. To change cylinders the user had to detach the drive belt and remove both the record and its carrying spool. The Juno was available "absolutely free" to agents who could sell nine pieces of jewelry provided by the British Premium Syndicate. [*TMR* #72 (April 1987) reproduces an undated advertisement, p. 2073.]

JURGENS, DICK, 1910–. American Big Band leader and trumpeter, born in Sacramento, California, on 9 Jan 1910. He organized his first orchestra in 1928 and achieved renown in San Francisco, then moved to the Aragon Ballroom in Chicago where he was a fixture during the 1930s. His group had a sweet, mellow sound, graced by fine vocalists Eddy Howard, Ronnie Kemper, Harry Cool, and Buddy Moreno. The band was popular until World War II.

Jurgens began recording in 1934 for Decca, but his important output was for Vocalion from 1938 to 1940, and for Okeh from 1940 to 1942. His biggest hits were the songs co-written by him: "It's a Hundred to One" (Vocalion #5063; 1939), "If I Knew Then" (Vocalion #5074; 1939), and "Careless" (Vocalion #5235; 1939), all with Eddy Howard singing; "Cecilia," sung by Ronnie Kemper (Vocalion #5405; 1940); "A Million Dreams Ago," sung by Harry Cool (Okeh #5628; 1940); and "One Dozen Roses" (Okeh #6636; 1942).

JURINAC, SENA, 1921– . Yugoslavian soprano, born Srebenka Jurinac in Tavnik on 24 Oct 1921. She studied in Zagreb and made her debut there as Mimi in 1942. Then she sang with the Vienna State Opera (1945), and went on to Salzburg, London, La Scala, and an American debut in San Francisco (1959). Although her repertoire covered Wagner, Puccini, Richard Strauss, Berg, and other modern works, Jurinac was particularly distinguished in Mozartean roles, from which most of the recordings were drawn. She was Donna Elvira in the complete *Don Giovanni* on Philips (#00280–82), and also in the LP on Decca (#302); the Countess in one *Nozze di Figaro* (Philips complete recording #00357–59) and Cherubino in another (Columbia #LWX 410–425). She also did a *Nozze* for Epic LP (#SC6022). With Fritz Busch at Glyndebourne, Jurinac created remarkable performances as Ilia in *Idomeneo* and Fiordiligi in *Così fan tutte*; these are sampled in a recent EMI Références CD (#H763199–2; 1990), which also offers Jurinac's fine rendition of Richard Strauss's four last songs, and works by Smetana and Tchaikovsky.

JVC. *See* JAPANESE VICTOR CO. (JVC).

KALAMAZOO NOVELTY CO. A firm located in Kalamazoo, Michigan, in 1906. It made the Duplexophone for the **Duplex Phonograph Co.**

KALLIOPE MUSIKWERKE AG. A German manufacturer of records, players, motors, and audio components, located in Leipzig. In the early years of the century the firm had branch factories in Dresden, Austria, Hungary, and Russia. They moved into the British market in 1912 under arrangements with Blum & Co., Ltd., of London. Stella was the record label used in the U.K., commencing in the summer of 1912; however, a prior use of that name, by Pathé in the U.K. required Blum to change the label name to Victory. In December 1912 Blum applied to have the trademark Kalliope registered for records, and on 2 Jan 1913 Kalliope, Ltd. was created, with the address 220 Old St., London. A suit was brought by Blum against Kalliope Musikwerke for breach of contract, with the result that Kalliope opened its own London office in competition with him; both firms were then selling the same products, but at different prices. In time Blum was enjoined against trading under the name Kalliope Co., Ltd. Thus Blum's headquarters, which had been called Kalliope House, was renamed Diploma House, and the Victory label was changed to Diploma in 1913. In addition to the Kalliope label, Kalliope Musikwerke used a label in Britain called Our Flag.

In Germany, Kalliope merged with Anker Phonogram GmbH in March 1913. The Anker name, anglicized to Anchor Gramophone Co., was successful in London selling 10-inch double-sided Kalliope label discs at one shilling. However the Kalliope firm became insolvent in 1913, although their associate Anker remained in business and continued to sell the Kalliope products. Then in 1916 the Anker business was bought by one Menzenhauer, who renamed the firm Kalliope, Menzenhauer & Schmidt. The Kalliope label remained in the German market until 1931, though it disappeared from Britain with the outbreak of World War I, except for some postwar imports. [Andrews 1988/10.]

KALTENBORN STRING QUARTET. An ensemble that made Edison cylinders in ca. 1912. The members were Frank Kaltenborn and Herman Kuhn, violins; Max Barr, viola; and Max Droge, cello.

KANSAS CITY SIX. A group of jazz musicians from the Count Basie band who made an important set of discs for Commodore on 8 Sep 1938. The artists were Buck Clayton, trumpet; Eddie Durham, trombone and electric guitar; Freddy Greene, guitar; Walter Page, string bass; Jo Jones, drums; and Lester Young. Young played a metal clarinet on most of these discs, rather than his usual tenor saxophone, showing remarkable inventiveness and facility on his second instrument. This session was also noted as the first to feature the electric guitar. The five works recorded were "Way Down Yonder in New Orleans" and "Pagin' the Devil" (featuring Page; #502), "Countless Blues" (referring to the absence of Basie, who could not play with the group for contractual reasons) and "I Want a Little Girl" (a particularly tender solo by Young; #509), and "Them There Eyes" (with a vocal by Greene; #511). There was also a Kansas City Five—the same musicians, minus Young, who did a Commodore session on 18 Mar 1938. A group of totally different membership was also called the Kansas City Five; they recorded for Pathé and Ajax in 1924 and 1925.

KANSAS PHONOGRAPH CO. One of the firms affiliated with the **North American Phonograph Co.** from 1890 to 1893, located in Topeka, Kansas. George E. Tewksbury was president in 1890 and general manager in 1892–1893. S.S. Ott was president in 1891–1892, and general manager in 1892–1893. A.B. Poole was secretary-treasurer in 1892.

KAPP, JACK, 1901–1949. American recording industry executive, born in Chicago on 15 June 1901. His father was a salesman for Columbia records, and Kapp began to work for the firm as a shipping clerk at age 14. He moved to Brunswick in 1926, in charge of the Vocalion label. In 1934 Kapp arranged with Edward R. Lewis, head of Decca Record Co., Ltd. (U.K.), to establish an American branch, and set up the Decca Record Co. on 4 Aug 1934 with himself as president; the new label became one of the best known and most profitable in the U.S. industry. Kapp was featured in a *Collier's Magazine* story of 1947, and titled "the biggest man in the record business." He died in New York on 25 Mar 1949.

KARAJAN, HERBERT VON, 1908–1989. Austrian conductor, born in Salzburg on 5 Apr 1908. He studied piano at the Mozarteum in Salzburg, then conducting in Vienna, making his debut there on 17 Dec 1928. Engagements in Ulm and Aachen followed, then important performances at the Vienna State Opera (1936) and the Berlin State Opera—in particular an acclaimed *Tristan* in 1937. Karajan was at La Scala in 1938, and was on his way to international stardom. His rise was interrupted by cloudy wartime experiences and politics, but by 1948 he was safely on his way once more, appointed to the directorship of the Vienna Symphony Orchestra (where he worked to 1960). La Scala made him music director in 1950, and he also was music director of the Philharmonia Orchestra of London. His final great appintment came in 1954, as music director of the Berlin Philharmonic Orchestra, where he remained until the year of his death. He also conducted at the Metropolitan Opera (1967) and in most of the world's leading concert halls and opera houses, gaining recognition as one of the finest conductors of the century. He died on 16 July 1989 in Anif, Austria.

Karajan's repertoire is well represented on records. He covered a vast range of symphonic and operatic literature, old and new. The composers with whom he became most closely identified were Verdi, Ravel, Beethoven, Bruckner, Mahler, Brahms, Wagner, and Shostakovich. A cross section of his art was offered in new DGG compact discs of 1989: *Ballo in maschera* with Placido Domingo and the Vienna Philharmonic Orchestra (DG #427635-2), the Bruckner Eighth Symphony with the Vienna Philharmonic (DG #427611-2), the four Brahms symphonies with the Berlin Philharmonic Orchestra (DG #427-602-2) and the nine Beethoven symphonies (DG #429036-2).

KARLE, THEO, 1893–1972. American concert and operatic tenor, born Theo Karle Johnston in Perry, Iowa, on 30 July 1893. He made his debut in New York in 1916, and sang on tour with the New York Philharmonic and other orchestras. A Brunswick recording artist from 1920 to 1925, Karle made more records for that label than anyone else. Earlier he had made a few Victor records, in 1916–1917. [Walsh 1972/9.]

KASSEL, ART, 1896–1965. American Big Band leader and songwriter, performer on clarinet, alto saxophone, and violin; born in Chicago on 18 Jan 1896. After military service in the first World War, he played with bands in Chicago and formed his own orchestra in 1924; one of the players for a time was Benny Goodman. He achieved success in a long run at the Bismarck Hotel in Chicago, and toured the Midwest. His band, known as Kassels in the Air, was a sweet dance ensemble. They recorded extensively, first for Victor in 1929 ("I Wish I Knew" #21885), then for Columbia from 1932 and Bluebird from 1934. His composition and theme song "Hell's Bells" was given an enterprising jazz-like recording (Columbia #2682; 1932). Kassel was active into the 1960s, mostly in West Coast appearances. He died in Van Nuys, California, on 3 Feb 1965.

KAUFMAN, IRVING, 1890–1976. Russian/American tenor and vaudeville artist, born Isidore Kaufman. His family emigrated to the U.S. when he was a child, and he began his career singing in the streets of Syracuse, New York, and passing the hat. Then he and his brothers Phil and Jack formed a vaudeville trio. In 1914 he began to record, for Edison Blue Amberol cylinders, with "I Love the Ladies." and he went on to a 17–year recording career with all the major labels. In addition to solo work, he was a member of the Avon Comedy Four, popular on stage and on records. The Victor 1917 catalog had 19 titles by him. During the period 1925–1930 Kaufman may have made more records than any other American singer, many under psuedonyms or anonymously. Among his best efforts were dance band vocals.

With the decline of the recording industry in the 1930s, Kaufman was occupied with radio broadcasts, including early singing commercials. Around 1950 he made Jewish dialect records, and in 1974 he recorded some songs in his home; but essentially he was in retirement from the mid-1940s, in California. He died on 3 Jan 1976. [Corenthal 1984 lists the Jewish dialect discs.]

KAUFMAN, LOUIS, 1905–. American violinist, born in Portland, Oregon, on 10 May 1905. He was acclaimed for his performances of contemporary music, as well as for his efforts to present baroque works in an authentic manner. He also played solo parts in numerous Hollywood films.

Kaufman recorded for many labels, especially for Capitol, Vox, Orion, and Concert Hall. He made one Edison Diamond Disc. His most important work was for Concert Hall LPs from 1949: the Violin Concerto of Khatchaturian (Concert Hall #126/9), and the Vivaldi 12 Concerti, opus 9 (Concert Hall set #1134). His interpretation of Torelli's 12 Concerti, opus 8,

appeared on L'Oiseau Lyre #LD 115/6. Orion cassettes issued good selections of his recordings in the 1980s, and Music and Arts/Harmonia Mundi offered a CD (#620) of 1954 recordings in 1990.

KAYE, SAMMY, 1910–1987. American dance band leader, born in Rocky River, Ohio, on 13 Mar 1910. Graduating from Ohio University in 1932, he formed a band and was successful in the Midwest, offering a notably sweet sound and the idea of "singing song titles"—announcements of the song name before the melody began. "Swing and Sway with Sammy Kaye" caught on as a slogan, and the band became one of the most popular for the longest time. A crisper sound emerged in the 1960s. Kaye's band continued to perform into the 1970s, after most of the Big Bands had long faded away. He died in Ridgewood, New Jersey, on 2 June 1987.

Kaye composed the wartime hit "Remember Pearl Harbor" almost immediately after the attack, and put it out on record with remarkable alacrity (Victor #27738; 17 Dec 1941). He had several other popular wartime songs, including "White Cliffs of Dover" (Victor #27704; 1941) and "I Left My Heart at the Stagedoor Canteen," featuring the outstanding vocalist Don Cornell (Victor #27932; 1942). His earliest record label was Vocalion, which issued his first hit: "Rosalie" (Vocalion #3700; 1937) . Among Kaye's many popular records were "Harbor Lights" (Columbia #38963; 1950), "Daddy" with vocal by the Kaye Choir (Victor #27391; 1941), and "There Will Never Be Another You" with vocal by Nancy Norman (Victor # 27949; 1942).

KEEN-O-PHONE (label). A vertical-cut record issued by the Keen-O-Phone Co., 227 S. Broad St., Philadelphia, from April 1913. In September 1913 the recording studios were at 1202 Walnut St., with Fred Hager in charge. The label was a successor to **Phono-cut**. In 1914 the label name was changed to **Rex**. The firm also made disc players, advertised in December 1911. Its machine was the feed-device type, which moved the turntable beneath the stylus. Keen-O-Phone was put into liquidation in 1914. [Andrews*; Blacker 1975.]

KEITH PROWSE (label). A record issued by the London music publishing firm, Keith Prowse & Co., Ltd. (21 Denmark St.), in 1927. There were just three issues, continuing a series sponsored by the firm but on the Parlophone label. The whole series was made up of jazz material from Okeh, Gennett, and Brunswick-Vocalion. The Black Bottom Stompers of Johnny Dodds, with Louis Armstrong and Earl Hines, are heard on two of the sides.

It is almost certain that the Prowse firm was the proprietor of the KP Music Recorded Library, a set of vinyl 78s made for use by the entertainment industry in the 1960s. A firm named KPM Recorded Library remains in the London telephone directory, at 23 Denmark St. [Andrews*; Rust 1978.]

KELL, REGINALD, 1906–1981. English clarinetist, born in York on 8 June 1906. He played in silent movie theaters, and studied at the Royal Academy of Music in London, later taught there. He was principal clarinetist for the Royal Philharmonic Orchestra, London Philharmonic, and London Symphony in the 1930s. He spent about 10 years in America before returning to London in 1958. He retired in 1966, and—having returned to the U.S.—died in Frankfort, Kentucky, on 5 Aug 1981.

Kell was among the first virtuosos to record the clarinet works of the masters. He was heard with the Busch Quartet in the Brahms *Quintet in B Minor* (Victor #M-491) and with Elisabeth Schumann in Schubert's *Hirt auf dem Felsen* (Victor #14815); he did the Schubert number also with Margaret Ritchie for HMV #C3688). His rendition of the Mozart Clarinet Quintet, with the Philharmonia Quartet (Columbia #CM-702) was especially notable.

KELLER, ARTHUR CHARLES, 1901–1983. American acoustical engineer, known for producing the first stereophonic recording. He was born in New York, and studied electrical engineering at the Cooper Union; then he took a master's degree at Yale University and did further work at Columbia University. While still a student he began a 48–year association with Bell Telephone Laboratories, working in the predecessor firm, Western Electric Engineering Dept. In 1923 he applied for his first of about 40 U.S. patents, having designed a vented enclosure for loudspeakers to enhance low-frequency response. Much of his subsequent research was concerned with audio systems.

In 1925, Keller commenced research that led to talking motion pictures based on film synchronized with discs. This was the system used in early talkies by Al Jolson, John Barrymore, etc. He later developed the stylus that made high fidelity records possible. His idea of recording two sound channels on the same disc opened the way for single-groove stereo disc recording. He was granted a basic patent for that invention and in 1931–1932 he and his associate, Irad S. Rafuse, made the first known stereo recordings of orchestral music (of the Philadelphia Orchestra in the Academy of Music). During World War II he worked on sonar systems for anti-submarine defense. When peace came he devoted his attention primarily to telephone switching apparatus. He retired in 1966. Keller died in Bronxville, New York, on 25 Aug 1983.

KELLY, DAN, 1843–1905. American vaudeville and recording artist of the 1890s, specializing in Irish dialect material. He was in the catalogs of the Ohio Phonograph Co. and in the 1893 Columbia catalog. More than 5,000 of his cylinders were sold in 1890–1892, a very high sales figure for that time. Kelly's most popular titles were in the Pat Brady series—"Pat Brady's Plea in His Own Defense," and "Pat Brady before the Election." [Brooks 1979.]

KELSO, MAY, 1867–1946. American actress, contralto, and vaudeville artist, born on 28 Feb 1867 in Dayton (or perhaps Columbus), Ohio. Her first name is variously May, Mary, Maym, and Mayme. (The death certificate identified her as Mary L. Bent—Bent was her married name—"also known as Maym Kelso.") Her stage and screen career extended from 1912 to 1927. She then retired, and died in South Pasadena, California, on 5 June 1946.

Kelso began to make Edison cylinders in 1899 with "Because" (#7176), singing a repertoire that included ballad and Negro dialect material. Her recording work ended in 1901, after 17 two-minute solo cylinders had been made, plus four duets with John Bieling. Later she made nine concert-size cylinders, covering much the same repertoire. A few few discs also appeared, from National Gramophone Co. in 1899 (a seven-inch version of "Kentucky Babe," #9418), and Zonophone in 1901 ("Kentucky Babe" again, plus "Stay in Your Own Backyard," #9414; and "Florida Flo," #9415). She did not record thereafter. [Walsh 1980/12, 1981/1.]

KEMP, HAL, 1905–1940. American Big Band leader, born James Harold Kemp in Marion, Alabama, on 27 Mar 1905. He organized a group while at the University of North Carolina, and then performed on ocean liners and in Britain. In 1927 he had a New York engagement, followed by important runs in Miami and Chicago. John Scott Trotter, pianist and arranger, was one of the notables in the band, which also had drummer-vocalist Skinnay Ennis, vocalist Smith Ballew, and sometimes Bunny Berigan. The Carolina Club Orchestra was the most used of several names for the group.

Kemp recorded in London for Columbia in 1924, then moved to Pathé, Vocalion, and many other labels in the 1920s. Brunswick was his major affiliation in the early 1930s, and Victor thereafter. His most popular record was "Got A Date with an Angel" and "Lamplight" both sung by Ennis (Victor #25651; 1937). Kemp was on radio and in motion pictures, and was at the peak of stardom when he was killed in an auto accident near Madera, California, on 21 Dec 1940.

KEMPFF, WILHELM, 1895–1991. German pianist, born in Jüterbog (Berlin) on 25 Nov 1895. At age nine he was a student in the Berlin Hochschule für Musik; in 1916 he began to concertize. He performed with the Berlin Philharmonic Orchestra in 1918—beginning a 60-year association—and toured Europe, Japan, and South America. His London debut was in 1951, his first appearance in America in 1964. Kempff specialized in Mozart, Beethoven, and Schubert. His Beethoven performances were widely regarded as definitive. His principal labels were Polydor, American Decca, and

Deutsche Grammophon. DG reissued recordings of 1951 in 1980, in LP album #2740 228, a 10-record set.

KENDZIORA, CARL, JR., 1921–1986. Historian of the record industry and discographer. He contributed regular columns, "Behind the Cobwebs," and articles to the journal *Record Research* from 1949 until he died. His major publications include a label list of Plaza (published 1961–1983 in *RR*) and "The Labels behind Black Swan" (*Record Changer* #14–1, 1955).

KENNEDY, WILLIAM A., ca. 1895–1958. Irish/American tenor, popular recording artist of the mid-1920s. He worked for Columbia, doing such familiar songs as "My Wild Irish Rose" (#33015; 1926) and lesser known items like "Little Town in the Ould County Down" (#33014; 1926).

KENTON, STAN, 1911–1979. American jazz bandleader and pianist, born Stanley Newcomb Kenton in Wichita, Kansas, on 19 Feb 1912. He grew up in Los Angeles, played and made arrangements for various groups there—Gus Arnheim's among them—in the 1930s. He formed is own Big Band in 1941, naming it the Artistry in Rhythm Orchestra. The group was quickly popular, making hit records like "And Her Tears Flowed Like Wine" (Capitol #166; 1944) and "Tampico" (Capitol #202; 1945). Kenton recorded for 27 years with Capitol, until 1970. Popular vocalists included Anita O'Day, Gene Howard, and June Christy. Star instrumentalists over the years included trombonist Kai Winding, alto saxophonists Art Pepper and Lee Konitz, tenor saxophonists Stan Getz and Zoot Sims, trumpeter Maynard Ferguson, and drummer Shelly Manne. Pete Rugolo joined Kenton as his arranger in 1945.

In 1949 Kenton performed in Carnegie Hall with a new orchestra, a 20-piece group he named Progressive Jazz—giving the name to the new jazz style. His largest orchestra was assembled in 1950, a 43-piece group he named Innovations in Modern Music Orchestra; it included strings. Kenton was especially popular on college campuses in the 1960s. His albums *West Side Story* (Capitol #T1609; 1961) and *Adventures in Jazz* (Capitol #T1796; 1962) won Grammy awards. He died in Los Angeles on 25 Aug 1979. [Jepsen 1962.]

KENTUCKY PHONOGRAPH CO. One of the affiliated firms of the North American Phonograph Co. from 1890 to 1893, based in Louisville. When North American ceased operations, the Kentucky firm remained active, finally closing in October 1909. J. R. Kincaid was president in 1891, and R. C. Kincaid was president in 1892. George W. Grant was general manager and secretary/treasurer in 1891, and George W. Seymour was general manager in 1892.

KERNS, GRACE, 1866–1936. American concert soprano, born in Norfolk, Virginia. Her surname is also seen as Kearns; she used pseudonyms Katherine Clark and Miriam Clark. In addition to solo work, she sang with the Columbia Ladies Quartet. Her first record was "My Beautiful Lady" for Columbia in September 1911. "Chinatown," a duet with John Barnes Wells, was a popular disc of 1915. Kerns ended her concert career in 1918 and went abroad to "minister to the needs of service men"; she also ceased recording, except for a few discs in 1919 for minor labels. Her biggest selling record was "Whispering Hope" with Mildred Potter (Columbia #2842, issued November 1918). She died in Williamsburg, Virginia, on 10 Sep 1936. [Brooks 1990; Walsh 1964/5–8.]

KEY (label). A British record sold by the Selfridge department store of London in 1933 and perhaps early 1934. About 30 releases are known, of dance and popular vocal material. Christopher Stone, the pioneer disc jockey, selected the works (from Panachord and Melotone catalogs) and was given credit on the labels. [Rust 1978.]

KICKER, KATE. A pianist who recorded for Berliner (e.g., #2547 "Piano Solo," 18 Apr 1896). She was the first female pianist heard on disc records.

KIDDY RECORD (label). A Mother Goose series of six discs advertised in *TMW* in October 1912, recorded by the Waldorf-Astoria Orchestra, with Gilbert Girard and a Miss C. M. Burd. James W. Ogden was president of the company. [Andrew*.]

KID-KORD (label). A seven-inch record issued by British Homophone Co., Ltd., in 1932, carrying material for children, such as nursery rhymes and animal stories. The discs, which had picture labels, were sold at 4s 6d in albums of six. When British Homophone ceased domestic trade in 1935 the trademark passed to Decca. [Andrews 1988/4.]

KILDARE (label). An obscure record issued in Britain (or perhaps Australia), in 1927 or 1928, with the word Kildare pasted over the Vocalion name that had marked the original release. One item is known to have had the Kildare name printed, rather than pasted, on the label. It may be that Kildare was "a continuation of the yellow-label Vocalion B series, marketed briefly after Vocalion itself was abandoned" or that the "Kildare sticker was used to disguise and thus dispose of out-of-date stock" (Rust). [Andrews*; Rust 1978.]

KIMMEL, JOHN J., 1866–1942. American accordionist, the first to record for a commercial label, born in Brooklyn on 13 Dec 1886; the name is also seen as Kimble and Kimmble. His initial recording was Zonophone #5996, a 10-inch disc of "Bedelia" issued in 1904. He was the first to record his instrument for Edison, beginning with "American Cake Walk" (#9341) in 1906, and continued with that label until 1929. Victor also had many of his records, from 1907 to 1928; Columbia and Emerson also issued Kimmel performances. He died on 18 Sep 1942 in Kings County, New York [Walsh 1958/2.]

KINCAID, WILLIAM MORRIS, 1895–1967. American flutist, born in Minneapolis on 26 Apr 1895. He studied in New York with George Barrère, and played in the New York Symphony Orchestra in 1914–1921. He became principal flutist of the Philadelphia Orchestra in 1921, remaining until his retirement in 1960. Kincaid recorded the Telemann Suite in A Minor with the Philadelphia Orchestra (Victor #VM890), bringing early attention to that composer as well as to the flute as a concert instrument. His recording of the Mozart Concerto No. 1 with the Philadelphia Orchestra remained in the Columbia catalog into the 1970s. He died in Philadelphia on 27 Mar 1967.

KINETOPHONE. The first device that added sound to motion pictures was developed by Thomas Edison and William Kennedy Dickson in 1889. It came to be called the Kinetophone. In a 1912 version the audio, using a Higham amplifier, was provided by large Blue Amberol cylinders, 4 3/8 inches in diameter and 7 1/4 inches long. The cylinder played up to six minutes, running 120 rpm, with groove pitch of 100 lines per inch. Kinetophone films (projected with the Kinetoscope) were single-reel shorts of six minutes or less in duration; they included "Sextette from Lucia," "Jack's Joke," "Scene from Julius Caesar," "Charge of the Light Brigade," and "Revenge of the Indian Girl." Synchronization of the cylinder with the film was the main problem. It required the record operator to observe certain cueing on the cylinder, then to start the machine at the right moment. Adjustments were possible once the film had started, but they needed to be made with great precision. Because Edison required users of the cylinders to be authorized purchasers of the entire audio-visual apparatus, his records were not widely sold. Theater managers were already showing films with costly projection equipment and were not inclined to duplicate it in order to acquire Edison cylinders. [Blacker 1981.] *See also* MOTION PICTURE SOUND RECORDING.

KING, B. B., 1925–. American blues singer and guitarist, born Riley B. King in Itta Bena, Mississippi, on 16 Sep 1925. He taught himself the guitar and made radio appearances; in 1952 he gained popularity with a record of "Three O'Clock Blues" (RPM #339), and by the early 1960s he had assumed a leading place among blues artists. He was able to blend jazz, rock, and blues styles successfully, as in "Rock Me Baby" (Kent #393; 1964), which was on the charts for 10 weeks. An outstanding hit was "I Like to Live the Love" (ABC #11406; 1973), 16 weeks on the charts. His album *There Must Be a Better World Somewhere* (MCA #5162) won a Grammy in 1981. He had two other Grammys, for the 1969 single "The Thrill is Gone" (BluesWay #61032), and for the 1985 album *My Guitar Sings the Blues.* Other outstanding albums included *Live in Cook County Jail* (ABC ABCS #723; 1971) and *To Know You is to Love You* (ABC ABCX #794; 1973).

KING, CAROLE, 1942–. American singer and writer of popular songs, born Carole Klein in Brooklyn on 9 Feb 1942. She composed successful songs for Black vocal groups in the 1960s, in the rhythm & blues and soul idioms. In the late 1960s she took up singing, achieving remarkable success with her second solo album *Tapestry,* which was among the all-time best sellers, appearing on the charts for 195 weeks beginning in 1971 (Ode #Sp 77009). *Tapestry* won two Grammys in 1971, and two other King records were winners in the same year: her composition "You've Got a Friend" was song of the year, and her single "It's Too Late" (Ode #66015) was record of the year. Other outstanding albums included *Fantasy* (Ode #SP77018; 1973), 34 chart weeks; *Music* (Ode #SP 77013; 1971), 38 weeks; *Rhymes and Reasons* (Ode #77016; 1972), 28 weeks; and *Writer* (Ode #SP 77006; 1971), 23 weeks.

KING, PEE WEE, 1914–. American country singer, born Julius Frank Anthony Kuczynski in Abrams, Wisconsin, on 18 Feb 1914. In 1934 he was performing with Gene Autry, and two years later he formed his own band, the Golden West Cowboys. The group was heard on *Grand Ole Opry* in 1937. King was co-composer with Redd Stewart of "Tennessee Waltz," which became one of the country music standards; he recorded it for Victor in 1947 (#202680). "Slow Poke" (Victor #210489) was on the charts 14 weeks in 1951. His group was the first to use electric instruments on *Grand Ole Opry* as Clel Summey played electric guitar from 1940. King was elected to the Country Music Hall of Fame in 1974.

KING, WAYNE, 1901–1985. American dance band leader, alto saxophonist and clarinetist, born in Savannah, Illinois, on 16 Feb 1901. He played in various Chicago bands and directed the Tivoli Theater orchestra until 1927, when he was invited to form a new group to open the Aragon Ballroom. He was identified with that venue for much of his career, playing languid dance numbers and waltzes; he acquired the sobriquet "Waltz King" and wrote an effective theme song, "The Waltz You Saved for Me" (Victor #22575; 1930). He won the *Radio Guide* prize as the most popular radio orchestra for seven years. In 1946 he began the Ziv Radio Series, doing 52 shows, all transcribed, and 26 more shows in 1947. Vocalist Nancy Evans, who started with King at age 17, remained with the band throughout its existence. Franklyn MacCormack provided poetic introductions to many of the numbers on the radio. He made a record in 1941 of "Melody of Love" with the King orchestra that achieved enormous success.

King's earliest recordings were for Vocalion in 1923 as a saxophonist/clarinetist with a group called Albert E. Short and his Tivoli Syncopators. On the Autograph label he appeared with the Del Lampe Trianon Orchestra in 1925. He recorded for Victor primarily, with some work for Brunswick in 1933. "Stardust" was an early hit (Victor 22656; 1931), and "Josephine"—another of his compositions—was one of his most popular records (Victor #25518; 1936). After military service in World War II, during which he reached the rank of major, he appeared on radio and television, and was active into the 1970s. *Dream Time* was a popular LP album of 1958 (Decca #DL 8663). King died in July 1985 in Paradise Valley, Arizona. [Kressley 1983 gives list of the Ziv transcriptions.]

KING (label). A record issued by King Records, Inc., Cincinnati, Ohio, located at 1540 Brewster St. Sydney Nathan was the founder and owner. The first records were made in 1944, by Black performers and country musicians. The venture was successful almost from the outset; in 1945, King was making 200 78s a day, but by 1949 the firm was selling six million discs a year. The Sensation label was acquired in 1948, and the Miracle label in 1950. Nathan was among the first to exploit the 45 rpm disc for popular repertoire. He was also quick to sign up rhythm & blues artists in the early 1950s, and in 1956 King acquired James Brown and

moved into soul music. Brown's many chart numbers were the mainstay of King, which began to lose ground in the 1960s as major labels competed strongly in the King specialties. With the death of Nathan in 1968, his family sold the company and it was soon dispersed. [Rotante 1945 has label listing.]

KINGSTON TRIO. American folk-singing group, established in San Francisco in 1957 by David Guard. John Stewart replaced Guard in 1961. Other members were Nick Reynolds and Bob Shane. They achieved popularity in campus and coffee house appearances in the San Francisco Bay area, and recorded a chart song "Tom Dooley" (Capitol #4049) in 1958; it took a Grammy award. Other hit records included "M.T.A." (Capitol #4221; 1959) and "Where Have All the Flowers Gone?" (Capitol #4671; 1962). The group had 18 chart singles, and 23 hit LP albums through 1965, nine of them gold; the most popular were *The Kingston Trio at the Hungry i* (Capitol #T 1107; 1959) and Grammy winner *Kingston Trio at Large* (Capitol #T 1199; 1959). The group was less successful after 1963, leading to a breakup in 1967. Then in the 1970s, both Shane and Reynolds led new groups using the Kingston Trio name. Finally in 1981, the original members came back together to make the album *The Kingston Trio: 15 Years Non-stop.*

KIPNIS, ALEXANDER, 1891–1978. Ukrainian/American bass, born in Zhitomir on 13 Feb 1891. He played the trombone and string bass in his youth; then graduated in conducting from the Warsaw Conservatory in 1912, and studied voice in Berlin. At the outbreak of World War I he was interned as an enemy alien, but was released and made his debut in Hamburg in 1915. Kipnis sang in many opera houses, including Baltimore 1923 (his U.S. debut), the Chicago Opera 1923–1932, Buenos Aires, and throughout Europe. He took American citizenship in 1931. From 1940 to 1946 he was with the Metropolitan Opera. He died in Westport, Connecticut, on 14 May 1978. His son Igor is a renowned harpsichordist.

Kipnis performed the whole bass repertoire, distinguishing himself in particular as Boris, Baron Ochs, Gurnemanz, Sarastro, Simon Boccanegra, and Wotan. His recording began in Germany in 1916 for Odeon. The first of the four works he inscribed was "Il etait temps" (in German) from *Faust* (#AA79397). He recorded during 1921–1922 for Deutsche Grammophon. In 1923 he made four sides for Homokord. He performed Lieder for U.S. Columbia in 1927.

Most of his discs were recorded for HMV (1929–1931) and Victor (1946–1948; 1955–1959). Two distinguished sets to which he contributed were the albums of the Hugo Wolf Society (Kipnis sang 13 songs) and the Brahms Society (24 songs). A CD resissue by Harmonia Mundi (#89019) presents 1930–1931 recordings, including the outstanding "Il lacerato spirito" (HMV #D2088) and "Herr Kavalier" from *Rosenkavalier* (#DB 1543). [Frankenstein 1974.]

KIPNIS, IGOR, 1930– . Harpsichordist, son of Alexander Kipnis, born in Berlin on 27 Sept 1930. The family transferred to the U.S., where he took up the piano and served as accompanist to his father's pupils. He studied harpischord with Fernando Valenti at Harvard University, graduating in 1952. After military service and odd jobs in New York, he made his debut as a harpsichordist in 1961. He quickly achieved recognition, and made world tours from 1967–1971. Kipnis helped to spread interest in the harpsichord, and also in the fortepiano. He recorded the Bach keyboard works for Columbia and Angel, as well as a set of six LPs that surveyed the harpsichord repertoire (Columbia #M3X-31521/25).

KIRK, ANDY, 1898–1992. American Big Band leader and bass saxophonist, born Andrew Dewey Kirk in Newport, Kentucky, on 28 May 1898. He grew up in Denver, Colorado, and played in George Morrison's band there from 1918. Moving to Dallas in 1925, he was with Terence Holder's "Dark Clouds of Joy" and took the leadership in 1929. He established the group Clouds of Joy, in Kansas City, and became one of the principal proponents of that city's jazz style. His wife, Mary Lou Williams, was pianist and arranger for the band, which continued until 1948. Later he worked with various groups, and performed in Europe during the 1960s. Among the many notable artists who were in his bands at one time or another

were Charlie Parker, Ben Webster, and Lester Young. He died in New York 11 Dec 1992.

Kirk recorded for Brunswick in 1930, inscribing "Dallas Blues" (#6129) and five other numbers. He then worked for Columbia and primarily for Decca. "Until the Real Thing Comes Along," with a vocal by baritone Pha Terrell (Decca #809), was a hit in 1936. LP albums were offered by several labels, including Ace of Hearts *Clouds of Joy* (#AH-110) and *Twelve Clouds of Joy* (#AH-160).

KIRKBY, STANLEY. English baritone, born James Baker, credited with the largest number of records in Britain from the 1900s–1930s. Charles Holland was one of his several pseudonyms. In 1913 he made a famous disc about the Scott Antarctic expedition, "Tis a Story That Shall Live For Ever" (Zonophone #1050). "It's a Long Way to Tipperary" was one of his best sellers in the U.S.

Kirkby was also one of the founders of the **Premier Manufacturing Co., Ltd.**

KIRKPATRICK, RALPH, 1911–1984. American harpsichordist and scholar, born 10 June 1911 in Leominster, Massachusetts. He graduated from Harvard College in 1931, and studied in Paris with Nadia Boulanger and Wanda Landowska. Then he toured Europe, performing and carrying out research into baroque performance practice. He became particularly expert on Domenico Scarlatti, and wrote the standard biography (1953). From 1940 to 1978 he taught at Yale University, then retired. Kirkpatrick edited works by several baroque masters, and performed them with great fidelity to the idiom of their day; he also played works by modern composers. His recordings of Bach and Scarlatti were issued on LP by Deutsche Grammophon and Odyssey.

KLEIBER, CARLOS, 1930– . German conductor, son of Erich Kleiber, born in Berlin on 3 July 1930. From 1935 to after World War II he lived with his parents in Argentina, studying music and making his first appearance as a pianist. Returning to Europe, he conducted in Munich in 1953, and secured numerous assignments in opera and the concert hall; however, he has not accepted any permanent post. His small number of recordings are highly regarded, including a *Rosenkavalier* (Philips CD #V072405; 1989), two complete CD performances of *Freischütz* (Denon 1985 and Decca 1986), a complete *Tristan* (DGG #413315; 1986), and a brilliant Beethoven Fifth Symphony with the Vienna Philharmonic Orchestra (DGG CD #415861; 1985).

KLEIBER, ERICH, 1890–1956. Austrian conductor, born in Vienna on 5 Aug 1890. He studied in Prague and commenced conducting there, at the National Theater. Then he held various posts with opera companies until 1923, when he was appointed director of the Berlin State Opera. He conducted the world premiere of *Wozzeck* there in 1925. In 1935 he left Germany for South America, and toured widely there and in the U.S. He was engaged again to direct the Berlin State Opera in 1954, but resigned in 1955. He died in Zurich on 27 Jan 1956. His son Carlos is also a noted conductor.

Kleiber made distinguished recordings of Mozart, Beethoven, and Richard Strauss, mostly for Decca in the last 10 years of his life. *Rosenkavalier* (Decca LXT2954/57, 1954; CD reissue #425950, 1990), with Sena Jurinac as Octavian, is considered to be a definitive interpretation; and his *Nozze di Figaro* is also at the highest level. The Kleiber Beethoven Fifth Symphony with the Royal Concertgebouw Orchestra (on Decca CD #417 637; 1987) is widely regarded as the finest version of that work, rivaled only by that of his son.

KLEMPERER, OTTO, 1885–1973. German conductor, born in Breslau on 14 May 1885. He studied in Frankfort and Berlin, and was conducting in Berlin at age 21. In 1910–1912 he conducted at the Hamburg Opera, in 1917 he was director of the Cologne Opera, and in 1924 he was director of the Wiesbaden Opera. Klemperer's American debut was in 1926 with the New York Symphony Orchestra. After a period in Germany, he returned to the U.S. as music director of the Los Angeles Philharmonic Orchestra in 1933. A brain tumor almost ended his career, but he recovered sufficiently to hold the post of director of the Budapest Opera from 1947–1950. He retired to Switzerland in 1972, and died in Zurich on 6 July 1973.

Klemperer recorded for Polydor in 1925–1933, doing the first and eighth Beethoven symphonies and a movement of Bruckner's Symphony No. 8, all with the Berlin State Opera Orchestra. He recorded further with the same label and ensemble until 1933, when he left Germany. In 1947 he worked for Vox, doing Beethoven, Mendelssohn, Bruckner, and Mahler with the Vienna Symphony Orchestra and the Pro Musica Orchestra. In the 1950s he recorded prolifically for EMI, with the Philharmonia Orchestra and the New Philharmonia Orchestra. He also made remarkable complete opera recordings, especially *Fidelio*. In 1962 he was awarded a Grammy for his recording of the Bach *St. Matthew Passion* with the Philharmonia Orchestra and Chorus, on the Angel label. EMI has released many of these interpretations on CD. [Heyworth 1983.]

KLINGSOR. A tradename (taken from the name of the sorcerer in *Parsifal*) used for gramophones and disc recordings, originating in Germany. The manufacturer in 1907 was Stephan Hain, of Krefeld. By 1912 the Klingsors were being made by the Polyphon Musikwerke AG in Leipzig, producers of the Polyphon label; Hermann Krebs and Heinrich Klenk were patentees. In 1912 *TMW* reported that the patent had been acquired by Theodore Isaac, to make and sell the instrument in Chicago. The Klingsor device was patented in the U.S., #899,491 (filed 28 Feb 1907; granted 22 Sept 1908).

The gramophone was remarkable for its "Saiten-Resonanz"—a harplike bank of steel strings that crossed the front of the instrument, at the loudspeaker opening. As the strings moved in sympathetic vibration to the speaker an enhanced sound resulted. Machines were still on the market in Britain in 1925, sold by J. G. Murdoch and Co. [*TMR* #13 (1971) has several photos and a short account.]

KNICKERBOCKER QUARTET. (I) An American vocal ensemble that recorded for Edison from 1908 to 1915, replacing the Edison Male Quartet. The original members were John Young, George M. Stricklett, Frederick Wheeler, and Gus Reed. After about 1912 the membership was frequently changed; among the singers at one time or another were Reinald

Werrenrath, Thomas Chalmers, Royal Fish, William S. Hooley, and Harvey Hindermyer. Four records are listed in Koenigsberg, of which the earliest was "Come Where My Love Lies Dreaming" (#9994; 1908). The group made seven Edison Diamond Discs, one with Elizabeth Spencer, in 1914–1915. [Koenigsberg 1987.]

KNICKERBOCKER QUARTET. (II) An American vocal group that recorded for the Columbia Graphophone Co. in 1917. Members were George Eldred, Lewis James, William Morgan, and Glenn Howard. One popular number was "Yaddie, Kaddie, Kiddie, Kaddie, Koo" (Columbia #47166).

KNICKERBOCKER QUINTET. An American vocal group that recorded for Edison. In 1905 the members were Parvin Witte, first tenor; Charles H. Bates, second tenor; Geoffrey O'Hara, baritone; Walter C. White, baritone, and Leon Parmet, bass. A popular two-minute cylinder by the Quintet was "The Rosary," (#9052; 1905).

KOCH, LUDWIG, 1881–1974. German bass, and recording executive in Germany and England, born on 13 Nov 1881 in Frankfurt. His father acquired an Edison "perfected phonograph" at the Leipzig Fair in 1889, and the boy began to collect famous voices on the cylinders. Among the persons he recorded were Hermann Helmholtz, the physicist and acoustician; Queen Victoria, Edward VII, Bismarck, and Hugo Wolf. He was also interested in animal sounds, and made the first bird song record in 1889, and went on to make many more in outdoor settings.

As a singer, Koch appeared in concert and opera, and recorded for Beka, but he ceased performing at the outset of World War I. He became an executive for German Odeon and the Parlophone Co. in 1928, made more animal records, and wrote 11 books. He was harrassed by the Nazis and eventually left the country, arriving in London in 1936. There he was assisted by Louis Sterling and others, and was able to continue recording bird songs. He was on the BBC staff in 1941–1943, and was heard on the radio through the 1950s.

Unfortunately, most of Koch's early cylinders were left behind when he fled Germany and were evidently destroyed. His 1889 bird song cylinder survived and has been played on BBC radio. [Carreck 1974.]

KOCH (AND S) CO. A New York firm, located at 296 Broadway, marketing in 1916 a disc player (Koch-O-Phone) in six models and vertical-cut Koch-O-Phone discs.

KOEHLER AND HINRICHS. A firm located in St. Paul, Minnesota, manufacturer of a record player combined with a clock and bookcase; this amalgamation sold for $100 in 1916.

KOERBER-BRENNER CO. A St. Louis firm, distributor of Victor products. In 1917 E. C. Rauth was vice president.

KOLODIN, IRVING, 1908–1988. Music critic and writer, born in New York on 22 Feb 1908. He studied at the Institute of Musical Art and became a critic for the *New York Sun* in 1932, remaining to 1950, having become its chief critic. Kolodin was music editor for *Saturday Review* from 1947 to 1982, gaining great influence. Kolodin was a historian of the Metropolitan Opera, having issued three editions of a standard narrative account beginning in 1883. He was given responsibility for assembling the classical recordings in the first official White House music library (1970).

In the 1950s he compiled record albums for RCA, including a *Critic's Choice* set and a five-record album entitled *50 Years of Great Operatic Singing*. He was among the earliest critics to concentrate on reviewing phonograph records. Among his many books are *Guide to Recorded Music* (1941; 3rd ed. 1950) and *Saturday Review Home Book of Recorded Music and Sound Reproduction* (1952; 2nd ed. 1956). He died in New York on 29 Apr 1988.

KONITZ, LEE, 1927–. American jazz alto saxophonist, born in Chicago on 13 Oct 1927. He began with the clarinet at age 11, then switched to the saxophone, playing with the Gay Claridge band in Chicago, then with Claude Thornhill (1947–1948) and Miles Davis (1948–1950). Later he worked with Lennie Tristano, and from 1952 to 1953 with Stan Kenton, performing in a quasi-bebop style. Konitz had his own combo in 1954, and toured widely in America and Europe. During the mid-1960s he turned to experimental jazz and cool jazz, influencing men like Art Pepper and Paul Desmond. His technique was smooth, with minimal vibrato. During the 1960s he settled on the West Coast, and remained active into the 1970s.

In 1949 Konitz and Miles Davis made an important album, *The Birth of the Cool* (Capitol #T-1974). *Intuition* was one of the significant albums made with Tristano (Capitol #1224; 1949). *The Real Lee Konitz* was issued in 1957 by Atlantic (#1273).

KORJUS, MILIZA, 1912?-1980. Swedish/Polish/Russian coloratura soprano, born in Warsaw of a Swedish father (a military attaché) and Polish/Russian mother. The facts of her birthplace and date are uncertain. She began singing in public as a child, and attracted the attention of Max von Schillings, who arranged for an appearance with the Berlin State Opera in 1934. After touring in Germany, she went to Hollywood to make the film *The Great Waltz* (1939). Then she toured Latin America, and in 1944 sang in Carnegie Hall. Not long after she retired from the stage.

Korjus recorded for Electrola in Berlin during 1934–1936, and for Victor in the U.S. from 1945–1947. Her discs display her remarkable virtuosity, especially the *Lakmé* Bell Song, variations by Adam on "Ah, vous dirai-je, maman?", and arias from *Entführung aus dem Serail* and *Zauberflöte*. EMI issued two LPs of her favorite numbers in 1979 (Electrola #147–30 819/20). [Pearmain 1964.]

KOSHETZ, NINA, 1894-1965. Ukrainian soprano, born in Kiev on 30 Dec 1894. She was daughter of a tenor at the Bolshoi Opera in Moscow; studied piano as a child (giving a recital at age nine), then singing. She toured Russia with Rachmaninoff, and became recognized as an interpreter of his songs. Her opera debut was on 22 Sep 1913 in Moscow, as Tatiana in *Eugene Onegin*; she sang there in the Russian, Italian, and French repertoires to 1919. Her American career began in 1920, and was al-most exclusively in the concert hall, where she specialized in Russian songs; however, she did sing in the premiere of *Love for Three Oranges* in Chicago, in 1921. In 1924–1931 she toured Europe, and in the late 1930s she was again in Hollywood. In 1941 she retired from the stage and settled in California, appeared in several motion pictures, and died in Santa Ana on 14 May 1965.

Koshetz recorded for Brunswick in 1922–1923, beginning with "None but the Lonely Heart" (#8720–2) and "At the Ball" by Tchaikovsky (#15029), and going on with other Russian and Ukrainian songs. She made 10 sides for Victor in 1926–1931, the most notable of which were arias from *Prince Igor* and *Sadko*. In 1939 she made an important four-disc album for G. Schirmer (#SCH-16), the New York music publisher, which has been reissued on LP by the International Piano Archives (#IPA-116; 1978); it includes songs by Tchaikovsky, Rachmaninoff, and Arensky, plus traditional gypsy airs. [Dangarfield 1991.]

KOSMOPHONE. A disc player sold by the New Polyphon Supply Co. in London in 1903, at a price of £3 2sh (including two Zonophone discs). The Kosmophone trademark was owned by the German firm Bumb and König in 1901. In September 1908 it was registered by the B.H. Han firm of Dresden, Germany, for machines and parts.

KOUSSEVITZKY, SERGE, 1874-1951. Russian conductor and string bass player, born in Vishy-Volochok on 26 July 1874. He learned trumpet as a child and played with a family ensemble at local events. After studying the string bass in Moscow he joined the Bolshoi Opera Theater orchestra in 1894, and became first chair in 1901. He gave recitals in Moscow and Berlin; and turned to conducting, leading the Berlin Philharmonic Orchestra in 1908, then forming his own orchestra in 1909. He toured Russia until the revolution, moved to Paris in 1920, then to America. In 1924 he was named director of the Boston Symphony Orchestra, a post he held for 25 years. Koussevitzky was a champion of new compositions, and commissioned many important works, including *Symphony of Psalms*. He established the Berkshire

Music Center (Tanglewood) in 1940. He retired in 1949, and died in Boston on 4 June 1951.

Koussevitzky was a Victor artist almost exclusively. During his tenure in Boston, the orchestra made only one commercial recording for another label, the Roy Harris *Symphony No. 1 (1933)* (Columbia album #M-191; 1934). His earliest recording was of his own *Concerto for Double Bass in F Minor*, with a piano accompaniment, not released at the time. (This and five other double bass performances by him were issued on Victor LP #LCT1145; 1954.) His first released recording was with the Boston Symphony, performing the *Petrouchka* Concert Suite (Victor album #M-49; 1929). Among his later records of distinction were *La mer* (Victor album #M-643; 1940), *La valse* (Victor album #DB 1541/2; 1931), and Tchaikovsky's symphonies No. 4 (Victor album #DM-1318; 1949) and No. 5 (Victor album #M-1057; 1946). [Young 1990.]

KRAINIS, BERNARD, 1924– . American recorder player, born in New Brunswick, New Jersey, on 28 Dec 1924. Although he did not begin to study the recorder until he was 21, he quickly became recognized as an outstanding virtuoso and brought the recorder repertoire to the attention of the public. He and Noah Greenberg established the **New York Pro Musica** in 1952. After 1959 Krainis left the Pro Musica group and toured with his own Krainis Baroque Ensemble, Krainis Trio, and Krainis Consort. He gave up extensive concertizing in 1970, taught at several colleges, and made records. An important album by his Consort was made for Kapp (#9034; 1960).

KREISLER, FRITZ, 1875–1962. Austrian/American violinist, born in Vienna on 2 Feb 1875. As a child he studied in Vienna, then went to Paris and graduated with highest honors from the Conservatory at age 12. He made his U.S. debut in 1888, and toured with great success. Kreisler then gave up performance to study medicine and art, and to serve as an officer in the Austrian army; he did not return to the stage until 1899 in Berlin. He toured again in America and Europe, gaining much acclaim. During World War I he returned to the Austrian army, continuing his musical career

after the Armistice. In 1943 he became a U.S. citizen. He died in New York on 29 Jan 1962.

Kreisler recorded first for G & T in 1904. He played five works: "Chant sans paroles" (Tchaikovsky; #2084), "Sarabande" (Sulzer; #2085), "Bagatelle" (Schubert; #2085), the first movement of Bach's *Partita No. 3*, and the Bach "Air on the G String" (#2087). Kreisler was known as a composer as well as a virtuoso: among his popular works are "Tambourin chinois," "Schön Rosmarin" "Caprice viennois," "Liebesfreud," and "Liebeslied." These pieces were among his early recordings, which included also many of his arrangements of compositions by Couperin, Tartini, Dvořák, and others. There were 50 solo records in the Victor 1917 catalog, mostly short concert pieces, plus duets with Geraldine Farrar, John McCormack, and Efrem Zimbalist.

Among the finest of his recordings were those he made in the late 1920s, while his technique was at its height. His Schubert and Grieg sonatas, with Sergei Rachmaninoff at the piano, are highly regarded (Victor albums # M-107 and M-45). The first recordings of the Beethoven, Brahms, and Mendelssohn concertos, with the London Philharmonic, are preferable to his later versions of them. Victor issued an album of recordings from 1924–1929 as *Fritz Kreisler Souvenirs* (Victrola #1372), and a CD from Pearl displayed performances from the same period (*Encores*; #GEMM CD9324; 1990). [Lewis, J. 1976.]

KRIPS, JOSEF, 1902–1974. Austrian conductor, born in Vienna on 8 Apr 1902. At age 16 he was a violinist with the Vienna Volksoper, and he made his conducting debut in 1921. He held various posts in Germany, then at the Vienna State Opera in 1933. From 1935 he was also a professor in the Vienna Academy of Music. During World War II he was unable to take part in musical life, but as soon as the conflict ended he was immediately active; Soviet authorities in Vienna gave him the task of restoring opera to the Staatsoper, and within two weeks after the fighting stopped he conducted *Fidelio* there. Krips remained in Vienna until 1950, when he took the directorship of the London Symphony Orchestra, staying until 1954. From 1954 to 1963 he was conductor of the Buffalo Philharmonic Orchestra, and from 1963 to 1970 of the San Francisco Symphony Orchestra. He died in Geneva on 13 Oct 1974.

Krips was most distinguished for his Mozart performances, and for interpretations of the other Viennese masters. But he was also a promoter of modern music. Among his best recordings were those made with the London Symphony for EMI and Decca. These included the Schubert Ninth Symphony (London #6061), all the Beethoven symphonies (on the Everest label), and numerous Mozart symphonies. Near the end of his life he began a series of Mozart symphony discs for Philips with the Royal Concertgebouw Orchestra, completing nine of them.

KRISTALL (label). (I) A German label, issued by the Kristall Schallplatten GmbH in 1929–1945.

KRISTALL (label). (II) A Swedish record issued in 1933–1939, affiliated with Sonora. In 1934 the releases were from Svenska Kristall Rex, a subsidiary of the German Kristall Schallplatten.

KRISTALL SCHALLPLATTEN GmbH. A Berlin firm founded in 1929 by Andreas Biele as a subsidiary of the Crystalate Gramophone Record Manufacturing Co. of London. It contracted with the American Record Corp. to issue matrices of various ARC labels, and issued also Vox records and Kristall records. **Carl Lindström**—then a part of EMI, Ltd.—took over the firm in 1938, and continued to use the Kristall label until 1945. [Sieben 1985.]

KRISTOFFERSON, KRIS, 1936– . American country singer and motion picture actor, born in Brownsville, Texas, on 22 June 1936. A Rhodes Scholar at Oxford (B.A., 1960) and an U.S. Army pilot, he turned to country music in Nashville and eventually began producing hit discs. "Why Me" (Monument #78571; 1973) was on the charts for 31 weeks; and there were five other chart singles by 1982. From 1971 to 1974 Kristofferson had six chart albums, most notably *Jesus was a Capricorn* (Monument #31909; 1972, 1973) which enjoyed 42 weeks on the list. An album with Rita Coolidge, *Full*

Moon (A & M #SP-4403), had 18 chart weeks in 1973.

Kristofferson was awarded a Grammy in 1973 for the single "Help Me Make It Through the Night." He and Rita Coolidge received Grammys for their duets "From the Bottle to the Bottom" (1973) and "Lover Please" (1975).

KRUESI, JOHN, 1843–1899. Swiss/American machinist, born in Speicher on 15 May 1843. He learned the machinist's trade in Zurich, and from 1867–1870 he worked in the Netherlands, Belgium, and France. In 1870 he crossed to America, taking a job with Singer Sewing Machine Co., then going to the Edison plant in Newark, New Jersey, in 1871. He became foreman of the machine shop, responsible for the mechanical execution of many Edison ideas. He assisted with the installation of the electric light system in New York; he patented the Kruesi Tube, an insulated underground cable. Kruesi and Charles Batchelor were responsible for the building of Edison's great plant in Schenectady, New York, which became the Edison General Electric Co.; in 1889 he became its assistant general manager. In 1895 he was appointed chief engineer of the new General Electric Co. He died on 22 Feb 1899 in Schenectady.

Kruesi is best known in the history of recorded sound as the man who made the first working model of the phonograph, following a sketch given to him (and Charles Batchelor) by Thomas Edison on 29 Nov 1877. Kruesi and Batchelor had the model ready on 6 December. An unfortunate error in dating the sketch has only recently been corrected (by Allen Koenigsberg in 1969); the mistake resulted from Edison's much later (ca. 1917) inscription on a copy of the drawing "Kreuzi make this Edison Aug 12/77." The inventor evidently forgot the date of his original instruction to Kruesi, and also the spelling of his machinist's name. Kruesi also made the patent model of the phonograph.

The spelling of Kruesi has had a varied history in the literature. It appears as Kreusi, Kreuzi, Krusci, and Kruesci in various respected sources. A photo of the Schenectady tombstone, reproduced in Betz clearly shows the correct spelling; but Betz's article presents a misspelled version in its very title. [Betz 1990; Biel in *ARSCJ* 13–2 (1981), p. 114.]

KRUPA, GENE, 1909–1973. American jazz drummer and Big Band leader, born in Chicago on 15 Jan 1909. He worked with the McKenzie-Condon Chicagoans and recorded with them in 1927–1928. Then he was with various groups, and in 1935 joined Benny Goodman. He was soon recognized as the premier drummer of jazz, providing virtuoso displays and lightning speed. In 1938 he left Goodman and formed several bands of his own to 1951. He toured with Jazz at the Philharmonic for 20 years. Krupa died in Yonkers, New York, on 16 Oct 73.

Among his famous discs are "After You've Gone," with Benny Goodman (Victor #25115; 1935), "Drummin' Man" (Columbia #35324; 1939), and "Drum Boogie" (Okeh #6046; 1941).

KUBELIK, JAN, 1880–1940. Bohemian violinist, born in Michle, near Prague, on 5 July 1880. He studied with Otakar Ševčik at the Prague Conservatory, and made his debut in Vienna in 1898. Then he toured Europe and the U.S., acclaimed as a new Paganini. His technique began to weaken in the 1930s, and after World War I he was less active; his final concert was in 1940. Kubelik died in Prague on 15 Dec 1940. He was father of the conductor Rafael Kubelik.

He was the first world-class violinist to record on disc, for G & T in 1902 (*see* VIOLIN RECORDINGS). He played František Drdla's "Serenade" (#7956) and arrangements of pieces from *Carmen* and of the *Lucia* Sextette. He was then heard on Victor Monarch records, in the 5000 series transferred from G & T, and on Fonotipia in 1905–1910. From 1911 to 1915 he recorded for HMV. He had eight solos in the Victor 1917 catalog, and duets with Nellie Melba. The principal acoustics were reissued on two Biddulph compact discs in 1991 (#LAB 033/4). Symposium Records issued the complete material of 1902–ca. 1934, including eight test pressings, in 1991 (CD #1072). [Lewis, J. 1981.]

KUBELIK, RAFAEL, 1914– . Bohemian conductor, born in Bychory on 29 June 1914. His father was the violinist Jan Kubelik. He studied at the Prague Conservatory, and made his debut with the Czech Philharmonic Orchestra in 1934, becoming its director in 1936. In 1948 he went to Britain, then to Switzerland (where he took citizenship in 1973). He was appointed conductor of the Chicago Symphony Orchestra and served from 1950 to 1953 in that post. In 1955–1958 he was director of Covent Garden; then for a year (1973) he was music director of the Metropolitan Opera Co. He was also director of the Bavarian Radio Orchestra, Munich.

Kubelik has made numerous outstanding recordings with the world's great orchestras. With the Chicago Symphony he is heard on Mercury recordings of—among others—Tchaikovsky, Brahms, and Smetana. DGG recorded his acclaimed renditions of the Mahler symphonies with the Bavarian Radio Symphony. Earlier, on 78s, he recorded Dvořák, Smetana, and Janáček with the Czech Philharmonic Orchestra for HMV. He directed the Vienna Philharmonic Orchestra in the Brahms symphonies for EMI. His DGG set of the Beethoven symphonies was made in the unusual manner of presenting each symphony by a different orchestra; among them were the Berlin Philharmonic, the Royal Concertgebouw, and the Cleveland orchestras.

Kunstkopf stereo. *See* DUMMY HEAD STEREO.

KUNZ, ERICH, 1909– . Austrian bass-baritone, born in Vienna on 20 May 1909. He studied at the Vienna Academy of Music, and sang with various opera companies; then went to the Vienna State Opera. He appeared in London, Tokyo, Salzburg, Bayreuth, and the Metropolitan Opera (debut on 26 Nov 52 as Leporello). Kunz was acclaimed primarily for his buffo roles and for his operetta interpretations. Many of his finest recordings—doing Papageno, Leporello, Figaro (Mozart's), Beckmesser, and Viennese light pieces—were reissued on two LPs (#1C 147–03) by EMI in 1980.

KURZ, SELMA, 1874–1933. Silesian coloratura soprano, born in Bielitz on 15 Nov 1874. Her first appearances were in Hamburg in 1895; she then went to the Vienna Court Opera from 1899 to 1926. In 1904 she was a great success as Gilda at Covent Garden. In the U.S. she was acclaimed as a concert singer. Kurz recorded for the Gramophone Co. in 1900, doing airs from *Mignon* and *Faust*. She made seven sides for International Zonophone Co. in Vienna in 1902, beginning with a seven-inch disc of the Brahms "Ständchen" (#10902). She was then a Gramophone Co. artist, doing the standard coloratura repertoire until 1914, and in 1923–1926. In ca. 1919 she worked with Deutsche Grammophon. A CD of her principal numbers was issued in 1990 by Club 99, #CL99–43. [Halban 1960; Kelly 1979.]

KYSER, KAY, 1906–1985. American Big Band leader, born in Rocky Mount, North Carolina, on 18 June 1906. He attended the University of North Carolina, earning a degree in 1928, and formed a dance band. He was engaged by the Blackhawk Restaurant in Chicago in 1934, and broadcast from there his popular *College of Musical Knowledge* radio show, in which people from the audience were brought to the stage to answer amusing questions. The program was carried to television in 1949–1951. Kyser made eight motion pictures before retiring in 1951. He did not play an instrument himself, but took the part of host and showman. He died in Chapel Hill, North Carolina, on 23 July 1985.

Kyser's ensemble was one of the smooth, sweet bands of the era, graced by outstanding vocalists, and sparked with some humorous and novelty arrangements. Often there were "singing song title" introductions. His orchestra recorded first for Victor in 1928, doing "Broken Dreams of Yesterday" and "Tell Her" (#V-40028). They were back on the Victor label for two sides in 1929, then did not record until 1935, for the Brunswick label. Star singer Ginny Simms joined the group then, and began a long series of successful ballad numbers; and Merwyn Bogue did many clown pieces as Ishkabibble. Wind player Sully Mason sang in novelty pieces. In 1938 Harry Babbitt joined the vocal forces, and he made a popular duet with Ginny Simms, "The Umbrella Man" (Brunswick #8225; 1938), with a charming solo, "Sixty Seconds Got Together," on the B side. "Three Little Fishies" was a hit of 1939, sung by Babbitt, Simms, and Bogue (Brunswick #8368). The orchestra signed with Columbia in 1939, and produced their greatest hits, of which only a few can be cited here: "On the Isle of May" sung by Simms and Babbitt (Columbia #35375; 1940), with "Playmates" sung by Sully Mason and chorus on the flip side; "Who Wouldn't Love You?" with Simms and Babbitt (Columbia #36526; 1942); and Sully Mason's lively "Got the Moon in My Pocket" backed by Babbitt's delicate solo of "Just Plain Lonesome" (Columbia # 36575; 1942).

LA BELLE (label). A record issued by the La Belle Phonograph Corp., New York, around 1919–1920. The discs were in fact Columbia records—and other labels later—with the La Belle stickers pasted over the original labels. [Rust 1978.]

LA SCALA. The principal opera theatre and opera company of Italy, full name Il Teatro alla Scala. It opened in Milan in 1778, was nearly destroyed in a bombing raid in 1943, and was rebuilt in 1946. Complete opera recordings by the La Scala company have been made since 1907. HMV and Columbia recorded more than 25 such sets by 1932, conducted by Carlo Sabajno or Lorenzo Molajoli. A number of superior artists who did not perform widely outside of Italy are heard on these discs, such as tenors Aureliano Pertile and Francesco Merli, and baritone Enrico Molinari. The La Scala chorus recorded for Odeon and Fonotipia, accompanying soloists or doing choral numbers. A 1990 CD reissue offered on 12 discs the complete *Pagliacci, Aida, Otello, Rigoletto, Trovatore*, and the Verdi *Requiem* (Harmonia Mundi #RPC 32539/50).

LABEL. (I) A paper attachment to a disc or cylinder, giving identification data on the music and or the performers. Before 1900 discs had no paper labels, but carried identification scratched into their surfaces. Eldridge Johnson began using paper labels on discs in 1900, and the practice soon became widespread.

LABEL. (II) The popular name for a record company or a division of a company that issues one or more series of records; for example, "the Brunswick label" refers to records released by the Brunswick-Balke-Collender Co.

LABIA, MARIA, 1880–1953. Italian soprano, born in Verona on 14 Feb 1880. She made her debut in Stockholm as Mimi on 19 May 1905, then sang with the Berlin Komische Oper from 1906 to 1908. She was with the Manhattan Opera Co., New York, until it folded in 1910, then appeared at the Vienna Opera. She died in Malcesine del Garda, Italy, on 10 Feb 1953.

Labia recorded for Odeon in Berlin in 1907–1910, doing dramatic arias (in German) from *Tosca, Carmen, Traviata,* and *Ballo in maschera*. In 1911 she sang in London for Edison wax Amberol cylinder #35021: "Voi lo sapete" (later Blue Amberol #28114; 1912 or 1913), "Ave Maria" from *Otello*, and "Non la sospiri" from *Tosca* (later Blue Amberol #28153, 1912 or 1913). There were also five numbers cut for Edison Diamond Discs, in 1912–1913: "Tre giorni son che Nina" (#82004, 82014, 82037), "Seconda mattinata" (#82010); "In quelle trine morbide" from *Manon Lescaut* (#82019, 82038), "Ballatella" from *Pagliacci* (#82021, 82035), and "Mi chiamano Mimi" (#82503).

Labyrinth. *See* LOUDSPEAKER, 5.

LACQUER DISC. Another name for the acetate disc; one usually made of metal, glass, or fiber, and coated one or both sides with a lacquer compound. Lacquers were used in home recording and in making instantaneous recordings between the introduction of electrical recording and the advent of the 1948 LP.

Around 1950 the industry generally began to abandon wax in favor of lacquer surfaces.

LAINE, FRANKIE, 1913–. American popular singer, born Frank Paul Lo Vecchio in Chicago on 30 Mar 1913. He sang in church, then at age 15 in clubs, then went on to radio. He developed a crooning, jazzy style said to be modeled on Louis Armstrong's singing. In 1946 he went to Hollywood, and contracted to record for Mercury. He scored a great success in 1947 with "That's My Desire" (Mercury # 5007), followed by another, "Mule Train" (Mercury #5345; 1949). In the 1950s and 1960s he put 21 singles on the charts, including "I Believe" (Columbia 39938; 1953) and "Moonlight Gambler" (Columbia #40780; 1956). His most popular album was *I'll Take Care of Your Cares* (ABC #604; 1967), 19 weeks on the charts.

LAMBERT, THOMAS BENNETT, 1862–1928. American inventor and recording company executive, born in Chicago. In 1900 he received British patent #13,344 for an "indestructible" cylinder record, and U.S. patent #645,920 (where the term used was "infrangible"). His process involved coating the usual wax master with a form of carbon, then depositing copper on it by electrolysis to make a shell. When the wax master was cooled and removed, a copper negative matrix remained; it was used to form duplicate cylinders in celluloid ("cellulose" was Lambert's term). The **Lambert Co.** was established in Chicago to produce and market the records. With the bankruptcy of that firm in 1906, Lambert turned to telephone research, then was vice president of the Marsh Laboratories in Chicago, producers of the earliest commercial electrical discs. He died on 9 Jan 1928. [Koenigsberg 1990.]

LAMBERT CO. The first company to mass-produce unbreakable cylinder records in the U.S., incorporated 5 Mar 1900 by brothers Albert D. and Brian F. Philpot, along with Varian M. Harris and others. The incorporation document stressed advertising purposes rather than the direct marketing of records for entertainment. (Thomas Lambert had been granted patents on a door-operated cylinder phonograph and a talking cigar cutter, and Balm & Harris offered their indestructible records as premiums for use with breakfast cereals.) Addresses of the firm at one time or another were 67–69 Lake St., 171 LaSalle St., 12 Sherman St., and 110–112 S. Jefferson St., Chicago.

Lambert cylinders were produced under U.S. patent #645,920, granted to **Thomas Bennett Lambert** 20 Mar 1900—though Lambert claimed in 1903 that the company had been named without his knowledge or consent. Only Lioret (in France) had produced commercial celluloid cylinders earlier. Thomas Lambert had experimentally molded celluloid records off and on during the 1890s, but did not file a successful patent application until 14 Aug 1899.

The first Lambert records to be sold (production began in May 1900) were white in color. They were formed from relatively thick-walled celluloid tubing and conformed to the overall dimensions of Edison brown-wax music cylinders.

Dyes were soon used to color the raw white celluloid and to reduce surface noise. Pink was used early on, but "Pink Lamberts" are seldom found today. Black dyes were in use by Fall 1903 and most surviving Lambert cylinders are black. A few brown ones have been reported. Orange was yet another color mentioned in court testimony, but examples are not known today.

Lambert cylinders initially had separate end flanges and three tiny sloping blocks of celluloid glued into the main tube "to guide the cylinder onto the phonograph mandrel." This was probably an attempt to circumvent the Edison tapered-bore cylinder patent (U.S. #382,418). Nonetheless, Edison's legal staff fought the Lambert Co., first in a 1902 patent interference suit regarding processes for duplicating records by molding (U.S. patent #713,209), and later in connection with the tapered-bore patent.

The guide blocks originally attached inside the title end were eventually dropped, leaving the end flanges to grip the mandrel at only two narrow support points. After the Edison tapered-bore patent expired in May 1905, some late black Lamberts were made with heavy plaster cores.

William F. Messer (a plumber by trade) has been credited with developing the improved steam-pressure record printing machines used by Lambert. Employed at the Lambert Co. from 1900 through part of 1902, Messer was allegedly *forced* to sign the associated patent application (filed 1 Feb 1902; U.S. patent #702,772, granted 29 July 1902) that covered integral end flanges to trap steam during molding. Thinner celluloid came into use at Lambert in 1902 in connection with these process developments, easing the previous relatively high material costs.

Thomas Lambert was included in the 1902 reorganization of the Lambert Co., but he and Lambert president Brian Philpot quit the company on 1 May 1902. (Company secretary Albert Philpot called this act "desertion.") Lambert, Messer, and Brian Philpot went to England in August 1902. During 1902–1904 ties were established with the Edison Bell Consolidated Phonograph Co., Ltd., for the manufacture of celluloid cylinders in Britain. After May 1904, the Lambert Co., Ltd., manufactured cored celluloid cylinders in England.

The Chicago staff struggled to continue production without some of their key employees. They added concert-size Lamberts, five inches in diameter, to their product line. Concert Lamberts were produced in both pink and black colorations from 1903 (in the U.S.); they are today among the rarest of all cylinder types. The Lambert record catalog eventually comprised some 1,200 typical popular selections (1,000 standard-size and 125 concert-size titles are known). Repertoire included band music, songs by Len Spencer, Harry MacDonough, Edward Favor, William F. Hooley, Steve Porter, Billy Murray, Emilio de Gogorza, and other prominent vocalists of the day; plus renditions by the American Quartet, "Uncle Josh" numbers by Cal Stewart, and instrumental pieces by Vess Ossman, and various unidentified performers on wind, brass, mandolin, etc. A disproportionately large number of Yiddish records appeared in a two-inch series.

The Lambert Co. also pressed records for other firms, including language lessons for the International Phonographic Language Schools of Chicago and exercise records under the Keating Talking Machine label. Both were black

in color. There was also an obscure Lambert medical series.

A Lioret patent date of 30 Oct 1894 appears on Lambert IPLS cylinders. This patent was purchased by the Lambert Co. on 23 Feb 1904, as part of its defense against the Edison molding-related lawsuits.

The Lambert Co. filed for bankruptcy in the U.S. in January 1906. A major competitive factor had been the gold-molded cylinders introduced by both Edison and Columbia in 1902, which were more durable and better sounding than the previous brown wax records. The last Lambert records were distributed by Beach & Beach, but their technological descendants continued in the products of the **Indestructible Phonographic Record Co.** and the **U-S Phonograph Co.**

In the first 11 months of production, only about 75,000 Lambert cylinders were made. This was a very small output (compared, for example, to the *daily* capacity of 120,000 Edison gold-molded records, claimed by National Phonograph Co. in 1907). Their relative scarcity today—along with the unusual variety of colors employed—accounts for the particular interest in Lambert records exhibited by many modern cylinder collectors. [Andrews 1974/4 relates the story of the British firm; Koenigsberg 1980; Koenigsberg 1990; Manzo 1980.]

Bill Klinger

LAND. A term for the surface of a record between adjacent grooves.

LAND-O-PHONE CO., INC. A New York firm, located in 1906 at 288 Fifth Ave. It manufactured the Land-0–Phone home recorder for discs, selling at $10. Blank discs, 10 1/2 inches in diameter, cost $.25.

LANDOWSKA, WANDA, 1879–1959. Polish pianist and harpsichordist, born in Warsaw on 5 July 1879. She studied piano at the Warsaw Conservatory, then in Berlin. She toured Europe as a pianist, but shifted her interest to the harpsichord. In 1913 she gave a special course on that instrument at the Berlin Hochschule für Musik. Landowska achieved acclaim and made her American debut with the Philadelphia Orchestra in 1923. In 1925 she established a school and concert center near Paris for the study of early music. She fled Europe during World War II, and settled in the U.S. in 1941. Her home was in Lakeville, Connecticut, where she died on 16 Aug 1959.

Landowska's work was the single most important factor in reviving interest in the harpsichord after 200 years of neglect. She recorded the instrument on four Red Seal sides for Victor in 1924, including "Harmonious Blacksmith" by Handel and the "Turkish March" from the Mozart A Major Sonata (#1193). Her most important records were of the "Goldberg Variations" by J.S. Bach, made for Victor in 1945 (#1650), and the six-disc album of the *Well Tempered Clavier* issued in the 1950s (Victor #26–35005). [Lewis, J. 1979.]

LANG, EDDIE, 1902–1933. American jazz guitarist, born Salvatore Massaro in Philadelphia on 25 Oct 1902. He studied violin and guitar, then teamed with his schoolmate Joe Venuti in performances during the 1920s. He was with the Mound City Blue Blowers in 1924, and worked with many major artists. Lang became recognized as the premier jazz guitarist. During the 1920s he made an important series of discs with Venuti, and in the 1930s he accompanied Bing Crosby. He died in New York on 26 Mar 1933.

Lang's first solo records, with piano accompaniment, were made for Okeh on 1 Apr 1927: "Eddie's Twister" and "April Kisses" (Okeh #40807). After five more solo sessions for Okeh, he recorded with his orchestra (including at times Tommy Dorsey and Jimmy Dorsey) for various labels through 1932. Among the fine records that came from the Lang-Venuti partnership were "Stringing the Blues" (Columbia #914D; 1926) and "Doin' Things" with "Goin' Places" (Okeh #40825; 1927).

LANGUAGE INSTRUCTION RECORDS. The earliest recorded language instruction is credited to **Cortina Academy of Languages,** which issued Spanish lessons on Edison cylinders in 1889. As early as April 1891 *Phonogram* carried notices of language cylinders available at $30 from Columbia, 24 records in each set, for French, German, Italian, or Spanish. Richard S. Rosenthal was the instructor; he named

his system Meisterschaft. **International Correspondence Schools** used the Edison phonograph for language courses from 1901. Language Phone Records were advertised in *TMW*, issued by the Language Phone Method Co. of New York in November 1916. That company filed for dissolution in 1921.

In Britain, Pathé recorded courses for the Modern Language Press, until the Russell Hunting Record Co., Ltd., took over in 1906, when the name was changed to the Linguaphone Co., Ltd. (Its successors are still in business, as the Linguaphone Institute.) Another early course was made for the Bizeray School of Languages by G & T through its Zonophone label in 1905. The International Correspondence Schools cylinders were also available in Britain, made by the Edison Works in the U.S., and are still on the market.

Language lessons appeared in the Victor catalog of 1938, with sets in French, German, Italian, and Spanish. At the peak of the LP era in 1979 there were courses from Cortina, Conversa-phone, and other labels on disc or cassette for 40 languages. On CD the number of vendors and languages has increased further, with a new emphasis on English instruction for speakers of other tongues. [Andrews*.]

LASERDISC. A digital recording format for audio/video marketed in the 1980s by Philips, Pioneer, Sharp, Sony, Yamaha, and several other manufacturers. It presents a high fidelity video program with audio, permitting variable speed play and scan, still-frame, and random access search and display of individual segments. Up to 60 minutes of program time per side is available on some formats, with 30 minutes as standard. Repertoire offered by various labels in 1990 included complete operas, motion pictures with second track commentaries, the live concert given at the Berlin Wall by various pop stars, and Madonna's *Blond Ambition* world tour.

Lateral alignment. *See* GAP ALIGNMENT.

LATERAL RECORDING. The process—also known as lateral cut or needle cut—of cutting records in which the vibrations are represented by sidewise deflections in a groove of uniform depth. It was developed commercially by Emile Berliner and was accepted widely in the U.S. and Europe by 1900. The other system, vertical cut, or "hill-and-dale," was preferred by a few labels, such as Pathé and Edison, into the 1920s, but the industry had standardized on lateral recording by the beginning of the 1930s. Both lateral-cut and vertical-cut recordings were made in the Volta Laboratories in the early 1880s, as shown by the notes of Charles Sumner Tainter. However the lateral method is not mentioned specifically in the key U.S. patent of Tainter and Chichester Bell, #341,214 (filed 27 June 1885; granted 4 May 1886). Berliner's method was not strictly a cutting, as it was the old method of acid etching. Berliner could not use a true cutting process because of the wax-cutting Bell and Tainter patent.

LAUDER, HARRY, Sir, 1870–1950.

Scottish singer and comedian, born in Portobello, near Edinburgh, on 4 Aug 1870. After a wretched childhood of work in mills and coal mines, he took to the stage at age 12, and at 20 was performing in a touring company. He formed his own group in 1897, and was famous through Scotland and Northern England in a few years. At age 30 he performed in London, offering songs in a rich dialect, and became "the hottest property in the British theatre" (Baker). His fame was soon international. He was knighted in 1919. The stage was his life until his 75th year, when he retired. He died on 26 Feb 1950, in Strathaven, Scotland, where he had built "Lauder Hall."

Lauder's discography covers 1902–1940. His first records were for Gramophone and Typewriter in February 1902; he made nine 10-inch sides in that session, with a piano accompaniment possibly by Landon Ronald. "To Jericho" was the first number (#2–2657). In December 1903 Lauder again recorded for G & T, in four sessions, and he went on with the label until August 1905, some of the titles appearing on the Zonophone label. In June 1906 he recorded for Pathé discs, "We Parted on the Shore" (#60286), and 13 other songs. In August he was back with G & T, to 1908. Lauder made Edison two-minute cylinders in London in March–June and July–September 1908, and four-minute cylinders in 1909. He began with Victor in New York in December 1909, and though he did return from time to time to Edison, his principal affiliation remained with Victor and HMV (and Zonophone, its subsidiary).

He achieved such popularity that several labels copied his repertoire, using Peter Dawson as an excellent imitator under the name of Hector Grant. With Victor, Lauder moved from the cheap black label to the more prestigious purple label. Four Victors made on 18 Oct 1911 were among the most popular discs issued by the firm before electric recording: "The Picnic" (#70060), "Roamin' in the Gloaming" (#70061), "Just a Wee Deoch an' Doris" (#70062), and "Breakfast in Bed on Sunday Morn" (#70063). The 35 titles in the Victor 1917 catalog were embellished by a "glossary of Scotch words used by Mr. Lauder, also phrases which might not be understood by our customers." The same catalog copy identified Lauder as "the highest salaried entertainer in the world." He wrote many of his hit songs.

In the 1927 catalog Victor had moved the Lauder repertoire to the Red Seal label. He still had 10 titles in the 1940 Red Seal section. Lauder records were reissued on numerous LP labels, and there were also reissues on Victor 45 rpm. Among the LP albums are Camden's *The Immortal Harry Lauder* (#CAL-479), EMI's *Golden Age of Harry Lauder* (# GX-2505) and Pearl's *I Love a Lassie* (#GEMM-169). RCA included him in its *Great Personalities of Broadway* album in 1970. Conifer #CDHD-164 is the first compact disc collection, *Sir Harry Lauder "Roamin' in the Gloamin."*

Lauder was also a film star, with appearances in 37 motion pictures of varying lengths, from 1904 to 1936. [Baker 1990.]

LAURI-VOLPI, GIACOMO, 1892–1979.

Italian tenor, born in Lanuvio, near Rome, on 11 Dec 1892. He studied law and voice in Rome, and served at the front during World War I. Then he made his debut in Viterbo (1919) and sang in Florence and at La Scala. On 26 Jan 1923 he appeared at the Metropolitan Opera as the Duke, remaining with the Company until 1933. Subsequently he returned to Europe, and resided in Spain. He died in Valencia on 17 Mar 1979.

Lauri-Volpi sang the standard tenor repertoire, but gained special praise for his interpretation of Raoul in *Ugonotti* (*Huguenots*)—a role he recorded in 1955 in the complete opera set issued by Golden Age of Opera (#EJS 116; taken from a radio broadcast). His other outstanding role was in *Guglielmo Tell*; he recorded two arias for Cetra in the 1930s: "O muto asil del pianto" and "O Matilde" (#LPV 45017). His earliest discs were Fonotipias, made in Milan in 1920. Later he was with the Brunswick label in the U.S. (1932–1936), Victor (1928–1930), and HMV (1934 and the 1940s). An important recording for Victor was the Nile Scene from *Aida*, with Elisabeth Rethberg and Giuseppe De Luca (#8206; 1930). Lauri-Volpi sang in the complete *Luisa Miller* recording for Cetra (#1221; 1951), and in *Trovatore* for the same label (#1226; 1951). He took part in a complete *Boheme* in 1952. A compact disc reissue on Harmonia Mundi (#89012; 1990) offers material from 1928 to 1934. [Williams, C. 1957/11.]

LAWRENCE, MARJORIE, 1907–1979. Australian soprano, born in Dean's Marsh, Victoria, on 17 Feb 1907. She studied in Melbourne and Paris, and made her Metropolitan Opera debut as Brünnhilde in *Walküre* on 18 Dec 1935; she stayed with the Metropolitan until 1941. In that year she contracted poliomyelitis in Mexico, and was not able to walk. Despite this disadvantage, Lawrence returned to the stage in the following year, singing while seated. Her last stage role came in 1943, but she was heard thereafter on radio.

Many of her recordings are of concert songs, by Brahms, Grieg, Mahler, Rachmaninoff, and so on. Her finest operatic records are from *Salome*, in which she earned great praise on stage. She recorded four arias from the opera, in French, for HMV in 1933–1934 (reissued on Harmonia Mundi CD #89011 in 1990). The same arias were in the Victor catalog as well. [Hogarth 1987.]

LAYERING. The practice employed by disc jockeys of playing several songs simultaneously.

LAZARO, HIPOLITO, 1887–1974. Spanish tenor, born in Barcelona. He studied in Milan, sang in Barcelona, then in 1912 in London. In 1913 he was at La Scala, and in 1918 he made his debut as the Duke at the Metropolitan Opera, remaining for two years. Later he sang throughout Europe and appeared in South America. Lazaro retired in 1950, and died in Madrid on 14 May 1974.

Most of Lazaro's records are Columbias made in 1916–1920 and (imported from Spain) 1925. He did the standard tenor arias, but was most acclaimed for two numbers from *Puritani*: "Vieni fra queste braccia" (Columbia #46752) and "A te o cara" (Columbia #48783)—the latter with a spectacular high D-flat. [Richards 1964.]

LEACHMAN, SILAS F., 1859–1936. American singer and comedian, born 20 Aug 1859. Chiefly a comic performer, noted for "coon songs," he rendered standard and patriotic songs as well. He was in politics, described in an article in the March 1888 *Scientific American* as "a 24th ward politician [with] a voice ranging from bass to first tenor." His first records were for the Chicago Talking Machine Co. in the early 1890s, and he remained with that label until about 1900; he had over 100 titles in the 1899 catalog, selling at $.75, while other cylinders in the same catalog were going at $.50. He was also in the Columbia 1894–1895 catalog. Victor recorded him in around 1902–1904, presenting about 50 numbers, but Leachman's popularity faded quickly and he was not in later catalogs. He died on 28 Apr 1936 in Chicago. [Walsh 1955/7–8.]

LEADBELLY, 1885–1949. American blues and folk singer, born as Huddie Ledbetter in Mooringsport, Louisiana, on 21 Jan 1885. He began performing as a teenager, and played a 12-string guitar in Dallas, accompanying Blind Lemon Jefferson. He spent 1918–1925 in prison, and again in 1930–1933—Alan Lomax discovered him there and arranged for his parole. From 1935–1940 Leadbelly recorded for the Library of Congress. He was a great success in New York clubs and on college campuses. "Goodnight Irene" (Asch #343–2; 1943) and "Rock Island Line" (Playboy #119; 1949) were two of his own compositions and were among his hit commercial records. Other important discs were "Match Box Blues" with "If It Wasn't for Dicky" (Elek #301; 1935), "Honey I'm All Out and Down" (Melotone #3327; 1935), and—perhaps his finest disc—"Good Morning Blues" (Bluebird #8791; 1940). He died in New York on 6 Dec 1949. A motion picture about his life was made in 1975. A multi-volume set by Folkways, *Leadbelly's Last Sessions*, displays the diversity of his music.

LEADER. A short length of uncoated tape attached to the beginning of a an open-reel magnetic tape or cassette tape to facilitate winding the recording tape on the take-up reel.

LEAD-IN GROOVE. The plain unrecorded groove that is found at the edge of a disc record; it has the function of guiding the stylus to the beginning of the recorded groove.

LEAD-OUT GROOVE. The plain groove that follows the recorded groove on a disc record; it has the function of keeping the stylus silently in place on the revolving disc until the machine's operation is terminated by the user.

LEANER, ERNEST, 1922–1990. Founder of the United Record Distributorship, Chicago, said to be the first major Black record distributor in the U.S. Leaner distributed the early records of the Supremes, Smokey Robinson, Stevie Wonder, and others. He carried Motown, Stax, Soul, VIP, Sceptor, Wand, and Cotillion labels. He also had recording studios at 1827 S. Michigan Ave., named One-Derful, and Toddlin' Town. Later he opened a shop, and the Record World chain of stores.

LEEDS (label). A record issued sometime between 1904 and 1906 by the Talk-o-phone Co., of Toledo, Ohio. It was single-sided, offering a routine repertoire of popular songs and instrumental solos.

LEEDS & CATLIN. A New York record manufacturer, located at 53 E. 11th St., with a plant in Middleton, Connecticut. The firm pioneered in making cylinder records for home entertainment, then turned to discs. Imperial was its own label; the Concert Records label was produced from its masters. The firm also supplied pressings for the Imperial, Nassau, Leeds, Sun, Talk-o-Phone, and other labels. After lengthy litigation for patent violations, Leeds & Catlin was finally forced into bankruptcy in the summer of 1909. Edward F. Leeds was president until his death in August 1908. After 1909, matrices of the firm continued to appear in Britain, pressed and to be found on some Britannic, Burlington, Pelican, The Leader, and probably other labels. [Andrews*.]

LEGGE, WALTER, 1905–1979. Record industry executive, with the Gramophone Co. and later with EMI from 1927 to 1964. He began as a writer of HMV liner notes, and became one of the great record producers. One of his innovations, in 1931, was the concept of **society records**—material of specialized interest sold by subscription. From 1945 until his retirement in 1964 he supervised recordings for EMI. He was married to the soprano Elisabeth Schwarzkopf, who collected some of his writings and various articles about him into a book, *On and Off the Record: A Memoir of Walter Legge* (New York: Scribner, 1982). [Sanders 1984.]

LEHMANN, LILLI, 1848–1929. German soprano, born in Würzburg on 24 Nov 1848. She studied in Prague as a child and made her debut there in October 1865; she then sang elsewhere and at the Berlin Opera from 1870. In Bayreuth she was coached by Richard Wagner, and created the roles of Wöglinde, Helmwige, and the Forest Bird. Her Metropolitan Opera debut was as Carmen, on 25 Nov 1885; she sang with the Metropolitan until 1890, doing the Wagner repertoire and Italian roles with Jean and Edouard De Reszke. Lehmann performed 170 different roles, and also gained distinction as a Lieder singer. She died in Berlin on 16 May 1929.

In 1905 and 1907 Lehmann recorded in Berlin for Odeon, beginning with the traditional love song "Long Long Ago" (#50071). She made discs of Verdi, Wagner, Mozart, and a particularly effective "Casta diva" (#52698). Other notable records, frequently reissued, included "O hätt ich Jubals Harf'" from Handel's *Joshua*, and "O glückliche Land" from *Hugenotten* (*Huguenots*). IRCC released 12 of her Odeons, and many appeared in LP reissues by Belcantodisc (U.K.); Concerteum (France); Eterna, Famous Records of the Past, Scala, and Top Artists Platters (U.S.); and Rococo Records (Canada.) [Dennis 1981/2.]

LEHMANN, LOTTE, 1888–1976. German/ American soprano, born in Perleberg on 27 Feb 1888. She studied in Berlin, made her debut in Hamburg in 1910, and was quickly recognized as a Wagner interpreter. In 1916 she was engaged by the Vienna Opera, where she gained fame for her Marschallin. Her U.S. debut was in 1930 in Chicago, as Sieglinde, a role she took to her Metropolitan Opera debut on 11 Jan 1934. American audiences also appreciated greatly her fine Lieder recitals. In 1945 she became a U.S. citizen; she settled in California, and died in Santa Barbara on 26 Aug 1976.

Lehmann's earliest recordings were on two vertical-cut sides for Pathé in 1914. She made a few Polydor and Odeon discs in 1927–1936, most notably the *Tosca* duet "Mario! Mario! Perchè chiuso?" sung with Jan Kiepura (Odeon #0–8743), one of the very few records she sang in Italian. EMI-Electrola #1C 30–704/5M is an LP album, *The Art of Lotte Lehmann*, issued in 1978; it spans her recording career of 1916–1932, primarily in opera. A CD *Song Recital* (RCA #GD 87809; 1990) offers Lieder from 1936 to 1950. [Jefferson 1988.]

LEIDER, FRIDA, 1888–1975. German soprano, born in Berlin on 18 Apr 1888. She studied in Berlin, and made a debut in Halle in 1915 as Venus. From 1923–1940 she was with the Berlin State Opera, and sang also in other major European houses. Her American debut was in Chicago as Brünnhilde in *Walküre*. At the Metropolitan Opera, 16 Jan 1933, she was heard as Isolde, a role that became associated with her. In 1934 she returned to Germany, and remained there despite problems with the Nazis. She died in Berlin on 3 June 1975.

Leider's recordings for Polydor in Berlin (1923–1926) included many notable items, such as the "Du bist der Lenz" duet with Lauritz Melchior (#72934). Her finest work was for HMV in 1927–1931, records made in London and Berlin. *Tristan* excerpts, including the love duet with Melchior (#D1723–24; 1929), "Ich sah das Kind" from *Parsifal* (#DB1545; 1932), and

"Or sai chi l'onore" from *Don Giovanni* with "Ah! si la liberté" from *Armide* (#D1547; 1929). The HMV material was reissued on CD #89004 in 1990. [Burros 1946.]

LEINSDORF, ERICH, 1912– . Austrian/ American conductor, born Erich Landauer in Vienna on 4 Feb 1912. He studied piano and cello, then made a conducting debut in Vienna in 1933. He secured the post of assistant to Bruno Walter and Arturo Toscanini at the Salzburg Festivals, and in 1937 was conducting at the Metropolitan Opera. He settled in the U.S., and became a citizen in 1942. Military service in 1943–1944 interrupted his new appointment to the directorship of the Cleveland Orchestra in 1943; he resumed work in Cleveland in 1945. He directed the Rochester Philharmonic Orchestra from 1947 to 1955, then the Boston Symphony Orchestra from 1962 to 1969. In 1977–1980 he was principal conductor of the (West) Berlin Radio Symphony Orchestra.

Leinsdorf has recorded extensively, having done all the major symphonies and about 20 complete operas. He has performed with the major world orchestras, and on many labels. He has won eight Grammys, five for operatic recordings (awarded in 1959 for *Nozze di Figaro*, in 1960 for *Turandot*, in 1963 for *Madama Butterfly*, in 1968 for *Così fan tutte*, and in 1971 for *Aida*) and three for orchestral records (in 1963 for the Bartók *Concerto for Orchestra*, in 1964 for the Mahler Fifth Symphony, and in 1966 for the Mahler Sixth Symphony).

LE MAIRE, PETE. American yodeler, whose name is also seen as Le Mar, La Mar, and Le Maur. He recorded for the United States Phonograph Co. of New Jersey and the Chicago Talking Machine Co. in the mid-1890s, and later made three titles for Columbia (in their 1897–1898 catalog). He was heard on U.S. and U.K. Zonophone also, and on Victor from 1901 to 1905. [Brooks 1979.]

LEMNITZ, TIANA, 1897– . German soprano, born in Metz on 26 Oct 1897. She sang with small companies until 1929, when she joined the Hanover Opera and remained to 1934. Then she was engaged by the Berlin State Opera, 1934–1957; she retired in 1957. Lemnitz sang across the repertoires, including Russian operas in Russian. She was heard in London and Buenos Aires. Her first records were for Polydor in 1934, beginning with "Wie nahte . . . leise, leise" from *Freischütz* (#15081)—one of her famous roles—and including two *Lohengrin* arias (#35081). From *Otello*, another of her fine showpieces, she sang four numbers for Electrola (HMV) in Germany (who recorded her in 1937–1948). Although sung in German, they represent her voice at its delicate best: the love duet (with Torsten Ralf) and the "Ave Maria." World Records issued a three-record LP album in 1978 that included the above-mentioned music (#SHB 47). A CD from Harmonia Mundi (#89025; 1990) included the *Otello* numbers, plus a splendid "Dich, teure Halle" from *Tannhäuser* and other material made for HMV in 1938–1939. [Seeliger 1963.]

LENOX (label). A rare American record issued briefly in the 1920s, perhaps affiliated with the Plaza Music Co. group of labels. Dance music and popular vocals were featured. [Rust 1978.]

LEVAPHONE (label). A British record issued in 1926 by **Levy's**, in London. It appeared in a pale lilac color, and also—for three items made from U.S. Vocalion matrices—a black label. Cliff Edwards was one of its better known artists. [Rust 1978.]

LEVEL. The intensity of output from an audio system, referring either to the signal or to noise; it is technically measured in decibels against a standard reference level (zero level) that is equivalent to a power of one milliwatt in a resistance of 600 ohms.

LEVINE, JAMES, 1943–. American conductor and pianist, born in Cincinnati, Ohio, on 23 June 1943. At age 10 he performed a concerto with the Cincinnati Symphony Orchestra, then studied piano with Rudolf Serkin. He graduated from the Juilliard School of Music in 1964, and served as assistant conductor of the Cleveland Orchestra in 1965–1970. Then he went to the Metropolitan Opera, as principal conductor in 1973–1974, and as music director from 1975. Levine has also conducted in Salzburg and Bayreuth, and is director of the Ravinia Festival, summer home of the Chicago Symphony Orchestra.

Levine's early recordings were primarily orchestral—with the Chicago, Philadelphia, and Vienna orchestras—rather than operatic. Among his finest discs are the Beethoven piano concertos, with Alfred Brendel soloist and the Chicago Symphony (Philips CD#412 787/788 and 411189; 1983–1985). Levine received a Grammy in 1983 for his conducting of the Chicago Symphony in the Mahler Seventh Symphony, and another for his *Carmina Burana* with the Chicago Symphony in 1986.

In the 1980s his important series of complete operas with the Metropolitan Opera began to appear on CD. (They are noted in the Metropolitan Opera entry.) The recording of *Walküre* won a Grammy in 1990.

LEVY, JULES, 1838–1903. British cornetist, born in London on 28 Apr 1838. He was the "most celebrated concert cornetist in history, playing for huge crowds and fantastic sums of money" (Brooks). He transferred to the U.S. in 1866. Levy is said to have made the first musical recording, when he performed "Yankee Doodle" at a public demonstration of the phonograph in New York, sometime in 1878. In the 1890s Levy made cylinder records for several companies: New England Phonograph Co. (1893), New York Phonograph Co. (ca. 1893), and Columbia (1895; he remained in the Columbia catalog to 1912). "Blue Bells of Scotland" and "My Country 'Tis of Thee" were among his Columbias, described as "played in four octaves"; he made 11 more, but none have survived. He made discs for Victor and Columbia from 1903. In the Victor catalog of 1917 he is listed with "Merry Birds—Solo with Variations" (#31176; 1904), the only Levy item in that catalog, retained "as a memorial of this great cornetist who died in 1905 [*sic*] although it is not up to our current standard of recording." Victor kept the memorial disc in print through 1919. Levy did two of the 14-inch records introduced by Victor in 1903. He died in Chicago on 28 Nov 1903. [Brooks 1979.]

LEVY'S. A jazz record shop, the first of its kind in Britain; located at 19–20 High St.,

Whitechapel, London. Advertisements announced that the establishment date was 1890. From ca. 1927, Levy's issued American import material from Vocalion and other U.S. labels. The firm also had its own labels for a time, the **Levaphone** (1926) and the **Oriole** (1927; 1931–1935).

LEWIS, EDWARD ROBERT, *Sir*, **1900–1980.** British recording industry executive. He attended Rugby and Trinity College, Cambridge. In 1929 he founded the **Decca Record Co., Ltd.**, in London, acquiring the Decca Gramophone Co., Ltd. (formerly Barnett Samuel and Sons). Entering the market in difficult times, Lewis acquired rights to American labels, made other foreign deals, and undersold his competitors. In 1934 Lewis organized the American counterpart firm, **Decca Record Co.**, and brought Jack Kapp from Brunswick to manage it. The subsequent history of the two Decca firms is told in the articles under their names. Lewis was knighted in 1960.

LHÉVINNE, JOSEF, 1874–1944. Russian pianist, born in Orel on 13 Dec 1874. He studied at the Moscow Conservatory, and even before graduating (1891) he performed the Emperor Concerto in concert, under Anton Rubinstein. He toured widely, and made his American debut in New York in 1906. In addition to concertizing, he and his wife Rosina established a teaching practice in New York. He died there on 2 Dec 1944.

Lhévinne was renowned for his virtuostic playing of the romantics, especially Chopin and Tchaikovsky. His performance of the Chopin B-Minor Etude, opus 25–10, was cited by Josef Hofmann as "the most colossal octave playing I have ever heard." Modern criticism has tended to agree with contemporary views of Lhévinne's masterful technique and sensitivity.

His first recordings were for Pathé in the U.S. in 1921. After that he worked only for Victor, producing a very small legacy: one item in 1928 and one in 1939, the others (including the Chopin piece mentioned by Hofmann) in 1935–1936. All his records have been reissued on one CD from Novello/BMG (#NVL CD902; 1989).

LIBERTY MUSIC SHOP. A New York record emporium, opened in January 1927. The shop began to issue records around 1933, featuring Broadway musicals, with some jazz and sophisticated vocal or dance material. About 214 78 rpm records were released under the Liberty Music Shop label, plus 10 LP reissues, through the late 1940s. Studio facilities were provided by Columbia and American Record Corp. The Shop had three locations in 1933: 10 E. 59th St., 795 Madison Ave., and 450 Madison Ave. Among the artists to appear on the label were Ethel Waters, Beatrice Lillie, Ethel Merman, Lee Wiley, Cy Walter, and Gracie Fields. [Raymond 1981 is a complete label list.]

LIBERTY PHONOGRAPH CO. A Cleveland firm, located at 1836 Euclid Ave. It first advertised discs with the Liberty Record label in February 1919. In March 1920 the company was renamed **Arrow Phonograph Co.**, and the name of the record label became Arrow. Laboratories were at 16–18 W. 39th St., New York. Both labels were announced to be "lateral" but not "lateral cut." The process, invented by F.W. Matthews, called for a ridge to be the recorded section of the master, with the recording done with a forked head instead of a cutting straight edge. Apparently these were the only discs made by that process. [Andrews*.]

LIBRARY OF CONGRESS. One of the three federally supported "national" libraries of the U.S., established in 1800. The Library's activities in the area of recorded sound began in the 1920s, as Carl Engel became chief of the Music Division. When his tenure commenced in 1922, the Library had but one recording, a cylinder made in 1904 of Kaiser Wilhelm II, received by donation. Since recordings were not at that time received by the U.S. Copyright Office (a unit within the Library of Congress), Engel made informal arrangements with the Victor Talking Machine Co. for donated copies of selected discs. Subsequently other labels began to supply the Library with much of their recorded output. These deposits are now required under copyright law.

In 1928 the Archive of Folk-Song was established, and became a principal focus of recordings (*see* AMERICAN FOLKLIFE

CENTER, the name taken in 1981). The principal resource for research is the Motion Picture, Broadcasting and Recorded Sound Division; it holds about 1.5 million recordings in all formats, including some 200,000 78 rpm discs. Access to these recorded materials for study—and to discographies and other reference books—is through the Recorded Sound Reference Center. One reference tool of particular interest is the **Rigler-Deutsch Index**, the major access guide to 78 rpm discs.

Two books are of special value to anyone who wishes to make use of the Library's holdings: *Special Collections in the Library of Congress: A Selective Guide* (Library of Congress, 1980) and *Scholar's Guide to Washington, D.C., Audio Resources*, by James R. Heintze (Smithsonian Institution Press, 1985). [Smart 1983.]

LIEBERSON, GODDARD, 1911–1977. British/American composer and record industry executive, born in Hanley, Staffordshire, England, on 5 Apr 1911. In 1915 the family moved to Seattle, Washington, and subsequently Lieberson graduated from the University of Washington. Then he studied at the Eastman School of Music, and wrote music criticism in Rochester. Lieberson moved to New York to work for the League of Composers, and founded the American Composer's Alliance. In 1939 he gained the post of assistant to the director of the Masterworks Division of Columbia Records, and three years later he was director. He quickly initiated pioneering projects during a time of economic turmoil for the label. Arnold Schoenberg's *Pierrot Lunaire* was one of his productions, and in 1940 he made recordings of Igor Stravinsky's music. In 1946 he became vice president of Columbia Records.

Lieberson also took up opera, making the first complete recording at the Metropolitan Opera House, *Hansel und Gretel* (1947). He succeeded with dramatic recordings, doing complete versions of several major plays, including *Who's Afraid of Virginia Woolf* by Edward Albee, for which he won the Grammy Award in 1963.

The new Columbia LP record of 1948 gave Lieberson the opportunity to expand the musical horizon of his firm, and of the American public; he gambled successfully on the public's

willingness to accept esoteric offerings by Charles Ives, Leonard Bernstein, Alban Berg, and other moderns. But his finest triumphs were made with cast recordings of Broadway musicals, beginning with *South Pacific* in 1949, and going on to the great hits *Camelot, My Fair Lady* (sales reported at more than six million copies), and *West Side Story*. He also established the profitable Columbia Record Club. In 1956 he became president of Columbia, and vice president of CBS, Inc. He became senior vice president of CBS in 1971, but returned to head Columbia Records in 1973 to replace Clive Davis—fired for improper handling of funds—and put the house in order. He retired in 1975; and died on 29 May 1977, in New York.

LIGHTOPHONE. A device invented by Arthur C. Ferguson for reproducing sound, accorded U.S. patent #595,053 (filed 17 Apr 1897, granted 7 Dec 1897). A diaphragm-controlled shutter varied a tiny light beam directed along a spiral path directed to a seven-inch glass plate coated with photographic emulsion. The plate was developed and transferred by photo engraving to a metal plate, etching a groove that was usable for reproducing sound with a gramophone-type player. Although Ferguson did not exploit the invention, the principle was taken up later for sound film.

LIMELIGHTERS. American folk singing group, formed in 1959. The members were Glenn Yarbrough, singer and guitarist; Alex Hassilev, singer; and Lou Gottlieb, bassist. They were successful with modernized folk material and topical songs. *Tonight in Person* was their first successful album (RCA #LPM 2272; 1961), charted for 40 weeks. Later in 1961 they made *The Slightly Fabulous Limelighters* (RCA #LPM 2393), which had 22 chart weeks. There were six other hit albums before the group broke up in the mid-1960s.

LIMITER. A circuit used in tuners and amplifiers to control the volume during signal peaks; it prevents overloading that would be caused by unwanted overmodulation.

LINCOLN (label). A record issued by the Lincoln Record Corp., New York, from 1924 to

1930, as a low-cost ($.50 per record) subsidiary of the **Cameo** label. Cameo material was used, with the real names of the artists suppressed. [Rust 1978.]

LINDSTRÖM (CARL) GmbH. A German firm established 1 Feb 1904, with Max Strauss as managing director. It was reorganized as Carl Lindström AG in June 1908, and joined with Beka Records AG in August 1910. In July 1911 the U.K. firm Fonotipia, Ltd., was acquired. At that point Lindström controlled these labels: Beka Grand, Beka Meister, Fonotipia, Jumbo, Odeon, and Parlophon; the firm had become a major competitor to the Gramophone Co. on the European market. Carl Lindström (London), Ltd., was formed on 26 Mar 1913. With the onset of World War I, the firm's fortunes were reversed. This British company, and Fonotipia, Ltd., were sold at public auction and acquired by the Hertford Record Co., Ltd., under restrictions established by His Majesty's government. Hertford was controlled by three staff members of the Columbia Graphophone Co., Ltd.; after the war Columbia acquired Hertford and all its assets.

Lindström's factories in France, Spain, Argentina, Chile, Italy, Switzerland, and Brazil were taken over by the Transoceanic Trading Co. (Netherlands) in 1920; that firm established Parlophone Co., Ltd., in London on 30 Aug 1923, and Parlophone passed to the control of the Columbia Graphophone Co., Ltd. in 1925. The name of Carl Lindström (London), Ltd., having done no business since its acquisition by the Hertford Record Co., Ltd., was finally struck from the register on 10 Dec 1927. Carl Lindström AG—changed again to Carl Lindström GmbH on 14 Oct 1969—was ultimately to combine with Electrola GmbH on 30 Mar 1972 to become the EMI Electrola GmbH. The important Odeon label had been produced constantly throughout the inter-war period. A label named Lindström American Record was recorded in the U.S. and pressed in Germany, sometime after the 1918 Armistice.

In America the General Phonograph Corp. of New York, established by Otto Heinemann in 1915 (owner of the Okeh and Odeon labels), was the Lindström affiliate, or had a contractual arrangement with Lindström. General's

Okeh label (1918) issued material from Fonotipia, Parlophon and Odeon. [Andrews*; Dearling 1984; Rust 1980.]

LINEAR PREDICTOR. A device that allows modification of one characteristic of speech sounds (e.g., pitch change) without altering other characteristics (e.g., duration). In terms of a recording, it permits playback at various speeds without changing pitch, or a shift in pitch without change of turntable or tape velocity.

LINK PIANO CO. A firm established in Binghamton, New York, by Edwin A. Link, Sr. in 1912, as successor to a bankrupt manufacturer of player pianos—the Binghamton Automatic Music Co.—that he had purchased two years earlier. Link's new company made player pianos and nickelodeons, and with considerable success; the Link Player Piano became one of the best known instruments in southern New York and Pennsylvania. Coin-operated pianos were a popular product. The firm also made pipe organs for movie palaces, mausoleums, and private homes, as far away as California. Link's son, Edwin A. Link, Jr., utilized his knowledge of the automatic piano's pneumatic mechanism as the foundation for his invention of the Link flight trainer.

LINOPHONE. The name given to a phonograph cylinder that was used as a dictation device to cue linotype operators; described in *TMW* 15 Oct 1907. It was in use at the London plant of a magazine named *Automobile Owner*.

LIN-O-TONE. A one-piece horn with no seams and no joints. It was advertised in May 1909 as usable on the Fireside model and other cylinder record players.

LIORET, HENRI JULES, 1848–1938. French clockmaker and manufacturer, born in Moret-sur-Loing on 26 June 1848. His clocks won the bronze medal at the 1878 Paris Exposition, where Thomas Edison had his exhibit; it is possible that Lioret became interested at that time in sound recording. He gained several important patents in the field: French brevet d'invention #230,177 (18 May 1893, with additions of 28 Nov 1893—covering the celluloid cylinder—and 5 Sep 1894), British patent #23,366 (1893), and U.S. patent #528,273 (filed 20 Dec 1893, granted 30 Oct 1894). He made a talking doll in 1893 for the Emile Jumeau doll manufacturer of Paris, sold successfully at 38 francs under the name of Bébé Jumeau. Having seen the Edison doll, Lioret improved on its weak points: the Edison cylinder could not be changed and it was too fragile. The Lioret doll operated with a spring mechanism and had unbreakable, interchangeable celluloid cylinders. In 1898 he used the mechanism in a talking clock. Visitors to Lioret's workshop at 18 rue Thibaud were greeted by a talking mechanical doorman. There was also a talking kiosk, developed by Lioret for advertising Chocolat Menier. His Lioretgraph No. 3 was a large weight-driven phonograph with oversized horn; he actually leased the Trocadéro auditorium in 1897 and brought in a substantial audience (to judge from a contemporary drawing) to admire it.

Lioret cylinders were duplicated by a complicated electroplating molding method. By 1900 he was able to produce a four-minute unbreakable record about 3 1/4 inches long, playable at 100 rpm on a phonograph—Lioret made these also, some weight-driven, with the tradename Lioretograph. He also made nonmolded brown wax cylinders, and vertical-cut discs. The Lambert Co. of Chicago purchased a Lioret patent and used it in defense against litigation brought by Edison over the molding process. Lioret was in business until 1911. He also collaborated with Léon Gaumont and others in motion picture work, and then turned to landscape painting. He died in Paris on 19 May 1938. [Koenigsberg 1990; Marty 1979 is a well illustrated account; *TMR* 56–57 (Feb.-April 1979), p. 1453, shows a phonograph and cylinders.]

LIPPINCOTT, JESSE H., 1842?–1894.

American recording industry executive. He apparently became interested in the audio business in 1887, when an associate, Thomas R. Lombard, was heading a syndicate that was negotiating with American Graphophone Co. to purchase sales rights for the graphophone. Lippincott, connected with a firm named American Electric Motor Co., was looking for a new industry for personal investment. By February 1888 it was he who led the negotiations with American Graphophone, and when a contract was signed on 29 Mar 1888 it was he who put up $200,000 for the sales rights. Lippincott then went after the other industry giant, Thomas Edison. For some $500,000 Lippincott purchased the stock of the Edison Phonograph Co. On 28 June 1888; he thereby gained control over the major phonograph interests in the U.S., and set up a new firm to engage in the rental of machines for business use: this was the American Phonograph Co., soon renamed the **North American Phonograph Co.** Lippincott's total investment in the new industry he wanted to control was about $1,329,000, including $250,000 he had paid to buy the Gilliland Sales Co. from Ezra Gilliland and John C. Tomlinson.

North American sold territorial rights to 33 companies for the rental of Edison phonographs and "phonograph-graphophones" and the sale of supplies. Lippincott was, however, the personal licensee of the American Graphophone Co. He contracted to purchase 5,000 graphophones per year. His agreement with that firm also required him to pay it a royalty on all machines and supplies. He soon ran into financial difficulty, one reason being the slow production and shipment of machines from the plant of American Graphophone and the Edison Phonograph Works. Another problem was the tendency of the machines to break down easily and few trained technicians available to do repairs. But basically there was just not much interest in the business offices of America in exchanging live stenographers for dubious gadgets. Common concerns of the North American affiliated companies were aired at the first convention of the local companies, as they formed the National Phonograph Association, in Chicago in 1890. In the fall of 1890 Lippincott, unable to meet his obligation to purchase 5,000 graphophones per year in the context of weak sales and rentals, declined in health. He was stricken with paralysis, and gave up control of North American to Edison, its principal stockholder and creditor, before dying in 1894.

Within two years the use of the phonograph for business purposes had yielded priority to the new idea of entertainment, or as North American expressed it in the November 1892 *Phonogram*, "for social purposes." Lippincott, had he lived, would have seen his dream come to nothing, or nothing in the direction he expected it to follow. [Koenigsberg 1987; Proceedings 1974.]

LITERARY RECORDINGS. Literary recordings include poetry, prose stories, and plays. (For the purposes of this article, speeches and comic monologs are not included.) The earliest recordings of literature were not meant for publication. Edwin Booth made two cylinders in March 1890, in Chicago. Those recordings of a speech from *Hamlet* and of Othello's speech to the senate were made for his daughter, Edwina. More than 40 years passed before those cylinders were duplicated on a 78 rpm record for mass distribution. Henry Irving recorded two passages from Shakespeare, the opening soliloquy from *Richard III* and Wolsey's long speech to Cromwell at the end of Act II of *Henry VIII*, at the home of Henry M. Stanley, the British explorer, for the entertainment of the Stanleys and their friends. The cylinders were not discovered and made available to a wider audience until over 60 years later (Gryphon #GR 900).

In 1899 Berliner became the first company to release a recording of an important Shakespearean performer, Ada Rehan. The sound quality of surviving examples is very poor, even on the re-recorded versions produced by the International Record Collector's Club in 1939 (IRCC #5000), but they still provide us an opportunity to hear the voice of an actress from the nineteenth century. The record is interesting as the first recording of a passage from *The Taming of the Shrew*, and also because it includes a passage from *The Country Girl* by William Wycherly, a Restoration playwright whose works were excluded from college textbooks until the second half of this century because they were considered excessively bawdy.

The last important examples of early literary recording are the five recordings made by Ellen Terry for Victor in 1911. That studio time was set aside for this important actress would suggest a carefully prepared set of recordings. However, the selections seem quite impulsively chosen and carelessly executed. Nevertheless, her recording of Portia's mercy speech reveals why she gained fame in that role (Victor #64194). The earliest examples of excerpts prepared for public distribution were probably produced by Columbia. As early as 1893 Columbia had coin-operated machines in Washington, D.C., with a recording by an imitator of Edwin Booth doing Othello's speech to the senate. Unfortunately, no example of the Columbia recording is known to exist. The first surviving recording of a carefully prepared extract was made in 1902 for G & T by Tyrone Power, Sr. His two recordings of passages from *Merchant of Venice* provide an impressive indication of the style of one of the most important actors of the turn of the century (Columbia #GC 1229/30). Frank Burbeck, an actor who never gained great fame but who had a long and honorable career, made five recordings of passages from Shakespeare. Among the other players who recorded carefully selected and prepared excerpts are Herbert Beerbohm-Tree, Ben Greet, Joseph Jefferson, and Henry Ainley. Special attention must be given to E.H. Sothern and Julia Marlowe, who produced 11 recordings for Victor in 1920 and 1921. Their carefully made recordings are among the first to use crowd noises and background music. Marlowe's performance of Juliet set the interpretation of that part for many decades, making the two sides given to the balcony scene of historical importance. Sothern's ponderous style is especially evident in his recordings of Antony's orations over the body of Caesar and his recording of Hamlet's soliloquy. Particularly noticeable is Sothern's use of the actor's tremolo, the vocal quavering that is used to suggest importance and dignity. The couple is shown to much better advantage in a scene between the Duke and Viola from *Twelfth Night* (Victor #74707; 1921).

Perhaps no Shakespearean actor has gained such fame on the basis of so few performances as John Barrymore. His 1920 production of *Richard III* and his 1922 production of *Hamlet* constituted his entire career on the Shakespearean stage. His readings of a soliloquy from *Hamlet* and a speech by Richard, Duke of Gloucester, from Act III of *Henry VI, Pt. 3* were later issued by Victor (#6827). In 1937 he starred in a series of 90 minute radio productions of Shakespearean plays. The recordings subsequently issued by Audio-Rarities of those performances are air checks that provide abundant evidence of Barrymore's carelessness in regard to meter but also his amazing vocal flexibility and ability to enter into a role. The recording of his *Twelfth Night*, in which he plays a number of voices, is exceptional (Audio Rarities #LPA 2280/1). Barrymore used the actor's tremolo only with characters who are pretentious and contemptible. After Barrymore's first performances the serious use of the tremolo rapidly died out.

In the early 1930s F.C. Packard, a professor of English at Harvard University, met the son of Edwin Booth and learned of the two cylinders in the possession of Edwina Booth. After her death in 1936 he gained permission to duplicate the recording of the speech from *Othello*. Perhaps Packard's recognition of the value of this important recording led him to set about issuing recordings of poets reading their own works and of noted readers interpreting the poems of the past. The Harvard-Vocarium recordings resulted, a mine of our poetic heritage, containing the first recordings of W.H. Auden (#1272/3), T.S. Eliot (#P1206/7), and many others. The series was the model for others issued by Yale University, Stanford University, the Library of Congress, and Caedmon.

Four other sets of excerpts from the 1930s deserve special mention. The Otis Skinner and Cornelia Otis Skinner recordings from early in that decade are particularly valuable (Victor #17762/4, 1811/3; reissued on Camden #CAL-190). The lecture demonstration by Johnston Forbes-Robertson for the International Educational Society series shows the work of a modern master of the pause of suspension. Linguaphone issued what seems to be the first album of readings of poetry, *Shakespearean Records* (#EEG.28E/38E), initiating the recording career of John Gielgud, who has recorded literature over a longer period of time than any other performer. Columbia issued two albums entitled *The Voice of Poetry*, one with Gielgud

(#M-419), the other with Edith Evans. About the same time as these albums were produced, five other recordings were released by an actor-director whose impact upon recordings of literature is unequaled by any other performer. Orson Welles, still in his early twenties, was catapulted to fame by his "anti-fascist" *Julius Caesar* produced at the Mercury Theatre. In 1938 he memorialized that production in a five-record set (Columbia #325). It was not a re-creation of the stage production. The performers were assigned different parts from those they had on the stage, and the play was greatly condensed. A piece of speech in one act was combined with a line from another act and another part; the entire murder scene from "The ides of March have come" to "Et tu Brute" lasted only 15 seconds. This was the first recording of a complete play in condensed form; it treated the recorded play as a new art form. After the production of this record and the shock of the radio production of *The War of the Worlds*, Welles was contacted by his prep school drama teacher, Roger Hill, who proposed to Welles the recording of each of the *Twelfth Night, Merchant of Venice, Julius Caesar.* and *Macbeth,* The four recordings were the first of full-length plays. They lacked the brilliance of Welles' short *Julius Caesar*, but they established the commercial viability of recording complete works. Of these four plays only the recording of *Julius Caesar* (Columbia album #C-10), was been reissued on LP (Entre #EL-53).

The extent of the challenge the Mercury Theatre recordings presented to the record industry was indicated a few years later when Victor issued *Macbeth* as a "Recordrama" (album #M 878). Stating that "it is neither practical nor necessarily desirable to record plays in their entirety," Victor separated the record sleeves with sheets containing photographs of scenes from the stage production and summaries of the events of play. The performances of Maurice Evans and Judith Anderson are impressive, but the first Recordrama was not followed by a second. Indeed, a year after Victor issued Macbeth, Columbia brought out *Othello* in three albums totaling 34 sides (#MM 554). The complete play had won the day; of course the performances of Paul Robeson, Jose

Ferrer, and Uta Hagen had something to do with the popularity of the set.

Early recordings of poetry included "Hiawatha" read by Harry Macdonough on a Lambert cylinder, and readings of Longfellow's "Paul Revere's Ride" and Thomas Buchanan Read's "The Rising of '76" by William Sterling Battis on a 12-inch Victor disc. More timebound—and therefore, in some ways, even more interesting—are Robert Hillyard's recordings of Sims' "Christmas Day in the Work-house," his recording of "The Littlest Girl" (drawn from Richard Harding Davis' story "Her First Appearance"), and Hillyard's own "A Fool There Was." These monologs are the sentimental ancestors of the more ironic and even satiric monodramas that made Ruth Draper an important figure in theatre and which are preserved on *The Art of Ruth Draper*, an album first issued by RCA Victor in 1954 (#LM-1895) and then on five LP's by Spoken Arts. Edgar Davenport's reading of Deprez' "Laska" was issued both on an Edison cylinder (#9087; 1905) and on several disc labels. It is an excellent example of the sentimental narrative poem, a genre which became identified with Edgar Guest. Guest, who gained fame writing verse for newspapers, issued a number of recordings on the Victor label. "The Old Wooden Tub" (#45360–B), and "The Boy and the Flag" (#45341–B), are among the best. Mention should also be made of Robert Service, who gained fame as a story teller in verse and who made only one record. However, a number of others, including the country singer Hank Snow, made recordings of his poems. Larry Allan Beck, who called himself the Bard of Alaska, demonstrated the vitality of the narrative verse tradition in the 1960s by issuing two vanity LPs of readings of Service and *Alaska, My Alaska*, collecting his readings of his own verse (Bard of Alaska #AMA-001-4).

The appeal of the introspective lyric is documented in the recording of poetry as well as books of verse. Perhaps the most significant readings—if not the best poetry—are excerpts from Walter Benton's *This Is My Beloved* (1943). Recordings were issued in an album of three 78 rpm records by Atlantic (#312), a company known primarily for jazz recordings. The reader was John Dall. This recording was reissued on

LP as Clarion #612. Another version was later produced with Alfred Ryder as the reader. In 1962 Laurence Harvey read a new version with background music by Herbie Mann; this was issued as Atlantic #1367. Then the singer Arthur Prysock did a reading with background music by Mort Garson, which was issued by MGM as Verve #V6–5070. After mid-century many records were produced that provided readings of poems focused on the intimate details of the experience of love, nearly always from the male point of view and nearly always heterosexual. *For Colored Girls Who Have Considered Suicide When the Rainbow is Enuf* by Ntozake Shange, recitations of introspective verse about the lives of women, was highly successful on the Broadway stage, and an effective recording was issued in 1976 (Buddah #DDS 95007–OC).

Until the 1950s spoken word recordings were produced by the same companies that were issuing records of dance music and opera. Decca issued a number of recordings by Carl Sandburg as well as *Medea* with Judith Anderson (#DAU 12; 1948) and *Death of a Salesman* with Thomas Mitchell (#DAU 774; 1950). Columbia issued a reading from Stephen Vincent Benet's *The Murder of Lidice* (#M536; 1942), and Victor issued *Dorothy Parker—Selected Poems and Prose* read by Ilka Chase (#M971). The major labels continued to produce literary recordings after the development of the LP. One of the most popular recordings was by the First Drama Quartette (Charles Boyer, Charles Laughton, Cedric Hardwicke, and Agnes Moorehead) doing *Don Juan in Hell*, a portion of George Bernard Shaw's *Man and Superman*. Even Atlantic, which rarely strayed from jazz, announced The Living Shakespeare Series and issued Margaret Webster's production of *Romeo and Juliet* with Eva Le Gallienne, Dennis King, and Richard Waring (Atlantic #401; 1951). However, spoken word recordings have increasingly became the province of specialized producers, such as Spoken Arts, **Argo**, and **Caedmon**. Argo's *Great Actors of the Past* (#SW 510), issued in 1977, provided access to the recordings of Edwin Booth, Henry Irving, Ellen Terry, Herbert Beerbohm-Tree, Constant Coquelin, and others; it includes what may be the most powerful reading ever recorded, Sarah Bernhardt doing Phedre's speech in which she acknowledges her incestuous love. Caedmon's creation of the Theatre Recording Society has resulted in an extraordinary collection of recordings, including classical plays of Sophocles and Aristophanes and contemporary plays. Also issued by Caedmon, the Shakespeare Recording Society's productions constitute one of the two great collections of Shakespeare's works. This collection should be compared to Works of Shakespeare performed by The Marlowe Dramatic Society and professional players, a series issued first by London and then by Argo. These two massive sets should put to rest questions regarding the desirability of issuing recordings of complete works, but that does not mean there is no place for abridgments. Two sets of abridgments of Shakespeare's plays deserve mention. For the series produced by Spoken Arts, three groups of players were used: the Swan Theatre Players directed by John Blatchley, the players of the Dublin Gate Theatre directed by Hinton Edwards, and a group called the Folio Theatre Players directed by Christopher Casson. For these recordings, the duration of each play was reduced to 50 minutes by shortening the scenes in such a way as to produce a continuous story. A similar technique was used in Bernard Grebanier's Living Shakespeare series.

The most striking recent development is the popularity of the recorded book, or **talking book**. Of the many companies active in this market, Books on Tape is probably the best known.

This article has focused on recordings of English and American literature by performers speaking English and from companies based in either Britain or America. Space does not permit attention to the extensive body of literary recordings produced in other countries. The first recording of a complete play was probably done in France. Italy has produced extensive recordings, including a complete version of Dante's *Divine Comedy*. Translations of passages from Shakespeare have been recorded in many lands, including the Soviet Union.

Regardless of the lack of attention given to recorded literature in academe, the body of material is large and growing. When Caedmon can expect to sell 100,000 copies of its most popular new issues, there is no reason to fear a decline in the production of audio-recordings of literature. Only a little attention is needed to reveal that literary recordings are important commercially as well as valuable historically and artistically. [Bebb 1972 discusses recordings of individual actors; Whittington 1981.]

Robert J. O'Brien

LITTLE CHAMPION (label). A record issued by J.E. Hough, Ltd., in London from December 1909 to about March 1910. It was a nine-inch, vertical-cut disc, made of a new compound named Vitaroid; price was 1s. 3d. [Andrews 1988/6.]

LITTLE MARVEL (label). A record issued by the Aeolian Co., Ltd., in Britain during the early 1920s. It was sold through the Woolworth stores. Size of the disc was 5 3/8 inches, later increased to six inches. A nursery series was included. Masters from Little Marvel were used to make records for other British stores.

LITTLE POP (label). A small-sized British record, issued by the Sound Recording Co., Ltd., from December 1921 to June 1922. About 100 titles were released, at one shilling each. [Andrews 1988/6.]

LITTLE TOTS' NURSERY TUNES (label). A British seven-inch disc issued in 1923–1924 by Plaza Music Co. (New York), handled in the U.K. by Barnett Samuel and Sons, Ltd. [Andrews 1988/6.]

LITTLE WALTER, 1930–1968. American blues singer and harmonica player, born Marion Walter Jacobs in Alexandria, Louisiana, on 1 May 1930. He taught himself the harmonica, and learned to play it with great expressiveness. He recorded successfully for Leonard Chess in the 1950s, notably "Mean Old World" (Checker #764; 1952), and "Blue Lights" (Checker #799; 1954). He and Muddy Waters made several distinguished duet records, including "All Night Long" (Chess #1509; 1952).

LITTLE WONDER (label). A 5 1/2 inch American record produced by Henry Waterson between 1914 and 1919; the recording and pressing were done by Columbia. The records were lateral cut, with a playing time of one minute and 45 seconds; they sold for $.15. A new record player was designed for the Little Wonder record, but standard phonographs could also accommodate it. Artists were anonymous, and the records had no paper labels (title and number were etched into the central area). By July 1915 the sales list showed disc numbers up to #183. The discs offered good reproduction of dance music and vocals, at a selling price of $.10. [Andrews*; Blacker 1983/3–4 to 1986/4 is a label list; Rust 1978.]

LIVE RECORDING. A recording made at an actual public performance rather than in the studio. In August 1888, recordings of an organ at Westminster Abbey, and at the Crystal Palace in London, were undertaken by Colonel Gouraud for the Edison Phonograph Co. to demonstrate the utility of the phonograph; parts of *Israel in Egypt* were inscribed (see OLDEST RECORDS.) The Mapleson cylinders of 1901 were the earliest series of live recordings, and the first live recordings made in the U.S.

Live studio. *See* REVERBERATION.

LOMAX, ALAN, 1915– . American folklorist and folk singer, son of John Avery Lomax, born in Austin, Texas, on 31 Jan 1915. He assisted his father in field work, and also studied at the University of Texas (B.A., 1936). From 1937 to 1942 he was assistant curator—to his father—of the Archive of Folk Song, Library of Congress. He collected folk songs in the Midwest and Southeast U.S. One of his important projects was to interview and record Jelly Roll Morton for the Library of Congress in 1938. He became director of folk music for Decca Record Co. after World War II, bringing that label to prominence in the field through the 1950s. Lomax also sang, and was heard on a 1958 LP from the Tradition label; then Kapp Records produced his album *Folk Song Saturday Night*. He performed on radio and at folk festivals. His books include collaborations with his father (see JOHN LOMAX), plus *Folk Songs of North America in the English Language* (1960), and *Hard Hitting Songs for Hard-Hit People*, with Woody Guthrie and Pete Seeger (1967).

LOMAX, JOHN AVERY, 1867–1948. American folklorist, born in Goodman, Mississippi, on 23 Sep 1867. His family moved to Texas when he was an infant, and he grew up in the ambience of cowboy songs and western folklore. After early schooling at Granbury College, and seven years of teaching, he attended Chautauqua (New York) summer schools and then went to the University of Texas (B.A., 1897). Working as a university administrator and teacher, he continued graduate study and earned master's degrees from University of Texas and from Harvard University. Supported by Harvard, he returned to Texas and made field recordings. He discovered songs such as "Git Along Little Dogies" and "Home on the Range," and published (with his son Alan Lomax) a collection, *Cowboy Songs and Other Frontier Ballads* (1910). A second collection appeared in 1919: *Songs of the Cattle Trail and Cow Camp*, but Lomax was able to give only a part of his time to folk song research, since he found it necessary to work in academic and banking positions. Finally, in 1932 he gained sufficient backing from the Macmillan Co. and from the Library of Congress to become a fulltime song collector, often assisted by his son Alan. He recorded more than 10,000 songs for the Archive of Folk Song at the Library of Congress, which he served as curator from 1934. The songs included his discoveries at an Arkansas penitentiary, "Rock Island Line" and "John Henry." Publication of his two collections, *American Ballads and Folk Songs* (1934) and *Our Singing Country* (1941) brought folk song into the American mainstream. His personal efforts achieved the release of Huddie Ledbetter (Leadbelly) from a Louisiana prison in 1933. The two Lomaxes published *The Leadbelly Legend: A Collection of World-Famous songs by Huddie Ledbetter* and *Negro Folk Songs as Sung by Lead Belly* (1936). Lomax was said to have traveled 300,000 miles in his field work. His last collection, in joint authorship with his son, was *Folk Song: U.S.A.* (1948). He also wrote an autobiography, *Adventures of a Ballad Hunter* (1947).

LOMBARD, THOMAS R. American recording industry executive. He was one of the organizers of the North American Phonograph Co., and served as president in 1893. A former mining prospector, he had worked with Jesse Lippincott, who planned and controlled the North American Phonograph Co.

LOMBARDO, GUY, 1902–1977. Canadian dance band leader, born Gaetano Lombardo in London, Ontario, on 19 June 1902. He studied violin, and formed a family performing group in London around 1917. By 1923 the ensemble was playing in the U.S., and a year later they made records for Gennett. Among the family members in the group were Carmen (saxophone and vocal), Lebert (trumpet), Victor (clarinet and saxophone), and Rose Marie (vocal). Guy Lombardo was leader, playing the violin on occasion. A tremulous, dulcet sound was developed, based on saxophones playing rather untuned vibrato, accompanied by a tinkling piano. The formula was greatly successful in the Granada Cafe, Chicago, in 1927–1928, then at the Roosevelt Grill in New York, where the orchestra—known as the Royal Canadians—played for 33 years. New Year's Eve radio shows from the Roosevelt, and later from the Waldorf-Astoria Hotel, established the Lombardo orchestra as a national tradition, playing "Auld Lang Syne" at midnight. The song was one of the popular Lombardo records (Decca #2478; 1939). "Boo Hoo" was another acclaimed number (Victor #25522; 1937). "Sweetest Music this Side of Heaven" was the nickname of the orchestra, which remained in the public eye through the 1960s.

Lombardo recorded for several labels, primarily Columbia (1927–1932), Brunswick (1932–1934), Decca (1934–1935), Victor (1935–1938), and Decca again from 1938. Carmen Lombardo's unique vocal style, characterized by a frail uncertainty, was well exemplified on "Little Lady Make Believe" (Victor #25823; 1938) and "When You Wish upon a Star" (Decca #2969; 1940). Carmen wrote many pleasing songs, among them "Boo Hoo," "Confucius Say" (Decca #2917; 1939) and "There Won't Be a Shortage of Love" (Decca #4199; 1942). Carmen Lombardo died in 1971; Guy Lombardo died in Houston on 5 Nov 1977.

LONDON (label). The record name given to exports from **Decca Record Co., Ltd.**, to the U.S. after World War II. In the U.K., the London label was used by Decca for 45 rpm, 78 rpm, and LPs, using material from American labels such as Atco, Atlantic, Cadence, Chess, Dot, Imperial, Liberty, Specialty, and Sun. The London label is still in use, for CDs released by Polygram (which acquired the label in 1980).

LONDON PHONOGRAPH CO. The firm operated by **J. E. Hough** in London from 1893 to 1896. It sold cylinders with the London Records label, as well as phonographs. Since the business was carried on in infringement of the rights in Edison patents and Bell-Tainter patents, legal action was taken by the patent owner, Edison Bell Phonograph Corp., Ltd. In October 1896 the London Phonograph Co. was enjoined, then renamed **Edisonia, Ltd.** [Andrews 1978/4.]

LONDON RECORDS (label). The cylinder record issued by the **London Phonograph Co.**, a firm owned by J.E. Hough, from December 1893. Releases continued under new management (Edisonia, Ltd., then Edison Bell Consolidated Phonograph Co., Ltd.) until at least September 1900. Among the artists were George Gaskin and Russell Hunting. [Andrews*; Andrews 1978/4.]

LONDON STEREOSCOPIC CO. The British firm licensed to utilize the Edison patents in the U.K., established in 1878. It offered machines in various models, including handcranks (one with a flywheel) and one operated by a falling weight.

LONG PLAYING RECORD. The early commercial cylinders had a two-minute playing time, a span insufficient for rendition of a typical song or instrumental work. Efforts began to extend playing time, both through the production of larger cylinders (e.g., five-inch "concert records") and through finer grooving. In 1895 Edison made cylinders with 400 threads per inch, 6.5 inches long; they played for eight minutes. Pathé in Paris made a cylinder 8 1/2 inches long (the Celeste) that played for four or five minutes.

Berliner's seven-inch discs of 1894 could play for two minutes. Various producers increased disc size: International Zonophone offered 10-inch discs in September 1901 in Europe, and in the U.S. Victor Monarchs in 10-inch size were sold in 1901. In 1903 discs of 12-inch diameter were marketed by Gramophone and Typewriter in the U.K. and the Victor Co. in the U.S. Pathé records in 1909 and Neophone records in 1905 reached 19 1/2 inches in diameter, but these were not available for long; in general the industry standardized with a 12-inch maximum.

Victor experimented in 1904 with a 14-inch disc that played for six minutes at a somewhat slower speed than 60 rpm, the ordinary record of the day. Columbia and Fonotipia had similar discs. None of these pioneer long-players were successful.

In Britain the **Marathon Records** of 1912–1915 and the constant linear surface speed records of the **World Record Co.** were important advances. Marathon 12-inch discs could play as long as 16 1/2 minutes, and some 12-inch World Records could play over 20 minutes. Vocalion Long-Playing Records used the World Record Co. process.

Brunswick announced in August 1925 its 40-minute (20 minutes per side) 12-inch electrically recorded discs; they had 500 grooves per inch.

The Edison 12-inch disc introduced in August 1926 could play 20 minutes per side, but it failed in the market because the grooves (450 per inch) were too thin for the heavy tone arms of the time, economic conditions dimmed interest in the purchase of new equipment needed to play the discs, and the repertoire was not ready to exploit the longer playing time. Victor failed with a 1931 long-play record—33 1/3 rpm—for similar reasons.

In Britain an advance was made with the **Broadcast** label in 1927. Fine grooving made possible a playing time of three minutes on an eight-inch disc; later there was a nine-inch disc, and then a 10-inch disc which could play up to six minutes.

Hit of the Week label introduced a tightly grooved 10-inch record in 1931 that played five or six minutes, but the extra time was not well used and the innovation was not impressive enough to forestall bankruptcy of the firm. The British counterpart label was **Durium**.

Columbia made 33 1/3 rpm records in 1932 for intermission music in motion picture theaters. The discs played from the center outward. A 12-inch record could play, like the later commercial LP, for 20 minutes.

The 33 1/3 rpm speed was found to be suitable also in adding sound when a motion picture film was projected, since a 20-inch diameter disc at that speed would cover the time used by one film reel, and gave respectable quality. Eventually that speed was employed by Columbia as it introduced the modern LP record, developed by Peter Goldmark and William S. Bachman, in 1948. It had between 250–400 grooves per inch, in contrast to the 96–125 grooves per inch of the standard 78 rpm record. Stylus diameter was .001 inch (one mill), and the stylus exerted only 6 grams of pressure, with a tip radius of less than 0.025 millimeters. This format became the new industry model, and remained so until the arrival of the compact disc. [Evans, R. 1979 is a brief account of long-play development; Fagan 1981 lists all the Victor 1931 long-play discs; Goldmark 1949.] *See also* COLUMBIA; DISC, 4; EDISON (label); INSTANTANEOUS RECORDINGS; TALKING BOOKS; TRANSCRIPTION DISCS.

LOOPING. A mixing technique used by disc jockeys to extend the playing time of a song by blending two records of it into a continuous play.

LOUDSPEAKER. (Often referred to as speaker.) This article consists of nine sections: 1. Introduction and terminology; 2. Completely closed box systems; 3. Bass reflex (vented) systems; 4. Passive radiator systems; 5. Transmission line loudspeakers; 6. Aperiodic systems; 7. Horn-loaded loudspeakers; 8. Electrostatic loudspeakers; and 9. Multi-way systems.

1. *Introduction.* The year 1925 heralded the most significant advance in the history of recorded sound, the commercial introduction of **electrical recording** and reproduction. Two technological developments made electrical recording feasible: the **transducer** and the vacuum tube **amplifier**. The transducer made it possible to convert mechanical energy into electric current and vice versa. Electrical re-

cording required two transducers: a **microphone** to convert sound vibrations into electricity, and an electrical disc **cutting head** to convert the electricity into a mechanical vibration that would cause a cutting stylus to cut a physical replica of the original sound wave into the record groove. On the reproduction end, a phonograph **cartridge** (pickup, as it was originally called), traced the mechanical picture contained in the record groove and converted the resulting vibration into electricity. Finally, the loudspeaker converted the electricity back into sound vibrations.

A microphone cannot provide sufficient voltage and current to feed a disc cutting head directly; the small signal from the microphone requires considerable amplification in order to drive the cutting apparatus. Similarly, the phonograph pickup is incapable of driving a loudspeaker. In both cases, the vacuum tube amplifier provides the means of increasing the voltage and current of the electrical signal provided by the first transducer to a level sufficient to drive the second transducer. Today, solid state amplifiers have generally replaced their tube counterparts, although equipment reviews in leading high end audio journals reveal that there is still a considerable interest in vacuum tube amplifiers.

The basic principles of the moving coil electrodynamic loudspeaker, often referred to as the dynamic loudspeaker, were first patented in Germany in 1874 by Werner von Siemens. In Britain John William Rayleigh described radiation theory for a circular diaphragm mounted in a baffle in his *Theory of Sound* (1877). In 1898 British physicist Oliver Lodge received a patent for a sound reproducer consisting of a moving coil attached to a wooden board. The modern dynamic loudspeaker is generally credited to C.W. Rice and E.W. Kellogg, who produced a working model in 1925. The essential elements of a modern moving coil loudspeaker, which has changed very little in its basic operation since Rice and Kellogg, are a coil of wire (the voice coil) surrounded by a magnetic field and attached to a vibrating diaphragm or cone. The voice coil and the cone are suspended by the "spider" at the rear of the cone, and the flexible rim suspension (the surround) at the front. As electric-

ity flows through the voice coil, the coil generates its own magnetic field which interacts with the field of the permanent magnet, causing the cone to move back and forth.

During the early days of radio and electrical phonographs, single full-range loudspeakers, which attempted to reproduce the entire range of frequencies available on recordings, were commonplace. Since the 1950s, however, nearly all loudspeaker systems claiming high fidelity performance have used more than one speaker to cover the entire audible frequency spectrum from 20Hz to 20,000Hz. The speaker enclosures described below are most commonly used with low frequency loudspeakers, normally called woofers. Separate speakers called midranges and tweeters are normally used for the middle and high frequency portions of the spectrum. These individual loudspeaker components are often called drivers. Prior to the widespread use of multi-way loudspeaker systems the enclosures described contained full-range speakers.

A moving coil loudspeaker normally radiates sound from front and rear, since the loudspeaker frame (basket) is open in the back. When the loudspeaker cone moves forward, a compression of air is produced in front of it, and a rarefaction is produced behind it. Conversely, when the loudspeaker cone moves backward, a rarefaction is produced in front of the loudspeaker, along with a compression at the rear. Thus, the radiation of sound waves from the front and the back of the speaker cone are out of phase with each other. At low frequencies the wavelengths reproduced are quite long with respect to the size of the cone. When the front and rear radiations meet, at the outer edge of the loudspeaker, cancellation occurs. This results in little low frequency output from the loudspeaker, despite large cone movement in this region.

Since the first use of dynamic loudspeakers, it has been necessary to isolate the front radiation of the cone from the back radiation. The simplest method is to mount the loudspeaker on a large, flat **baffle**. The distance from the front of the speaker, around the baffle to the rear of the driver, determines the low frequency cut-off point for the system. When the distance is less than 1/4 wavelength of the frequency being reproduced, the output from the system is greatly reduced. Many early radio receivers and phonographs used flat-baffled loudspeakers, as well as the variant open back enclosure. Early radios and electric phonographs were often housed in five-sided wooden boxes that contained both the electronics and the loudspeaker. Open back cabinets provided sufficient distance between the front and rear of the driver, but with a much smaller front profile. Such enclosures usually had cabinet resonance problems, causing uneven low frequency response. Generally, the deeper the cabinet, the more serious the resonance problems become. Furthermore, the baffle size required to handle satisfactorily a 25 Hz low frequency would have been too large to be practical (11 feet four inches square). Fully enclosed boxes were necessary to achieve accurate bass was with a front baffle of manageable size.

One choice which must be made in designing an enclosed box loudspeaker enclosure concerns the rear radiation of the loudspeaker cone. There are two possibilities: the rear radiation can be completely absorbed inside the enclosure; or a portion of the rear radiation can emerge, through a port or vent, to reinforce the front radiation at low frequencies. The major types of loudspeaker enclosures, beginning with those which completely absorb the rear radiation of the driver.

2. *Completely closed box systems.* The infinite baffle enclosure was popular through the mid-1950s. A true infinite baffle would isolate the front radiation of the driver from the rear radiation at the lowest operating frequencies. Since it has never been possible to build a baffle of infinite size, such an enclosure was always approximated using a box of manageable proportions. One common approach to building an infinite baffle was to mount the driver on the wall of a room, in which case the room at the rear of the loudspeaker became the enclosure and the room at the front of the driver became the listening room. It was also common to mount loudspeakers on closet doors. Very large, stand-alone enclosures were built by a number of manufacturers, which approximated infinite baffles. During the 1950s, Bozak was a leading proponent of such enclosures,

exemplified by its B-310 loudspeaker system. The B-310 contained four 12-inch woofers housed in an enclosure with an internal volume of nearly 18 cubic feet. Electro-Voice manufactured a loudspeaker system known as the Patrician, the second version of which contained a single 30-inch woofer in an enclosure of comparable size.

In 1949, Harry F. Olson and J. Preston received a patent on what they called the air suspension loudspeaker. The air suspension loudspeaker contained a woofer mounted in a small, sealed enclosure in which the air became part of the cone's suspension. The RCA LC-1 loudspeaker system was the first commercial product based on the Olson and Preston patent. It is important to note that the woofers used by Olson were not substantially different than those used in large infinite baffles or open-back enclosures; they had relatively stiff suspensions, with a resulting high free-air resonant frequency. When such drivers are placed in a small enclosure, the system resonance will be even higher than that of the driver in free air, resulting in relatively weak low bass, unless extremely large woofers are used.

Perhaps the most significant development in the history of the high fidelity loudspeaker occurred in 1953 when American designer Edgar Villchur built his first acoustic suspension loudspeaker. What distinguished Villchur's loudspeaker from Olson's air suspension design was the use of the first high compliance woofer. Villchur's first such woofer was a Western Electric 728B, a 12-inch driver that he modified by replacing the stiff outer suspension with a loose cloth surround. The new surround was made out of the ticking from an old mattress edge, sealed with butyl rubber to prevent air leaks. Such modifications of existing drivers were hardly practical for production, so the modified 728B became the model for the first high compliance woofer manufactured **Acoustic Research, Inc.,** founded by Villchur and Henry Kloss. The high compliance woofer had a very low free-air resonance frequency of less than 15 Hz. When it was placed in a sealed box of 1.7 cubic feet, a low frequency cutoff point of 38 Hz was achieved. The trapped air inside the small, airtight enclosure provided most of the support for the woofer cone, and served as a restoring force for the cone at frequencies near system resonance. In an infinite baffle loudspeaker, as in Olson's air suspension designs, the compliance of the air inside the enclosure is greater than that of the driver's suspension. In an acoustic suspension loudspeaker the situation is reversed, the compliance of the air being less than that of the driver suspension. Prior to the development of the acoustic suspension loudspeaker, a low frequency cutoff of 38 Hz was unheard of in such a small enclosure.

These small-box systems became known as bookshelf loudspeakers and their introduction played a major role in public acceptance of stereophonic recording. When high fidelity enthusiasts contemplated converting their monaural systems to stereo, adding a second 18 cubic foot enclosure to their living rooms was, in most cases, an unwelcome prospect. The compact size of the acoustic suspension loudspeakers made installing a pair of them extremely practical. One negative characteristic of acoustic suspension loudspeakers is their relative insensitivity (often referred to as inefficiency), that is, more amplifier power is required for a given playback level. As a result, a trend toward higher powered amplification began in the late 1950s. In 1955, a 25 watt amplifier was considered a power house; today, amplifiers delivering 10 times that power are not uncommon. Acoustic Research's first commercial acoustic suspension loudspeaker system was the model AR-1, a prototype being introduced in 1954 at the New York Audio Fair. The AR-1 that arrived on the market in 1955 was a two-way loudspeaker using a Western Electric 755A eight-inch full range driver as a tweeter, with Villchur's 12-inch high compliance woofer. Another model, the AR-1W, was also introduced in 1955. The AR-1W contained only the woofer from the AR-1, without the 755A tweeter. For those who desired a better tweeter, the Janszen 1–30, a four-element electrostatic array, could be placed on top of the AR-1W enclosure.

In 1957 a second Boston firm, KLH, was formed by Henry Kloss and Tony Hofmann. The KLH-1 of 1958, manufactured under license from Acoustic Research, contained two 12-inch, high compliance woofers in a floor

standing enclosure, along with a cutout for the same Janszen electrostatic elements used with the AR-1W. Throughout the 1960s the AR and KLH loudspeaker systems were known for their very low sonic coloration and high accuracy, characteristics that became known as the "New England Sound" and the "Cambridge Sound." The AR-3A and the KLH-6 were, for many years, standards by which other dynamic bookshelf loudspeaker systems were judged.

In 1962 **Electro-Voice, Inc.**, introduced a bookshelf loudspeaker using a high compliance woofer called an air suspension loudspeaker. Following patent litigation brought by Acoustic Research, court rulings established the acoustic suspension principle as a public domain invention. The original formulas for acoustic suspension loudspeaker design were developed by Tony Hofmann. In 1972 the mathematics of closed box loudspeaker design was analyzed and described by Richard Small in a series of landmark articles that formed the basis for most later designs (Small 1972).

3. *Bass reflex (vented) systems*. The bass reflex loudspeaker uses a fully enclosed box, except for a small port or vent, usually placed on the front baffle board below the woofer. Some of the back radiation from the woofer cone emerges from the port in phase with the front radiation, reinforcing the low frequencies. The first experiments with ported loudspeaker enclosures were performed by A.C. Thuras of Bell Laboratories in 1930. His model was based on the Helmholz resonator. The Thuras patent application (1932) described the interaction of the driver and the port. Similar work was done in the early 1930s by Voight in England and Olson in the United States; then in 1937 Jensen introduced the first modern bass reflex loudspeaker system. Early bass reflex loudspeakers had highly inaccurate low frequency response (by today's standards), and their excessive output at resonance made them sound like 'boom boxes." Nevertheless, they were extremely popular during the days of low power amplifiers due to their relatively high sensitivity. During the 1950s more precise mathematical models were developed by L.L. Beranek, B.N. Locanthi, R.H. Lyon, and J.F. Novak, but the modern vented loudspeaker

was first portrayed by Australian A N. Thiele in 1961. Thiele described vented loudspeakers in terms of their electrical equivalent circuits, and showed that it was possible to achieve a smooth low frequency response, equivalent to an ideal electrical high pass filter. Thiele's work did not receive wide attention until 1971 when his paper was reprinted in the U.S. (Thiele 1971). Richard Small did much to enhance the work of Thiele, showing that the vented loudspeaker was a fourth order high pass filter, and that the filter could be adjusted for a wide variety of mathematically predictable response characteristics. He also showed the effect of enclosure losses on the performance of the loudspeaker system, and presented the mathematics for matching an enclosure design to a specific driver, using the driver's electrical and mechanical specifications (Small 1973). These driver specifications are now universally known as Thiele/Small parameters. Modern terminology refers to the bass reflex as the design type that preceded Thiele and Small, and to the vented loudspeaker as the type that followed their work.

4. *Passive radiator systems.* This category of loudspeakers is related to vented designs. A passive radiator system actually contains two woofers, one with the usual voice coil and magnet structure, and the other without. The passive driver is acoustically coupled to the active loudspeaker at low frequencies. The two speakers contribute as much to the output at low frequencies as the vent does in a vented design. One advantage of passive radiator systems is the absence of wind noise and pipe resonances sometimes found in vented systems. Harry F. Olson received the first patent on these systems in 1935, and followed his original work with research published in 1954 (Olson 1954). He referred to the passive drivers as "drone cones." Most of today's passive radiator systems use an active driver smaller than the passive unit, for example, an eight-inch active loudspeaker coupled to a ten-inch passive driver. Today, the best known commercial proponent of passive radiator systems is Polk Audio, an American firm based in Baltimore. It typically uses multiple 6 1/2 inch active drivers with much larger passive units.

5. *Transmission line loudspeakers.* The transmission line loudspeaker is a refined descendant of the Stromberg-Carlson acoustic labyrinth, which was invented by Benjamin Olney in 1936. The acoustic labyrinth is a long pipe into which the back radiation of the woofer is loaded. The length of the pipe is normally a quarter wavelength of the woofer's free air resonant frequency, which produces a pressure node at resonance, controlling the cone motion of the woofer. Since the labyrinth is a completely open pipe, except for a lining of fiberglass, a substantial amount of sound emerges from the end of the tube. The modern transmission line loudspeaker was first described by A.R. Bailey in 1965 (Bailey 1965; Galo 1982). Although superficially resembling the acoustic labyrinth, the transmission line operates quite differently. A classic transmission line is completely filled with absorbent material, either long fiber wool or dacron polyester. That damping material acts as an acoustic low pass filter, effectively increasing the length of the line as the frequency drops. At the lowest operating frequencies the woofer is mass-loaded by the air in most of the length of the line. This results in excellent woofer control at low frequencies. The transmission line is a theoretically non-resonant enclosure, and the internal pressures found in closed box designs are nearly absent in a well-designed system. In a classic transmission line, all of the back radiation from the driver is absorbed in the line, but some variations on this concept have made use of a portion of the back radiation. A negative side effect is the relatively poor control of the woofer cone below the system cut-off frequency.

The transmission line is probably the least scientific of all present day loudspeaker enclosures, and there are no hard and fast formulas for determining line length and stuffing density. Recent research by Robert Bullock and Peter Hillman (Bullock 1986; Hillman 1989) has led to a more precise understanding of the transmission line, but designs are not as mathematically predictable as they are for closed and vented boxes. Since 1965 only a handful of commercial designs have employed transmission lines, their relatively large size and complex internal construction making them somewhat expensive and impractical. Among home loudspeaker builders they have attained a kind of cult status. Irving M. Fried is the best known commercial proponent of the transmission line, having marketed many such systems under the brand names of IMF and Fried Products.

6. *Aperiodic systems.* The aperiodic loudspeaker is a closed box system that contains a vent stuffed with damping material. The stuffing, usually foam or fiberglass, provides a pressure release for the system at low frequencies. The term aperiodic literally means an absence of resonances at any specific frequency or multiples thereof. Aperiodic damping is defined as "damping of such a high degree that the damped system, after disturbance, comes to rest without oscillation or hunting" (Turner 1988). In a standard acoustic suspension system the trapped air in the box is quite reactive, or springy, at very low frequencies. The reactive nature of the air will cause excessive cone excursion at system resonance. Adding an aperiodic vent to the system releases internal pressure at resonance, resulting in better control of the cone motion at very low frequencies. The aperiodic loudspeaker offers some of the performance advantages of the transmission line in terms of excellent woofer control and a reduction in internal pressure at frequencies near system resonance, but with enclosures much more manageable in size. It is important to note that no sound emerges from an aperiodic vent, so this design does not resemble a vented loudspeaker in any way.

The first patent on such a loudspeaker enclosure was issued in 1936 to Marvel W. Scheldorf, an engineer for RCA; he described his invention as an acoustic resistance device. Scandinavian firms have shown the greatest interest in this concept. In 1969 Dynaco introduced the model A-25, the first in a series aperiodic loudspeakers made for them in Denmark by Seas. The Dynaco A-25 was considered, by many reviewers, to be the best bookshelf loudspeaker since Acoustic Research introduced the model 3A. Today another Danish firm, Dynaudio, is the leading advocate of aperiodic loading. For many years it has manufactured a device called a Variovent, which contains tightly packed fiberglass stuffing held in place by a plastic grill and frame. A third

Danish firm, Scan-Speak, manufactures a similar device. Audio Concepts, an American loudspeaker manufacturer based in LaCrosse, Wisconsin, also manufactures loudspeakers with aperiodic loading, including the Sapphire II, introduced in 1990.

7. *Horn-loaded loudspeakers.* Since the first acoustical phonographs appeared, horns have been used as acoustic amplifiers. A **horn** functions as an acoustical impedance matching device, coupling the relatively small surface area of the radiator to the large volume of air in the room. The size of the mouth opening determines the low frequency cutoff for the horn. Horn shapes on acoustic phonographs made prior to 1925 were determined largely by trial and error. No mathematical procedures had been developed for determining the size and rate of expansion between the throat and the mouth, and the horns usually had very uneven frequency response. In 1919 the American physicist Arthur G. Webster received a patent for the first exponential horn. As the name implies, the cross-sectional area of the horn increases exponentially with distance from the throat, resulting in a more uniform frequency response. Webster's work failed to have an impact on the phonograph industry until 1925, when acoustical recording was abandoned in favor of the electrical process. The Orthophonic Victrola was the first commercial phonograph to incorporate an exponential horn. It was also the first to use a folded horn design. An exponential horn with low frequency response adequate for the reproduction of electrical recordings required a large mouth opening, and consequently had to be quite long. The folded horn reduced the size to manageable proportions.

The first experiments with horns coupled to dynamic loudspeakers were conducted by Rice and Kellogg in 1925. Because of the very high efficiency of horn-loaded loudspeakers, they were highly effective where large rooms had to be filled with a high volume of sound. This made them especially suitable for use in talking motion picture theaters, since the vacuum tube amplifiers available at that time had very limited power output capability. Although horn systems were used extensively in theaters during the 1930s, their large dimensions made them impractical for home use. That situation changed in 1940 when the American engineer Paul W. Klipsch invented the corner horn loudspeaker, a complex folded horn design in which the walls of the room form the mouth of the horn. The Klipschorn loudspeaker in production today is still based on the original 1940 model, using a horn midrange and tweeter to fill out the remainder of the audible spectrum. (Klipsch was not the first engineer to advocate corner placement of loudspeakers. The first corner loudspeaker patent application was made by M. Weil in 1925; his patent was issued in 1931.) Today, Klipsch is the only major manufacturer of home high fidelity loudspeakers that continues to advocate horn designs over all other types. However, due to their exceptionally high efficiency, horn systems continue to be the preferred loudspeakers for sound reinforcement and motion picture applications.

8. *Electrostatic loudspeakers.* Unlike the dynamic speaker, an electrostatic loudspeaker does not make use of electromagnetism; instead it uses a thin plastic sheet, stretched over a rectangular frame, as the vibrating diaphragm. The plastic sheet is coated with a conductive material, connected to a high voltage power supply that charges the diaphragm to a potential of between 2,000 and 3,000 volts negative DC. Suspended on either side of the plastic diaphragm are a pair of metal screens, called stators, to which the audio signal is applied. The output from the amplifier is connected, through a transformer, to the two screens, allowing it to interact electrostatically with the polarities of the signals on the screens. When the audio signal on the front screen is positive, the signal on the rear screen will be negative. The negatively charged diaphragm will be attracted toward the positively charged screen, and repelled by the negative screen. When the audio signal reverses polarity, the opposite will occur, with the diaphragm moving back toward the rear (positive) screen and away from the front (negative) screen. The acoustical output from the two sides of the loudspeaker are out of phase with respect to each other. This type of loudspeaker, known as a dipole, has no enclosure.

Because of the absence of an enclosure, low bass information is normally weak due to cancelation. To overcome this problem, electrostatic panels for low frequency reproduction are usually very large, floor-standing arrangements. Smaller electrostatic elements are usually used in conjunction with the large panels for midrange and high frequency coverage. The earliest electrostatic loudspeakers were small units used only for high frequency reproduction. They were normally used in conjunction with a conventional dynamic woofer forming a two-way system.

During the 1920s there was a considerable amount of experimentation with electrostatic loudspeakers, particularly in Britain and Germany, but there were few commercial products. Among the first was the Kyle condenser loudspeaker, which was used by Peerless in a radio receiver introduced around 1930. The **Automatic Musical Instrument Co.** used one of the first electrostatic loudspeakers in a juke box, also introduced in 1930. These early electrostatic speakers employed a single screen, in front of the diaphragm, and were enclosed at the rear. Hence, they were not dipoles. The first modern dipole electrostatic loudspeaker was the Quad, introduced in 1958 by Acoustical Manufacturing Co., Ltd. The following year, KLH introduced the Model 9 electrostatic loudspeaker, with two tall dipole speakers, held at a fixed angle by a pair of brackets. A stereo installation, therefore, required the use of four panels. Because of the extremely low mass of the plastic diaphragm, electrostatic loudspeakers are capable of exceptional clarity and inner detail in the midrange and high frequencies. However, since electrostatic speakers often suffer from a lack of extreme low bass, many designs use a conventional dynamic woofer system, coupled to electrostatic elements for the midrange and high frequencies. Since electrostatic dipoles are completely free of enclosure-related resonance problems, successful integration with dynamic woofer systems is difficult and rare.

A related category is the planar loudspeaker. It is nearly identical to an electrostatic, having a large, thin plastic diaphragm as the vibrating element. However, planar speakers use conventional magnetic principles, and are, therefore, dynamic loudspeakers. Thin wires are embedded into the plastic diaphragm, forming the equivalent of a voice coil. Magnetic strips are placed in the front and back of the diaphragm, where the stators would be in an electrostatic loudspeaker. Magnetic rather than electrostatic interaction causes the diaphragm to vibrate. Magneplan, a Minnesota firm, is the best-known manufacturer of planar loudspeakers. Its first such speaker, designed by company founder Jim Winey, was the Magneplanar Tympani I of 1971. It contained three tall panels that operated as dipoles.

9. *Multi-way loudspeakers*. As early as 1925, Rice and Kellogg realized that the very large loudspeakers suitable for low frequency reproduction were far from optimum for reproducing the midrange and high frequencies. Their first multi-way system, developed that year, consisted of three horn-loaded drivers, each dedicated to a limited portion of the frequency spectrum. There was little practical use for such a system until the sound motion picture industry was formed, since most early electric phonographs and radios used single drivers to cover the entire available range. In 1934 Shearer and Hilliard built the first modern two-way horn loudspeaker system for the MGM studios in Culver City, California. Until the late 1950s, multi-way systems for home use employed either small direct radiator cone drivers for the midrange and treble (a direct radiator is a loudspeaker that radiates directly into the room, without any horn loading to improve efficiency), or cone drivers with horns attached. Then in 1958 Villchur and Roy Allison introduced the dome tweeter, bringing several advantages over the cone drivers previously used. Because of its physical shape, the dome was more rigid than the cone, resulting in less distortion at high frequencies. In addition, the small size of the dome (typically one inch or less in today's systems) results in much wider dispersion at high frequencies, giving a uniform frequency response in a large number of listening positions. By the mid-1960s, dome drivers had also become common for midrange reproduction.

Today's high performance multi-way dynamic loudspeaker systems usually employ small dome drivers as tweeters, and either dome or cone drivers for the midrange. Dome drivers are typically manufactured as sealed, self-contained units, and do not require the construction of any enclosure. Cone midrange drivers, typically four to five inches in diameter, are not sealed at the rear and will normally require some kind of sub-enclosure which can be incorporated into the complete system. Sub-enclosures for midrange drivers can be either closed, aperiodic or vented boxes, depending on the driver used and the preference of the system designer. Transmission line loading, though less popular, has also been used effectively with midrange loudspeakers.

Multi-way loudspeaker systems require the use of a combination of filters which, together, form the crossover network. In a two-way system, a low-pass filter feeds the low frequencies to the woofer and a high-pass filter sends the high frequencies to the tweeter. A three-way system contains both of these filters, plus a band-pass filter to feed the middle portion of the frequency spectrum to a dedicated midrange driver. The earliest multi-way crossover networks were based on the theories of Bell Telephone engineers G.A. Campbell and O.J. Zobel. Their crossovers were known as constant-K and M-derived designs, in which each filter section was designed individually, matching electrical impedance to the other sections. The constant-K and M-derived filters were replaced by Butterworth filters in the 1950s. Butterworth filters, using calculus-based network theory, were designed as a whole, allowing simpler and more precise matching of the filter sections.

A crossover that uses filters rolling off at the rate of six decibels per octave outside of the passband (6dB/octave) yields minimum phase response across the entire spectrum, but this rate of attenuation is not sufficient to insure low distortion with many drivers. In 1971 Richard Small indicated that a 12dB/octave rolloff was the minimum necessary in order to reduce driver distortion. Since the 12dB/octave crossover has both amplitude and phase problems, many engineers in agreement with Small's premise have sought higher rates of attenuation. Siegfried Linkwitz introduced the 24dB/octave all-pass crossovers in 1976. Known as Linkwitz-Riley crossovers, they have received wide acceptance due to their symmetrical vertical radiation pattern (Linkwitz 1976).

The effects of improper time alignment were analyzed in 1956 by C.P. Boegli. Time alignment of the drivers in a multi-way system has become a major concern during the past two decades, but there is no consensus today among loudspeaker engineers as to the relative importance of flat amplitude response versus time alignment of drivers and minimum phase response across the audible spectrum. Nor is there consensus on which type of crossover roll-off characteristic is best. Every loudspeaker system is the result of compromises, each engineer has a preference regarding which compromises to make.

The personal computer has revolutionized loudspeaker design during the past decade, and is now considered an essential tool for loudspeaker engineers and manufacturers. A large quantity of software has been written for both crossover and enclosure design, bringing sophisticated loudspeaker design within the reach of the non-mathematician, while enabling those who are mathematically inclined to work in a fraction of the time which would otherwise be required. With an appropriate interface card and software, the computer can also function as a test and measurement system. The Maximum-Length Sequence System Analyzer (MLSSA), developed and marketed by DRA Laboratories, is an example, and has become a de facto standard for loudspeaker measurements.

(The author wishes to express his gratitude to C. Victor Campos for providing a large quantity of unpublished historical information on the acoustic suspension loudspeaker. Mr. Campos was a member of the technical departments at Acoustic Research and KLH during the 1960s and 1970s, and since 1986 he has been Director of Product Development for Adcom, an audio equipment firm based in East Brunswick, New Jersey.) [Audio 1969; Badmaieff 1966; Bailey 1965; Borwick, 1988; Bullock 1986; Dickason 1987; Eargle 1977; Galo 1982; Hillman 1989; Linkwitz 1976; Olson, M. 1947; Olson, M. 1954; Small 1972; Small 1973; Thiele 1971; Turner 1988; Villchur 1965; White 1987.]

Gary A. Galo

LOUISIANA FIVE. One of the pioneer jazz groups, active in 1918–1920. Members were Alcide Nunez, clarinet; Charlie Panelli, trombone; Joe Cawley, piano; Karl Berger, banjo; and Anton Lada, drums (and leader). They recorded for Emerson in December 1918, making five sides; the first was "Heart Sickness Blues" (#9150). In 1919 they continued with Emerson, and also made three Edison Diamond Discs (beginning with "Foot Warmer" and "B-Hap-E"; #50569, also on Blue Amberol cylinders #3843, #3789). There were also some Columbias and Okehs; then the group returned to Emerson for its final sessions, in December 1919 and January 1920. Rust says that a Lyric record of September 1920, although carrying the Louisiana Five identification, was "almost certainly . . . made by a different personnel." [Dethlefson 1991 has a photo of the group, p. 56; Rust 1969.]

LOUISIANA PHONOGRAPH CO. A New Orleans firm, located at 128 Gravier St. It was established ca. 1891, as one of the affiliates of the **North American Phonograph Co.** The company took an independent stance, and not only leased business machines but sold cylinders and phonographs, leased coin-ops, and made records for sale. In 1891 it was making about $500 a month from each coin-op on location. The firm's own records featured Paoletti's Southern Band, performing marches, waltzes, polkas, and the like. And there was a series of "Brudder Rasmus Sermons" delivered by Louis Vasnier ("very humorous," stated one advertisement, and "faithful reproductions of a dusky style of pulpit oratory that is rapidly passing away"). H.T. Howard was president of the firm in 1891–1893.

LOVIN' SPOONFUL. American rock group established in 1965. Members were John Sebastian (singer, guitarist, harmonica player), Zalman Yanovsky (singer, lead guitarist), Steve Boone (bass guitarist), and Joe Butler (drummer). The group balanced quiet tunes and humor with raucous rock styles. Successful albums included *Do You Believe in Magic?* (Kama Sutra #KLP 8050; 1965), *Hums of the Lovin' Spoonful* (Kama Sutra #KLP 8054; 1966), *Daydream* (Kama Sutra #KLP 8051), and—31 weeks on the charts—*Best of the Lovin' Spoonful* (Kama

Sutra #KLP8056). There were also 14 chart singles, and two major motion picture appearances. The group broke up in late 1967.

LOWE, CHARLES P. American vaudeville and concert performer on xylophone and bells. He recorded widely in the 1890s and early 1900s, beginning with New Jersey Phonograph Co. in 1892. Between 1896 and 1900 he made 28 xylophone cylinders for Columbia, beginning with "Home, Sweet Home" (#12,000), and including a variety of pieces such as "Carnival of Venice," "Charleston Blues," and "Cordelia Polka." He started with Victor in September 1900 with "Carnival of Venice" (#V-205) on the xylophone, and continued with the label to November 1904, making a total of 35 records. Lowe also worked for other labels until he quit recording in about 1905. [Brooks 1979.]

LP record. *See* LONG PLAYING RECORD.

LUCKY 13 PHONOGRAPH CO. A New York firm, located in 1916 at 3 E. 12th St. It was established in 1915, as manufacturer of the Cleartone and Lucky 13 lines of disc players, in 33 different models. Advertising in *TMW* continued through November 1919.

LUDGATE RECORDS (label). A British record issued from 1921 to 1924, offering dance and popular music. The owner was Dollond & Co., Ltd., a very old scientific optics firm. Records were drawn from the stock of the Universal Music Co., Ltd., which held the Gennett matrices that had belonged to Invicta Record Co., Ltd. (Invicta had exchanged certain matrices with the Starr Piano Co.) and Vocalion material that had come through the Aeolian Co., Ltd., and then the Vocalion Gramophone Co., Ltd. [Andrews*.]

LUNCEFORD, JIMMIE, 1902–1947. American jazz saxophonist and Big Band leader, born James Melvin Lunceford in Fulton, Missouri, on 6 June 1902. He learned the saxophone, trombone, flute, and guitar as a youth, and performed while attending Fisk University. In 1929 he organized his own band. The ensemble benefited from Sy Oliver's arrangements in 1933–1939, and created a powerful swing ef-

fect. Willie Smith led the reed section, Oliver the trumpets. The band had an important Cotton Club engagement in 1934, gaining acclaim for the hot style of numbers such as "White Heat" (Victor #24586; 1934) and Lunceford's theme song, "Jazznocracy" (Victor #24522; 1934). Lunceford had made two Victor sides earlier, in Memphis in 1930; but 1934 marked the start of his long series of regular recordings. He was one of the early Decca artists, making hits with "Organ Grinder's Swing" (#908; 1935), and "Margie" (#1617; 1938). In 1939 the band recorded for Vocalion, then in 1940 for Columbia. They were back with Decca in 1941, at the peak of their popularity, then they declined in public interest, along with most of the Big Bands after the World War II. Lunceford died in Seaside, Oregon, on 12 July 1947.

LYNN, LORETTA, 1935– . American country singer, born Loretta Webb in Butcher Hollow, Kentucky, on 14 Apr 1935.; a coal miner's daughter. She taught herself guitar as a child, and also learned about marriage at an early age, taking Oliver Lynn as her husband when she was 13. The couple moved to Bellingham, Washington, where she sang on radio and in clubs. She was noticed by an executive from Zero records, and contracted with the label, making the successful "I'm a Honky Tonk Girl" (Zero #1011; 1960). She toured, and then sang in Nashville, moving there in the early 1960s. In 1961 she began to record for Decca, and had a hit with "I Walked Away from the Wreck" (#31323). Chart songs followed every year, as Lynn appeared on *Grand Ole Opry*, and toured Canada and Europe. She recorded duets with Ernest Tubbs and with Conway Twitty, and was acclaimed as the top country female artist. She made LP albums in the 1960s and 1970s for MCA and Decca. The title of Lynn's most famous song, "Coal Miner's Daughter" (Decca #32749; 1970), was used for her autobiography and for a 1980 film about her life.

LYRADION MANUFACTURING CO. An Indiana firm, located in Mishawaka. It marketed a radio-phonograph console, wired for its own receiver or for Westinghouse receivers, in 1923. *TMW* reported the firm had declared bankruptcy in April 1924.

LYRAPHONE CO. OF AMERICA. An American firm, first advertising as the Lyraphone Co., 220 Fifth Ave., New York, in 1915. In July 1917, by then renamed Lyraphone Co. of America, it had the address 12–14 W. 37th St., with a factory at 31–45 Steuben St., Brooklyn. It was located at 117 Mechanic St., Newark, New Jersey, from August 1919 to early 1921. With the acquisition of the American Piston Ring Co., Lyraphone moved part of its operations into that firm's factory at 704 S. 11th St., in May 1921. The company produced three labels, Lyraphone, Lyric Record, and Lyric. It also sold a circular gramophone with a rubber tone arm.

Lyric Records were announced in July 1917, vertical cut, in 10- and 12-inch sizes. A thousand titles were available by September, including material in 17 languages. Most of the offerings were popular songs and dance music, but there were some classical items. Mario Rodolfi sang "E lucevan le stelle" on #7102. And in 1919 the president, M. J. Samuels, announced that the visiting Sistine Chapel Quartette (from the Sistine Choir of the Vatican) would record for Lyric Records.

The label name was changed to Lyric, and the record label was redesigned, around 1919. It was identified as lateral cut.

A Canadian factory opened in Toronto in April 1920. Another label, Lyraphone, was introduced ca. 1921, using Paramount material. On 24 Oct 1921 Lyraphone went into receivership, but operations continued for some time. [Andrews*; Rust 1978.

LYRIC (label). Records made to order by Estella Mann's Lyric Phonograph Co., 1270 Broadway, New York, the principal performers being her Lyric Trio, in 1898. Other offerings included band and violin selections, and talking records by Harry B. Norman. *See also* LYRAPHONE CO. OF AMERICA.

LYRIC MALE QUARTET. The name taken for certain Edison Diamond Disc recordings by the **Shannon Four.**

LYRIC QUARTET. A mixed vocal group that recorded for Victor in 1906–1918. Members were Harry Macdonough, tenor; Elise Stevenson, soprano (replaced by Olive Kline in 1910); Corinne Morgan, contralto (replaced by Elsie Baker in 1910); and Frank C. Stanley, bass (died in 1910; replaced by William F. Hooley or Reinald Werrenrath). There were 38 numbers by the quartet in the 1917 Victor catalog, displaying their varied repertoire. "Asleep in Jesus" (#17389), "Gloria" from Mozart's 12th Mass (#31589), "My Bonnie Lass She Smileth" (#18146), and "You're in Love" (#18260) are among the selections. Most of the records were still listed in the 1922 catalog, but all had been cut out by 1927.

Lyric Record. *See* LYRAPHONE CO. OF AMERICA.

LYRIC TRIO. (I) A mixed vocal group that recorded for several cylinder labels from ca. 1898. It was perhaps the first recorded trio with a female voice. Original members were Estella Louise Mann, mezzo-soprano; John C. Havens, tenor; and William F. Hooley, bass. Cylinders were made for the Babson Brothers Co., Chicago, ca. 1898 (listed in their 1899 catalog), then for Columbia ca. 1899. Later the group worked for Edison (as the Original Lyric Trio), Berliner, Victor (1900–1901), and others to ca. 1901. Singers on the first Victors were Grace Spencer, Harry Macdonough, and Hooley. While most of the material performed was light opera and popular material, the Trio did venture into grand opera; for example, Edison #7385 was a trio from *Faust*. [Brooks 1979.]

LYRIC TRIO. (II) A male group that recorded for Columbia in 1914–1915, unusual in having only high voices. Members were Will Oakland, countertenor; Albert Campbell and Henry Burr, tenors. Two of their numbers were "Dear Love Days" (#39467; 1915) and "Everything Reminds Me of that Old Sweetheart of Mine" (#39468; 1915).

Lyrics. *See* DRUG LYRICS; SEXUALLY ORIENTED LYRICS.

M

MAAZEL, LORIN, 1930– . American conductor, born of American parents in Neuilly, France, on 6 Mar 1930. He was taken to the U.S. as an infant, and studied violin and piano in Los Angeles. At age eight he conducted a performance of the visiting orchestra from the University of Idaho, and in 1939 he conducted the National Music Camp Orchestra (Interlochen, Michigan) at the New York World's Fair. At age 11 he conducted the NBC Symphony Orchestra, and a year later the New York Philharmonic Orchestra. Then he modestly left conducting and played as a violinist with the Pittsburgh Symphony Orchestra. With a Fulbright Grant to Italy, he conducted various groups there in 1953–1955, then toured Europe and South America. He was the first American to conduct at Bayreuth (1960). In 1962 he conducted at the Metropolitan Opera, and returned to Europe to direct various ensembles. Maazel succeeded George Szell as music director of the Cleveland Orchestra in 1972, remaining to 1982. He took the post of artistic director of the Vienna State Opera in 1982.

Among Maazel's distinguished recordings are the Beethoven Ninth Symphony with the Cleveland Orchestra (CBS #MK 76999), the Mahler symphonies with the Vienna Philharmonic Orchestra, also for CBS, and complete operas *Carmen* (Erato #880373) and *Luisa Miller* (DGG #415 366–2GH).

MACDONALD, THOMAS HOOD, 1859–1911. American inventor, born in Marysville, California. He was a research scientist at the Bridgeport, Connecticut, plant of the American Graphophone Co., and developed many key devices in the cylinder and disc fields. Macdonald was granted 54 individual patents, and two as joint inventor with Frank L. Capps. His most important ones were for the Graphophone, Type N—the "Bijou" (*see* COLUMBIA RECORD PLAYERS for details on this and the other models mentioned here); it was U.S. patent #569,290 (filed 2 Nov 1895; granted 13 Oct 1896). Later he filed for the double-spring "Eagle" Graphophone, on 16 Sept 1897; patent #680,794 granted 20 August 1901). A toy Graphophone, marketed 1899, had patent #683,130 (filed 21 Feb 1899; granted 24 Sept 1901). An invention of special interest was the Multiple Graphophone, marketed as the Multiplex Grand; Macdonald received patent #711,706 for it (filed 11 June 1898; granted 21 Oct 1902). This was the first attempt at stereo recording, using three separately recorded tracks on the same cylinder. As all the records have been lost, it cannot be ascertained how well the process worked, but it was shown at the Paris Exposition of 1900. Macdonald went to England to organize Columbia's British factory at Earlsfield, Surrey, in 1905; cylinder and disc records were produced there. He died on 3 Dec 1911. [Koenigsberg 1990.]

MACDONOUGH, HARRY, 1871–1931. Canadian tenor, born as John Scantlebury MacDonald, on 30 May 1871 in Windsor, Ontario. He was one of the most popular early recording artists, having made cylinders before 1900 for the Michigan Electric Co. (to be played in **coin-ops**) and for Edison. His surname was misspelled as Macdonough on his first cylinder label, and he decided to leave it that way; then he deliberately changed the first name. Ralph Raymond was another performing name he used. His first Edison record was "Good-Bye, Sweet Dream, Good-Bye" (#6500; 1898); he made 105 Edison cylinders by 1912, all popular ballads of the day. He began working with Victor in 1903, making "No One to Love" (#2183), and made some 350 records by 1908. "The Holy City" was his greatest Victor hit (#94; 1903). Macdonough was a member of the Schubert Trio, and of the Edison Quartet (also known as the Haydn Quartet) until it disbanded in 1914. Then he sang with Orpheus Quartet and the Lyric Quartet. He made duets with Grace Spencer and many other star performers. The "Miserere" duet from *Trovatore*, with Olive Kline, was long one of the most popular Victor offerings. There were still 77 titles in the 1917 Victor catalog, but the number had dropped to four ("Miserere" one of them) by 1927.

Macdonough was also active in the Victor business office, as assistant recording director. He carried on with both executive and performing work from the early 1900s to 1920, then quit recording but remained as an executive until 1925, at which time he moved to Columbia as director of recording studios. He died on 26 Sep 1931. [Walsh 1943/11–12; 1952/5.]

MADISON (label). An American record issued from about 1926 to 1931; it was an affiliate of Grey Gull. Although "Madison Record Co." appears on the labels, "the firm had no corporate existence" (Rust). It was the Woolworth stores that distributed them for $.10 each. A few interesting jazz numbers are found, but nearly all the material is standard dance and popular song. [Barr 1982; Rust 1978.]

MAGNAVOX CONSUMER ELECTRONICS CO. Magnavox is the familiar name of this American firm, though it was renamed in 1985 to NAP Consumer Electronics Corp. It is now a subsidiary of North American Philips Corp. It was located in 1991 at POB 6950, Knoxville, Tennessee. Originally the Magnavox Corp., it was a well-known maker of radios and phonographs, having begun as a manufacturer of

amplifiers for projection of recordings or live voices to large audiences (thus the company name). The amplifier—as described in *TMW* April 1920—was called a Telemegafone; it had 100 times the volume of an ordinary player, operating with a storage battery and external horn.

MAGNETIC RECORDING. Varying magnetic patterns, which correspond to sound waves, can be imposed on a moving magnetizable surface. Such patterns can be played back; the magnetic patterns can be read and transduced to sound waves. This principle, which underlies all modern tape recording systems, was discovered independently by several 19th-century inventors. Thomas Edison, while working on the cylinder phonograph in the late 1870s, observed that it would be possible to magnetize indented tracks on a tinfoil cylinder, then to record in the tracks, and read the deformations in the foil with an electromagnet. He did not develop that idea, but Charles Sumner Tainter did some experiments in the Volta Laboratory. Tainter's approach was to propose a fountain pen attached to the recording diaphragm, the pen to carry ink that contained bits of iron; the pen would then write on a paper covered cylinder in response to the sound signal. He filed on 29 August 1885 for a patent, which was granted (U.S. #341,287; 4 May 1886), but decided to concentrate on mechanical cylinder recording instead of pursuing the electromagnetic trail.

An article by Oberlin Smith, "Some Possible Form of Phonograph," appeared in *Electrical World* on 8 Sep 1888; in it Smith proposed that particles of steel, carried by cotton or silk thread, could serve as the magnetized medium for recording telephone speech. Those particles could be scanned by an electromagnet. But Smith did not develop the notion into a patent.

The first working magnetic recorder was the **Telegraphone** of the Danish engineer **Valdemar Poulsen**, dating from 1898. That device looked something like a cylinder phonograph, with its cylinder grooved to hold a carbon steel wire. An electric motor rotated the cylinder at 84 inches per second, running the wire past the poles of an electromagnet. Signals were indeed inscribed on that wire; one message remains playable to this day. But there was a lack of amplification, and a major obstacle of short playing time—limited to no more than a minute per length of wire. One of Paulsen's patents suggested variant media, such as a band (steel tape) machine, and a paper strip coated with magnetizable metal dust. Later he and Oscar Pedersen did construct a usable wire machine for dictation, with 20 minutes playing time. Both the British Post Office and War Office—and the U.S. Navy— bought these devices before and during World War I.

Lee De Forest suggested in 1924 the possible application of his amplifier to the wire recording process, thus allowing music reproduction, but he did not follow up on the concept. A year later Henry C. Bullis got a U.S. patent (#1,213,150) for the application of magnetic recording in motion pictures; this concept was not immediately developed either. A strong deterrent to all magnetic systems designers was the success of the talking machine in both its cylinder and disc formats. In the years before World War I improvements in recording machines and media poured from hundreds of thriving manufacturers, and the public in America and Europe was apparently insatiable for the products.

Nevertheless research continued. W. L. Carlson and G. W. Carpenter patented their substitution of high-frequency bias in place of direct-current bias applied to the recording head in 1921 (U.S. #1,640,881). And in Germany, Kurt Stille made diverse ameliorations and innovations. He developed a finer wire, capable of longer duration; and a steel-tape recording machine with sprocket holes in the tape, the purpose being synchronization with motion picture film. His wire machine had a cartridge containing supply and take-up reels, on the order of today's cassette. It was patented in U.K. (#331,859; 1928). He described it in a 1930 article, under the name of Dailygraph, and saw it receive some commercial production: rights were acquired by the International Telephone and Telegraph Co. in 1932, who redesigned it and produced it in Germany as the Textophone (1933).

Stille's steel tape machine was noisy and erratic, and ran too fast (six feet per second) to be practical. A demonstration in London in 1929, by film producer Ludwig Blattner, was not successful in blending film and speech. Blattner—who had acquired the rights from Stille by license—persisted with this sound carrier, and sold some devices to the British Broadcasting Corp. in 1930. New models were devised with playing time up to 30 minutes per spool, and a British Blattnerphone Co. was chartered. Later the rights passed to Guglielmo Marconi's Wireless Telegraph Co., where further improvements were forthcoming, sufficient to make the machines usable at the BBC into the 1950s. A comparable machine was developed by the C. Lorenz AG in Germany and adopted by the German radio system.

Military research in World War II led to American wire recorder models with 0.1 millimeter stainless steel wire moving at 30 inches/ second; one spool could run 60 minutes. Commercially available recorders were made by the Brush Development Co. and Western Electric Co., both with steel tapes. Marvin Camras, of Armour Research Foundation (Chicago), received many patents in the early 1940s, and saw production of steel wire machines by General Electric Co. Wire recording reached high quality in the late 1940s, notably with an Armour Research model and the Magnecorder in the U.S., and a Boosey & Hawkes device in Britain. However, the rapid improvements in plastic tape recording soon eclipsed the wire machines.

Fritz Pfleumer, of Dresden, brought to a practical stage the idea of a paper or plastic base for a recording tape. He began experiments in 1927, using soft iron powder as the magnetic coat, attaching it to the base with sugar or other organic binders. Pfleumer received German patents #500,900 and #544,302, then U.K. patent #333,154 (1928). Various improvements in the tape were made in Germany through the 1930s. By 1934 the Badische Anilin und Soda Fabrik was producing cellulose acetate tapes coated with ferric oxide. The Allgemeine Elektrizitäts Gesellschaft (AEG) was able to record a symphonic concert on their **Magnetophon** in 1936, albeit not very

satisfactorily. It took another two years of research by AEG before a machine suitable for
broadcasting was available, and music could
at last be presented in decent rendition, with a
frequency response of 50–6,000 Hz.

In the postwar period tape recording
spread throughout the world. The introduction of Mylar as a thinner, durable base accompanied numerous technical refinements. The
Ampex Corp. was the first to market high
quality tape equipment in the U.S. (1948). Sales
of pre-recorded **reel to reel tape** began around
1954, but the medium was not commercially
successful because of the clumsy manual process required to thread a tape onto the take-up
reel. Quality did reach high levels, and tapes
were soon utilized by record companies as the
original recording media, with the signal later
transferred to disc.

A monumental stride was taken by Philips
in 1963, with the introduction of the audiocassette (see CASSETTE) and its compact portable
recorder. Improvements in fidelity followed.
Then in 1986 Sony brought out the **DAT** (Digital Audio Tape), transforming the field. [Hoover
1971 has illustrations of reel-to-reel and cassette formats, p. 125; Jansen 1983; Magnetic
1982.] *See also* TAPE; TAPE RECORDING.

MAGNETOPHON. The magnetic tape recorder first made by Allgemeine Elektrizitäts
Gesellschaft (AEG) in 1935. It was demonstrated at the Berlin Radio Fair, showing the
new cellulose acetate base tapes coated with
ferric oxide. Although intended for business
dictation, the machine was used also for musical recording. When Thomas Beecham and the
London Philharmonic Orchestra performed in
Germany in 1936 the Magnetophon recorded
the concert. In 1938 AEG produced an improved version, type K4. It had a frequency
response of 50–6,000 Hz, adequate for radio
use. In 1942 another improved version, type
HTS, was put into service; it carried the frequency range of 50–9,000 Hz, while reducing
distortion characteristics and signal to noise
ratio. During the Second World War the machine was used for broadcasting taped concerts, with a fidelity that puzzled listeners outside Germany; when the Allies captured Radio

Luxembourg on 11 Sep 1944 they found the
Magnetophon, in the last version, type K7. It
ran the tape at 30.31 inches/second (77 centi-
meters/second), and gave up to 10,000 Hz in
response. It had facilities for editing, a time
clock, and a means of running two or more
machines in synchronization for continuous
play. One tape reel ran 22 minutes.

Manufacture of high quality machines
based on the Magnetophon began outside Germany in 1947—one of the first was the EMI's
BTR1. In America the design was modified by
Jack Mullin and Ampex Corp.

MAGNOLA TALKING MACHINE CO. A
Chicago firm, located in 1916–1923 at 711 Milwaukee Ave. It made the Magnola line of record
players, with five models advertised in *TMW*
of January 1917. An advertisement in the January 1923 *TMW* reported the "7th year of steady
success."

Main amplifier. *See* POWER AMPLIFIER.

MAJESTIC (label). (I) A seven-inch vertical-
cut record offered for $.25 by the Majestic
Phonograph Co., Inc., of 247–253 W. 19th St.,
New York, in 1916–1917. Advertising in *TMW*
for October 1916 gave the firm's name as Majestic Record Corp., 37 E. 28th St., New York.
Playing time was said to be "as long as any 10-
inch record," and a nine-inch disc to play 4 1/
2 minutes was announced for November 1916
at $.50. Thirty new titles were marketed each
month in 1916: classical, popular and dance,
humor, and sacred numbers. There were 100
titles in the catalog by November 1916. A bankruptcy petition was filed on 27 Aug 1917, and
the stock of 700 titles was offered at a bargain
sale.

A rare disc today, Majestic had an etched
design instead of a paper label. [Rust 1978.]

MAJESTIC (label). (II) An American record
produced ca. 1923 by the Olympic Disc Record
Corp. for sale in Ross Stores, Inc. The catalog
series is the same as that of the **Olympic** label,
suggesting an affiliation between Olympic and
Majestic, but they did not entirely duplicate
each other. [Rust 1978.]

MAJESTIC (label). (III) An American record issued by Majestic Records, Inc., 29 W. 57th St., New York, a subsidiary of the Majestic Radio and Television Co. (St. Charles, Illinois), from 1945 to 1947. The output consisted of pop, jazz, country and western, and gospel material. Majestic bought the Hit label (the Classic Record Co.) from Eli Oberstein and continued issuing Hit concurrently with the new Majestic, while also reissuing Hit material on Majestic. The new label was immediately successful, sparked by the Eddy Howard recording of "To Each His Own" (#1070; 1946). Other artists on Majestic included Louis Prima, Ray McKinley, Jimmie Lunceford, Jack Leonard, Ella Logan, and Jimmie Durante. Former New York Mayor Jimmy Walker was president of Majestic Records, Inc.; **John Hammond** was recording director from 1946. Around 1949 Mercury Records acquired the Majestic catalog. [Porter 1978 is a label listing.]

MAJESTIC PHONOGRAPH CO. A Chicago firm established in 1916, maker of the Majestic line of record players in five models. Location was 218 S. Wabash Ave. The firm was not listed in the Chicago directory after 1916.

MALE QUARTETS. The early use of the talking machine for reproducing music coincided with the peak of America's male quartet movement. The first quartet to record (1891) was the **Manhasset Quartet**. Many of the earliest male recording artists were not only vocal soloists, but also members of quartets. Henry Burr, Albert Campbell, Billy Murray, Arthur Collins, Steve Porter, and William Hooley were some of the better known artists who doubled as soloists and harmony singers. The songs of the times as recorded by the male quartets stimulated the art of quartetting around the country because many of these tunes could be readily harmonized by average singers applying "ear harmonies" to the recorded songs.

Early recording artists were sturdy, intrepid vocalists. Singing into the horns was vocally demanding, since the master records they made around 1900 would only produce 25 to 50 cylinder pressings before wearing out. If a particular recording was selling well, the artists would have to make further masters.

Even multiple horns, which cut up to seven masters per take, did not relieve the tedium. There was no **crooning** in the pre-microphone days prior to 1925, and singers had to possess durable voices to sustain the rigors of the recording session. The quartet men were also versatile, often singing more than one part as they went from session to session: here a duet, there a trio; then a quartet, maybe a quintet; yesterday a soloist, tomorrow a choralist.

Victor had the finest catalog of male ensembles, notably the **Hayden Quartet, Peerless Quartet**, and the **American Quartet**. Quartets often used different names when recording for different companies. Thus the American Quartet became the **Premier Quartet** for Edison; the **Shannon Four** became the Singing Sophomores when doing college songs for Columbia, and then became the **Revelers** for modern cabaret style songs on Victor.

The Peerless Quartet was an offshoot of the Columbia Quartet, which can be traced to the Invincible Quartet, also known as the Invincible Four. It was one of the more stable groups, in a time when the genealogy of quartets was a tangled web of personnel changes, with singers moving frequently from group to group. Henry Burr provided continuity for Peerless, as well as management, for almost 20 years.

Between them, Henry Burr and Billy Murray, lead singers for the Peerless and American Quartets, recorded about 16,000 songs through the years, including solos, duets, trios, and other combinations. (By comparison, Bing Crosby and Frank Sinatra recorded about 3,600 songs between them.)

A dramatic change in vocal style arrived with the microphone in the mid-1920s. Where the horn had required singers to push their voices, the electric recording process allowed them to croon softly. Gene Austin, Rudy Vallee, and Bing Crosby replaced the old time singers like Burr and Murray. By the end of the 1920s most of the recording quartets of the acoustic era had broken up; a few like the Maple City Four and some vaudeville foursomes survived. (There were still 10 sides by the Peerless and eight sides by the Shannon in the 1940 Victor catalog.) In the 1940s there were only a few significant ensembles, such as the **Ink Spots**, the **Mills Brothers,** The Sportsmen, and the Golden Gate Quartet.

Val Hicks

MALNECK, MATTY, 1904–1981. American jazz violinist, Big Band leader, and composer, born in Newark, New Jersey, on 10 Dec 1904. He played violin and made arrangements for the Paul Whiteman orchestra in 1927–1938. Later he had his own orchestra, which was on the Dick Powell radio program and other shows in 1942–1943. Malneck's most popular composition was "Stairway to the Stars" (1939). Among his more interesting recordings were "Londonderry Air" / "Listen to the Mocking Bird" (Brunswick # 8413; 1939) and "Carnival of Venice" / "William Tell Overture" (Columbia #35299; 1939).

MAMAS AND THE PAPAS. American rock group of the mid-1960s, consisting of John Phillips, Dennis Doherty, (Ms.) Cass Elliott, and Michelle Gilliam Phillips. It was unusual among rock ensembles in having a balance of male and female performers. The group made 14 chart singles in 1966–1967, beginning with "California Dreamin'" (Dunhill #4020; 1966). "Monday, Monday" (Dunhill #4026; 1966) was said to have sold 160,000 copies the day it appeared in the shops. There were seven chart albums in the 1960s, of which the most popular were *If You Can Believe Your Eyes and Ears* (Dunhill #D 50006; 1966) and *The Mamas and the Papas* (Dunhill # D 500010). The group broke up in 1968, but several successful albums of their 1960s material appeared later, the last in 1973. John Phillips brought together a new ensemble under the name Mamas and the Papas in 1982 and achieved modest popularity but had no chart records.

MANCINI, HENRY, 1924– . American composer and orchestra leader, born in Cleveland on 16 Apr 1924. After study at the Juilliard School he played piano in dance bands. In the late 1940s he was arranging for Tex Beneke's band. He was in Hollywood writing movie scores in the 1950s, and also composed music for television programs. In 1961 he wrote "Moon River" and in 1962 "Days of Wine and Roses"; both songs won Academy Awards. As a con-

ductor he made 14 chart singles of his own compositions and other works, and 30 chart albums. *Peter Gunn* (RCA LPM#1956; 1959) and *The Pink Panther* (RCA LPM #2795; 1964) were the greatest sellers of his many successful LPs.

MANDEL (label). A lateral-cut record of the **Mandel Manufacturing Co.,** 1455 W. Congress St., Chicago, issued from January 1921. Masters came from Arto, Lyric, and other sources supplied by the Standard Records brokering agency of New York. The material was popular vocal and dance numbers. Mandel was only advertised once, in April 1921, with a selling price of $1.00. [Rust 1978; a label list appeared in *RR* #88 (January 1968).]

MANDEL MANUFACTURING CO. A Chicago firm, established in 1915, located in 1916 at 501 Laflin St., in 1921 at 1455 W. Congress St. Louis Mandel was one of the owners. Joseph F. Grossman was president, J. H. Hupp was secretary, and Raymond T. Bell works superintendent. The Mandel line of disc players was on sale in 1916, in four models. The **Mandel label** record appeared in 1921. In June 1921 liquidation proceedings were reported. Louis and Nathan Mandel were listed as proprietors of the Mandel Phono Parts Co., 1539 Milwaukee Ave., in the Chicago 1923 directory. That firm was not listed in subsequent directories.

MANDOLIN RECORDINGS. In July 1899 there was an anonymous rendition of "D'amor passaggero" on Gramophone Co. record #57351, made in Naples. Two Neapolitan mandolinists made 11 Gramophone discs in Naples in 1900: Professor Giandolfi and Professor Pallavicini; among the latter's performances were "Polka con variazioni" (#57358) and "Trionfo mandolinistico" (#57361). Guido Volpe recorded one side for G & T in London, "Sylvia Ballet: Pizzicato" (#37350; 1902).

Edison cylinders presented mandolin playing as early as 1899, the earliest number being #7233: "Pixies," performed by W. C. Townsend. The same artist was heard on another four cylinders, and Samuel S. Siegel was heard on 10, one a duet with guitarist M. L. Wolf, "Autumn Evening" (#9014; 1905). There were six mandolin solos in the Victor 1917 catalog, performed by Clarence Penney or William Place, Jr. Mandolins in groups of guitars were featured on 11 other Victor discs, with Samuel S. Siegel performing on several of them. In the 1922 Victor catalog there were only four solos and five records of mandolins with guitar(s). By 1927 the category had disappeared from the Victor catalog. Mandolin records were not listed in the later Victor catalogs, nor in the Columbia catalogs of the 1940s. In the early LP era a few recordings by the Mandolin Orchestra of Paris appeared on the Period label.

MANHASSET (MANHANSETT) QUARTETTE. A studio vocal group of the 1890s, formed expressly for recordings; "possibly the first vocal group to record under its own name" (Brooks). Membership varied; the original group consisted of John Bieling, tenor; George Gaskin, second tenor; Joe Riley, baritone; and Jim Cherry, bass. Later Cherry was replaced by Walter Snow, and for a time by a bass named Evans. The quartet's first Edison recording, "Reception Medley," was made on 27 Sept 1891. They made 19 other cylinders on that day. In 1892 they sang for the New Jersey Phonograph Co., and for Boswell; they worked also for Columbia, Berliner, Zonophone, and Leeds & Catlin. The group broke up in 1896, succeeded by the Edison Quartet. [Brooks 1979; Walsh 1962/10.]

MANHATTAN LADIES QUARTET. A vocal group that recorded for Edison after 1912. It consisted of Irene Cummings, Mabel Meade Davis, Annie Laurie McCorkle, and Anne Winkoop. [Walsh 1962/10.]

MANHATTAN QUARTET. A male vocal group that recorded chiefly for Edison and Victor from ca. 1912 to 1929. The singers identified were Henry Weiman, Arthur Hall, Nick Latterner, and Frank Schwarz. Victor's 1912 catalog was the first to list them, as singers of German language material. During World War I this was understandably an untenable specialty in the U.S., but the quartet was in the catalog again after the Armistice. "Deutschland über Alles" (Edison Diamond Disc #50187; 1914) was cut out of the Edison catalog on 12

July 1918 "for patriotic reasons." Of the 14 Diamond Discs by the Manhattan Quartet the "most amusing title" (Walsh) appeared in 1927; it was a dance-tempo version of "Studentenlieder" / "Volkslieder" (#57023). [Walsh 1962/10; Walsh 1972/12.]

MANILOW, BARRY, 1946–. American vocalist, pianist, accordionist, arranger, and composer of popular songs; born in Brooklyn on 17 June 1946. He began as a performer, then made arrangements and composed television and radio commercials. His composition "Mandy" was a hit in 1974 (Bell #45613); he followed it with "It's a Miracle" (Arista #0108; 1975), "I Write the Songs" (Arista #0157; 1975), "Looks Like We Made It" (Arista # 244; 1977), and "Can't Smile without You" (Arista #0305; 1978). Manilow had 18 albums on the charts between 1975 and 1985; those with the longest chart life were *Tryin' to Get the Feeling* (Arista #AB4060; 1975), 93 weeks; *This One's for You* (Arista #AB4090; 1976), 92 weeks; and *Live* (Arista #AL8050), 87 weeks.

MANN, ESTELLA LOUISE, 1871–1947. American soprano, born in Nashville, Tennessee, on 1 Nov 1871. She was the first woman to make a career of recording, doing grand opera to coon songs. Mann's solo and ensemble records came from Columbia in the late 1890s. She also made discs for Berliner, and at least one Zonophone, "Prince of Peace" (#9461; 1900). She also sang with the Lyric Trio. Mann was also the first woman to own a share of a record company, the **Lyric Phonograph Co.** She died in Evansville, Indiana, on 24 Aug 1947. [Brooks 1979; Walsh 1952/4. A photograph of her making a record in 1898 appears in Hoover 1971.]

MANN, HERBIE, 1930–. American jazz flutist, born in New York on 16 April 1930. He studied at the Manhattan School of Music, and performed with major symphony orchestras. He made popular records in 1968 ("Unchain My Heart"; A&M #896) and 1969 ("Memphis Underground"; Atlantic #2621), then was less prominent until the mid-1970s. The single "Hi Jack" (Atlantic #3246; 1975) was on the charts 14 weeks. Mann had four chart albums between 1975 and 1979, and another with Fire Island. *Discotheque* was the album with the longest chart life, 17 weeks.

MANNE, SHELLY, 1920–1984. American jazz drummer, born Sheldon Manne in New York on 11 June 1920. As a young man he played saxophone in New York clubs and on transatlantic ships. At age 18 he changed from saxophone to drums. He was with the Raymond Scott and Will Bradley bands in 1941–1942, then with Les Brown in 1942. There were important records with Coleman Hawkins and Woody Herman in 1948–1949. "The Man I Love" (Signature #9001) with Hawkins, Eddie Heywood and Oscar Pettiford showed his skills to great advantage. After military service he joined Stan Kenton (1946–1947, and at intervals to 1952), then worked with various bands and combos. He recorded for Decca, Capitol, and several other labels. Manne absorbed the new bebop style, teaming with Dizzy Gillespie in 1945, but he preferred a cooler approach and became one of the forces behind West Coast jazz. He played in trios with André Previn and with Ornette Coleman. Manne's Capitol records with Stan Kenton were popular (notably "Artistry in Percussion," #289; 1946), and his LPs for Contemporary—reissued on Fantasy CD—(*Shelly Manne and His Friends, My Fair Lady* (made with Previn in 1956), and *My Son the Drummer*) presented some of his best work. In 1984 he backed Barry Manilow in the chart album *2:00 AM Paradise Cafe* (Arista #AL8–8245. Manne won the *Downbeat* and *Metronome* polls many times during 1947–1960 as the favorite jazz drummer. He operated a popular club in Hollywood, Shelly's Manne-Hole, from 1960 to 1974. Manne died 26 Sep 1984 in Los Angeles.

MANOIL (JAMES) CO., INC. A firm established in Newburgh, New York, in 1916. It made the Manophone, a disc player, in six models.

MANONE, WINGY, 1904–1982. American jazz trumpeter and vocalist, born Joseph Mannone on 13 Feb 1904 in New Orleans. He lost his right arm in an accident as a child, and learned to play the trumpet with the left. He played in riverboats as a teenager, moved to Mobile, Alabama, and then to St. Louis. He had his own band by 1926, performing in the South and in the early 1930s in Chicago and New York. In 1935 he made a hit record, singing a spoof on "Isle of Capri" (Vocalion #2913). He was featured in the Bing Crosby motion picture *Rhythm on the River* in 1940 and recorded the title song for Bluebird (#B-10844; 1940); later he appeared frequently with Crosby. Manone's Big Band of 1941 had Mel Powell at piano and Zutty Singleton on drums; they made some fine sides for Bluebird, like "The Boogie Beat'll Getcha" (#B-11298). His later work, based in Las Vegas, tended to be more comical than jazzy. He continued performing into the 1970s. Manone died in Las Vegas on 9 July 1982.

MANTELLI, EUGENIA, 1860–1926. Italian soprano, also mezzo-soprano. Her debut was at Lisbon in 1883. In 1894 she sang at the Bolshoi Opera, as Mantelli-Mantovani, then toured Russia with Francesco Tamagno. She was at the Metropolitan Opera in 1894–1900, and in 1902–1903. Bettini recorded four numbers by her in 1899. She also worked for Zonophone ca. 1905. IRCC reissued four of the arias made at that time on a seven-inch LP (#7007; 1955). "Una voce poco fa" is perhaps the most distinguished of that group.

MANTOVANI, ANNUNZIO PAOLO, 1905–1980. Italian/British conductor, born in Venice on 15 Nov 1905. He went to London as a youth and attended Trinity College of Music. At 18 he formed an orchestra in Birmingham, and achieved popularity on the radio and on tours of Britain. He became a British subject in 1933. After World War II he concentrated on radio and recording, gaining world fame for his cascading string sound. The orchestra toured the U.S. and Canada in 1956. Mantovani died in Tunbridge Wells, England, on 29 Mar 1980.

Mantovani recorded first in the 1920s as a violinist, often as Signor Gandini. He was heard on Columbia, Crystalate, British Homophone, and Decca records with various orchestras. It was with Decca in the 1940s that he developed the lush orchestral sound that made him famous. He went on to make 50 chart albums, all for the London label, between 1955 and 1971, of which the most popular was *Exodus* (London #LL3321; 1960), 43 weeks.

MANUAL SEQUENCE. Also known as standard sequence. The recording sequence of 78 rpm or LP discs in an album in which the material flows from disc one, side one, to disc one, side two; thence to disc two, side one, etc. With the advent of automatic record changers, manufacturers provided alternative sequencing that would keep the material in order when the discs dropped one after the other onto the turntable; in that "automatic sequence" the material flowed from disc one, side one, to disc two, side one, etc. Album numbers showed the distinction: e.g., for Columbia Masterworks, M or X prefixes denoted manual sequence and MM or MX denoted automatic sequence.

MAPLESON CYLINDERS. Lionel S. Mapleson (1865–1937), nephew of impresario "Colonel" James Henry Mapleson, was librarian of the Metropolitan Opera Co. in 1889–1937. On 20 Mar 1900 he purchased an Edison "Home" Model A phonograph, for $30.00, and on 21 March he made a cylinder of Suzanne Adams singing "Valse," a song written by her husband Leo Stern. On 30 or 31 Mar 1900 Mapleson recorded the voice of Marcella Sembrich. During the seasons of 1901–1902 and 1902–1903, Mapleson recorded on 120 cylinders segments of live performances at the Metropolitan Opera, at first not too successfully from the prompter's box, then with better results with a six-foot horn from a vantage point over the stage. More than 60 records from the 1902–1903 season survive: "remarkably consistent in quality and often genuinely impressive" (Hall).

The cylinders remained in the Mapleson family until 1937, when William H. Seltsam acquired 124 of them. Through the initiative of Seltsam and his International Record Collectors' Club, reissues of 64 cylinders were prepared and released on nineteen 78s and five LPs from 1939 to 1966. Other cylinders were discovered and reissued on LP: 10 through Aida Favia-Artsay came out under the name *Met Stars 1901–02* in 1959. Altogether 136 cylinders are extant today, 117 of vocal operatic selections, four of non-operatic vocal material,

and 11 of instrumental music. These are the survivals of Mapleson's activity. He made many more records, which he took back to his family in London and which disappeared without a trace.

The principal artists heard on these cylinders include several for whom there are no surviving commercial recordings: Georg Anthes (tenor), Lucienne Bréval (soprano), Luigi Mancinelli (conductor), Emilio de Marchi (tenor), Luise Reuss-Belce (contralto), Albert Saléza (tenor), Thomas Salignac (tenor), Fritzi Scheff (soprano), and Milka Ternina (soprano). The other major artists are Suzanne Adams (soprano), Albert Alvarez (tenor), Alexander von Bandrowski (tenor), David Bispham (baritone), Robert Blass (bass), Alois Burgstaller (tenor), Emma Calvé (soprano), Giuseppe Campanari (baritone), Walter Damrosch (conductor), Carlo Dani (tenor), Jean de Reszke (tenor), Andreas Dippel (tenor), Emma Eames (soprano), Johanna Gadski (soprano), Emil Gerhäuser (tenor), Charles Gilbert (baritone), Alfred Hertz (conductor), Louise Homer (contralto), Marcel Journet (bass), Nellie Melba (soprano), Adolph Mühlmann (baritone), Lillian Nordica (soprano), Pol Plançon (bass), Edouard de Reszke (bass), Ernestine Schumann-Heink (contralto), Antonio Scotti (baritone), Marcella Sembrich (soprano), and Anton van Rooy (baritone).

Of all these luminaries, Jean de Reszke is of the greatest interest, for the legendary tenor cannot be heard satisfactorily elsewhere. He is very faint in airs from *L'africaine, Le Cid,* and *Huguenots;* more distinguishable in *Siegfried* Act I. (The IRCC reissue of "Schmiede, mein Hammer" is however wrongly attributed to De Reszke; it is sung by Anthes.)

Five excellent recordings were made of *Götterdämmerung* with Lillian Nordica, and five others give strong documentation of the *Tosca* of 3 January 1903, with Emilio de Marchi and Emma Eames. Two fine cylinders were made of *Fille du régiment,* with Sembrich, Thomas Salignac, and Charles Gilbert.

After years of restoration and research work at the New York Public Library, an LP was issued in 1986 by the Library, distributed by the Metropolitan Opera Guild, of "all the known playable recordings and fragments" made by

Mapleson. Credit for final transfer of the cylinder tapes to LP belongs to engineer Tom Owen and producer David Hamilton. David Hall, who retired as curator of the Rodgers and Hammerstein Archives in 1983, did the basic research and, with Owen, the initial transfer to tape. [Hall 1981/1; 1981/2; Hall 1982/1; Hall 1982/7; Hall 1984; Hall*; Taylor 1987.]

MARATHON (label). An American record marketed by the Nutmeg Record Corp. in November 1928—a seven-inch disc that played as long as a standard 10–inch disc. Distortions in the output affected public interest in the record, which was accordingly discontinued in a few months. [Rust 1978.]

MARATHON RECORD (label). A British issue of the **National Gramophone Co., Ltd.,** in 1912 and National Gramophone Co. (1913), Ltd., in 1913. It was a vertical-cut disc, offered in both 10–inch and 12–inch sizes. The grooves were narrow enough to produce "the first real long play record" (Walsh); at 80 rpm, the discs played five minutes 40 seconds per 10–inch side, and eight minutes 12 seconds per 12–inch side. Marathon #2042 (December 1913) was advertised as "the longest record ever made"; it contained four songs by Tom Kinniburgh. There were "nearly 30 hits on one disc," a dance medley (#2050). A special soundbox was sold to give the records "a clearer tone, and greater volume." The 10–inch discs appeared with numbers 101 to 473, the 12–inch discs with numbers from 2001 to 2065. National Gramophone Co.(1913), Ltd., experienced a financial crisis in 1914, and went into receivership. No new Marathon records were issued after March 1915. [Andrews 1987/4.]

MARCONI, FRANCESCO, 1855–1916. Italian tenor, born in Rome on 14 May 1855. He made his debut in Madrid in the 1878–1879 season as Faust, then sang in Rome and (1880) at La Scala. He gained great popularity throughout Europe, notably in Russia, as well as in South America. His voice was said to be unequaled in Italy before the advent of Enrico Caruso. Unfortunately his recordings were made after his vocal prime. He worked for G & T in Milan, 1903–1904, beginning with #52016,

"Dai campi, dai prati" from *Mefistofele*. Another group of records was made in Milan for the same label in 1908, including an outstanding "Tu che a Dio" from *Lucia*, "Invan, invan" from *Nerone*, and "Vieni fra queste braccia" from *Puritani*; these were reissued by Top Artists Platters in 1959–1961 (#303, 321, 326). Marconi died in Rome on 5 Feb 1916.

MARCONI VELVET TONE (label). In 1906 Guglielmo Marconi, the Italian scientist and developer of radio, visited the American Graphophone Co. plant in Bridgeport, Connecticut, and became a consultant for the firm. October 1907 saw his idea of a thin, flexible, laminated disc with a paper core and plastic surface produced as Columbia's Marconi Velvet-Tone label. Although the disc was a "half century ahead of its time" (Rust) it had to be played with gold-plated needles, each one good for only 12 plays. The public bypassed the new silent surfaces of Velvet Tone because of this considerable cost increment over standard (noisy) discs they were used to. The record was also available in Britain, through an agent. [Rust 1978.]

MARGIN CONTROL. A disc recording technique developed in the early 1950s which controlled groove spacing one revolution ahead of the signal being recorded; it utilized an extra head on the tape reproducer.

MARRINER, NEVILLE, *Sir*, **1924–** . British violinist and conductor, born in Lincoln on 15 Apr 1924. He studied at the Royal College of Music in London, and at the Paris Conservatory. He was a violinist with the Martin String Quartet in 1946–1953, then with the London Symphony Orchestra in 1956–1968. In 1959 he formed a chamber orchestra in London with the name Academy of St. Martin-in-the-Fields (in the Trafalgar Square church), and achieved international stature with performances of music from the baroque to the 20th century. Successful recordings were made for Argo, Philips, and EMI. Marriner formed a similar orchestra in the U.S., the Los Angeles Chamber Orchestra, then another in Australia. He was appointed to the directorship of the Minnesota Orchestra in 1978, and remained to 1985. He directed the Academy group in the Mozart music of the motion picture *Amadeus*; the soundtrack album was on the charts 45 weeks (Fantasy #WAM-1791; 1984). Marriner was knighted in 1985.

MARSALIS, WYNTON, 1961– . American trumpeter, born in New Orleans on 18 Oct 1961, son of jazz pianist Ellis Marsalis. At 14 he won a competition and played the Haydn Trumpet Concerto with the New Orleans Philharmonic Orchestra. He studied at Juilliard School, then played with Art Blakey's Jazz Messengers and toured with a quintet that included his brother Branford, saxophonist. He also worked with Miles Davis. Marsalis has kept classical and jazz careers at international levels; in 1983 he won Grammy's for both categories, and he plays regularly with major symphony orchestras. His best known jazz album was *Hot House Flowers* (Columbia #FC 39530; 1984, and CBS/Sony CD #32DP 183); he had four other chart albums by 1985, all for Columbia.

MARSH LABORATORIES, INC. A Chicago firm established ca. 1921 by Orlando Marsh (1881–1938); successor to Cullen, Marsh & Co. The first address was Suite 625 in the Kimball Building on Wabash Ave., with a move by 1927 to the Lyon & Healy Building at 78 E. Jackson Blvd. A 1931 advertisement again gives the 306 S. Wabash address. T. B. Lambert—"almost certainly the same Lambert of celluloid record fame some two decades earlier" (Bryan)—was vice-president, Marsh was president, though at first Marsh was listed as vice president, and Harve [*sic*] J. Badgerow was president and treasurer. The same advertisement states that "seventeen years ago Orlando R. Marsh instituted the first electrical recording laboratory in the world." If that is accurate, it would date the founding of the Marsh Laboratories (or perhaps Cullen, Marsh & Co.) at 1914, earlier than has been supposed. The principal claim to fame of the laboratories was the creation and production of the first **electrical recordings**, issued on the **Autograph** label in 1924. In 1931 the firm was engaged in "electrical transcription service," providing material for radio stations. While there is no terminal date available

for the firm, Marsh himself was known to be active in the recording business until at least 1936. [Bryan 1990.]

MARSPEN (label). A British record of the mid-1920s, issued in two sizes: 5 3/8 inches and six inches in diameter. It was made by the Edison Bell Works of J. E Hough, Ltd., and also by the Crystalate Gramophone Record Manufacturing Co., Ltd., from the masters of both firms, for distribution by the Marks and Spencer chain of stores. [Andrews*.]

MARTIN, FREDDY, 1906–1983. American dance band leader, born on 9 Dec 1906 in Cleveland. He played tenor saxophone in his youth, and formed a band while still in high school. In 1932 he organized a professional band and had early engagements at the Hotel Bossert in Brooklyn, the Hotel Roosevelt, Waldorf Astoria and other major New York ballrooms. He was also popular in Chicago, and became a fixture in the late 1930s at the Coconut Grove in Los Angeles. Martin's band was featured on radio shows in the 1930s, Success was greatly expanded in 1941 with a hit recording of "Tonight We Love," an adaptation of the first theme of Tchaikovsky's B-Flat Piano Concerto, arranged by Ray Austin and played by Jack Fina (Bluebird #11211). Martin followed that with an adaptation of a theme from the Grieg Concerto (Bluebird #11430). With vocalist Merv Griffin he had a 1948 hit record, "I've Got a Lovely Bunch of Coconuts" (Victor #20-3554). During the 1940s his band appeared in several motion pictures, and he remained active into the 1970s.

MARTIN, RICCARDO, 1874–1952. American tenor, born Hugh Whitfield Martin on 18 Nov 1874 in Hopkinsville, Kentucky. He studied violin and piano as a child, then had some vocal training in Europe. Returning to America, he took up composition under Edward MacDowell at Columbia University (1896). But his singing attracted more notice than his compositions, and he returned to Europe to study in Paris, making his debut in October 1904 in Nantes, as Faust. After further study in Italy, he sang in Verona on 4 Nov 1905, took the name Riccardo Martin, and appeared in Milan, then joined the San Carlo Opera Co. In 1906–1907 he took part in a U.S. tour with the troupe, and on 20 Nov 1907 he made his debut at the Metropolitan Opera Co. as Faust. He remained nine seasons—missing 1916–1917 to sing with the Boston Grand Opera—doing 159 appearances in 17 roles. He was the first American-born tenor to achieve operatic eminence. After his years at the Metropolitan Martin sang with the Chicago Opera Co. in 1920–1922, then settled in New York as a teacher. He died there on 11 Aug 1952.

Martin recorded for Edison in 1908, making "Vesti la giubba" (#B-160) and four other arias, plus Francesco Tosti's "Goodbye." He sang for Victor from 24 Feb 1910 to 8 Dec 1910, doing eight numbers; the first was "Als die alte Mutter" ("Songs My Mother Taught Me") by Dvořák (#87051), and the last the "Addio alla madre" from Cavalleria rusticana (#88277). There was also one Operaphone record, on an eight-inch vertical-cut disc, of "Amarella." [Bott 1980.]

MARTIN, TONY, 1912– . American popular vocalist, born Alvin Morris in Oakland, California, on Christmas day 1912. He sang with various orchestras, including Ray Noble's, and appeared in motion pictures from 1936. He was prominent on radio in the 1940s, then on television, and was a well-known night club performer in the 1970s. Among his notable discs were "Begin the Beguine" / "September Song" (Decca #2375; 1939), "All the Things You Are" (Decca #2932; 1939), and "I Get Ideas" (Victor #20-4141; 1950).

MARTINELLI, GIOVANNI, 1885–1969. Italian tenor, born in Montagnana, near Padua, on 22 Oct 1885. He played clarinet in the town band, then went to study voice in Milan and made his debut there on 3 Dec 1910 in the Rossini Stabat Mater, followed by his operatic debut as Ernani. Puccini heard him sing, and gave him the role of Dick Johnson in the premiere of Fanciulla del West in Rome, on 12 June 1911. He sang at Covent Garden and in Philadelphia, then at the Metropolitan Opera as Rodolfo on 20 Nov 1913, remaining 30 years. His farewell concert was on 8 Mar 1945, but he

sang on, making his final appearance in Turandot (Seattle, 1967) at age 82.

At the Metropolitan he sang Radames 126 times, and Don José 75 times. Wagner was not in his regular repertoire, though he did sing Tristan in German in Chicago opposite Kirsten Flagstad in 1939.

Martinelli recorded prolifically from 1912 through 1968; the discography in Collins 1979 has 202 numbered entries, including broadcasts. In 1913 he made eight Edison Diamond Discs, singing the main tenor arias from Aida, Boheme, Gioconda, Manon Lescaut, Martha, Rigoletto, and Tosca. From 1913 to 1929 he worked with Victor, performing the Italian/French repertoire. The most elegant recordings of that period may be the Aida duets with Rosa Ponselle (1924–1926) and the Carmen duets with Geraldine Farrar (1915). He participated in outstanding ensemble recordings from Forza del destino with Ponselle, Giuseppe de Luca, and Ezio Pinza (1927–1928); and from Faust with Frances Alda and Marcel Journet in 1919. His "Miserere" (Trovatore) duet with Ponselle (Victor #8097; 1928) is widely admired. "O muto asil" from Guillaume Tell (Victor #6212; 1923) and "Come rugiada al cespite" from Ernani (Victor #64514, 737; 1915) are highly regarded by collectors.

From 1935 to 1939 Martinelli made seven selections from Otello with the Metropolitan Opera, Helen Jepson, and Lawrence Tibbett. He made 12 Vitaphone soundtracks during 1926–1927, recorded by Victor on 16-inch discs. These were short subjects, lasting about eight minutes, filmed at the old Manhattan Opera House. With his voice in decline, Martinelli continued to record, and in 1948–1968 made LPs for various labels.

A Nimbus CD of 1989 presented the Verdi ensemble numbers mentioned above, the Guillaume Tell aria, and the tenor showpieces from Pagliacci, Cavalleria rusticana, Fedora, and Eugene Onegin. Martinelli died in New York on 2 Feb 1969. [Collins 1979; Wile 1971/2.]

MASCOT TALKING MACHINE CO. A New York firm, established in 1916 at 66 W. 37th St. It offered the "Mascot" line of record players in seven models.

MASKING. The addition of one sound signal to another in order to raise the threshold of hearing of the first one.

MASTER. The copper or nickel shell made from an original disc or tape recording, from which copies are made, leading to the final pressing. It is also known as a "metal master." It may also be a lacquer disc (in instantaneous recording). In the early days of recording, the master was usually of wax for cylinders and discs. (See also DISC, 1; RECORDING PRACTICE.)

MASTER (label). An American record issued from February 1937, lasting less than one year. It was marketed by the music publisher Irving Mills, who issued the Variety label at the same time. Jazz was the featured material, with artists like Duke Ellington, Cab Calloway, and the Raymond Scott Quintet included. [Rust 1978.]

MASTER TONE (label). A department store label distributed by Kaufmann & Baer Co., Pittsburgh, in the early 1920s. The record was apparently produced by the Bridgeport Die and Machine Co., Bridgeport, Connecticut. Material was popular dance and vocal. [Kendziora 1987/3.]

MASTERPHONE CO. A New York firm, advertising in TMW for May 1914 the sale of a device to "clarify and amplify record tone." Location was 187 Broadway, and later 61 Broadway.

MASTER-PHONE CORP. A New York firm, located in 1915 at 286 Fifth Ave. In January 1915 there was advertising for the "red needle," a composition of improved fibre that promised five to 10 plays, with no wear and no "muffled sound." An announcement in TMW for 15 Sep 1915 stated that a patent for this needle had been acquired by the Phonograph Accessories Corp.

MASTERS, FRANKIE, 1904–1990. American Big Band leader, born 12 Apr 1904 in St. Mary's, West Virginia. He attended Indiana University and played in a dance orchestra there, then moved to Chicago and worked in various the-atres. He attracted attention in the later 1930s and had a radio show in 1937. His orchestra was of the sweet variety, in demand for hotel and ballroom engagements. He co-composed the hit song "Scatterbrain" in 1939 (Vocalion #4915). David Rose became the band's arranger in the 1940s; there were many radio shows and long engagements at Chicago hotels. Vocalist Phyllis Miles was featured on a number of fine discs, such as "Blue Champagne" / "Harbor of Dreams" (Okeh #6279; 1941).

MATHIS, JOHNNY, 1935– . American popular singer, born in San Francisco on 30 Sept 1935. After training as a classical singer, he turned to nightclub work and became an international star. Between 1957 and 1974 he made 39 chart singles, among them "It's Not for Me to Say" (Columbia #40851; 1957) and "Too Much, Too Little, Too Late" (Columbia #10693; 1978). He also had 54 chart albums by 1974, such as Heavenly (Columbia #1251, 8152; 1959), on the lists 56 weeks.

MATLOCK, MATTY, 1909–1978. American jazz clarinetist, born Julian C. Matlock in Paducah, Kentucky, on 27 Apr 1909. He grew up in Nashville and played there in the 1920s, then joined Ben Pollack's band in 1929, replacing Benny Goodman. He was one of the original members of the Bob Crosby band in 1935, and became its arranger; then arranged for Red Nichols, Pee Wee Hunt, and others. He is heard on many Bob Crosby records, of which "March of the Bob Cats" (his composition) may be mentioned (Decca #1865; 1938). Matlock made several LP albums with his own groups, including Pete Kelly's Blues—the name of a motion picture in which he was featured—(Columbia #CL-690). When he left Bob Crosby in 1942 he went to Hollywood, working in radio and television; he led successful groups in the 1960s, with a long run in Las Vegas and dates in Lake Tahoe, as well as a tour of the Far East. He died in Van Nuys, California, on 14 June 1978.

MATRIX. (I) An alternative term for master.

MATRIX. (II) A circuit in an electrical system that mixes or separates signals.

MATRIX NUMBER. A serial number engraved or embossed on each side of a disc record by the manufacturer, usually near the center; or on the circumference of a cylinder record. This number is a guide to the date of the record; it may indicate which take or performance is on the record; and it may provide other data as well. The matrix number is sometimes useful in the case of reissues, as it suggests whether or not the reissue does in fact offer the identical take as the earlier record.

MATZENAUER, MARGARETE, 1881–1963. Hungarian contralto/soprano, born in Temesvár on 1 Jan 1881. She grew up in a musical family; and studied in Graz, Berlin, and Munich. On 15 Sep 1901 she joined the Strasbourg Opera, then in 1904–1911 she was with the Munich Court Opera. She sang in Bayreuth in 1911, and made her Metropolitan Opera debut on 13 Nov 1911 as Aida; she remained with the company until 1930, while singing also in Europe. Matzenauer had a remarkable vocal range, and was able to sing both the soprano and contralto repertoires throughout her career. She retired in 1938, and died in Van Nuys, Calif., on 19 May 1963.

Matzenauer made relatively few records: 86 are enumerated in Miller 1976. She recorded for G & T in Munich during 1906–1909. "Ach, mein Sohn" ("Ah, mon fils") and "O gebt, o gebt" ("Donnez, donnez") from *Prophète* (#043079 and #043080) are among her finest records of that period. She was with Victor in the U.S. during 1912–1913, singing Verdi, Wagner, and other roles in German, Italian, and French; and again with Victor in 1924–1926. A favorite among collectors in "Nobles seigneurs, salut!" from *Huguenots* (Victor #6471). "Ah, mon fils" was recorded again in 1925 (#6531). She also made Edison Diamond Discs from 1919 to 1922, among them a *Lucia* Sextette with an ensemble comprising Thomas Chalmers, Marie Rappold, Giovanni Zenatello, Enrico Baroni, and Arthur Middleton. Top Artists Platters and Collectors Guild reissued many of her arias on LP in 1959 and 1960. [Miller 1976.]

MAUREL, VICTOR, 1848–1923. French baritone, born in Marseilles on 17 June 1848. He studied at the Paris Conservatory, and made his debut at the Paris Opéra in 1868; then sang throughout Europe and the U.S. From 1879 to 1894 he was a member of the Opéra, after which he sang at the Metropolitan Opera from 3 Dec 1894 (debut as Iago) to 1896. He was back in Paris until 1904, then transferred permanently to America in 1909. Maurel was most distinguished in Wagnerian and Verdian roles. He created Iago (5 Feb 1887) and Falstaff (9 Feb 1893). He died in New York on 22 Oct 1923.

Maurel recorded for G & T in Paris in 1903, doing "Sogno di Iago" (#2–32814) and an air from Gluck. In 1904 and again in 1907 he was with Fonotipia in Milan, singing the "Serenata" of *Don Giovanni* (#39041), "Era la notte" from *Otello*, and "Quand'ero paggio" from *Falstaff*. His few recordings were reissued by various labels, including IRCC, Scala, Olympus, Belcantodisc, and Top Artists Platters.

MAURO, PHILIP. Legal counsel for the American Graphophone Co. in the 1890s and early 1900s. The graphophone patent #569,290, granted to Thomas A. Macdonald on 13 Oct 1896, was acquired in part because of the arguments of Mauro and his fellow attorney Pollok; the patent examiner had at first cited a German and an American patent as prior conceptions. Mauro became known for aggressive patent litigation, and won injunctions against Hawthorne & Sheble, Frank Seaman, and Emile Berliner. American Graphophone Co. was enabled to produce disc records in 1901–1906 on the strength of Mauro's case for the validity of the Joseph Jones patent; he had to rewrite the claims several times to demonstrate their novelty to a skeptical patent examiner. On 31 Jan 1899 he gave a "brilliant paper" (Read) before the Washington Academy of Sciences, "Development of the Art of Recording and Reproducing of Sound," and repeated it for the Franklin Institute in Philadelphia; he credited Macdonald and American Graphophone scientists for the invention and improvement of the talking machine.

MAXICUT PROCESS. A technique developed by EMI, Ltd., using an electronic logic circuit in the preview computer, to recognize frequencies and levels otherwise difficult for average record players to reproduce.

MAYFAIR (label). A British record made from Edison Bell Winner, Panachord, or Piccadilly masters, offered in exchange for coupons found in Ardath cigarettes, in 1931–1933. All artists used pseudonyms, including such American performers as Joe Venuti, Benny Goodman, and Red Nichols. [Andrews*; Rust 1978.]

MCA, INC. (MUSIC CORPORATION OF AMERICA). An entertainment industry conglomerate, established in Chicago in 1924 by Jules C. Stein; it is now located in Universal City, California. Originally the firm was a booking agency for jazz and swing bands; by 1927 it represented about 40 of them. Two-thirds of the active bands were MCA clients by the late 1930s. Moving to California in 1937, MCA expanded its interests to booking of movie actors and to acquisition of other talent agencies. Television booking and production was added to the firm's activities in 1949, with great success and profits.

Universal Studios was acquired in 1959, and MCA, Inc. was organized to replace the Music Corporation of America. Decca Records, Inc. was purchased in 1962. Shortly after, the firm gave up its talent booking and concentrated on feature film production (Universal) as well as other entertainment production, including recordings. Other labels acquired were Coral, Kapp, and UNI; these were merged into the single MCA label. ABC-Dunhill was acquired in February 1979. The company also distributes Chess, Dot, Gold Mountain, Hughes Music, Motown (a substantial share of that company was acquired in 1988), Silver Eagle, and Zebra. MCA Records, Inc., is the name of the firm that handles all recordings.

McCARTNEY, PAUL, 1942– . British popular singer and songwriter, born James Paul McCartney in Liverpool on 18 June 1942. While a member of the **Beatles**, he—along with John Lennon—wrote most of the group's material. In his first solo album *McCartney* (U.K. release

Apple #PCS 7102; 1970; U.S. release Apple #STAO 3363; 1970), he sang and played all instruments himself, with some harmonizing vocal accompaniment from his wife Linda. He and his wife formed the group Wings in 1971; the group stayed together until 1981, with many personnel changes over the years. The first album credited to Wings, *Wild Life* (U.K. release Apple #PCS 7142; 1971; U.S. release Apple #SW 3386; 1971), took approximately three days to record. One of the most widely acclaimed Wings albums (credited to Paul McCartney and Wings) was *Band on the Run* (U.K. release Apple #PAS 10007; 1973; U.S. release Apple #SO 3415; 1973), which was recorded in Lagos, Nigeria, and featured McCartney on vocals, drums, bass, guitar, and synthesizer. The only others appearing on the album were Linda McCartney and guitarist Denny Laine—the remaining Wings members left the group before recording was to commence. Wings albums that reached number one on the *Billboard* charts include *Red Rose Speedway* (Apple #3409; 1973), *Venus and Mars* (Capitol #11419; 1975), *Wings at the Speed of Sound* (Capitol #11525; 1976), *Band on the Run*, and *Wings Over America*.

McCartney has recorded his albums for Apple, Capitol/EMI, and Columbia. During his solo career, he has released recordings credited to Paul McCartney; Paul & Linda McCartney; Wings; and Paul McCartney and Wings. His first number-one album since the break-up of Wings, *Tug of War* (Columbia #37462; 1982), was a critical success.

He issued an album intended for release only in the Soviet Union, *Cnoba B CCCP* (literal translation is "Again in the U.S.S.R." — Melodiya #A60 00415 006; 1989), which contains 13 rock and roll songs that McCartney considers classics.

He made two world tours since embarking on a solo career. A recording of his 1976 tour was released as *Wings Over America* (Capitol #11593; 1976) and his 1989/1990 world tour album was *Tripping the Live Fantastic* (Capitol #94778; 1990).

On 25 Jan 1991, McCartney and his band taped a performance for the MTV program *Unplugged*, playing live acoustic music at the Limehouse Studios, Wembley, London. The concert was recorded and released as *Unplugged (The Official Bootleg)* (Capitol cassette #C4–96413; compact disc #7964132; Hispavox LP #7964131; 1991). A limited edition of numbered copies was produced.

In addition to rock music, McCartney has also written in the classical genre. His *Liverpool Oratorio*, which was written with Carl Davis, was commissioned for the 150th anniversary of the Royal Liverpool Philharmonic Orchestra. It premiered 28 June 1991 at the Anglican cathedral in Liverpool. Artists included soprano Kiri Te Kanawa, tenor Jerry Hadley, mezzo-soprano Sally Burgess, bass Willard White, the Royal Liverpool Philharmonic Orchestra and Choir, and the Liverpool Cathedral Boys' Choir. The performance was recorded for release in September 1991, in Britain on EMI Records and on Angel Records in the U.S. [Gambaccini 1976; Salewicz 1986.]

Felicia Reilly

MC CORMACK, JOHN, 1884–1945. Irish/American tenor, born in Athlone on 14 June 1884. He sang in the St. Patrick's (Dublin) cathedral choir, won a national singing competition in 1903, studied voice in Milan (1905), and made his opera debut in 1906 in Savona. He then sang in Ireland, and at Covent Garden in October 1907 in *Cavalleria*. He was a great success with the San Carlo Company in Naples, as Alfredo and the Duke. His American debut was at the Manhattan Opera Co. on 10 Nov 1909, in *Traviata*. He was with the Metropolitan Opera from 29 Nov 1910, singing in the 1912–1914 and 1917–1919 seasons. In 1910–1911 he was with the Chicago Opera. On the crest of world fame, he toured Australia with Nellie Melba in 1911, and appeared in Europe and South America. He became an American citizen in 1919. After 1920 he McCormack devoted himself mostly to concertizing throughout the world. He did sing Wagner in Los Angeles in 1928, and starred in the motion picture *Song of My Heart* in 1919. His last tours were in the late 1930s and early 1940s, after which he made radio broadcasts for the BBC. He died near Dublin on 16 Sep 1945.

McCormack's pure light voice—representing "the last link with 18th century vocalism" (Johnston)—was ideally displayed in Mozartean roles and in Rossini, though he excelled also in the rest of the lyric repertoire. On the concert stage he presented a repertoire of Irish and British songs, as well as art songs of Europe and the United States.

His earliest records were made in London in 1904. He recorded Irish material for on seven-inch and 10–inch discs for G & T, on 19 September and again on the 23rd, 24th, and 26th of the month. At the same time (21–23 September) he was making cylinders for the National Phonograph Co., Ltd. "The Snowy Breasted Pearl" was the first cylinder (#13124); there were nine other Irish songs in that session. In November 1904 he made two-minute cylinders for Edison Bell (three sessions of Irish songs), then he worked with Sterling Records in July 1906, making more two-minute cylinders, and with Pathé. For the Odeon label in 1906–1909 he extended his repertoire to include Italian and French arias, making about 80 sides; they were issued by Sterling and Hunting, Ltd., and some were later reissued by the American Odeon Corp. of New York.

Victor signed McCormack in 1910, starting a long association on Red Seal records. He began with the *Lucia* Tomb Scene (#C8535–1). His most famous and most popular disc was "I Hear You Calling Me" (#64120; 1910). By 1917 he had 130 solo numbers in the Victor catalog, plus duets with various artists and the great recording of the *Rigoletto* Quartet with Lucrezia Bori, Josephine Jacoby, and Reinald Werrenrath (#89080; 1914). "Il mio tesoro" (Victor #74484; 1916) was voted the favorite tenor acoustic record by collectors, as reported in *Hobbies* magazine, March 1947. "Oh Sleep, Why Dost Thou Leave Me?" from *Semele*, is another perennial favorite (#66096; 1920) among numerous remarkable discs. McCormack recorded for HMV in 1924–1942, making 220 discs in Britain for that label, and for many smaller labels. He took part in the Hugo Wolf Society issues in 1932. There were many LP reissues, by Victor, Scala, Belcantodisc, Top Artists Platters, HMV, and others. [Johnston 1988; Mathews 1986; Worth 1986.]

MC GILVRA, J. H. American record industry executive. He was president of the Old Dominion Phonograph Co., Roanoke, Virginia; and an official of the Volta Graphophone Co. At the first convention of the National Phonograph Association, in 1890, he was elected temporary chairman.

MC GREAL, LAWRENCE. American record industry jobber, doing business in Milwaukee from ca. 1911 to his bankruptcy in 1915. In July 1911 it was announced that he was the new president of the National Association of Talking Machine Jobbers.

MC KENZIE, RED, 1899–1948. American jazz bandleader and singer, born in St. Louis on 14 Oct 1899. He grew up in Washington, D.C., then returned to St. Louis and formed the Mound City Blue Blowers in 1923. This was a novel group, with McKenzie playing a comb, Dick Slevin playing the kazoo, and Jack Bland playing banjo; they got a Brunswick contract and began to record in 1924 with "Arkansaw [sic] Blues" / "Blue Blues" (#2581). Outstanding artists joined this bizarre ensemble in the next few years, including Frankie Trumbauer, Eddie Lang, Eddie Condon, Gene Krupa, Jack Teagarden, Glenn Miller, Pee Wee Russell, Coleman Hawkins, Muggsy Spanier, Jimmy Dorsey, Bunny Berigan, and Dave Tough—but through all that talent Mc Kenzie (who did not play a regular instrument) performed on his comb. He also sang, as in "Georgia on My Mind" / "I Can't Believe That You're in Love with Me" (Okeh #41515; 1931). He was less active after the Blowers disbanded in the late 1930s.

MC KINLEY, RAY, 1910– . American jazz drummer, vocalist, and Big Band leader, born in Fort Worth, Texas, on 18 June 1910. After playing with various groups he joined the Dorsey Brothers band in 1934. In 1942 he formed his own band and was quickly successful, featured in a motion picture in 1943, *Hit Parade*. During the War he was with Glenn Miller's Air Force Band, and became co-leader of that ensemble upon Miller's death. In 1956 he led the Glenn Miller orchestra, playing the old hits as well as new material. He was less active after 1965.

Ray McKinley's band recorded for Decca in 1936, then for Capitol, Hit, Victor, Majestic

and Jazz Club. "Fingerwave" for Decca (#1020) is a typical number. He made LPs of the Glenn Miller orchestra for Victor, and with the Air Force Band.

MC KUEN, ROD, 1933– . American singer, composer, poet, and actor, born in Oakland, California, on 29 Apr 1933. Before he was 20 he was a disc jockey on Oakland radio and author of a syndicated newspaper column. During military service in Korea he appeared as a singer in a Tokyo supper club and in several motion pictures, and after leaving the army he made several films for Universal in Hollywood. He wrote and sang songs in New York, Paris, London, and throughout the world; he gave command performances in U.K., Korea, and the White House. His most successful album was *Rod McKuen at Carnegie Hall* (Warner #2WS 1794; 1969). Among his most popular compositions was "The World I Used to Know," which was a chart record by Jimmie Rodgers (Dot #16595; 1964).

MC PARTLAND, JIMMY, 1907–1991. American jazz cornetist, born James Dougald McPartland in Chicago on 15 Mar 1907. He studied violin and cornet, then founded and played in the Austin High Gang, young white self-taught musicians who built on the Black New Orleans Dixieland style. He was soon performing with Bix Beiderbecke, whose style was similar to his own, and whom he replaced in the Wolverines when he was just 17 years old. McPartland was a key artist in the development of the Chicago jazz style. He was in the bands of Art Kassel and Ben Pollack during the late 1920s. In the 1930s he was with Horace Heidt, led his own groups; he had a year with Jack Teagarden, 1941–1942, then went into military service. He met and married Marian Turner, jazz pianist; later divorced and remarried her before he died. They played in Chicago groups together. He was active into the 1980s. He died on 13 Mar 1991.

McPartland was heard on the last Wolverine recordings, made in December 1924: "When My Sugar Walks down the Street" and "A Prince of Wails" (Gennett #5620). He recorded with McKenzie and Condon's Chicagoans in 1927, on four sides for Okeh. "Singapore Sorrows" was one of his discs with Ben Pollack (Victor #21437; 1928). With his own orchestra in 1939 he made "Jazz Me Blues" / "China Boy" (Decca #18042) and "The World is Waiting for the Sunrise" / "Sugar" (Decca #18043). There were LP albums for a half dozen labels, of which the most notable was MCA #2–4110 (1956).

MC PARTLAND, MARIAN, 1920– . British jazz pianist, born Margaret Marian Turner near Windsor on 20 Mar 1920. She studied violin, then piano at the Guildhall School of Music in London. Turning from classical to jazz piano, she performed in music halls. Having met and married Jimmy McPartland in 1945, she returned to the U.S. with him and worked with him in Chicago groups. In 1951 she began to perform with her own trio, developing a sophisticated style with classical elements, and became popular in quality jazz clubs. She has remained active, and in 1992 was hosting a radio program, *Piano Jazz*. Her major recordings have been on LP, with such albums as *Marian McPartland Trio* (Capitol #T-785) and *At the London House* (Argo #640). She also recorded two albums with her husband, *The Middle Road* (Jazztone #J-1227) and *Dixieland Now and Then* (Jazztone #J-1241).

MECHANICAL ELECTRICAL ANALOGIES. The properties that determine the passage of an electric current are analogous to properties concerning mechanical motion. The analogies are: (1) inductance = mass; (2) capacitance = compliance; (3) resistance = friction or viscosity. Thus for every mechanical situation there is an equivalent electric circuit situation, and the solution of a problem in one medium is equivalent to the solution in the other. This fortunate fact of nature makes possible, among other things, electrical recording of sound.

Mechanical recording. *See* ACOUSTIC RECORDING.

MEDALLION (label). An American record, trademarked in 1919 by the Baldwin Piano Co. of Cincinnati. Emerson masters were used for the issues, which were nearly all dance numbers. Some vocal pieces were released, such as

"When You're Gone I Won't Forget" by the Shannon Four (#8245), and some sacred items. Emerson artists often used pseudonyms on Medallion. There were no issues after 1921. [Hinze 1977; Rust 1978.]

MEEKER, EDWARD WARREN, 1874–1937. American comedian and singer, also animal imitator and announcer; born in Orange, New Jersey, on 22 Jan 1874. He made cylinders for Edison from March 1906, beginning with "What's the Use of Knocking When a Man is Down" (#9234); and made many coon songs and Irish dialect records. He was with Edison for 32 years. Meeker was the announcer for hundreds of records up to 1908, when announcements were dropped. His final Edison recordings were Diamond Discs "Mr. Gallagher and Mr. Shean" with Steve Porter (#50970; 1922) and "He's Living the Life of Reilly" (#51040; 1923). He also imitated animals and did background bits in assistance of other artists. Meeker died in Newark, New Jersey, on 19 April 1937. [Koenigsberg 1987; Walsh 1946/2–4; 1971/4.]

MEEKLENS, BESSIE. Saxophonist, the first to record the instrument. She made 12 cylinders for Edison on 23 April 1892, with piano accompaniment, beginning with "Ave Maria." [Koenigsberg 1987.]

MEHTA, ZUBIN, 1936–   . Indian conductor, born in Bombay on 29 Apr 1936. He studied violin and piano; went to Vienna and played double bass as well. Then he took up conducting, and when he graduated from the Vienna Academy of Music in 1957 he made his debut directing the Tonkünstler Orchestra in the Musikverein. In 1960 he became director of the Montreal Symphony Orchestra, then conducted the Los Angeles Philharmonic Orchestra concurrently; and was named director of the Israel Philharmonic Orchestra in 1977. In 1978 he became music director of the New York Philharmonic Orchestra. Mehta's discs with the Los Angeles Philharmonic were rather numerous; they covered-20th century composers like Ives and Varèse as well as the standard repertoire. With the New York Philharmonic for CBS Records he recorded *Symphonie fantastique* plus the Beethoven and Brahms symphonies. Mehta has conducted at the Metropolitan Opera, and recorded complete versions of *Turandot, Tosca, Aida*, and *Trovatore*.

MEISSELBACH (A. F.) AND BRO., INC. A Newark, New Jersey, firm, established in 1887. In 1916, from a location at 29 Congress St., it sold sapphire and diamond point needles.

MELBA, NELLIE, *Dame*, **1861–1931.** Australian soprano, born Nellie Mitchell near Richmond on 19 May 1861. She studied piano, violin, and harp; and she played organ in church. After her marriage in 1882 she took up singing, studying in London and Paris. Her operatic debut was as Gilda in Brussels on 13 Oct 1887; it created a sensation. Triumphs throughout Europe followed, and a Metropolitan Opera debut on 4 Dec 1893 as Lucia. She was widely regarded as the greatest of coloraturas. Melba sang her farewell concert at Covent Garden on 8 June 1926, and retired to Australia. She died in Sydney on 23 Feb 1931.

Melba had a long recording career. She was first recorded by Mapleson on stage at the Metropolitan in 1901, doing nine arias. Her earliest commercial discs were for the Gramophone Co. in London, March 1904, beginning with Francesco Tosti's "Mattinata" (#03015); she continued with that label to 1907, making 56 records altogether. Then she worked with Victor in New York and Camden, in 1907, making 23 sides. One of those was the "Soave fanciulla" duet from *Boheme* with Enrico Caruso (#85200); she also did two other arias from that opera. Melba recorded in Europe and America from 1908–1921, making 86 more records, some with John McCormack and Mario Sammarco. Her Covent Garden farewell on 8 June 1926 was recorded live, including her speech; then she sang a final studio recording session on 17 Dec 1926, from which four records were made.

A special label, lilac in color, was made for her by G & T; she also bargained for unusually high royalties. Her discs sold at premium prices, but very successfully. Among the most popular was "Caro nome" (Victor #88078 or #6213). An EMI Références CD (#H761070–2; 1989) presents a good selection of her arias. [Harvey 1949; Hogarth 1982; Moran 1984/1.]

MELCHIOR, LAURITZ, 1890–1973. Danish/American tenor, born in Copenhagen on 20 Mar 1890. His early singing was as a baritone, and it was in that aspect that he made his debut in 1913 at the Copenhagen Royal Opera. By 1918 he had changed focus and begun to sing the dramatic tenor repertoire, though his voice always retained a shading from the lower range. He was soon recognized as an outstanding interpreter of Wagner, and remains today the legendary Heldentenor. From 1924 to 1931 he was a regular performer in Bayreuth. On 17 Feb 1926 he made his Metropolitan Opera debut as Tannhäuser, and stayed with the company until 1950, missing only the 1927–1928 season. He took American citizenship in 1947 and settled in California, where he died (in Santa Monica) on 18 Mar 1973.

It was as a baritone (Germont, in Danish) that Melchior made his earliest record, for Odeon in Denmark during 1913. He was still making records 40 years later, on several labels. HMV recorded him in a few songs during 1913, then Polyphon recorded his tenor voice (*Lohengrin, Walküre*, and *Tosca*) in 1920–1921. In 1924 he sang in Germany for DGG, then for Parlophon in 1925–1926. After his arrival in America he made one record for Brunswick: "Winterstürme" and the Prize Song (#50085; 1926). Melchior's major block of recording was for HMV and Victor beginning in 1928, almost exclusively from the Wagner operas. (He was the consummate specialist: he did Tristan more than 200 times; at the Metropolitan, during 24 seasons, he sang only seven roles.)

Pearl and Seraphim released LP versions of his major arias. On CD there is an EMI Références item, #H7–69789 (1989) that selects from his releases of the early 1930's. Other CDs include RCA #GD87914 (1990) of material from the later 1930s and 1940—including outstanding duets with Kirsten Flagstad. Another RCA CD (#GD87915), of Wagnerian scenes, is mostly for Flagstad, but includes fine duets with Melchior. [Hansen 1972.]

MELODIYA (label). The official record of the Soviet Union, issued by a state agency on Tverskoy Boulevard, Moscow. Production of LPs reached 120 million per year in the 1980s, and there were also 8 million cassettes. Seventy percent of the sales (60%-65% of the output) was in the popular field. The first Melodiya compact discs (65 items) appeared in April 1990. Record pressing plants were in Riga, Leningrad, Apulevka, Moscow, Tbilsi, and Tashkent. [Bennett, J. 1981.]

MELODISC RECORDS (label). An American disc marketed in 1921 by the **Emerson Phonograph Co.**, 206 Fifth Ave., New York. The records were seven inches in diameter, selling for $.35. Although advertising in *TMW* claimed great success for the Melodisc, it appeared at an infelicitous time, while the Emerson firm was in receivership and reorganization. The record was not advertised after 1921. [Andrews*.]

MELODOGRAPH CORP. A New York firm established in 1916, located at 142 W. 14th St. The Melodograph disc player was advertised in *Cosmopolitan* magazine for November 1916, selling for $10 by mail order. It was said to be made of a "secret process composition of metals" which cannot warp and will not rust. Using any kind of needle, it could play either vertical or lateral-cut records (by turning the soundbox). The firm also issued some vertical-cut discs of their own, with the Melodograph label, in seven-inch size. The firm petitioned for bankruptcy on 5 Sep 1917. [*NAG* 36 (Spring 1981) reproduces the *Cosmopolitan* advertisement on p. 12; Rust 1978.]

MELODY (label). (I) A British record, 10–inch and 12–inch size, issued in December 1918 by Morgan, Scott & Co., Ltd., religious music publishers. The discs were made by the Crystalate Record Manufacturing Co., Ltd., from **Guardsman** matrices of the Invicta Record Co., Ltd. [Andrews*.]

MELODY (label). (II) An American label, issued briefly during 1923. Masters were from Olympic. [Rust 1978.]

MELODY THREE. A male trio, also known as the Men About Town, who recorded for various labels in the late 1920s. Members were Jack Parker, Will Donaldson, and Phil Duey (Dewey). Frank Luther took the place of

Donaldson later. Among their three Victor records of 1928–1929 was "Remember Me to Mary" / "Pals, Just Pals" (#21754; 1928).

MELOGRAPH (label). A double-sided lateral-cut German record, of the Melograph Record GmbH, sold from Liverpool by the Melograph Disc Record Co., Ltd., from October 1907. Both 10–inch and 12–inch records were offered, until World War I made it impossible to continue by making supplies unobtainable from an enemy country. [Andrews*.]

MELOPHONE TALKING MACHINE CO. A New York firm established in 1915, located at 376 Lafayette St. Advertising of 1916 offered the Melophone line of inexpensive disc players in four models, selling from $7.50 to $15.

MELOTO (label). A British issue of the Meloto Co., Ltd., London, (controlled by Aeolian Co., Ltd.) on sale by March 1922 to about 1927. Distribution was not through shops, but through a system that required buyers to take an initial 12 records to qualify for the loan of a cabinet gramophone; the machine became the buyer's property following the purchase of another eight discs per month for a further 23 months. Nearly 700 records were released in 10–inch size (there were also 12–inch records), drawn from **Aco** material. While most of the output was dance music and popular vocals, there were some jazz items that had originated in the Gennett catalog. [Andrews*; Rust 1978.]

MELOTONE (label). An American record, the inexpensive ($.50, later $.35) Brunswick (Warner Brothers) subsidiary, issued from 13 Nov 1930 to spring of 1938. Jazz reissues and originals are found, and music by good dance bands. The country repertoire was well covered by Tex Ritter, Gene Autry, Red Foley, and others. Josh White, Leadbelly and Bing Crosby appeared on Melotone. Mexican, Cajun, and Hawaiian series were offered. Many Melotone recordings appeared in Britain on the **Panachord** label. [Rust 1978.]

MELTON, JAMES, 1904–1961. American tenor, born in Moultrie, Georgia, on 2 Jan 1904. He played saxophone in college groups, at the

University of Georgia, then studied voice and sang on radio. His concert debut was on 22 Apr 1932 in New York; his opera debut in Cincinnati on 28 June 1938. From 7 Dec 1942 into the 1950s he sang with the Metropolitan Opera. Although primarily a classical singer, he crossed over to popular styles where he achieved national renown. He was with the Revelers male quartet, and made solo records for Victor, Columbia, and others of love songs and show tunes. His first popular Victor was "There's Danger in Your Eyes, Cherie" / "A Year from Today" (#22335; 1930). He appeared on the *Voice of Firestone* and other radio programs, and was seen in several motion pictures. Melton introduced the song "September in the Rain" and recorded it for Decca (#1247; 1937). One of his favored operatic roles was Pinkerton; he is heard in the Flower Duet with Licia Albanese on Victor #VM-1068, three 12–inch discs. LP reissues included *James Melton Sings* (Mayfair #9609) and *James Melton Sings George Gershwin and Cole Porter Favorites* (Craftsman #8031).

MELVA (label). A disc issued by the Melva Record Co., Brooklyn, apparently in 1922. Only 20 records are known to have been released. [Rust 1978.]

MENDELSSOHN MIXED QUARTETTE. A vocal group that recorded for Edison in 1903 and 1904. Members were Edith Chapman, Corinne Morgan, George Morgan Stricklett, and Frank C. Stanley. Eight two-minute cylinders are listed by Koenigsberg, beginning with "Good Night, Good Night, Beloved" (#8321) and concluding with "What Shall the Harvest Be?" (#8834). [Koenigsberg 1987.]

MENGELBERG, WILLEM, 1871–1951. Dutch conductor, born in Utrecht on 28 Mar 1871. He studied in Holland and in Cologne, and at age 20 was music director in Lucerne. From 1895 to 1945 he was conductor of the (Royal) Concertgebouw Orchestra in Amsterdam, bringing it to world acclaim. He specialized in the music of Beethoven, Mahler, and Strauss. CD reissues from Teldec and EMI have covered the principal Mengelberg recordings from 1926 to 1944, although many of them are technically unsatisfactory. Mengelberg was accused of being a Nazi sympathizer and exiled to Switzerland by his government, cutting off the possibility of high quality post-War recordings. He died in Chur, Switzerland, on 21 Mar 1951. [Wolf 1971.]

MENUHIN, YEHUDI, *Sir,* **1916–** . American violinist and conductor, born in New York on 22 Apr 1916. His family took him to San Francisco, where he studied for his debut, which took place in Oakland when he was seven years old. He played a New York recital at age nine, then studied in Paris with Georges Enesco. He made a sensational appearance in 1927 with the New York Symphony Orchestra, performing the Beethoven Concerto. Thereafter he made world tours, and also directed the Bath Festivals in 1959–1968, and the Windsor Festival in 1969–1972. He was awarded an honorary knighthood in 1965.

Menuhin's first records were made for Victor while he was yet eleven years old, as two engineers crossed the continent to Oakland just for one session and four short pieces with the prodigy. By age 15 he was able to record the Bruch Concerto in G Minor with mature artistry (Victor #DB1611; 1932). Biddulph CD #LAB 031 presents early recordings in *The Young Yehudi Menuhin* (1991). In 1932 he performed and recorded the Elgar Concerto with the composer conducting (Victor album # M174). In the 1938 Victor catalog he has 11 concertos plus many shorter pieces, in addition to duets with his pianist-sister Hephzibah. He and Georges Enesco also recorded, making the Bach Concerto for Two Violins (Victor #7732, 77r33). Perhaps his finest recording was of the Beethoven Concerto with the Vienna Philharmonic Orchestra in 1960, reissued on CD by EMI in 1990. Over the years Menuhin has recorded virtually the entire standard repertoire for his instrument, and also works by modern composers such as Francis Poulenc, Paul Ben Haim, Lukas Foss, and Aram Khachaturian. And in a crossover spirit he recorded swing pieces with Stéphane Grappelli, and made an album with Ravi Shankar.

As a conductor Menuhin appears on record with the Bath Festival Orchestra of the 1960s, the English Chamber Orchestra, the Royal Philharmonic Orchestra, and other ensembles. He is active in the concert hall and recording studio; his most recent discs being of Elgar (for Virgin Classics) the Beethoven Fifth (for Pickwick) and—with the Warsaw Sinfonia—the Mozart G Minor Symphony (for Virgin).

MERCURY (label). An American record issued from 1945, commencing with three popular series. The label was a subsidiary of the Mercury Radio and Television Corporation. Offices were at 839 S. Wabash and 328 N. La Salle St., Chicago. Popular artists included Tony Martin, Frances Langford, Buddy Rich, Connie Haines, Vincent Lopez, Harry Babbitt, Erroll Garner, Frankie Laine, Vic Damone, Art Kassel, Ted Weems, Rex Stewart, and Dinah Washington.

Mercury's classical recording activity had its origin in the 1948 takeover of Keynote Records, then headed by **John Hammond.** A Mercury office was established in New York with Hammond in charge as vice-president. He had already produced, in company with Mitch Miller, Stravinsky's *Dumbarton Oaks Concerto* with Miller as soloist and Daniel Saidenberg conducting, plus recordings of Vivaldi with Alexander Schneider, and Mozart with the Miller-Saidenberg combination. Two Brahms piano quartets with Mieczyslaw Horszowski, Schneider, Milton Katims, and Frank Miller; plus the Schubert *Death and the Maiden* string quartet, and the Shostakovich Quartet No. 3, with the Fine Arts Quartet, were also among the Hammond-Miller productions that appeared on the new Mercury classics label.

Hammond invited David Hall to take charge of classical artists and repertoire in the spring of 1948, and a catalog was built up from both domestically produced chamber music and solo instrumental discs, including the Brahms clarinet sonatas with Reginald Kell and Horszowski; the complete Bach solo violin partitas and sonatas with Schneider; organ discs by Ernest White, at New York's Church of St. Mary the Virgin; and piano recordings by Abram Chasins and Constance Keene. The initial building of a symphonic catalog was accomplished through licensing deals abroad, beginning with the Khachaturian Violin Concerto with David Oistrakh, the composer con-

ducting, arranged by Hammond through sources in the Soviet Union. Until Mercury began its American symphony orchestra recording program in late 1950, its symphonic catalog grew out of licensed acquisitions from Czechoslovakia and the Bavarian Radio. Mercury was the first label, in 1949, to arrange with Columbia for use of its LP technology.

Large scale domestic symphony recording by Mercury began with the Louisville Orchestra, featuring the William Schuman dance scores *Judith* (commissioned by Louisville and conducted by Robert Whitney) and *Undertow* (conducted by the composer). C. Robert Fine was the guiding engineering genius for Mercury's domestic program, producing the Louisville disc with a single Telefunken U47 microphone. Late April 1951 saw the Mercury production team of David Hall (producer), Fine, and George Piros in Orchestra Hall, Chicago. Rafael Kubelik and the Chicago Symphony Orchestra taped the Mussorgsky-Ravel *Pictures at an Exhibition*, along with works of Bloch and Bartók. Out of the laudatory *New York Times* review of the Mussorgsky came the term adopted by Mercury for its domestic symphonic series: "Living Presence."

Thus began a long line of distinguished recorded performances that included the Minneapolis Symphony under Antal Dorati and the Detroit Symphony under Paul Paray, plus an extensive American music program with the Eastman-Rochester Symphony Orchestra under Howard Hanson and the Eastman Wind Ensemble under Frederick Fennell. Many "firsts" came out of these programs: the Schoenberg *Five Pieces for Orchestra* and the three great Tchaikovsky ballet scores were recorded in their entirety; and the *1812 Overture* complete with the cannon and bells called for by the composer.

By the time of the initial Chicago recordings, the Mercury New York staff had been joined by Wilma Cozart, who had come from the Dallas Symphony Orchestra staff with an excellent working background in orchestra management and administration. She eventually assumed the administrative chores of the Mercury Classical operation, as well as much of the packaging work; and with Hall's departure for Denmark on a Fulbright grant in mid-

1956 she was named vice-president, a first for her gender with a major record firm. Under her regime, Mercury continued its domestic program but expanded its reach abroad, recording extensively in London, and carrying out the first recordings done by an American team in the Soviet Union. While emphasis at Mercury had been on the symphony orchestra, chamber music and solo instrumental recording continued, producing among other items a first integral recording of the Charles Ives violin sonatas, with Rafael Druian and John Simms. The Roth String Quartet and the Albeneri Trio were among the ensembles added to the roster, and in later years Joseph Szigeti did a substantial amount of recording.

The Mercury symphonic recording enterprise with Robert Fine and Wilma Cozart (who had become Mrs. Fine) came to an end for all intents and purposes in mid-1963. Mercury had been taken over by the multinational firm Philips in June of 1961, and for a time the Cozart-Fine combination functioned with little interference; but hard times in the record business forced cutbacks all along the line, including the rigorous quality standards originally established. In February 1964 Cozart resigned. It was not until 1990 that she was invited by Polygram to resurrect the Living Presence line in the CD format. [Novitsky 1988.]

David Hall

MERITT (label). A short-lived American record issued by the Kansas City music store Winston Holmes in the late 1920s. Perhaps only a dozen or so issues appeared, some of them with interesting material such as blues numbers by local Black artists and sides by George E. Lee and his Orchestra. [Rust 1978.]

MERLI, FRANCESCO, 1887–1976. Italian tenor, born in Milan on 27 Jan 1887. He sang as a youth in Italian provincial opera houses, finished second to Beniamino Gigli in a competition in 1914, then began singing at La Scala in 1916, where he remained to 1946. He also appeared in Covent Garden, Teatro Colón in Buenos Aires, and the Metropolitan Opera (where he made his debut as Radames on 2 Mar 1932). He retired in 1950, and died on 11 Dec 1976 in Milan.

Merli sang the lyric roles in his early career, then more dramatic parts. He was distinguished for his Otello, Manrico, Des Grieux in *Manon Lescaut*, and Canio. His recording career, mostly with Columbia, began ca. 1924 in Milan, with duets from *Forza del destino*. His most important discs were the complete operas he recorded with the La Scala company: *Manon Lescaut*, *Pagliacci*, and *Trovatore*. LP reissues appeared on several labels, including Top Artists Platters.

MERRIMAN, HORACE OWEN, 1888–1972. Canadian audio engineer, born 21 Nov 1888 in Hamilton, Ontario. He received a B.A. in science from the University of Toronto. During World War I he and Guest were engaged in efforts to enhance air to ground communication via electric loudspeakers; with the Armistice they turned to other applications and decided to develop a method of making phonograph records electrically. After considerable experimentation, in later stages at the studio of Columbia Graphophone Co., Ltd., in London, they produced the moving coil recording head for electric disc recording (British patent # 141,790; 1920). He and Guest recorded a part of the Ceremony of Burial of the Unknown Warrior, in Westminster Abbey (London), on 11 Nov 1920. Microphones and signal buttons were placed at three points in the Abbey, wired to a sound recording van located near the south transept entrance. Although an attempt to record the entire ceremony was made, only two hymns were well enough transcribed to be issued commercially (by Columbia Graphophone Co., Ltd.: Kipling's "Recessional" and "Abide with Me." These recordings were the first to be sold using any type of electrical process. Merriman later served as engineer in charge of the Interference Section, Radio Branch, Dept. of Transport, until his retirement in 1954. [*TMR* #40 (June 1976) carries Merriman's own account of the Westminster Abbey project.] *See also* ELECTRICAL RECORDING.

Metaphone. *See* ECHOPHONE.

METEOR (label). An American record issued by an unidentified firm in Piqua, Ohio, in 1919 or 1920. It was affiliated with Arto. Some items by Earl Fuller's Novelty Orchestra are of interest, but most releases were of little musical value. [Kendziora 1987/10; Rust 1978.]

METRO (label). (I) An American record issued by the Metropolitan Record Co., New York, in the early 1920s. All the known releases are of Irish material, and the record itself bears an Irish label motif.

METRO (label). (II) An American record, like the preceding label devoted to Irish music, produced in the 1920s for Tom Ennis, an Irish pipes player. The two Metro labels were not connected. [Rust 1978.]

METRO-GOLDWYN-MAYER (label). An American record, produced by Columbia "exclusively for Loew's Theatres everywhere"— as the label reads—from ca. 1928. The material was drawn from M-G-M motion pictures. It was not connected to the later MGM label.

METROPOLE (label). (I) A British record issued by the Metropole Gramophone Co., Ltd., Finsbury Square, London; later by Metropole Industries, Ltd., from April 1928 to ca. 1930. Those two firms had taken over the former Hertford Town factory whose previous occupant had been the Parlophone Co., Ltd. (under Columbia's control). About 300 discs were released; some were offered free with the purchase of the firm's Metrophone portable and console record players. American material from Grey Gull was used on about 50 of the records, and much of the material was shared with the Piccadilly label, from the associated firm Piccadilly Records, Ltd. [Andrews*; Rust 1978.]

METROPOLITAN BAND. A group directed by "Signor G. Pelaso" that made 179 brown wax cylinders for the Norcross Phonograph Co. in 1898.

METROPOLITAN ENTERTAINERS. A vocal trio that recorded one Edison Diamond Disc, "Too Many Parties and Too Many Pals" (#51681), in 1926. It consisted of Elizabeth Spencer, Charles Harrison, and Ernest Hare.

METROPOLITAN MIXED TRIO. A vocal group that recorded for Edison, in 1903. Members were Corinne Morgan, George S. Lenox, and Frank C. Stanley. Later, on other labels, the members were Elise Stevenson, Henry Burr, and Stanley. The same singers were also identified on some Edison records as the Manhattan Trio.

METROPOLITAN OPERA COMPANY. A New York Company that gave its first season in 1883–1884, and has achieved universal recognition as one of the world's superior ensembles. Nearly all the great singers and operatic conductors have appeared on its programs. Saturday afternoon broadcasts—constituting the longest running radio show under one sponsor in U.S. history—have brought the Metropolitan into millions of homes. In 1991 the artistic director of the company was James Levine.

Lionel Mapleson made the first recordings of the Metropolitan Opera, on his famous cylinders of 1901–1903. These records were made without commercial intent, and were not marketed. (See MAPLESON CYLINDERS.) A catalog from Leeds & Catlin, dated 1902, offered 19 recordings made by the "Metropolitan Opera House String Orchestra" directed by Nahan [misspelled Nathan] Franko, one of the conductors for that season. All these records, of instrumental parts from opera and some nonoperatic selections, have been lost.

Apparently the earliest commercial record dates from 1906, a Victor issue that for some reason identified the Metropolitan chorus as the "New York Grand Opera Chorus" (Victor #64049; session of 8 June 1906). The number sung was "Scorrendo uniti" from *Rigoletto*. In other sessions of June 1906 another five chorus numbers were recorded, again with the name New York Grand Opera Chorus. Not until January 1910 was there a recording session with identified soloists: the "Miserere" sung by Frances Alda and Enrico Caruso (Victor #89030; 1910). By the end of 1916 40 records had been made by Victor, but in the 1917 Victor catalog there is no specific entry in the artist's section for the company. From 1918 to 1920 Columbia recorded the Metropolitan Orchestra, without vocalists, since most of the singers had Victor contracts.

The great period of records was 1927–1930, some 70 sides for Victor. Star performers offered much of the French/Italian repertoire, and in many cases made definitive interpretations, e.g., the "Miserere" by Rosa Ponselle and Giovanni Martinelli (#8097; 1928), the "Vergine degli angeli" duet from *Forza del destino*, by Ponselle and Ezio Pinza (#8097; 1928), *Rigoletto* duets by Amelita Galli-Curci and Giuseppe De Luca, and the *Rigoletto* Quartet by Galli-Curci, Louise Homer, Beniamino Gigli, and De Luca.

From 1930 to 1938 only 11 recordings were made, but in 1939 there was renewed activity, notably with an *Otello* set, featuring Martinelli, Lawrence Tibbett, and Helen Jepson. In 1940 there was a set of *Tristan* discs, with Rose Bampton and Arthur Carron. A *Tannhäuser* set followed, and then a *Lohengrin*, with the same lead singers. Victor catalogs had begun listing the chorus and orchestra in the Red Seal artist section.

In 1941 the company began to record for Columbia, and made the first complete opera recordings in the U.S., as well as several extended excerpt sets. Among these the *Carmen* set attracted special attention, featuring the new favorite interpreter of the role, Risë Stevens (Columbia album M-607; 1946). But it was *Hänsel und Gretel* that marked the beginning of complete recordings, a set made on 24 sides with Risë Stevens and Nadine Conner as the children (Columbia #MOP-26; 1947). *La Boheme* was next recorded in its entirety, with Richard Tucker, Bidú Sayão, Mimi Benzell, and Francesco Valentino (Columbia #OP-27; 1948). When *Madama Butterfly* was recorded complete, with Eleanor Steber and Richard Tucker, it was released on LP as well as 78 rpm (Columbia LP #SL4; 78 #MOP-30; 3 Oct 1949).

Victor resumed recording of the Metropolitan in 1955, making a series of extended excerpts. Commercial recordings of the company ceased after the DGG release of a complete *Carmen*, with Marilyn Horne, James McCracken, and Tom Krause (DGG #2709 043; 1972).

A special project of 1940 should be mentioned. More than 80 sides of popular opera numbers were sold through newspapers, with the artists and even the company shrouded in anonymity. Victor did the recording, in an arrangement with the Publishers Service Co., Inc., and the National Music Appreciation Committee.

Nineteen recordings were made in 1956–1957 jointly with the Book-of-the-Month Club. These were extended excerpt sets, offered to the public through an organization named the Metropolitan Opera Record Club.

The high costs involved in making records of the company were responsible for the suspension of that activity after 1972. A total of 477 commercial recordings issued by that time are listed by Fellers. Then in 1990 *Walküre* was recorded complete on four CDs, with Hildegard Behrens, Jessye Norman, Christa Ludwig, Gary Lakes, and James Morris, with James Levine conducting (DG #423389–2), winning a Grammy. In 1991 *Rheingold* was recorded complete on three CDs, with James Morris, Christa Ludwig, and Siegfried Jerusalem (conducted by James Levine); and this recording also won the Grammy award for best operatic recording of the year (DG #427–607–2). Another Grammy came in 1991, with the recording of *Götterdämmerung* (Behrens, Reiner Goldberg, and Matti Salminen, with Levine conducting) on four CDs (#429–3852). The next recording, *Siegfried*, was announced in 1991. [Fellers 1984, a complete discography of the commercial issues; Hamilton, D. 1984 is a useful review of Fellers; Gray 1975 is an account of the 1940 project.]

METROPOLITAN PHONOGRAPH CO. (I) One of the 33 companies affiliated with the **North American Phonograph Co.**; founded in 1888. Charles A. Cheever was president; Felix Gottschalk was secretary. At the 1890 convention of the National Phonograph Association, Cheever stated that Metropolitan had 325 [Edison] phonographs leased in the New York area, and about 50 or 60 graphophones. In Fall 1890 the firm merged with the New York Phonograph Co. [Brooks 1979.]

METROPOLITAN PHONOGRAPH CO. (II) A firm established on 5 Oct 1914 in New York, located at 9 W. 23rd St. William S. Finberg was president.

METROPOLITAN QUARTETTE. A mixed vocal group that recorded for Edison cylinders in 1909–1911, and later on Diamond Discs. The original members were Florence Hinkle, Margaret Keyes, John Young, and Frederick Wheeler. Later members included Elizabeth Spencer, Thomas Chalmers, and Mary Jordan. "Darling Nellie Gray" was their first issue (#10053). [Koenigsberg 1987.]

MEYER, JOHN H., 1877–1949. American bass singer, born in New York on 12 July 1877. He was also a pianist and arranger. His first record was a hymn for U-S Everlasting cylinders in 1908: "Why Do You Wait" (#217). Most of his recording was in groups.

He succeeded Frank C. Stanley as bass in the Peerless Quartet in 1911; and he was a member of the Sterling Trio and the Eight Famous Victor Artists. Later he made duets for Grey Gull and Gennett discs. He should not be confused with his contemporary, John W. Myers. His death came in Flushing, New York, on 3 May 1949. [Walsh 1972/8.]

MGM (label). (I) An American record issued from 1947, initially from 701 Seventh Ave., New York. Pop, jazz, country, classsical, children's, sacred, and gospel material were issued. MGM absorbed Verve in 1960. On 5 May 1972 MGM was sold to Polydor (Polygram). The 1991 distributor was the Polygram Group, New York.

MGM (label). (II) A British issue that appeared in 1949, produced by EMI, Ltd., under the registered trademark of Loew's, Inc., of the U.S., whose matrices were used. The trademark showed the familiar Metro-Goldwyn-Mayer lion. [Andrews*.]

MICHIGAN PHONOGRAPH CO. A Detroit firm, established in 1890 as one of the **North American Phonograph Co.** affiliates; it was located in the Opera House building. C. C. Bowen was president in 1890–1893. Charles Swift, who was secretary in 1890 and a member of the board of directors, was a "champion in the cause of unification among phonograph interests" (Read).

MICKEL, GEORGE E. American record industry executive, also in the bicycle business. He was elected vice president of the National Association of Talking Machine Jobbers in 1912 and reelected in 1913. In 1914 he was president of the Nebraska Cycle Co. of Omaha.

MICROCASSETTE. A small version of the audiocassette, using tape 1/8 inch wide and moving at a speed of 15/16 inches per second. Its case is 5.5 by 3.3 by 0.7 centimeters (2 3/16 by 1 5/16 by 9/32 inches). It is used in telephone answering machines and for other business functions, and to a limited extent for musical programming.

Microgroove record. *See* LONG PLAYING RECORD.

MICROPHONE. This article consists of seven sections:

1. Types of microphone
2. First microphones: 1870s to 1920s
3. The radio age
4. The post-war boom
5. The rock era: 1960s
6. The golden era: 1970s
7. Modern microphones

1. *Types of microphone.* A microphone changes sound energy into electrical energy. There are several basic types. Carbon microphones use pellets, rods, or granules of carbon sandwiched between two electrodes. A DC current passes through the carbon, while a diaphragm vibrates, compressing the carbon, which causes a change in the electrical resistance of the carbon, creating an AC voltage component across the electrodes.

Piezoelectric microphones rely on the properties of certain materials that create a voltage when they are mechanically distorted. A diaphragm vibrates, bending the piezoelectric material, creating an AC voltage. Crystal microphones use Rochelle salts, a naturally occurring piezoelectric substance. Ceramic microphones use a synthetic material which is more rugged. More recently, certain plastics, such as Kynar or PVDF, have been used. Piezoelectrics are inexpensive, but somewhat fragile.

Dynamic microphones work much like an electrical generator. The diaphragm is attached to a coil of wire suspended between the poles of a magnet. As the diaphragm vibrates, the coil cuts the magnetic field, generating an AC voltage. Ribbon microphones work like dynamics, but use a pleated metal ribbon suspended between a horseshoe magnet's poles. Ribbons are more frail than dynamics and have lower output voltages. Ribbon microphones are also called velocity microphones.

Condenser microphones consist of a capacitor having one fixed electrode and one movable electrode serving as the diaphragm. A DC bias voltage is applied to both electrodes. As the diaphragm electrode vibrates, the change in capacitance caused by its movement creates an AC voltage. Electret microphones are permanently charged, but still require a supply of electricity, usually a penlight battery, to power a circuit used to convert their very high impedance to a lower impedance to minimize noise and loss of high frequencies. "Condenser" is an older name for a capacitor; some newer designs use the term capacitor microphone.

Some microphones are sensitive to sound equally in all directions, while others exhibit directionality, especially at higher frequencies. Cardioid microphones are more sensitive to sound arriving from the front, less so from the sides, and lesser still from the rear. Cardioid means "heart shaped"; the term refers to the shape of a graph of its directional sensitivity. Supercardioid microphones are more directional cardioids. Bidirectional, or figure eight, microphones are sensitive mainly from the front and rear, and much less so from the sides. Ribbons are the most common bidirectional types. Shotgun microphones use an interference tube for a highly directional pickup pattern. More directional still are parabolic microphones, which use a curved dish to focus sound energy onto the microphone diaphragm.

Contact microphones use rubber discs or solid rods to sense vibrations in solid materials, such as walls or rock. Hydrophones are underwater microphones.

2. *First Microphones: 1870s to 1920s.* The very first microphones were designed for use in telephones. As such, they were called transmitters, not microphones. Alexander Graham Bell's design of April 1876 used a carbon rod suspended vertically in a pool of diluted sulfuric acid to cause a change in resistance to a DC voltage, creating what he called "undulating current." A diaphragm of sheepskin mounted horizontally at the bottom of a funnel vibrated the carbon rod. This "liquid" microphone was a meager success, and was quickly superseded because of the hazards involved with the open cup of acid. Later that year, Bell's improved design used a diaphragm that pressed a small platinum button against a carbon block to create the varying resistances. All the principal manufacturers of transmitters followed this pattern, including Ader, Berliner, and Edison. Batteries supplied the DC voltages.

Another design used in many early Bell telephones was the "magnetic" transmitter. This design was the same as a telephone receiver: a coil of wire was wound around the end of a magnet. A steel diaphragm was placed at the end of the magnet by the coil. As it vibrated, it induced a weak AC voltage in the coil. Although this simplified telephone design allowed the same device to send and receive, it limited the telephone's range and usefulness, and the design was quickly superseded by battery-driven carbon microphones. Carbon microphones developed higher voltages in the era before electronic amplifiers existed.

By 1880, carbon rods began to substitute for carbon blocks, improving reliability and sensitivity. It was with a rod-type carbon microphone that Bell demonstrated **binaural** sound, with a pair of transmitters placed on either side of a mannequin's head. In a separate room, "auditors" experienced "binaural audition" by listening to a pair of receivers, much like modern headphones. In 1881, Clément Ader placed pairs of his transmitters in the footlights of the Paris Opéra. Visitors to the Electrical Exhibition Hall 10 miles away could hear the opera through pairs of receivers, connected by telephone circuits to the transmitters there.

The year 1885 brought the Blake transmitter, which for the first time used carbon granules instead of rods or blocks. The White transmitter of 1890 placed the carbon microphone in its familiar, modern form. Called the "solid back" transmitter, it allowed vertical mounting for the first time, and greatly reduced the "packing" of the carbon granules that plagued earlier designs.

Various improvements in materials, manufacturing, and power supply occurred up to the 1920s, but no major improvements in sound quality derived, because the sole application of microphones was in telephone systems.

3. *The radio age.* The advent of radio, talking movies, and electronic amplifiers in the 1920s gave impetus for better designs to meet the greater quality demands of these applications. Whereas telephones were concerned with speaking voice only, radio and the movies often included music.

Although the very first radio microphones were still carbon types, new designs quickly arrived. The first condenser microphones were simultaneously developed by Bell Laboratories in the United States, Telefunken in Germany, and AKG in Austria, during 1923 and 1924. Bell Laboratories' Model 103 was used in their early experiments into "wide-range electrical recording," and the 1932 landmark stereophonic recording experiments in Philadelphia with Leopold Stokowski. The Radio Corporation of America (RCA) seven-inch square box condenser and the Western Electric cathedral-shaped model became standards of film and broadcasting.

The 1930s were an era of rapid improvements in microphone design and use. Bell Laboratories upgraded its condenser models, largely because of recording experiments begun in the late 1920s. In England, Alan Dower Blumlein employed ribbons in his experiments, leading to his pioneering successful stereo recordings.

Other ribbon microphones gained rapid acceptance too, most visibly by the distinctive angular RCA Model 44, and models by Shure Brothers, Electro-Voice, and others. Huge cylindrical Telefunken microphones festooned the podium during rousing speeches by Adolf Hitler. Crystal microphones, such as those made by Astatic, Amperite, and Brush, adorned the podiums of less grandiose public address systems.

Western Electric marketed the first cardioid microphone, their model 639 "birdcage," which used a ribbon and omnidirectional dynamic inside the same housing. A switch could select only the ribbon element for bidirectional pickup, only the dynamic element for omnidirectional pickup, or both to create a cardioid pickup. Their models 630 "8–ball" and 633 "saltshaker" also became mainstays.

Dynamic microphones arrived with the discovery of better magnetic materials. Besides RCA, Shure, Electro-Voice, AKG, and Calrec, less costly models were marketed by companies such as Turner, Universal Microphone Company, and American Microphone Company.

During the Second World War, microphone development continued. The huge Telefunken U-27 became a world standard following the War. RCA's innovative model 77 ribbon became almost universal in film and radio, and later in television. Adjustable vanes inside the "time capsule" shaped perforated metal housing allowed it to be bidirectional, cardioid, or nearly omnidirectional. RCA 77s are still sought after today.

4. *The post war boom.* The arrival in America and Europe of German tape recording technology in the late 1940s brought fresh demand for even higher quality microphones. Electro-Voice created a cardioid dynamic that vented the rear of the diaphragm, creating partial cancellation of the sound resulting in a cardioid pickup pattern. This technique became quickly copied, and is the method still most used cardioid microphones.

Radio, stereophonic movies, television, and home tape recording led to a proliferation of microphone designs. In 1956, court actions forced the divestiture of Western Electric's microphone division to speaker giant Altec. Telefunken introduced their classic U-47, a condenser in which a pair of elements was electronically switched to create different pickup patterns. Other models came into being: Electro-Voice 635, 644, and 664; Shure 515, 545, and the 55, associated with the birth of rock and roll; and AKG C-12, recently brought back as "The Tube." Many of these are still made today.

5. *The rock era: 1960s.* Improved materials, lower manufacturing costs, and a proliferation of models characterized the 1960s. Neumann (formerly Telefunken), Schoeps, AKG, Shure,

Electro-Voice, Altec, Peavey, and Calrec marketed a wide range of successful models, primarily dynamic and condenser types. Carbon microphones remained in telephones, and crystal types became used only in the cheapest home models. Neumann updated the Telefunken U-47. B&K (Bruel & Kjaer), introducing what many claim is the best microphone ever created. Sennheiser and Electro-Voice marketed their very rugged designs. Nearly all quality microphones were dynamics or condensers.

Pressure from the demands of television and movie sound brought the lavaliere microphone, inconspicuously worn around the speaker's neck.

6. *The "golden era": 1970s.* New technologies arrived in the 1970s. Electro-Voice marketed the Mike Mouse, an innovative product based on research into boundary layer effects. An omnidirectional microphone was placed inside a specially shaped foam windscreen and laid on the floor. This eliminated the comb filter effect that occurs when sound from a nearby floor or wall arrives at the microphone, blends with direct sounds, and causes partial cancellations. Crown took this idea a step further with their Pressure Zone Microphone, or PZM. A PZM mounted a tiny condenser upside down a very short distance from a metal boundary plate. The unique configuration duplicated the Mike Mouse but gave greater freedom of placement.

The Electret microphone was introduced, in which the "bias" DC voltage was replaced by a permanent static charge. Nearly every recorder manufacturer could then offer quality condenser models. Studio and broadcast microphones dropped in cost. Electrets were built into portable cassette recorders. Lavaliere microphones using electrets became so small as to be nearly invisible. Electrets replaced crystals in low cost models, and were used in telephones.

Piezoelectric models using conductive plastics, such as Kynar or PVDF, were introduced in operator's headsets, music instrument pickups, hydrophones, ultrasound microphones, and contact microphones.

The **direct-to-disc** audiophile record craze brought a generation of transformerless condensers. Originally modifications of existing units, they improved transient response by eliminating losses caused by transformer core saturation.

AKG C-414, C-451, and C-461 condensers became popular and the cosmetically distinctive D-190 dynamic became one of the most visible European models. AKG two-way dynamic models D-200 and D-202, with separate high/low frequency dynamic elements, gave condenser-like quality. Neumann transistorized the U-47, which became the U-87. Shure SM-57 and SM-58 cardioids became arguably the two most visible public address microphones.

7. *Modern Microphones.* In the 1980s, rare-earth magnets led to a new generation of dynamic microphones. Electro-Voice marketed the N-Dym line, and Shure the Beta line. Their neodymium magnets created such high magnetic flux that they exhibited a clarity normally associated with condensers, along with higher output. Digital microphones built the quantization circuits into condenser microphones to attain remarkable results. Great improvements in wireless microphone technology occurred.

In 1991 innovations were appearing quickly. One was B & K's "Ball" accessory for the 4000 series omnidirectional condensers. The seven-centimeter diameter solid plastic ball made the omnidirectional microphone into a somewhat cardioid pattern. [Borwick 1987; Borwick 1990; Ford 1962; Klinger*; Olson, H. 1977.]. *See also* ELECTRICAL RECORDING; RECORDING PRACTICE.

Kermit V. Gray

MICRO-PHONOGRAPH. The name given by **Gianni Bettini** to his cylinder recording/playing device, patented in 1889.

MIDDLE-OF-THE-ROAD (MOR). A popular music style said to be of interest primarily to women (Denisoff says "married women over the age of 24"), emphasizing nostalgic and romantic material. Among the favorite performers have been Michael Jackson, Barry

Manilow, Kenny Rogers, and Dionne Warwick. [Denisoff 1975.]

MIGNON (label). A British record of 1912, made by Beka Records division of Carl Lindström (London), Ltd. It was a six-inch, double-sided disc, sold with a small record player to accommodate it. There was little promotion after the first advertisements, and then the War stopped imports. [Andrews*.]

MIL. One-thousandth of an inch. A measure used to describe the thickness of the base in a magnetic tape, stylus dimensions, groove dimensions, etc.

MILANOV, ZINKA, 1906–1989. Croatian soprano, born in Zagreb on 17 May 1906. After study in Zagreb, she made her professional debut with the Ljubljana Opera in 1927, then went to Hamburg and Vienna. In 1937 she was acclaimed for her singing in the Verdi *Requiem* under Arturo Toscanini in Salzburg. Her Metropolitan Opera debut was on 17 Dec 1937, in *Trovatore*; she remained to 1966, but not without interruptions; and also appeared internationally. The role of Aida, her second at the Metropolitan (sung first on 2 Feb 1928) became one of her outstanding interpretations; she also excelled in *Gioconda* and *Cavalleria rusticana*.

Milanov was a Victor artist. Among her important recordings were many complete opera recordings: *Trovatore*, *Tosca*, *Cavalleria* (these with Jussi Björling); *Aida*, *Forza del destino*, and *Gioconda* (all with Giuseppe Di Stefano). "Voi lo sapete" (Victor #11–8927) represents her voice at its peak. [Einstein 1968.]

MILITARY BAND RECORDINGS. In Britain and in continental Europe military bands of the various army regiments and some naval establishments formed the backbones of many record catalogs, from the earliest days of the industry until the end of the First World War. Their repertoires, which covered a great range of popular and light classical material in addition to marches, was later undertaken by studio orchestras and then by established symphony and concert orchestras.

The popularity of military bands in the U.S. during the later 19th century and early 20th century was immense. Such bands flourished in communities across the nation, playing all categories of popular music in addition to marches. The early record companies, cylinder and disc, gave high priority to band music. An Edison recording session of June 1889 brought forth six numbers by Duffy and Imgrund's Fifth Regiment Band, an ensemble that returned about 20 times to the Edison studio by 1892. The 12–piece band of **Patrick S. Gilmore** was recorded by Edison on 17 Dec 1891, doing 19 numbers of various types, some featuring cornetist **Tom Clark**. Voss' First Regiment Band was another Edison group of the period. The first Edison Diamond Discs made by military bands were done in 1913, by the National Promenade Band and the New York Military Band; later by the Edison Concert Band (the material recorded was dance and pop as well as march).

Columbia signed **John Philip Sousa** and his **United States Marine Band** to an exclusive contract as soon as the firm began to make entertainment records in 1889. The 1891 Columbia sales list included 27 marches plus 23 other orchestral items. Sousa had a new ensemble in the 1895 catalog, the Grand Concert Band, featuring the famous trombonist **Arthur Pryor**.

A list of Columbia brown-wax two-minute cylinders issued from 1896 to 1900 shows the United States Marine Band playing "Washington Post March" (#1; 1896), followed by close to a hundred other numbers. Many were marches, e.g., "Columbia Phonograph March" (#58) and Columbia Phonograph Co. March" (#63); others were waltzes, overtures, operatic potpourris, medleys of national airs, patriotic songs, and even "Safe in the Arms of Jesus" (#378). Sousa's Grand Concert Band made many Columbia cylinders from 1895 to 1900, including popular songs, marches, and two solo items by Arthur Pryor. The year 1896 also saw the beginning of series by the Washington Military Concert Band, Gilmore's Band, The Old Guard Band (New York), and the Twenty-third Regiment Band (New York). Columbia continued to record military bands when it phased into the disc format (from 1902; Columbia cylinder sales ceased in 1912). A house group, the Columbia Band, made a series of overtures and operatic excerpts in 1904, and continued to 1909. Many other bands were recording for the label too: Prince's Military Band, Rena Military Band, British Grenadiers Band, etc. The interest in band music continued into the electrical recording era (from 1925), with the **Grenadier Guards Band** and the Highland Military Band among others on Columbia.

Berliner's earliest seven-inch discs included material by Sousa's Band, Victor Herbert's 22nd Regiment Band, the United States Marine Band, and various unnamed bands. More than 1,000 Berliner discs with bands or band members as soloists had appeared by 1900.

Sousa's Band had six sessions for Victor in October 1900, making 167 takes, of which 84 were released. Their repertoire included marches, gallops, waltzes, polkas, musical show tunes, etc. "Hands across the Sea March" started the first session, released as #300. By the end of 1902 another 375 releases were credited to the Sousa Band. Kendle's First Regiment Band was in the Victor studio eleven times in 1901 and 1902; other bands of the period on Victor were Kilties Band of Canada (with bagpipes), the American Band of Providence, Rhode Island (directed by cornetist **Herbert L. Clarke**), and Pryor's Band—a Victor house organization established 1903. The Pryor Band output was unmatched by any group: more than 2,000 titles emerged from 5,000 takes. In Williams 1972 it is suggested "that the Pryor recordings began to represent the bread and butter sales of the company." Sousa's was more famous, but less active in recording. The **Garde Republicaine Band**, of France, made Victor records in New York in October 1904, producing 20 titles. After 1912 there was less work by the Pryor and Sousa bands, as Victor formed a new house organization, the Victor Band. This group ran into the dance craze of the pre-War period, and recorded mostly in that genre. The Marine Band was with Victor for two sessions, in one of which (15 Oct 1906) it recorded the first U.S. version of Scott Joplin's "Maple Leaf Rag." When the Original Dixieland Jass Band made its famous first disc on 26 Feb 1917 (Victor #18255), the realm of dance and pop music began to pass from military bands to jazz/pop/swing ensembles. Although the wartime interest in military matters sustained further recording of marches, there was a quick decline of public interest in the military band in the 1920s. Records by the Victor Band were fewer each year: down to four in 1930, and none in 1931. Only a few more discs came out in the 1930s from one band or another. There were still about 100 titles listed under Band Music in the 1940 Victor catalog.

In the late 1940s Columbia was listing fewer than 40 singles and four or five band music albums, mostly by the Goldman Band and the Band of H. M. Grenadier Guards.

With the advent of LP, a new flowering of military band music appeared. During the 1950s around 90 military or marching bands made records; among them were old familiar groups like the Band of the Coldstream Guards, the Garde Republicaine, the Goldman Band, and the Grenadier Guards. Interesting new groups included German military ensembles, and others from Sweden, Spain, Austria, Wales, and Holland. Much of the LP repertoire has carried into CD, and CD has also brought reissues of early material such as Herbert L. Clarke directing the Sousa Band (1909–1921). [Boots 1981; Smart 1970; Williams F. 1972.]

MILLER, EDDIE, 1911– . American tenor saxophonist and clarinetist, born in New Orleans on 23 June 1911. He played locally until 1930, then went to New York. He spent four years with Ben Pollack, then joined the new Bob Crosby band, becoming its most featured soloist. Miller's style remained in a joyous Dixieland mode (although the sax was not a regular part of the traditional New Orleans groups), with lean, elegant improvisations, as in "Till We Meet Again" (Decca #2825; 1939) with Bob Crosby's Bob Cats. In "Milenberg Joys" he took part in a remarkable four-way improvisation (Decca #25293; 1942). In 1944 he played a memorable counterpoint for Martha Tilton's popular "Stranger in Town." He freelanced after military service, and played again with Crosby groups and with him on television. He made hundreds of records with many ensembles and for numerous labels. Miller continued playing, mostly in New Orleans, into the 1980s, then suffered a debilitating stroke in 1988.

MILLER, GLENN, 1904–1944. American Big Band leader and trombonist, born Alton Glenn Miller in Clarinda, Iowa, on 1 Mar 1904. He attended the University of Colorado, then left to pursue a musical career. After some time on the West Coast he joined Ben Pollack's band in Chicago in 1926. From 1928 he was a freelance trombonist in New York, then he was with Smith Ballew as arranger in 1932–1934. He was briefly with the Dorsey Brothers, then with Ray Noble's first American band in 1935. In 1937 he organized his own band, and began recording for Decca and Brunswick; financial difficulties led to dissolution of that group, but he founded another in 1938 and became recognized by 1939 for his splendid arrangements, gaining a Bluebird contract. "Moonlight Serenade," his composition and his theme song, was an early hit record (Bluebird #10214; 1939). Another was "In the Mood" (Bluebird #10416; 1939). Miller had a radio show in 1939–1942. Ray Eberle and Marion Hutton were the principal vocalists; in the band there were outstanding men like Tex Beneke, Billy May, and Hal McIntyre. In 1941 the band acquired a stylish vocal quartet, the Modernaires. They made a motion picture that year, *Sun Valley Serenade*, and recorded a great hit from it, "Chattanooga Choo Choo" (Bluebird #11230; 1941).

From 1941 to September 1942 the Miller band grew in stature, and was widely judged to be the finest of its kind. "Elmer's Tune" (Bluebird #11274; 1941), "String of Pearls" (Bluebird # 11382; 1941), and "Skylark" (Bluebird #11462; 1941) had great popularity. Other hit records—on the Victor label, as a prestige move—included "I've Got a Gal in Kalamazoo," Tex Beneke singing, with "At Last" (Victor #27935; 1942), and "Serenade in Blue" (Victor #27995; 1942; all these coming from his other film, *Orchestra Wives*; and the instrumental "American Patrol" (Victor #27873; 1942).

Miller enlisted in the Army Air Force in September 1942, and was tasked with direction of the AAF Dance Band. That group made regular radio broadcasts and V-Discs; it included other militarized swing/jazz performers, such as Mel Powell and Ray McKinley. When Miller was killed as his plane went down between Britain and France, on 16 Dec 1944, the AAF band was taken over by McKinley and arranger Jerry Gray. In the postwar years various musicians led members of the old Miller band: among them Tex Beneke, Ralph Flanagan, Ray Anthony, Ray McKinley, and Buddy De Franco; it continued performing into the 1970s.

There were many LP reissues of the Miller recordings, including *The Complete Glenn Miller* (1976). On CD many of the hits are on RCA's #PCD1–5459, *Unforgettable Glenn Miller*, made from the 78s with no remastering. Another important CD is *Glenn Miller in Hollywood* (Mercury 826 635–2), taken from soundtracks of his films. [Flower 1972; Polic 1989.]

MILLER, POLK, 1844–1913. American popular singer, born in Grape Lawn, Virginia, on 2 Aug 1844. He served in the Civil War, then became a drugstore owner; organized a quartet of Black singers named Miller's Old South Quartet, or the Old South Quartet. He and his group made Edison cylinders in 1910; those listed in Koenigsberg 1987 are "Rise and Shine" (#10332), "Old Time Religion" (#10333), and "Jerusalem Mournin'" (#10334). Miller played banjo with the quartet, of which James L. Stamper, bass, and Randall Graves are the only identified members. Miller died in Richmond on 20 Oct 1913. [Koenigsberg 1987; Walsh 1960/ 1; 1962/10.]

MILLER, REED, 1880–1943. American tenor, born in Anderson, South Carolina, on 29 Feb 1880. He was "the finest oratorio singer of his day" (Walsh), with records for the major labels. Miller's earliest recordings were made in 1904 for Zonophone, under the name of James Reed; the first was "Teasing" (#6035). His first Edison cylinder was "Birds in Georgia Sing of Tennessee" (#9658; 1907). He went to Victor in 1910, and Columbia in 1914 (an excerpt from *Elijah*). Opera arias, in English, were among his 27 Edison Diamond Discs of 1913–1921: "Vesti la giubba" / "Siciliana" (#82031). He also made duets with Fred Wheeler, and sang with the Stellar Quartet and the Frank Croxton Quartet. His recording ceased after 1921. Miller's wife, Nevada Van der Veer, was a contralto who also made early records. He died in New York on 29 Dec 1943. [Walsh 1958/3.]

MILLER, ROGER, 1936–1992. American country singer, instrumentalist, and songwriter, born in Fort Worth, Texas, on 2 Jan 1936. He was a cowboy and rodeo performer as a youth, while learning to play the guitar, banjo, and piano. After military service in the 1950s, and various odd jobs, he went to Nashville to concentrate on a musical career. He achieved great success in the 1960s and 1970s, with 43 chart singles and six chart albums. "When Two Worlds Collide" (Victor #7868; 1961) was his first national hit, with 22 weeks on the charts. "King of the Road" (Smash #1965; 1965), his own composition, was his signature song; and there were five other chart records in the same year. Smash, Victor, Mercury, and Columbia were the labels he worked with. Miller won 11 Grammy awards in 1965–1966. He died on 25 Oct 1992.

MILLER, WALTER. American recording engineer and inventor, an associate of Thomas Edison from ca. 1888 to 1929. He had various duties, including direction of research, supervision of and entertainment cylinder production, and general supervision of recording. Miller had 18 U.S. patents in the area of sound recording between 1898 and 1904, five of them in his name alone, and the others with Jonas W. Aylsworth or Alexander N. Pierman. His principal invention was the molding technology that made mass production of cylinders possible; it was covered in several patents with Pierman: #726,965 (filed 21 Nov 1902; granted 5 May 1903), and #785,510 (filed 26 Feb 1903; granted 21 Mar 1905), etc.

MILLS BROTHERS. A popular male vocal group, consisting of four Ohio-born brothers: Herbert, Harry, Donald, and John; they flourished in the 1930s and 1940s, and remained active into the 1970s. After local work in Cincinnati they went to New York for radio shows in 1930. Their smooth, relaxed idiom weathered the various style changes of their time. "Paper Doll" was their greatest hit (Decca #18318; 1943); "Lazy River" was another notable success (Decca #28458; 1952). "Glow Worm" was on the charts for 18 weeks in 1952 (Decca #28384). In 1968 they recorded their final chart song, "Cab Driver" (Dot #17041).

There have been many LP albums as well, at least seven on the Dot label. *Fortuosity* (Dot #DLPS 25835; 1968) was on the charts 15 weeks.

MILLS NOVELTY CO. A Chicago firm, located at Jackson Blvd. and Green St., maker of slot machines and amusement devices, and the popular **coin-op**, Violano-Virtuoso. This was an electric powered violin-playing machine, representing both violin and piano accompaniment on paper music rolls. About 5,000 were made from 1909 to 1930, primarily for restaurants and taverns. There had been an earlier automatic violin advertised, the Virtuosa, in 1907. One version for theatre use had four different rolls, allowing the projectionist to select the music. Mills also made a theatre instrument called the Mills Melody Violin: it allowed violins to be played from a keyboard. In 1929 Mills was located at 410 W. Fullerton. It marketed the Dance Master, a disc coin-op with 12 selections, each on a separate turntable in a ferris wheel arrangement (similar to the cylinder **Multiphone**). Later the firm went into juke box manufacture; their post-War Constellation model had 20 records and 40 selections.

MILWAUKEE TALKING MACHINE MANUFACTURING CO. A firm established in 1915, located at 418 4th St., Milwaukee. In 1916 it offered the Perfectrola line of record players, in seven models.

MIMOSA (label). A British record, single-sided, 5 3/8 inches and six inches in size, made by Crystalate Gramophone Record Manufacturing Co., Ltd., and sold by Sound Recording Co., Ltd. and Woolworth's, from 1921. Material was military music, dance music and popular songs. Later the record was issued double-sided. Mimosa masters were used for other labels, e.g., Kiddyphone, Pigmy, Oliver, Marspen, Beacon, Butterfly, and Savana. [Andrews*.]

MINGUS, CHARLES, 1922–1979. American jazz bass player and composer, born in Nogales, Arizona, on 22 Apr 1922. He studied cello and bass while in his teens, and played with several bands: Lee Young, Louis Armstrong, and Lionel Hampton. His first recording was with the

Russell Jacquet orchestra in 1945, for the Globe label. An important record, "Mingus Fingus," was made with Hampton in 1947 (Decca #24428). He was a member of the Red Norvo Trio, recording for the Discovery label in 1950–1951. Mingus was peripatetic most of his career, never long with one group of colleagues. He formed a sextet in 1964, with Eric Dolphy (alto sax, bass clarinet, flute), Clifford Jordan (tenor sax), and Danny Richmond (drums), Johnny Coles (trumpet), and Jaki Byard (piano); and made the three-album set *The Great Concert* in Paris (America #AM003–05). His last records were done in January 1978, in three sessions for Atlantic. Appropriately his final number was "Farewell, Farewell" (Atlantic #SD 8805).

The CDs *Black Saint and the Sinner Lady* (MCA Impulse #MCAD 5649) and *Mingus Revisited* (EmArcy #826 498, originally recorded 1960) offer a wide selection of his work and the many musicians he teamed with. He died in Cuernavaca, Mexico, on 5 Jan 1979. [Ruppli 1981.]

MINNESOTA MINING AND MANUFACTURING CO. (3M). A diversified American firm, established in 1902, located in St. Paul. 3M is of interest in the sound recording field for its development of magnetic tape players and (1947) "Scotch" recording tapes. Research under direction of Wilfred W. Wetzel led to an improved magnetic tape with an iron oxide coating; this was the Scotch tape. It reached a high frequency of 15,000 Hz, moving at 7 1/2 inches per second. When this tape went into production in 1947 it almost immediately replaced discs in professional work, such as making of radio transcriptions. The firm also makes video tapes. In 1989 3M had factories in 41 countries and annual sales, of all products, of $11.9 billion.

MINNESOTA PHONOGRAPH CO. A Minneapolis firm, established in 1890 as one of the **North American Phonograph Co.** affiliates; it was located at 108 Rochester Block. C. H. Chadbourne (or C. N. Chadbourn) was general manager in 1890 and president in 1892.

MINSTREL RECORDINGS. Minstrel shows—variety dance/comedy/musical productions by white artists in blackface, later by Black artists—were a popular genre in America from the mid-19th century. The Virginia Minstrels, organized by Edwin Pearce Christy, were the first troupe of minstrels, appearing in New York in February 1843, and creating a sudden sensation. Renamed as Christy's Minstrels, they began a New York run on 27 Apr 1846 and performed every night until 13 July 1854. Stephen Foster songs were featured by the group. When E. P. Christy died in 1862 his son George kept the company going for some time, but it closed down finally in 1865. A characteristic element in the shows was the humor drawn from players who portrayed stupid Blacks and made absurd responses to questions posed by a player representing the superior white man. This curious format dominated American theater (with great success in Britain also) into the 1890s, when vaudeville, burlesque, and the Broadway revue took over much of its audience.

Early recordings made much of the white person's image of the dimwitted Black, and of the self-deprecating Negro, as in **coon songs** and foolish dialogues. Minstrel recordings were made by white and Black artists; among them (in the 18 items of the Victor 1917 catalog) Billy Murray, the Peerless Quartet, and the American Quartet. On Edison cylinders there was the Billy Heins Ancient City Quartet recording in 1898; and there were the Edison Minstrels, recording from ca. 1899 on five-inch Concert cylinders. From 1903 there were two-minute cylinders by the same group, also known as the Edison Modern Minstrels. On Columbia Twentieth Century cylinders there was a group named the Rambler Minstrels in 1907.

Victor's Evening with the Minstrels series of eight discs began in 1902, and ran to 1909. A confusion of titles was attached to many of the early Victor releases, as Olden Time Minstrels, Victor Minstrels, and Matinee Minstrels were names given to the same ensembles. In 1907 a group taking the name of the long defunct Christy Minstrels made four records.

Victor's 1922 catalog still carried a section of 15 Minstrel Records, by the Victor Minstrel Co., Peerless Quartet, Billy Murray, and a few others. But by 1927 the category had been dropped from the catalog.

In Britain there were recordings by the Excelsior Minstrels on Edison Bell cylinders, and by the Black Diamonds Minstrels (formed by Russell Hunting, who took part) on Sterling, Pathé, and Odeon records. The Coontown Minstrels were on the Jumbo label. Popular minstrel troupes were heard on almost all makes of disc in Britain up until the First World War. The Kentucky Minstrels recorded for HMV in the 1930s. After the Second World War the Black and White Minstrel Show recorded and gave live performances. [Andrews 1977/1 has a selective discography of British issues; Koenigsberg 1987; Leonard 1986; Fagan 1983.]

MISSOURI PHONOGRAPH CO. A St. Louis firm, one of the **North American Phonograph Co.** affiliates, established in 1890. A. W. Clancy was vice president in 1890, and president in 1891–1893. J. C. Wood was general manager in 1891–1893, and vice-president in 1892–1893. The firm had about 50 multiple-tube **coin-ops** on location in 1891, earning about $100/week from each one.

MITCHELL RECORD (label). An American record issued in 1924–1926 by the Mitchell Phonograph Corp. of 3000 Gratiot Ave., Detroit. Masters came first from the Emerson family of labels, then from Grey Gull. Production of Mitchell records was effected by the Bridgeport Die and Machine Co. until it dissolved in 1925. [Rust 1978.]

MITROPOULOS, DIMITRI, 1896–1960. Greek/American conductor and pianist, born in Athens on 1 Mar 1896. He studied in Athens and Brussels, then piano with Ferruccio Busoni in Berlin. He was assistant conductor of the Berlin Opera from 1921 to 1924. His Paris debut in 1932 was a notable success; he then conducted in many cities, and made an American debut in 1937 with the Boston Symphony Orchestra. Mitropoulos was appointed director of the Minneapolis Symphony Orchestra, and held the post from 1937 to 1949. He became an

American citizen in 1946. From 1950 to 1958 he directed the New York Philharmonic Orchestra, conducting also at the Metropolitan Opera and various other orchestras and opera companies. He died on 2 Nov 1960, while rehearsing the La Scala Orchestra in Milan.

Among his fine recordings the most famous was the Mahler First Symphony, with the New York Philharmonic (Columbia album #SL 118), which he had also done with the Minneapolis Symphony in 1941 (Columbia album #469). His most acclaimed operatic recordings were *Boris Godunov* (Victor #LM-6063; 1956) and *Vanessa* (Victor #LM-6138; 1958), with the Metropolitan Opera Company.

MIXDOWN. A reduction in the number of channels from the original recording, as signals are transferred from a multi-track reproducer to a two-track master record, or to a monaural master, etc. *See also* MIXER.

MIXER. A device that blends two or more recorded signals. In recording, the mixer permits a manipulation of outputs from several channels, so that they may be faded, selected, or combined in any combination and in any arrangement of volumes. *See also* MIXDOWN.

MOBLEY, EDWIN H. American inventor, holder of nine early patents in sound recording: diaphragms, soundboxes, a turntable for discs, and a phonograph-reproducer (U.S. patent # 690,069; filed 3 July 1901; granted 31 Dec 1901) that improved stylus tracking and volume of the Edison Automatic Reproducer. Edison sued him successfully on the grounds that Mobley had no right to alter Edison's patented device. [Koenigsberg 1990.]

MODERN JAZZ QUARTET. A group formed by vibraphonist Milt Jackson in 1952, successor to his own Milt Jackson Quartet of 1947. Members were Jackson, pianist John Lewis, drummer Kenny Clarke, and bassist Percy Heath. Clarke was replaced by Connie Kay in 1955. They began to record for Blue Note in 1952, moving to Atlantic in 1956, and established a reputation for structured performance with a classical aspect. The men wore evening dress and played to adult audiences. The MJQ has performed with major symphony orchestras and with string quartets. When Jackson departed in 1974 the quartet dissolved, but got together again in 1981. They were performing in England and Scotland in 1991. The CD *Echoes* offers music recorded in 1984, after the group was reunited (Pablo #3112–41); it includes some outstanding original treatments in "Watergate Blues" and "Hornpipe." A four-CD set on Atlantic (the group's label since 1956) surveys their career (#MJQ 40; 1991).

MODULATION. The technique of varying a characteristic (i.e., amplitude) of a wave (the carrier) as a function of the instantaneous value of another wave (the modulator). Amplitude modulation (AM) and frequency modulation (FM) are basic to radio broadcasting. Modulation is also a factor in acoustic and electrical recording, telephony, etc. [Isom*.]

MONARCH RECORD (label). An American label of the Victor Talking Machine Co., also titled Victor Monarch Record; issued from 3 Jan 1901. These were the earliest 10–inch discs from any firm. Earlier Victors had been seven-inch size. Some 585 seven-inch Victors had already appeared before the Monarch 10–inch was introduced, and the name Victor was retained for the smaller records. Many of the same titles were duplicated in both series. Victors—phased out by 1906—sold for $.50, Monarchs for $1. It was on the Victor Monarch Record that the **Nipper** trademark first appeared in the U.S. A special series of Monarch imports began with material originating in London, Milan, Paris, and St. Petersburg in 1901 and 1902, with a red label (announced as "imported Red Seal Records"). When Victor initiated its American-made Red Seals in 1903, the Monarch imports (they were in a 5000 series) were renumbered into the 91000 series. Monarch as a label name was carried into Victor's 1904 catalog, then dropped. The reason Victor abandoned the Monarch name was to avoid confusion with the Gramophone Monarch Record, introduced in June 1903 by the associated G & T. [Fagan 1983.]

MONAURAL. Single-channel sound transmission or recording, another term for monopho-

nic; it is often shortened to "mono." To the listener, monaural recordings give the effect of listening with one ear only.

MONK, THELONIOUS, 1917–1982. American jazz pianist, born in Rocky Mount, North Carolina, on 10 Oct 1917. His family moved to New York, where he learned to play the piano and worked at Minton's Playhouse ("the cradle of modern jazz"). In 1944 he made records with Coleman Hawkins, presenting his personal style that did not fit the current bebop phase. He worked for the Blue Note label, then Prestige, before moving to Riverside and a successful album, *Brilliant Corners* (1956; on Riverside CD #VDJ 1526); this was followed by further Riverside discs that established his reputation for originality. *The Complete Riverside Recordings* (Riverside #RCD-022–2) is a 15–CD (or 22–LP) set of 153 numbers, Monk's complete Riverside output of 1955–1961. Monk died in Englewood, New Jersey, on 17 Feb 1982.

Mono. *See* MONAURAL.

Monophonic. *See* MONAURAL.

MONROE, BILL, 1911– . American country singer and "Father of Bluegrass Music," born in Rosine, Kentucky, on 13 Sep 1911. He played fiddle tunes on the mandolin (the only instrument available to him) as a youth in a family group. In 1938 he organized the Blue Grass Boys, and developed the new bluegrass style; he was on *Grand Ole Opry* in October 1939, and became nationally acclaimed. The Blue Grass Boys had an unusual instrumentation for country music, including a plucked string bass as well as the Monroe mandolin. It had an up-tempo beat, bringing it close to jazz. He built the Bluegrass Hall of Fame and Museum in Nashville, later moving it to Hendersonville. After stardom in country music during the 1940s, Monroe was overshadowed by musicians he had trained: Lester Flatt and Earl Scruggs. But in the 1970s his innovative style was again recognized (he was elected to the Country Music Hall of Fame in 1970) and he remained in the vanguard of bluegrass performers. He presents a hard-blues sound, sung in a high tenor wail, accompanied on his mandolin.

Monroe recorded 109 pieces for Decca from 1950 to 1958; all are included on Bear Family #BCD 15423, four CDs (1990). He has continued performing, and recording for Decca (and its successor MCA), with undiminished creative powers.

MONTANA, PATSY, 1914– . American country singer, guitarist, and songwriter, born Ruby Blevins in Hot Springs, Arkansas, on 30 Oct 1914. She began her singing career in her teens, and was lead vocalist with a group called the Prairie Ramblers from 1934 to 1948, touring widely, and appearing on the *National Barn Dance* radio show. Known as "The Cowboy's Sweetheart" or "The Yodeling Cowgirl," she was one of the mainstays of the *Barn Dance* for about 25 years, and had her own radio program as well. She sang with the influential string band named The Prairie Ramblers (Chick Hurt, Jack Taylor, Tex Atchison, and Salty Holmes). Montana's radio appearances and recordings were instrumental in the establishing of country music as a prime force in American life. She recorded extensively from 1932 to 1959 on various labels, including Columbia, Decca, Surf, Victor, and Vocalion. An early Victor was typical of her enduring popular discs: "I Love My Daddy Too" / "When the Flowers of Montana Were Blooming" (# 23760; 1932).

Montana has never retired; she has composed more than 200 songs, and continues making appearances, sometimes with her two daughters. In 1989 she released a new album, *The Cowboy's Sweetheart*, on the Flying Fish label, and she performed in the annual University of Chicago Folk Festival.

MONTANA PHONOGRAPH CO. A firm established in 1890, one of the affiliates of the **North American Phonograph Co.**; location was Helena, Montana. The president in 1892 was E. D. Edgerton. The firm was still in business, as an Edison distributor, as late as October 1925.

MONTAUK TRIO. An instrumental group that made one Edison Diamond Disc in 1923: "You Wanted Someone to Play With" / "Somebody's Wrong" (#51228). Members were Walter Wooley, piano; Henry L. Taylor, banjo; and Stanley Brooks, saxophone.

MONTEUX, PIERRE, 1875–1964. French conductor, violinist, and violist, born in Paris on 4 Apr 1875. He played viola in various orchestras, then in 1911 became conductor for the Ballets Russes. He was on the podium during the riotous premiere of *Sacre du printemps* in 1913, calmly taking the piece to its final bar in the midst of pandemonium. He also directed the world premieres of *Petrouchka, Daphnis et Chloe,* and other works. From 1917 to 1919 he was a conductor at the Metropolitan Opera; then he conducted the Boston Symphony Orchestra from 1919 to 1924. He went to the Concertgebouw Orchestra as an associate conductor with Willem Mengelberg in 1924–1934, then was principal conductor of the Orchestre Symphonique de Paris during 1929–1938. Monteux was director of the San Francisco Symphony Orchestra from 1936 to 1952, and of the London Symphony Orchestra from 1961 to 1964. He died in Hancock, Maine, on 1 July 1964.

His first discs were made with the Paris orchestra in the 1930s. With the San Francisco orchestra he recorded the standard symphonies, plus Stravinsky and Ravel, for RCA Victor. Thereafter he recorded for many labels with many orchestras. His most appreciated records have been those of Stravinsky and Ravel, notably *Sacre du printemps* with the Paris Conservatory Orchestra (on 78s as London #ST55–1538; LP as Decca #ECS 750; 1957) and *Daphnis et Chloe Suite* with the London Symphony Orchestra (on 78s as London #STS 15090; LP as Decca #JB69; 1959).

MONTGOMERY, WES, 1925–1968. American jazz guitarist, born John Leslie Montgomery in Indianapolis, Indiana, on 6 Mar 1925. He is regarded as the successor to Charlie Christian, achieving a "vocalized expression" with the instrument, playing with thumb instead of a pick. He was with Lionel Hampton in 1948–1950, then returned to Indianapolis for local work. In 1959 he signed with the Riverside label and did his best jazz playing. Later albums for Verve and A&M show him in lush orchestral settings, with less jazz character.

These later albums were highly popular; seven were on the charts in 1966–1968, most notably *A Day in the Life* (A&M #LP-2001, SP-3001; 1967), which had 30 chart weeks (CD reissue as A&M #75021). Of the many fine CDs available, *Round Midnight* (originally from 1965; Affinity #C 13) and *Full House* (recorded 1962; Riverside # VDJ-1508) show him at his best. Fantasy has reissued the extensive Riverside material on compact disc. Montgomery died in Indianapolis on 15 June 1968.

MONTGOMERY WARD AND CO., INC. A Chicago-based retailer, beginning as a mail-order house in 1872. As early as 1898 the firm was offering Edison cylinder phonographs and Berliner gramophones, as well as records for them. In the 1930s the firm began to issue records under its own label, Montgomery Ward; at first these were pressed by Victor using Victor or Bluebird masters, offering good jazz and country material. During 1939–1940 there was a series from the Varsity label. In 1988 the firm discontinued catalog sales and the use of house brand products.

MOOGK, EDWARD B., 1914–1979. Canadian librarian and discographer, born in Weston, Ontario, on 15 July 1914. Moogk had a career as a drummer with dance bands. He founded and developed the recorded sound collection at the National Library of Canada. From 1945 to 1970 he had a radio show that featured old recordings. From the name of the show he took the title of his acclaimed book, *Roll Back the Years / En remontant les années* (1975), a detailed history of recorded sound in Canada up to 1930. He died before he could complete a second volume, on 18 Dec 1979, in London, Ontario.

MOONLIGHT TRIO. A vocal group that recorded two Edison Diamond Discs in 1918. "Rose of No Man's Land" was one of them (#80434). Members were Gladys Rice, George Wilton Ballard, and Thomas Chalmers.

MORGAN, CORINNE, ca. 1874–1950. American contralto, singer of opera, operetta, and popular songs. She recorded for Edison from 1902, beginning with "Whisper and I Shall Hear" (#8223); by 1905 she had 20 other solos

plus duets with Frank Stanley, all of these being popular songs. She also made 17 Columbia 10-inch discs during 1902–1906, and around 50 Victor discs between 1903 and 1908. Zonophone also recorded Morgan, with 17 discs in 1902–1905. There were two Busy Bee cylinders also, in 1904–1905. Her final records were for Emerson in 1921.

On Victor she did opera and oratorio numbers as well as pop material. One of the best received Victors was "When You and I Were Young, Maggie" with Frank Stanley (#2533). She also recorded as a member of the Lyric Quartet in 1906–1910, and with the Peerless Quartet. [Walsh 1971/7–9.]

MORRIS, ELIDA, 1886–1977. American soprano and comedienne, born in Philadelphia on 12 Nov 1886. She started out in minstrel shows, then went on the Keith vaudeville circuit doing Negro dialect songs; thence to the opera stage. In 1913 she scored a great success in a 10-week run in Britain, and for several years after that she divided her time between Britain and America; she also toured South Africa. Her first records were for Columbia in 1910, beginning with "You'll Come Back" (#A 826). In August 1910 she recorded for Victor, "Angel Eyes"—a duet with Billy Murray (#5782). Her most famous record for Victor was "Stop! Stop! Stop!" (#16687; 1911); she did the same piece for Columbia (#A953; 1912). Morris left Victor in 1913, and worked for Pathé and Columbia. She had a hit record in 1914: "High Cost of Loving" / "I Want to go Back to Michigan" (Columbia #A 1592). Morris continued on stage into the 1960s. She died in Santa Barbara, California, on Christmas day, 1977. [Walsh 1963/1–4.]

MORTON, EDDIE, 1870–1938. American comedian, born in Philadelphia on 15 May 1870. He was a policeman in Philadelphia, and was known as "the singing cop" in vaudeville. He recorded for Victor from 1907–1913, beginning with "Mariutch" (#5220) and "That's Gratitude" (#31661). "Don't Take Me Home" was a Morgan favorite that he offered on Edison #9949 (1908) and for Columbia, Victor, and Zonophone). One of his funniest records was "If He Comes In I'm Goin' Out" (Victor #16650).

His all-time best seller was "Oceana Roll" (#16908; 1911)—but much of the sales impetus came from the B side, "Alexander's Ragtime Band" by Arthur Collins and Byron Harlan. Morton's last Victor record was one of the best: "Noodle Soup Rag" / "Isch ka bibble"; he made a final Columbia in 1914, then some Emersons in 1916. He died in Wildwood, New Jersey, on 11 Apr 1938.

MORTON, JELLY ROLL, 1890–1941. American jazz pianist, one of the pioneers of jazz composition and arrangement, born Ferdinand Joseph LeMenthe (Morton was his stepfather's name) in Gulfport, Louisiana, on 20 Oct 1890. He played in the brothels of New Orleans until around 1906, then moved up to New York by 1911 and Chicago by 1914. After further travel he settled in Chicago in 1923. Morton began to record in 1923, with an orchestra of his own, doing "Big Foot Ham" for Paramount (#12050; June 1923) followed by "Muddy Water Blues"; and then appearing with the New Orleans Rhythm Kings in "Sobbin' Blues" (Gennett #5219; 17 July 1923), followed by "Clarinet Marmalade" and "Mr. Jelly Lord" on the same date. He did more Gennett records in Richmond, Indiana, on the next day, then went on to work for various labels.

Morton was one of the first artists to make electrical recordings, for the **Autograph** label in 1924. From 1926 he was with Victor in Chicago with his Red Hot Peppers group and made his finest discs. "Black Bottom Stomp" has become legendary (Victor #20221; 1926), and most of his records of that period are classics. The 111 performances of the *Jelly Roll Morton Centennial: His Complete Victor Recordings* (Bluebird #2361–2RB; 1980, five CDs) include much of his great work. Morton died in Los Angeles on 10 July 1941. [Davies 1968.]

MOSAIC (label). An American record issued by Mosaic Records, 197 Strawberry Hill Ave., Stamford, Connecticut. The specialty is reissues of jazz classics, including Thelonious Monk, Charles Mingus, Jerry Mulligan, Sidney Bechet, and James P. Johnson. An important recent release was a box of 21 LPs covering

nearly all the jazz matrices recorded by the Keynote label in 1941–1947.

MOTEN, BENNIE, 1894–1935. American jazz pianist and bandleader, born in Kansas City, Missouri, on 13 Nov 1894. His ensemble, established 1923, was "progenitor of the black swing-era orchestras, as epitomized by the Basie band in the mid-to-late 1930s" (Schuller). Moten and Basie were the bands that carried on the Kansas City style. (Basie was pianist with Moten before setting up his own group.) Ben Webster, Walter Page, and Jimmy Rushing were among the artists in the Moten band of 1932, when they recorded their most remarkable sides, all for Victor on 13 December: "Toby" / "Moten Swing" (Victor #23384), "Blue Room" (#24381), and seven others. Upon Moten's premature death in 1935, Basie took over the ensemble, then formed his own band, using some of the Moten personnel.

MOTHER GOOSE BOOK. A children's book including two unbreakable six-inch discs, sold for $.50 in November 1921 by the Cabinet and Accessories Co., 140 E. 34th St., New York. Oliver Goldsmith was president of the company. [Andrews*.]

MOTHER GOOSE RECORDS. In 1920 the Talking Book Corp. of New York released sets of records with books for children. The records were pressed in Atlanta by the Southern States Phonograph Co. and distributed by the Emerson Phonograph Co. Imported to Britain and sold there by the Herman Darewski Publishing Co., they were still being marketed in 1922. [Andrews*.] *See also* KIDDY RECORD (label).

MOTION PICTURE MUSIC. There were various systems in the early days of the film that provided mood music related to action on the screen. The photoplayer arrived around 1912. It was an orchestrion with various special effects under operator control. These were made by the North Tonawanda Musical Instrument Co., **Rudolph Wurlitzer Co., Justus Seeburg,** American Photoplayer Co., The Operators Piano Co., Chicago, Lyon & Healy, and the Automatic Music Co. (later the Link Piano Co.) The photoplayer thrived until around 1923. Only a few of the thousands made have survived.

MOTION PICTURE SOUND RECORDING.

The first motion pictures with any kind of sound added to them were shown in the Edison laboratory, West Orange, New Jersey, on 6 Oct 1889. The system, developed by **William Kennedy Dickson**, used a cylinder synchronization device. Running about 12 seconds, at 46 frames per second, the resulting films included Dickson's own voice giving a greeting to Edison. That was the forerunner of Edison's **Kinetophone**, developed in a 1912 version to the point of making short subjects and selling the system to theatres.

In 1897 George W. Brown claimed invention of a device to synchronize the projector with the phonograph; in 1900 Léon Gaumont made the first practical synchronizer, linking the projector and phonograph electrically. He presented a filmed speech to the Société Française de la Photographie in November 1902, with a type of **Auxetophone** amplifier. (His product was sold in America by the Gaumont Co., 124 E. 25th St., New York, under the tradename Chronophone, in 1904.) Oskar Messter in Germany had similar success in 1903–1904. Other systems of synchronizers were Viviphone (1907), Cameraphone (1908), Synchronoscope (1908), and Cinephone (Britain, 1909). All these early systems faced the same problems: getting the synchronization exactly right and keeping it so throughout the showing; coping with the short playing time of early records; and finding ways to enhance the phonographic volume to fill a theatre. While these difficulties were being researched, the main use of the phonograph in the early theatres was to bring customers in as it played through large horns that projected through the wall into the street.

In 1903 Eugen Lauste demonstrated a method of getting sound from film through photographed sound waves, with the light passing through the film onto a selenium cell. He gained British patents and gave successful demonstrations, but did not do well commercially. The soundtrack idea, with the sound inscribed on the film with the pictures, was patented in 1919 by Theodore W. Case. Lee De Forest joined in the research, acquiring the Case patent and improving the quality of voice and music reproduction. He made a stock of short films by comedians and musicians, under the name of Phonofilms, by 1925, including one by Al Jolson, "Sonny Boy." The first Mickey Mouse cartoon with sound, *Steamboat Willie* (1928), used this method. William Fox used the system in Movietone News short subjects, shown first in 1927 in New York and London. The British Talking Picture Corp. used the De Forest system in early Pathé newsreels. The concept of the soundtrack (a strip on the film, 0.1 inch wide) replaced the idea of the synchronized disc by 1928.

Edison's sound film research was detoured by a fire in the plant in 1914, plus difficulties with the unions and Edison's own multiple activities. He had lost interest in the Kineteophone project by 1915.

Bell Telephone Laboratories made some improvements; one was the reduction of record speed from 78 rpm to 33 1/3 rpm to give more playing time in the synchronized system; and they developed amplifiers and large horns to extend the sound range. Bell's process was called Vitaphone, an inadvertent use of an old company name. Vitaphone discs were lateral cut, center-start, 12 to 16 inches in diameter, running 33 1/3 rpm. The **Vitaphone Corp.**, under contract with Warner Brothers, made a series of short subjects (four to 10 minutes) between 1926 and 1932; they included work by Giovanni Martinelli, Mischa Elman, Harold Bauer, and Efrem Zimbalist. Vitaphones were shown in New York in February 1926; and on 6 Oct 1927 the famous Al Jolson film *The Jazz Singer* was premiered. This feature length motion picture, the first with speech, ushered in the era of talking pictures. When it was released there were about 100 theatres in the U.S. that were equipped to show sound films, out of about 7,500 Warner Brothers houses. By the end of 1929 there were some 4,000 theatres with sound installation.

During the 1930s there were many areas of progress. Reliable film-drive systems were developed, noise reduction was achieved, post-synchronizing in the studio rather than on location, and various improvements in theatre installations and in sound reproducing apparatus. After World War II magnetic recording became operational for motion picture use. When wide-screen films were made in the early 1950s, soundtracks were made on a separate three-track magnetic coated film. Those soundtracks were then dubbed onto the film print itself. Cinemascope carried three tracks 63 mils wide and one track 29 mils wide. The Todd-A-O system used six magnetic tracks on 70 mm film. [Ford 1962; Geduld 1975; Shaman 1991.]

MOTOWN (label). An American record produced in Detroit by the Motown Recording Corp. from 1959 to 1972, then from a base in Los Angeles. **Berry Gordy, Jr.,** was the founder; he set up shop at 2648 W. Grand Blvd., in a building known as Hitsville, USA. Barrett Strong's "Money" was the first record made there, a chart hit in 1960. "Anna" and "Tamla" were early names for the records, giving way to the Motown name. The label became famous for its recording of Black artists who became accepted by white audiences: Stevie Wonder, Diana Ross, Marvin Gaye, the Supremes, etc. Michael Jackson began making Motown records at age nine.

The original Detroit studio site is now occupied by the Motown Museum Historical Foundation. It was proclaimed a historical site by the governor of Michigan in 1987. [Bianco 1988 is a history and discography.]

MOUTRIE (S.) AND CO., LTD. According to a notice in *TMW* in 1906, a jobber with an office in Shanghai; he was an agent for Victor, and perhaps other firms.

MOXIE (label). An American record, known in just one issue. It was an advertising record for a soft drink named Moxie, made by Gennett in New York in late 1921. Arthur Fields sings on one side, and Harry Raderman's orchestra does a dance number on the flip side. A bottle of the beverage is shown on the label. [Rust 1978.]

MOYSE, MARCEL, 1889–1984. French flutist and conductor, born in Saint Amour on 17 May 1889, one of the leading performers on the instrument in the 20th century. He studied at the Paris Conservatory from age 15, then—after playing in several orchestras—he returned there as a professor in 1932. Meanwhile he was flutist for the Opéra-Comique in Paris in 1913–1938. In 1913 he accompanied Nellie Melba on a tour of the U.S. During the 1920s he gave the premieres of works by Ravel, Debussy, and Ibert. His earliest records were made in 1926. He and Adolph Busch revived several works by J. S. Bach in the 1930s, and recorded them: the second orchestral suite (Victor #11996; 1936) and the fifth *Brandenburg Concerto* (Columbia #68442; 1935) among them. He performed in a trio with Busch and Rudolf Serkin. In 1949 he moved to the U.S. and helped organize the Marlboro Festival in Vermont. He was still conducting when in his nineties. Death came in Brattleboro, Vermont, on 1 Nov 1984. Moyse's major recordings were reissued on Seraphim #60357 (in America) and World Records #SHB-68 (Britain).

MOZART TALKING MACHINE CO. A St. Louis firm established in 1916. It made the Mozart line of record players in seven models, and a vertical-cut record with the label name Mozart.

MUCK, KARL, 1859–1940. German conductor, born in Darmstadt on 22 Oct 1859. He pursued an academic course and took a doctorate in classical philology, also studying piano at Leipzig Conservatory. After conducting in several opera houses, he became first conductor of the Berlin Opera in 1892. Muck was conductor of the Wagnerian repertoire at Covent Garden in 1899, and director of *Parsifal* at Bayreuth in 1901 (he directed most of the *Parsifal* performances there until 1930). From 1906 to 1908 he directed the Boston Symphony Orchestra, then returned to Germany, and returned to a permanent appointment in Boston in 1912. There was concern about his German sympathies, and he was interned as an enemy alien in 1918. After the War he returned to Germany, directing the Hamburg Philharmonic in 1922–1933. He also conducted at Bayreuth. Then he went to Stuttgart, where he died on 3 Mar 1940.

Muck's fame on stage and in recordings rests with his Wagnerian interpretations. His finest records are the *Parsifal* excerpts made in Bayreuth in 1927 for Columbia (#L2007–2011), reissued on Pearl (CD #OPALCDS 9843; 1990). But he had begun to record 10 years earlier, for Victor, with the Boston Symphony. The first disc was the Tchaikovsky Symphony No. 4 Finale (Victor #74553). From 1927 to 1929 Muck worked for HMV in Berlin. He recorded numbers from seven Wagner operas. [Dyment 1977.]

MULTINOLA. An automatic record player, advertised in 1909 as capable of handling 16 four-minute cylinder records in succession. The user had a choice of hearing one of the cylinders, or a disc record. In 1911 The American Multinola Co., The Arcade [Euclid Ave.], Cleveland, was named as the manufacturer. It sold home models as well as **coin-ops**.

MULTIPHONE. The first selective **coin-op** phonograph, available in Britain from the late 1890s into the early 1900s, and in the U.S. from 1905. W. Mayer and Co., trading as the Multiphone Co., sold the machines in U.K. Multiphones had five-inch mandrels to accommodate six-inch long cylinders. The Multiphone Operating Co., New York, sold the machines in the U.S. They each held 24 cylinders on a ferris wheel device, in a cabinet around seven feet high. John C. Dunton was the inventor of the feed mechanism (U.S. patent #797,102; filed 28 Nov 1904; granted 15 Aug 1905). A patron could crank the wheel to the desired cylinder, crank up the spring motor, then insert a coin to hear the selection. The lack of an electric motor contributed to the failure of the enterprise in 1908 or 1909. [Hoover 1971 has illustrations; Koenigsberg 1990.]

MULTIPLEX GRAND. The earliest multi-track recording device, shown by Columbia at the Paris Exposition of June 1900. It was an invention of **Thomas Hood Macdonald** (U.S. patent # 711,706; filed 11 June 1898; granted 21 Oct 1902), the "first attempt at single-record stereo recording" (Koenigsberg). The machine "simultaneously recorded three separately spaced tracks and played them back on a five-inch diameter cylinder (14 inches long) through

three 56-inch long brass horns" (Koenigsberg). None of the records made are extant, and only parts of one machine are known to survive. The Shah of Iran bought one in 1901, for $1,000. [Koenigsberg 1990.]

MULTIPLEXER. A switching circuit in an audio system that makes possible the serial transfer of signals from various sources in a defined sequence intended for a single output.

MULTITRACK RECORDING. A technique of studio recording in which microphones are placed close to each instrument or group of instruments; in the control room the engineer mixes all the outputs to achieve a desired balance. The microphone outputs may as an alternative be directed to 24 or more tracks on a tape recorder, stored for later mixing. *See also* RECORDING PRACTICE.

MUNCH, CHARLES, 1891–1968. Alsatian conductor, born in Strasbourg on 26 Sep 1891. He studied violin, then conducting with Wilhelm Furtwängler. During the First World War he was gassed and wounded, but resumed his career as concertmaster of the Strasbourg orchestra and of the Gewandhaus Orchestra in Leipzig. He went to Paris, organized and conducted an orchestra in 1935–1938. Then he directed the Paris Conservatory Orchestra in 1938–1946. His U.S. debut was with the Boston Symphony Orchestra in 1946; he became its permanent conductor in 1949. Munch left Boston in 1962, and became founding director of the Orchestre de Paris. He died during a tour with that ensemble in America, on 6 Nov 1968 in Richmond, Virginia.

While he was with the Paris Conservatory Orchestra Munch made his first recordings, for HMV and Columbia. Over a period of 33 years he recorded more than 200 works by 64 composers. After World War II he worked for Decca, and made one disc that was particularly acclaimed: *Daphnis et Chloe* Suite number 2 (#K1585–1586). With the Boston orchestra he recorded extensively for RCA Victor, specializing in French composers. He made further discs of French music after leaving Boston, with several European orchestras. Several CDs have been released that cover outstanding

Munch performances, including *Symphonie fantastique* (RCA #7735–2–RV); *La mer* and *Nuages* (RCA #6719–2); and above all *Daphnis et Chloe* (RCA #60469–2–RG).

MURDOCH (JOHN G.) AND CO., LTD. A British wholesale distributor of various record labels, and also operator of a recording studio in the firm's main building in the Farringdon Road, London. The composer Albert W. Ketelbey was recording director. Columbia Indestructible [cylinder] Records were sold from July 1909, and Bel Canto was one of the disc labels handled. Murdoch supplemented the American repertoire coming on Indestructible by recording British artists. The early cylinders were two-minute, 100 threads/inch. In September 1910 the new four-minute, 200 threads/inch records went on sale. An Argosy phonograph, imported from Germany by Murdoch, was sold as well, from January 1911; there were two models, each able to play both types of cylinder records. After May 1910 the Columbia name was dropped from Murdoch's advertising, but he continued to sell the indestructible records until at least 1913. [Andrews*.] *See also* INDESTRUCTIBLE PHONOGRAPHIC RECORD CO. (III).

MURPHY, LAMBERT, 1885–1954. American tenor, born in Springfield, Massachusetts, on 15 Apr 1885. He was a versatile artist, performing in popular quartets, church choirs, and opera. He made a debut at the Metropolitan Opera on 17 Nov 1911, and was with the company four years; his repertoire there included Wagner, and the new American operas *Mona* and *Cyrano de Bergerac*. Murphy was a leading tenor on Victor records for almost 20 years, from 1911. His first solo record was "Hmm, She Is the One Girl," sung under the name of Raymond Dixon; he made more than 200 other records for the label. Best sellers included "Mavourneen Roamin" and "Sunshine of Your Smile" (1916). In 1927 he was moved to the Red Seal series, but not long after that he was dropped from the catalog. He then sang with the American Singers on radio and records, into the early 1930s. Murphy died in Hancock, New Jersey, on 24 July 1954.

MURRAY, BILLY, 1877–1954. American singing comedian, born in Philadelphia. He is recognized as the greatest performer of his kind, having started out humbly enough in a road show based in Denver. In 1897 he made his earliest records, for Peter Bacigalupi in the Edison San Francisco office, doing duets with Matt Keefe. His first Edison solo was "I'm Thinkin' of You All the While" (#8452; 1903). He was with Field's Minstrels on the East Coast in 1903, doing ballads and coon songs, and making records for various labels. With Victor in 1904 he made the firm's all-time best seller (up to that time): "Yankee Doodle Boy" (#4229)—but he bested that sales feat in 1906 with "You're a Grand Old Flag" (#4634) and had a second great hit that year with "Cheyenne" (#4719). In 1907 he began making duets with Ada Jones. Another "all-time best seller" was recorded for Victor and Edison, "Casey Jones" with the American Quartet (Victor #16483; Edison #10499; 1911). Murray was one of the Eight Famous Victor Artists, and had a joint exclusive contract with Victor and Edison in 1909; this became a Victor exclusive in around 1922, remaining so until 1928. From 1914 to 1918 he made Edison Diamond Discs.

In the 1917 Victor catalog there are over 100 titles by Murray. However, he did not adjust to electrical recording and the new **crooning** style, and his popularity waned after 1925. In his last years with Victor he formed Murray's Trio, with Carl Mathieu and Monroe Silver. His Victor contract not renewed in 1928, he turned to Edison again, and Brunswick, Pathé, and others, and continued to make records until 1932. Later he was a radio actor. He made a brief comeback in 1940 for Bluebird, singing "It's the Same Old Shillelagh" and a few more old favorites.

MUSE (label). An American record produced by the American Record Manufacturing Co. of Framingham, Massachusetts, in 1922. It used masters from Cameo for about 100 issues, then from Plaza-Banner, Emerson, and Grey Gull. The highest Muse number was 429. Possibly the label changed name to Tremont after the Muse distributor, Kress Stores, dropped the line. [Rust 1978.]

Music Corporation of America. *See* MCA, INC.

MUSICAL HERITAGE SOCIETY. An American organization established in 1963 to market records by mail. Material came from Europe under license arrangements. At first the specialty was early music, but the repertoire expanded to cover all periods and even jazz and folk music. More than 3,000 titles have appeared. Among the major projects completed were the issue of all 107 Haydn symphonies on 49 LPs (#MHS 201–MHS 249; 1968–1970), and all the Bach organ works on 25 discs. In the 1980s a label presenting original material (classical and jazz) was made available in retail stores, named Musicmasters. The address is 1710 Highway 35, Ocean, New Jersey.

MUSICAL THEATRE RECORDINGS. Recorded musical theatre tends to divide into three categories, according to the performers:

(1) Cast recordings—those performed by members of the original, revival, or foreign cast productions in which they sang the material; (2) Composer recordings—show material performed by the song's composer or lyricist; and (3) Studio recordings—material from stage shows recorded by performers who had no connection with a production.

Recordings from all three categories have appeared from almost the beginning of recorded sound, in all of the formats known: cylinders, discs of all speeds, piano rolls, tapes, films, video tapes and videodiscs, and compact discs. All have accomplished the historical benefit of preserving the sound of the world's musical theatre. In some cases, where sheet music, scores, and libretti of a production have not survived, recordings are the only remaining documentation.

The earliest preserved sounds from the stage were spoken excerpts or speeches from plays, recorded either by the actors who had spoken the lines onstage or by studio speakers like Len Spencer and Russell Hunting. (*See* LITERARY RECORDINGS.) Then the fledgling recording companies began to record songs that were current hits on the stage. Singers like Ada Jones and Arthur Collins, and staff ensembles like the Edison Concert Band and the Peerless Orchestra, recorded individual songs or medleys from popular musical comedies in New York. In London, the early recording companies seemed to be more interested than their American counterparts in bringing to the studio singing artists from the theatre. One reason for reluctance of American labels to make cast recordings was probably expense; the stage artists could demand a higher salary than the house performers for their services. Thomas Edison may have been particularly conscious of this, for very few cast performances were made by his company. However, the earliest musical selection recorded by a stage performer was made for Edison in 1893, when Edward M. Favor recorded "The Commodore Song" from the musical play *Ship Ahoy* (1890) and "Whisper Love" from *1492* (1893), in which he appeared. Favor soon devoted much more of his time to being a recording artist than a stage artist.

In 1898 the recording of musical theatre by cast performers took a more conscious direction. A Frenchman, Maurice Farkoa, had appeared in 1895 on both the London and New York stages in a musical comedy entitled *An Artist's Model*, in which he had a famous laughing song, "Le fou rire." Farkoa recorded this number several times, first in 1896 for Berliner in Washington, D.C., and subsequently in London in 1898 and 1899, in both French and English versions. At the same time, current members of the Savoy Theatre Co. were recording selections from Gilbert and Sullivan operas. And the smash hit of the 1899 season in London, *Florodora*, had 12 numbers of the score recorded by original cast artists on Berliner discs. In America in 1898, Berliner enticed several members of The Bostonians company into his studio, where they recorded four selections from the current Victor Herbert hit, *The Fortune Teller*; these performers included Alice Nielson and Eugene Cowles. Jessie Bartlett Davis, another member of The Bostonians, introduced—and recorded in 1898—the endurable "O Promise Me" from the score of Reginald De Koven's *Robin Hood* (1891). Other excerpts were made by Pathé with the revival cast of 1919.

Victor Herbert was probably the first artist in the composer recording category. With the orchestra to which he gave his name (although his actual presence in the recording studio is disputed), he recorded a number of selections and medleys (which were often called "selections" or "fantasias") from his hit shows during the first decade of the century. The first of these was a medley from *Mlle. Modiste* (1905), recorded in 1909. His orchestra recorded many other selections, by Herbert and by other composers, in the next decades.

After the turn of the century, individual musical theatre selections were being recorded with some regularity. Such artists as the team of Williams and Walker, Henry Tally, Ralph Herz, Blanche Ring, Nora Bayes, and Grace Cameron (in the United States), and Edna May, Ellaline Terris, George Grossmith, Jr., and Gertie Millar (in London) recorded examples of their stage successes.

The *Florodora* experiment in England in 1900 caused no similar attempt in the United States for almost four decades. Not until 1938 was an original cast collection of all the major numbers from an American musical recorded, and it was done by a new independent company, Musicraft. On seven 12–inch 78 rpm discs (#1075/81), this company recorded most of the songs from Marc Blitzstein's *The Cradle Will Rock*, performed by the original artists, including the composer. It was the cast recording of Rodgers and Hammerstein's *Oklahoma!* in 1943 by Decca (album #DL-8000) that started the recording landslide which continues today.

Many of these records have now been reissued on LP and compact discs, by the major record companies and by smaller companies like Totem, World Records, Pelican, and the Smithsonian Institution who specialize in this area. Sources for reissues are often private collectors, who have located original cylinders and discs and added them to their collections, rather than from the original recording companies, which in some cases have since disappeared or whose master recordings have been destroyed or lost. A great deal of the sound of musical theatre before the LP era would have been permanently lost, had it not been for such collectors as Jack Raymond, David Hummel, Miles Kruger, and Allen Debus.

In the CD era virtually all important new musical productions and revivals are recorded by original casts as well as by studio artists.

Musical theatre can now live for the future, instead of for only one night.

Notes On the Recordings Cited:

1. Edward Favor's recording of "The Commodore Song" was issued on North American Phonograph Company cylinder #772; "Whisper Love" was issued on North American Phonograph Company cylinder #972. A fragment of the latter appears on a seven-inch flexible LP, APM #1: *APM Celebrates "A Century Of Sound"*, issued by Allen Koenigsberg.

2. Maurice Farkoa's first recording of "Le fou rire" was issued on Berliner #1302. Subsequent recordings of the song in French and in English also appeared on Berliner discs.

3. The original cast performances from *Florodora* all appeared first on Berliner records. Their LP reissue is on Opal #835: *Florodora*; there is a CD also, Opal #9835.

4. Some of the original performers' recordings from *The Fortune Teller* on Berliner records were reissued on the Smithsonian release #R-017: *Music of Victor Herbert*.

5. Jessie Bartlett Davis' recording of "O Promise Me" appeared first on Berliner #5524; it has been reissued on LP on Mark 56 Records #828: *First Disc Recordings*.

6. The selection of melodies from *Mlle. Modiste*, played by Victor Herbert's Orchestra, appeared on a four-minute Edison cylinder #4M-195.

7. *The Cradle Will Rock* was originally issued Musicraft Album #18, on seven 12-inch 78 rpm discs; its LP reissue is on American Legacy #T-1001. Polydor #827927 is the CD.

8. The first album issue of *Oklahoma!* was Decca #359. A second collection of three additional songs from the show was issued shortly after, in Decca album #383. Decca reissued the first set many times. But it was not until the issue of a boxed set of LPs devoted to Rodgers and Hammerstein (Time-Life #STL-AM01) that both of the original recordings were issued together. [Atchison 1988; Bloom 1986; Bordman 1978; Bunnett 1984; Green 1976; Green 1987; Hummel 1984; Lewine 1984; Lynch 1987; Pinne 1984; Raymond 1982; Rust 1977; Seeley 1989; Smolian 1970; Warner 1984.]. *See also* GILBERT AND SULLIVAN OPERAS.

Larry Warner

MUSICASSETTE. The enclosed cassette launched by Philips in a compact cassette portable recorder in 1963.

MUSICRAFT (label). An American record issued from the late 1930s to 1948 by Musicraft Corp., 40 W. 46th St. (later 245 E. 23rd St.), New York. It offered pop, jazz, classical, country, Latin, folk, children's, and gospel material. An important series of organ music, performed by Carl Weinrich, was released beginning in 1937. In 1938 Musicraft issued the first original cast album of a Broadway musical, *The Cradle Will Rock* (#1075/81 in album #18).

MUTE. To silence, to reduce, to soften the output of an audio instrument. *See also* MUTING CIRCUIT.

MUTE (label). The largest **independent** label in U.K. After 10 years without affiliation, it merged with the U.S. **Enigma** in 1988.

MUTI, RICCARDO, 1941– . Italian conductor, born in Naples on 28 July 1941. He studied violin and piano, then composition at the Naples Conservatory, then went to Milan to take up conducting. In 1967 he won the Guido Cantelli competition and had several important engagements with Italian orchestras. He was named principal conductor of the Teatro Comunale, Florence, in 1970; performances in Salzburg followed, with both the Berlin Philharmonic Orchestra and the Vienna Philharmonic Orchestra. Muti's American debut was with the Philadelphia Orchestra on 27 Oct 1972. He was named principal conductor of the Philharmonia Orchestra, London, and remained 10 years (1973–1982). Then he succeeded Eugene Ormandy as conductor of the Philadelphia Orchestra in 1982. He also became music director at La Scala in 1986. In 1990 his retirement from Philadelphia was announced, effective 1992.

Muti has been an exclusive EMI artist since 1975. His most acclaimed records with the Philadelphia Orchestra have been of Beethoven, Mahler, Stravinsky, Scriabin, and Tchaikovsky. In 1991 he recorded CDs for EMI of the Tchaikovsky fourth and sixth symphonies, with the Philadelphia Orchestra.

MUTING CIRCUIT. In an audio system, the circuit that silences audible sound during the change cycle of a record player, or in a tape deck when the tape is rewinding or fast-forwarding, or in a radio receiver when it is tuned across the band.

MUTUAL TALKING MACHINE CO. A New York firm, established in 1916, located at 145 W. 45th St. The Mutual line of record players was offered.

MUZAK CORP. An American firm, established 1934, with headquarters in Seattle. It provides recorded music as a background sound to public places and work environments. In 1990 Muzak was being piped in to 130,000 U.S. locations, and was heard by an estimated 80 million persons daily. The Muzak selections (5,000 songs) are all soothingly arranged and recorded by house musicians, who present songs with the lyrics removed and the overall effect softened. Tapes are used at present, but before that format arrived RCA pressed vinyl discs for Muzak, vertical cut. The concept underlying Muzak dates back to the 1906 **Ampliphone**.

MUZIO, CLAUDIA, 1889–1936. Italian soprano, born Claudina Muzzio in Pavia on 7 Feb 1889. She studied in Milan and made her debut in Arezzo in *Manon Lescaut* on 15 Jan 1910. Her Metropolitan Opera debut was in a *Tosca* of 4 Dec 1916, with Enrico Caruso and Antonio Scotti. She stayed with the Metropolitan to Spring 1922, then sang in Chicago to 1932. The Metropolitan saw her for one more season, 1933–1934, then she returned to Italy. Muzio died in Rome on 24 May 1936.

Among her first recordings, for HMV in Milan, 1911 and 1914, were several fine examples of her art: "La mamma morta" from *Andrea Chenier* (#82224), "Sorgi, o padre" from Bellini's *Bianca e Fernando* (#82267), and "Spiagge amate" from Gluck's *Paride ed Elena* (#82267). IRCC reissued the Bellini and Gluck arias on #192. She auditioned for an Edison representative in London, but was not accepted, so went to Pathé; for that label she recorded 40 sides during the First World War. Edison then decided to engage her for a fine series of Diamond Discs between 1920 and 1925. Selections from the 1920–1921 Diamond Discs appear on Odyssey LP #Y33793; one is the "Mamma morta" aria she had done for HMV. Some of her greatest singing is Tatiana's aria from *Eugene Onegin* (Diamond Disc #82224; 1921) and the Bird Song from *Pagliacci* (Diamond Disc #82232; 1921). The Edisons appear on Cantabile/Harmonia Mundi compact disc #BIM 705–2.

Muzio's Columbia electrical recordings of 1934–1935 have been reissued on EMI Références CD #H7 69790–2. One of the most remarkable is Stefano Donaudy's song, "O del mio amato ben" (#BX 1376; 1935).

MYERS, JOHN W., ca. 1864–   ?. Welsh baritone, also a theatre manager. He came to the U.S. at age 12, and became a successful singer. He began recording ca. 1892 for the New Jersey Phonograph Co., then for Columbia and other labels, and was one of the most popular recording artists at the turn of the century. There were 22 Edison cylinders, the first being "Light of the Sea" (#7820; 1901). For Columbia two-minute cylinders, ca. 1896–1900, Myers sang such numbers as "Beer, Beer, Glorious Beer" (#6012), "The Star Spangled Banner" (#6015), and "Sweet Rosie O'Grady" (#6036). Myers founded the Globe Phonograph Record Co. in 1897, a maker of brown wax cylinders. He was usually identified on records as J. W. Myers; he should not be confused with his contemporary, John H. Meyer. He quit recording in 1907, except for a few discs about 10 years later. [Brooks 1979; Koenigsberg*; Walsh 1944/7.]

N

NADSCO (label). An American record, one of the Grey Gull affiliates, issued from around 1922 to sometime after 1925. Material was dance music and popular vocals. [Barr 1982; Rust 1978.]

NAKAMICHI. A Japanese manufacturer of audio (especially cassette) equipment. The firm has pioneered many technical developments that have made high quality cassette recording possible. The 1000 Model digital tape player (1989) sold for $10,000. A compact disc system named MusicBank appeared in 1990, allowing user selection of any track from any of six discs.

NANES ART FURNITURE CO. A New York firm established in 1915, located on Grand St. at the East River. Disc players in five models were sold under the tradename Savoy.

NAPOLEON, PHIL, 1901– . American jazz trumpet player, born Filippo Napoli in Boston on 2 Sep 1901. He began performing in public as a young child, and in 1916 recorded as a cornet soloist. Napoleon and Frank Signorelli founded the **Original Memphis Five,** one of the earliest Dixieland groups, in 1922. He also had his own band, recording for Pathé, Edison, and Victor in 1926–1927. Napoleon's Emperors was the name of his ensemble that recorded for Victor in 1929; it included Jimmy Dorsey, Tommy Dorsey, Joe Venuti, and Eddie Lang. "Mean to Me" (Victor #V-38057) and "Anything" (#V-38069) were two notable discs. He had another band in 1937, and made four sides for the Victory label.

NARELLE, MARIE, 1874?–1941. Australian soprano, born Marie Ryan in Combanning Station. She studied in Australia, London, and Paris. Her acclaimed debut was in London in 1902, sharing the program with Adelina Patti. She gave a command performance. Then she sang in concerts with John McCormack; both made their U.S. debuts at the St. Louis Exposition in 1904, and they toured the U.S. in 1909–1911. Narelle became known as the "Queen of Irish Song." She began to record for Edison in September 1905, with "Killarney" (#9081; later as Amberol #495), making cylinders and Diamond Discs until 1914. Later she worked for Pathé, singing "Dear Old Honolulu" (#20134; 1916); she may have recorded also under the name Marie Ryan. Her last stage appearances were in 1931. Narelle died in Chipping Norton, England, on 25 Jan 1941. [Walsh 1964/2–3.]

NASSAU (label). An American record of 1906, masters from Imperial, pressed by the Leeds and Catlin Co., sold by Macy's department store. A record player named Nassau was also available through Macy's. [Andrews 1984/12.]

NATIONAL (label). (I) A record issued by the National Certificate Co., New York, in the early 1920s. Pressing was done by the Bridgeport Die and Machine Co. [Rust 1978.]

NATIONAL (label).(II) A record produced in the early 1920s by the National Record Exchange Co., Iowa City, Iowa. It was linked with Paramount. Some good jazz material was included, but most of the output was dance music and popular vocals. [Rust 1978.]

NATIONAL (label).(III) A record credited to the National Record Co., New York, issued in 1925; it was one of the Emerson-Consolidated group, with matrix numbers paralleling those on the Clover label. [Kendziora 1988/11; Rust 1978.]

NATIONAL (label). (IV) A Paramount subsidiary record, issued from October 1944. National Disc Sales, Inc., 1841 Broadway, New York, was the distributor. Material was pop, race, and hillbilly. Among the artists were Raymond Scott, Vincent Lopez, Al Trace, Pete Johnson, Billy Eckstine, Kate Smith, Red Mc Kenzie, and Charlie Ventura. Savoy acquired the label in 1957. [Porter 1977.]

NATIONAL ACADEMY OF RECORDING ARTS AND SCIENCES (NARAS). An organization established in 1957 to promote creative and technical progress in the sound recording field. The membership consists of performers, producers, engineers, and others engaged in the industry; there were 6,500 members in 1991. From 1958 NARAS has presented the annual **Grammy** awards for outstanding recordings. The NARAS Hall of Fame was established to honor records issued before the Grammys began. In 1991 the executive vice-president was Christine M. Farnon. The office is at 303 N. Glenoaks Blvd., Burbank, California.

NATIONAL ASSOCIATION OF TALKING MACHINE JOBBERS. A U.S. trade organization established in 1907 (originally the Talking Machine Jobbers National Association; new name first cited in *TMW* of 15 June 1908). W.D. Andrews was the first vice president. The officers in 1908–1909 were James Bowers, president; W.D. Andrews, vice president; Louis Buehn, treasurer; and Perry B. Whitsit, secretary. New officers elected at the third convention of the association, July 1909, were Whitsit, president; J. Newcomb Blackman, vice president; Buehn, treasurer; and Joseph C. Roush, secretary. The fourth convention was held in

Atlantic City, New Jersey, in July 1910, with all the officers reelected. A new president, Lawrence McGreal, was elected at the fifth convention, in Milwaukee, July 1911; E.F. Taft became vice president; Roush, treasurer, and William F. Miller, treasurer.

At the sixth convention, Atlantic City, July 1912, Blackman was elected president; George E. Mickel, vice president; Buehn, secretary; John B. Miller, treasurer. Roush was the new president in July 1913, elected at the seventh convention in Niagara Falls, New York. Mickel became vice president; W.H. Reynalds [*sic*], treasurer; Whitsit, secretary. In July 1914, at the eighth convention in Atlantic City, Mickel was president, E. F. Taft, vice president; E. C. Rauth, secretary; and W. H. Reynalds, treasurer.

Andrew G. McCarthy was the new president in 1915, elected at the ninth convention, in San Francisco. H.F. Miller was vice president; Reynalds, treasurer; Rauth, secretary. At the tenth convention, in July 1916 in Atlantic City, Rauth was president, H. A. Winkelman, vice president; L. C. Wiswell, secretary; and Reynalds, treasurer.

The 11th convention was in Atlantic City in July 1917. Blackman became president; I Son Cohen [sic], vice president; Arthur A. Trostler, treasurer; and Roush, secretary. There was no convention in 1918, but the executive committee met in Philadelphia. The *TMW* story of the 12th convention, Atlantic City, 1919, refers to the group for the first time as "Victor jobbers." Mickel was elected president; Thomas H. Green, vice president; Trostler, secretary; and Reynalds, treasurer. At the 14th convention, Atlantic City, 1920, Wiswell became president; Buehn, vice president; Trostler, secretary; and Reynalds, treasurer. The organization met in Colorado Springs, Colorado, in July 1921, for its 15th convention; Buehn was elected president; Trostler, vice president; Charles K. Bennett, secretary; and George A. Mairs, treasurer.

At the 16th convention, Atlantic City, June 1922, Trostler was elected president; Thomas Green, vice president; W.F. Davidson, secretary; and Mairs, treasurer. The executive committee met in July 1922 and voted to dissolve the association.

Nothing further was said about the group in *TMW*.

NATIONAL AUTOMATIC MUSIC CO. An American firm, affiliated with the **Automatic Musical Instrument Co.** It provided **coin-op** pianos to places of entertainment, having 4,200 of them on location in 1925.

NATIONAL BARN DANCE. A country music radio show broadcast from WLS, Chicago, in 1924–1960, and from WGN, Chicago, in 1960–1970. Under director George D. Hay (who later went to Nashville to form the **Grand Ole Opry**), the *Barn Dance* became the first nationally known program of its type, and was a major force in the acceptance of the country genre in mainstream America. Among the artists who began great careers in the Eighth Street Theatre (venue of the WLS program) were Gene Autry, Bob Atcher, Patsy Montana, Lulu Belle and Scotty, and Red Foley. Over the years nearly every significant country artist appeared on the program. Sears, Roebuck and Co., the first sponsor, promoted recordings by the country stars in its mail order catalogs.

NATIONAL GRAMOPHONE CO. A firm established on 19 Oct 1896 by Frank Seaman, at 874 Broadway, New York, succeeding his New York Gramophone Co.; in advertising it was styled the National Gram-o-phone Co. It was eventually succeeded by the **National Gramophone Corp.**, another Seaman firm established in March 1899. Seaman had contracted personally with Berliner Gramophone Co. for U.S. sales rights—except for Washington, D.C.—to Berliner products, and he set up the National Gramophone Co. to handle sales. After an unsuccessful first year, business improved greatly. In 1897 the firm was advertising the "Gram-o-phone Zon-o-phone"—in fact a Berliner gramophone—and the "Improved Gram-o-phone Zon-o-phone." Sherman, Clay & Co., San Francisco, was the Pacific Coast agent. Sale price of the record player in an October 1898 advertisement was $25.00. Records were selling at $.50 each. The April 1899 catalog of the firm included material by the Sousa Band, the Banda Rossa, Cal Stewart, Albert C. Campbell, Vess L. Ossman (banjo),

W. Paris Chambers (cornet), Henry A. Higgins (cornet), and George Graham (humorist). F.M. Prescott was noted as the "sole export agent."

However there were legal problems, as American Graphophone Co., led by Philip Mauro, brought litigation over alleged infringement of its Bell-Tainter patents. There was also a dispute between Seaman and Berliner, based on Seaman's failed effort to have Berliner take on more cheaply made gramophones. Seaman finally stopped ordering gramophones in October 1899. Berliner refused to supply Seaman with discs, so National Gramophone Co. had no Berliner products to sell and was phased out of business. Seaman's second firm, National Gramophone Corp., was left to deal with the American Graphophone Co. litigation. [Andrews*; Wile 1991.]

NATIONAL GRAMOPHONE CORP. Frank Seaman, who had been operating the **National Gramophone Co.** since 19 Oct 1896, established a second firm on 10 March 1899. The purpose of the National Gramophone Corp. was to be the sales agency of the new distinctive **Zonophone** disc players being developed by L.P. Valiquet and manufactured by the **Universal Talking Machine Co.** The first Zonophones were merely clones of the Berliner gramophone, and Seaman knew that he could not carry on indefinitely with that product. As it happened, problems developed with Berliner in 1899 and came to a head just at the time (late 1899) when the new Zonophone products—record players and discs—were ready. The early firm, National Gramophone Co., was phased out, and Seaman concentrated his plans on the new corporation. Frank J. Dunham was its president, Orville La Dow its secretary; Seaman was treasurer.

The patent conflict with the Columbia interests (American Graphophone) remained to hinder sales of the new Zonophones. Seaman's strategy was to admit infringement of the Columbia patents, but to devise a cross-licensing agreement whereby he could continue to make and sell the new Zonophones, and Columbia (which did not yet have its own disc machines) could also handle them. With the cross-licensing agreement in effect, from May 1900, Columbia was able to drop the Vitaphone line of machines and discs that had been operating under Columbia protective licensing.

Advertising by the National Gramophone Corp. in November 1900 promoted the "Zon-o-phone (substituted for our Gram-o-phone which is abandoned)." All these machinations came to a dismal end for Seaman, for the Zonophone venture did not prosper, and by March 1901 the National Gramophone Corp. was in difficulties from which it could not recover; it was put into liquidation in September 1901. In 1903 the Zonophone tradename and the Universal Talking Machine Co. assets passed to the Victor Talking Machine Co. [Andrews*; Wile 1991.]

NATIONAL GRAMOPHONE CO., LTD. A British firm established at 13A, New Street Hill, London, in 1911, certificated to do business as of 3 Aug. Later it moved to 15 City Road. Directors were P.J. Packman, James Albert Corey, Walter Amelius Cloud, Robert Crawford Lees, and Walter Hansen Rawles. After some litigation brought by the National Phonograph Co., Ltd., over the prior use of the name "National" in Britain, the plaintiff firm determined to withdraw its complaint and change its own name to Thomas A. Edison, Ltd. (August 1912). Nevertheless the National Gramophone Co., Ltd., decided not to go ahead with plans to issue a disc labelled "National," and advertised (for the first time in July 1912) one named **Marathon Record**. This was a narrow-grooved vertical cut record with longer playing time than typical discs of the time.

A new company was created on 2 Jan 1913, named the National Gramophone Co. (1913), Ltd. It took over Marathon Records and Marathon record players. Business was excellent in 1913, but there was a financial crisis in early 1914, and the firm went into receivership in March 1915. The last additions to the Marathon Records catalog came in March 1915. Apparently the **Orchestrelle Co., Ltd.**, of London, acquired some or all of the National assets. [Andrews 1987/4.]

NATIONAL MALE QUARTET. A vocal group that recorded for Edison Diamond Discs in 1924–1927. Members were Clarence da Silva, tenor (replaced in 1926 by Arthur Hall); Lloyd Wiley, tenor (replaced in 1926 by John Ryan); Harry Jockin, baritone; and Harry Donaghy, bass. The group's best record was "Yankee Rose" (#51967; 1927). Another popular disc was "Bye, Bye, Blackbird" / "Honey Bunch" (#51758; 1926).

NATIONAL MUSIC LOVERS, INC. (label). An American record of 1922–ca. 1927. issued by an organization of that name at 354 Fourth Ave., New York (later 327 W. 36th St). Material came from Paramount, Emerson, Olympic, and Plaza-Banner; it included dance music, novelty items, band and concert music, sacred music, Irish numbers, songs, and operatic items. Some well-known artists appeared under pseudonyms, such as the California Ramblers and Fletcher Henderson. These records were available by mail order, with a money-back guarantee of satisfaction. [Cotter 1975 is a complete label list.]

NATIONAL PHONOGRAPH ASSOCIATION. A trade organization formed by the 33 regional affiliates of the **North American Phonograph Co.** A convention was held in Chicago on 28–29 May 1890, chaired by J.H. McGilvra of the Volta Graphophone Co. Edward Easton called the convention to order. R.F. Cromelin was secretary. Among the issues discussed were the poor performance of graphophones, and the need for a single standardized instrument (association members were selling both the graphophone and the Edison phonograph); and the problem of hostility between the interests of Charles Sumner Tainter and Thomas Edison. The principal business of the regional affiliates at the time was in leasing instruments for business use. But a number of the members were also involved with musical cylinders placed on location in coin-operated machines. At the second convention, New York, June 1891, only 19 companies were represented. A.W. Clancy was elected president, and Easton, vice president. There were 22 firms represented at the third convention, held in Detroit in 1893. Clancy was re-elected president. In 1894, as Edison liquidated the North American Phonograph Co., the National Phonograph Association ceased to function. Then there was a new assembly, in Cincinnati on 25 Sep 1900; Henry D. Goodwin was chairman, and James L. Andem the secretary at that meeting. [Proceedings 1974.]

NATIONAL PHONOGRAPH CO. The firm established by Thomas Edison in Orange, New Jersey, in January 1896 to manufacture and distribute spring-driven cylinder phonographs for home use. This firm also held the relevant Edison patents. The first products were the Edison Home Phonograph, sold for $40, and the Edison Standard Phonograph, sold for $20. Manufacturing of the machines was carried out in Orange, in the Edison Phonograph Works. Concentrating on mail order sales to the rural market, the enterprise provided the first successful competition for the graphophone. By 1901 there were offices in New York (83 Chambers St.), Chicago (144 Wabash Ave.), and San Francisco (933 Market St.).

A European headquarters was set up in Antwerp (it moved to London in 1904). Branch offices were established in Paris, Berlin, Brussels, Vienna, and Milan. These overseas activities were coordinated by Will Hayes. Recording began in London in May 1903, at 52 Grays Inn Road, then in new premises in the Clerkenwell Road in January 1904. The European factories had closed by 1908, but recording studios and sales agencies remained open. Machines and records were manufactured in the U.S. after 1911.

Production figures for Edison cylinders show a steady increase from 1896 to 1904. For the year ending 28 February, the records manufactured were:

1897	None
1898	87,690
1899	428,310
1900	1,886,137
1901	2,080,132
1902	1,976,645
1903	4,382,802
1904	7,663,142

In 1905–1907 there were about 12,000 Edison dealers in the U.S. When Edison established **Thomas A. Edison, Inc.** in 1910, the National Phonograph Co. was absorbed into it, along with the Edison Phonograph Works. [*APM* 1–10 (December 1973): 3, gives the production figures.]

NATIONAL PHONOGRAPH CO., LTD. The only British firm authorized to distribute genuine Edison goods wholesale; established in London in March 1902 by J.L. Young and E. Sinclair. It was independent of the Edison business at first, but was engaged by Edison's attorney in July 1902 to handle the Edison interests in Britain. The address then was 55–56 Chancery Lane. By May 1903 the firm had moved to 25 Clerkenwell Road. The record master-making plant was at 52 Gray's Inn Road, London. In August 1912, the company was absorbed into the new firm, **Thomas A. Edison, Ltd.** [Andrews*.]

NATIONAL SOUND ARCHIVE (NSA). A unit in the British Library since 1983, originally (1947) the British Institute of Recorded Sound. NSA is located at 29 Exhibition Road, London. The Archive holds about 750,000 discs of all kinds, and over 35,000 hours of recorded tape. Member companies of the British Phonographic Industry send two copies of about 75 percent of their releases for deposit to NSA. The collections illustrate the development of recorded sound in all formats, and in all categories. There are important holdings in Western art music (including BBC broadcast material not otherwise available); traditional music from most countries of the world (including hundreds of hours of field recordings, some dating back to the late 1890s); The Library of Wildlife Sounds; drama (including the repertoires of the Royal Shakespeare Co. and other national groups, as well as radio plays); spoken literature; jazz and popular music, British and imported (including live sessions and concerts broadcast by the BBC). A free listening service is provided by appointment to any member of the public, and reference service through a comprehensive library.

NSA is much concerned with restoration and transfer of materials from temporary media like acetate tapes to more permanent sound carriers. A recent development of that effort is the Computer Enhanced Digital Audio Restoration system (**CEDAR**). [Borwick 1989/7.]

NATIONAL TALKING MACHINE CO. A New York firm, established in 1916 at 118 E. 28th St. The Bluebird line of record players, in four models, was marketed in 1916.

NATIONAL VOICE LIBRARY. A unit of the Michigan State University Library, East Lansing, Michigan, also known as the G. Robert Vincent Voice Library. Documentary and historical recordings are collected. A printed catalog of the collection—all of which is in tape format—was published in 1975 by G.K. Hall (Boston); it presented about 7,000 catalog cards. [Vincent 1975.]

NATION'S FORUM (label). An American record, produced by Columbia for Nation's Forum—an historical society founded in 1918 by St. Louis attorney Guy Golterman, with cooperation of the U.S. State Department, to preserve the voices of statesmen and prominent leaders. The address was 33 W. 42nd St., New York. In 1918 the first series of discs appeared, 10–inch records, not sold commercially. The second series, 12–inch records, appeared in 1919–1920. Among the voices heard were Calvin Coolidge, General George Pershing, Eamon de Valera, and Samuel Gompers. As radio became available in 1920 (presidential election results were broadcast in November), the public interest in such records—slight as it had been—disappeared, and the project ceased. [Andrews*; Rust 1978.]

NATUS, JOE, 1860–1917. American singer and comedian, born in Detroit on 1 Mar 1860. He performed alone and with minstrel groups, and began to record for Edison in about 1900, making 36 vaudeville numbers and solo ballads, plus 19 duets with Arthur Collins. He also worked for Lambert, Zonophone, Victor (and Monarch), and Columbia (to 1907). Among his Columbia two-minute cylinders were "Sweet Annie Moore" (#31584) and "Wrap Me in the Stars and Stripes" (#31587). He died in Rome, New York, on 21 Apr 1917.

NAXOS (label). A CD record established in 1987 by Klaus Heymann, headquartered in Hong Kong. It is a budget label, a companion to Heymann's Marco Polo label. There were more than 350 titles in the Naxos catalog at the end of 1990, with some 3 million total sales. Naxos of America opened its office in Cherry Hill, New Jersey, in 1991, marking its entry into the U.S. market. In Britain, Woolworth's was the first outlet, but Naxos discs are now stocked by the regular record shops.

NEBRASKA PHONOGRAPH CO. One of the 33 affiliates of the **North American Phonograph Co.**, established in 1890 in Omaha. E.A. Benson was president in 1890 and 1892; H.E. Cary was vice president and general manager in 1891–1892. The company continued to 1893. Leon F. Douglass began his career with the firm; he went on to success as an inventor and joined Eldridge Johnson's Consolidated Talking Machine Co.

NEEDLE CHATTER. Vibration of the pickup in a disc player, caused by insufficient vertical compliance of its moving parts.

Needle cut. *See* LATERAL RECORDING.

NEEDLE TINS. During the 78 rpm era, phonograph needles were sold in tin boxes, often bearing colorful designs; they have become collectors' items. Many of the needles were made by record manufacturers, and carry the same logo as the disc labels of those companies. For example, **Nipper** appears on HMV needle tins, and the two-note Columbia trademark on its tins. Not all needles were sold in tins; there were also various kinds of paper boxes and even aluminum boxes. [Lambert, R. 1985 gives numerous illustrations.]

NEEDLES. Replaceable needles were a hallmark of the 78 rpm period. They were made of various materials: steel, chrome, fibers, thorn, cactus, sapphire, and diamond. Some needles were designed for a single play only (e.g., the Beltona), others played as many as 10 records (e.g., the Petmecky) and some went on to 20 or more performances (e.g., the Euphonic). With the popularity of the juke box in the 1930s there was improved needle design: alloy tipped shockproof needles came into use, capable of many plays. The diamond needle was theoretically non-wearable. And some sapphires, such as the one marketed by Neophone in 1905, were also "permanent"—advertised to play from 500–800 times.

As early as 1906 there were nine types of needle available: three to play quietly, three to play at medium volume, and three types for loud playback. (These were sold by Universal Talking Machine Co. of New York.) Loud needles had rounded tips, and softer-sound needles had sharper tips. The problem with all metal and jewel needles was that they chewed up the record grooves. Fiber, thorn, and cactus needles were popular with collectors in the 1930s and 1940s because they produced minimal record wear, but of course the needles themselves wore out instead. They could be shaved for replay, and shaving devices something like pencil sharpeners were sold for the purpose. Victor sold a fiber "needle cutter" in 1909 that used a plunger action, "enabling you to use each fiber needle at least ten times." Major manufacturers offered a choice of materials; for example in 1924 HMV was advertising steel, fiber, and "tungstyle"—said to be semi-permanent—varieties.

The **Petmecky Co.** had the favorite brandname needles of the acoustic period, made by the **W. H. Bagshaw Co.**, of Lowell, Massachusetts. In the electric era the Recoton brand was among the most popular in America.

With the arrival of LP records, the lightweight **stylus** took the place of the needle.

NEGATIVE FEEDBACK. The inversion and return of a portion of an amplifier's output to its input. It is used intentionally to reduce distortion and to provide more predictable amplification and response. Since negative feedback also reduces **gain**, the amplifier must have a greater **open-loop gain** to compensate for this factor. But the considerable improvement in many other characteristics often outweighs the reduction in gain. [Klinger*.] *See also* ACOUSTIC FEEDBACK.

NELSON, RICK, 1940–1985. American rock singer, born Eric Hilliard Nelson on 8 May 1940 in Teaneck, New Jersey. At age 12 he began to take part (as Ricky) in his parents' television show, the *Adventures of Ozzie and Harriet*. In 1957 he started singing on the pro-

gram, and made his first hit records, "Be-Bop Baby" / "Have I Told You Lately That I Love You" (Imperial #5463) and "I'm Walking" (Verve #10047). Nelson was able to promote his records by presenting the material on the television show, and had a series of 45 chart singles by 1965. Following a dip in popularity, as the Ozzie and Harriet program went off the air, he moved to a country rock style and achieved new successes. "Garden Party," with his country group the Stone Canyon Band, was a gold single of 1972, 18 weeks on the charts (Decca #32980). Nelson was again out of public favor in the later 1970s, but made another comeback in 1981, with the chart album *Playing to Win* (Capitol #SOO 12109). He was killed in a Texas plane crash on New Year's Eve, 1985.

NELSON, WILLIE, 1933– . American country singer, guitarist, and songwriter, born in Abbott, Texas, on 30 Apr 1933. He was a disc jockey in Texas and on the West Coast, and sang in various locales before moving to Nashville in 1960. There he established himself as a composer, with such songs as "Crazy"—made into a hit record by Patsy Cline. He did not succeed as a singer in Nashville, and moved to Austin, Texas, where he adopted a more exuberant, rock-oriented style and in 1973 recorded a successful album, *Shotgun Willie* (Atlantic #7262; 1973). In 1975 his song "Blue Eyes Crying in the Rain" was the best-selling country record (Columbia #10176; also in the album *Red-headed Stranger* [Columbia # KC33482; 1975]). Between 1975 and 1985 Nelson had 25 chart albums on his own, plus others with Waylon Jennings, Kris Kristofferson, Johnny Cash, Ray Price, or Leon Russell. *Willie Nelson's Greatest Hits* (Columbia # KC2–37542; 1981) was on the charts 112 weeks.

NEOPHONE CO., LTD. A British manufacturer, located at Finsbury Square, London, incorporated 10 Oct 1904. William Michaelis was founder and general manager; E.J. Sabine was assistant manager. The new firm took over the business of a previous one operated by Michaelis, the Neophone Disc Phonograph Co. Vertical-cut discs (German-made at first) of various sizes were offered, some of 20-inch diameter with about 10 minutes playing time per side.

Made of a material called Neolite, the large black records were playable on any machine; but the smaller nine-inch white discs (made of pressed paper with a white enamel surface) required a sapphire reproducer. The white discs were unbreakable, but the black ones were breakable.

A line of Neophone record players was sold to accommodate the firm's discs, and in 1905 an attachment was sold that would make it possible to play the vertical-cut discs on regular talking machines. Another interesting product was a home disc recorder, first in the industry, offered in 1905 (*TMR* #52–53, 6 June 1978, reproduced an advertisement for it).

Neophone was very successful, and in 1905 had established branches in France, Italy, Germany, Russia, Austria, and Belgium. Artists from La Scala were among those available on Neophone records. Nevertheless it was decided to put the company into liquidation, and to replace it with one named Neophone (1905) Ltd., incorporated on 22 Sep 1905, at 22 Philpot Lane, London. William Michaelis was principal shareholder and a director of the new company. In February 1906 there were seven types of Neophone discs on sale, from nine inches to 20 inches in size, covering operatic works (some in a series that had labels autographed by the artists) and popular repertoire.

"Neolite Disc Phonograph Records"—12 inches, double sided—were first issued in June 1906, along with Neolite Universal Reproducers that could be adjusted to play vertical or lateral-cut records. Offices in New York, Toronto, Paris, Brussels, Berlin, Milan, Australia and Japan were reported during 1906.

On 4 Feb 1907 a subsidiary company was registered in Britain to handle sales everywhere except in the U.K.: International Neophone Co. (2 Tabernacle St., London). Then Neophone was acquired by the General Phonograph Co., Ltd., in July 1907. That firm resolved to wind up its affairs on 13 Apr 1908, and the Neophone trademark disappeared. The International Neophone Co., Ltd., was stricken from the U.K. Companies Register on 21 Feb 1911. [Andrews 1978/3 is a history and label list.]

NEVEU, GINETTE, 1919–1949. French violinist, born in Paris on 11 Aug 1919. She made her debut at age seven with the Colonne Orchestra of Paris, playing the Bruch First Concerto. Then she took first prize at the Paris Conservatory at age 14, and won the Wieniawski Grand Prize Competition in Warsaw (defeating, among others, David Oistrakh), in 1934. Carl Flesch and Georges Enesco were among her teachers. Neveu's U.S. debut was with the Boston Symphony Orchestra in 1947. She was a world success, at the peak of her career, when she died in an air disaster in the Azores, on 28 Oct 1949. Her few recordings display a sensitive virtuosity, in particular with French composers. EMI Références CD #H& 63493–2 (1990) includes her Debussy Violin Sonata (HMV #ALP 1520; 1957), the Ravel *Tzigane* (HMV #DB6907/08; 1949), Chausson's "Poème" (HMV #ALP 1520; 1957), and the Richard Strauss Violin Sonata in E-Flat (HMV # DB4663/6; 1948).

NEW CHRISTY MINSTRELS. American folk and popular singing group, formed in 1961 by Randy Sparks, named for the 19th-century troupe of E.P. Christy. Much of their material was composed for them but in a folklike idiom. The group disbanded in the mid-1970s, having sold more than 13 million albums. Their greatest hits were made in 1962–1964, among them *Ramblin* (Columbia #CL2055; 1963), 41 weeks on the charts; and *Today* (Columbia # CL 2159; 1964), 32 weeks.

NEW COMFORT RECORDS (label). A disc issued by New Comfort Talking Machine Co., Cedar Rapids, Iowa, in 1921. The firm advertised its discs and phonographs in *TMW*, and announced its incorporation in June 1921, but there is no further information about its products. Rust says the record was "a rare member of the Grey Gull complex" about which little is known other than its numbering in a 5000 series. [Andrews*; Rust 1978.]

NEW ENGLAND PHONOGRAPH CO. An affiliate of the **North American Phonograph Co.**, established in 1890 in the Boylston Building, Boston. General A.P. Martin was president in 1892; Charles A. Cheever and Jesse Lippincott were among the directors. Russell Hunting and W.F. Denny were the leading artists.

NEW FLEXO (label). A record issued from early 1925 to autumn of the same year, by the Warner Record Co. of Kansas City, Missouri. Flexible discs without paper labels, many survive in illegible form. No well-known artists have been identified as performers. [Rust 1978.]

NEW GRAMOPHONE. A disc player marketed in 1925 by the Gramophone Co. in the U.K., for use with the new electric recordings. It replaced the standard pre-electric instruments, as the Victor Orthophonic did in America. [There is a photo in Andrews 1985/6.]

NEW JERSEY PHONOGRAPH CO. One of the affiliates of the **North American Phonograph Co.**, established in 1890 at 758 Broad St., Newark. George Frelinghuysen was president in 1892, and Nicholas Murray Butler was vice president. General manager was Victor H. Emerson. Frank L. Capps was an employee when he invented the three-spring motor that was used on the Edison Concert Phonograph and other machines.

A catalog issued before November 1891 offered 499 brown wax cylinders. The repertoire included band selections, "parlor orchestra" works, instrumental solos with piano accompaniment (piccolo, clarinet, cornet, xylophone), vocal solos (comic, coon songs, sentimental, and so forth), and vocal ensembles. There were also bird imitations and some anecdotes. George W. Johnson made his earliest appearance for this label, singing "Whistling Coon" (#423) and "Laughing Song" (#424).

In 1893 the firm was succeeded by the U.S. Phonograph Co. of New Jersey.

[*TMR* #10 (June 1971) reprinted the catalog cited above; *TMR* #20–21 (Feb-April 1973) printed date information supplied by Raymond Wile.]

NEW JERSEY SHEET METAL CO. A firm located at 9–11 Crawford St., Newark. In 1907

it marketed the Ajax horn of "rust proof sheet steel" and the collapsible Kompakt horn.

NEW MUSIC QUARTERLY RECORDINGS (label). A record issued in 1933–1948 by *New Music Quarterly*, a publication devoted to contemporary American music. After 1940 the label was named New Music Recordings. There were 64 sides in toto, offering 62 titles by 38 composers; all were first recordings. In 1978 eight sides were reissued on LP by Composers Recordings, Inc. Orion issued an LP in 1971, with works of Charles Ives and Carl Ruggles; and New World Records issued Ives's *General William Booth Enters into Heaven* in 1976 as part of a large anthology. Among the 83 artists on the NMQR records were flutist Georges Barrère, pianists Leonard Bernstein and Aaron Copland, violist/composer Quincy Porter, harpist Carlos Salzédo, conductor Nicolas Slonimsky—presenting the earliest Ives orchestral music on record—and violinist Joseph Szigeti in the initial recording of the Ives Violin Sonata No. 4.

Before the NMQR records appeared, there had been virtually no commercial recording of contemporary American music; the available repertoire had included major works by George Gershwin, Ferde Grofé, John Alden Carpenter, and a few others.

Composers Henry Cowell, Charles Ives, and Otto Luening were principal supporters of the enterprise. When it folded, the matrices found their way through Theodore Presser Music Co. to (1977) Composers Recordings, Inc., of New York. [Hall 1984/1 is a history and label list.]

NEW ORLEANS RHYTHM KINGS (NORK). An ensemble established in Chicago in the early 1920s by trumpeter Paul Mares, trombonist Georg Brunis,, and clarinetist Leon Roppolo [spelling usually seen as Rappolo], white men from New Orleans. Their group, which included seven or eight other musicians, performed 17 months at Friar's Inn, and was at first known as the Friar's Society Orchestra. They were quickly famous, rivalling the older great white group, the Original Dixieland Jazz Band. They disbanded in 1924, revived a year later, then broke up permanently.

NORK recorded for Gennett in 1922, beginning with "Eccentric" (#5009). "Panama" / "Tiger Rag" was a showpiece for Roppolo (Gennett #4968; 1922), who was also brilliant in "Wolverine Blues" (Gennett #5102; 1923). In 1925 NORK recorded for Okeh and Bluebird. Altogether they only recorded 28 titles.

This group should not be confused with two later ones of the same name, headed by Wingy Manone and Muggsy Spanier.

NEW PHONIC (label). A record issued by Carl Henry, Inc., of New York, in 1927–1928. Matrices came from Plaza-Banner, with the artists disguised by pseudonyms. It is a rare label, with only a few copies known. [Kendziora 1989/4; Rust 1978.]

NEW WORLD RECORDS (label). An American record of 1975, founded with a grant from the Rockefeller Foundation. The benefaction was intended to produce a representative collection of recordings of American music for presentation to libraries and schools. About 100 discs resulted.

NEW YORK GRAMOPHONE CO. The firm operated by **Frank Seaman** from 7 Feb 1896, prior to the formation of his National Gramophone Co. on 19 Oct 1896. It implemented Seaman's sales rights for Berliner Gramophone Co. products in New York and New Jersey.

NEW YORK PHILHARMONIC ORCHESTRA. Founded in 1842 as the Philharmonic Symphony Society of New York, this is the oldest continuous major orchestra in the U.S. There were various conductors at first, with no permanent director. Then Theodore Eisfeld was appointed director in 1852, remaining until 1865. He was followed by Carl Bergmann (1855–1876), Theodore Thomas (1877–1891), Anton Seidl (1891–1898), Emil Paur (1898–1902), Walter Damrosch (1902–1903), Vasily Safonov (1906–1909), Gustav Mahler (1909–1911), Josef Stransky (1911–1922), Willem Mengelberg (1921–1930), Willem van Hoogstraten (1923–1925), Wilhelm Furtwängler (1925–1927), Arturo Toscanini (1927–1936), John Barbirolli (1936–1943), Artur Rodzinski (1943–1947),

Bruno Walter (1947–1949), Dimitri Mitropoulos (1949–1957), Leonard Bernstein (1958–1969), Pierre Boulez (1971–1978), Zubin Mehta (1978–1990), and Kurt Masur (1990–.). There were also a number of regular conductors who shared principal duties, and prominent guest conductors; e.g., George Szell was music adviser and senior guest conductor from 1969 to 1971.

In 1928 the Philharmonic merged with Damrosch's Symphony Society orchestra, and took the name Philharmonic-Symphony Society Orchestra. The orchestra now gives more than 200 concerts per year. It is recognized as one of the premier ensembles of the nation. Recordings of the orchestra are cited in the articles about the conductors.

NEW YORK PHONOGRAPH CO. An affiliate of the **North American Phonograph Co.**, established in 1890 at 257 Fifth Ave., New York. John P. Haines was president in 1890–1892. Recording studios were set up around 1890 to make brown wax cylinders. **Coin-op** machines were a major enterprise; there were 175 of them leased in 1891. In 1906 the firm brought an action against the National Phonograph Co., with a successful outcome in 1908.

NEW YORK PRO MUSICA. An ensemble established in New York by Noah Greenberg in 1952; it was originally named the Pro Musica Antiqua, suggesting its focus on music of the Middle Ages, Renaissance, and baroque periods. Great acclaim followed its performance in 1957–1958 of the medieval *Play of Daniel*, performed in the appropriate surroundings of the Cloisters (a monastery that is part of the Metropolitan Museum of Art). When Greenberg died in 1966, J.R. White became director (1966–1970), followed by Paul Maynard (1970–1972), and George Houle (1972–1974). The group disbanded in 1974.

Recordings of the Pro Musica were important in creating audiences for early music, and for the acceptance of authentic instruments in modern performance. As their work coincided with the emergence of the LP record, they achieved popularity through that medium. Among their outstanding recordings were the *Play of Daniel* (MCA #2504) and the *Play of Herod* (MCA #2-10008).

NEW YORK RECORDING LABORATO-RIES. A record manufacturer established in 1916, with an executive office not in New York but in Port Washington, Wisconsin. Studios were at 1140 Broadway, New York; and the pressing plant was in Grafton, New York. Much recording was done in Chicago, and from late 1929 also in Grafton. Paramount was the principal label produced (1916–1932), along with its various affiliate labels such as Broadway, Famous, and Puritan. [Rust 1978.]

NEW YORK TALKING MACHINE CO. A firm located at 83 Chambers St., New York, established as a successor to the Victor Distributing and Export Co. in 1910. A 1911 advertisement described the company as an exclusive Victor wholesaler. Later locations were 119 W. 40th St., and (1921) 521 W. 57th St. H.D. Geissler was president in 1920.

NEW YORK TRIO. An chamber ensemble that recorded for Edison Diamond Discs in 1928. It consisted of Louis Edlin, violin; Cornelius Van Vliet, cello; and Clarence Adler, piano.

NEW YORKERS. A vocal quintet that recorded three Edison Diamond Discs in 1929. Members were Ed Smalle, Colin O'More, Harry Donaghy, and two men known only by their last names: Mr. Shope and Mr. Preston.

NEW ZEALAND. The history of sound recording in New Zealand is inevitably of a more modest nature than that of **Australia**, largely due to the substantial difference in the size of population (approximately one-fifth that of Australia). During the 19th and early 20th centuries mechanical instruments played a part in New Zealand musical life, just as they did in that of Australia. There are a number of accounts of pianolas in the hands of private persons, and various forms of musical automata were in existence. Advertisements from around 1905 show that companies like Charles Begg & Co, Ltd. and the Dresden Piano Co. stocked a wide range of talking machines and records, primarily from Gramophone and Typewriter Ltd., in England. An advertisement for His Master's Voice, with the familiar **Nipper** pho-

tograph, appeared in the *N. Z. Free Lance* (Wellington) in November 1905. Despite the appearance of discs, Edison phonographs and cylinders were still imported, and in 1910 were still extensively promoted in New Zealand. The Cecil Zonophone, from America, appeared in 1910.

His Master's Voice (N.Z.), Ltd., was incorporated on 10 May 1926, although recordings and equipment were still imported. Only occasionally were records actually made in New Zealand. Such was the case in June 1930 when recordings of the Rotorua Maori Choir were made in the Tunihopua Meeting House at the suggestion of W.A. Donner, of the Columbia Graphophone Co., Australia, after he had visited Rotorua. The discs were subsequently given world-wide distribution. In the 78 era New Zealand artists frequently recorded at the Australian HMV studios at Homebush.

Until the late 1980s the industry was dominated by six firms who accounted for over 90 percent of record sales. These were CBS, EMI, Festival, Polygram, RCA, and WEA. EMI and Polygram owned record clubs. Several local companies produced and distributed records by New Zealand artists, among them Viking and Kiwi Pacific. More than 90 percent of records sold were made from imported masters, pressed locally at the plants of EMI and Polygram. In 1978 sales of records and tapes in the country amounted to about NZ$34.5 million. Over 5 million LPs were produced, and about 1.6 million cassettes. National economic conditions forced EMI to close its pressing plant in 1988. No CDs are currently produced in New Zealand. Works by New Zealand composers and artists are recorded locally and master tapes are sent overseas for processing. There are many independent labels in the main cities.

A special role in sound recording history has been played by the New Zealand Broadcasting Corp. (now Radio New Zealand), established in 1936, and by the National Orchestra (1946). An important repository is the Radio New Zealand Sound Archive (1956), with rare recordings of Polynesian and Pacific music, complementing holdings of the Archive of Maori and Pacific Music at the University of Auckland. There are also important materials in the Sound and Music Centre, and in the Alexander Turnbull Library, both units of the National Library; and in the Hocken Library, Dunedin. (Acknowledgements: Beverley Anscombe, Music Librarian, University of Auckland; Auckland Public Library; Tony Chance, Recording Industry Association of New Zealand, Inc.; Roger Flury, Librarian, Sound and Music Centre; Hocken Library; Radio New Zealand; Jill Palmer, Music Librarian, Alexander Turnbull Library.)

Gerald R. Seaman

NEWARK TINWARE AND METAL WORKS. A manufacturer of talking machine horns, advertising in 1907 a line made of simulated wood. Location was 53 Nurr Ave., Newark, New Jersey.

NICHOLS, RED, 1905–1965. American jazz trumpeter, born Ernest Loring Nichols in Ogden, Utah, on 8 May 1905. His father taught him cornet and gave him a place in his brass band; from there Nichols went on to play in theater orchestras and, at age 17, with a dance band in Ohio named the Syncopating Five. In 1923 he was playing in the New York areas with various groups. During the 1920s he was with Vincent Lopez, Sam Lanin, Harry Reser, the California Ramblers, and Paul Whiteman. He formed his own group, Red Nichols and His Five Pennies, in 1926. This ensemble varied in number and membership; it included—in recording sessions of December 1926 and January 1927—such luminaries as Jimmy Dorsey, Eddie Lang, Miff Mole, and Joe Venuti. Later on Pee Wee Russell, Benny Goodman, Glenn Miller, Jack Teagarden, Bud Freeman, Dave Tough, Red McKenzie, Tommy Dorsey, Gene Krupa, Ray McKinley, and Will Bradley were in the Pennies; and there were vocalists such as Dick Robertson, Smith Ballew, and the Boswell Sisters. As the size of the group grew to as many as 14 artists, it was in fact a Big Band, and was identified as an orchestra on some recordings.

Nichols was popular on radio through the 1930s. After World War II he led another group in long engagements at California venues. A 1959 motion picture based on his life, *The Five Pennies*, with Danny Kaye playing Nichols,

gave him a late career boost. He died in Las Vegas on 28 June 1965.

Nichols recorded prolifically, beginning as a sideman with Sam Lanin in 1924, and continuing with various Lanin groups to 1931. He cut four sides with Red and Miff's Stompers (the Miff being Miff Mole) for Edison Diamond Discs in October 1926. With the Pennies he recorded from December 1926 to October 1963, mostly on Brunswick, Victor, Bluebird, and Capitol. "Sometimes I'm Happy" / "Hallelujah!" (Brunswick #4701; 1930) was a typical disc of the smaller ensemble (with both the Dorseys and Gene Krupa). The larger group is well displayed in "Love Is Like That" (Brunswick #6118; 1931), with a Ballew vocal. Material of 1926–1930 was reissued on LP in Brunswick album #LAT 8307. Capitol released several other LP albums, covering work of the 1950s. [Backensto 1969 is a memorial issue of *RR*, with the Lanin-Nichols discography and a list of the Nichols records after 1956.]

NICOLE (label). A cylinder and disc record issued by Nicole Frères, Ltd., a firm that can be traced back to a family of music box makers in Switzerland. The business passed from family hands and was established in Britain in the late 19th century. Music boxes were replaced by gramophones and Edison phonographs in the London manifestation. In 1901 the firm switched from Gramophone Co. products to those of International Zonophone Co., Berlin. Because of lack of supplies from Germany, Nicole Frères, Ltd., began to make its own records, unbreakable paper-based discs, in seven- and 10–inch sizes. The Nicole Record Co., Ltd., was formed to manufacture the discs.

At the close of 1905 cylinder records were made. Nicole had an international repertoire of material, much of it acquired by recording engineer Steve Porter, who journeyed as far as India to make records. In 1906 the Disc Record Co., Ltd., of Stockport, Cheshire, acquired all the Nicole masters, which it used to press shellac records for clients, later on the clients' own labels. [Andrews*; Catalogue 1971.]

NIELSEN, ALICE, ca.1868–1943. American soprano, born in Nashville, Tennessee; her birthdate is usually given as 7 June 1876, but her death record shows age 74, which would place the birthdate ca. 1868. She sang in church choirs, then toured for two years with a light opera company. Two of Victor Herbert's operettas were composed for her, *Fortune Teller* (1898), and *Singing Girl* (1899). Her grand opera debut was in Naples as Marguerite, on 6 Dec 1903. She sang Mimi opposite Enrico Caruso at Covent Garden. Her first American appearance was in New York in November 1905, then she toured with the San Carlo Opera Co. From 1909 to 1913 Nielsen sang with the Boston Opera Co. and from time to time with the Metropolitan Opera. Norina in *Don Pasquale* and Mimi were two Metropolitan roles; but she was overshadowed there by Emmy Destinn, Lucrezia Bori, Frances Alda, and Frida Hempel. She retired from the stage and taught voice in New York, where she died on 8 Mar 1943.

Nielsen sang with the Alice Nielsen Quartet on Berliner records in the 1890s, and for other labels. She made landmark Berliners in 1898, participating in the first U.S. cast recordings of a musical (*Fortune Teller*). Her first Victor was "Addio del passato" (64068; 1907); she had five solos and five duets with tenor Florencio Constantino in the Victor 1917 catalog. A favorite record with collectors is her "Last Rose of Summer" which appeared on Victor #74121 and Columbia #A5283.

NIKISCH, ARTHUR, 1855–1922. Hungarian conductor, born in Szentmiklós on 12 Oct 1855. He studied violin at the Vienna Conservatory; after graduating in 1874 he played in orchestras in Vienna and Leipzig. From 1882 to 1889 he was first conductor at the Leipzig Theater. Appointed to conduct the Boston Symphony Orchestra, he served in that post from 1889 to 1893. Then he returned to conduct in Budapest, and to lead the Gewandhaus Concerts in Leipzig. He was a visiting conductor with the Berlin Philharmonic Orchestra and the London Symphony Orchestra. Nikisch was greatly influential in establishing the primary role of the conductor. He died in Leipzig on 23 Jan 1922.

In the history of recorded sound, Nikisch occupies a significant place as the first great conductor of the first (almost) complete symphony played by a major orchestra. This was

the Beethoven Fifth Symphony, performed by the Berlin Philharmonic Orchestra in 1909, issued on eight single-sided discs by the Gramophone Co. during 1914. These discs (HMV #040784/91) were greatly popular, despite the alterations in the scoring necessitated by acoustic recording limitations, and led to a flow of symphony records from the U.K., Germany, and America. (This was not, however, the earliest symphonic recording; *see* ORCHESTRA RECORDINGS.) Symposium has issued a set of two compact discs (#1087/8; 1991) including all the Nikisch recordings with the Berlin Philharmonic and London Symphony of 1913–1921, in works by Beethoven, Berlioz, Liszt, Mozart, and Weber. [Shawe-Taylor 1961.]

NILES, JOHN JACOB, 1892–1980. American folksong collector, singer, and composer, born in Louisville, Kentucky, on 28 Apr 1892. He studied at the Cincinnati Conservatory of Music, and collected folksongs in the Southern Appalachian region. He arranged songs for publication, and also wrote songs in folk style. During the 1930s he was popular as a singer; he made an album for Victor in 1939 entitled *Early American Ballads*. Many singles and albums followed, into the 1960s. In 1965 Victor issued an LP, *John Jacob Niles: Folk Balladeer*. Niles died on his farm near Lexington, Kentucky, on 1 Mar 1980.

NIMBUS (label). A British record, issued by Nimbus Records, Ltd., Monmouth; the American distributor is Nimbus Records, Inc., Charlottesville, Virginia. A speciality is CD reissues of early material, primarily vocal. The Prima Voce series has included material by Enrico Caruso, Giovanni Martinelli, and Rosa Ponselle; plus anthology records like *Divas 1906–1935*. There is also an extensive catalog of current recordings.

The Nimbus company developed the **Ambisonics** technique of recording. An Ambisonic microphone is also used in transferring acoustic material to contemporary formats. [Andrews*.]

NIPPER, 1884–1895. A white fox terrier with black markings, the dog in the painting "His Master's Voice" by **Francis Barraud,** famous as the Victor/Gramophone Co. trademark. Born in Bristol, Nipper was owned first by the painter's brother, Mark Henry Barraud. When Mark Henry died in 1887, Nipper moved in with Francis, in Liverpool, and the painting followed at some uncertain date. He was seen in advertising by Emile Berliner, who registered the trademark with the U.S. Patent Office in July 1900; and by Eldridge Johnson's Consolidated Talking Machine Co., in 1900. The dog was next seen on Victor Monarch record labels from January 1902, and on Gramophone Co. labels from February 1909. He appeared in other countries as well, wherever Gramophone affiliates were found, with the text translated appropriately into "Die Stimme seines Herrn," "La Voce del Padrone," etc. In Germany the dog trademark was used by the affiliate until 1949, while the Gramophone Co. branch, Electrola (established 1926) used it only on products sold outside Germany until 1949, when EMI gained control of the trademark and used it on early LPs in Germany.

In 1949 a plaque was placed (according to undocumented reports) over Nipper's supposed grave, near a mulberry tree on Eden St., Kingston-on-Thames. That was the place of employment of Mark Barraud, nephew of the painter and son of Nipper's first owner; he took the dog to work with him each day. However, later developments in that location have resulted in a parking lot, under which Nipper apparently lies. The property, now addressed as 83 Clarence St., belongs to Lloyds Bank. A marker was laid in the parking area on 15 Aug 1984, by David Johnson, Chairman of HMV Shops, Ltd., and a memorial plaque was placed in the foyer of the bank. Nipper's birth and death dates as given above, are taken from the memorial plaque and marker, which are illustrated in *TMR* #70 (December 1985): 1948–1949.

As for the current use of the trademark, a letter from J.P.D. Patrick, vice president for international marketing for EMI Classics, stated that "Nipper is alive and well and to be found in all the territories where EMI have the right to use the trademark. This right does not, however, apply worldwide (not in the USA and the Far East, for instance). . . . Nipper will continue to grace tape and LP releases in the relevant territories . . . and is also appearing on CDs conceived for, and distributed by, specific territories: an example is West German EMI Electrola's current Meisterwerk series" (*Gramophone*, November 1989, p. 822).

In late 1990 RCA began to use two "Nippers"—a grown dog and a puppy—in advertising its new line of television models and camcorders. RCA was acquired from General Electric by Thomson Consumer Electronics, a French company, in 1987. Thomson has the right to use the Nipper symbol and so does General Electric. The latter firm owns the four green stained glass windows—circular, 14 1/2 feet in diameter—now in the nine-story tower in Camden, New Jersey, which was for years the centerpiece of Victor's vast establishment there. Eldridge Johnson commissioned Nicola D'Ascenzo Studios of Philadelphia to make the windows in 1915. They remained in place until the late 1960s, when RCA changed its logo and donated three of the windows to the Smithsonian Institution, Widener College, and Pennsylvania State University. The fourth window was stored by RCA until 1988, when it was given to Camden County Historical Society. A revival of interest in Nipper resulted in a fresh commission by RCA to D'Ascenzo in 1979, and four new windows, copies of the originals, were installed. [Berliner 1977; Hoover 1971 has full-page photographs of the 1915 windows, on pp. 48–49; Petts 1983.]

NIPPON COLUMBIA CO., LTD. A Japanese firm, located in Tokyo, maker of Denon products and other audio items. In the U.K. the distributor is Hayden Laboratories.

NIPPONOPHONE CO., LTD. A Japanese firm, the pioneer of the talking machine industry in that country, established in 1911. The head office was at 1 Chome, Ginza, Tokyo; there were branches all over Japan. In June 1912 the company published the fourth edition of its machine catalog; this was reprinted in *TMR* #75 (Autumn 1988). Records made in Tokyo were marketed, as well as American and European imported material. In 1921 it was noted in *TMW* that Russell Hunting, Jr., was head of recording. In May 1927, *TMW* announced that the Columbia Phonograph Co. had acquired control of Nipponophone.

NOBLE, RAY, 1903–1978. British Big Band leader and composer, born in Brighton on 17 Dec 1903. He studied music at Cambridge University, then formed a dance band in London. In 1929–1934 he was musical director for HMV in London. He transferred to the U.S. in 1934, and with Glenn Miller's assistance he established a band in New York. On 1 June 1935 he opened at the Rainbow Room, atop Rockefeller Center, and was highly successful there with a sweet-swing style; he also began regular appearances on radio. The 1935 ensemble included outstanding artists, e.g., Charlie Spivak, Pee Wee Ervin, Glenn Miller, Will Bradley, Bud Freeman, Claude Thornhill, and vocalist Al Bowlly. They began recording in February 1935 for Victor, remaining with that label until 1937. Noble's composition, "The Touch of Your Lips," with vocal by Bowlly, was a great success in 1936 (Victor #25277).

With Bowlly's return to England in 1936 Noble's stellar assemblage had begun to dissolve; he broke up the band in early 1937, then reorganized and switched to Brunswick records (from January 1938), with new vocalist Tony Martin making a fine disc of the Noble song "I Hadn't Anyone Till You" (Brunswick #8079; 1938). In October 1938 the group recorded another Noble hit, "Cherokee" (Brunswick # 8247). Other songs by Ray Noble became popular records by his band, on the Columbia label from 1939: "The Very Thought of You" / "Goodnight, Sweetheart" (Columbia #36546, vocals by the composer). The Noble orchestra was featured in four motion pictures between 1935 and 1945, and was much on radio. In the mid-1950s Noble retired. He died in London on 2 Apr 1978. Six LP albums by HMV were issued, covering much of his distinguished work.

NOISE. (I) Any undesired signal in a recording or transmission system; an interfering disturbance. *See also* DISTORTION.

NOISE. (II) In acoustics, noise is a sound with a large number of frequencies outside the harmonic series of the fundamental.

NOISE. (III) White noise is a random signal, having the same energy level at all frequencies, sometime used as a mask to conceal disagreeable sounds.

NOISE. (IV) Pink noise is a band-limited random signal with the same amount of energy in each octave.

NOISE. (V) Ambient noise is the total of the undesired signals in the listening environment. It renders inaudible the desired portion of a received signal that falls below a certain decibel level; in an average home situation, it is estimated that signals of volume below 30 dB are not actually heard because of ambient noise.

NOISE. (VI) Surface noise is the result of friction between a record surface and the playback stylus, friction that is enhanced and more audible when the surface is scratched or damaged or when the stylus is worn. But even with all elements in perfect condition, there was an audible hissing noise in playback of 78 rpm records. LP records in fine condition, played with proper lightweight styli, were for practical purposes free of surface noise. Some cylinder records had extremely quiet surfaces when new. *See also* NOISE REDUCTION SYSTEMS; SIGNAL TO NOISE RATIO.

Noise filter. *See* SCRATCH FILTER.

NOISE REDUCTION SYSTEMS. Surface noise was a nuisance from the beginning of the sound recording industry. Early discs were so noisy from the contact of hard needles with gritty grooves that the desired performance signals could nearly disappear into the background. Improvements in materials lessened the seriousness of this problem, which in any case appeared to have been solved in the advertising of the manufacturers—who promoted "silent surfaces" long before such things were practical; and indeed the audience for 78s did learn to listen through the surface noises to a certain extent, ignoring them somewhat like white noise (*see* NOISE, III). The best Edison Diamond Discs possessed nearly silent surfaces, and other good discs could be rendered almost free of noise when played with fiber, thorn, or cactus needles. Tape recording brought its own noise, tape hiss.

Real work on noise reduction through technical means began in the 1950s. D.T. N. Williamson gave a lecture in Britain in 1953 on "Suppression of Surface Noise," using a capacitor/inductor delay line and valve equipment. His ideas were employed by the Garrard MRM/101 of 1978, intended to cancel clicks on stereo LPs. Essentially the system analyzed waveforms as they occurred, delayed those with frequencies that matched click frequencies, shunted them out of the signal, and returned the entire cleaned signal to its place in the audio stream. This approach to noise reduction, the "dynamic noise filter," has been used in most of the popular modern systems: Burwen, SAE, SEA, Dolby, MicMix, dbx, and Packburn. Another approach, the "static filter," was adapted by Owl, Orban, UREI, and Pultec.

Digital processing has opened a new pathway to noise reduction. A computer with appropriate instructions can translate a sound signal into digital (numerical) form, sample it for specific patterns named in its program, eliminate those patterns that have been designated as unwanted, and replace them with the average of neighboring number patterns. CEDAR is a functioning digital system which operates along the line just described. It is also able to compare several records of similar content, to find the points where there is least noise, and to produce a new combined recording with the best characteristics of all of them and the fewest intrusive sounds. [Klinger*; Tuddenham 1988.]

See also CEDAR; dbx; DOLBY NOISE REDUCTION SYSTEMS; PACKBURN AUDIO NOISE SUPPRESSOR; SONIC RESTORATION.

NON-MAGNETIC TAPE RECORDING. The

idea of cutting a groove into a ribbon of some kind, by acoustical means, is an old one. Thomas Edison's first reproduction of sound in fact took place on a paper ribbon, and he alluded to this kind of medium, and other sound carrier formats, in his British patent #1644. U.S. patent # 944,608 was granted to Franklin C. Goodale on 28 Dec 1909; it was for a talking

machine based on a celluloid tape instead of a cylinder. Frank E. Holman had a U.S. patent granted on 9 Nov 1909 for a talking machine with a belt for a carrier; it was claimed to play for 50 minutes.

Optical (photographic) sound recording on film was another non-magnetic approach; it was developed by Frenchmen Eugene Lauste and Eugene Boyer before 1913. These early systems failed to replace the short-playing noisy discs because they lacked amplification devices, and their unamplified playback was very weak. With the development of electron tubes by Lee de Forest optical systems became significant, especially in motion picture sound. In the U.K., **British Ozaphane, Ltd.** used sound films without pictures, offering an eight-millimeter film soundtrack with playing time up to 90 minutes. The Dutch Gramofilm of 1934 was similar in concept; and there were comparable devices in other countries.

The many promising features of the non-magnetic systems were eclipsed by the arrival of magnetic recording, first on wire, then in its several tape manifestations. [Jansen 1983.]

NOONE, JIMMIE, 1895–1944. American jazz clarinetist and saxophonist, born in Cut-Off, Louisiana on 23 April 1895. He played guitar first, then went to the clarinet, perhaps studying with Sidney Bechet in New Orleans and playing there with his group. He then performed in Chicago with various bands, and was successful at the Apex Club there from 1926 with his own Apex Club Orchestra, which included Earl Hines at the piano. Noone made his first records—an important series—with that ensemble, for Vocalion in 1928: "I Know That You Know" / "Sweet Sue" (#1184), and continued with the label to January 1931. "Apex Blues" (Vocalion #1207; 1928) and "Four or Five Times" (Vocalion #1185; 1928) were outstanding numbers. Mildred Bailey was vocalist on the final Vocalion cuts, "He's Not Worth Your Tears" / "Trav'lin' All Alone" (#1580). His later records were for Brunswick, Vocalion again, Decca, and Bluebird. The Australian Swaggie label recorded his quartet in a Chicago session in 1941.

LPs of the Apex material were issued by Decca (#DL 9235) and Ace of Hearts (#AH-84).

His records demonstrate his place as a link between the New Orleans jazz style and the Chicago swing style of clarinet playing. Noone died in Los Angeles on 19 Apr 1944.

NORCROSS PHONOGRAPH CO. Isaac W. Norcross, Jr. was an entrepreneur of the brown-wax cylinder era. During the late 1890s, he marketed his own pantographically-duplicated records from the New Zealand Building, Rooms 10–14, 125 West 37th Street, New York City. Both standard and concert-size cylinders were offered. An advertisement in the July 1898 *Phonoscope* offered 179 brown wax cylinders recorded by the Metropolitan Band, directed by G. Peluso. Jumbo was the label name. Norcross also featured phonograph parlors "open every day."

Norcross persisted with duplicated brown-wax records well beyond the beginning (1902) of the mass-produced gold-molded records. He sometimes operated at the fringes of the law, supplying information and equipment to others wishing to duplicate cylinder records. He developed his own "Norcross Attachment" for use in recording master cylinders. In 1908, he offered a Norcross Reproducer made "especially for Indestructible Records."

In August 1909, at his laboratory in the New Lang Building (662 Sixth Avenue, New York) he recorded master records for use by the **U-S Phonograph Co.** of Cleveland. They proved unsatisfactory and Charles Hibbard (of U-S) had replaced Norcross as laboratory manager by November 1909. John Kaiser (formerly of Harms, Kaiser & Hagen) also served as a recording expert for U-S Phonograph at the same location.

Norcross left New York around March 1910 and was living in Los Angeles in 1912.

Bill Klinger

NORDICA, LILLIAN, 1857–1914. American soprano, born Lillian Norton in Farmington, Maine, on 12 Dec 1857. She studied in Boston and made her debut there in 1876. She was a soloist with Gilmore's Band in 1878. Then she studied in Milan, and took the name Nordica for her debut there as Elvira, on 8 Mar 1879. Tours of Europe, including Russia, followed; and on 18 Dec 1891 she appeared as Valentine in *Huguenots* at the Metropolitan Opera. Subsequently she specialized in Wagnerian roles, remaining at the Metropolitan intermittently to 1909. She died on 10 May 1914, in Batavia, Java.

Nordica's recordings were few. **Mapleson cylinders** of 1901–1903 display her voice in Wagner fragments. She then worked for Columbia in 1906–1911, making a fine "Liebestod" (#30652; 1911) and a collector's favorite, Elisabeth's aria from *Hunyadi László* by Erkel, sung in Hungarian. There were also arias from *Mignon, Madama Butterfly, Tannhäuser,* and *Gioconda.* [Dennis 1951/9; Moran 1963.]

NORDSKOG (label). An American record, claimed to be the first from the Pacific Coast, issued from 1921–to ca. 1923 by the Nordskog Phonograph Recording Co., main office in Santa Monica, California. Andrae Nordskog was founder and head of the firm. Only 27 issues are known, but they have interesting material. Abe Lyman recorded first for Nordskog, and Eva Tanguay made her only record for the label. Kid Ory's Jazz Band made six sides. Ory's discs—issued with the Sunshine label pasted over the Nordskog label—were the first made by a Black New Orleans jazz group. In addition to original recordings, Nordskog released material from Arto masters; this was done as part of an exchange agreement with Arto, which did the Nordskog pressing at first, and which also distributed Nordskog material under its own label. Some artists lost their names in these transcontinental trips; for example, the Original Memphis Five on Arto became the Hollywood Syncopators on Nordskog #3013. [Kendziora 1968/7; Rust 1978.]

NORTH AMERICAN PHONOGRAPH CO. A firm established by **Jesse H. Lippincott**—originally named the American Phonograph Co.—on 14 July 1888 as the sole outlet for the graphophone and sole sales agency for Edison phonograph products. Patents of the Edison Phonograph Co. were acquired, but not the Bell-Tainter graphophone patents. Lippincott's associates were Thomas R. Lombard, George S. Evans, George H. Fitzwilson, and John Robinson. They capitalized the company at

$4,000,000. Offices were in the Edison Building (44 Broad St.), New York, and the Masonic Temple, Chicago.

North American engaged in leasing phonographs and "phonograph-graphophones" to business offices for dictation purposes, selling supplies, leasing coin-ops for entertainment, and selling entertainment cylinders for the home market. Thirty-three regional companies were appointed as franchises to handle all leases and sales in specific territories, under strict rules. The member companies bought their stock from North American at a discount of about 30 percent, and took the responsibility for their own marketing. There were 34 U.S. affiliates (two of them merged ca. 1890) and a Canadian agent.

These were the member firms of the early 1890s: Alabama Phonograph Co., Central Nebraska Phonograph Co. (including the western part of the state), Chicago Central Phonograph Co. (covering Cook County), Colorado and Utah Phonograph Co., Columbia Phonograph Co., Eastern Pennsylvania Phonograph Co., Florida Phonograph Co., Georgia Phonograph Co., Holland Brothers (the Canadian agents), Iowa Phonograph Co., Kansas Phonograph Co. (including New Mexico), Kentucky Phonograph Co., Leeds and Co. (for Indiana), Louisiana Phonograph Co., Metropolitan Phonograph Co. (merged with New York Phonograph Co. ca. 1890), Michigan Phonograph Co., Minnesota Phonograph Co., Missouri Phonograph Co. (including Arkansas and Indian Territories), Montana Phonograph Co., Nebraska Phonograph Co. (for Eastern Nebraska), New England Phonograph Co., New Jersey Phonograph Co., New York Phonograph Co., Ohio Phonograph Co., Old Dominion Phonograph Co. (for Virginia, North Carolina, and South Carolina), Pacific Phonograph Co. (for Arizona, California, and Nevada), South Dakota Phonograph Co., Spokane Phonograph Co. (covering Oregon, Idaho, and Eastern Washington), State Phonograph Co. of Illinois (covering the state except for Cook County), Tennessee Phonograph Co., Texas Phonograph Co., West Coast Phonograph Co. (for Western Oregon and Western Washington), Western Pennsylvania Phonograph Co. (covering Western Pennsylvania and West Virginia), Wisconsin Phonograph Co., and Wyoming Phonograph Co. (See individual articles on the firms for details of location, dates of operation, etc.) The companies deployed themselves in a trade organization called the National Phonograph Association in 1890 and met for annual conventions.

It should be noted that one of the member companies was in a unique position: Columbia Phonograph Co. had been established before North American, in 1888 (incorporated 1889). Its directors had arranged with American Graphophone Co. (licensee of the Volta Graphophone Co.) to have graphophone sales rights to the territory of Washington, D.C., Maryland, and Delaware. Columbia was the only one of the regional franchises to survive unscathed the termination of North American. Several other companies limped along for a few years, some with new names.

A trade journal, *Phonogram*, was published by North American from January 1891 to 1893. In April 1892 the company began to emphasize entertainment cylinders for the home market. The main problem faced was that not many homes were ready to spend $150 or more for a phonograph; another problem was the difficulty in making satisfactory duplicates from the original cylinders. Nevertheless the first edition of the *Catalogue of Musical Phonograms* had appeared in 1890, and more than 1,400 selections were available within two years. These were the Edison "2-minute" brown wax cylinders (*see* CYLINDER, 2). Some of the member companies began to compete with the parent firm by producing their own cylinders: Columbia, Louisiana, New England, Ohio, and the Canadian Holland Brothers.

Samuel Insull was president in 1892, and Thomas Lombard was president in 1893. Following early successes and later financial difficulties North American Phonograph Co. was bankrupt in August 1894, and its assets went into receivership in 1896. Lippincott died in 1894. The stock and assets were auctioned by court order, and Thomas Edison himself bought everything, "becoming for the first time sole proprietor of his phonographic enterprise" (Read). [Andrews 1976/2; Klinger*; Koenigsberg 1987; Wile 1972/2.]

NORVO, RED, 1908– . American jazz xylophonist, pianist, and Big Band leader, born Kenneth Norville in Beardstown, Illinois, on 31 Mar 1908. He studied at the University of Missouri during 1926–1927, and played locally; was with Paul Ash's group at the Oriental Theater in Chicago; had a band in Milwaukee in 1928. In the early 1930s he joined Paul Whiteman (and married feature singer Mildred Bailey). He put together a band in 1935, with Bailey as vocalist, and was successful in New York. Eddie Sauter did arrangements, George Wettling was the drummer. Later he was with the Benny Goodman Quintet and Sextet (1944–1945), and with Woody Herman (1945–1946). He was pioneer on the xylophone in jazz context, and also performed on the vibraphone. Norvo made numerous world tours, and was seen on television; during the 1960s he was popular on the West Coast and in Las Vegas.

Norvo's early recordings, in small groups that included Jimmy Dorsey and Benny Goodman, were made in New York for Brunswick in 1933. "Knockin' on Wood" / "Hole in the Wall" was the first (#6652). Then he recorded with his own septet, octet, and—from January 1936—with his orchestra. Among the fine records made by the orchestra, those with Mildred Bailey's vocals stand out, e.g., "I've Got My Love to Keep Me Warm" (Brunswick #7813; 1937) and "Love is Here to Stay" (Brunswick #8068; 1938). Norvo's band also recorded for Vocalion and Columbia.

NOVOTNA, JARMILA, 1907– . Czech soprano, born in Prague on 23 Sep 1907. She studied with Emmy Destinn, and made her debut in Prague as Violetta on 27 June 1926. Then she joined the Berlin State Opera. Her American debut was in San Francisco in 1939. She was heard first at the Metropolitan Opera as Mimi on 5 Jan 1940, remaining to 1951, and returning for the 1952–1956 seasons. Then she retired to Vienna.

Her best roles were Cherubino, Mimi, Elvira, Euridice, Pamina, Violetta, Marenka in *Bartered Bride*, and Octavian. She began recording for Columbia in 1925, doing "Caro nome" and three other arias, all in Czech. Two HMV acoustics, not issued until 1926, presented her in two Czech arias. In April 1931 she was recording for HMV in Germany, singing in German or Czech four numbers from *Traviata*. She did more German and Czech pieces for Electrola in June 1931, and for Odeon; then sang Czech folk songs for Victor in 1942 with Jan Masaryk at the piano (three-disc album #M-936; later on LP as #1383, 1969). [Frankenstein 1979.]

OAKLAND, WILL, 1880–1956. American countertenor, born Herman Hinrichs in Jersey City, New Jersey, on 15 Jan 1880. Rust observes that he had the highest male voice ever heard on stage (Rust 1989). His specialties were the sentimental song and the Civil War ballad. Oakland first recorded for Edison in 1908, with "When the Autumn Moon is Creeping Thro' the Woodlands" (#9902), and made his first Victor disc a year later: "When You and I Were Young, Maggie" (#5682; 1909). He had 13 solo items in the Victor 1917 catalog, plus numbers with the Heidelberg Quintette. He recorded many solos and quartet numbers for Edison, Columbia, U-S Everlasting, and other labels until 1926. His final issue was "Let's Grow Old Together" / "Gone" (Harmony #162–H; 1926). Oakland went into radio and became famous; he was voted the most popular radio singer in a 1926 poll. He also appeared in vaudeville and operated a night club. He died on a bus going to Newark, New Jersey, on 15 May 1956. [Walsh 1949/11.]

OAKLEY, OLLY. British banjoist, a pioneer recording artist for that instrument; real name James Sharpe. He recorded for G & T beginning in 1901, with "Rugby Parade March" (#6334), again in 1902 (11 numbers) and then to 1904. Rust identifies "Whistling Rufus" (#6374;1903) as "early ragtime." The disc is of further interest for its piano accompaniment, by Landon Ronald. Oakley went on to record prolifically for many cylinder and disc labels.

OBERLIN, RUSSELL, 1928–. American countertenor, born in Akron, Ohio, on 11 Oct 1928.

He studied at Juilliard School in New York, graduating in 1951. He was a founding member, with Noah Greenberg, of the **New York Pro Musica**, and did much to popularize the countertenor voice in America along with its repertoire. From 1971 he was a professor of music at Hunter College, New York.

OBERSTEIN, ELI, ca. 1902–1960. American record industry executive. In 1939 he set up the United States Record Co., making Varsity and Royale labels. Masters came from Crown, Gennett, and others. Risque "party" records were among the popular issues. In 1940 the company name was changed to Independent Record Co., and the Top Hat label emerged. During the recording ban of 1942, Oberstein continued to issue new material, on the Hit label; he gained the reputation of "pirate" and was ousted from the American Federation of Musicians, which had imposed the ban. Other positions held by Oberstein included vice president of RCA Victor, and treasurer of Columbia Phonograph Co. When he died, in Westport, Connecticut, on 13 June 1960, he held the presidency of Rondo Record Corp., New York. [Blacker 1977/10.]

OCARINA. A globe-shaped flute, invented by Giuseppe Donati, made of various materials and in various sizes. It is also known as a sweet potato, because of its shape. A Berliner record of 29 Aug 1898, "Whistling Coon," offered an ocarina with banjo, by performers identified as Mays and Hunter. In February 1906 Edison issued an ocarina solo by Eugene C. Rose, "Genevieve Waltz Medley" (#9197). The celebrated ocarina player on British and European records was Mose Tapiero of Italy. He recorded classical and semi-classical works for many labels.

O'CONNELL, CHARLES, 1900–1962. American recording industry executive, and conductor, born in Chicopee, Massachusetts, on 22 Apr 1900. He studied organ in Paris with Charles-Marie Widor, and was A & R head for Victor, with responsibility for Red Seal records, 1930–1944. From 1944 to 1947 he headed the masterworks division of Columbia Records. He was conductor of studio orchestras for both labels. O'Connell wrote the *Victor Book of the Symphony* (1934) and contributed to revisions of the *Victor Book of the Opera*. He died in New York on 1 Sep 1962.

O'CONNOR, GEORGE H., JR., 1874–1946. American tenor/baritone, born in Washington, D.C., on 20 Aug 1874. He studied voice and dancing as a child, and appeared in *Pirates of Penzance*; then sang in the Georgetown University Glee Club. His local fame reached the White House, and he became known as the favorite entertainer there, singing for Presidents McKinley, Theodore Roosevelt, Taft, Wilson, Harding, and Coolidge. While his specialty was the coon song and other dialect numbers, he also sang ballads. O'Connor was a lawyer, admitted to the D.C. bar in 1895.

His first Columbia record, which O'Connor considered his finest, was "Mississippi Barbecue" / "Alabama Jamboree" (#A1669; 1915). In 1916 Columbia released what proved to be the most popular of his discs, "Nigger Blues" (#A2064). Another great hit was the humorous "I Ain't Prepared for That" of 1917. Many of his discs had flip sides by Al Jolson, which helped the sales. His final release was "Jazzin' the Cotton Town Blues" / "There's Always Something Doin' Down in Dixie" (Columbia #A2507; 1918). O'Connor died on 28 Sep 1946. [Walsh 1955/1–2–3.]

O'DAY, ANITA, 1919– . American popular singer, born Anita Belle Colton in Kansas City, Missouri, on 18 Oct 1919. She began singing professionally in Chicago as a teen, and joined Gene Krupa's band in 1941, remaining to 1943.

Then she was with Stan Kenton in 1944–1945, returned to Krupa (1945–1946), and went freelance. O'Day became famous as a singer of jazz, with improvisation and scat singing that were comparable to instrumental performance. She was a sensation at the Newport Festival of 1958, and sang throughout America and Europe. In 1985 she gave a Carnegie Hall concert, to observe her 50th year as a performer.

O'Day's records with Krupa include "Let Me Off Uptown"—her biggest hit, with Roy Eldridge's trumpet in counterpoint—(Okeh #6210; 1941), "Skylark" (Okeh #6607; 1941), and "Side by Side" (Columbia # 36726; 1942). She released several important LP albums, including *Anita* (Verve #2000; 1955) and *Live at the City* (Emily #102479; 1979). Emily was her own label.

ODEON RECORD (label). A record first issued in Germany by the **International Talking Machine Co. mbH**, the firm organized by Frederick M. Prescott to replace his lost control over the International Zonophone Co. The label name Odeon was taken from the name of a famous theater in Paris. Odeon was assiduous in seeking out European opera stars (Lilli Lehmann, Emmy Destinn, John McCormack) to record. Odeon discs were recorded and marketed in many countries; and marketed briefly by Columbia in the U.S. from 1908 to 1910.

Odeon Records were made in several metric sizes: 19 cm (7 1/2 inches), 27 centimeters (10 3/4 inches), 30 centimeters (12 inches), and 35 centimeters (13 1/2 inches), all but the last being double-sided. Those were the first double-faced records marketed in Europe (Zonophone had marketed double-faced records in South America in 1902). When the patent claim for double-sided records, by Prescott and Ademor Petit, was defeated in an Austrian court on a challenge from the Favorite Schallplatten Fabrik (1907), Odeon was deprived of a desirable monopoly.

Before Fonotipia, Ltd., of England, acquired a controlling interest in Odeon Records (International Talking Machine Co.) during 1906, the **American Record Co.** issued blue discs with the American label, showing an American Indian on the label. The firm carried out special 27–centimeter pressings for Prescott's business in Europe, the discs being labelled American Odeon Record. The export records were also blue, and carried the Indian picture. In 1908 there was another Odeon subsidiary, the Jumbo Record Fabrik, which marketed Jumbo and Jumbola Records. Many were later converted to "Blue-labelled Odeon Records." Otto Heinemann, a founder-director of International Talking Machine, was involved.

From July 1911, the business of Fonotipia, Ltd., was acquired by Carl Lindström AG (Beka and Parlophon records), giving Lindström the Odeon, Jumbo, Jumbola, and Fonotipia labels. In 1925 the Odeon label became a part of the Columbia business in Europe (not in the U.S.), which eventually passed to EMI, Ltd., in 1931. The label remains today one of the EMI trademarks.

In the U.S. the Columbia Phonograph Co. concession for Odeon discs terminated in 1910, and the label was no longer generally available in America until January 1921. At that time an American agency of Lindström, the **American Odeon Corp.** began selling Odeon and Fonotipia discs with American and international repertoires in 21 languages. Newly recorded American Odeon Records (10 inches, $.85) appeared in March 1921. In June 1921 the firm had either changed its name to the American Odeon Phonograph Corp., or the business had passed into new management; the address was unchanged: 100 W. 21st St., New York. Records of such stars as John McCormack, Emmy Destinn, and Lilli Lehmann became available in America from the Odeon European backlog catalogs.

Another name change was reported in July 1921, to American Odeon Record Corp.; but the trading name was American Odeon Corp. by September 1921. All "the latest popular hits" were then available on the label, with some foreign language catalogs. On 31 Dec 1921 the firm decided to go out of business.

Meanwhile Otto Heinemann's **General Phonograph Corp.** had announced (November 1920) that it had secured access to Lindström's catalogs, including Dacapo, Beka, Favorite, Fonotipia, Lyrophon, Parlophon, and Odeon. That material was issued on the Okeh label until January 1922, when the Odeon name

began to appear (with the takeover by General of the American Odeon Corp. business). Upon the acquisition by the British-controlled Columbia Phonograph Co., Inc. of the disc business of General Phonograph, the enterprise was renamed **Okeh Phonograph Record Corp.** Odeon Records seem to have vanished from the U.S. with the Columbia take-over, although the name was revived with a label circulating to the West Coast trade in 1929 as Odeon Electric Records. [Andrews*.]

ODETTA, 1930– . American folk singer and guitarist, born Odetta Holmes Felious Gordon in Birmingham, Alabama, on 31 Dec 1930. She studied music at Los Angeles City College, and began performing in California in her teens. She sang Afro/American work songs, spirituals, and blues, becoming a key figure in the folksong revival of the 1950s, with acclaimed appearances at such venues as the Blue Angel in New York and the Gate of Horn in Chicago. Odetta toured widely, and gave recitals at Town Hall and Carnegie Hall. She was one of the performers at the Newport Folk Festival of 1959. Her first album, on the Tradition label, was *Odetta Sings Ballads and Blues* (1956). Among her favorite songs were "He's Got the Whole Wide World in His Hands" and "Take This Hammer," both of which were included in a 1957 LP, *Odetta at the Gate of Horn*. *Odetta at Town Hall* (Vanguard #VRS-9103; 1961), and *One Grain of Sand* (Vanguard # VRS-9137; 1963) were two other successful albums. She continued performing into the 1980s, on television, stage, and in motion pictures.

O'DOWD RECORD (label). An American disc advertised in February 1922, featuring Irish material. It was obtainable from Thomas O'Dowd, 60 E. 129th St., New York. Artists included O'Dowd himself and James O'Neill. [Andrews*.]

OFFSET. (I) The slight inward slant of the mounting of the headshell on a phonograph pivoted tone arm. Its purpose is to minimize the angle of the stylus in the groove.

OFFSET. (II) In a CD system, the difference between access time and start time.

O'HARA, GEOFFREY, 1882–1967. Canadian/American tenor and composer, born in Chatham, Ontario, on 2 Feb 1882. He transferred to the U.S. in 1904 and became a citizen in 1922. O'Hara was highly versatile, appearing in minstrel shows and vaudeville, as well as operettas. He was also a church organist. He composed "Your Eyes Have Told Me," recorded by Enrico Caruso; and he sang American Indian songs. "K-K-K-Katy" was the most popular of his 300 songs. His first record was an Edison cylinder in 1905, "The Rosary" with the Knickerbocker Quintet (#9052). Then he sang for Zonophone in 1906–1907 as a member of the Criterion Quartet. He went to Victor in 1916. Victor #17635 (also on Edison Blue Amberol #2451) presented O'Hara in Indian songs with tom-tom accompaniment. His best-selling record was "They Made It Twice as Nice as Paradise and They Called It Dixieland" (Victor #18051; 1916). O'Hara died in St. Petersburg, Florida, on 31 Jan 1967. [Walsh 1960/2.]

OHIO PHONOGRAPH CO. One of the affiliates of the **North American Phonograph Co.**, situated at 220 Walnut St., Cincinnati, from 1890 to 1897. **James Andem**, a pioneer in the entertainment use of the phonograph, was president in 1890–1893. The firm was one that produced its own records, in addition to selling those from the parent company. Dan Kelly was a leading artist, maker of the "Pat Brady" series of records. In May 1897 the company was succeeded by the Edison Phonograph Co., with Andem as general manager. **Calvin Child** gained his early experience with the company.

OISEAU-LYRE (label). A French record, established at 122 rue de Grenelle, Paris, in 1933. Louise Dyer, an Australian, founded the company for the issue of early music. Printed scores and recordings (made at the Pathé studios) were offered. The catalog is a small one, but of great interest for music by lesser known composers. Interesting LPs were made by Christopher Hogwood and the Academy of Ancient Music. Among the CD releases (distributed by Polygram) are Carl Orff's *Carmina Burana* by the New London Consort (1990) and *Sylvan and Oceanic Delights of Posillipo; Italian Renais-* *sance Dances, Songs, and Instrumental Pieces* (1990). [Andrews*.]

OISTRAKH, DAVID, 1908–1974. Russian violinist, born in Odessa on 30 Sep 1908. He studied in Odessa and made his debut in Kiev, playing the Glazunov Concerto under the composer's baton. In 1928 he went to Moscow, and in 1934 was appointed to the faculty of the Moscow Conservatory. He won a major competition in Brussels in 1937, leading to appearances in European capitals and (1955) in the U.S. He died in Amsterdam on 24 Oct 1974. His son Igor also achieved international fame.

Oistrakh's recordings, with many great orchestras, span the concerto repertoire. Among the notable albums (reissued on CD) are those made with the Philadelphia Orchestra under Eugene Ormandy, including the Sibelius Concerto (Odyssey #Y-30489; 1961) and the Tchaikovsky Concerto (Odyssey #Y-30312). He also recorded a brilliant Brahms Concerto (Angel #S-36033; 1970) and Brahms Double Concerto with Mstislav Rostropovich (Angel #Y-36032; 1970), both with the Cleveland Orchestra under George Szell. Igor Oistrakh recorded several works with his father, including the J.S. Bach Concerto for Two Violins.

OKEH (label). An American record first produced by the Otto Heinemann Phonograph Supply Co., Inc., 25 W. 45th St., New York. Heinemann had resigned in December 1915 from his post as managing director of Carl Lindström AG, and set up this new firm; it had a factory in Elyria, Ohio, and an office in Chicago. In May 1916 he was selling talking machines with the tradename Vanophone. By October 1917 the company declared itself to be the world's largest manufacturer of talking machine supplies.

Okeh records were on sale in May 1918, 10-inch, vertical-cut discs for $.75 each. The label was written in various ways, commencing as "OkeH" then going to all capitals with the middle letters smaller. By 1921 the form was Okeh, with only the initial capitalized. "OKeh" is also seen. The name supposedly came from Otto Heinemann's initials combined with an Indian word meaning "It is so." Material on the label included outstanding jazz and blues items, and folk music of various nations. "Ja Da" (#1155) and "Ole Miss" (#1156), issued in 1919, are described by Rust as "the only genuine New Orleans jazz on records at that time other than the music of the Original Dixieland Jazz Band." Jimmy Durante led a group named the New Orleans Jazz Band. Mamie Smith made her first record for Okeh in 1920, "You Can't Keep a Good Man Down" (#4113), leading to the Okeh race series that started in 1921. Louis Armstrong's earliest discs under his own name were Okeh. Later there were great popular artists of all kinds, including Duke Ellington, Smith Ballew, and Vernon Dalhart.

A complete Okeh catalog appeared in October 1918. The price of records went up to $.85 by December 1918. During 1919 about 25 new records came out each month. Agents in London were appointed in April 1919, and Okeh records were sold there from 1920.

After 1 Oct 1919 the Heinemann company came to be known as the **General Phonograph Corp.**, with Heinemann as president and general manager. The first lateral-cut Okeh records were advertised in December 1919. The General Phonograph Corp. of Canada, Ltd., was organized in Toronto.

General announced in November 1920 that it had secured access to the recorded repertoire of Carl Lindström AG, including the catalogs of Beka, Dacapo, Favorite, Fonotipia, Lyrophon, Odeon, and Parlophone. These were to become the Okeh "Foreign Records" series. American Odeon Corp. issued its last two lists in November 1921, of Odeon and Fonotipia releases; from January 1922 General issued Odeon and Fonotipia with their label names.

Okeh material was used in Britain by the Parlophone Co., Ltd. from 1923. Some Okeh masters were used by Parlophone to press Ariel Grand Records for the mail order house of John G. Graves, Ltd.

A new "red label" record using the "Truetone process"—evidently electric—was announced in February 1926, and the word Truetone appeared on labels. Columbia Phonograph Co. acquired Okeh in October 1926 and Heinemann was made president of a new Columbia subsidiary, the Okeh Phonograph Corp. (25 W. 24th St. New York), in November 1926. Many label designs followed, in numer-

ous colors, but the same jazz and swing repertoire continued. From 1935 to 1940 there was no Okeh label, but then CBS revived the Columbia label and Columbia changed its old subsidiary Vocalion into a new Okeh. It carried pop, jazz, gospel, country, sacred, and rhythm and blues material.

Okeh remains in the CBS group, now owned by Sony. In Britain Parlophone has been the Okeh outlet. [Andrews*.]

OLCOTT, CHAUNCEY, 1860–1932. American composer and tenor, born in Buffalo, New York, on 21 July 1860. He was probably the most popular stage performer in Irish background plays and musical shows, and the most renowned Irish tenor of his day. He composed the songs "When Irish Eyes Are Smiling," "My Wild Irish Rose," and "Mother Machree," all of which became staples of the Irish song repertoire. Olcott recorded first for Columbia in June 1913, singing "My Wild Irish Rose" (#A1308). He also recorded his other compositions, and many other songs, until his last issues in March 1922. Olcott died on 18 Mar 1932 in Monte Carlo.

OLD DOMINION PHONOGRAPH CO. One of the **North American Phonograph Co.** affiliates, located in Roanoke, Virginia (Masonic Temple Building). It was established in 1890, with J.H. McGilvra as president. In June 1891 the firm had 142 **coin-op** machines leased to customers.

OLD GUARD BAND. A New York ensemble, one of the early instrumental groups to record. They were heard on Columbia two-minute cylinders in 1896, playing eight numbers. "Rastus on Parade March" was the first (#1801). Operatic medleys were performed also, from *Lohengrin*, *Prophète*, and *Tannhäuser*.

OLDEST PERSON TO RECORD. By this is meant the person with the earliest birthdate, not the person of most advanced age at the time of recording. The *Phonogram* reported that the manager of the Ohio Phonograph Co., Arthur Smith, had visited the home of Horatio Perry, a Cleveland centenarian, and made a record of his voice. Perry was born in 1790—so for a year he was a contemporary of Mozart. An even earlier birthdate is ascribed to one Peggy O'Leary, who sang an Irish melody into a phonograph in 1900; she was said to be 112 years old at the time, placing her birthdate in 1787 or 1788 (this was reported in *HN* #131, April 1983, by John S. Dales, who quoted a contemporary magazine account of the O'Leary rendition). Ms. O'Leary would almost surely be the earliest-born person to make a record. It seems that among professional singers, the earliest birthdate belongs to Peter Schram, a Danish baritone born in 1819. As reported in *Recorded Sound* 85 (January 1984) he made a private record in Copenhagen in 1889.

Among well-known persons to record (non-commercially), the oldest was Cardinal John Henry Newman (born 1801), who is known to have made a cylinder in the late 1880s (reported by Peter Martland in *HN* #131, April 1983).

The earliest born national leader to make a record was Lajos Kossuth (1802–1894) of Hungary. His address in Turin, Italy, on 20 Oct 1890, was recorded and a broken cylinder remains in the National Library in Budapest. Fragments of the speech are discernible. In 1977 a 45 rpm disc containing the fragment, plus the full speech read by an actor, was issued by Hungaroton.

On commercial recordings, the recording artist with the earliest birthdate seems to be J. G. Tollemache Sinclair, who did recitations for G & T, Columbia (in London) and for Odeon. His declamation of "La jeune fille mourante" (G & T #1333) dates from November 1906. His birth took place in Edinburgh on 11 Aug 1825. Josef Joachim (born 1831) seems to have been the instrumentalist with earliest birthdate to record commercially, for G & T. Gustave Walter and Charles Santley (both born 1834) were apparently the earliest-born singers on commercial discs, recording for G & T in the 1900s. Santley's rendition of "Non piu andrai" (G & T #05200; 1903) marked him as the earliest born singer to record an opera aria. Walter was the earliest born signer to record an aria in German: "Leb' wohl, Mignon" ("Adieu, Mignon") from *Mignon*; (G & T #3–42154; 1905). [Johnson, Colin, 1983.]

OLDEST RECORDS. The oldest known record in existence today is one made in 1878 by Augustus Stroh (inventor of the Stroh violin). Still on the mandrel of his machine, and never played, it was reported in *Sound Box*, November 1990, and *ARSC Journal* 22–1 (Spring 1991). Among extant records that have been played, the oldest may be an engraved metal cylinder made by Frank Lambert in 1878 or 1879. It was intended to be the sound track in a talking clock, and offers the hours: "One o'clock, two o'clock, three o'clock . . ." through twelve o'clock, with ten o'clock for some reason omitted. A very interesting account of the discovery and explication of this unusual artifact appears in Cramer 1992. Another venerable record is the white wax cylinder made by composer Arthur Sullivan, praising Thomas Edison for inventing the phonograph, but saying he shudders to think how much horrible music it will cause to be recorded. Jim Walsh (*Hobbies* April 1965) gives the date of that record as 5 Oct 1888.

Another group of cylinders from 1888 was reported to be at the Edison National Historic Site, West Orange, New Jersey, in 1988 (*NAG* #65, July 1988). It consists of 22 records, 21 in white wax, made by Colonel Gouraud in London, during August 1888. They include a whistling number by "Mrs. Shaw," a "letter from Col. Gouraud to Mr. Edison," three live recordings of a Handel Festival at the Crystal Palace, and an "organ solo played on the grand organ at Westminster Abbey by Prof. Bridge." There was no announced plan by officials at the Historic Site to play or reissue the cylinders, and it was not stated when (if ever) the records had been played in the past. [Cramer 1992.]

OLIVER, KING, 1885–1938. American jazz cornetist and band leader, born Joseph Oliver on a plantation near Abend, Louisiana, on 11 May 1885. He played in New Orleans brothels, and formed a group that became the Creole Jazz Band. In 1918 he moved to Chicago and in 1922 invited Louis Armstrong to join his Creoles. Historic recordings followed in 1923 (discussed in the article on Armstrong), showing Oliver at his peak, especially in two-cornet work with Armstrong. After Armstrong left in 1924, Oliver's group moved toward a smoother style, featuring Barney Bigard, Albert Nicholas, Kid Ory, and Omer Simeon. Fine recordings were made in 1926–1927 in Chicago, including "Someday, Sweetheart" (Vocalion #1059; 1926) and "Black Snake Blues" (Vocalion # 1112; 1927). The ensemble was then titled King Oliver and His Dixie Syncopators. A sophisticated sound developed in the next few years, in part because of the arrival of trombonist J.C. Higginbotham who replaced Kid Ory. "Speakeasy Blues" (Vocalion #1225; 1928) is a good example. Oliver recorded for Victor in 1929–1930, then for Brunswick and again for Vocalion (his final recordings) in 1931. Among several LP reissues, Coral #LRA 10020 is of interest for its 1929–1931 material. Oliver died in Savannah, Georgia, on 8 Apr 1938. [Allen, W. 1955.]

OLIVER, SY, 1910–1988. American trumpeter, arranger, and composer, born in Battle Creek, Michigan, on 17 Dec 1910. He played with various bands in his teens, and was with Jimmie Lunceford in 1933 as performer and arranger. Oliver's arrangements for Lunceford were outstanding, giving that ensemble a unique and sophisticated timbre. "The magical way in which Sy Oliver could blend harmony and instrumental color with his own unique brand of relaxed swing is shown to perfect effect on 'Dream of You' " (Schuller). Oliver arranged for Tommy Dorsey in 1939–1943, doing his most famous work ("Yes Indeed," "Opus No. 1," "Well, Git It," etc.). In a "dramatic overnight impact" (Schuller) he produced a jazz-based sound for Dorsey. Oliver was a music director and producer for Decca Records, breaking the color line in the music industry. He led his own band at times, notably in the late 1970s when he was installed at the Rainbow Room in New York. He also composed for Hollywood and for television programs. His death came on 27 May 1988 in New York.

OLYMPIC (label). An American record issued from April or May 1921 by the Olympic Disc Record Corp., a subsidiary of the **Remington Phonograph Corp.** Phil E. Remington was president of Olympic, J.S. Holmes was vice-president, Everett H. Holmes was treasurer, John Fletcher was secretary. Matrices and

equipment acquired from the Operaphone Co. formed the basis of the business, which was at 1666 Broadway, New York; there was also a recording studio in Brooklyn. Material included dance and popular vocal numbers, plus Hawaiian, operatic, and sacred items. Issues ceased after December 1921, when Remington and Olympic went bankrupt. A revival of the label took place in 1922–1923, by the Fletcher Record Co., Inc., of New York. John Fletcher—once vice president of Operaphone and secretary of Olympic Disc Record Corp.—and Harry Pace of the Pace Phonograph Co. were the men who formed that company, through purchase of the Olympic plant. The new company was located at 156 Meadow St., Long Island City. Pace was president of the Pace Phonograph Record Corp., from which **Black Swan** discs emanated. The Fletcher Co. pressed Black Swan records, and the two labels shared many of the same matrices (contrary to Black Swan's avowed intention of publishing records only by Black artists). The firm announced bankruptcy in December 1923.

The Capitol Roll and Record Co., Chicago, revived the label briefly in 1924. Matrices were brought from Long Island by John Fletcher. A production plant was located at 721 N. Kedzie Ave. One hundred selections were available in November 1924. [Andrews*; Kendziora 1986/ 4; Kunstadt 1987; Rust 1978.]

OLYMPIC RECORD (label). A British issue, not connected with the American Olympic label, registered as a trademark by the Sound Recording Co., Ltd., in 1912. Exclusive use of the label was taken by Levy's of Whitechapel, London, which enjoyed rights in the label even after the trademark passed to the Crystalate Manufacturing Co., Ltd., and then to the Crystalate Gramophone Record Manufacturing Co., Ltd. Masters came from Grammavox, Popular, and Imperial. Some Olympics had stuck-on labels over Grammavox and Popular labels. There were 10-inch and 10 1/4-inch sizes, double-faced. [Andrews*.]

ONEGIN, SIGRID, 1889–1943. Swedish contralto, born in Stockholm as Elizabeth Elfriede Emile Sigrid Onegin on 1 June 1889. She studied in Frankfurt, Munich, and Milan, and made her debut in recital (using the name Lily Hoffmann) in Wiesbaden on 10 Sep 1911. Her first operatic role was Carmen, in Stuttgart on 4 Oct 1912. She made her Metropolitan Opera debut as Amneris on 22 Nov 1922. In 1931 she retired to Switzerland, and died there on 16 June 1943, in Magliaso.

Onegin recorded for Polydor in Germany in 1921–1925, singing Carmen, Delilah, and several Verdi and Wagner roles, all in German. She was also recording a similar repertoire in English for Brunswick, in the U.S. During the electric era she was with Brunswick, Victor, and HMV. Among her outstanding discs are three *Carmen* numbers on Brunswick # 15128 and 50077 (1927), "Mon coeur s'ouvre à ta voix" in German (HMV #DB 1420; 1929), and "Ah! mon fils" from *Prophète* (HMV #DB 1190; 1929). These and several other arias are included on the Harmonia Mundi CD #89027; 1991). In a review of this disc, John B. Steane observed that "there is probably no more beautiful contralto voice on record than Onegin's" (*Gramophone*, February 1991). [Dennis 1950/10.]

O'NEILL, ARTHUR J., 1868–1916. American record industry executive, one of the founders of the **O'Neill-James Co.** of Chicago in 1904. He gained a U.S. patent (#874,985) for a talking machine with a three-inch diameter turntable spindle (filed 11 Apr 1907, granted 31 Dec 1907), and developed discs with large center holes to play on them. He also started another firm, **Aretino Co., Inc.,** then merged the two companies in 1910. He continued in the business until 1915, then became the first Pathé representative in Chicago, trading under the name of State Street Pathéphone Co. He died in Chicago in October 1916. [Fabrizio 1979; Koenigsberg 1990.]

O'NEILL-JAMES CO. A Chicago firm, established on 22 Apr 1904 by **Arthur J. O'Neill,** Winifred B. James, and Sherwin N. Bisbee. It dealt in various products, from an address at 185 Dearborn St., but soon came to specialize in talking machines and discs. Its record label was **Busy Bee,** the name taken from Bisbee's surname. A partner firm was set up in 1907, **Aretino Co., Inc.,** to trade in talking machines

of a sort invented by Arthur O'Neill, with a large spindle, manufactured by Columbia and by Hawthorne & Sheble. Indeed the spindle was large enough (three inches) to accommodate the various large-holed discs on sale (Standard and Diamond, 9/16 inch; Harmony, 3/4 inch; United, 1 1/2 inch), and even normal discs (with an adaptor ring). Thus the firm had a universal talking machine, and it was that product upon which attention became concentrated. But Victor forced Hawthorne & Sheble out of business in 1909, requiring Aretino to turn to Columbia for its machines and adding to the cost of operations. O'Neill merged his two firms, but was unable to stay in business beyond 1915. [Fabrizio 1979; Fabrizio 1980.]

ONE-STOP OUTLET. The name given to a record wholesaler who handles all labels.

OPEN LOOP GAIN. The added gain before feedback, required of an amplifier to compensate for negative feedback amplification loss.

Open reel tape. *See* REEL TO REEL TAPE.

OPERA DISC MUSICA (label). An unauthorized record, using Gramophone Co. masters that had been held by Deutsche Grammophon AG when the First World War broke out. After the war the records were issued in Germany until stopped by legal action. The Opera Disc Distributing Co., 25 W. 18th St., New York, issued in 1921 a 32-page catalog of about 1,000 items by about 500 star singers. Victor litigation put an end to the business in March 1923. [*Hobbies* lists the offerings, in 1943/4–5, 1944/3–4.]

OPERA RECORDINGS. This article is in two parts: (1) Single numbers; (2) Complete sets.

1. *Single numbers.* Before 1900 the cylinder manufacturers took three approaches to operatic material. They offered instrumental selections (overtures and arrangements of the vocal numbers), arias translated into English, and (occasionally) arias in their original languages. In most cases truncations were required to fit the numbers into the typical two-minute time of the brown wax cylinders. On 25 May 1889 Alfred Amrhein recorded a violin solo version

of the overture to *Fra diavolo* on a cylinder for Thomas Edison's North American Phonograph Co. A few days later, on 28 May 1889, cornetist John Mittauer performed "Rigoletto." Selections from *Faust* were recorded on 29 May 1889 by flutist C. Aug. Joepel and clarinetist Henry Giese. Similar performances followed, by various instrumentalists.

Among the first renditions by Issler's Orchestra was "Selection" from *Mikado*, made for Edison on 13 Nov 1889. A "Polka" from *Paul et Virginie* (by Victor Massé) was inscribed by the Fifth Regiment Band in an Edison session on 29 July 1891.

Nineteenth-century vocal cylinders by the major labels were few. Thomas Bott sang "Song of the Toreador" on Edison #353, announced in September 1898. Frank C. Stanley sang the "Armorer's Song" from Reginald De Koven's *Robin Hood* on a five-inch Concert cylinder for Edison (#B97; 1898). Bernard Bégué made 10 Columbia cylinders in 1898 and several Edison records ca. 1899. Henri Weber was active for Pathé in Paris from 1897, making at least 42 records by 1900. Fifteen of those cylinders were French opera arias.

The cylinders made by **Gianni Bettini** in New York in the late 1890s included an extensive selection of arias by recognized opera singers. Bettini's May 1897 catalog listed baritone numbers by Alberto de Bassini, from *Carmen*, *Nozze di Figaro*, *Traviata*, *Pagliacci*, *Rigoletto*, *Ballo in maschera*, *Favorite*, *Barbiere di Siviglia*, *Lucia di Lamermoor*, *Ernani*, and *Trovatore*. Soprano Gertrude Sylva had 12 arias listed in that catalog; contralto Carlotta Desvignes had three arias; tenor Dante del Papa had 19 arias. Other major voices included baritone Mario Ancona (four arias), bass Pol Plançon (two arias), soprano Rosalia Chalia (five arias), baritone Giuseppe Campanari (five arias), soprano Frances Saville (two arias), and soprano Marie Engle (one aria). Later American catalogs issued by Bettini (1898, 1899) offered more material by those artists, and a few new ones. The most interesting addition in the 1899 was baritone Anton van Rooy, the first Wagnerian singer to record. Soprano Marcella Sembrich appeared in the 1900 catalog.

When Bettini moved to Paris in 1901 he continued making opera cylinders (and discs

dubbed from them), engaging prominent artists from the Paris Opéra and Opéra-Comique. By that time there were also discs from the two firms that were to become the leaders of operatic recording, the Gramophone Co. in Britain and the Victor Talking Machine Co. (and its predecessors, Berliner Gramophone Co., and the Consolidated Talking Machine Co.).

Fred Gaisberg, as a young employee of Emile Berliner, heard tenor Ferruccio Giannini singing in Atlantic City, and brought him to the Berliner studio to record. The result was "La donna è mobile," apparently the earliest aria on disc (#967; 21 Jan 1896). Giannini made at least 21 other discs by 1899, and also recorded for Columbia, Victor, and Zonophone.

The Berliner, Gramophone, and Zonophone seven-inch discs made in Britain from August 1898 included various operatic items. The Hotel Cecil Orchestra played the *Trovatore* "Miserere" (#504; 2 Sep 1898) and the *Mignon* "Polonaise" (#513; 8 Sep 1898). James Norrie sang "Then You'll Remember Me" from *Bohemian Girl* (#2031; 8 Sep 1898), and Tom Bryce sang an English version of the "Drinking Song" (Brindisi) from *Cavalleria rusticana* (#2058; 22 Sep 1898). Montague Borwell sang the "Toreador Song" (#2080; 4 Oct 1898).

As a result of Fred Gaisberg's recruiting, G & T recorded the world's leading operatic artists. By the time of its February 1904 catalog, the firm was offering arias by such luminaries as Emma Albani, Suzanne Adams, Mattia Battistini, Emma Calvé, Enrico Caruso, Feodor Chaliapin, Giuseppe De Luca, Fernando De Lucia, Victor Maurel, Pol Plançon, Maurice Renaud, Mario Sammarco, Antonio Scotti, Francesco Tamagno, and Anton Van Rooy. Red Label records made by those artists were later available in America as Victor Red Seal records.

Victor's earliest opera recordings came before the firm was established, on the labels of the predecessor Eldridge Johnson firms. On 14 July 1900, Johnson's Improved Gramophone Record label recorded the Voss' First Regiment Band performing the *Zampa* overture; on 18 Oct 1900 violinist Charles D'Almaine playing the "Miserere." The first opera vocals on a Johnson label were made in June and July 1900. They were "Mephisto Serenade" from *Faust* and "Who Treads the Path of Duty" from *Magic Flute*, sung by George Broderick. Emilio de Gogorza, one of the most recorded baritones of the early years, sang the *Martha* Drinking Song in July 1900, and "Di provenza il mar" with "Dio possente" from *Faust* in October 1900.

The first female opera singers on the Johnson label were Marie Romaine, interpreting "Then You'll Remember Me" from *Bohemian Girl* (2 July 1900), and Rosalia Chalia, who sang three arias on 30 October 1900: "Ah fors è lui," Addio del passato," and "Una voce poco fa."

Victor began recording its counterpart to the Gramophone Red Labels in May 1903. They were the Red Seals, of which the first to represent opera were "Connais tu le pays?" and "Habanera" sung by Zélie de Lussan (#M-2188; 17 May 1903). The Red Seal catalog grew to encompass all the great names of the operatic universe. Victor's 1917 catalog included interpretations by the artists already mentioned, plus sopranos Frances Alda, Blanche Arral, Celestina Boninsegna, Lucrezia Bori, Emmy Destinn, Emma Eames, Geraldine Farrar, Johanna Gadski, Amelita Galli-Curci, Alma Gluck, Nellie Melba, Alice Nielsen, Adelina Patti, Marcella Sembrich, and Luisa Tetrazzini. Among the contraltos were Clara Butt, Julia Culp, Maria Galvany, Jeanne Gerville-Réache, Louise Homer, Margarete Matzenauer, and Ernestine Schumann-Heink. Tenors included Enrico Caruso, Edmond Clément, Hipolito Lazaro, Fernando de Lucia, Francesco Marconi, Riccardo Martin, Giovanni Martinelli, John McCormack, Leo Slezak, and Evan Williams. The principal baritones were Pasquale Amato, Emilio de Gogorza, Giuseppe de Luca, and Titta Ruffo. Marcel Journet was among the bass voices.

Through the acoustic era and the pre-LP electrical era, Victor and the Gramophone Co. (EMI from 1931) remained dominant in opera. The list of great singers recruited by 1940 is too long to give here; a few of the most important names only are mentioned. Sopranos: Kirsten Flagstad, Lotte Lehmann, Lily Pons, Rosa Ponselle, Elisabeth Rethberg, Bidú Sayão, and Helen Traubel. Mezzo-sopranos and contraltos: Gladys Swarthout, Kerstin Thorberg. Tenors: Jussi Björling, Beniamino Gigli, Giacomo Lauri-Volpi, Giovanni Martinelli, Lauritz Melchior, Aureliano Pertile, Tito Schipa. Baritones: Friedrich Schorr, Lawrence Tibbett, Leonard Warren. Basses: Alexander Kipnis, Ezio Pinza.

The Columbia Phonograph Co. also recruited noted singers, albeit never so many as Victor, and issued a catalog in spring 1903 of "Columbia Grand Opera Disc" records—that was the style of the labels. Those discs were made in New York in late 1902 or early 1903, and marketed the first time in March 1903. Artists in the series included Suzanne Adams, Antonio Scotti, Edouard de Reszke, Giuseppe Campanari, Marcella Sembrich, and Ernestine Schumann-Heink.

Edison Diamond Discs did not feature opera, but did include some fine recordings (from 1913) by Alessandro Bonci, Lucrezia Bori, Anna Case, Emmy Destinn, Charles Hackett, Frieda Hempel, Maria Labia, Giovanni Martinelli, Margarete Matzenauer, Claudia Muzio, Marie Narelle, Marie Rappold, Jacques Urlus, Alice Verlet, and Giovanni Zenatello.

With the introduction of the larger size discs, 10-inch (1901) and 12-inch discs (1903, with perhaps a few earlier), longer numbers were recorded and more complete versions of arias that had appeared in cut form were presented.

It is of interest that "star albums" were not made for individual singers during the 78 era. Victor did produce *Stars of the Metropolitan*, a two-volume set that included arias and duets by many of their famous artists. The LP brought a sudden profusion of new performers, and of individual albums for them. Among the outstanding names of the 1950s and 1960s were Carlo Bergonzi, Montserrat Caballé, Maria Callas, Franco Corelli, Mario del Monaco, Victoria de los Angeles, Giuseppe di Stefano, Placido Domingo, Dietrich Fischer-Dieskau, Mirella Freni, Nicolai Gedda, Nicolai Ghiaurov, Tito Gobbi, Marilyn Horne, Sena Jurinac, Alfredo Kraus, Erich Kunz, George London, Christa Ludwig, Cornell MacNeil, James McCracken, Robert Merrill, Sherill Milnes, Anna Moffo, Birgit Nilsson, Luciano Pavarotti, Jan Peerce, Leontyne Price, Elisabeth Schwarzkopf, Renata Scotto, Cesare Siepi, Beverly Sills, Giulietta Simionato, Joan

Sutherland, Renata Tebaldi, Giorgio Tozzi, Richard Tucker, Jon Vickers, Ljuba Welitsch, Wolfgang Windgassen, and Fritz Wunderlich. Victor no longer controlled the world opera scene, as the labels brought forward by the LP contracted many leading singers. Callas and Schwartzkopf, for example, were on Angel; Del Monaco, Pavarotti, Sutherland, and Tebaldi on London; Fischer-Dieskau on Deutsche Grammophon. Most of the LP artists had albums of their favorite arias.

The 1970s and 1980s saw the rise of such individuals as Thomas Allen, Agnes Baltsa, Kathleen Battle, Hildegard Behrens, José Carreras, Edita Gruberova, Siegfried Jerusalem, Tom Krause, Eva Martón, Kurt Moll, Jessye Norman, Leo Nucci, Elena Obraztsova, Lucia Popp, Herman Prey, Samuel Ramey, Katia Ricciarelli, Matti Salminen, Martti Talvela, Kiri Te Kanawa, and Frederica von Stade. In this group also, a variety of record labels are found.

There are separate entries in this Encyclopedia for many of the artists cited above.

2. *Complete sets.* One of the earliest efforts, perhaps the first, to record a substantial portion of an opera was an *Aida* on the Zonophone label (#12664/78, #24017, #24019/25) recorded in Milan in 1906 and 1907. The cast included no names of international stature: Teresa Chelotti and Elvira Magliuolo shared the role of Aida (the former participated only in Aida's two arias and the duet with Amonasro); Virginia Colombati (Amneris), Orazio Cosentino (Rhadames), Giovanni Novelli (Amonasro), Alfredo Brondi (Ramfis) are the other named participants. That this recording contained substantial cuts is revealed by the absence of the Preludio and by the limitation of both "Ritorna, vincitor" and "O cieli azzurri" to one side each. The chorus in the "Gloria all'Egitto" is identified as that of La Scala, an ascription not to be taken too literally, while the single orchestral excerpt, the "Marcia trionfale," is performed by what is called the Banda di Milano.

In 1907 there was also the more plausible choice (because of its brevity) of *Pagliacci* (G & T #54338/39, #052163/63, #052166/68, #053150, #054146/55) as a step in the direction of recording complete operas. This version had the marked advantage of Leoncavallo's per-

sonal supervision, although the conductor in charge was Carlo Sabajno. The cast for this effort included more notable singers than the *Aida* mentioned above: Giuseppina (Josefina) Huguet (Nedda), Antonio Paoli (Canio), Francesco Cigada (Tonio), Gaetano Pini-Corsi (Beppe), and Ernesto Badini (Silvio). The project had originally started out using the tenor Augusto Barbaini as Canio, but the five sides he recorded with the other cast members listed above were shortly re-made with Paoli. Because this attempt at a complete recording was not issued as a separately packaged set, it would be theoretically possible to compile some parts of it with alternate leading tenors.

After these first Italian efforts, endeavors began in Berlin from 1907 with Johann Strauss's *Fledermaus* (G & T #41971/74 (dialogue), #2–40543 (overture), #043074, #2–44213/22, #44624, #044059/61, #3–42789; 1907) on 21 sides, including four devoted to dialogue. The cast contained some popular local figures in this repertory: Emilie Herzog (Rosalinde), Marie Dietrich (Adele), Robert Philipp (Eisenstein), and Julius Lieban (doubling the roles of Alfred and Dr. Blind). The following year two French operas were recorded complete in German translations: *Carmen* (Gramophone Co. Pre-Dog #2–40829/31, #4–42181/82, #2–43199/201, #042180, #053109, #44690, #2–44464/74, #044093/104, #044505/06; 1908—36 sides) and *Faust* (Gramophone Co. Pre-Dog #4–42075/79, #2–43095/96, #040521/23, #042163/64, #043101/02, #2–44366/80, #044081/85; 1908—34 sides). These sets offer the fascination of Emmy Destinn months before her Metropolitan Opera debut in two roles (Carmen and Margarethe) which she never performed in the U.S. Her tenor partner in both works was Carl Jörn, who sang at the Metropolitan in 1909–1914. Other notable singers in these casts were Minnie Nast (who would create Sophie in *Rosenkavalier*) as Micaela, and Paul Knupfer as Mephistopheles. Besides the relative celebrity of the major participants, these sets have much to reveal about the German-language performing traditions of these two works in the first decade of the century (e.g., many high notes were added). The impetus of these German recordings led in 1909 to the first major attempt upon the Wagnerian repertory: the complete second act of *Tannhäuser* (Odeon #50699/710, #76125/26, #80046/48, #80051/53) in the Dresden version, performed by Anny Krull (in her only known recordings; she created the role of Elektra in the same year), the tenors Fritz Vogelstrom and Walter Kirchhoff (as Walter von der Vogelweide), the baritone Hermann Weil, and the American bass Leon Rains. Many years would elapse before a Wagnerian opera was preserved complete.

Even more enterprising than these German discs was a series of full-length operas undertaken by the French firm of Pathé Frères starting in 1912, carried out under the generic title of *Le théatre chez soi*. This collection would by 1923 include relatively complete recordings of *Romeo et Juliette* (Pathé #1501/27; 1912), *Rigoletto* (Pathé #1536/50; 1912), *Favorite* (Pathé #1551/71; 1912), *Galathée* (Pathé #1572/86; 1912) of Victor Massé, *Traviata* (Pathé #1587/1602; 1912), *Trouvère* [*Trovatore*] (Pathé #1603/21; 1912), *Faust* (Pathé #1622/49; 1912), *Carmen* (Pathé #1650/67; 1912), *Noces de Jeannette* (Pathé #1708/17; 1921) of Massé, and *Manon* (Pathé #1718/41; 1923). Although they are sonically unappealing, particularly the earlier sets, these contain much of interest.

Outside of France Donizetti's *Favorite* is almost always performed in an inaccurate Italian version. The work was originally written for the Opéra (2 Dec 1840) and remained on both Parisian and French provincial stages for more than 70 years. The Pathé *Favorite* preserves that performing tradition, as nearly as we have come to understand it today. The *Trouvère* sequence (36 sides) documents the version that Verdi arranged for the Paris Opéra in 1857, which contains some fascinating changes as well as an expanded ending to the final scene. *Traviata* presents us with the French adaptation made for the Théatre-Lyrique and introduced there in 1864 as *Violetta*, with the 21–year-old Christine Nilsson making her operatic debut, singing a French translation by Edouard Duprez, the brother of the famous tenor. *Romeo*, dating from 1912, comes from a time when the influence of Gounod still made itself felt only 19 years after his death. The two opéras-comiques of Massé, although they have disappeared from the international repertoire,

provide fascinating souvenirs of a performance style that would otherwise have disappeared.

Today, when anything approaching authentic French style is rarely to be encountered, this Pathé series offers much information to the serious student. The singers who participate in these performances are largely unfamiliar today, as relatively few appeared on other than French-language stages, but there are some notable examples of adroit, stylish singing to be found here. The *Romeo*, for instance, offers the 27–year old Yvonne Gall as Juliette, the robust tenor of Agustarello Affre as Romeo, the great Marcel Journet as Frère Laurent, Henri Albers as Capulet, Alexis Boyer as Mercutio, and even the veteran Hippolyte Belhomme in the small role of Gregorio. The *Manon* is Fanny Heldy, and the title role in *Noces de Jeannette* is sung by the much-recorded Ninon Vallin. The role of Pygmalion in the other Massé work was originally written for mezzo-soprano, but later adapted by the composer for bass; in this series that part is assigned to the sonorous voice of André Gresse, who also sings Mephisto in the *Faust* set. The firm foundation of this series is provided by two baritones: Henri Albers and Jean Noté; the former contributes an aristocratic Alphonse (*Favorite*), d'Orbel (i.e., Germont), and a vigorous Escamillo; the latter, Rigoletto, di Luna, and Valentin. The historical value of this series far outweighs its sonic deficiencies.

In Italy in 1916 and 1917 there appeared two *Rigolettos*, with traditional cuts and others as well, featuring two prominent baritones in their youthful heydays, Cesare Formichi on the earlier (Columbia #D16346/362; 1916) and Giuseppe Danise on the later (HMV #7–254023/34, #2–0252004/05, #2–0254014/28, #2–254511; 1917), but the casts are otherwise ordinary. Another complete *Rigoletto* (Phonotype #1566/67, #1592, #1777, #1795/96, and also #1795/take 3, #1875, #1883/87, #1910/23, #1929/36, #1939, #2299; 1918), most of which was recorded in Naples in 1918, but using some material from earlier sessions, features the 52 year-old Fernando De Lucia as the Duke, availing himself of convenient transpositions, and surrounded by a local cast. In the summer of that same 1918, De Lucia, who had made his debut in 1884, incised his Count Almaviva in a full-length *Barbiere* (Phonotype #1924, #1942/50, #1962/70, #1983/91, #1996/99, #2015, #2067/69, #2297/98, #2337, #2000/02; 1918) again with largely nondescript partners. These two De Lucia sets, idiosyncratic and uneven as they are, preserve in complete roles the highly individual art of one of the first generation of recorded singers and are of indubitable historic interest.

The immediate post-World War I acoustic era saw the major Italian companies returning to a limited number of complete sets. From 1918, there is a *Traviata* on 22 sides (HMV #5620/41; 1918); from 1919 another *Barbiere*, this one with Ernesto Badini as Figaro standing out from a generally lackluster entourage. In 1920 there was a single-cast *Aida* (HMV #S5150/80; 1920) from Voce del Padrone that superseded a 1912 version from Columbia (Columbia Zonophone #12664/678, #24017/25; 1912) that had been patched together with four Aidas while four mezzo-sopranos shared the role of Amneris, and two tenors sang Rhadames. Columbia issued an Italian *Carmen* (Columbia #D4620/43; 1920) with Fanny Anitua in the title role and Luigi Bolis as José. The first full-length Puccini recordings are another feature of this period: *Boheme* (HMV #S5056/78; 1918) and *Tosca* in two versions (Columbia (1918) and Voce del Padrone (HMV #S5701–24; 1920).

One other phenomenon of the later acoustic and early electric period deserves mention. This was a series of semi-complete operas in English. Among them is to be found the first recorded *Madama Butterfly* (HMV #D893/906), with British artists Rosina Buckman, Nellie Walker, Tudor Davies, and Frederick Ranalow in the leading parts, and Eugene Goossens at the musical helm. This tradition was carried on with an English *Pagliacci* (Columbia #4347/58; 1927) with Frank Mullings singing "On with the Motley," and a restrained *Cavalleria* (Columbia #5127/36; 1927). The most interesting one of this group is an abridged *Faust* (Columbia #DX 88–103; 1929–30), conducted by Thomas Beecham, with a cast headed by Miriam Licette and Heddle Nash.

That more complete sets were not made in the period 1918–1925 may be explained in part by the rumors of the improved electric recording method then under development. Certainly,

once the new technique became established, there was a rush both in Italy and France to replace older sets with modern ones and to explore some new territory. Both Columbia and Voce del Padrone produced rival sets of the standard works, and in the then more rarified field of the final Verdi, they divided the honors: Columbia with *Falstaff* (Columbia #GQX 10563/576; 1930) and Voce del Padrone producing *Otello* (HMV #S 10350/65; 1931). These sets reflect the performing practices of the period: e.g., the regulation cuts and traditional *oppure*. Unlike some recent complete recordings, they present seasoned (if not invariably pleasing) performers of their parts. Particular highpoints are the Rhadames (HMV #AW 23/41; 1928) and Manrico (HMV #AW 224/38; 1930) of Aureliano Pertile, the *Barbiere* Figaro (Columbia; #D 14565/79; 1929) and Rigoletto (Columbia; #GQX 10028/42; 1930) of Riccardo Stracciari, and the Tonio (Columbia QCX 10016/24; 1930) and Germont (Columbia #D 14479/93; 1928) of Carlo Galeffi. There are also agreeable surprises: the Azucena of Irene Minghini-Cattaneo, and the Count di Luna and Iago of Apollo Granforte.

In Italy this was not merely a period of recapitulating what had already been done. There was also the treasurable *Don Pasquale* (HMV #1410/24; 1932) which contains Tito Schipa's only complete, commercially recorded role, as Ernesto. Columbia was even more venturesome, producing *Gioconda* (Columbia #GQX 10600/18; 1928) with Giannina Arangi-Lombardi in the title role, and Boito's *Mefistofele* (Columbia #GQX 10619/35; 1932) with Nazzareno De Angelis as the devil and a youthful Mafalda Favero as Margherita. There is even a *Fedora* (Columbia #GQX 10496/506; 1931), blemished for some tastes by the damaged voice of Gilda Dalla Rizza in the title role, but redeemed from another point of view by being recorded when the *verismo* tradition still maintained some echoes of its original vitality.

The French studios were also active. From 1928 there is a *Carmen* (Columbia #9527/41; 1928) with an almost impeccable José from Georges Thill. From 1931 came the famous version of *Faust* (HMV #C2122/41; 1931), with Cesar Vezzani in the title role, the veteran Journet as Mephisto, Mirielle Berthon as Marguerite, and the eloquent Louis Musy as Valentin, conducted by Henri Busser. One of the finest recordings of any period is the complete *Werther* (Columbia; #LFX 151/65; 1933) that boasts Ninon Vallin and Thill in leading parts. More than a bit of memorable stylishness is to be found in *Manon* (Columbia #D 15156/73; 1932) with Germaine Feraldy as Manon and the poetic Rogatchewsky as Des Grieux. Besides these sets, there are some abridged versions of the same period that should not be overlooked; the *Mignon* (Columbia #CM-Op #19) from the Monnaie that preserves most of the mellifluous Wilhelm of André d'Arkor, and the *Louise* (Columbia #CM-Op 12; 1934), abridged by the composer, Gustave Charpentier, with Vallin and Thill. Far more enjoyable to listen to than the ground-breaking Pathé series of 20 years earlier, these sets as a whole are required listening for anyone wanting to understand the French style.

There was no comparable spurt of activity in German studios. Although there were a number of versions of highlights the sheer length of the Wagner operas made them a financial risk. Two important examples, however, deserve mention. One is the 1928 set of *Meistersinger* (IGI #298; 1928) from Berlin, with Leo Blech conducting and Friedrich Schorr as Hans Sachs. The other is the famous *Rosenkavalier* from Vienna (Victor #VM-196; 1933), presenting about two-thirds of the whole score. Lotte Lehmann was the Marschallin, Maria Olszewka was Octavian, Elisabeth Schumann was Sophie, and Richard Mayr was Ochs.

Nor should it be overlooked that in these years around 1930 from Bayreuth there appeared two historic recordings, the first festival recordings since the piano-accompanied excerpts from 1904. An abridged *Tristan* (Columbia #L2187/206) from 1928 contained only about half the score; it had an experienced Isolde in the rather impersonal Nanny Larsen-Todsen. It was followed by a nearly complete *Tannhäuser*, Paris version (Columbia #LFX 102/119; 1930). The first move toward a substantial recording of the *Ring* had been in England, with scenes from *Götterdämmerung* (HMV #D1572/87; 1928) sung in English. In a project divided between Berlin and London, with mixed casts and two conductors, about two-thirds of *Siegfried* was recorded (Victor #VM-83, 20 sides; #VM-161, 12 sides; #VM-167, eight sides; 1928–1933), dominated by Melchior's heroic Siegfried. A project to record *Walküre* (Victor #VM-298; 1935) began in Vienna in 1935, with Bruno Walter leading Lehmann, Melchior and Emanuel List. A healthy start was made on Act II (Victor #VM-582; 1937–38) by the same forces, but the Second World War intervened and the missing sections were filled in from Berlin. The war prevented the completion of the project from its original source, but U.S. Columbia produced Act III (Columbia #CBS 32260018E; 1945) with a vintage Metropolitan Opera cast (Helen Traubel as Brünnhilde, Herbert Janssen as Wotan, and Irene Jessner as Sieglinde), under Artur Rodzinski's leadership.

Probably the most significant and influential series of 78 rpm electric recordings of complete operas were the three Mozart recordings from the Glyndebourne Festival directed by Fritz Busch. That there were serious questions about the viability of such a project in mid-Depression is revealed by the form in which the first of them, the *Figaro* (HMV #DB 2474/79, #DB 2583/93, 1934) of 1934, was produced. It appeared in three volumes, one devoted to the larger ensembles, the other two containing arias and duets, but without any of the *recitativo secco*. Even without any sense of dramatic continuity, the music rather than the drab singing of it seemed like rain in mid-Sahara. The following year saw a *Così fan tutte* (Victor #VM-812/813/814; 1935) and the year after that a *Don Giovanni* (Victor #VM-423/424/425; 1936), both produced in correct sequence. It is no exaggeration to claim that these three recordings, plus Beecham's Berlin *Zauberflöte* (Victor #VM-541/542; 1937)—even without the dialogue—played a key part in preparing the ground for the general appreciation of Mozart's primacy as an opera composer.

Contemporary with these Mozart recordings, there were important recordings in Italy of Beniamino Gigli. He was heard in *Pagliacci* (HMV #DB 2229/307; 1934) in 1934, and Puccini's three masterworks (*Boheme* (HMV #DB 3448/60; 1938); *Tosca* (HMV #DB 3562/75; 1938); and *Madama Butterfly* (HMV #DB

3859/74; 1939). In the following year, he sang Turridu in the 50th anniversary *Cavalleria* (HMV #DB 3960/70; 1940), plus a Verdi *Requiem*, *Andrea Chenier* (HMV #DB 5423/35; 1940), and *Aida* (HMV #DB 6392/411; 1942). Finally there was a *Ballo in maschera* (HMV #DM 0100/16; 1943).

Cetra began its important series of full-length operas with the first recordings of *Norma* (1937) and *Turandot* (1938), both featuring Gina Cigna in the title roles. By that time the notion of recording operas with international celebrities was fairly established.

The LP record of 1948, and the change from acetate discs to magnetic tapes for the original recording media changed and simplified the process of recording complete operas. Cetra exploited the technological advances with a stream of firsts. Among them were *Sonnambula* with Lina Pagliughi, Ferruccio Tagliavini and Cesare Siepi; *Ernani, Nabucco, Forza del destino, Simon Boccanegra, Don Carlos, L'amico Fritz, Adriana Lecouvreur, Fanciulla del West*, and *L'amore dei tre re*. After recording a few sets for Cetra, Maria Callas was signed up by the company known in the U.S. as Angel, while London embarked upon a rival series starring Renata Tebaldi. The famous Toscanini series of opera broadcasts with the NBC Symphony from the 1940s was released by RCA in the 1950s. In the years since, there has been a proliferation of sets of an ever-widening repertory that extends from Jacopo Peri, Claudio Monteverdi, and Pier Cavalli to Benjamin Britten, Hans Werner Henze, and Karlheinz Stockhausen. The ever-widening range of available material is enriched by the choice between studio and live recordings, the latter promulgated by both commercial and private enterprises.

Now, in the CD period, a great deal of out-of-print material is emerging. VCR and the laserdisc are providing access to the visible aspects of opera. [Blyth 1979.] *See also* LA SCALA; METROPOLITAN OPERA CO.

William Ashbrook [section 2]

OPERAPHONE (label). An American vertical-cut (with some lateral cuts) record made by the Operaphone Manufacturing Corp., New York, in 1916 and 1917, then by the Operaphone Co., Inc., from April 1918 to December 1920. John Fletcher was the organizer and vice president of the firm, which was established in 1914. When the company filed for trademark registration, for the Operaphone name, on 13 Sep 1919, it was identified as the Operaphone Co., Inc., located at Creek and Meadow Streets in Queens, New York City. That application stated that the corporation had been using the trademark continuously since 1 Mar 1915.

The earliest advertisement for Operaphone records appeared in January 1916, announcing eight-inch double-sided discs, said to play as long as 12-inch discs, at $.35 each. At that time the company office was at 2 Rector St., New York. By April 1916 there were 144 titles available on 72 discs, and 12 new discs (24 selections) were being released each month. A different address was given, Fifth Ave. Building, Madison Square, New York City. There were 200 titles issued by September 1916, but advertising in *TMW* ceased after February 1917.

In April 1918 the label was again mentioned, as coming from the Operaphone Co., Inc., Creek and Meadow Streets, Long Island City, New York. By July 1918 there were 300 selections in the catalog. A series of 10-inch lateral-cut records was released from September 1919 to December 1920. Advertising in July 1920 gave the price per disc as $1. The repertoire at that time was popular vocal, dance, and light orchestral material; there were no opera numbers on Operaphone. Among the artists in 1920 were Sam Ash, the Harmonizers, Ernest Hare, Lewis James, Billy Jones, Billy Murray, Al Bernard, and the Orpheus Trio. Al Ofman's Dance Orchestra and the Novelty Dance Orchestra provided the dance items. "Music for Everybody" was the slogan seen on the record labels.

It was reported in March 1921 that the company was going to withdraw from the record field. The business was acquired by the **Remington Phonograph Corp.**, which reorganized it as the **Olympic Disc Record Co.** [Andrews*; Kunstadt 1986/4.]

OPTICAL RECORDING. (I) A system of recording sound on film through a photographic process. The sound signal activates a light valve, causing variations in the light that falls upon and exposes the film as it moves past the valve. The changes in density that result are analogs to the frequency and amplitude of the original signal. Playback is achieved by drawing the film between a photoelectric cell and a light source, producing a fluctuation that is converted back into sound. Because the fidelity of this kind of recording is inferior to that of other processes, magnetic recording is used on film sound tracks for improved reproduction. The idea of recording with light beams is an old one, traceable to the **Photophone** of 1879. *TMW* described such a process in May 1912. *See also* MOTION PICTURE SOUND RECORDING.

OPTICAL RECORDING. (II) In CD systems, optical recording has a wide application, meaning any kind of medium using laser light to convey data to or from the disc.

OPTICAL SOUND TRACK. On a motion picture film, the narrow band that carries a photographic record of sound. *See* OPTICAL RECORDING (I).

ORCHESTRA RECORDINGS. The history of orchestral recording is discussed here in five periods on the basis of the medium used to preserve sound:

1. Beginnings (1877)—the era of the two-minute cylinder and the five- to seven-inch disc;

2. No longer a toy (1901)—the period of the first "long-playing" records (from the 10-inch disc of 1901 to Edison's genuine LPs of 1926) and of the first multi-disc album sets of longer works;

3. The microphone (1925)—the period that saw the introduction of electrical recording bring the gramophone to something like maturity as a means for the transmission of serious music;

4. Tape and the rebirth of LP (1948)—the flowering of half a century of experiment that freed the record listener from "maddening interruptions [imposed] upon the continuity of an extended piece of music" (Sackville-West 1951);

5. The compact disc (1982).

1. *Beginnings.* Commercial recording of orchestral music began in the final decade of the 19th century, but little remains with which to document the earliest period, apart from lists and catalogues published by the fledgling companies then active. On the evidence of these paper survivals, selections seem to have been drawn from programmes of contemporary theatre and restaurant ensembles: dance music by the Strauss family and others, *morceaux de salon* and potpourris from current operettas, a repertoire of light classics that was to remain popular (and hence saleable) for the next 50 years.

Sound recording might have been "the wonder of the age," but it was still a carnival wonder, a toy dismissed by most musicians and music lovers. It was not until the turn of the century that the names of established orchestras (from St. Petersburg, Warsaw and New York) began to appear in catalogues. Of these, only one series was wholly devoted to music from the standard repertoire: the Leeds & Catlin cylinders of the "Metropolitan Opera House String Orchestra" under its concertmaster, Nahan Franko. These were made during the period of Lionel Mapleson's experiments with live recording of actual performances in the Metropolitan Opera House itself. Played on modern equipment, some orchestrals that have survived from this period can sound remarkably vivid; but acoustical reproduction could distort orchestral sound far more than did the initial acoustical recording process, and at the time technology agreed with public taste: despite occasional and short-lived exceptions, "orchestra" was synonymous with "wind band."

2. *No longer a toy.* Although the earliest technological advances had little immediate influence on the kind of music recorded, the development of records more durable, less cumbersome and with a longer playing time than the two-minute wax cylinder and the seven-inch disc laid the foundations for a gradual revolution. Up to 1898, the longest orchestral work to have been issued was a suite of dances from Edward German's incidental music for Shakespeare's *Henry VIII* (on three seven-inch Berliners, #570–X and #573/74). By 1903, the Victor Company had managed to get all three dances onto one 14-inch side, playing at 60 rpm (De Luxe #2036) and had attempted

Beethoven's *Egmont Overture* (De Luxe #2010). It was not until 1905 that a more ambitious project was undertaken: the recording of the entire Overture to Rossini's *William Tell*, by the Orchestra of La Scala, Milan (G & T #50516, #50500/02).

It was operatic celebrities, such as Mattia Battistini, Enrico Caruso, Feodor Chaliapin, Nellie Melba, and Adelina Patti, who brought artistic respectability and commercial viability to the recording industry; but it was operatic routiniers—reliable artists of less than stellar rank—who initiated the trend that was to establish the gramophone as transmitter of the musical culture of an age. Costly celebrities could be engaged only "to do star turns," isolated arias requiring only one record side (at most, two); but less expensive singers were available to exploit the appetite for more extensive operatic recordings whetted by the hearing of a single aria. By 1903 Gramophone and Typewriter had begun to assemble generous abridgements (10 to 15 sides) of popular Italian operas, all recorded by La Scala forces. Discs could always be purchased singly, but the abridgements were marketed as sets. In 1906 Handel's *Messiah* was issued in London on 25 single-sided discs; by 1907 when Leoncavallo's *Pagliacci* (supervised by the composer) appeared in Milan on 21 sides and Lehár's *Lustige Witwe* in Berlin on 32 sides, such sets of compositions presented as "complete" and in their own albums were becoming a gramophonic commonplace. (*See* OPERA RECORDINGS, 2.)

The immediate result of these operatic ventures was the publication, beginning in 1905, of the first musically significant recordings of orchestral music. The Scala Symphony Orchestra, playing under Carlo Sabajno, the conductor who usually led them in operatic accompaniments, demonstrated that recordings could provide a passable echo of what was to be heard in the theatre and the concert hall—even of music by Wagner and Richard Strauss. What Caruso's 1902 series had done to encourage the finest voices of the day to appear before the recording horn, these La Scala performances seem to have accomplished (on a far more modest scale) for the orchestra.

In 1907, the Gramophone Co. in Paris issued a group of Emil Waldteufel's waltzes conducted by the composer and Pathé Frères recorded Edouard Colonne and his orchestra (so well that the discs were still available 15 years after the conductor's death). The next year, Odeon published records conducted by Léon Jéhin in Monte Carlo. By the end of 1909, Victor Herbert's Orchestra had begun to appear on Edison cylinders (the orchestra, possibly conducted by Herbert, had made Victor records in 1903, the year of its formation, and returned to Victor in 1911). **Landon Ronald,** with the New Symphony Orchestra he had just been appointed to conduct, began their uniquely important association with the gramophone with two movements from the Grieg Concerto; the soloist was Wilhelm Backhaus (Gramophone Co. #05523/24, December 1909); and the International Talking Machine Company (Odeon) had made history by issuing Tchaikovsky's *Nutcracker Suite*, the first extended work recorded by an orchestra (the London Palace [Theatre] Orchestra, under Herman Finck) and presented in an album (#0475/78, April 1909). A year later, Mendelssohn's music for *Midsummer Night's Dream* was issued under the same auspices and in the same format (#0641/44). And by the autumn of 1911 (two and one-half years before Arthur Nikisch's more famous recording appeared in February, 1914 [HMV #040784/91]), the "Grosses Odeon-Streichorchester" could be heard playing Beethoven's Fifth Symphony (#XX76147/53). Within two years, Beethoven's Sixth Symphony (#XX76292/301), Haydn's "Surprise Symphony" (#XX76312/17) and the 39th and 40th symphonies of Mozart (#XX76331/36, #XX76325/30) could all be had, anonymously conducted but complete, on Odeon records.

From this point onward, hardly a month was to pass without the announcement in London or Berlin of a first recording of a standard orchestral work. Riga and St. Petersburg supplemented those vocal offerings with orchestral music by Russian composers—years (in some cases, decades) before any of these works appeared in Western lists. Many performances were truncated and most were rescored. Except in Germany, a market for long orchestral works occupying several discs was slow to develop; even the attempts made to lengthen the playing time of record sides (such as the short-lived experiments sponsored in the U.K. by the National Gramophone Company in 1912–1915 (see MARATHON RECORD), and World Records, 1922–1923) proved unsuccessful. And the acoustical process could accommodate an orchestra only with difficulty:

> since the distal diameter of the [recording] horns was limited, a wide arc of players was impossible, so there was inevitable overcrowding towards the centre of the horn face. . . . Low frequencies from stringed instruments and those of soft attack—such as the bass drum at anything less than fortissimo—were particularly difficult [to record, as were] large numbers of middle and upper strings. . . . Cellos and basses might be [replaced by] bassoons, perhaps supported by one cello. . . . No more than half-a-dozen violins would be needed . . . boosted by a couple of Stroh violins, and the violas [could be] replaced by the Stroh viola and a clarinet or two. . . . The woodwind—particularly the oboes—would be pressed up behind the strings seated immediately before the recording horns while the bass sounding instruments would often be beneath these horns and facing the strings. . . . Mirrors [provided] the only means of their seeing the conductor placed high above and behind them. Similarly the orchestral horns were elevated further back with the rest of the brass, perhaps five or six feet above the rest of the players but, since their bells point behind them, they had to face away from the recording horns so that their bells were directed at those horns. Here came into operation another set of mirrors so that they too could see the conductor (Melville-Mason 1977).

The small size of recording orchestras (50 players constituted a large band; most records were made with half that number), the readiness of gramophone companies to employ "house conductors" and sponsor "house orchestras" (composed of musicians experienced in coping with the intricacies of the recording process), the reedy, brassy characteristic of many records made acoustically—all these are clarified by the foregoing quotation. What remains astonishing in the light of it is the fact that nearly all of the major orchestras and conductors of reputation active in Germany, the U.K. and the U.S. in the period from 1910 to 1925 did in fact make records.

The contribution of American companies was primarily technological; recordings made in the U.S., especially from 1916 on, were often characterized by excellent sound (the Columbias full and resonant, the Victors and Brunswicks admirable in detail). There were some abbreviated firsts in the U.S.: Columbia's Schubert "Unfinished Symphony" (Prince's Symphony Orchestra [#A5267, April 1911]); and a Victor series: two symphonies by the Victor Concert Orchestra (Haydn's "Military Symphony" [#35311; April 1913 and #35520; May 1916] and Mozart's "Jupiter Symphony" ([#17707 and #35430; March-April 1915) and two works of Bach: the Double Concerto (Fritz Kreisler and Efrem Zimbalist (#76028/30, March 1915) and the Suite No. 3 (Josef Pasternack and the Victor Concert Orchestra (#35656, #35669; November-December 1917). But only four extended works were recorded complete in the U.S. during the acoustic period, all by Victor: Beethoven's Symphony No. 5, with Josef Pasternack and the Victor Concert Orchestra (#18124, October 1916; #35580, November 1916; #18278, September 1917; #35637, October 1917), Liszt's *Les préludes* with Willem Mengelberg and the New York Philharmonic (#74780/82 and #66131; January-April 1923), Schubert's "Unfinished" and Stravinsky's *Firebird Suite* with Leopold Stokowski and the Philadelphia Orchestra (#6459/61, December 1924; and #6492/93, February 1925). Stokowski's first attempt to record Rachmaninoff's Concerto No. 2 with the composer as soloist was not satisfactory, and only two movements were published (#8064/66; May 1924). Apart from these (and Columbia's ground-breaking series with Modest Altschuler's Russian Symphony Orchestra,

1911–1912), most American recordings merely introduced to trans-Atlantic listeners short works and fragments already available in Europe.

What was accomplished in Europe, especially after 1916, was remarkable: Bach's *Brandenburg Concerto No. 3*, the keyboard Concerto in D Minor, BWV 1052; the solo Violin Concerto in E Major, BWV 1042; the Double Concerto and the second orchestral suite; all of the symphonies of Beethoven (in 36 different sets, nine of them devoted to the Fifth), the Violin Concerto and four of the five piano concerti; Berlioz' *Symphonie fantastique*; the first and second symphonies of Brahms; Bruch's Violin Concerto No. 1; Bruckner's Seventh Symphony; Dvořák's *New World*; most of the major orchestral works of Edward Elgar, conducted by the composer; Franck's Symphony in D Minor and the *Variations symphoniques*; four symphonies of Haydn (nos. 45, 88, 92 and 94); *The Planets* of Gustav Holst; Lalo's *Symphonie espagnole*; three symphonic poems, the Hungarian Fantasy and both the piano concerti of Liszt; Mahler's "Resurrection Symphony"; the Violin Concerto, first Piano Concerto and the "Italian Symphony" of Mendelssohn; three violin concerti (K. 216, K. 218, K. 219), two serenades (K. 375, K. 388) and three symphonies (K. 543, K. 550, K. 551) of Mozart; Ravel's *Ma mère l'oye* and *Tombeau de Couperin*; Rimsky-Korsakov's *Capriccio espagnole*, *Russian Easter Overture*, *Scheherazade*, and the suite from his *Golden Cockerel*; Saint-Saens' *Carnival of the Animals*; and Schubert's "Unfinished" (in a total of 17 recordings, eight of them complete, with Stokowski's American set making a ninth). There were also issues of Schumann's Piano Concerto and three of his four symphonies; Scriabin's *Poem of Ecstasy*, Smetana's *Moldau*; nine tone poems of Richard Strauss (of which only *Also sprach Zarathustra* was abbreviated); Stravinsky's *Petrushka* and two versions of his *Firebird Suite* in addition to Stokowski's; and Tchaikovsky's *Francesca da Rimini*, first Piano Concerto and fifth and sixth symphonies (the Violin Concerto was recorded but remained unpublished). The preludes and orchestral interludes from Wagner's music dramas appeared, together with his *Siegfried Idyll* (two recordings of the original version for chamber orchestra and six of the version for large orchestra).

Many of these works (and more than this partial list suggests) were available in a number of alternative versions, and many of the most important sets date from the years immediately preceding the introduction of electrical recording. That momentous development did not enforce radically new decisions about what to record but rather confirmed decisions already made.

3. *The Microphone.* The first electrical orchestral records were issued in the United States in July, 1925 (Columbia #50014–D and Victor #6505); the first such issue in Europe (August 1925) was also an American recording (HMV #C1210, an experimental Victor published only in the U.K.). By the following October, The Gramophone Co. was able to issue selections from *La boutique fantasque* (#D1018), an electrical remake of a record (#D572) issued exactly four years earlier. In December HMV #D1037/41 appeared: Tchaikovsky's Symphony No. 4, a work never before issued in complete form, and the first electrical recording of a symphony to be published. In March 1926 Columbia announced Berlioz's *Symphonie fantastique* conducted by Felix Weingartner, a work that Weingartner had already recorded acoustically for Columbia (unpublished) and which had only recently become available in complete (but acoustical) versions conducted by Rhené-Baton (HMV #W608/13; April 1925) and Frieder Weissmann (Parlophon #P1934/39; May 1925), and the slightly abridged version by Oskar Fried (Polydor #69808/11; September 1925).

Fried's recording was reissued, with the missing movement supplied (Polydor #66356/60), four months after the Weingartner set went on sale, for during this transitional period acoustical recordings continued to be issued side-by-side with the electricals: Alfred Hertz's *Fra diavolo* overture (Victor #6506; July 1925) with Stokowski's *Danse macabre* (#6505); Elgar's first recording of his Symphony No. 2 (HMV #D1012/17; September 1925) with the first electricals by Vladimir de Pachmann (HMV# DB861) and Albert Coates (HMV# E397); Dan Godfrey's set of the Vaughan Williams *London Symphony* (Columbia #1717/22; April 1926) a month after Weingartner's *Symphonie fantastique* (#L1708/13); Oskar Fried's first electrical *Eine kleine Nachtmusik* (Polydor #69826/27; January 1926) two months before Hans Pfitzner's acoustical version of Schumann's Symphony No. 2 (#69828/32).

The foregoing survey encapsulates roughly the first decade of the "age of the microphone." Some "old process" recordings intended for publication remained in the vaults while others continued to be issued until the end of 1926, only to yield to "new process" replacements as these became available. In the case of the Tchaikovsky Piano Concerto, this happened only seven months after the initial acoustical issue; Bruckner's Symphony No. 7 had to wait four years. By the time new versions had been prepared of Mahler's "Resurrection Symphony" (1935), Strauss's *Also sprach Zarathustra* (1935), *Alpine Symphony* (1941), and *Macbeth* (1950), the acoustical sets had long since disappeared.

Initial reaction to the new technology was mixed. An early review could praise one disc for reproducing "the different tone colours . . . with astonishing truth" while dismissing another for its "coarse and distorted" tone despite its great volume and "very clear" definition (H. Wild, in *Sound Wave*, November 1925). But the ultimate verdict was expressed by Ernest Newman:

> It is now [1926] possible, by virtue of the new methods of recording that have come into use, for the gramophone listener to get the thrill of the real thing as he knows it in the concert-room. . . . At last an orchestra really sounds like an orchestra. Those records bring with them the very blood and nerves of the orchestra and the theatre (quoted by Lawrence Gilman in his "Foreword" to Darrell 1936).

Such statements could be made because the microphone had freed the recording process from the constraints of half a century and enabled it to be undertaken in the theatre and concert room, capturing the sound of an orchestra playing with its full complement music as scored by the composer.

One of the more significant consequences of this liberation was the virtual disappearance of the "house orchestra" and "house conductor" except for the recording of "light music." The first decades of the century saw the emergence of the "star" conductor; now technology enabled record producers to offer the Maestro the kind of prominence they had previously accorded the Diva. Many names already familiar continued to appear in the catalogues—Leo Blech, Adrian Boult, Albert Coates, Hamilton Harty, Alfred Hertz, Landon Ronald, Frederick Stock, Frieder Weissman, Henry Wood—but the new age belonged to Thomas Beecham, Wilhelm Furtwängler, Serge Koussevitzky, Willem Mengelberg, Stokowski, Arturo Toscanini, Bruno Walter, and Weingartner, to whom the most important projects were committed. All (save Furtwängler and Koussevitzky) had recorded before; but it was the microphone (more through discs, arguably, than through radio broadcasting) that gave more flattering display to their talents, made them international celebrities, and established their performances as formative for the taste of an international audience.

The presence of some of them (Koussevitzky, Stokowski and Toscanini, primarily, supervising orchestras of unsurpassed technical proficiency) helped the United States emerge as an important source of recordings, even before the outbreak of war in 1939—the event which forced the American market, largely supplied from Europe in the lean years after 1930, to depend on domestic sources.

This wholesale involvement of celebrities produced an expansion of repertoire at once vast and restricted. The gramophone became a close monitor of the careers of the great as virtually every work they performed in public concerts found its way onto discs. Multiple versions of the classics from Beethoven onwards came to abound as younger artists established themselves and technological advances rendered earlier recordings obsolete. Some of the "new music" was recorded as it began to find an audience; Stravinsky and Hindemith were invited to join Elgar and Richard Strauss in conducting their own music; a society was formed (by the Gramophone Co.) to issue the works of Sibelius by subscription after the Finnish government sponsored recordings of his first two symphonies; in

Beecham Frederick Delius found a champion, as did Prokofiev in Koussevitzky and Shostakovich in Stokowski.

Yet among composers before 1800, only Bach, Handel and Haydn were even comparatively well represented in catalogues, and only Mozart could boast a discography that included most of his major works. Twentieth-century composers suffered from a similarly selective representation. Undoubtedly these omissions would have been supplied in time; but until the middle 1940s, the large, established companies (Deutsche Grammophon, and EMI with its American affiliates) tended to give only cursory attention to works of any period which lay outside the main stream of concert programming, and for which there was no assured market. Apart from subscription issues of the kind already mentioned (*see* SOCIETY RECORDS), it was left to small companies (the National Gramophonic Society and Decca in the U.K., Éditions de l'Oiseau-Lyre in France, and to a lesser extent Musicraft in the U.S.) to record material deemed more esoteric.

Then in the midst of the postwar revival, a technological innovation as dramatic as the microphone intervened to transform the medium.

4. Tape and the rebirth of LP. Although "longplaying" discs were used successfully as early as 1926 to provide sound for motion pictures and for radio broadcasting, Thomas Edison's attempts to introduce the record-buying public to the microgroove LP in 1926 failed as did RCA Victor's 33–1/3 rpm "program transcriptions" in 1931. (*See* LONG PLAYING RECORDS.) However, the microgroove record that American Columbia introduced in June, 1948—a time of prosperity and unprecedented interest in recordings—was greatly successful. In many cases the LPs even sounded better than the 78s which they were intended to supersede:

Columbia's LPs were not obvious patchups from noisy four-minute shellac pressings. Many years before, in anticipation of LP, the Columbia engineers had started recording a duplicate set of masters at each session in large acetate transcription blanks; by 1948 there existed a valuable backlog of high-quality, noisefree recordings readily transferable to LP(Gelatt 1955).

Each company had its own backlog; and as one after another they committed themselves to the new medium (Decca/London and Vox in 1949, RCA Victor in 1950, EMI in 1952), a significant portion of the post-war orchestral catalogue was transferred to LP.

Stereophonic recording, introduced in the middle 1950s, gradually drove virtually all monophonic issues into the cut-out bin or onto budget status, a category that some companies (notably CBS, Deutsche Grammophon, EMI, and RCA) augmented with transcriptions of much earlier material. Thus pre-war recordings by Furtwängler, Hamilton Harty, Koussevitzky, Mengelberg, Frederick Stock, Stokowski, Toscanini, Bruno Walter, and Weingartner all returned to circulation during the 1950s and 1960s. While many of these restorations were sonic failures, some gave "new bloom" (in that favourite phrase of the critics) to what had seemed still saleable but faded performances. Interest in historical reissues began to spread from the legacies of famous singers to include the orchestra, especially when a composer's own interpretation (or that of an eminent soloist in a concerto) could be rescued; and so Elgar, Holst, and Richard Strauss all reappeared to join the company of Pablo Casals, Emanuel Feuermann, Jascha Heifetz, Bronislaw Hubermann, Fritz Kreisler, Rachmaninoff, Albert Sammons, and Joseph Szigeti. By the end of the 1960s, improvements in sound reproduction had drawn engineers to experiment with pre-electrical recordings; composers again (Elgar, German, and Stanford), conductors (Beecham, Fried, Otto Klemperer, Nikisch, and Toscanini); and a concerto performance of outstanding merit (Kreisler and Eugene Goossens in a previously unpublished version of Bruch's Opus 26). When the centenary of Edison's phonograph was celebrated in 1977, the gramophone could claim to have presented to contemporary listeners the broad spectrum of its own past.

Of far greater significance, however, was the attention that could then be paid to the present, and to the past before the 19th century in which sound recording began. The expansion of repertoire on electrical 78s, which had seemed "vast" when compared with the products of the acoustical era, was dwarfed by the LP explosion. Integral recordings of the symphonies of Bruckner and Mahler became more numerous than integral recordings of the Beethoven symphonies had been on 78s; and the Beethoven cycle threatened to become a test piece for every ambitious conductor to record and re-record. By the 1970s one could expect to find the works of most of the major composers since the time of Bach available in complete or nearly complete editions. In addition, the widest conceivable variety of new music was being committed to discs, together with works unheard for centuries. The musical culture of the 19th century was ceasing to be the centre of interest; and the deaths of Furtwängler (1954), Toscanini (1957), Beecham (1961) and Walter (1963) marked the passing of an era that ended with the autumnal careers of Otto Klemperer and Adrian Boult. None of the new generation of conductors—not even Von Karajan or Leonard Bernstein—won the esteem accorded their predecessors.

Paradoxically, the very technology that enabled recordings to do something like justice to gargantuan forces under the control of a virtuoso conductor was helping to bring the "age of the conductor" to a close. That technology was at the same time changing the relation between recordings and music heard in public concerts. The substitution of one late 19th-century invention for another in the initial recording process—magnetised tape for wax blanks—meant that wherever music could be played and heard, recordings of it could be made. This simplification, felt especially in the preservation of live performances, meant also that works known only to musicologists and accessible only to a specialised audience could be modestly profitable ventures for even a small company to sponsor. Baroque music, whether performed on modern or "authentic" instruments, owed much of its popularity to the gramophone.

The use of tape also made it possible to edit recorded material, eliminating passages imperfectly registered and splicing in improvements. What ultimately emerged from the loudspeakers might thus be an amalgam of several different performances, one more perfect than any of its sources. Although misgivings eventually prompted experiments with direct to disc recording and digital computerization, the fact remained that recordings had become (and would remain), not an echo of the public concert, but medium of musical communication quite distinct.

5. *The compact disc.* The reappearance of the single-sided disc approximately five inches in diameter indicates how far sound recording has come in a century. Playing time has been extended from just over 90 seconds to just under 90 minutes; the full audible range has been captured and, through computer technology, extraneous noise has been eliminated. The weakest link in the recording chain, the needle connecting disc to play-back unit, has been replaced by a laser beam promising absolutely faithful, wear-free reproduction. The LP with its turntable has joined the 78 with its gramophone and the cylinder with its phonograph in the museum of the outmoded.

While the CD revolution has followed the pattern of the earlier microphone and LP revolutions, during its first decade it has proved itself less adventurous than either of its predecessors. As in the late 1920s, an entire catalogue has been replaced; and as in the early 1950s, much of this has been done by transferring previously available performances to the new format. But the extraordinary achievements of the period from 1950 to 1985 have left little in the orchestral repertoire for CD to explore that LP had not already mapped. History has been served, however, in some important releases of unpublished material from company archives and radio broadcasts. [Darrell 1936; Gelatt 1977; Melville-Mason 1977.] *See also* entries for the individual conductors and orchestras mentioned.

Claude G. Arnold

ORCHESTRELLE CO., LTD. A British firm established 1 July 1912, superseding the London branch of the American firm Orchestrelle Co. It took control of several other companies that had been subsidiaries of the American firm. It was the business of the Orchestrelle companies to market musical instruments, including Aeolian organs, pianos, pianolas, harps, etc., and piano rolls. In 1915 the company advertised the new Aeolian Vocalion talking machine, with the innovative **Graduola** control; possibly the machines were assembled in Britain from American components. Musola and Phoneto record labels were introduced in October 1916, and exported to Australia by Orchestrelle Co., Ltd. The firm opened its own recording laboratories in February 1917. Later that year the **Aeolian Co., Ltd.**, absorbed Orchestrelle. *See also* AEOLIAN CO. [Andrews 1980/10.]

ORCHESTROPE. A **coin-op** disc player made by the **Capehart Co.** in 1928. It offered 56 titles, but was not selective.

ORGAN RECORDINGS. Until the introduction of electrical recording in the mid-1920s there was very little recording of the solo pipe organ. The earliest known is a cylinder made by Colonel Gouraud at Westminster Abbey in 1888 (*see* OLDEST RECORDS), the organist being "Prof. Bridge." There was organ accompaniment for a series of 15 sacred songs on Columbia two-minute cylinders made in early 1901. S. C. Porter was the singer, but the organist is not named. The first of the series was "Nearer My God, to Thee" (#31356). Apparently the earliest solo organ record was an Edison cylinder of August 1909, Albert Benzler playing "Abide with Me" (#10180).

J. J. McClellan was recorded at the Salt Lake City (Utah) Mormon Tabernacle organ by Columbia in 1911, both as soloist and accompanying a violinist. In 1912–1913 Welte-Mignon made organ rolls in Freiburg, Germany, including 20 compositions of organist Eugène Gigout and his contemporaries; these were released on two LP records by Fulton Productions of Tulare, California (#UF-4 and #UF-5). In 1913 Easthope Martin, the composer, recorded on a grand organ at least 10 sides for HMV.

The 1917 Victor catalog announced that efforts to record the organ had "met with little success until the recent series of experiments by the Victor"; but only one disc was offered, #35547, presenting the Chopin "Funeral March" played by Richard K. Biggs, and the

"Hallelujah Chorus" played by Reginald L. McAll, both on an Estey pipe organ. The 1922 catalog carried the same lone example of the King of Instruments, and even the 1927 catalog had just one organ disc, albeit a different one.

Before World War I Pathé, in England, had installed an instrument from the Positive Organ Co. and recorded it with Reginald Goss Custard, organist of St. Margaret's in Westminster. William Ditcham and F. R. Kinkee also recorded organ solos before the War. Albert W. Ketelbey performed solo items for Columbia in 1909, and Omar Letorey of Paris recorded for Odeon well before 1914.

Electrical recording involved the organ from its inception. The first electric to be released was Columbia Graphophone's live inscription of the Westminster Abbey ceremony in November 1920, engineered by H.O. Merriman and Lionel Guest. When Autograph initiated commercial electrics in Chicago, in 1924, organ music was a specialty. Milton Charles and Jesse Crawford performed on instruments in two Chicago movie houses. In the succeeding decade a considerable assemblage of organ recordings was issued in America and Britain, and the problem became less technical and more one of repertoire. A writer in *Gramophone* of August 1932 grumbled that "a glance at the bulky but heterogeneous lists of organ records shows clearly that instead of a coherent and carefully planned repertoire of legitimate organ music, a mere jumble of assorted musical confectionery has come, bit by bit, into being." He noted the lack of recording of major composers like Rheinberger and Vierne, and even English composers like Parry and Stanford. Vierne had in fact recorded some of his pieces, at Notre Dame in December 1928, but for Odeon (#166149 and #171074), presumably not available yet in the U.K.

It was in the 1930s that the organ took its rightful place among other instruments on record. Charles Widor recorded his own works in 1932 at St. Sulpice (HMV # DB4856). Performers like Marcel Dupré (nine titles in the 1938 Victor catalog, most of them by J. S. Bach), Albert Schweitzer (one Bach Prelude and Fugue in the Victor 1938 catalog, and four albums for Columbia by 1943), Alfred Sittard, and Mark Andrews—the most recorded artist in the 1938

Victor list, with 33 items, mostly hymns—began to make up for the long neglect of the organ by the record companies. There were 24 "grand organists" listed in the HMV catalog for 1937–1938; four in the Columbia catalog, eight in the Parlophone catalog, and five in the 1941 Decca catalog; not to mention numerous theatre organists on all labels.

Nevertheless it was a slow march. David Hall wrote in the 1942 edition of *The Record Book* that "prior to 1937 . . . there was not an organ recording in the domestic catalogues worth having." He mentioned the twin technical challenges: the need to make records in vast echoing churches, and the trouble with capturing the sweeping dynamic range of the instruments without distortion. For example, fine performances of Albert Schweitzer were "badly over-amplified, resulting in tremendous tonal blurs." But the young Musicraft label began in 1937 to get good technical results, and they had the outstanding organist Carl Weinrich. Then Technichord recorded E. Power Biggs on the baroque organ in Harvard's Germanic Museum, with splendid success. Use of smaller instruments was rare in this period however, which preferred the grand organs of great churches.

The LP introduced a complete change in the types of music recorded and the styles of instruments used. Small tracker-action instruments became popular, and sometimes the record jackets gave their actual specifications and lists of the stops used in the performance. Chorale preludes, hitherto conspicuously absent, suddenly became important. Recording techniques advanced to permit even the loudest passages to be recognizably recorded. There came also a vogue for recording on old instruments that existed at the time of the composition being played; for example a number of Bach works were rendered on a Silbermann organ. Another plan was to take a single organist and record him in different cities and churches, often in different countries (Biggs was the major exponent of this approach, while an English organist, Peter Hurford, recorded in Canada and Australia).

With advantages of improved techniques, organ concerti joined the record lists. Handel had been standard for years; now other composers such as contemporary Malcolm Williamson were included the catalogs. There were also recordings of the pipe organ with other solo instruments. Electronic organs have not found much favor on record, except in popular music.

Compact discs have already built a respectable repertoire of organ music. Artists like Carlo Curley, Michael Murray, Simon Preston, and John Rose have presented the instrument in all its infinite variety and splendor. A fine series of CDs entitled Historic American Organs provides the sounds of old instruments in various regions. Great European Organs is a colossal series of compact discs from the Priory label, with 23 volumes released by summer 1991. [Carreck 1960.]

E. T. Bryant, revised

ORIGINAL DIXIELAND JAZZ BAND. A pioneer ensemble of white performers, responsible for much of the early interest in jazz and for the first commercial recordings. Members were Nick La Rocca, cornet; Larry Shields, clarinet; Eddie Edwards, trombone; Henry Ragas, piano; and Tony Sbarbaro [later Spargo], drums. The spelling "jass" is found in early issues. The ODJB originated in New Orleans, played in Chicago in 1916, then went on to great success in New York at Reisenweber's Restaurant in January 1917. They made the first jazz recordings in jazz style, "Livery Stable Blues" and "Dixie Jass Band One-Step" on 26 Feb 1917 (Victor # 18255). On 31 May 1917 the group recorded "Darktown Strutters' Ball" / "Indiana" for Columbia (#A-2297). They went on to record prolifically, with personnel changes, for Victor and finally with Bluebird in 1938. Records were made in London also, for Columbia, in April, May, and August 1919, and again in January and May, 1920. The group disbanded after 1938. It was at its best in vigorous spirited numbers like "Tiger Rag" (Victor #18483; 1918). [Enderman 1989 is a complete discography.]

Original Lyric Trio. *See* LYRIC TRIO.

ORIGINAL MEMPHIS FIVE. A group consisting of Phil Napoleon, trumpet; Miff Mole, trombone; Jimmy Lytell, clarinet; Frank

Signorelli, piano; and Jack Roth, drums. Napoleon and Signorelli were the founders of the band and its chief performers. OMF was the most prolific of the ensembles working in the mode of the Original Dixieland Jazz Band, and even took that name for a period and on their first recordings: "Gypsy Blues" / "My Honey's Lovin' Arms" (Arto 9140; 1922). They went on with Arto, and also Pathé Actuelle, Vocalion, Victor, Edison, and many other labels. Before they stopped recording in 1931, the group had included a number of other performers, among them Red Nichols, Tommy Dorsey, and Jimmy Dorsey. Folkways #RBF26 is an LP release of material from 1922–1924.

ORIGINAL NEW ORLEANS JAZZ BAND. A group consisting of Frank Christian, cornet; Frank Lhotak, trombone; Achille Baquet, clarinet; Jimmy Durante, piano; and Arnold Loyacano, drums. In 1918 they cut two sides for Okeh, then they went to Gennett for four sides in 1919. "Ja Da," recorded for both labels, was a popular number (Okeh #1156; Gennett #4508).

ORIGINAL PIANO TRIO. A group that recorded two sides for Edison Diamond Discs in 1922. Members were George Dilworth, Edgar Fairchild, and Herbert Clair. Their record contained "Apache Love" and "Bimini Bay" (#50888).

Original Wolverines. *See* WOLVERINES.

ORIOLE (label). (I) An American record, sold for $.25 in McCrory's dime stores from 1921 to 1938. Matrices came from several sources: Grey Gull, Emerson, Plaza-Banner, and American Record Corp. Material was dance and popular vocal, with some race and hillbilly items. Many recordings were identical to issues from the Jewel label. [Rust 1978.]

ORIOLE (label). (II) A British record issued by **Levy's** of Whitechapel, London, in 1927, featuring important blues and jazz material, mostly from the American Vocalion catalog. Levy's Sound Studios, Ltd., was opened in Regent St. in the 1930s by Jack Levy. Trading as Levy's Public Phono & Cycle Stores, the firm made Levaphone records and Oriole. In a series started in 1931, Oriole included material by the new Quintette of the Hot Club of France, and by Duke Ellington. That second series from Levy's ended in 1935. [Rust 1978.]

ORIOLE (label). (III) In 1949 there was another series of **Levy's** Orioles, including London-made pressings as well as American imports. Jack Levy, whose sound studios were used to record the earlier British Oriole, also made that label, from a new address in Bond St. Those Orioles were mentioned in *Gramophone* in September 1949, and continued to be sold, as 78s, into early 1961.

In 1954, then at Oxford St., Oriole was registered with Embassy and Allegro labels. Oriole was taken over by CBS Records, which used the name for low-cost line in Australia. CBS also took Oriole's registered trademarks Plaza, Time Oriole, Realm, and Senator. [Andrews*.]

ORMANDY, EUGENE, 1899–1985. Hungarian/American conductor and violinist, born in Budapest on 18 Nov 1899, as Eugene Blau. He studied at the Royal Academy of Music in Budapest at age five, and with Jenö Hubay at age nine. He was 15 when he took his diploma and began recitals and orchestra playing. He transferred to the U.S. in 1921, taking a post as concertmaster, then conductor, of the Capitol Theater Orchestra in New York. In 1927 he became a U.S. citizen. He was appointed music director of the Minneapolis Symphony Orchestra in 1931, then left to become associate director of the Philadelphia Orchestra (with Leopold Stokowski) in 1936. He succeeded Stokowski to the directorship in 1938, and remained with orchestra until 1980. Under his baton the Philadelphia Orchestra developed further the magnificent unique sound created by Stokowski, and was recognized as one of the preeminent ensembles of the world. Ormandy specialized in works of the 19th century. He died on 12 Mar 1985.

Ormandy's earliest recordings were two violin solos with piano accompaniment for Cameo (#465; 1923), made while he was with the Capitol Theater Orchestra. He played "Hymn to the Sun" and "Song of India" by

Rimsky-Korsakoff. From 1924 to 1930 Ormandy recorded as a violin soloist in the popular repertoire for Okeh, with the Capitol Orchestra, with the Dorsey Brothers Orchestra (1928), and with his own salon orchestra. Ormandy seems to have been the earliest crossover conductor, making a remarkable transition from directing Phil Napoleon, Tommy Dorsey, Glenn Miller, Jimmy Dorsey, Eddie Lang, and Smith Ballew to the Minneapolis Symphony Orchestra.

His classical recording career began in Minneapolis, where Victor discs brought him a national reputation in such works as Mahler's Second Symphony, the Sibelius First Symphony, and Schoenberg's *Verklärte Nacht*. With the Philadelphia Orchestra, for Victor and Columbia, he inscribed a huge repertoire from 1936 to 1986. Among the Philadelphia records reissued on CD are the Tchaikovsky Sixth Symphony; the Sibelius Violin Concerto, with Dylana Jenson; Bartók's *Music for Strings, Percussion and Celeste*; and Benjamin Britten's *Young Person's Guide to the Orchestra* with narration by David Bowie. [Williams, F. 1985.]

ORPHEUS QUARTET. A vocal group that recorded for Victor from 1911–1918; they were also known as the Victor Male Quartet. Members were Lambert Murphy, Harry Macdonough, Reinald Werrenrath, and William F. Hooley. In Britain there was a group named Orpheus Quartette, which recorded on Twin Double Sided Disc Records in 1908; they were a different foursome whose membership is not known. [Andrews*.]

ORTHOPHONIC. The Victor gramophone introduced in 1925 to play the new electric records. *See* VICTROLA.

ORTOFON. A Danish firm established 9 Oct 1918 in Copenhagen, by Axel Petersen and Arnold Poulsen, to develop sound motion pictures. By 1923 they were able to demonstrate a sound film, using the "variable area" method that required two films run simultaneously—one carrying the audio, the other the video. The method was accepted and licensed in Europe and America (*see* MOTION PICTURE SOUND RECORDING). Later the firm developed new

disc cutterheads and amplifying systems, with records issued by Tono. Improvements were made also in tape recording and in recording long-playing microgroove discs. Ortofon moving coil pickup cartridges became universally praised, and the firm's stereo cutterhead was used everywhere. High quality audio equipment is still being produced. In Britain the agent is Ortofon, Ltd., located in Twyford, Berkshire.

ORY, KID, 1886–1973. American jazz trumpeter and band leader, born as Edward Ory in La Place, Louisiana, on Christmas day 1886. He played banjo, then turned to the trombone (developing the so-called tailgate style), but also played alto saxophone, cornet, and string bass. In 1912–1919 he led bands in New Orleans, with sidemen including at times King Oliver, Louis Armstrong, Johnny Dodds, Sidney Bechet, and Jimmie Noone. He was on the West Coast from 1919 to 1925, and made there one of the first jazz records to be cut by Black artists ("Ory's Creole Trombone" / "Society Blues"; *see* SUNSHINE label); then went to Chicago and recorded with Louis Armstrong's Hot Five and Hot Seven. Ory was with King Oliver's group during 1925–1927, then toured widely and freelanced. In 1926 he composed the jazz standard "Muskrat Ramble." From 1933 to 1942 he left music to be a chicken farmer and office worker, but returned in a combo with Barney Bigard in Los Angeles in 1942. Again he formed his own group, the Creole Jazz Band, and toured Europe with it in 1956–1959, then was less active, finally retiring to Hawaii in 1966. He died in Honolulu on 23 Jan 1973.

Ory's Creole Jazz Band made outstanding records in 1944–1945, such as "Do What Ory Say" / "Careless Love" (Cres #5; 1945) and "Blues for Jimmy Noone" featuring clarinetist Omer Simeon (Cres #2; 1944). Ory's band made an important series with Red Allen in 1959. There have been LP and compact disc reissues of these, on the Good Time Jazz label, and most of his other recordings.

OSSMAN, VESS, 1868–1923. American banjoist, born Sylvester Louis Ossman in Hudson, New York, on 21 Aug 1868. He started playing at 12 years of age, and by 1898 was an established international artist (with a command performance for King Edward VII in 1903), doing Negro songs, ragtime, marches, and so forth. Ossman, "the banjo king," was "probably the leading instrumental soloist on record in the 1890s and early 1900s" (Brooks). He started with Edison around 1893, then played for all the labels, disc and cylinder, mostly before 1911. He had 15 records in the Columbia 1896 catalog, and was an exclusive for the label for a few years. He also worked for Bettini, and Berliner, and was one of the first Victor artists. In 1899 he began to accompany Len Spencer, and Arthur Collins in his Negro songs. Ossman's best seller was "Turkey in the Straw Medley" / "Dixie" (Victor #4424; 1905; also on other labels).

In 1906 he organized the Ossman-Dudley Trio (with Audley Dudley, mandolin; and George F. Dudley, harp and guitar) and made a hit ragtime record for Victor, "St. Louis Tickle" (#4624).

Between 1911 and 1916 he made only a few records, among them numbers for the U-S Phonograph Co. indestructible cylinders. Back in action in 1916, he had another Victor hit in "Good Scout—One Step," then established a Banjo Orchestra (really two banjos, with piano, saxophone and drums). Later he was one of the Eight Famous Victor Artists. "Buffalo Rag" was the last of his records kept in the Victor catalog, until 1924. After Ossman died, in Minneapolis on 8 Dec 1923, many of his numbers were re-recorded by Fred Van Epps. [Brooks 1979; Walsh 1948/9–10–11; 1949/1–2; corrections in 1952/5.]

OUT OF PHASE. The term given to the situation when the moving elements of two loudspeakers, in response to a simultaneous identical signal, move in opposite directions.

OUTPUT. In an audio system, any signal leaving any component.

OUT-TAKE. Material that is recorded (or filmed) but not retained in the final master.

Overload. *See* DISTORTION, III, VI.

OVERSAMPLING. In a CD system the process of enhancing the signal for improved detail. The more times a signal is oversampled, the cleaner the resulting sound. In 1989 less expensive players included two-times oversampling, and highest price players had eight times oversampling.

OWEN, WILLIAM BARRY. American record company executive, born in New Bedford, Massachusetts. He was a director of the National Gramophone Co. from October 1896, and was sent to London in 1897 by Emile Berliner to demonstrate the Improved Gramophone and sell rights. He established the **Gramophone Co.** in April 1898, to import gramophones and make recordings. He served as managing director of the new enterprise, located in London's Maiden Lane. In 1899 he purchased the **Nipper** painting from Francis Barraud.

Owen made an unfortunate decision to diversify in 1900, and began to deal in typewriters; the company name was changed to the Gramophone and Typewriter, Ltd. With the market failure of his typewriter, Owen resigned and was succeeded by Theodore Birnbaum in 1904. He then retired to Martha's Vineyard, Massachusetts, to raise chickens, and died there on 19 Mar 1914.

OXFORD (label). (I) An American record, marketed by mail-order by Sears, Roebuck and Co., from ca. 1900 to ca. 1918. There were only a few issues before 1911, when the main series began. Masters came from Zonophone, Victor, Leeds & Catlin, and Columbia. Major artists were included, such as Emilio de Gogorza and Bert Williams, but frequently the artists' names were omitted from the label. In 1911 10-inch discs were selling at $.30. In 1915 12-inch discs were also sold, at $.50. Sears replaced the Oxford label with the new Silvertone records in 1912, but in fall 1917 there was a resurgence of Oxford when the supply of Silvertone paper labels was temporarily exhausted. [Bryan 1975 is a complete list.]

OZAWA, SEIJI, 1935– . Japanese conductor, born in Hoten, Manchuria, on 1 Sep 1935. He

studied piano, composition, and conducting in
Tokyo, then went to Europe to seek his fortune.
He supported himself at first by selling motor
scooters in France and Italy. He won a major
competition for conductors in 1959, and was
given a scholarship to study with Herbert von
Karajan and the Berlin Philharmonic Orchestra. Leonard Bernstein engaged him as assistant conductor of the New York Philharmonic
Orchestra in 1961. From 1970 to 1976 he directed the San Francisco Symphony Orchestra;
in 1973 he was named music director of the
Boston Symphony Orchestra.

Ozawa has a wide, eclectic repertoire, and
has recorded (for many labels) major works
from all periods. An outstanding series was the
Beethoven piano concertos with Rudolf Serkin
(on Telarc #10062). Another acclaimed disc
presented the Berg and Stravinsky violin concertos with Itzhak Perlman (DGG #413725-2).
These have been reissued on compact disc.

P CHANNEL. On a compact disc, a subcode (inaudible) channel used for carrying information on lead-in, lead-out, and playing areas.

PACIFIC PHONOGRAPH CO. One of the affiliated firms that comprised the **North American Phonograph Co.**, later independent; it was established 7 Jan 1889. Location was 323 Pine St., San Francisco in 1890, at which time **Louis Glass** was general manager. Glass developed the **coin-op** cylinder phonograph, and leasing models of it was a prime occupation of the company. The first coin-op on location seems to have been at the Palais Royal saloon, in San Francisco, on 23 Nov 1889. After the break-up of North American, the Pacific Phonograph Co. continued in business. A notice in *TMW* for June 1915 states that it had moved to the Sachs Building, 140 Geary St., San Francisco, and that the "head" was A. R. Pommer.

PACKAGED SYSTEM. A complete audio playback system, also known as a rack system, including all components with necessary connections. During the early hi-fi period of the 1950s, enthusiasts preferred to have separate components. But modern packaged systems demonstrate quality equivalent to that of assembled sets of components, and they may be harmoniously clustered as well as less costly.

PACKARD MANUFACTURING CO. A firm established in 1932 by **Homer Capehart**, in Indianapolis, Indiana. It made **coin-op** phonographs for a few years after World War II, including the Manhattan jukebox.

PACKBURN AUDIO NOISE SUPPRESSOR. A device designed to suppress transient noises (ticks, pops, clicks, crackle, scratch, etc.) in phonograph records, mono or stereo, wherever or however made, as well as the audible hiss characteristic of all audio media prior to the development of successful encode/decode noise suppression systems, and more recently, digital audio. This article describes Model 323A, which has three principal components: a switcher, a blanker, and a continuous noise suppressor.

The switcher is designed specifically for the reduction of transient noises in monophonic disc and cylinder records by taking advantage of the circumstance that, whereas the same signal is engraved on each side of the groove wall, the noises caused by dirt, mildew, scratches, cracks, particulate matter in the record material, etc., are not the same on each side of the groove wall.

Prior to the development of the Packburn switcher, a monophonic disk or cylinder was best reproduced for stereo by summing (in the appropriate polarity) the signals from the left and right channels. The switcher also does this, in the rest position. However, at any moment when the reproduction from the left or right channel is more noise-free than the sum signal (by a user-adjustable threshold amount), the switcher can reproduce from the quieter groove wall only. At frequencies lower than 300 Hz, where switching would not accomplish anything, the two channels are mixed to minimize rumble. The switching process is applicable to vertical-cut recordings as well as to lateral-cut records, as a correct playback stylus rides on the side walls of the groove; it is, however, more effective with lateral records.

The switching process is the least compromising mode of noise reduction, as it has no effect on the fidelity of reproduction and does not introduce distortion or have any other undesirable side effect. In fact, its audible effect is one of decreased distortion in the reproduction of records that have any substantial amount of transient noises. The output of the process is a monophonic signal in which the noise content consists of the residual noise that has survived the switcher's three-way choice.

Stereo records, monophonic tape recordings, and broadcasts cannot be processed with the switcher. For these the blanker is used.

The blanker is designed to cope with transient noises from any source: the output of the switcher, a stereo disc, a tape, compact disc, or broadcasts. It will usually be most effective in dealing with an original record, as copying and broadcasting processes, which typically employ filtering, compression and limiting, tend to reduce the amplitude of a noise transient, and thus lower its detectability by the blanker circuitry. Transient noise suppression is achieved by clipping the amplitude of each individual positive-going and negative-going pulsation of a noise transient whenever the amplitude of the transient exceeds a threshold value determined by the peak program level in the vicinity of the transient; and by the setting of the "blanker rate" control. The blanker does not attempt to eliminate the totality of the transient, which would require momentarily reducing the signal level to zero. Therefore, a slight ghost of lower frequency components of certain noise transients will sometimes remain. Cracks, pits, gouges, dents or bumps may still be audibly detectable but as low frequency thumps which normally will not be painful to listen to.

Once the switcher and blanker have completed their tasks—to cope with transient noise—there remains the need to reduce audible hiss. This is accomplished by the continuous noise suppressor. In the case of recordings containing no transient noises, such as master tapes or copies thereof, the continuous noise suppressor will be the only processor needed.

The Packburn continuous noise suppressor is classified as a dynamic noise suppressor. In such devices the cutoff frequency of a variable low-pass filter varies with the dynamics of the program material in such a way that audible noise is minimized with a zero or minimal degradation of the perceived fidelity of reproduction and without introducing extraneous noises as a result of the dynamics of the filter operation. The success of such a device is crucially dependent on the design of its sensing and control circuits and on the user-operated controls that are provided. The operation of the filter in the Packburn continuous noise suppressor is controlled as follows:

a. The signal amplitude in the frequency range of 1.7 kHz to 3.4 kHz is employed as an index of the high frequency content of the signal in the audible range;

b. The time rate of change of the total signal-plus-noise is employed as an index of the audible surface noise;

c. A voltage derived from the ratio of measurements (a) and (b) is employed to control the width of the pass band;

d. Separate user-adjustable controls are provided to select the minimum cutoff frequency in quiet passages and the maximum cutoff frequency in loud passages;

e. User-adjustable means are provided for a rapid increase of the pass band width at the onset of signal transients.

As the continuous noise suppressor functions best if it "hears" the program material with the same treble equalization that one chooses for listening, the Packburn unit provides a treble equalization switch that allows one to select the RIAA curve or one of five other equalization curves that match those historically used in cutting records prior to the standardization of the RIAA curve by the record industry in 1953.

Other controls are provided in the Packburn 323A to assist in obtaining optimum results. Meters assure proper adjustment of the input level, and a frequency meter reads out the fluctuating value of the cutoff frequency as the continuous noise suppressor operates. The user can audition the separate groove walls of a record, which can be of assistance in selecting the optimum size stylus for record playing;

and can audition the vertical component of lateral-cut records as well as the lateral component of vertical-cut records.

The channel balance control, which is important in adjusting the switching process, also serves as a canting control for vertical-cut records.

To accommodate stereo recordings, Model 323A is provided with two blankers, two treble equalization networks, and two continuous noise processors. it is designed to interface with contemporary stereo playback systems. It can be inserted in a tape loop of a preamplifier, amplifier or receiver, or it can be interposed after the preamplifier.

In professional installations, the Packburn Audio Noise Suppressor is used immediately after the stereo preamplifier and prior to such devices as equalizers, filters, volume expanders, reverberation synthesizers, etc., save that, in record restoration work, one may prefer to utilize the continuous noise suppressor in the final stage of processing.

(Packburn is registered with U.S. Patent and Trademark Office.) *See also* NOISE REDUCTION SYSTEMS.

Richard C. Burns and Thomas N. Packard

PADEREWSKI, IGNACE, 1860–1941. Polish pianist and composer, born in Kurylowka, Podolia (Russian Poland) on 18 Nov 1860. He performed in public as a child, and was sent to Warsaw Conservatory by wealthy patrons. On graduation in 1878 he joined the piano faculty. After further study with Theodor Leschetizky he gave recitals in Paris and Vienna (1888), then London (1890) and New York (1891). His playing and his personality brought him great adulation in America.

Paderewski was also an assiduous composer, though only one minor piece, the "Minuet in G," remains in the repertoire. And he was the first celebrated musician to occupy a high political post, being prime minister of the Polish Republic in 1919, and later his country's delegate to the League of Nations. In 1940 he was named president of the Polish parliament in exile. He died in New York on 29 June 1941.

His earliest records were made in Switzerland for HMV in 1911: seven numbers including his own "Minuet" (#045530), "Hark! Hark! The Lark" by Schubert/Liszt (#045532) and five Chopin pieces. All were reissued by Victor. Another group was made in Paris in 1912, for HMV (not issued with Victor numbers); six Chopin items, and pieces by Mendelssohn, Debussy, Paderewski, and Liszt, along with another "Hark! Hark! The Lark." There were another 13 HMV recordings, then Paderewski recorded for Victor, a series of works from his usual limited repertoire. The 1917 Victor catalog carried five sides by him.

He continued recording Chopin and other romantics through the acoustic period and into the electric era, becoming somewhat more adventurous in the 1930s with Wagner transcriptions, Brahms, Mozart, and Beethoven. His final session was on 15 Nov 1938. [Methuen-Campbell 1984.]

PAGE, PATTI, 1927– . American popular singer, born Clara Ann Fowler in Claremore, Oklahoma, on 8 Nov 1927. She grew up in Tulsa, Oklahoma, singing in church and on local radio. Moving to Chicago, she did club and radio engagements, and began to record for Mercury in the late 1940s. She had a long series of hit records, beginning with her most enduring favorite, "Tennessee Waltz" (Mercury #5534; 1950). Among her 35 other chart songs through the 1960s were "I Went to Your Wedding" (Mercury #5899; 1952) and "How Much Is That Doggie in the Window" (Mercury #70070; 1953). Page had three best-selling LP albums in the 1960s, notably *Hush, Hush, Sweet Charlotte* (Columbia #CL 2353; 1965). In the early 1970s, after an inactive period, she entered the country field and enjoyed another string of hit records, including "Make Me Your Kind of Woman" (Mercury #73199; 1971).

PAGLIUGHI, LINA, 1907–1980. American soprano, born in New York of Italian parents on 27 May 1907. At age six she gave a recital in San Francisco. Encouraged by Luisa Tetrazzini, she studied in Milan, and made her debut there as Gilda in 1927. From 1930 to 1947 she appeared at La Scala, then with Italian Radio. Her light childlike voice was best suited to delicate roles like Gilda, Rosina, and Lucia. She retired in 1956, and died in Rubicone, Italy, on 2 Oct 1980.

Pagliughi recorded in Milan during 1928–1930 for HMV, for Parlophone (Italy) in 1932–1934, and then for Cetra in 1935–1943, standard coloratura numbers and several arias from Rossini and Bellini. She made four sides for Victor in 1940, the most popular being "Carnival of Venice," in which she sang a duet with a flute (Victor #2061). Her finest recording was the complete *Rigoletto* (Victor set #M-32; 1928), with the La Scala company. She also recorded a complete *Lucia*. [Di Cave 1973.]

PALACE TRIO. An instrumental group that recorded for Victor and other labels in the 1920s. Members were Rudy Wiedoeft, saxophone; Mario Perry, accordion; and J. Russell Robinson, piano.

PALEY, WILLIAM SAMUEL, 1901–1990. American radio and television executive, born 28 Sep 1901 in Chicago. He graduated in 1922 from the Wharton School of Finance, University of Pennsylvania, and went into his father's cigar business. Attracted to the new radio field, he acquired in 1928 a small chain of stations that had been set up in 1927 by Arthur Judson as the United Independent Broadcasters, Inc. (UIB). UIB had been in immediate financial difficulty, and had sold its operating rights to the Columbia Phonograph Co., which had renamed it the Columbia Phonograph Broadcasting System. In 1928 Columbia Phonograph sold UIB's operating rights back to it, and it changed itself to the Columbia Broadcasting System (CBS) in time for Paley to invest $400,000 in it and take over as president. By 1930 CBS had expanded from 16 to 70 stations across the U.S. CBS began its weekly broadcasts of the New York Philharmonic-Symphony Orchestra concerts in 1930. Important popular artists like Kate Smith and Bing Crosby were also featured.

Columbia Phonograph Co. was acquired when CBS bought the American Record Corp. in 1938. The Columbia Recording Co. was then the manufacturing arm; later the name of the enterprise became Columbia Records, Inc. Paley wished to revive the famous Columbia label, which had barely survived a decade of being passed among indifferent owners, and hired **Edward Wallerstein** to manage the unit. The result was a grand renaissance for the label, including a triumph with the new microgroove LP record in 1948. It was after Laurence A. Tisch became CEO of CBS that the Columbia label (changed to CBS Records in 1979) was sold to Sony Corp. (1986).

Paley had a distinguished military career in World War II, as a civilian assigned to reconstruct the Italian radio network, then as a colonel in the Psychological Warfare Division. He earned decorations from several nations. After the War, CBS pioneered in regularly scheduled television broadcasting and in the development of color television. Paley turned over the presidency to Frank Stanton in 1946, remaining as chairman of the board. He died in New York on 26 Oct 1990.

PALLATROPE. The 1925 Brunswick system for making discs, adapted from Charles A. Hoxie's **Photophone** idea. It was a "light ray" recording process, using a microphone, a crystal mirror, a light source, and a photo-electric cell. The spellings Pallotrope and Palatrope are also seen.

PALOMA QUARTET. The first women's group to record. They had three titles in the Victor catalog of February 1903: "La Paloma" (#1887), "Medley" (#1889), and "The Waterfall" (#1900). Walsh says he never heard any of these, nor had anyone else he knew of; and that they "must be among the rarest records." [Walsh 1965/5.]

PAN (label). An American record issued ca. 1920, of which only nine examples are known. The material includes Sousa marches, operatic arias, and violin solos (by Vera Barstow). Labels were triangular. The Pan Phonograph Co. is identified as the source. Lyric seems to have supplied the masters. [Rust 1978.]

PANACHORD (label). A British record issued by Warner-Brunswick, Ltd., of London, from May 1931 to December 1939. Masters were from Melotone, Decca, and Brunswick in the U.S.; from Broadcast, Decca, Brunswick, and Imperial in Britain; and also from Polydor in Germany. In 1933 Decca Record Co., Ltd., took over the label. Material was varied, lying primarily in the popular, dance, and country fields. Tex Ritter, Chick Webb, Woody Herman, and Ted Weems were among the artists represented. The most important releases were of Joe Venuti and Eddie Lang with their All Star Orchestra (#25151 and #25168; 1931), issued in the U.S. on Vocalion and Melotone. [Mitchell, R. 1966; Rust 1978.]

PANAMA-PACIFIC EXPOSITION, SAN FRANCISCO, 1915. A world's fair with important exhibits of talking machines. Victor had its own "Temple" for displays. John Gabel's Automatic Entertainer was shown. Thomas Edison had a Panama Canal display with special recorded narration. Awards won by the Columbia Graphophone Co. led to its issue of special "banner" discs, which were Columbia Records with a simulated award ribbon across the label.

PANATROPE. The all-electric record playback machine marketed by Brunswick in 1925. Developed in cooperation with RCA, General Electric, and Westinghouse engineers, it provided an extended frequency range (hence the name "pan" meaning all, "trope" meaning scale)—said to reach 16,000 Hz. The system used a horsehoe magnetic pickup, a vacuum-tube amplifier, and a dynamic loudspeaker (the first available for domestic use). The reproducer was modelled on the Victor Orthophonic. Records were made by a light-ray system. *See also* PALLATROPE.

PANHELLENION PHONOGRAPH RECORD (label). A New York disc issued around 1922, from an address at 48 W. 39th St. The specialty was Greek language material, plus opera and songs performed by Greek artists. [Andrews*.]

PANORAMIC POTENTIOMETER. A device used in multichannel recording to locate the signal from each channel into the stereo field. It is also called a Panpot.

PARABOLIC REFLECTOR. A curved sound reflector, intended to direct signals to a microphone.

PARAMETRIC EQUALIZER. A type of **equalizer** that allows a boost or cutout of any frequency or any bandwidth.

PARAMOUNT (label). An American record issued by New York Recording Laboratories, Inc., first reported in *TMW* in March 1918. The firm had offices in Port Washington, Wisconsin, studios at 1140 Broadway, New York, and a pressing plant in Grafton, Wisconsin. Early discs were vertical cut, but by the end of 1919 all issues were lateral cut. A. J. Baum was in charge of the New York Recording Laboratories in May 1921. Charles A. Prince was musical director there in December 1922, with Al Housman as his assistant; in February 1923 Housman was reported to be the recorder.

Important material appeared on the label, notably blues and jazz. Artists included Big Bill Broonzy, Alberta Hunter, Blind Blake, Fletcher Henderson, Jelly Roll Morton, Trixie Smith, King Oliver, Ethel Waters, Ida Cox, Elmo Tanner, Blind Lemon Jefferson (with a special label of his own once, #12650; 1928), and Ma Rainey (also with a personalized label for one release, #12098; 1924).

In April 1924 Paramount took over the **Black Swan** label, and in June issued a joint catalog of the two labels (reprinted in *Record Changer* of June 1950). **Race records** became the predominant category in the Paramount output. Paramount masters were used for Broadway, Famous, and Puritan records.

Paramount is credited with the first live recording of a sports event, namely the Jack Dempsey-Gene Tunney boxing championship bout from Soldier Field, Chicago, on 22 Sep 1927. It occupied 10 sides (#12534–12538), selling for $3.75. This was the regular price for Paramounts, $.75 each (after an initial price of $.85). The final Paramounts came out in summer 1932. [Andrews*; Rust 1978; Vreede 1971 gives label list of the 12000/13000 race series.]

PARIS EXPOSITION, 1889. The world's fair named Exposition Universelle ran only six months, from 6 May 1889 to 6 Nov 1889, but attracted some 25 million visitors. Thomas Edison had a major 9,000 square foot exhibit there, displaying 45 phonographs. Sarah

Bernhardt and other celebrities were featured making records. The public could hear recordings through ear tubes. Edison presented a phonograph to Gustave Eiffel, who installed it in his apartment on the third level of the Tower. There was also an exhibit of the graphophone by Charles Tainter, but it was a less elaborate display. Henri Lioret had an exhibit of his clocks at the fair, and became interested in the talking machine; it is believed that the stimulus of meeting Thomas Edison and hearing the phonograph inspired his own work in the field. Valdemar Poulsen's **Telegraphone** was also exhibited.

PARKER, CHARLIE, 1920–1955. American jazz saxophonist, born Charles Christopher Parker in Kansas City, Missouri, on 29 Aug 1920. He is known also as "Bird" or "Yardbird." He played both alto and tenor saxophone, and composed; Parker was one of the pioneer figures of the **bebop** style. A self-taught musician, he left school at age 15 to make his way. He first recorded in 1940 in Wichita, Kansas, with the Jay McShann orchestra. "Coquette" was the most interesting number, suggestive of Parker's emerging mode. In 1943 he made a few more sides with McShann, notably "Jump the Blues" (Decca #4418). His innovative improvisations received national attention after the end of the U.S. record industry recording ban in November 1944, when he recorded 37 titles. "Ko-Ko" was one of the outstanding pieces of that period (Savoy #597; 1945). Later he recorded for Dial, Mercury, Clef, and Verve. For Jazz at the Philharmonic he did an outstanding version of "Lady Be Good" (Disc #2005). Between 1947 and 1951 he was often in the studio, recording his own quintet as well as other groups. Most of the Parker recorded output has been reissued. *The Original Bird* CD from Savoy; Mosaic's release of Parker solos set in wax by his disciple Dean Benedetti; *The Very Best of Bird*, featuring the Dial releases of 1946 and 1947 (Warner); *Bird: The Complete Charlie Parker on Verve*, a set of 10 CDs; and *Compact Jazz* (Verve/Polygram).

In 1988 the film *Bird* appeared, directed by Clint Eastwood, introducing a novel recording approach. Parker's solos were extracted from their old discs, and set into the context of new performances overdubbed by different sidemen. Sound quality was enhanced in comparison with the original records, but the result was, according to one critic "hopelessly anachronistic, because these present-day boppers are playing in a now somewhat dated style that Parker was still in the process of defining." The soundtrack record of the film (Columbia) was criticized for its artificiality. [Koster 1974.]

PARLIAMENT (label). A low-price American record, issued from 1959 by Parliament Records, 600 Fifth Ave., New York. Material issued was classical. **Artia** was the parent label.

PARLOPHONE (label). (I) A British record issued from 1923, by the Parlophone Co., Ltd., of London. Its origin was Parlophon, used by the Carl Lindström workshop as a model name for one of its manufactured phonographs. After the Lindström business was taken over and Carl Lindström AG formed, the Beka Record business was absorbed. The 12-inch Beka Meister Records were renamed Parlophon in Germany, and the name spread throughout a number of European catalogs. In Britain, "Parlophone" had been registered to some other concern, so Lindström continued (from 1910) with the Beka Meister name for its 12-inch discs. That label continued in the U.K., with fresh imports from Germany, after the First World War.

A Dutch subsidiary of Carl Lindström AG was given control of the Lindström overseas enterprises, and it was through that company that Lindström was able to regain a foothold in Britain, in 1923, with the formation of the Parlophone Co., Ltd. That firm produced Parlophone record players and discs in 10- and 12-inch sizes. Parlophone was the initial label; later there was also a label styled Parlophone Odeon Series.

In October 1925 Columbia Graphophone Co., Ltd., took a controlling interest in Carl Lindström AG, the Dutch company (Trans-Oceanic Trading Co.) and the Columbia Phonograph Co., Inc., of the U.S., and formed Columbia (International), Ltd. Parlophone was then controlled by Columbia in Britain, and Parlophon elsewhere. When British-owned Columbia Phonograph Co., Inc., acquired the Okeh label from Otto Heinemann, the Okeh repertoire was allowed to continue coming on Parlophone and Parlophon records.

Material on Parlophone included interesting jazz and blues from Okeh, with artists' names changed and even some of the titles altered to avoid possible offense. Unusual offerings included a "Laughing Record" (#E-5500; 1925) and a best-selling Hawaiian number by Kanui and Lula (#R-1614). The Beatles' earliest British recording was done for Parlophone. [Andrews*; Rust 1978.]

PARLOPHONE (label). (II) An American record issued from 1929 to 1931. It was a Columbia-Okeh affiliate, distinguished by smooth surfaces. Material was dance and jazz, much of it by pseudonymous artists. [Rust 1978.]

PAR-O-KET (label). An American record made by the Paroquette Manufacturing Co., Inc., New York, in 1916–1917. The firm was incorporated in 1915 by James A. Clancy, Frank J. O'Brien, and Arthur P. O'Brien. Henry Burr, the famous tenor, organized the company, which was said to be owned and operated by the recording artists themselves. The first discs were announced in October 1916. They were seven-inch and 10-inch vertical-cut records, sold for $.25 and $.35. Paroquette was not successful, and in May 1918 the complete plant was sold at public auction for the benefit of its creditors. In January 1919 all the seven-inch masters were advertised for sale in *TMW*. [Andrews*; Rust 1978.]

PARSONS, CHARLES ALGERNON, *Sir*, **1854–1931.** British engineer and inventor, born in London. He studied at Cambridge University, then apprenticed in Newcastle-upon-Tyne. He set up a turbine generator business, and worked also with marine equipment. As a diversion, he experimented with sound amplification, and developed the **Auxetophone,** gaining three British patents for it: #10468 (1903), #10469 (1903), and #20892 (1904). He demonstrated the device for the Royal Society in May 1904, and sold the gramophone rights to G & T sometime before 21 Mar 1905.

PARTON, DOLLY, 1946–. American country singer, songwriter, and guitarist, born Rebecca

Parton in Locust Ridge, Tennessee, on 19 Jan 1946. Living with an uncle in Nashville, she sang locally and played guitar as a child, and signed a contract with the Monument label at age 20. "Dumb Blonde" was an early chart single (Monument #982; 1967), followed by another, "Why, Why, Why" (Monument #1032; 1967). Parton began a 10-year association with Porter Wagoner in 1967, producing 22 chart songs, among them "Lost Forever in Your Kiss" (RCA #0675; 1972) and "Please Don't Stop Loving Me" (RCA #10010; 1974). Parton's greatest solo hits were "Coat of Many Colors" (RCA #0538; 1971), and "Jolene" (RCA #0145; 1973). There were many popular albums in the 1970s. The Country Music Association voted Parton female vocalist of the year in 1975 and 1976. She reached a wide audience in a motion picture, *9 to 5* (1980), composing the title song and winning a Grammy for it; the single was on the charts 13 weeks (RCA #12133; 1980). Monument has reissued her early material on CD, and RCA has reissued other songs in a series of "Best of" CDs. *Rainbow* was a compact disc favorite of 1988 (Columbia #CK 40968).

PARVIS, TAURINO, 1879–1957. Italian baritone, born in Torino on 15 Sep 1879. He sang at La Scala, and was with the Metropolitan Opera in 1904–1906. Parvis recorded on single-faced Zonophones, in the U.S., during 1904–1906, including an outstanding "La ci darem la mano" with Eugenia Mantelli (#12573). He went to Columbia cylinders and discs, from 1905 to 1914, and worked also for Pathé in Milan in 1913, making about 25 arias and duets. In 1918 he recorded for Edison Diamond Discs.

PASTERNACK, JOSEF ALEXANDER, 1881–1940. Polish/American conductor, born in Czestochowa on 1 July 1881. He entered the Warsaw Conservatory at age 10, studying piano and composition, and learned to play virtually every orchestral instrument. At age 15 he transferred to the U.S., touring as a pianist; then played viola in the Metropolitan Opera Orchestra from 1900 to 1909, and served as assistant conductor of the orchestra in 1910–1912. He then returned to Europe and conducted both opera and symphony concerts. Back in the U.S., he conducted the Century

Opera Co. in New York, and various orchestras. In 1916 Pasternack became musical director of the Victor Talking Machine Co., a position that including conducting house orchestras. He remained with Victor until 1927. From 1928 until his death he was in demand as a conductor on the radio and as a composer for motion pictures. Pasternack died in Chicago on 29 Apr 1940.

PATCH. To patch is to connect items of equipment, as in an audio system, with cords and plugs. Such connections are usually controlled by break-jacks. The cord used for patching is the patch cord.

PATENTS. Millions of patents of all kinds have been issued since the birth of the U.S. patent system in 1790 (over 5 million since the Patent Office began its current consecutive system of numbering). Originally, working models of each invention were required by the examiners, but this condition was cancelled by Congressional Statute on 8 July 1870 and by Office Rule on 1 Mar 1889, saving the potential inventors some precious funds, and lessening massive storage problems for the Patent Office and the National Archives. Many of the wood and metal models were destroyed by neglect and fire, especially in 1836 and 1877. Others were sold off and dispersed in 1925–1926, but a number still exist today in private collections and institutions.

After six days of intensive labor, **John Kruesi** completed the first working cylinder phonograph—invented by Thomas Edison—on 6 Dec 1877; on the seventh day, he constructed the still-required model for submission to the Patent Office. It was returned to Edison on 22 June 1926, and is preserved today at the Henry Ford restoration of Menlo Park in Greenfield Village, Dearborn, Michigan. The model had been sent to Washington with the formal application less than three months after the devastating Patent Office fire of 24 Sep 1877, in which over 76,000 models were destroyed (about one-third of the total then existing).

Between 1877 and 1912 (when the external horn machines lost their popularity) the U.S. Patent Office granted over 2,000 Utility (invention) Patents to about 1,000 inventors in the sound recording field, and more than 70 Design Patents. A patent remained in force for 17 years from the date of the grant and could not be extended, except under extraordinary circumstances. In the patent titles the word "phonograph" outnumbered "graphophone" five to one, although the subclass headings themselves used the latter term more often. "Talking machine" was a distant third. Although the "paper average" was about two phonograph patents per inventor, the reality was quite different. Thirty-two inventors received—either singly or jointly—10 or more patents apiece. Although numbering only about 3 percent of the inventors surveyed, they received more than 33 percent of the patents. In that sense, the field became dominated by relatively few inventors, financed by the larger companies. Yet others who received only one or two patents— **Charles Batchelor**, John B. Browning, Heinrich Klenk, **Henri Lioret**, William F. Messer, Stanislaus Moss, and Werner Suess, for example—still managed to make a substantial impact.

These were the most prolific U.S. phonograph invention/design patentees, from 1877 to 1912, with the number of patents they received:

Thomas A. Edison, 134
Thomas H. Macdonald, 56
Eldridge R. Johnson, 54
Jonas W. Aylsworth, 38
Louis Valiquet, 33
John C. English, 31
Peter Weber, 27
Charles S. Tainter, 25
Ademor N. Petit, 23
Alexander N. Pierman, 22
Edward L. Aiken, 18
Walter H. Miller, 18
Thomas Kraemer, 15
Gianni Bettini, 14
Frank L. Capps, 14
George K. Cheney, 14
Victor H. Emerson, 14
Isidor Kitsee, 14
Horace Sheble, 14
Leon F. Douglass, 13
Emile Berliner, 12
Edward D. Gleason, 12

Edward H. Amet, 11
Robert L. Gibson, 11
Joseph W. Jones, 11
Wilburn N. Dennison, 10
Alexander Fischer, 10
George W. Gomber, 10
Luther T. Haile, 10
Frederick Myers, 10
John F. Ott, 10
William W. Young, 10

Edison's personal involvement with the field was the longest of any inventor, spanning 1877 to 1930. Ironically, his first U.S. phonograph patent, which established the industry, had little importance in the subsequent commercial development because of an unfortunate choice of words. Although Edison was aware that his first recorder would engrave paraffined paper in 1877, he had difficulties with wax clogging the stylus, and his lawyer failed to mention this detail in the original U.S. application, specifying "indentation" rather than "engraving." This lack of foresight would cost Edison dearly in the later struggles with Columbia.

Although millions of dollars were invested on the strength of a handful of major patents, other entrepreneurs gambled smaller sums—but frequently everything they had—on a single clever idea. For example, Louis Glass built and applied for a patent on the first U.S. coin-operated phonograph in 1889. Edward Amet constructed the first spring-wound motor for phonographs by 1891 (probably brought to market in mid-1894), and **Thomas Lambert** developed the first standard-size, unbreakable (celluloid) cylinder record by mid-1900.

A number of patentees were known in other, though allied, fields. Recording artist **Steve Porter** (Stephen C. Porter) had already been a founder of the American Phonograph Record Co. in 1901 when he later received a phonograph patent himself (#1,012,910). The only other singer with a patent was Berliner artist James K. Reynard (#666,819 and #776,941), but Hulbert A. Yerkes, Columbia's later jazz band director and vice-president, received a design patent on a Grafonola (#41,902) and two other invention patents after 1912. **Byron G. Harlan** was the one-fifth as-

signee of Rudolph Klein's double-volute disc (#814,053), and the famed Victor recording engineer (and Berliner alumnus) William Sinkler Darby also managed to obtain one: #786,347. The keeper of Edison's musical accounts book from 1889 to 1892, and the world's first recording director, Adelbert Theo Wangemann, later received two patents (#872,592 and #913,930)—but both posthumously.

Patents and the suits fought over them often changed the form of competing products. The early Echophones of Edward Amet had deeply indented mandrels, thus to avoid Edison's patent on the continuously tapered interior of a cylinder record. Thomas Lambert had to remove the little angular guide blocks from the title end of his first (hollow) white and pink celluloid cylinders. Columbia's Type AZ Graphophone with its fixed frame and Lyre Reproducer was only permitted on the market in late 1904 when Edison's patent #430,278 was held invalid. U-S Phonograph's unusual coiled-tube tone arm cylinder phonographs, developed by Harry McNulty and Thomas Towell with a double feedscrew, successfully avoided Victor's patent on the solid tapering tone arm and Edison's two-minute to four-minute gear-shifting devices.

Some inventions and ideas that later became important in the industry were buried in earlier applications. For example, although Ademor Petit received a patent for a two-sided disc record in 1904 (#749,092), this very feature was mentioned as early as 1891 in the U.S., by Joseph Wassenich (#505,910), and also indicated by Edison in his British Patent #1644 of 1878, not to mention the 1878 abandoned patent application of William Hollingshead which fortuitously survived. Even the concept of a cabinet-styled phonograph with concealed horn slowly emerged in 1899 with a music box mechanism (J. Philips. #632,925), but eventually, after years of litigation (and assistance from Keen-O-Phone and Brunswick) it was John Bailey Browning in 1927 who finally received credit for his prior conception of the **Victrola**. Other ideas, such as tapered tone arms, radial tracking, anti-skating devices, magnetic recording, tone-modifiers, disc-changing mechanisms, and the ideal horn weave their way through the work of many inventors.

Extended litigation over patents marked the early years of the industry; much of it was brought on by brazen, unauthorized imitations. After the Victor Talking Machine Co. had spent $1 million buying and defending Emile Berliner's pivotal patents (especially for the groove-driven reproducer), Eldridge Johnson (in the May 1909 issue of *TMW*) reacted to his own Supreme Court victory on this issue over Leeds & Catlin on 19 Apr by commenting on patent infringers: "Injunctions, fines, and even danger of imprisonment do not stop them. People infected with this curious spell seem more like the followers of some strenuous religious belief than simple business men who are working for a livelihood."

Research into the formative decades of the phonograph is greatly facilitated by use of Patent Office documents. Copies of the original applications are still available on request from the U.S. Patent and Trademark Office, Washington, D.C. 20231, at a cost of $1.50 each.

Patents issued by European countries followed various principles, bringing about a number of challenges for American inventors and firms. Foreign patents had varying terms, and many were subject to renewal. U.S. Statutes limited the American patent to the term of the inventor's shortest-running foreign counterpart (a practice not ended until the implementation of the Treaty of Brussels). The situation became so complex that some patents filed before 1898 expired before they were granted! American practice demanded that a U.S. citizen apply for a patent simultaneously in the U.S. and in any foreign country chosen. Edison's failure to file a U.S. application in 1878 (or promptly convert his March caveat) at the same time as his second English phonograph patent (Series 1878, 24 Apr and 22 Oct 1878, #1644) led to denial of the American patent application filed 15 Dec 1878 on the grounds of prior publication. Edison tried to repair the damage by reapplying, to no avail. Partly as a result, American Graphophone Co. was able to negotiate a royalty of $10 for every Edison machine sold until 1894.

Some of the pivotal names in European recorded sound had their patent histories. Léon Scott's important phonautographic patent was registered in France on 25 Mar 1857 (#17.897/31.470), with illustrations showing a flat recording surface; the 29 July 1859 amendment displayed the familiar traveling drum inspired by Young, Duhamel, and Wertheim. **Charles Cros** did not register a formal patent on his sealed Paleophone description of 16 Apr 1877 (opened 3 Dec) until 28 Apr/1 May and 2–3 Aug 1878 (French patent #124.313) and as far as is known never "reduced the idea to practice," built a model, nor even made a drawing. His explicator, Abbé Lenoir, did use the word "phonograph" in the 10 Oct 1877 issue of *La semaine du clergé*. However, the word had been previously used by Edison in August, and long before—in the 1840s—by Isaac and Benn Pitman to describe their newly-invented system of shorthand transcription.

Allen Koenigsberg

(The above text is a modified version of introductory material in Koenigsberg's *Patent History of the Phonograph 1877–1912* [1990], used by permission. Copyright © 1989 by Allen Koenigsberg. All rights reserved.)

A number of significant patents were granted after 1912. Electrical recording systems were made possible by the prior invention of the Audion—British patent #1427, issued in 1908—and the single-stage amplifier—U.S. #841,387; 1907—by **Lee De Forest**. Among the great innovations of the 1920s was the pioneer moving-coil recording head for disc recording, patented by **Horace Owen Merriman** and **Lionel Guest** (British patent #141,790; 1920).

Alan Dower Blumlein and H. E. Holman developed the moving-coil microphone in the 1930s, gaining a patent from Britain, #350,998. They also patented a single-turn moving-coil cutting head (British patents #350,954 and #350,998).

At **Bell Telephone Laboratories** in the U.S. the research of Joseph P. Maxfield and Henry C. Harrison led to several related patents in 1923: U.S. #1,562,165; #1,663,884; #1,663,885; #1,678,116; and #1,709,571; plus British patent #262,839. **Microphone** research at Bell led to the patents for several instruments (U.S. #1,333,744; #1,456,538; #1,603,300; #1,611, 870; #1,675,853; British #134,872). The so-called rubber-line electrical recorder, designed to give a flat, extended range frequency response, also came from Bell Laboratories, in 1923 (U.S. #1,562,165; #1,663,884; #1,663,885; #1,678,116; #1,709,571; British #262,839). Advances in microphone design came from RCA in 1931, with the ribbon microphone (U.S. #1,885,001; British #386,478); there were numerous further developments of microphone design.

Full frequency range records (ffrr), introduced by Decca Record Co., Ltd., around 1945, was the result of **Arthur Haddy**'s research; it ushered in the age of high fidelity.

In magnetic recording, based on the early work of **Valdemar Poulsen** (first British patent #8,961; 1899), progress was slow. Among the key patents of the 1920s were one for applying bias by W. L. Carlson and G. W. Carpenter in 1921 (U.S. #1,640,881), and Curt Stille's steel tape recorder (British #331,859; 1928). The **Blattnerphone** of the late 1920s was improved and patented by Guglielmo Marconi (British #458,255 and #467,105). Wire recording developments in the 1940s were largely credited to **Marvin Camras** of the Armour Research Foundation in Chicago. Among his patents were U.S. #2,351,003 and #2,351,007, filed in 1942. The use of coated tape as the magnetic medium was first patented in Germany in 1928 (#500,900 and #544,302; then British #333,154) by Fritz Pfleumer.

Stereophonic recording began with the work of W. Bartlett Jones, who patented in 1928 his idea of putting two channels into a single groove (U.S. #1,855,150), but he did not develop the concept into production. Alan Blumlein was researching the subject also, and put many basic ideas into his patent applications of December 1931 (British #394,325; U.S. #2,095,540). He laid the foundations of the modern stereo disc. Blumlein thought of spacing pressure microphones to provide the listener with localizing ability (British #394,325; 429,022).

Peter Maxfield's successful **long-playing record,** issued by Columbia in 1948, was based on a combination of ideas and processes previously patented, as well as some new ones. For example W.S. Bachman's U.S. patent #2,738,385, for a variable-pitch system of re-

cording, allowed the extension of recording time to 30 minutes per side of the 12-inch LP.

PATHÉ FRÈRES COMPAGNIE. A firm established by Charles Pathé and Emile Pathé in Paris, in 1896. It succeeded their earlier company, Les Phonographes Pathé (1894). Address was 72 Cours de Vincennes. The Pathé brothers had seen an Edison phonograph demonstration and had begun to put on exhibitions themselves. They went on to wholesale Edison machines, and to market their own cylinders for it. They also became interested in motion pictures. The Compagnie Général des Cinématographes, Phonographes et Pellicules was registered in December 1897, with an address at 98 rue de Richelieu. Four years later the name was elaborated to Compagnie Général de Phonographes, Cinématographes et Appareils de Précision. In 1898 the Pathé brothers issued a catalog of their cylinders, offering nearly 800 recordings. "Celeste Aida" was number one in the catalog; like most of the records, it bore no artist's name; however announcements on the records did reveal the identity of the performers. The cylinders were made of perishable light-brown wax compounds, and only a few have survived.

Pathé's second catalog, 1899, continued with the same repertoire, which was basically classical and largely operatic. There were also popular songs, religious items, spoken records, children's songs, national anthems, and material in Italian, Spanish, German, and Russian.

Deluxe cylinders with prominent artists were offered from late 1901 or 1902, in competition with G & T's Red Label records. However the composition of the cylinder was unchanged. The "Céleste" five-minute cylinder was issued in 1903–1905, to counter G & T's new 12-inch discs. Because it required a new playback machine, the innovation was not a market success. In about 1903 Pathé abandoned its brown wax formula for the more durable black wax. In November 1906 the firm introduced its disc records, vertical cut, with shallow, wide grooves. They started at the center and played outward, using a sapphire stylus. Because the wide grooves reduced playing time, the disc diameter was larger than the conventional discs of G & T and other firms: up to 14 inches at first, then to 20 inches by 1909. All discs were in fact made to metric dimensions, although in Britain the sizes were expressed in Imperial measures, and later there were 10- and 12-inch discs there.

Pathé gave up its cylinders in Britain in 1906 (carrying on with them a few more years in France) and concentrated on disc production.

Pathé was also active in the sale of record players, cylinder at first, then (from 1906) both disc players (Pathéphones) and cylinder players. It sold Edison machines, and Columbia Graphophones, at one time relabeling the Graphophone Eagle as their own Le Coq. The firm also produced its own brand of players, and in time discontinued the import of American machines. A line of office dictating machines, named Ronéophone, was available as well. The Pathé cylinder machines were of high quality, but the disc players were prevented from attaining the standard of Victor machines because of the Victor patent on the tapered tone arm.

This is a list of Pathé cylinder phonographs:

Model	Year	Illustrated in:
0	1904	Marty 1979, p. 94
1	1904	Marty 1979, p. 88
2	1904	Marty 1979, p. 88
3	1904	Marty 1979, p. 88
4	1904	Marty 1979, p. 94

The above were also identified as Nouveau Phonographe Pathé. They all played standard cylinders and 9.5-centimeter "Inter" cylinders. Model 4 also played the larger Stentor records.

Aiglon   before 1903   Marty 1979, p. 89
An adaptation of the Graphophone.

Céleste   ca. 1900   Marty 1979, p. 91
The largest Pathé phonograph, an adaptation of the Graphophone; it played cylinders of 8.2 inches x 4.1 inches (21 centimeters x 10.5 centimeters). Selling price was 1,000 francs. A lighter model came out in 1903 for 600 francs.

Chant-Clair   ca. 1905   Marty 1979, pp. 86–87
For Concert-size cylinders. Some models had cardboard horns, others aluminum horns.

Coq   before 1899   Marty 1979, p. 94
Packaged for travel; it was a copy of the Graphophone Eagle. The cock was the Pathé trademark.

Coquet   before 1903   Marty 1979, p. 94
A smaller Coq, with an aluminum horn.

Français   before 1903
An adaptation of the Graphophone.

Gaulois   before 1903   Marty 1979, pp. 92–93
Discontinued after 1903.

Stentor   ca. 1900

These are Pathé gramophones (all with internal horn unless noted):

A   1905   Marty 1979, p. 95

Actuelle 1920   TMR 60–61, cover
A console with lid and doors.

Aida   1912   TMR #19
The top of the line deluxe console, of mahogany, inlaid; could play discs up to 20 inches in diameter; spring motor ran 20 minutes. Sold in Britain for 60 guineas.

Carmen 1912   TMR #19
A console, with 10-minute spring motor; made of mahogany, inlaid. Sold in Britain for 20 guineas.

Cert   1912   TMR #18
A table model without a lid, with 10-minute spring motor. Sold in Britain for £2/5/0.

Concert   Marty 1979, p. 102
A large instrument for public entertainment, coin operated. Electric motor. Could play the large 20-inch diameter records.

Coronet 1912   TMR #18
An external brass horn table model, in oak or mahogany, with 12-minute spring motor. Sold in Britain for £6/10/0.

Diamond   Marty 1979, p. 103
A portable that folded into a box.

Difusor ca. 1922   TMR #60–61, p. 1610
Table model and console, with a large conical diaphragm at the rear of the apparatus to diffuse the sound. Sold in France for 575 and 650 francs.

Duplex 1912   TMR #19
A double table model, with two complete turntable-motor-reproducer mechanisms. The purpose was to permit playing album sets, such as "Complete Opera at Home," without interruption. With 12-inch turntable, it sold in Britain for £13/10/0. A cheaper model with 10-inch turntable cost £9/10/0.

Elf   1912   TMR #18
A table model with lid, 10-minute spring motor. Sold in Britain for £1/17/6.

Hamlet 1912 *TMR* #19

A console, with 12-minute spring motor. Sold in Britain for 35 guineas.

Gioconda 1912 *TMR* #19

An elegant console in mahogany, inlaid, with 20-minute spring motor. Sold in Britain for 45 guineas.

Ideal 1912 *TMR* #18

A table model with carrying case. Sold in Britain for £2/15/0.

Jeunesse 1910 Marty 1979, p. 100

Smallest of the table models, without lid; it played only the 21- and 24-centimeter records. Sold in France for 25 francs.

Leader 1912 *TMR* #18

The least expensive external horn table model; sold in Britain for £2/2/0.

Louise 1912 *TMR* #19

A table model with cover, made of mahogany, inlaid. Sold in Britain for £12/12/0.

Martha 1912 *TMR* #19

A console, of mahogany, with 25-minute spring motor. Sold in Britain for 30 guineas. Described in the 1912 catalog as being in "Hettelwhite" style.

Omnibus 1908 Marty 1979, p. 97

A table model with exterior horn. Sold in France for 35 francs.

Onward 1912 *TMR* #18

A table model with interior horn, said to have a hinged lid (not shown in the illustration). Sold in Britain for £3/15/0.

Orpheus 1912 *TMR* #18

A table model with lid, and two front doors for volume control. Sold in Britain for £7/15/0.

Oxford 1912 *TMR* #18

An interior horn table model, with two front doors. Sold in Britain for £7/15/0.

Pathéphone: the generic name for Pathé disc players.

Romeo 1912 *TMR* #19

A console in mahogany, with 12-minute spring motor. Sold in Britain for 40 guineas.

Ronéophone

A disc dictating machine for business use. A large wax disc was provided, which could be shaved for re-use. Spring motor and electric motor versions were available. The name came from the Ronéo firm, makers of office equipment, which joined with Pathé in this effort.

Scout 1912 *TMR* #18

An external horn table model, available with brass or wood horn. Sold in Britain for £3/13/0 (brass) or £3/15/0 (wood).

Success 1912 *TMR* #18

An internal horn table model, in oak. Sold in Britain for £5/5/0.

Tosca 1912 *TMR* #19

A deluxe console in mahogany, with 12-minute spring motor. Sold in Britain for 20 guineas.

Zampa 1912 *TMR* #19

A console, in oak, with 10-minute spring motor. Sold in Britain for 18 guineas.

The company was highly successful throughout Europe, and had branch offices in many countries before 1910. Pathé Frères (London), Ltd., was established in 1902, at 14-16-18 Lamb's Conduit St.; it issued a catalog of cylinders in 1904 and a catalog of record players on sale in 1906. Hurteau and Co. of Montreal were the agents for Pathé goods in Quebec. There were other factors elsewhere in Canada. In New York there was already a Pathé address, at 42 E. 23rd St. In September 1917 it moved to 41 W. 25th St. (*see* PATHÉ FRÈRES PHONOGRAPH CO., INC.).

Rights for France and the colonies (not the U.S.) were acquired by Columbia Graphophone Co., Ltd., in October 1928. Discs with the Pathé label were still made in France until 1932, although the company had been absorbed by the Société Pathé Marconi, which brought together the French interests of the Gramophone Co., Columbia, and Pathé. All became part of EMI, Ltd., in 1931.

[Andrews*; Girard 1964 chronicles the company's history in the cylinder period; Watts 1989; *TMR* #58 (June 1979) reproduced a 1904 cylinder catalog.]

PATHÉ FRÈRES PHONOGRAPH CO., INC.

A New York firm established in late 1911 or January 1912, incorporated in Delaware. The arrangement with the French firm, **Pathé Frères Compagnie**, allowed the American company to buy and market Pathé goods. Emil Pathé was consulting engineer for the American firm. In March 1913 Pathé products were demonstrated in New York, including Pathéphones,

Pathégraphs, twin-turntabled Duplex Pathéphones, and a Pathé Reflex machine, along with Pathé discs. In May 1914 it was reported that the firm had leased the entire second floor of a newly erected building at 29-33 W. 38th St., New York. **Russell Hunting** was named director of recording at a new pressing plant to be constructed.

Record sizes and prices in September 1914 were 11 1/2-inch ($2), 14-inch ($2.50), and 20-inch ($4). In subsequent months, as shipments continued to arrive from Europe despite the War, dealers were named in several American cities. The O'Neill-James Co. assumed responsibility for Chicago and the West. The State Street Pathéphone Co. was established in Chicago by **Arthur J. O'Neill**. In New York, **Eugene A. Widmann** was reported to be general manager and treasurer. A $200 record player was marketed, with gold-plated parts and a four-spring motor. Later there was a Sheraton Pathéphone, with an electric (battery) motor, selling for $300. An extensive factory was occupied in Belleville, New Jersey, responding to great demand for Pathé discs. In July 1915 the American firm claimed to command the largest record catalog in the world, with over 96,000 selections.

Frank L. Capps became production manager in October 1915, in charge of all experimental, mechanical, and development work. The Pathé Pathéphone Shop opened opposite the New York Public Library on Fifth Ave. at 42nd St.

The center-start records were replaced by standard outside-start records in February 1916. Record labels bore the characteristic rooster trademark. The Pathé Frères Pathéphone Co., Ltd., of Canada was established, with a factory in Toronto. An agreement was made with Brunswick-Balke-Collender in 1916; Brunswick to make record players for Pathé, and Pathé to supply discs to be sold through Brunswick dealers. In February 1917 the New York office moved from 29 W. 38th St. to a new building at Grand Ave. and Flushing Ave., Brooklyn. George W. Lyle, for many years vice president and general manager of Columbia Graphophone Co., was appointed assistant manager to Widmann. Walter L. Eckert, late chief of Thomas Edison's financial department,

joined Pathé as general auditor and office manager. Pathé's output in 1917 was reported to have increased 500 percent over the previous year.

A revolutionary new record player, the Actuelle, was demonstrated. It had a cone-shaped parchment diaphragm fitted into a gold-plated aluminum frame and attached to the needle holder by a wire. It could play either vertical-cut or lateral discs with a twist of the needle. Two doors on one side of the cabinet and a device with a wire (a remote) were used to control the volume.

In November 1918 the Pathé Military Band marched on Fifth Ave. as part of Peace Day celebrations, joined by the office staff and administration; Widmann acted as parade marshall. One of the Pathé artists, Kathleen Howard, sang the national anthem on the Public Library steps. *Pathé News*, a house organ, was published from June 1919.

Widmann announced that from July 1919 the American firm would control the stock, plant and policy of the British Pathé company, as well as other companies in the Western Hemisphere. (The British firm was sold in 1921 to the Compagnie Général des Machines Parlantes, Pathé Frères, Paris.)

Among the star artists on the Pathé label in 1919 were Eddie Cantor, Rudolf Ganz, Claudia Muzio, Tito Schipa, and Jacques Thibaud. The **Actuelle (label)**, lateral cut, was introduced in the U.S. and Britain. There were popular series, including dance records, race records, comedy songs, Hawaiian, sacred, and standard vocal material. Pathé jazz and pop artists included Red Nichols, Duke Ellington, Annette Hanshaw, the California Ramblers (as the Golden Gate Orchestra), Lee Morse, and Cliff Edwards. Maurice Chevalier and other French performers were available from masters cut in Paris.

Eugene A. Widmann became chairman of the board, succeeded as president by W. W. Chase. Financial difficulties arose in 1921 due to influx of radio. Widmann resigned as chairman of the board in December. Receivers in equity were appointed to take charge of the firm and deal with the claims of its creditors. A reorganization emerged, and a name change took place in August 1922, to Pathé Sound

Wave Corp. In November 1922 the name was changed to Pathé Frères Phonograph and Radio Corp. Emil Pathé was director of the new entity, and Widmann returned to the presidency. Actuelle discs were still selling well, at $.55 each. And a new subsidiary was set up, called Perfect Record Co. **Perfect** lateral discs were issued around September 1922, at $.50 each. Vertical-cut discs were no longer advertised.

The New York offices moved to 150 E. 53rd St. in August 1923. A radio division was created, headed by James Watters. Throughout 1924 the company advertised Pathéphones, Pathé radios, and lateral-cut discs.

Widmann announced in September 1925 a new process of recording, based on extensive research in electrical and photoelectrical soundwave reproducing methods—a system differing from any other. It was not an electric process, but by 1927 a new Pathéphonic electrical method was in use. James E. Macpherson was president of the firm in 1928, and of the associated Pathé Record Corp. In 1928 Pathé and **Cameo Record Corp.** merged. Many records were then issued on both labels simultaneously.

The record industry was in economic crisis in 1929. Pathé was among the companies that were merged into the new **American Record Corp.** in August. Actuelle records were no longer produced, but Perfect continued, pressed from Cameo masters. until 1938. Pathé and Perfect masters were used in Britain to produce some of the Pathé discs there, and for Actuelles and Pathé Perfect; and also for subcontracted work to Homochord, Grafton High Grade Record, Scala Record (7000 series), and Scala Ideal Record. Through further subcontracting, it was also used for Gamage and Vox Humana records. [Andrews*.]

PATRIA RECORDS (label). An American 10-inch disc issued in 1917 by the Patria Records Corp., 32 E. 23rd St., New York. Phillip Waldman was general manager. A war message by President Woodrow Wilson was advertised in May. [Andrews*.]

PATTI, ADELINA, 1843–1919. Spanish soprano, born in Madrid as Adela Juana Maria Patti on 10 Feb 1843. She was the daughter of two Italian singers, who took her to New York as a child. She began singing in recitals there in 1851, and made a formal debut as Lucia in 1859. A juvenile sensation, she was acclaimed in Covent Garden and Paris. In 1877 she sang Violetta at La Scala, and in 1892 was heard at the Metropolitan Opera. She retired in 1895, to Craig Y Nos, a Welsh castle, but returned to sing a farewell concert in 1906 and a Red Cross benefit in 1914. She died in Brecknock, Wales, on 27 Sep 1919.

Patti's sensational career, featuring 30 roles, was not marked by a flow of great recordings, as she was reluctant to make records. Possibly her first effort displeased her: a cylinder made in London in 1895 of "Éclat de rire" (a laughing song) from Auber's opera *Manon Lescaut* (released on disc in 1943 as IRCC #219). She was finally persuaded in 1905 by the Gramophone Co. to have recording equipment installed in her castle, and made 14 sides—accompanied by Landon Ronald—that were issued on a special pink Patti label. In 1906 she added a few more sides, bringing her total number of different pieces recorded on disc to 21. Her records were sold at premium prices in Britain (one guinea) and in America ($5 each by Victor). As a woman of 62 and 63 years when she made these records, following a 50-year public career, she did not sound at her greatest on them. EMI issued the Patti material on LP in 1974, and Pearl presented a CD of all her disc recordings in 1990 (#GEMMCD 9312). [Williams, C. 1956 is a complete discography.]

PAUL, LES, 1916– . American guitarist, born in Waukesha, Wisconsin, on 9 June 1916. He was on radio from the early 1930s, and was featured on the Fred Waring show in 1938–1941. After the War he led his own trio, then found success in the 1950s using a multichannel recording process to present himself playing several guitar parts in backup to the vocals of his wife, Mary Ford. "How High the Moon" (Capitol #1451; 1951) and "Mocking Bird Hill" (Capitol #1373; 1951) were early chart singles. There were a dozen others in the next ten years, notably "Vaya con Dios" (Capitol #2486; 1953) which was on the charts 22 weeks. The couple also had a pair of best-selling LP albums, in

1955 and 1959, and appeared on television. Paul was still performing in 1992.

PAVAROTTI, LUCIANO, 1935– . Italian tenor, born in Modena on 12 Oct 1935. He taught school and sold insurance while taking voice lessons, and made his debut in Reggio Emilia in 1961 as Rodolfo. His success was immediate, and soon he was singing in all the major houses of Europe. In 1968 he appeared at the Metropolitan Opera as Rodolfo; by then he was already recognized as one of the preeminent singers of the century. Pavarotti has recorded extensively, covering the Italian/French repertoire, most notably in complete Verdi operas for Decca with Joan Sutherland and in numerous recital records. By 1985 he had placed eight albums on the best seller charts, all on the London label. He received Grammys for three albums (1978, 1979, 1988). The 1990 album *Carreras, Domingo, Pavarotti in Concert* (London #430433-2; with José Carreras and Placido Domingo) sold around 5,700,000 copies. [Pavarotti 1981 contains a complete discography up to time of publication.]

PAYOLA. The name given to illegal promotional payments given by record companies or artists to disk jockeys. It was a special problem in America in the 1950s, peaking at the 1959 national disc jockey convention in Miami Beach, styled by *Time* magazine as an event of "booze, broads, and payola." Major scandals led to government investigations, and tighter controls by radio and television stations, though problems remained into the 1970s. Columbia was involved in a 1973 scandal centered on Clive Davis (indicted but not convicted). Another key figure in payola history was **Dick Clark**, but he was never indicted. **Alan Freed** was the most well-known disc jockey to be convicted of accepting payola.

PEACOCK (label). A British record issued in the mid 1930s, through Peacock Stores. British Homophone and Decca/Panachord masters were used. Repertoire was light popular, and the artists were pseudonymous. Peacock Stores, Ltd., is in business today, but does not issue records. [Andrews*; Rust 1978.]

PEAK. The maximum numerical value for any given event; in audio systems usually applied to the maximum instantaneous output (peak output) of a given component. Usually the peak is occasioned by a musical fortissimo.

PEARL (label). A British record of Pavilion Records, Ltd., distributed by Harmonia Mundi and H. R. Taylor, Ltd., in the U.K. and by Koch International in the U.S.; by other distributors worldwide. The firm specializes in reissues, many from Columbia and HMV/Victor matrices. Important material by such artists as Enrico Caruso, Pablo Casals, Fritz Kreisler, and Artur Schnabel has appeared. CD transfers are widely acclaimed for their technical excellence. Flapper and Opal are associated labels.

PEERCE, JAN, 1904–1984. American tenor, born Jacob Pincus Perelmuth in New York on 3 June 1904. He played violin and sang with dance bands in New York, and appeared in Radio City Music Hall from 1933 to 1941. He made his opera debut in Philadelphia, as the Duke, in 1938. His Metropolitan Opera career extended form 1941 to 1968. Arturo Toscanini chose him to sing in the NBC broadcast of the Beethoven Ninth Symphony in 1938; Toscanini referred to Peerce as his "favorite tenor." Peerce appeared with major opera companies and in recital worldwide. He suffered a stroke in 1982, and died in New York on 15 Dec 1984.

It is uncertain whether Peerce is the unidentified singer on Grey Gull disc #1505 of ca. 1927: "My Ohio Home" / "There Never Was a Gal like My Daddy's Gal." His first definite recordings were under the names Pinkie, Pinky, or Jack Pearl, for the Perfect label in 1931. (Another pseudonym used was Randolph Joyce.) He was then heard on various labels, singing the light repertoire and operatic numbers. "Bluebird of Happiness" was a favorite with his fans (W.B. transcription #500–622); ca. 1934). He recorded the Toscanini-Beethoven symphony cited above in 1938 for ATRA (#3007). Peerce made 24 LP albums. [Pinta 1987.]

PEERLESS (label). An American record, pressed by the Starr Piano Co. from Gennett masters. Only a few issues are known, from 1922. [Rust 1978.]

PEERLESS ORCHESTRA. An ensemble that recorded about 150 numbers for Edison cylinders before 1912. It also made many records, from overtures to ragtime, for Zonophone in Britain, in 1910–1922. [Koenigsberg 1987.]

PEERLESS PHONOGRAPH CO. A New York firm, established in 1915 to handle Pathé products. Location was 132nd and Brown Place. Ben H. Janssen was president.

PEERLESS RECORD (label). An American disc supplied by Leeds & Catlin in the first decade of the century. It was a double-sided record, 10-inch size. [Andrews*.]

PEERLESS QUARTET. A male vocal ensemble active from 1906 to 1928. It was organized by Frank C. Stanley, who sang bass until his death in December 1910. The other members were Albert Campbell, tenor; Henry Burr, lead tenor; and Steve Porter, baritone. In 1910 Burr became manager, John H. Meyer took the bass line (also acting as arranger), and Arthur Collins replaced Steve Porter as baritone. Having begun as an offshoot of the Columbia Quartet (which came from the Invincible Quartet or Invincible Four), they retained that name for Columbia records until 1912, when they became the Peerless on that label also. They made thousands of records for all labels, including eight Edison cylinders in 1909–1910, four Edison Diamond Discs in 1914–1915, and a great quantity of discs for Victor (125 titles in the 1917 catalog), with whom they signed as exclusive artists in 1920.

In 1917 the members were Campbell, Burr, Meyer, and Frank Croxton; this was the peak period for the group. Another personnel change took place in 1926, as Carl Mathieu replaced Campbell, Stanley Baughman replaced Meyer, and James Stanley replaced Croxton; this left Henry Burr as the only original member to remain with the quartet until it disbanded, in 1928. Their final Victor was made on 11 Sep 1927: "Old Names of Old Flames" (#21079). In 1940 Victor still carried nine of their sides in the catalog, including "Darling Nellie Gray"

(#19887) and the ever popular "Sweet Adeline" (#20055). [Walsh 1969/12.]

PEERLESS TRIO. A male vocal ensemble that recorded for Indestructible Records in 1907–1908, and for Victor. Members were Billy Murray, Byron C. Harlan, and Steve Porter. They were known as the Victor Vaudeville Co. on Victor discs, of which there were three in the 1917 catalog, two 10-inch and one 12-inch ("Court Scene in Carolina" / "Darktown Campmeetin' Experiences"; #35609).

PENNINGTON (label). An American record issued by the Bridgeport Die and Machine Co. in 1924 and 1925, marketed by the L. Bamberger & Co. department stores. Masters came mostly from Paramount, Emerson, Olympic, and Blu-Disc. Releases ceased when Bridgeport Die and Machine went bankrupt in 1925. [Kendziora 1991/1; Rust 1978.]

PERCUSSION INSTRUMENT RECORDINGS. The only known drum solo on acoustic records is "Ragtime Drummer," played by James I. Lent. It was issued on G & T, and on Victor (#17092), Indestructible Cylinders (#689), and Emerson (#779), in 1904. During the swing era drummers became established as key sidemen and often as soloists. Among the names that stand out are Louis Bellson, **Sonny Greer** (with Duke Ellington), **Jo Jones** (with Count Basie), **Gene Krupa, Ray McKinley** (with Jimmy Dorsey), Buddy Rich (with Bunny Berigan), **Shelly Manne, Dave Tough** (with Benny Goodman), **Chick Webb,** and George Wettling (with Red Norvo). Ringo Starr was the most acclaimed drummer of the rock era, as the driving force of the Beatles.

For information on non-drummer percussionists *see* LIONEL HAMPTON; MILT JACKSON; RED NORVO.

PERFECT (label). An American record issued by Pathé (but shown as coming from the Perfect Record Co., Brooklyn) from sometime between July and September 1922; the final releases were in April 1938, when the label belonged to the American Record Corp., which had taken over Pathé Frères Phonograph Co, Inc., in 1929. Much of the early output (until

1929) corresponded to the material on Pathé's Actuelle label. Perfect was a low-price record, selling for $.50 at first, then dropping as low as $.25; the regular price of standard labels in the 1920s was $.75. Like other cut-rate labels from major companies, Perfect kept its artist names secret, using pseudonyms. Thus the California Ramblers appeared as the Golden Gate Orchestra, Fletcher Henderson as the Lenox Dance Orchestra or the Southampton Society Orchestra, etc. Some real names were given in the later years of the label.

Series issued on Perfect were race, standard vocal and standard instrumental, opera-classical, star series, popular vocal, and dance music. Discs were made at the Pathé studio at 18 W. 42nd St, then at 150 E. 53rd St. The label itself had several designs, of which the most striking featured two nude women apparently worshipping a perfect sunrise.

In Britain (1928) the Perfect label was an outwardly Pathé product, using mostly American Pathé matrices. It terminated with the takeover of Pathé in Europe by Columbia (International), Ltd. [Andrews*; Kendziora 1963/5–6 is a label list of the dance and race series; Rust 1978.]

PERFORMANCE RIGHTS. In January 1851, the Société des Auteurs, Compositeurs et Éditeurs de Musique was established in Paris to work for the recognition of rights and to assist in the prosecution of infringers. Similar organizations were founded in other countries. France had the first laws (1905) to protect the producers of recordings against unwarranted reproductions. The Société demanded royalties on all records sold, and despite some setbacks, like the 1906 decision in Belgium against copyright holders, the movement took hold. In Italy in 1906 a composer society won a suit for royalties on record sales. In the U.S. the Copyright Act of 1909 included coverage of recordings, calling for a $.02 royalty; enforcement then became the main problem, and it remains so today. *See also* COPYRIGHT; PIRATED RECORDS.

Periodicals. *See* SOUND RECORDING PERIODICALS.

PERMANENT NEEDLE SALES CO. A Chicago firm, located in 1910 at 14 State St. Advertising in *TMW* offered the first permanent jewel disc needle, which required no changing and no sharpening. It was available in loud, medium, and soft volume designs.

PERSONICS. The practice of making customized tapes for clients.

PERTILE, AURELIANO, 1885–1952. Italian tenor, born in Montagnana on 9 Nov 1885. He made his debut in *Martha* in Vicenza in 1911, sang in various Italian houses, and appeared at La Scala in 1916. His one season at the Metropolitan was 1921–1922, after which he settled at La Scala until 1937. He performed the Italian/French dramatic tenor repertoire, plus Lohengrin, and was acknowledged to be among the finest interpreters of his time. He died in Milan on 11 Jan 1952.

Pertile recorded for Pathé in Milan in 1923–1926, beginning with "Donna non vidi mai" from *Manon Lescaut* (#10371). "Cielo e mar" (#74949), and "Una vergine" from *Favorita* (#10411) were outstanding among these early numbers. Later he went to Fonotipia (1927), Columbia (1927–1931), and HMV (1928–1932). "Quando le sere" from *Luisa Miller* (HMV #DB1111; 1928) was one of his highly praised early electrics. He was heard in the complete recordings of *Aida* and *Carmen*. There were many LP reissues, and a CD of 1990 carried material from HMV, including the above cited arias (the Pathés in later re-recordings), from the 1928–1932 period. [Morby 1952 is a complete discography.]

PETER, PAUL, AND MARY. An American vocal and instrumental folk group, consisting of Peter Yarrow, Noel Paul Stookey, and Mary Ellin Travers. They began to perform together in New York in 1962, and were successful on a national tour. Having signed a Warner label contract, they quickly made a best-selling album that was on the charts for two years, *Peter, Paul and Mary* (Warner #W1449; 1962), and followed it a few months later with *Movin'* (Warner #W1473; 1963); it was a chart album for 76 weeks. Their outstanding singles of the period were Grammy Award winning "Blowin' in the Wind" (Warner #5268; 1963), and "Puff the Magic Dragon"—written by Yarrow—(Warner #5348; 1963). "Leaving on a Jet Plane" (Warner # 7340; 1969) was one of the many later hit singles by the group. They appeared on major television shows in the 1960s and also in clubs and in concert. In the 1970s they were less active, but made one more chart album, *Reunion* (Warner #BSK 3212; 1978). The trio gave a concert in the Chicago area in August 1991.

PETERSON, OSCAR, 1925– . Canadian jazz pianist, born in Montreal on 15 Aug 1925. He performed on Canadian radio, then went to New York in 1949. He gained a reputation as a soloist and for his tasteful accompaniments; and formed an outstanding trio, with Ray Brown, bass, and Herb Ellis, guitar; in 1958 replacing Ellis with a drummer, Ed Thigpen. The biggest hit of their many albums was *Oscar Peterson Trio + 1* (Mercury #MG 20975; 1964). Brown and Thigpen left in 1965. In 1990 the original threesome came back together, and recorded *The Legendary Oscar Peterson Trio* for the Telarc Jazz label.

PETMECKY CO. A firm located in Kansas City, Missouri; and in 1907 at 506a New York Life Building. They manufactured Multi-Tone needles, which played loudly or softly depending on their placement in the reproducer. Petmecky needles were claimed to "improve the record."

PETMECKY SUPPLY CO., INC. A Texas firm, incorporated in Austin in December 1909, licensed to distribute Victor products in Texas and Oklahoma. Fred Petmecky was president; B.F. Reeves was vice president and general manager.

PHANTASIE CONCERT RECORD (label). A rare American record of 1921, and perhaps early 1922. Material (dance, blues, and novelty items) came from Lyric, Olympic or Criterion. Issues by a singer named Josephine Baker were not by the famous artist of that name. [Kendziora 1984/6; Rust 1978.]

PHASE INVERTER. A circuit in an amplifier that derives the opposing voltage polarity required to drive the push-pull output stage.

PHASE SHIFT. A distortion in an audio system produced when signals originally simultaneous are heard with a small delay between them. This delay, often occasioned by ultrasonic filters in modern systems, may be as tiny as a thousandth of a second, but it will result in a mismatch of the signal peaks. If the signal peaks are at exact opposite stages of their cycles, they are 180 degrees out of phase, and cancel each other out. Out-of-phase program material is a particular problem in stereo playback, as it may cause loudspeakers to vibrate out of step with each other. However, some out-of-phase programming is fundamental to the stereo effect: when signals are separately reproduced through different loudspeakers it is phase shift (at very low frequencies) that suggests to the listener that the sound is coming from somewhere between the two speakers. It seems that among audio components it is the loudspeakers that have the potential to create sufficient phase shift to be audible. *See also* PHASING; PHASING SWITCH.

PHASING. (I) The correlation between cone movement in one loudspeaker with respect to that in another loudspeaker. *See also* PHASE SHIFT; PHASING SWITCH.

PHASING. (II) A special effect obtained in the sound studio by dividing a signal between two tape machines or networks, and subjecting one to a minuscule time delay. *See also* FLANGING.

PHASING SWITCH. A control on an amplifier, also known as the phase reversal switch, that reverses the leads to one loudspeaker, thus changing its relative phase. *See also* PHASE SHIFT.

PHILADELPHIA ORCHESTRA. An ensemble established in 1900, succeeding an amateur orchestra that had played under the conductor W. W. Gilchrist. Fritz Scheel was the director until he died in 1907. Carl Pohlig headed the orchestra until 1912, when he resigned and was succeeded by Leopold Stokowski. Under Stokowski the resonant, glowing "Philadelphia sound" was developed, and with it world eminence. Eugene Ormandy was conductor from 1938 to 1980, further perfecting the ensemble timbre, when Riccardo Muti took the podium. Muti's resignation, effective in 1992, brought an unexpected successor in Wolfgang Sawallisch.

The orchestra made its first Victor records in 1917, and became a mainstay of the label. By the time of the 1940 catalog there were about 360 titles recorded. A number of events in recording history were centered on the orchestra. Victor's first orchestral electric recording was *Danse macabre* (#6505; 1925). And Victor's 1931 initiative with long-playing records included the Philadelphians playing the first complete symphony for LP (albeit 78 rpm, not microgroove 33 1/3), Beethoven's Fifth. In 1932 Bell Laboratories conducted experiments in the Academy of Music, leading to recording the orchestra under Stokowski with two microphones; the signals were etched into parallel grooves on 78 rpm discs, giving a stereophonic effect that was demonstrated successfully at the Chicago Century of Progress Exposition in 1933. In 1940 the Disney film *Fantasia* featured the orchestra in a multiple-track recording that gave theatre-goers a preview of surround-sound.

For other notable discs made by the Philadelphia Orchestra, *see* RICCARDO MUTI; EUGENE ORMANDY; LEOPOLD STOKOWSKI.

PHILHARMONIA (label). An American disc issued during 1951–1954 from Philharmonia Records Corp., 65 Montague St., Brooklyn. The material was classical.

PHILHARMONIC (label). (I) A British disc issued in 1913–1914 from a company of the same name, pressed from Favorite Record matrices. [Andrews*.]

PHILHARMONIC (label). (II) An American record, produced by Varsity for Firestone Tires in 1939–1940. Masters came from Columbia, Victor, and HMV. Material included some good jazz items, e.g., by W. C. Handy and Jack Teagarden. [Rust 1978.]

PHILHARMONIC STRING QUARTET. An ensemble that recorded for Edison in 1928. Members were Scipione Guidi, and Arthur Lichstein, violins; Leon E. Barzin, viola; and Oswaldo Mazzucchi, cello. Ensembles of the same name recorded for Columbia and HMV in Britain in the 1920s.

PHILIPS (label). One of the record brands sold by Polygram (PolyGram) International, so named from the Polygram parent firm, Philips NV. Recording under this label name began in the Netherlands in 1950, and branched out into Germany, Austria, Belgium, and (upon acquisition of the French Polydor Co.) in France. Reciprocal agreements were made with Columbia in the U.S. in 1951, and Philips repertoire appeared in America on the Epic label (a Columbia subsidiary) from 1955. Repertoire from Columbia was provided to Philips, rather than EMI, Ltd. In 1961 there was an exchange of material between Philips and Mercury Records. There were 78 rpm Philips records in Britain in January 1953.

Philips Phonographic Industries (PPI) and Deutsche Grammophon Gesellschaft (DGG) merged interests, each taking 50 percent of the other's shares. On 3 Jan 1972 PPI was renamed Phonogram International, becoming a subsidiary of the new conglomerate **PolyGram International**, which acquired Decca in England on 17 Jan 1980. [Andrews*.]

PHILLIPS, JOSEPH A., ca. 1880–1958. American baritone, born in Buffalo, New York. He sang in Europe as well as the U.S., doing a repertoire of ballads, popular material, and operetta. He began to record for Victor in 1911, with "All That I Ask Is Love" (#5806). Then he worked for Edison from 1912 to 1923. "Mary Was My Mother's Name" (Edison #988; 1912) was a notable success. He made a number of well-received duet records with Helen Clark. On Pathé records he was "Justice Lewis"; on Okeh he was sometimes "Franklyn Kent." Phillips died in Buffalo on 25 July 1958. [Walsh 1972/10–11.]

PHONADISC (label). A British record issued by **Edison Bell** in 1908 and 1909. It was 8 1/2 inches in size, vertical cut.

PHONAUTOGRAPH. The device invented by **Léon Scott** in 1857 to record (but not reproduce) sound signals on a lampblack-covered cylinder. Emile Berliner adapted the principle in his gramophone.

PHONET. In Thomas Edison's early terminology, the stylus/diaphragm assembly of the phonograph.

PHONO-CUT. Another name for vertical cut, the process of inscribing sound signals on record surfaces through an up and down movement of the cutting stylus.

PHONO-CUT (label). (I) A vertical-cut record issued by the Phono-Cut Record Co. of Boston, a subsidiary of the Boston Talking Machine Co., ca. 1912. The label was sold to a Mr. Keen in 1913, and became **Keen-o-phone.**

PHONO-CUT (label). (II) An American record of the Phono-Cut Record Co., offered in 1916. It was a 10-inch disc, selling at first for $.65, then for $.25. In April 1916 the record was available from the Wonder Talking Machine Co., 113-119 Fourth Ave., New York. [Andrews*.]

PHONOGRAM. (I) The original name given by Thomas Edison to his cylinder records, suggesting their intended use for business purposes. Later, musical cylinders were called "records."

PHONOGRAM. (II) The name of an early trade periodical; *see* SOUND RECORDING PERIODICALS.

Phonogram International. *See* POLYGRAM INTERNATIONAL.

PHONOGRAPH. In current terminology, any disc or cylinder record player. Originally it meant only the cylinder player, while the disc player was a **gramophone,** but that distinction faded early in the U.S. In Britain the specific terminology was retained through the 78 rpm

era, and lingers today in some contexts, e.g. the name of the principal sound recording journal, *Gramophone.* For history and technical aspects of the cylinder phonograph, *see* CYLINDER and THOMAS A. EDISON. *See also* GRAPHOPHONE.

PHONOGRAPH ACCESSORIES CORP. A New York firm, located at 25 Broad St. In 1915 it was announced acquisition of the patent for the "red needle" from the Master-Phone Corp.

PHONOGRAPH AND RECORDING CO. A New York firm, advertising in November 1921 from 260 W. 42nd St. It made records to order, for customers' own labels. [Andrews*.]

PHONOGRAPH MANUFACTURERS NATIONAL ASSOCIATION. A trade organization established in Chicago on 19 Feb 1925. President was M. C. Schaff (or Schiff); vice president was Otto Heinemann.

PHONOGRAPH PARLORS. Establishments that provided coin-op phonographs for public listening, popular in the U.S. after 1889, and then worldwide. Notable parlors were the Pathé **Salon du Phonographe** in Paris and a similar establishment in London; and the lobby of the Vitascope Hall motion picture theatre in Buffalo, New York (the first deluxe movie house in the U.S.), where 28 Edison phonographs were deployed. In Italy, the parlor was known as the Bar Automatico. Parlors declined in popularity with the introduction of automatic pianos and music boxes, but they persisted for years, often grouped with other coin machines in penny arcades.

PHONOGRAPH RECORDING CO. OF SAN FRANCISCO. A firm that made disc records to order; it was active in ca. 1926–1927. Only one example has been noticed in the literature. [Kendziora 1990/5–6; Rust 1978.]

PHONOGRAPH-GRAPHOPHONE. The commercial designation first given to the instrument of Chichester Bell and Charles Tainter when it was leased by the North American Phonograph Co. Later it was simply the **Graphophone,** the name they had given to their original experimental models, and later still it was the Columbia Graphophone.

PHONOGRAPHIC MUSIC CO. A Brooklyn firm, located in 1907 at 39 S. Ninth St. It advertised the Phonometer, a speed meter for disc players, in 1907.

PHONOLAMP. A device invented by George E. Emerson, marketed in the U.S. in 1916 by the Electric Phonograph Corp. of 29 W. 34th St., New York. It was an electric lamp with an electric motor phonograph in the lamp base. Doors in the base opened to give access to the turntable and reproducer, from which "the tone is carried upwards through the stem of the lamp, which acts as a concealed horn, and at the top is reflected downward by means of a globe and thereby producing a tone of unusual clarity"—this according to a *TMW* advertisement of 15 June 1916. The apparatus appeared in at least five models, selling from $75 to $200. A record with the same label name was produced by the Grey Gull organization, and given to purchasers of the lamp. [Kendziora 1988/2.]

Phonometer. *See* PHONOGRAPHIC MUSIC CO.

PHONOTHÈQUE NATIONALE. The French national record archive, established as a section of the Bibliothèque Nationale (Paris) in 1938.

PHONOTYPE RECORDS (label). A record made in Italy, trademarked by the Italian Book Co. of 145-147 Mulberry St., New York. It was later known as Fonotype. *TMW* advertising from January 1922 to September 1925 offered Italian language comic material and Italian popular music, on 10-inch discs for $.65 (later $.75) and 12-inch discs for $1.25. Matrices were put on sale in October 1926. [Andrews*.]

PHOTOPHONE. A light-ray system of sound recording, invented by Charles A. Hoxie, based on experiments of Alexander Graham Bell in 1879. The Bell concept was not practical at the time, because electronic amplification was not yet available. The principle was later adapted by General Electric for the Brunswick Pallatrope system of 1925.

PIAF, EDITH, 1915–1963. French popular singer, born Giovanna Gassion in Paris on 19 Dec 1915. She took the first name Edith from Edith Cavell, and was nicknamed Piaf (sparrow) by people who saw her singing in the streets—her first musical venue. She went on to become a highly praised nightclub singer, noted for sad, sentimental ballads. She was discovered by Polydor in 1936, and signed to a contract. Her first record was made in Paris, "La java de Cezique" (Polydor #2203; 1936), a song with accordion accompaniment. She stayed with Polydor until 1944, when Philips took over the label. Polydor leased U.S. rights to Vox, which then issued her earliest American records on 78 rpm in the early 1940s, then on LP and EP. "L'accordioniste" (Polydor #5360; 1940) was one of her great hits; it appears on a CD reissue by EMI in 1990 (#CZ 315) with 19 other numbers. She also worked for Columbia, producing her greatest hit, her own composition, "La vie en rose" (Columbia #4014-F). Piaf continued singing in Paris until her health failed in 1963; she died that year in Paris, on 11 October. [Rotante 1983.]

PIANO RECORDINGS. This article, generally limited to acoustic recordings, has five sections:

1. Technical problems
2. Cylinders
3. Discs
4. Performance practice
5. Historical reissues

1. *Technical problems.* Popular as the piano was in the home and in public recitals around 1900, it appeared as a solo instrument in very few recordings. Cylinders and discs of the time emphasized the vocal repertory and utilized the piano as an accompaniment only. Although there were gradual improvements in recording techniques, a pianist had problems in making acoustic recordings, whether as accompanist or soloist. Placement of the recording horn relative to the piano was critical to prevent loud playing from "blasting" and soft passages from vanishing in the surface noise. Even with ideal horn placement—which required

the piano to be mounted on a platform—the pianist was normally constrained to a narrow dynamic range that obstructed musical expression. Furthermore, speed control of the recording was often irregular, resulting in a noticeably wavering piano tone.

Other inhibiting factors were the necessity to fit a composition (or part of one) onto a disc or cylinder with no more than four minutes playing time; the lack of an audience to induce spur-of-the-moment inspiration; and the concern that any slip or artistic flaw would be preserved for posterity. Many pianists found making records under such conditions to be a repugnant and difficult task, while some artists demanded perfection by repeating the same piece over and over; **Artur Schnabel** once did 29 takes before he was satisfied with a recording. **Vladimir de Pachmann** often demanded that the piano be moved, the lights be turned off, and an audience be found.

The versatile and accessible piano was the accompaniment on early recordings for most of the solo instrumentalists (especially violinists) and numerous vocalists in popular and art song. It also served as an economical orchestra substitute in opera and oratorio arias. The earliest commercial recordings in the 1890s often presented local accompanists who were not famous or even well enough known in many cases to be named in the cylinder catalogs, or on the etched disc label; or accompanists might be designated only by a surname, like the "Mr. Guttinguer" on an early Pathé cylinder Many pianists of great ability recorded accompaniments on prominent labels like Victor, Columbia, and HMV; e.g., **Landon Ronald, André Benoist,** Frank La Forge (1879–1953), and conductor **Arthur Nikisch.** The great HMV executive **Fred Gaisberg** is heard accompanying singers on many early records.

2. *Cylinders.* The first significant recordings of a famous musician were non-commercial private two-minute wax cylinders (mentioned in letters but unfortunately lost or destroyed) recorded by the 12-year old prodigy pianist **Josef Hofmann** during a visit to Edison's laboratory in 1888. In 1889, Johannes Brahms became the first major composer known to have made a cylinder, recorded during a visit to Vienna by an agent of Edison. Although the

fidelity of this important historical document of a fragment of his Hungarian Dance No. 1 (preserved only in a 1935 dubbing) was exceedingly poor, the announcement "Herr Brahms" is plainly audible. It was issued on LP by the International Piano Archive, IPA #117.

Before mass production of cylinders was possible (*see* CYLINDER, 3) they had to be individually inscribed; thus multiple copies could only be made by setting up a row of recording machines, into which the performer played the same piece over and over. Thus not all copies made at the same session were identical, though they carried the same catalog number. Pianists listed in **Bettini** catalogs who each made a dozen such cylinders around 1898 in New York were Aimé Lachaume (playing pieces of Beethoven, Chopin, Godard, Debussy, Liszt, and the pianist's own works) and Joseph Pizzarello (playing Chopin, Godard, Grieg, Hofmann, Liszt, Moszkowski, Paderewski, Schumann and the pianist's "Gavotte"). Because of limited production, fragile construction (*see* CYLINDER, 2), and the destruction of stock during World War I, few of these Bettini cylinders are known to still exist even as unique copies. (*See* Moran 1965/2.)

Edison cylinders were manufactured over a longer period than any others (1889–1929) and many have survived. Pianists in the Edison catalogs included **Frank Banta, Sr.; Frank Banta, Jr.; André Benoist; Albert Benzler;** Karee Bondam, Walter Chapman, **Zez Confrey, Ferdinand Himmelreich,** Henry W. Lange, Constance Mering, **Ernest L. Stevens,** Donald Voorhees (-1989), and Victor Young (1889–1968).

Except for a few classical favorites such as Chopin Mazurkas and Liszt's "Liebestraum" played by Walter Chapman, almost all of the repertoire consisted of accompaniments and/or popular music. Some piano cylinders were also produced by other companies, such as the Pathé recordings of Lucien Lambert (1858–1945), made around 1905.

3. *Discs.* Few piano solo recordings were available at the turn of the century. Eldridge Johnson's "Improved Gram-o-phone" catalog (the predecessor of Victor) listed only three, all recorded in 1900: "A Cork Dance" (#A407), composed and played by **Arthur Pryor** (fa-

mous as a trombonist and bandmaster rather than as a pianist); "Hello Ma Baby" (#A402), an original fantasie by Frank P. Banta, Sr.; and "Variations on the Mariner's Hymn," played by the composer C.H.H. Booth (#A434).

The earliest significant commercial solo piano records were about 100 discs made by The Gramophone Co. (from 12 Dec 1900 to 18 Nov 1907 the Gramophone & Typewriter, Ltd.) in major European cities. The repertoire consisted almost exclusively of works by such 19th-century composers as Brahms, Chabrier, Chopin, Godard, Grieg, Liszt, Massenet, Mendelssohn, Rachmaninoff, Raff, Schubert, Schumann, and Volkmann. There were arrangements of J. Strauss and Wagner, and a few examples of 18th-century favorites (Handel and Scarlatti) originally for harpsichord. Most of the pioneering performances listed in Gramophone Co. catalogs were made in London by **Wilhelm Backhaus** (eight discs in 1908), Ilona Eibenschütz (1873–1967, three discs), **Percy Grainger** (three discs), Nathalie Janotha (1856–1932, four discs, including Chopin's Fugue in A Minor, from the manuscript then owned by the pianist), **Vladimir de Pachmann** (six discs, of which five were by Chopin), Landon Ronald (two discs), and **Lillian Bryant**—the first female solo pianist to record commercially. Raoul Pugno (1852–1914) made 17 discs in Paris in 1903, Louis Diémer (1843–1919) made five, and Franz Rummel (1853–1901) made one. Alfred Grünfeld (1852–1924) made 23 discs in Vienna; Josef Hofmann recorded four numbers in Berlin; Alexander Michalowski (1851–1938) made one in Warsaw. One disc was known to come from St. Petersburg, by a pianist named P. P. Gross.

Of particular importance on G & T were pianist-composers who recorded only their own compositions: Camille Saint-Saëns (1835–1921, considered the earliest-born major pianist to make commercial discs, in 1904); Edvard Grieg, on five and nine discs, respectively, all recorded in Paris in April 1903; and Cécile Chaminade on six discs made in London in November 1901.

Fonotipia issued about 10 discs recorded ca. 1905 in Paris by Maria Roger-Miclos (1860?-?) of compositions by Chopin, Godard, Liszt, Mendelssohn, and Schumann.

The heavy predominance of 19th-century romantic repertoire in these earliest discs, with special emphasis on Chopin and Liszt and assorted salon-type offerings, continued throughout the entire acoustic era.

Only a few world-renowned pianists made solo Edison Diamond Discs, the most significant being (in 1919) the first recordings by **Sergei Rachmaninoff**: Liszt's Hungarian Rhapsody No. 2 on three sides of Edison #82169/70; Scarlatti-Tausig's *Pastorale* (as a filler on Edison #82170); the first movement of Mozart's Sonata in A Major, K. 331; two Chopin waltzes, and the composer's own *Polka de W.R.*, Barcarolle, op. 10, and the renowned Prelude in C Sharp Minor, op. 3. Rachmaninoff, soon lured over to Victor, made numerous records documenting his art until just before his death.

Other well known Edison keyboard artists were E. Robert Schmitz (1889–1949) in a 1914 disc of Chopin's "Valse Posthume" and the great **Moriz Rosenthal** in several 1929 experimental electric lateral-cut discs (issued on LP, Mark 56 #723 and #725) of Chopin compositions inscribed just before Edison ceased recording. Particularly well known as an accompanist, André Benoist also recorded a few solos for Edison around 1918–1920. However, Edison's catalog included mostly lesser-known pianists. The great inventor's personal prolific staff-pianist-arranger, Ernest L. Stevens, claimed to have made over 600 records (including experimental discs) most of them as an accompanist or ensemble pianist, many under pseudonyms.

Famous pianists who recorded in Europe often appeared on Victor, Columbia, and Brunswick American releases from ca. 1910 to 1925. Victor's most prestigious artists, issued on the Red Seal label series, included **Wilhelm Backhaus**, Harold Bauer (1873–1951), **Alfred Cortot**, De Pachmann, Ossip Gabrilowitsch (1878–1936), Guiomar Novães (1895–1979), **Ignace Jan Paderewski**, Rachmaninoff, and Olga Samaroff (1882–1948). Less celebrated pianists on the less expensive blue, purple, and black labels included Frank La Forge, Ferdinand Himmelreich, Alfred Grünfeld, Charles Gilbert Spross (1874–1961, who also recorded accompaniments), Julius L. Schendel, Benno Moiseiwitsch (1890–1963, who later advanced to Red Seal status), and "Master" Shura Cherkassky (1911– ; "recorded at the age of eleven" according to the labels on 10-in. blue-label Victor #45394 which included the prodigy's own *Prelude Pathetique*).

Although some of the repertoire seems rather frivolous by today's standards (e.g., transcriptions of popular songs like "Listen to the Mocking Bird," and "Silver Threads Among the Gold," or "Carnival of Venice Variations," or a piano transcription of the *Lucia* Sextette— all played by Himmelreich), concert miniatures composed by Beethoven, Moszkowski, Chaminade, Chopin, Gottschalk, Godard, Mendelssohn, Sinding, Liszt, Rachmaninoff, and Poldini were issued. The first piano record of a work by Debussy, *En bateau* played by Spross, appeared about 1911. Pianists playing popular music also appeared on the non-red labels, such as Felix Arndt (1889–1918, famous for the song "Nola").

Columbia's impressive but somewhat smaller roster included Arthur Friedheim (1859–1932), **Ignaz Friedman**, **Leopold Godowsky**, Percy Grainger, Josef Hofmann, Mischa Levitski (1898–1941), and Xaver Scharwenka (1850–1924).

In the early 1920s, Brunswick acoustics presented important performances by Godowsky and Hofmann, and issues by Elly Ney (1882–1968). Other companies also offered major pianists, such as the Russian Vassily Sapelnikoff (1868–1941) on Vocalion.

Although most discs were lateral-cut, Pathé issued **vertical-cut** piano records. Among the most important were those of Bernhard Stavenhagen (1862–1914), performing Chopin's Nocturne in D-Flat, op. 27, no. 2. Other Pathé pianists were Edouard Risler (1873–1929, Paris, 1917), **Josef Lhévinne** (U.S.A., 1921), and Rudolf Ganz (1877–1972, U.S.A., 1916–1918, who made some Pathé cylinders that were transcribed onto disc on the Actuelle label).

The piano concerto repertory was even more limited than solo piano in the acoustic era, the first piano concerto recording having been made by Wilhelm Backhaus of the Grieg Concerto by HMV in 1910. In the Victor catalog, there were just a few favorites, all in truncated form, such as the "Adagio" from the Grieg Concerto (#70043) and "Adagio" from

the Beethoven Emperor Concerto (#55030), both played by La Forge; the Grieg (Victor #55154/5) and Saint-Saëns Second Concerto (Victor #55160/1) both played by Arthur De Greef (1862–1940). These were on non-red labels; however, Rachmaninoff's first recording of a concerto, his own second, the second and third movements only (Victor #8064/6; 1924)) did appear on Red Seal. And the composer's authoritative performances of all four concertos, and the *Rhapsody on a Theme of Paganini*, were issued later on electrical recordings. Sapelnikoff, who had played the Tchaikovsky First Concerto under the composer, recorded it on an abbreviated late acoustic Vocalion, in London, February 1926.

After 1925, the rapidly expanding electrically recorded piano catalogs of Victor, Columbia, and other companies provided a relatively generous choice of artists, genre (solo, chamber, and concerto), repertory, multiple versions, and multi-record sets. Although the Victor Red Seal catalog tended to predominate in the U.S. (with some acoustic period artists such as Rachmaninoff, Paderewski and Cortot for Victor and Godowsky for both Columbia and Brunswick continuing to be active), some important artists were heard on the non-red labels, such as Hans Barth (1897–1956), a student of Reinecke, Hoagy Carmichael (1899–1981) and **Fats Waller**. European labels such as HMV (which exchanged some releases with its American affiliate Victor), Parlophone, and Odeon (some licensed to American Decca), Polydor (some licensed to Brunswick), Homocord, and others brought out important releases. Smaller companies such as Musicraft, Concert Hall, and Vox presented innovative material, often by artists who later became world famous. The exponential expansion of post-war piano records on LPs and compact discs is for the most part beyond the limited scope of this brief overview. Duet performances appeared rarely in the early period. One example was the Berliner disc recorded in 1899 by Jeanne Douste (ca. 1870–ca. 1936) and her sister Irene Douste playing an arrangement from *Così fan tutte* and Rubinstein's *Toreador*.

Two-piano acoustic recordings were also very few in number, examples being by Schnabel students Guy Maier (1891–1956) and

Lee Pattison (1890–1966) on Blue Label Victor. Two-piano married teams that later became well known on electric 78s included Matthay students Ethel Bartlett (1896–1978) and Rae Robertson (1893–1956); Pierre Luboschutz (1891–1971, an Edouard Risler student) and Genia Nemenoff (1905–); and Schnabel students Vitya Vronsky (1909–) and Victor Babin (1908–1972), especially remembered for several superb recordings of the two Rachmaninoff Suites.

4. *Performance Practice.* Time constraints of acoustic 78 rpm sides posed a major limitation to piano (and other) early recordings; longer works (if recorded at all) were often truncated. That repeats were seldom observed (except "da capo" repeats) would thus not provide a reliable clue as to whether repeats were observed in concert. Relatively few of the late acoustics (after about 1920) even devoted both sides of a double-sided disc to one composition, since most were couplings of different works issued earlier as single-sided disc. Truncations did not merely consist of omitting repetitions. Beethoven's 32 *Variations in C Minor*, as recorded in 1925 by Rachmaninoff, utilized two sides but was still truncated since six variations were omitted. Three early acoustics of Mendelssohn's *Rondo Capriccio op. 14*, as recorded by Maria Roger-Miclos (Fonotipia #39256; ca. 1905), Josef Hofmann (Columbia #A6078; ca. 1915), as well as the early 1920s recording by Alfred Cortot (Victor #74810), all omit the 26-measure lyrical "andante" introduction. Roger-Miclos also omits 30 measures just before the broken octave coda. In comparison, Hofmann's 1913 Welte-Mignon roll (#3031) is uncut. Tempos, especially if fast and scrambled, were as likely dictated by time limits as by artistic conception. Most truncations were well planned to sound as inconspicuous as possible, but the Louis Diémer disc of Chopin's Nocturne op. 27 no. 2 in D-Flat (G & T #35544; ca. 1903) finishes before the piece finishes, with the last measures conspicuously missing. Conversely, a composition was occasionally expanded or markedly varied. Because Goossens' "Casperle Theatre" ("The Punch and Judy Show, op. 18 no. 6" from *Kaleidoscope*), a sprightly half-minute work, did not fill a side, Eugène d'Albert's recording

(Deutsche Grammophon #B 27045, reissued on LP Veritas #VM 110) repeated the piece after the recording technicians (and perhaps the pianist?) provided some applause and laughter. When Harold Bauer recorded two of the Brahms waltzes op. 39 he played No. 15, followed by No. 16 (Schirmer Records #2004, reissued on LP Veritas #VM 108), and then repeated No. 15 to create the effect of an ABA structure.

Performances from the 78 era may provide reliable clues to the performance practices of the late 19th century because mature artists tended to reflect approaches taught to them, or performances heard while their own personal styles were being formed. This residue from the previous generation may often raise questions about the borderlines between artistic imagination and grotesque distortion. Early 20th-century piano recordings frequently present aspects of style and execution that stand out as striking or eccentric to modern listeners. These include modifications and variants from the score, such as playing single notes as octaves; adding ornamentation, scales, and parallel scales (especially in thirds); interpolating extra measures and cadenzas; spreading or arpeggiating chords and adding arpeggios and chords; playing the left-hand bass slightly before the right or letting the right hand be slightly delayed; pedaling in extremes—from little or none for clear counterpoint to blurred for sonorous effect; producing tone (difficult to describe) that is singing, ringing (bell like), bright, brittle, or ethereal; phrasing and articulating imaginatively; bringing out inner voices; introducing unmarked tempo changes, retards, or accelerandos; and altering rhythm with exaggerated rubato.

Although most of the surprising, fascinating, and distinctive traits heard in early piano recordings are not easily described, the following examples will try to document the observations noted above.

Multiple versions of a work by one performer often vary appreciably. Alexander Michalowski's paraphrase on Chopin's "Minute Waltz" (Polish Columbia #DMX 258) and a quite different longer version (Polish Syrena #6578; ca. 1930)—both reissued on LP Veritas #VM 115—expand and elaborate the short work with intricate introductory, developmental, and coda material. Fortunately for comparison, Michalowski also recorded a relatively straightforward version (G & T #25601; ca. 1904–1905). Vladimir de Pachmann's first disc of the "Minute Waltz" (G & T #5566; ca. 1907) adds a quick ascending and descending D-Flat scale run between the trio and the return of section A, but Pachmann's reproducing roll made about the same time lacks this added flourish, ending instead with several extra cadential chords. Ignaz Friedman's Duo-Art reproducing roll (#67220) adds a rapid brusquely rolled chord in the left hand before the return of the first theme and delightfully varies the downward scale at the end by playing it in thirds. Outdoing all other Minute Waltzes, Josef Hofmann's concert performance (Casimir Hall concert of 7 Apr 1938, on LP IPA #5007–5008) surpasses Friedman by playing the entire return of the first section in thirds.

Chopin's Waltz op. 42 in A-Flat performed by Rachmaninoff (Edison Diamond Disc #82197; 1919) adds ritardandos at the ends of phrases, stretches or lengthens the A-Flat trill on the upbeat to the next phrase, and adds parallel notes to an upward right-hand scale leading to the coda. Ferruccio Busoni (1866–1924) linked two Chopin works together by playing at a fast tempo the Prelude Opus 28 No. 7 in A Major with a repeat (not in the score) followed by a short bridge passage leading directly into the Etude Op. 10 No. 5 in G-Flat Major ("Black Key Etude") which concludes with two extra measures of echo-effect figuration inserted just before the concluding downward double octaves (British Columbia #L 1476, reissued on IPL #104).

Chopin's Nocturne Op. 9 No. 2 in E-Flat played by Raoul Koczalski (1884–1948) uses variant right-hand ornamentation learned from annotations reportedly written by Chopin in the score of Karol Mikuli (1819–1897), a student of Chopin and the teacher of Koczalski. [Methuen-Campbell, p. 75] Chopin's Etude Op. 25 No. 2 in F Minor played by Francis Planté (1839–1934) at age 90 in 1928 (French Columbia #D 13060, reissued on LP IPL #101) has the closing downward run starting an octave higher than written so as to be executed twice as fast with twice as many notes as are in the score

(giving a stretto effect). Liszt's etude *La leggierezza* interpreted by Paderewski (reissued on LP Camden #310) adds a little-known elaborate Leschetizky cadenza that blends into the style of the work. Liszt's Hungarian Rhapsody No. 2 recorded by Rachmaninoff in 1919 incorporates an apparently improvised (unpublished) two-minute cadenza.

Arthur Friedheim's performance of Liszt's *La campanella* (Columbia #517; 1913) adds an upward glissando, an extra measure of the "bell" figuration (the title means "the bell"), and a sudden accelerando and ritardando in a measure of right-hand tremolo octaves. Schubert's Impromptu in F-Minor Op. 142 No. 4 was played by Eugène d'Albert (1864–1932) (Deutsche Grammophon #65516; ca. 1916; on LP Veritas #VM 110) at an extremely fast tempo to fit the disc's time limit. The pianist omitted several whole note (i.e., whole measure) rests with fermatas.

5. *Historical Reissues.* Numerous LP and CD reissues and first issues have been made of historical piano recordings. For examples, RCA and its budget subsidiaries RCA Camden and RCA Victrola, have provided a significant sampling of the vast Victor heritage, the most monumental single release having been the complete known extant recorded performances by Sergei Rachmaninoff in five volumes (15 LPs issued ca. 1973) which included some test pressings released for the first time. Other commercial labels, particularly Veritas, Rococo, Pearl, Opal, and Music and Arts have made available significant historical materials. The International Piano Archives at Maryland (IPAM), previously known as the International Piano Archive (IPA) and the International Piano Library (IPL), has produced important material. Sources other than early commercial cylinders and discs include private recordings (made at concerts, social gatherings, etc.) and off-the-air broadcasts that allowed significant piano recordings to be issued for the first time on LP and CD.

Examples of such important historical offerings include the cylinder by Brahms already mentioned and one by Isaac Albéniz (1860–1909) of two improvisations recorded in 1903—both issued on IPA #109. Privately recorded concert performances have also seen the first light of day on LP and CD, such as Josef Hofmann's Golden Jubilee concert on 28 Nov 1937 on the 50th anniversary of his American debut (IPA #5001–5002). Two versions of the Grieg Concerto in A Minor played by Percy Grainger (from 1945 and 1956) filled out by the commercial 1908 cadenza excerpt (G & T #5570), made only a few years after Grieg coached the young performer in its interpretation, appeared on IPA #508. Paderewski's student Sigismund Stojowski (1869–1946) played Stojowski and Chopin (IPA #115) obtained from a 1944 broadcast. Previously unpublished commercial discs that were eventually issued include Josef Hofmann's 1935 RCA test pressings (LP Victrola #VIC 1550).

Such LPs and CDs provide a great service to pianists, musicologists, and others who wish to hear and study performance style and tradition of the past, and they insure the preservation and survival for posterity of the valuable sonic information. Originals are often unavailable even in major archives.

Pianists who recorded in the acoustic era rarely hesitated to infuse their playing with personal ideas and interpolated liberties in the grand 19th-century romantic tradition. Later generations of pianists preferred to display virtuosity by demonstrating how precisely an artist could adhere to the printed score—though many older editions used by recording artists were over edited with misleading indications. Currently, pyrotechnical display has to be executed with precision to be considered acceptable. Expanded exposure to records, radio, and video formats has contributed significantly to homogenizing interpretative style (analogous to minimizing regional dialects and accents). [Basart 1985; Capes 1956; Crutchfield 1986; Dubal 1989; Edison 1987; Fagan 1983; Ferrara 1975; Girard 1971; Holcman 1960; Holcman 1961/11; Holcman 1961/12; Holcman 1961/13; Holcman 1962; International 1983; Lewis, J. 1988; Matthews 1977; Methuen-Campbell 1981; Methuen-Campbell 1983; Methuen-Campbell 1984; Perkins 1981; Sitsky 1986; Sitsky 1990; Wodehouse 1977.] For recordings after the acoustic period, see entries for individual pianists: CLAUDIO ARRAU; DANIEL BARENBOIM; JORGE BOLET; ALFRED CORTOT; EDWIN FISCHER; WALTER GIESEKING; LEOPOLD GODOWSKY; GLENN GOULD; MYRA HESS; VLADIMIR HOROWITZ; JOSÉ ITURBI; WILHELM KEMPFF; WANDA LANDOWSKA; IGNACE PADEREWSKI; ARTUR RUBINSTEIN; ARTUR SCHNABEL; RUDOLF SERKIN; GEORG SOLTI. See also JAZZ RECORDINGS; REPRODUCING PIANO ROLLS.

Steven Permut

PIANOLA. The trade name of the inner player manufactured by the **Aeolian Co.** Weber was the most popular model; others were the Steck, the Wheelock, and the Stuyvesant. Dimensions of the Stuyvesant were typical of the inner player: 61 inches long, 29 1/2 inches deep, 56 1/2 inches tall; with a boxed weight of about 1,000 pounds. Pianola became widely used as a generic name for player pianos of all brands.

PICCADILLY (label). A British record issued from 1928 to 1932 by Piccadilly Records, Ltd., a firm with commercial connections to Metropole Gramophone Co., Ltd. (later Metropole Industries, Ltd.). Metropole's English matrices and imported Emerson and Grey Gull matrices were used. There were low-cost records and "Celebrity" red-labelled records. The Piccadilly records continued after Metropole went out of business. Piccadilly had gained ownership of the Hertford Town factory, which had belonged to the Hertford Record Co., Columbia Graphophone Co., Ltd., Parlophone Co., Ltd., and Metropole Gramophone Co. [Andrews*.]

PICCOLO RECORDINGS. George Schweinfest was the first identified piccolo player on record, making 36 numbers for Columbia in 1897–1898; the earliest was "Golden Robin Polka" (#23500). Berliner recorded some piccolo solos and duets in September and October 1898, the players not identified, but Rust suggests that one of the artists was the flutist A. Fransella. [Rust 1981.]

PICKUP. The electrical counterpart of the acoustic soundbox, the device that translates groove undulations into audio signals; also known as a **cartridge.**

PICTURE DISCS. Records with illustrations on their labels and/or playing surfaces, issued by many companies from 1905 as **postcard records**, then by **Talk-O-Photo** in 1920, and as Emerson children's records in 1922 (six inches in diameter, with color pictures on one side). In 1932–1933 there were 30 items by Victor, including sides with photos of Enrico Caruso and Jimmie Rodgers. A recent price guide lists about 6,000 picture discs, worldwide. The most famous label in the picture field was **Vogue**, in 1946–1947. [Lindsay 1990.]

PICTURIZED PHONOGRAPHS. Devices that showed illustrations as accompaniment to records played in **coin-op** phonographs during the early years of the 20th century. Some of the brand names were Illustraphone (Hawthorne & Sheble), Cailophone, and Scopephone (both by Caille Brothers), and the Illustrated Song Machine (Rosenfield Co., New York). The Discophone was the first in use with disc players in the U.S.; it was made by the Valiquet Novelty Co., Newark, New Jersey.

PIED PIPERS. American popular vocal group, formed in the 1930s, prominent in the early 1940s with the Tommy Dorsey orchestra. Members were John Huddleston, Chuck Lowry, Hal Hopper, Woody Newbury, Whit Whittinghill, Bud Hervey, and George Tait. Huddleston's wife, **Jo Stafford**, sang with them later. There were various other artists in the group from time to time. Having left Dorsey in 1942, the Pied Pipers appeared on many radio shows, including the *Lucky Strike Hit Parade*, and made motion pictures. They were active through the 1950s.

Most of the Pied Piper records were for Victor and Capitol. They backed up Frank Sinatra on his first hit solo with Tommy Dorsey, "I'll Never Smile Again" (Victor #26628; 1940), and in the fine arrangement of "There Are Such Things" (Victor #27974; 1942). Among their popular LP albums was Capitol #T-907, *Accent-tchu-ate the Positive*, with Johnny Mercer.

PIERCE, WEBB, 1926– . American country singer, guitarist, songwriter, and publisher, born in West Monroe, Louisiana, on 8 Aug 1926. After local performances, he appeared on the *Louisiana Hayride* radio program in 1950 and gained recording contracts with several labels, including Decca. He was successful with a nasal voice that helped to establish the so-called honky-tonk style. His first hit records were "Wondering" (Decca #46364; 1952) and "Back Street Affair" (Decca #28369; 1952). "Slowly" (Decca #28991; 1954) and "In the Jailhouse Now" (Decca #29391; 1955) were important records of the mid-1950s, when Pierce was featured on *Grand Ole Opry*. He established a Nashville publishing firm, Cedarwood Music, in 1953, and made a success of it while continuing his performances and recordings. By 1976 he had recorded 84 country chart songs. After the 1970s he was less active.

PIKE, ERNEST. British tenor, said to be King Edward's favorite; he was the son of one of the Royal bakers. For a time his popularity was as great as Peter Dawson's. As early as April 1904 Pike recorded for G & T, singing "Take a Pair of Sparkling Eyes" from *Gondoliers*, (#2-2465; August 1904) and two other numbers in the same session. Pike recorded also for the Gramophone Co. Zonophone label and the Columbia Regal label. He made Edison two-minute cylinders in London in 1907, and four-minute cylinders later (to 1910), beginning with "When the Berry's on the Holly" (#13769). On some Edisons, such as #13769, he was identified as Herbert Payne. Among his other noms du disque were David Boyd, Arthur Brett, Eric Courtland, Alan Dale, Arthur Gray, Jack Henty, Sam Hovey, Herbert Payne, and Richard Pembroke. He was the Murray of "Murray and Denton." Pike remained popular in Britain into the 1920s.

PINCH EFFECT. In disc recording, the situation caused by the fact that the cutting stylus does not twist to face the groove direction, while the reproducing stylus does; thus points of contact between the one stylus and the groove are not identical to the points of contact of the other stylus and the groove. The result is tracing distortion (*see* DISTORTION, XIII). [Frederick 1932 gives illustrations.]

PING PONG EFFECT. A stereophonic separation of signals in which the sound output appears to come from one or the other of the loudspeakers, rather than from the space between or around them; the term coming from the alternating sounds of table tennis rackets striking the ball.

PINI-CORSI, ANTONIO, 1858–1918. Italian baritone, born in Zara in June 1858. After a debut in Cremona in 1878, he sang in many Italian houses. Chosen by Verdi, he created the role of Ford in *Falstaff* at La Scala in 1893. He was with the Metropolitan Opera from 1899 to 1901 and 1909 to 1914, recognized as one of the greatest portrayers of buffo roles like Leporello and Dr. Bartolo, as well as Ford. He died 22 Apr 1918 in Milan.

Pini-Corsi recorded for Pathé cylinders and discs in Paris, in 1905 and 1912. His first record was #4134, "Manca un foglio" from *Barbiere di Siviglia*. In 1912 he sang Ford's principal aria, "Quand'ero paggio" (#84542). He is also heard on Columbia records made in Milan in 1904, including his fine "Largo al factotum" (#10245); and on G & T from 1903 to 1909, including much material from *Don Pasquale*. There have been numerous LP reissues, on Classic Edition, Belcantodisc, Top Artists Platters, Olympus, and Heritage labels. Most of the reissues are from *Barbiere di Siviglia*.

Pink noise. *See* NOISE, IV.

PINNOCK, TREVOR, 1946– . English harpsichordist and conductor, born in Canterbury on 16 Dec 1946. He studied at the Royal College of Music in London, and toured with the Academy of St. Martin-in-the-Fields. In 1973 he established the English Concert, a group devoted to early music and authentic performance. He and the Concert have won many important awards, including the Grand Prix du Disque and the Gramophone Award (for *Messiah*). As soloist Pinnock has recorded the complete J. S. Bach toccatas, the "Goldberg Variations," and an album of popular harpsichord pieces named *The Harmonious Blacksmith*; all are on Deutsche Grammophon/Archiv label.

PINZA, EZIO, 1892–1957. Italian bass-baritone, born in Rome on 18 May 1892. He studied engineering, then turned to singing and made his operatic debut in 1914 in Soncino, doing Oroveso in *Norma*. After military service with the Italian army he went to La Scala, and was heard in the world premiere of Boito's *Nerone*. His Metropolitan Opera debut was in *Vestale* on 1 Nov 1926; he remained with the company until 1947. Pinza's greatest roles, establishing him as the leading interpreter of the bass-baritone repertoire, were Mephistofeles, Don Giovanni, and Boris. But his most wonderful characterization was a crossover into the Broadway musical, as he sang opposite Mary Martin in *South Pacific* (1949). In 1954 he appeared in another Broadway show, **Fanny.** He died in Stamford, Connecticut, on 9 May 1957.

Pinza recorded for HMV in 1923–1924, and again in 1929 and 1939. He was with Victor in 1927–1940, and 1950–1954; then with U.S. Columbia in 1944–1950. His first disc was one of his acclaimed arias, "Il lacerato spirito" (HMV #2-052240; 1923). Among his outstanding recordings were two of the Verdi *Requiem*, one made at La Scala for Victor (#V-9831-30; 1929), the other—with Beniamino Gigli and Maria Caniglia—at the Royal Opera House, Rome (Victor #DB 6210-19; 1939). He was in the *Lucia* Sextette made for Victor, with Amelita Galli-Curci, Louise Homer, Gigli, Giuseppe De Luca, and Angelo Bada (#10012). His popular album *Falling in Love with Love* included selections from Hollywood musicals (Victor # 10-3282). *South Pacific* was in a Columbia album (#MM 850; 1949); its "Some Enchanted Evening," remarkably phrased by Pinza, is on Columbia #41190-1A. CDs include BMG #MOIR 404 and Club 99 #CL 99-12, both from 1991; the latter has much of the acoustic material. [Richards 1980.]

PIONEER ELECTRONICS (USA), INC. A firm located in Long Beach, California, noted for high end components, especially receivers.

PIRATED RECORDS. Records copied and sold without authorization, also known as bootlegs. The practice began in the cylinder era, as the blanks were easily obtained and copying devices were available; the quality of copies was hard to distinguish at first from the quality of originals, neither being outstanding. But by 1902 the superiority of factory-made cylinders was clear, and pirating diminished. It resumed in the disc period as recording from radio ("air shots" or "air checks") became practical, and flowered with the LP and the tape master. Live concerts and operas were recorded surreptitiously on the scene and sold, often rather brazenly. And American labels copied material from European socialist countries without payment (for example, Colosseum label reissued many Russian, Czech, and Polish recordings). Jolly Roger and many other labels copied Victor and Columbia jazz performances. Among the most notorious pirated records were those made of Maria Callas in *Traviata*, a role she had not (for various odd reasons) recorded "legally" for EMI. In March 1966, her Covent Garden performance of 1958 materialized on LP, complete, thanks to an obscure label named FWR. Another bootleg Callas Violetta (from La Scala in 1955) appeared in 1972; and a Mexico City performance of 1952 came out in 1973, issued by the most famous bootlegger, Edward J. Smith. (EMI finally did issue a Callas Violetta, from 1958, the "Lisbon Traviata."

Cassette tapes have proved the easiest format to copy and distribute illegally. There was already a $100 million market in the U.S. for bootleg cassettes in 1971, according to a story in *Business Week* magazine. The Recording Industry Association of America (RIAA) took steps to combat piracy through legislation, and succeeded in getting laws against it passed in several states. Then Congress passed the revised Copyright Act (1978), giving protection—legal, at least—to the original makers of recordings.

In 1981 and 1982 investigative reporting brought to light the pirating activities of the Aries Records firm in California. Uncommon modern works were recorded by the label from broadcasts or illegal tape copies, artists' names were changed (in most cases), and the records were boldly marketed along with those of legitimate producers.

A report from the International Federation of the Phonographic Industry (IFPI) in 1991 pointed out that worldwide piracy is continuing on a massive scale. For 1989 bootlegs were said to have caused losses to the industry of £568 million. On the world map, the centers of illegality have been Southeast Asia, India, and Latin America. In Africa the legitimate music industry is said to be on the verge of collapse because of incursions by pirates; and IFPI reports greatly increasing problems in newly liberated Eastern Europe. In Western Europe the situation has stabilized, with losses around £1 million per year. However the compact disc is proving to be another easy format to work with, and more than a third of the CD sales in Germany, for example, are attributed to illegal issues. [*Gramophone* report in April 1991, p. 1785; Wile 1985.]

PITCH. (I) The property of musical tone that is determined by the frequency of the sound wave that produces it. In order for musicians to play in ensemble, an agreement is necessary among them regarding the pitch to be sounded for each note of the score. Various standards for pitch have been in use, though none have found universal adoption. These agreements have gradually resulted in a raising of the pitch standard; it is believed now that musicians of the 18th century played any given note about a semitone lower than the same note would be played today. In the early 19th century, pitch in European opera houses was 425.5 cycles per second for the note A in the treble staff. A Paris agreement of 1859 established that the note A would be played at 435 cycles per second (435 Hz). In 1939 an international agreement set the pitch of A at 440 hz, and this remains the most accepted norm.

Pitch in recording is affected by the speed at which the cylinder or disc rotates, the factor being applicable both in making the record and in playing it back. A 6 percent deviation in playing speed results in a change in pitch by a semitone: 6 percent faster meaning the pitch rises a semitone, 6 percent slower that it falls a semitone. A 6 percent deviation is achieved on a 78 rpm disc by 4 1/2 revolutions per minute on either side of the correct rotation rate, and by only two rpm for an LP record. Early discs made to be played at speeds above 78 rpm (e.g., at 80 or 82 rpm) will result in a noticeably lower (flattened) pitch when the playback turntable is set for 78 rpm. These problems have been a prime concern to those who reissue acoustic discs in LP or CD format. As examples of artists whose records need careful speed monitoring, *see* ENRICO CARUSO; BING CROSBY. *See also* SONIC RESTORATION; STROBOSCOPIC DISC; TUNING BAND.

PITCH. (II). The distance between tracks on a recording medium. For example on a compact disc it is 1.6 microns.

PITCH. (III). The number of grooves (i.e., turns, or threads) per inch on a cylinder or disc record, expressed as a decimal; "0.1 inch pitch" refers to a configuration of 10 grooves per inch. Most cylinder records of the early 1890s had 1.0 pitch, or 100 grooves per inch. Standard 78 rpm discs have a pitch of 0.9 to 1.2. Microgroove LPs have a pitch of 2. to 3. *See also* CYLINDER, 4; DISC, 5.

PITS. The bumps on a **compact disc**, carriers of the signal. They are read by the laser pickup by diffracting the light they receive and decreasing the light returned to the pickup according to the characteristics of the signals they represent.

PIZZARELLO, JOSEPH. One of the earliest pianists identified on records, with 12 numbers in the **Bettini** catalog of May 1897, and 12 in Bettini's 1898 catalog.

PLANÇON, POL, 1851–1914. French bass, born Pol-Henri Plançon in Fumay on 12 June 1851. His opera debut was in Lyons in 1877. In 1883 he sang Mephistopheles at the Paris Opéra, the first of more than 100 times he would perform that role there in 10 seasons. He appeared first at the Metropolitan Opera in 1893, and remained to 1908. Plançon had more than 50 roles, including Wagnerian parts and the bass-baritone repertoire of the French/Italian composers. He died in Paris on 12 Aug 1914.

His first records were for **Bettini**; there were listings in the three known catalogs from 1897 to 1898, a total of five songs and two arias. "Air du tambour-major" from *Le Caid* by Thomas was particularly notable, and he recorded it later for G & T (#2-2664; 1902) and Victor (#85019; 1903 and 1906). He made Zonophone discs in Paris in 1901–1902; and G & T's in London in 1902. Most of his output was in the U.S. for Victor during 1903–1908. There were 20 solos in the 1917 Victor catalog. Perhaps the finest of his discs is the "Serenade" from *Damnation du Faust* (Victor #81034; 1904 and 1906). There were many 78 rpm reissues, on IRCC, HMV Archive, and Historic Record Society; and numerous LP reissues as well, on most of the reprint labels. [Hervingham-Root 1953 is a complete discography.]

PLATE. The name given to the early hard rubber disc recordings made by Emile Berliner, issued by the U.S. Gramophone Co. in 1894. Berliner continued referring to his discs as plates until 1896.

PLATE PHONOGRAPH. A tinfoil disc player, marketed in Paris in 1879 by Ducretet et Cie.

PLATTER. A phonograph disc record.

PLAYBACK CURVE. The reciprocal of the **recording curve** in an audio system; the degree of frequency compensation or equalization required in playback.

PLAYBACK HEAD. The element of a **tape deck** that generates electric currents from the recorded pattern on the tape passing by it; it may be the same head as the **recording head**.

PLAYBACK LOSS. The difference between recorded and reproduced levels at a given point on a disc record. It results from the variance in formation between the two walls of the modulated groove (one side being concave, the other convex).

PLAYBOY. A juke box introduced by Seeburg in 1939; it was the first to have a wall box with selections in it, separated from the speaker apparatus.

PLAYERPHONE TALKING MACHINE CO. A Chicago firm, established in 1916 at 21 S. Wabash Ave. It advertised the Playerphone disc player, available in six models. The firm was reported bankrupt in February 1922. There was a vertical-cut record with the label name Playerphone for a time. [Rust 1978.]

Playing speeds. *See* PITCH; SPEEDS.

Plays. *See* LITERARY RECORDINGS.

PLAYTIME (label). A children's record, in seven-inch diameter, issued by American Record Corp. and then by CBS in 1932 and 1941. [Rust 1978.]

PLAZA (label). A British record issued from 1933 to 1935 by **British Homophone Co., Ltd.** It was an eight-inch disc, but had a long playing time equal to standard records; price was 6 pence.

PLAZA MUSIC CO. A New York firm, established in 1911 as a music publisher. In September 1919 Plaza was advertising "Perfection" albums, from 18 W. 20th St. Bankruptcy was announced in December 1920, but by April 1921 it was back in business. Discs with the **Banner Record** label were announced in January 1922. In March 1922 Plaza reported having acquired the Repeat-O-Voice business, with its six-inch, double-sided metal discs for home recording. Plaza continued dealing in sheet music, and sold phonographs and accessories.

Banner was the principal Plaza label for 14 years. At first Plaza drew on other firms for its matrices, for example, Paramount and Emerson, but in 1923 began to record in its own studio. Among its own labels, there was considerable duplication of material, often with names of artists changed. The Plaza output was primarily dance music and popular vocals; there were also some light classical records, and miscellaneous ethnic and folk music. Noted artists like Vernon Dalhart, Billy Jones, Ernest Hare, Fletcher Henderson, and the Original Memphis Five appeared on the Banner label. Little Tots' Nursery Tunes was another Plaza label.

Conqueror label was introduced in 1926, and was issued until 1942. It used Banner material, with the artists under pseudonyms. **Domino** was another label in the Plaza group, issued from 1924 to 1933. In the mid-1920s

Plaza material was used for the **Homestead** label, distributed by the Chicago Mail Order Co. From 1927 to 1932 there was also the **Jewel** label. **Lenox** was a rare label with Plaza material. **Oriole** was issued from 1921 to 1938. Plaza masters were used by **Regal** from 1923 to 1931, Regal Record Co. being a Plaza subsidiary. The Regal Record Co. came under control of the Crystalate Gramophone Record Manufacturing Co., Ltd., of the U.K. in 1929, as the first step in the formation of the American Record Corp. [Andrews*; *RR* carried a long series of lists from the Plaza 5000 series, beginning in the #36 issue (1961), and continuing to 1983; Rust 1980.]

Poetry. *See* LITERARY RECORDINGS.

Pole face alignment. *See* GAP ALIGNMENT.

POLLACK, BEN, 1903–1971. American Big Band leader and drummer, born in Chicago on 22 June 1903. He played in various Dixieland combos, mainly the New Orleans Rhythm Kings in Chicago. He organized his first band in 1924, and began to attract star sidemen, many of whom went on to form their own orchestras: Benny Goodman, Glenn Miller, Charlie Spivak, Harry James, Jimmy McPartland, among others. In the 1920s he had one of the outstanding white ensembles, with engagements at the Blackhawk Restaurant and Southmoor Hotel in Chicago and the Park Central Hotel in New York. After 1940 he was less active for a time, but returned to prominence in the 1950s on the West Coast, and appeared in a 1956 motion picture about Benny Goodman. He died on 7 June 1971 in Palm Springs, California.

Pollack's band recorded first for Victor, making "When I First Met Mary" (#20394) in December 1926; the group at that time was known as Ben Pollack and His Californians. As the Park Central Orchestra they recorded in 1928–1929, with Smith Ballew, Scrappy Lambert, and the popular tenor Franklyn Baur as vocalists (Ballew and Lambert under pseudonyms). After 1930 the band left Victor and worked with numerous labels, notably Banner and Columbia. They made their final discs in 1938 for Decca.

POLONIA PHONOGRAPH CO. A Milwaukee, Wisconsin, firm, active in 1921. It made machines and records, with a repertoire of interest to Polish immigrants. There was a recording laboratory in New York City, and a pressing plant at Grove St., Milwaukee. [Andrews*.]

POLYDOR (label). A German record made by Deutsche Grammophon Gesellschaft, Berlin and Hanover, from 1921. The label was used only for exports, and although DGG originated as the German branch of the Gramophone Co., and had the right to use the Gramophone Co. trademarks in Germany, the export label did not carry the **Nipper** picture nor was it identified with "Die Stimme seines Herrn." Polydor exports to the U.S., handled by Brunswick and sold by them as Polydor/Brunswick records, included a roster of great artists (such as Wilhelm Furtwängler and the Berlin Philharmonic Orchestra). Polydor was also established in other countries, and was greatly successful until the economic crisis of 1929. During the 1930s there was a Decca Polydor label marketed by British Decca, in U.K. The French Polydor record was sold to Philips in 1950. U.S. Decca released Polydor recordings in America. Polydor was among the 11 labels listed in the first LP catalog (predecessor to *Schwann*), issued October 1949. With the establishment of the new DGG label in 1952, Polydor was assigned to light music. After 1955 Polydor was marketed in Britain by Heliodor Record Co., Ltd. CD Polydors are now distributed by Polygram.

See also POLYGRAM INTERNATIONAL; DEUTSCHE GRAMMOPHON GESELLSCHAFT.

POLYGRAM INTERNATIONAL. A firm established on 3 Jan 1972, owned by Philips NV, merging Polydor International and Phonogram International. The name is printed as PolyGram, better suggesting the roots of the enterprise in Polyphon Musikwerke (Leipzig, 1911) and the Gramophone Co. (although the suffix may have come from phono*gram*). PolyGram Records, the record distributing arm, handles the firms's labels, including Atlanta Artists, Casablanca, Chocolate City, Compleat, Decca (U.K.), De-

Lite, Deram, Emarcy, Enja, Gramavision, Lection, London, Mercury, MGM, Millenium, MPS, Oasis, Philips, Polydor, Riva, RSO, Threshold, Total Experience, 21, Vertigo, and Verve.

In 1990 PolyGram reported worldwide sales of £1,634,000,000. Compact discs accounted for 62 percent of records sold.

POLYPHON (label). A lateral-cut, double-sided 10-inch disc on sale in Britain in 1908, presenting German repertoire. The first London agent was J. A. Williams, 92 Hatton Garden. In July 1910 the agency was Klingsor Works, London. With the September 1910 issues, the label name had been changed to Klingsor, but the Polyphon trademark remained. **Polyphon Musikwerke AG** established its own British branch and began selling Polyphon Records from January 1913 (the Klingsors having been discontinued). In June 1913 the label name changed again, to "Pilot Record—Formerly Polyphon Record." The label ceased with the outbreak of World War I in 1914. [Andrews*.]

POLYPHON MUSIKWERKE AG. A German firm, established in Leipzig around 1890 as a music box maker. It began to issue disc records with the **Polyphon** label in 1905, and also made talking machines. By act of the German government, it took over the holdings of Deutsche Grammophon AG, the German branch of the Gramophone Co., on 24 Apr 1917. In 1924 the Anglo-German Arbitration Tribunal restored privileges to Deutsche Grammophon.

POLYPHONE. A phonograph with two sapphire-stylus reproducers, each tracking the same groove but 3/8 to 1/2 inch apart. Leon Douglass was the inventor. The manufacturer named in an 1899 *Phonoscope* advertisement was Polyphone Co., 107 Madison St., Chicago. It was marketed by H. B. Babson and the Talking Machine Co. of Chicago.

PONS, LILY, 1898–1976. French soprano, born Alice Josephine Pons in Draguignan on 12 Apr 1898. She made her debut in Mulhouse in 1927, as Lakmé, a role that came to be associated with her. She sang elsewhere in France, then at the

Metropolitan Opera on 3 Jan 1931—singing another of her great roles, Lucia. Pons remained with the Metropolitan until 1958, in some 180 performances, appearing also in the major houses of Europe and Latin America. During the 1930s she made motion pictures as well. Her second marriage was to the conductor Andre Kostelanetz. She died on 13 Feb 1976 in Dallas.

Pons recorded for Odeon in France., 1928–1929, notably with airs from *Lakmé* and "Una voce poco fa." She worked for HMV and Victor in 1930–1940, and for Columbia in the U.S. from 1941 to 1954. "Ardon gl'incensi," the Mad Scene from *Lucia*, was inscribed in 1930 (#7369) for Victor, and remained in the catalog into the 1940s; it was transferred to the LP album *Arias* (#1473). The Bell Song from *Lakmé* was one of her most famous records (Columbia #71640-D; 1944). Most of her other 78 rpm work was also reissued on LP.

She was Rosina in the complete Metropolitan Opera live recording of *Barbiere di Siviglia* of 1938, Lakmé in the 1940 performance, and Gilda in the 1939 performance of *Rigoletto*; all these were issued on Golden Age of Opera records. Pons had the role of Adele in the complete recording of *Fledermaus* made in 1950 by the Metropolitan Opera under Eugene Ormandy (#78245). In 1954 she recorded a complete *Lucia* for Columbia (#SL 127). A CBS compact disc of 1990 (#45694) presented many of her favorite arias, with Kostelanetz conducting some of them. [Park 1960 is a complete discography.]

PONSELLE, ROSA, 1897–1981. American soprano, born in Meriden, Connecticut, on 22 Jan 1897. She sang in church, and then as a teen in a duo with her sister Carmela, "Italian Girls," or the Ponzillo Sisters (Ponzillo being the original family name). The sister act reached the New York Palace Theatre, performing material like "Kiss Me Again" and "Comin' thro' the Rye." She was brought to the attention of Enrico Caruso, who arranged an audition at the Metropolitan Opera, and was catapulted from vaudeville to the opera stage at age 21. Her debut was in *Forza del destino*, with Caruso and Giuseppe De Luca; it was a great success.

Ponselle remained with the Company until 1937, establishing herself as one of the leading dramatic sopranos in *Norma, Ernani, Trovatore, Aida*, etc. She retired in 1937, to live in Maryland, and died in her villa near Baltimore on 25 May 1981.

Ponselle made Columbia records from 1919 to 1923, and Victors from 1923 to 1929. Her Columbias are best played at 80 rpm, to get the correct pitches; an 82 rpm playback is needed for "D'amor sull' ali rose" from *Trovatore*, Columbia #49559. Carmela and Rosa Ponselle made several records from their vaudeville repertoire on Columbia. For Victor her finest solo disc was probably "Pace, pace, mio Dio" (#6440; 74866). The *Forza del destino* trio, with Ezio Pinza and Giovanni Martinelli (Victor #8104) is another prized interpretation. Other notable offerings were the "Ave Maria" from *Otello* (Victor #6474; Columbia #98029) and "Casta diva" (Columbia #49720). Ponselle is heard on complete opera recordings taken from Metropolitan Opera performances of 1935–1936, in *Carmen* and *Traviata*; these came out on Golden Age of Opera records. LP releases appeared on all the reissue labels. Nimbus made a CD (#N 17805) of mostly Verdi numbers (including the *Forza* trio; plus "Casta diva" and "Mira, O Norma" with Marion Telva and several concert songs. "Pace, pace" appeared on an RCA CD (#GD 87810) in 1990, along with "Casta diva" and the familiar Verdi material. [Park 1982 is a complete discography.]

PORT. A vent or auxiliary opening in a bass reflex **baffle**. It must be precisely located and of correct dimension to allow passage of rear sound waves through the enclosure while keeping them in phase with the front waves.

PORTABLE RECORD PLAYERS. The Decca portable gramophone, introduced in 1912 and made popular at the front in World War I, was the first famous portable. But the Pigmy model of the Gramophone Co., introduced in 1909, was the earliest of the genre. Of modern portable audio players, the most important has been the Sony Walkman, a cassette machine small enough to fit in the palm, used for headphone listening.

PORTER, STEVE, 1862–1936. American baritone, born Stephen Porter in Buffalo, New York. He sang in vaudeville, doing solo and ensemble work, appearing with Lillian Russell, the Diamond Comedy Four, and the American Quartet, all before or near the turn of the century. In 1906 he was one of the original members of the Peerless Quartet. His recording activities, from 1895 for Berliner, covered many labels and types of song. He did ballads, comic turns, sacred numbers, Irish monologs, and occasionally opera ("Toreador Song" is Columbia cylinder #4538, ca. 1898). After 1900 he was heard mostly on ensemble records, with the Spencer Trio, American Quartet, Greater New York Quartet, etc. The 1917 Victor catalog had 21 titles by Porter, who continued to make records into the 1920s, some with a new group called the Harmonizers.

Porter and three colleagues established the American Phonograph Record Co. in 1901, to make cylinder records on demand. When that venture failed, Porter sailed for England and was engaged by Waterfield, Clifford and Co. of London as recording expert for their New Century Cylinder Record, for which he also performed. He moved to Nicole Records, Ltd., on formation of that company in 1903, as expert and performer. When Nicole Frères (India), Ltd., was established, Porter went to India as recording expert. By 1910 he was back in America, and remained until his death in New York, on 13 Jan 1936. [Andrews*; Brooks 1979; Walsh 1943/7, 10; 1952/5.]

PORTLAND (label). A British record of Curry's stores, issued in 1923–1924. Fewer than 100 releases are known, from matrices of Edison Bell. Some of the material was from Gennett. [Rust 1978.]

POST SYNC. New audio material added in synchronization to a previously filmed motion picture.

POSTAGE STAMPS. The earliest stamps to illustrate a phonograph record were issued in Argentina in 1939 (Scott catalog #470 and #472); they were promoting the use of flexible discs for mailing messages. A number of commemorative stamps that showed audio equipment or personalities of sound recording history were printed for the phonograph centenary year of 1977. The audio category is considered here to be separate from the much larger category of music and musicians on stamps.

Charles Cros appeared on a French stamp issued 3 Dec 1977 (Scott #B502). The U.S. issued a foolish stamp on 23 Mar 1977 (Scott #1705), showing a "phonograph unlike any ever seen before" (Brooks). Edison was also blasphemed by a 1977 stamp from Afars et Issas—a French territory in East Africa, now Djibouti—(Scott #C104 and C105) that presented him listening to a lateral-cut disc, the format he fought nearly all his life. India #764 pictured an early Berliner gramophone. Surinam #476 and #477 showed a tinfoil phonograph in one denomination, and a modern turntable in another.

Uruguay issued a stamp with a picture of Edison's 1878 phonograph in 1977 (#1003). An American stamp of 6 Oct 1977 honored *The Jazz Singer* with a correct illustration of a Vitaphone projector and disc playing mechanism (#1727).

It is also of interest that a postage stamp commemorating folk songs, playable on a standard LP phonograph, was issued by Bhutan in 1973; Scott did not give it a number. [Brooks 1979/2.]

POSTCARD RECORDS. Max Ettlinger & Co., of Long Acre, England, marketed Discal postcards in March 1905. In June of the same year Zonophone GmbH advertised singing postcards, and a few days later there was advertising from M. Taubert & Co. of Berlin for postcard records. Ettlinger was still selling the cards in May 1908. Such cards could be played on a standard turntable, but needed a clamp to keep them from slipping. Postcard records became common throughout the industry, and were issued in both 33 1/3 and 45 rpm speeds. [Andrews, communication to *HN* #155, p. 173.]

Pot. *See* POTENTIOMETER.

POTENTIOMETER. In an amplifier, the variable attenuator, or potential divider, used to control volume; it is often referred to as a pot.

POULSEN, VALDEMAR, 1869–1942. Danish inventor and engineer, credited with the development of magnetic wire recording around 1898. His machine was named the **Telegraphone**, first patented in Britain (#8961) in 1899. He also invented a process for magnetic recording on iron discs and metal tape, but did not exploit it. Poulsen set up a corporation to hold his patents: A/S Telegraphonen Patent Poulsen; and a manufacturing firm: Dansk Telegraphone Fabrik A/S (1903). He showed his recorder at the Paris Exposition of 1900, and registered the voice of Emperor Franz Joseph. Later he recorded King Edward VII, and presented the wire to Queen Alexandra (its whereabouts are not known). In 1905 he sold those interests to the Telegraphone Corp. (U.S.A.) and the American Telegraphone Co. became the manufacturer. Among Poulsen's eight American patents, #661,619 (filed 8 July 1899, granted 13 Nov 1900) was most important, as the bearer of his basic ideas for wire recording.

POWELL, MAUD, 1868–1920. American violinist, born in Peru, Illinois, on 22 Aug 1868. She studied in Leipzig and Paris, then returned to American and gave recitals. Female violinists were not often seen at that time, which was one reason she was a favorite with audiences; but she also played elegantly. Powell performed at the Columbian Exposition in Chicago in 1893. She recorded for Victor from 1904 to 1917, placing 50 solos in the 1917 catalog. Many of her recordings were arrangements, but among them were the Wieniawski *Polonaise* (#81052), Sarasate's *Zigeunerweisen* (Victor #64262) and two movements from the J. S. Bach Sonata in C Minor (Victor #64618/19). She died in Uniontown, Pennsylvania, on 8 Jan 1920.

POWELL, MEL, 1923– . American composer and jazz pianist, born in New York on 12 Feb 1923. He began as a jazz and swing player, with Benny Goodman; but also studied composition with Paul Hindemith, and took a music degree from Yale in 1952. He was on the Yale faculty from 1957 to 1969, and then went to the California Institute of Arts as Dean, remaining to 1975. He has a long catalog of classical compositions, a number of which have been recorded on LP and CD.

Powell formed a jazz trio with Ruby Braff and drummer Bobby Donaldson, and made some brilliant recordings in 1954 for Vanguard, bringing classical and jazz ideas together. For instance "Bouquet" and "You're My Thrill" are Debussian. Powell did not stay long in jazz, however, and did not record the genre after the mid-1950s.

POWER AMPLIFIER. The main amplifier, or basic amplifier; the device that boosts the voltage supplied by the pre-amplifier to the level required to drive a loudspeaker. *See also* AMPLIFIER.

PREAMPLIFIER. A device, commonly known as a preamp, added to an amplifier to accommodate the very low voltage output from pickups and tape recorders and to raise that voltage to a point that will drive the amplifier. For example the output level of a cartridge may be 1–5 millivolts; the preamplifier could raise it to 1–1.5 volts. The preamp may also provide frequency-response equalization, and may have other functions as well. It may be built into the turntable or the amplifier, or may appear as a separate component. *See also* AMPLIFIER; CONTROLS.

PRE-EMPHASIS. A process used in radio or recording systems to increase the relative intensity of weaker frequencies, to improve signal-to-noise ratio, or to reduce distortion. *See also* DE-EMPHASIS.

PREMIER. The "Columbia Gold Moulded" cylinder records, six inches long, announced in April 1905. (There had been prior demonstrations.) Because of the enhanced volume produced—by the Higham mechanical amplifier built into the reproducer mechanism—the player marketed for these records was called the Loud Speaking Graphophone; it cost $100 minus horn; later the name Twentieth Century Graphophone was given to the machine, and to the records. The cylinders were issued to April 1909, despite poor sales. [Bryan 1982; Klinger*.]

PREMIER CABINET CO. A firm located in 1916 in Williamsport, Pennsylvania. It offered the Premier line of disc players in 10 models.

PREMIER MANUFACTURING CO., LTD. A British firm, located at 81 City Road, London; maker of the Clarion cylinder ca. 1907. They also made the Clarion disc from 1908, and Ebonoid discs from 1909. The Ebonoid discs, like the Ebonoid Gold Moulded Cylinders, played up to five minutes. [Andrews*.]

PREMIER QUARTET. A vocal ensemble, also known (on Victor records) as the American Quartet. Steve Porter, Thomas Chalmers, John Young, and Billy Murray were the original members. They made 40 Edison Diamond Discs between 1915 and 1918. Their material included items connected to the World War I, such as "Bing! Bang! Bing 'Em on the Rhine" (Edison #50489; 1918) and "Submarine Attack" (Edison #50490; 1918). In 1925 the American Quartet had the same membership except for John Ryan, a tenor who replaced Young. One of their popular Victor discs was "That Certain Party" / "Tomorrow Morning" (1925).

PRESCOTT, FREDERICK MARION, 1866–1923. American record company executive. He and his brothers began as general import/export traders in New York, emphasizing products of the Universal Talking Machine Co. They also stocked Graphophone Grands. In 1898 Prescott was trading as the Edison Phonograph Agency, and in 1899 was sole sales exporter for Frank Seaman's National Gramophone Co., getting Zonophones into Britain and Europe.

Prescott visited Britain in 1898, and returned to the New York business, handling machines and records from all companies. The firm issued more catalogs than any other in the trade. Prescott's 40-inch horns were used with Graphophone Grands in Koster and Bial's Music Hall, in New York. In addition to American, British, and Spanish phonographic materials, the firm handled motion pictures, bicycles, watches, and novelties. Prescott imported concert-size Pathé cylinders, and stocked all sizes of Pathé records.

Undertaking another European voyage, Prescott had contracts in Britain and agents in Germany, and Austria-Hungary for Zonophone Products. In March 1901 the **International Zonophone Co.** was established, with Prescott as managing director to 1903, when Gramophone Co. took over the firm. He then became founding president and general manager of the **International Talking Machine Co. mbH** in Berlin, marketing Odeon products.

The **American Record Co.** was set up in 1904 by International Talking Machine, through Hawthorne & Sheble with Frederick Prescott; the plant was in Springfield, Massachusetts. John Prescott (one of Frederick's brothers) was manager.

In 1920 Frederick Prescott was living in Pompton Lakes, New Jersey, and advertising himself as a consultant to disc record manufacturers, promising to help any firm to increase record production. He died on 30 July 1923. [Andrews*.]

PRESENCE. (I) The impression given to the listener of an audio system that the original program source is actually present.

PRESENCE. (II) A boost given to frequencies in the region of 2,000–8,000 Hz, intended to enhance the forwardness of a recorded signal on playback, thus to give a greater impression of presence.

PRESERVATION OF SOUND RECORDINGS. This article has five sections:
1. General considerations
2. Phonograph records
3. Magnetic recordings
4. Compact discs
5. Archival work

1. *General considerations.* In the history of communication, the invention of sound recordings can be considered comparable to the invention of the printing press. It permitted people to preserve oral material so that it can be heard in aural form again and again, just as the printing press has enabled people to preserve oral material in written form, available to those who can read. Today the sound record-

ing is as important an information medium as the written word. Collections of sound recordings are a heavily used part of library and archival collections, yet less is known about the preservation of sound recordings than of printed materials.

Recorded materials come in a variety of formats, all of which are unstable and impermanent. The physical nature of each of these formats is discussed elsewhere in this encyclopedia, and will not be dwelt upon here. (*See* CYLINDER; DISC; and TAPE.) When establishing policies for the storage, handling, and use of sound recordings, it is important to determine whether the material is to be preserved for archival purposes or will be available for use by the general public.

Preservation is commonly defined as the maintenance of objects as closely as possible to their original condition through proper collection management, repair, and physical treatment. The goal of preserving sound recordings is to maintain the aural quality as closely as possible to the quality when the recording was made. Proper housing and storage in a stable environment will retard the deterioration of sound recordings. Proper handling will also preserve the physical recording and its sound quality. However, a library has no control over the conditions under which circulated material will be housed and played when it has left the building. Therefore, sound recordings in circulating collections should be considered impermanent. Rare and unique recordings should never be housed in collections that circulate to the public.

A clean, well-ventilated environment will extend the life of sound recordings and playback equipment. Discs and tapes are especially sensitive to the effects of heat, relative humidity, particulate matter, and light. Audio materials in circulating collections should be housed in an area with a constant temperature of approximately 68 degrees fahrenheit, with a fluctuation of plus or minus five degrees, and a relative humidity range of 40 percent to 50 percent. The critical factor is the stability of temperature and relative humidity; rapid fluctuations in temperature and/or relative humidity can cause irreparable damage to most sound recordings within a short period of time.

Fluctuations of plus or minus five degrees are tolerable. Sound recordings should be housed well removed from heat sources; direct exposure to heat will distort and destroy them. Discs and magnetic media are especially susceptible to damage from particulate matter, air pollution, and smoke; they must be protected from unnecessary exposure to these hazards. Smoking should never be permitted in a library or sound archive.

Archival collections should be stored in a controlled environment. Current research indicates that sound recordings are extremely sensitive to their environment, especially those that are paper-based, such as tapes and some discs. These materials should be stored under special conditions, with a cooler environment, as low as possible, and a relative humidity range of between 25 percent and 35 percent. If possible, rare and unique sound recordings, especially tapes, should be housed in a vault designed for the purpose. Recordings, on the rare occasion that originals are used, need to be acclimated for 24 to 36 hours before playback; the time for acclimation will depend upon the medium.

At present there is considerable research underway, in the United States and elsewhere, into the physical nature of sound recordings and the environmental requirements for their long-term preservation in original format. American sound archivists are active in their professional organization, the **Association for Recorded Sound Collections** (ARSC) and in international organizations, such as the International Council on Archives (ICA), concerned with the preservation of sound recordings. If collections of recorded sound are to be preserved, it is important that their custodians keep up with research in the field.

2. Phonograph records. The earliest recorded sound was transcribed on cylinders made of a variety of compounds. These early recordings are rare and fragile. They must be stored in a secure, controlled environment with rigid temperature, humidity and pollution controls. Cylinders, and other early recordings in a variety of unusual formats, are rarely, if ever, played.

The phonodisc (phonograph record) is a flat disc, made of a wide variety of materials.

The physical nature of phonograph records is described elsewhere. What is important to understand when dealing with the preservation of these materials is that we do not know precisely what most of them are made of, nor how long they will last. Certainly many have lasted, in reasonably good condition, far longer than most specialists have expected. Research is underway to identify the processes used to manufacture discs, and the ingredients in them, to determine the optimum method, or methods, for the storage and preservation of original phonograph records in archives.

Discs, whether they be housed in archives or circulating collections, should be placed on baked enamel shelves in an upright position. Shelves should not be tightly packed, but discs should be placed close enough together so that each disc is upright. Phonodiscs that are askew on the shelves will warp within a short period of time. This will cause deterioration and sound distortion and will make the disc unplayable. Partitions placed every four to six inches along the shelf will help hold phonograph records in an upright position. Wooden shelves are not recommended for the housing of sound recordings, for the acids in wood may react adversely with the properties within the discs and accelerate deterioration. Metal shelves coated with baked enamel are recommended for the storage of library and archival materials, including sound recordings. If a new storage area is to be created, research on appropriate shelving will ensure that a collection survives for a long time.

Discs should be removed from the sleeves that contain them and placed in protective sleeves or envelopes. Most of the original envelopes for phonodiscs are made of acidic board, harmful to the recordings they house. (However, original envelopes often are preserved for their informational and artifactual value.) Protective sleeves can be obtained from suppliers of archival materials. The original plastic wrapping (shrink wrap) that surrounds the envelope and disc should be removed immediately and discarded. If it is not removed promptly, it will continue to shrink and can cause distortion of the disc. Also, this plastic, and the plastics used commercially for sleeves within the envelope, are chemically unstable and can damage the recording. Sound archivists do not agree on the most suitable protective sleeves for archival recordings. If an archival collection is to be rehoused, it is advisable to seek advice from the Library of Congress Motion Picture, Broadcasting and Recorded Sound Division, or, through the Association for Recorded Sound Collections, to hire a consultant to help set up a rehousing program.

Discs should be cleaned before each use (*see* CLEANING).

The study of sound recordings undertaken by A.G. Pickett and M.M. Lemcoe (Pickett 1959) remains the most useful source of information on disc properties, stability, and longevity.

3. *Magnetic recordings.* The development and physical nature of magnetic media are described elsewhere in this encyclopedia (*see* MAGNETIC RECORDING). **Reel to reel tape** recordings provide the best stability and fidelity, but they are not appropriate for circulating collections of recordings; they are more appropriately housed in research and/or archival collections. To prevent deterioration, magnetic recordings of archival value are often placed in cold storage with a controlled relative humidity to ensure their long-term preservation. Research is underway to determine the optimum storage conditions for magnetic tape; it is an extremely fragile medium. Surrogate copies should be made for general use.

The audiocassette is especially popular because each cassette is a contained unit, resistant to mishandling and simple to use, although its sound quality is inferior to that of reel to reel tape and it is not a stable or permanent medium. Cassette technology is also ephemeral, but this need not be a consideration in collections where the cassettes will wear out before they become obsolete and present playback problems. As users of circulating sound collections usually do not demand the finest quality of reproduction, the tape cassette is a convenient way to provide access to aural performances (information) while preserving original material in original format.

A major problem with cassette recordings is non-alignment of the tape within the cassette when the tape is wound too loosely on its spool or the tension varies. Cassettes should be checked after each use to be sure that the tape is wound properly or soon distortion will become obvious. If the cassette is played on poorly maintained equipment, it can be damaged.

The **print-through** phenomenon is an effect caused by a combination of inferior tapes, improper rewinding, and improper storage. Proper storage of cassettes can somewhat lessen the risk of print-through.

It is important to house circulating collections of tape and video cassettes in an environmentally controlled area if they are to be preserved for any length of time. Fluctuations in temperature and relative humidity can quickly cause the tape and its sound quality to distort. High relative humidity will cause the stretching and warping of the tape. The binders will degenerate, ooze, and migrate, causing adjacent layers to stick together. Oxide coatings will come loose and can shed completely in playback. Affected tapes will leave a gummy residue on the tape transports and heads of the playback equipment, causing further distortion (*see* TAPE DECK). Dust and particulate matter are especially harmful. Tape cassettes should be stored in plastic cases that offer support and protection from particulate matter. Paper-based archival storage boxes for cassettes are not recommended because the paper itself is a cause of particulate matter which can affect the tape. Appropriate storage containers are available from archival suppliers.

The careful maintenance of playback equipment in a sound collection is essential. Equipment should be checked and cleaned after each use. Unfortunately, librarians have no control over the playback equipment upon which circulating tapes will be played. However, tapes can and should be inspected for damage upon return to the library.

4. *Compact Discs.* Compact discs are easy to handle and are relatively impervious to damage by users and other hazards that threatened earlier discs. Originally, compact discs were advertized as "permanent." While they do offer considerable protection from the risks of rough handling and playback, their ingredients are not stable and will deteriorate over time. In addition to problems that are attributed to poor quality control in manufacture, sound archivists are beginning to recognize other problems with the medium. One cause of deterioration is the ink used on the labels placed on some discs, which may react with the materials in the composition of the disc. This reaction appears to be accelerated when discs are stored in high relative humidity. Studies are underway to identify other causes of CD deterioration. Compact discs, and their playback equipment, are as sensitive as other media to fluctuations in temperature and relative humidity, and to dirt and air pollution. They require a controlled environment for storage and playback. Librarians should follow guidelines for the housing and storage of other sound media at this time.

Digital recording is a complex process, and many of the early compact discs were defective. Quality control in production is better today than it was a decade ago, but optical disc technology is constantly evolving. There are no standards for this medium. At present compact discs are suitable for circulating collections, but they present real and continuing problems for archival collections. The compact disc is considered a transitional medium. It is ideal for the transmission of information, but it is not the medium for storage of information. Compact discs will present serious challenges for the sound archivist in the not-too-distant future.

5. *Archival work.* The curator of a collection of sound recordings needs to evaluate the use that the material will receive, then determine how it can best be preserved, through proper storage, handling, and use, for as long as possible. It is advisable to learn as much as possible about the media in the collections, from the professional literature of the sound archivist and that of the new technologies.

As the technology of sound recording is evolving at a rapid rate and there are few standards, a recording technology and its playback equipment can become obsolete within a short period of time. This problem plagues circulating collections as well as sound archives. Much early material has deteriorated so badly that it can no longer be used, and playback equipment is no longer available to retrieve the sound of some recordings. Maintaining playback equipment is a challenge that can be met by only a few sound archives in the world.

The re-recording (reformatting) of material is possible, but it is expensive and time-consuming. Re-recording the older sound recordings in a suitable format, without enhancements, for playback, is a preferred method for preservation and access in archival collections. Of concern is the fact that there are, at present, no standards for the re-recording of sound recordings into a newer medium for playback. When dealing with the preservation of aural materials, the goal is to retain the quality of the sound as closely as possible to the original, blips and all, not to enhance the quality of the sound (see SONIC RESTORATION). Sound archivists and audio librarians follow the same principle of preservation as curators of collections of printed materials.

Good housekeeping practices, a stable environment, and the proper maintenance of playback equipment will help extend the life of a collection, but an institution has no control over the conditions under which its material will be played once it leaves the library. Circulating collections must be considered impermanent. Printed guidelines for handling and playback of materials can be distributed with the recordings when they circulate; this can help to curtail abuses, and preserve materials for future users.

(The author wishes to acknowledge the assistance of Gerald Gibson, Motion Picture, Broadcasting, and Recorded Sound Division, Library of Congress; Vincent Pelote, Institute of Jazz Studies, Rutgers University; and Christopher Ann Paton, Popular Music Collection, Georgia State University, in the preparation of this essay.) [Association 1987; Brownstein 1990; Day 1989; Geller 1983; Gibson 1991; Griffin 1985; Isom 1972; Knight, G. 1977; McWilliams, J. 1979; McWilliams, J. 1983; Pickett 1959; Smolian 1987; Swartzburg 1991; Ward 1990.] *See also* SOUND RECORDINGS AND THE LIBRARY.

Susan Swartzburg

PRESIDENTS ON RECORD. The first U.S. president to make a record was Rutherford B. Hayes, when Thomas Edison took a tinfoil phonograph to the White House for a demonstration on 18 Apr 1878. Benjamin Harrison was the first to make a commercial record, for Bettini; but the record was never described or listed in a Bettini catalog; no copy is known to exist.

No live recording was made of William McKinley's last speech, 5 Sep 1901, just before his assassination, but many records were marketed with parts of the speech read by recording artists (Frank C. Stanley, William F. Hooley, Len Spencer, etc.).

William Howard Taft made a number of recordings while campaigning for the presidency in August 1908: 12 Edison cylinders, 13 Victor/HMV discs, and 15 Columbia discs, three of them repeated on cylinder. As president he made seven Victors, on 1 Oct 1912, speaking on issues of the day (peace, prosperity, tariff, etc.); these were the first commercially released records by a president in office. Earlier in 1912 ex-president Theodore Roosevelt and candidate Woodrow Wilson made records.

With the advent of radio, and then of talking motion picture newsreels in the 1920s, the magic of a president's voice was lessened, and only a few made commercial recordings. The most interesting was Franklin Roosevelt's "War Message to Congress and the Nation" of 8 Dec 1941, declaring war on Japan, and defining 7 December as a "day that will live in infamy" (Columbia #36516; 1941).

PRESLEY, ELVIS ARON, 1935–1977. American rock singer and actor, born on 8 Jan 1935 in Tupelo, Mississippi. Referred to as the "King of Rock and Roll," Presley was one of the first singers to define and shape the rock and roll sound, which was a mixture of rhythm and blues, country, and gospel. His success and popularity were unprecedented, with audiences made up primarily of teenagers. He began playing guitar when he was 11. At 13, he and his parents moved to Memphis, Tennessee. Upon graduation from high school, Presley became a truck driver. Sun Studios in Memphis, owned by Sam Phillips, was where he made his early recordings. His first recording was "Blue Moon of Kentucky," backed with "That's All Right" (Sun #209; 1954), and the second was "I Don't Care if the Sun Don't Shine," / "Good Rockin' Tonight" (Sun #210;

1954). These met with success on the local charts.

RCA signed him on 22 Nov 1955. His first LP was *Elvis Presley* (RCA #LPM 1254; 1956), which became RCA's best-selling album up to that time. Presley recordings have appeared on the Sun, RCA, RCA/Pickwick, RCA/Camden, and Readers Digest labels.

Among his many radio and television appearances were performances on *Grand Ole Opry, Louisiana Hayride,* and the *Ed Sullivan Show.* Tapes in 10-inch format of the *Louisiana Hayride* radio programs, including Presley performances, are housed at the Archives of the State of Louisiana.

Presley released 131 singles, with 18 number one hits—"Heartbreak Hotel" (RCA #6420; 1956) was his first number one single and "Suspicious Minds" (RCA #9764; 1969) was his last. His biggest selling disc was "It's Now or Never" (RCA #7777; 1960), with sales above 20 million copies worldwide.

A poll of U.S. juke box owner-operators, reported in *Variety* (3 Aug 1988) concluded that "Hound Dog" / "Don't Be Cruel" (RCA #6604; 1956) is the most popular juke box record of all time.

Ninety-three albums were released (both before and after his death), with nine reaching the number one position on the *Billboard* charts. His most popular albums were two from film soundtracks that he made after leaving military service: *G.I. Blues* (RCA #LPM 2256; 1960) and *Blue Hawaii* (RCA #LPM 2426; 1961).

Presley toured only in the United States. He later performed in shows in Las Vegas. He appeared in 34 movies, commencing with *Love Me Tender* (1956), usually singing in them, with motion picture soundtracks released to coincide with the pictures.

Since Presley's death on 16 Aug 1977, many novelty recordings and also tributes to him have been released. [Foerster 1987; Whisler 1981.]

Felicia Reilly

PRESSING. (I) The final form of the disc, made from the stamper; it is the form that is sold to the end user (see DISC, I).

PRESSING. (II) As a verb, the process of molding the biscuit as it is kneaded and squeezed flat between warmed bed plates (*see* DISC, 3).

PRESTIGE (label). An American record issued from 1949 to 1971 from 745 Tenth Ave., New York, then 446 W. 50th St., New York; later (from 1967) located at 203 S. Washington Ave., Bergenfield, New Jersey. Bob Weinstock was the founder. The label was significant for its issues of the **cool jazz** school of the 1950s and 1960s. Sessions included such artists as Miles Davis, Stan Getz, Lee Konitz, Modern Jazz Quartet, Thelonious Monk, and Lennie Tristano. John Coltrane, Barry Harris, and Pat Martino also appeared on Prestige. In addition to their original pressings, Prestige leased classic sessions from other labels for reissue. In May 1971 the label was sold to Fantasy, in San Francisco, which concentrated on LP reissues of the early Prestige material. [Ruppli 1980 is a complete label list.]

PREVIN, ANDRÉ, 1929–. German/American pianist, composer, and conductor, born on 6 Apr 1929 in Berlin. At age six he entered the Hochschule für Musik, Berlin; in 1938 his (Jewish) family had to leave Germany and took up residence in Paris. Previn studied at the Conservatory there, and had lessons from Marcel Dupré. In 1939 the family transferred to Los Angeles, where Previn continued his studies and took American citizenship in 1943. He worked as an orchestrator and music director for MGM in Hollywood, and also performed as a jazz and concert pianist. He won Academy Awards for scoring the films *Gigi* (1958), *Porgy and Bess* (1959), *Irma la douce* (1963), and *My Fair Lady* (1964).

Previn's conducting career began with a concert of the St. Louis Symphony Orchestra. In 1967–1969 he was conductor of the Houston Symphony Orchestra, then he directed the London Symphony Orchestra from 1968 to 1979. Previn also led the Pittsburgh Symphony Orchestra from 1976 to 1982, and both the Royal Philharmonic Orchestra and the Los Angeles Philharmonic Orchestra from 1982; he resigned from the Royal Philharmonic in 1986.

Previn has a special affinity for English composers, and has made notable discs of several important works. Benjamin Britten's *Spring Symphony* (EMI CD #C747667-2) and the Vaughan Williams symphonies for RCA, all with the London Symphony, are fine examples. His most popular jazz recording was *My Fair Lady*, a 1964 album (Columbia #CL 2195) with Shelly Manne that featured a remarkable version of "I Could Have Danced All Night." The single "Like Young" with the David Rose orchestra was on the charts 14 weeks in 1959 (MGM #12792), and won a Grammy as best popular orchestral record. Previn also received Grammys for two jazz albums on the Contemporary label, the 1960 *West Side Story*, and the 1961 *André Previn Plays Harold Arlen*. Three other albums were chart successes between 1959 and 1964.

PRIDE, CHARLEY, 1938–. American country singer and guitarist, born in Sledge, Mississippi, on 18 Mar 1938. He taught himself guitar while engaged in miscellaneous occupations, and moved to Nashville in 1963. Signing with RCA Victor in 1964, he was the first Black country artist to be heard on a major label (although his race was at first concealed by Victor). His list of 51 country chart singles began with "Just between You and Me" (Victor #9000; 1966). Other great successes came with "Afraid of Losing You Again" (Victor #0265; 1969), "All I Have to Offer You' (Victor 0167; 1969), "Is Anybody Goin' to San Antone?" (Victor #9806; 1970), and "Honky Tonk Blues" (Victor #11913; 1980).

PRIMROSE, WILLIAM, 1903–1982. Scottish violist, born in Glasgow on 23 Aug 1903. He studied violin in Glasgow, then took lessons in Belgium from Ysaÿe, who recommended a change to the viola. He played viola with the London String Quartet from 1930 to 1935. Settling in the U.S. in 1937, he became active as a soloist and ensemble player, then held the post of principal violist in the NBC Symphony Orchestra under Toscanini to 1942. Later he taught in several universities while maintaining a concert schedule. His activities were valuable in bringing the viola to wide audiences; and he

was the major exponent of the instrument on Victor records during the 1930s (appearing also on Columbia). He had five numbers in the 1940 Victor catalog, where he was described as *the* violist. Primrose also recorded the violin, for Columbia, Decca, and HMV, including the Bach Partita No. 3 and Sonata No. 2. He died in Provo, Utah, on 1 May 1982.

PRINCE, 1958–. American rock singer, born in Minneapolis on 7 June 1958. His full name is Prince Rogers Nelson, taken from the Prince Rogers Trio, a jazz group led by his father. As a child he learned to play all the instruments of a pop ensemble, and when he made his demo tape he sang and performed all the parts. Between 1979 and 1985 he made six remarkably successful multi-channel albums, in which he was composer, singer, and instrumentalist. The three most popular were on the Warner Brothers label: *Prince* (#BSK 3366; 1979), 29 weeks on the charts; *1999* (#9-23720-1F; 1982), 162 weeks; and *Purple Rain* (#25110-1; 1984), more than 78 weeks. The album *Dirty Mind* (# BSK3478; 1980) aroused controversy over its "X-rated" lyrics, and many AOR stations refused to broadcast it. Among the most popular Prince singles were "I Wanna Be Your Lover" from the album *Prince*, "Little Red Corvette" from *1999*, and the 1986 hit "Kiss," from the *Parade* album. *Purple Rain*, the soundtrack album from a motion picture, is said to have sold more than 11 million copies.

PRINCE, ALEXANDER. British performer on the concertina, among the earliest to record the instrument. He made five records with orchestral accompaniment for the Zonophone label (of G & T) in February 1906, beginning with "Life in Vienna" (#49106). Three more discs were dated from 4 Feb 1908 in the ledger of G & T with Zonophone numbers #49110–49112; they were concertina solos. [Walsh 1953/3.]

PRINCE, CHARLES ADAM, 1869–1937. American military band director, pianist, and organist; born in California. He was musical director for Columbia from the late 1890s, and conductor of the Columbia Orchestra / Columbia Band to 1905. After 1905 he directed

Prince's Band and Prince's Orchestra. He retired to California in the late 1920s, and died in San Francisco on 10 Oct 1937.

The Columbia Orchestra made more than 200 cylinder records between 1896 and 1900, beginning with "Honeymoon March" (#15000). Their repertoire covered marches, waltzes, polkas, ballads, and novelty numbers. In 1906 Prince's Band and Orchestra recorded extensively on the larger Twentieth-century cylinders, in the same popular repertoire. Columbia's first attempt at serious classical music was with Wagner's "Rienzi Overture," by the Columbia Orchestra conducted by Prince (#A6006; 1917), on a double-faced 12-inch disc. His last Columbia disc was made in 1922, after which he moved to the Puritan label briefly, then went to Victor. [Walsh 1952/12; 1953/1.]

PRINCESS SAPPHIRE RECORD (label). An American record issued by the Sapphire Record and Talking Machine Co., New York, probably between 1917 and 1920. "Little is known about them. They are very rare" (Rust). [Rust 1978.]

PRINT-THROUGH. The transferral of signal information from one portion of a magnetic tape to another portion, with the effect of simultaneous playback of the transferred signal and the signal already present. This is a major problem of the format, arising from the tight winding of tape on its reel, tape coercivity, or temperature aberrations. Thickness of the base is an important factor also.

Print-through is most likely to occur immediately after recording, and becomes less likely with the passage of time. It may be helpful to rewind a freshly recorded tape a few times before playback. Annual winding of little used tapes—fast forward and slow reverse—is recommended by some authorities as a means of reducing the tendency of tape layers to adhere to each other. However, "winding retightens the tape-pack and this freshly accumulated tension restarts the tape stretching cycle anew. Thus ritual rewinding may cause more ills than it cures" (Smolian). There is no device or method that will remove print-through once it has occurred. [Smolian 1987.] *See also* PRESERVATION OF SOUND RECORDINGS.

Production master. *See* MASTER.

PRYOR, ARTHUR, 1870–1942. American trombonist; a "youthful sensation of the band world in the 1890s" (Brooks). He played with the Liberati Band in 1889 and then with the Sousa Band from 1892. He became assistant conductor, and directed most of the recordings made by the Sousa Band. In 1903 he left Sousa to form his own band, and toured extensively. His band flourished until he died.

Pryor recorded first for Columbia cylinders in 1895. He did solos with Sousa's Band on Columbia cylinders #516 and #517, "Say Au Revoir but Not Good-Bye" and "Little Marcia Marie Polka." In October 1900 he did his first Victor solo, again with Sousa's Band, playing his own arrangement of "Fanny Waltz" (#V-309). One of the four solos in the Victor 1917 catalog—reflecting Pryor's lifelong love of opera—was "Celeste Aida" (#35030). His band and his orchestra were also in the catalog, and he was identified as composer of 10 numbers. He recorded into the late 1920s, and was well represented (32 titles) in the 1940 catalog. [Brooks 1979.]

PSEUDONYMS. Recording artists have frequently used more than one stage name (nom du disque) in their studio work. One reason was to avoid contractual difficulties when they wished to work with one label while signed up as an exclusive to another. A second reason was that record companies wanted to simulate a long list of artists when they did not have such; if they gave each person three names it quickly tripled the list without extra cost. Some of the invented names taken by the more prominent performers are given below. Where the real name in parentheses is marked with an asterisk, that name is itself a stage name. Pseudonyms for orchestras and large ensembles are not included here as they would be too numerous; for example Ben Selvin's orchestra recorded under at least 23 different names. [Principal sources: Bayly 1976/12; Lumpe 1990; Rust 1969; Rust 1989; Sutton 1991 (the most exhaustive and well-researched list for American records, with label names given for each pseudonym); Walsh 1944/5; 1952/5; 1962/11; 1970/6.]

Adams and Clark
(Frank Luther* and
Carson Robison)

Adams, Charles
(Charles A. Prince)

Adams, Joe (Frank
Luther*)

Ahern, James (Vernon
Dalhart*)

Alexander, Alfred
(Henry Burr*)

Alexander, George
(Clifford Wiley)

Alix, May (Alberta
Hunter)

Allen, Edward (Arthur
Middleton)

Allen, Gary (Len
Spencer)

Allen, Mack (Vernon
Dalhart*)

Ames, Molly (Beulah
Gaylord Young)

Anderson, Charles
(Elliott Shaw)

Anderson, Ernie (Fred
J. Bacon)

Andrew, Merry
(Charles Penrose)

Andrews, Jim (Arthur
Fields* or Irving
Kaufman)

Anthony, Harry (John
C. Young)

Astor, Paul (Easthope
Martin)

Atkinson, George
(Burt Shepard)

Aubrey, Charles
(Wilfred Glenn)

Aunt Jemima (Tess
Gardella)

Austin, Gene (Charles
Keene or Gene
Lucas)

Baker, Donald (Arthur
Fields*)

Baldwin, Arthur
(Arthur Fields*)

Ball, Ray (Frank
Marvin)

Ballard, George
Wilton (George
Wilton)

Ballard, Wolfe
(Vernon Dalhart*)

Balzer, Joseph (Gustav
Görlich, Robert
Heger, Artur
Rother)

Barr, Harry (Henry
Burr*)

Barrel House Pete (Art
Gillham)

Barrett, Betty (Marie
Tiffany)

Bartle, S. (Alexander
Prince)

Beason, Kitty (Delores
Valesco)

Beat Brothers (Beatles)

Beatty, Josephine
(Alberta Hunter)

Beaver, George (Irving
Kaufman)

Beaver, Harry (Irving
Kaufman)

Bellwood and Burr
(Albert Campbell
and Henry Burr*)

Belmont, Joe (Joseph
Walter Fulton)

Bennett Brothers
(Victor Arden and
Wheeler
Wadsworth)

Bennett, John (Al
Bernard)

Bergere, Bettina
(Gladys Rice)

Bernie, D. Bud (Arthur
Fields*)

Big Boy and Shorty
(Phil Cook and
Victor Fleming)

Billings Brothers
(Frank Luther* and
Carson Robison)

Billings, Bud (Frank
Luther*)

Billings, Joe (Carson
Robison)

Bingham, Ethel
(Annette Hanshaw)

Birmingham Bud
(Frank Luther*)

Black and White (Billy
Jones and Ernest
Hare)

Black Brothers (Frank
Luther* and Carson
Robison)

Black, Herbert (Frank
Luther*, Charles
Hart, Elliott Shaw,
or Charles
Harrison)

Blake, Harry (Billy
Jones)

Blanchard, Dan (Frank
Luther*)

Blue Ridge Duo
(George Reneau
and Gene Austin)

Blue, Bob (Smith
Ballew)

Blue, Buddy (Smith
Ballew)

Bluebird Trio (Billy
Jones, Ernest Hare,
and piano)

Bolton, Joe (Joe Batten)

Bonner, William
(William A.
Kennedy)

Boynton, Edward
(Fred Van Eps)

Britt, Andy (Arthur
Fields*)

Britten, Ford (Arthur
Fields)

Bronson, George
(Irving Kaufman,
Arthur Fields*, or
Lewis James)

Brown and Edwards
(Boudini Brothers)

Brown, Arthur (Irving
Kaufman)

Brown, Betty (Vaughn
De Leath)

Brown, Edna (Elsie
Baker)

Brown, William
(Scrappy Lambert)

Bruce, Robert (Lewis
James or Henry
Burr*)

Buckley, Eugene
(Arthur Fields*)

Burke, Edward (Elliott
Shaw)

Burns, Arthur (Colin
O'More)

Burr, Henry (Harry H.
McClaskey)

Burton, Billy (Charles
Harrison)

Burton, Howard
(Arthur Hall*)

Burton, Sammy
(Irving Kaufman,
Billy Jones, or
Ernest Hare)

Butler, Frank (George
Baker)

Calhoun and Leavitt
(Frank Luther* and
Carson Robison)

Calhoun, Jeff (Vernon
Dalhart*)

Calhoun, Jess (Vernon
Dalhart*)

Cannon, Jimmy
(Vernon Dalhart*)

Careau, Franklin
(Frank Croxton?)

Carson, Cal (Carson
Robison or Frank
Luther*)

Casey, Michael
(Russell Hunting)

Chappell, Miss (Edith
Chapman)

Charles, Harold
(Irving Kaufman)

Chester and Rollins
(Frank Luther* and
Carson Robison)

Christy Brothers
(Irving Kaufman
and Jack Kaufman,
or Arthur Fields

and Charles
Harrison)
Christy, Frank (Irving
Kaufman)
Cinway, Charles
(Charles Hart)
Clare and Mann (Al
Bernard and Ernest
Hare)
Clare, Jack (Al
Bernard)
Clark, James (Carson
Robison)
Clark, Katherine
(Grace Kerns)
Clark, Miriam (Grace
Kerns?)
Clarke, Billy (Irving
Kaufman)
Clarke, Catherine
(Grace Kerns)
Clarke, Glory (Vaughn
De Leath)
Clarke, Jane (Grace
Kerns)
Clayton, Bob (Gene
Autry)
Clifford, Arthur
(George
Alexander*)
Clifford, Ed (Cliff
Edwards or Vernon
Dalhart*)
Clifton, Edward (Cliff
Edwards)
Collins and Reynolds
(Henry Burr* and
Jack Kaufman)
Collins, Bill (Gene
Austin)
Collins, Charlie (Harry
Fay)
Collins, Jane (Helen
Clark)
Collins, Kitty (June
Kirkby or Eleanor
Jones-Hudson)
Collins, Sallie (Helen
Clark)
Combs, Irving (Irving
Kaufman)

Confidential Charley
(Ernest Hare or
Irving Kaufman)
Conrad, Louise
(Louise Gaisberg)
Cook, Tom (Frank
Luther*)
Courtland, Eric
(Ernest Pike)
Craig, Al (Arthur
Hall*)
Craig, Allen (Irving
Kaufman)
Cramer Brothers
(Vernon Dalhart*
and Carson
Robison)
Cramer, Al (Vernon
Dalhart*)
Crange, George
(Irving Kaufman)
Crane, Harry (Arthur
Fields*)
Craver and Wells
(Vernon Dalhart*
and Carson
Robison)
Craver, Al (Vernon
Dalhart*)
Cummings, James
(Vernon Dalhart*)
Curtis, Harry (Charles
Hart or Charles
Harrison)
Dale, Charles (Arthur
Fields*, Lewis
James, Franklyn
Baur, Arthur Hall*,
or Irving
Kaufman))
Dale, Edward (Charles
Hackett)
Dale, Edwin (Charles
Hackett)
Dale, Walter H.
(Arthur Fields*)
Dalhart, Vernon
(Marion Try
Slaughter)
Dalton, Charles
(Vernon Dalhart*)

Dalton, Jack (Jack
Kaufman)
Daniels, Wallace
(Ernest Hare)
Daniels, Walter (Frank
Luther*)
Dare, Dot (Annette
Hanshaw)
Davies, Fred (Peter
Dawson)
Dawson, Leonard
(Peter Dawson)
De Kyzer, Marie
(Marie Kaiser)
De Marco, Angelina
(Vaughn De Leath)
De Rex, Billy (Billy
Jones)
De Wees, George
(Irving Kaufman)
Del Campo, A.
(Alberto de Bassini)
Dell, Vernon (Vernon
Dalhart*)
Destinova, Emmy
(Emmy Destinn)
Dexter, Charles
(Arthur Fields*)
Dickson, Charles
(Irving Kaufman)
Dittman, Evans (Paul
Althouse?)
Dixie Stars (Al
Bernard and J.
Russell Robinson)
Dixon and Andrews
(Vernon Dalhart*
and Carson
Robison)
Dixon, Charles (Irving
Kaufman)
Dixon, Martin (Vernon
Dalhart*)
Dixon, Raymond
(Lambert Murphy)
Donivetti, Hugo
(Charles Harrison)
Donovan, Hugh
(Charles Harrison,
Arthur Fields*, or
Ernest Hare)

Dooley and Shea (Billy
Jones and Ernest
Hare)
Dudley, S. H. (Samuel
Holland Rous)
Duffy, Tom (Irving
Kaufman)
Dwyer, Gertrude
(Vaughn De Leath)
Edwards, A. (Ernest
Pike)
Edwards, Billy
(Arthur Fields*)
Edwards, Thomas
(Billy Jones)
Edwards, Thomas
(Elliott Shaw, or
Arthur Fields)*)
Edwards, Tom (Irving
Kaufman)
Eide, Kaja (Eidé
Norena)
Elliott and Spencer
(Ed Smalle and
Gerald Underhill)
Elliott, Joseph (Vernon
Dalhart*, Arthur
Fields*, Charles
Harrison, Ernest
Hare, Billy Jones, or
Charles Hart)
Elliott, Joseph and
Samuel Spencer
(Billy Jones and
Ernest Hare)
Ellis, Gay (Annette
Hanshaw)
Ely, Carl (Walter Van
Brunt?)
Epstein, George
(Irving Kaufman)
Evans and Clarke
(Vernon Dalhart*
and Carson
Robison)
Evans, Francis (Frank
Luther*)
Evans, Frank (Vernon
Dalhart*, Frank
Luther*, Carson
Robison, Arthur
Fields*)

Evans, Franklin
(Carson Robison)
Evans, Hal (Vernon
Dalhart*)
Evans, Harry (Evan
Williams)
Evans, Henry (Evan
Williams)
Evans, William T.
(Evan Williams)
Everett, Elliot
(Wilhelm Kempff?)
Faber, Ed (Carson
Robison)
Farkas, A. (Andor
Földes)
Fernand, M. (Emilio
de Gogorza)
Fields, Arthur (Abe
Finkelstein)
Florio, Nino
(Giuseppe di
Stefano)
Flynn, Jimmy (Irving
Kaufman)
Foster, Al (Sid Gary)
Foster, Charles (Fred
Hillerbrand)
Francisco, Carlos
(Emilio de
Gogorza)
Francisco, E. (Emilio
de Gogorza)
Francisco, Signor
(Emilio de
Gogorza)
Franklin, Ed (Emilio
De Gogorza)
Frawley, Tom (Irving
Kaufman)
Fredericks, William
(Frank C. Stanley?)
French, George
(Arthur Fields*)
Fuller, Jeff (Vernon
Dalhart*)
Fuller, Jep (Vernon
Dalhart*)
Gardiner, Arthur
(Arthur Tracy)

Gargolo, Ugeso (Billy
Jones)
Garland, Dorothy
(Delores Valesco)
Geer, Georgia
(Vaughn De Leath)
Geer, Gloria (Vaughn
De Leath)
George, Arthur
(George Baker)
Gilbert, Lawrence E.
(Thomas Chalmers)
Gillette, Irving (Henry
Burr*)
Goddard, Herbert
(Emilio de
Gogorza)
Gold Dust Twins (Earl
Tuckerman and
Harvey
Hindermyer)
Gordon, Charles
(Percy Hemus)
Gordon, George
(Charles Hart)
Grant, Arthur (Arthur
Hall* or Ernest
Hare)
Grant, Hector (Peter
Dawson)
Grant, Rachel (Gladys
Rice)
Gray, Henry (Arthur
Fields*)
Green, Alice (Olive
Kline)
Green, Bert (Jack
Kaufman)
Green, Marion
(Wilfred Glenn)
Green, Rosa (Rosa
Henderson)
Green, Sadie (Vaughn
De Leath)
Grimes, Betty
(Vaughn De Leath)
Guenther, Felix (John
Bath)
Gunboat Billy and the
Sparrow (Arthur

Fields* and Fred
Hall)
Haines, Ralph
(Scrappy Lambert)
Haley, Harry (Henry
Burr*)
Hall, Arthur (Adolph
J. Hahl)
Hall, Edgar (Andrea
Sarto)
Hall, Freddy (Billy
Jones)
Hall, James (Andrea
Sarto)
Hamilton, Edward
(Reinald
Werrenrath)
Hancock, Billy
(Johnny Marvin)
Happiness Boys (Billy
Jones and Ernest
Hare)
Hardy, John (Gene
Autry)
Hardy, Paul (William
Wheeler)
Harmony Broadcast-
ers (Billy Jones and
Ernest Hare)
Harmony Brothers
(Frank Luther* and
Carson Robison)
Harold, Eugene (Billy
Jones)
Harper, Billy (Irving
Kaufman)
Harris and Smith
(Charles Hart and
Elliott Shaw)
Harris, David (Billy
Jones, Irving
Kaufman, Vernon
Dalhart*, Ernest
Hare, Elliott Shaw,
Walter Van Brunt,
Charles Harrison)
Harris, Frank (Irving
Kaufman)
Harris, Harry (Vernon
Dalhart* or Cliff
Edwards)

Harris, Henry (Vernon
Dalhart*)
Harris, Mae (Rosa
Henderson)
Harrison, James F.
(Frederick J.
Wheeler)
Hartley, Lester
(Franklyn Baur)
Harrow, David and
Thomas Edwards
(Billy Jones and
Ernest Hare)
Harvey, Harold
(Lewis James)
Hayes, Lou (Vernon
Dalhart*)
Henry, Albert (Albert
Benzler?)
Henty, Jack (Ernest
Pike)
Herold, Francis
(Arthur Fields*)
Hill, Murry K. (Joseph
T. Pope, Jr.)
Hill, Sam (Gene
Autry)
Hilton, Charles
(Charles Harrison)
Hilly, Dan (Arthur
Fields*)
Hobbs, Herb (Arthur
Fields*)
Holland, Byron (Byron
G. Harlan)
Holland, Charles
(Stanley Kirkby)
Holmes, Dick (Jack
Kaufman)
Holmes, John (Irving
Kaufman)
Holt, Arthur (Irving
Kaufman)
Holton, Larry (Arthur
Fields* or Scrappy
Lambert)
Hometowners (Arthur
Fields* and Fred
Hall)

Honey Duke and His
Uke (Johnny
Marvin)
Howard, Anna (Lucy
Isabelle Marsh)
Howard, Frank
(Albert Campbell
or Arthur Hall*)
Hughes, Dan (Billy
Murray)
Hunter, James (Arthur
Fields*)
Hüttner, Maria
(Margot Pinter)
Incognita, L'
[Zonophone]
(Violet Mount)
Ireland, S. (Stanley
Kirkby)
Irving, Henry (Irving
Kaufman)
Irving, John (Irving
Kaufman)
Jack, Arizona (Alf
Gordon)
Jackson, Happy (Frank
Luther*)
James, Morton
(Morton Downey)
Jamieson and Turner
(Charles Hart and
Elliott Shaw)
Jefferies, Walter
(George Baker)
Jeffries, Jack (Harry
Fay)
Jewel Trio (Vernon
Dalhart*, Carson
Robison, and
Adelyn Hood)
Jimson Brothers
(Frank Luther* and
Carson Robison)
Johnson, Emma
(Helen Clark)
Johnson, Gene (Gene
Autry)
Johnson, Harold (John
Harrison)
Johnson, Murray
(Stanley Kirkby)

Johnson, Sara (Rosa
Henderson)
Johnson, William
(Billy Jones)
Jolly Jester (Charles
Penrose / Billy
Whitlock)
Jones and White
(Ernest Hare and
Al Bernard)
Jones Brothers
(Vernon Dalhart*
and Carson
Robison)
Jones, Duncan (Cal
Stewart)
Jones, Harry (Carson
Robison)
Jones, Henry (Ernest
Hare)
Jones, Mamie (Aileen
Stanley)
Jones, Mr. (Billy Jones)
Jones, Reese (Billy
Jones)
Jones, Willy (Billy
Jones)
Jordan Brothers
(Charles Hart and
Elliott Shaw)
Jordan, Henry
(Charles Hart)
Jordan, James (Elliott
Shaw or Charles
Hart)
Joyce, Randolph (Jan
Peerce)
Judson, Robert (Ernest
Hare)
Keene, Charles (Gene
Austin)
Kelly, John (Billy
Jones)
Kent, Franklyn
(Joseph A. Phillips)
Kern, Jimmy (Arthur
Fields*)
Kernell, Frank (S. H.
Dudley*)

Killeen, Pete (Irving
Kaufman)
Kimmble, John J. (John
J. Kimmel)
Kincaid, Joe (Vernon
Dalhart*)
King, Al (Henry Burr*)
King, Daisy (Vaughn
De Leath)
King, Fred (Vernon
Dalhart*)
King, Henry (Arthur
Fields*)
King, Martin (Scrappy
Lambert)
Kingston, Kathleen
(Mary Carson)
Kirkby, Stanley (James
Baker)
Knapp, Frank (Henry
Burr*)
Lambert, Fred (Fred
Duprez?)
Lance, Roland
(Scrappy Lambert)
Lane, Jack (Johnny
Marvin)
Latimer, Hugh
(Vernon Dalhart*)
Lawrence, Harry
(Joseph A. Phillips)
Lazy Larry (Frank
Marvin)
Le Fevre, Edward
(Edward M. Favor)
Lee, Mabel (Annie
Rees)
Lee, Mamie (Vaughn
De Leath)
Lee, Marion (Annette
Hanshaw)
Lee, Virginia (Vaughn
De Leath)
Lenox, Ruth (Helen
Clark?)
Leon, Albert (Ernest
Hare)
Leonard, Larry (Len
Spencer)
Leslie, Walter (Ernest
Hare)

Lewis and Scott (Billy
Jones and Ernest
Hare)
Lewis, Howard
(Arthur Hall*)
Lewis, Justice (Joseph
A. Phillips)
Lewis, Robert (Lewis
James)
Lewis, Rodman
(Scrappy Lambert)
Lewis, William
(Arthur Fields*)
Lincoln, Chester
(Byron G. Harlan)
List, Karl (Karl Böhm,
Alfons Dressel, or
Oswald Kabasta)
Litchfield, Ben
(Franklyn Baur?)
Little, Tobe (Vernon
Dalhart*)
Livingston, ___ (John
Bieling)
Lloyd, Arthur (Burt
Shepard)
Loew, Jack (Irving
Kaufman or Jack
Kaufman)
Lone Star Ranger
(Vernon Dalhart*
or Arthur Fields*)
Long, Tom (Gene
Autry)
Lord, Jack (Scrappy
Lambert)
Lorin, Burt (Scrappy
Lambert)
Lumberjacks (Arthur
Fields* and Fred
Hall)
Luther and Faber
(Frank Luther* and
Carson Robison)
Luther Brothers
(Frank Luther* and
Carson Robison)
Luther, Francis (Frank
Luther*)
Luther, Frank (Francis
Luther Crow)

Lyons and Heilman (Billy Jones and Ernest Hare)

Lyons, Billy (Billy Jones)

Macdonough, Harry (John S. MacDonald)

MacFarland, Bob (Irving Kaufman)

Mack, Arthur (Arthur Fields*)

Mander, Ambrose (Arthur Fields*)

Mann, Frank (Ernest Hare)

Mark, Freddie (Irving Kaufman)

Marron, John (Ernest Hare)

Marsden, Victoria (Gladys Rice)

Martin, Happy (Jack Kaufman)

Martin, Jack (Arthur Fields*)

Massey, Bob (Vernon Dalhart*)

Martini, Enrico (John Charles Thomas)

Massey, Guy (Vernon Dalhart*)

Matthew, J. (Henry Burr*)

Maxwell, P. (Harry Fay)

May, Jimmie (Johnny Marvin)

McAfee, Billy (Vernon Dalhart*)

McClaskey and Meyers (Henry Burr* and John H. Meyer)

McClaskey, Shamus (Henry Burr*)

McHugh, Martin (Walter Van Brunt)

McLaughlin, George (Vernon Dalhart*)

Meadows, Arthur (Arthur Fields*)

Meredith, May (Helen Clark)

Merritt, G. (Stewart Gardner)

Meyer, Saul (Monroe Silver)

Middlestadt, Edouard (Arthur Middleton)

Miller, Kenneth (Charles Harrison)

Miller, Walter (Stanley Kirkby)

Mitchell and White (Vernon Dalhart* and Ed Smalle)

Mitchell, Sidney (Irving Kaufman)

Mitchell, Warren (Vernon Dalhart*)

Mme. X [Pathé] (Alice Verlet)

Moore, Buddy (Al Bernard)

Moore, Harry A. (Vernon Dalhart* or Charles Harrison)

Moore, Tom (Billy Jones)

Moreley, Herbert (Morton Harvey)

Morgan, John (Stanley Kirkby)

Morley, Herbert (Harvey Morton)

Morris, William (Billy Jones)

Morse, Dick (Vernon Dalhart*)

Morton, James (Morton Downey)

Mr. X (Arthur Fields or Vernon Dalhart*)

Murphy and Shea (Albert Campbell and Jack Kaufman)

Myers, John (John H. Meyer)

Nash, Grace (Louise MacMahon)

Nelson and Gwynne (George Ballard and William Wheeler)

Nelson, Gerald (Scrappy Lambert)

Nelson, Grace (Grace Hornby)

Nesbit, Henry (Harvey N. Emmons)

Nevill, Tom (Irving Kaufman)

Nichols, Frank (Arthur Hall*)

Nielson, Varna (Aileen Stanley)

Noble, Harold (Scrappy Lambert)

Norton, Walter (Arthur Fields*)

Oakley, Olly (James Sharpe)

O'Brien, John (Walter Van Brunt)

O'Brien, Padric (Arthur Fields*)

O'Malley, Dennis (Billy Jones)

Odde, Erik (Jussi Björling)

Old King Cole (Bob Pierce)

Old Pop Collins (Fred Hall)

Oliver, Paul (Frank Munn)

Oriole Trio (Vernon Dalhart*, Carson Robison, and Adelyn Hood)

Osborne, James (Peter Dawson)

Palmer and Oliver (Virginia Rea and Frank Munn)

Palmer, Olive (Virginia Rea)

Pampini, Carlo (Guido Deiro)

Parker, H. C. (Frank C. Stanley)

Parsons, Happy Jim (Irving Kaufman)

Patterson, Lila (Ma Rainey)

Patti, Orville (Irving Kaufman)

Paula, Madame (Billy Whitlock)

Payne, Herbert (Ernest Pike)

Pearl, Jack (Jan Peerce)

Pearl, Pinky (Jan Peerce)

Perry, George (Arthur Hall*)

Peters and Jones (Vernon Dalhart* and Carson Robison)

Peters, Sam (Vernon Dalhart*)

Phillips, Curt (Ernest Hare)

Pietro (Pietro Deiro)

Pinckney, Henry (Reed Miller)

Pippins, Cyrus (Byron G. Harlan)

Pitkin, Cy (Billy Murray)

Post, Irving (Franklyn Baur or Irving Kaufman)

Price, Jimmy (Frank Marvin)

Prime, Alberta (Alberta Hunter)

Radio Aces (Gerald Underhill Macy and Ed Smalle)

Radio Boys (Arthur Hall* and John Ryan?)

Radio Franks (Frank Bessinger and Frank White)

Radio Girl (Vaughn De Leath)

Radio Imps (Gerald Underhill Macy and Ed Smalle)

Radio Joe (Ernest Hare)

Radio Kings (Billy Jones and Ernest Hare, or Frank Bessinger and Frank Wright)

Radio Red (Wendell Hall)

Randall, Roy (Arthur Fields*)

Raymond, Harry (Vernon Dalhart*)

Raymond, Ralph (Harry Macdonough)

Red-Masked Baritone (Wendell Hall)

Reed and Griffin (Billy Jones and Ernest Hare)

Reed, James (Reed Miller)

Rees, William (Billy Jones)

Reese, William (Billy Jones)

Reeve, Arthur (Edgar Coyle)

Reeve, Floyd (Steve Porter)

Regal Rascals (Vernon Dalhart*, Carson Robison, and Adelyn Hood)

Rice, Robert (Henry Burr*)

Richards, Charles (Arthur Fields*)

Richards, Daisy (Vaughn De Leath)

Ritz, Sally (Rosa Henderson)

Roberts, Charles (Smith Ballew)

Roberts, Ed (Irving Kaufman)

Roberts, John (Scrappy Lambert)

Roberts, Roy (Ernest Hare)

Roberts, Victor (Billy Jones)

Rodolfi, Mario (Mario Chamlee)

Roe, Turner (Elliott Shaw?)

Rogers, Gene (Harvey Morton)

Romeo Boys (Billy Jones and Ernest Hare)

Roy, Dudley (Billy Whitlock)

Rubahn, Gerd (Karl Böhm)

Rundle, William (Charles Harrison)

Russell, Al (Irving Kaufman)

Russell, Roy (Scrappy Lambert)

Ryan, Jimmy (Arthur Fields*)

Sampson, Sammy (Bill Broonzy)

Samuels, Claude (Carson Robison)

Sanborn, Dave (Al Bernard)

Sanders, Bessie (Alberta Jones)

Saunders and White (Billy Murray and Walter Scanlan*)

Scanlan, Walter (Walter Van Brunt)

Scott, Henry (Vernon Dalhart*)

Scott, Herbert (Walter Van Brunt)

Seelig, Arthur (Arthur Fields*)

Seward, Hatch (Meade Lux Lewis)

Shannon, Thomas (Charles Harrison or Walter Van Brunt)

Shaw, Janet (Annette Hanshaw)

Shea, Jack (Jack Kaufman)

Silver, Erik (Wilhelm Backhaus, Leonid Hambro, or Helmut Roloff)

Silver Masked Tenor (Joseph M. White)

Simpson, Al (Al Bernard)

Sims, Skeeter (Al Bernard)

Sloane, John (Arthur Fields*)

Smith, Anne (Ma Rainey)

Smith, Bertram (Billy Jones)

Smith, Harry (Irving Kaufman)

Smith, Josephus (Vernon Dalhart*)

Smith, Oliver (Frank Munn)

Sorano, Madame (E. Pett)

Southerners (Frank Luther* and Carson Robison)

Spence, Elton (Johnny Marvin)

Spencer and Harris (Billy Jones and Ernest Hare)

Spencer, Ernie (Ernest Hare)

Spencer, Samuel (Cliff Edwards, Arthur Fields*, or Billy Jones))

Stanley, Frank C. (William Stanley Grinsted)

Stebbins, Cy (Byron G. Harlan)

Stehl, George (George Steel)

Stein, Gerhard (Wilhelm Backhaus or Friedrich Wührer)

Stell, George (George Steel)

Stendahl, Mr. (Leon Beyle)

Sterling, Frank (Elliott Shaw)

Stewart, Cliff (Arthur Hall*, Vernon Dalhart*, or Arthur Fields*)

Stoddard, Edgar (Andrea Sarto)

Stone, Edward (Vernon Dalhart* or Charles Hart)

Stone, Fred (Arthur Fields*)

Street Singer (Arthur Tracy)

Strong, Arthur (Joseph A. Phillips)

Strong, Will (Peter Dawson)

Stuart, Billy (Vernon Dalhart*)

Sullivan, Walter (Charles Harrison)

Taylor, Harry (Burt Shepard?)

Taylor, Noel (Irving Kaufman)

Terrill, Norman (Charles Harrison)

Terry, Bert (Byron G. Harlan)

Terry, Will (Vernon Dalhart*)

Thomas and West (Billy Jones and Ernest Hare)

Thomas, Bob (Arthur Fields* or Ernest Hare)

Thomas, Fred (Art Gillham)

Thomas, John (Ernest Hare)

Thomas, Josephine (Rosa Henderson)

Thompson, Bob (Billy Jones)

Thompson, Bud (Frank Luther*)

Thompson, Madge (Vaughn De Leath)

Three Kaufields (Arthur Fields*, Irving Kaufman, and Jack Kaufman)

Tillotson, Merle (Merle Alcock)

Topnotchers (Billy Jones and Ernest Hare)

Townson, Joe (Stanley Kirkby)

Treadway, Deacon (Byron G. Harlan)

Turner, Allen (Ernest Hare, Vernon Dalhart*, Charles Hart, or Elliott Shaw)

Turner, Fred (Olly Oakley*)

Turner, Hobo Jack (Ernest Hare)

Turner, Sid (Vernon Dalhart*)

Turney Brothers (Frank Luther* and Carson Robison)

Tuttle, Frank (Frank Luther* or Vernon Dalhart*)

Twitchell, Atwood (George Alexander*?)

Two Kaufields (Arthur Fields* and either Jack Kaufman or Irving Kaufman)

Ukulele Ike (Cliff Edwards)

Uncle Billy (Billy Jones)

Uncle Ernest (Ernest Hare)

Uncle Ernie (Ernest Hare)

Uncle Joe (Al Bernard)

Uncle Josh (Cal Stewart)

Uncle Lewis (Lewis James)

Vaughn, Caroline (Beulah G. Young)

Vernon, Bill(y) (Vernon Dalhart*)

Vernon, Fred (Harry Fay)

Vernon, Herbert (Vernon Dalhart*)

Vernon, Walter (Billy Jones)

Vernon, Will (Vernon Dalhart*)

Veteran, Vel (Arthur Fields* and others)

Vincent, Sam (Fred Van Eps)

Wainwright Sisters (Brox Sisters)

Wallace, Frankie (Frankie Marvin)

Wallace, Ken (Johnny Marvin)

Walters, Nat (Ernest Hare)

Warfield, Lewis (Frank Marvin)

Warner, Florence (Aileen Stanley)

Warner, Yodlin' Jimmy (Frank Marvin)

Warren, Charles (Charles Hart)

Warren, G. P. (Fred Gaisberg)

Watson, Nora (Elsie Baker)

Watson, Tom (Vernon Dalhart*)

Watt, Brian (Irving Kaufman)

Weary Willie (Jack Kaufman, Frank Marvin, Frank Luther*, or Carson Robison)

Webster Brothers (Billy Jones and Ernest Hare)

Webster, Frank (Albert Campbell)

Wells, Charley (Carson Robison)

Wells, Lorenzo (Percy Hemus)

Welsh, Corinne (Corinne Morgan)

Welsh, George (Peter Dawson)

West, Billy (Billy Jones)

West, Jack (Frank Marvin)

West, Mabel (Elsie Baker)

West, William (Billy Jones)

Wheeler and Morse (Henry Burr* and Jack Kaufman)

Whispering Pianist (Art Gillham)

White, Bob (Vernon Dalhart*)

White, George (Frank Marvin, Vernon Dalhart*)

White, Gladys (Rosa Henderson)

White, Jerry (Jack Kaufman)

White, Joe (Billy Jones)

White, Robert (Vernon Dalhart*)

White, Slim (Al Bernard)

Whitlock, Walter (Vernon Dalhart*)

Wiggins, Pete (Frank Luther*?)

Wilbur, John (John H. Meyer)

Williams Brothers (Frank Luther* and Carson Robison)

Williams, Bessie (Rosa Henderson)

Williams, Carlton (Billy Jones)

Williams, Frank (Stanley Kirkby, Billy Jones, or Dan Quinn)

Williams, George S. (William Stanley Grinsted)

Wilmott, Leo (Fred Van Eps)

Wilson, Arthur (Charles Hart)

Wilson, Harvey (Harvey Hindermyer)

Wilton, George (George Wilton Ballard)

Windy City Duo (Vernon Dalhart* and Ed Smalle)

Winslow, Alice (Edith Clegg)

Winters, Horace (Irving Kaufman)

Wood, Robert (Arthur Fields*)

Woods, George (Vernon Dalhart*)

Woods, Gladys (Vaughn De Leath)

Woods, Grace (Helen Clark)

Woolf, Walter (Irving Kaufman)

X, Mr. (Vernon Dalhart* or Arthur Fields*)

Young, Blanche (Bessie Jones)

Young, Marvin (Irving Kaufman)

Young, Patsy (Annette Hanshaw)

PUBLISHERS' SERVICE CO., INC. An American firm that carried out a national campaign in the U.S. in 1939, involving a newspaper in each community. A record player was offered to buyers of 10 record albums at $3 each. The albums were entitled *World's Greatest Music*. Performers were not named.

PUBLIX (label). An American record issued by Paramount Pictures to promote music from their films of the 1930s. Columbia did the pressings. [Rust 1978.]

Puck. *See* CAPSTAN.

PURETONE (label). An American record issued by the Bridgeport Die and Machine Co., Bridgeport, Connecticut, in the mid-1920s. Matrices came from Paramount. [Rust 1978.]

PURITAN RECORD (label). An American vertical-cut (lateral-cut from December 1919) record made at United Phonographs Corp., Sheboygan, Wisconsin, from 1918 to February 1922, and at Bridgeport Die and Machine Co.,

Bridgeport, Connecticut, from March 1922 to 1925. Matrices, from Paramount and Plaza, included jazz and blues, by King Oliver, the Original Memphis Five, and other admired groups. The label continued to 1927. [Rust 1978.]

PURITONE (label). An American record pressed from Columbia's Harmony masters for Strauss and Schram, Inc., a Chicago mail order house, in 1928–1929. Dance and popular vocals made up the repertoire. [Rust 1978.]

PUSH-UP PLAYER. The type of 1890s piano roll player that was mechanically independent of the piano, and had to be pushed up to it in order to function. Aeolian Company's **Pianola** was the most popular, and gave its name to the genre.

PYE RECORDS, LTD. A British audio firm, located in Cambridge. It had the Pye, Marble Arch, and Virtuoso labels by 1968. In 1972 Pye was among the first firms to enter the quadraphonic field, using the Sansui QS system.

Q CHANNEL. An inaudible subcode channel on a compact disc that carries information on tracks, index numbers, product codes, and the like.

QRS C0. A Chicago firm established ca. 1903 to make piano rolls; it was still producing them on a limited scale in the 1980s. QRS was a subsidiary or sister-company of the **Melville Clark Piano Co.**, maker of player pianos. Ernest G. Clark, brother of Melville Clark, was the first president, and Edwin F. Clark was secretary. In 1904 C. O. Baughman became secretary. The first location was in the Fine Arts building on Michigan Ave. An address at 615 S. Wabash Ave. was given in the 1913 city directory, but in the 1916 directory the location was again Fine Arts building. In 1923 the directory address was 306 S. Wabash Ave. (Kimball Building).

Later the owners of the firm were Max Korlander and J. Lawrence Cook. In November 1926 the firm was at its peak of success, having acquired the U.S. Music Roll Co. The two manufacturers had a combined output of 8,700,000 rolls per year. Talking machines were produced for the first time in summer 1928. At that time QRS was located at 333 N. Michigan Ave. In April 1929 QRS merged with the DeVry Corp., an audio-visual equipment manufacturer.

QRS also marketed disc records for a time in 1923, using Gennett matrices. And a few years later they again entered the disc market, using Gennett-made records intended wholly for QRS use. A third series of discs, recorded and manufactured by the Cova Recording Corp.

of New York, appeared around 1929 and was issued for about a year. Some were released on the Goodson label in U.K.

The most renowned artist on the QRS rolls was Fats Waller; he made 22 of them between 1923 and 1927, beginning with "Got to Cool My Doggies Now." In a biography of Waller by his son (1977), there is offered a solution to the puzzle of what the letters QRS stand for: "Quality Reigns Supreme." Other speculations on the letters may be entertained, since "the factory has no notion today" of the original meaning (Ord-Hume) and the company archives contain no clues. In radio code QRS means "Shall I transmit more slowly?" or "Please transmit more slowly"; and the firm did make radio tubes. "Quality Real Special" has also been suggested, inelegant as it may be. [Goslin 1983; Ord-Hume 1984; Rust 1978; Rust 1980.]

Quad. *See* QUADRAPHONIC RECORDING.

QUAD ELECTROACOUSTICAL, LTD. A British audio firm, established in the mid-1930s as Acoustical Manufacturing Co., Ltd. It pioneered in the production of electrostatic loudspeakers.

QUADRAPHONIC RECORDING. Also Quadrophonic, Quadrasonic, or Quad. A four-channel sound reproduction system, intended to give the impression of concert hall ambience. Four microphones are used in recording, and four loudspeakers—one in each corner—have to be set up in the listening room. Acoustic Research, Inc., of Boston seems to have made the first quad recordings, in 1968. British-made quad records appeared in U.K. in 1970.

There were market difficulties from the beginning. The cost of buying a four-channel amplifier and two additional speakers was sufficient to keep most audiophiles at bay. Loudspeaker placement was also a problem in most home situations. Then there was the nuisance of incompatible rival systems being offered by major firms. For example, EMI used the CBS matrix system, while Pye and others took the Sansui QS system. Record companies waited to see which system would prevail before investing in record production. The public also waited, and meanwhile sales were too small to form the basis for commercial viability.

Nevertheless, the concept was useful; for a pair of speakers cannot reproduce the entire performance environment. Four-channel sound, correctly executed, is impressively realistic. In the late 1980s there was a rebirth of interest in quad, under the new name of **surround sound**. [Bauer, B. 1971.]

Quadrasonic. *See* QUADRAPHONIC RECORDING.

Quarter track. *See* TAPE.

QUINN, DAN W., ca. 1859–1938. American tenor and comedian, born in San Francisco. He sang in New York, and made his first records there in 1892, for the New York Phonograph Co.; he was among the earliest singers on record, and one of the three most prolific recording artists of the 1890s (with George Gaskin and Len Spencer). He did show tunes, coon songs, Irish songs, war songs, and standard popular numbers—about 2,500 titles in all. On record

he was often accompanied by Frank Banta, Sr. Quinn appeared in the New Jersey Phonograph Co. catalog of 1893, and Columbia catalogs of 1895–1899, with hundreds of two-minute cylinders. He made about 250 items for Edison from before 1899 to December 1902, beginning with "All Coons Look Alike to Me" (#1001). Quinn was among the first artists on the Victor label, making the #9 matrix on 29 June 1900, "Strike up the Band" and 11 other sides on that day and the following one. His final Victor was made in 1916, his last record (for Gennett) in 1918. Quinn's popularity faded after 1910; only one of his records remained in the 1917 Victor catalog: "At the Fountain of Youth" / "Hello Boys! I'm Back Again" (#17935). He died on 7 Nov 1938. [Brooks 1979; Walsh 1945/3–5.]

QUINTET OF THE HOT CLUB OF FRANCE. A jazz ensemble formed in 1934 in Paris, the principal non-American group of its kind. **Stéphane Grappelli**, organizer of the quintet and its violinist, and **Django Reinhardt**, guitarist, were the star performers. The other members were Roger Chaput and Joseph Reinhardt, guitarists, and Louis Vola, bass. Various personnel changes took place later. The quintet made fine recordings for Ultraphon, HMV, Decca, and the Swing label. Its first issue, "Dinah" (Ultraphon #AP-1422; 1934) and the second, "Tiger Rag" (Ultraphon #1423; 1934) were immediate sensations. Among the outstanding later discs were "Limehouse Blues" (HMV #K-7706; 1936), "Appel Direct" (Decca #F-6875; 1938), and "Billet doux" (Decca #F-7568; 1938). After Grappelli left the group in 1940, he was replaced by clarinetist Hubert Rostaing, and the quintet continued performing into the 1940s. An LP reissue by Eclipse (#ECM 2051) carries important material from the 1935–1939 period.

R & B. *See* RHYTHM AND BLUES RECORDINGS.

RACE RECORDS. The term given by American record companies to recordings by Black performers intended for the Black buyer, in use from about 1921 until the early 1940s. Okeh was the first label to use the term in advertising: "All the greatest Race phonograph stars can be heard on Okeh records.... Ask your neighborhood dealer for a complete list of Okeh race records" (*Chicago Defender*, January 1922). "Race" was an accepted way for Black people to refer to their community, so there was nothing shameful about the designation. By the end of 1922 Okeh had issued 40 records in the 8000 series, featuring "The World's Greatest Race Artists on the World's Greatest Race Records." The material included blues songs, jazz instrumentals, and male quartet pieces. At first Black Swan and Arto were the only serious competitors to Okeh in the race area. Arto closed down in 1923. Then Paramount initiated a special series in 1923 for its Black talent, the 12000 series. Okeh described its 8000s as "The original race record" while Paramount called its 12000s "the popular race record." Columbia entered the field and had a hit with **Bessie Smith**'s first recording, "Down Hearted Blues" (#A3844; 1923), but the company was in financial trouble and had difficulty sustaining its new 14000 race series.

In 1924 Paramount acquired Black Swan, a label that had intended to record Black artists exclusively, and was able to produce about one race disc a week in that year. Okeh was flourishing also, with around 100 new race records a year in the mid-1920s. Victor (19000 series, and—from 1929—the V-38500 series) and Edison joined the race labels in 1923. Gennett (the only firm to print the words "race record" on the disc labels), Ajax (of Compo in Canada), and Vocalion introduced race series. Vocalion had the greatest success (1000 series), guided by Jack Kapp, head of the Race Division from March 1926. **Ethel Waters** sang for Vocalion; **Blind Lemon Jefferson** for Paramount; the Birmingham Jubilee Singers were a major boost for Columbia in 1926, which also scored with sermons by Rev. J. M. Gates (who then went on to Victor). The Black Patti label was active for a short time in 1927. Pathé's Perfect label had a race series that included Rev. Gates and Rosa Henderson. QRS had a race series in 1928–1929. In 1927 there were about 500 race records issued annually by all the labels.

During the 1930s, a disastrous period for the record industry, the flow of race records nearly stopped at the major labels. Paramount concluded its long-running 12000 race series, and the Gennett label was discontinued. Okeh went on, under its new owner, Grigsby-Grunow, but with only a record a month. Race records made up about 1 percent of industry sales in 1931, a drop from 5 percent in the mid-1920s. In this gloomy period, the American Record Corp. (ARC) began to release race discs on several of the labels it had acquired: Oriole, Perfect, Romeo, and Banner. With **Big Bill Broonzy** and the Famous Garland Jubilee Singers signed on, ARC kept active and promised the only real competition to Vocalion; this competition became muted when

Vocalion's parent firm, Brunswick, and ARC were both taken over by Consolidated Film Industries in 1930.

Bluebird entered the race field in 1933. At the end of 1934 there were just a few other companies still active in the race market: ARC/Vocalion, Columbia, and Victor. The new American firm, Decca, hired Jack Kapp (who had headed the Vocalion race series) and Mayo Williams, a prominent talent scout for race artists. Decca's 7000 series was soon established as a major force. All promoted the urban blues style, which had been replacing the traditional blues. Joe Pullum (Victor-Bluebird) and Leroy Carr (Vocalion) were stars of the mid-1930s. In 1937 there were revival signs in the industry, and race records began to emerge again in quantity: urban blues, gospel quartet music, and sermons. Washboard Sam (Robert Brown) enlivened the Bluebird list in the late 1930s.

World War II brought relief from the Depression, but also restrictions on the use of shellac—resulting in cutbacks of special severity in the race series. And the American Federation of Musicians recording ban of 1942 hurt the genre badly. Victor's December 1941 catalog had about 350 race items, a number that diminished to 75 in May 1943. Decca had no race category in its 1944 catalog, and by 1945 Victor had dropped the race section from its catalog. The term "race record" was generally abandoned, replaced to some extent by **rhythm and blues**; and the making of discs aimed at the Black buyer began to pass from the major companies to new independent labels like Chess. Essentially however, the Black artist had found a place in the white mainstream, in the **Big Bands**. And the Black record buyer became less differentiated from the white buyer, as both sought the offerings of blues singers and Black jazzmen.

Dixon and Godrich estimate that "between 1920 and 1942 about 5,500 blues and 1,250 gospel records had been issued, involving all told about 1,200 artists." [Dixon 1970.] *See also* BLUES RECORDINGS.

RACHMANINOFF, SERGEI VASILYEVICH, 1873–1943.

Russian pianist, conductor, and composer, born in Semyonovo on 1 Apr 1973. He studied at the St. Petersburg and Moscow conservatories, winning the composition prize for his opera *Aleko* (1892). At that time he also wrote his most famous work, the Prelude in C-Sharp Minor for piano. In 1891 he performed his Second Piano Concerto.

From 1904 to 1906 he conducted the Bolshoi Opera; in 1909 he toured the U.S. During the Russian Revolution he lived in Sweden, then Denmark, and finally New York. Throughout the 1930s he toured widely, living most of the time in New York, and continuing to compose. In 1942 he retired to Beverly Hills, California, where he died on 28 Mar 1943.

Rachmaninoff's first recordings were 10 sides for Edison Diamond Discs in 1919–1920. Franz Liszt's three Hungarian Rhapsodies (opus 2) were the initial efforts, on discs #82169 and #82170. The artist had to use an upright piano in the studio, and the whole outcome was weak. Another of the Diamond Discs was the Prelude in C-Sharp Minor (#82202; 1920). He recorded for Ampico piano rolls in the same year, and worked with them intermittently for 10 years. In 1920 Rachmaninoff became a Victor artist, and stayed with the label until his death.

Among the principal Rachmaninoff recordings are those he made with the Philadelphia Orchestra, under Eugene Ormandy, of his own compositions. The Piano Concerto No. 2 was inscribed in April 1929 (Victor #8148-52, album #M-58), and the *Rhapsody on a Theme of Paganini* was done in December 1934 (Victor #8553-55, album #M-250). Several years later he recorded Concerto No. 1 (Victor #18374–76, album #M-865; 1939), and Concerto No. 4 (Victor #11-8611-14, album #M-972; 1941). In 1973 Victor issued *The Complete Rachmaninoff* in five albums holding 15 LPs. Melodiya produced an eight-record set, *The Art of Sergei Vasilevich Rachmaninov*, encompassing all the solo works. A CD of nearly all the solo electrical recordings that the composer made of his own music, plus works of seven other composers, appeared on RCA CD #GD 87766 in 1990. [Palmieri 1985 has a detailed discography.]

RACK JOBBER.

In the American popular record industry, the person who provides a stock of current recordings to a discount store, drug store, supermarket, etc. Elliot Wexler of Philadelphia is believed to have been the first rack jobber, followed by David Handleman in Detroit. Although **cutouts** are basic to the inventory, the rack jobber will also acquire items on the charts—enjoying preferential terms from the major companies. Majors have also produced low-cost albums intended for the racks. In the early 1970s about 80 percent of all record sales were by these jobbers, who had moved into the department stores as well as smaller outlets, and who were in fact dominating pop/rock record distribution. [Denisoff 1986.] *See also* DUMPING.

RADIEX (label). An American record of the 1920s, a subsidiary of Grey Gull. Advertising in *TMW* during 1924 gave the address Radiex Dept., 598 Columbia Road, Boston. The disc price was $.25. Material was popular vocals and dance music; matrices were from Emerson, Paramount, and Plaza. The final issues were in 1930. [Andrews*; Rust 1978.]

RADIO FRANKS. A trio made up of Frank Wright, Frank Bessinger, and Frank White, who sang on the radio and recorded for Brunswick and other labels in the mid-1920s.

RADIO PHONOGRAPHS. The rise of radio in America from 1921 severely damaged the phonograph industry (*see* DISC, 6). The idea of combining the competing formats into one cabinet, a radio phonograph, was articulated first in advertising of August 1922, by **Jewett Radio and Phonograph Co.** of Detroit. The only other firm to advertise a combination in 1922 was George A. Long Cabinet Co., Hanover, Pennsylvania. Emerson announced its new PhonoRadio in January 1924. In all these early combinations it was necessary to remove the phonograph reproducer and attach a radio receiver in order to hear radio stations through the phonograph horn. But a *TMW* advertisement of February 1924 offered a model with a switch, by the Oro-Tone Co., of Chicago. Sonora then marketed its Sonoradio, also with a switch controlling the two functions.

It was the RCA 1924 product, Radiola, that dominated the combination market in the 1920s, and the model name became a convenient generic term for all radio phonographs. Brunswick announced a similar machine in July 1924. The Gramophone Co. marketed its table model Lumiere around that time, containing a crystal radio set and a folding external horn. Phonograph attachments for radio sets were a later approach; these were called Radiograms, a name also given to radio phonograph combinations.

RADIO PROGRAM RECORDINGS. This article has 13 parts: 1. Overview; 2. Comedies; 3. Adventures and mysteries; 4. Detective stories; 5. Dramas; 6. Soap operas; 7. Music and variety shows; 8. Science fiction; 9. Children's programs; 10. Quiz shows; 11. Westerns; 12. Collectors and collections; and 13. Producers and distributors.

1. *Overview.* By the late 1930s almost all urban homes (and the majority of rural homes) in the U.S. had radio sets and played them an average of five or more hours a day. Yet radio's reign as the popular culture center of America was very brief. The "golden age of radio" lasted only about 20 years—from the emergence of Eddie Cantor as the first national radio figure in the fall of 1931, to Milton Berle as the first national television figure in the early 1950s.

The Bing Crosby Show was the first radio program broadcast from **transcription discs**, from fall 1946. Crosby refused to do a live show each week, and as a result almost all of his programs are available on tape today, along with more than 50,000 other shows from over 2,200 different series. Recordings range from a single 15–minute episode of *The Black Hood*, a program about a comic book super-hero whose adventures were broadcast over the Mutual Network in 1943–1945, to over 800 episodes— out of 7,000 broadcasts—of the comedy show *Fibber McGee & Molly* (NBC, 1935–1959).

Although thousands of radio shows have been lost, thousands of others are available— on reel to reel or cassette tape recordings, on long-playing records, or on compact discs. In addition, compilation albums are for sale from several small firms that have been licensed by copyright owners. For example, *Radio Cliff Hangers*, offering episodes of Flash Gordon, Little Orphan Annie, Charlie Chan, etc., is offered by Radiola in a two-record set. About a dozen LPs each have been produced of radio performances of Bing Crosby, Judy Garland, and Al Jolson.

The most important radio programs for which recordings are available are mentioned below, by type of program. All shows were 30 minutes long, unless otherwise noted.

2. *Comedy.* The most consistently popular type of programming in radio was comedy. Many episodes are available on records:

The Abbott and Costello Program (NBC, 1942–1949), *The Adventures of Ozzie and Harriett,* (CBS, 1944–1954), *The Alan Young Show* (ABC, 1944–1949), *The Aldrich Family* (NBC, 1939–1951), *Amos 'n' Andy* (NBC/CBS, 1928–1960), *The Baby Snooks Show* (CBS, 1937–1951), *Beulah* (CBS/ABC, 1945–1954), *Blondie* (CBS, 1939–1950), *The Bob Hope Show* (NBC, 1934–1953), *The Bob & Ray Show* (NBC/CBS, 1948–1960, 15 min.), *The Burns and Allen Show* (CBS, 1932–1958), *The Charlie McCarthy Show* (NBC, 1937–1956), *A Date with Judy* (NBC, 1943–1949), *Duffy's Tavern* (NBC/ABC, 1940–1951), *Easy Aces* (NBC/CBS, 1931–1945, 15 min.), *The Eddie Cantor Show,* (NBC, 1931–1954), *The Fred Allen Show* (CBS, 1932–1949), *The Great Gildersleeve* (NBC, 1941–1958), *The Halls of Ivy,* 1949–1952), *The Jack Benny Program* (CBS/NBC/CBS, 1932–1955), *The Jack Carson Show* (CBS, 1943–1956), *The Judy Canova Show* (CBS/NBC, 1943–1953), *The Life of Riley* (NBC, 1944–1951), *Life with Luigi* (CBS, 1948–1952), *Lum and Abner* (NBC/CBS/ABC/Mutual, 1931–1953), *Meet Corliss Archer* (CBS/ABC, 1943–1955), *My Friend Irma* (CBS, 1947–1954), *Our Miss Brooks* (CBS, 1948–1957), *The Phil Harris-Alice Faye Show* (NBC, 1948–1954), and *The Red Skelton Show* (NBC, 1941–1953).

3. *Adventures and mysteries.* Beginning with *Empire Builder* in 1928–1929, sponsored by the Great Northern Railroad, old-time radio abounded with thriller drama, and many people today remember radio most vividly for its many adventure and mystery series. Golden age radio was the era of the adventurer, the spy, and tales of crime, horror, and suspense. The best—and some of the most artistic—are available on tape: *The Big Story* (NBC, 1947–1955), *Big Town* (CBS/NBC, 1937–1954), *The Black Castle* (Mutual, 1943–1944, 15 min.), *The Black Museum* (Mutual, 1951–1052), *Bold Venture* (Syndicated, 1951–1952), *Box 13* (Mutual, 1948–

1949), *Casey, Crime Photographer* (CBS, 1946–1955), *The Clock* (ABC, 1946–1948), *Crime Club* (Mutual, 1935–1947), *Dangerous Assignment* (NBC, 1950–1954), *David Harding, Counterspy* (ABC, 1942–1957), *Escape* (CBS, 1947–1954), *The Hermit's Cave* (Syndicated, 1940–1943), *I Love A Mystery* (NBC Red/Mutual/CBS, 1939–1952, 15–30 min.), *Inner Sanctum* (NBC Blue, 1941–1952), *Jason and the Golden Fleece* (NBC, 1952–1953), *Lights Out* (NBC, 1938–1946), *The Lone Wolf* (Mutual, 1948–1949), *The Man Called X* (ABC, 1944–1948), *Mr. District Attorney* (NBC, 1939–1954), *Mollé Mystery Theatre* (NBC, 1943–1948), *The Mysterious Traveler* (Mutual, 1943–1952), *Mystery in the Air* (NBC, 1945–1947), *Night Beat* (ABC, 1950–1952), *Quiet, Please* (Mutual/ABC, 1947–1949), *The Scarlet Pimpernel* (NBC, 1952–1953), *The Shadow* (CBS/NBC/Mutual, 1930–1954), *Suspense* (CBS, 1942–1962), *The Whistler* (CBS, 1942–1955), and *The Witch's Tale* (Mutual, 1931–1938).

4. *Detective stories.* Inexpensive to produce and attractive to listeners, the radio detective story as a separate genre emerged around 1930 (*True Detective Mysteries* was broadcast during the 1929–1930 season.) The detective program quickly became one of the most common types of evening radio broadcasting. Many episodes of the following programs are available: *The Adventures of Nero Wolfe* (ABC, 1943–1951), *Boston Blackie* (NBC, 1944–1948), *Broadway Is My Beat* (CBS, 1949–1954), *Candy Matson, Yukon 28209* (NBC, 1949–1951), *Dick Tracy* (ABC, 1943–1948, 15 min.), *Dragnet* (NBC, 1949–1956), *Ellery Queen* (CBS/NBC/ABC, 1939–1948), *The Falcon* (Mutual/NBC/Mutual, 1945–1954), *The Fat Man* (ABC, 1946–1951), *Hercule Poirot* (Mutual, 1945–1947), *Let George Do It* (CBS, 1946–1954), *The Green Hornet* (Mutual/ABC, 1936–1952), *The Line-Up* (CBS, 1950–1953), *Mr. and Mrs. North* (NBC/CBS, 1942–1955), *Mr. Chameleon* (CBS, 1948–1952), *Mr. Keen, Tracer of Lost Persons* (NBC, 1937–1954), *Nick Carter, Master Detective* (Mutual, 1943–1955), *Pat Novak for Hire* (ABC, 1946–1949), *Perry Mason* (CBS, 1943–1955, 15 min.), *Philip Marlowe* (NBC/CBS, 1947–1951), *Philo Vance* (NBC, 1945, 1948–1950), *Richard Diamond, Private Detective* (NBC, 1949–1953), *Rogue's Gallery* (ABC, 1945–1952), *The Saint* (NBC, 1945–1951), *Sam Spade* (ABC/CBS/NBC, 1946–1951), *The Thin Man* (NBC, 1941–1950),

and *Yours Truly, Johnny Dollar* (CBS, 1949–1962).

5. *Dramas.* Of the various program types drama had the slowest start, but it came to embody the most artistic achievements of radio. Although the quality was uneven, there were prestige offerings each season. For example, in prime time each week *Cavalcade of America* (CBS/NBC, 1935–1953), entertained and educated listeners for 18 seasons (781 programs). With star performers and original scripts written by authors such as Maxwell Anderson, Stephen Vincent Benét, and Robert Sherwood, *Cavalcade of America* was radio at its finest. Of the 781 programs broadcast, more than 400 are available on cassettes. Other available dramatic programs are listed below.

Academy Award Theatre (CBS, 1946), *Brownstone Theatre* (Mutual, 1945–1946), *CBS Radio Workshop* (CBS, 1956–1957), *Campbell Playhouse* (CBS, 1938–1940), *Curtain Time* (Mutual/ABC/NBC, 1938–1950), *Damon Runyon Theater* (Syndicated, 1949–1950), *Family Theatre* (Mutual, 1947–1957), *Favorite Story* (Syndicated, 1946–1949), *The First Nighter* (NBC/CBS/Mutual/CBS, 1930–1949), *Ford Theatre* (NBC/CBS, 1947–1949, 60 min.), *Hallmark Playhouse* (CBS, 1948–1953), *Hollywood Theater of Stars* (NBC, 1946–1948), *Lux Radio Theater of the Air* (CBS/NBC, 1936–1955, 60 min.), *The Mercury Theatre of the Air* (CBS, 1938, 60 min.), *Screen Director's Playhouse* (NBC, 1949–1951), *Screen Guild Theater* (CBS/NBC/ABC, 1939–1951), *Studio One* (CBS, 1947–1948, 60 min.), *Theatre Guild of the Air/The U.S. Steel Hour* (ABC, 1945–1954, 60 min.), and *Whispering Streets* (ABC/CBS, 1952–1960).

6. *Soap operas.* Often the object of contempt, daytime serial dramas were significant sources of revenue for the networks. Inexpensive to produce, they also allotted a greater percentage of time for advertising than the average comedy or drama program. Long runs of these programs are widely available, for example, more than 350 episodes of *One Man's Family* (NBC, 1932–1959, 15 min.), the popular and long-running serial, have been preserved. Other soap operas on record are: *Backstage Wife* (Mutual/NBC, 1935–1959, 15 min.), *Big Sister* (CBS, 1936–1952, 15 min.), *The Brighter Day* (NBC/CBS, 1948–

1956, 15 min.), *David Harum* (NBC/CBS, 1936–1950, 15 min.), *Front Page Farrell* (Mutual/NBC, 1941–1954, 15 min.), *The Goldbergs* (NBC/Mutual/CBS, 1929–1950, 15–30 min.), *Guiding Light* (NBC/CBS, 1937–1956, 15 min.), *Just Plain Bill* (NBC/CBS, 1936–1955, 15 min.), *Life Can Be Beautiful* (CBS/NBC, 1938–1954, 15 min.), *Lorenzo Jones* (NBC, 1937–1955 15 min.), *Ma Perkins* (NBC/CBS, 1933–1960, 15 min.), *Our Gal Sunday* (CBS, 1937–1959, 15 min.), *Pepper Young's Family* (NBC, 1936–1059, 15 min.), *Portia Faces Life* (CBS/NBC, 1940–1951, 15 min.), *Right to Happiness* (NBC Blue/CBS, 1939–1960, 15 min.), *Road of Life* (CBS/NBC, 1937–1959, 15 min.), *The Romance of Helen Trent* (CBS, 1933–1960, 15 min.), *Scattergood Baines* (CBS/Mutual, 1937–1950, 15–30 min.), *Stella Dallas* (NBC, 1937–1955, 15 min.), *Vic and Sade* (NBC Blue/Mutual, 1932–1944, 15 min.), *When A Girl Marries* (CBS/NBC/ABC, 1939–1958, 15 min.), and *Young Widder Brown* (NBC, 1938–1956, 15 min.).

7. *Music and variety programs.* The bulk of broadcasting time was filled with music and variety offerings. From the early 1920s music programs were the mainstay (with regard to hours aired per week) of both networks and independent stations, and variety shows grew in number during the late 1920s and early 1930s. Some of the most popular ones available are: *Arthur Godfrey Talent Scouts* (CBS, 1946–1958), *The Bing Crosby Show* (ABC/CBS, 1946–1956), *Carnation Contented Hour* (NBC, 1932–1951), *The Fitch Bandwagon* (NBC, 1937–1948), *The Fleischmann's Hour* (NBC, 1929–1936, 60 min.), *The Frank Sinatra Old Gold Show* (CBS, 1945–1947), *The Fred Waring Show* (NBC/CBS/NBC/ABC, 1931–1957, various formats), *Grand Ole Opry* (NBC, 1925–present, 30–60 min. segments), *House Party* (CBS, 1944–1967), *The Kate Smith Show* (CBS, 1936–1958), *Kraft Music Hall* (NBC, 1936–1948), *Manhattan Merry-Go-Round* (NBC, 1933–1949), *NBC Bandstand* (NBC, 1956–1957, 60 min.), *The National Barn Dance* (NBC, 1933–1950), *Philco Radio Time* (ABC, 1946–1949), *The Railroad Hour* (ABC/NBC, 1948–1954, various formats), *The Rudy Vallee Show* (NBC, 1944–1947), *Shell Chateau* (CBS, 1935–1937, 60 min.), and *Your Hit Parade* (NBC/CBS/NBC, 1935–1959, various formats).

8. *Science fiction.* Originally a children's genre in the 1930s (Flash Gordon and Buck Rogers), science fiction shows for an adult audience did not appear until the early 1950s. On 8 Apr 1950 *The Outer Limit* by Graham Doar was presented on *Dimension X*, ushering in a new era in science fiction programming. With the presentation of stories by authors such as Isaac Asimov, Ray Bradbury, and Robert Heinlein, adult science fiction stories were introduced to the listening public. Episodes available today are from the following programs: *Beyond Tomorrow* (CBS, 1950), *Buck Rogers in the 25th Century* (Mutual, 1931–1947, 15 min.), *Destination Space* (NBC, 1947–1949), *Dimension X* (NBC, 1950–1951), *Exploring Tomorrow* (Mutual, 1957–1958), *Flash Gordon* (Mutual, 1935–1936, 15 min.), *Space Patrol* (ABC, 1950–1955), *Starr of Space* (ABC, 1953–1954), *Tales of Tomorrow* (ABC/CBS, 1953), *Tom Corbett—Space Cadet* (NBC, 1952), *2000 Plus* (Mutual, 1950), and *X Minus One* (NBC, 1955–1958).

9. *Children's programs.* Children's programs typically were aired in the afternoon hours after school, on Saturday mornings, and during the week in the early evening. *Little Orphan Annie*, based on the popular comic strip, began in 1931, the first of the adventure serial dramas for children. Others quickly followed. These programs were regular radio fare in the 1930s and 1940s. Some of the more popular ones are available: *Abbott and Costello Children's Show* (ABC, 1947–1949), *Archie Andrews* (Mutual, 1943–1953), *Big Jon and Sparky/No School Today* (ABC, 1950–1958, 60 min.), *Captain Midnight* (Mutual, 1939–1949, 15 min.), *The Challenge of the Yukon/Sergeant Preston* (ABC/Mutual, 1947–1955; an earlier 15–min. version, 1938–1947, had been broadcast from Station WXYZ in Detroit), *Chick Carter, Boy Detective* (Mutual, 1943–1944, 15 min.), *Don Winslow of the Navy* (NBC Blue, 1942–1943), *Hop Harrigan* (ABC/Mutual, 1942–1948, 15 min.), *Jack Armstrong, the All/American Boy* (CBS, 1933–1950, 15 min.), *Jungle Jim* (Syndicated, 1935–1952), *Land of the Lost* (Mutual, 1943–1948), *Lassie* (ABC, 1947–1950, 15 min.), *Let's Pretend* (CBS, 1931–1954), *Little Orphan Annie* (NBC Blue/Mutual, 1931–1943, 15 min.), *Mandrake the Magician* (Mutual, 1940–1942, 15 min.), *Mark Trail* (Mutual, 1950–

1953), *The Sea Hound* (ABC, 1942–1948), *Sky King* (ABC/Mutual, 1946–1954, 15–30 min.), *Smilin' Ed's Buster Brown Gang* (NBC, 1944–1952), *Superman* (Syndicated/Mutual/ABC, 1938–1951, 15 min.), *Terry and the Pirates* (NBC/ABC, 1937–1948, 15 min.), *Tom Mix* (NBC/Mutual, 1933–1950, 15 min.), and *The Voyage of the Scarlet Queen* (Mutual, 1947–1948).

10. *Quiz shows.* By 1938 network radio was filled with quiz shows adapted to every type of program: sports, news, mystery, and even parodies of quiz shows (for example, *It Pays to Be Ignorant* (CBS, 1942–1949). Some of the programs were very popular. The success of *Stop the Music!* (ABC/CBS, 1948–1954, 60–75 min.) with a Hooper rating of 20.0 in its first season was a major factor in the demise of Fred Allen's career (Allen's show had a Hooper rating of 11.2 during the 1948–1949 season). Other quiz shows, currently available on cassette tape, are: *Beat the Band* (NBC, 1940–1944), *Break the Bank* (Mutual/ABC/NBC, 1945–1955, 30 min), *Can You Top This?* (Mutual/NBC/ABC, 1940–1954), *Dr. I.Q.* (NBC/ABC, 1939–1950), *Earn Your Vacation* (CBS, 1948–1949), *Information, Please!* (NBC/CBS/Mutual, 1938–1948, 60 min.), *Kay Kyser's Kollege of Musical Knowledge* (NBC/ABC, 1938–1949, 60 min.), *You Bet Your Life* (ABC/CBS/NBC, 1947–1959), and *Quiz Kids* (ABC/NBC/CBS, 1940–1953).

11. *Westerns.* The most underdeveloped popular genre in radio was the western. Although *Death Valley Days* began in 1930, until the 1950s only a few westerns were broadcast; and these were designed primarily for children. Some did appeal to adults, and one, *The Lone Ranger*, was instrumental in the formation of the Mutual Broadcasting System in 1934. When *Gunsmoke* and other more realistic radio shows were developed in the early 1950s, radio was already becoming secondary to television as a main entertainment medium. Indeed, competition from television is one of the reasons that westerns and other radio shows were improved so much in the early 1950s. Those available on record are: *The Cisco Kid* (Mutual, 1942–1943), *Fort Laramie* (CBS, 1956) starring Raymond Burr, *Frontier Gentleman* (CBS, 1958), *Gene Autry's Melody Ranch* (CBS, 1940–1956), *Gunsmoke* (CBS, 1952–

1961), *Have Gun, Will Travel* (CBS, 1958–1960), *Hopalong Cassidy* (Syndicated, 1950–1952) starring William Boyd, *The Lone Ranger* (Mutual/ABC, 1933–1955), *Red Ryder* (Syndicated, 1942–1952), *The Roy Rogers Radio Show* (Mutual, 1944–1955), *The Six Shooter* (NBC, 1953–1954) starring James Stewart, *Straight Arrow* (Mutual, 1948–1951), *Tales of the Texas Rangers* (NBC, 1950–1952), starring Joel McCrea, *Tennessee Jed* (ABC, 1945–1947, 15 min.), and *Wild Bill Hickock* (ABC, 1951–1956) starring Guy Madison and Andy Devine.

12. *Collections and collectors.* It has been estimated that there are about 1,500 serious collectors of old-time radio (OTR) in the U.S. In addition to collecting OTR, many of the serious collectors also compile logs (necessary for identifying the titles and airing dates of specific shows), produce newsletters that inform other collectors about the field, hold conventions, and trade (and sell) programs. Among the major collectors are:

Jim Harmon (634 South Orchard Drive, Burbank, California 91506), a producer of radio programs and a writer/dealer in nostalgia, has authored several books, including *The Great Radio Comedians* and *The Great Radio Heroes*.

Jay Hickerson (POB 4321, Hamden, Connecticut 06514) is a musician/entertainer with over 8,000 general interest shows in his collection. He has published an OTR newsletter (*Hello Again*) since 1970, and since 1971 has helped run an annual OTR convention near his home.

Walter M. Keepers, Jr. (6341 Glenloch Street, Philadelphia, Pennsylvania 19135) has a very large collection of Big Bands and vocalists and also has one of the largest collections of video cassettes.

Terry Salomonson (Audio Classics, POB 1135, St. Charles, Missouri 63302) has a large general collection and has written logs on radio shows broadcast by WXYZ in Detroit: *The Lone Ranger, The Green Hornet,* and *Challenge of the Yukon.*

David S. Siegel (POB 610, Croton-on-Hudson, New York 10520) describes his collection as consisting of over 100,000 shows (over 50,000 hours). By comparison, the Library of Congress has only about 500,000 shows in its collection.

Raymond Stanich (173 Columbia Heights, Brooklyn, New York 11201) conducts research on OTR and has authored many logs. His book (with Francis M. Nevins, Jr.), *The Sound of Detection: Ellery Queen's Adventures in Radio,* was published in 1983 by Brownstone Books (1711 Clifty Drive, Madison, Indiana 47250).

13. *Producers and distributors.* Sandy Hook Records, distributed by Radiola (Box C, Sandy Hook, Connecticut 06482) releases long-playing records of OTR shows that have been remastered: *Kate Smith on the Air!* (radio recordings of Kate Smith from the 1930s and 1940s, including the first broadcast, in 1938, of "God Bless America"), *The Big Broadcast of 1932* (original soundtrack album with George Burns & Gracie Allen, Bing Crosby, The Boswell Sisters, The Mills Brothers, Kate Smith, Cab Calloway, etc.), *Jeanette MacDonald & Nelson Eddy in "Sweethearts"* (a 1946 Screen Guild radio broadcast of the famous operetta, plus 1944–1948 radio recordings of Eddy and MacDonald doing many of the songs they made famous), and *Dick Tracy in B Flat* (the "first comic strip operetta of all time," complete as broadcast 15 Feb 1945, with Bing Crosby, Bob Hope, Frank Sinatra, Judy Garland, Dinah Shore, Jimmy Durante, etc.), among many others.

Other tape and record sources are Memories of Radio (Dick Judge), 362 Browncroft Boulevard, Rochester, New York 14609; Old Time Radio (Carl Frolich, Jr.), 2 Heritage Farm Drive, New Freedom, Pennsylvania 17349; BRC Productions (Bob Burnham), P.O. Box 2645, Livonia, Michigan 48151); Publishers Central Bureau, Department 349, 1 Champion Avenue, Avenel, New Jersey 07001; BWP Radio, Inc. (Bob Gilchrist), Suite 9-E, 1105 N. Main Street, Gainesville, Florida 32601; Radio Memories from the Attic (George Barker), 1000 Augusta Avenue, Elgin, Illinois 60120; and Vintage Broadcasts (A. W. Blatt), 42 Bowling Green, Staten Island, New York 10314.

All of the producers/distributors listed above have catalogs that they will provide free or for a nominal fee. [MacDonald 1982; Pitts 1986; Slide 1982; Smart 1982; Sterling 1978; Summers 1958; Swartz 1992.]

Jon D. Swartz and Robert C. Reinehr

Radiogram. *See* RADIO PHONOGRAPHS.

Radiola. *See* RADIO PHONOGRAPHS.

RAGTIME RECORDINGS. The ragtime style of music was highly popular in the U.S. from the mid-1890s to the early 1920s. It was characterized by syncopated rhythm, and usually marked by improvisation; thus it was easily reshaped into jazz. Although there were ragtime vocals and ragtime instrumental ensembles, the main format for the style was the piano. Performers at the World's Columbian Exposition in Chicago, 1893, brought the style to wide attention, and the ragtime craze swept the country in the next few years.

"All Coons Look Alike to Me," an 1896 song popularized by Dan W. Quinn on Edison cylinder #1001, included a "rag accompaniment," a designation that appeared on other coon songs later. Composer-pianists Tom Turpin and **Scott Joplin**, based in St. Louis, brought the ragtime style to a height of ingenuity and sophistication. Joplin's "Maple Leaf Rag" was a great success in 1899. Gradually ragtime gave way to jazz, as ragtime pianists like Jelly Roll Morton expanded their stylistic repertoires.

A revival of interest in the early ragtime style began in the 1960s, through the work of Joshua Rifkin and Gunther Schuller, and through the impact of a motion picture that featured Scott Joplin's music, *The Sting* (1974). Modern composers like William Bolcom began to compose in ragtime, merging it with modern idioms.

Performances by the early ragtime piano artists were infrequently recorded. Scott Joplin made piano rolls from 1899–1914, reissued by Riverside on LP #RLP 8815. The earliest disc of piano ragtime is "Creole Belles" (Victor matrix #A-1079; 1901) played by Christopher H. H. Booth. It was the Columbia recordings of 1912 by Mike Bernard that initiated a more generous output by the record companies: there were about 100 titles under "ragtime" in the Victor 1917 catalog, for example, played by banjo, accordion, and Pryor's Band; sung by Al Jolson, Billy Murray, and the Peerless Quartet. But by then the classic ragtime had nearly run its course, soon to be replaced by so-called novelty

rags and by jazz. The 1922 Victor catalog had just 25 ragtime titles, and the 1927 catalog listed none.

Early recordings were made by performers on many instruments: saxophone (Rudy Wiedoeft), accordion (Guido and Pietro Deiro), piccolo (George Schweinfest), flute (Frank Mazziotta), banjo (Vess Ossman, Olly Oakley, Fred Van Eps), and trombone (Arthur Pryor). Ossman is credited with the first ragtime disc record, for Berliner in 1897. Berliner then recorded the United States Marine Band in September 1899 playing "You Got to Play Ragtime" followed by banjoist Richard L. Weaver doing "Ragtime Dance" on 14 Dec 1899. In 1899 Fred Gaisberg recorded a guitar and mandolin performance by the Musical Avolos—a march from *Rice's Ragtime Opera*—which was the first European disc to bear any reference to ragtime. Victor made "Ragtime Skedaddle" by flutist Frank Mazziotta (#4033; 1904). Ossman's Victor record of "St. Louis Tickle" with the Ossman-Dudley Trio (#4624; 1906) was a best seller.

Ragtime was often played by military bands. A Berliner record of 1897 offered ragtime by a studio band, then by the Sousa Band. Arthur Pryor, who led the Sousa Band on records, was also the major composer of ragtime pieces for bands to play.

In the 1940s the piano finally took center stage, with such ragtime artists as Wally Rose and Joe "Fingers" Carr (Lou Busch) bringing about a renewed interest in the form through their recordings. Pee Wee Hunt's 1948 recording of "Twelfth Street Rag" was a great best seller, in the most frequently recorded of all rags. Joshua Rifkin, who endeavors to play the rags as written, offered a splendid album in 1969: *Piano Rags by Scott Joplin* (Nonesuch #H71248). *Pastimes and Piano Rags* was an important album by William Bolcom, including rags by James Scott and Artie Matthews (Nonesuch #H71299; 1973). Dick Hyman recorded all the Joplin rags in a five-disc set (Victor #ARL 5-1106). The soundtrack recording of *The Sting* (MCA #390; 1974) was on the charts for 47 weeks. [Hasse 1985; Jasen 1973.]

RAINBOW (label). An American record devoted to sacred music, issued in the 1920s by the Rodeheaver Record Co. (named for trombonist and gospel singer Homer Rodeheaver) of Chicago. The Rodeheaver firm was listed in the Chicago directory of 1915, with addresses at 440 S. Dearborn St. and 900 N. LaSalle St. There was a branch in Philadelphia, at 114 Walnut St. In June 1921 there was an address at 219 E. 39th St., New York. It was reported in October 1921 that C. R. "Johnnie" Johnston, the recording expert who had inscribed the voices of Florence Nightingale and Alfred Tennyson in 1888, had joined Rainbow Records. Thomas P. Ratcliff was the general manager, with an office then located at 150 E. 41st St., New York. Ratcliff left Rainbow in April 1922 to join the Aeolian Co. L. E. Gillingham was reported to be general manager of the Rodeheaver Record Co. in July 1922.

In the 1923 Chicago directory the firm's location was given as 218 S. Wabash Ave., and the same address appeared in the 1928–1929 directory. Rodeheaver was not listed in the 1929–1930 directory. [Andrews*; Rust 1978.]

RAINEY, MA, 1886–1939. American blues singer, born Gertrude Pridgett in Columbus, Georgia, on 26 Apr 1886. She began singing in public at 12. In 1904 she married Will "Pa" Rainey and toured with him with the Rabbit Foot Minstrels, Tolliver's Circus, and other shows. She then established her Georgia Jazz Band. Rainey began to record in 1923 for Paramount, achieving great acclaim with "Boweavil Blues" (#12080) and "Moonshine Blues" (#12083). She was a mainstay of Paramount's 12000 series of "popular race records," with such hits as "Stormy Sea Blues" / "Levee Camp Moan" with the Georgia Jazz Band (#12295; 1925). Probably her greatest work on record was in "See See Rider" (#12252; 1924) and "Soon This Morning" (#12438; 1927). She was an influence on Bessie Smith and other later blues artists. Rainey retired in about 1933, and died in Rome, Georgia, on 22 Dec 1939. [Lieb 1983 has a discography; Vreede 1971 is a Paramount discography with illustrations of Rainey advertisements.]

RAISA, ROSA, 1893–1963. Polish/American soprano, born in Bialystok. She studied in Naples, and appeared in Rome in 1912. The next year she made her opera debut in Parma, singing in Verdi's *Oberto*. She then sang in Chicago, London, Paris, and Buenos Aires, and was for several seasons with La Scala. Her American performances were mostly in Chicago; when she retired in 1937 she remained in the city, opening a school for singers. Raisa died in Los Angeles on 29 Sep 1963.

Aida was her great role, and extracts from the opera are among her finest recordings; she did "La fatal pietra" and "O terra addio" for Vocalion, plus 13 other arias in the 1920–1924 period. She made five sides for Pathé in 1924, and then five for Brunswick in 1928–1930. Her last discs, for HMV in 1933, included "Vissi d'arte" (#DB 2122) and "Voi lo sapete" (#DB 2123). IRRC, Scala, and RCA offered reissues.

RAMBLER MINSTREL CO. A male quartet that recorded ca. 1906–1907, also known as the Victor Minstrel Co. (in 1907), the Colonial Quartet, and the Zonophone Quartet. Members were Byron G. Harlan, Billy Murray, Arthur Collins, and Steve Porter.

RAMPAL, JEAN-PIERRE, 1922– . French flutist, born in Marseilles on 7 Jan 1922. He studied at the Paris conservatory (and was a professor there from 1968), played in the orchestra of the Vichy Opéra, then at the Paris Opéra. To him and James Galway go the credit for bringing a wide flute repertoire to the attention of world audiences. He recorded first for the Boite à Musique label in the late 1940s, performing baroque and classical material. Rampal also performs in the popular vein, and had a *Cash Box* chart album (the first for any flutist) in 1976 with Claude Bolling, doing Bolling's *Suite for Flute and Jazz Piano* (Columbia #M33233).

RAPKE (VICTOR H.) CO. A New York firm, located at 255 E. 86th St. in 1907. It advertised the Rapke horn and horn crane, said to be "free of foreign noises and rattle."

RAPPOLD, MARIE, ca. 1873–1957. British soprano, born Marie Winterroth in London, of German parents. The family transferred to the U.S. when she was a child, settling in New York; she studied there, and made her debut at the Metropolitan Opera on 22 Nov 1905. She sang with that company until 1920, then moved to Los Angeles. She died on 12 May 1957 in North Hollywood.

Rappold began recording on two-minute Edison "gold moulded" cylinders in 1906–1907 with three numbers. "Ave Maria" (#B21), "Euch lüften die mein Klagen" from *Lohengrin* (#B33), and Elisabeth's Prayer from *Tannhäuser* (#B43). She was heard on four-minute cylinders from 1910 to 1912, in 11 arias and songs, then made Diamond Discs from 1915 to 1922. Among her later records were a *Lucia* sextet with Margarete Matzenauer and Giovanni Zenatello (#82266), and Wagner numbers with Jacques Urlus.

RARITIES. Among the rarest and sought after disc labels—with the fewest extant specimens—are **Autograph** and **Black Patti**. The early Berliner discs, such as those made for the toy machine of 1890, are collector's items. Discs made by certain artists are scarce and valuable today, among them Gemma Bellincioni (G & T), Enrico Caruso (Zonophone), Feodor Chaliapin (G & T), Mary Garden (G & T), Victor Maurel (G & T), and Pol Plançon (Zonophone). Certain oddities, equivalent to postage stamps incorrectly printed, become rare for the mishaps they immortalize, such as Nellie Melba's "Sweet Bird" take on which she is heard to say "I'm sorry to be such a fool; we must begin it all over again."

All white wax cylinders are rare. Among the major cylinder labels, the records of **Bettini** are highly prized.

RAY, JOHNNY, 1927–1990. American popular singer. He developed a style that blended R & B, country, and gospel idioms, adding to them some heartfelt sobbing; he earned the sobriquet "Prince of Wails." His first chart record, "Cry" (Okeh #6840; 1951) was an enormous success, and may have sold 25 million copies. "Little White Cloud That Cried" (1952) was featured in the film *There's No Business Like Show Business*; it was 14 weeks on the charts. Ray had 10 other chart singles in the 1950s. He continued performing until 1989, including tours of Britain and Australia, but never reached the recording heights again. He died in February 1990.

RCA (label). A British record sold in U.K. by Decca Record Co., Ltd., from 1957, in 78 rpm, 45 rpm. and LP formats. (Andrews*.]

RCA (RADIO CORPORATION OF AMERICA). An American firm established on 17 Oct 1919 in New York. It had an early association with Victor Talking Machine Co. in 1925, through an arrangement for RCA radios to be included in certain Victrola record player models. Then, on 4 Jan 1929, RCA bought Victor. The Victor label name was retained, with RCA added, and the record remained in the forefront of the industry. On 15 Apr 1986, RCA became part of the **Bertelsmann** conglomerate. For the history of RCA, *see* VICTOR TALKING MACHINE CO., II.

RCA VICTOR (label). The name given to the **Victor** label after **RCA** acquired the Victor Talking Machine Co. in 1929. With the transfer of the RCA record business to **Bertelsmann** in 1986, the several RCA label series remained distinct, within the BMG Classics group.

REA, VIRGINIA. American popular singer, born in Louisville, Kentucky. She studied in France, and is said to have successfully auditioned by telephone for The American Opera Co., New York. She sang with various companies in the 1920s, then turned to radio in 1925 and found her niche. Under the name Olive Palmer, she became one of the most acclaimed radio vocalists in the 1930s, as the "Olive Palmolive Girl" on the Palmolive soap program, then on the Goodyear and Buick programs. She dropped out of sight in 1937, however, and did not return to public performance.

Rea recorded for Edison, Brunswick, Columbia, and Victor. Her Brunswick work was the most extensive, covering six years and a wide repertoire. For both Columbia and Victor she was a studio artist, singing in diverse ensembles as needed. She worked for Edison Diamond Discs, as Virginia Rea, in 1920–1923, and again in 1929 as Olive Palmer. The early sessions produced three vocal waltzes in Italian—"Se saran rose," "La zingarella," and "La capinera" (#80731, #80524, #80705)—and

"Goodbye, Beloved" with the Lyric Male Quartet (#80746). Only one disc was released from her 1929 sessions, "On the Beautiful Blue Danube" and "Indian Love Call" (#52633). [Ferrara 1988/1.]

REAL TIME SPECTRUM ANALYZER. An instrument that displays signal strength "in the frequency domain," plotting level versus frequency. It is especially useful for making accurate frequency measurements of weak signals in the presence of stronger signals. It can be used to identify rumbles, ticks, pops, and surface noise. [Klinger*.]

RECEIVER. A unit in an audio system that incorporates the tuner and the amplifier.

Rechanneled stereo. *See* REPROCESSED STEREO.

RECORD BOYS. A male ensemble that broadcast regularly on radio stations WJZ and WRC (New York) in 1926–1927. Members were Al Bernard, Frank Kamplain, and Sam Stept. A popular recording was "Hokum" (Vocalion #15308, and other labels). Kamplain, a yodeler and singer, started a new group of the same name when the original one dissolved in 1927. It included baritone Tom Ford and pianist Lew Cobey; they recorded for Brunswick, and made one Edison Diamond Disc.

RECORD CATALOGS. The first printed catalog of a record company was that of the **North American Phonograph Co.** in 1890. Columbia's first catalog came out later in the same year. *See also* DISCOGRAPHY.

RECORD CHANGER. A turntable and tone arm assembly that stacks records and plays them in succession; also known as an automatic turntable. A disc changer was described in *Scientific American* in 1921, but none reached the market until 1927, sold by Victor. A model of the Victor Orthophonic Victrola played 12 discs, on one side only, holding the stack at a 60 degree angle; it shut off after the last disc was played. The first British disc changer was made by Garrard; the same firm produced the first changer that could play both sides of each

record in the stack, in 1938. Garrard machines (and their counterparts by the **Capehart Co.** in America) actually turned each record over; another approach was illustrated by the Sharp player of 1981, which held the disc vertically and played each side with its own tone arm assembly.

In most record changers of the 78 rpm and LP eras, the stack of discs to be played was directly above the turntable and parallel to it. The records were held in a level position by a record leveler arm (or record support arm, or record balance arm). The same arm activated the shut-off mechanism after the final disc had been played. Breakage of the 78s was avoided on the drop from the stack because there was a cushion of air that developed and provided a reasonably soft landing. Other formats existed: for example there were the machines that pushed each record off the turntable after playing it, into a hopper of some kind (the records awaiting play were stacked on the turntable).

Some record changers were able to handle only six records, but most could play 12. It seemed that 12 was the maximum because as the fallen discs piled up on the turntable, the tone arm had to reach up to play the top one, creating an awkward playing angle. Records also tended to slide around on each other, especially if any were warped.

Finally there should be mention of the RCA novelty of 1949, the 45 rpm disc and its compact record changer. It was a high speed operator, and reasonably quiet about it, but only in the wildest fancy could anyone have expected it to equal the speed of an LP moving from one band to the next. [Dezettel 1968; Hoover 1971, pp. 82–83, illustrates the Automatic Orthophonic; Kogen 1977.]

RECORD CLUBS. Entities established by record manufacturers to promote mail order sales; they were introduced by Victor in 1934, in a plan that required participants to buy a record every month for one year. Other labels followed. Consumers were given certain bargains and bonuses to inspire participation. The clubs were affected by retailer objections, and by a 1962 Federal Trade Commission ruling that clubs must make available material from other labels as well as their own. There were also customer concerns about the practice of clubs that involved shipping records every month unless they were specifically rejected in advance by the club member. Yet club sales accounted for about 9 percent of the American market in the mid-1980s. [Denisoff 1986.] *See also* SOCIETY RECORDINGS.

Record collecting. *See* COLLECTING AND COLLECTORS.

RECORD CONDITION. Applied to 78 rpm and LP discs, the term mint (M) or near mint (NM) describes records never played, in mint condition. M is never a certainty, since the usual sign of an unplayed record is its factory packaging, but a record may have been removed from its package and resealed into it. Very good condition (VG) is the state of a record free from marks and scratches, although showing evidence of some playing; it is practically as good as new, but not NM. A good record (G) has been played but is not badly worn or damaged. A record in fair (F) condition has had heavy play but is usable. One in poor (P) condition is virtually unplayable, and would be kept for historical reasons only.

Such designations have not been applied to tapes or to CDs, where noticeable wear or damage is not a factor of concern. Tapes do develop problems such as **print through**, or simple breakage, but these are not gradual forms of decay—they exist or do not. CDs have not evidenced operational wearability.

RECORD CORP. OF AMERICA. A firm located in Union City, New Jersey, from 1951 to ca. 1957. It issued dubbed classical material on several labels: Allegro/Elite, Allegro/Royale, Concertone, Gramophone, Halo, **King, Royale,** and **Varsity.** Artists were given pseudonyms, or in some cases were incorrectly attributed. [Lumpe 1990.]

Record label. *See* LABEL.

RECORD OUT SWITCH. A control in a recording system that permits the recording of one signal while listening to another signal.

RECORD PLAYER. A device consisting of components necessary to play and listen to a sound recording. For a cylinder record, it consists essentially of a mandrel to support and rotate the cylinder, a **reproducer** to track the grooves and produce vibrations, a motor or handcrank, and a **horn** to amplify the vibrations so they can be heard. For a disc record, an acoustic record player consists of a **turntable** to spin the record, a soundbox and needle to track the grooves and produce vibrations, and a **tone arm** to hold the soundbox and carry the vibrations to the horn. An electric record player translates the vibrations to electrical impulses in a **cartridge** (pickup), enhances their volume in an **amplifier,** and then translates them back to audible sound vibrations in the **loudspeaker**(s).

In a CD record player a spindle drive rotates the disc, a laser beam pickup reads the pits on the record, and one or two D/A converters translate the digital signals to stereo analog signals that can be enhanced in the same kind of amplifier and loudspeaker that is used in an LP player. [Klinger*.]

RECORD REPEATER CO. A New York firm, located at 432 Fifth Ave. in 1915. In January 1915 it advertised a "Rek-Rep" device for **automatic stop** or **automatic replay** in a disc record player.

RECORD SALES AGENCY. A New York firm, located at 25 W. 42nd St., advertised in *TMW* in 1921. It had been pressing its own labelled discs, and discs for owners of other labels, for two years. [Andrews*.]

RECORD SHOPS. Cylinder records were sold by mail order as early as the 1890s, but were also available in record company offices and phonograph parlors. Columbia records had a first location at 5th St. and Louisiana Ave. in Washington, D.C.—which may have been the original record outlet. Their later phonograph parlor was at 919 Pennsylvania Ave. Affiliates of the **North American Phonograph Co.,** throughout the U.S., had offices from which cylinder records and phonograph products could be purchased.

The first retail store to sell disc records to the public was established by Emile Berliner in Philadelphia in 1895; **Alfred C. Clark** was the proprietor of the shop.

As the industry grew, the number of retail shops increased, aa well as the number of record departments in larger stores. The practice of trying out records before purchase was common, but it was usually executed by shop personnel (a so-called record girl played the record for the customer). An innovation of 1921 was the notion of self-service trials in private listening booths; this was the American pattern through the 78 rpm era. (A secondary trend surfaced in 1924: listening stations with earphones in place of booths. However it did not take root, and such stations never became popular except in libraries.)

Certain shops gained attention for their enterprising activities beyond sales of records, such as the **Commodore Music Shop** (1924) and the **Liberty Music Shop** (1927) in New York, both of which issued recordings; the H. Royer Smith Co. in Philadelphia (1907), which issued a record review periodical from 1930–1987; and the **Gramophone Shop** in New York (1928), which published an early unified catalog of available recordings.

In the 1990s major North American and British cities have a great variety of record shops. Significant chain stores operating in more than one city include Tower Records and Sam Goody. The Princeton Record Exchange is located in Princeton, New Jersey, between New York and Philadelphia. Serenade is one of the popular Washington stores. Chicago has Rose Records, established 1932, and now operating 30 stores. In Toronto there is L'Atelier Grigorian; in Montreal and other Canadian cities there are the Archambault stores.

Squires Gate (Blackpool) and Harold Moore's Records (London) are two of Britain's major outlets. The Music Discount Centre, with several London locations, is the first substantial discount shop in the city. Tower Records has three London shops. Among other European emporia of distinction, the 60-year-old Discos Castello in Barcelona should be mentioned.

RECORDER. The **soundbox** and cutting stylus used to make cylinder records.

Recording characteristic. *See* RECORDING CURVE.

RECORDING CURVE. Also known as recording characteristic. A plot of the relative emphasis given to the various frequencies in the audio spectrum. Lower frequencies have to be recorded at lower volume levels than higher frequencies, because they already seem louder to the ear, and—on discs—to prevent cutting into adjacent grooves. Standards for the curve have been established by the **Recording Industry Association of America (RIAA)**. *See also* AUDIO FREQUENCY; EQUALIZATION; PLAYBACK CURVE.

RECORDING HEAD. In a tape recorder, the electromagnetic device that impresses the signal, by means of a varying magnetic field, on the tape surface. It may be the same head as the **playback head**.

RECORDING INDUSTRY. For historical accounts see CYLINDER, 6, and DISC, 6. Modern studio practice is discussed at RECORDING PRACTICE. Sources for research into the history of the industry are described in Brooks 1979. See also names of individuals, listed in the index under Executives and other officials.

RECORDING INDUSTRY ASSOCIATION OF AMERICA (RIAA). A trade organization established in 1952, located (1991) at 1020 19th St., NW, Washington, D.C. Its purpose is to promote the interests of the industry and to "foster good relations among all concerned" with it. Among its active concerns are record piracy, technical standards, and rewards for achievement. RIAA designates as Gold records those that sell 1 million copies (for singles), 500,000 copies (for albums) or 250,000 copies (boxed sets). Platinum records are those that sell 2 million copies (singles), 1 million (albums), or 500,000 (boxed sets).

RECORDING INDUSTRY CHARTS. The charting of sound recordings was inevitable in American society, where competition is a birthright and trivia—such as that included in countless best-selling "book of lists" publications—has become a national obsession. Charting appears to have begun shortly after Thomas Edison filed for a patent to his phonograph on 24 Dec 1877. Its prime purposes then—as now—were to promote the recording industry by focusing interest on new releases, and to provide retailers a gauge of relative demand.

Phonogram, an early record industry periodical established in 1891, anticipated charting by including ongoing mention of top popular recordings. *The Phonoscope* featured monthly listings (though not in precise rank order) during the 1896–1899 period. Data on sheet music sales, and lists of popular song releases from ASCAP and the leading record labels served as early chart prototypes.

Billboard, the bible of the recording industry throughout most of the 20th century, instituted weekly lists of sheet music in 1913, and published lists of the most popular songs in vaudeville in 1913–1918. During 1914–1921, the major record companies provided *Talking Machine World* with monthly lists of their best-selling records. *Variety* advanced the practice to a considerable degree with more systematic listings from late 1929.

By 1934, both *Billboard* and *Variety* were regularly charting the top songs in radio airplay and sheet music sales. From November 1934 through early 1938, *Billboard* carried the best-selling charts of the individual record labels, and in late 1938 instituted weekly surveys of the most popular records in juke boxes. As a result, two separate weekly charts emerged within the industry at this time: best-selling records, and radio airplay-sheet music sales. As far as the general public was concerned, however, the long-running radio show, *Your Hit Parade*, provided the principal format for top hits; it continued to be influential on television during the 1950s. A similar top ten countdown was employed by Dick Clark on *American Bandstand*.

During the early 1940s, the pace-setting *Billboard* evolved the triad of charts that dominated the industry until the late 1950s: "Best Sellers in Stores" (20 July 1940–4 Oct 1958), the first comprehensive listing combining data from all labels; "Most Played By Disc Jockeys" (1945–19 July 1958); and the previously instituted "Most Played in Juke Boxes" (which ran until 12 June 1958). After World War II, *Billboard* began running supplementary charts to focus further the industry picture; for example, "Up & Coming Hits" (1947–1948), "Regional and Up & Coming Hits" (1952–1954), and the "Honor Roll of Hits" (which ran through 16 Nov 1963—a compilation of tunes rather than individual records).

With *Billboard*'s publication of the weekly "Hot 100" (of 45s) beginning on 18 Aug 1958, the industry could look to one chart for a combined factual account of a single's popularity. Similar listings soon appeared for other genres (country, rhythm & blues, classical, etc.) and formats (long-playing albums).

In the meantime, many radio stations and retail outlets began producing their own charts as a marketing tool (for example, to encourage listening to their local count-down programs). These proved particularly useful in spotting local talent and regional break-out hits. While initially available only by mail or pick-up at the local outlets, the industry trade publications began running selected charts of key markets in the 1960s based on such listings.

The late 1970s and 1980s saw the widespread proliferation of charts to include the important new genres and formats appearing at the time. These included disco/dance/ 12-inch singles, rap music, college/alternative rock, new age, easy listening, album-oriented radio, videotapes, videodiscs, video clips, computer software, video games, and compact discs (until subsumed by the mainstream pop album charts). One particular marketing stratagem, midline catalog albums (i.e., older classic releases still popular with buyers), proved sufficiently successful in the early 1980s to have its own chart for a time within the trade.

Industry trades journals, which have long dominated the chart sector, have included *Billboard*, *Cash Box*, *Variety*, and *Record World* (which ceased publication in the early 1980s). In recent years, a number of fanzines and serious music journals (for example, *Rolling Stone*) have begun including their own listings as well. The various charts in both *Billboard* and *Cash Box* have been compiled in book form by Joel Whitburn's Record Research, and Scarecrow Press, respectively.

As of late 1991, charting remained an essential component of the industry. In an effort to counteract criticisms that the charts were either falsified to reflect the interests of the highest bidder, or grossly inaccurate in reflecting actual performance (particularly sales), *Billboard* instituted its SoundScan service (beginning with the "Hot 100" singles and "Top 200" albums) in its 25 May 1991 issue. SoundScan compiled computerized bar-code information from store registers. The sudden rise of country recordings, and corresponding fall of many alternative music titles, led many industry insiders to deride the system because it tended to be concentrated in large retail chains that catered more to middle-of-the-road/rural customers, rather than independent and specialty record stores. Despite such criticism, computerized tabulation appears to be the wave of the future, as it provides accurate unit sales figures as the basis for determining chart rankings.

These charts were included in the 26 Oct 1991 issue of *Billboard*:

TOP ALBUMS—The Billboard 200, Contemporary Christian, Country, Gospel, Latin, Modern Rock Tracks, New Age, R & B, Rock Tracks, World Music;

HOT SINGLES—Adult Contemporary, Country, Dance, Hot 100, Hot 100 Singles Action, R & B, R & B Singles Action, Rap, Top 40 Radio Monitor, Top POS Singles Sales. [Hoffmann 1981; Hoffmann 1983; Hoffmann 1984; Hoffmann 1986/1; Hoffmann 1987; Hoffmann 1988; Hoffmann 1989/1; Hoffmann 1989/2; Whitburn 1982; Whitburn 1986.]

Frank Hoffmann

RECORDING PRACTICE. The genesis of any commercial recording project is the careful selection of artist and repertoire. Once these artistic considerations have been determined, it is the task of the producer to make all the necessary musical, technical, physical, and monetary arrangements for the recording.

When searching for the proper venue to make the recording, the first decision the producer must make is where—in a studio, or on location—the session should be held. This prompts a fundamental question: "Where will be music be performed to best advantage?" If the answer is that a recital or concert hall, a nightclub or cocktail lounge, or any other "real" environment is where the performers and their music are most comfortable, this is where the producer will consider scheduling the recording session—keeping in mind, however, that there are technical considerations which might also influence the decision. For example, a noisy room, acceptable for a live performance with an audience, may not prove satisfactory for a recording because the other aural and visual stimuli of the live experience will not be present to "mask" the record listeners' awareness of the intruding noise. Recording studios, on the other hand, generally offer a very controlled acoustical environment—in most modern studios this is usually means rather dry acoustics, so that any sense of "liveness" will need to be added artificially during recording.

Technical and other cost factors will also be considered: on-location sessions often cost more than in-studio sessions because all of the equipment needs to be brought to the site, set up, calibrated and tested prior to recording, and then it must all be removed at the end. In addition, risers, chairs, stands and instruments (and sometimes even acoustical treatment) also need to be brought to the site. All these technical factors aside, sometimes the music will "just sound better" when recorded on location. These, and numerous other tradeoffs between cost and result will all be evaluated when making the decision.

Today, digital recording formats are readily available in both direct-to-stereo and **multitrack** processes (see below) and the costs are no longer so widely different as they were in earlier days of digital recording. Since both formats can be used to produce analog or digital products (LPs, cassettes, or CDs) the primary factors involved in choosing the recording format will be based on the "sound" of the recording and the preferences of the producer.

The next decision the producer will need to make is whether to record direct-to-stereo (two-track) or to use a multitrack process. Both methods have their advantages as well as disadvantages. The decision between the two approaches will be determined primarily by the type of music being recorded and, to a lesser degree, by the capabilities of the performers and the recording facility. Music intended to be played "live" (classical, folk, small jazz ensembles, and the like) will frequently be recorded direct-to-stereo. Contemporary recording practices, however, generally tend toward multi-microphone, multitrack methods to avoid problems with musical balance. Thus, even if a direct-to-stereo mix is recorded, a multitrack "protection" tape will be made simultaneously.

Direct-to-stereo is a time-proven method for recording music that can be performed in "real time," as in a live performance. The recording techniques are, generally, less complex than multitrack, and when properly implemented, will result in a realistic, lifelike sound.

Complex musical performances (Broadway musicals, opera, and so forth.), "popular" genres (rock, rap, and so forth.), electronic music, or other musical formats requiring "layering" or "over-dubs" will almost always be recorded via a multitrack process. Multitrack recording is employed whenever the artistic intent is to create a "new reality" that does not exist (either conveniently or at all) in real time or space. Multitracking becomes a necessity when overdubbing or layering parts, or where performance difficulties or the instrumentation dictate that a proper musical blend cannot easily be achieved in actual performance. Multitracking also affords the opportunity for electronic manipulation of existing sounds to create new sounds, or for the replacement of one voice or line with another. It gives the producer and performers, therefore, the ability to "bend reality" to suit their art. This is the primary benefit of, and reason for, multitrack recording: the ability to mix or re-mix the individual voices (tracks) after the initial recording session, to achieve the exact balance desired.

Cost factors differ widely between the two approaches, and since producers are always concerned with money, this will also be considered when making the decision. Direct-to-stereo recording sessions take much less time, and when they are finished, the basic recording is complete. Multitrack sessions not only take much more time during the initial recording (and usually at much higher hourly rates), but the result is not yet a finished recording. The producer must then spend additional time to **mixdown** the multitrack tape in order to produce the final stereo master tape. As a general rule, the total time required to complete a multitrack recording will be at least six to eight times that of a direct-to-stereo session.

During the recording sessions, whether direct-to-stereo or multitrack, the performances are generally accomplished in individual takes. Each **take** is a segment of the entire musical piece. With some forms of music—particularly classical music or short songs—a take of a complete movement or song will be made, in order to provide a sense of continuity. Then, if needed, short segments ("pickups" or "inserts") will be recorded to replace spots that did not go well during the full recording.

With multitrack sessions, it is quite common for individual instruments, groups of instruments, or vocalists to be recorded separately. Sometimes, these are recorded at widely different times, or even in entirely different locations, depending on the availability of the performers or instruments. This process is called **tracking**, since each part is recorded to a separate track on the tape. A related process, called overdubbing, comes into play when one performer is required to record more than one part or line of the musical composition. In both processes, the original track is played back to the performer, via headphones, and the new part is performed onto another track in synchronization with the original. During the mixing process the two or more parts are mixed together to provide the complex texture so vital to modern musical performances.

Once the session master tape has been recorded, the next step in the process is post production. In editing, the first stage, the individual takes are selected and combined (spliced together) to produce a finished performance of each piece; these pieces are then sequenced to produce the complete recording as it will be released. Numerous artistic and technical processes are involved in this stage, depending on the final release format for the recording.

As mentioned earlier, multitrack recordings must also be mixed-down to a stereo master. This usually occurs after the editing, although some producers prefer to mix first, and then edit. In popular music, special signal processing (compression, equalization, reverberation, phasing, etc.) effects are frequently employed during the mixing process to augment or enhance the texture.

The days of the vinyl LP having passed, smaller projects are now usually produced only as cassettes. Compact discs are the other common release format. The cost of CD production has fallen while the availability of production facilities has risen, so that the CD is nearly as viable as the cassette for most recording projects today.

Editing and mixing a recording can be done in either the analog or the digital domain, and the decision as to how to proceed will usually follow the format of the original recording. Sometimes, particularly with lower-budget projects, analog copies of digital tapes will be made for post production purposes, since considerable cost savings can be achieved during these stages. The edited analog tape will then be used as the final production master.

The total time available on the various release formats will frequently dictate that different "duplication masters" be created for each. Cassette sides generally have a maximum running time of 45 minutes; two sides afford a total program length of 90 minutes. Compact discs provide a total playing time of around 72 minutes. Thus, the different program lengths will determine how the tapes are edited.

Dynamic range of the release format will also play an important role in the mastering process: cassettes have a limited dynamic range. The technical limitations of the different release formats will also be taken into consideration when producing these duplication masters. For cassettes, this master will be an equalized, often compressed, stereo master tape. (For LPs, the final master was a lacquer disc.) For compact discs, the duplicating-master will be a digital tape, containing the program, timecode, and all of the special codes necessary to indicate track numbers, timings, table of contents, and so forth.

During the preparation of these final duplicating masters the producer has a last chance to change the sound or order of the recording. Once the duplicating master has been made, the remainder of the process is just mechanical duplication. [Borwick 1987.] *See also* DISC, 3.

Ron Streicher

RECORDING STUDIOS. Early American recording studios, often called laboratories, were those of Thomas Edison (1887), A.T.T. Wangemann (a New Jersey studio for Edison, opened May 1889), and the New York Phonograph Co. (1890). In Britain the first studio was in Queen Victoria St., in the City of London, established by Colonel Gouraud's **Edison Phonograph Co.** in 1888; it moved to Edison House, Northumberland Ave., W.C., by 1890 when the company passed to the Edison United Phonograph Co. of Newark, New Jersey. (Clients paid to be recorded.) The next London studio was in Fore St., E.C., where J.L. Young, ex-manager of the Edison Phonograph Co., set up his own business in 1893, with a studio to record and sell items performed by British artists. **J.E. Hough** began recording his London label cylinders in 1894, from his Broad St. premises.

Emile Berliner was making discs in the U.S. as early as June 1892, in a laboratory housed with his first American firm, the American Gramophone Co. The first British disc recording studio was opened by the Gramophone Co., in Maiden Lane, London (1898). Thereafter all major labels had their own studios, while most independent labels had their recording done for them. Among the most notable studios of today are the **Abbey Road** complex of EMI and **Cherokee Ranch** in Hollywood. The *Billboard International Directory* provides a yearly list of studios in operation. The periodical *Mix* gives details in each issue about a selected group of active studios. [Andrews*.]

RECORDITE CO. A New York firm, established in 1907, located at 1905 Park Ave. It advertised in 1907 a disc record cleaning fluid named Recordite.

RECORDOL CO. A New York firm, located at 108 E. 125th St. In 1907 it marketed a cleaning fluid for cylinder records, named Recordol.

RED LABEL RECORDS. Disc records with paper labels of red color have been intended to suggest high quality deluxe productions since the early years of the industry. G & T issued such discs in 1901, carrying voices of the Russian Imperial Opera (Chaliapin among them); they sold for $5.00. Red labels became a major series for G & T (the Gramophone Co.), carrying their great singers and instrumentalists, from 1902. Victor negotiated with G & T to issue the red labels in America, calling them Red Seals. Later Victor recorded its own Red Seals, but the two companies continued to share material. Victor's 10-inch Red Seals appeared in April 1903; the 12-inch Red Seals came out in September 1903. The public was receptive: 306,312 Red Seals were sold by the end of the year. Other companies used red labels later to present series of special interest, such as Decca's Personality Series; but in other cases the firms just had red or maroon colored labels for all their discs (for example, Nadsco or Romeo).

RED NEEDLE. A fiber needle made and patented by the Master-Phone Corp. in 1915, and patented by them; the patent was sold in summer 1915 to the **Phonograph Accessories Corp.** The needle was said to give five to 10 plays without record wear, and without "muffled tone."

Red Seal records. *See* RED LABEL RECORDS; VICTOR TALKING MACHINE CO.

REDDING, OTIS, 1941–1967. American popular singer, born in Dawson, Georgia, on 9 Sep 1941. He sang in church and revival meetings, and adopted a shouting style of projection that he later refined. In the mid-1960s Redding was greatly acclaimed, producing 29 chart singles and 10 chart albums, several of them posthumously released.

Dictionary of Soul (Volt #S-415; 1966) was among the most highly regarded of these. Atco assembled *The Best of Otis Redding* in 1972 (#SD-2-801). He was killed in an air crash near Madison, Wisconsin, on 10 Dec 1967.

REDMAN, DON, 1900–1964. American jazz saxophonist, Big Band leader, and arranger; born Donald Matthew Redman in Piedmont, West Virginia, on 29 July 1900. He learned to play all the wind instruments, and to make outstanding jazz/swing arrangements. He worked with Fletcher Henderson, Louis Armstrong, Paul Whiteman, Jimmy Dorsey, Ben Pollack, and others. He had his own band from time to time in the 1930s and 1940s. Redman's group recorded for Brunswick in 1931–1933, then for various labels. (An LP selection of material from 1932–1937 appeared on CBS #E-52539.) But Redman's lasting value was as an arranger, as one who shaped sophisticated sound profiles. He took the Henderson band from blandness to exciting complexity in just a year or two (1923–1924), and when he left in 1927 the group lost its focus. He led McKinney's Cotton Pickers in 1928–1931, then formed his own band. Notable examples of his work are heard in the Henderson records of "Copenhagen" (Vocalion #14926; 1924) and "Rocky Mountain Blues" (Columbia #970-D; 1927). His design of "Deep Purple" for Jimmy Dorsey and Bob Eberle (Decca #2295; 1939) was an outstanding specimen of his ballad style. Redman toured Europe with a band in 1946–1947, then was less active. He died in New York on 30 Nov 1964.

REDUCTION. The combination of tracks from a multitrack recording into a lesser number of tracks, such as for a stereophonic or quadraphonic record.

REED, PETER HUGH, 1892–1969. American record critic and journalist, born in Washington, D.C., on 16 June 1892. He studied voice in Italy, but his career hopes were abandoned after he was gassed in World War I. He took up criticism, and was a pioneer in radio reviews of recordings. In 1935 he was founder-editor of the *American Music Lover* (renamed *American Record Guide* in 1944)), the only significant record review journal of its time in the U.S. He retired in 1957, succeeded as editor by James Lyons. Reed died on 25 Sep 1969 in Wingdale, New York.

REED, SUSAN, 1927– . American folk singer, harpist, and zither player, born in Columbia, South Carolina. As a child she learned traditional Irish songs from Abbey Theatre players who visited her family home, and she took up the Irish harp; she also learned the autoharp and zither. She sang professionally in New York as a teenager, and after success in the Cafe Society Uptown she toured the U.S. A Town Hall recital followed in 1946, then radio and television appearances. During the 1950s Reed recorded for Victor, Columbia, and other labels, doing Irish material and other traditional songs. Elektra issued an LP album in 1954 entitled *Old Airs from Ireland, Scotland and England,* and Columbia released *Folk Songs* in 1958. Her work did much to bring Irish and Appalachian folk music to a wide audience.

REED, DAWSON AND CO. An American firm with offices at 516 Broad St., Newark, and 74 Cortland St., New York, active in the late 1890s. It issued brown wax cylinders and catalogs. In 1899 issues of *Phonoscope* the firm advertised "the only successful violin records—loud, clear and distinct," played by T. Herbert Read. Other artists on the records—"strictly first class originals"—included Billy Golden, Dan Quinn, Vess Ossman, William Hooley, S. H. Dudley, Harry Macdonough, the Lyric Trio, Cal Stewart, the original American Quartet, and Estella Mann. [Klinger*.]

REEL TO REEL TAPE. A magnetic tape format, also known as open reel tape, popular in the 1950s and 1960s, in which the recorded tape is played back by attaching its end to an empty take-up reel and running it past the playback head. After play, the tape is rewound to its original feed reel. A reel seven inches in diameter contains about 1,200 feet of tape, and plays at 7 1/2 inches per second, for a total playing time of about 30 minutes. Although the running time of such a tape exceeded that of an LP record side, sales for pre-recorded open reel tapes were poor. The use made of

them was in home recording and in making copies of disc material. Open reels were also used in professional studio work, to make the original recording from which the disc masters, stampers, etc. were prepared. With the introduction of cassettes in 1963, interest in reel to reel taping virtually vanished in the U.S. *See also* MAGNETIC RECORDING; and TAPE.

RE-ENTRANT GRAMOPHONE. The British version of the Victor Orthophonic record player, introduced in October 1927 by the Gramophone Co.

REEVES, AL, 1864–1940. American vaudeville and minstrel show performer, singer and banjoist, known in the 1880s and 1890s as the "King of Burlesque." The only records he seems to have made were cylinders for Columbia in 1892. [Brooks 1979.]

REEVES, JIM, 1924–1964. American country singer, guitarist, and composer, born in Panola County, Texas, 20 Aug 1924. He intended to make a career in professional baseball, but was injured in a game and did not recover properly. Turning to music, he performed on radio and made some records, one of which—"Mexican Joe"—brought him considerable attention. He had success with singles on the Fairways label and on the Fabor label, then was offered a contract with RCA. Reeves made at least one hit record every year. After his death, in a private plane crash on 31 July 1964, his wife arranged for posthumous issue of material not yet released. The *Cash Box* country singles charts included 64 of his discs between 1958 and 1980. "I Guess I'm Crazy" (RCA # 8383; 1964) and "I Won't Come In While He's There" (RCA #9057; 1967) are among the most noteworthy of his successes. The album *Best of Jim Reeves* (RCA #LPM2980) was on the charts 23 weeks in 1964. He was elected to the Country Music Hall of Fame in 1967.

REGAL (label). (I) A British low-priced record issued by Columbia Phonograph Co., General—London, and then by the Columbia Graphophone Co., Ltd., from 1914 to 1931. Material was greatly varied: popular dance and vocals, and John McCormack, sacred pieces, spoken records and country/western numbers. Material came from the U.S., Britain, and the continent. With the EMI merger of 1931, Regal was attached to the HMV low-priced record, Zonophone, and the result was Regal-Zonophone, a label that continued to 1949, and was revived by EMI in the 1960s and again in 1980 for a few rock items. [Andrews*; Badrock 1991.]

REGAL (label). (II) An American low-priced record, not related to the British one above, made from Emerson and Plaza masters. The Regal Record Co. was at 266 Fifth Ave., New York in February 1922. At first (1921) it sold records, for $.50 each, to department stores, but in 1922 the discs were offered to merchant dealers. Important artists appeared on Regal, including the Original Memphis Five, Noble Sissle, Eubie Blake, Cab Calloway, Duke Ellington, Ben Selvin, and Vincent Lopez. Little Tots' Nursery Tunes was a series of seven-inch records, three in an album, sold in March 1923; at that time the claim was made that Regals were being made in the world's third-largest record factory.

It appears that sometime in 1924 the **Plaza Music Co.** acquired Regal Record Co. Regal's Playtime line was advertised by Plaza in December 1924. Then in January 1929 it was reported that the **Crystalate Gramophone Record Manufacturing Co., Ltd.,** had purchased the Regal Record Co., Inc., from Plaza. Subsequently Regal was combined with Cameo Records, Inc., and the Scranton Button Co. to the **American Record Corp.** Production of the Regal label then ceased. [Andrews *; Rust 1978.]

REGINA MUSIC BOX CO. A firm established in 1892 in Rahway, New Jersey, with offices later at Broadway and 17th St., New York; and 259 Wabash Ave., Chicago. A German named Brachausen formed the company. He was one of the founders of the Polyphonmusikwerke in Germany a few years earlier, and had been employed by the German company that made the Symphonion brand of music boxes. Regina music boxes were essentially Polyphon music boxes at first. In 1898 Regina was marketing **coin-op** music boxes. The Regina Disc Changer

of ca. 1900 played a dozen two-minute steel tune discs. The Reginaphone could play either gramophone records or steel tune discs, and the Automatic Reginaphone of 1905 was able to play six cylinder records consecutively, one for each coin inserted. A selective coin-op, the **Hexaphone,** was offered in 1906. The Reginapiano (an inner player) was another product, vacuum cleaners still another.

In 1909 the firm name was shortened to the Regina Co. It had addresses at 47 W. 34th St., New York, and 218 S. Wabash, Chicago, plus a factory in Rahway. A contract with Columbia Phonograph Co. allowed the two firms to distribute each other's products, so Regina began to sell Columbia records. Regina was bankrupt in 1922. [Andrews*; Hoover 1971 has illustrations of the Hexaphone (pp. 36–37) and Reginaphone (pp. 40–41).]

REINER, FRITZ, 1888–1963. Hungarian conductor and pianist, born in Budapest on 19 Dec 1888. His professional debut was as a pianist, playing a Mozart concerto at age 13. He studied at the Budapest Academy of Music, coached and conducted opera in Budapest, then from 1914 to 1921 directed the Court Opera in Dresden. Reiner developed a close association with Richard Strauss in Dresden (where nine of his operas had their premieres). He also conducted as a guest in many European cities. He transferred to the U.S. in 1922 to conduct the Cincinnati Symphony Orchestra for nine years, teaching also at the Curtis Institute in Philadelphia (Leonard Bernstein was among his pupils). From 1938 to 1948 he was music director of the Pittsburgh Symphony Orchestra. He then moved to the Metropolitan Opera for five years, beginning with an acclaimed performance of *Salome* with Ljuba Welitsch. In 1953 he took the post of music director of the Chicago Symphony Orchestra, remaining to 1962, and raising that ensemble to world class status. He died in New York on 15 Nov 1963, while preparing a Metropolitan Opera performance of *Götterdämmerung*.

Many of Reiner's early recordings are not on commercial records. He did not record at all with the Cincinnati Orchestra. His first conducting discs were experimentals made by Western Electric in the Academy of Music,

Philadelphia in 1931–1932. Although Leopold Stokowski was on the podium for most of the sessions, Reiner directed three performances, which remain in the Bell Laboratories archive. EMI recorded some Royal Opera performances in 1936–1937 at Covent Garden, but did not gain the approval of Reiner to release them; the sessions (segments of *Tristan, Fliegende Holländer,* and *Parsifal*) have been sold in the underground market. There are also air shots available from Reiner's broadcast operas from San Francisco in 1936–1938.

Finally in 1938 there were some authorized commercial records by Reiner, for the World's Greatest Music series—he directed the New York Philharmonic Symphony Orchestra in six discs, which were issued without artist identification. While he was with the Pittsburgh Symphony Reiner at last conducted for the first time commercially with his name given on the discs: Columbia contracted with him in 1938. Important recordings emerged, as Reiner brought that ensemble to a high level of polish, notably in Strauss works, Bartók, Mahler, Falla, and Shostakovich.

Reiner went to RCA Victor in 1950, and soon began a legendary series of records with the Chicago Symphony Orchestra. His first CSO recording was *Ein Heldenleben,* on 6 Mar 1954. Among the great performances captured on disc are the Bartók *Concerto for Orchestra* (1955), *La mer* and *Rapsodie espagnole* (1956–1957), the Rachmaninoff Second Concerto with Artur Rubinstein (1956), the Tchaikovsky Violin Concerto with Jascha Heifetz (1957), Prokofiev's *Alexander Nevsky* (1959), a group of Johann Strauss waltzes (1960), and the Second Piano Concerto of Brahms, with Van Cliburn (1961). These were all reissued in 1990 on RCA compact discs #GD 60175, #GD 60176, and #GD 60179. The only complete, approved, commercially issued opera recording by Reiner is *Carmen,* done at the Metropolitan Opera in 1952, with Risë Stevens, Jan Peerce, and Robert Merrill; it is regarded as the finest recorded version of the work (reissued on RCA CD #7981-2-RG; 1989). [Hart, P. 1987; Helmbrecht 1978]

REINHARDT, DJANGO, 1910–1953. Belgian jazz guitarist, born in Liberchies on 23 Jan 1910. He played in Paris from 1922, with Jean Sablon and Stéphane Grappelli, and in 1934 formed the Quintet of the Hot Club of France. He was said to have the "fastest technique in the history of guitar playing" (Stroff) despite a mutilated left hand. He also overcame an inability to read music (he could hardly read French either). After he played for the last time with Grappelli in 1949, Reinhardt embraced the electric guitar and experimented with new styles. His death, on 15 May 1953, in Paris, brought a great display of mourning and a lavish funeral.

A Pathé-Marconi CD, #746-5012, includes some of his work of 1928 with Sablon and Charles Trenet, and some of the 1940s amplified guitar material. LP reissues covered all his important output, including performances with Coleman Hawkins and Benny Carter on *Django Reinhardt and the American Jazz Giants* (Prestige #PR-7633). Quintet records are noted in the article about them. [Stroff 1988/5.]

REISMAN, LEO, 1897–1961. American dance band leader and violinist, born in Boston. He studied to be a concert violinist, then directed a salon orchestra and gained success with it, mostly in Boston during the 1920s. The Reisman orchestra was one of the finest in the "sweet band" category, playing without tricks or excess sentimentality. They first recorded for Columbia in 1921, and had an immediate hit with "Bright Eyes" (#A-3366). In the late 1920s the Reisman specialty had become Broadway and Hollywood show tunes. Fred and Adele Astaire were heard on 1931 Reisman recordings from *The Band Wagon,* and Noel Coward in a medley of his songs. Astaire returned to sing "Cheek to Cheek" in 1935 (Brunswick #7486). Among the men who played in the orchestra were Eddie Duchin (piano) and Adrian Rollini (saxophone). Smith Ballew, Frank Luther, Lee Wiley, Dick Robertson, Clifton Webb, and Anita Boyer were among the vocalists. Several of the early Victor long-playing records of the 1930s featured Reisman. In 1935 he left Victor for Brunswick, but did not carry his success with him; the swing bands were rising in public interest, and there was the general slump of the Depression to deal with. Reisman was back with Victor in the late 1930s, and became identified with the "society orchestra" group, those that played for gatherings of the wealthy.

In the mid-1940s Reisman moved to Decca, and was active until the early 1950s. He died 18 Dec 1961.

REMINGTON PHONOGRAPH CORP. An American firm established in Philadelphia in 1919. It moved to New York in 1920, setting up an office at 1666 Broadway, manufacturing phonographs and (by November 1920) disc records. Remington operated the Olympic Disc Record Corp., which was formed in March 1921, issuing **Olympic** label records. Philo E. Remington was president of Olympic. With the bankruptcy of Remington and Olympic in December 1921, some of the assets passed to the Fletcher Record Co., which revived the Olympic label for a time in December 1922. [Andrews*.]

REMOTE CONTROL. The earliest example of controlling an audio system from a distance was the 1931 HMV device that had a 12-foot cord. Sophisticated remote control without a cord had to wait for the 1950s, when such features became available for television. There were infrared LED remotes in the mid-1970s. Remotes for the videocassette player and the record player followed. Remotes in the early 1990s offered a full command of all audio and video functions, making it virtually unnecessary for the user ever to approach the sound source directly. [Klinger*.]

RENA MANUFACTURING CO., LTD. A British firm established 12 Nov 1908, at 27-29 Worship Street, London; **Louis Sterling** was general manager. Double-sided lateral-cut discs, from Columbia matrices, were sold in 10-inch and 12-inch sizes. In March 1909 the firm offered six models of its Rena record player; in July it also marketed Sonola machines. But in November of 1909 the company was out of business. Columbia took over the disc assets, and also the Rena offices and sales rooms. [Andrews 1986/11.]

RENAUD, MAURICE, 1861–1933. French bass-baritone, born in Bordeaux on 24 July 1861. He studied in Paris and Brussels, and sang at the Monnaie in Brussels from 1883 to 1890. Then he was with the Opéra-Comique in Paris, 1890–1891, and the Opéra in 1891–1902. He was a favorite at the Manhattan Opera from 1906 to 1909, then had a season in Chicago, and was at the Metropolitan Opera in 1910–1912. He was heard in about 60 operas. He died in Paris on 16 Oct 1933.

Renaud recorded nine titles for G & T in Paris in 1901, beginning with "Leonor viens" from *Favorite* (#32076). In the following year he appeared on the new red label series, with the Paris recordings reissued and five new items, notably "Evening Star" (#2-2704). He made another red label group of about 17 titles, in Paris in 1906; and a last set of 10 sides, on black label, in 1908. The black labels included "Voici des roses" from *Damnation de Faust* (#032041). Renaud was also on Pathé cylinders and discs, in 1903, beginning with the Toreador Song (master #3381). [De Cock 1957.]

REPROCESSED STEREO. Simulated stereophonic recordings made from monophonic masters; also known as electronically reprocessed stereo, electronic stereo, rechanneled stereo, simulated stereo, enhanced recordings, and enhanced stereo. *See also* SONIC RESTORATION.

REPRODUCER. The name given during the acoustic period to the pickup and its assembly; also known as the **soundbox.** Weight varied, always with the intent of achieving the lightest pickup that would track the grooves properly; in the Victor Orthophonic the reproducer weighed 142 grams (about five ounces).

REPRODUCING PIANO ROLLS. The reproducing piano differed from the music box and the player piano or **Pianola**, being designed to play back the notes, rhythm, dynamics, and tonal characteristics captured in a pianist's performance. The pianist performed on a special reproducing piano which marked a master roll to be punched later and replicated for distribution. In comparison to a standard player piano, the reproducing piano had additional pneumatics, activated by "expression holes" in the rolls.

The three famous major brands of reproducing pianos were Welte-Mignon (named after Edwin Welte) appearing about

1904, **Duo-Art** appearing about 1913, and **Ampico** (short for American Piano Company) appearing about 1916, the most sophisticated and accurate system of its time. The rolls for one system were not compatible with the others, and Welte-Mignon produced three types of rolls which were not even compatible with each other. Smaller, less widely known brands included Duca, Hupfeld, Artecho (also known as Celco or Apollo), Artrio-Angelus, Recordo, Pleyela, Empeco, and Stella. After a successful quarter century, the reproducing piano firms were nearly all out of business by 1930.

Reproduction mechanisms were pneumatic systems manufactured in two basic configurations: units built inside of the piano (mostly grands but sometimes in uprights) and units used outside the piano. The external system, called a Vorsetzer (German for "one who sits in front of") was a cabinet containing padded mechanical fingers for depressing each key.

Relatively few reproducing pianos were manufactured and very few survive in good condition. Since a reproducing piano needs to be finely tuned and painstakingly adjusted to provide a reasonable illusion of a live performance, an inadequately maintained instrument, containing many moving parts and intricate pneumatic tubing, could easily give a poor impression of what had been a nuanced performance.

Generally, virtuoso showpieces reproduced better than slow lyrical works in which any lack of subtle voicing and nuance became obvious, although mechanisms could not always adequately reproduce quick repeated notes. Like modern recordings mastered on magnetic tape, rolls could be edited to correct wrong notes, uneven passage work, and other technical shortcomings on the part of a pianist. Furthermore, the tempo of a performance could be accelerated (or retarded) without alteration of pitch; therefore original performance tempos are suspect. Dynamics could also be unreliable. (Several Josef Hofmann rolls were advertised to have been directed and approved by the artist, who had notated the score to guide the dynamic-range manipulation of the engineers.)

Reproducing pianos utilizing recent scientific developments have been made in limited quantities in recent years. In the 1970s, an invention called the Pianorecorder used computer digital technology to provide the means to transfer piano rolls onto magnetic tape cassettes. In the 1980s, a computer driven record/playback system producing extremely realistic results was available installed in Bösendorfer pianos.

The number of pianists and choice of repertoire was much greater for reproducing rolls than for acoustic discs. Many of the same pianists who made acoustic and electric recordings also made reproducing rolls, such as: Eugène d'Albert (1864–1932), Conrad Ansorge (1862–1930), **Wilhelm Backhaus,** Hans Barth (1897–1956), Harold Bauer (1873–1951), Alexander Brailovsky (1896–1976), Conrad van Bos (1875–1955), Una Bourne (1882–1974), Robert Casadesus (1899–19720, Cécile Chaminade (1857–1944), Harriet Cohen (1895–1967), **Alfred Cortot,** Fanny Davies (1861–1934), **Vladimir de Pachmann,** Louis Diémer (1843–1919), **Edwin Fischer,** Frank La Forge (1879–1953), Arthur Friedheim (1859–1932), **Ignaz Friedman,** Ossip Gabrilowitsch (1878–1936), Rudolph Ganz (1877–1972), **Walter Gieseking, Leopold Godowsky, Percy Grainger,** Arthur de Greef (1862–1940), Alfred Grünfeld (1852–1924), Mark Hambourg (1879–1960), **Myra Hess, Ferdinand Himmelreich, Josef Hofmann, Vladimir Horowitz,** José Iturbi, Raoul von Koczalski (1884–1948), Alexander Lambert (1862–1929), Frederic Lamond (1868–1948), Ethel Leginska (1886–1970), Mischa Levitzki (1898–1941), **Josef Lhévinne,** Arthur Loesser (1894–1969), Marguerite Long (1874–1966), Robert Lortat (1885–1938), Guy Maier (1891–1956), Frank Marshall (1883–1959), Yolanda Merö (1887–1963), Benno Moiseiwitsch (1890–1963), Vianna da Motta (1868–1948), William Murdoch (1882–1942), Elly Ney (1882–1968), Guiomar Novães (1895–1979), **Ignace Paderewski,** Egon Petri (1881–1962), Isidor Philipp (1863–1958), Francis Planté (1839–1934), Leff Pouishnoff (1891–1959), Raoul Pugno (1852–1914), Edouard Risler (1873–1929), Maria Roger-Miclos (b. 1860?), **Moriz Rosenthal, Artur Rubinstein,** Beryl

Rubinstein (1898–1952), Harold Samuel (1879–1937), Vasili Sapelnikoff (1868–1941), Emil von Sauer (1862–1942), Irene Scharrer (1888–1971), Xaver Scharwenka (1850–1924), Julius Schendel, E. Robert Schmitz (1889–1949), **Artur Schnabel, Rudolf Serkin,** Charles Gilbert Spross (1874–1961), Bernhard Stavenhagen (1862–1914), Sigismund Stojowski (1869–1946), Karol Szreter (1898–1933), Paul Wittgenstein (1887–1961), and Michael Zadora (1882–1946).

Notable popular music and ragtime pianists who made rolls included Felix Arndt (1889–1918), **Eubie Blake, Zez Confrey, Scott Joplin, and James P. Johnson.**

Significant pianists who are not known to have made cylinders or discs but left rolls as documents were Fanny Bloomfield-Zeisler (1863–1927), Teresa Carreño (1853–1917), Anna Essipoff (1851–1914), Theodor Leschetizky (1830–1915, best known as a teacher), Sophie Menter (1846–1918, who studied with Liszt and Tausig), Willy Rehberg (1863–1937), Alfred Reisenauer (1863–1907, a Liszt student), Alexander Siloti (1863–1945, disc test pressing rumored to exist), and Constantin Sternberg (1852–1924).

Recording-roll documents were made by numerous composers, listed here by nationality (some also made discs).

(1) *American composers.* Victor Herbert (1859–1924), Carrie Jacobs-Bond (1862–1946), Rudolf Friml (1879–1972), Charles Wakefield Cadman (1881–1946), Nathaniel Dett (1882–1943), John Powell (1882–1963), Charles Tomlinson Griffes (1884–1920), Ernst Toch (1887–1964), Ferde Grofé (1892–1972), George Gershwin (1898–1937), Aaron Copland (1900–1990), Morton Gould (1913–).

(2) *Austrian composers.* Oscar Straus (1870–1954), Erich Wolfgang Korngold (1897–1957).

(3) *British composers.* John Ireland (1879–1962), Cyril Scott (1879–1970).

(4) *French composers.* Camille Saint-Saëns (1835–1921), Gabriel Fauré (1845–1924), Vincent D'Indy (1851–1931), Cécile Chaminade (1857–1944), Claude Debussy (1862–1918), Gabriel Pierne (1863–1937), Albert Roussel (1869–1937), Florent Schmitt (1870–1958), Reynaldo Hahn (1874–1947), Maurice Ravel (1875–1937), Arthur Honegger (1892–1955), Darius Milhaud (1892–1974).

(5) *German composers.* Carl Reinecke (1824–1910, the earliest born significant composer to make any type of recording, although not known to have made cylinders or discs), Max Bruch (1838–1920), Engelbert Humperdinck (1854–1921), Gustav Mahler (1860–1911), Richard Strauss (1864–1949), Ferruccio Busoni (1866–1924), Max Schillings (1868–1933), Hans Pfitzner (1869–1949), Max Reger (1873–1916).

(6) *Hungarian composers.* Ernö von Dohnányi (1877–1960), **Béla Bartók.**

(7) *Italian composers.* Ruggero Leoncavallo (1857–1919), Pietro Mascagni (1863–1945), Alfredo Casella (1883–1947).

(8) *Russian composers.* Sergei Liapunov (1859–1924), Alexander Glazunov (1865–1936), Alexander Scriabin (1872–1915), **Sergei Rachmaninoff,** Nicolai Medtner (1880–1951), Igor Stravinsky (1882–1971), Serge Prokofiev (1891–1953).

(9) *Spanish composers.* Enrique Granados (1867–1916), Manuel de Falla (1876–1946).

Other significant composers on reproducing rolls include Ernesto Lecuona (Cuban, 1896–1963), Ludvig Schytte (Danish, 1848–1909), Manuel Ponce (Mexican, 1882–1948), Alexandre Tansman (Polish, 1897–1986), Georges Enesco (Romanian, 1881–1955), and Wilhelm Stenhammer (Swedish, 1871–1927).

Most composers recorded primarily their own works, both original piano compositions and transcriptions of orchestral and vocal works. The composer's rendition, even if reduced to a piano version, provides valuable clues to performance practice.

Compositions were written expressly for player pianos (not meant to be interpreted or even playable by a human) by composers such as Paul Hindemith (1895–1963), Nikolai Lopatnikoff (1903–1976), Stravinsky, and Ernst Toch. Recently there have been numerous works by Conlon Nancarrow (1912–).

Conductors who made reproducing rolls (of less significance since they also made orchestral discs) included **Arthur Nikisch,** Walter Damrosch (1862–1950), **Felix Weingartner,** Leo Blech (1871–1958), Ernest Schelling (1876–1939), Désiré Inghelbrecht (1880–1965), Eugene Goossens (1893–1962), Werner Janssen (1899–1990), and pianist-conductor Carlo Zecchi (1903–).

Reproducing rolls were not exclusively solo performances, since some famous pianists performed duets. Examples listed in catalogs include Casella and Respighi playing a transcription of *Fountains of Rome*, and Bauer and Gabrilowitsch playing the Arensky Waltz from the Suite op. 15 (also recorded as an electric disc, Victor #8162).

Numerous rolls can be heard and studied from transfers onto commercial recordings. Although a few 78 rpm transfers were issued by American Decca, the first large sampling was a five-LP anthology (Welte-Mignon material recorded under adverse conditions just after World War II) by Columbia (#ML4291–ML4295). Several record labels devoted almost exclusively to such transfers were Distinguished, Welte Treasury, and Klavier. Major classical labels that issued important roll releases included Argo, Oiseau-Lyre, Telefunken, and Everest. Quality of the roll-to-disc transfers varied considerably, depending primarily on the variations among instruments and piano technicians.

Comparisons can be made of some pianists who recorded the same work on disc and roll, an example being Josef Lhévinne's magnificent performances of the Schulz-Evler paraphrase of Strauss's *Blue Danube* waltz. The electric disc (Victor #6840) compares very favorably to the Ampico roll (issued on Argo #DA 41) although it is a slightly different and longer version. Reproducing rolls and their recorded transfers, so readily available to students and scholars, should not be forgotten or summarily dismissed; they offer important information to be weighed in the study of historic performance practice. [Farmer 1967; Sitsky 1990.]

Steven Permut

RESONA (label). An American record of the early 1920s, pressed by the Bridgeport Die and Machine Co. from Paramount masters, then (1923) from Federal masters. The Charles Williams Stores are named on the later labels. After spring 1924 Emerson and Plaza supplied the masters, all of which were popular dance and vocal numbers. There were no issues after 1925. [Rust 1978.]

RESONANCE. (I) A vibration in a sound system that results from a relatively small periodic stimulus having the same or similar period as the natural vibration period of the system.

RESONANCE. (II) The intensification of a musical signal by supplementary vibration of the same frequency.

Restoration. *See* SONIC RESTORATION OF HISTORIC RECORDINGS.

RETHBERG, ELISABETH, 1894–1976. German soprano, born on 22 Sep 1894 in Schwarzenberg. A lyric and dramatic singer, she could also sing coloratura parts. She had been a piano prodigy, but decided to study voice. Fritz Reiner heard her in 1915 and arranged for a Dresden Opera audition; it resulted in her debut there on 22 June 1915 in *Zigeunerbaron*; she remained in Dresden to 1922, singing also in Berlin and Vienna. On 22 Nov 1922 she made her Metropolitan Opera debut as Aida, with Giovanni Martinelli, and remained with the company to 1942. Aida is considered to have been her finest role; she often sang it opposite Martinelli. Her repertoire encompassed Verdi, Mozart, Wagner, Puccini, and Weber. Rethberg was also a fine performer of the art song, with about 1,000 of them in her repertoire. Arturo Toscanini named her the "greatest living soprano" when she appeared under his direction at La Scala in 1929, and Willem Mengelberg said she had the most beautiful voice in the world. Though her prime was in the 1920s, she continued into the 1940s with no loss of strength. Her final public appearance was in Town Hall, New York, doing a Lieder recital, on 20 Apr 1944. She died in Yorktown Heights, New York, on 6 June 1976.

Rethberg's first recording was for Odeon in 1920, singing "Pastorale" by Bizet (#76215); she made 14 other Odeons, including five duets with Richard Tauber. In 1924–1925 she worked for Brunswick in Chicago, then she recorded for HMV and Odeon in Berlin. She became a Victor artist in 1929, beginning with six numbers from *Aida*, and principal airs from *Ballo in maschera, Meistersinger, Faust, Otello, Don*

Giovanni, Attila, and *Lombardi.* Her final recordings were Mozart duets with Ezio Pinza, with whom she toured extensively in America, Europe, and Australia. She also made four sides for the Hugo Wolf Society ca. 1932 (issued 1935). Golden Age of Opera recorded her in complete operas from the stage of the Metropolitan: *Lohengrin* (EJS #135; 1940 performance), *Nozze di Figaro* (EJS #118; 1940), *Otello* (EJS #181, 1938; #106, 1940), and *Simon Boccanegra* (EJS #177, 1935; #108; 1939). There were numerous LP reissues of her 78s, by RCA Victor, Top Artists Platters, and others. [Richards, J. 1948/2; Richards, J. 1950.]

REVELERS. A male vocal quartet/quintet with piano, an outgrowth of the Shannon Four (established 1917), active from 1925 to ca. 1940. Original members were Franklyn Baur, first tenor; Lewis James, second tenor; Elliott Shaw, baritone; Wilfred Glenn, bass (also the organizer and manager); and Frank Banta, Jr., piano. Carson Robison sometimes whistled and played the guitar. Other artists in the Revelers at one time or another included James Melton, Charles Harrison, Sam Ash, Billy Jones, Frank Parker, and Robert Simmons (tenors); Phil Duey (baritone); Ed Smalle (tenor, pianist, arranger) and Frank Black (pianist). In response to changing musical tastes in America, the Revelers essayed a new quartet style, informal and swinging. They were highly popular on the radio in the U.S. and a great success on a European tour of 1926, particularly in London where a Command Performance was the highlight. They toured Europe annually into the 1930s.

The group was heard on many record labels, most prominently on Victor, where they began with "Just a Bundle of Sunshine" / "Every Sunday Afternoon" (#19731; 1925). In their next Victor session, there were five vocalists, as Smalle sang while playing the piano; "Dinah"—one of their great hits—and "I'm Gonna Charleston Back to Charleston" were recorded (#19778 and #19796; 1925). Other favorite records were "Birth of the Blues" (Victor #20111; 1926) and "Nola" with James Melton as first tenor (Victor #21100; 1927). They recorded extensively for Victor until 1934, finishing with "The Last Round-Up." The Revelers had a plethora of pseudonyms, including Acme Quartet, Aeolian Quartet, Cathedral Quartet, Gounod Quartet, Lyric Male Quartet, and Vocalion Quartet. On Columbia the group was named Singing Sophomores; on Brunswick they were the Merrymakers. In addition they were the main voices in a number of choruses, such as the Victor Mixed Chorus and Trinity Choir. The group did not disband until 1954, when Glenn retired. [Riggs 1970.]

REVERBERATION. Multiple reflections of sound waves within a closed space, resulting in echo effects that may be heard along with the original signals. The time taken up between the introduction of a sound wave to the closed space and the return of the reverberation to the point of introduction is the reverberation time. A room, or recording studio, is said to be "live" if it has a comparatively long reverberation time; "dead" if the reverberation time is comparatively slow. Reverberation can be created artificially with electromechanical devices or electronic circuits. *See also* RESONANCE; ROOM ACOUSTICS.

Reverse equalization. *See* EQUALIZATION.

Reviews. *See* CRITICISM.

Re-voicing. *See* DUBBING.

REX (label). (I) A cylinder record sold in Britain by the Lambert Co., Ltd., after May 1904. [Andrews*.]

REX (label). (II) A 10-inch disc sold in Britain ca. 1906 to 1914, pressed from matrices owned by the Disc Record Co., Ltd. [Andrews*.]

REX (Label). (III) Possibly the label of the New Rex Record Co., of London, which advertised in *TMW* from January 1907 to September 1907, stating that its records had preferential tariffs in the British colonies (probably directed to Canadian dealers). [Andrews*.]

REX (label). (IV) An American vertical-cut disc record of 1914, based in Philadelphia. It was issued by the new Rex Talking Machine Co., which succeeded the liquidated **Keen-O-Phone**

Co. Fred Hager, from Keen-O-Phone, and Charles L. Hibbard were in charge of recording. Apparently this was the first American firm to offer customers a record player under an agreement to purchase discs at given intervals.

Most of the material was dance music and popular songs, with light classics; but there was some good piano ragtime as well. Ferruccio Giannini and Ellen Beach Yaw were also heard on Rex.

A report of September 1916 stated that 1,200 titles were available, in 10-inch size for $.75 and 12-inch size for $1.25, all vertical cut, to be played with a jewel stylus. Then the company went into liquidation, in October 1916, and was acquired by the Imperial Talking Machine Co. in May 1917. [Andrews*; Blacker 1975/1; Rust 1978.]

REX (label). (V) A British disc record, registered to the Vocalion Gramophone Co., Ltd., then owned by the Crystalate Record Manufacturing Co., Ltd., when it acquired the Vocalion business. The first releases appeared in September 1933. In 1935 the record was priced at 1 shilling. "I'm Popeye the Sailor Man" was one of the 1935 discs (#8536). From April 1937 Rex records were issued by new owners, the Decca Record Co., Ltd., which had acquired the record side of Crystalate's business. American Brunswick and Vocalion matrices became available to the Rex label through the American Record Corp. Under Crystalate, Rex had access to Regal (of U.S.) matrices, as Crystalate owned Regal Record Co., Inc., then a part of the American Record Corp. The final Rex issues were in March 1948. [Andrews*; Hayes, J. 1974.]

REYNALDS, W.H. (The name is also seen spelled Reynolds.) American record company owner. His Reynalds Music Co. was located in Mobile, Alabama. Reynalds was active in the National Association of Talking Machine Jobbers, serving as treasurer for most of the time between 1913 and 1920.

RHYTHM AND BLUES RECORDINGS. The term rhythm & blues (r & b) emerged as the most acceptable designation for the music that had developed out of pre-World War II blues styles, for the most distinctive new element in this genre was the addition of a dance beat. The expression first appeared in formal usage in the late 1940s as the name of RCA's division that served the Black audience; other alternatives at the time included "ebony" (MGM) and "sepia" (Decca and Capitol). Prior to the rise of rock 'n' roll, r & b had already evolved into a wide variety of subgenres, including:

(1) The self-confident, assertive dancehall blues which, in turn, encompassed (a) big band blues (for example, Lucky Millinder, Tiny Bradshaw); (b) shout, scream, and cry blues (for example, Wynonie Harris, Joe Turner, Big Maybelle, Ruth Brown, LaVern Baker, Roy Brown); and (c) combo blues or jump blues. Combo blues had a number of regional strains in addition to the cosmopolitan style exemplified by Louis Jordan: West Coast (for example, Roy Milton, Amos Milbern, T-Bone Walker), Mississippi Delta (for example, Ike Turner's Kings of Rhythm), New Orleans (for example, **Fats Domino**, Professor Longhair) and Eastern Seaboard (for example, Chuck Willis, Wilbert Harrison).

(2) The quieter, more despondent club blues (for example, Charles Brown, Cecil Gant, Ivory Joe Hunter).

(3) The country-tinged bar blues (usually centered in either the Mississippi Delta or Chicago). Chief exponents included **Muddy Waters, Howlin' Wolf,** Elmore James, and John Lee Hooker.

(4) Vocal group singing, which was subdivided into (a) the cool style (for example, The Orioles, The Cardinals, The Spaniels); (b) the dramatic style (for example, The Moonglows, The Flamingos, The Platters); (c) the romantics (for example, The Harptones); (d) the cool style with a strong blues emphasis (for example, The Clovers, The Drifters); and (e) the sing-along novelty approach geared to mainstream pop acceptance (for example, The Crows, The Penguins, Frankie Lymon & The Teenagers).

(5) Gospel-based styles, which possessed three major strains: (a) spiritual singing, with the focus upon the quality of the voice (for example, **Mahalia Jackson**); (b) gospel singing, with its concentration on the interplay between

voices, which were often deliberately coarsened to stress the emotional conviction of the singers (for example, Rosetta Tharpe, the Dixie Hummingbirds); and (c) preacher singing, with its tendency to speak the message in an urgent near-shout which often revealed the phrasing and timing of singing minus the melodic dimension.

It soon became evident, musically speaking, that "rhythm & blues" was a less than satisfactory name for at least two of the most important stylistic innovations of the 1950s, the various vocal group styles and the gospel-based styles, which were to become increasingly popular as rock 'n' roll began to siphon off the unique spirit of previous r & b forms. For instance, the new vocal groups invariably based their approach on the style of two black ballad-singing aggregates who had proven to be successful with the easy listening audience, the **Mills Brothers** and the **Ink Spots**. Both groups sang in the close harmony "barbershop" style, accompanied by a light rhythm section. They were similar in the ease with which they timed their harmonies, and the purity of their voices.

Of course, these characteristics were a far cry from those comprising the classic r & b style. Therefore, the term "rhythm & blues" became most useful as a market designation; i.e., an indication that the performer was Black, recording for the Black audience. As noted by Gillett, there was ample justification—at least until 1956—for classifying the Black market separately. The Black audience was interested almost exclusively in Black performers; only five recordings by white acts reached the r & b top ten between 1950 and 1955, and three of those were rock 'n' roll records (Bill Haley's "Dim the Lights" and "Rock Around the Clock," and Boyd Bennett's "Seventeen"). Few white singers had either the interest of the cultural experience necessary to appeal to the Black audience's taste—until rock 'n' roll changed the equation, resulting in a new type of white performer.

Lacking the financial resources and industry connections of white pop acts, r & b artists displayed impressive persistence and creativity. The Harptones' doo-wop rendition of "The Shrine of St. Cecilia" (Rama #221; 1956) represents a case in point. Taking a well-known tune, the group overcame the shortage of studio resources by intoning the "tick-tocks" of a clock and "ding-dongs" of bells; the sincerity of the delivery managed to make dated lyrics sound relevant and meaningful.

Motown Records played the pivotal role in the development of r & b into a mainstream genre. The product of the vision of one man, owner and founder Berry Gordy, the label sculpted a mainstream pop sound out of gospel and blues roots which reflected the vision of upward mobility and wholesome fun held by young Blacks in the 1960s. Motown's stars were groomed to offend no one; the songs they sang were had romantic lyrics that could appeal to practically anyone; and the music itself was rarely demanding, or even aggressive in the tradition of Southern soul. The closest thing to an overt political statement released by Motown in the mid-1960s was Stevie Wonder's "Blowing' In the Wind" (Tamla #54136; 1966).

Although the assembly-line approach employed by Motown led to criticism for monotony, the label released a remarkably diverse array of recordings, varying in sound, arrangement and feel. This diversity—reinforced by Motown's mainstream commercial success—proved to be the launching pad for many of the Black music styles that evolved after the mid-sixties. Virtually all Black musicians were influenced by the Motown Sound.

A host of regional independent labels producing soul music in the 1960s sought to control production values and nurture available talent with an eye to the long-term payoff, including Vee-Jay and Chess/Checker (Chicago), Stax/Volt/Enterprise, Goldwax and Hi (Memphis), Philadelphia International, Philly Groove and Avco (Philadelphia) and Fame (Muscle Shoals, Alabama). Funk, disco and the dance-oriented styles of the eighties such as go-go music also owed much to Motown.

The rich diversification of styles and comparatively rapid rate of change characteristic of Black popular music in the post-World War II era stands in bold contrast to the chief white-dominated genre indigenous to the United States, country music. Gillett offers the following rationale for this situation:

> This is partly because several white southern styles have never been widely popular with the national American audience, so that singers did not continually have to invent styles that would be special to their local audiences—those invented thirty or forty years ago were still special to a local area, or to the white south. In contrast, almost every black southern style has proved to have universal qualities that attract national and international audiences, and this situation has placed continual pressure on singers to come up with new styles that are not already widely known and that the local audience can feel to be its own. And invariably, musicians and singers have responded positively to such pressure.

This predisposition for change has proven to be at once a strength and a weakness. It has enabled Black contemporary to remain a dynamic genre, ever responsive to the needs and interests of its core audience. However, it has also discouraged participation on the part of the uninitiated. who are confused by the rapid succession of fads and fashions.

The following chronology identifies the key events in the history of r & b:

1946. *Billboard* begins charting the sale of records in the "Negro" market, employing the heading, "Harlem Hit Parade." The weekly listing is eventually renamed "Race Records."

1948. **Atlantic** Records is formed. The label has shown a flair for assessing performing styles and audience tastes that has been unmatched in the post-World War II era of popular music. Beginning with a roster of performers randomly collected from individuals without contracts, Atlantic acquired a succession of singers from various sources and with various styles. By the mid-fifties the company's artists included Joe Turner, Ruth Brown, LaVern Baker, Clyde McPhatter, Ray Charles, Ivory Joe Hunter, Chuck Willis, The Cardinals, The Clovers, The Drifters, The Coasters, and Bobby Darin. With these performers Atlantic's share of the r & b market grew from three Top Ten records in 1950 to 17 (out of 81) in 1956. Though no longer independent, Atlantic continues to thrive as part of the WCI family.

17 June 1949. *Billboard*, without any editorial comment, begins employing the term "rhythm & blues" in reference to the Black charts.

6 Mar 1959. "There Goes My Baby" is recorded by The Drifters (Atlantic #2025). It was one of the first rhythm & blues discs to use strings. Its combined artistic and commercial success inspired an upsurge in the development of sophisticated recording techniques for Black music, culminating in the "Golden Age of Soul" (1964–1968).

12 Mar 1960. *Cash Box* combines its pop and r & b charts. In an editorial appearing on the front page of that issue, the magazine justifies this decision by noting the similarity between the pop and r & b charts; that is, the r & b listing was at that time almost 90 percent pop in nature. *Cash Box* evidently had second thoughts about this policy, and reinstated the separate r & b compilation on 17 Dec 1960 ("Top 50 in Locations"). *Billboard* used the same reasoning in deleting its r & b singles charts between 23 Nov 1963 and 30 Jan 1965. *Billboard* ultimately returned to the two-chart system.

16 Feb 1961. The Miracles' "Shop Around" (Tamla #54034) reaches number one, remaining three weeks. The song was the first major hit for Motown.

26 Aug 1961. The Mar-Keys' "Last Night" becomes the first Stax production to reach number one. Stax—and later in the decade, the Muscle Shoals, Alabama, studio headed by Rick Hall—offered a rawer, more spontaneous, gospel-influenced alternative to the Motown sound. The Mar-Keys (whose rhythm section also recorded as Booker T. & the M.G.'s) backed most of the label's artists, including Sam and Dave, **Otis Redding**, Eddie Floyd, Rufus Thomas, Carla Thomas, and Johnnie Taylor.

26 May 1962. **Ray Charles'** country-influenced "I Can't Stop Loving You" (ABC #10330) begins the first of its 11 consecutive weeks at the top of the r & b charts. The song typified—in dramatic fashion due to its incredible

commercial success—the inclination of talented Black performers to favor sweet and sentimental sounds over personal expression in order to achieve mainstream pop impact. Similar career moves were taken by Sam Cooke, Jackie Wilson, Brook Benton, and others. Yet Black singers such as Wilson Pickett and **Aretha Franklin** were able to attain pop music success in the late 1960s while remaining true to their cultural roots.

12 Oct 1963. "Cry Baby," by Garnett Mimms & The Enchanters (United Artists #629) begins the first of two weeks at number one. "Cry Baby" was among the earliest—and certainly the most successful commercially—of the gospel-styled songs to have an accompaniment that was not slightly adapted from some other genre of music. Unlike most records, with their slow, gentle, lilting, "Cry Baby" offered an uncompromising expression of ecstasy. On other "gospel revivalist" records, the strong rhythms meant that the impact was absorbed physically by the listener and not on a purely emotional level as was the case with "Cry Baby." In short, the song possessed all the prime ingredients characterizing the classic soul genre.

11 Mar 1967. Dyke & The Blazers' "Funky Broadway" (Original Sound #64) enters the r & b charts, remaining there 27 weeks, peaking at number 11. The word "funk" didn't become part of the legitimate radio jargon until the song had "bubbled under" for so long that disc jockeys were forced to play it and say the word. Though nobody knows who coined the term, "funk" simply was not a word used in polite society. But "Funky Broadway" changed all that.

11 Mar 1967. Aretha Franklin's "I Never Loved a Man" (Atlantic #2386) reaches number one, remaining there for seven weeks. In a kind of soul-waltz time, the record built up from a quiet but dramatic opening organ figure into a hammering, screaming, but always firmly controlled yell of delight, as a brilliantly organized band fed more and more to support the singer's emotion. It was the first of Franklin's 18 number one songs on the r & b charts, more than any other artist between 1960 and 1985. Noteworthy commercial success

combined with impeccable artistry earned her the sobriquet, "Queen of Soul."

10 Feb 1968. Sly & The Family Stone's first hit, "Dance to the Music" (Epic #10256) enters the r & b charts, eventually peaking at number three. The song shook off the assumptions about the separate roles of voices and instruments as sources of rhythm and harmony, alternating them and blending them yet never losing either melody or dance beat. The adventurousness of the sound was recognized by the white audience who had tended to deride soul arrangements as being overly simple. As Sly began employing increasingly personal lyrics, the social consciousness school of funk was created.

12 Oct 1968. "Say It Loud, I'm Black and I'm Proud" (King #12715) by "Soul Brother Number One," **James Brown**, tops the charts. "Say It Loud" was merely the most successful of the wave of political slogan songs exploiting Black pride.

23 Aug 1969. *Billboard* declares rhythm & blues officially dead by renaming its list of best-selling records for that market "Best-Selling Soul Singles." Ironically, there was every sign that the new euphemism for "black"—which had been widely used during most of the sixties—would soon be musically outdated, and its successor defied prophesy.

9 June 1973. Manu Dibango's "Soul Makossa" (Atlantic #2971) enters the r & b charts, eventually reaching the Top 20. Recorded by an African in Paris, "Soul Makossa" was imported into the U.S. when its enormous popularity in discos made domestic release seem like a good business proposition. Thus, the first disco pop hit was born.

29 July 1978. "Soft and Wet," the first hit by **Prince**, (Warner #8619), enters the charts, eventually reaching number nine. Prince's combination of street-level hipness and musical inventiveness propelled him to the vanguard of Black music in the 1980s. His seemingly boundless energy spawned a new school of stars, including The Time, Vanity, Andre Cymone, and Sheila E.

10 Apr 1982. *Cash Box* first employs the term "Black Contemporary" in the heading of its Black charts (that is, "Top 100 Black

Contemporary Singles"). The term has gained nearly universal acceptance both inside and outside the music industry. Black Contemporary encompasses the full range of Black pop music (dance music, easy listening, jazz fusions, and so forth) as well as white releases that are expected to appeal to the Black audience.

[Gillett 1970; Hirshey 1984; Hoffmann 1986; Rolling 1980.] *See also* BLUES RECORDINGS; RACE RECORDS; SOUL MUSIC.

Frank Hoffmann

RIALTO (label). (I) An American record produced by the U.S. Record Manufacturing Corp. of Long Island City, New York, in 1921. It shared material with another record by the same firm, Hits. There was no connection with the later label of the same name. Only a few issues are known. [Kendziora 1962/11; Rust 1978.]

RIALTO (label). (II) A Chicago record sold by the Rialto Music House, a store at 330 S. State St., in 1924. Possibly the label and the store were named for the Rialto vaudeville-burlesque theater across the street. The records were made by Orlando Marsh, but whether the process was electric (like other Marsh issues of the time) or acoustic is not known. Rust has found only one specimen: "London Blues" played by Jelly Roll Morton, with a song by Frank Collins on the flip side; it has no number.

The music store remained in business at the same address through at least 1929–1930. In the Chicago directory of that year it had two other locations as well: 168 N. State St., and 409 E. 47th St. [Rust 1978.]

RICE, GLADYS, ca. 1896–?. American popular singer, born in Philadelphia. She sometimes used the names Rachel Grant and Bettina Bergere. Rice began to record for Edison in 1916, in a duet with Irving Kaufman, "My Hula Maid" (Edison Diamond Disc #50297; Blue Amberol cylinder #2759). Duets with various artists were a specialty; Billy Murray was her main partner after 1917. Her last Edison disc—of 59 in all—was a duet with Murray made in late summer 1929, a month before Edison ceased

all recording activity ("That's You Baby"; #52642). She was also a member of the Homestead Trio from 1917 to 1921, and of the Moonlight Trio. Rice sang popular and comic songs for most of the labels into the early 1930s. [Wile 1976.]

RICH-TONE (label). An American record sold in 1921 and 1922 by the Phonograph Record Exchange of America, Chicago. About 50 releases are known, sold for $.85 (more costly by $.10 than the discs of major firms at the time). Material was from Gennett masters, with artists using pseudonyms. [Kendziora 1988/6; Rust 1978.]

RIGLER AND DEUTSCH INDEX. A compilation of information about 78 rpm recordings, the result of a project undertaken by the Associated Audio Archives, of the **Association for Recorded Sound Collections, Inc. (ARSC).** Planning for the project began in 1974, and work began in 1981 with support from the National Endowment for the Humanities, the Hewlett Foundation, and the Ledler Foundation. By 1984 a set of microfilm photographs and indexes were made available for purchase. Free consultation of the index is possible at the five participating libraries: Library of Congress, Rodgers and Hammerstein Archives of Recorded Sound at the New York Public Library, Belfer Audio Laboratory and Archive of Syracuse University, the Archive of Recorded Sound of Stanford University, and the Yale Collection of Historical Sound Recordings of Yale University.

The Rigler and Deutsch Index consists of 1,230,000 microfilm photographs, on 946 reels, of the labels of 615,000 78 rpm records belonging to the member libraries. The index is computer accessible by title, composer, performer, label, record number, matrix number, and library.

RIMINI, GIACOMO, 1888–1952. Italian baritone, born 22 Mar 1888 in Verona. He sang in various Italian houses, then in Rome as Scarpia and Germont in 1915. He won acclaim for his lively Falstaff, under Arturo Toscanini in Milan; and Falstaff became his signature role, sung throughout Europe and the U.S., as well as South America.

Rimini made four Pathé discs in 1917, beginning with "Invocazione" from *Faust* / "Brindisi" from *Otello* (#60052). He worked for Vocalion in 1918–1924, then for Brunswick to 1935. Columbia recorded him in a complete *Falstaff* album in 1932 (#10564/576, also released on LP in 1955).

RISHELL PHONOGRAPH CO. A firm established in 1867 as the Rishell Furniture Co., in Williamsport, Pennsylvania. In 1916 it offered the Rishell line of record players in eight models, all in the upper price range. At about the same time the firm produced records with the Rishell label, using material from Okeh and Imperial-Rex-Empire-Playerphone. As late as April 1924 Rishell was offering talking machines for sale. [Andrews*; Rust 1978.]

RITTER, TEX, 1907–1974. American country singer, born in Panola County, Texas, on 12 Jan 1907. He grew up as a cowboy, then studied law at the University of Texas, and later at Northwestern University near Chicago; but also sang and lectured on the cowboy traditions. He gained popularity in the 1930s in New York, as a stage actor and radio performer, then went to Hollywood to make many western films in the 1940s and 1950s. He was elected to the Country Music Hall of Fame in 1964. His death came on 2 Jan 1974.

After recording for Columbia (one disc in 1931) and Decca (11 issues in 1937–1939), Ritter became a Capitol artist, recording extensively from 1942 until he died. Among his chart singles the most popular was "Hillbilly Heaven" (Capitol #4567; 1961). [Toborg 1970 and Toborg 1979 give a complete discography.]

RIVERSIDE (label). An American record, one of the principal jazz independents of the late 1940s and 1950s. Riverside was notable for its transfer to disc of Imperial piano rolls (1953) and its reissue of 78 rpm jazz material from Paramount, Black Swan, Broadway, Famous, and Puritan labels. All the Gennett discs and documents were acquired for reissue, and the lists from Champion, Supertone, and Circle labels.

ROBERTS, ROBERT, 1879–1930. American baritone and comedian, known as Bob Roberts or Ragtime Robert, born in Cincinnati. He was a popular recording artist in the early years of the century, beginning with Columbia in 1902 with a hit rendition of "Ain't Dat a Shame?" He was successful also with "Woodchuck Song" on both Victor and Edison (1904). For Edison he made about 60 cylinders from 1904 to 1908. Roberts' greatest hit was "He Walked Right In, Turned Around and Walked Right Out Again," made for Victor in 1906. "Ragtime Cowboy Joe" (#17090; 1912) was one of two items still in the Victor catalog in 1917. Roberts dropped out of sight thereafter. He died in Cincinnati on 21 Jan 1930. [Walsh 1944/4.]

ROBESON, PAUL, 1898–1976. American bass singer, born in Princeton, New Jersey, on 9 Apr 1898. He took a law degree from Columbia University in 1923, then turned to acting, on the New York and London stage. He gave a song recital, of spirituals, in New York in 1925, then toured Europe as a singer. His acting career did not cease; he played Othello in London in 1930, for example. But neither the vocal nor dramatic paths were fully developed, because his Marxist politics—openly expressed—led to resistance in America and Western Europe during a period of Communism-phobia. He died in Philadelphia on 23 Jan 1976.

Robeson recorded in 1920 for Black Swan, two sides as a member of the Four Harmony Kings (#2016). Then he became a Victor/HMV artist, making remarkable discs of traditional and spiritual melodies. "Water Boy" (Victor #19824), "Swing Low, Sweet Chariot" (Victor #20068), and "Sometimes I Feel Like a Motherless Child" (HMV #B8604) exemplify his art. His "Ol Man River" from *Show Boat* remains definitive; it was coupled on Victor #B8497 with a charming duet, "Ah Still Suits Me"—with Elizabeth Welch—from the same show, but often cut. His Stephen Foster songs are also exemplary, but he lacked the style for some of the pop/swing numbers he tried now and then. *Ballad for Americans* was a popular Victor album in 1940 (#P20), many times reissued. Columbia made a number of Robeson recordings too, notably his dramatic lead in *Othello* (complete set, album #SL 153) and the complete music to *Show Boat* (#C-55, reissue of Brunswick's 1932 cast recording). Robeson did not record grand opera material. The Pearl CD #GEMMCD 9356 (1989) offered songs from the 1920s and 1930s. [Davis, L. 1983]

ROBISON, CARSON J., 1890–1957. American country singer, guitarist, whistler, and composer; born 4 Aug 1890 in Chetopa, Kansas. He was singing professionally at age 15, and was an early radio performer (WDAF, Kansas City, 1922). He went to New York in 1924, and was signed by Victor. He specialized in duets, with Wendell Hall or Vernon Dalhart. "Song Birds of Georgia" was his first duet release, with Hall (Victor #19338; 1924). In 1926–1928 he also recorded Edison Diamond Discs, including four with Dalhart. Robison was a valuable studio musician for Victor, contributing his guitar accompaniments and whistling obbligatos to the songs of artists like Gene Austin, Frank Crumit, Aileen Stanley, and The Revelers. He backed up Dalhart on the great hit record of the "Prisoner's Song" and "Wreck of the Old '97" in 1924.

In 1928 Robison broke off his association with Dalhart and formed the Carson Robison Trio; his partners were Frank Luther (recording as Bud Billings) and Phil Crow. They made a number of best sellers, notably "When the Bloom is on the Sage" (Victor #V-40282; 1930). In 1932 and in 1939 he toured the U.K. as Carson Robison and His Pioneers, and recorded there for many labels. He also broadcast from Radio Luxembourg, as Carson Robison and his Oxydol Pioneers.

As a composer, Robison wrote more than 300 songs. Among them were specimens of the popular genre, disaster chronicles. During World War II he contributed topical songs. A later group of his was the Pleasant Valley Boys, recorded on MGM. His Old Timers recorded for Columbia. Robison died in Poughkeepsie, New York, on 24 Mar 1957. [Morritt 1979.]

ROBYN, WILLIAM, 1894– . Latvian/American tenor, born in 1894. He recorded more than 300 sides for Victor, Columbia, Cameo, and around 50 other labels between 1919 and 1931. His repertoire of popular and ethnic songs was in great demand on the "dime store labels." Robyn had more than 50 noms du disque. On stage and radio he appeared as Wee Willie Robyn, a member of *Roxy's Gang*—one of the most successful variety shows of the period. Later he became a cantor. Robyn was still alive in July 1991. [Brooks*.]

ROCK MUSIC RECORDINGS. "If one had to pick the recording session at which rock 'n' roll was born, it would be the date of April 12, 1954, at Pythia Temple on Manhattan's West Side at which **Bill Haley** and The Comets cut "Rock Around the Clock." (Shaw 1974). Yet rock 'n' roll songs existed before Haley's song topped the charts in 1955 (Decca #29124). Some historians have singled out The Crows, whose uptempo **rhythm and blues** (r & b) recording, "Gee" (Rama #5) scored heavily on the pop charts in early 1954. As early as 1951 Jackie Brenston had a number one hit with "Rocket 88" (Chess #1458), which featured a wild saxophone solo, a boogie-woogie beat carried by an overamplified electric guitar, and lyrics celebrating the automobile. Haley himself "covered" the song and by 1952 was recording full-fledged rock material like "Rock the Joint" (Essex #303). Still, the fact remains that these and other r & b prototypes appear in retrospect as oddities that were briefly popular and then disappeared. "Rock Around the Clock," in contrast to these hits, inspired a movement. (The fact that the song was featured in a popular movie was no small factor; *Blackboard Jungle* caused riots among youth worldwide and its title song inspired countless imitations.) But Haley was a temporary phenomenon; he accumulated only three top ten hits during his long career. Not until the rise of **Elvis Presley** to superstar status, beginning with television appearances in 1956, that the commercial preeminence of rock 'n' roll was assured.

The revolutionary nature of Presley's career cannot be fully appreciated without consideration of the countless disciples his success engendered. Artists like Jerry Lee Lewis, **Buddy Holly**, Eddie Cochran, **Rick Nelson, Conway Twitty,** Gene Vincent, Jack Scott, Roy Orbison, **Johnny Cash**, Bob Luman, Frankie Avalon,

Bobby Rydell, Fabian, and Bobby Darin affected the structure of the American record industry. A & R men who had dominated the first half of the 20th century gave way to freelance songwriters who were close to their audience both in age and outlook. Often the singers themselves wrote and produced their own songs. Despite the resistance of the older record labels (whose control of the industry had been broken by the independent companies recording rock), the American Society of Composers, Authors, and Publishers (whose music sales were being eroded by Broadcast Music Incorporated's virtual monopoly of country and western, r & b, and rock 'n' roll material), and various conservative groups, the rock genre emerged intact.

Rock styles and developments are listed below, with the persons associated with them.

1. Gestation Period (pre-1956)
   Clyde McPhatter and the Drifters; **Fats Domino; Hank Williams; Bill Haley** and His Comets
2. The Beat Era (1956–1958)
   Elvis Presley; **Chuck Berry;** Buddy Holly
   a. Doo-Wop (1954–1957)—Coasters; Penguins
   b. New-Doo-Wop (1958–1965)—Diamonds; Danny and the Juniors
3. Brill Building Era (1959–1965)
   a. Teen Idols / American Bandstand Phenomenon (1959–1963)—Frankie Avalon; Fabian; **Rick Nelson**
   b. Dance Crazes (1960–1965)—**Chubby Checker;** Joey Dee and the Starliters
   c. Instrumentals—Duane Eddy; Ventures
   d. Novelty Songs—Chipmunks; Ray Stevens
   e. Payola Scandal—**Dick Clark; Alan Freed**
   f. Commercial Folk (1958–1963)—**Kingston Trio; Peter, Paul and Mary**
      1. **Calypso (1957–1958)—Harry Belafonte**
      2. Hootenanny (1963)—Rooftop Singers
   g. Spector Sound (1958–1966)—Ronettes; Righteous Brothers; Crystals
   h. Girl Groups—Shirelles; Chiffons
4. The British Invasion (1964–)
   a. British Scene prior to 1964—Cliff Richard
   b. First Wave (1964–1965)—**Beatles;** Dave Clark Five; **Rolling Stones**
   c. Second Wave (1966–1970)—Bee Gees; **Cream**
   d. Third Wave (1971–1975)—**Elton John;** Thin Lizzy
   e. Commonwealth Contributions—Guess Who
5. American Renaissance (1965–1966)
   a. California Sound
      1) Surf Sound (1962–1964)—**Beach Boys;** Jan & Dean
      2) Car Songs—Rip Chords; Ronnie & The Daytonas
   b. Folk Rock (1965–1966)—Byrds; Turtles
      1) Protest—**Bob Dylan;** Phil Ochs
   c. **Soul Music (1964–75)**
      1) Chicago Sound (1958–)—Jerry Butler; Impressions
      2) Motown Sound (1960–)—**Supremes;** Temptations
      3) Memphis Sound (1961–)—Booker T & The M)G)'s; Sam & Dave
      4) Muscle Shoals Sound (1966–)—Percy Sledge; **Aretha Franklin**
      5) Philadelphia Sound (1968–)—The O'Jays; Stylistics
      6) Blue-Eyed Soul—Rascals; Hall & Oates
6. Era of Specialization
   a. Other Regional Styles
      1) New Orleans Sound (1954–)—Huey "Piano" Smith; Lee Dorsey
      2) Cajun Rock—Doug Kershaw
      3) Zydeco—Clifton Chenier
      4) Tex-Mex (1956–)—Richie Valens
      5) Detroit Sound (1966–)—Mitch Ryder & The Detroit Wheels
      6) San Francisco Sound (1966–)—**Jefferson Airplane;** Grateful Dead
      7) Bosstown Sound (1967–1969)—Beacon Street Union; Earth Opera
      8) Sounds of the South (1970–)—Allman Brothers Band; Lynyrd Skynyrd
      9) Ska / Rock Steady / Reggae (1964/1966/1970–)—Millie Small/Desmond Dekker/Bob Marley and The Wailers
      10) Salsa—Ray Barretto

11) Junkanoo—KC & The Sunshine Band
b. Hybrid Children of Rock
   1) Punk Rock (1966–1967)—Seeds; Standells
   2) Acid Rock/Psychedelia (1966–1968)—Doors; Iron Butterfly
   3) Symphonic Rock/Classical Rock (1967)—Moody Blues; Electric Light Orchestra
   4) Progressive Rock (1967–)—Pink Floyd; Traffic
   5) Latin Rock (1969–)—Santana
   6) Big Band Rock (1969–)—Chicago; Blood, Sweat & Tears
   7) Heavy Metal Rock (1969–)—Black Sabbath; Grand Funk Railroad
   8) Jazz-Rock (1970–)—Mahavishnu Orchestra; Weather Report
   9) Pub Rock (1971–1975)—Graham Parker & The Rumour
   10) Glitter Rock (1972–1975)—Alice Cooper; Suzi Quatro
   11) Afro-Rock (1972–)—Osibisa
   12) Euro-Pop/Euro-Rock (1973–)—Abba/Focus; Golden Earring
   13) Christian Rock—Stryper; Amy Grant
   14) Bubblegum (1967–)—Tommy James & The Shondells; Archies
   15) Album-Oriented Rock (1967–)—Led Zeppelin; Aerosmith
7. Nostalgia (1963–)
   a. Oldies But Goodies (1963–)
   b. Rock and Roll Revival (1969–1974)—Sha Na Na; Flash Cadillac & The Continental Kids
   c. Blues Revival (1965–)—Paul Butterfield Blues Band; Blues Project
      1) Rhythm and Blues Revival (1968–)—**Creedence Clearwater Revival**; J. Geils Band
      2) English R & B Revival (1960–)—Joe Cocker; Dr. Feelgood
   d. Neo-Rockabilly (1980–1983)—Stray Cats
8. Softer Sounds
   a. Soft Rock (1966–1970)—**Mamas and The Papas**; Fifth Dimension

   1) Pop-Rock (1971–1979)—Helen Reddy; Olivia Newton-John
   2) Adult Contemporary (1980–)—Lionel Richie; Laura Branigan
   b. Country Rock (1968–)—Flying Burrito Brothers; Poco
   c. Singer/Songwriter Tradition (1970–)—James Taylor; **Carole King**
9. Black Contemporary (1975–)—Luther Vandross; Teddy Pendergrass
   a. Funk (1975–)—Ohio Players; Earth, Wind, and Fire
   b. **Disco** (1974–1980)—Barry White; Trammps
   c. Dance-Oriented Rock (1981–)—**Prince**
      1) Hip-Hop (New York)—Time Zone; Shango
      2) Go-Go (Washington, D.C.)—E.U.; Trouble Funk
   d. Rap (1979–)—Grand Master Flash; Run-D.M.C., Public Enemy, M.C. Hammer
10. New Wave (1975–)
   a. Punk Revival (1975–1979)—Ramones; Sex Pistols
   b. Power Pop (1973–)—Raspberries; Nick Lowe
   c. Hardcore (1980–)—Husker Du; Dead Kennedys
   d. Funk-Punk (1978–)—Rick James
   e. Oi—Cockney Rejects
   f. Techno-Pop—Kraftwerk; Human League
   g. The New Romantics/Blitz—Duran Duran; Thompson Twins
   h. Industrial/Material Music—Throbbing Gristle; Cabaret Voltaire
   i. Ska/Bluebeat Revival—Specials; Madness
   j. Neo-Psychedelia—Cult; Three O'Clock
   k. Avant-Garde (1970–)—Laurie Anderson; Eno

Rock 'n' roll is teenage music. It reflects themes such as the problems of young love, rebellion against the establishment (in the fifties and early sixties this usually meant parental authority), preoccupation with dress styles and recreational pursuits (for example, cars, surfing, dancing). However, as the teens who had experienced the early halcyon years of rock 'n' roll matured into adults, the music took on an increasingly sophisticated character. With the appearance of adult themes such as ecology, personal fulfillment, and the inhumanity of war, the essence of rock (the term that had gained widespread use by the mid-1960s) became clearer; that is, it represents a willingness by writers and performers to take chances artistically, and it contains a healthy dash of irreverence for established social mores.

The disinclination of the major record labels in the mid-1970s to sign fresh talent, particularly new wave acts, left the field open for the appearance of hundreds of independent labels dedicated to filling this gap (a situation roughly parallel to that of the early 1950s in which the "indies" took the lead in disseminating rock 'n' roll to the American consumer). The independents avoided mistakes made by established labels that had resulted in an industry-wide recession beginning in the late 1970s; such as the astronomical cash advances given to high status acts such as the Rolling Stones, **Paul McCartney**, and **Stevie Wonder**, whose most creative work was felt to be in the past. The practice of shipping quantities of record albums to retailers far in excess of projected demand was equally unenlightened. (While an announcement that a superstar's latest recording had been certified gold prior to its release date may have contributed to the general hype considered a necessary precondition to the enormous success sought by the majors, the losses resulting from the return of unsold products severely depleted profits throughout the industry.)

Forced to economize, and cognizant of the modest success enjoyed by the independents, the majors were attracted to acts that required minimal time and resources to produce a record. Those artists without sufficient material for an album were encouraged to release either a mini-LP. (usually three to six songs on a 12-inch disc) or a 12-inch single. These new configurations, with enhanced sonic qualities and a lower price tag, helped to revitalize the industry. Disco, the dominant genre, became increasingly discredited by costly studio budget overruns and public reaction to its formulaic musical approach and show business excesses.

New wave came to be seen by industry insiders as combining the best of two earlier eras: the raw energy and spontaneous excitement of the fifties and the integrity and sense of purpose characterizing the sixties. As the new wave's top artists matured musically and became adept at media manipulation, its hegemony—both in aesthetic and commercial terms—was assured.

The development of rock was, as Chambers (1985) has noted,

> encouraged by technological possibilities that had become available in the recording studio. The studio had rapidly become the privileged, if not unique, composition space for pop. Technological factors, due to their integral role as productive musical elements (echo, double-tracking, phasing, editing, etc.), have never been external but always "within" pop music's history; there at the "interface where the economics of capital and libido interlock." In fact, the full flowering of progressive rock at the end of the 1960s was directly involved in the second major turning point in the post-war history of sound recording. After the introduction of recording tape and the ensuing flexibilities that were increasingly exploited in pop through the 1950s and early 1960s, it was the introduction of multiple track recorders that led to a further revolution in recording in general, and producing pop music in particular. These new machines were initially four track, but there quickly followed in rapid succession eight, twelve, sixteen, and a little later twenty-four, track recording studios.

Balanced between increasingly sophisticated electronic hardware and a cultural impetus to establish the LP at the apex of pop music recording, the recording studio further advanced its importance in the making of the music. Record producers and engineers like Jimmy Miller, Shel Talmy, and Glyn Johns rose to become the equivalent of recording stars in their own right. Even the peculiar sound characteristics of particular studios acquired their own individual fame and clientele. All this was deeply stimulated by the now widespread availability of relatively inexpensive hi-fi equipment and the universal adoption of the stereo LP by the end of the 1960s.

Perhaps the most significant bond between rock and the record industry has resulted from the former's development as the first truly urban form of folk music. What started as the language of teenagers now embraces virtually all of Western society, reflecting its needs and aspirations. Its universal coinage is largely due to the dissemination of rock on sound recordings, at home and virtually everywhere else via the phonograph and tape players. The mass media have also contributed to this process, creating a global consciousness (often, as a result, undermining lingering prejudices and misconceptions) and speeding up the exchange of information. Rock has been arguably the greatest success story in the history of show business. Rock artists like **Bruce Springsteen** and **Michael Jackson** command the wealth and public attention accorded opera singers and film stars in previous generations. [Chambers 1985; Shaw 1974.]

Frank Hoffmann

ROCKOLA, DAVID C., 1897– . Canadian business executive, born in Virden, Manitoba. Before the age of 20 he was in the food processing business, manufacturing coolers. In 1924 he began distributing vending machines and scales, and patented a new scale mechanism. In 1932 he established the Rock-Ola Manufacturing Corp. in Chicago. (Address in 1945 was 800 N. Kedzie.) His firm acquired the patents of John Gabel, and began leasing the Entertainer instruments in 1934. A dial device for selection of tunes was added later, permitting a choice among 12 discs. Rockola was one of the four successful juke box companies in the 1930s.

Rockola was one of those visionaries who believed that people would pay to telephone a central record center and request music to be played; he designed a "mystic music" service to accomplish this, but it failed to attract customers. He tried another remote system during World War II, which was also unsuccessful. After the War he developed the very popular Magic-Glo juke box. He had a 200-selection box in operation in 1958. He was still listed as chairman of the board of the Rock-ola Manufacturing Co., now located in Addison, Illinois, in a 1991 directory. [Hoover 1971, p. 113, illustrates a 1935 Rock-Ola juke box.]

ROCOCO (label). A Canadian LP record, based at 3244 Younge St., Toronto, specializing in vocal reissues of material not otherwise available.

RODGERS, JIMMIE, 1897–1933. American country-western singer, known as "The Singing Brakeman," born in Mendoza, Mississippi, on 8 Sep 1897. Rodgers is regarded as the "founding father of modern country and western patterns" (Stambler). His main work as a young man was not musical: he was a cowboy, then a railroad brakeman. In the mid-1920s, his health too poor to continue railroad work, he formed a group called the Jimmie Rodgers Entertainers and performed at rural fairs, not too successfully. When his financial situation had become desperate, in August 1927, he went to Bristol, Tennessee, for an audition with Victor; he—and the Carter Family, present at the same time—found success with the company. He cut "The Soldier's Sweetheart" / "Sleep, Baby, Sleep" on 4 Aug (#20864), and was on his way to stardom. A 15-minute film, *The Singing Brakeman* (1929), was probably the earliest country music motion picture.

By early 1933, he was said to have sold 20 million records. His nine "Blue Yodel" songs were among the most acclaimed of his discs. Victor issued one of its picture discs depicting him, made in his session of 17 May 1933 ("Barefoot Blues" / "Cowhand's Last Ride"; #18-6000). A few days later he died of tuberculosis, in New York, on 26 May 1933. Rodgers was the first person elected to the Country Music Hall of Fame, in 1961. The U.S. Postal Service issued a commemorative stamp to observe his 80th birthday, in 1977. [Bond 1978.]

RODGERS AND HAMMERSTEIN ARCHIVES OF RECORDED SOUND. The research facility for sound recordings in the New York Public Library, located in the Library and Museum of the Performing Arts, Lincoln Center. It is a unit of the Music Division, but has holdings in non-musical fields as well, such as drama and documentation of special events. The Archives opened to the public in November 1965, named for the Rodgers and Hammerstein Foundation which helped to support it. Jean Bowen was first head of the Archives, succeeded by David Hall. Donald McCormick is the present head.

The collections of the Archives are second in size and importance only to those of the Library of Congress. There are about a half million discs, tapes, cylinders and videotapes, in addition to printed research materials. Among the special collections are the **Mapleson cylinders**, Metropolitan Opera archives, and the Jan Holcman collection of recorded piano music. The Archives participated in the important **Rigler and Deutsch Index** project. [Hall 1974.]

ROGERS, KENNY, 1939– . American pop/rock singer, born Kenneth Roy Rogers in Houston, Texas, on 2 Aug 1939. He sang with the Bobby Doyle Jazz Trio, then with the New Christy Minstrels and with the rock group First Edition. After 1975 he pursued a solo career, and in 10 years had produced 22 chart albums, plus others with Dolly Parton. The most durable of those records were *The Gambler* (United Artist #UA-LA 934; 1978), 125 weeks on the charts; and *Greatest Hits* (Liberty #LOO-1072; 1980), 164 weeks. "Lucille" was among his noteworthy hit singles; it was on the charts 18 weeks, and won a Grammy award in 1977 (United Artist #929).

ROGERS, ROY, 1912– . American country/western singer, born Leonard Slye in Cincinnati, 5 Nov 1912. He taught himself the guitar and began to perform locally, then—having hitched a ride to California—organized a group called the Rocky Mountaineers, then another called the International Cowboys. When those failed, he joined the Sons of the Pioneers, which was beginning its climb to stardom. He auditioned for a movie part in Hollywood, and got the lead in *Under Western Stars*. Subsequently he was featured in more than 100 motion pictures,

often with his wife, Dale Evans. He was also prominent on radio and television.

Rogers had a long recording career, with many hits for Victor, Decca, Vocalion, and other labels. He was still on the charts in the 1970s, with four albums, and made a chart LP in 1980, *Ride Concrete Cowboy* (MCA #41294). One of his best singles was "Happy, Gene and Me" (1974), which was used as the title for an album in the following year; both single and LP were on the 20th Century label.

ROGERS, WALTER BOWMAN, 1865–1939. American cornetist and then musical director for Victor, born in Delphi, Indiana, on 14 Oct 1865. He studied at the Cincinnati Conservatory of Music, then went to New York and became cornet soloist with Cappa's Seventh Regiment Band; in 1899 he joined the Sousa Band, remaining to 1904. At that time he accepted an invitation to be musical director for Victor Talking Machine Co. He also made records for the firm, beginning in 1902, as cornetist accompanied by the Sousa Band or by a pianist. Rogers was one of the first artists to appear on 12-inch Victors, when that size was launched in 1903, playing "The Harp that Once through Tara's Halls" (#31110). He had two duets with Arthur Pryor, trombonist, in the Victor 1909 catalog; one of them, "Miserere," remained until the 1922 catalog (#16794).

As musical director he made arrangements and conducted dance records, organized the Victor Light Opera Co. and the Victor Opera Co. In 1916 he left Victor to be manager of Paroquette, and then went to Brunswick as recording director, remaining until about 1929. He died in Brooklyn on 24 Dec 1939. [Walsh 1959/2.]

ROLLING STONE (periodical). Beginning in the modest manner of a **fanzine** in November 1967—the first issue sold 6,000 of its 45,000 copy run—*Rolling Stone* became the primary journal of American pop/rock. Although the title seems connected with the Rolling Stones group, it was in fact drawn from the proverb "A rolling stone gathers no moss" (this from the announcement in the first issue; but the announcement also refers to the Muddy Waters song of the same name, and to the first record of Bob Dylan, and to the Stones group). Covering the entire youth culture as well as its music, the journal filled a niche in the publishing scene and was able to shed an early image of being a trade magazine for the music industry; in the late 1980s circulation had reached 400,000. Over the years the association with rock music faded, and the audience age level rose; content became generalized, but the reviews of new pop/rock records, a feature since the early days, remain influential.

ROLLING STONES. British rock group, formed in 1962, also known as the Stones. Members were Mick Jagger (lead vocals), Keith Richards (born Keith Richard, lead guitar), Bill Wyman (bass guitar), Brian Jones (rhythm guitar, 1962–1969), Mick Taylor (rhythm guitar, 1969–1975), Ron Wood (rhythm guitar, 1975–present), and Charlie Watts (drums). They were influenced by blues singer/guitarists, including Robert Johnson and Muddy Waters. They favored rhythm and blues records, particularly those of the Chicago-based Chess label. The Rolling Stones themselves recorded at the Chess studios in 1964, notably "2120 S. Michigan," which is the studio's address. They recorded for the London label until a controversy over the album *Beggar's Banquet* (London #PS 539; 1968)—the group wanted a cover depicting a public bathroom, but the company refused, and the Stones founded their own production firm. Their recordings were manufactured and distributed by Atlantic Records, but released on their own label Rolling Stones Records (which was headed by Marshall Chess, son of Leonard Chess, founder of the Chess label in Chicago). There was further controversy when the group recorded "Let's Spend the Night Together" (London #904; 1967) Andrew Loog Oldham became their manager and sometime producer in 1963, while Eric Easton became their assistant manager. In 1969, the Stones offered a free concert at the Altamont Raceway near Livermore, California, and attracted 300,000 people. The group was criticized later for using the event as background for the filming of their movie *Gimme Shelter*. Their September 1981 tour of 20 cities brought $25 million in ticket sales, reviving the momentum

of rock music after several halting years for the genre. Other albums include *Their Satanic Majesties Request* (London #NP-2; NPS-2; 1967), *Let It Bleed* (London #NPS-4; 1969), *Sticky Fingers* (Atco #COC 59100; 1971), *Exile on Main Street* (Rolling Stones #COC-2-2900; 1972), *Hot Rocks* (London #2PS 606/7; 1972, on the charts 94 weeks), *Some Girls* (Rolling Stones #COC 39108; 1978), *Black and Blue* (Rolling Stones #COC 79104; 1976), and *Emotional Rescue* (Rolling Stones #COC 16015; 1980). Mick Jagger and Keith Richards write most of the group's material. Much of the band's recording has been done at Regent Sound Studios in London. [Appli 1987; Benson 1986; Palmer 1983.]

Felicia Reilly

ROLLINI, ADRIAN, 1904–1956. American jazz musician, performer on various instruments, born in New York on 28 June 1904. He was a piano prodigy, and made about 30 piano rolls for the Republic and Mel-O-Dee labels in 1920–1921; but became better known as a bass saxophonist. From 1924 to 1927 he was with the California Ramblers, then he performed for two years in the Savoy Hotel ballroom, in London. In the 1930s he was with Leo Reisman and Richard Himber, then led studio groups of major jazzmen. Rollini concentrated on vibes in the late 1930s, appearing frequently on radio. He settled in Florida and continued playing until 1955. He died in Homestead, Florida, on 15 May 1956.

Many of Rollini's records were made with numerous orchestras and partners, including Bix Beiderbecke, Frankie Trumbauer, Joe Venuti, and Red Nichols. Working on his own, he recorded for several labels in greatly varied material. "Isle of Capri" / "Girl with the Light Blue Hair" (Okeh #5979; 1941) was a notable single. On LP, Mercury recorded the *Adrian Rollini Trio* (#MG 20011). [Montgomery 1975 lists the piano rolls.]

ROLLINS, SONNY, 1929– . American tenor saxophonist, born Theodore Walter Rollins in New York on 7 Sep 1929. He started on piano, then alto saxophone, and switched in 1946 to the tenor. In the late 1940s he worked with Art Blakey in New York, then went on to play with Bud Powell, Fats Navarro, Miles Davis, Charlie

Parker, Thelonious Monk, and others. He performed also with the Modern Jazz Quartet. His style was staccato and slurring, in contrast to the legato approach of his great contemporary John Coltrane. In the 1960s he had his own groups, playing often at the Village Vanguard in New York. *A Night at the Village Vanguard* (Blue Note #BST 81581; 1957) was a major album, with the notable renditions of "I Can't Get Started," "Old Devil Moon," and "Sonnymoon for Two" included.

ROMAIN, MANUEL, 1870–1926. Spanish tenor and vaudeville artist. He was in the U.S. as a minstrel show performer and vaudeville singer by the early 1900s, and began to record in 1907. He made about 40 Edison cylinders in 1907–1910, the first being "When the Blue Birds Nest Again" (#9628). He was the first singer on the Amberol records, singing "Roses Bring Dreams of You" (#2). In 1909 Romain made three discs for Victor, and in 1911 he was with Columbia, doing "Let's Grow Old Together, Honey" on #A1192. For Edison Diamond Discs he contributed two Irish songs (#50230; 1915). After working for Emerson in 1916–1917, he became an Edison exclusive artist. He died in Quincy, Massachusetts, on 22 Dec 1926.

ROMEO (label). An American record issued from 1926 to 1939, originally a subsidiary of **Cameo**, sold through the S. H. Kress chain stores for $.25. American Record Corp. absorbed Romeo in 1931, and kept it going for eight years, presenting some 2,300 issues. Many of the artists—popular and dance performers—used pseudonyms. [Rust 1978.]

RONALD, LANDON, *Sir*, **1873–1938.** British pianist and conductor, born L.R. Russell in London on 7 June 1873. He studied composition and piano at the Royal College of Music in London, then began conducting light opera and summer concerts. In 1909 he became director of the New Symphony Orchestra. From 1910 to 1938 he was principal of the Guildhall School of Music. He was knighted in 1922. Ronald died in London on 14 Aug 1938.

Ronald had a long association with the gramophone. He accompanied recording sessions of the musical show *Florodora* in 1900,

in the Maiden Lane studios of the Gramophone Co., and in the same session made some piano solo records. The Gramophone Company then engaged him as musical adviser and accompanist. He was also a talent scout, and in that capacity persuaded Emma Calvè to record, and played the piano accompaniment for her. He also brought Nellie Melba into the studio, in 1904. His triumph was to arrange for recording of Adelina Patti in her Welsh castle; she did so only on condition that he should be her accompanist.

With the New Symphony Orchestra he achieved a significant recording first, making the earliest disc of a piano concerto—the Grieg work, with Wilhelm Backhaus as soloist (January 1910). He conducted the allegro movement from the Saint-Saëns B Minor Concerto, with pianist Irene Scharrer, on 13 Nov 1915 (HMV #E2-055500). In 1917 he negotiated a contract with the D'Oyly Carte Opera Co. He was also responsible for bringing Edward Elgar and the Gramophone Co. together, in a relationship fruitful for both over many years.

Ronald's orchestral records were highly acclaimed. Among them were important concertos with such soloists as Fritz Kreisler, Yehudi Menuhin, and Alfred Cortot. [Duckenfield 1990.]

RONSTADT, LINDA, 1946– . American country and popular singer, born in Tuscon, Arizona, on 15 July 1946. She sang locally, then went to Los Angeles, forming a group called the Stone Poneys. She was successful in the country-western idiom, Motown, and New Wave, and in 1980 also in Gilbert and Sullivan (*Pirates of Penzance* on Broadway). She was invited to sing at the inauguration of Jimmy Carter, and had invitations from California governor Jerry Brown. Ronstadt had 14 chart albums between 1975 and 1985, of which the most popular were *Simple Dreams* (Asylum #6E-104; 1977) and *Greatest Hits* (Asylum #7E-1092; 1980). There was also a string of chart singles with the Stone Poneys, 20 songs in the 1970s; of them "Love Has No Pride" (Asylum #11026; 1973) and "That'll Be the Day" (Asylum #45340; 1976) are perhaps the most noteworthy.

ROOM ACOUSTICS. The size and shape of the space in which one listens to an audio system has a considerable impact upon the quality of the perceived sound. A large room requires greater acoustic output from the loudspeakers. A room with curtains and carpets tends to be "dead" (non-reverberating) and requires more acoustic output than a "live" room. Higher frequencies are damped by such furnishings. Room shape contributes to the creation of standing waves: the result of enforcing (or weakening) certain wavelengths that are sub-multiples of the distance between two opposite surfaces. The least desirable room for audio listening is a small one in the shape of a perfect cube. The larger the room, the less impact there is from these resonances. In some cases the poor effects of standing waves can be dealt with by shifting the location of the loudspeakers or by use of separate subwoofer speaker.

Reflective surfaces also have an impact on speaker performance, by enhancing low-frequency output. Speakers should be located at least a foot from walls, and should be on stands that keep them from floor contact. Whatever is done about these matters, there will remain better and worse places to sit while listening; usually the listener should be positioned equidistant from both speakers, forming one tip of an equilateral triangle with them. [Masters 1990.]

ROSE, EUGENE C., 1866–1961. Flutist, born in Danzig on 26 July 1866. He played at the Paris Exposition of 1889, and with the Sousa Band. From 1911 to 1917 he played in the orchestra of the Metropolitan Opera. One of the earliest recording artists, he recorded for Edison cylinders in 1889, performing in a flute trio. Rose recorded later for many labels. His best seller was "Genevieve Waltz Medley", an ocarina solo (Edison #9197; 1906). He died in Freeport, New York, on 21 Aug 1961. [Walsh 1947/10–11; 1952/5.]

ROSENTHAL, MORIZ, 1862–1946. Polish pianist, born in Lwow on 17 Dec 1862. He studied with Karol Mikuli, a pupil of Chopin; later with Rafael Joseffy and Franz Liszt. He became one of the world's leading virtuosi, specializing in Chopin. He settled in the U.S. in 1938, and died in New York on 3 Sep 1946.

Rosenthal began to record in 1929 for Parlophone/Odeon, playing a Chopin Mazurka and a Chopin/Liszt transcription. He remained with Parlophone into 1931, doing many Chopin works, including the first concerto with the Berlin State Opera (#38839/40; #21695/98; 1930). He worked for Edison in 1929, making two Chopin sides (Diamond Disc #82353), and for Victor in 1928, 1939, and 1942. His final record was of the same work with which he began his recording career, the Chopin/Liszt "My Joys" from "Chants polonais"; with it was the Chopin "Tarantelle in A-Flat" (Camden #CAL 377; released on LP). Pearl offered a CD selection of his work in 1989 (#GEMM CD 9339), all recorded when he was over 65 years of age, but lacking nothing in technical command. [Methuen-Campbell 1984.]

ROSENTHAL, RICHARD S. An early promoter of language instruction by phonograph; he spoke on the subject at the 1893 convention of the National Phonograph Association. Rosenthal's organization, the International College of Languages, sent out sets of pre-recorded cylinders to students, with blanks for return of their recitations. Others followed this example—the "Languagephone Method"—in the cylinder era, but in the advanced technological age that followed instruction, ironically, became unilateral.

ROSS, DIANA, 1944– . American soul singer, born in Detroit on 26 Mar 1944. She sang for social events in Detroit, then formed her trio, The **Supremes**, with Florence Ballard and Mary Wilson. Ross left the trio to have a solo career in 1970, and achieved national stardom in Las Vegas, in films (*Lady Sings the Blues*, about Billy Holiday), and on television. She had 23 chart LPs by 1985, nearly all on the Motown label, of which the most popular was the soundtrack from the movie *Lady Sings the Blues* (Motown #M7581). Her 58th album appeared in 1991, *The Force behind the Power.*

ROSS (label). An American record issued through Ross Stores in 1924–1925; Bridgeport Die and Machine Co. made the discs. Matrices came from Paramount, Emerson, and probably Banner. Surviving specimens are rare. One item was "She Loves Me," sung by Arthur Hall with the Golden Gate Orchestra (#11410). [Rust 1978.]

ROSWAENGE, HELGE, 1897–1972. Danish tenor, born in Copenhagen on 29 Aug 1897. He studied engineering, then voice, and made successful concert tours of Europe. From 1929 to 1945 he was with the Berlin State Opera, and again from 1949. He also appeared with the Vienna State Opera in 1936–1958, and sang often in Bayreuth and Salzburg. Roswaenge was greatly acclaimed, and was compared favorably to Enrico Caruso. Among his hundred roles, Radames and Canio were outstanding, but he also gave remarkable interpretations in *Fidelio* and in lesser known operas such as *Ivan Susanin* and Wille's *Königsballade*. He died in Munich on 19 June 1972.

Roswaenge recorded in 1927 for Grammophon/Polydor in Berlin, beginning with a German version of "Che gelida manina" (#B22434) and two arias from *Tosca*. He also recorded four sides for HMV/Electrola in 1927, then six sides for Parlophone/Odeon in 1928. During 1928–1932 Roswaenge was active for Polydor in Berlin, recording 131 numbers. Among eight arias he made for Telefunken (Berlin) in 1932, the "Preislied" (#018795) was particularly elegant. His German "O paradiso" of 1933 (Telefunken #018978) was also noteworthy. He worked for Polydor and HMV/Electrola in 1935. The most enduring of his single discs was Sobinin's Aria from *Ivan Susanin* (HMV/Electrola #DB5563; 1940). His rendition of Tamino in the HMV *Zauberflöte*—with Thomas Beecham and the Berlin Philharmonic Orchestra—is regarded as the finest interpretation of the role on record.

A good selection of his favorite arias (including the numbers cited above) appears on a CD from Harmonia Mundi (#89018; 1990). Material from the 1920s and 1930s—Mozart, Puccini, Verdi, Bizet, Beethoven—appeared on CD in 1990 (Pearl #GEMM CD 9394). [Dennis 1976.]

ROYAL (label). (I) A lateral-cut, double-sided British record sold by the City Manufacturing Co., London, in 1908.

ROYAL (label). (II) An American record sold by the Royal Record Co. ca. 1921–1922. Material, which was popular and dance music, paralleled offerings on several other labels, but with artists' names changed. The matrices were shared with Cardinal, Clarion, Melva, Phantasie Concert Record, Symphony Concert Record, Cleartone, and others. [Kendziora 1988/11.]

ROYAL CONCERTGEBOUW ORCHESTRA AMSTERDAM. One of the premier orchestras of Europe, known as the Concertgebouw Orchestra until 1988, when it was renamed by royal decree in honor of its 100th anniversary. Willem Kes was the first conductor, succeeded in 1895 by **Willem Mengelberg**, who remained in the post until 1941, bringing the orchestra to world renown. Eduard van Beinum was conductor from 1941 to 1961, followed by **Bernard Haitink** (who shared the post with Eugen Jochum until 1964). Riccardo Chailly became conductor in the 1988–1989 season. The orchestra's name comes from the hall in which it has played since its inception, the Amsterdam Concertgebouw.

Mengelberg conducted for the first Concertgebouw recording, of the *Tannhäuser* Overture, in May 1926 (Columbia set #X-27), and recorded for Columbia until 1936; 11 works were listed in the 1943 Columbia catalog, including the Brahms third and fourth symphonies. Telefunken recorded the orchestra after that time until the 1940s, when DG/Polydor and Decca made some issues. Philips recorded the Concertgebouw in stereo from 1957.

A 10-CD Teldec set of Mengelberg's Telefunken material has been issued, but because of engineering problems with it the older LP reissues on Past Masters label may be preferable. Several other CD releases have been criticized on sonic grounds as well. [Van Bart 1989 is a discography of the orchestra; in a review of the book, Bob Benson discusses the infelicities noted above in CD reissues (*ARSCJ* 20–2 [Fall 1989]: 198–201).]

ROYAL TALKING MACHINE CO., INC. A Chicago firm, established in 1918. Columbia disc players were sold, some with one-half inch spindles like those on players of the **Standard Talking Machine Co.** Royal did not issue discs.

ROYALE (label). An American record introduced in fall 1939 by **Eli Oberstein.** The issuing organization was the United States Record Corp. Original material on Royale— jazz, gospel, and classical—included cuts by Richard Himber and Johnny Green. Reissues included sides by the Quintet of the Hot Club of France. Jan Peerce and the Don Cossack Chorus were also heard on Royale.

In 1951 the United States Record Corp. was absorbed by the Record Corp. of America, which continued the Royale label name. An important series of operatic and symphonic material appeared, apparently made from radio broadcasts of the late 1940s in Germany and perhaps Italy. Artists were given pseudonyms. The label ceased around 1957. [Lumpe 1990.]

ROYALTIES AND FEES. In the current American pop/rock field, artists usually receive about 7 percent of the list price of each record sold, though the percentage may reach twice that amount for star performers. Customarily the artist's income is reduced at the source, by company deductions for promotion fees, costs of album graphics, and tour costs not made up by admission intake. Records sent out to the media for promotion purposes do not earn royalties, nor do **cutouts.** Publishers and songwriters receive small royalties on records sold, based on the number of their songs in an album, around 0.3 percent each, per song. And the producer receives about 3 percent. The system makes it difficult for the pop performer to cull huge profits, even from a record on the charts. **Francesco Tamagno** is believed to have been the first recording artist to insist on and receive royalties for discs sold, in 1903. [Andrews*; Denisoff 1986]

ROYALTY RECORDINGS. It appears that the earliest surviving recording in any format made by a monarch is one made by Queen Victoria in Balmoral Castle, Scotland, in 1888, on a Bell-Tainter graphophone carried there by a solicitor on behalf of **Henry Edmunds,** the American Graphophone Co. representative in Britain. A broadcast of that recording—now in the Science Museum, London—was made on 10 Nov 1991. A few words in the Queen's voice were heard, speaking about the tomatoes growing at Balmoral. It is reported that another record was made by Queen Victoria, in 1896— a cylinder sent by her with a message to the Emperor of Ethiopia, with instructions that it should be destroyed after he had heard it. There is no verification for the existence nor for the destruction of the record.

The earliest royalty recording on a magnetic medium was taken by the Poulsen Telegrafon in 1900, of Emperor Franz Joseph; that wire recording was transferred to an LP disc. King Edward VII also made a wire recording, but it has been lost.

Among disc recordings, the oldest royal survivor is HMV #1235 (1903), on which Queen Elizabeth of Romania recited five of her own poems, including one in English, entitled "A Friend." Her name on the recording, which was made in Bucharest, was given as Carmen Sylva. Kaiser Wilhelm is said to have made a 1904 record.

Princess Peara Nene (Waiata Na Rangatira Peara Nene), a Maori princess of New Zealand, recorded two songs for Sound Recording Co., Ltd., on its Grammavox Record label #D25, ca. 1911.

In 1923 King George V and Queen Mary recorded an "Empire Day Message to the Boys and Girls of the British Empire" for HMV (#19072).

ROYCROFT (label). An American record distributed in 1927–1928 by William H. Wise and Co., 50 W. 47th St., New York, for a society named Roycrofters. The material consisted of English madrigals, carols, and folk songs, performed by a group identified as the English Singers. A 12–record set, the *Roycroft Album*, was apparently the first multi-disc non-operatic album to be marketed in the U.S.; but the records were also sold singly. The labels carry the legend: "Roycroft Living Tone Record; Microphone Recording; The Roycrofters, East Aurora, N.Y." [Blacker 1972/8; Blacker 1984.]

RUBINSTEIN, ARTUR, 1887–1982. Polish/ American pianist, born in Lodz on 28 Jan 1887. He was a piano prodigy born into a non-musical family. After public performances at age seven, he was sent to Berlin for study and made a formal debut there at age 13. In 1903 he took lessons from Ignace Paderewski; but he was for the most part self-taught. Rubinstein played in Carnegie Hall on 8 Jan 1906 with the Philadelphia Orchestra, then toured Europe and South America, gaining recognition as one of the two premier pianists of his time. Chopin was the composer he performed most definitively, but he was renowned also for his Brahms, Beethoven, Spanish composers, and contemporaries. He made motion pictures in the 1940s, recorded and concertized widely, with intervals taken for intensive practice to correct his occasionally erratic technique. In 1946 he became an American citizen. He was given the U.S. Medal of Freedom in 1976, the year of his final recital. He died in Geneva on 20 Dec 1982.

Rubinstein's recordings, from the 1930s to the 1970s, span the repertoire of the instrument. After some work for Odeon, he became a Victor artist. His Chopin albums—mazurkas, nocturnes, scherzos, concertos, polonaises— remain the touchstone for pianists today. In addition to his solo work, he was distinguished in chamber music; a fine example is the Brahms Cello Sonata, with Gregor Piatigorsky (Album # M-564). Odeon reissued some of the earlier recordings in 1987, on #C 2LP 137 and #LC 137. They included his performance of the Cesar Franck Violin Sonata with Jascha Heifetz, and his Tchaikovsky Concerto No. 1 with Barbirolli, made in 1932 (Victor #7802-05) and still an unsurpassed rendition of that oft-recorded masterpiece.[Manildi 1983.]

RUFFO, TITTA, 1877–1953. Italian baritone, born in Pisa on 9 June 1877, as Ruffo Cafiero Titta (he later chose to reverse the elements of his name). He studied in Rome and Milan, and made a debut in Rome as the Herald in *Lohengrin* (1898). Then he appeared throughout Italy, in Rio de Janeiro, Vienna, Paris, London, and Philadelphia. Finally he was heard at the Metropolitan Opera on 19 Jan 1922, as Figaro in *Barbiere di Siviglia;* he remained with the company to 1928. He returned to Rome, and then settled in Florence, where he died on 5 July 1953.

Ruffo recorded first for Pathé cylinders in ca. 1904–1906, beginning with "Buona Zazà" from Leoncavallo's opera *Zazà* (#4200). He did 14 numbers, mostly standard baritone items. Thereafter he was a Victor/HMV artist, recording a wide French/Italian repertoire from 1907 to 1933. He had 40 solos in the Victor 1917 catalog, plus duets with Enrico Caruso (a Caruso duet, from *Otello*, was still in the catalog of 1940, with Ruffo's final recording, "Nemico della patria" / "Adamastor" from *L'africaine* (#7153; 1929), and the *Otello* "Credo"). The "Brindisi" from *Hamlet* (Victor #6266, #18140, #88619; first made for HMV #052188; 1907) is a favorite among collectors. LPs by all the major reissue labels covered most of Ruffo's output. [Moran 1984; 2 has a complete discography.]

RUMBLE. A low-frequency noise, usually between 20 and 35 Hz, brought about in a phonograph by motor or transport vibrations. In some cases rumble originates in the recording mechanism, and is thus a part of the recorded signal. Aside from motor rumble there is the possibility of rumble caused by resonance in the springs which keep the idler wheel in contact with the turntable rim. Rumble also occurs in cylinder playback. A rumble filter is a control on an amplifier that may reduce audible rumble that originates in the turntable or record changer.

RUSSELL, PEE WEE, 1906–1969. American jazz clarinetist, born Charles Ellsworth Russell in Maplewood, Missouri, on 27 Mar 1906. He played violin, piano, and drums as a youth, then turned to the clarinet. After some time at the University of Missouri he played in Texas with Jack Teagarden and in St. Louis with Bix Beiderbecke; in 1927 he went to New York, teaming with Red Nichols, Bobby Hackett, Eddie Condon, and others. Later he freelanced, concentrating first on the dixieland style, then experimenting with modern jazzmen like Thelonious Monk and John Coltrane. He was active into the 1960s—appearing at the 1963 Newport Jazz Festival—and died in Alexandria, Virginia, on 15 Feb 1969.

An outstanding early recording was made with his group called the Rhythmakers (including James P. Johnson, piano, and Zutty Singleton, drums) for the Hot Record Society in 1938: "Dinah" / "Baby Won't You Please Come Home" (HRS #1000). "A Ghost of a Chance" with Buddy Hackett's band (Vocalion #4565; 1938) was a notable effort as sideman.

He had a fine session on 29 Mar 1960 with Buck Clayton, trumpet; Tommy Flanagan, piano; Wendell Marshall, bass; and Osie Johnson, drums. Russell's lyrical gift is displayed in "The Very Thought of You," and his quick rhythmic manner in "Lulu's Back in Town"; the session was reissued on Fontana #68840-403ZL.

SABINE, E. J. Record industry executive. He was with the Columbia Phonograph Co., General—London, the new British branch of the Columbia Phonograph Co., in 1900; thence he went on to the Berlin branch. Later he was associated with the **National Phonograph Co., Ltd.** In 1904 he joined William Michaelis as assistant manager of the new **Neophone Co., Ltd.**, in London. After a turn in Brussels as manager of the Neophone office there he returned to the U.K. to manage the firm's wholesale depot in Manchester. When Neophone closed down in February 1907, Sabine went to the newly formed International Neophone Co., Ltd., as one of the directors. In July 1907 he joined **Aldridge, Salmon and Co., Ltd.** That firm opened a record department as the **Universal Talking Machine Co.**; it handled the Columbia, Pathé, and Favorite lines, and had its own Elephone Records (10-inch, double-sided discs).

SADLER, JOSIE. American vaudeville artist, participant in the Ziegfeld Follies of 1912. She recorded five two-minute cylinders for Edison in 1909–1910, beginning with "He Falls for the Ladies Every Time" (#10179; 1909) in German dialect. She tried Dutch dialect in "Come and Hear the Orchestra" (Amberol #184; 1909). Sadler also recorded for Victor, and the 1917 catalog carried her comic view of "Hilda Loses Her Job" (#16783).

SAFRANSKI, EDDIE, 1918–1974. American jazz string bassist, born in Pittsburgh on 25 Dec 1918. He played with many bands, most prominently in the 1940s with Hal McIntyre and Stan Kenton. He won the *Downbeat* poll every year from 1946 to 1952 as the favorite bassist. In 1951 he was with the Benny Goodman Sextet. Later he was a freelancer with many radio and television appearances. He died on 10 Jan 1974, in Los Angeles. Among his notable discs were "Safranski" (Capitol #20088; 1946) with Kenton, and "Farewell Blues" with the Goodman Sextet (Columbia #39564; 1951).

ST. LOUIS EXPOSITION, 1904. At this world's fair there was competition between Victor and Columbia products for the premium awards; both had large exhibits. Afterwards Victor claimed to be the winner, and advertised accordingly. But it was Columbia who had won, so it sued Victor and the Exposition to prevent false claims of victory. Then Columbia added an award banner to its record label, naming the prizes received. Read (1976) observes that the chairman of the talking machine competition at the fair was an official of the Columbia Phonograph Co.

The **Multiplex Grand** cylinder and the **Higham Amplifier** were exhibited at the fair; and John McCormack was among the artists who performed.

ST. LOUIS TALKING MACHINE CO. A firm located in 1907 at 7th and St. Charles St. O. A. Gressing was reported to be the new general manager in March 1908.

SALÉZA, ALBERT, 1867–1916. Belgian tenor, born in Bruges on 18 Oct 1867. He studied at the Paris Conservatory, and made his debut at the Opéra-Comique on 19 July 1888; then sang in

Nice and Monte Carlo. He returned to Paris, performed in Brussels, then at the Metropolitan Opera from 1898 to 1901, and again in 1904–1905. Among his roles at the Metropolitan were Radames, Rodolfo, Edgar, and Faust, the last three sung opposite Nellie Melba. He became a professor at the Paris Conservatory in 1911. Saléza died in Paris on 26 Nov 1916.

He was recorded by **Bettini** in 1898 or 1899, producing six cylinders. "Morir si pura e bella" from *Aida* was the first. He was also heard on **Mapleson cylinders** made in 1901, doing the *Faust* finale with Melba and Edouard de Reszke; "Verranno a te sull'aure," a duet with Melba from *Lucia*; and "Che gelida manina." He made no regular commercial records.

SALON DU PHONOGRAPHE. A phonograph parlor operated by **Pathé Frères Compagnie**, located on Boulevard des Italiens, Paris, around the turn of the century. It followed the practice of a century later in inviting customers to order selections through a speaking tube, upon which the record would be played in another room and heard by the customer through ear tubes. There were said to be 1,500 cylinders in the Salon collection. In a sense it was the earliest record library.

SALVINI, TOMMASO, 1829–1916. Italian actor, famous for his Shakespearean roles. He toured the U.K. and U.S., and while in New York in 1897 recorded for **Bettini**, making a cylinder entitled "A Dramatic Phrase."

SAMMARCO, MARIO, 1868–1930. Italian baritone, born in Palermo on 13 Dec 1868. He made his debut in Palermo as Faust in 1888, then sang in many European houses including La Scala. A great success in Covent Garden, he appeared there every season from 1905 to 1913, and again in 1919. His American appearances were with the Manhattan Opera (1906–1910) and Chicago Opera (1910–1914). His repertoire encompassed the standard French/Italian works, plus English, Spanish, and Russian material. He retired in 1919, and died in Milan on 24 Jan 1930.

Sammarco recorded for G & T in Milan in 1902–1904, making 18 sides; the first was "Racconto" from Franchetti's *Germania* (#52371). Then he was with Fonotipia in 1905–1906, for about 40 sides. Victor and HMV recorded him in 1910–1911. Sammarco also recorded for Pathé discs, ca. 1912 in Milan. "Di provenza il mar" was the first record (#86398), followed by nine popular arias. Among his finest discs were "Ah Mimi! tu piu non torni," with John McCormack (Victor #89044; 1911), the *Rigoletto* Quartet, with McCormack and Melba (HMV #2-054025; 1911) and "Numero quindici" from *Barbiere di Siviglia*, with McCormack (HMV #2-054021; 1911). These and many others were released on LP, by the major reissue labels.

SAMPLING FREQUENCY. In compact disc technology, the frequency at which an analog signal is measured and quantized to a digital number during recording; it is 44,100 samples per second, (44.1 Khz). [Klinger*.]

SAMUEL (BARNETT) AND SONS, LTD. A British musical instrument firm, located in 1903 at 32 Worship St., London. Barnett Samuel was a wholesale merchant, dealing in musical items among other things, from 1832. The firm was one of the first in London to take up phonographs and gramophones, toward the end of the 19th century. It was announced in *TMN* during 1903 that the shop had 100,000 records in stock. Products of Columbia, Zonophone, and Edison were handled. In 1908 the firm was appointed sole agent in the U.K. for Odeon, Fonotipia, and Jumbo Records of Fonotipia, Ltd. The most successful item marketed by Samuel was its own "Dulcephone Decca" portable (1914). The firm withdrew from the talking machine industry in summer 1928, its business converted into a public company called the **Decca Gramophone Co. Ltd.**, after the brand name of its phonographs of that period. In 1929 the company was acquired by the new **Decca Record Co., Ltd.** [Andrews*.]

SANTLEY, CHARLES, *Sir*, **1834–1922.** British baritone, born in Liverpool on 28 Feb 1834. He studied in Milan, and made his debut at Pavia in 1857, singing a minor role in *Traviata*. He sang mostly in oratorios and concert for several years, then joined the Covent Garden company and stayed until 1863; thence he went to Mapleson's company. Valentine in *Faust* was a part which brought him much acclaim; indeed Gounod wrote for him the famous aria "Avant de quitter ces lieux," for the 1864 London production. Subsequently Santley toured the U.S., and joined the Carl Rosa Opera group. On 1 May 1907 he sang a jubilee concert and was knighted later that year. He died in London on 22 Sep 1922.

Santley was the second earliest born singer to record an opera aria: "Non piu andrai" (G & T 052000; 1903); he was 69 years old at the time. At the same session (3 June 1903) he cut four other sides for G & T, all concert songs, discs that are scarce today. He did not record again until 1913, when he had a final session for Columbia. [Moran 1977/4.]

SAPPHIRE RECORD AND TALKING MA-CHINE CO. A New York firm. It was acquired by the **Indestructible Phonographic Record Co.** in 1911.

SARGENT, MALCOLM, *Sir.*, 1895–1967. British conductor, born Harold Malcolm Sargent in Stamford on 29 Apr 1895. He studied organ, then served in the infantry during World War I. In 1921 he began conducting, and during the 1920s led the D'Oyly Carte Opera Co. and the Ballets Russes, plus the Royal Choral Society from 1928. Sargent directed the Halle Orchestra in 1939–1942, the Liverpool Philharmonic Orchestra in 1942–1948, and the BBC Symphony Orchestra in 1950–1957. He also directed the Promenade Concerts in London from 1948 to 1966. There were numerous world tours with his various orchestras. He died in London on 3 Oct 1967.

Sargent recorded across a wide repertoire, for Victor. HMV, and Columbia. Among his notable discs were the Beethoven Piano Concertos No. 1 and No. 5, with Artur Schnabel (Victor albums #M-158 and #M-155) and the London Symphony Orchestra; and the other three Beethoven concertos with Schnabel and the London Philharmonic Orchestra (Victor albums #295, #194, and #156). For Columbia he led the D'Oyly Carte Opera Co. in definitive recordings of many Gilbert and Sullivan light operas, made in the late 1920s and early 1930s.

(These have been reissued on CD by Arabesque.) His support for English composers resulted in a few important discs, e.g., the Vaughan Williams "Lark Ascending" with the Liverpool Orchestra (Columbia #DX-1386/7) and "Fantasia on Greensleeves" with the Halle Orchestra (Columbia #DX 1087).

SAUTER, EDDIE, 1914–1981. American jazz trumpeter, Big Band leader, and arranger, born in Brooklyn on 2 Dec 1914. He studied at Columbia and the Juilliard School, and played in various dance bands. In 1935 he joined Charlie Barnet, then went to Red Norvo in 1936 as trumpeter and mellophone player. For Norvo he made outstanding arrangements, including those for Mildred Bailey, and gained fame for his original and resourceful orchestrations. Almost all Norvo's records during 1936–1939 were Sauter designs. Then he became Benny Goodman's arranger, in 1939, and continued to expand his instrumental colors. He made about 60 arrangements that Goodman recorded (many with Helen Forrest's vocals) before the 1942 Petrillo ban, establishing the orchestra on a new sophisticated level. "How High the Moon" (Columbia #35391; 1940), "The Man I Love" (Columbia #55001; 1940), and "Cocoanut Grove" (Columbia #35527; 1940) exemplify his art. His setting of "My Old Flame" for Peggy Lee (Columbia #36379; 1941) was a "masterpiece of the genre" (Schuller).

Sauter's later work was with many top bands, including Artie Shaw, Tommy Dorsey, Woody Herman, and Ray McKinley; then he formed a new group, with Bill Finegan: the Sauter-Finegan Band. When that ensemble dissolved in 1957, Sauter worked in German radio for two years, then went into television production in New York, and arranged for Broadway shows. He was active into the 1970s. [Schuller 1989.]

SAVANA (label). A British record of the 1920s, produced in 5 1/2-inch, six-inch, and 10-inch sizes. Proprietors were Rose, Morris and Co. (a firm still in business in 1990). Discs were pressed from Edison Bell and Crystalate masters, used on Bell, Imperial, and Mimosa discs, some matrices being American imports from Plaza Music Co. of New York. Material was dance music, popular vocals, and instrumentals. [Andrews⁺; Rust 1978.]

SAVILLE, FRANCES, 1863–1935. American soprano, born in San Francisco on 6 Jan 1863. She sang oratorio in Australia, studied in Paris, and made her opera debut in Brussels; afterwards sang in many European houses. Her Metropolitan Opera debut was as Juliette, opposite Jean de Reszke, on 18 Nov 1895. She also sang Manon and Elisabeth in *Tannhäuser*. After the 1898–1899 season she went to sing in Vienna, then retired to California, where she died (in Burlingame) on 8 Nov 1935.

Saville's only records were for **Bettini**. In his 1897 catalog she was listed singing "Caro nome" and an aria (not named but presumably Micaela's aria) from *Carmen*. Bettini's 1899 catalog carried the "Caro nome" but not the *Carmen* piece; it added the Brahms "Wiegenlied."

SAVITT, JAN, 1913–1948. Russian / American violinist and Big Band leader, born in Petrograd, Russia, on 4 Sep 1913. He grew up in Philadelphia and studied at the Curtis Institute, then played violin in the Philadelphia Orchestra. In the 1930s he was a musical director on a Philadelphia radio station, then formed a dance band for broadcasting. He took the band on tour, and gained a fine reputation for attractive swing and dance arrangements. He died in Sacramento, California, on 4 Oct 1948.

Savitt made a few early records for the Variety label in 1937, then recorded for Bluebird (1937–1938), Decca (1939–1941), and Victor from 1941. "It's a Wonderful World," his own composition, was a popular disc (Decca #2836; 1939); "720 in the Books," another Savitt tune, was also successful (Decca #2771; 1939); both were sung by Johnny Watson. Gloria DeHaven was vocalist with Savitt for a time, and did a fine rendition of "If You Ever, Ever Loved Me" (Bluebird #B-11548; 1942).

SAVOY (label). An American record, issued from 1942 by the Savoy Record Co., Newark, New Jersey. Herman Lubinsky (1896–1974) was owner of the firm until his death. With the benefit of **A & R** man Tony Reig, Savoy signed important musicians of the bebop movement: Charlie Parker, Miles Davis, Stan Getz, Dexter Gordon, Ray Brown, Sonny Stitt, Fats Navarro, Kay Winding, and many others. Fred Mendelssohn joined the organization in the late 1940s, and developed a great list of gospel singers. Rhythm and blues artists were recruited by Lee Magid, who also discovered Della Reese. Under A & R man Ozzier Cadena, Savoy produced the first records of Cannonball Adderley and Charlie Byrd, and outstanding work of Milt Jackson.

Savoy was one of the first jazz labels to release 12-inch LPs, from 1955 in the MG 12000 series. However the label lost momentum in the 1960s, and was acquired in 1975 by Arista Records. Muse Records, New York, was the Savoy distributor in 1991. [Ruppli 1980/1.]

SAVOY GRAMOPHONE CO. A subsidiary of the **Nanes Art Furniture Co.** of New York.

SAXOPHONE RECORDINGS. Evidently the earliest person to record the saxophone (sax) was a woman, Bessie Meeklens, who made 12 Edison wax cylinders with piano accompaniment on 23 Apr 1892. Her first number was "Ave Maria." Eugene Coffin was the earliest Columbia saxophonist, performing "Rocked in the Cradle of the Deep" and seven other pieces in 1896. Jean-Baptiste Moeremans, of the United States Marine Band, recorded ca. 1899 for Columbia cylinders, doing "The Heart Bowed Down" (#12700) and two other numbers. He was also with Victor from 1900 to 1911.

A saxophone quartet from Sousa's Band recorded three items for Victor discs in August 1902, and returned to the studio in September 1903. Other early artists included F. Wheeler Wadsworth, Nathan Glantz (of the Van Eps Trio), Duane Sawyer, the **Six Brown Brothers** (sextet), H. Benne Henton, and Steve Porpora.

The minuscule classical repertoire for the instrument inhibited the growth of that genre of recording, but there was no shortage of jazz performances. New Orleans Dixieland bands did not use saxophones; but as the dixie style expanded the instrument appeared in ensembles of the 1920s. **Don Redman** played alto saxophone (and clarinet) with the Fletcher Henderson Dance Orchestra on their earliest recordings, for Brunswick in 1921. He was joined by **Coleman Hawkins** in the reed section in 1923, and Allie Ross in 1924. Paul Whiteman's 1920 lineup had three saxophone players, Ross Gorman, Don Clark, and Hale Byers, clarinetists who doubled on altos and tenors when needed. By the mid-1920s Whiteman had a full choir of saxophones. **Frankie Trumbauer** was featured with Whiteman from 1927 to the mid-1930s. Art Hickman's orchestra had three or four saxophones in 1919.

Harlan Leonard, alto saxophone (also soprano saxophone, and clarinet), was one of the artists added when Bennie Moten increased the size of his orchestra in 1924. Otto Hardwick, a clarinetist who played alto and baritone saxophone as well, was with the Duke Ellington band of 1924; and Prince Robinson, clarinet and tenor sax, was added to the Ellington band in 1925. Don Redman was with Ellington in 1926. The 1928 Ellington band included **Barney Bigard** and **Johnny Hodges**, both men playing sax as well as clarinet—a combination that became standard in the swing bands.

Herschel Evans played a melodic and fluent tenor saxophone with Troy Floyd's Plaza Hotel Orchestra; he can be heard on "Dreamland Blues" (Okeh #8719; 1928). An early soprano saxophone solo—by Siki Collins—appeared on Floyd's only other record, "Shadowland Blues" (Okeh #8571; 1928). Walter Page, trumpet virtuoso, played a baritone saxophone on a recording of "Squabblin'" made by his Blue Devils (Vocalion #1463; 1929).

From such initiatives it was the alto sax and tenor sax that entered the jazz/swing mainstream. In the 1930s the great name was Coleman Hawkins, tenor. His influence embraced nearly all who followed, such as Budd Johnson, Don Byas, **Willie Smith**, **Charlie Barnet**, **Ben Webster**, and Flip Phillips. The next great innovator was **Lester Young.**

Among the many fine sax players with the Big Bands, a few can be cited here. Count Basie had Lester Young and Herschel Evans; Bob Crosby had **Eddie Miller**; Jimmy Dorsey had Herbie Haymer; Benny Goodman had **Bud Freeman**; Harry James had Willie Smith (in 1944–1954, with interruptions) Guy Lombardo had Carmen Lombardo; Jimmie Lunceford had Willie Smith (1929–1942); Artie Shaw had Tony Pastor.

During the bebop era **John Coltrane** was a leading saxophone artist, playing tenor and soprano; **Gerry Mulligan** was a master of the baritone sax; Dexter Gordon, Cannonball Adderly, and **Stan Getz** of the tenor; **Charlie Parker** and **Paul Desmond** of the alto.

SAYÃO, BIDÚ, 1902–. Brazilian soprano, born Baluina de Oliveira Sayão near Rio de Janeiro on 11 May 1902. She studied in France with Jean de Reszke, returned to Brazil and made a concert debut in 1925. A year later she appeared as Rosina in her opera debut, and became a favorite in that and other coloratura and lyric roles. She sang throughout Europe opposite great artists like Beniamino Gigli, Aureliano Pertile, Titta Ruffo, and Jan Kiepura. In 1931 she sang Juliette with Georges Thill at the Paris Opéra. Arturo Toscanini invited her to sing with the New York Philharmonic Symphony, leading to a highly successful American debut. She began with the Metropolitan Opera on 14 Feb 1937, as Manon, and remained 15 seasons until she retired in 1952. Sayão was renowned for her interpretations of Gilda, Mimi, Violetta, and Cio Cio San. In addition to opera, she was a brilliant concert artist, excelling in the French art song.

Sayão's recordings began with Victor, in Brazil, where she sang arias from *Guarany* (Victor #11561) and seven other numbers in 1935. She continued with Victor in the U.S., doing one side in 1938 and two others in 1940; then went to Columbia for her principal output, from 1944 to ca. 1948. Ten records covered her outstanding arias; they were reissued on LP by Columbia, Philips, and several other labels. Air shots from Metropolitan Opera performances were released by Golden Age of Opera, displaying her art in the complete *Boheme, Don Giovanni, Don Pasquale, Nozze di Figaro,* and *Romeo et Juliette;* there was also a complete *Manon* from San Francisco, plus several extended excerpt albums. Odyssey issued an album (#Y33130) of her concert songs in 1977. [Léon 1960.]

SCALA (label). A British record issued from 1911 to 1927. In 1912 the source firm was Scala

Record Co., Ltd., 80 City Road, London. Pressings were from Germany until World War I (masters from Beka and others), then made in London as well. A number of American masters were used, including Vocalion and Gennett, in producing a popular dance and vocal repertoire. A second label, Scala Ideal, appeared from the same company during 1923–1927, offering the same popular material. [Rust 1978.]

SCHIØTZ, AKSEL, 1906–1975. Danish tenor, later a baritone, born in Roskilde on 1 Sep 1906. He studied languages at the University of Copenhagen, taking a master's degree in 1929; at the same time he pursued vocal studies. He made his opera debut in Copenhagen, in *Così fan tutte* (1939), commencing a career in which the Mozart roles were greatly admired. He specialized also in Lieder, and was instrumental in popularizing the Schubert cycles through his recordings with pianist Gerald Moore. In the U.S. from 1948, he taught voice at several universities before retiring to Denmark in 1968. He died in Copenhagen on 19 Apr 1975.

The great Schiøtz/Moore interpetations of Schubert included the *Schöne Müllerin* on HMV (set #GM-407) plus individual songs from other cycles. Schiotz also recorded several Mozart arias, e.g., "Dalla sua pace" (HMV #DB-2564), and "Una aura amorosa" from *Così fan tutte* (HMV #DB 5265).

SCHIPA, TITO, 1888–1965. Italian tenor, born Raffaele Attilio Amadeo Schipa in Lecce on 2 Jan 1888. He was a composer first, then took up singing; he made his debut in Vercelli as Alfredo in 1910. Then he sang throughout Europe, and with the Chicago Opera Co. from 1919 to 1932. His Metropolitan Opera debut was on 23 Nov 1932, as Nemorino; he remained with the company until 1935, achieving great success even in competition with Beniamino Gigli and Giovanni Martinelli, although his vocal prime had been in the 1920s. His lyric roles were the finest, not only in the usual Verdi, Rossini, and Mozart repertoire, but also in such operas as *Mignon*, *Werther*, and Cilea's *Arlesiana*. After world tours in the 1930s he settled in Italy, retired from opera in 1954, but continued giving recitals until 1963. He died in New York on 16 Dec 1965.

Schipa's earliest records were for HMV in Milan in 1913–1914. He first sang two arias from *Cavalleria rusticana* (#252127 and #252128), and numbers from *Gioconda, Lucia, Faust,* plus Verdi-Puccini material. In 1916–1919 he worked for Pathé in Milan, doing among other arias his greatly acclaimed "Questa o quella" (#10316; later recorded also for Victor) backed by "La donna è mobile." Victor recorded Schipa in America during 1922–1926, including duets with Amelita Galli-Curci and Lucrezia Bori. A number of CD reissues have covered most of the Schipa output, including RCA #GD 87969 (among them arias and Spanish songs, done in the 1920s and 1930s, and duets with Galli-Curci from *Lucia* and *Traviata*); EMI Références #CD H763200–2, on which one can hear the marvelous rendition of "Una furtiva lagrima" and the earliest Milan HMV's; and a complete *Don Pasquale* from 1933 at La Scala (EMI #CHS7 63241–2, in which Schipa displays the bel canto style to perfection. [D'Andrea 1981; Hutchinson 1960.]

SCHNABEL, ARTUR, 1882–1951. Austrian/American pianist, born in Lipnik on 17 Apr 1882. A child prodigy, he studied with Theodor Leschetitzky from 1891 to 1897, and began public performances. He lived in Berlin and concertized there, playing recitals with violinist Carl Flesch, then teaching at the Hochschule für Musik. His American debut was in 1921. Schnabel was universally acclaimed for his Beethoven and Mozart interpretations. He lived in New York from 1939, taking American citizenship in 1944, but finally returned to Europe. He died in Morschach, Switzerland, on 15 Aug 1951.

Schnabel did not like to record, and made no discs until he was 50 years old, slightly after his prime. He worked for Victor/HMV, doing the Beethoven concertos with Malcolm Sargent, Beethoven and Mozart sonatas, and works of Schubert and J. S. Bach.

Harmonia Mundi issued a CD in 1990 of Mozart works (#Z6590/93; later released by EMI, Références #CHS7 63703-2) that offered some uneven technical results and infelicitous orchestral partnerships. Schnabel's superior Beethoven sonata interpetations appear on another EMI Références CD, #CHS7 63765-2. [Bloesch 1986.]

SCHOETTEL (E. A. AND A. G.) CO. A New York firm, located in 1907 in Queens. They marketed the Mega horn, and other gramophone horns made of papier-maché.

SCHORR, FRIEDRICH, 1888–1953. Hungarian/American baritone, born in Nagyvarád on 2 Sep 1888. He studied law in Vienna, and took voice lessons. He made his opera debut in Graz and remained with the company five seasons. He also appeared with the Chicago Opera in 1911–1912, then returned to Europe. He sang in Graz, Prague, and Cologne; then joined the Berlin State Opera and remained from 1923 to 1931. Schorr was with the Metropolitan Opera in 1924–1943, singing also in Bayreuth in 1925, 1927, 1928, and 1930. He was famed for his Wagnerian interpretations, notably Hans Sachs and Wotan, but was also distinguished as Amonasro and in the Richard Strauss operas. He later taught at the Manhattan School of Music. Schorr died in Farmington, Connecticut, on 14 Aug 1953.

Schorr recorded for HMV, Brunswick, and Polydor (DG Schallplatte) in the 1920s. The earliest record was "Wotan's Abschied" from *Walküre* (Polydor #1108; 1921). Schorr made 26 sides, most of them Wagnerian, in 1921–1922. He went to Brunswick in 1924 and sang six numbers; the one of most interest to collectors was "Sonst spielt' ich" from Lortzing's *Zar und Zimmermann* (#15088). Electrola (the Berlin HMV branch) recorded Schorr in 1927–1929, 26 items plus 31 sides from a live performance of *Meistersinger* at the Berlin State Opera (Electrola #EJ 277/86).

Outstanding discs were made by HMV in London in 1929–1931. The finest were 13 arias, duets, and the Quintet from *Meistersinger*; Lauritz Melchior was his partner for "Abendlich glühend" (#D2000; 1931). Melchior also sang with Schorr in a scene from *Götterdämmerung*, "Hast du, Gunther, ein Weib?" (#D1700; 1929). In the 1930s Schorr was in Metropolitan performances that were recorded from radio broadcasts by the Golden

Age of Opera label: *Siegfried* (EJS #173; 1937), *Rosenkavalier* (EJS #496; 1937), and *Walküre* (EJS #178; 1940). The same label also produced a *Meistersinger* (EJS #224; 1939). [Dennis 1971 is a complete discography.]

SCHUBERT RECORD (label). An American record, vertical cut, offered 1917– ca. 1918 by the Bell Talking Machine Corp., New York. Twenty to 30 new selections were issued monthly, on 10-inch discs selling for $.75 each. Franz Schubert's portrait graced the labels. The records were still on sale in December 1918, after which date there was no further advertising. [Andrews*; Rust 1978.]

SCHUBERT TRIO. A mixed vocal group that recorded briefly for Victor. On 12 June 1906 they sang "Praise Ye" from Verdi's *Attila* (#4776). Members were Elise Stevenson, soprano; Harry Macdonough, tenor; and Frank C. Stanley, bass. There was no listing for the trio in the Victor 1917 catalog.

SCHUMANN, ELISABETH, 1888–1952. German/American soprano, born in Merseburg on 13 June 1888. She studied in Dresden, Berlin, and Hamburg; then made her debut in Hamburg on 2 Sep 1909 as the Shepherd in *Tannhäuser* and remained with the company there until 1919. She sang one season at the Metropolitan Opera (1914–1915), making her debut as Sophie, a role that brought her much acclaim. She was also noted for her Mozartian roles. Then Schumann spent 20 years with the Vienna State Opera before returning to the U.S. She became an American citizen in 1944. She taught at the Curtis Institute of Music, and gave outstanding Lieder recitals. On 23 Apr 1952 she died in New York.

Schumann recorded for Favorite in Germany in 1913, then for Edison Diamond Discs in 1915 and 1922. Her other records were made in Europe in the early 1920s, for Polydor in Berlin and for HMV. "Vedrai, carino" (HMV #DA 845) and "Batti, batti" (HMV #946) were among her fine Mozart selections (she also sang the arias in German, for Polydor); they were reissued by Top Artists Platters. *Rosenkavalier* was captured in a Sofia performance by HMV (#DB 2060/72) and reissued on LP #COLH 110/1 in 1962. Two compact discs covering her Schubert song cycles were released in 1990 by EMI (Références #CHS7 63040-2). Preiser issued a CD in 1991 that featured Mozart arias, plus several Lieder by Richard Strauss, Mahler, and Robert Schumann (#89031). [Owen, H. 1952 is a discography.]

SCHUMANN-HEINK, ERNESTINE, 1861–1936.

Czech contralto/mezzo-soprano, born in Ernestine Rössler in Lieben, near Prague, on 15 June 1861. She studied in Graz, and made her opera debut in Dresden, remaining with the company from 1878 to 1882. Then she appeared in Hamburg and Bayreuth, establishing herself as a Wagner specialist (Erda, Fricka, Brangaene) as well as in the Verdi repertoire and as Carmen. She was heard at the Metropolitan Opera on 9 Jan 1899 as Ortrud, in a cast that included the two De Reszke's, and quickly became an American favorite—not only in opera but as a concert singer. Schumann-Heink (whose stage name was a combination of the surnames of her first two husbands, both of whom died) sang until age 70 and gave a farewell Metropolitan appearance as Erda in *Siegfried* on 11 Mar 1932. She died in Hollywood on 17 Nov 1936.

Schumann-Heink began to record ca. 1899, with two Zonophone seven-inch discs, private recordings, one being a message to her children. She made her first commercial records for Columbia in 1903, five numbers beginning with "Ah mon fils" from *Prophete*. She was heard on **Mapleson cylinders** in the same year, in three Wagner fragments. Then she became a Victor artist, from 1906, beginning with "Mon coeur s'ouvre" in German (#85094), one of her most popular arias. In September 1906 she recorded an enduring hit, Brahms' "Wiegenlied" (#81085). In the 1917 Victor catalog she is represented by 40 solos, plus a duet with Enrico Caruso, "Ai nostri monti" (#89060; 1913), and a duet with Geraldine Farrar, "Wanderers Nachtlied," by Anton Rubinstein (#87504; 1913). "The Rosary" was perhaps her most appreciated solo record of that period (#87221 on 10-inch Red Seal, and #88108 on 12-inch; 1908). The Victor 1940 catalog still carried 15 of her Red Seals, including the acclaimed Christmas songs "Stille Nacht"/"Weih-

nachten" (#6723; 1926). Her final recording sessions were in January 1931. [McPherson 1967; Moran 1977/5.]

SCHWANN CATALOGS. The earliest published catalog of long-playing records was issued by William Schwann in Boston, October 1949. Entitled *Long Playing Record Catalog*, it consisted of 26 pages, typed out by Schwann himself, listing the LP output of 11 labels available in the U.S. Subsequently this modest publication grew into the respected Schwann catalog series, listing each month the records available in the U.S., with coverage of LP discs and tapes, and most recently of CDs. Name changes have been a frustrating characteristic of the series, which now (1992) carries these titles: *Opus* (classical material; quarterly), *Spectrum* (pop material, spoken, children's; quarterly), and an annual *Artist Issue* (all formats arranged by performers), plus a monthly update service. In 1992 the publisher was Schwann Publications, with editorial offices at 535 Boylston St., Boston.

SCHWARZKOPF, ELISABETH, 1915– . German soprano, born in Jarotschin on 9 Dec 1915. She studied in Berlin, and made her debut with the Deutsche Oper in 1938. Then she went to the Vienna State Opera, and Salzburg, becoming famous for her Mozartean roles. A great sensation at Covent Garden, she sang there from 1947 to 1951. She created the role of Anne Truelove in *Rake's Progress* in Venice, 1951. Schwarzkopf was immediately popular in the U.S. after her Carnegie Hall recital of 25 Oct 1953. She appeared with the San Francisco Opera and Chicago Lyric Opera, then from 1964 to 1966 at the Metropolitan Opera. The Marschallin was her Metropolitan debut role, and one that she made a favorite. She made a farewell tour of America in 1975 and settled in Switzerland. Her husband Walter Legge was the subject of her book, *On and Off the Record* (1982).

Bridging the 78-LP eras, Schwarzkopf recorded for Columbia in London during 1946–1954, doing Mozart, Verdi, Puccini, Wagner, *Fidelio*, and *Hänsel und Gretel*. She continued with U.S. Columbia in the 1950s and early 1960s. The gems among her records are the complete operas, including Richard Strauss works and Mozart; also *Falstaff* (she sings Alice) and *Meistersinger* (Eva). In 1952 she was in a complete *Dido and Aeneas* made for HMV (#ALP 10026). She has an extensive CD discography, nearly all of it from EMI. [*Gramophone*, December 1990, listed her compact discs.]

SCHWEINFEST, GEORGE, ca. 1862–1949. Pianist, flutist, and performer on nearly all the other instruments; one of the earliest and most prolific recording artists. He began with Edison on 28 Aug 1889, playing the piano in "Sea Breeze Polka" and six similar numbers. On 9 Sep 1889 he played the flute and piccolo in 11 numbers, beginning with "Etude de Concert" (flute); Edward Issler accompanied on the piano. The same duo returned for sessions on the next four days. On 8–9–10 Oct Schweinfest was piano accompanist for clarinetist William Tuson. In November he was pianist and also violinist; and he played flute for a recording by Issler's Orchestra. In 1890 he made more records on those instruments; in 1893 he was with the New Jersey Phonograph Co., playing the piccolo, then he worked for Berliner.

In 1897–1898 Schweinfest made a series of 37 piccolo cylinders for Columbia (#23500–23536); these were mostly polkas and similar dance numbers. On Victor records he confined himself to flute and piccolo, beginning with a series made in September 1900, repeating his dance repertoire. His final records were a Victor disc of 1902 (a remake of "Ben Bolt"), Columbia discs of ca. 1902, and a Columbia cylinder of 1906. He was also a member of Issler's Orchestra and the Columbia Orchestra. [Brooks 1979.]

SCOTT, LÉON, 1817–1879. French inventor, printer, and librarian; born Edouard-Léon Scott de Martinville. His work in the printing trade gave him the opportunity to read scientific treatises, leading to an interest in invention. He developed the **Phonautograph** in 1857, a device that recorded sound but did not play it back. Although he patented the invention (#17.897/31.470; 25 Mar 1857) he was unable to market it. He became a librarian, and wrote several books unrelated to recorded sound. When Edison's phonograph was announced

in 1877, Scott claimed recognition for his prior work, but unsuccessfully; he was by then reduced to selling prints in a stall behind 9 rue Vivienne, Paris. He died on 26 Apr 1879, poor and forgotten.

SCOTT, ROBERT FALCON, 1868–1912. British explorer. He is of interest in the history of recorded sound because the Gramophone Co. gave him two record players to take on his Antarctic expedition of 1910–1913, with several hundred discs. Accounts from expedition members indicate that the machines were in constant use. Among the artists heard by the explorers were Enrico Caruso, Nellie Melba, Luisa Tetrazzini, Geraldine Farrar, Clara Butt, and Harry Lauder. In May 1913 Diploma Records issued an account of the expedition. [Taylor 1988/8.]

SCOTTI, ANTONIO, 1866–1936. Italian baritone, born in Naples on 25 Jan 1866. He made his debut in Naples in 1889, then toured Europe and South America. In 1899 he was acclaimed for his Don Giovanni at Covent Garden, and repeated the success on 27 Dec 1899 at the Metropolitan Opera, where he remained on the roster for 33 years. His great roles were Don Giovanni, Scarpia, Iago, Rigoletto, and Falstaff. He died on 29 Feb 1926.

Scotti was heard on **Bettini** cylinders, singing "Serenata" and "Fin ch' han del vino" from *Don Giovanni*, and "Bella siccome un angelo" from *Don Pasquale*. Fragments from *Ernani*, *Pagliacci* and *Tosca* were recorded from the Metropolitan stage in 1901–1903 on **Mapleson cylinders**. In 1902 Scotti made five sides for G & T in London. Then he made three Columbia records in 1903 before beginning a Victor career in 1903. He recorded six Edison two-minute cylinders in 1906–1908. One of them, "Vi ravviso" from *Sonnambula*, was a lifelong favorite, recorded later for Victor (#87034). The best recording results came from his first U.S. issues of 1904, with piano accompaniment (the 81000–85000 series), although these were withdrawn when Scotti re-recorded the material with orchestral accompaniments beginning in 1906 (87000–88000 series). There was a distinguished duet with Enrico Caruso, "Solenne in quest'ora" (#89001), and another outstanding duet, with Geraldine Farrar, "La ci darem la mano" (#89015). He was in two Victor recordings of the *Rigoletto* Quartet, both with Caruso, and in the definitive version of the *Lucia* Sextet, with Caruso, Marcella Sembrich, and Marcel Journet in the cast (#96200). Thee were 13 solos in the 1917 catalog, plus the ensemble pieces. Most of the 78 rpm and LP reissue labels offered Scotti material.

SCOTTISH GRAMOPHONE MANUFACTURING CO., LTD. A Glasgow firm, established ca. 1917, incorporated 12 Apr 1919. At least two types of gramophone were made, a table grand and an upright cabinet model. The firm was dissolved on 15 Feb 1943. [Hamilton, C. 1986.]

SCRANTON BUTTON WORKS. A Scranton, Pennsylvania, firm established in 1915. It pressed records for the dime store trade. Scranton combined with Cameo Records, Inc., and Regal Record Co., Inc. (owned by the Crystalate Gramophone Record Manufacturing Co., Ltd., of Britain; formerly belonging to the Plaza Music Co.) to form the **American Record Corp. (ARC).** Pressing for ARC labels was done by the Scranton Button Works. [Andrews*.]

SCRATCH FILTER. A control on an amplifier that serves to reduce the noise on a disc with scratches or other surface defects.

SCROLL. An inaudible segment of the groove on a recorded disc, used to separate and link the recorded bands. It would only be needed when a side carried more than one song or instrumental piece, so it was not much used in the acoustic era. The earliest example noted in the literature was Victor #16863 (1911), which has two songs by Henry Allan on side A, and five "Mother Goose Songs" by Elizabeth Wheeler on the flip side. Another Wheeler disc of Mother Goose songs, with separation scrolls, was #35225 (1912).

A French language set issued by HMV in 1927 (#C-1353+) had such dividers for lessons. The HMV *Instruments of the Orchestra* had scrolls that were "locked," so that the needle would not pass to the next band without human inter-

vention; evidently the purpose was to give a teacher time to talk about the instruments as they were illustrated (HMV #C-1311+; 1927). In 1932 and 1933 the British labels Durium and Broadcast Four-Tune used scroll separators. Scrolls became standard on LP records. [Copeland, P. 1990.]

SCRUGGS, EARL, 1924– . American country singer and banjo player, born in Flint Hill, North Carolina, on 6 Jan 1924. He played banjo as a child, developing a three-finger style, and joined Bill Monroe's Blue Grass Boys, and in 1944 performed with them at the Grand Ole Opry. He then teamed with **Lester Flatt**, guitarist, and formed the Foggy Mountain Boys (1948). He remained with Flatt until 1969, then Scruggs set up another group, the Earl Scruggs Review, moving to a country-rock style. That ensemble made a chart album, *Earl Scruggs Revue Anniversary* in 1975 (Columbia #33416) and another in 1976, *Earl Scruggs Revue* (Columbia #34090). Scruggs starred in the motion picture *Banjo Man* (1975).

SEAMAN, FRANK. American record company executive, one of the pioneer builders of the industry. He was owner of the **New York Gramophone Co.**, which sold products made by Emile Berliner in New York and New Jersey up to 1896. Then he established and became president of the **National Gramophone Co.** in 1896. Seaman had personally contracted with Berliner for U.S. sales rights (except for Washington, D.C.), and did well after a slow first year. The **Universal Talking Machine Co.** was set up on 10 Feb 1898 to manufacture machines—which the Berliner Gramophone Co. refused to accept, or allow Seaman to stock. Litigation ensued over Seaman's alleged infringement of Bell-Tainter patents, both Seaman and his company being defendants in the proceedings. A new firm, National Gramophone Corp., was set up in March 1899; through this firm, and Universal, Seaman manufactured an unauthorized Berliner-clone machine named the **Zonophone.** The earlier National Gramophone Co. went into liquidation.

Berliner broke with Seaman, and Seaman replied with a petition to have the Berliner Gramophone Co. prohibited from using the name "gramophone" on the basis of Seaman's own exclusive contract to do so. This bizarre approach was successful: Berliner was enjoined not to use the name gramophone in June, 1900, and Eldridge Johnson was similarly restricted on 1 Mar 1901. However Seaman was sued by the graphophone interests for infringement of the Bell-Tainter patents, bringing about a consent agreement in which Columbia gained the assets of the Universal Talking Machine Co. and was able to market disc players with the Zonophone name.

Eldridge Johnson devised an improved recording process and record player, and marketed them over Seaman's claim that he was still sole sales agent for the gramophone. The court supported Johnson, who removed the "gramophone" name from his record labels in favor of the "Improved Record." The National Gramophone Corp. folded in September 1901; Universal Talking Machine Co. held a sheriff's sale of patents and equipment on 28 Oct 1901. The Zonophone business was reorganized under the name Universal Talking Machine Manufacturing Co. on 19 Dec 1901. (The earlier Universal retained its corporate existence for a time, acting as sales agent for the new one.) The new company made machines (claiming 700 per week) and discs (2,000 per day), but Seaman had lost the assets of his National Gramophone Corp. and Universal Talking Machine Co. and had to accept from Victor an out of court settlement of $25,000 in 1903 (from his suit against Eldridge Johnson and Berliner). He left the sound recording field in late 1903. He was not mentioned as an officer of either Universal company when G & T acquired the stock of both companies in June 1903. [Andrews*.]

SEARCHLIGHT HORN CO. A Brooklyn firm, located at 753 Lexington Ave. in 1906. It advertised a horn designed "on the principle of the searchlight" that could play "louder and clearer than any other." Following that promotion in June 1906, there was a September advertisement claiming sales of 10,000 per month. A 1907 advertisement touted a "knock-down" model, "easily taken apart."

SEARS, ROEBUCK AND CO. A Chicago firm, established with that name in 1893, succeeding a number of other companies. At first Sears was devoted entirely to mail order sales of a wide variety of products. In the mid-1920s retail stores were opened, and the sale of goods under several house tradenames (Allstate first; later Craftsman, Kenmore, etc.) began. In time Sears became the largest retailer in the world, with 500,000 employees and $53 billion in sales (1989). Headquarters is in the Sears Tower, with new offices being developed in the Chicago suburb of Hoffmann Estates.

The 1897 mail order catalog (#104) offered cylinder phonographs and records. The Columbia Type A Graphophone sold for $25, or with a package of 12 records and a hearing tube for $35. The talking machine product line expanded in subsequent catalogs. Catalog #111, 1902, offered the Columbia Graphophone Model AB, under the name of "Gem Graphophone," for $10. An "exhibition outfit" was available with the machine, including a large horn, admission tickets, advertising posters, etc., all for $23.75. A Columbia Grand, with five-inch cylinders, was available in that catalog for $50. A large selection of cylinder records was also sold, at $.50 each. In 1902 disc record players were offered as well, under the names "Regina Graphophone" and "Regal Graphophone Grand." Ten-inch Climax records were sold for $1, and seven-inch discs with the name Acme for $.50.

In later catalogs Sears marketed discs under various names: **Silvertone, Challenge, Conqueror,** and **Supertone** labels; masters came from nearly every major record company in the 1920s. The firm was the first sponsor of the *National Barn Dance* radio program (1924), and subsequently featured recordings of country artists in its catalogs. In the mid-1920s the catalog offered dance and vocal records on the brown-label Silvertone Record, at $.49 plus postage. Needles, phono parts, empty albums, etc. were sold as well. Phonographs cost from $3.49 to $19.95.

In the catalog of Fall-Winter 1926–1927 the price of Silvertones was $.39. "Selections by Negro Artists" included Alberta Jones and Jelly Roll Morton. The Challenge label was added to catalog in Fall 1927, at $.24. Silvertone was discontinued in Spring 1929, displaced by the Challenge (three for $.65 post paid; label discontinued in 1932)) and a new one, Conqueror (three for $.89 post paid), and also new Supertone (at $.43 each post paid; discontinued in 1932). A successful **race record** of 1930 was Conqueror #7081 by Mandy Lee, "I Needs Plenty Grease In My Frying Pan"; it remained in the catalog until 1936. In spring 1934 the price of Conqueror was down to $.19 in lots of ten, or $.21 each. Josh White appeared on three country blues items in 1934. By 1938 the catalogs had dropped all country blues records and race records. [Charters 1960.]

SEEBURG, JUSTUS, 1871–1958. Swedish/American industrialist, born in Gothenburg. After technical training there, he transferred to the U.S. in 1886. He worked in a piano factory in Chicago, and became superintendent of Cable Piano; then he was co-founder of Kurz-Seeburg Co., Rockford, Illinois, which made piano actions. He sold his interest in 1902, and established the Seeburg Piano Co. in Chicago, 1907. That firm made coin-op pianos with electrically driven bellows and perforated paper rolls. A line of Orchestrions appeared in 1910, used in silent film theaters.

In 1927 Seeburg began to manufacture automatic electric **coin-op** phonographs. He discontinued the Orchestrion with the arrival of sound films. Two interesting products followed: the Audiophone, with eight turntables for selective play (1928), and the Melophone, allowing 12 selections (1930). In 1935 the **Selectophone** and the **Symphonola** were introduced. A wall-mounted juke box, the Playboy, was introduced in 1939. The firm was in receivership during the 1930s, and diversified to other products. Finally the family sold out in 1956 to Fort Pitt Industries.

SEEGER, PETE, 1919– . American folksinger and songwriter, born Peter R. Seeger in Patterson, New York, on 3 May 1919. He was the son of musicologist Charles Louis Seeger. After two years at Harvard University he left academe to pursue a career playing banjo and singing folk music. He was in a group named the Almanac Singers in the early 1940s, and in 1949 joined the **Weavers.** He continued to perform solo as well, concentrating on songs of social content. As a composer, he had several successes, including "If I Had a Hammer," "Kisses Sweeter Than Wine," and "Where Have All the Flowers Gone?" He was co-lyricist of the civil rights song, "We Shall Overcome." His record of "Little Boxes" (Columbia #42940; 1964) was a chart hit. An album, *We Shall Overcome* (Columbia #CL 2101; 1964) was on the charts 18 weeks. He and Arlo Guthrie made a successful album in 1975: *Together in Concert* (Warner #2R 2214). Seeger also wrote a standard instruction manual for the five-string banjo, and edited several song collections.

SEGOVIA, ANDRÉS, 1893–1987. Spanish guitarist, born in Linares on 21 Feb 1893. He was self-taught, making a debut in Granada at age 16, then going on to play in Madrid, Barcelona, and South America. He was the first artist to elevate the Spanish guitar to the category of a concert instrument. Albert Roussel wrote a composition for him, entitled "Segovia," which he played in Paris in 1924. Segovia appeared in Carnegie Hall on 8 Jan 1928, and continued performing everywhere into the 1980s. He died in Madrid on 2 June 1987.

The earliest recordings date from 1927, on HMV. They include some of the J. S. Bach transcriptions for which Segovia was much admired. Much of his performing and recorded repertoire was made up of his arrangements. He remained with HMV to 1939, then recorded for Decca and Victor Among the remarkable sides cut for HMV were "Recuerdos de la Alhambra" by Francisco Tárrega (#D1395; 1928), and "Theme varié" (#D1255) by Fernando Sor. Two works by Manuel Ponce—the "Theme, Variations, and Fugue" and the *Suite*, were brilliantly recorded in 1932 and 1941. A set of two compact discs in the EMI Références series presents much of the 1927–1939 material (#CHS 61047-2). [Wade 1983.]

SELECTOPHONE. A Seeburg jukebox, 1935, developed by Wilcox. It had many turntables on a single revolving shaft.

SELTSAM, WILLIAM, 1897–1968. American writer on music and founder of the International Record Collectors Club (IRCC). He began a career as a musician, but was afflicted with hearing loss and went into office work. In 1932 he enlarged on a longtime interest in phonograph records by launching the IRCC, devoted to reissue of important vocal (and a few instrumental) recordings from the golden age. He was scrupulous in labeling and documentation of his records, giving exact recording dates and re-recording dates, and endeavored to determine proper record speed and pitch. From 1937 to 1939 Seltsam supervised the transfer of **Mapleson cylinder** material to IRCC discs. One of his discoveries was the first recording by Ernestine Schumann-Heink, a seven-inch privately made disc of ca. 1899; he reissued it on IRCC ("Wie ein Grüssen").

As an author, Seltsam is known for *Metropolitan Opera Annals* (New York: H. W. Wilson, 1947) and its two supplements. The three volumes cover all Metropolitan Opera New York performances from 1883/84 through 1966.

SEMBRICH, MARCELLA, 1858–1935. Polish soprano, born Prakseda Marcelina Kochanska in Wisniewczyk on 15 Feb 1858. Her father taught her violin and piano, and a friend of the family helped finance further instruction. She studied in Vienna, and turned to voice; made her debut in Athens on 3 June 1877 in *Puritani*, using her mother's maiden name then and thereafter. In 1878 she sang Lucia in Dresden and in 1880 at Covent Garden. Her Metropolitan Opera debut was on 24 Oct 1883, the second night of the company's first season. She was a great success as a singer, but showed her early training in a remarkable concert in which she played parts of a violin concerto and a Chopin mazurka, also singing some of Rosina's arias from *Barbiere di Siviglia*. She was a favorite with the Metropolitan until 1909; then gave song recitals until 1917. She also headed the voice department at the Curtis Institute of Music, Philadelphia. She died in New York on 11 Jan 1935.

Her main roles were Lucia, Violetta, Gilda, Rosina, Mimi (she was Puccini's personal favorite in the role), Zerlina, Susanna, and Queen of the Night. Unfortunately her voice did not record well. Her first records were three **Bettini** cylinders in 1900. She is heard on four **Mapleson** cylinders of 1902 and 1903, singing fragments of *Fille du régiment*, *Zauberflöte*, *Ernani*, and *Traviata*, plus Johann Strauss's "Voices of Spring." All of these were issued on IRCC discs. After three Columbia sides in 1903, Sembrich began recording for Victor in November 1904, singing "Ah! Fors' è lui" (#85035), and continued with the label. There were 25 solos in the 1917 Victor catalog, duets with Emma Eames and Antonio Scotti; a premium priced *Rigoletto* Quartet with Enrico Caruso and Antonio Scotti (#96001, selling for $6) and a premium *Lucia* Sextet, with Caruso, Scotti, and Marcel Journet among the cast (#96200; at $7). Her finest coloratura disc was "Ah non giunge" from *Sonnambula* (#81047; 1904—reissued on IRCC #8). She made her last discs in 1919. Reissues appeared on most of the 78 rpm and LP reprint labels. [Owen, H. 1969.]

SENSITIVITY. In an audio system, the response-signal ratio of a microphone or other transducer, taken under specified conditions.

SEPARATION. (I) The ability of a microphone to accept signals from certain sources and not from other sources.

SEPARATION. (II) In elements of a stereo system, the degree to which individual channels are kept distinct.

SEPARATION RECORDING. A method of recording which assigns microphones to each performer or group of performers in an ensemble, inscribing their contributions independently of the other participants. The separate signals are mixed in the control room, not necessarily in a manner to duplicate the original event. Elements may also be recorded at different sessions, and combined later in a mixdown.

SERIAL COPY MANAGEMENT SYSTEM (SCMS). A method of controlling the copying of compact discs through a device in the tape recorder. This device permits the making of unlimited copies onto tapes from a CD, but tags each tape to prevent it from being copied to yet another tape. Thus a first-generation copy is possible, but not a second-generation copy. This system, replacing the **Copycode** that had brought the DAT industry to a standstill, was agreed upon by representatives of the recording and consumer electronics industries.

SERKIN, RUDOLF, 1903–1991. Bohemian pianist, born in Eger on 28 Mar 1903. He studied in Vienna, both piano and composition (with Arnold Schoenberg), and began a concert career in 1920. Many of his appearances were with violinist Adolf Busch, and it was with him that Serkin made his American debut in 1933. He was appointed to the faculty of the Curtis Institute of Music in Philadelphia in 1939, and served as director from 1968 to 1976. He was an active performer until the year of his death, widely acclaimed as one of the world's great interpreters of the Viennese repertoire. His son Peter is also a renowned pianist.

From the numerous recordings of highest quality that Serkin left, possibly the set of Beethoven concertos, made with Eugene Ormandy and the Philadelphia Orchestra in 1966, stands out. (Four were reissued in 1991 on CD by CBS Masterworks, #CD 42259, 42260.) He also recorded peerless renditions of the Beethoven sonatas, for Columbia; and of the Brahms and Schumann concertos, with the Cleveland and Philadelphia Orchestras, also for Columbia. The two Brahms concertos were reissued by CBS Masterworks on CD #42261 and #42262 in 1991. Serkin and Busch recorded the Beethoven "Kreutzer Sonata" for Columbia, as well as other chamber works. He and Mstislav Rostropovich won a Grammy for their 1983 recording of Brahms cellos sonatas (Deutsche Grammophon #25320).

SESSION. The event of actual recording, in a studio or on location. Sessions comprise a variable number of **takes**. The date of a session, which occupies no more than one day, is important in discography as an aid to establishment of precedence and the identification of personnel.

SESSION TAPE. The tape of all the material performed during a recording **session**, including both the accepted material that appears on the master, and the rejected (out-take) material.

SEXUALLY ORIENTED LYRICS. During the 78 rpm era there were few recorded songs with overtly sexual lyrics, except for "under the counter" party records and some blues and "race" material. A number of blues songs had suggestive words and double meanings, such as (in "Mill Man Blues") "Now, lady, I ain't no mill man / Just the mill man's son / But I can do your grinding / Till the mill man comes." Innuendos in **race records** of the late 1920s did appear frequently enough for Vocalion to tag their releases "Better and Cleaner Race Records"—but that label was turning out as many suggestive titles and texts as any other (e.g., Tampa Red's "It's Tight Like That" (Vocalion #1216; 1928). Later blues lyrics focused more on sexual relationships than on sexual relations.

Love songs—the staple of the mainstream popular repertoire—contented themselves with talk about kisses. But in pop/rock songs of the 1960s lyrics tended to become sexually explicit, leading to consumer complaint and various attempts to restrict access. The very term "rock and roll" has a sexual connotation, although it has been interpreted simply as having a party or as dancing. Suggestive lyrics were found in the preceeding rhythm & blues period ("Roll All Night Long," "Work with Me, Annie"), but the idiom did not become pervasive until the 1960s and 1970s. Such lyrics, especially when melded with the bump and grind mannerism popularized by Elvis Presley (whose lyrics were only mildly suggestive in themselves), resulted in public performances of plain eroticism. Noted representatives of this mode have been the Rolling Stones; The Fugs ("Wet Dream"); David Bowie; and the Doors, with Jim Morrison as the highly sensual lead singer ("Light My Fire"). Morrison was described by the *Miami Herald* as the "king of orgasmic rock." Protest movements arose in 1969–1970, as various "decency rallies" were held without great impact.

In the late 1980s the lyrics associated with "rap music" were preponderantly sexual. Recordings by the group 2 Live Crew were actually judged to be obscene by courts in some U.S. jurisdictions, but the performers were found innocent by higher courts. Their album *Nasty as You Wanna Be* appeared to break all earlier taboos for language and content. One shopkeeper in Florida who carried *Nasty* was in fact convicted of selling obscene material.

The addition of the visual element, in music videos, brought another area of concern. The popular videos (and live performances) of the singer Madonna were widely criticized in the 1980s and 1990s, and even **Michael Jackson** contributed a controversial video in 1991.

In the 1980s the U.S. record industry responded to pressure from parent groups by affixing warning stickers on certain albums, reading "Parental Advisory—Explicit Lyrics."

SHAMROCK STORE (label). An American record, issued between 1928 and 1936 by the Shamrock Store, 1334 Third Ave., New York. Material was of Irish interest; some of the masters came from Plaza. [Rust 1978.]

SHANNON FOUR. A male vocal quartet that recorded for Victor from 1917, and for various labels under various pseudonyms. Later they called themselves the Shannon Quartet, and made Victors until 1928. The original membership was Charles Hart, and Harvey Hindermyer, tenors; Elliott Shaw, baritone; and Wilfred Glenn, bass. who organized the group. In 1918 Lewis James replaced Hindermyer. Hart was replaced by James Melton; others who sang tenor were Franklyn Baur, Charles Harrison, Frank Parker, and Robert Simmons. Ed Smalle joined the group at times, singing and/or playing the piano accompaniment. In 1925 the Victor recordings were made by Baur, James, Shaw, and Glenn. In that year the group took the name **The Revelers**, although they also continued with the Shannon name. The Shannon sang a more traditional quartet style; the Revelers a jazzy modern style.

Other names for the Shannon group were the Lyric Male Quartet (on Harmony, Edison Blue Amberol, and Edison Diamond Disc), Acme Male Quartet or Hudson Male Quartet (on Pathé), Campus Glee Club (on Cameo), Cathedral Quartet or Liberty Quartet (on Emerson), and the Peerless Four (on Okeh and Gennett).

SHAVERS. Cylinder record blanks had to be turned smooth for both initial use and for re-use, this task being accomplished by a shaver. Edison's British patent #17175 (1887) included such a device, attached to the carrier arm of the New Phonograph. Later the shaver (or planer, or parer) had a separate existence, which might have been powered by a treadle (1890s to ca. 1905; based on U.S. patent #375,579 by Charles S. Tainter) or by electricity (from ca. 1897). An electric drive could spin a cylinder under the planer at 1,500 rpm to 2,800 rpm. In March 1908 Edison marketed his Universal Shaving Machine, usable on both regular size and six-inch business cylinders. A simple hand-cranked machine was available in 1912, employing a steel blade that could smooth a cylinder with just a few turns. [Klinger*; Frow 1978.]

SHAW, ARTIE, 1910– . American jazz clarinetist and Big Band leader, born Arthur Jacob Arshawsky in New York on 23 May 1910. He began playing in a band in New Haven, Connecticut, his instrument being the alto saxophone. He turned to the clarinet, then played tenor sax in Irving Aaronson's band. He was freelancing in New York in 1931–1935, and formed a group in 1936 that had a string quartet in it—an unusual sound that was widely appreciated. He began recording for Brunswick, and performed at the Lexington Hotel in New York until 1937. He regrouped, forming a conventional swing band, engaged Helen Forrest as vocalist, and produced his first and perhaps greatest record, "Begin the Beguine" (Bluebird #7746; 1938), an arrangement by Jerry Gray. "All the Things You Are," sung by Forrest, was one of his finer ballad records (Bluebird #10492; 1939). Among the artists who played in his bands at that time were Billy Butterfield, trumpet; Johnny Guarnieri, piano and harpsichord; Ray Coniff, trombone; Tony Pastor, tenor sax; and Buddy Rich and Dave Tough, drums.

Shaw's second great hit was "Frenesi" (Victor #26542; 1940), again with an orchestra including a string section. Emulating Benny Goodman, Shaw formed a small hot group from his band, the Gramercy Five; they made an acclaimed record for Victor, "Summit Ridge Drive" (#26763; 1940). During the Second World War Shaw enlisted in the Navy and was asked to lead a band to entertain the troops in the Pacific. In 1944 he put together a strong jazz band, with Roy Eldridge; and he also engaged the classical repertoire for clarinet, with a Carnegie Hall appearance and some recordings. He retired in 1954, then returned for another round of performances in 1983.

Among the LP reissues of earlier material there was a fine Sunbeam album (#SB207) that included sessions of 1936–1937, notably "Sweet Lorraine" and "Streamline." The Bluebird recordings were reissued by RCA; they cover 1938–1939, when Billie Holiday was briefly singing with the group, sparkling in "Any Old Time." Most of the Gramercy Five recordings reappeared on LP (RCA #LSA 3087).

SHAW, ELLIOTT, ca. 1887–1973. American baritone, known as a member of numerous male quartets in the 1920s. He began with the Shannon Four in 1918; continued with the same men as they formed The Revelers; and sang also with the Crescent Trio. On Pathé records he was known as Frank Sterling. Shaw retired to Sharon, Connecticut, and died in Bronxville, New York, on 13 Aug 1973.

SHAW, ROBERT, 1916– . American choral and orchestra conductor, born in Red Bluff, California, on 30 Apr 1916. He conducted his college glee club, and then the Fred Waring Glee Club (1938–1945). In 1948 he founded the Robert Shaw Chorale and conducted it for 20 years; it became recognized as one of the major choral groups of the world, making extended tours under auspices of the U.S. Department of State. From 1956 to 1967 Shaw was associate conductor of the Cleveland Orchestra, and then he became director of the Atlanta (Georgia) Symphony Orchestra. Under his leadership the Atlanta Orchestra and its Chorus achieved a high level of excellence. Shaw has won 10 Grammys (1961–1989) for performances with the Atlanta Symphony and Chorus, including definitive renditions of the requiems of Berlioz, Verdi, and Britten. Telarc compact discs have issued those works, and other masterpieces of the choral repertoire, from *Messiah* to *Carmina Burana*.

SHEARING, GEORGE ALBERT, 1919– . British/American jazz pianist, born in London on 13 Aug 1919. Blind from birth, he learned music from braille notation. Transferring to the U.S., he was greatly successful with an unusual piano style (locked hand, thick chords in parallel motion) and his gift for interpolating classical, contrapuntal elements into his improvisations. His George Shearing Quintet was highly popular from 1949 into the 1970s, featuring vibes and guitar blending with the piano line. He composed "Lullaby of Birdland," a major hit, and recorded it on MGM #11354. He had six chart albums for Capitol in the 1950s and 1960s, including *Shearing on Stage* (Capitol #ST 1187; 1959). In the 1980s he made a remarkable series of appearances and recordings with **Mel Tormé**. *An Evening with George Shearing and Mel Tormé* (Concord Jazz #190; 1982) won a Grammy.

SHEBLE, HORACE. Philadelphia recording industry executive and inventor, a partner in **Hawthorne & Sheble** with Ellsworth A. Hawthorne. He held 14 patents in the audio field, notably U.S. #701,769 (filed 15 June 1901, granted 3 June 1902) for a talking machine cabinet in which the gramophone was in a sliding drawer; and U.S. #872,586 (filed 21 Dec 1906; granted 3 Dec 1907) for a tone arm. The tone arm was Sheble's answer to the patented tapered tone arm of Eldridge Johnson; it was a "sound-conveying tube consisting of a plurality of sections of progressively increasing cross-sectional area." This configuration was used on the Hawthorne & Sheble Star Talking Machine. Sheble went to work for Columbia Phonograph Co. in 1911. [Koenigsberg 1990.]

SHEIP AND VANDEGRIFT, INC. A Philadelphia firm, stemming from the Henry Sheip Manufacturing Co., which had built cabinets for Berliner and Victor from 1900–ca. 1906. When Victor began making its own cabinets in 1907, the firm made wooden horns; they advertised in *TMW* of March 1910 as a maker of Musicmaster horns, in oak, mahogany or spruce.

SHELLAC. The name given to the compound that was used to make most disc records from about 1896 to about 1948. Shellac is also the name of the principal ingredient in the compound. Shellac is a resinous compound secreted by the lac, a tree insect native to India, Burma, and Thailand. The secretion is utilized to form a protective shell for the insect and for its unhatched eggs, such shells being about the size of a grain of wheat. This shell-lac is scraped from twigs and branches, and shipped in dry powder form. For the disc record application in its developed state, shellac itself formed 13.6 percent of the shellac compound. Other ingredients were vinsol (8.7 percent), Congo gum (.92 percent), white filler (37.4 percent), red filler (37.4 percent), carbon black (1.3 percent) and zinc stearate (.49 percent). It was Fred Gaisberg who discovered the utility of the shellac compound for discs, in 1896; he found it being used for button making by the **Duranoid Co.**, of Newark, New Jersey.

Problems in the use of shellac for records included the uncertain quality of the shellac itself, which was often loaded with impurities; the variable inclusion of scrap (including, in times of shortage, old records returned for recycling) in the compound by different manufacturers; and the basic difficulty of getting enough of the material from India. During the Second World War the supply was virtually cut off. But even under the best conditions, shellac was subject to gross surface noise produced by the abrasive filler—most of it limestone. Another great problem was the brittleness of the record, requiring great care and cost in handling, packaging, and shipping.

Lamination of the final shellac disc, initiated and produced briefly by Columbia in 1906 (see MARCONI VELVET TONE label), reduced surface noise. Columbia returned to the laminated record in 1922, and presented a technically superior product that worked well later with juke boxes, and which sustained the label through the shellac shortage of World War II (since lamination reduced the need for so much shellac).

Shellac was finally replaced as a disc ingredient by **vinyl**, introduced in the 1930s, and rendered ubiquitous by the LP record. [Isom 1977.]

SHEPARD, BURT. American born comedian and singer, especially popular on the British stage. He was one of the Berliner recording artists, having recorded from November 1898.

His first rendition was a "Parody on 'Home Sweet Home'" (#2151). As Berliner became the Gramophone Co. (and G & T), Shepard continued to make recordings, in ever increasing numbers, often as Charles Foster. Rust speculates that another popular name on early HMV, Harry Taylor, was in fact Shepard. His "Laughing Song"—imitating the version of composer George Washington Johnson—was one of the great successes of the Gramophone Co., selling more than a million copies throughout the world. He worked for Victor from July 1901 to November 1906, beginning with "Limburger Cheese" (#V7); and he appeared in Pathé's 1904 catalog.

SHERMAN, CLAY AND CO. A San Francisco firm, located in 1929 at Kearny and Sutter Streets. It sold Steinways and other pianos, phonographs, radios, and records.

SHONK (CHARLES W.) CO. A Chicago firm, established in 1877. It manufactured the Mag-Ni-Phone disc player in 1916.

SHORE, DINAH, 1917– . American popular singer, born Frances Rose Shore on 1 Mar 1917 in Winchester, Tennessee. She studied sociology at Vanderbilt University, Nashville (B.A., 1938), and sang on local radio. Moving to New York to pursue a musical career, she sang on WNEW and performed with the Xavier Cugat orchestra, taking the name Dinah from the title of a song she often sang. By 1940 she was well known; made records for Bluebird and appeared on the Eddie Cantor radio show. Soon she was the top female vocalist on radio and recordings. Shore had her own television shows after the War, achieving highest audience ratings. In the 1960s her popularity faded, but she remained active as a television special hostess and guest.

Shore's early records were made with Cugat; they included an evocative "Breeze and I" (Victor #26641; 1940). Her first independent recording was a great hit: "Yes, My Darling Daughter" (Bluebird #10920; 1940). Other important discs were "Blues in the Night" (Bluebird #B-11436; 1942), "Sleigh Ride in July" / "Like Someone in Love" (Victor #20-1617; 1945), and "Buttons and Bows" (Columbia #38284;

1948). Her last hit single was "Scene of the Crime" (Victor #7349; 1958). She made LP albums for Victor, Columbia, and several other labels. [Greenfield 1982.]

SHURE BROTHERS. American audio firm located at 222 Hartrey Ave., Evanston, Illinois; established as Shure Radio Co. in 1925 by S. N. Shure. In 1926 the name was changed to Shure Brothers as the founder's brother, S. J. Shure, joined in. A major product was the two-button carbon microphone, followed by other innovative microphone designs. The first single-element unidirectional microphone was introduced in 1939. Late designs, such as the SM57 and SM58 models, are used internationally for recording rock and pop concerts. Recently the firm has developed a line of high-quality cartridges, mostly of the moving magnet type. The Ultra 500 cartridge was acclaimed for its ability to track high velocity grooves while maintaining a flat frequency response. Shure's important V15 series of cartridges was used as the basis for a more affordable series that appeared in 1988, the VST series, described by a reviewer as "the finest performing cartridge available at its price." [Hirsch 1988, source of the quote; Whyte 1986/4.]

SIEGEL, SAMUEL, ca. 1876–1948. Mandolin player, among the first to record the instrument. He was heard on seven-inch Berliners, and on the Improved Record of Eldridge Johnson's Consolidated Talking Machine Co. ("Medley of Coon Songs"; #A-449). He made 10 Edison cylinders, one a duet with guitarist M. L. Wolf, "Autumn Evening" (#9014; 1905). As the mandolin faded from popularity in the 1920s. his records were deleted. There were two left in the 1922 Victor catalog, duets with a guitarist named Butin, but none remained in the 1927 catalog. Siegel died in Burbank, California, on 11 Jan 1948.

SIGNAL. In audio terminology, the complex of sound waves that is introduced to the recording system to be captured and reproduced.

SIGNAL-TO-NOISE RATIO. In an audio system, the ratio between the level of the desired input signal and the extraneous audible material (such as hum, surface scratch, vibrations from components, etc.). It is usually expressed in decibels (dB): for instance a ratio of 10 dB means that the signal is 10 dB louder than the extraneous noise. Obviously the higher the ratio, the better the result. Early equipment and record materials yielded very low ratios; for example, Berliner's hard rubber discs offered unpleasant data: "in terms of signal-to-noise ratio, the best probably did not exceed 6 dB and the average was very near unity." The shellac record was better, but "the best signal-to-noise ratio never exceeded 32 dB; 28 dB was a high average performance." With the vinyl record, 55 dB to 60 dB ratios were reached. A good CD player has a ratio of at least 110 dB. Ideally there should be no noise at all in a CD output, but the optimal situation is not achieved in practice because of noise in the analog circuitry. [Isom 1977, source of the quotations; Pohlmann 1989.]

SIGNATURE (label). An American record issued from the mid-1940s, by the Signature Recording Corp., 601 W. 26th St., New York. The firm was owned by Bob Thiele. Jazz and some boogie-woogie appeared in early issues, then a wider repertoire of popular material. Artists in 1946 included Ray Bloch (who was also music director), Harry Cool, Hazel Scott, and Will Bradley. Releases continued through 1959. [Porter 1980.]

SILVER, MONROE, 1875–1947. Yiddish dialect comedian, born in New York on 21 Dec 1875. He was a prolific recording artist, making Victor records from 1911 to 1926, and working for many other labels. He began with "Abie, Take an Example from You Fader" (#16841; 1911), and ended with a duet sung with Billy Murray, "I Ate the Baloney!" (#20096; 1926). His most famous series was about Cohen: "Cohen Gets Married," "Cohen on His Honeymoon," etc., which he inscribed for Victor beginning in 1918, and for Edison Diamond Discs (and Blue Amberols) in 1920. Silver replaced Byron G. Harlan in the Eight Famous Victor Artists in 1918 or 1919. After his recording career ended he continued with night club work and on radio. He died in New York on 3 May 1947. [Walsh 1972/3.]

Silverton (label). *See* DIXI (label).

SILVERTONE (label). (I) An American record issued by **Sears, Roebuck and Co.** from ca. 1916 to ca. 1941. Masters were from Columbia at first, then from a variety of labels (Plaza, Paramount, Gennett, etc.). Sears also used the name Silvertone for its radios and phonographs, marketed from 1911. [Rust 1978.]

SILVERTONE (label). (II) A British label of Cooper Brothers, Ltd. It used matrices of Carl Lindström (London) and Fonotipia, Ltd., from December 1916. [Andrews*.]

SILVERTONE (label). (III) An eight-inch British label made for Selfridge department stores by the British Homophone co., Ltd., from its Solex matrices of 1930/1931. [Andrews*.]

SIMON AND GARFUNKEL. American popular singing/guitar duo, consisting of Paul Simon (1941–) and Art Garfunkel (1941–). They did some early work together, then went their separate ways. Teaming again in 1964, they were soon greatly successful with "Sounds of Silence" (Columbia #43396; 1965), and the album of the same name in the following year. Ten other chart albums followed by 1974, notably *Parsley, Sage, Rosemary and Thyme* (Columbia #CS 9363; 1966, 1968), and *Bridge over Troubled Water* (Columbia #CS 9914; 1970) which was 87 weeks on the charts and sold 2 million copies. Simon's composition "Mrs. Robinson" was part of the soundtrack for the motion picture *The Graduate* (1968).

The pair split in the 1970s, each pursuing solo careers with great success. *Still Crazy after All These Years* was a Simon chart album of 1975 (Columbia #PC 33540). Garfunkel's principal solo success was *Breakaway* (Columbia # PC 33700; 1975). There have been periodical reunions of the team for concerts and recordings, most recently in Chicago, August 1991.

SIMS, ZOOT, 1925–1985. American jazz tenor saxophonist, born John Haley Sims in Inglewood, California, on 29 Oct 1925. He played professionally as a teen, and at age 18 was performing with Benny Goodman. From 1947 to 1949 he was with Woody Herman.

Later he was in Stan Kenton's band and with various ensembles headed by Gerry Mulligan. He continued playing and recording in the U.S. and Europe, taking up the soprano saxophone along with the familiar tenor. *Down Home* was a quartet album recorded in 1960 featuring some elegant examples of Sims' mellow extemporization, as in "Avalon" and "Goodnight, Sweetheart" (Bethlehem #BCP 6051).

Simulated stereo. *See* REPROCESSED STEREO.

SINATRA, FRANK, 1915– . American popular singer and actor, born Francis Albert Sinatra in Hoboken, New Jersey, on 12 Dec 1915. With no musical training, he gained acceptance as a radio singer in New York, and was invited to join the Harry James band in 1939. During the next few years, with Tommy Dorsey (1940–1942) and then as a soloist, he rocketed to national fame, becoming an icon in particular for pre-teen girls who literally swooned at his concerts. He faded in the late 1940s, but returned to public notice with a highly successful film appearance (non-singing) in *From Here to Eternity* (Academy Award 1953). Then he signed with Capitol Records and began a series of hits, adopting a more swinging style than he had in the 1940s. By 1960 he was again established as the most popular male vocalist and also as a Hollywood actor. Sinatra retired in 1971, but continued performing and recording thereafter. In 1985 he was awarded the Presidential Medal of Freedom.

Sinatra's first record was a demo made on 3 Feb 1939, "Our Love," with Frank Manne's orchestra; tape copies exist, but the acetate has been lost. His first commercial recording was "From the Bottom of My Heart" / "Melancholy Mood" (Brunswick #8443; 1939), with Harry James. One of his outstanding discs in the James period was "All or Nothing at All" (Columbia #35587; 1939); upon reissue in 1943 it became his first million-selling disc. There were many superb sides made with Tommy Dorsey, but the greatest success was achieved by "I'll Never Smile Again"—sung with the Pied Pipers (Victor #26628; 1940). Later Dorsey hits included "Stardust," also with the Pied Pipers (Victor #27233; 1940), "Violets for Your

Furs" (Victor #27690; 1941), and "There Are Such Things"—again with the Pied Pipers (Victor #27974; 1942). In 1942 Sinatra also made some records on his own, for Bluebird, one of them the elegant "Lamplighter's Serenade."

Signing with Columbia in 1943, Sinatra made a fine record of "A Lovely Way to Spend an Evening" (#36687); then in 1945 "Dream" (#36797) and "Nancy" (#36868). One of the fine arrangements made for him by Axel Stordahl was "If You Are But a Dream" (#36814; 1944). He also made a number of important V-Discs during the Second World War.

Nelson Riddle wrote outstanding arrangements for Sinatra, among them "I've Got You Under My Skin" (Capitol #W-653; 1956). Sinatra's cool, easy style was exemplified in "Lady is a Tramp," which he sang in the film *Pal Joey* (1956). "All the Way" (Capitol 3793; 1957) was another splendid ballad of the time, arranged by Riddle. There were 54 chart singles from 1950 to 1981.

Later hits included "Strangers in the Night" (Reprise #0470; 1966), winner of four Grammy Awards; "Something Stupid" with his daughter Nancy (Reprise #0561; 1967), "My Way" (Reprise #0817; 1969)—the all-time best seller in Britain—and "New York, New York" (Warner #49233; 1980). Reprise was his own company, formed in 1961, and sold to Warner Brothers in 1963. Sinatra had 51 solo albums on the charts in 1955–1974, plus many others with such artists as Count Basie, Duke Ellington, Bing Crosby, and Antonio Carlos Jobim. His final chart album was *She Shot Me Down* (Reprise #FS 2305; 1981). He made no records after 1986, other than a special cut of "The Gentleman is a Champ" to honor Lew Wasserman of MCA Universal, although he was heard (doing earlier records) on soundtracks in 1988 and 1989. Dozens of CDs have appeared, from EMI and Reprise, documenting a major portion of the Sinatra output. [Kline 1989; Lonstein 1979; O'Brien 1992; Oprisko 1990.]

SINGLETON, ZUTTY, 1898–1975. American jazz drummer, born Arthur James Singleton in Bunkie, Louisiana, on 14 May 1898. He played with New Orleans bands as a youth, worked on riverboats and in St. Louis, then moved to Chicago. He became an innovative force in jazz

through appearances and recordings with Louis Armstrong's Hot Five (1928), Jelly Roll Morton, and Barney Bigard (1929). His techniques included use of wire brushes, the sock cymbals (later to be the hi hat), ride patterns and offbeat bass accents. In the 1930s he worked with such artists as Sidney Bechet and Roy Eldridge; in the 1940s he recorded with Charlie Parker and Dizzy Gillespie. He remained active later in New York clubs. Singleton died in New York on 14 July 1975.

Examples of his notable discs are "Muggles" with Armstrong (Okeh #8703; 1928), and "My Little Dixie Home" with Morton (Victor #38601; 1929). He recorded with groups of his own in 1935 and 1940 for Decca; the only 1940 item was "King Porter Stomp" / "Shim-Me-Sha-Wabble" (#18093).

SIR HENRI (label). An American record known by only a few issues, dating from ca. 1910. Material came from Imperial. [Rust 1978.]

SISTER TEAMS. A duo-piano sister team, Jeanne and Irene Douste, recorded one side for Berliner in 1899. Recorded vocal duet performances by sisters apparently began in about 1917, as Fanny and Kitty Watson sang for Okeh and Columbia, continuing until 1920. The Farber Sisters worked for Columbia and Pathé, and the Heart Sisters for Columbia; the Brox Sisters for Victor and Emerson, the Dennis and the MacDowell Sisters for Edison—these among others in the 1920s. Among the most acclaimed of the early popular duos were the Trix Sisters (*see* **Helen Trix**). In the 1930s the **Boswell Sisters** and the **Andrews Sisters** were the most famous. **Rosa Ponselle**'s opera career was preceded by vaudeville performances with her sister Carmela, in a team billed as the Italian Girls.

SIX BROWN BROTHERS. A saxophone ensemble, originally the Five Brown Brothers, who recorded ca. 1912 on U-S Everlasting cylinders. From 1914 to 1920 they worked for Victor, then (1921–1924) for Emerson. Five of them were true Browns: Alec, William, Vern, Fred, and Tom; the other, Harry Finkelstein, was not related to them. Others who were in the group at one time or another were Guy

Shrigley, James White, and Sunny Clapp. [Rust*.]

SIZES. Cylinder sizes are given in the article CYLINDER, 4. Disc record sizes are in DISC, 4. In general disc diameters increased over the years, from (approximately) three and five inches in Berliner's first toy and doll records, to seven-inch records by Berliner, 10-inch by Victor in 1901, and 12-inch by Victor in 1903. Larger sizes were found sporadically later. *See also* SMALL RECORDS.

SKATING FORCE. The tendency of a spinning disc to draw the cartridge and **tone arm** toward its center. Anti-skating mechanisms are often used on pivoted tone arms. A tangential tone arm eliminates skating force.

SKELLY MANUFACTURING CO. Thomas V. Skelly (of Downers Grove, Illinois) was president of Victor Novelty Works (1905–1909) and the Skelly Manufacturing Co. (1907–1909), both in Chicago. He designed the little-known Skelly Concertophone, a 1906 multi-cylinder, **coin-op** adaptation of the Columbia 20th-Century BC Graphophone. The Concertophone played 25 six-inch cylinders, arranged Ferris-wheel-style, and was meant for use in noisy public locations, benefitting from the **Higham amplifier.** Various models could play standard two-minute records and the three-minute Columbia 20th-Century cylinders, or (after 1908) even four-minute records.

Skelly obtained at least three U.S. patents of a phonographic nature: #874548, for a "Record Holding & Shifting Attachment for Phonographs," applied for on 25 May 1906 and granted on 24 Dec 1907; #854002, for a "Phonograph-Record Holder" (the special Concertophone mandrel), applied for on 11 Feb 1907 and granted on 21 May 1907—a remarkably short period of examination; and #915231, for a "Coin-Detector," applied for 8 Apr 1907 and granted 16 Mar 1909.

Skelly Manufacturing Co. was listed in the Chicago city directories of 1907–1909, with a location at 79 S. Jefferson St. There was no directory listing in 1910. The 1911 and 1912 directories had listings for Thomas V. Skelly, at 528 W. Jackson Blvd., but no listing for the firm.

Bill Klinger

SLEEVE. The jacket or envelope used for protecting, storing, or marketing a disc recording; also known as a slipcase or record cover. Usually the material is paper or cardboard. Often there is a second envelope inside the sleeve, made of paper or mylar, intended to give the surface additional protection. Sleeves may do more harm than good to their records, however; this point is discussed in PRESERVATION OF SOUND RECORDINGS.

SLEZAK, LEO, 1873–1946. Austrian tenor, born in Mährisch-Schönberg on 18 Aug 1873. He sang as a youth in the opera chorus in Brno, then made his debut there as Lohengrin on 17 Mar 1896. From there he went to the Vienna Opera (1901–1926), and sang throughout Europe. His Lohengrin at Covent Garden, 18 May 1900, was greatly acclaimed. Slezak's Metropolitan Opera debut was as Otello on 17 Nov 1909; he remained with the company through 1913. Subsequently he toured Europe and Russia, gave recitals and made motion pictures. He was known for his sharp sense of humor, exemplified in his famous (perhaps apocryphal) improvisation during a *Lohengrin* performance when the mechanical swan departed the stage without him: "When does the next swan leave?". He died in Egern, Bavaria, on 1 June 1946. His son Walter became a famous movie actor.

Slezak's early records were for Zonophone in Vienna, made in 1901: German versions of "Ah! Dispar, vision" from *Manon* and of "Vesti la giubba" (#1665, #1667). He also worked for G & T from 1901, producing a large number of numbers from a wide repertoire, all in German. Slezak recorded for Pathé in Vienna in 1903–1904, making cylinders and discs. The first two numbers (both reissued by IRCC) were "Auftrittslied des Raoul" from *Huguenots* and "O Mathilde" from *Guillaume Tell* (#19050 and 19051, both sung in German). He did six other arias for Pathé, then worked with Columbia and Odeon in Vienna, Edison in the U.S. (1908–ca.1912), and for Victor. An important Edison Blue Amberol cylinder was "E lucevan le stelle" (#28146; 1912 or 1913). Among the finest tenor records of the acoustic era are Slezak's renditions of "Komm holde Dame" from *Weisse Dame* (G & T #042017; 1903) and "Magische Töne" from *Königin von Saba* (G & T #38002; 1905).

There were five numbers in the Victor 1917 catalog, and two in the 1922 catalog. Slezak continued recording until at least 1921, for Polydor in Germany. His records have been widely reissued by the LP and 78 rpm reissue labels. Many of his G & T records were reissued on CD #89020 from Preiser in 1990. [Kaufman 1964.]

SMALL RECORDS. Disc records of lesser diameter than the typical 10-inch size of the 78 rpm era have appeared from time to time in the U.S., more commonly in Britain and Germany. The smallest playable record known was made for Queen Mary's doll house, 1924; it measured one and 5/16 inches. (However see the Bhutan postage stamp record, in POSTAGE STAMPS.) Among the diminutive British and German labels were Baby Odeon, Beka, Broadcast Jr., Crown, Crystalate, Favorite, G & T, Globe, Homo Baby, Homophon, Kiddyphone, Little Marvel, Little Wonder, Marspen, Mimosa, Nicole, Neophone, Odeon, Oliver, Pathé, Phonadisc, and The Bell (some of those labels produced standard size records as well). In American the Harper Bubble Books appeared in 1920–1921, and were marketed also in Britain, as Hodder-Columbia Books that Sing. Little Tots' Nursery Tunes were published in New York by Plaza Music Co. in 1923–1924. [Andrews 1988/4.]

SMALLE, ED, 1887–1968. American singer, pianist, arranger, and conductor, born in Roxbury, Massachusetts, on 2 Nov 1887. He was a highly versatile artist, best known for his singing as soloist and ensemble performer. He recorded for many labels with many groups. In the 1920s he performed with The Revelers, as pianist and singer. King George invited him to a command performance in 1928. His Leaders Trio recorded for broadcast in the U.K., Australia, and Canada. CBS radio featured his Vagabond Glee Club, and in 1935 he was in the motion picture *Radio Nuts*. He made duet records with Billy Murray in 1919 for Edison Diamond Discs, and in 1925 for Victor. He and Vernon Dalhart recorded five duets for Edison Diamond Discs in 1924. After an illness Smalle left the mainstream, then returned to local radio in Westerly, Rhode Island. He died there on 23 Nov 1968. [Rust*; Walsh 1955/5–6; 1969/5.]

SMIRNOV, DMITRI, 1882–1944. Russian tenor, born in Moscow on 19 Nov 1882. He was with the Bolshoi Theater from 1904, and also the Maryinsky Opera in St. Petersburg. Then he appeared in Paris, and on 30 Dec 1910 at the Metropolitan Opera, as the Duke, remaining through 1912. Then he returned to Europe, singing the Russian repertoire, plus Faust, Don José, Canio, and Rodolfo with great effect. In 1909 he recorded for G & T in Moscow, singing airs from *Rigoletto* ("Parmi veder le lagrime," #022132) and seven other operas. From 1912 to ca. 1922 he worked for HMV. One of his finest discs emerged from that period, "Mi par d'udir ancora" from *Pecheurs du perles* (#DB 583, Victor #74741; 1921). Smirnov died in Riga on 27 Apr 1944. [Stratton 1973.]

SMITH, ARTHUR, 1898–1971. American country fiddler, born in Bold Springs, Tennessee, on 10 Apr 1898. He did railroad work, learning country music from his father and playing in his spare time. Then he formed a trio called the Dixieliners in 1932, a string band that performed locally and then advanced to Grand Ole Opry. He gained national fame in 1936 with the recording of "There's More Pretty Girls Than One" (Bluebird #6322). Known as the King of Fiddlers, Smith developed a sophisticated variation of the old country fiddle mode that greatly influenced later country and bluegrass artists. His records were mostly Bluebirds, but he also recorded for Capitol, Folkways, and other labels. He retired in the 1950s but made a comeback in the folk music revival of the 1960s. He was elected to the Fiddler's Hall of Fame in 1982.

SMITH, BESSIE, 1894–1937. American blues and jazz singer, born in Chattanooga, Tennessee, on 15 Apr 1894. She performed with touring minstrel shows as a teenager, and in Atlanta. Pianist Clarence Williams arranged for her to make records for Columbia, and her first disc established her as a major artist: "Downhearted Blues" (#A3844). The first important jazz singer, and one of the first to record vocal blues, she is regarded as the greatest classic blues artist, the "Empress of the Blues." Her tours and recordings continued through 1931, when she faded from sight for two years. John Hammond brought her back in 1933 for an important session on Okeh (#8945 and #8949) with Jack Teagarden, Benny Goodman, and other jazz stars; she made no further records. She made public appearances for a few more years. Smith died in Clarksdale, Mississippi, on 26 Sep 1937.

Among Smith's finest solo records were "Back Water Blues" (Columbia #14195; 1927), "After You've Gone" (Columbia #14197; 1927), and "Nobody Knows You When You're Down and Out" (Columbia #14451; 1929). Her skill at jazz improvisation is illustrated in "A Good Man is Hard to Find" (Columbia #14250; 1927). She also made remarkable duets with Louis Armstrong on cornet, for example, "St. Louis Blues"/"Cold in Hand Blues" (Columbia #14064; 1925). In "J. C. Holmes Blues" her voice was embellished by Charlie Green's trombone, weaving a background with the Armstrong cornet, both muted (Columbia #14095-D; 1925). A total of 159 recordings are listed in the discography by E. Brooks. Smith was largely responsible for the emergence of Columbia as a race label; she was the best selling blues artist of the era. [Brooks, E. 1982; Schuller 1968.]

SMITH, H. ROYER. Philadelphia music merchant and Victor record dealer. In 1919, after working six years for Lyon and Healy, he bought the Drew Music House, located at 10th and Walnut Streets, and opened his own shop. The H. Royer Smith Co. was the prominent Philadelphia record store of the 78 rpm era. In 1930–1933 the record review monthly *Disques* was issued by Smith; the name changed to *The New Records* in 1933. It was published until 1987, widely respected by librarians and collectors.

SMITH, KATE, 1909–1986. American popular singer, born Kathryn Elizabeth Smith in Greenville, Virginia, on 1 May 1909. She sang in church, then went to New York and appeared in several musicals, beginning with *Honeymoon Lane* (1926). She was soon engaged for radio and recording work as well. Smith was one of the first to have a theme song or signature song, "When the Moon Comes over the Mountain"—it was one of her best records (Victor #25760; 1937). She began to record for Columbia in 1926, doing numbers from *Honeymoon Lane,* and stayed with the label (or its subsidiary, Harmony) until 1932. Then she worked for Brunswick, Decca, and Victor through 1939, before returning to Columbia. Her repertoire consisted of love songs and traditional melodies. In 1939 she recorded her greatest hit, "God Bless America," Irving Berlin's "national anthem" (Victor #26198). Smith continued recording until 1976. She died on 17 June 1986. [Hayes, R. 1977; Pitts 1988.]

SMITH, MAMIE, 1883–1946. American jazz and blues singer, born Mamie Robinson in Cincinnati on 26 May 1883. As a teen she toured as a dancer, then went to Harlem and established herself as a vocalist. Her record of "That Thing Called Love," / "You Can't Keep a Good Man Down" was the first vocal blues record, and the first record by a Black jazz/blues singer (Okeh/Phonola #4113; 14 Feb 1920). "Crazy Blues," made in her second record session, was a great success (Okeh/Phonola #4169; 10 Aug 1920), selling a million copies in six months. Smith became nationally famous, touring widely and appearing in films through the 1930s. In a fresh approach to singing "she delivered her songs with a reckless abandon and a wide-open shouting style that was worlds removed from the whimpering balladeers of the day" (Schuller). She continued to record for Okeh, making many fine discs with her Jazz Hounds ensemble, the membership of which has not been established (trumpeter Johnny Dunn was one player, and Coleman Hawkins was with the group in the early 1920s). Smith remained with Okeh, and that label was a leader in the switch from jazz to blues effected by the major companies. She died on 30 Oct 1946.

SMITH, PINE TOP, 1904–1929. American blues singer and pianist, born Clarence Smith in Troy, Alabama, on 11 June 1904. As a teenager he toured as a pianist and dancer, developing a new style that came to be called **Boogie-Woogie.** His recording of "Pine Top's Boogie-Woogie" (Vocalion #1245; 1928) defined the mode and set the standard for others to follow. He also sang effectively on the B side, doing "Pine Top's Blues." Just as his career was blossoming he was killed during a brawl that took place while he was performing in Chicago, on 15 Mar 1929.

SMITH, WILLIE, 1897–1973. American jazz pianist, born William Henry Joseph Bonaparte Bertholoff in Goshen, New York, on 24 Nov 1897; known as Willie the Lion. He grew up in Newark, New Jersey, and played the piano as a young child. As a teenager he was performing in Harlem, developing the new stride piano style. During World War I he earned his Lion nickname through valor in action. He became famous when he started to record in 1935, beginning with "There's Gonna Be the Devil to Pay" (Decca #7073). His masterful solo series with Commodore in 1939, performing his own compositions "Echoes of Spring" (#521) and "Finger Buster" (#522), with standards like "Stormy Weather" (#519), combined stride with classical elements, counterpoint and impressionistic harmonies. His peak of popularity was in the late 1940s, when he toured Europe. He died in New York on 18 Apr 1973.

SMITH, WILLIE, 1910–1967. American jazz alto saxophonist, born William McLeish in Charleston, South Carolina, on 15 Nov 1910. He performed while in college in Nashville, and was heard by Jimmie Lunceford, who invited him to join his band. He was with Lunceford from 1929 to 1942, arranging as well as playing sax and sometimes doing vocals. In the 1940s and 1950s he was with Charlie Spivak, Harry James, and Duke Ellington, and led his own groups. He became recognized as one of the three or four outstanding alto soloists. "Sophisticated Lady," with Lunceford, was a good early example of his art (Decca #129; 1934). "Who's Sorry Now," with Harry James, was an outstanding record of the 1940s (Columbia #36973; 1945). Smith died in Los Angeles on 7 Mar 1967.

SMITH REPEATOSTOP CO. A Chicago firm, located in the Hartford Building in 1911. It made the Repeatostop device, which either repeated or stopped a disc after it had played one time. R. B. Smith was the inventor, holding U.S. patent #906,319 (filed 16 Sep 1908; granted 8 Dec 1908).

SMITHSONIAN INSTITUTION. The American national museum, founded in 1846, now consisting of several component museums, most of them in Washington, D.C. The National Museum of American History (NMAH) has a collection of recordings and artifacts pertaining to recorded sound. Included are a **Phonautograph;** an 1877 Thomas Edison **tin-foil phonograph;** a cylinder ostensibly recorded by Alexander Graham Bell in the Volta Laboratory, 1881; an Emile Berliner photo-engraved record dated 26 July 1887 and a Berliner gramophone of 1888. The Department of Social and Cultural History of NMAH holds important collections of jazz, popular, blues, and country records dating from 1903; there are more than 1,000 artists represented. Armed Forces Radio and Television Service transcription discs are there, plus the series **Hit of the Week** records.

The Department of History of Science in NMAH has Columbia's experimental microgroove recordings of 1943–1946. It also has numerous records of geophysical phenomena, such as radio noise from Jupiter, and tapes representing engineering standards. Examples showing the development of audio components are found, including complete phonographs, headphones, tone arms, loudspeakers, receivers, magnetic recording devices, and microphones. Early recordings and early record players are abundant.

In the NMAH Department of National History there is a collection of radio transcription discs from the World War II period. There is also a collection of recordings from political campaigns, from 1896.

The Smithsonian has issued many recordings, including the Smithsonian Collection of Classic Jazz (1973), consisting of six 12-inch LPs. This was enlarged and remastered on five CDs in 1989. Individual albums have been released on country, jazz, and swing artists, and for American musicals. *Voices of the Civil Rights Movement: Black American Freedom Songs, 1960–1966* is an important contribution. A recreation of the Paul Whiteman 1924 concert in Aeolian Hall (which featured the premiere of *Rhapsody in Blue*) was issued on two LPs. Another CD album of special interest is *American Popular Song*, a collection of 110 selections by 62 artists, covering six decades on five compact discs (1988). *Big Band Jazz* won a Grammy in 1984 as the best historical album. [Heintze 1985 gives details on audio materials in all Washington institutions.]

SOBINOV, LEONID, 1872–1934. Russian tenor, born in Yaroslavl on 7 June 1872. He studied law in Moscow, graduating in 1894, but also travelled with an Italian opera troupe, and decided to make singing his career. His debut was in 1897 at the Bolshoi, and he remained with that company through his career, singing also at the Maryinsky Theater in St. Petersburg, and throughout Europe. He was at La Scala in 1904–1906. His great roles were Lenski in *Eugene Onegin*, Faust, Des Grieux, and Alfredo. Sobinov also excelled in solo recitals (Nicolas Slonimsky was his accompanist during 1918–1919), and was idolized by the public, especially by young girls. He died in Riga on 14 Oct 1934.

Sobinov was recorded first by Fred Gaisberg for G & T in St. Petersburg and Moscow in 1901, presenting 26 numbers, mostly Russian opera arias. In 1904 he made another set of G & T discs in St. Petersburg, this time including in the 21 sides a large measure of French/Italian repertoire, sung in Russian. He worked for Pathé also, in 1908, St. Petersburg, offering 10 items on vertical-cut discs. In 1910 he was back with Gaisberg and the Gramophone Co. (in Moscow) for 11 arias, Russian and Western. His last sessions were in 1911, in St. Petersburg and Moscow. Reissues appeared on the Russian Gramplasttrecht label, and later on Melodiya. All the major reissue labels in the U.S. and U.K. have covered his repertoire. Among his outstanding records were the arioso of Lenski from *Eugene Onegin* (HMV #2-22649; 1904), "Salut demeure" (#022078; 1904), and "Mein lieber Schwann" (#022137; 1910). [Robertson, J. 1978.]

SOCIETÀ ITALIANA DI FONOTIPIA. An Italian firm, established in Milan in 1904. The original owner was Michaelis, Foa and Co. Ownership passed to **Fonotipia, Ltd.**, in 1906, then to **Carl Lindström AG** of Berlin, in 1911. The Transoceanic Trading Co., Netherlands, acquired the firm in 1920. It came under control of the Columbia Graphophone Co., Ltd., in 1925, and thence went to EMI, Ltd., in 1931.

Fonotipia was set up to compete with the Gramophone Co. (Italy), Ltd., of which Alfred Michaelis had been general manager. He left in summer 1904, under disagreable circumstances, and created the Fonotipia rival ca. October 1904, with engineer Dino Foa as his partner. It seems that the new firm was also the Italian agent for F. M. Prescott's Odeon records. Fonotipia's first records, 11 single-sided discs, appeared in 1905. It produced some 360 sides by November 1905. Artists included Alessandro Bonci, Victor Maurel, Giovanni Zenatello, and violinist Jan Kubelik.

See FONOTIPIA, LTD. for the continuation of the account of this label.

SOCIETY RECORDS. It occurred to **Walter Legge**, at the Gramophone Co., that a marketable idea in the dismal 1930s would be to issue discs in subscription sets. HMV established various "societies" that involved an advance purchase commitment by the consumer for a series of records of special interest. In 1931 HMV announced the first society set, six albums of songs by Hugo Wolf—sung by Alexander Kipnis, John McCormack, and others—and 500 subscriptions were eventually received. After the Wolf issue appeared in April 1932, a Beethoven/Schnabel set was announced, in 15 albums of six or seven records each. Other society sets that emerged from EMI and its American affiliates included J.S. Bach Cello Suites (Pablo Casals), "Goldberg Variations" (Wanda Landowska), Organ Music (Albert Schweitzer), *Art of the Fugue* (Roth

Quartet), and *Wohltemperierte Klavier* (Edwin Fischer). Brahms songs were interpreted by Alexander Kipnis. Delius works were conducted by Thomas Beecham. The Haydn quartets were played by the Pro Arte Quartet. Landowska also did the Scarlatti sonatas. Glyndebourne performances of Mozart operas were made, under direction of Fritz Busch and Beecham. Most of the society releases have been reissued on LP.

SODERO, CESARE, 1886–1947. Italian conductor, born in Naples on 2 Aug 1886. He was a cellist and conductor in Naples from age 15, and conducted widely in Europe while very young. In 1906 he was at the Manhattan Opera as soloist and conductor, and worked also with other companies. Sodero was director of recording and staff conductor for Edison from 1914 to 1929, responsible for more than 11,000 records. He was staff conductor for NBC from 1925 to 1934. From 1942 to 1947, the year of his death, he was a conductor with the Metropolitan Opera.

SOLEX (label). A British record introduced by **British Homophone Co., Ltd.**, in September 1930. It was a fine-grooved disc, eight inches in diameter, said to play as long as a normal 10-inch disc. Matrices were contracted to Selfridge's, who sold them under the label name Silvertone. The eight-inch discs ceased after April 1931. A 10-inch record was introduced in January 1935, but it was only sold for four months. After 1935 there were no further issues. [Andrews 1986/4.]

SOLID STATE. A term applied to various semiconductor devices, for example, the transistor, to distinguish them from their electron tube counterparts.

SOLO ART (label). An American record, issued in limited quantities during 1939–1940 by Solo Art Recordings, 1000 Broadway, New York. Producer was Dan Qualey, who recorded the work of jazz pianists he liked best: Albert Ammons, Meade "Lux" Lewis, and Jimmy Yancey. There were about 20–30 issues, on 10-inch and 12-inch records. [Rust 1978.]

SOLOPHONE CO. An American firm, located in Harrison, New Jersey. In 1916 it advertised Solophone disc players, in three models that sold from $90 to $175.

SOLTI, GEORG, Sir, 1912– . Hungarian-English conductor and pianist, born György Solti in Budapest on 21 Oct 1912. He played the piano in public at age 12, and studied at the Liszt Academy (with teachers Ernö Dohnányi, Béla Bartók, and Zoltán Kodály). He was accompanist at Salzburg in 1936 and 1937, under Arturo Toscanini, and made his conducting debut in Budapest in 1938. He spent the World War I years in Switzerland, then became conductor of the State Opera in Munich, remaining to 1952. From there he went to Frankfurt, directing symphonic and operatic activity. In 1960, following appearances at the Metropolitan Opera and San Francisco Opera, Solti became director of the Dallas Symphony Orchestra, but after a year went to Covent Garden where he was music director until 1971. He took British citizenship and was knighted in 1972. From 1969 to 1990 he was music director of the Chicago Symphony Orchestra, achieving world recognition for himself and the ensemble; he and the orchestra won 20 Grammy Awards. He was also principal conductor of the London Philharmonic Orchestra in 1979–1983. He retired from the Chicago post in 1990, having passed the baton to his chosen heir, Daniel Barenboim.

Solti's outstanding recordings are numerous. He conducted the *Ring* in the famous **John Culshaw** recording of 1966 (available on Decca CD #414 100-2DM15; 1989, 15 discs), and also collaborated with Culshaw in *Salome*. A good selection of Solti's orchestral specialties, most of them with the CSO, appeared on Decca CD #430 635-2DM12, a 12-disc set (1991). The set includes acclaimed interpretations of Richard Strauss tone poems, the Brahms Fourth Symphony, Mahler's Fifth Symphony, and Holst's *The Planets*. [Marsh, R. 1984 is a discography of the CSO records.]

SONIC RESTORATION OF HISTORICAL RECORDINGS. This article has 19 sections: 1. Introduction; 2. Record condition; 3. Turntable speed and pitch; 4. Cartridges and styli; 5. Tone arm, turntable, and tracking; 6. Cartridge hookup; 7. Equalization; 8. Noise; 9. Resonance and parametrics; 10. Non-linearity and selective gain riding; 11. Dynamic expansion; 12. Phase effects; 13. Spectrum analyzers; 14. High and low frequency enhancement; 15. Reverberation, time-delay, and ambience; 16. Compression, limiting, and de-essing; 17. Editing; 18. Quasi-stereo; and 19. Processing sequence.

1. *Introduction.* The sonic restoration of historical recordings is both art and science. This condensed discussion will be limited to a large extent to currently available state-of-the-art equipment and its use in the field. Let us first define and clarify a few terms which are often misunderstood. An historical recording is one that is not currently available in the marketplace in its original format. This includes virtually all recordings on cylinders, 78s, wire, open-reel tape, and broadcast transcriptions as well as many LPs, movie and TV sound tracks, and private recordings. We use historical recording in a more limited sense to mean any recording of important content or performance which in sound quality does not adequately represent the performance. Dubbings or dubs (transfers) are mechanically or electrically made copies of an original recording. Duplication of cylinders was originally done by mechanical dubbing and the copies made were inferior to the original as is the case with most electric dubs of 78s. However, the transfers of early vocal records done by the HMV engineers in the 1940s are an excellent exception and show what could be done with care and effort. A re-pressing, as the name implies, is a new record made from an original metal part (stamper). If the metal part has not deteriorated due to age or wear, the new pressing can be superior to the original issue since modern vinyl takes a better impression and is much quieter than shellac. Reissue is a confusing term which can mean either re-pressing or dub.

There are three interrelated concepts in the field which are often confused with each other and need clarification. Sonic preservation is done by sound archives, universities and others to preserve the sound of an original source which may be deteriorating. The main consid-

erations are long storage time and no alteration of the original sound or at least none which cannot be undone. The common method is two-track analog tape recording using modern low-print-through tapes (such as AGFA 468), and documenting everything that is done, including stylus size, turntable speed and, inherent (playback) equalization, if any. Some noise reduction may be achieved, using a device like the Packburn Transient Noise Suppressor, but nothing must be allowed to alter the sound of the source in any way. For the purist, the less done the better. Additionally, the original source will be treated with the greatest care possible, for example, records kept in acid free sleeves and stored at 65 degrees Fahrenheit and 40 percent humidity.

Sonic enhancement is the process of altering a sound source to produce a desired result; it may or may not accurately represent the sound of the original performance. Its criteria are subjective, usually commercial, and often reflective of current ideas regarding good sound or consumer preferences. Sonic restoration is similar to sonic enhancement in many of its techniques but more specific in its main objective, which is authenticity to the original performance. Authenticity is the central problem in sonic restoration, especially with acoustically recorded material. While the sound of such recordings gives some idea of what the original performance was like, the many technical limitations of acoustic recording may leave an incomplete or deceptive impression. The same is true of early electrical recordings but to a much lesser extent. The objective of the sonic restorer of historical recordings is to determine insofar as possible what the sound of the original performance was really like, and then to make all modifications with this in mind. Of course all three, sonic preservation, enhancement, and restoration, are interrelated and overlap to some extent; and there may sometimes be disagreement as to which of the three a given piece of work belongs. Our discussion will be devoted primarily to sonic restoration of 78 rpm discs.

2. *Record condition.* It goes without saying that the condition of the sound source is of the greatest importance in restoration work. While recent LPs and CDs have been standardized,

78s were pressed on different materials (*see* DISC, 3), were made in various sizes (*see* DISC, 4), and recorded at variable speeds (*see* DISC, 4). They first appeared in 1894 (*see* BERLINER [label]) and were marketed into the late 1950s (*see* DISC, 6). Most 78s were made of **shellac** compounds, and were vulnerable to dirt, warps, digs or gouges; to aging, moisture damage, and simple wear from ordinary use. Many have cracks, and some discs presented for restoration are broken. Discs were frequently pressed off-center.

Usually the first step in restoration is **cleaning**. Then warps are dealt with. Often a warped disc can be flattened between glass plates using carefully applied amounts of heat and pressure. With off-center records, the center hole can be enlarged and the record carefully recentered on the spinning turntable. Broken records, if the break is clean, can sometimes be glued or taped back together with the tape on the reverse side. For bad gouges and digs, a temporary but useful technique is to fill in the damaged area using softened wax and play the filled-in area of the record, before it becomes too firm, at a **tracking force** greater than normal. If the **anti-skating force** is perfectly balanced and the missing area is not too large, temporary groove walls will be formed that match up with the existing grooves. While this technique does not give permanent results, it is fast and usually enables the record to be played for restoration purposes. (Extensive record repairs are only justified if the recording is very valuable or one of a kind. With most common records undergoing restoration, the best solution is simply to find a better copy in an archive or private collection.)

3. *Turntable speeds and pitch*. Many so-called 78s were not recorded at 78 rpm. They vary from the low 60s to over 100 rpm (*see* DISC, 4). When a restoration or reissue is made, the original recording speed of the source disc must be observed. A deviation from the original speed results in a change of pitch (*see* PITCH, II), destroying the integrity of the performance. Thus a high quality variable speed turntable, equipped with a multi-speed strobe or digital speed readout, is essential. However, the real problem lies in determining the original speed of the source recording. Some guidelines are

helpful. The older records were generally recorded at lower speeds. Victor acoustics were most often recorded around 76 rpm, and their electrics prior to 1930 were also often at 76 or 77 rpm. Many European electric discs were recorded at 80 rpm, with Pathés at about 90 rpm. Edison Diamond Discs were consistently made at 80 rpm. G & Ts were recorded in the low 70s or even 60s.

One technique useful with records made using cutter tables and amplifiers using alternating current is to synchronize with the AC hum frequency (60 Hz in the U.S., 50 Hz in Europe), using a sharply spiked filter to exaggerate the hum frequency. An accurate digital counter can set the spike to the frequency of the original recording's alternating current. Then adjustments in the turntable speed make possible tuning for maximum hum and hence the correct pitch of the original. Comparing the sound of a 78 with a modern recording of the same music can be a good reference to correct the pitch to A-440, if A-440 was the pitch in use when the original was made. Care with LPs is necessary too, as not all such discs which might be used for comparison are at exactly 33 1/3 rpm. A pitch pipe, electronic synthesizer, or properly tuned piano, in conjunction with the musical score, may serve as useful references.

Early vocal records present a serious problem because songs and arias were frequently transposed to suit individual singers. Biographical and discographical sources may suggest the preferred keys of certain singers. Some old records have a playback speed printed right on the label but this, as well as published listings of correct speeds, should always be viewed with caution. Finally it must be remembered that standard concert pitch has changed during the history of sound recording (*see* PITCH, I).

4. *Cartridges and styli*. A superb cartridge for 78 rpm playback is the Shure V15 type V used with the Shure VN578E stylus assembly, but even better sound is obtained by using the VN578E assembly with the Shure Ultra 500 cartridge body. This combination is truly amazing. Moving-coil cartridges, as opposed to the moving-magnet types, can offer somewhat better sound and in particular better transient response. However, because a wide range of

stylus sizes is necessary to play various 78s properly, moving coil cartridges—which would require frequent changes of stylus—are not suitable. The dynamic stabilizer brush in the Shure VN578E dramatically aids tracking of 78s with warps or broken-down groove walls. This feature plus very high stylus compliance makes Shure the cartridge of choice. The elliptical stylus mounted on the VN578E assemblies (0.5 by 2.5 mils) is excellent for playing 78s of the 1940s and 1950s but not suitable for many earlier ones. Figure 1 gives our recommendations on stylus sizes; generally the earlier records take the larger sizes. Styli should be made in a truncated format (cut off on the bottom), as this minimizes noise pick-up from the bottom of the groove.

All styli ought to be diamond, but with the very large sizes necessary to play some vertical-cut records, cost may dictate the use of sapphire. The criterion on stylus selection for any given record is to choose one that gives the cleanest, least distorted sound, not the least surface noise. Surface noise is much easier to deal with than distortion. Expert Stylus Co. is one firm that can supply a wide variety of elliptical truncated styli mounted on Shure VN578E stylus assemblies.

5. *Tone arm, turntable, and tracking.* A high quality tone arm long enough to play 16-inch transcriptions, combined with a quality variable speed turntable, is essential. We recommend the Diapason transcription turntable with digital speed read-out of its continuously variable speeds from 16 to 120 rpm plus the ability to play records up to 20" in diameter. Correct geometry is also very important. The overhang, azimuth, and lateral and vertical tracking angles must all be easily adjustable. They should be normally optimized for 12 inch LPs, but with problem records the adjustments may have to be altered to even make tracking possible. (Vertical tracking angle is now very common at 20 degrees for LPs, whereas for 78s it is theoretically zero degrees.) For Pathé records, with their very shallow grooves, and for "center start" records, the ability to adjust anti-skating force can be crucial. The optimization for Pathé's, and other apparently unplayable records, is to put the problem record on the turntable at its correct speed then, with the stylus force reduced to almost nothing, gently lower the stylus to a position on the record about halfway through. The stylus will probably start skating across the record toward the inside or outside. The anti-skating force is then set higher or lower until the stylus remains stationary without skating, then increased to normal.

6. *Cartridge hookup.* For best results in playing 78s, the cartridge should be connected in a normal stereo configuration and fed into a stereo preamp. Once the signal is amplified to line level, a "canting control" can be used. To make this control, a ganged audio-taper potentiometer is wired so that the center point of rotation gives equal amounts of left and right channel output. For vertical-cut (hill and dale) records, a simple phase-reversal, two-pole, double-throw toggle switch can be used in the cartridge leads of one channel to obtain the required vertical signal. Phase reversal and a form of canting can be found already built into the Packburn Audio Noise Suppressor, which will be discussed under Noise.

7. *Equalization.* The multi-graphic equalizer, now quite popular, divides the frequency spectrum into discrete frequency bands, each individually adjustable in gain. The term "graphic" refers to the position of the slide potentiometers as they show peaks or dips in the sound spectrum as if they were plotted on a graph. The simplest multi-graphics are five-band equalizers with each band being two octaves wide. The one-octave and third-octave units are common in professional recording consoles and even sixth-octave equalizers are becoming more common. In sound work as the number of bands increases the multi-graphic equalizer becomes more complex to use. The one-octave (10-band) multi-graphic is a good choice for home audio systems but for restoration work the half- or third-octave unit is preferred.

Most versatile of all equalizers, the parametric is somewhat similar to the multi-graphic equalizer in that it divides the audio spectrum into frequency bands and the level or amplitude of each band can be separately controlled. Unlike the multi-graphics, where each band is fixed in frequency, the parametric can shift this band (within limits) higher or lower in frequency. In addition, the shape (broadness or narrowness, also known as "Q") of the affected band can be controlled from very broad (several octaves) to very narrow (notch). These three variable parameters (level, frequency, and "Q") give the parametric equalizer tremendous capabilities in dealing with difficult problems such as the resonances in acoustically made recordings. Results with parametrics, such as the Orban Model 642B, can be spectacular.

The adjustable notch-filter is a very useful type of specialized equalizer. With its very narrow bandwidth and deep cut (40 or more dB) it can remove 60- or 120-cycle AC hum as well as cutter whistle, a problem on many early electric recordings, and can do this without apparent effect on the overall sound. It should be a basic premise of restoration work that if the listener is aware of electronic processing then the restorer has made a mistake. These various adjustable sound-shaping equalizers are indispensable in working with 78s and many early LPs and may also be useful in undoing some of the excessive enhancement of modern recordings, especially pop.

LP records currently follow standard recording **equalization** (EQ) curves of the Recording Industry Association of America (RIAA) in the U.S., or the similar International Electrotechnical Commission (IEC) curve used mostly in Europe and the Far East. Acoustic records made before the development of the electrical process in 1925 were recorded mechanically and inherent in that process is a theoretical constant-velocity response of the cutter. Since there was insufficient musical energy to overcome the mass of the linkage between horn and cutter, the result was not a true constant velocity output in the lower frequencies and we call the result inherent mechanical equalization. In the acoustic process, low frequencies, what there were of them, had large cutter excursions which decrease as frequency increases. With the development of the electrical process and its greater frequency range, problems appeared. The much lower frequencies could then be recorded, but had too great a cutter excursion, and the greatly extended higher frequencies had such small excursions that they were lost in the system

noise. By changing from a constant velocity characteristic at some point in the frequency spectrum to a constant amplitude characteristic (which the electric process made possible), the problem could be solved, provided that the playback machine did the same in reverse. The point in the frequency spectrum where this change takes place is the turnover frequency. Additionally, it became possible to boost the higher frequencies when recording and that, in turn, required a corresponding high frequency cut or rolloff in playback. The result of all this was that it became possible to get extended high frequency response, which was not lost in the surface noise, and extended low frequency response, which did not break across into adjacent record groove walls. The combination of turnover and rolloff characteristics became known as the recording curve or inherent equalization curve, and it has taken almost half a century before everything finally settled down into the international standard of the RIAA curve.

A major problem for the sonic restorer of 78s and early LPs is the very great variety of recording equalization curves used by different companies from 1925 through the early 1950s. Many different curves were required by the playback equipment to inversely match the original recording curves, which were widely variable. In most modern audio systems for playing analog recordings, the playback equalization is now truly locked into the standard curve and it is impossible with this equalization to play most 78s and many early LPs properly.

One approach to solving this problem is to use a multi-graphic equalizer to undo the gross distortions of the RIAA curve and simulate the various older equalization curves. It works after a fashion but takes considerable time and is definitely awkward. The best approach is to use The Re-Equalizer by Esoteric Sound. Connected at the output of a pre-amp with RIAA equalization, it undoes the RIAA curve and offers six positions of turnover and six positions of rolloff. Its 36 possible EQ combinations can duplicate almost any of the old curves that will be encountered.

Acoustic records should be played back with a 250 Hz or higher turnover. Otherwise the bass, which was greatly attenuated by the mechanical equalization of the primitive recording process, will be almost non-existent. At the lowest frequencies, where **rumble** may become severe, a high-pass filter may be employed as needed. Additionally, some slight rolloff of the high frequencies might be used, perhaps 5 dB at 10 kHz but rarely more. In the field of sonic preservation, as opposed to sonic restoration, an argument can be made for using no inherent electrical equalization (no turnover) on acoustics, but we much prefer 250 Hz or higher with clear documentation as to what was done.

Electrical recordings have never been controversial regarding the need for using playback equalization, but there is still some disagreement as to what specific curves to use on which company's records made at what time. Based on the published curves, the McIntosh chart, information from record manufacturers and many years of experience with old recordings, we have developed a the following list of recommended turnover and roll-off characteristics for playing most old recordings:

8. *Noise.* **Noise reduction systems** are of two types: double ended or closed type (sometimes called encode/decode) where something is done during the recording and undone during playback, and the much more difficult single ended or open type where only the playback can be affected. Most commercially available systems of the single ended type, which are essential for 78s, are of little use in sonic restoration work. A notable exception is the Packburn Audio Noise Suppressor, with three noise reduction circuits designed to handle the different types of noise found on historical recordings. Commensurate with not degrading the sound, it is the most effective noise reduction system available.

For maximum hiss reduction the Dynafex Audio Noise Reduction System is even a bit more effective than the Packburn's Continuous Noise Suppressor, although—unlike the Packburn—it colors the bass sound slightly (a problem that can be reduced with parametrics).

In Britain the National Sound Archive, jointly with the Department of Engineering at Cambridge University, has developed **CEDAR** (Computer Enhanced Digital Audio Restoration). Both CEDAR and the Sonic Solutions NoNoise process seem effective on click and pop reduction if less so on hiss reduction. We believe, however, that such automatic programs are not as satisfactory as digital editing click removal, on a click-by-click basis.

The RCA / **Soundstream** digital restorations were concerned primarily with adjusting the unnatural resonances of acoustic recordings. However, in taking out the unnatural resonances, for example on Enrico Caruso records, the process also took out most of the natural resonances of that magnificent voice. It may have been good digital electronics, but in our opinion, it was a musical disaster and a disservice to the artist.

9. *Resonance and parametrics.* Unnatural resonances can be eliminated with parametric equalization. An example may be useful. A typical Victor acoustic record generally has one of its strongest resonant peaks in the area of 3,100 Hz; the precise frequency will vary from one record to another. By adjusting a parametric band for a narrow positive spike and sweeping the frequency back and forth while listening for the worst sound we can easily find the exact center frequency of the resonant peak. It is always easier to find a resonant peak by exaggerating it rather than notching it out. Having found the exact center of the resonant peak, we lower the gain of the parametric band to create a deep notch. The result will sound much better. Reduction of the notch increases the gain and brings back some of the ugly sound; further adjustment of the bandwidth will locate the best sound. The resulting signal will be a smooth response without any loss of natural sound qualities. In the cited example we may need to repeat the process on a lesser scale at the second harmonic of 6,200 Hz and even at the subharmonic of 1,550 Hz. If an electric 78 had this 3,100 Hz resonance, it might require additional work at the third harmonic, 9,300 Hz. In addition to eliminating unnatural resonances, parametric equalizers, such as the Orban 642B, can serve as excellent notch filters and are very important as phase modifying devices. Furthermore, they can aid in reducing surface noise in conjunction with the Packburn. Almost anything that other equalizers can do, parametrics can do as

Suggested Inherent Record EQ Settings

Label	Speed (RPM)	Turnover (Hz)	Roll-Off at 10KHz in DB
All records since 1955	33, 45, 78	500	13.7
Acoustics and cylinders	78	250 (or as needed)	5
Records Made between 1925 and 1955			
Transcriptions	33, 78	500	16
Cameo Pathe			
Oriole Romeo			
Banner Perfect	78	Inconsistent (as needed)	
Allegro	33	750	16
American Record Society	33	500	12
Angel	33	500	12
Atlantic	33	500	16
Bach Guild Banner	33	750	16
Bartok Boston	33	630	16
Blue Bird	78	800	10
Blue Note	33	400	12
Brunswick (early)	78	1000	8.5
Brunswick (late)	78	300	16
Caedmon	33	630	11
Capitol	45	500	12
Capitol	33, 78	400	12
Canyon			
Capitol-Cetra			
Colosseum	33	400	12
Cetra-Soria			
Columbia	33	750	16
Columbia	45	500	16
Columbia (USA)	78	300	16
Columbia (European)	78	300	5
Concert Hall			
Contemporary			
Coral	33	400	12
Cook	33	500	12
Coral	78	750	16
Decca	33, 45, 78	750	16
Decca (Engl.)			
FFRR	78	250	5
Deutsche Gramophone	78	300	5
Dial	33	750	16
Disc			
Diva (See Harmony)	78	300	16
Electra	33	630	16
Electrola	78	800	10
EMS	33	400	12
Epic	33	750	16
Esoteric	33	500	12
Festival	33	750	16
Folkways	33	630	16
Good Time Jazz	33, 78	400	12

Label	Speed (RPM)	Turnover (Hz)	Roll-Off at 10KHz in DB
Gramophone	78	300	8.5
Handel Soc.			
Haydn Society	33	750	16
Harmony	78	300	16
records are acoustic			
through August 1929			
Hit of the Week	78	500	5
HMV	33, 78	800	10
King	78	500	16
London	33	750	10
London FFRR	78	250	5
Lyrichord	33	630	16
Majestic	78	500	16
Mercury	33, 45, 78	400	12
MGM			
Montilla	33, 45, 78	500	12
Musicraft	78	750	14
New Records			
Oceanic			
Oxford	33	750	16
Odeon*			
Okeh*			
Parlophone*	33, 78	300	8.5
Period	33	500	16
Philharmonia	33	400	12
Polydor	33, 78	300	8.5
Rachmaninoff Society	33	750	16
Victor and RCA Victor	33, 45, 78	800	10
Remington	33	500	16
Renaissance	33	750	12
Schirmer	78	1000	24
Stradivari	33	750	16
Supraphone	78	400	0
Technichord	78	800	12
Telefunken			
Radiofunken	33, 78	400	0
Urania (old)	33	750	16
Urania (new)	33	400	12
Ultraphome	33, 78	400	0
Vanguard			
Vox			
Westminster	33, 78	750	16
Velvet Tone	78	300	16
records are acoustic			
through August 1929			
Vitaphone	33	950	18.5

Notes

78 means 78.26 rpm (recorded/60Hz) or
77.92 rpm (recorded/50 Hz).
Earliest "78's" are 60 to 100 rpm.

Speeds listed 33 are 33 1/3 rpm.
EQ on 78's marked * may be:

(very early)	250	0
(very late)	500	

well or better, but the amount of work is formidable.

10. *Non-linearity and selective gain riding.* Another serious problem on acoustics records, almost never encountered on electrics, is that of non-linearity in the treble frequencies, a result of mechanical hysteresis (slop or play) in the linkage between the horn and the cutting stylus. Hence the higher frequencies, insofar as they could be recorded, reproduce well on loud passages, but poorly on soft passages. Among collectors of acoustic records, this is thought of as a "blasting" effect, that is, if the treble sound is relatively bright on normal passages, then the loud peaks usually come blasting through in an irritating way. The sound is similar to over-modulation on electric recordings. This non-linear or blasting phenomenon on acoustics is aggravated by unnatural resonances and internal phase shift problems, but even when these are removed with parametrics, the original problem remains.

The best way of handling non-linearity or blasting is downward gain riding of selected treble EQ on the loud passages while keeping the full treble EQ for normal and softer passages. It may be helpful to use upward gain riding of treble EQ in exceptionally quiet passages. After selecting the appropriate EQ, the procedure is to play the record a number of times, practicing the EQ gain riding, until it can be done smoothly and imperceptibly, before making a final tape. Records with a relatively narrow dynamic range are not likely to have the non-linearity problem. It is most noticeable with singers, particularly singers with powerful voices, such as Marcella Sembrich or Ernestine Schumann-Heink. Most recordings of such singers cannot be successfully restored without this frequency-selective gain-riding technique.

In a similar way, although not for the same reasons, selected bass EQ gain-riding can be of great help on many acoustics and some electric recordings. Sometimes, rumble filters, even when combined with low frequency gating, as with the old Phase Linear 1000, cannot totally eliminate rumble without cutting into the sound. In these cases the bass should be set for the best sound at loud and medium levels, and downward gain riding used on the softer pas-

sages where the masking effect of the music is absent. Again, careful discrimination is needed so that the results are inaudible to the listener. Most difficult of all are recordings where selective gain riding is necessary on both high and low frequencies. Dynamic parametrics such as the Troisi dQ 520 offer the possibility of great help with non-linearity and gain riding problems. Its parametric setting comes into play gradually at a preset threshold and may enable some gain riding operations to be done on an automatic or semi-automatic basis.

11. *Dynamic expansion.* On most electric 78s dynamic expansion can greatly enhance the sense of life and realism. Even acoustic records may need some expansion as the recording horn and system of mechanical recording compressed the sound in unnatural ways. If the non-linearity problems are corrected, then three to six dB of expansion may be of great help. Noise pumping must be avoided at all costs, but proper noise-reduction techniques usually reduce noise pumping to inaudible levels except on records in really bad condition. Downward expansion of quiet passages may also improve realism and additionally can further reduce noise. Again, subtlety is the watchword. There are a number of excellent professional dynamic expansion systems, but where subtle downward expansion must be used we employ the Dynafex DX-1.

12. *Phase effects.* **Phase shift** in music is a displacement in time of one tone with respect to another. It is normally expressed in degrees of a circle with 180 degrees being out of phase (cancellation) and 360 degrees being a return to the in phase (reinforcing) condition. When phase shift exceeds 360 degrees it is usually thought of as "time delay" of the signal and expressed as a unit of time, for example, 10 micro-seconds or 10 milli-seconds (ms) and so on. When two tones are separated by less than 30 ms most people perceive them as a single tone (this is known as the Haas effect). Because much phase shift encountered is only a fraction of a cycle it has been widely believed and repeatedly stated in technical literature that the ear is relatively insensitive to phase shift. Fortunately that idea is now changing. The ear may be relatively insensitive, for example, to a 90 degree phase shift between the simulta-

neous playing of tones on a violin and a horn, but the effects of phase shift in audio systems and recordings, especially multiply mixed recordings, is readily apparent.

Natural phase shifts surround us all the time and are part of our natural sonic environment but much of the artificially and accidentally created phase shifts of modern recordings can be very irritating. On example after example paralleling the left and right outputs of a stereo recording results in a disappearance of bass from phase shift cancellation. All audio systems introduce some phase shift but the less the better. Confused phase relationships may explain much of the muddiness and sonic graininess of many modern recordings when the different tracks are mixed down into the final product.

We have observed that with some acoustic records undergoing restoration, the normal bass and treble controls (or the gain of adjacent parametric bands) seem to operate in reverse. Increasing the bass level seems to produces less bass; decreasing the treble level seems to increase treble, etc. We have observed this strange phenomenon in varying degrees quite a number of times, always on acoustics and never on electrics. Assuming proper operation and use of the electronic equipment, there seems to be some form of phase cancellation or augmentation between the effect of the equalizer control and acoustic recording horn resonances. There may also be interaction between the phase shifts inherent in analog equalizers and the resonances unique to acoustic records.

Digital equalizers, without the inherent analog phase shifts, may solve this problem. While some are available now, their sound quality does not yet seem comparable to the analog units. The physics of the complex phase and resonance relationships on acoustic records seems to defy analysis. For now, the problems can only be treated empirically—by trial and error. Without doubt this is the most complex area in sonic restoration. It is the reason that work on acoustics is so much more difficult than on electrics.

13. *Spectrum analyzers.* A third-octave (or narrower), real-time spectrum analyzer can be a very useful tool. It should have storage capability, a fast sampling rate with peak and aver-

aging display modes covering up to four or five seconds—perhaps longer. It is useful in locating resonant peaks, checking inherent record EQ, rebalancing of weak treble or bass and many other applications. We use the Gold Line 30, which can store the waveform of the sound, at any of six moments in time, as selected by the user. These can then be recalled from memory at a later time and compared with each other as desired. For example, if we are working on the 1928 recording of Richard Strauss conducting the Berlin Philharmonic in Beethoven's Fifth Symphony, we might store in memory the spectral pattern of the very first opening chord. Then by similarly storing that same chord from a modern recording or a number of modern recordings, we can compare the 1928 spectral pattern with modern ones having much better sound, and thereby get an idea of where the sonic problems lie and what to do about them.

14. *High and low frequency enhancement.* There are several devices on the market which can be used to enhance the weak higher frequencies on old records. The BBE Model 422A Sonic Maximizer breaks the sound into three frequency bands at 150 Hz and 1.2 kHz, introduces small time delays to the lower bands, and uses a voltage-controlled amplifier to alter the apparent level of the highest band based on the content of the middle band. It is effective and unobtrusive on most sound sources, giving better apparent highs and improved clarity. Its low-band level control enables the user to correspondingly increase the bass frequencies.

15. *Reverberation, time delay, and ambience.* Even when all the techniques discussed so far are employed, there is still something missing from the sound of early electric 78s and even more so with acoustics. Sound exists in some kind of environment —an acoustic space. The sonic reflections of the recording hall or acoustic recording studio are weak or missing on old records. A quality reverberation, time-delay, and ambience system used with discretion may be of great aid in restoring the sense of acoustic space. Acoustic records were very close miked, or should we say "close horned"? It was the only way to get enough energy to drive the mechanical cutters. The medium and long room

reflections, associated with a good music environment, are almost entirely missing, with only a few of the shorter room reflections being present. This results in an extremely "dead" sound. What is needed is to introduce a fair amount of the longer reflections and an even larger amount of the medium delays. We use the ADS Model 10 Acoustic Dimension Synthesizer. No longer available, it was a home entertainment system, not terribly flexible in its use with tape recording, so a few interface modifications were needed. However, it was more natural sounding than some professional units costing three or four times as much. There are also some currently available reverberation, time-delay, and ambience systems by Yamaha, Lexicon, JVC and others which are well worth investigating. Reverberation, time-delay and ambience can be very useful in reducing the dry, dead sound of many historical recordings, but the result should never sound like many excessively reverberant modern recordings.

16. *Compression, limiting, and de-essing*. The more these three processes can be avoided, the better, but sometimes they are necessary. In the acoustic era a form of mechanical compression was sometimes used with singers with very powerful voices. The singer moved up close to the recording horn before singing very soft passages and backed away rapidly before singing very loud ones. Electronic compression is the reduction in the level of loud passages in a graduated manner, and it is the opposite of dynamic expansion. With wide dynamic-range recordings a small amount of compression may be needed, especially if the results are going on cassettes. Limiting, the abrupt stop of level increases beyond a preset point, should generally be avoided in restoration work. In a few cases limiting helps to minimize the non-linearity problem with acoustics, discussed in the earlier section. It should be used in addition to, but not to replace, selective-EQ gain-riding. De-essing, which minimizes the sibilants associated with the "S" sound on vocals, is usually not needed on 78s with their limited frequency range, but there is one exception. Worn records that sound "edgy" on highs may be helped since distortion, barring actual sound breakup, is worse on the transient or attack where de-

essers function. We use Orban's Model 424A Gated Compressor Limiter/De-esser, and find it a useful, subtle, and natural sounding unit when used with discretion.

17. *Editing*. The standard editing method is the old mechanical process of tape cutting and splicing. In length, 78s are generally less than four minutes per side, and with long musical works, the unavoidable interruptions to change record sides are awkward and disconcerting. Where direct splicing, instead of cross-fading, is used to join sides, it is best done on the start of a note or possibly on the end of a note from the previous side; it should never be done in the middle of a pause as the shift in background hiss would be very disconcerting. A splicing block with a very gradual two-inch cutting groove can be helpful in making splices less noticeable. When editing sides together, a gradual decrease in treble at the end of a record is sometimes audible on early records. This is inherent in the nature of disc recording and was compensated for, in later recordings, by diameter equalization, which was a gradual increase in treble added on the inner grooves. When this treble-loss problem is encountered, the restorer can add diameter equalization with a gradual increase of three to five dB of treble on the inner grooves, followed by a return to normal before the start of the next side.

An interesting editing approach to clicks, pops, thumps, and swish has been developed by Richard C. Burns. It is to use tiny bits of splicing tape on the oxide surface of the tape to create artificial **dropouts**. This approach gives no alteration of the timing and permits control of the degree of dropout by using one or more layers of splicing tape. Of course, exact location of the click, pop, thump, or swish is necessary, but this is no more difficult than with the traditional tape cutting and splicing method. A further advantage is that correction of a mistake only involves carefully removal of splicing tape, rather than splicing back in the portion of tape removed, as is the case in the cut-and-splice method. Swish is usually too lengthy to be removed by tape cutting and splicing, but can be handled, by this technique, using a compromise between degree of dropout and loss of high frequency. In some cases of swish, where even a single layer of splicing tape causes too great a dropout, Burns recommends using a china marker on the oxide surface and lightly coating this with baby powder to prevent the tape sticking to the recorder heads.

The new digital, stereo-editing work stations offer greater flexibility, accuracy, and speed. They enable the restorer to try the blending of 78 sides by direct connections or cross fades in any place and with any blending slope. The work can be tried time after time until the results are perfect, without any mechanical cutting of tape. Digital editing of any click or pop residuals, which the Packburn might leave, becomes relatively simple. In mechanical editing there are many occasions where audible clicks and pops are masked by the sound which is heard, at the very low tape speeds encountered while "rocking reels" on a recorder. The great difficulty of finding the precise location of a defect on the tape is much lessened through digital editing.

18. *Quasi-stereo*. Artificially synthesized stereo from a mono source does not work out very well. The Orban 245F creates pseudo-stereo by the use of phase filters and shifters, but even when the control settings are set very low, the results are audible and do not sound very natural. Orban's broadcast version with more bands is a bit more subtle but it still sounds artificial. The Studio Technologies AN-2 Stereo Simulator works on the same principle and with the same problems as the Orban units but with more control over the various parameters. We have never heard any synthesized stereo that did not sound better when the channels were paralleled to produce mono. A very subtle and natural quasi-stereo-spread can be produced by using slightly different settings on parametrics to create two channels. A somewhat fuller and richer sound can be achieved this way without any artificial quality. Mixing in some of the stereo output of a reverberation, time-delay, and ambience system can also be useful in achieving a natural stereo effect.

The listener must never be aware of the use of electronic processors as such, and subtlety is the watchword. New equipment is leading to exciting possibilities in restoration. For example, a new breed of digital processors can recall previous complex parametric settings with the push of a button. The possibilities ahead are endless, but mere equipment will never replace skill, dedication, and good judgment.

19. *Processing sequence.* We have found that best results are obtained when we follow these steps in the restoration procedure:

1. Clean the record and make any repairs.

2. Play the record, adjusting for optimum stylus size, geometry, tracking force, and turntable speed to insure correct pitch.

3. Adjust inherent EQ for best sound using, the record EQ chart above as a starting point.

4. Adjust for best noise reduction.

5. Do preliminary sound rebalancing with a multi-graphic equalizer.

6. Carefully study the results for unnatural resonances, blasting, and other problems.

7. Work with parametrics for best sound.

8. Work with high frequency enhancement and selective-EQ gain-riding as needed.

9. Work with dynamic expansion and/or compression if needed.

10. Work with reverberation, time delay, and ambience as needed.

11. Work with quasi-stereo if appropriate.

12. Carefully listen to how all the processing interrelates and adjust to eliminate poor interactions. Also check to see if it is possible to eliminate the use of any processor! Theoretically, the fewer of these the better.

13. Repeat steps 2 through 12 until no further improvement occurs.

14. Document the audio chain sequence and all control settings.

15. Put the resulting work aside for a day or two, then come back and listen again to see if it still sounds the same; if not adjust as needed. In difficult cases, it may be necessary to start all over again from the beginning.

16. When we are satisfied, we tape the results at 15 IPS to create a working or edit-master tape. It may be necessary to make this tape several times until any selective EQ gain riding is imperceptible.

17. Edit the edit-master tape as needed.

18. Using the edit-master tape as a source, repeat any of the above processing steps that yield further improvement.

19. Check and adjust for best absolute polarity.

20. Tape the final result, which becomes the copy master tape, and is the source of all user records, cassettes, CDs, etc.

(Without the help of my associate, Mr. Donald H. Holmes, this article would have been impossible. His years of experience with parametrics and many useful suggestions on restoration proved invaluable. Also, I am greatly indebted to Richard C. Burns of Packburn Electronics and Carl J. Malone of Specialty Audio for their review and suggestions. A longer version of this article appeared in the June and July 1991 issues of *Audio* magazine. The full-length version, dealing with more equipment, sources, and the artistic elements, is available at nominal cost from the author (1782 Manor Dr., Vista, CA 92084).

Michael R. Lane

SONORA (label). (I) An American disc record issued by the **Sonora Phonograph Co.** (previously the Sonora Chime Co.), 76 Reade St., New York, and later by the Sonora Record Co., from May 1910 to 1948.

SONORA (label). (II) A Swedish label issued from ca. 1935.

SONORA PHONOGRAPH CO. A New York firm, successor to Sonora Chime Co., established in 1910. The address was 76 Reade St. The company issued vertical-cut discs from May 1910, and also made record players for both vertical and lateral-cut discs. Some of the record players had the new **automatic stop** feature. Victor sued them for violation, in the record players, of their old Berliner patent #534,543 (covering the groove-driven stylus), and gained an injunction; the injunction was later vacated (and the patent expired in February 1912), but meanwhile Sonora was bankrupt. However, it reorganized, and was again offering the Sonora line of 11 models, at $45–$1,000, by 1916. One model had a "tone modifier" control. Jewel needles were provided. Another dispute with Victor in 1916, over the right to make an enclosed horn machine, was settled with Victor selling Sonora a license to continue.

In March 1921 it was announced, by company president S. E. Brightson, that Sonora records would be launched by the new Sonora Record Corp. Perhaps the most expensive record player of the 78 era, the Bardini, was offered in 1921; it sold for $5,000. Sonora also manufactured player pianos in the 1920s. In January 1922 it constructed the "largest sign in the world" along the New York Central Railroad tracks between Albany and New York City; it was 800 feet long. A Chicago office was operating at 64 E. Jackson in 1928, while the executive headquarters were at 50 W. 57th St. in New York. The Federal Radio Corp. acquired a controlling interest in Sonora in 1929.

During 1944–1948 a final series of Sonora discs appeared. The firm at that time was named Sonora Record Co., with offices at 77 W. Washington Blvd., Chicago, and 730 Fifth Ave., New York. The material offered on the label was popular, country, r & b, jazz, classical, and children's. The successor to that company, Sonora Radio and Television Corp., 325 N. Hoyne Ave., Chicago, did not deal in phonograph records.

SONS OF THE PIONEERS. American country group formed in 1933 as the Pioneer Trio. Members were **Roy Rogers** (then using the name Dick Weston), Bob Nolan, and Tim Spencer. In 1934 fiddler Hugh Farr joined in, and his brother Karl Farr made it a quintet in 1935. Decca recorded the Pioneers from 1934, in their quickly famous renditions of "Tumbling Tumbleweeds (#46027; 1934)," and "Cool Water" (#5939; 1935), (both written by Nolan). Many other classics followed, on Decca, then Victor. It was through the work of the ensemble that the romantic cowboy image was widely disseminated, and their harmony singing inspired many imitators.

The Pioneers were a great success in Hollywood, appearing in more than 100 western films. Rogers left the group to concentrate on the movies in 1937; he and the Pioneers made two successful motion pictures together in 1941. There were many changes in membership which complicated the task of the Country Music Hall of Fame when it was decided to induct the group in 1980. It was determined to include six men in the honor, Rogers, Spencer, Nolan, the Farrs, and Lloyd Perryman. Still active in the 1980s, the group retained its basic style and repertoire.

SONY CORPORATION. A Japanese firm established in 1946 as Tokyo Telecommunications Engineering (current name taken in 1958) in the bombed-out shell of a department store on the Ginza street. It made audio components, and experimented constantly to find new products and applications. Sony marketed the first Japanese tape recorder in 1950, and the world's first transistor radio in 1955, and went on to miniaturize other components; their pocket radio came out in 1957, gaining great popularity in world markets. Sony transistor television was introduced in 1959, and the solid state video recorder in 1961. Other successful innovations included the desktop electronic calculator (1964), the Trinitron color television tube (1968), and the Walkman (1979). From 300 employees in the early 1950s, the firm went to 4,400 employees in 1961, 22,000 by 1975, and 26,000 by 1980.

In the audio field, Sony joined with Philips in developing **compact disc** technology, and has become the market leader in CD players. The firm has invested heavily in **DAT** and high definition television. Sony acquired CBS Records from CBS in 1988, for $2 billion, and Columbia Pictures from Coca Cola in 1989 for $4.9 billion. The Sony Classical label has taken the place of the venerable Columbia name on compact discs issued by the firm.

SORIA, DARIO, 1912–1980. Italian/American recording industry executive, born in Rome on 21 May 1912. He took an economics degree from the University of Rome in 1934. His family fled Italy in 1939 and came to America. Soria worked for the U.S. Office of War Information during World War II, becoming a citizen in 1945. He was head of overseas news broadcasting for CBS (1943–1948). In that period he organized the Cetra-Soria label, drawing on the Cetra matrices, which offered a major catalog of operatic material.

Artists on the Cetra-Soria label included Maria Callas, Cesare Siepi, Ferruccio Tagliavini, and Italo Tajo. Sixteen complete Verdi operas were issued over a seven-year period. In 1953 Soria sold the label to Capitol, and assumed leadership of a new EMI American subsidiary which revived the Angel label. He was responsible for elegant packaging as well as high quality material on Angel until 1961, when he moved to RCA Victor as vice-president of the international division. From 1970 he was managing director of the Metropolitan Opera Guild. When he died, in New York on 28 Mar 1980, Soria was at work on a planned release of a Metropolitan Opera historic broadcast of *Ballo in maschera*.

SOUL MUSIC RECORDINGS. Soul began in the early 1960s as a vehicle for compositions and performances by Black Americans, the term generally replacing **rhythm and blues**, which in turn had replaced race music. The style is based on impassioned expression, and such vocal devices as falsetto, sobs, and shouts. The label that carried much of the early soul was **Atlantic** (**Ray Charles, Aretha Franklin, Otis Redding**). Subsidiary labels to Atlantic included Stax and Volt. **Motown** Records was the other major label to specialize in soul music (Smokey Robinson, **Diana Ross** and the **Supremes**, and the **Temptations**). In the 1970s the popularity of soul faded; it was to some extent replaced by **disco**, and then by rap music.

SOUND EFFECTS RECORDINGS. Radio programs required the use of simulated sounds to accompany dramatic programs, and these were created in the studio via ingenious means. That task was simplified as phonograph records appeared in the late 1920s. It seems that the earliest specimen was "London Street Sounds," made by Columbia Graphophone Co., Ltd., in 1928. Major labels offered sound effects discs in the 1930s, covering such typical needs as fire engines, crowd noises, storms, and horses. Victor had an elaborate set of records in the 1940 catalog that allowed the user to choose, for example, between a train approaching and passing a point, passing a station, entering a tunnel, coming to a stop, or running at constant speed. Mumbling was available, either by mixed voices or by females alone. The BBC sound effects catalog is now the world's most comprehensive, making 450 effects available on ten compact discs, at a cost in 1990 of £199.

Purchasers will hear the sound of a dental drill (high or low speed), a TV screen being smashed by a cricket ball, birds and sheep on a Welsh hillside, the sounds of a public library in action, bread being sliced, a Rolls Royce door opening and closing, three rams bleating, 40 children on wet gravel, a kiss, a burp, and even a flying saucer taking off.

SOUND RECORDING. The process of registering and reproducing sonic signals. Various means and devices have been applied to this task, beginning with the **Phonautograph** of 1857, proceeding through cylinder phonographs and disc gramophones, wire and tape recordings, cassettes, compact discs and DAT. A description of the way each of those recordings is made is given in the appropriate article. See especially CYLINDER; DISC; and RECORDING PRACTICE.

SOUND RECORDING CO., LTD. A firm established in March 1910 on Swallow St., Piccadilly, London, to make discs for use with motion picture films. Grammavox was the first label; other labels made later included Champion, Standard, Beacon, Butterfly, Popular, and Stavophone. Imperial was the final label issued, as successor to Popular. The company was absorbed by Crystalate Gramophone Record Manufacturing Co., Ltd., in July 1925. [Andrews*.]

SOUND RECORDING PERIODICALS. Journal articles about sound recording began to appear in many countries from the 1870s, as news of Thomas Edison's invention spread rapidly around the world. In Russia, in 1878, three articles dealing with the phonograph appeared: "Eshche o govoriashchei mashine ii fonografe Edissona," (*Svet*, no. 6); "Fonograf," (*Tekhnicheskii sbornik*, nos. 5–6; "Fonograf, govoriashchaia mashina," (*Zhurnal dlia vsekh*, T. 2). In 1894, an article on Thomas Edison appeared in the *Repertorio Colombiano*, from Bogotá, Colombia. By 1902 Russia had a magazine devoted to the gramophone, *Grammofon i fonograf*. Several other Russian magazines began publication in the next few years, including *Grammofonnyi mir*, *Grammofonnaia zhisn*, and *Novosti grammofona*.

In the United States, *Phonogram* appeared in 1891 and *The Phonoscope*—"the first independent publication to be devoted primarily to the phonograph field" (Read 1976) in 1896. *Talking Machine World* (U.S., 1905) was one of the most valuable periodicals for research into the industry. *Phonographische Zeitschrift* was the first German trade journal (1900). *Rivista fonografica italiana* was published in Milan from 1900.

Early recording magazines from England were *Phonogram*, which appeared ca. 1893, *Sound Wave* (1906), and *Talking Machine News* (1906). In France, *Bulletin phonographique et cinématographique* appeared ca. 1899, *Phono-ciné-gazette* in 1905, and *Musique et instruments* in 1911.

Lists of new records in turn-of-the-century phonograph/gramophone magazines serve as an interesting chronicle of the entertainment tastes of the times (see CYLINDER, 7, and DISC, 7.) Many of the early publications contained illustrated interviews with leading personalities. They also offered technical material regarding the history and development of talking machines. In these early magazines, one can trace the rapid growth and expansion of the industry, through articles and reports about record production plants that opened around the world.

A number of more general American periodicals carried information on talking machines. These included *Scientific American* (1845–), *Electrical World* (1885–), *American Machinist* (1877–), *North American Review* (1815–), and the *Journal of the Franklin Institute* (1826–). Similar British periodicals included *Electrician* (1862–), *Electrical Review* (1872–), *Musical Opinion and Musical Trades Review* (1877–), and *Nature* (1870–). In Germany there were such titles as *Elektrische Nachrichtentechnik* (1924–) and *Elektrotechnische Zeitschrift* (1880–). Publications from France that presented material on talking machines included: *L'illustration: journal universel* (1843–), *Les inventions illustrées: sciences, industrie, finance* (1899–), *La nature: revue des sciences et de leurs applications aux arts et à l'industrie* (1873–), *La science et la vie: maga-*

zine des sciences et de leurs applications à la vie moderne (1913–), La science illustrée (1887–), and Science pour tous: revue populaire de vulgarisation scientifique (1856–).

Russian publications that contained references to early talking machines were: Zhurnal noveishikh otkrytii i izobretenii (1896–), Zapiski russkogo tekhnicheskogo obshchestva (1867–), Nauka i zabava (1893–), Niva: il. zhurnal lit., politiki i sobr. zhizn' (1870–), Ogonek: khudozhestv.-lit. zhurnal (1899–), Elektrichestvo (1880–), Elektrichestvo i zhisn' (1910–), Elektrotekhnik (1897–), and Elektrotekhnicheskii vestnik (1894–).

In the 1920s, sound recording periodicals continued to flourish and proliferate. One early magazine, Gramophone, which began in Britain in 1923, is still published, and so is American Record Guide (1935–). Another early American title, New Records (1933), continued publication until 1987. The French magazine, Musique et instruments, which underwent various title changes, and which eventually incorporated Machines parlantes & radio, began publication in 1911 and continued into the 1980s. As technical advances in sound reproduction increased, more new magazines appeared, recounting developments in sound recording, such as the advent of LPs, 45s, stereo, eight-track tapes, cassettes, CDs, digital audio tapes, etc. Magazines became more specialized to suit the varied needs of record dealers and buyers.

There have been magazines for classical music record collectors, such as: Fanfare (U.S.A.), Record Collector (England), Vocal Art (U.K.), Diapason (France), Stimmen, die um die Welt gingen... (Germany), and Musica (Italy), as well as magazines for popular music collectors, such as: Discoveries (U.S.A.), Goldmine (U.S.A.), Footnote (later: New Orleans Music) (U.K.), Memory Lane (U.K.), and Bulletin du Hot club de France (France). Special interest periodicals have included The Picture-disk Collector (Netherlands), Soundtrack (Belgium), Show Music (U.S.A.), Antique Phonograph Monthly (U.S.A.), Jocks (for disc jockeys; U.K.), Metal Hammer/Crash (for heavy metal rock; Germany), The Beat (for reggae, Caribbean, African; U.S.A.), and Sound Choice (for new age music; U.S.A.).

For audiophiles, such magazines as Absolute Sound (U.S.A.), Audio (U.S.A.), Audio Amateur (U.S.A.), Audio Critic (U.S.A.), Stereophile (U.S.A.), Audio (Germany), Hi-Fi Stereophonie (Germany), and High Fidelity (Denmark) appeared. Other magazines had some technical articles along with extensive record reviews, such as High Fidelity (U.S.A.), Stereo Review (U.S.A.), Gramophone (U.K.), Hi-Fi News (later: Hi-fi News & Record Review) (U.K.), Diapason/Harmonie (France), Fono Forum (Germany), Luister (Netherlands), and Playback and Fast Forward (India).

Various associations have published their own journals, such as: ARSC Journal (Association for Recorded Sound Collections), B.A.S. Speaker (Boston Audio Society), British Institute of Recorded Sound Bulletin (superseded by Recorded Sound), In the Groove (Michigan Antique Phonograph Society), Phonographic Bulletin (International Association of Sound Archives), and The Phonographic Record (Vintage Phonographic Society of New Zealand).

As popular musical styles changed and evolved, sound recording magazines documented the various trends. There were magazines featuring salon dance music, Big Bands, blues, jazz, rock 'n' roll, disco, calypso, country, rock, heavy metal, reggae, new age etc.

In the U.S., libraries with substantial collections of sound recording publications include New York Public Library— Rodgers & Hammerstein Archives of Recorded Sound, Library of Congress, Yale University (Historical Sound Recordings Collection), and Stanford University Archive of Recorded Sound.

The list of titles that follows is a preliminary checklist of serial publication in the field of recorded sound. It is international in scope, but emphasizes U.S. periodicals. British and Canadian titles are well represented. Items from other countries are included if they appear in the New York Public Library catalogs or in standard English-language reference works, such as the Union List of Serials. The checklist includes house organs of record companies as well as independently produced publications. The periodicals appear in chronological order according to the dates of their first issues. Dates, country of publication, frequency, publisher, title variants, and content annotations are given whenever possible. A title index follows the chronological list.

1. *Phonogram*; A monthly magazine devoted to the science of sound and recording of speech. 1891–1893. New York. Monthly. "Official organ of the phonograph companies of the United States." *See also #8.*

2. *The Phonogram*; A monthly journal devoted to the science of sound and recording of speech. 1893–? London. Monthly. The Phonogram Co., Ltd. Includes articles on the development of the phonograph and how to work it, lists of famous voices recorded by the phonograph, the uses put to the phonograph by actors and actresses, etc.

3. *Billboard.* Monthly (Nov. 1894–May 1900); weekly (June 1900–date). Cincinnati, etc. Title varies: *Billboard Music Week* (v. 73–74, 1961–1962). Material in the earliest years of the publication dealt with theatrical news, including columns highlighting the current theatrical activities and performers from Berlin, London, and Paris. There were also articles on vaudeville, carnivals, fairs, tent shows, and poultry shows; along with skating rink news, film advertisements, film reviews, and some musical news. Articles dealing with sound recordings and record reviews did not appear until the 1930s.

4. *Music, Art and Trade Journal and Talking Machine Review.* 1895–1930. London. Earlier title (1895–1925): *Music.* Merged into: *Music Dealer and Radio-Gramophone Review* (#46).

5. *The Phonoscope*: A monthly journal devoted to scientific and amusement inventions appertaining to sound & sight. Nov. 1896–June 1900. New York. Monthly. Phonoscope Publishing Co. Includes illustrated articles on talking machines, inventors, artists etc. Also mentions recordings of such persons as Sarah Bernhardt, Nellie Melba, Mark Twain, Lillie Langtry, and Ellen Terry. Includes articles on the autograph, zerograph, radiophone, megaphone and cathoscope; x-rays; automatic slot machines; "picture projecting devices" such as: vitascope, phantoscope, eidoloscope, biograph, cinematographe, theatrograph & kineopticon. Contains brief reviews of films for "screen machines." Includes listings of new records with artist & record company; no record numbers. Listings of the latest popular songs and successes

are given as well as listings of new films for projecting devices.

6. *Vsemirnoe tekhnicheskoe obozrenie*: Ezhemesiachnyi politekhnicheskii zhurnal. 1898–1917. Saint Petersburg, Russia. Monthly.

7. *Bulletin phonographique et cinématographique.* 1899?–1900? Paris. M. Siry, director.

8. *Phonogram*; Printed monthly for those interested in phones, graphs, grams & scopes. "Devoted to the arts of recording and reproducing sound." May 1900–December 1902. New York. Monthly. Includes gramophone riddles, poems, cartoons, articles dealing with various uses for the phonograph, listings of Edison concert records with label numbers, including spoken word, songs sung in French, Italian, Yiddish, Latin, Swedish etc., historical articles (example: "The Story of the Phonograph. History: Ancient, Medieval and Modern"), articles on popular theatrical artists. *See also #1, #17.*

9. *Canadian Music and Trades Journal.* 1900–? Toronto, Canada. Irregular. Later titles: *Canadian Music Trades Journal* (ca. 1907–1929); *Canadian Music and Radio Trades* (1931).

10. *Phonographische Zeitschrift; Fachblatt für die gesamte Musik-und Sprechmaschinen-Industrie.* 1900–1938. Berlin. Frequency varies. Organ of Internationaler Verein für Phonographisches Wissen, Reichsverband des Deutschen Sprechmaschinen-und Schallplatten-H andels, and others. Later titles: *Phonographische und Radio-Zeitschrift; Phonographische, Radio und Musikinstrumenten Zeitschrift.*

11. *Rivista fonografica italiana*; Periodico mensile illustrato. 1900–? Milan, Italy. Monthly.

12. *Grammofon i fonograf.* 1902–1906. Saint Petersburg, Russia. Tipografiia N.N. Klobukova. Weekly. Includes listings of newly released recordings, historical surveys of the phonograph/gramophone industry, illustrated biographical articles of important persons in the gramophone industry, illustrated articles of early Russian gramophone apparatus, including factories, libretti of popular recorded songs and arias, illustrated vignettes of well known artists. Later titles: *Svet i zvuk* (#21); *Grammofon i fotografiia.*

13. *The Columbia Record.* 1903–? New York. Columbia Phonograph Co. Monthly. Includes

news of various early graphophone dealers and stores, technical articles, interviews with performers, brief record reviews, etc.

14. *Edison Amberola Monthly. See: Edison Phonograph Monthly* (#15).

15. *Edison Phonograph Monthly.* 1903–? Orange, New Jersey. Monthly. Published for trade use only by the National Phonograph Co. Includes advance listings of new Edison molded records with artists and label numbers, sales information, and lists of U.S. and Canadian jobbers of phonographs and records. *See also* #17.

16. *The Talking Machine News.* May 1903–? London. Original title: *Talking Machine News and Record Exchange* (nos. 1–2), followed by *Talking Machine News and Cinematograph Chronicle* (nos. 3–29). Subtitles dropped with no. 30 (October 1905). From no. 157 to no. 177? titled *Talking Machine News and Journal of Amusements* (#28). Publication continued into 1930s. Monthly and semimonthly. "The recognised organ of the trade." Includes illustrated articles on popular artists, historical articles, record reviews, technical articles dealing with the upkeep and proper use of talking machines and recordings, and trade articles.

17. *The New Phonogram.* 1904? Orange, New Jersey. Monthly. The National Phonograph Co. Variant title: *The Phonogram.* Includes listings of new Edison records with label numbers, artists and capsule reviews, phonograph cartoons, and poems. *See also* #1, #8, #15.

18. *Phono-ciné-gazette;* Revue illustrée des questions intéressant le phonographe, le gramophone. 1905–1908? Paris. Bi-monthly. Edmond Benoit Lévy, director. Contains record reviews, concert reviews, listings of spectacles (theatre, music hall etc.), phonograph poems, cartoons, illustrations of artists. theatre news, and film news.

19. Entry deleted.

20. *Die Sprechmaschine;* Fachzeitschrift für die gesamte Sprechmaschinen-Industrie des In- und Auslandes. 1905–1914. Berlin. Bi-weekly.

21. *Svet i zvuk.* 1905–1906. Saint Petersburg, Russia. Monthly. Formerly: *Grammofon i fonograf* (#12). Includes illustrated technical articles, historical gramophone articles, lyrics of popular arias, and current happenings in the talking machine industry.

22. *The Talking Machine World.* 1905–1934. New York. Later titles: *Talking Machine World & Radio Music Merchant* (from January 1929), *Radio-Music Merchant.*

23. *Sound Wave;* The gramophone journal. 1906–1941. Finsbury, England. Monthly. Variant title: *The Sound Wave and Talking Machine Record.* Incorporates: *The Phono Trader & Recorder.* Includes articles on popular artists, listings of recordings from various companies such as: Gramophone Co., Edison, Sterling, Columbia, Odeon, Zonophone, Beka, Neophone, Imperial, and Edison Bell, giving label numbers, composers and artists; large section of record reviews, technical articles dealing with fine points of recording and playback, articles dealing with novel uses for the phonograph, such as street gospel meetings, the improvement of Jewish synagogue singers, etc.

24. *The Voice of the Victor;* The trade journal of the Victor Talking Machine Co. 1906–1930? Camden, New Jersey. Monthly. Includes industry news, articles dealing with different uses for the gramophone, listings of new recordings with label numbers, and reviews.

25. *Novosti grammofona* [Gramophone news]. 1907–1908. Saint Petersburg, Russia. Monthly. Includes record listings with label numbers, artists and repertoire, illustrated technical articles, illustrated vignettes of artists, texts of recorded songs and arias, etc.

26. *Gramophone & Talking Machine News;* A musical paper for all. 1908?–1928? London. Monthly. Includes articles on recording artists, listings of new recordings with company and label numbers, illustrated technical articles, opera synopses, and record reviews.

27. *Ofitsial'nye izvestiia aktsionernogo obshchestva grammofon.* [Gramophone Co. news] 1908–1910. Moscow. Monthly. Continues as: *Pishushchii amur i grammofonnye novosti* (#31) in 1910. Includes listings of recommended and best new recordings, articles on the gramophone industry, Zonophone news, small record reviews, articles dealing with grammophone libraries, Grammophone Co. news from around the world, and humorous gramophone cartoons.

28. *The Talking Machine News and Journal of Amusements.* 1908?–? London. Monthly. Supersedes:

The Talking Machine News (#16). Consecutive numbers are odd-numbered only. Includes illustrated articles on popular artists, record reviews, musical articles, a column written by Mikhail Mordkin entitled: "The art of dancing and the talking machine," illustrated technical articles.

29. *Unterricht und Sprechmaschine.* 1908?–1914? Stuttgart, Germany. Publisher: Wilhelm Violet.

30. *Grammofonnyi mir/die Grammophon-Welt* [Gramophone World]. 1910–1917. Saint Petersburg, Russia. Monthly. Includes articles in German and Russian, capsule record reviews, technical articles, and illustrated sketches of artists.

31. *Pishushchii amur i grammofonnye novosti.* 1910–1911. Moscow. Formerly: *Ofitsial'nye izvestiia aktsionernogo obshchestva Grammofon* (#27).

32. *Die Stimme seines Herrn.* 1910–1916. Berlin. Monthly. Issued by the German branch of the Gramophone Co. Includes record listings with label numbers, illustrated historical articles, illustrated articles on popular performers, and record reviews.

33. *Grammofonnia zhizn'* [Gramophone Life]. 1911–1912. Moscow. Bi-weekly. Fabrikant i optovik. Includes listings of new recordings, illustrated technical and historical articles, concert, opera and operetta reviews, illustrated articles about popular artists, and capsule record reviews.

34. *Musique et instruments*; Revue générale de l'industrie et du commerce de la musique, des machines parlantes et de la radio. 1911–1984? Paris. Weekly, bi-monthly. Auguste Bosc, director. Later title: *Musique et radio.* Absorbed in September 1939: *Machines parlantes & radio* (#72).

35. *Duo-Art Music.* 1913?–1930?. New York. Monthly. Aeolian Co.

36. *Musique-adresses*; Annuaire français de la facture instrumentale, de l'édition musicale et des industries qui s'y rattachent. 1913–? Paris. Annual. Auguste Bosc, director. Title variant: *Annuaire O.G.M.*

37. *Muzykal'noe ekho.* 1914. Vilna, Lithuania. Organ of Posviashchennyi grammofonnoi promyshlennosti.

38. *Pishuschii amur*; Zhurnal torgovykh izvesti obshchestva "Grammofon." 1914–1916.

Petrograd, Russia. Amur Company. Includes copious illustrations of early Russian gramophone factories and their various operational activities, illustrated articles of popular artists, and listings of new recordings with artists and label numbers. Articles dealing with various uses of the gramophone include "The Gramophone in the Monastery."

39. *Edison Diamond Points.* 1915–? Orange, New Jersey. Monthly. "Devoted entirely to the Edison Diamond Disc Phonograph and record business." Includes industry articles, music articles, and capsule record reviews.

40. *Along Broadway*; The Edison musical magazine. 1916–? Orange, New Jersey. Monthly. Thomas A. Edison, Inc. Includes illustrated articles on popular artists, musical articles, and record reviews.

41. *The Phonograph*; A musical news weekly. 1916–1978. New York. Weekly. Later titles: *Phonograph and Talking Machine Weekly* (July 1919–September 5, 1928); *Talking Machine and Radio Weekly* (September 12, 1928–December 6, 1933); *Radio Weekly* (December 13, 1933–April 26, 1939); *Radio and Television Weekly* (May 3, 1939–1978). Includes mainly news of the recording industry.

42. *The Talking Machine Journal*; The national journal of the talking machine industry. 1916–1957. New York. Monthly. Later titles: *The Talking Machine and Radio Journal*; *Radio & Electric Appliance Journal*; *Radio-Television Journal*; *Radio-Television Journal & The Talking Machine World*; *Radio Journal*; *Radio Television Journal*; *Radio and Appliance Journal*; *RTJ* (Radio and Television Journal). Issues for May 1919–June 1923 include listing of "latest record releases." Includes industry news, record statistics (example: "The fastest selling Victor records"), and historical articles.

43. *Victor Educational Bulletin.* 1916–1918. Camden, New Jersey.

44. *The Voice*; The magazine of the Gramophone Co., Ltd. 1916–? Hayes, Middlesex, England. Irregular.

44a. *Audio.* 1917–1935. San Francisco, New York, etc. Suspended publication June 1917–December 1919. Variant titles: *Pacific Radio News* (January 1917–October 1921), *Radio*; *Audio Engineering*.

45. *The Tonearm.* 1918?–1919? Bridgeport, Connecticut. Monthly. Columbia Phonograph Co., Inc., American Graphophone Co., Columbia Graphophone Manufacturing Co.

46. *Revue des machines parlantes.* 1919–1929. Paris. Monthly. Later title: *Machines parlantes et radio* (#72). Edité par L'Office de la Musique.

47. *The Victor Tourist.* 1919?–? For the Victor traveling staff. Camden, New Jersey.

48. *Weekly Bulletin.* [Victor] 1919?–?

49. *Phono-radio-musique;* Radiophonie, Phonographie, Télévision. 1920?–1937? Paris. Monthly. Organe de la Chambre Syndicale de L'Industrie et du Commerce Français des Machines Parlantes. J.M. Gilbert, director.

50. *Record Review.* 1920?–1921? New York. Bimonthly. Columbia Graphophone Co., Educational Department.

51. *The Total Eclipse.* 1920?–? U.S. Monthly. "Published monthly by the Eclipse Musical Company in the interests of Victor merchants."

52. *Better Selling Bulletin.* 1921?–1923? U.S. Later title: *Better Letters Bulletin.* Weekly. Includes letters to Penn-Victor dealers from the Penn Phonograph Co.

53. *The Gramophone.* 1923– . London. Monthly. Title variants: *The Radio Gramophone* (v.7, no.84–v.8, no.89), *Gramophone*. Includes music articles, listings of recommended recordings, record society articles, and comprehensive record reviews and criticism.

54. *Power; RCA Victor Service Notes.* 1923–1945? Camden, New Jersey. RCA Victor Company, Inc. Irregular.

55. *Elektrische Nachrichtentechnik.* 1924–1943? Berlin. Monthly? Publisher: K. W. Wagner.

56. Entry deleted.

57. *Australasian Phonograph Monthly.* 1925–1927. Sydney, Australia. Publisher: Count L. de Noskowski. Includes articles, and record reviews of such labels as Apex, Brunswick, Columbia, HMV, Parlophone, Edison Diamond Discs, and Polydor.

58. *Jahrbuch für Phonotechnik und Phonokunst.* 1925–1927? Berlin. Variant title: *Internationales Jahrbuch für Phonotechnik und Phonokunst.*

59. *Listener In.* 1925–? Melbourne, Australia. Monthly. Adgar H. Baillie, United Propriety, Ltd. "The wireless journal of Australia."

60. *Radio matériel.* 1925. Paris. Monthly. Later title: *Radio et phono matériel; Revue mensuelle des négociants en T.S.F. et machines parlantes.*

61. *Music Lovers' Phonograph Monthly Review.* 1926–1932. Boston. Monthly. The Phonograph Publishing Co., Inc. "An American magazine for amateurs interested in phonographic music and its development—only American magazine of its kind." Title variant: *The Phonograph Monthly Review* (Oct. 1926–June 1927). Superseded by: *Music Lover's Guide* (#78). Includes technical articles with illustrations, articles on recording personalities, the recording industry, comprehensive record reviews, reports from phonograph societies, and listings of new releases with company and label information.

62. *L'édition musicale vivante; Études critiques de la musique enregistrée: disques, rouleaux perforés, etc.* 1927–1933. Paris. Monthly. Superseded by: *Sélection de la vie artistique* (1934–1935).

63. *The Music Seller Reference Book.* 1927–1936? London. Annual. Evan Bros., Ltd. Variant title: *Music Seller and Radio Music Trader.* "Records and music issued..." Includes factors (agents) of gramophone records, addresses of record manufacturers, alphabetical index to separate numbers of operas and oratorios, alphabetical listings of gramophone records with title, artist, record company and label number, music publisher, addresses of music publishers, list of published sheet music, and classified index of manufacturers and suppliers.

64. *Musique; Revue d'histoire, de critique, d'esthétique et d'informations musicales.* 1927–1930? Paris. Monthly. Robert Lyon, director. Marc Pincherle, editor-in-chief. Includes music articles, phonograph articles, book reviews, record reviews, concert reviews, etc.

65. *The Gramophone Review.* 1928–1929. London.

66. *Gramophone World and Record Times.* 1928–? London.

67. *Le phono.* 1928–? Paris. Weekly.

68. *Phono-magazine.* 1928–? Paris. Monthly.

68a. *Die Tonwiedergabe.* 1928–1938? Vienna. Fachblatt für Industrie, Handel und Export aller an der Tonwiedergabe interessierten Kreise.

69. *Grammotechnik.* 1929?–1932? Prague, Czechoslovakia. Verband für Industrie und Handel

der Grammophon- und Musikinstrumenten-Branche in der CSSR, Prag.

70. *De gramophoon revue.* 1929–1933. Amsterdam, Netherlands. Monthly. Absorbed by: *Schijven schouw.* Published by A.J.G. Strensholt en Allert de Lange. Includes articles on popular recording artists, illustrated technical articles, listings of recordings with label numbers from different companies, and record reviews, both pop and classical.

71. *Kultur und Schallplatte.* 1929–1931? Berlin. Monthly. "Mitteilungen der Carl Lindström AG, Kulturabteilung." Includes music articles, record releases, and record reviews.

72. *Machines parlantes & radio.* 1929–1939. Continues numbering of *Revue des machines parlantes* (#45). Paris. Monthly. Absorbed by: *Musique et instruments* (#34).

73. *Phono-revue.* 1929–? Paris. Monthly.

74. Entry deleted.

75. *Disques.* 1930–1933. Philadelphia. Monthly. Superseded by: *The New Records* (#82).

75a. *Sprechmaschinen-Radio-Zeitung.* 1930–1932. Berlin. Variant title: *Radio und Sprechmaschine-Zeitung.* A supplement to *Musik-Instrumenten Zeitung.*

76. *International Record Collector's Club. Bulletin.* 1932–1956. Bridgeport, Connecticut.

77. Entry deleted.

78. *Music Lovers' Guide.* 1932–1935. New York. Monthly.

79. *Wurlitzer's Record Notes.* 1932–1935. U.S. Monthly.

80. *The Gramophone Record.* 1933–? London. Continues as: *Gramophone Record Review* (#136).

81. *Record Review.* 1933–1953. Truro, U.K. Title varies: *Gramophone Record and Home Musician; Gramophone Record* (1949?–1953), *Gramophone Record Review* (1953).

82. *The New Records.* 1933–1987. Philadelphia. Monthly. H. Royer Smith Company. Supersedes *Disques* (#75).

83. *Recorded Music.* Privately printed in the interests of and dedicated to the gramophoniac at large. 1933–1934. New York. Monthly.

84. *American Record Guide.* 1935– . Milbrook, New York. Bi-monthly. Former titles: *The American Music Lover; The Listener's Record Guide; Music Lovers' Guide.* Absorbed: *The American Tape Guide.*

85. *Disques.* 1935?–1962? Paris. Originally a monthly supplement to: *Phono-radio-musique* (#49), then became an independent title.

86. *The Monthly Letter.* (E.M.G. Hand-Made Gramophones, Ltd.) 1936–1980. London. Monthly.

87. *H.R.S. Society Rag.* 1938–1941? U.S.

88. *Victor Record Review.* May 1938–February 1949. Camden, New Jersey. Monthly. Continued by: *RCA Victor Record Review* (#115). Combined with: *RCA Victor's In the Groove* (#105).

89. *Gateway to Music, Los Angeles. On the Record.* 1939–1947. U.S. Monthly.

90. *Records; A monthly review.* 1939–1940. New York. Monthly.

91. *The Steinway Review of Permanent Music* (November 1939–January 1942). Variant titles: *Review of Permanent Music* (February 1942–December 1949), *Review of Recorded Music* (January 1950–May 1958).

92. *Listen.* Guide to Good Music. 1940–1950? New York. Monthly.

93. *Co-Art Turntable.* 1941–1943. Beverly Hills, California. Monthly.

94. *Cash Box.* 1941– . New York. Weekly. Identifies and lists most popular recordings, from March 25, 1950.

95. *The Record Changer.* 1942–1957. New York [varies]. Monthly.

95a. *International Records Agency. Bulletin.* 1942–1950. Richmond Hill, New York. Bulletin. Modern imported and domestic phonograph records.

96. *Coda.* 1943–1946. U.S. Monthly. Columbia Records. Superseded by *Columbia's Disc Digest* (#103).

97. *The Jazz Record.* 1943–1947. New York. Monthly.

98. *Music Views.* 1943–1959. Hollywood, California. Capitol Records. Variant titles: *Capitol News; Music News; Capitol; News from Hollywood.*

99. *Record Retailing.* 1943–1954. U.S. Monthly. Continued by: *Record and Sound Retailing* (#150).

100. *Musica e dischi.* 1945–1986. Milan, Italy. Monthly. Variant title (v. 1. no. 1): *Musica; Rassegna della vita musicale italiana.* Superseded by: *M & D* (#521).

100a. *A. J. Q. Handbook.* (Australian Jazz Quarterly.) 1945– ? Australia. Quarterly.

101. *Record Review.* 1945–1947. New York: G. Schirmer. Monthly.

101a. *Audio Record.* (Audio Devices, Inc.) 1945– ?. New York.

102. *Columbia Promotion News.* 1946–1950. U.S. Monthly.

102a. *Disc.* 1946– ?. Mt. Morris, Illinois.

103. *Columbia's Disc Digest.* 1946–1947. U.S. Monthly. Supersedes: *Coda* (#96).

104. Entry deleted.

105. *RCA Victor's In the Groove.* 1946–1949? U.S. Monthly. *See also* #88.

106. *The Record Collector.* 1946– . Ipswich, Suffolk [etc.] England. Monthly. James F. E. Dennis, editor. Includes extensive discographies on early singers. Variant titles: *Bulletin* (v. 1, nos. 1–4), *Record Collector's Bulletin* (v. 1, nos. 508).

107. *Record World.* 1946?–1982. U.S. Weekly.

107a. *Disc.* 1947–? . Bristol, England: City of Bristol Gramophone Society.

108. *Audio.* 1947– . Philadelphia. Monthly. Formerly: *Audio Engineering.*

109. Entry deleted.

110. *Critique; A review of gramophone records.* 1943–1955. London: Gramophone Exchange. Monthly.

111. Entry deleted.

112. *Swing Journal.* 1947– . Japan. Monthly. Jazz recordings.

113. *The Discophile.* 1948–1958. London. Bimonthly. Absorbed (January 1959) by: *Matrix* (#148).

113a. *Phonolog Reporter.* 1948– . San Diego: Trade Service Publications, Inc.. Title varies. Weekly. A loose-leaf service, maintaining a 6,000-page list of 1 million current recordings, classical and popular.

114. *Just Records.* (Elaine Music Shop.) 1948–1950? New York. Monthly.

115. *RCA Victor Record Review.* (RCA Victor) v. 1, no. 1, April 1949–v. 1, no. 6, September 1949. Camden, New Jersey. Former title: *Victor Record Review* (#88). Superseded by: *RCA Victor Picture Record Review* (#118).

116. Entry deleted.

117. *Ceskoslovenská diskografie; Gramofonové závody.* 1949– . Prague, Czechoslovakia.

118. *RCA Victor Picture Record Review.* 1949–1953. Camden, New Jersey. Monthly. Supersedes *RCA Victor Record Review* (#115).

119. *Record Letter.* 1949–1950. Kirkland, Washington. Irregular. Superseded by: *American Record Letter* (#122) and *International Record Letter* (#124).

120. *Record News.* 1949–1951. Brighton, England. Monthly.

121. *Schwann Long Playing Record Catalog.* 1949–1989. Boston. Monthly [varies]. Title varies: *Schwann Record & Tape Guide* (1971–1984; issued in parts: *Schwann 1* and *Schwann 2*), *The New Schwann Record and Tape Guide* (1984), *Super Schwann* (1987, quarterly), *Schwann* (1988–1990, quarterly), *Schwann Compact Disc Catalog* (1985–1989), *Schwann CD* (1989). Cover titles do not always correspond to title-page titles. Superseded by *Opus* (#561, classical music, quarterly), *Spectrum* (#563, popular music, quarterly), *In Music* (#559, monthly). The popular and classical catalogs currently list about 90,000 recordings.

121a. *Tonband-Aufnahmen.* 1950–1967. Germany. Monthly. Superseded by: *Tonband und Schallplatte* (#256).

122. *American Record Letter.* 1950–? Kirkland, Washington. Monthly. Supersedes *Record Letter* (#119).

123. *Revue des disques.* 1950–?. Belgium. Monthly. Later title (July 1964): *Revue des disques et de la haute-fidelité* (#446).

124. *International Record Letter: A monthly listing of new or unusual records of concert, folk and ethnic music, literary readings, and discs from the theater.* October 1950–1952. Kirkland, Washington: B. Richardson [etc.]. Monthly. Supersedes: *American Record Letter* (#122).

125. *The Forty-Five.* (Le Mire Products.) 1951–1957. New York. Monthly.

125a. *Record Year; A guide to the year's gramophone records.* 1951. London. Annual.

126. *High Fidelity.* 1951–1989. Great Barrington, Massachusetts [etc.]. Monthly. Merged with *Musical America* in 1965 to form: *High Fidelity and Musical America.* The two periodicals were issued separately as well as bound together. *High Fidelity* was absorbed by *Stereo Review* (#178) in 1989.

126a. *Disc Collector.* 1951– . Palmer, Michigan. Monthly. Issues 1–11 from the National Hillbilly Record Collectors Exchange.

127. *Almanach du disque.* 1951–1958? Paris. Annual.

128. *Bulletin du Hot Club de France.* 1952?– . France. Monthly.

129. *Les cahiers du disque.* 1952–1955? Paris: I.M.E. Pathé-Marconi. Irregular.

130. *Luister.* 1952– . Amersfoort, Netherlands. Monthly.

131. Entry deleted.

132. *Audio Engineering Society.Journal.* 1953–1985. New York. Monthly.

133. *Bielefelder Katalog. Katalog der Schallplatten klassischer Musik.* 1953– . Bielefeld, Germany. Semiannual.

133a. *Harrison Tape Catalog.* 1953–1972. New York: Weiss Publishing Corp. Bi-monthly. Title, imprint, and frequency vary. Each issue presented some 20,000 tape titles, covering all formats, including classical and pop. Continued as: *Harrison Tape Guide* (#304a).

134. *Jazz Discography* (Cassell & Co.) 1953–? London.

135. *Gramophone Classical Catalogue.* 1953– . Harrow, England: General Gramophone Publications, Ltd. Quarterly. Title varies.

136. Entry deleted.

137. Revue du son. 1953– . Paris. 11 per year. Later title: *Nouvelle revue du son.*

138. *Record News.* 1953–1959. London. Monthly. Later title (April 1958–March 1959): *Record News and Stereo Disc.* Absorbed by: *Hi-Fi News* (#163).

139. Entry deleted.

140. *Schwann Artist Issue.* 1953–1982. Boston. Formerly: *Schwann Long Playing Record Catalog. Artist Listing; Schwann Catalog. Artist Issue.* Continued by: *The New Schwann Artist Issue* (#507).

141. *Theme.* 1953–1957. U.S. Monthly. Supersedes: *Record Exchange.*

142. *Vocal Art.* 1953–1971? London. Irregular.

143. *Audio League. Report.* 1954–1957. Pleasantville, New York. Irregular.

144. Entry deleted.

145. *Broadcast Music, Inc. Record Catalog Supplement.* 1954?–1964? New York. Irregular.

146. *For the Record.* (Book of the Month Club.) 1954–1960. U.S. Monthly.

147. *Hi-Fi Music at Home.* 1954–1959. New York. Bi-monthly; Monthly. Absorbed by: *High Fidelity* (#532).

148. *Matrix; Jazz record research magazine.* 1954–1975. London. Bi-monthly. Absorbed: *The Discophile* (#113), in January 1959.

149. *Phono: Internationale Schallplatten-Zeitschrift.* 1954–1966. Vienna. Quarterly. Incorporated in: *Oesterreichischer Musikzeitschrift.*

150. *Record and Sound Retailing.* 1954–1962. New York: M. and N. Harrison. Monthly. Formerly: *Record Retailing* (#99). Superseded by: *Home Entertainment Retailing* (#217).

150a. *Recordland.* 1954– . Chicago.

151. *Audiocraft.* 1955–1958. Great Barrington, Vermont. Monthly. Variant title: *Audiocraft for the Hi Fi Hobbyist.* Absorbed by: *High Fidelity* (#126).

152. *Columbia Record Club Magazine.* 1955–1959. New York. Monthly. Continued by *Columbia Record Club Magazine* (Monophonic), 1959–1967, and *Columbia Record Club Magazine* (Stereo), 1959–1973. Variant title: *Columbia LP Record Club Magazine.*

153. *Better Listening.* 1955–1963? Los Angeles. Irregular. Variant title: *Better Listening through High Fidelity.*

154. *GTJ & CR News.* (Good Time Jazz Record Company.) 1955–1961. Los Angeles. Bi-monthly.

155. *High Fidelity Record Annual.* 1955–1956. Philadelphia. Annual. Collection of record reviews from *High Fidelity* (#126). Continued by: *Records in Review* (#157).

156. *Record Research.* 1955– . Brooklyn, New York. Bi-monthly with some irregularities. Important articles on early record labels, many by Carl Kendziora or George Blacker. Extensive label lists.

157. *Records in Review.* 1955–1981. Great Barrington, Massachusetts: Wyeth Press. Annual. Reviews of classical and semi-classical records and tapes from *High Fidelity* (#532) magazine.

158. *Record Monthly.* (New Zealand Federation of Recorded Music Societies.) 1956– . Christchurch, New Zealand.

159. *British Institute of Recorded Sound. Bulletin.* 1956–1960. London. Irregular. Superseded by: *Recorded Sound* (#202).

160. *Diapason; La revue du disque microsillon.* 1956–1984. Paris. Monthly. Superseded by: *Diapason-harmonie* (#501).

161. *Fono Forum;* Zeitschrift für Schallplatte, Musik, HiFi-Technik. 1956– . Bielefeld, Germany. Monthly.

162. Entry deleted.

163. *Hi-Fi News.* 1956–1970. London. Monthly. Superseded by: *HiFi News and Record Review* (#274).

164. *Record News;* The magazine for record collectors. 1956–1961. Toronto, Canada. Monthly.

165. *Collectors Item.* (New York Gramophone Society.) 1956–1957? New York. Irregular.

166. *Alta fedeltà.* 1957– . Milan, Italy. Monthly.

167. *High Fidelity Trade News.* 1957–1981? New York. Monthly.

168. *Klassiska skivspegeln.* 1957–1960. Sweden. Superseded by: *Skivspegeln.*

169. *Records and Recording.* 1957–1982. London. Monthly. Title from February 1967: *Records and Recording and Record Times.* Absorbed by: *Music and Musicians.*

170. *Stereo Review's Stereo Buyers Guide.* 1957– . New York. Annual. Former titles: *Stereo Directory* and *Buying Guide.*

171. *Tape Recording and Hi-Fi Magazine.* 1957–1960. London. Monthly. Variant titles: *Tape Recording and Reproduction Magazine; Tape Recording & High Fidelity Reproduction Magazine.* Superseded by: *Tape Recording Fortnightly* (#199).

171a. *Audio Cardalog.* 1958–1969? Albany, New York. Monthly.

172. *Harrison Catalog of Stereophonic Records.* 1958–1959? New York. Monthly. Variant title: *This Month's Records.*

172a. *Il disco.* 1958?–1970. Milan, Italy. Bi-monthly.

173. *Great Music.* (Book-of-the-Month Club, RCA Victor Society of Great Music.) 1958–1959? New York. Monthly.

173a. *Phonoprisma.* 1958–1963. Kassel, Germany: Bärenreiter Verlag. Bi-monthly. Formerly: *Musica Schallplatte* (#175). Issued as a supplement to : *Musica (Cassel).*

174. *Hi Fi Review.* 1958–1960. Chicago. Monthly. Superseded by: *Hi Fi/Stereo Review* (#193).

174a. *Recorded Folk Music;* A review of British and foreign folk music recordings. 1958– . London.

175. *Musica Schallplatte.* 1958–1961. Germany. Bi-monthly. Superseded by: *Phonoprisma* (#211).

175a. *Record Times.* (EMI, Ltd.) 1958– . London.

176. *Philips Music Herald.* 1958–1970? Baarn, Netherlands. Irregular.

177. *Records Magazine.* (Decca Record Co., Ltd.) 1958–1966? London. Monthly.

177a. *Allen's Poop Sheet.* 1958–1974/1975? U.S. Irregular.

178. *Stereo Review.* 1958– . New York. Monthly. Absorbed *High Fidelity* (#126) 1989.

179. *Das Ton Magazine.* 1958?–1963? Germany. 6 per year.

180. *Modern Hi-Fi.* 1958–1970? New York. Irregular. Superseded by: *Modern Hi-Fi & Stereo Guide* (#290).

181. *Blues Research.* 1959–1974? Brooklyn, New York. Irregular.

181a. *Audio Times.* 1959– . New York. Semi-monthly.

182. *Discoteca hi fi.* 1959–1960. Milan, Italy. Monthly. Continued by: *Discoteca alta fedeltà;* (#192).

183. *Das gesprochene Wort.* 1959–1966. Leipzig, Germany. Annual. A section of the national bibliography.

184. *Der Jazz Freund.* 1959?–1982? Menden, Germany. Quarterly.

185. Entry deleted.

186. *Music Week.* 1959– . London. Weekly. Former titles: *Music and Video Week; Music Week: Record Retailer.*

187. *Musik och ljudteknik.* 1959–1975. Stockholm, Sweden. Irregular. Superseded by: *Musiktidningen.*

188. *Der Musikmarkt.* 1959– . Starnberg, Germany: Josef Keller Verlag. Semi-monthly.

189. *Studio Sound & Broadcasting Engineering.* 1959– . England. Monthly. Former titles: *Studio Sound and Broadcasting; Studio Sound.* Incorporates: *Sound International.*

190. *Your One-Spot Numerical Reporter.* 1959–? U.S. Irregular.

190a. *Records on Review;* A survey of recent record releases. (Gregg Sherman.) 1959– . U.S.

191. *Discographical Forum;* A bi-monthly of jazz and blues research. 1960–? England. Bi-monthly.

192. *Discoteca alta fedeltà.* 1960–1978. Monthly. Supersedes: *Discoteca hi fi* (#182).

193. *Hi-Fi Stereo Review.* 1960–1968. U.S. Monthly. Formerly: *Hi Fi Review* (#174). Absorbed by: *Stereo Review* (#178).

194. *Hillandale News* (Official Journal of the City of London Phonograph & Gramophone Society). 1960– . London. England. Bi-monthly. Research journal covering all aspects of re-

corded sound: labels, artists, firms, etc., emphasizing British aspects. Includes contributions by Peter Adamson, Frank Andrews, Peter Copeland, George Frow, George Taylor, and other leading scholars.

195. *Jazz-Disco.* 1960?-? Malmö, Sweden. Bi-monthly.

196. *Jazz Report*; The record collector's magazine. 1960–1982? Ventura, California. Irregular.

197. *Der Plattenteller.* 1960?–1964. Munich, Germany. Monthly.

198. *Stereo.* 1960–1968. U.S. Quarterly.

199. *Tape Recording Fortnightly.* 1960–1961. London. Monthly. Supersedes: *Tape Recording and Hi-Fi Magazine* (#171). Superseded by: *Tape Recording Magazine* (#214).

200. *Audio and Record Review.* 1961–1969. London. Monthly. Later titles: *Audio Record Review* (1966–1969), *Record Review* (#278). United with: *Hi-Fi News* (#163), in 1970, to form: *Hi-Fi News and Record Review* (#274).

201. *Disk.* 1961–? Amersfoort, Netherlands. Monthly.

202. *Recorded Sound.* (Journal of the British Institute of Recorded Sound.) 1961–1984. London. Irregular. Supersedes: *British Institute of Recorded Sound, London. Bulletin* (#159).

203. *Classical Recordaid.* 1962–1977. U.S. Irregular.

204. *Columbia Stereo Tape Club. Magazine.* 1962–1973. U.S. Monthly.

205. *Country & Western Roundabout.* 1962–1968. Loughton, U.K. Irregular.

206. *Gramophone Popular Record Catalogue.* 1962–1987. Harrow, England: General Gramophone Publications, Ltd. Quarterly.

207. *HIP*; The jazz record digest. 1962–1971? U.S.

208. *Hi-Fi Stereophonie.* 1962–1983. Stuttgart, Germany. Monthly. Merged with: *Stereoplay* (#500).

209. *Hillbilly.* 1962–1971? Basel, Switzerland. Quarterly.

210. *Mezhdunarodnaia kniga. Katalog dolgoigraiushchie gramplastinok.* 1958–1977? Moscow. Monthly. Title varies. A catalog of recordings available for purchase outside the USSR, issued in English and Russian. Works are listed by genre, with indexes by composer and artist. There was an earlier series, from 1936.

211. Entry deleted.

212. *Ragtime Review.* 1962–1966. U.S. Quarterly.

213. *The Stereophile.* 1962– . Santa Fe, New Mexico. 8 per year.

214. *Tape Recording Magazine.* 1962–1971. London. Monthly. Formerly: *Tape Recording Fortnightly* (#199). Superseded by: *Sound & Picture Tape Recording* (#297).

215. *Harrison Catalog of Stereophonic Tapes.* 1962?–1969. New York. Title varies. 5 per year.

216. *Deutsches Rundfunkarchiv, Frankfurt am Main. Hinweisdienst: Musik.* 1963–1964. Germany. Monthly.

217. *Home Entertainment Retailing.* 1963–1964? U.S. Irregular. Formerly: *Record and Sound Retailing* (#150).

218. *Deutsches Rundfunkarchiv, Frankfurt am Main. Hinweisdienst: Wort.* 1963–1964? Frankfurt, Germany. Monthly.

219. *RPM Music Weekly.* 1963– . Toronto, Canada. Weekly.

219a. *Reader's Digest Music Guide.* 1962–1964. U.S. Monthly. Superseded by: *Music Guide; The magazine of the RCA Victor Record Club* (#235).

220. *Paris. Phonothèque Nationale. Bulletin.* 1963–? Paris. Irregular.

221. *Sound Industry Directory.* 1963– . New York: St. Regis Publications. Annual.

222. *Stereo.* 1963– . Japan. Monthly.

223. *Diapason microsillon*; Catalogue général des disques microsillon. Disques classsiques. 1964– . Paris. Annual.

223a. *Phonolog List of Tapes.* 1964–1989. Los Angeles: Trade Services Publications, Inc. [varies]. Quarterly.

223b. *Phonolog Tape Parade.* 1964– ?. Los Angeles. Monthly.

224. *Disc Collector Newsletter.* 1964–1980. U.S. Irregular. Superseded by: *Disc Collector* (#466).

224a. *Record Preview.* (Billboard Publishing Co.) 1964– . New York. Monthly.

225. *Le grand baton.* (Journal of the Sir Thomas Beecham Society.) 1964?– . Redondo Beach, California. Irregular.

225a. *Country Corner.* 1964?–1981? Bremen, Germany. 5 per year.

226. *Indiana University. Archives of Folk and Primitive Music. Report.* 1964–1965. Bloomington, Indiana. 3 per year. Superseded by: *Indiana University. Archives of Traditional Music. Trimester Report* (#233).

227. *Audiofan.* 1965–1967. New York: St. Regis Publications. Monthly. Merged with: *Audio* (#108) in 1968.

227a. *Schwann's Children's Records.* 1965–1981. Boston. Annual. Variant titles: *Schwann Children's Record & Tape Catalog; Schwann Children's & Christmas Record & Tape Guide.*

228. *Collector.* 1965–1967? Italy. Bi-monthly.

229. *Federation of British Tape Recordists. Recording News.* 1965– . Essex, England. Bi-monthly. Formerly: *Federation of British Tape Recordists. News and Views.*

230. *Harmonie.* 1965?–1980. France. Monthly. Superseded by: *Harmonie hi-fi conseil* (#444).

231. *High Fidelity and Musical America.* 1965–1986. U.S. Monthly. Formerly: *High Fidelity* (#126). In 1987, split again into the original magazines: *High Fidelity* and *Musical America. High Fidelity* was then absorbed by *Stereo Review* (#178) in 1989.

232. *High Fidelity Jahrbuch.* 1965?–1980. Düsseldorf, Germany. Annual. Variant title: *Deutsches High Fidelity Jahrbuch.* Superseded by: *HiFi Jahrbuch.*

233. *Indiana University. Archives of Traditional Music. Trimester Report.* 1965–1971. Bloomington, Indiana.. 3 per year. Formerly: *Indiana. University. Archives of Folk and Primitive Music. Report* (#226).

234. *JEMF Quarterly.* 1965–1985. Los Angeles: John Edwards Memorial Foundation. Quarterly. Formerly: *JEMF Newsletter* (1965–1968). Superseded by: *American Vernacular Music.*

235. *Music Guide.* (RCA Victor Record Club.) 1965–1966. Indianapolis, Indiana [etc.]. 13 per year. Supersedes: *Reader's Digest Music Guide* (#221).

236. *The Phonographic Record.* (Journal of the Vintage Phonographic Society of New Zealand.) 1965?–1980? Christchurch, New Zealand. Irregular.

237. *Recording Rights Journal.* (Mechanical Copyright Protection Society.) 1965–1968. London. Quarterly.

238. *Storyville.* 1965– . London. Bi-monthly. Jazz and blues.

239. *Arturo Toscanini Society. Newsletter.* 196?–?. U.S. Irregular.

240. *Record Beat.* 1966?– . New York: Record Beat Publishing Co.

240a. *Schwann Country and Western Catalog.* 1966–1970? Boston. Annual.

240b. *Harrison Catalog of Stereo and Tape Cartridges.* 1966–1969. New York. Bi-monthly.

241. *Discografia internazionale.* 1966–1972. Milan, Italy. Irregular.

242. *Hi-Fi Stereo Buyers' Guide.* 1966?–1981. U.S. Bi-monthly.

243. *Record of the Month.* 1967– . London: Sinclair's Publications, Ltd. Monthly.

244. *BN: Blues News.* 1967?– . Helsinki, Finland. Bi-monthly.

245. *db; The sound engineering magazine.* 1967– . U.S. Monthly.

245a. *The Discographer.* 1967–1971? Fresno, California: George C. Collings. Irregular.

246. *High Fidelity.* 1967?– . Denmark. Monthly.

247. *I A J R C Journal.* (Journal of the International Association of Jazz Record Collectors.) 1967–? U.S.

248. *International Piano Library. Bulletin.* 1967–1971. New York. Quarterly.

249. *R S V P: the magazine for record collectors.* 1967?–? London. Monthly.

250. *ARSC Bulletin.* (Association for Recorded Sound Collections.) Nos. 1–21, 1968–1989. Annual. Absorbed by *ARSC Journal* (#250b).

250a. *ARSC Journal.* (Association for Recorded Sound Collections.) 1968– . Silver Spring, Maryland [varies]. Semiannual. An important journal of research in all areas of recorded sound. Includes extensive annotated bibliographies, by Tim Brooks, of writings in other periodicals. Reviews of books and of sound recordings. Recent issues have included articles by such scholars as John F. N. Francis, Donald McCormick, Gerald Parker, Steven Smolian, and Ray Wile.

251. *Hi-Fi Sound.* 1968?–1977. London. Monthly. Superseded by: *Popular Hi-Fi & Sound.*

252. *Kounty Korral Magazine.* 1968– . Sweden. 4–6 per year. Includes country music record reviews and discographies.

253. *Musica e nastri.* (Supplement to: *Musica e dischi,* #100) 1968–1970? Milan, Italy.

254. *New Amberola Graphic.* 1968– . St. Johnsbury, Vermont: New Amberola Graphic Phonograph Co. Quarterly. Edited by Martin Bryan. An important journal for collectors, presenting authoritative research about phonographs and gramophones, as well as recording art-

ists. Illustrations are a useful feature, many of them reproductions from old magazines and sales materials. Tim Brooks, George Paul, and Ray Wile are among the scholars represented in recent issues.

255. *Svensk ton pa skiva* [Swedish music on records]. 1968–1981. Sweden. Biennial.

256. *Tonband und Schallplatte.* 1968–1969? Germany. Monthly. Formerly: *Tonband-Aufnahmen* (#180).

257. *UE-Hi-Fi Vision.* (Unterhaltungs-Elektronik): das schweizer Monatsmagazin für Unterhaltungselektronik und Musik. 1968– . Goldach, Switzerland. Monthly. Formerly: *Unterhaltungs-Elektronik.*

258. *The Collecta.* 1969?–1976. Watford, Herts., England. Irregular. Edited by Derek Spruce.

259. *Columbia Stereo Tape Cartridge Bulletin.* 1969?–1971? U.S. Monthly.

260. *Sound Canada.* 1969– . Toronto. Monthly. Continues as *Sound & Vision* (1984).

261. *Discography Series.* 1969– . Utica, New York. Irregular. J. F. Weber, editor and publisher.

262. *Gramophone Spoken Word and Miscellaneous Catalogue.* 1969– . Harrow, Middlesex, England: General Gramophone Publications, Ltd. Annual. Lists discs and tapes of language courses and material in foreign languages, children's material, documentary recordings, instructional recordings, sound effects material, and miscellaneous entertainment items. Indexes of authors, artists, and anthologies.

263. *The Gunn Report.* 1969?– . England. Irregular.

264. *The Maestro.* (Journal of the Arturo Toscanini Society.) 1969–1975? Dumas, Texas. Irregular.

264a. *Record Buyer.* (World Distributors [Manchester], Ltd.) 1969?– . Manchester, England. Monthly.

265. *Memory Lane*; Britain's no. 1 magazine for nostalgia. 1969– . Hadleigh, Benfleet, Essex, England. Quarterly. Incorporating: *The Al Bowlly Circle.*

266. *Record Exchanger.* 1969–1983. Anaheim, California: Art Turco. Irregular. Concerned with rock music and performers; includes an auction section.

267. *Danske grammofonplader.* 1969– . Copenhagen, Denmark: Nationalmusset, Nationaldiskoteket. Annual. Lists Danish recordings (mu-

sic of all countries), including cassettes after 1975. Arranged by genre, with artist index.

268. *Talking Machine Review International.* 1969–1988. Bournemouth, England. 6 per yr.; irregular. Title varies. Numbers 1–57: *Talking Machine Review.* Edited by Ernie Bayly. An important journal dealing with all aspects of recorded sound. with emphasis on label lists and histories of British firms. Among the scholars represented: Frank Andrews, Arthur Badrock, John Dales, (Michael Kinnear), and Brian Rust. Outstanding illustrative material was featured, with reproductions from old catalogs and periodicals. Publication ceased with number 75. A continuation began in 1989, as *International Talking Machine Review*, edited by John W. Booth (Gillingham, England).

269. *Audio Amateur.* (E. T. Dell.) 1970– . Swarthmore, Pennsylvania; later Peterborough, New Hampshire. 4–5 per year.

270. *Australian Hi-Fi.* 1970?–1975? Australia. Bimonthly.

271. *Bomp.* 1970?–1979? U.S. Bi-monthly. Formerly: *Who Put the Bomp.*

271a. *After Beat.* 1970–1972. U.S. Monthly. Big Band discographies and articles.

272. *Bruno Walter Society & Sound Archive. Information Bulletin.* 1970–? U.S. Irregular.

273. Entry deleted.

274. *Hi-Fi News and Record Review.* October 1970– . London. Monthly. A merger of *Hi-Fi News* (#163) and *Record Review* (#278).

275. *International Federation of Record Libraries. Cahiers.* 1970–? Paris: Phonethèque Nationale.

276. *Journal of Country Music.* 1970– . Nashville: Country Music Foundation. Quarterly. Continues numbering of *Country Music Foundation. Newsletter.*

277. *Listening Post; A selective list of new or recently released recordings published monthly by the Audiovisual Division of Bro-Dart.* 1970–1976. U.S. Irregular.

278. *Record Review.* January 1970–September 1970. London. Monthly. Formerly: *Audio and Record Review* (#200). United with: *Hi-Fi News* (#163) in October 1970 to form: *Hi-Fi News and Record Review* (#274).

279. *Recording Engineer/Producer.* 1970?– . Overland Park, Kansas. Monthly.

280. *Sound Verdict.* 1970?–1981? London. Annual. Index to audio articles and equipment reviews.

281. *Stereo Sound.* 197?– . Japan. Quarterly.

282. *The Street Singer, and Stars of the Thirties.* 1970?–1974. London. Irregular. Absorbed by: *Nostalgia Magazine* (#361).

283. *What Hi-Fi?* 1970– . Middlesex, England. Monthly.

284. *Arhoolie Occasional.* 1971–1973. U.S. Irregular. Superseded by: *The Lightning Express* (#385).

285. *Bim Bam Boom.* 1971–1973. U.S. Irregular.

286. *Commodore; Light music on 78s.* 1971–1974. Kent, England. Quarterly. Superseded by: *Vintage Light Music* (#369).

287. *Creative World.* 1971?–1978? U.S. Irregular.

288. *Deltio kritikes diskographias.* 1971–1976? Athens, Greece. Irregular.

289. *Disc.* 1971–1975. England. Weekly. Superseded by *Record Mirror & Disc* (#365).

290. *Modern Hi-Fi & Stereo Guide.* 1971–1974. Formerly: *Modern Hi-Fi* (#185). Superseded by: *Modern Hi-Fi and Music* (#358).

291. *Old Time Music.* 1971– . London. Quarterly.

292. *Phonogram.* 1971?–1981? Doveton: Phonograph Society of Australia. Bi-monthly.

293. *Phonograph Record Magazine.* 1971?–1978? Hollywood, California.

294. *Phonographic Bulletin.* 1971– . Utrecht, Netherlands [varies]: International Association of Sound Archives. Irregular. Emphasis is on archive organization and on preservation problems.

295. *Popular Hi-Fi.* 1971?–1976?. London. Monthly. Variant title: *Popular Hi-Fi & Sound.* Absorbed by *What Hi-Fi?* (#393).

296. *Soul Bag.* 1971?– . Paris: Comité de Liaison des Amateurs de Rhythm & Blues. Monthly.

297. *Sound and Picture Tape Recording.* 1971–1973. London. Monthly. Formerly: *Tape Recording Magazine* (#214). Superseded by: *Tape and Hi-Fi Test* (#332).

298. *Studies in Jazz Discography.* (Institute of Jazz Studies, Rutgers University.) 1971–1973? U.S.A. Irregular. Continued by: *Journal of Jazz Studies* (#324).

299. *Stereo Review's Tape Recording & Buying Guide.* 1971–1984. New York. Annual.

300. *Suono stereo hi-fi.* 1971?–1980. Italy. Monthly. Superseded by: *Suono* (#460).

301. *Vintage Record Mart.* 1971–1981? England. Bi-monthly.

302. *Antique Records.* 1972– . Ditton, England.

303. *B.A.S.Speaker.* (Boston Audio Society.) 1972– . Boston. Monthly.

304. *Discolandia continental.* 1972– . Mexico. Monthly.

304a. *Harrison Tape Guide.* 1972–1976. U.S. Bi-monthly. Continues: *Harrison Tape Catalog* (#133a).

305. *The Horn Speaker.* 1972– . U.S. 10 per year.

306. *Hot Buttered Soul.* 1972?–1976. England. Monthly. Absorbed by: *SMG* (#346).

307. *Jazz Digest.* 1972–1974. U.S. Monthly. Formerly: *HIP-the Jazz Record Digest* (#207).

308. *Micrography.* 1972?– . Amsterdam, Netherlands. Irregular. Edited by Erik M. Bakker. Jazz and blues discographies on LP.

309. *Music Retailer.* 1972–1979? U.S. Monthly.

310. *RPM: Record Trading Magazine.* 1972–? Poole, Dorset, England. Irregular.

311. *S/N Signals and Noise.* (Newsletter of the New York Audio Society.) 1972–? New York.

311a. *Audio-cassette Newsletter.* 1972– . Glendale, California: Cassette Information Services. Quarterly.

312. *Sir Thomas Beecham Society. Bulletin.* 1972– . U.S. Irregular.

313. *Stereo-Video Guide.* 1972– . Toronto, Canada. 6 per year.

314. *Stereoplay. Il piu diffuso mensile di hi-fi, dischi e musica.* 1972– . Rome. Monthly.

315. *Who Put the Bomp.* 1972–1976. U.S. Quarterly. Superseded by: *Bomp* (#271).

316. *Whole Lotta Rockin'.* 1972–1976? Rune Halland, Norway: Rock 'n' Roll Society of Scandinavia. 4 per year.

317. *Antique Phonograph Monthly.* 1973– . Brooklyn, New York. Quarterly. Edited by Allen Koenigsberg. An important collectors' journal, emphasizing material on the cylinder phonograph. Scholars represented in recent issues include Tim Brooks, Joe Klee, Bill Klinger, George Paul, and Michael Sherman.

318. *Bruno Walter Society & Sound Archive. Newsletter.* 1973–1974? U.S.. Irregular.

319. *Different Drummer.* 1973–1975. U.S. Monthly.

320. *Hi-Fi Answers.* 1973–1982? London. Monthly.

321. *Hi-Fi for Pleasure.* 1973–1980? London. Monthly.

322. *HiFi Stereophonie Testjahrbuch.* 1973–1983. Germany. Annual. Superseded by: *HiFi Stereophonie Test* (#484).

323. *High Fidelity's Test Reports.* 1973–1981. New York. Annual.

323a. *Forever;* The first rock 'n' roll collectors' magazine in Japan. 1973?-? Japan. Quarterly?

324. *Journal of Jazz Studies.* 1973–1979. New Brunswick, New Jersey: Institute of Jazz Studies. Irregular. Continues: *Studies in Jazz Discography* (#298). Superseded by: *Annual Review of Jazz Studies* (#472). Significant research on jazz artists and their recordings. Reprinted by Scarecrow Press, Metuchen, New Jersey.

325. *Media Review Digest.* 1973–1974. U.S.. Formerly: *Multi Media Reviews Index.*

325a. *Audiovisione.* 1973– . Rome.

326. *Not Fade Away.* 1973–1981. England. Vintage Rock 'n' Roll Appreciation Society. Bi-monthly.

326a. *Absolute Sound;* The High End Journal. 1973– . Sea Cliff, New York. Bi-monthly. Technical articles and reviews of new equipment in upper price ranges.

327. *Radio & Records.* 1973– . U.S. Weekly.

328. *Record Monthly.* 1973– . Japan. Monthly.

329. *Rumble;* Magazine for collectors of instrumental records. 1973–1977. England. Quarterly.

330. *Sono.* 1973–1978. Canada.

331. *Stereo.* 1973– . Germany. Monthly.

332. *Tape and Hi-Fi Test.* 1973–1975. Title variant: *Tape.* Absorbed: *Sound and Picture Tape Recording* (#297).

333. *Aware.* 1974?-? U.S. Irregular. Formerly: *Rock-It-with-Aware.*

333a. *Audio Scene Canada.* 1974–1980. Canada. Monthly. Superseded by: *Audio Video Canada* (#464).

334. *Bielefelder Katalog. Verzeichnis der Jazz Schallplatten.* 1974–1983. Bielefeld, Germany. Continues: *Katalog der Jazzschallplatten.* Continued by *Bielefelder Katalog: Jazz.*

334a. *Melting Pot.* (National Association of Discotheque Disc Jockeys.) 1974?-? U.S. Irregular.

335. *Blues Link.* 1974?–1975. England. Absorbed: *Blues World.* Superseded by: *Talking Blues* (#391).

336. *Deutsche Bibliographie. Schallplatten-Verzeichnis.* 1974–1977. Bielefeld, Germany. Quarterly with annual index. Continued by *Deutsche Bibliographie. Musiktonträger-Verzeichnis* (#416). Lists all classical and popular recordings issued in the Federal Republic of Germany, with full contents of each disc. Indexes by manufacturer number, title, topic, and artist. A section of the national bibliography.

337. *Goldmine;.* The record collector's marketplace. 1974– . Fraser, Michigan. Bi-weekly; varies. All facets of rock music history and discography, with record auction supplement.

338. *Hi-Fi World.* 1974–? U.S. Irregular. Formerly: *The Hi-Fi Newsletter.*

339. *IMDT Newsletter.* (International Institute for Music, Dance and Theatre in the Audio-Visual Media, Vienna.) 1974?-? Vienna. Irregular.

339a. *For the Record. News from the National Academy of Recording Arts and Sciences (NARAS).* 1974–1982? U.S. Irregular.

340. *Jazz Times.* 1974– . U.S. Monthly. Formerly: *Radio Free Jazz; Sabin's Radio Free Jazz! USA.*

341. *Klassiek journal.* 1974?-? Netherlands. Irregular.

342. *Music Master.* 1974– . England. Annual. Catalogue of recordings currently in print in the United Kingdom. Other publications include: *Music Master CD Index; Music Master Labels List; Music Master Prefix List; Music Master Supplement; Music Master Title Index; Music Master Tracks Catalogue; Music Master Yearbook.*

343. *Musician's Guide.* 1974–1978? U.S. Monthly.

344. *RTS Music Gazette.* 1974– . U.S. Monthly [varies].

345. *Recording Locator.* 1974–? San Jose, California. Quarterly. Deals with recorded religious music.

346. *SMG: a magazine for record collectors.* 1974?-? England. Monthly. Absorbed: *Hot Buttered Soul* (#306) in 1976.

347. *Tape Deck Quarterly.* (FM music program guide.) 1974–1977. U.S. Quarterly.

348. *Trouser Press.* 1974?–1984. U.S. Monthly. Formerly: *Transoceanic Trouser Press.*

349. *Audio Video Magazine.* 1975– . Paris. Monthly. Formerly: *Audio Magazine.*

350. *Australian Hi-Fi Annual.* 1975?-? Australia. Annual.

351. *Band-Amatoren.* 1975–1980? Denmark. Monthly.

351a. *Fritz Reiner Society. Newsletter.* 1975–1982. U.S. Irregular.

352. *Basic Repertoire.* (Stereo Review.) 1975?–1980? U.S. Annual.

353. *Blitz;* The rock and roll magazine for thinking people. 1975– . Los Angeles, California. Bimonthly.

354. *Diapason. Discopop.* 1975–1977. Paris.

354a. *Adagio.* 1975?-? Quebec, Canada. Bi-monthly.

355. *Hifi Stereo.* 1975–1981? Paris. 11 per year.

355a. *Canadian LP & Tape Catalog.* 1975– . Ottawa.

356. *International Musician and Recording World.* 1975?–. England. Incorporated: *One Two Testing Zig Zag.*

357. *Jazz Records.* 1975–1983? Tokyo. Annual supplement to: *Swing Journal* (#112).

358. *Modern Hi-Fi and Music.* 1975–1977. U.S. Formerly: *Modern Hi-Fi and Stereo Guide* (#290).

359. *Modern Recording.* 1975–1980. U.S. Bi-monthly; monthly. Superseded by: *Modern Recording & Music* (#451).

360. *Musik-Informationen.* 1975–1984. Germany. Monthly. Superseded by: *Musik-Info* (#496).

361. *Nostalgia Magazine.* 1975–? England. Incorporating: *The Street Singer, and Stars of the Thirties* (#282).

362. *Paul's Record Magazine.* 1975–? Hartford, Connecticut: Paul Bezanker. Irregular. Features extensive rock discographies.

363. *Recommended Recordings.* 1975– . London. Semiannual.

364. *The Record Collector's Journal.* 1975–1976. U.S. Monthly. Absorbed by: *Goldmine* (#337).

365. *Record Mirror and Disc.* 1975–76. London. Weekly. Formerly: *Disc* (#289). Superseded by: *Record Mirror* (#411).

366. *Soundtrack Collector's Newsletter.* 1975. Belgium. Quarterly. Superseded by: *Soundtrack! The Collector's Quarterly* (#457).

367. *Stereopus.* 1975–1977. U.S. Quarterly.

368. *Time Barrier Express.* 1975?–1980? U.S. Irregular.

369. *Vintage Light Music.* 1975– . England. Quarterly. Formerly: *Commodore;* For the enthusiast of light music on 78s (#286).

370. *Yesterday's Memories.* 1975–1977. U.S. Quarterly. Rhythm & blues; rock 'n' roll.

371. *L'anno discografico.* 1976–1979. Rome. Annual.

372. *Audio & Electronics Digest.* (Society of Audio Consultants.) 1976–1983? Beverly Hills, California. Monthly. Supersedes: *Audio Digest and Personal Communications.*

373. *Audiogram.* 1976–1982?. U.S. Irregular.

374. *The Big Beat of the 50's.* 1976?–1982? Australia. Irregular.

375. *Blitz.* 1976?–1979? U.S. Irregular. Formerly: *Ballroom Blitz.*

376. *Cadence;* American review of jazz and blues. 1976– . Redwood, New York. Edited by Bob Rusch. Irregular.

377. *Disco World.* 1976–? U.S. Monthly.

378. *Harmonie;* Catalogue général classique. 1976–1979. France. Annual.

379. *Hi-fi conseils.* 1976–1980. France. 10 per year. Superseded by: *Harmonie hi-fi conseil* (#444).

380. *Hifi Report.* 1976–1980. Germany. Annual.

381. *High Fidelity Musica;* Mensile di alta fedeltà, video, attualità e cultura. 1976– . Rome. Monthly.

382. *High Fidelity's Buying Guide to Speaker Systems.* 1976–1981? U.S. Annual.

383. *IAR: International Audio Review.* 1976–1980? U.S. Irregular.

383a. *Kastlemusick Exchange.* 1976. U.S. Monthly. Continued as: *Kastlemusick Monthly Bulletin* (#384).

384. *Kastlemusick Monthly Bulletin.* 1976–1983. Wilmington, Delaware. Monthly. Edited by Robert A. Hill. Formerly: *Kastlemusick Exchange* (#383a).

385. *The Lightning Express;* An occasional newspaper devoted to America's music. 1976–? U.S. Irregular. Incorporating: *The Arhoolie Occasional* (#284).

386. *Mean Mountain Music.* 1976–? U.S. Features country, rock 'n' roll artist and label discographies.

387. *Music Week Directory.* 1976– . London. Annual. Former titles: *Music and Video Week Directory; Music and Video Week Yearbook; Music Week Industry Year Book.*

388. *New on the Charts.* 1976–1986. U.S. Monthly.

389. *Rockin' 50's;* Dedicated to the true rock 'n' roll era. (Buddy Holly Memorial Society.) 1976– . U.S. Bi-monthly.

390. *The Sensible Sound.* 1976– . U.S. Quarterly.

391. *Talking Blues.* 1976–1977? England. Irregular. Formerly: *Blues Link* (#335).

392. *Waxpaper.* 1976–1979. U.S.A. Monthly [varies]. Warner Brothers records. Superseded by: *Warner World* (#437).

393. *What Hi-Fi?* 1976–1982? London. Monthly. Absorbed: *Popular Hi-Fi* (#295).

393a. *Canadian Independent Record Producer Association. Newsletter. (CIRPA).* 1976– . Toronto. Irregular.

394. *World Pop News.* 1976–1977? Netherlands. Irregular.

394a. *ARSC Newsletter.* (Association for Recorded Sound Collections.) 1977– . Silver Spring, Maryland [varies]. Quarterly.

395. *Anno discografico.* 1977– . Milan, Italy. Monthly.

396. *The Audio Critic.* 1977– . Bronxville, New York. Irregular.

397. *L'audio giornale;* Il mensile professionale del mercato hi-fi e discografico. 1977– . Rome. Monthly.

398. *Audio Update.* 1977–1981. U.S. Bi-monthly.

399. *BPI Year Book.* (British Phonographic Industry) 1977– . England. Annual.

400. *Disc-o-graph.* 1977?–1978? U.S. Irregular.

401. *Fanfare;* The magazine for serious record collectors. 1977– . Tenafly, New Jersey. Bi-monthly. An important source of reviews of new classical recordings.

402. *Gramophone News.* 1977–? U.S. Monthly.

403. *HiFi Stereophonie. Schallplattenkritik.* 1977–1983? Germany. Annual.

403a. *Recording Industry Index.* 1977– . Cherry Hill, New Jersey: National Association of Recording Merchandisers. Annual.

404. *Inside Stanyan.* (Stanyan Record Co.) 1977–? U.S. Irregular.

405. *Keynote.* 1977–1990. U.S. Monthly. Included the WNCN-FM Program Guide.

406. *The Mix;* The recording industry magazine. 1977– . Emeryville, California. Monthly. Includes descriptions of recording studios, in regional groupings.

407. *Musica;* Bimestrale di informazione musicale e discografica. 1977– . Milan, Italy. Bi-monthly.

408. *Musical Heritage Review Magazine.* 1977– . U.S. 18 per year.

409. *NARAS Institute Journal.* (National Academy of Recording Arts and Sciences.) 1977–? Atlanta. Semi-annual.

410. *Progressive Platter.* 1977?– . Boston. Irregular.

411. *Record Mirror.* 1977–1985. London. Weekly. Formerly: *Record Mirror and Disc* (#365). Superseded by: *rm* (#509).

412. *Record Review.* 1977–1984. U.S. Bi-monthly.

413. *Rockingchair;* Review newsletter for librarians who buy records. 1977–1982. U.S. Monthly.

414. *Stereoguida;* Il trimestrale hi-fi per non sbagliare l'acquisto. 1977– . Rome. Quarterly.

415. *Audio.* 1978?– . Germany. Monthly.

416. *Deutsche Bibliographie. Musiktonträger-Verzeichnis.* 1978– . Germany. Monthly. Formerly: *Deutsche Bibliographie. Schallplatten-Verzeichnis* (#336).

417. *High Fidelity's Buying Guide to Tape Systems.* 1978– . New York. Annual. Formerly: *Buyer's Guide to the World of Tape.*

418. *International Musician and Recording World.* 1978–1981. U.S. Irregular.

419. *Outlet.* 1978– . England. Irregular.

419a. *Mr. Audio's Bimonthly.* 1978?–? U.S. Irregular.

420. *Record Finder.* 1978– . U.S. Irregular.

421. *Trouser Press Collectors' Magazine.* 1978?–1980? U.S. Annual.

422. *Australian Sound & Broadcast.* 1979– . Sydney. Bi-monthly.

423. *Discoveries.* 1979– . U.S. Irregular. Editor: Michael Gray.

423a. *Full Blast.* 1979– . U.S. Irregular. Includes rock music record reviews, discographies, and articles.

424. *I.A.S.A. (Australia) Newsletter.* 1979–1986. Australia. Irregular. Variant title: *I.A.S.A. Australian Branch Newsletter.* Superseded by: *Australasian Sound Archive* (#440).

425. *Music;* Mensile di musica ed alta fedeltà. 1979– . Rome. Monthly.

426. *Music Hall.* 1979–1980. England. Bi-monthly. Formerly: *Music Hall Records.*

427. *Music World.* 1979–1981? U.S. Formerly: *Music World and Record Digest Weekly News* (#429).

428. *Music World & Record Digest.* Mar. 1979–? U.S. Weekly. Superseded by: *Music World and Record Digest Weekly News* (#429).

429. *Music World and Record Digest Weekly News.* 1979–? U.S. Weekly. Formerly: *Music World & Record Digest* (#428). Superseded by: *Music World* (#427).

430. *Overtures;* A magazine devoted to the musical on stage and record. 1979?–1981. England. Bi-monthly.

430a. *Tape Deck.* 1979– . New York. Annual.

431. *Pro Sound News.* 1979?– . Carle Place, New York. Monthly.

432. *Rock & Roll: Musik-Magazine.* 1979?– . Germany. Bi-monthly. Formerly: *Rock.*

432a. *Stereo Test Reports.* 1979– . New York. Irregular.

433. *Sound International.* 1979?–? England. Monthly.

434. *Sounds Vintage.* 1979–1983. England. Bi-Monthly.

435. *Superstereo Audio Magazine.* 1979– . Milan, Italy. Monthly.

436. *Tarakan Music Letter.* 1979–1985. U.S. Irregular.

437. *Warner World.* 1979–1981? U.S. Monthly. Formerly: *Waxpaper* (#392).

438. *Audio South Africa.* 198?– . Johannesburg, South Africa. Bi-monthly.

439. *Audio universal.* 198?–. Buenos Aires, Argentina. Monthly.

440. *Australasian Sound Archive.* (International Association of Sound Archives) 1980– . Australia. Quarterly. Formerly: *I A S A Australian Branch Newsletter* (#424).

441. *Disc'ribe; A journal of discographical information.* 1980– . Los Angeles, California. Irregular.

442. *Early Music Record Services. Monthly Review.* 1980– . Essex, England. Monthly.

443. *Guia da audio.* 198?– . Buenos Aires, Argentina. Annual.

444. *Harmonie hi-fi conseil.* 1980–1981. France. Monthly. Supersedes: *Hi-fi conseils* (#379). Superseded by: *Harmonie-opera hi-fi conseil* (#469).

445. *Hi-Fi & Elektronik.* 1980– . Copenhagen, Denmark. Monthly.

446. *Hifi musique.* 1980–? Belgium. Irregular. Formerly: *Revue des disques et de la haute fidelité* (#139).

447. *High Fidelity's Buying Guide to Stereo Components.* 1980–? New York. Annual.

448. *HiVi.* 198?– . Japan. Monthly. Formerly: *Sound Boy.*

449. *IAR Hotline.* (International Audio Review.) 1980– . Berkeley, California. Irregular.

450. *Library of Congress. National Library Service for the Blind and Physically Handicapped. Instructional Disc Recordings Catalog.* 1980?– . Washington. Annual.

451. *Modern Recording & Music.* 1980–1986. U.S. Monthly. Supersedes: *Modern Recording* (#359).

452. *Ovation.* 1980–1990. New York. Monthly. Contains WQXR (New York) Program Guide.

453. *Le petit baton.* 1980– . Redondo Beach, California. The Sir Thomas Beecham Society. Irregular.

454. *Pro Sound.* 198?– . Japan. Bi-monthly. Formerly: *Tape Sound.*

455. *Recordings of Experimental Music.* 1980?–? U.S.. 6 per year.

456. *Rhythm & News.* 1980–1982. U.S. Superseded by: *Whiskey, Women and...* (#490).

457. *Soundtrack! The Collector's Quarterly.* 1980– . Belgium. Quarterly. Formerly: *Soundtrack Collector's Newsletter* (#366).

458. *Speaker Builder.* 1980?– . Peterborough, New Hampshire. Quarterly.

459. *Stereo Review Compact Disc Buyers Guide.* 198?– . U.S. Semi-Annual.

460. *Suono.* 1980–1985. Italy. Monthly. Formerly: *Suono stereo hi-fi* (#300).

461. *Vocal Collector's Monthly.* 1980–? New York. Irregular.

462. *L'audio giornale review; Rivista di elettroacustica ed alta fedeltà.* 1981– . Rome. Monthly.

463. *Audio Review.* 1981– . Rome. Monthly. Variant title: *Audioreview.*

464. *Audio Video Canada.* 1981–? Canada. Monthly. Formerly: *Audio Scene Canada* (#333a).

465. *Australian Music Directory.* 1981?–? Australia. Annual.

466. *Disc Collector.* 1981– . U.S. Monthly; varies. Formerly: *Disc Collector Newsletter* (#224).

467. *Discophiliac; A newsletter for serious collectors of classical music.* 1981–1984? U.S. Irregular.

468. *Guide to Recording in the UK.* (Association of Professional Recording Studios) 1981– . Rickmansworth, England. Annual. Formerly: *Guide to A P R S Member Studios.*

469. *Harmonie-opéra hi-fi conseil.* 1981–1982. France. Monthly. Formerly: *Harmonie hi-fi conseil* (#444). Superseded by: *Harmonie panorama musique* (#483).

470. *High Performance Review.* 1981– . Stamford, Connecticut. Quarterly.

471. *Show Music.* 1981– . U.S. Irregular.

472. *Annual Review of Jazz Studies*. 1982– . New Brunswick, New Jersey: Institute of Jazz Studies. Published by Scarecrow Press, Metuchen, New Jersey. Irregular. Volumes issued: 1982, 1983, 1985, 1988, 1991. Continues: *Journal of Jazz Studies* (#324). A major outlet for scholarly research in jazz.

473. *The Coop*. 1982?– . U.S. Irregular. Each issue includes a recording.

474. *The International Music Review*. 1982–1983. U.S. Irregular.

475. *International Records News*. 1982–? Italy. Monthly.

476. *Joslin's Jazz Journal*; Dedicated to the glory of record collecting. 1982– . U.S. Quarterly.

477. *Maximum Rock 'n' Roll*. 1982– . Berkeley, California. 6 per year.

478. *Record Collector's Monthly*. 1982– . U.S. Monthly.

479. *Annual Chart Summaries*. 1983– . Cambridge, England. Annual.

480. *CD Review Digest Annual*. 1983– . U.S. Annual.

481. *E A R for Children*. (Evaluation of audio recordings.) 1983– . Roslyn Heights, New York: Sound Advice Enterprises. Quarterly.

481a. *Record & Tape Buyers Guide*. 1983– . Toronto. Annual.

482. *Grammy*. 1983– . U.S. Bi-monthly.

482a. *Sound & Video Contractor*. 1983– . Overland Park, Kansas. Monthly.

483. *Harmonie panorama musique*. 1983–1984. France. Monthly. Supersedes: *Harmonie-opéra-Hi-fi conseil* (#469). Superseded by: *Diapason-harmonie* (#501).

484. *HiFi Stereophonie Test*. 1983–1984? Germany. Annual. Formerly: *HiFi Stereophonie Testjahrbuch* (#322).

485. *IFPI Newsletter*. (International Federation of Phonogram and Videogram Producers.) 1983– . England. 6 per year.

486. *IJS Jazz Register and Indexes*. 1983– . New Brunswick, New Jersey: Institute of Jazz Studies, Rutgers University.

487. *Pulse*. (Tower Records) 1983– . West Sacramento, California: MTS. Monthly..

488. *Rockin' Fifties*. 1983?– . Germany. 5 per year.

489. *Stimmen die um die Welt gingen.*. 1983– . Germany. 4 per year. Discographies and articles on early opera & operetta singers.

490. *Whiskey, Women, and ...*; The blues & rhythm jubilee. 1983–1984? U.S. Irregular. Continues: *Rhythm & News* (#456).

491. *Digital Audio*. 1984–1985. U.S. Monthly. Superseded by: *Digital Audio & Compact Disc Review* (#502). Variant title: *Digital Audio. The Compact Disc Review*.

492. *Hi-Fi Sound Magazine*. 1984?– . Quebec, Canada. Bi-monthly.

493. *In the Groove*. 1984– . U.S. Michigan Antique Phonograph Society. Monthly.

493a. *Recording World*. 1984– . New York. Quarterly.

494. *Jazziz*. 1984– . U.S. Bi-monthly.

494a. *Journal of the Phonograph Society of New South Wales*. 1984– . Georges Hall, Australia. Quarterly. Title from 1990: *Sound Record*.

495. *The Laser Disc Newsletter*. 1984– . U.S. Monthly.

496. *Musik-Info*. 1984–1986. Germany. Monthly. Superseded by: *Siegert's Fachmagazine für die Unterhaltungs-Gastronomie*.

497. *Opus*. 1984–1988. U.S. Bi-monthly. Incorporated into: *Musical America*.

498. *Retro-Rock Review*. 1984–1985. U.S. Quarterly. Superseded by: *Retro-Rock* (#526).

499. *Sound Scrutiny Guides*. 1984– . England.

499a. *Audio*. 1984– . Durango, Colorado: Orion Research Corp. Annual. Former title: *Audio Reference Guide*.

500. *Stereoplay*. 1984– . Germany. Monthly. Merged with: *HiFi Stereophonie* (#208).

500a. *Illustrated Audio Buyers Guide*. 1984– . Shawnee Mission, Kansas. Annual.

500b. *Illustrated Audio Equipment Reference Catalog*. 1984– . Shawnee Mission, Kansas. Annual.

501. *Diapason-harmonie*. 1985– . Paris. Monthly. Formed by the merger of: *Diapason* (#160) and *Harmonie panorama musique* (#483).

502. *Digital Audio & Compact Disc Review*. 1985–1988. Farmingdale, New York. Monthly. Continued by: *Digital Audio* (#491). Superseded by: *Digital Audio's CD Review* (#552).

503. *Gramophone Compact Disc Digital Audio Guide and Catalogue*. 1985– . Harrow, Middlesex, England: General Gramophone Publications, Ltd. Quarterly. Title varies.

504. *Juke Blues*. 1985?– . London. Quarterly.

505. *The Music Video Leader*. (RCA/Columbia Pictures Home Video) 1985– . U.S. Irregular.

506. *Names & Numbers*. 1985– . Netherlands. Irregular.

507. *The New Schwann Artist Issue*. 1985– . U.S.A. Irregular. Formerly: *Schwann Artist Issue* (#140).

508. *Option*. 1985– . U.S. Bi-monthly. Covers non-mainstream music.

509. *rm*. 1985–1990. England. Weekly. Formerly; *Record Mirror* (#411). In 1990, title changed back again to: *Record Mirror*.

510. *Sonics*. 1985– . Australia. Bi-monthly.

511. *Sound Choice*. 1985–. U.S. Quarterly. Reviews electronic, ethnic, experimental, industrial, jazz, rock, new age, etc. music.

512. *Entertainment Merchandising*. 1986–1988. Duluth, Minnesota. Monthly.

513. Entry deleted.

514. *Compact Disc*. 1986– . New York. Quarterly.

515. *Country Sounds*. 1986–1987. U.S. Monthly.

516. *The Green Compact Disc Catalog*. 1986–1987. Peterborough, New Hampshire. Bi-monthly. Superseded by: *The Green CD Guide* (#543).

517. *The Historic Record*. 1986– . England. Quarterly.

518. *Jazz Archivist*. 1986– . New Orleans, Louisiana: Hogan Jazz Archive, Howard-Tilton Memorial Library, Tulane University. Semi-annual.

519. *Jocks*; The UK's top selling DJ magazine. 1986– . London, Monthly.

520. *Ken's Kompendium of Reviews of Classical Compact Discs*. 1986–1987. U.S. Quarterly. Superseded by: *Ken's Kompendium of Award-Winning Classical CD's* (#536).

521. *M & D*. 1986– . Milan, Italy. Monthly. Formerly: *Musica e dischi* (#100).

522. *Music & Media*. 1986– . Netherlands. 50 per year. Formerly: *Eurotipsheet*. Features European top hit record charts.

523. *Needle Time*. 1986?– . England. Bi-monthly.

524. *Playback and Fast Forward*. 1986– . India. Monthly.

525. *Pro Sound News (Europe)*. 1986– . England. Monthly.

526. *Retro-Rock*. 1986– . U.S. Quarterly. Formerly: *Retro-Rock Review* (#498).

527. *BBC Sound Archive. Index*. 1987– . London.

528. *CD classica*; Mensile di musica classica su compact disc. 1987–. Florence, Italy. Monthly.

529. *CD Review Digest*. 1987–1989. U.S. Quarterly. Superseded by: *CD Review Digest—Classical* (#549) and *CD Review Digest—Jazz, Popular, etc.* (#550).

530. *Compact*; La revue du disque laser. 1987– . Paris. Monthly.

531. *Cymbiosis*. 1987– . U.S. Bi-monthly. Each issue includes a cassette.

532. *High Fidelity*. 1987–1989. U.S. Monthly. Absorbed by *Stereo Review* (#178) in 1989.

533. *Home Recording*. 1987–1989. U.S. 6 per year. Superseded by: *EQ* (#558).

534. *IPAM Newsletter*. (International Piano Archives at Maryland.) 1987– . College Park, Maryland. Irregular.

535. *Jazzthetik*. 1987– . Germany. Monthly.

535a. *What CD?* 1987?–. Peterborough, New Hampshire. Bi-monthly.

536. *Ken's Kompendium of Award-Winning Classical CD's*. 1987– . U.S.A. Semi-Annual. Formerly: *Ken's Kompendium of Reviews of Classical Compact Discs* (#520).

537. *Music-Shop*. 1987– . Germany. 10 per year.

538. *Notizie dall'archivio sonoro della musica contemporanea*. 1987– . Rome. Bi-monthly.

539. *Osborne Report of New Releases*. 1987–1989. U.S. Monthly.

539a. *DJ: Disc Jockey*. 1987?– . London. Monthly.

540. *Announced*; This month in classical recordings. 1988– . U.S. Monthly.

540a. *Audio Video*. 1988?– . South Africa. 11 per year.

541. *Digital Audio Club*; La prima rivista di hi-fi e musica digitale. 1988– . Rome. Monthly.

542. *Discoveries*. 1988– . U.S. Bi-monthly. Includes country, jazz, rock 'n' roll, etc., discographies, record reviews, record sales, concert reviews, books, magazines, articles, interviews.

543. *Green CD Guide*. Jan./Feb.1988–June 1988. U.S. Bi-monthly. Continues: *Green Compact Disc Catalog* (#516). Absorbed by: *Digital Audio Yearbook*.

544. *Home & Studio Recording*. 1988– . Canoga Park, California. Monthly.

545. *Hungaroton*. 1988– . Paris. Irregular. Specializing in Hungarian artists and recordings.

545a. *D & J Mix*; Journal des disc-jockeys. 1988? France. Monthly.

546. *Audio Carpaetorium*. 1989– . U.S. Irregular.

547. *Australian Record & Music Review*. 1989– . Australia. Quarterly.

548. *CD Review*. 1989–. U.S.A. Monthly. Formerly: *Digital Audio's CD Review* (#552).

549. *CD Review Digest—Classical.* 1989–. U.S. Quarterly. Formerly: *CD Review Digest* (#529).

550. *CD Review Digest—Jazz, Popular etc.* 1989–. U.S.A. Quarterly. Formerly: *CD Review Digest* (#529).

551. *Classical.* 1989–. New York. Monthly. With WNCN & WQXR program guides as well as updates to the *Stevenson Classical Compact Disc Guide.*

552. *Digital Audio's CD Review.* v. 5, no. 5, Jan. 1989–v. 5, no. 7, Mar. 1989. Farmingdale, New York. Monthly. Continues: *Digital Audio & Compact Disc Review* (#502). Superseded by: *CD Review* (#548).

553. *Ecouter voir.* (Association pour la Cooperation de l'Interprofession Musicale.) 1989–. France. Quarterly.

554. *New Orleans Music.* 1989–. England. Bimonthly. Formerly: *Footnote.*

555. *The Picture-Disk Collector.* 1989–. Netherlands. Quarterly.

556. *Sound & Vision;* The international record collector for all collectors of records and memorabilia. 1989–. Rome. Monthly.

557. *The Beat.* 1990–. U.S. Bi-monthly. Includes reviews of African, Brazilian, Caribbean, and reggae recordings.

558. *EQ: the creative recording* magazine. 1990–. U.S. Bi-monthly. Formerly: *Home Recording* (#533).

558a. *Audiophile;* With Hi-Fi Answers. 1990–. England. Monthly.

559. *In Music.* 1990–1991. Boston. Monthly. Latest new releases. One of the three publications that continued *Schwann CD* (#121). *See also* #561, #563.

561. *Opus.* 1990–. Boston. Quarterly. Classical music guide. One of the three publications that continued *Schwann CD* (#121). *See also* #559, #563.

561a. *Substance.* 1990–. Edinburgh, Scotland. Irregular. Rock music articles and reviews.

562. *Record Mirror.* 1990–. England. Weekly. Formerly: *rm* (#509).

563. *Spectrum.* 1990–. Boston. Quarterly. Popular music guide. One of the three publications that continued *Schwann CD* (#121). *See also* #559, #561.

564. *Turok's Choice.* 1990–. New York. 11 per year.

565. *A.V. Collector;* An occasional periodical. 1991–. England. Irregular.

Title Index
(compiled by Joanne Giese)

The titles are alphabetized word by word, with initial articles omitted. Hyphenated words are filed as though they were single words. The symbol "&" files ahead of the word "and."

This article is a revised, updated, and expanded version of "Sound Recording Periodicals: 1890–1929" (*Performing Arts Resources*, 1989). Information has been gathered from the New York Public Library catalogs, *Union List of Serials*, *New Serial Titles*, *Ulrich's Periodicals Directory*, *Serials Directory* (Ebsco), and various specialized sources. I would like to thank the following individuals and institutions for their kind assistance in the compilation of this listing: Gary-Gabriel Gisondi, Rodgers & Hammerstein Archives of Recorded Sound, New York Public Library (whose publication, "Sound Recordings Periodicals, a Preliminary Union Catalog of Pre-LP-related Holdings in Member Libraries of the Associated Audio Archives" (*ARSC Journal* 10 [1978]) was a great source of information; Donald McCormick, Rodgers & Hammerstein Archives of Recorded Sound, New York Public Library; Richard Warren and his staff, Yale University, Historical Sound Recordings Collection; General Research Division and the Annex, New York Public Library; Detroit Public Library; National Library of Canada, Music Division; National Archives of Canada, Moving Image and Sound Archives; Vancouver Public Library; National Film & Sound Archive, Canberra, Australia; National Library of Australia; The British Library, National Sound Archive; The British Library, Bibliographical Information Service; Staatliches Institut für Musikforschung Preussischer Kulturbesitz, Berlin; Staatsbibliothek Preussischer Kulturbesitz, Berlin; Phonogrammarchiv der Oesterrichischen Akademie der Wissenschaften, Vienna; Bibliothèque Nationale, Département de la Phonothèque Nationale et de l'Audiovisuel, Paris; Casalini Libri, Florence; M. E. Saltykov-Shchedrin State Public Library, Leningrad; Lenin State Public Library, Moscow.

As the list of titles is no more than a preliminary checklist, additions and corrections from readers are invited.

Sara Velez

SOUND RECORDINGS AND THE LIBRARY. This article is in five parts: 1. Background; 2. Collection development; 3. Cataloging; 4. Classification; and 5. Equipment.

1. *Background.* Guido Biagi, Librarian of the Royal Library at Florence, predicted in a talk at the 1904 conference of the American Library Association that

there will be a few readers but an infinite number of hearers, who will listen from their own homes to the spoken paper, to the spoken book. University students will listen to their lectures while they lie in bed, and, as now with us, will not know their professors even by sight. But even if the graphophone does not produce so profound a transformation as to cause the alphabet to become extinct and effect an injury to culture itself . . . still, these discs, now so much derided, will form a very large part of the future library (Phonographs 1909).

In the years since his prediction, print has not been replaced by sound recordings, but recordings have become an important part of most libraries.

The first account of sound recordings in an American library was of the piano roll collection in the Evanston (Illinois) Public Library in 1907. Apparently the earliest library to include sound recordings other than piano rolls was the Academy of Sciences at Vienna, which initiated in 1909 its famous phonographic archives.

American libraries soon took interest in recordings, too. The earliest accounts of phonograph records being used in American libraries are sketchy, but it seems that they entered the library early in the 20th century. The Music Teachers National Association reported in 1913 that collections of piano rolls could be found in seven New York libraries, and collections of gramophone records could be found in seven New York and four California libraries. The Forbes Library of Northampton, Massachusetts, reported in 1912 that it had bought one of the popular graphophone cylinder machines. One of the first libraries to collect and circulate phonograph records was the St. Paul Library whose collection—for educational purposes only—began in 1914. Obviously the collection was well used, for it reported holdings in 1919 of nearly 600 records which accounted for a circulation of 3,505 for the year. These early accounts point to a growing interest in developing collections of sound recordings. The demands upon public libraries overcame the objections that recordings were fragile and easily damaged, that their sound quality was poor and deteriorated with use, and that they were very expensive for only three minutes of sound.

The earliest documented collection of sound recordings in an academic library was started in 1915 at the University of Wisconsin, in Madison. The earliest detailed information about the beginnings of a record collection in an academic environment refers to a gift from the Antioch College Class of 1928 that provided a fund, a portion of which was "allotted for the purchase of phonograph albums, which would circulate from the college library on the same basis as books." (Lyle 1934). There were collections of recordings in colleges in that period, but that they were generally restricted to students in music appreciation courses. Therefore, the institution of a circulating collection in a college library was innovative, and according to the report, successful. By 1930 the Antioch collection consisted of about 125 albums with a circulation rate of about 400 albums per month.

A review of the status of record collections in U.S. university libraries in the mid-1950s stated that "it is fruitless to look for uniformity in a field so tied up with technological changes and the rapidly fluctuating economy of record production. The administration of record collection will remain one of the frontier areas in librarianship for many years to come" (Duckles 1955). A survey sent to 500 diverse American libraries in 1960 found that most sound recording collections were less than 15 years old and averaged in size between 100 and 1,000 recordings (Davis 1960).

In 1965, a meeting at the Henry Ford Museum in Dearborn, Michigan, by librarians of sound recording collections and private collectors led to the formation of the **Association for Recorded Sound Collections (ARSC)** in the following year. Other organizations that facilitate dialog among conservators of sound recording collections are the Record Libraries Commission of the International Association of Music Libraries (IAML) founded in 1951 and the **International Association of Sound Archives (IASA)** founded in 1969. Reports of the work of the Record Libraries Commission, often as summaries of the annual meetings, appear in issues of *Fontes Artis Musicae*. Since its founding, IASA has met annually with IAML, and there is an overlap of membership with the Record Libraries Commission.

In 1974 representatives of Stanford University, Yale University, the New York Public Library, and the Library of Congress met in New York to discuss means of facilitating the cataloging of their sound recording collections. This meeting led to the formation of the Associated Audio Archives (AAA) which was expanded to include the sound archives of Syracuse University and for a time the University of Toronto. The AAA has produced a set of cataloging rules, a union list of periodicals, and a union list of record manufacturers' catalogs. It developed and tested an innovative technique for cataloging sound recordings using micro-photography with computer indexing, and produced the **Rigler and Deutsch Index**, which gives access to a majority of the extant 78 rpm recordings.

2. *Collection development.* In colleges and universities most users of a recording collection are from the music department or school; other departments and programs, however, also use sound recordings in their curriculum. The aims and needs of these users determine in large part the recordings which should be selected. While faculty and student requests for recordings are the most significant forces in the selection of the recordings for an academic library collection, the selection librarian has to serve as the central focus in the process, mediating between many pressures in order to serve all needs within the constraints of the institutional budget. Consequently, the librarian must have a thorough understanding of institutional objectives and faculty preferences in order to maintain a well-balanced collection responsive to its users.

In public libraries there is likely to be demand for recordings of popular music, leading to concerns about quality, costs, and in some cases community objections (*see* SEXUALLY ORIENTED LYRICS).

Selection of materials requires access to discographical listings and review media (*see* DISCOGRAPHY; SOUND RECORDING PERIODICALS).

3. *Cataloging.* Before 1942 the cataloging of record collections was based on local rules; there existed no "official" cataloging code for recordings.

The first cataloging rules for recordings appeared in 1942 as a result of the work of a Music Library Association committee. Those rules were revised by a joint committee of the Music Library Association and the American Library Association, and reissued in 1958 (Music 1958). In 1967 the first full integration of the rules for cataloging recordings and books appeared, as the *Anglo/American Cataloguing Rules* (AACR).

Many variant catalog codes for recordings resulted during the long, slow process of establishing a national standard. In the chaos of multiple cataloging codes, there is a dichotomy between those intended for predominately popular collections and those intended for "classical" collections. The latter codes are generally based upon rules used for books, and their products may be easily integrated into catalogs with book materials. Those codes based upon the perspective of stand-alone catalogs of popular music generally specify an abbreviated catalog record and a unit entry based upon the recording's title.

The printing of Library of Congress cataloging cards for recordings, begun in 1953, has had an important impact upon the development of cataloging. For the first time, cataloging copy for recordings was readily available, and its availability tended to establish a standard for cataloging. Though the Library of Congress has repeatedly stated that it catalogs only for itself, it has over the years come to recognize that its policies have a profound impact upon other libraries.

As a result of discussions between the Library of Congress and the Cataloging Committee of the Music Library Association, it was agreed that the cataloging of seven (later nine) selected libraries would be included in the *National Union Catalog* beginning in 1973. One of the criteria for selection of a library to participate in this project was the agreement to provide analytics for every work on a recording. As a result of further discussions, the Library of Congress has agreed to provide analytics to recordings for up to 25 works. The ideal of shared cataloging was becoming a reality.

There have been four important developments in the cataloging of recordings since 1967: the development of the MARC (machine readable) format for music and sound recordings, the development of international standard bibliographic descriptions for non-book materials, ISBD(NBM), the revision of AACR (Anglo 1978), and the development of ARSC rules for cataloging archival collections (Rules 1978).

The MARC music format was first implemented by OCLC, the largest bibliographic utility, in 1977. Music librarians formed the Music OCLC Users' Group (MOUG) with the intention of sharing cataloging and related policies so that maximum use could be made of the machine-readable cataloging data. However, many of the promises of shared cataloging remained unfulfilled. MOUG is only an advisory forum, and many libraries do not wish to change their local practices to conform with national standards. The fact that OCLC contains many types of libraries also contributes to an inconsistency of cataloging policy; small public libraries often have different requirements for the cataloging of sound recordings than do academic libraries. Much of the cataloging in the OCLC data base requires local correction and augmentation.

ISBD(NBM) was issued by the International Federation of Library Associations (IFLA) in 1977 as part of its program for Universal Bibliographic Control (UBC). It was intended to provide a standard for the preparation of national bibliographies of non-book materials, excluding maps, and was based upon the principles of ISBD(General). Although ISBD standards are internationally accepted and consequently can provide the basis for international shared cataloging, the ISBD(NBM) guidelines are inadequate because they were developed solely in the forum of IFLA with little consultation with record librarians and catalogers. The general acceptance of ISBD principles by the Anglo/American cataloging community during AACR2 revision extended the importance of ISBD(NBM) beyond its capabilities.

The provisions for the bibliographic description of sound recordings in the second edition of *Anglo/American Cataloguing Rules* (AACR2) were based in part upon ISBD(NBM) because of its appearance as an international standard. The process of developing AACR2 was inadequate in the area of sound recordings. Such rules were discussed at the very end of the revision process, almost at the publication deadline. Consequently, many doubtful decisions were made. Because this component of AACR2 was inadequately formulated, sound recording librarians have not fully supported it, and it has not had the effect that was intended. Each country that has implemented the code has variously interpreted the rules to accommodate its needs.

The ARSC cataloging rules are compatible with AACR2 for historical sound recordings cataloging, and have been adopted by the Library of Congress.

Sound recordings are expensive to catalog because of the need to provide access to performers as well as the composers and titles of the recorded works. Instead of three or four access points commonly found for most printed materials, sound recordings typically require 12 or more. Only through the use of a set of standardized cataloging rules and the ready availability of shared cataloging, preferably in machine readable form, can sound recordings be economically cataloged. AACR2 is being revised; with reliance upon sound recording catalogers and a more reasoned consideration of the basic principles of cataloging and the needs of the catalog's users, a strong and useful code should result.

4. Classification. Little has changed since the first survey by the Music Library Association published in 1937 showed that there were four principal methods of organizing recordings in collections: by composer, by form, by record company name and number, and by accession number. At that time most libraries shelved their recordings by form or by record company number; the Music Library Association report, however, urged that records be shelved by accession number. An alternative point of view is that " classification should place the materials on the shelf in an order which reflects some informational pattern. It will thus not only locate an item but, to some extent, describe it. In this manner the call number becomes more than an abstract symbol, and the usefulness of an open-shelf policy becomes evident" (DeLerma 1969). The choice of classification method has definite implications for service, especially for large and actively growing collections. In open-shelf collections, composer or form classifications assist users in finding what they want. But such classifications have one major deficiency: the inability to adequately classify LP recordings that contain the works of several composers, or multiple forms.

Many public libraries and some academic libraries use variations of the Dewey Decimal Classification to shelve their recordings, and a number of academic libraries use variations of the Library of Congress classification. The use of the Library of Congress classification was encouraged when classification numbers began appearing on printed Library of Congress cards in January 1972. While the Library of Congress does not shelve its own recordings by these numbers, it provides them because of demand from purchasers of its cards.

Manufacturer or accession number schemes are not true classifications, but they are probably the most common schemes used in shelving recordings in academic libraries. Accession shelf arrangement eliminates the need to shift recordings as a collection grows, and it uses shelving efficiently. Though often used for small, open collections, it does not lend itself to easy browsing. Its principal advantage to the browser is in finding the newest recordings in the collection. The card catalog or computer catalog is the principal means of access to a closed collection arranged by accession number, and because the user will not have physical access to the recordings and the information contained upon them, the catalog must be as complete and current as possible.

Manufacturer's numbers are most commonly used as a shelving classification by very large collections of sound recordings and sound archives. It is an effective interim means of providing access to collections which are largely uncataloged. Most discographies and catalogs of sound recordings specify manufacturer's label name and issue number; requests for a specific record can be serviced by simply looking on the shelves.

Little change is expected to occur in the wide use of variant classification schemes for academic collections of sound recordings. Each collection has its own rationale for existence and service, and the classification scheme chosen reflects the orientation of the library.

5. *Equipment.* Playback equipment should reproduce the sound as accurately as possible. Depending upon the philosophy of the collection and the budgetary constraints under which it operates, an academic library may have equipment available for individual patron use or for use only by staff.

Equipment necessary to operate a sound recording collection consists of three parts: amplification equipment (for example, preamplifiers, amplifiers, or consoles to direct the sound to various listening locations), playback equipment (for example, disc, cassette, or reel-to-reel tape machines), and sound generation equipment (for example, headphones or speakers). The library's choice of the kind of equipment they acquire is dictated by the available budget and the operating philosophy of the collection. Size and activity of the library's clientele determine the size and quality of a playback facility; for example, a circulating collection does not require as extensive a playback setup as a noncirculating collection.

There are few equipment standards available for sound recording libraries or archives other than very general or out-of-date specifications. Changes in equipment preclude the suggestion of any but the most general guidelines for equipment characteristics. Depending upon an institution's budgetary resources, the choice of equipment for a playback facility will depend upon the expertise of the librarian or an outside consultant, and the facility will contain anything from a few pieces of amateur stereo equipment to an elaborate multi-station playback center that permits listening to compact discs, LPs, 78s, and tape formats.

Sound reproduction equipment typically consists of headphones or loudspeakers. Speakers must be used in sound-proof listening rooms, while most headphones can be used anywhere in the library because they reproduce the sound directly into the listener's ears. This characteristic of headphones can, however, lead to ear damage if sound levels are too loud. Any installation which uses headphones should take care to insure that their headphones will not play at too high a level.

Aids to the selection of sound recording equipment are various, and range widely in quality. Some of the best sources are regular reviews in *Audio, Consumer Reports,* and *Stereo Review.* Because of the continual improvement in the quality of audio equipment, installation choices in the library need to be carefully researched. [Buth 1975; Davis 1960; DeLerma 1969; Duckles 1955; Gaeddert 1977; Lyle 1934; Phonographs 1909; Rules 1978] *See also* COLLECTORS AND COLLECTING; PRESERVATION OF SOUND RECORDINGS. to disk.

Garrett H. Bowles

SOUND REPRODUCTION CO. A New York firm, located at 56 Liberty St. in 1916. It made the Maestrola disc player, sold for $12.

SOUNDBOX. A common designation for the reproducer of an acoustic phonograph; it is usually applied to disc machines. Its parts are the diaphragm, needle arm and screw, spring, cushions, casing, and gasket. It was supplanted in the electric era by the cartridge, or pickup.

SOUNDSTREAM. A system of sonic enhancement for acoustic records, invented by Thomas Stockham. Using digital technology, Soundstream adds harmonics that were not produced in the original recording by means of a parallel modern recording of the same work. It reduces surface noise, and brings the singer's voice forward; but also increases the presence of low pitched rumble. The most notable Soundstream recordings are those of Enrico Caruso, issued by RCA. *See also* SONIC RESTORATION OF HISTORICAL RECORDINGS.

SOUSA, JOHN PHILIP, 1854–1932. American bandmaster, violinist, and composer, born in Washington, D.C., on 6 Nov 1854. He studied violin, then the wind instruments, and played with the United States Marine Band at age 13; in 1880 he became its director. He resigned in 1892 to form his own Grand Concert Band, with which he became world famous. The band performed at the Columbian Exposition in Chicago, 1893, and at the Paris Exposition of 1900; it made European tours and a world tour in 1910–1911. Sousa continued band work into the 1920s. His death came in Reading, Pennsylvania, on 6 Mar 1932.

Sousa was a pioneer recording artist, with Columbia cylinders from 1890; in the earliest known record sales list there are 59 cylinders by the Marine Band, consisting of 23 marches, five waltzes, nine polkas, and 22 miscellaneous pieces. Only a small complement of the ensemble was involved in the studio recording, as few as 16 or 17 players. Sousa did not participate in recording, being a skeptic about the whole business ("the menace of mechanical music" as he termed it in a magazine article). When his own band began to record, he let other men do the conducting of it, usually Arthur Pryor.

In 1893 the New Jersey Phonograph Co. began to record the new Grand Concert Band, and listed 23 cylinders; however none has come to light. The band recorded Columbia cylinders from 1895 to 1899, making 52 records. Four undated catalogs of the Chicago Talking Machine Co., issued before 1900, included 29 records by the Sousa Band; one scholar speculates that the recordings date from May 1895 (Smart 1970). Other labels with Sousa material that was not simply copied from Columbia records include D. E. Boswell Co., Chicago (eight records), the U-S Phonograph Co., Newark (19 records), Victor (542 sides during 1900–1902), and Edison (36 cylinders in 1909–1910). After 1911 the band became a Victor exclusive ensemble. There were still 14 titles by the band in the 1940 catalog, including the most enduring of the great Sousa compositions, "Stars and Stripes Forever" (#20132) and "Washington Post" (#20191). [Smart 1970.]

SOUTH DAKOTA PHONOGRAPH CO. One of the affiliates of the North American Phonograph Co., established in 1890 in Sioux Falls. Henry Lacey was general manager.

Southern Four. *See* FISK JUBILEE QUARTET.

SOVEREIGN (label). A British record, unbreakable and double-sided, offered by British Sonogram, Ltd., in 1907. It was made by the Disc Record Co., Ltd., of Stockport, Cheshire. [Andrews*.]

SPALDING, ALBERT, 1888–1953. American violinist, born in Chicago on 15 Aug 1888. He studied as a child in Florence and Paris, and made his debut in Paris on 6 June 1905, playing the Saint Saëns Third Concerto to great critical acclaim. He played the same concerto in his first "official" U.S. appearance, with the New York Symphony Orchestra on 8 Nov 1908 (he had performed earlier, as a guest soloist at the Metropolitan Opera House, 29 Nov 1908). He toured Europe; served in the U.S. Army during the First World War, then concertized extensively and appeared on the radio; in 1941 he had his own CBS program. During the Second World War Spalding was again in the service, and was for a time head of Radio Rome (for the Allied forces). He was decorated by three governments for his military accomplishments. After five more years of concerts, he retired in 1950, and died on 26 May 1953 in New York.

Spalding was one of several violinists to record for Edison, but the only one with a wide following; he made cylinders in 1909, and Edison Diamond Discs from 1913 to 1929. In 1926 he was briefly with Brunswick. Victor signed him for the 1930s.

The first Edison was a four-minute Amberol cylinder dating from August 1909, the Wieniawski "Polonaise in D-Major" (#177). Later he made a popular cylinder (#3815) and Diamond Disc record (#82536; 1915) of Gounod's "Ave Maria" with soprano Marie Rappold; the disc was used in **tone tests**. (In 1953 Spalding said of the tone tests that nobody could have distinguished between the live artist and the record; but that on modern records anybody could!) Other singers with whom he collaborated on Edison were Claudia Muzio and Frieda Hempel.

More than 70 Spalding records, concert standards and arrangements of songs, were listed in the 1925 Edison catalog. With Victor he began to deal with the solid repertoire, including the sonatas of Franck, Brahms, Tartini, and Handel. His accompanist of more than 40 years, Andre Benoist, was his partner in those sonatas. A particularly notable disc was the Ludwig Spohr Concerto No. 8, with Eugene Ormandy and the Philadelphia Orchestra (#15355/56; album #M-544). [Ferrara 1988/7; Walsh 1954/2–3.]

SPANIER, MUGGSY, 1906–1967. American jazz cornetist, born Francis Joseph Spanier in Chicago on 9 Nov 1906. He played drums as a child, then cornet in school band and then in various Chicago groups. In 1929 he was invited to join the Ted Lewis orchestra, remaining to 1936; then he was with Ben Pollack two years. His subsequent moves were numerous, including time with Bob Crosby, Miff Mole, and Earl Hines. He retired for health reasons in 1964, and died in Sausalito, California, on 12 Feb 1967.

Spanier's first records were made for Gennett in 1924 with a group he called the Bucktown Five; "Hot Mittens" (#5518) and "Buddy's Habits" (#5418) were the most interesting of the seven sides. In 1939 he recorded again, for Bluebird in four sessions. This time he had his Ragtime Band, and the presentations were in the general style of Bob Crosby's Bobcats, a little out of step with the jazz/swing bands of the period. "Dippermouth Blues" (#B-10506) was an imitation of the King Oliver 1923 disc, and "Livery Stable Blues" (#B-10518) was not unlike the version by the Original Dixieland Jazz Band (1917). The best of eight sides made for Decca in 1942, with a large orchestra, were "Chicago" / "Can't We Be Friends?" (#4168). A Riverside LP reissued the Bucktown material (#RLP 1035); a CMS LP (#FL 20009) covered the 1939 records; and Avalon LP #12 reissued the 1942 material.

SPECIAL RECORD (label). A series produced by Columbia/Harmony in the late 1920s especially for use by stage and motion picture theaters; the idea was to promote songs that were in the day's performance. Fine artists and a high standard of recording mark the label. [Rust 1978.]

SPECTACLE. A combination **recorder** and **reproducer** assembly invented by Thomas Edison (U.S. patent #386,974; filed 26 Nov 1887; granted 31 July 1888) with improvements by **Ezra Gilliland** (U.S. patent #393,640; filed 7 June 1888; granted 27 Nov 1888). The device enabled the user to make a record and then play it back quickly on the same machine, simply by pivoting the spectacle, which held—in a form similar to a pair of eye-glasses—the recorder diaphragm and stylus along with the counterparts of the reproducer. The spectacle was first marketed in Edison's Perfected Phonograph of 1888. [Klinger*.]

SPEEDS. A major challenge to all forms of sound recording has been to establish the optimal speed of the medium as it spins on a turntable, turns on a mandrel, or passes a given point. A speed that is too slow will result in unacceptable distortions, one that is too quick will use up the recording surface in a short time. Another problem is to see that the playback speed is exactly the same as the recording speed; if it is not, there will be a change in musical pitch (on a disc, a deviation of four rpm will cause a semitone rise or fall).

The experiments and conclusions of recording manufacturers are outlined in the articles CYLINDER, 5 and DISC, 4. Discs are supposed to rotate at a constant number of revolutions per minute (rpm); they operate as CAV systems (constant angular velocity). There was a fair range of standardization among principal manufacturers of discs during the acoustic period. Following Victor's lead, most American labels were recording at 78–80 rpm shortly after the turn of the century. However 75 rpm was the norm for Columbia acoustics made in France, Italy, and Spain; and for Odeon acoustics in all countries. Parlophone used 75 rpm for one series, and 80 rpm for another. (Victor itself announced in its May 1917 catalog that "all records should be played at a speed of 76"; however, the November 1917 catalog gives the correct speed as 78, suggesting the possibility of a misprint in the May edition.) Other labels showed similar variations from the "standard" 78 rpm. Even the first electrics may be odd. Ault reports on his study of Columbia set #X 198 (1927) of *Les Préludes* by Felix Weingartner and the London Symphony: "The four sides were recorded at four different speeds, the first side at about 74 rpm, with each side a little faster until the last side was at about 77 rpm." Ault also points out the slow recording speed for the first Bing Crosby record (70 rpm) and the fast speed (83 rpm) of Columbia #50-D, of the Original Memphis Five (1924). Variations in speed were found from one session to another in the same studio.

In modern discographies of old records, the compiler often endeavors to indicate the correct recording (and playback) speed of each disc. John Bolig's *Recordings of Enrico Caruso*, for example, notes all the correct speeds, which range from 75 to 80 rpm.

The **Phonometer** was a 1907 device intended to monitor turntable speed.

Long-playing 33 1/3 rpm microgroove discs and 45 rpm discs maintained the advertised speeds.

Compact discs operate on a different system, which requires a varying number of rpm to maintain a constant relative velocity between pickup and track across the disc radius (a CLV system, "constant linear velocity"). CDs rotate from 200 to 500 rpm.

Another aspect of the question has to do with the travel speed of a stylus as it moves along a disc groove from the outside to the inside of the record. [Ault 1987; Brooks*] *See also* SURFACE SPEED; TUNING BAND.

SPENCER, ELIZABETH, 1875–1930. American mezzo-soprano, born Elizabeth Dickerson in Denver, Colorado. She sang in vaudeville and concert, and recorded from 1911 for Edison, who regarded her as his "favorite soprano." She did ballads, some opera ("Hear Me, Norma" on Amberol #629; "My Heart at thy Sweet Voice," on Diamond Disc #82512), duets (with Charles Harrison, Henry Burr, John Young, Walter Van Brunt, and others), and sang with the Homestead Trio (1921–1925), Metropolitan Quartet, and the Edison Mixed Quartet. Her best-selling record was the B side of Diamond Disc #80160 where she sang "On the Banks of the Brandywine," happily combined with Edison's greatest hit, "I'll Take You Home Again, Kathleen," by Van Brunt. Spencer was one of the Edison **tone test** artists.

In 1917 she turned to Victor and became their exclusive. "A Perfect Day" (#18250) was her first record; her most popular Victor was her last one: "Let the Rest of the World Go By," a duet with Charles Hart (1923). Then she worked for Emerson, Regal, and Banner; and returned to Edison in 1921. In 1926 she recorded as one of the Metropolitan Entertainers. Spencer died in Denver in April 1930. [Walsh 1951/8–9.]

SPENCER, GRACE, 1872–1952. American soprano, one of the earliest recording artists; known as the "First Lady of the Phonograph." She recorded five duets with Harry Macdonough in 1900, on Edison brown-wax cylinders, beginning with "Life's Dream is O'er" (#7559); made a nine-inch Zonophone disc ca. 1900 ("I Will Magnify Thee O God"); and began to record for Victor on 10 July 1901, in Macdonough duets, the first being "When We

Are Married" (#V-904). Her first Victor solo, recorded in the same session, and the first by a woman on the label, was "Queen of the Philippine Islands." Spencer had been heard even earlier on Victor, as a member of the Lyric Trio; that group rendered a trio from Verdi's *Attila* on 15 June 1900. [Walsh 1948/4–5.]

SPENCER, LEN, 1867–1914. American baritone and comedian, born Leonard Garfield Spencer in Washington, D.C., on 12 Feb 1867. He worked in his father's business school and was attracted by the Columbia "Office Graphophones" there. On an errand to the Columbia establishment, he made some song recordings, and was drawn to a recording career; he became Len Spencer, the singer, and Leonard G. Spencer, the interpreter of famous speeches. He also spoke the announcements on Columbia cylinders and discs. Spencer made more than 50 cylinders for the New Jersey Phonograph Co. by 1893. He made Berliner discs, and recorded for Edison. Then he signed an exclusive contract with Columbia in May 1898. Soon he was one of the leading figures in the new industry.

Spencer's repertoire was greatly varied. In 1898 for Columbia brown-wax cylinders he did **coon songs** and sentimental ballads; he sang duets with Roger Harding, covering a spectrum from "Nearer My God, to Thee" (#8415) to "The Broadway Swell and the Bowery Bum" (#8402). The **Spencer Trio** was active in the same period.

In 1901 Spencer appeared on Victor discs, in coon and minstrel duets with Vess Ossman. Accompanied by Parke Hunter's banjo, Spencer made his most famous record for Victor on 25 Sep 1903: the comic sketch "Arkansaw Traveler" (#1101). It was still in the catalog in 1922, along with such favorites as "Auction Sale of Household Goods" (#857; 1904) and "Barnyard Serenade" (#4562; 1905). "Arkansaw" had appeared earlier as an Edison cylinder, #8202 (1902); "Barnyard" was also an Edison cylinder (# 9191; 1906).

There were also duets with Ada Jones in 1905–1906, Bowery sketches, coon skits, Jewish and Irish routines. Spencer's fine speaking voice was heard in renditions of President McKinley's final speech in 1901, Lincoln's

Gettysburg address, and William Jennings Bryan's renowned "Cross of Gold" oration. Jim Walsh cites "Little Arrow and Big Chief Greasepaint" as "one of the funniest things ever cut into wax"; it remained in the Edison catalog until 1929. Spencer's final recording, his only Edison Diamond Disc, was "Uncle Fritz and the Children's Orchestra" (#50196; 1914). He also ran a booking agency in New York, Len Spencer's Lyceum. He died on 15 Dec 1914. [Brooks 1979; Walsh 1947/3–8.]

SPENCER TRIO. A male vocal ensemble that recorded for Columbia cylinders ca. 1897–1898, and for Victor discs in 1903–1904. The membership varied: Len Spencer was always one of the three, with (for Victor) Billy Golden and Steve Porter; or (for Columbia) Billy Golden, Billy Williams, Roger Harding, or Steve Porter. A whistler named Chalfont joined for some records in 1897. "Mocking Bird Medley" (Victor #V-1946; 1903) brought forth whistling by Golden. "Alpine Specialty" was first done for Columbia cylinders, then for Victor discs. [Brooks 1979.]

SPINDLE. (I) The vertical post at the center of a gramophone turntable. It keeps the disc in position during play, and in certain types of **record changer** it holds the stack of records to be played, or which have been played. The standard size in the 78 era was 0.25 inches in diameter; this was the size used by Berliner in his original instruments. Other sizes were used, among smaller manufacturers in the early 1900s, notably those based in Chicago: 1/2 inch and even three inches. (See for example ARETINO and UNITED TALKING MACHINE CO.) The RCA 45 rpm record player of 1948 had a 1 3/8 inch spindle to accommodate the little vinyl discs; spindles of that diameter were later available as attachments to LP record players.

SPINDLE. (II) On a compact disc player, the spindle is the part of the drive that spins the disc.

SPIVAK, CHARLIE, 1905–1982. Russian/American trumpeter, born in Trilsey on 17 Feb 1905. Coming early to the U.S., he played with many ensembles, notably Ben Pollack in 1931–1934, the Dorsey Brothers, Jack Teagarden, and Ray Noble. In 1935 he was with Glenn Miller. He was recognized as a melody performer, rather than a jazz improviser, having a particularly lush tone. In the 1940s he led his own band, identifying himself as "the sweetest trumpet in the world." Many agreed, selecting him through the *Metronome* poll as trumpet player of the year in 1940. Willie Smith, alto sax, and Dave Tough, drums, were in the band, and June Hutton was one of the vocalists; a later singer was Irene Daye. His orchestra won the 1944 *Downbeat* poll as the most popular "sweet or dance band." Popularity of the group continued into the late 1940s, after which time Spivak concentrated on smaller combo work. He died in Cleveland on 1 Mar 1982.

The Spivak orchestra recorded for Okeh in 1941–1942. One of their popular discs was "Star Dreams" (Okeh #6546; 1941). Columbia recorded Spivak's trumpet version of the "Elegy" of Jules Massenet (#36596; 1942).

SPLICING TAPE. An adhesive tape used in editing recorded tapes; it is not magnetized. Sizes for open-reel tapes and cassettes are available. In studio work a splicing machine applies the tape.

SPLITDORF RADIO CORP. A Newark, New Jersey, firm, formed as a division of the Splitdorf Bethlehem Electrical Co. in June 1927. Splitdorf had been licensed by RCA and Westinghouse in April 1927. Thomas Edison acquired Splitdorf Radio in December 1928, as a means of access to the radio industry. He renamed the Splitdorf radio as Edison radio, and sold three models in 1929; two of them were radio-phonograph combinations that played Diamond Discs or lateral-cut discs.

SPOKANE PHONOGRAPH CO. One of the affiliated companies of the **North American Phonograph Co.**, established in 1890 in Spokane Falls, Washington. J.W. Wilson was manager in 1891. Louis Glass was one of the directors; he took the most active role in promoting the firm, in particular his **coin-op** machines.

Spoken word recordings. *See* LITERARY RECORDINGS.

SPRING MOTOR RECORD PLAYERS. Because early sources of electrical power were expensive and/or unreliable, most of the pioneer phonograph and gramophone makers used spring motors to rotate their mandrels and turntables. The first such motor was developed by **Edward H. Amet** (U.S. patent application filed in 1891) and used on the Edison Class M phonograph of 1894. **Frank L. Capps** invented a motor with three springs (patented 1896) that was used with the Edison Concert machine of 1899. The motor of J. E. Greenhill was perhaps the first to be used in a phonograph (1893). Henri Lioret made a talking doll in 1893 with his own spring mechanism. Columbia's first spring motor phonograph was the Type F Graphophone of 1894.

The earliest spring motor for a disc machine was patented buy Levi H. Montross (U.S. #598,529; filed 8 Oct 1896; granted 8 Feb 1898). He sold these in Camden. Eldridge Johnson used the Montross motor in the 200 gramophones he manufactured for the U.S. Gramophone Co. (Berliner's firm) in 1896. He then took an order for another 3,500 machines. An improved governor, invented by Johnson, was used in the Berliner "trademark" model, the Improved Gramophone.

Even after the use of electric power became convenient, spring motors were used to drive portable 78 rpm disc players and cylinder or disc machines used in **field recordings**. [Koenigsberg*; Koenigsberg 1990; Paul 1991/2.]

SPRINGSTEEN, BRUCE, 1949– . American rock singer, born in Freehold, New Jersey, on 23 Sep 1949. He sang and played guitar in Greenwich Village clubs, and became known for his songs of discontent and social comment. In 1975 he rose to national fame with three chart albums for Columbia: *The Wild, The Innocent and the E Street Shuffle* (#KC 32432), *Greetings from Asbury Park* (#KC 31903), and *Born to Run* (#PC 33795). Of eight other hit albums through 1985, the most popular was *Born in the*

U.S.A. (Columbia #QC 38653), which was on the charts more than 80 weeks.

STACY, JESS, 1904– . American jazz pianist and Big Band leader, born in Cape Girardeau, Missouri, on 4 Aug 1904. He played piano on the riverboats, then in Chicago with various bands from 1926 to 1929. He was acclaimed for his virtuosity, lyricism, and splendid tone. Then he joined Benny Goodman for the first of three partnerships in 1935–1939 (the later associations were 1942–1944 and 1946–1947). Stacy was with Bob Crosby from 1939 to 1942. In four consecutive years, 1940–1943, Stacy was winner of the *Downbeat* poll as most popular jazz pianist. He had his own band in 1945–1946, featuring his wife **Lee Wiley** as vocalist. After 1960 he was inactive.

Stacy's greatest records were made as soloist, accompanied by Gene Krupa and a string bass, from 1935 to 1939, and as a sideman with Goodman. Of the solo discs, the standouts are "Barrelhouse" (Parlophone #R-2187; 1935), "Candlelights" (Commodore #517; 1939), and "Ec-Stacy" (Commodore #1503; 1939). His most inspired improvisation on record may be in "Sing, Sing, Sing" with Goodman at the Carnegie Hall concert of 16 Jan 1938 (Columbia LP #SL 160).

STAFFORD, JO, 1920– . American popular vocalist, born in Coalinga, California, on 12 Nov 1920. She and her sister made youthful appearances on radio as a singing team; then she joined the **Pied Pipers** and sang with them in the Tommy Dorsey band from 1940. Later she was a soloist with Dorsey, left in 1942 to freelance, and made many radio appearances, notably on *Your Hit Parade*. In 1943 and 1945 she was winner of the *Downbeat* poll as favorite female vocalist. She was married to **Paul Weston**, and made several entertaining parody records with him. After 1960 she was less active.

With Dorsey there were fine ballad records, notably "He's My Guy" (Victor #27941; 1942). From 1950 to 1957 Stafford had nine chart singles, including "Shrimp Boats" (Columbia #39581; 1951) and "You Belong to Me" (Columbia #39811; 1952). Among her spoof records were several with Red Ingle, the best being "Tim-Tayshun" (Capitol #412); and several gems with Weston—who masqueraded as Jonathan Edwards—such as "Carioca." Her most popular LP album was *Ski Trails* (Columbia #CL 910; 1956). The "Jonathan Edwards" material is in Columbia album #CL-1024.

STAMPER. The mold part in the disc record making process that is used to create the final pressing. *See also* DISC, 3.

STANDARD (label). A record made by the **Standard Talking Machine Co.** of Chicago from 1903. The discs, surplus items from Columbia, were modified by expansion of their center holes to 9/16 inch. From March 1918 the label was issued by the Consolidated Talking Machine Co. of Chicago. [Rust 1978.]

STANDARD GRAMOPHONE APPLIANCE CO. A New York firm, located in 1912 at 173 Lafayette St. It advertised the Simplex stop and start attachment for disc players.

STANDARD METAL MANUFACTURING CO. A New York firm, located in 1907 at 10 Warren St. It made Standard Horns.

STANDARD PLAY. A designation for the 78 rpm disc, in contrast to the 33 1/3 rpm LP microgroove disc.

STANDARD PNEUMATIC ACTION CO. A New York firm, located in the 1920s at 638 W. 52nd St. Primarily a maker of player piano actions of the inner type, their products were used in over 100 brand name pianos. One model included a built-in disc phonograph.

STANDARD QUARTETTE. A male vocal group that recorded for Columbia cylinders. They were announced on the records as "gentlemen of color"—"which, if true, would seem to make them the first Black group ever to record" (Brooks). Among their presentations in the 1894–1896 period were "Swing Low," "Nationality Medley," and old fashioned jubilee songs. [Brooks 1979.]

Standard sequence. *See* MANUAL SEQUENCE.

STANDARD TALKING MACHINE CO. A Chicago firm established in October 1901 at 198–202 Monroe St. It was apparently a branch of the East Liverpool China Co. (established 1901). It sold discs with the label name **Standard**, and Standard brand talking machines to play them. The discs had 9/16 inch spindle holes, and the record players had spindles to match. Both discs and machines were modified Columbia products. The machines came from the Bridgeport factory, some carrying that information stamped on them. The first to be marketed by Standard, ca. 1903, was identical to the Columbia AU model, with a seven-inch turntable; later there was a similar machine with a 10-inch turntable. In 1913 Standard absorbed the **Great Northern Manufacturing Co.**, formalizing a long association. Standard was succeeded by **Consolidated Talking Machine Co.** of Chicago; that firm issued 10-inch records with the Standard label in March 1918. [Fabrizio 1980.]

STANDING WAVES. A vibrational mode that may result in a small room when audio equipment produces tones of certain frequencies. The second octave, from 32 Hz to 64 Hz, is the range usually affected, since 32 Hz has a wave length of 35 feet and 64 Hz has a wave length of 17.5 feet. Room dimensions that are one-half or one-quarter of those wave lengths will act to enhance the volume of tones in that segment of the audio range, with the effect of distorted loudness balance, exaggerating the bass tones. [Klinger*.] *See also* ROOM ACOUSTICS.

STANFORD ARCHIVE OF RECORDED SOUND (StARS). The Archive of Recorded Sound at Stanford University, Palo Alto, California, was established in 1958 as a unit of the Stanford University Libraries. It was one of the first major institutional sound collections devoted to the acquisition, preservation, and dissemination of historically and artistically significant sound recordings. Curatorship for the Archive was endowed in 1988. The Stanford University Libraries pioneered in understanding that recordings of many kinds embody an historical immediacy unparalleled by the written word, and recognizing recordings as aural documents which should be an integral part of a university's scholarly resources.

Because there had been little attempt at systematic organization of materials relative to, and the actual preservation of the many formats in which recorded sound can be stored, scholars in many fields were (and often still are) unaware of the vast areas of documentary resources that exist. Students of history, music, drama, literature, and communications can draw on a variety of resources in the Archive (some of which date back 100 years), and in matters of performance practice and expression can reflect even earlier times. Biographers can often listen to the voices of their subjects and their contemporaries; musicians can hear composers interpret their own works (*see* COMPOSER RECORDINGS). Singers and instrumentalists can listen to performances by those artists for whom the compositions were written (by Verdi, Puccini, Ravel, Massenet, and so forth.). Such recordings provide authenticity available in no other form.

The Stanford Archive houses more than 200,000 recordings of classical and popular music, literature, drama, interviews, public addresses, and radio broadcasts in formats ranging from wax cylinders to compact discs. Commercial 78 rpm and LP discs, as well as private tape recordings, comprise the largest portion of the holdings. Special collections include the Stanford Department of Music concert tape collection, the Stanford speech collection, the Pryor collection of early World War II newscasts, the Richard Crooks collection, the Kirsten Flagstad collection, the Richard Bonelli collection, and recordings donated by the families of such singers as Mario Ancona, Lawrence Tibbett, and Mario Chamlee. The Benjamin Lincoln jazz collection is at Stanford, as well as recordings from Project South (interviews with participants in the civil rights movement), the Monterey Jazz Festival archives, the Carmel Bach Festival tape archives, the Djerassi Foundation tape archives, and the Stanford Program for Recordings in Sound literary series.

The Archive also maintains an extensive reference collection of books and periodicals on the history and development of the sound recording industry and its major figures. A wide range of discographies covering specific manufacturers, performers, performance media, and chronological periods is included in this collection. Original manufacturers' catalogs as well as photographs and clippings are available to researchers.

The **Rigler and Deutsch Index** provides access to the Archive's 78 rpm recordings as well as to those held by four other archives. The reference collection and those LP and CD recordings purchased for StARS are available through Stanford's online public catalog. For the large number of Archive holdings not yet formally cataloged, in-house finding aids and other reference guides are available to help locate recordings.

StARS is located on the lower level of the Braun Music Center in an environmentally controlled area. There are closed stacks for the sound recordings, while the reference collection is in a public reading area. Sound recordings are handled only by the staff, to ensure both proper care and correct playback for researchers. An audio room is equipped to handle playback of the many formats; it is large enough for small classes and seminars.

All Archive collections are non-circulating. The staff can prepare tape copies for faculty or student to borrow for prolonged study or classroom presentation. Tape duplication of holdings not under copyright or other specific restrictions imposed by donors can often be arranged for non-Stanford scholars. Specific requests should be addressed to the Archivist. The Archive is open to the public Monday-Friday, 1:00–5:00 PM, or by appointment. Listening appointments are encouraged, with advance notice from scholars planning to do extended work.

The Archive offers for sale some of its holdings in disc and facsimile reprint formats. For additional information one may write to the Archivist, Stanford Archive of Recorded Sound, Braun Music Center, Stanford, California 94305–3076. The telephone is (415) 723-9312.

A major project in which the Archive is involved is *The Encyclopedic Discography of Victor Recordings*, a work in progress since 1963. Ted Fagan and William R. Moran commenced the task of listing Victor Red Seal recordings, and enjoyed the cooperation of George Marek,

then president of RCA. It was soon found that much more was involved than simple copying of existing Victor files, and that many of the files had already deteriorated seriously. The authors decided that unless their effort could be extended to cover all Victor recordings, in a few years much valuable information would be lost forever. So a complete catalog was proposed, one that would list systematically the entire 78 rpm output of the firm, its predecessors and successors, covering 1900 to ca. 1950.

More than 20 years were expended in transcribing and re-organizing the necessary information before the first volume was published in 1983: *The Encyclopedic Discography of Victor Recordings: Pre-Matrix Series* (Westport, Connecticut.: Greenwood Press). That 393-page volume covered all Victor records (published and unpublished) produced from 12 Jan 1900 to 23 Apr 1903, at which date Victor revised its identification system with the introduction of **matrix numbers**. That system, with only minor modifications, stayed in use to the end of the 78 era. The first volume also contained—as a special appendix—a history of the Victor Talking Machine Co. by B. L. Aldridge, a work never before publicly available; a discussion, with illustrations, of the Victor label, as well as the evolution of the catalog numbering system; a chronological listing of recording sessions; and an indexes of artists and titles for the period.

Greenwood published the second volume, in 648 pages, at the end of 1986. In addition to introductory historical material and illustrations of Victor labels used during the period, it listed by matrix number all recordings made from number 1 (14 Apr 1903) to number 4999 (7 Jan 1908). There were also "overseas" recordings, plus 28 pages of detailed notes on specific discs, a chronological list of sessions, and indexes by artist and title. Suggested playing speeds were given for many of the records.

The authors then decided to break the ongoing matrix volumes for a massive catalog number index volume, to list the equivalent matrix and/or import data for all catalog numbers used in the many Victor series from 1900 through 1925 (the advent of electrical recording). This has proved to be an immensely difficult project, its realization unfortunately prolonged by the untimely death of the junior author, Ted Fagan, in 1987. But the two authors had recognized that the project was too large to be completed in their own lifetimes, and had arranged for the partial transfer of the enterprise to the Stanford Archive. The assistant archivist, Richard Koprowski, was appointed assistant editor of the Victor project after Fagan's death. At this writing (1991) standardization of computer programs is under way and data are being entered for the third volume of the series. This Catalog Number volume was to be ready for the publisher in 1991. Subsequent volumes will return to the Matrix Series, carrying on from matrix number 5000 (1908). It is anticipated that the project when complete will occupy some 25 volumes.

William R. Moran

STANLEY, AILEEN, 1893–1982. American vaudeville singer, born Maude Elsie Aileen Muggeridge in Chicago. She and her brother Stanley—whose name she later took for her stage name—were performing in public when she was five years old. Her career went on from there to cover 50 years in America and Britain, rising from dingy small-town theaters to private parties in London attended by the Prince of Wales. Stanley was a featured performer in the Keith-Albee circuit, and a radio artist from the early days of the medium, with Rudy Vallee and Paul Whiteman. She appeared in three Broadway musicals, *Silks and Satins* (1920), *Pleasure Bound* (1929), and *Artists and Models of 1930* (1930).

Known as "The Victrola Girl" ("The Gramophone Girl" in the U.K.), Stanley recorded prolifically for Victor/HMV from 1920 (after a few sides for Pathé). "Broadway Blues" / "My Little Bimbo Down on the Bamboo Isle" (from *Silks and Satins*) was her first Victor (#18691; 1920). She also worked for Okeh, Vocalion, Gennett, Edison, and other labels in the 1920s, making a total of 215 recordings. Sales of her discs were reported to have reached 25 million copies.

She and Billy Murray made popular duets for Victor, the best being "Any Ice Today, Lady?" / "Whadda You Say We Get Together?" (#20065; 1926). Another was a sensation: "Bridget O'Flynn" / "Who Could Be More

Wonderful Than You?" (Victor #20240; 1926). Stanley made few records after 1930, but continued on stage in U.S. and U.K. Her final disc was "It Looks Like Rain in Cherry Blossom Lane" / "I've Got My Love to Keep Me Warm" (HMV #BD444; 1937). She died in Los Angeles on 24 Mar 1982. [Walsh 1963/10–11–12; 1964/1.]

STANLEY, FRANK C., 1868–1910. American bass singer, born William Stanley Grinsted in Orange, New Jersey, on 29 Dec 1868. He was one of the most prolific recording artists, with thousands of discs and cylinders on many labels, while also pursuing a career in politics (as an alderman in Newark, New Jersey). He started recording as a banjo player for Edison in 1891, under his real name, inscribing "Lumber Yard Jig" and 11 other numbers. As a singer he was heard in numerous ensembles, among them the **Columbia Male Quartet**, the **Invincible Four**, and the **Metropolitan Mixed Trio**. He made about 70 records for Edison from 1899, beginning with "If You Love as I Love" (#7322). He had many duet partners, including Byron Harlan, Henry Burr, Harry Macdonough, and Corinne Morgan.

In 1906 Stanley initiated a series of duets with Elise Stevenson on Victor and Columbia, then from 1909 on Edison. The two were also members of the **Schubert Trio** in 1906. Stanley was the first to record songs from *Merry Widow*, with eight Indestructible Cylinders in February 1908.

Stanley was at the peak of his popularity in 1906, when he organized the **Peerless Quartet** (originally the Columbia Male Quartet) and managed it until his death. His final solo record was "Boy O' Mine" for Edison in October 1910. He died in Newark on 12 Dec of that year.

STAR (label). (I) A British cylinder record issued from 1904–1907 by the Phonograph Exchange Co., 4 White Lion St., Norwich; and from September 1905 at 73 Farringdon St., London. One of the early issues was of the bells of St. Peter Mancroft Church, in Norwich, recorded in the belfry. An important artist was Maude Dewey, "champion lady whistler of the world," recording bird songs. The Welsh Bethesda choir was also recorded. Most of the repertoire was however of the music hall type. [Andrews 1979/10.]

STAR (label).   (II) An American disc record first advertised in March 1907, made by **Hawthorne & Sheble**. Matrices were from Columbia. Production ceased with the demise of H & S in 1909, but sales continued in U.K. for a time.

STARCK (label). An American record issued in 1926–1927 by the Starck music stores. There were about 100 items, from Pathé masters. [Rust 1978.]

STARR (label). An American record issued by the **Starr Piano Co.**, of Richmond, Indiana, in 1916; the name was changed to Gennett in the following year for the U.S. market, but remained Starr in Canada. [Rust 1978.]

STARR PIANO CO. A firm established in 1872 in Richmond, Indiana, and incorporated in 1878, by James and Benjamin Starr. The first piano was produced in 1873, and was successful; the company was turning out 15 instruments a week by 1884. There was a new incorporation in 1893, with Benjamin Starr as president. Henry Gennett joined the firm that year; when he became president in 1906 the firm had grown to 600 employees. They had made 90,000 pianos by 1912, and were finishing 40 per day. There were more than 30 buildings in the Starr complex in Richmond.

A new structure was built in 1916 for the manufacture of disc records (first advertised in October 1916) and record players. The records were 10-inch, vertical-cut, playing four to five minutes per side; they sold for $.65 to $4 each. The long playing time was achieved by fine grooving (150 turns per inch). A new main office was opened in Cincinnati, at 27 W. 4th Ave. West, in October 1916. Starr was the first label name, then—from September 1917— **Gennett**. In March 1919 Gennett records were advertised as lateral cut. There was a New York address for Starr's Gennett Records division, at 9 E. 37th St. Clarence Gennett was treasurer and retail manager at the time, and Henry Gennett the factory manager. R. C. Mayer

was head of the recording laboratories, with Fred Myer factory superintendent.

Starr disc players were sold from August 1915, with 11 models available in 1916. Under the Gennett name the company achieved great commercial success (3 million records per year in the mid-1920s) and considerable artistic success. A legal battle with Victor had to be endured for years (1918–1922), over the alleged infringement of Victor's patent for a lateral record-cutting stylus; but in the end Starr was upheld. Starr cut 1,250 masters in 1928, comparing favorably to giant Victor's 1,900. It had a Canadian affiliate, Starr Co. of Canada. W.D. Stevenson, vice president of the Canadian company, was named vice president of the U.S. company in 1925 (the only non-family member in a senior position at Starr).

Pianos were not neglected by Starr; there were still 15,000 per year being produced in the mid-1920s. But 35,000 record players were made as well. In March 1926 Starr took on the manufacture of the Portophon Portable record players, having acquired the patents, machinery, parts, and drawings from the liquidator of the Thomas Manufacturing Co. Then the Depression forced the Gennett label to cease; but the factories continued to make pianos and to press records for other firms. Eventually even the piano manufacture stopped (1949), and finally the Starr property was acquired for salvage by a local business man who demolished it after 1978. The original 1872 building has been spared. [Andrews*; Klein 1983.]

STATE PHONOGRAPH CO. OF ILLINOIS. One of the affiliates of the **North American Phonograph Co.**, established in 1890 in the Home Insurance Building, Chicago. Granger Farwell was president in 1892.

STEGER AND SONS. A Chicago manufacturer of reproducing grand pianos, established 1879. In addition to player actions, the firm made talking machines beginning in 1919. Models offered in 1920 were in all price ranges, including a "Gothic" at $1,250 and a $60 table model. Tone arms were devised with adjustable pressure for playback of vertical-cut and lateral-cut discs; and advertising stated that "no other phonograph has this pressure adjustment." Location of the company during 1916–1922 was at Wabash Ave. and Jackson Blvd., in its own Steger Building; factories were in Steger, Illinois. In 1923 the firm was at 1541 E. 60th St., on the South Side of the city. The 1929 Chicago directory shows Steger back downtown at 238 S. Wabash Ave. In 1932, the final appearance of a Steger piano firm in the telephone directory, the company name was F. L. Steger, the address was 3317 Hernden.

STEREOPHONIC RECORDING. Usually referred to as stereo. The process of recording two signals from the sound source, in a manner that will produce on playback an impression on the listener of an arc of sound between the two required loudspeakers. Stereo is based on the theory first propounded by **Alan D. Blumlein**, to the effect that the human binaural hearing mechanism could be imitated by a pair of left-right microphones. The stereo effect creates far greater realism than monaural recording, producing an illusion of depth that may be compared to the effect of stereoscopic photography.

Stereo works because the brain compares the intensities of incoming sounds and contrasts the input received by each ear. It notes the arrival time from right and left sources, the reverberations, the intensities; and thus is able to determine source direction as well as distance instantaneously (and unconsciously). (*See* HEARING.)

In disc recording the twin signals are cut into the same record groove, at an axis of operation of 45/45 degrees. This was one of the Blumlein methods, later to become the industry standard. Westrex and **Bell Telephone Laboratories** received a U.S. patent for the 45/45 discs in 1957. With each sidewall of the disc groove impressed with one program channel, the stereo cartridge distinguishes between them as it picks them up and sends one to each loudspeaker.

Early experiments with **binaural** sound transmission preceded the phonograph; there were such efforts in Britain in 1876, by Lord Rayleigh. Silvanus Thompson of Bristol University carried on in 1877–1878. The use of two listening tubes, spaced like human ears, was found to produce a certain localizing ability of the source signals on the part of the listener. Alexander Graham Bell in America was also interested in "stereophonic phenomena"—apparently he was the first to use the term. In Paris, 1881, Clément Ader demonstrated two-channel telephone transmission for a large enthusiastic audience in the Opéra auditorium. Listeners wore pairs of headphones.

Thomas Edison's second British phonographic patent (#1644; 1878) referred to multiple soundboxes on a single cylinder or disc, probably an effort to secure greater volume in reproduction, rather than a stereo effect. (The Columbia **Multiplex Grand** Graphophone of 1898 utilized the concept.)

Real efforts to record stereophonically began with the work of W. Bartlett Jones in the U.S. He patented the idea of putting the left and right sound signals in adjacent grooves of the disc or on opposite sides of the record (U.S. patent #1,855,149). Both methods required two replay styli, and difficulties of synchronizing these were a serious flaw in the design. (A curiosity in this genre was the perhaps unintentional stereo recording made by **Duke Ellington** in 1929.) Jones then patented (#1,855,150) a single groove, single stylus system. Simultaneous vertical and lateral modulation of the groove was involved. This idea was not developed commercially at the time.

Then came the Blumlein approach, already mentioned. His patent applications of 1931 established all later practice (U.K. #394,325; U.S. #2,095,540). EMI made experimental 78 rpm stereo discs at the Abbey Road studios in 1933. Pressings of these test discs (one of them Thomas Beecham conducting the Mozart Jupiter Symphony) exist, and sound effective. Other important research was carried out by **Arthur Charles Haddy** and colleagues of the Decca Record Co., Ltd., in London. Haddy's work, and that carried on in Germany by Teldec, led to an increased frequency spectrum in stereo playback, and to solving the problems of groove spacing so that space on the disc was not wasted by the dual signals. In the U.S. there was experimental stereo recording in March 1922 in the Philadelphia Academy of Music, as **Arthur Charles Keller** and a Bell Telephone Laboratories team made records of the Philadelphia

Orchestra with two microphones. The output was on two parallel vertically-cut tracks in 78 rpm discs. They were demonstrated at the Century of Progress Exposition in Chicago, 1933.

RCA initiated commercial recording in stereo in Boston's Symphony Hall on 21–22 Feb 1954, inscribing the *Damnation of Faust*. They followed that with a recording of the Chicago Symphony Orchestra under Fritz Reiner. EMI unveiled its "stereosonic" records in April 1955. Decca's first commercial recording in stereo—using the three-microphone "Tree" assembly—took place in Geneva, with the Orchestre de la Suisse Romande, in May 1954. Decca began to use extra microphones, "outriggers," to capture flanking sounds from the boundaries of the orchestra. Eventually Decca recorded the famous Georg Solti *Rheingold* in 1958 "where a KM-56 Tree captured the main orchestral sound" with a "six-channel unit augmented by a three-input outboard mixer and a single-channel pan-potted amp, a total of just 10 mikes to record what is universally recognized as a landmark achievement in stereo production" (Gray). In May 1958 the first 45/45 stereo discs were marketed in the U.S., by three independent labels: Audio-Fidelity, Urania, and Counterpoint. That summer RCA and Columbia came out with their discs. The Recording Industry Association of America (RIAA) had finally determined which of all the systems to endorse, and worldwide mass production followed. Pye issued the first commercial stereo discs in the U.K. in June 1958.

Multi-channel optical motion picture recording was first used commercially by Walt Disney studios in *Fantasia* (1940). It had a four-track sound film, derived from eight recording channels. It could best be described in today's terms as **surround sound**, rather than stereo, since it did not observe the natural sound perspectives of stereo. Cinemascope, developed by Bell Telephone Laboratories and demonstrated in January 1953, was an attempt to created true stereophonic sound on film.

Two-channel tape recording was also produced in the Bell Laboratories. At the New York World's Fair, 1939, demonstration tapes of Vicalloy were successfully displayed. Further important work in stereo tape was carried out by **Marvin Camras**, with a three-channel wire recorder. Domestic stereo tapes were introduced commercially by EMI in October 1955—a two-track system, also labelled "stereosonic"—with a two-tape set of *Nozze di Figaro* performed at the Glyndebourne Festival. RCA's four-track system appeared in 1958. For several years the companies produced their releases in both monaural and stereo versions, to accommodate users who did not have the new stereo playback equipment. Then compatible systems were developed, with which a stereo disc could be played as if it were only monaural (i.e., without the twin loudspeakers and stereo amplifier). Thus the user without the means or desire to acquire a stereo system could buy stereo records, and the need for manufacturing monaural records evaporated. By the end of the 1960s virtually all commercial recording on disc and tape was stereophonic. [Borwick 1982; Crowhurst 1960; Davis 1958; Ford 1962; Gray 1986; Klinger*; Kogen 1968.] *See also* RECORDING PRACTICE.

STERLING, LOUIS, *Sir*, **1879–1958.** American/British record industry executive, born 16 May 1879. He was born into a family of humble means, and had to sell newspapers in New York. But by 1900 he was in the export business; and in 1903 he was in England, working for **Gramophone & Typewriter, Ltd.**, who appointed him manager of the **British Zonophone Co.**, its newly-established outlet for its International Zonophone Co. of Germany. Sterling resigned to set up his own **Sterling Record Co., Ltd.**, in December 1904, to make cylinder records. **Russell Hunting**, director of his recording department, was his partner. On 18 Mar 1905 the firm was renamed the **Russell Hunting Record Co., Ltd.** It marketed the Sterling Gold Moulded Cylinder record, and was appointed British agent for products of Fonotipia, Ltd. A new company was formed in August 1906, **Sterling and Hunting, Ltd.**; it took on the Fonotipia agency from 17 Sep 1906, and began to sell Odeon and Fonotipia discs and cylinders made for the Linguaphone Co., Ltd. It also sold the Sterling records made by the Russell Hunting Record Co., Ltd., and marketed by that company until Sterling and Hunting, Ltd., was formed.

Sterling resigned from Sterling and Hunting, Ltd., in April 1908. The Russell Hunting Record Co., Ltd., went into liquidation that year. Sterling set up the new **Rena Manufacturing Co., Ltd.**, with N. D. Rodkinson as his partner, on 12 Nov 1908. Rena sold double-sided discs—the first in Britain—from Columbia matrices, plus Rena record players. Sterling was successful with Rena, and was asked to join the **Columbia** Phonograph Co., General—London, so he closed down his company, letting Columbia have the Rena records business and becoming manager of the Columbia activity on a commission basis. Columbia changed its name to Columbia Graphophone Co. (January 1913), and Sterling became European manager (December 1914). He began a vigorous campaign to record symphonic music and chamber music, repertoires not previously emphasized by the record labels.

Due to World War I, Columbia had to establish itself as a self-sufficient British company, and Sterling was instrumental in founding the Columbia Graphophone Co., Ltd., in February 1917—which became British-owned in April 1923. Sterling was able to take control of the British firm, and then to gain a controlling interest also in the failing American firm, on 31 Mar 1925. The American company had reorganized as the Columbia Phonograph Co., Inc., in February 1924, and that company had passed into the hands of Columbia (International) Ltd., upon its formation by Sterling's Columbia company on 3 Oct 1925.

Sterling had taken an early interest in electrical recording, as witnessed by Columbia's cooperation in the Westminster Abbey effort of November 1920 by **Lionel Guest** and **H. O. Merriman**. When the new Western Electric system was offered to Victor, which hesitated, and when Sterling got some of the electric masters from Russell Hunting, he went at once to New York, leaving 26 Dec 1924, to obtain the Western Electric license. He had to acquire the Columbia Phonograph Co., Inc.—which had been licensed—to achieve this. Victor came around, so the two rivals shared the electric system.

The merger of 1931 which created EMI, Ltd., gave Sterling yet another high post: he was a director of the new conglomerate. In June of that year he was knighted, the first person from the record industry to be so honored.

Sterling resigned from EMI before World War II. He died on 3 June 1958. [Andrews*.]

STERLING (label). A British cylinder record of the Russell Hunting Record Co., Ltd., Sterling and Hunting, Ltd., and Russell Hunting and Co., issued from June 1905 to February 1909. In 1907, at the peak of the cylinder business in Britain, Sterling was highly successful; as many as 3 million cylinders were sold in a 12-month period. Issues covered popular music of the day, operatic numbers, Irish and Scottish material. However there were no new issues after February 1909, the records having been undercut in price by the Edison Bell and Clarion cylinder records. The label was revived briefly in 1909 by **James Edward Hough**, who purchased the Sterling business after a fire had destroyed the cylinder manufacturing capacity of the Edison Bell plant. [Andrews*; Carter 1975 is a label list.]

STERLING AND HUNTING, LTD. A British firm, formed by the **Russell Hunting Record Co., Ltd.**, on 27 Aug 1906, to be the British sales agency for the Odeon and Fonotipia discs of Fonotipia, Ltd. The new firm also acted as sales agency for the Sterling cylinder records, for the recording and manufacturing company, and for the Sterling-made Linguaphone Language Course cylinders of the International Linguaphone Co., Ltd. **Louis Sterling** was general manager. The company was successful at first, in large part because of aggressive advertising; one promotional effort sent a balloon flying over London. The company claimed in February 1907 that it had shipped 80,000 records on a single day. Catalogs covered operatic material, popular music of the day, plus Irish and Scottish items. However it was unable to meet the competition—in a period of economic depression—of records coming from Edison Bell and Clarion, selling for 25 percent less than the Sterling. The firm folded by October 1908, and was dissolved 6 Aug 1909. Sterling had already departed, and set up in business as the **Rena Manufacturing Co., Ltd.** [Andrews*.]

STERLING RECORD CO., LTD. A British firm established 17 Dec 1904 by **Louis Sterling** and **Russell Hunting**, to manufacture and sell phonographs and gramophones. Charles Stroh, son of the inventor of the **Stroh violin**, was on the board, and Russell Hunting was director of the recording department. Address was Bishop Road, Cambridge Heath, London.

The firm changed its name on 18 Mar 1905 to **Russell Hunting Record Co., Ltd.**, which stayed in business until 10 Dec 1908. [Andrews*.]

STERLING TRIO. A male vocal group that recorded for many labels from 1916–1920, then exclusively for Victor in 1920–1925. In 1926 they worked for Gennett. Members were Albert Campbell, Henry Burr, and John H. Meyer. (Henry Moeller probably took the place of Burr in 1926.) There were 18 sides in the Victor 1917 catalog, many with geographical themes like "Georgia Moon" (#17927) and In Florida Among the Palms" (#18138). "Down Deep in an Irishman's Heart" was their final Victor effort (#19749; 1925).

STERN, ISAAC, 1920– . Russian/American violinist, born in Kremenetz on 21 July 1920. He was taken to the U.S. as a child, studied violin at the San Francisco Conservatory of Music (1928–1931) and made his debut with the San Francisco Symphony Orchestra at age 11. Then he toured Australia and Europe, establishing himself as one of the world's major artists. From 1955 he was part of an important trio, with pianist Eugene Istomin and cellist Leonard Rose. He is also distinguished for his humanitarian activities, and for his successful efforts to save Carnegie Hall from destruction. Stern has reduced his concert schedule in recent years, but still plays more than once a week.

A Columbia artist, Stern has recorded for that label a wide repertoire of solo music, all the major concertos, and chamber works—most notably the Beethoven trios—with Istomin and Rose. Among his fine discs are the Brahms sonatas, and the sonatas of Debussy and Franck, all with Alexander Zakin; the Sibelius, Brahms, and Bartók (first) concertos with the Philadelphia Orchestra; and the Samuel Barber and Bartók (second) concertos with the New York Philharmonic Orchestra. He inscribed the Copland Sonata, with the composer at the piano.

Isaac Stern won five Grammy awards, for discs of 1961, 1962, 1964, 1970, and (his 50th anniversary album) 1981. A CD of the Brahms trios, Schubert trios, and Mendelssohn's first trio was issued by Sony Classical in 1991 (#CD 46425, three discs).

STERNO (label). (I) A British label made for the **British Homophone Co., Ltd.**, by the Gramophone Co., Ltd., some of whose matrices it used—with others specially recorded—in 1926. The disc, named after W. D. Sternberg, founder of British Homophone and the Sterno Manufacturing Co., was 10-inch size; the label was grey, blue, black, and white. The rarity of Sterno discs in Britain suggests that they were exported to countries where the Homochord label and trade mark belonged to others, for these Sternos had equivalent Homochord issues in U.K. No issues have been found later than those of Homochord in December 1926. [Andrews*.]

STERNO (label). (II) A British label manufactured and sold by **British Homophone Co., Ltd.**, from February 1929 to April 1935. There was a 10-inch disc with a red and gold label, and later a 12-inch disc with a magenta label. [Andrews*.]

STEVENS, ERNEST LINWOOD, 1893–1981. American pianist, born in Elizabeth, New Jersey, on 15 Dec 1893. He was performing publicly in high school. In 1919 he made a test recording for Edison, and was engaged as his personal pianist. He tried out new music, and experimented with placement of the piano in recordings. Stevens also made numerous records, as soloist, with his "Recording Orchestra," and with the Ernest L. Stevens Trio, which had a banjo (M. Aron) and saxophone (Charles J. Murray), with various other members (including at one time John Sorin, performing on a Chinese block). Most of his commercial records were made in the experimental studio in West Orange, New Jersey. He retired to private teaching, and had an active studio into the 1980s. Stevens died on 6 Apr 1981, in Montclair, New Jersey.

The first of his Edison Diamond Discs was "Ma!—Medley Fox Trot" (#50929; 1922). Among his other Diamond Discs of interest were the piano solo "All Over Nothing At All" (#50987; 1922), and "Keep on Building Castles in the Air" (#51016; 1922), with the trio. His first disc with the dance orchestra was "Twilight on the Nile" (#51157; 1923). He used pseudonyms on some records, e.g. , Franz Falkenburg and Harry Osborne. The last record by Stevens was "Sun Is at My Window" / "I Loved You Then" (#52526; 1929). [Grable 1979.]

STEVENSON, ELISE, 1878–1967. British soprano, born Alice C. Stevenson in Liverpool, on 9 Feb 1878. She was a church and concert singer, with a brief but very active recording career from 1906 to 1911. Her first record was a duet for Victor with tenor Harry Macdonough, "Cross Your Heart" (1906). Later in the same year she did the same song with bass Frank C. Stanley (#4776). Her first solo record was "Last Rose of Summer" for Victor in June 1906. She made 19 other Victor discs to December 1907. She was also heard in the Victor Trinity Choir and the Victor Light Opera Co.

Stevenson made two duets for Edison cylinders in 1909–1910, with Stanley and Macdonough, and took a part in one record by the Manhattan Mixed Trio (with Irving Gillette [Henry Burr] and Stanley). In that month she did a song with the Schubert Trio. She made some Zonophones, then went to Columbia for her best hits, from February 1907, most of them with Stanley, who was also her manager. Her final successful record was a duet with Henry Burr, "Love is Like a Red Red, Rose" (Columbia #16854; 1911). She then had a baby, and gave up her career for motherhood. She died in South Laguna, California, on 18 Nov 1967.

STEWART, CAL, 1856–1919. American humorist, born in Virginia. He was a favorite recording artist from ca. 1897, beginning with Edison and Berliner, then going to Columbia, Victor, and other labels. He was most famous for his series of monologs and skits about Uncle Josh. The Columbia 14000 series had 32 cylinders about that colorful character (1898–1900),

beginning with "Uncle Josh's Arrival in New York." There were 14 Josh items in the Victor 1902 catalog, and 42 in the Victor 1917 catalog. Edison had 15 records by Stewart in 1898, and 57 by 1912. A special favorite was "Uncle Josh Rides a Bus on Fifth Ave." (Edison #3883; before 1899). Victor records often identified the hero as Uncle Josh Weathersby; but it seems that he was drawn from a creation of Denman Thompson, named Uncle Josh Whitcomb.

Stewart signed an exclusive contract with Columbia in 1903, leading to the rise of imitators on the other labels. By 1906 he had made 37 discs for Columbia; then he was free to return to Victor and Edison in 1907–1908. Edison got an exclusive contract in 1911, but Victor signed Stewart again in 1915, in time for his best seller "Uncle Josh Buys an Automobile." He continued with Edison, making 14 Diamond discs between 1915 and 1924. In his last year, 1919, Stewart was working for Columbia, recording as many as five monologs per day. He died on 7 Dec 1919 in Chicago. A number of his records were not issued until after 1925, on Harmony, Diva, Silvertone, and Velvet Tone labels. [Betz 1976; Brooks 1979; Petty 1976; Walsh 1951/1–4; 1952/5.]

STEWART, REX, 1907–1967. American jazz cornetist, born on 22 Feb 1907 in Philadelphia. He grew up in Washington, and was playing on Potomac riverboats in his teens. In New York during the 1920s he was with Fletcher Henderson, and McKinney's Cotton Pickers. In the mid 1930s he had his own band, then joined Duke Ellington in 1934, remaining to 1945. Later he toured Europe and Australia. Stewart was also a disc jockey and writer on jazz. He died on 7 Sep 1967 in Los Angeles.

His first records were noteworthy, made with a pick-up group before he joined Ellington in 1934: "Stingaree" / "Baby, Ain't You Satisfied?" (Vocalion #2880). Stewart's fine recordings include one of his own composition, "Rexatious" with his Fifty-Second Street Stompers (Variety #517; 1936). With Ellington he made the acclaimed "Boy Meets Horn" (another of his own compositions), on Brunswick #8306; 1938. LP reissues cover all the above titles; the most comprehensive being *Rex Stewart Memorial* (CBS Realm #E-52628).

STEWART, SLAM, 1914– . American jazz string bassist, born Leroy Stewart in Englewood, New Jersey, on 21 Sep 1914. He studied in Boston, and played with various groups there. He was in New York in the 1930s, and teamed with guitarist Slim Gaillard to form Slim and Slam, a novelty/jazz group. Then in the 1940s he performed with Art Tatum, Benny Goodman, and his own trio; and made a fine series of records with Dizzy Gillespie and Charlie Parker. He did important work with Roy Eldridge in the 1950s. During the 1960s he toured Europe. In 1973 he was again with Goodman, in the Rainbow Room, New York.

Slim and Slam had a popular record in "Flat Foot Floogie with a Floy Floy" (Vocalion #4021; 1938). Some of Stewart's finest efforts were heard on the seminal Charlie Parker recordings of 1945, "Hallelujah!" and "Slam Slam Blues" (reissued on Jazztone #J1204), and in Dizzy Gillespie's brilliant "Groovin' High," "Dizzy Atmosphere," and "All the Things You Are" of 1945 (reissued on Savoy #MG 12020).

STEWART PHONOGRAPH CORP. A Chicago firm, established in 1916 at 2815–2853 N. Lincoln Ave. It advertised the Stewart disc player at $6.50, a wind-up table model said to handle any type or make of record. The firm was listed in the 1917 city directory, but did not appear in later directories.

STILLSON (label). An American record, issued briefly in 1923 or 1924 from the Gennett studios; it was part of a projected "personal series." The label name was from the orchestra leader Ray Stillson. Only a few were issued, in 1924. [Kendziora 1960/3; Rust 1978.]

STITT, SONNY, 1924–1982. American jazz saxophonist, born Edward Stitt in Boston, on 2 Feb 1924. He was a Big Band alto saxophone performer in his teens, joining Billy Eckstine in 1945, and the Dizzy Gillespie band in 1946. He led and played with many groups, among them the Miles Davis Quintet. Stitt developed a style drawn from Charlie Parker's, but produced more original material when he took up the tenor saxophone around 1950. Two of his important LP albums were *Sonny Stitt Sits in*

with the Oscar Peterson Trio (Verve #8344; 1959) and *Stitt Plays Bird* (Atlantic #1418; 1963). He died in Washington, D.C., on 22 July 1982.

STOCK, FREDERICK AUGUST, 1872–1942. German/American conductor, born in Jülich on 11 Nov 1872. He studied in Cologne and played violin in the orchestra there, then was invited by Theodore Thomas to join the Thomas Symphony Orchestra (to become the Chicago Symphony Orchestra in 1912) in 1895 as first violist. He was assistant conductor in 1899, and conductor in 1905, remaining in the post until his death. He promoted contemporary composers, instituted children's concerts, created the Chicago Civic Orchestra (a training ensemble for the CSO), and initiated a recording program. Stock became an American citizen in 1919. He died in Chicago on 20 Oct 1942.

Under Stock the CSO was the first major orchestra to make commercial recordings under its regular conductor. Victor recorded the ensemble in New York in May 1916, then in Chicago from 1925, and remained the orchestra's label through the Stock tenure. Interesting items in the 1940 catalog include the J. S. Bach *Suite in B-Minor* and some of Edward MacDowell's *Woodland Sketches* arranged by Stock for orchestra. A low-price black label set of the Mozart 40th Symphony was offered as album G-3 (for $2.50, while Red Seal albums were selling at $3.50).

STOKOWSKI, LEOPOLD, 1882–1977. British/American conductor, born of Polish parents as Antoni Stanislaw Boleslawowich in London on 18 Apr 1882. He played violin, piano, and organ as a child, and was the youngest student ever admitted to the Royal College of Music (1895). He was organist of St. James, Piccadilly, and in 1905 at St. Bartholomew's in New York. Stokowski made his debut as a conductor in Paris in 1908, and was heard by representatives of the Cincinnati Symphony Orchestra who were searching for a new conductor. He directed the Cincinnati Symphony from 1909 to 1912, then went to the Philadelphia Orchestra for 25 years, and international fame. In 1915 he became an American citizen.

Stokowski was renowned for developing the unique sound of the Philadelphia Orchestra, for his energetic promotion of new compositions (he directed more than 2,000 premieres), and for his flamboyant personality. He appeared in the motion picture *One Hundred Men and a Girl* (1940), and was responsible for the music performed in *Fantasia* (1940). His transcriptions of organ works by J.S. Bach helped to shape the baroque revival that blossomed in the late 1940s. After leaving the Philadelphia Orchestra he formed the All/American Youth Orchestra (1940), and conducted the Houston Symphony Orchestra in 1955–1960. He continued conducting in Europe and America, and recording, until the year of his death, which came on 13 Sep 1977 in Nether Wallop, England.

The Victor catalog of 1940 had five pages of Stokowski/Philadelphia Orchestra listings, displaying the major orchestral repertoire from the 18th to the 20th century. Among the jewels in that array are the Rachmaninoff Second Concerto, performed by the composer (album #M-58), the first and fifth symphonies of Shostakovich (#M-192, M-619), Toccata and Fugue in D Minor of Bach, in Stokowski's resonant transcription (#8697), and brilliant excerpts from Wagner operas. Stokowski's 1965 recording of the Symphony No. 4 by Charles Ives won a Grammy award. (See also the recordings cited in the article on the Philadelphia Orchestra.) The Leopold Stokowski Society was established in 1979 in Britain; it has reissued a number of the maestro's recordings under its own label. The latest release is of Sibelius performances, taken from HMV sessions of the 1950s. [Lewis, J. 1977.]

STOLLWERK CHOCOLATE RECORD. A vertical-cut disc issued by Gebrüder Stollwerk AG, a firm that had acquired Edison patents for Germany ca. 1898. Remarkably, the records were made of chocolate, with a foil covering. Other records were also made by Stollwerk, in wax or on a coated, compressed card base. In 1903 the firm produced spring motor disc players.

Storage of recordings. *See* PRESERVATION OF SOUND RECORDINGS.

STRACCIARI, RICCARDO, 1875–1955. Italian baritone, born in Casalecchio on 26 June 1875. He studied in Bologna and made his debut there in 1898, as Marcello. From 1904 to 1906 he was with La Scala; in 1905 he sang at Covent Garden. His Metropolitan Opera debut was as Germont on 1 Dec 1906; he remained through 1908 with the company, then went to Europe and South America. The 1917–1918 season found him in Chicago, after which he sang widely in the U.S. and Europe to 1942. He died in Rome on 10 Oct 1955.

Figaro in *Barbiere* was Stracciari's most famous role, the "Largo al factotum" recorded acoustically for Columbia in America (#49181; ca. 1917) and again in Milan (#D14652) with about 30 other arias ca. 1925. Other outstanding records include "Lo vedremo" and "O dei verd'anni miei" from *Ernani*, among his earliest discs on the Fonotipia label (#69153, #69154; 1910). His very first disc was "Cruda, funesta smania" from *Lucia* (Fonotipia #39058; 1904). Stracciari starred in two complete opera recordings, *Barbiere di Siviglia* (Columbia #14564/79; 1929) and *Rigoletto* (Columbia #GQX 10028/42; 1930). His 78's were made available by all the principal LP reissue labels, and a compact disc of his 1925 Columbia records appeared in 1990 from Preiser (#89003). [Peel 1985.]

STRAKOSCH, MADAME. A mezzo-soprano who recorded for **Bettini.** She had 12 cylinders in his 1898 catalog, including "Swanee River," "Home Sweet Home," and "I Dreamt I Dwelled in Marble Halls." It is not impossible that she was Clara Louise Kellogg, the soprano (1842–1916), who had retired in 1887 and married Karl Strakosch.

Strand Quartet. *See* CRITERION QUARTET.

STREISAND, BARBRA, 1942– . American popular singer and actress, born in New York on 24 Apr 1942; her given name was spelled in the usual Barbara way, but she later dropped an A. She studied acting, and appeared as a singer in Greenwich Village. At age 20 she made her Broadway debut in the musical *I Can Get It for You Wholesale*. National fame arrived with the show *Funny Girl* (1964), and the film of it which earned her an Academy Award in 1968. The cast album won a Grammy. Streisand's hit albums include three named for herself, in 1963 and 1964 (all on Columbia), *People* (Columbia #CL 2215; 1964, with her great hit song "People"—also a Grammy winner), *Color Me Barbra* (Columbia #CL2478; 1966), and *The Way We Were* (Columbia #PC 32801; 1974). Her last great hit album was *Memories* (Columbia #TC 37678; 1983). She has had 36 chart albums in all, and eight Grammy awards.

STRING QUARTET RECORDINGS.

By about 1910 the major problems of recording strings had been solved, and a few record companies formed quartets that performed arrangements. Already in 1905 an ensemble named the Renard Trio and Quartette had recorded a number of pieces. The American String Quartette played "Solitude of the Shepherdess" on Edison cylinder #10100 in 1909; and the Vienna Instrumental Quartet played "In Vienna—Serenade" and "Tin Soldier" for Edison cylinders in 1910–1911 (#10520, #10304).

Mischa Elman and three artists from the Boston Symphony Orchestra played for Victor, as the Elman String Quartet, placing three numbers in the 1917 catalog: the Theme and Variations from Haydn's Emperor Quartet (#74516), and movements from quartets by Mozart and von Dittersdorf. Several other items by this group were added in the 1922 catalog. There was also the Victor String Quartet, offering three Beethoven movements and several other works in the 1917 catalog. The appearance of the **Flonzaley Quartet** on Victor, from 1918, marked the beginning of a new era; this was the first recognized string quartet to record. By 1922 it had 14 numbers in the catalog, most of them movements from the quartet literature.

In the 1920s and 1930s other important ensembles began to record for Victor: the **Busch Quartet**, the Pro Arte Quartet, the Quartetto di Roma, and above all the **Budapest Quartet.** Columbia had the Roth Quartet, the Lener Quartet, and at times the Budapest Quartet. By the end of the 78 era, most of the important repertoire had been recorded.

STROBOSCOPIC DISC. A special record or printed disc used to check the speed of a turntable. Radial lines on the disc appear to be stationary if the turntable is rotating at true speed. Some commercial discs carrying normal programming have also served as stroboscopics, via an edge marking to assist in turntable speed adjustment; W.D. Sternberg used this device on records issued by British Homophone Co. in 1930 (4 in 1, Plaza, and Sterno labels). The British label Great Scott had strobe marks on the edges of 1934 releases. Decca had a similar marking on certain 1938 discs, and DGG had an edge pattern used, even on LPs, into the mid-1960s.

STROH, JOHN MATTHIAS AUGUSTUS, 1828–1914. German inventor, born in Frankfurt-am-Main. A British Post Office employee, he made a cylinder phonograph for the chief engineer of the General Post Office and demonstrated it to the Royal Institution on 1 Feb 1878. He then designed various improvements to steady the cylinder movement with counterweights and a clockwork train. His most renowned invention was the **Stroh violin.** His son Charles was an industry executive, a director with the Russell Hunting Record Co., Ltd., and a manufacturer of the Stroh violin.

STROH VIOLIN. The instrument invented by **John Matthias Augustus Stroh** for use in acoustic recording, and used widely by the industry for about 10 years from 1904. His son Charles was the first manufacturer. It had the strings of a violin, but instead of a soundbox it had a diaphragm and metal trumpet; these changes presented an amplified, if rather artificial, sound to the recording horn. The first commercial record on which a Stroh violin is heard was Victor #2828, **Charles d'Almaine** performing "Military Serenade" (23 Apr 1904); the instrument was identified as a "viol-horn." In *TMW* for 1909 there were various advertisements by George Evans, 4 Albany St., Regents Park, London, claiming to be the sole maker of the Stroh violin, as successors to Charles Stroh. [Hoover 1971 has a clear illustration.]

STRONG (label). An American record issued by the Strong Record Co., Inc., 206 Fifth Ave.,

New York, in just a few issues during 1923. The records was advertised as flexible, unbreakable, non-chippable and non-warping. Material was popular and blues. The firm also offered to make records for clients. Adolf Hawerlander was president of Strong, with Henry Glaue the products manager and A. Lawrence—formerly with Edison—the recorder at the laboratory. Abe Schwartz was the musical director. In December 1923 it was reported that the company had applied for receivership. There was a reorganization and a plan to pay off the creditors, but further information is lacking. [Andrews*.]

STUMPF, CARL, 1848–1936. German psychologist, born in Wiesentheid on 21 Apr 1848. He earned a doctorate in 1870, and was a professor at Würzburg in 1873. Later he taught in Prague, Halle, and Munich. In 1893 he established the Psychological Institute at the University of Berlin for research into musical perception. He was also interested in the music of other cultures, which led him to make a cylinder recording of the court orchestra of Siam, as they visited Berlin in 1900. He deposited this and other records in the **Berlin Phonogramm-Archiv**, established by him in 1905. He died in Berlin on 25 Dec 1936.

STYLUS. The jewel or metallic element or **needle** in a **cartridge** that tracks the record groove; it is attached by a stylus shank to the magnet in the cartridge. The term needle was applied to this element through the 78 era, when steel needles were the norm. There were sapphire needles and diamond needles, as well as fibers and alloys; they were spherical or conical. The microgroove LP record (1948) required a lightweight tracking device, leading to the various kinds of cartridge and their stylus tips. To avoid surface noise from the groove bottom, styli were often truncated.

Stylus types in use at the end of the LP era (late 1980s) were spherical (conical), suitable to early LP records; elliptical, used with later lighter tone arms; hyper-elliptical, with a wider and thinner contact area to improve high-frequency response; and micro-ridge, with the smallest contact area. Diamond styli (1,000+ hours of playing time) were common, with tips almost invisible to the naked eye. Sapphire tips (about 40 hours of playing time) were a second choice; other materials included tungsten carbide, osmium, and various alloys.

The standard dimensions of styli used on LPs were 0.001 inches (0.6 millimeters) radius and 40–50 degrees included angle. With a 90-degree groove angle, such a tip had an effective radius at the point of contact of 0.0007 inches. Despite close similarity in dimensions, actual standardization of LP styli never occurred. Every manufacturer had slight modifications that made replacement of worn styli a matter of finding specific type numbers in a cross reference list bearing hundreds of types. [Blacker 1978.]

SUBCODE. Data encoded on a compact disc with miscellaneous inaudible information, e.g., track numbers, copyright, copy inhibit codes.

SUN (label). (I) An American record issued ca. 1907 by **Leeds & Catlin.**

SUN (label). (II) A record issued from 1953 to 1959 by Sun Record Co., Inc., 706 Union Ave., Memphis, Tennessee.. It was a cradle of the rockabilly style, and was first to record Johnny Cash and Elvis Presley.

SUNRISE (label). (I) An American record produced by **Grey Gull Record Co.** ca. 1929; it had a subtitle "The Record of Today." It offered dance music and popular vocals, with some jazz numbers.

SUNRISE (label). (II) A low-priced RCA record issued in 1933–1934. Material duplicated that of Bluebird, and the price was the same for both labels, $.35. [Rust 1978.]

SUNSET RECORD (label). An American record issued by an unidentified company in California between 1924 and 1926. California artists were featured. [Rust 1978.]

SUNSHINE (label). (I) A paste-over title added to six sides of Nordskog records in 1922 for performances by Kid Ory's Jazz Band. The group was identified as Spike's Seven Pods of Pepper Orchestra. "Ory's Creole Trombone" and "Society Blues" were the principal numbers; they were among the first jazz records cut by Black artists. [Rust 1978.]

SUNSHINE (label).(II) A record issued by the Sunshine Phonograph and Record Co., St. Petersburg, Florida, in early 1925. Masters came from Okeh. [Kendziora 1987/6.]

SUPERIOR (label). A record made by the **Starr Piano Co.** from December 1930 to June 1932. There were 339 issues, drawing on Gennett material. Vernon Dalhart and Carson Robison were among the better known artists. [Kay 1961; Rust 1978.]

SUPERTONE (label). (I) A record issued by Brunswick in 1930–1931, using Brunswick masters.

SUPERTONE (label). (II) Four slightly different labels issued by the Straus and Schram store, Chicago. Material came from Pathé, Grey Gull, Columbia, and Paramount.

SUPERTONE (label). (III) Two similar labels sold by Sears, Roebuck and Co. by mail order in the 1920s. The first had material from Olympic and Paramount; it was on sale in 1924. The second had material from Gennett, and was sold from 1928 to 1930. [Kendziora 1967/1; Rust 1978.]

SUPERTONE TALKING MACHINE CO. A New York firm, established in 1916 at 8 W. 20th St. It sold the Supertone line of disc players, in three models, ranging from $15 to $100. A report of February 1921 stated that the company was to be reorganized by its creditors.

SUPERVIA, CONCHITA, 1895–1936. Spanish soprano and mezzo-soprano, born in Barcelona on 9 Dec 1895. She studied in Barcelona, then travelled to South America and made her debut at the Teatro Colón in Buenos Aires on 1 Oct 1910. She sang in Italy, Havana (1914), Chicago (1915–1916), and from 1924 at La Scala. She died after childbirth in London on 30 Mar 1936.

Supervia was a famous Carmen, Rosina, Mignon, and Musetta; she excelled in roles that brought out her vivacious and elegant style. To many hearers that style was marred by an excessive vibrato. She began recording in 1927, for Fonotipia in Italy, Odeon in Spain, and Parlophone in Spain, singing airs from *Italiana in Algeri* as well as her Carmen and Rosina specialties. Those were her labels through her brief recording career, which ceased in 1934. The outstanding numbers were "Una voce poco fa" (Parlophone #R20074; 1929), several *Carmen* pieces also on Parlophone, made in 1931 and 1934, "Connais-tu le pays" (Parlophone #20192; 1930), and Musetta's Waltz (Parlophone #20180; 1932). There were LP versions by all the microgroove reissue labels. Three CDs appeared in 1990, one each from EMI, Preiser, and Club 99; among them they comprise the essential Supervia collection. [Barnes, H. 1951.]

SUPRAPHON (label). A Czech record, issued from the 1950s. In 1991 the American distributor was Koch International.

SUPREME (label). An American record issued in the late 1920s, one of the low-priced Grey Gull affiliates. Material was dance music and popular vocals. [Rust 1978.]

SUPREMES. A female popular vocal trio established in 1964 by **Diana Ross**; the other members were Florence Ballard (replaced in 1967 by Cindy Birdsong) and Mary Wilson. The group sang in the new **soul music** style for Motown records, achieving great success and making 18 chart albums by 1976. *Where Did Our Love Go* (Motown #MM 621; 1964) was the most acclaimed, on the charts for about a year. When Ross left in 1970, the Supremes lost their edge and began to decline in popularity.

SURFACE NOISE. The unwanted sound heard in playback of 78 rpm discs, and to a lesser extent in playback of LPs, sometimes caused by mistakes in cutting, mastering, and plating; but especially by abrasives in the shellac compound, and by wear in the grooves and/or playback needle or stylus. Some surface noise can be suppressed as original records are transferred, by means of equalizer and dynamic static filters. *See also* PACKBURN AUDIO NOISE SUPPRESSOR; SONIC RESTORATION OF HISTORIC RECORDINGS.

SURFACE SPEED. In contrast to turntable speed, this is a measure of the velocity of the stylus as it moves through the groove of a disc record. The velocity increases as the groove diameter diminishes toward the center of the record. It was this factor that influenced Thomas Edison to hold to the cylinder record, where surface speed is constant. Charles Tainter applied for a patent in 1887 for a device that maintained uniform surface speed on discs, but he did not follow it with commercial production. Discs issued in the U.K. in 1922–1924, by the **World Record Co.**, played at constant surface speed; this was achieved by a record controller device, one that was made available for standard gramophones by Noel Pemberton Billing (British patents #195,673 and 204,728). *See also* DISC, 4; SPEEDS; and TURNTABLE.

SURROUND SOUND. An improved reincarnation of the **quadraphonic recording** concept, and of the approach taken in the film *Fantasia* (1940). It was introduced in the 1980s, based on the Dolby Surround system. This system uses four to six loudspeakers, operated by several amplifiers, the whole assemblage driven by a computer decoder that analyzes the input signals and steers the output to the correct location of the listening environment. The four channels of sound are front, center, rear, and surround. In 1990 surround sound was available through major manufacturers like Yamaha, Lexicon, and Toshiba, in the high-end price range (Shure Brothers complete HTS Reference System sold for $9,600). Simulated spatial environments are a by-product of surround sound: Toshiba, for example, offered sound modes such as "cathedral" and "space fantasy."

SUTHERLAND, JOAN, *Dame*, 1926– . Australian soprano, born in Sydney on 7 Nov 1926. She made her debut in a concert performance of *Dido and Aeneas* in Sydney in 1947. She went to London in 1951, and appeared at Covent Garden, gaining great praise for her performance as Lucia in 1959. Sutherland sang Lucia at the Metropolitan Opera on 26 Nov 1961, and achieved renown for her coloratura, lyric, dramatic and Wagnerian roles. In 1978 she was made a Dame Commander of the British Empire.

Sutherland's recordings span the repertoire. She is featured in complete operas by Bellini, Bizet, Donizetti, Gounod, Meyerbeer, Mozart, Offenbach, Puccini, Rossini, Thomas, Verdi, and Wagner. Her album *Art of the Prima Donna* (London #1214; 1961) won a Grammy as best classical vocal disc.

SWARF. In the recording process, the material cut or scraped from the surface of a record by the cutting stylus. *See also* CHIP.

SWINGER. A disc record whose spindle hole is not at the geometric center of the disc circle. In playback a wobbling of pitch results. The same result may occur if a spindle is undersized, allowing loose movement of the disc around it.

SWINGLE SINGERS. A French popular vocal group, greatly successful in the 1960s with swinging arrangements of baroque and other classical compositions. They produced the instrumental lines vocally—with varying degrees of pitch accuracy—and added jazz bass and percussion. The eight members were brought together in Paris in 1962 by Ward Lemar Swingle and Christiane Legrande. They won a Grammy as best new artists of 1963, and for their album of that year, *Bach's Greatest Hits* (Philips #PHM 200-097), which was on the charts 35 weeks. There were three other Grammys, for *Going Baroque* (Philips #PHM 200-133; 1964), *Anyone for Mozart* (Philips #PHM 200-149; 1965), and for a rendition of Luciano Berio's *Sinfonia* in 1969. The group disbanded in 1973.

SYLVA, GERTRUDE. A soprano who sang for **Bettini** cylinders; she had 15 solo arias and songs in the 1897 catalog, plus four numbers with flute and piano; and 13 solos in the 1898 catalog, plus four others with flute. "The Last

Rose of Summer" had an accompaniment of piano, violin, and flute.

SYMPHONIC PHONE-NEEDLE CO. A New York firm that advertised in *TMW* during 1906 from a location at 1907 Park Ave. It marketed the Symphonic needle, said to play 500–800 times.

SYMPHONOLA. A **coin-op** produced by Seeburg in the mid 1930s. It operated with a single turntable, which moved to play up to 20 different records.

SYMPHONOLA (label). An American record distributed by the Larkin Co. department store in Buffalo, New York, ca. 1919–1920. Matrices were from Emerson and Pathé. Most of the output consisted of popular vocal and dance numbers, but there were some sides by Tito Schipa and soprano Yvonne Gall. [Kendziora 1989/9; Rust 1978.]

SYMPOSIUM RECORDS. A British firm, located at 110 Derwent Ave., East Barnet, Hertfordshire. It offers important compact disc reissues of historical material. A 1991 list included the complete early recordings by Jan Kubelik, and another of Arthur Nikisch.

SYNCHROPHONE, LTD. A British firm (23 Berners St., London) that made in 1931 a combination gramophone, radio, and motion picture projector, sold as the Synchrophone. Hans Knudsen, inventor of the machine, had tried to promote it through an earlier firm, Synchrophone Co., Ltd. (1919–1928). Twelve-inch records, with the label name Synchrophone Record, were produced to give sound to the silent films projected. The user was required to start the record and film at the same time, guided by appropriate markings. The company was in liquidation in October 1935. Arthur Woollacott bought the business on 3 Jan 1936 and set up the Synchrophone (1936) Co. It was the earliest label to have a female as recording expert, Ursula Greville. [Andrews*; *TMR* #46 (June 1977) presented an extended advertisement of the firm, from which some of the above text has been drawn.]

SYRACUSE AUDIO ARCHIVES. A library of sound recordings and text documentation, part of Syracuse University, Syracuse, New York. It is officially the Belfer Audio Library and Archive. A major collection, it participated in the **Rigler and Deutsch** project to list all known 78 rpm records.

SZELL, GEORGE, 1897–1970. Hungarian/American conductor and pianist, born in Budapest on 7 June 1897. He grew up in Vienna, studied piano and composition there, and made his debut in a concert of his own music at age 11. Five years later he conducted the Vienna Symphony Orchestra; then the Berlin Philharmonic Orchestra. In 1915 he was engaged by Richard Strauss to conduct at the Berlin Staatsoper, and was soon in demand as a conductor of opera and symphony throughout Europe. His American debut was in St. Louis on 24 Jan 1930. From 1942 to 1946 he conducted at the Metropolitan Opera; in 1946 he became an American citizen. In 1946 he was appointed music director of the Cleveland Orchestra, remaining in that post until his death, which came on 29 July 1970.

Under Szell the Cleveland Orchestra, with a remarkable sound balance that was often likened to chamber music, came to be regarded as one of the world's greatest ensembles, touring Europe and the Far East. Szell specialized in the Austro-German composers, with relatively little attention to contemporaries other than Bartók. Szell and the Cleveland Orchestra recorded for CBS, Epic, and Angel. The clarity of the orchestra's sound is heard to advantage in the Mozart symphonies, of which numbers 35, 39, 40, and 41 were grouped in Columbia album #MG 30368, and in Mozart's "Eine kleine Nachtmusik" (Columbia #MS 7273). Among their outstanding collaborative discs were Mozart Concertos 21 and 24 with Robert Casadesus (Columbia # MS 6695; 1965), the Brahms Violin Concerto with David Oistrakh (Angel #32096; 1970), and the Brahms Double Concerto with Oistrakh and Mstislav Rostropovich (Angel #36032; 1970). CD reissues appeared in 1991 from Sony, covering Haydn (#46332) and Mozart (#46333) material.

SZIGETI, JOSEPH, 1892–1973. Hungarian/American violinist, born in Budapest on 19 Feb 1892. He studied with Jenö Hubay, and performed in public in 1905. He made his London debut in 1907 and remained in Britain until 1913. He was in Geneva to 1924, toured in Europe, and appeared in Philadelphia in 1925. World concert tours followed. Szigeti's friendship with Bartók led to his performance, with Benny Goodman (who commissioned the work) and the composer, of the first hearing of "Contrasts" in Carnegie Hall, 1940 (Columbia #70362/3, set #X-178). He settled in the U.S. and became a citizen in 1951. After 1960 he was less active, living mostly in Switzerland.

Szigeti's repertoire was extensive, but he was most renowned for his performances of J.S. Bach's unaccompanied sonatas and partitas; and for his reading of the Beethoven Concerto. His first recording was for the Gramophone Co. in 1908. He did the Prelude from Bach's sixth sonata (#07911), "Zéphire" by Hubay (#07913), and Anton Rubinstein's "Romance" (#07914). In 1926 he became a Columbia exclusive artist, doing the Bach solo works from 1928 to 1932, and the Brahms third sonata with Egon Petri in 1938, among other fine interpretations that were all reissued on two compact discs by Biddulph in 1990 (#LAB 005/06). His pianist partners in the Beethoven sonatas included Claudio Arrau, Béla Bartók, and Artur Schnabel. Stern did the Beethoven Concerto with Bruno Walter in 1932 (Columbia set #M-177).

T

TAFT, WILLIAM HOWARD, 1857–1930.
Twenty-seventh president of the United States
(term of office 1909–1913). He is the earliest
president whose voice is known to be preserved on record, beginning with campaign
speeches of August 1908. *See also* PRESIDENTS
ON RECORD.

TAGLIAVINI, FERRUCCIO, 1913– . Italian
tenor, born in Reggio nell' Emilia on 14 Aug
1913. He made his debut as Rodolfo in Florence
in 1938, and soon gained recognition as one of
the leading interpreters of the lyric repertoire.
On 10 Jan 1947 he made his Metropolitan Opera debut as Rodolfo, and remained to 1954,
returning in 1961–1962. Rossini, Bellini, and
Donizetti roles were his specialties. He also
sang successfully in concert, applying his bel
canto to Italian and French songs. Tagliavini's
most popular recording was the complete *Lucia*,
with Maria Callas (HMV #5166; 1960) He retired in 1965.

TAINTER, CHARLES SUMNER, 1854–1940.
British instrument maker and inventor. In 1879
he began working with Alexander Graham
Bell in a research facility in Washington, D.C.,
and in 1881 he was invited by Bell to join him
and with **Chichester Bell** in the formation of
the Volta Laboratory Association. The purpose
of Volta was to carry out acoustical and electrical research. Tainter was probably responsible
for the emphasis on developing a talking machine that would improve on Edison's tinfoil
phonograph. He applied the principle of engraving into wax as early as 1881, and created
a demonstration cylinder that was sealed in the

Smithsonian Institution; the record—presenting the voice of **Alexander Graham Bell**—was
apparently played for the first time in public, at
the Smithsonian, in 1937; documentation of the
event is not positive. Tainter eventually filed
on 27 June 1885 a patent application (U.S. #
341,214; granted 4 May 1886) for his method of
"recording and reproducing speech and other
sounds." His application specified that the recording surface was solid beeswax and paraffin, and that the signal vibrations were inscribed vertically (hill and dale); but the word
cylinder did not appear. Another patent application, for a machine with a removable wax-
coated cardboard cylinder, was filed on 4 Dec
1885 (U.S. patent #341,288; granted 4 May 1886).
The instrument he developed came to be called
the **graphophone**, giving its name to the new
organization established in 1886 by him and
the Bells: **Volta Graphophone Co.**

Tainter's notebooks show diverse experimentation. He worked on a variable-speed
turntable to derive constant **surface speed** in
disc recording on lateral-cut records, and on a
wax paper strip medium. On 7 July 1887 he
filed for a U.S. patent on a foot-treadle
graphophone that turned the cylinder at 200
rpm (#375,579; granted 27 Dec 1887); it used a
wax-coated cardboard cylinder, six by 1 and 5/
16 inches. Although the treadle feature (an
adaptation of the Howe sewing machine) did
not succeed commercially with the graphophone, it was used later in **shavers**. A **coin-op**
graphophone was developed and patented in
time for exhibition at the World's Columbian
Exposition, Chicago, 1893 (U.S. #506,348; filed
27 Apr 1893; granted 10 Oct 1893); it became

the Columbia Graphophone Type AS (1897; *see* COLUMBIA RECORD PLAYERS). Tainter received a total of 25 U.S. patents in the phonograph field.

TAKE. The name given to the smallest identifiable unit of a recording **session**. In the early period of recording, before the use of magnetic tape to receive the original impression of the signal, a take necessarily included an entire presentation: a song, instrumental composition or discrete movement of a large composition, literary reading, etc. With modern technology, a take may include a minute portion of a presentation, and many takes of the same portion may be made. The best takes are then edited into a satisfactory whole version of the signal presentation, and used to make the negative master. (*See* DISC, 1.) Takes that are not used to make masters are called out-takes.

Record manufacturers sometimes give identification numbers to takes, possibly as parts of matrix numbers. Out-takes are sometimes preserved, and may be used later to make pressings when it is desired to have complete documentation of a performer's work. *See also* RECORDING PRACTICE.

TALKER. A talking machine (phonograph or gramophone). The terms was widely used in dealer and trade-press jargon during the early years of the industry.

TALKING BOOK. The name given to the recorded version of a book. Originally talking books were discs made for blind persons. They appeared in Britain in 1934, made by Decca and EMI for the National Institute for the Blind, using slows speeds, such as 24 rpm. Talking books are circulated in the U.S. by the Library of Congress through a network of local libraries. Cassette tapes replaced the discs in the 1960s, and a wider audience was identified as cassette players became common in automobiles. By the 1980s a large repertoire of fiction and non-fiction works was available on cassette. In most cases long books are abridged on record, but some firms specialize in complete texts. Readings are done by actors who sometimes dramatize fiction material by using different voices for the characters; and many talking books have sound effects and/or background music, simulating radio dramas. "Bookcassettes" marketed by the Brilliance Corp., Grand Haven, Michigan, do not have sound effects or music; they use digital speech compression to achieve a quick reading speed, and use four tracks of a stereo cassette to increase the capacity of their monophonic recordings. The firm Books on Tape, of Newport Beach, California, advertises itself as having the "world's largest selection of audio books." *See also* LITERARY RECORDINGS.

TALKING DOLLS. This medium was the earliest format for entertainment records. Thomas Edison's U.S. patent #423,039 (filed 2 July 1889; granted 11 Mar 1890) was for a doll with a cylinder record. The Edison talking doll was shown at the Paris Universal Exposition of 1889, and first sold to the public in April 1890, in New York. The doll was not a commercial success, with only about 500 eventually sold, at $10–$25, and many returned by unsatisfied buyers. Twelve pre-recorded records were available. (*See* EDISON PHONOGRAPH TOY MANUFACTURING CO.)

Emile Berliner's 1889 doll used a disc record; it was also unsuccessful. Maison Jumeau, established 1842, was the most famous dollmaker. The firm produced dolls for a world market, with the most exotic creations emanating from the 1860s through the 1890s, a "golden age" of French dollmaking. The dolls were called Poupées (lady-types) and Bébés (child-types). A successful line of the Bébés (at 38 francs), offered in 1896, was fitted with a talking mechanism made by Henri Lioret. [Koenigsberg 1990; Marty 1979 shows three Bébés on p. 74.]

TALKING MACHINE. The generic term for the phonograph, and later for the gramophone, as used in the trade literature and in company names from the early days of the industry into the 1920s. This designation was sometimes abbreviated to "talker."

Talking Machine Co. *See* CHICAGO TALKING MACHINE CO.

TALKING MACHINE JOBBERS' NATIONAL ASSOCIATION. A trade organization formed in September 1907, through a merger of the Eastern and Central States associations. In 1908 the name was changed to the National Association of Talking Machine Jobbers.

TALK-O-PHONE. A disc record player (sometimes spelled "Talkaphone") marketed in Britain by the Talkophone Syndicate (established July 1903 in London), and in the U.S. by the Talk-o-Phone Co. of 35 Bond St., Toledo, Ohio (established 1904). By January 1905 the headquarters was in New York City, and there were branches in Chicago and San Francisco. A. L. Irish was president and treasurer, C. G. Metzger was vice-president, and R. A. Fuller and O. C. Reed were directors.

The price of the American product, shown in an advertisement of 1905 or 1906, was $18–$50 for various models. There were also Talk-o-phone disc records sold in America. Leeds was a label name used. It was claimed that the Toledo firm sold more than 25,000 of the record players in its first year, its factory working double shifts to meet the demand. The Chicago branch moved to larger premises in Steinway Hall on Van Buren St. Talk-o-phone machines were used as premiums in promotional campaigns of the Los Angeles Record and the San Francisco Call newspapers.

In fall 1905 litigation ensued, as the Victor Talking Machine Co. alleged infringement of its Berliner patent for the groove-driven reproducer. Then the Toledo works brought out, in November 1905, a new machine which fed the tone arm across the disc by a mechanical feed device beneath the turntable. Reports of great success for the new record player—selling for $1 to $5—appeared in January 1906.

Nevertheless the company was reorganized in August 1906, as new capital entered the business; a firm called the Atlantic Phonograph Co. emerged in New York, apparently the heir to the Talk-o-phone products. [Andrews*; Andrews 1984/13.]

TALK-O-PHOTO (label). A single-sided six-inch record issued by the Talking Photo Corp. of 334 Fifth Ave., New York, in 1919–1920. The discs featured photographs of the recording artists (in the known issues, all were movie stars) on one side and performances by them on the other. Emerson cut the masters. Items listed by Blacker appear to be spoken material, for example "How to Become a Star" by David Powell; "My Real Self," by Mae Murray; and "Happiness" by Gloria Swanson. There were 91 records in the series, but only 16 have been identified and just three have been seen and discussed in the literature. Robert B. "Patti" Wheelan was president of Talking Photo Corp. in 1920. [Blacker 1990.]

TALLY, HARRY, 1866–1939. American tenor, born in Memphis, Tennessee, on 30 June 1866. The name was also spelled Talley. He was a vaudeville performer, featured on the Orpheum circuit for 25 years.

Tally began recording in 1902 for Columbia, going unidentified on early issues, and remained with the label to 1911. A popular item was the **coon song** "Love Me, Phoebe" (#203). He made three Edison cylinders in 1903–1904: "My Little Coney Isle" (#8483; 1903), "There's Music in the Air" (#8518; 1903), and "Seminole," (#8808; 1904), which appeared later on a Victor disc. His early cylinders were not successful, but he returned to make five popular Edison Diamond Discs, all duets with Harry Mayo; the finest were "At the Ball, That's All" (#50238; 1915) and "Piney Ridge" (#50315; 1915). Tally appeared in Edison **tone tests,** singing along with these discs. He was also heard on some Zonophone records of 1905.

The first three of his 38 Victor records were made on 1 July 1904. They were "Mandy, Won't You Let Me Be Your Beau?" (#2936), "Seminole" (#2937), and "If I Were Only You" (#2938). On 26 July 1907 Tally made his last Victor disc, "Take Me Back to New York Town" (#5230). His popularity was ending by 1917, when there were only two items in the Victor catalog; by 1922 he was not to be found there.

TAMAGNO, FRANCESCO, 1850–1905. Italian tenor, born in Turin on 28 Dec 1850. He worked as a baker, and as a locksmith, but also studied at the Turin Conservatory and in 1873 sang in an opera in the Teatro Regio. Rapid success came to him. He performed in several houses and was at La Scala in 1877; he then earned international acclaim in Europe and South America. *Aida, Don Carlo,* and *L'africaine* were among his greatest triumphs. In 1887 he created the role of Otello, and took it—with the other Verdi operas—to the stages of the world. He last performed in Naples in 1904, and died in Varese on 31 Aug 1905.

Tamagno was signed by G & T in 1903, with the first royalty contract in the industry (10% of retail sales, and a £2,000 advance, equivalent of $10,000 at that time). He made 19 records, five in the new 12-inch size. His red label discs cost £1 each (or $5.00 for the American Red Seals) while regular red labels were selling for half that, 10 shillings. Among the most admired of Tamagno's records were the *Otello* death scene (HMV #DS-100) and other numbers from that opera, "Di quella pira" (HMV #52670; 1903), and "Muto asil" from *Guillaume Tell* (HMV #052103; 1905). The 12-inch HMV records of 1904–1905 are considered superior to the 1903 10-inch discs, but Victor released only the 10-inch material in the U.S. All five were carried into the 1922 catalog, but none survived to 1927. Reissues appeared on all the major LP reissue labels. [Favia-Artsay 1952; Moran 1977/6.]

TANGENTIAL TONE ARM. Also called a linear tracking arm. A type of **tone arm** that moves straight across a disc record along the disc's radius, rather than in an arc. It is designed to eliminate **skating** and **horizontal tracking error.**

TAPE. In common audio terminology, a strip of thin plastic, coated with iron oxide or similar substance, that may be magnetized to record sounds. (*See also* NON-MAGNETIC TAPE.) Through the 1950s tapes had an acetate base, and tended to become brittle with age and to break easily. More recent tapes have a polyester base, such as mylar; they do not grow brittle, though their elasticity may be a problem (better tapes are pretensilized to overcome this).

The widely used iron oxide coating was improved upon by Dupont in the late 1960s with the development of chromium dioxide coatings. Better response at high recording levels was achieved in 1978 as 3M introduced pure metal particle (non-oxide iron) tape. For nomenclature of current tape types *see* CASSETTE.

Tape thickness is 1.5 or 1.0 mils (38 or 25.4 micrometers) for the **open-reel** variety; 0.47 or 0.31 mils for cassette type.

See also MAGNETIC RECORDING; PRESERVATION OF SOUND RECORDINGS; TAPE DECK; TAPE RECORDER; TAPE RECORDING.

TAPE DECK. The mechanical element of a **tape recorder,** including its motors, reels, linkages, recording head, erase head, and playback head; but not including the electronic components and electric circuits. It is also known as a tape transport. A deck must be connected to an amplifier in order to drive a loudspeaker. The use of separate tape decks arose in the high fidelity period (1950s), when users began to demand distinct components in the audio system. A tape deck may accommodate open-reel tapes or cassette tapes.

A conventional grading of tape decks assigns them to one of three categories: professional, semiprofessional or audiophile, and consumer. Libraries use good consumer-grade decks, while sound archives use only professional or semiprofessional grade. There is no significant difference in performance between the two better grades, but the professional grade is more rugged and reliable. Among the makers of professional-grade tape decks marketed in America are Ampex, 3M, Scully, Crown, and Studer. Widely used semiprofessional decks come from Revox, Tandberg, Sony, and TEAC. Sony and TEAC are also major producers of consumer-grade decks.

Refinements in the basic mechanism were offered by various firms. Ampex developed an automatic threader for open-reel tapes. Bell and Howell marketed a "tape inhaler" that pulled the tape to the take-up reel with a vacuum. Sony marketed at one time a tape changer for four open-reel tapes, with a total playing time of 60 hours. [Klinger*.]

TAPE GUIDES. In a tape deck, the rollers or posts that keep the tape in proper position as it moves across the heads.

TAPE LEADER. The section of a tape that precedes the part with the program material. It may be magnetic, carrying technical signals and production information. Or it may be a plain paper or plastic attachment to the magnetized tape, intended merely to aid in the affixing of the tape end to the take-up reel, and to protect the recorded portion in storage.

TAPE PACK. The name given to the fully wound tape on its reel, or to the portion of tape that is wound on the reel.

TAPE RECORDER. A machine that converts audio (or video) signals into magnetic variations on a tape, and is usually able to reproduce the recorded signals. It includes all necessary mechanical, electrical, and electronic components. A tape recorder can also be used to record computer data, readings from scientific instruments, signals that activate other machines, etc. See also ALIGNMENT; MAGNETIC RECORDING; TAPE DECK; TAPE RECORDING.

TAPE RECORDING. Although it could be applied to audio recording on **non-magnetic tape**, the term is used today only to describe **magnetic recording** on plastic tapes (acetate, mylar, etc.) that are coated with particles suitable for magnetization. The process typically involves a **microphone** to convert sound vibrations into electrical impulses, an **amplifier** to strengthen them, and a **recording head** to induce these signals onto the plastic **tape** by magnetizing the particles in the tape coating in corresponding patterns. As current flows through the recording head it establishes a magnetic field around a minute gap in the electromagnet; the magnetic field acts on the segment of the tape passing the recording head. In playback, the magnetic patterns generate electric signals in the **playback head**; these are enhanced by the amplifier, then converted by **loudspeakers** into a replica of the original sound signals.

Tape recording may operate by either an analog or a digital process.   In **analog recording**, the magnetic particles are magnetized in a continuum of magnetic strengths that correspond to the levels of the input sound signals. The wave forms of the original sound are represented in the magnetic medium in a way that mimics their form. In **digital recording**, electrical signals from the microphone are converted to a quantized numerical code for storage on the tape; the tape then carries a representation of the input signal, but does not mimic its form. This digital technology is also used in making compact discs. An important difference between analog and digital recording is that there is virtually no loss in signal fidelity in successive generations of digitally-made tape copies.

Whether analog or digital, the tape recording process usually requires two reels for the tape; one is the supply reel on which the tape is stored, and the other the take-up reel that receives the tape as it moves past the heads. (Endless loop cassettes and eight-track cartridges have just one reel.) The tape is set in motion by the **capstan**, which is rotated by a motor; often the same motor also turns the take-up reel, so that the tape is wound smoothly on the reel. Before it reaches the take-up reel, the tape passes the heads of the machine. In recording, it is the recording head that is activated: it magnetizes the particles. In playback, the playback head is activated: it reads the magnetic patterns back into electrical pulses. The **erase head** is used to neutralize any previous recording on a tape before the tape reaches the recording head, or just to create a blank tape. In consumer-grade **tape decks** the heads may be combined into one device, but in professional and semiprofessional-grade tape decks the heads are separate.

Recording takes place at different tape speeds for different purposes (*see* TAPE SPEED). There are also different widths of magnetic tape in use, most commonly 1/4 inch. Wider tapes are used in multitrack studio recording, as the tapes must carry much more than a few tracks of signal information. Two-inch-wide tapes can carry up to 24 tracks.

Tape recording has been widely used since the 1950s in studio recording (*see* RECORDING PRACTICE) and in radio broadcasting. **Stereophonic recording** has been the norm since the mid-1950s. **Noise reduction systems,** and the development of chromium dioxide and other metallic tape coatings have led to great improvements in tape recording performance. The **cassette** revolutionized tape recording in the 1960s, and **DAT** is poised to create another industry transformation in the 1990s. [Klinger*; McWilliams, A. 1964.] *See also* DISC, 6, for historical aspects of the tape recording industry.

TAPE SPEED. The rate of tape motion, usually stated in inches per second (IPS), of a **magnetic tape** as it passes the recording or playback head of a **tape recorder** or **tape deck**. In the U.S., professional tape speeds have been 30 IPS and 15 IPS. Consumer recording has been at 7 1/2 IPS or 3 3/4 IPS, although 1 7/8 IPS and the higher speeds are sometimes available. In the Philips audiocassette the tape travels at 1 7/8 IPS. Microcassette recorders use a speed of 15/16 IPS.

Tape transport. *See* TAPE DECK.

TATE, ALFRED O. An associate of Thomas Edison. He was Edison's personal representative at the convention of the National Phonograph Association in 1893. Tate served as secretary of the **Edison Phonograph Works** and the Edison Manufacturing Co. In 1887 he became Edison's private secretary. He emerged as a dissident within the Edison circle, and provided his employer with crucial misinformation in the 1888 controversy involving **Ezra Gilliland**; as a result he came between Edison and his trusted colleague **Charles Batchelor.** [Welch 1972.]

TATUM, ART, 1910–1956. American jazz pianist, born Arthur Tatum on 13 Oct 1910 in Toledo, Ohio. He was blind in one eye, and only partly sighted in the other, so he learned music from braille notation. At age 16 he was playing in local clubs, and by 1922 he was in New York, a great success on radio, developing a perfect stride style which he mingled with torrents of notes from his right hand. Tatum was a sensation in New York in 1937 and Britain in 1938. In 1943 he formed a trio with Tiny Grimes, guitar, and Slam Stewart, bass; but he was essentially a soloist, one who did not change with style movements in jazz. His prodigious technique prompted many crit-

ics to compare him with the great virtuoso pianists like Vladimir Horowitz. At the same time he was criticized for filling every measure with crowds of notes. He did work in a simpler vein during the 1940s. He died in Los Angeles on 5 Nov 1956.

Tatum's outstanding records include "Tea for Two" (Brunswick #6553; 1933), "Stormy Weather" (Brunswick #80159; 1937), "Gone with the Wind" (Decca #1603; 1937), and "Lonesome Graveyard" with trumpet counterpoint from Joe Thomas (Decca #8563; 1941). In the 1950s he was with the Clef label, doing splendid numbers like "Ain't Misbehavin'" (#659; 1953). Tatum's output was vast: *The Tatum Solo Masterpieces* was an LP set of 13 discs. Compact discs on the Pablo and Capitol labels have covered most of his material. In 1973 the Tatum album *God is in the House* (Onyx Label) won a Grammy award. [Laubich 1982.]

TAUBER, RICHARD. 1892–1948. Austrian/British tenor, born in Linz on 16 May 1892. He studied in Frankfurt, and made his debut in Chemnitz as Tamino on 2 Mar 1913. He was engaged by the Dresden Opera, but turned to operetta, specializing in Lehár's works and to song recitals. A great success in a New York recital in 1931, he went on to triumphs in England and Australia. He took British citizenship in 1940. Tauber's final appearance in America was a Carnegie Hall recital on 30 Mar 1947. He died in London on 8 Jan 1948.

Tauber began recording for Odeon (Germany) in 1919, with four songs, a German version of "M'appari" and five other arias; plus four selections from Schumann's *Dichterliebe*. Arias from *Mignon* were among the finest of his opera discs (#81938 and #81941). Lenski's aria from *Eugene Onegin* (#80956) and "Wintersturme" (#81042) were other outstanding excerpts from opera. Tauber also worked for German Odeon in 1926–1930; Austrian Odeon, 1934–1935; and British Parlophone-Odeon, 1934–1946. A total of 735 sides are known.

Tauber's Lieder performances were issued by Parlophone records, among them elegant songs from Schubert's *Winterreise* (#RO 20037/42; 1928). He was also acclaimed for German folk songs, such as those recorded in 1934

(Parlophone #RO 20241/46). These and others are on Pearl CD #GEMM CD 9370 (1990). For Odeon he made an outstanding "Heiden-röslein" (Schubert; sung in French, #250,849; 1933). Schumann's "Die beiden Grenadiere" has been a favorite with collectors (1927). Perhaps his most acclaimed discs were "Dein ist mein ganzes Herz" (#0-4949) and "Adieu, mein kleiner Gardeoffizier" (#0-4983).

Operetta remains Tauber's greatest contribution; he recorded the Viennese and Hungarian masterworks for Odeon and Parlophone. A CD from EMI (#CDH7 69787-2; 1989) offers a fine selection. His opera repertoire is sampled by a Pearl compact disc (#GEMM CD 9327; 1989) presenting him in Mozart airs sung in his prime (1922) in addition to Wagner, Verdi and Puccini. There is more opera on EMI CD #M7 69476-2, but it is less well recorded and edited. [Abell 1969 is a complete discography.]

TAYLOR TRIO. A string trio that recorded for various labels ca. 1904. Membership was not fixed; one group included Alexander Hackel, violin; Albert W. Taylor, cello; and William E. Berge, piano. Alexander Drasein was another violinist, and Oscar W. Friberg another pianist.

TE KANAWA, KIRI, 1944– . New Zealand soprano, born in Gisborne on 6 Mar 1944. She won a radio prize in Melbourne, and remained there, singing at social functions. Then she gained a study grant to London in 1966, and made her debut as the Countess in *Nozze di Figaro* in 1970; this became one of her finest roles. In 1972 she appeared in San Francisco, and on 9 Feb 1974 at the Metropolitan Opera in an emergency substitution for Teresa Stratas in *Otello*. Verdi and Mozart were her great vehicles, and also her most acclaimed recordings (complete *Nozze di Figaro* (Decca CD #410-150-2DH3; 1984) and *Simon Boccanegra* (London #2-425628; 1990). She also made outstanding complete recordings of Puccini's *Manon Lescaut* (London #2-421426-1LH2) and *Rondine* (CBS #2-M2K-37852); and a notable version of the Mahler Fourth Symphony with Georg Solti (Decca CD #410 188-2DH; 1984). An interesting crossover singer, Te Kanawa has also inscribed an album with Nelson Riddle, *Blue Skies* (London #44666-2), with such numbers as "Here's That Rainy Day" and "How High the Moon."

TEAGARDEN, JACK, 1905–1964. American jazz trombonist and blues singer, born Weldon Leo Teagarden in Vernon, Texas, on 29 Aug 1905. He played piano as a young child, then took up the trombone at age 10. After playing in San Antonio, Texas, he went on to New York and Chicago. He joined Ben Pollack's band in 1928, but also played with Red Nichols, Louis Armstrong, Eddie Condon, and others. In 1933 he went to Paul Whiteman's orchestra, and was a featured soloist until 1938, when he left to organize his own band. In 1947 he was with the Louis Armstrong All Stars; then he led an All Star ensemble of his own and remained actively performing until his death, in New Orleans on 15 Jan 1964.

Teagarden was among the few white musicians to excel in the blues, which he performed with virtuosity (for example, brilliant trills). He was also a fine jazz vocalist. He began to record in the late 1920s, with Condon, Pollack, Armstrong, and others. "Makin' Friends" with Condon (Okeh #41142; 1928) and "Knockin' a Jug" with Armstrong (Okeh #8703; 1929) are representative of his work in that period. His singing is heard to advantage in "Stars Fell on Alabama" (Brunswick #6993; 1934) and "I Gotta Right to Sing the Blues" (Brunswick #8397; 1939). In 1946 he made some records on a label named for him, Teagarden Presents. Grudge, Jazzology, and Savoy Jazz are among the labels that have issued Teagarden material on compact discs.

TEBALDI, RENATA, 1922– . Italian soprano, born in Pesaro on 1 Feb 1922. She studied at the Parma Conservatory at age 16, and made her debut in *Mefistofele* in Rovigo in 1944. Chosen by Arturo Toscanini to sing at the re-opening of La Scala after the World War II, she remained with the company, singing also throughout Europe and South America. On 31 Jan 1955 she was heard at the Metropolitan Opera as Desdemona, and appeared regularly there to 1973. Her great roles were Aida, Desdemona, Leonora, Violetta, Mimi, Cio Cio San, Tosca, Eva in *Meistersinger*, and Gioconda. Tebaldi has been acclaimed for the beauty and control of her voice, as well as for her dramatic skills.

Tebaldi has made numerous complete opera sets, all of them remarkable and many definitive. In the Decca LXT series she took part in *Aida, Andrea Chenier, Boheme, Fanciulla del West, Forza del destino, Madama Butterfly, Manon Lescaut, Otello, Tosca, Traviata, Trittico, Trovatore,* and *Turandot.* She recorded *Cavalleria rusticana* and *Turandot* for RCA Victor. Her recital album of 1958 won the Grammy for best classical vocal disc. [Segond 1981.]

TEFIFON. A phonographic device that recorded sound on an endless band of 35 millimeter film—up to 100 feet long—inscribing lateral grooves on the film with a stylus. The film was housed in a cartridge, and played back at 7 1/2 inches per second with a sapphire needle and a crystal pickup. Tefifon was marketed in Germany from about 1950, though the development of it is traced to the 1920s; the main work was carried out by Karl Daniel (1905–1979) of Cologne, who organized a company to handle it: Tefi-Apparatebau. Because of its long playing time—an hour for a small cartridge, up to four hours for larger cartridges—the device appeared to have a promising future, even in competition with the new LP disc. A catalog was issued in 1954 with 264 prerecorded tapes listed, mostly light music. Inability of the firm to secure the services of major artists, who were under contract to the record labels, prevented the Tefifon from achieving long prosperity, and it passed from the scene ca. 1960. [Czada 1983.]

TELDEC (label). A record belonging to the Time Warner conglomerate, affiliated since January 1988 with its **WCI**, marketed and distributed by Warner Classics in the U.K. and Elektra International Classics in U.S. Teldec succeeded **Telefunken**, and continues to specialize in German recordings, its traditional strength since the 1920s. The Esprit line is a low-cost Teldec. Among the artists on recent CDs are the Leipzig Gewandhaus, the Berlin Philharmonic Orchestra, the Mozarteum Orchestra of Salzburg, and the Vienna Concentus Musicus under Nikolaus Harnoncourt.

TELEFUNKEN (label). A German record made by Telefunkenplatte GmbH, Berlin, from the 1920s. Supraphon was its Czech subsidiary, Ultraphon its French affiliate. Polydor was the related American label in the early LP period, one of the group of 11 labels listed in the first Schwann catalog (1949). The first video audio discs were demonstrated at the Telefunken building in Berlin on 24 June 1970. **Teldec** is the current name of the label.

TELEGRAPHONE. The magnetic wire recorder developed by **Valdemar Poulsen** ca. 1898. It used steel piano wire of 0.01 inch diameter, moving past the recording head at 84 inches (213 centimeters) per second. Poulsen's concept included the possibility of magnetic recording on coated paper strips and even discs, and these alternatives were cited in his British patent #8961; 1899). The telegraphone was patented in the U.S. (#661,619; filed 8 July 1899, granted 13 Nov 1900) and in a dozen other countries. It was demonstrated at the Paris Exposition of 1900, and used to record the voice of Emperor Franz Joseph I in Vienna (the recording still exists, in the Danish Technical Museum, Hellerup). King Edward VII recorded words of appreciation for the invention, and the wire was given to Queen Alexandra, but its whereabouts are unknown.

Despite its early fame, the telegraphone proved unable to compete with the cylinder phonograph because its playback sound was very faint (there were then no adequate means of amplification), its playing time per spool of wire was very brief because of the high speeds required, and the wire tended to tangle in transport to its take-up reel. Later Poulsen and Oscar Pedersen worked out a longer playing wire machine that would run 20 minutes, and some of them were used by the British Post Office and the War Office during World War I, and by the U.S. Navy. But the telegraphone was a commercial failure, and little was heard about it after 1910. [Hoover 1971 has an illustration on p. 124.] *See also* MAGNETIC RECORDING.

TELEPHON-FABRIK BERLINER. The J. Berliner Telephon-Fabrik, established in Hanover in 1881 by **Joseph Berliner** and **Emile Berliner**. It was there that the first records of the Gramophone Co. of London were pressed.

TEMPTATIONS. American popular vocal group, organized in 1960 as successor to the Primes, which had been established in 1959. The original members were Otis Williams, Melvin Franklin, Paul Williams, Eddie Kendricks, and David Ruffin. Singing rhythm and blues for Motown's Gordy label, the group scored with several singles in the early 1960s, made a number-one hit disc, "My Girl" in 1965 (Gordy #7038), and had a series of 46 chart songs in the next 15 years. They won two Grammys for "Cloud Nine" (Gordy #7081; 1968) and another for "Papa was a Rolling Stone (Gordy #7121; 1972). The most successful of the group's 33 chart albums were two volumes of *Temptations' Greatest Hits* (Gordy #GM919; 1966 and Gordy #GS954; 1970).

TENNESSEE PHONOGRAPH CO. One of the affiliated firms of the **North American Phonograph Co.**, established in 1890. The address was 5 Noel Block, Nashville; general manager in 1890 was J. Balleran.

TETRAZZINI, LUISA, 1871–1940. Italian soprano, born in Florence on 28 June 1871. She studied in Florence, and made her debut there in *L'africaine* in 1890. She sang in South America and Europe, and in 1904 in San Francisco. Then she went to Covent Garden, and the Manhattan Opera (1908–1910), with one season at the Metropolitan Opera after her debut there—to mixed notices—as Lucia on 27 Dec 1911. Tetrazzini appeared later in Chicago, Boston, and Philadelphia; then returned to Italy where she entertained soldiers during the First World War. Subsequently she concentrated on recitals, in Britain and America, until 1931, when she retired to Milan. She died there on 28 Apr 1940.

On 8 Sep 1904 Tetrazzini recorded for the Zonophone label, singing the Mad Scene from *Lucia* first (#10000), and "Caro nome," "Una voce poco fa," Juliette's Waltz, and "Ah, non giunge" from *Sonnambula*. She made many discs for the Gramophone Co. in London from 1907 to 1913, repeating her Zonophone material and adding much of the coloratura repertoire. Her later work was for Victor in 1911–1920. Among her outstanding discs are "Saper vorreste" from *Ballo in maschera* (Victor #88304; 1911), and the *Lakme* "Bell Song" (Victor #88297, #6340; 1911). She participated in a renowned version of the *Lucia* Sextette, with Enrico Caruso, Pasquale Amato, and Marcel Journet (Victor #96201). Her sisters Eva and Elvira were also recording artists. (The Columbia and Phonadisc issues by "E. Tetrazzini" are by Elvira.) There were numerous LPs released by all the reissue labels. A five-CD set by Pearl in 1989 offered the "complete known recordings." [Richards 1949 is a discography.]

TEWKSBURY, GEORGE E. Recording industry executive. He was president of the Kansas Phonograph Co. in 1890, and general manager in 1892–1893. In 1894–1895 he managed the **U-S Phonograph Co.**, Newark, New Jersey. Tewksbury held a basic **coin-op** patent, U.S. #523,556 (filed 13 Dec 1893; granted 24 July 1894). He became general sales agent for the **National Phonograph Co.**, Thomas Edison's organization (1896–1897), but had a falling out with Edison and died shortly after, afflicted with a form of insanity. He was author of *A Complete Manual of the Edison Phonograph* (1897).

TEXAS PHONOGRAPH CO. One of the affiliated firms of the **North American Phonograph Co.**, established in Galveston in 1890. H.L. Sellers was president in 1890, and H.E. Landes was president in 1892. General manager was Thomas Coyngton.

TEYTE, MAGGIE, 1888–1976. English soprano, born Maggie Tate in Wolverhampton, 17 Apr 1888. She studied in London, then with Jean de Reszke in Paris, changing the spelling of her name to suit French pronunciation. Her debut was as Zerlina at Monte Carlo, 1907. She was greatly successful in song recitals, often accompanied by Debussy at the piano, and becoming recognized as an outstanding interpreter of French *mélodie*. Teyte continued operatic work as well, at the Opéra-Comique in 1908–1910; and in London, Chicago, Boston, etc. Melisande was her favored role. After 1917 she turned more definitely toward a career as recitalist, and remained active through World War II. She died in London on 26 May 1976.

Her earliest recording was made in 1907 for HMV, "Because" (#3729). She worked for Columbia in 1914–1916, doing mostly English concert numbers. Teyte recorded for Edison Diamond Discs in 1919, presenting some unlikely repertoire; her first piece was "I'se Gwine Back to Dixie" with the Lyric Male Quartet (#82159), which had a solo on the B side, "Ma Curly-Headed Baby." Then she made five other sides, concert songs in English, the last in 1924.

The most important Teyte records were made much later, in the 1940s, when she was "discovered" in America, much to the credit of Joseph Brogan, proprietor of the Gramophone Shop in New York. These records were her true repertoire: French songs, selections from *Pelléas*, and a fine English recital. EMI offered an extensive selection on four LPs (#RLS 716) in 1976. [Tron 1954 is a discography.]

THAT GIRL QUARTET. A female vocal group, the "most successful women's recording ensemble" (Walsh); active from ca. 1910 on many labels. The members were Harriet Keys, Allie Thomas, Presis (or Precis) Thompson, and Helen Summers. They made U-S Everlasting cylinders, then worked for Victor, beginning with "Silver Bell" (#16695; 1911). Edison recorded them also, beginning with "Honeymoon Honey in Bombay" (#10494; 1911). There were six titles in the Victor 1917 catalog, four titles in 1922, but none in 1927. The group may have been the one known as the Savoy Girl Quartet on Columbia records of 1911. [Walsh 1973/1.]

THIBAUD, JACQUES, 1880–1953. French violinist, born in Bordeaux on 27 Sep 1880. He took first prize at the Paris Conservatory at age 16, and began to concertize extensively while in his teens. In 1898 he gave 54 recitals in Paris, then played through Europe, and toured in America in 1903. Highly regarded as a soloist, he was perhaps even more noteworthy in chamber music, particularly in the famous trio he formed in 1904 with Alfred Cortot and Pablo Casals. He had another fine collaborator in pianist Marguerite Long. Thibaud's long ca-

reer ended in an air crash in the French Alps on 1 Sep 1953.

His earliest records were for Fonotipia around 1905: he began with the *Thaïs* "Meditation" (#39054) and did five other concert pieces. Later he worked for Pathé, HMV, and others. His greatest records were with the trio, including material by Schumann, Mendelssohn, Schubert, and Beethoven. In 1940 he participated in a superlative recording of the Fauré Piano Quartet No. 2, made in Paris with Long, Maurice Vieux (viola), and Pierre Fournier (cello; HMV #DB 5103/6). Long and Thibaud recorded Mozart violin sonatas 26 and 34. He and Casals did the Brahms Double Concerto on Victor #8208/11, with Cortot conducting the Barcelona Symphony. An Angel LP, made rather poorly in Japan, reissued a selection of Thibaud's solo work from the 1930s (#GR 2079; 1979). [Lewis, J. 1981.]

THILL, GEORGES, 1887–1984. French tenor, born in Paris on 14 Dec 1887. He was a student of Fernando de Lucia in Naples, and sang at the Opéra-Comique on 15 May 1918 as Don José. His first appearance at the Opéra, in *Thaïs*, was a great success; he became the leading tenor of the company and remained (with interruption by the First World War) until the 1940s. Thill had special acclaim for his roles in *Werther*, *Carmen*, *Faust*, *Turandot*, and Wagnerian works. He was at the Metropolitan Opera in 1930–1932, at La Scala and in Buenos Aires. He died on 17 Oct 1984, at his home in Draguignan, France.

Thill recorded for Columbia in Paris and Milan during the 1926–1933 period. His major accomplishment was in the complete recording of *Werther*, made in 1931, with Ninon Vallin. The CD reissue of this classic (EMI Références #CHS7 63195-2; 1990) won the *Gramophone* magazine award as best recording of its type in 1990. A selection of Thill's arias and songs was offered on four LPs by French EMI (#2C 153-16211/4; 1979).

THIRD STREAM. A style of composing and performing that blends jazz/popular idioms with the techniques of classical music. **Benny Goodman** may be identified as the earliest

Third Stream musician. Later manifestations appeared in the work of such artists as **George Shearing, Marian McPartland, Dave Brubeck**, and the **Modern Jazz Quartet**.

THOMAS, JOHN CHARLES, 1891–1960. American baritone, born in Meyersdale, Pennsylvania, on 6 Sep 1891. He studied at the Peabody Conservatory in Baltimore, then sang in New York musicals. Turning to the concert stage he found immediate success. He also sang opera in Brussels, Covent Garden, Chicago, and elsewhere; then at the Metropolitan Opera, with a debut on 2 Feb 1934 as Germont, and a stay of 20 years. Thomas retired to California, and died in Apple Valley on 13 Dec 1960.

His recording career began with Edison Diamond Discs in 1914, but none of the vocal numbers he made were ever issued. His spoken voice was heard on five discs that were released, giving explanatory talks about the artists who performed on the other sides of the discs. In 1916 he was with the Lyric label, making the *Forza del destino* duet under the name of Enrico Martini, with Mario Chamlee, who appeared as Mario Rodolfi; (Lyric #7016A). He moved to Vocalion and made 36 records from 1920 to 1923; those were mostly ballads and light opera numbers. Brunswick recorded Thomas from ca. 1924 to 1929, continuing the concert repertoire. For Victor, from 1931 to 1934, he added several operatic excerpts, from *Tannhäuser*, *Traviata*, *Herodiade*, and *Hamlet*; but he also sang popular and novelty pieces like "The Green Eyed Dragon" (#1655; 1933). In a final group for Victor, in 1938–1944, there were more opera and concert arias, and also a successful series of Broadway musical numbers. He made about 250 records of hymns, for Air Arts, Inc., a firm of which he was half owner. Thomas was seen and heard on three Vitaphone short subjects of 1927, and took part in two complete opera recordings for the Unique Opera label: *Barbiere di Siviglia*, with Lily Pons and Ezio Pinza (#129; 1938), and *Traviata*, with Vina Bovy and Nino Martini (#285; 1937). [Morgan 1979.]

THOMAS MANUFACTURING CO. A Dayton, Ohio, firm, established in 1903. A catalog of September 1913 (reprinted in *TMR* #54–55) described numerous products: Dayton phonograph motors, Dayton tone arms, and Dayton soundboxes. The Orchestrola and Armoniola disc players were marketed in 1916, in seven models, priced from $15–$200. Later Thomas made the Portophon portable machines. When the company failed in 1926, Starr Piano Co. purchased the drawings, patents, machinery, and plant from the liquidator. [Andrews*.]

THOMPSON, HANK, 1925–. American country singer and guitarist, born in Waco, Texas, on 3 Sep 1925. He taught himself harmonica and guitar as a child, and performed on a Waco radio station before joining the Navy in 1943. After the War he returned to radio, forming his own group, the Brazos Valley Boys. Capitol Records signed him and began a fruitful 18-year association; his total record sales came to more than 30 million. He had early hits with compositions of his own, "Humpty Dumpty Heart" and "Today" (1948) and went on to about 70 chart records. Among his great singles were "I've Run Out of Tomorrows" (Capitol #4085; 1958) and "She's Just a Whole Lot Like You" (Capitol 4386; 1960). After 1966 he moved to Warner Records, and in 1968 he went to the Dot label.

THOMPSON, WILLIAM H., 1873–1945. American baritone and vaudeville artist, one of the early performers on Edison cylinders. He made about 40 of them as a soloist from 1902 to 1911, and also duets with Albert Campbell. The Edison 1902 list included "Sadie, Say You Won't Say Nay" (#8037), plus "In the Moonlight with the Girl You Love" (#8044), and two others. There were further duets on Edison cylinders, with Will Oakland and Albert Campbell, then recordings for U-S Everlasting Records, with Frank Coombs. Thompson cut 14 sides for Victor, in two sessions: 30 Nov 1903 and 21 June 1904. He did not record after 1913. He died on 24 July 1945 in Chicago. [Walsh 1951/5.]

THORBORG, KERSTIN, 1896–1970. Swedish contralto, born in Venjan on 19 May 1896. She studied and made her debut in Stockholm, and was with the Royal Opera in 1924–1930.

Then she sang in Berlin and Vienna, and at the Metropolitan Opera as Fricka on 21 Dec 1936, remaining to 1950 (except for the 1946–1947 season). She gave many recitals across the U.S. and Canada before retiring to Sweden, where she died on 13 Apr 1970, in Hedemora.

She began recording for HMV in 1928, with "Mon coeur s'ouvre a ta voix" (#1626-2), and three other arias. For Odeon she sang 22 numbers, mostly in Swedish, in 1928–1933. Columbia recorded her in *Das Lied von der Erde* (album #M-300) in 1936. Thorborg was renowned for her Wagnerian roles, which she finally recorded for Victor in 1940–1945. Brangaene's air from *Tristan* was an outstanding example (#CS 048862; 1940). Most of the LP reissue labels offered Thorborg material. She is also heard on several air shot releases from the Metropolitan Opera, including complete versions of *Lohengrin*, *Siegfried* and *Walküre*. Thorborg was one of those who sang in Arturo Toscanini's acclaimed rendition of the Beethoven Ninth Symphony in 1938, with Jan Peerce and Ezio Pinza. [Frankenstein 1978 is a discography.]

THORN-EMI. The parent firm of EMI Records, Ltd., since November 1979. EMI Records, Ltd., was successor to **EMI, Ltd.**

THORNHILL, CLAUDE, 1909–1965. American pianist and Big Band leader, born in Terre Haute, Indiana, on 10 Aug 1909. He studied at the Cincinnati Conservatory and the Curtis Institute of Music, while also playing on a riverboat. He worked for Hal Kemp, and settled in New York around 1931. Then he played in Freddy Martin's band, and Paul Whiteman's. Thornhill moved frequently thereafter, performing with Benny Goodman, Leo Reisman, Ray Noble, and Andre Kostelanetz. He had a band briefly in 1937 before moving to Hollywood to freelance there. He started another band in 1940, and reorganized it after military service. In the 1950s and 1960s he led small groups. Thornhill died in New York on 1 July 1965.

His 1937 band recorded two sessions, one for Vocalion and one for Brunswick. The 1940 group was with Okeh, then Columbia. "Snowfall" (Columbia #36268; 1941) and "Autumn Nocturne" (Columbia #36435; 1941) were highly popular. In 1946 there was a hit with Fran Warren's vocal of "Sunday Kind of Love" (Columbia #37219).

THREE KAUFIELDS. A male vocal trio that recorded for Emerson around 1919. Members were Irving Kaufman, Jack Kaufman, and Arthur Fields.

TIBBETT, LAWRENCE, 1896–1960. American baritone, born in Bakersfield, California, on 16 Nov 1896. His surname was Tibbet, but he gracefully accepted the extra "t" when it appeared as a misprint in an opera program. He was a sheriff's son, and worked as a cowboy. Then he took up Shakespearean acting, served in the Navy during World War I, and became a singer. He made his Metropolitan Opera debut on 24 Jan 1923, and remained with the company to 1950. Tibbett sang 396 times with the Metropolitan in New York and 163 times on tour with them. He portrayed 52 different roles in his lifetime, 48 of them at the Metropolitan. In addition to his star roles as Escamillo, Rigoletto, Scarpia, Ford, Tonio, and Iago, he performed in the premieres of significant American works: *Merry Mount*, *Emperor Jones*, *Peter Ibbetson*, and *King's Henchman*. He made three motion pictures: *Metropolitan*, *New Moon*, and *Under Your Spell*. In the 1940s he crossed over to the radio program *Your Hit Parade*, giving uneven renditions of such material as "Accentuate the Positive" and "Don't Fence Me In"; unfortunately his magnificent voice had begun to crumble by then.

Tibbett's first records were made in 1927 for Victor: "Believe Me, If All Those Endearing Young Charms" (#1238), "Calm as the Night" (#3043), "Drink to Me Only With Thine Eyes" (#1238) and the "Prologo" from *Pagliacci*. In 1929–1930 he sang arias from *King's Henchman*, and a powerful "Te Deum" from *Tosca* coupled with the "Toreador Song," splendidly demonstrating the smokey resonance of his voice. A fine series of airs from John Stainer's oratorio *The Crucifixion* was made in 1929. "Standin' in the Need of Prayer" from *Emperor Jones* was a remarkable disc of 1934 (#7959). Tibbett also inscribed a Wagnerian set in 1934, excerpts from Act III of *Walküre*, with Leopold Stokowski and the Philadelphia Orchestra. "Without a Song" (#1507; 1931) was a popular light number. From *Porgy and Bess* there were memorable renditions of "It Ain't Necessarily So (#11878), "I Got Plenty o' Nuttin'" (#11880), and an ineffable duet with Helen Jepson, "Bess, You Is My Woman Now." A compact disc of his greatest operatic material (*Porgy* included) appeared in 1990 from RCA (#GD87808); and another, from Pearl (#GEMM CDS 9452), in 1991. [Bullard 1977; Moran 1977/8.]

TILTON, MARTHA, 1918– . American popular vocalist. She began professionally on radio in Los Angeles in 1935, and joined Jimmy Dorsey for a time in 1936. In 1937 she became a member of Benny Goodman's band, and made the hit record "And the Angels Sing" (Victor #26170). In the 1940s she freelanced, and made some fine discs like "I'll Walk Alone" (Capitol #157; 1944) and "Stranger in Town" / "I Should Care" (Capitol # 184; 1944). Tilton was on the radio show *Your Hit Parade* in 1947, and in the 1956 film *Benny Goodman Story*.

TIM. See TRANSIENT INTERMODULATION DISTORTION.

TIMBRE. The tone color or tone quality of a musical sound. Timbre varies with different patterns of harmonics generated as a tone is produced; it is the principal basis for the audible differences among musical instruments when they play the same pitches. Since many of the harmonics that give specific instruments their identifiable tone color are in the upper range of the audio spectrum, early acoustic recordings (unable to capture that portion of the range) failed to give recognizable representations of numerous instruments, the piano among them. While today's studio recording apparatus is capable of dealing with all timbre problems, some playback equipment may be so poor —for example, cheap portable cassette players—as to recall the performance limitations of the acoustic era.

TIME WARNER, INC. The world's largest media and entertainment conglomerate, created by the merger of **WCI** (Warner Communications) and Time, Inc., on 10 Jan 1990. Head-

quarters is in the Time & Life Building, New York. Time, Inc. was a major publisher of magazines (*Time, Life, People, Money, Fortune*) and had entered the cable television market in 1972 with its Home Box Office. Warner originated with Warner Brothers studios, one of the principal Hollywood enterprises of the 1930s.

The record labels owned by Time Warner include Atlantic, Nashville, Reprise, and Warner Brothers Records.

TIMELY TUNES (label). A low-priced label ($.35) introduced by RCA Victor in April 1931, offering dance music and some jazz. Issues ceased three months later. Most artists appeared under pseudonyms. [Rust 1978.]

TINFOIL PHONOGRAPH. The first cylinder **phonograph of Thomas A. Edison**, constructed according to his design by **John Kruesi** and **Charles Batchelor** between 4–6 Dec 1877. Edison's basic sketch was completed on 29 Nov 1877. "Mary Had a Little Lamb" was the first phrase successfully repeated by the tinfoil phonograph. Edison filed a patent application for the device on 24 Dec 1877, and received U.S. patent #200,521 on 19 Feb 1878. *See also* CYLINDER, 1. [Koenigsberg 1987.]

TOLLEFSEN TRIO. An instrumental group that recorded for Edison Diamond Discs in 1915. They were Carl Henry Tollefsen, violin; Augusta Tollefsen, piano; and Michael Penha, cello. One number is listed in Wile (1990), "Pastel—Menuet" (#80241).

TONE ARM. Often written as one word, tonearm. The pivoted device in a modern disc playback system that holds the **cartridge**; it is propelled across the record surface by the groove wall. In acoustic systems the hollow tone arm carried the needle/diaphragm vibrations to the horn. In electrical systems the tone arm includes wires that conduct transmits the electrical signals generated in the cartridge to the amplifier. A pivot point allows the stylus free play, but it has to have a certain amount of friction to keep the stylus from jumping across the grooves. Normally the downward stylus tracking force has been between two and 10 grams; this permits proper **tracking** without bringing damaging pressures to bear on the grooves.

The position of the tone arm should ensure that it locates the stylus on a tangent to the record groove. This is not completely possible in practice, since the tangent achieved at the outer rim of the disc will not be maintained as the stylus approaches the inner grooves; the technical compromise has been to use a bent tone arm, one that keeps the stylus nearly tangent all the way across the disc. The vertical tracking angle—that angle with which the stylus meets the groove—should be 15 degrees from the vertical.

A tone arm may be an integral part of the turntable or separate from it; separate tone arms can give superior performance but are expensive and relatively difficult to install. It must be, in either case, free of audible resonances, or sympathetic vibrations may arise.

The earliest phonograph with a distinct tone arm, as opposed to a stylus/diaphragm attached directly to the horn, was the Echophone invented in 1895. Eldridge Johnson made a key improvement by inventing the tapered tone arm (U.S. patent #814,786; filed 12 Feb 1903; granted 13 Mar 1906), allowing "the sound waves to advance with a regular, steady, and natural increase in their wave fronts in a manner somewhat similar to ordinary musical instruments." The tapered arm patent was held by Victor, which used it in constant litigation against imitators. The arm was first used on the Victor IV of April 1903. February 1905 advertising from Zonophone announced its "Gibson Patent Tapering Sound Arm."

Major advances in tone arm design followed the research of Percy Wilson in the early 1920s; he attacked the problem of tracking error through mathematical analysis, devising an "overlap and offset" method for achieving the correct offset angle and overhang. E.G. Löfgren, H.G. Baerwald, B.B. Bauer, J.D. Seagrave, and J.K. Stevenson wrote significant papers on the same problem of tracking distortion in the 1938–1966 period. Frederick Hunt, although writing primarily on record wear, contributed important findings on tracking force in a 1962 paper. Skating force was effectively addressed by weighting the rear of the tone arm (among other elegant solutions). Linear tracking arms became available in the 1960s. Garrard introduced articulated tone arms in record changers, to give near-zero lateral tracking angle error. The radial tone arm, which rides on a straight rail instead of pivoting in an arc from its base at the corner of the turntable, was made commercially viable in the early 1980s, combining low mass and straight-line tracking, but in practice it was not judged to be audibly superior to the finest pivoting arms.

Other features in modern tone arms include cuing mechanisms, height adjustments, vertical tracking angle adjustments, and damping mechanisms. The overall trend in design was toward lower mass. A problem not fully dealt with at the end of the LP era was the electrostatic attraction of the tone arm by the records in the stack of a record changer. An equipment review of 1986 announced the remarkable specifications of the SME V, "the ultimate tonearm"; it had virtually no tracking error or other disturbing features—other than the price ($1,200). [Klinger*; Kogen 1977; Long 1986 (the SME V review); Mitchell 1982 (these papers give numerous references to the research literature).]

TONE CONTROL. A knob or switch on an amplifier that adjust the relative degree of treble or bass passed to the output. It can be used to adjust minor imbalances in recording, or such as are produced by the loudspeakers. In early usage of the acoustic period, a "tone control" was more accurately volume control. [Klinger*.]

TONE TESTS. A puzzling phenomenon of recording history, consisting of recitals sponsored by the Thomas A. Edison Co. to illustrate the quality of Edison Diamond Discs. In those recitals, which were held from 1915 to 1925, singers or instrumentalists would perform a program in partnership with Diamond Disc recordings and would from time to time cease their live performance, allowing the disc to continue the music. A darkened stage permitted the performer to slip away, and the audience would not have been aware of that departure until the lights went back on. The point was to demonstrate that the audience would be unable to distinguish between the live performance and the recorded version. Difficult as it is for those of a later generation to believe that such suspension of disbelief might have occurred on the wide scale that it apparently did, all contemporary reports testify that the illusion was remarkable.

Although special pressings were made of the Diamond Discs used in the tone tests, to minimize the surface noise that plagued regular issues until about 1924, there was no way to improve upon the limited **audio frequency** range of the acoustic process: about 1,000 to 2,000 or 3,000 Hz.

The earliest test to be reported in the press was held in February 1915 in New York. Participants were Christine Miller, Elizabeth Spencer, Donald Chalmers, and John Young. It was organized by a man named Hallowell, who was succeeded by Verdi E.B. Fuller, a superintendent for Thomas A. Edison, Inc. There was then a test held for a dealers' group in August 1915, followed by a series of national tests. Alice Verlet sang a tone test recital in Orchestra Hall, Chicago; as reported in *TMW* of 15 Dec 1915 there was no claim that the audience was unable to distinguish between voice and machine. But an advertisement in *TMW* on 15 Jan 1916 stated that observers found it "almost impossible" to tell the difference; and by 15 May 1916 the Edison advertisements were saying that audiences found it "impossible" to make the distinction.

Newspaper critics offered glowing praise, in statements that were quoted in Edison promotional material. Among the quotations given in a 1919 publication were: "Impossible to distinguish between the singer's living voice and its re-creation by the musical instrument...." (Boston *Herald*); "No one in the audience... could tell which was the real and which the reproduced" (Brooklyn *Daily Eagle*); "A convincing demonstration of the power of a man to produce tone from an instrument so perfectly as to defy detection when compared side by side with the tone of the original producing artists" (*Musical America*).

Artists who engaged in tone tests included Anna Case, Thomas Chalmers, Arthur Collins, Byron G. Harlan, Frieda Hempel, Mario Laurenti, Margarete Matzenauer, Arthur Middleton, Marie Rappold, Elizabeth Spencer,

Maggie Teyte, Jacques Urlus, Alice Verlet, and Giovanni Zenatello. It was during a tone test that Arthur Collins fell into a trap door on the darkened stage, sustaining injuries that affected his career.

Albany, New York, was the site of the largest tone test audience, as 6,000 teachers heard Laurenti sing in the State Armory in the early 1920s; they were reportedly unable to detect any difference between the disc and the person. More than 4,000 tests were held by the end of 1920. Overseas tests were reported from Liverpool (England) in 1923, and Melbourne (Australia) in 1924. Mexico City was a site in 1923. The final notice of one of these events appeared in the *TMW* of 15 Aug 1925.

One of the tone test singers may have offered a partial solution to the puzzle of the illusion created by the tone tests, in saying that the performers endeavored to imitate the records. This possibility was explicitly denied in Edison promotional material. Surely there was at least imitation of volume. A remarkable comment by Albert Spalding is more directed toward the persuasiveness of the recordings themselves: he observed that nobody could have distinguished between the live artist and the record, but that on modern records (he was speaking in 1953) anybody could. Frow suggests that the illusion was accomplished because it "the world was a simpler place, people were simpler too."

On occasion Brunswick and other labels conducted demonstrations of their products in live/recorded recitals, but it is not reported that they carried out the dramatic lights-out routine of the Edison tests. [Frow 1982.]

TORMÉ, MEL, 1925– . American popular singer, born in Chicago on 13 Sep 1925. He played piano and drums, and composed, performing as a child in vaudeville and then on radio. After military service in World War II he achieved popularity as a solo singer, nicknamed the "Velvet Fog." In later years he developed a jazzy scat style and his greatest successes, capped by a brilliant series of appearances and records with George Shearing in the mid-1980s. "Try a Little Tenderness" (Musicraft #381; 1946) exemplified his "foggy" lyric style; "One for My Baby" (Musicraft

#15107; 1947) was his famous dialogue with bartender Joe. "Stranger in Town," one of his two most acclaimed compositions—the other was "The Christmas Song"—was recorded for Capitol (#2529) in 1953. Tormé's continuing popularity is demonstrated by the presence of 20 compact discs in the 1991 catalog. His work with Shearing is on five CD's from the Concord Jazz label. *An Evening with George Shearing and Mel Tormé* (Concord Jazz #190; 1982) was a Grammy winner. Tormé received another Grammy, as best male jazz vocalist, for his 1983 "Top Drawer."

TORRIANI, MADAME. A soprano who recorded for **Bettini**. In the June 1898 catalog she had 12 numbers, beginning with "Chimes of Normandy" and including arias from five operas; eight of those numbers appeared again in the 1899 catalog.

TORTELIER, PAUL, 1914–1990. French cellist, born in Paris on 24 Mar 1914. He took first prize at the Paris Conservatory at age 16, and made his debut at 17. He was first cellist in the orchestra at Monte Carlo from 1935 to 1937, then played with the Boston Symphony Orchestra in 1937–1939. Tortelier performed widely as a soloist and in chamber ensembles. He lived in Israel in 1955–1956, then joined the faculty of the Paris Conservatory. Tortelier made an acclaimed recording of the Elgar Concerto, with Malcolm Sargent and the London Philharmonic Orchestra (Angel #S-37029), and another of the Brahms Double Concerto with Christian Ferras (Seraphim #S-60048). His Fauré sonatas with Jean Hubeau, and Vivaldi sonatas with Robert Veyron-Lacroix (recorded for Erato) were outstanding, and his *Don Quixote* for HMV with Thomas Beecham was definitive (now on EMI compact disc #CDH7 63106-2; 1989). He continued performing into an advanced age, and died at Manoir de Villarceaux, near Paris, on 18 Dec 1990.

TOSCANINI, ARTURO, 1867–1957. Italian conductor and cellist, born in Parma on 25 Mar 1867. He entered the Parma Conservatory at age nine, and graduated with a first prize in cello in 1885. He was cellist with an Italian opera troupe in Rio de Janeiro, in 1886, when he had the opportunity to substitute for the regular conductor in a performance of *Aida*; from then he pursued a conducting career. Back in Italy he conducted the 1892 premiere of *Pagliacci*, and the 1896 premiere of *Boheme*. His genius was recognized by an appointment as chief conductor of La Scala at age 31; a post he held from 1898 to 1903, and again from 1906 to 1908. He was principal conductor at the Metropolitan Opera from 1908 to 1913, and also conducted orchestral concerts in New York. Toscanini returned to La Scala as artistic director in 1921–1929; but he was again invited to America and conducted the newly merged New York Philharmonic-Symphony Orchestra from 1928 to 1936. Meanwhile he had been the first non-German to conduct at Bayreuth, in 1930–1931. The NBC Symphony Orchestra was formed for him to conduct in 1937, and he brought it to world stature, remaining with it to 1954, when he retired. When died in New York on 16 Jan 1957, he was widely considered to have been the greatest conductor of his time.

Toscanini's major accomplishments were in performances and recordings of Beethoven, Brahms, Verdi, and Wagner. His repertoire was limited in the moderns, though he did make a definitive disc of Samuel Barber's *Adagio for Strings*. In 1921 he began recording for Victor, with the La Scala Orchestra, doing a miscellaneous group of ten 12-inch and six 10-inch sides. The first item was Ildebrando Pizzetti's "Quay of the Port of Famagusta" (#64952). There were two Beethoven movements and two Mozart movements; the other material was of a lighter character. Beethoven symphonies were recorded in the 1930s and in the 1950s, seven of them at least twice, giving collectors much ground for comparison and speculation. Toscanini never had a perfect combination of a great orchestra with a great hall to record in; Carnegie Hall and the NBC studio 8H being deficient in spaciousness. He apparently preferred faster tempos as he grew older, though it could be said that he had become more passionate about the scores. Those who wish to examine such questions have the RCA CD set of five records (#GD60324; 1990) which gives all the symphonies in performances from 1939 to 1952. Definitive Verdi recordings are also on RCA CD (#GD 60326, seven discs;

1990): *Falstaff* (from radio broadcasts of 1950; *Aida* (from broadcasts of 1949); and the *Requiem* (from a 1951 broadcast, with the Robert Shaw Chorale).

Outstanding interpretations of the Brahms orchestral works were made in the 1940s and 1950s, reissued on an RCA CD set of four discs (#GD 60325; 1990). But the grandest Toscanini reissue is in progress at this writing (1991): it is the BMG Classics project to release the entire Victor output on about 80 compact discs. Even that massive production will not capture all of the maestro's recorded legacy, a large portion of which has been acquired by the Arturo Toscanini Society, founded in 1968, collector of a huge body of material from American and European air shots. There were 800 tapes and 1,000 transcriptions in the society's library, according to a 1973 account.

The largest Toscanini collection is at the New York Public Library, Performing Arts Research Center (Lincoln Center); that collection is "one of the greatest archives ever to document a single career" (McCormick). Assembled in the family home at Riverdale, New York, the collection was deposited with the library in 1970. It was not until 1985 that negotiations between the library and the family were completed, and funding was received, from Wanda Toscanini Horowitz, to begin work on processing the archive. It includes such unique items as 4,600 acetate discs of rehearsals and performances; 1,789 test pressings of released performances and 799 test pressings of unreleased performances; and several thousand tape reels of rehearsals, air shots, and concerts. There is also an enormous documentation of published and manuscript material. [Dyment 1986; Gray 1973 describes the Arturo Toscanini Society; McCormick 1989 describes the New York archive.]

TOUGH, DAVE, 1908–1948. American jazz drummer, born in Oak Park, Illinois, on 26 Apr 1908. In his student days he played with the Austin High School Gang and then with various Chicago groups. In 1927 he went to Europe and freelanced. In the 1930s he was with Benny Goodman occasionally and with Tommy Dorsey for two years. Tough was afflicted with ill health and hardly ever stayed long with one group. His finest period was with Woody Herman in 1944–1945; he took the *Downbeat* award in 1945 and 1946. He died in Newark, New Jersey, on 6 Dec 1948.

Tough's brilliant work with Herman is heard to advantage in "Caldonia" / "Happiness is Just a Thing Called Joe" (Columbia #36789; 1945) and "Bijou" / "Put that Ring on My Finger" (Columbia #36861; 1945). Columbia reissued the Herman sessions on LP #CL-6049. In 1947 he made a fine disc of "Stop 'n' Go" / "Piña Colada" with the progressive jazz group of Charlie Ventura (National #9066).

TOUREL, JENNIE, 1903?–1973. Russian-American soprano and mezzo-soprano, born Jennie Davidovich in St. Petersburg on 15 June 1903 (the place and date of her birth are uncertain). She studied flute and piano, and after the Revolution went to Paris, beginning vocal studies. Inspired by her teacher, Anna El-Tour, she took a stage name from hers. In 1930 she made her opera debut in Chicago, singing a role in the American premiere of *Lorenzaccio* by Ernest Moret; in 1931 she made her European opera debut in Paris, and sang in many European houses. Her Metropolitan Opera debut, as Mignon, was on 15 May 1937. She remained in America, taking citizenship in 1946, and sang with the Metropolitan in 1943–1945 and 1946–1947. She portrayed Mignon, Carmen, and Rosina in her last season. Tourel was brilliant in recitals, specializing in Rachmaninoff and other Russian song composers and in the French repertoire. She also taught at the Juilliard School. Death came in New York on 23 Nov 1973.

Two LP discs from Odyssey (#Y2 32880; 1976) cover important material from Tourel's wide repertoire. *Carmen* arias, Debussy songs, and Rossini numbers are included. Missing from that memorial issue were her remarkable Rachmaninoff songs, with Erich Itor-Kahn at the piano, recorded for Columbia in set #M-625. Another fine Columbia recording was *Alexander Nevsky* with the Philadelphia Orchestra and Westminster Choir (#M-580).

TOURNAPHONE. A German disc player marketed in Britain in 1906. Three models are illustrated in Chew 1981, one of them the Baby Tournaphone.

TOY RECORDS. Small discs (usually five to seven inches in diameter) intended for children, often sold with small record players. Thomas Edison held a patent for toy and doll cylinder phonographs (U.S. #423,039; filed 2 July 1889; granted 11 Mar 1890), but exploited only the doll. Emile Berliner marketed toy gramophones in 1889 in Germany, with five-inch "plates" (see BERLINER (LABEL). In view of the repertoire on those plates, it may be that the product was miniature in size but not necessarily for children. In December 1900 the Consolidated Talking Machine Co., immediate predecessor of Victor, advertised a Toy Gram-O-Phone for $3, with six records and 100 needles included.

After World War I there were several sets of toy records in the U.S. **Mother Goose Records** were distributed by Emerson Phonograph Co. in 1920. Harper Brothers issued **Bubble Books** in 1919. Both the Emerson and the Harper releases were combinations of children's books with small discs.

In Britain there were numerous examples in the 1920s. The **Bob-o-Link Talking Book** was offered from 1922. Other labels in the field included **Little Marvel**, Kiddyphone, **Mimosa**, **Victory**, Broadcast Junior, HMV (Nursery Series), Homo Baby, **Savana**, Pigmy Gramophone, and **The Bell**. J. E. Hough offered The Bell, whose matrices were used to press under other labels as well, namely **Marspen**, Savana, Boots the Chemists, The Little Briton, **John Bull Record**, The Dinky, and The Fairy.

The smallest discs (diameter 15/16 inches) were the HMV records made for the Queen Mary's Doll House gramophone, shown at the Wembley Empire Exhibition in 1924.

Little Tots' Nursery Tunes records appeared in 1923, with releases in Britain and the U.S. HMV presented a series of seven-inch records of children's material in 1924, featuring Auntie and Uncle characters. Another seven-inch children's issue in U.K. was on the Goodson label 1930. In the same year Crystalate offered a Nursery Rhymes series. Other nursery rhymes were issued on the **Durium** label in 1932. **Kid-Kord** was another seven-inch label of 1932.

LP toy records appeared from Oriole Records, Ltd., in about 1951. Others came from the Children's Record Co., London (the Cricket label), Selcol Products, Ltd. (Gala Nursery Records), Lumar, Ltd., of Swansea, Wales (Kiddietunes—Extra Long Play), and Pickwick International, Inc. (G.B.), Ltd. (Happy Time Records).

Many small records were not intended for children, but carried regular repertoire; both adult and children's small discs are discussed in Andrews 1988/4. [Andrews*; Andrews 1988/4; Haines 1973, with reader comments in *TMR* #24 (October 1973), pp. 255–256.] *See also* CHILDREN'S RECORDS.

TRACING. The movement of the **needle** or **stylus** as it follows the modulations of the record groove. Failure of the stylus to follow the groove variations closely results in **tracing distortion.** *See also* TRACKING FORCE.

TRACING DISTORTION. A type of nonlinear distortion that results when the curve traced by a reproducing **stylus** is not the exact replica of the groove. (*See* DISTORTION, VII.) It is caused by the differences in shape between the cutting and reproducing styli, and it increases as the radius of the groove spiral shortens and the **groove speed** lessens. Ten percent is the maximum acceptable tracing distortion for the seven-inch 45, 20 percent is the maximum for the 12-inch LP, and 30 percent for the extended-play (EP) long-playing record. Optimum playback stylus shape, size, and contact angle, as well as the counter distortion of the input signal to the cutting stylus are interdependent and dependent factors that contribute to the amount of distortion and are not subject to complete neutralization. [Isom*.]

TRACK. The path on a magnetic tape that is used for recording and playback. Full track means that the entire width of the tape is used; dual track means that half the width of the tape is used for each continuous signal. An eight-track tape employs eight side-by-side tracks, representing four separate stereo pairs of two channels each, or two of four channels each. [Isom*.] *See also* MULTITRACK RECORDING.

TRACKING FORCE. In disc playback, the force exerted by the **cartridge** (pickup) on the **stylus.** A low tracking force is advantageous in terms of disc wear, but too little tracking force will allow the stylus to bounce in the groove, leading to disc wear and to distortion. Modern LP cartridges track at two grams—some at one gram. [Isom*.]

TRANSCRIPTION DISCS. Large diameter (between 16 and 20 inches) **lacquer** (acetate), later vinyl, discs used in film recording and in radio, in the 1930s. A vertical-cut disc came from Bell Telephone Laboratories, playing at 33 1/3 rpm, with 200 grooves to the inch; it had a thin wax cover on an aluminum backing, with gold sputtering. Playback discs were translucent acetate, later vinyl. [Kunstadt 1988.] *See also* DISC 1, 4; INSTANTANEOUS RECORDINGS; RADIO PROGRAMS RECORDED.

TRANSDUCER. Any device that converts one form of energy to another. In an electrical audio recording system such conversions occur as input signals (mechanical energy) are changed to electrical energy by the microphone, then back to mechanical energy by the cutting head as it creates the groove pattern. The sequence is reversed in playback. *See also* DISC, 3; MECHANICAL ELECTRICAL ANALOGIES; MICROPHONE.

TRANSIENT INTERMODULATION DISTORTION (TIM). The type of distortion in playback of an audio system that follows sudden overloads of the amplifier, too quick for the compensating negative feedback to counteract it. A loud sforzando in a musical work, like those in Haydn's "Surprise Symphony," is a typical cause. The result is a ringing effect or, in piano recording, a ping sound. *See also* TRANSIENT RESPONSE.

TRANSIENT RESPONSE. In audio playback, the reaction of the system to a sudden change in amplitude of the signal, or of its frequency. Poor transient response, often caused by loud-speaker inadequacy, brings a boom in the bass or an edgy sound at the top of the spectrum. *See also* TRANSIENT INTERMODULATION DISTORTION (TIM).

TRANSISTOR. A semiconductor device that can amplify or (with power gain) switch electrical signals. Transistors generally replaced vacuum tubes in audio systems during the 1960s.

TRANSPORT. The element in a CD player that spins the disc while isolating it from vibration.

TRAUBEL, HELEN, 1899–1972. American soprano, born in St. Louis on 20 June 1899. She studied singing as a child, and made a concert debut with the St. Louis Symphony Orchestra on 13 Dec 1923, performing in the Mahler Fourth Symphony. She continued singing and studying locally, and then sang at the Metropolitan Opera in a minor role on 12 May 1937. After singing her first major part, as Sieglinde on 28 Dec 1939, she was quickly identified as the prime American Wagnerian soprano. She was Kirsten Flagstad's successor as Brünnhilde, Elsa, Isolde, and the other Wagner heroines. She was also outstanding as the Marschallin, and occasionally ventured into the Italian repertoire with fine results. An early operatic crossover singer, she enjoyed working in New York nightclubs; objections from the Metropolitan management in 1953 led her to quit the opera company and remain with the popular idiom. Traubel then performed on Broadway, in films and on television. She died in Santa Monica, California, on 28 July 1972.

Her records were for Victor (1940 and 1947) and Columbia (1945–1949). Traubel's remarkable Isolde is illustrated in the 1945 Columbia set #MM 573, including the Narrative and the Liebestod, and in the 1947 duet with Torsten Ralf (set #X 286). Perhaps her greatest discs were the Act I duets from *Walküre* and the Dawn Duet from *Götterdämmerung* with Lauritz Melchior, under Arturo Toscanini (Victor #LM 2452; 1941). RCA compact disc #60264 (1991) reissued the *Walküre* material, but as of summer 1991 neither the *Tristan* nor the

Götterdämmerung interpretations were in the catalog.

TRAVIS, MERLE, 1917–1983. American country singer and guitarist, born in Rosewood, Kentucky, on 29 Nov 1917. He learned banjo first, and transferred some of the technique to the guitar (thumb picking on top of the melody line). He played on Indiana radio, then on WLW in Cincinnati. Fame arrived with a move to California in 1944, as he signed with Capitol Records and made discs of some of his own compositions: "No Vacancy" (Capitol #258; 1946), "Divorce Me C.O.D." (Capitol # 290; 1946), "So Round, So Firm, So Fully Packed" (Capitol # 349; 1946), and above all "Sixteen Tons" (in Capitol album #50; 1947). A later composition, "Smoke, Smoke, Smoke that Cigarette," was made into a hit record by Tex Williams. Travis was elected to the Country Music Hall of Fame in 1977. He died on 20 Oct 1983, in Tahlequah, Oklahoma.

TREMONT (label). An American record of the mid-1920s, produced by the American Record Manufacturing Co., of Framingham, Massachusetts. Masters were from Cameo. [Rust 1978.]

TRIANGLE (label). An American record made by **Bridgeport Die and Machine Co.** from September 1922 to 1925. Paramount and Emerson provided most of the masters. The price was $.50. [Rust 1978.]

TRIO DE LUTECE. An instrumental ensemble that recorded for Columbia in 1916. Members were George Barrere, flute; Carlos Salzedo, harp; and Paul Kefer, cello. "Chant sans paroles" of Tchaikovsky and "Serenade" by Widor were played on #2684.

TRISTANO, LENNIE, 1919–1978. American jazz pianist, born Leonard Joseph Tristano in Chicago on 19 Mar 1919. He became blind in childhood, but went ahead with his planned career, studying at the American Conservatory of Music in Chicago (B.Mus., 1943). He was highly praised for his club performances. In 1949 he made a fine LP for Prestige with Lee Konitz (#7250). A 1955 Atlantic record, *Lines*,

offered Tristano solos; among the most enduring are "These Foolish Things" and "You Go to My Head." "Turkish Mambo" demonstrated his skill with rhythmic complexities. He died in New York on 18 Nov 1978.

TRITON PHONOGRAPH CO. A New York firm, established in 1913. Location was 137 Fifth Ave. in 1916, when five models of the Triton disc player were marketed, selling for $10 to $50.

TRIX, HELEN, ca. 1892–1951. American vaudeville singer, born in Newmanstown, Pennsylvania, date uncertain. She recorded early for Edison cylinders, with six solos and an ensemble number in 1906–1907, the first being "Is Your Mother In, Molly Malone?" in Irish dialect (#9365; 1906). Her biggest hit for Edison was "The Bird on Nellie's Hat" (#9450; 1907); it was also recorded for Victor in 1907. In the 1920s she and her sister Josephine were on stage together, gaining acclaim in the U.K. and the U.S. She made records for HMV in the early 1920s, and later made electrics for Columbia in Britain. She remained active until after the Second World War. Trix died in New York on 18 Nov 1951. [Brooks 1990; Walsh 1954/4–5.]

TROCADERO ORCHESTRA. A London hotel ensemble that recorded for the Gramophone Co. in 1898 and 1899, producing some of the earliest dance music on record. They also played marches, and selections from opera, beginning with "Hip Hip Hurrah March." The Trocadero recordings of "La Marseillaise" and of the Austrian and Prussian national anthems (all in September 1898) appear to be the earliest disc recordings of that genre.

TROMBONE RECORDINGS. Early trombone cylinders were made for Edison in 1898–1903, by Nicholas Scholl and Leo A. Zimmerman. "Five Hundred Thousand Devils" (by Scholl; #5600) was the first of the group of 10 items. Zimmerman also played on Columbia cylinders ca. 1900, and did a solo with Gilmore's Band in 1903. He recorded for Electric cylinders and Odeon Records when Sousa's Band visited England in the first decade of the century. Because of the British brass band movement, many trombone works were recorded in the U.K.: solos, duets, and combinations with cornets. An unnamed artist performed six solos for Berliner discs in October 1898, beginning with "Rocked in the Cradle of the Deep."

The lack of an interesting repertoire has inhibited the appearance of international concert artists on the trombone. However the instrument is vital in jazz and swing music, beginning with early Dixieland style. It was Eddie Edwards who was heard on the first jazz record to be issued, by the Original Dixieland Jazz Band. Miff Mole played with the Original Memphis Five in the 1920s; Bill Rank was with Bix Beiderbecke and Frank Trumbauer. Kid Ory was a skillful handler of the instrument's brazen sound. Jack Teagarden was the principal virtuoso of the 1930s.

Great trombonists of the swing era included Tommy Dorsey, who developed a uniquely dulcet legato; J.. Higginbotham, Bill Harris, and J.J. Johnson. Glenn Miller was a trombonist, and so was Will Bradley. Other featured trombone artists in the Big Bands included Benny Morton (Count Basie), Ray Coniff (Bunny Berigan), and Pee Wee Hunt (Glen Gray).

TRUETONE NEEDLES.
A brand of needle produced by the New York Disc Needle Co. In 1916 they advertised a variety of needles, categorized as loud, extra loud, opera, medium tone, and soft tone.

TRUMBAUER, FRANKIE, 1901–1956.
American jazz saxophonist, born in Carbondale, Illinois, on 30 May 1901. After military service in World War I he went to Chicago and played with various groups. In 1925–1926 he had his own band in St. Louis, with Bix Beiderbecke; the two of them went on to Paul Whiteman's orchestra in 1927. Trumbauer, Beiderbecke, and guitarist Eddie Lang made an important group of Okeh recordings, including "Wringin' and Twistin'" (Okeh #40916). Trumbauer also recorded with his own band, with varying personnel, but featuring Beiderbecke; Jimmy Dorsey, Adrian Rollini, Jack Teagarden, Matty Malneck, and Eddie Lang are among the men heard on Okeh discs made in 1927–1930. Smith

Ballew and Johnny Mercer did some of the vocals. "Trumbology" (Okeh 40871; 1927), "Singin' the Blues" (Okeh #40772; 1927), and "I'm Coming, Virginia" / "Way Down Yonder in New Orleans" (Okeh #40843; 1927) were among the best of the records. Trumbauer left the music field in 1940, for aviation; he was a test pilot in World War II. He died in Kansas City on 11 June 1956.

TRUMPET RECORDINGS.
It was the cornet that was used in early recordings, and sometimes the bugle, rather than the trumpet. The cornet and trumpet are very similar, but the cornet, with a slightly more conical bore, is easier to play and gives a more mellow tone. Emil Cassi, of Theodore Roosevelt's Rough Riders, did offer some bugle calls on the trumpet (according to Koenigsberg 1987) on an Edison cylinder made before May 1899. In Dixieland jazz groups, cornets were typically present. In the mid-1920s the trumpet took the place of the cornet in jazz and dance ensembles. Recordings of 1927–1929 illustrate the changeover, as major groups turned to the trumpet sound and distinguished performers appeared. The California Ramblers had Chelsea Quealey; Red Nichols played trumpet with Miff Mole and His Molers; Manny Klein was with Jack Teagarden and Gene Prince with Andy Kirk. King Oliver, famous as a cornetist, played trumpet in 1929 recordings. There were three trumpets in the Fletcher Henderson band of 1927, setting the pattern for the Big Bands of the 1930s. Edna White was a noted soloist of the 1920s, not a member of a Big Band.

Those Bands had many outstanding trumpeters, among them several future Band leaders. Charley Teagarden was with Paul Whiteman; Buck Clayton was with Count Basie; Bunny Berigan and Charlie Spivak were with Tommy Dorsey; Cootie Williams and Rex Stewart were with Duke Ellington. Benny Goodman had Harry James and Ziggy Elman. Jimmie Lunceford had Sy Oliver.

Other soloists who emerged in the late 1940s and 1950s include Roy Eldridge, Charlie Shavers, Maynard Ferguson, Miles Davis (who dominated the 1960s as well), Chet Baker, and Dizzy Gillespie.

On the classical side there have been a number of prominent soloists, despite the paucity of repertoire. Among the more prolific recording artists are Maurice André, Gerard Schwarz, and Thomas Stevens. **Wynton Marsalis** is the most renowned crossover trumpeter, with important recordings in the classical and popular catalogs.

TUBA RECORDINGS. This instrument is heard to best advantage in the band or orchestra, rather than as a solo performer; indeed there is virtually no concert literature for it. An unidentified artist played "Rocked in the Cradle of the Deep" on a Columbia cylinder ca. 1900 (#29200) with a piano accompaniment. There were several LP records by classical tuba players, such as Harvey Phillips and Roger Bobo. Ralph Vaughan Williams wrote a concerto for the instrument, performed on an RCA LP (#LSC-3281) by John Fletcher. "Tubby the Tuba" was a children's disc by Danny Kaye, recorded later by Carol Channing.

TUBB, ERNEST, 1914–1984. American country singer, songwriter, and guitarist, born in Crisp, Texas, on 9 Feb 1914. He developed a distinctive deep drawling vocal tone and gained success on several radio stations in Texas. He appeared at the Grand Ole Opry from 1942, becoming a regular performer there, then formed a group called the Texas Troubadours and toured with them. A honky-tonk variant of country music emerged from their work. Tubb performed at Carnegie Hall in 1947, in the first country program to be presented in that auditorium. He had a record shop in Nashville, and broadcast a program from there: *Midnight Jamboree*. The young Elvis Presley was among the singers presented. Tubb was one of the great names in country music for a half century. He used an electric guitar, and he fostered the use of the term "country" in place of the derogatory "hillbilly." He was elected to the Country Music Hall of Fame in 1965. Death came in Nashville on 6 Sep 1984.

Tubb's recordings were consistent hits from the 1940s until the 1980s. An early chart song was a duet with Red Foley, "Goodnight, Irene" (Decca #46255; 1950). Among 35 *Cash Box* country single chart numbers in 1958–1982, perhaps the most appreciated were "I Cried a Tear" (Decca #30872; 1959), "Next Time" (Decca #30952; 1959), and "Thanks a Lot" (Decca #31526; 1963). He had several successful duet discs with Loretta Lynn, the most popular being "Mr. and Mrs. Used to Be" (Decca #31643; 1964). Most of his career was with Decca, but he made some 1979 discs for the Cachet label.

TUCKER, RICHARD, 1913–1975. American tenor, born Reuben Ticker on 28 Aug 1913 in Brooklyn. As a child he sang in the synagogue and on radio. In 1943 he made his opera debut with the Salmaggi Co. in New York, as Alfredo. He joined the Metropolitan Opera on 25 Jan 1945, as Enzo, and stayed 30 years as one of the tenor mainstays of the company. He excelled in the Verdi and Puccini roles. In 1947 Tucker made his European debut in Verona, in a performance with Maria Callas, making her Italian debut. He was heard subsequently in Covent Garden, La Scala, Vienna, etc. He died in Kalamazoo, Michigan, on 8 Jan 1975.

The Tucker recorded legacy is strongest in the complete opera sets he made for Columbia and Victor. *Forza del destino* was among his finest, recorded in 1955 with Callas (HMV #SLS 5120) and again in 1965 with Shirley Verrett for Victor (#SER 5527/30). His other complete opera sets were of *Aida, Boheme, Cavalleria rusticana, Così fan tutte, Lucia, Madama Butterfly, Pagliacci, Rigoletto, Traviata,* and *Trovatore.*

TUCKER, SOPHIE, 1884–1966. Russian/American vaudeville performer and popular singer, known as the "Last of the Red Hot Mamas." She was brought to America at age three, and did her first work as a waitress in her father's restaurant in Hartford, Connecticut. She went to New York and got various singing jobs in vaudeville and burlesque. She was in the *Ziegfeld Follies of 1909,* but did not attract much notice.

Her earliest records were six Edison cylinders made in 1910, among them "My Husband's in the City" (#10366) and "That Loving Soul Kiss" (#10493). She was a "coon shouter" in the early days, with suggestive lyrics; later she sang in a cabaret style. offering more sophisticated material. She had her own group, Five

Kings of Syncopation, in the early 1920s, and made some records with them for Arto and Okeh. "After You've Gone" (Okeh #40837; 1927) was accompanied by Miff Mole's Molers. Her all-time favorite disc was "Some of These Days," recorded with Ted Lewis in 1926 (Columbia #826-D); recorded again for Victor in 1929 (#22049). "There'll Be Some Changes Made" (Okeh #40921) was another great success. Tucker was a popular motion picture actress from 1929 to 1945, and she had star billing in several Broadway revues. As her voice faded in the 1950s and 1960s she developed a quiet talking style of presentation. She died on 9 Feb 1966.

TUNER. In an radio **receiver**, the device that selectively converts radio signals to audio signals. It is often a separate component in an audio system, used with an audio amplifier. [Klinger*.]

TUNING BAND. On certain early discs, a band that followed the program material; it reproduced a fixed pitch, for the purpose of setting the correct turntable speed. A 1904 G & T record, #053048 (a song by Giordano sung by a soprano named Frascani) and a 1909 Gramophone Concert Record, #GC-37851 ("Ave Maria" for cello and piano) had such bands, termed "key-notes" by G & T. Fonotipia copied the device, but gave it up following protests from the Gramophone Co. (Italy), Ltd..

TURNER, ALAN. British baritone. He sang with various opera companies in the U.K., and in Chicago and Philadelphia. Turner made many opera and operetta recordings for Edison, Victor, Gramophone Co., Odeon, Edison Bell, Marathon, Operaphone, Pathé, and others. He organized his own Alan Turner Opera Co. and toured widely in the 1930s. His Edison cylinders were "In Happy Moments" (#9291; 1906), "Queen of the Earth" (#9876; 1908), and "Goodbye, Sweetheart, Goodbye" (#9843; 1908). In 1906 he made four records for G & T, including the "Toreador Song" (#3-2455) and the *Pagliacci* "Prologo" (#02081). He was pictured in the 1915 *Victor Book of the Opera* clad as Count di Luna, and a number from *Trovatore* was among the 25 listings for him in the 1922

Victor catalog; but he disappeared quickly with the arrival of electrical recording—there was no sign of him in the Victor 1927 catalog.

TURNER, EVA, 1892–1990. British soprano, born in Oldham on 10 Mar 1892. She sang in the chorus of the Carl Rosa Opera Co., then had solo roles and was heard by someone who arranged for an audition with Arturo Toscanini in Milan. As a result she was engaged at La Scala for Wagnerian roles, and began an international career. Turandot became the role most associated with her, and also Aida—performed with great success in Chicago in 1928–1930—but she retained her Wagner connections, doing an acclaimed *Tristan* under Albert Coates in London, in 1937. Turner died in London, on 15 June 1990.

She recorded exclusively for Columbia, making 30 sides in Italy (1927–1928), and London (1928, 1933, 1938). Turner's finest records include "In questa reggia" from *Turandot* (Columbia #D 1619, replaced by #D1631, in U.S. #D12588; 1928) and "Ritorna vincitor" (Columbia #D1578, in U.S. #12587; 1928), and "Oh patria mia" (#L1976, U.S. #D16404; 1927). All were reissued by Columbia on LP. [Richards 1957 is a discography.]

TURNTABLE. The platter or platform on which discs are rotated in recording or playback; by extension the term is applied to the complete assembly: platter, spindle, driving components, and motor. An ideal turntable has a constant accurate speed of rotation, without **rumble**, and without effects from outside vibrations or feedback. These desired conditions were hardly to be found in the early turntables of Emile Berliner, operated by hand cranking, or later models with treadle power. **Spring motor phonographs** ran more dependably, and finally electric mains power made constant speed possible.

Two types of operation are found: belt drive, in which a resilient belt connects the motor to the turntable platter; and direct drive, in which a motor shaft or roller is directly coupled to the platter's center or rim. (Although there was no motor but the human engine involved, Berliner record players can be classed as both belt driven and direct; some had a belt to carry the cranking energy to the platter, some had the crank attached to the platter.) Either belt drive or direct drive can give satisfactory results, but direct drive has been preferred in professional work.

Heavy turntables (about eight pounds) offer greater stability and are used in studio work, but they require a stronger motor than consumer turntables (weighing about four pounds).

Felt covering was used on turntables in the 1890s. The first advertising for velvet covered turntables appeared in 1921. Recent mats for turntables have emphasized anti-static qualities and non-conductivity.

In the best of LP turntables, beginning in the 1960s with Acoustic Research, Inc., products, and exemplified today by the Yamaha PF-800, there is a suspended subchassis isolation system, to prevent any unwanted movements. On the direct drive Diapason Archive Turntable, a readout provides continual monitoring of the playing speed; the turntable can be set to any speed from 16 rpm to 120 rpm. [Kogen 1977.] *See also* FLUTTER; PITCH; TONE ARM; and WOW.

TWEAKING. A method of suppressing resonances and vibrations in audio playback by the placement of dampers under components. The dampers, made of various kinds of absorbent materials, are sometimes called isolation feet. Good results have been reported with such feet positioned beneath a turntable. [Whyte 1989.]

TWEETER. A high frequency (treble) **loudspeaker.**

TWENTIETH CENTURY GRAPHOPHONE. Columbia's 1905 model BC and the 1906 model BCG were identified as Twentieth Century machines (*see* COLUMBIA RECORD PLAYERS).

TWIN DOUBLE SIDED DISC RECORD (label). A British record, often referred to as the Twin, sold from June 1908. It was made by the Gramophone Co., Ltd., from its own matrices and those of its sister companies. They were the firm's first double-sided discs in Britain (there were already double-sided Gramophone concert records on sale in Europe), sold behind the facade of "The Twin Record Co.," a subdivision of Gramophone Co. with its own headquarters office (later registered in 1910 as a private limited company, with all shares held by the parent company).

Twin discs had their own single-face number series, quite separate from Gramophone Concert discs, and from Zonophone single-sided discs (which had "X" prefixed single-face numbers in repertoire blocks). The **British Zonophone Co.** had been set up earlier by G & T to handle British issues of Zonophone Records and machines from the G & T German subsidiary, International Zonophone Co. (In 1910 British Zonophone also became an independent private limited company, as a subsidiary of the Gramophone Co., Ltd.) The two labels came together in May 1911, the Zonophones having been sold under British Zonophone since February 1904 and the Twin since June 1908. The new label of the combined catalogs was "Zonophone Record—The Twin." It bore the twin cherubs design, a registered trademark. The Twin label was used in India after the First World War, by the Gramophone Co. India, Ltd. [Andrews*.]

TWITTY, CONWAY, 1933– . American country and rock singer, born Harold Lloyd Jenkins in Friars Point, Mississippi, on 1 Sep 1933. He took his stage name from the names of two southern towns. He performed with a group he formed at age 10, then was in military service from 1954 to 1956. In 1958 he signed with Mercury Records and made a hit with "I Need Your Lovin'" (#71086; 1957). "It's Only Make Believe" was his first chart song on the MGM label, which recorded him to 1961 (#12677; 1958). Twitty was a rock star, but he departed from that style as the hits tapered off in the 1960s; by 1965 he had become a country singer. A new group, the Lonely Blue Boys, was a great success in the 1970s, with more than 40 chart singles. "You've Never Been This Far Before" (MCA #40094; 1973) was one of his finer solos of that time. His duets with Loretta Lynn were particularly popular, for example, "As Soon As I Hang Up the Phone" (MCA #40251; 1974) and Grammy winner "After the Fire is Gone" (Decca #32776; 1971). MCA was

his label through the 1970s; in the 1980s he was
with Elektra.

TWO KAUFIELDS. A male vocal duo who
recorded for Emerson in 1919. Members were
Arthur Fields and either Irving Kaufman or
Jack Kaufman.

.

U

U.S. Everlasting Record. *See* U-S EVERLASTING RECORD.

U.S. PHONOGRAPH CO. Edison's phonograph export agency during the 1890s, located in Newark, New Jersey. (This was a brown-wax era firm, with no connection to the later **U-S Phonograph Co.** of Cleveland.)

U.S. Phonograph Co. began in the spring of 1893 as a successor to the **New Jersey Phonograph Co.**, one of the North American Phonograph Co. local companies, and was reorganized in January 1894. **Victor H. Emerson** served as general manager from the beginning, and as president from January 1894. **George Tewksbury**, formerly of the Kansas Phonograph Co., was another executive of the firm. **Frank L. Capps** invented the early U.S. spring motor in 1895. These men were to become influential personalities in the recording industry.

U.S. Phonograph produced a variety of musical and spoken-word selections on cylinders by mechanical duplication in their laboratory at 87-91 Orange Street, Newark. Popular artists included Russell Hunting, Dan W. Quinn, Len Spencer, John Yorke AtLee and Issler's Orchestra.

When Edison organized his **National Phonograph Co.** in January 1896, he was not in a position to meet the demand for entertainment records. U.S. Phonograph Co. supplied master cylinders to Edison until U.S. Phonograph was bought out by National Phonograph in late 1897. [Annand 1970.]

Bill Klinger

U.S. Phonograph Co. (Cleveland). *See* U-S PHONOGRAPH CO.

ULTONA. The **reproducer** marketed by the **Brunswick-Balke-Collender Co.** in 1916. It could play vertical-cut or lateral-cut discs.

UNITED (label). An American record issued ca. 1911–ca. 1913 by the **United Talking Machine Co.** of Chicago (608 S. Dearborn St.), a division of the **Great Northern Manufacturing Co.** The material consisted of Columbia overstock, modified with larger spindle holes (1 1/2 inches) and pasteover labels. Playback required access to a machine made by the Great Northern Manufacturing Co. When United Talking Machine was succeeded by the **Consolidated Talking Machine Co.**, sometime before March 1918, the United label was continued by Consolidated. [Rust 1978.]

UNITED HEBREW DISK RECORDS. An American label issued by the United Hebrew Disk and Cylinder Co., 257–261 Grand St., New York. Advertising appeared from January to November 1905. Pierre Long was manager of the firm. [Andrews*.]

UNITED HOT CLUBS OF AMERICA (UHCA). A record issued by the **Commodore Music Shop** in New York from 1936 to ca. 1941. It was a reissue label for jazz classics that were no longer available through normal channels. Rust has accounted for 86 sides in all. [Rust 1978.]

UNITED STATES GRAMOPHONE CO. The second American firm established by Emile Berliner, succeeding his American Gramophone Co. in April 1893. Address was 1410 Pennsylvania Ave., Washington, D.C. Gramophones were marketed, and also one-sided seven-inch discs with the Berliner label. The machines produced included hand-driven models and battery-operated models; about 1,000 were sold in 1894. In fall 1894 a factory and salesroom opened in Baltimore. The **Berliner Gramophone Co.** took over both manufacturing and sales of all products (except for the District of Columbia region). United States Gramophone Co. continued to hold the Berliner patents. [Wile 1979/2.]

UNITED STATES MARINE BAND. One of the principal musical ensembles of the 19th century, greatly acclaimed under the direction of **John Philip Sousa.** The band was one of the leading groups on early records, beginning with work for Columbia cylinders in 1890. (Only a small number of the musicians—as few as a dozen of them—actually made the studio recordings.) When Sousa resigned in 1892, Francesco Fanciulli succeeded him, and directed the record sessions to 1897; William H. Santelmann followed Fanciulli. On Columbia the band had a wide repertoire apart from marches: two-steps, polkas, waltzes, ballads, hymns, etc. Berliner recorded the Marine Band in September 1899, as they rendered "You Got to Play Ragtime." From 1909 the band was also heard on Edison cylinders (20 numbers by 1912), Edison Diamond Discs (11 sides by 1925), and then on Victor discs, from 1906 to 1927. There were 13 sides in the Victor 1917 catalog, directed by Santelmann; one of them the "Maple Leaf Rag." [Hoover 1971, p. 73, shows about 14 members of the band, identified as "Sousa's Band," in the studio in 1891.]

United States Phonograph Co. *See* U-S PHONOGRAPH CO.

UNITED STATES RECORD MANUFACTURING CO. A firm established in 1920 in Long Island City, New York. Victor H. Emerson was president. It was announced in March 1921 that the company was prepared to press

10-inch discs in substantial quantities and to supply stock matrices for the presses of others. Addresses given in advertising of April 1921 were the main office at 48 E. 34th St., New York City, and the factory at 8th-9th Avenues, Long Island City. Thomas H. McClain, an engineer formerly with Thomas Edison, supervised the factory. A label named H.I.T.S. was advertised by the firm in September 1921, stemming from its "Hits Department" at 249 W. 34th St. [Andrews*.]

UNITED STATES TALKING MACHINE CO. (I) A Chicago firm active in 1897. It sold a finger-wound disc player at a cost of $3, and records for it (disguised Berliner discs). Joseph N. Brown was the inventor of the machine (U.S. patent #653,654, filed 22 Apr 1897; granted 17 July 1900), which had a wooden tone arm, steel needle, and gutta percha listening tubes. Despite its low selling price, and a manufacturing cost of only 12 1/2 cents per unit, the device was a market failure and remainders were sold off at $.98 each. [Koenigsberg 1990.]

UNITED STATES TALKING MACHINE CO. (II) A Newark, New Jersey, firm established in 1916. It advertised in that year a line of Ideal disc players, in eight models, selling from $12 to $85.

UNITED TALKING MACHINE CO. A Chicago firm, established in 1911 as a division of the **Great Northern Manufacturing Co.** Location was 608 S. Dearborn St. Record players were sold under the Symphony name, and discs with the **United** label. The players had 1 1/2 inch spindles, to accommodate the extra large spindle holes that were cut into the discs (which were Columbia overstock records, relabelled by United). The firm seems to have been absorbed by the **Consolidated Talking Machine Co.** sometime before March 1918. [Fabrizio 1980.]

UNIVERSAL PHONOGRAPH CO. A New York firm, located at 34 E. 21st St. In the January 1899 *Phonoscope* it advertised records guaranteed to be original, and invited clients to "come and take the records off the rack as they are being made." Material included "catchy music" as well as selections from "works of Wagner, Meyerbeer, etc." George Rosey and his orchestra, and Albert Campbell were artists identified in the promotion copy. Joseph W. Stern was proprietor, and Mitchell Marks was manager.

UNIVERSAL QUARTET. A male vocal ensemble who recorded for Zonophone around 1905. Tentative identification of the membership, by Walsh, mentions Geoffrey O'Hara, tenor; Reinald Werrenrath, baritone; and Walter MacPherson, bass. [Walsh 1962/10.]

UNIVERSAL TALKING MACHINE CO. A firm which **Frank Seaman** took part in establishing on 10 Feb 1898, with Orville La Dow as president. Its record plant was at 152 E. 23rd St., New York, and its machine factory at 517 E. 132nd St. The purpose of Universal was to make machines for Frank Seaman's **National Gramophone Co.** Seaman was sole sales agent for Berliner gramophones and discs, and the Berliner Gramophone Co. objected to Seaman's attempts to handle alternative cheaper machines. As a consequence, Seaman took part in organizing the **National Gramophone Corp.** (on 10 Mar 1899), as sales outlet for the Universal Talking Machine Co. machines (called Zonophones) as soon as they would be in production. In fact, the first Zonophone products (1898) had been unauthorized, disguised Berliner items, contributing to the eventual break between Berliner and Seaman. Successful litigation by the Columbia (Graphophone) interests against Seaman's company for infringements of their Bell-Tainter patents was followed by a cross-licensing agreement between the producers of the Zonophone and Columbia products. When the National Gramophone Corp. failed in fall 1901, the Universal Talking Machine Co. held a sheriff's sale of patents and equipment and took on the role of sales outlet for the Zonophone lines. A new company, Universal Talking Machine Manufacturing Co., was formed on 19 Dec 1901 to take over the production of those lines. (It was not licensed by the Graphophone people.) This was the third Zonophone firm, along with the Univer-

sal Talking Machine Co., and the International Zonophone Co. that had been founded in spring 1901.

The original Universal Talking Machine Co. kept its corporate existence to 6 June 1903, when its share stock was acquired by G & T, along with the share stock of Universal Talking Machine Manufacturing Co. and that of the American and German International Zonophone Co. In September 1903 G & T sold the Universal assets to Victor.

As a Victor subsidiary the Universal firm continued to produce the Zonophone line of discs and players. In 1908 it offered five discs by Luisa Tetrazzini, in nine-inch size for $.75, and in 11-inch size for $1.25. The address of the UTMMC was given in a July 1911 advertisement as 4th and Race Streets, Philadelphia. Columbia successfully litigated UTMMC out of business in 1912, on grounds of patent infringement, as it had never been licensed by Columbia. All masters and factory stock of American-made Zonophone records had to be destroyed by court order.

The American company was not related to the British Universal Talking Machine Co., Ltd. [Andrews*.]

UNIVERSAL TALKING MACHINE CO., LTD. A British firm, not related to the American company of like name, registered on 9 Nov 1907, addressed at Fenchurch Ave., London. It was a successor to the gramophone branch of **Aldridge, Salmon and Co., Ltd.** British gramophones were sold. The firm wound up operations on 5 May 1908, then reorganized and continued in business under the same name. **E.J. Sabine** and Thomas F. Bragg were among the directors, while controlling interest was held by Aldridge, Salmon and Co., Ltd. A record with the Elephone label was issued from November 1908, at which time the firm was at 37 Curtain Road. Liquidation came on 6 June 1909. The Universal name was used for a time in 1910 by **William Andrew Barraud**, before he gave his company his own name. [Andrews 1990/6.]

Universal Talking Machine Manufacturing Co. *See* UNIVERSAL TALKING MACHINE CO.

UP-TO-DATE (label). A rare American record of ca. 1924, apparently related to the **Blu-Disc.** Record #2019 was a vocal by Florence Bristol accompanied by Duke Ellington. [Rust 1978.]

URLUS, JACQUES, 1867–1935. German tenor, born near Aachen on 9 Jan 1867. His family moved to the Netherlands when he was 10 years old. He studied engineering, then voice, and sang in a minor operatic role in 1894, with the National Opera at Amsterdam. He continued with the company to 1899, becoming a leading tenor, then sang in Leipzig from 1900 to 1915. Urlus became known as one of the finest Wagner tenors, performing at Bayreuth (1911–1914) and singing Tristan with great success at Covent Garden in 1910. He was the leading heldentenor at the Metropolitan Opera in 1913–1917. He sang through Europe, and retired after a final performance in Amsterdam in 1932. Urlus died in Noordwijk, Netherlands, on 6 June 1935.

Pathé cylinders and discs of 1903, sung in Dutch, marked the beginning of his recording career. He did 15 Wagner numbers, plus tenor arias by Mascagni, Leoncavallo, Verdi, Gounod, Bizet, and Meyerbeer. In 1907 he recorded in Leipzig for Grammophon, beginning with a German version of "O paradiso" (#3-42898). He recorded a total of 76 numbers for Gramophone Co. labels, the last being in 1912. Thereafter he sang for Edison Diamond Discs from 1914 to 1925, doing 30 solos and three duets with Marie Rappold.

Urlus recorded in 1923 for Deutsche Grammophon, on the Musica or Polydor labels (11 items); for Odeon, in Germany, in 1924 (17 items). His final recording session was on 25 Jan 1927. Several of his great Wagner arias were reissued by the Club 99 on LP (1962), including "Wintersturme" from *Walkure*, and "Preislied" from *Meistersinger*. [Dennis, P. 1981.]

U-S EVERLASTING RECORD. A brand and type of cylinder record manufactured by the **U-S Phonograph Co.** of Cleveland, Ohio. The cylinder was formed from thin sheet celluloid, rolled into a tube and butt-joined. After pressing under steam heat and pressure in a metal matrix, the still-warm molded record was slipped over a core of wax-impregnated wood pulp. This "unbreakable" construction proved less vulnerable to the effects of atmospheric moisture and temperature changes than most other forms of celluloid cylinders. The end rims of standard-production U-S Everlasting records are all impressed with a patent grant date of 11 Dec 1906, identifying the record construction developed by Varian M. Harris.

Some 1,100 U-S Everlasting and Lakeside titles were issued between 1910 and 1913. It is likely that all were recorded in New York City. The catalog included separately-numbered series for Grand Opera and Foreign Language items. A generous proportion of "cultural" titles were offered in the U-S catalogs, compared to the typical range of popular material then being recorded by the major cylinder record companies.

Bill Klinger

U-S PHONOGRAPH CO. The last firm to challenge Edison's market dominance in the cylinder field, originally formed in August 1908 as the Cleveland Phonograph Record Co. The corporate name was changed to United States Phonograph Co. on 14 July 1909 and to U.S. Phonograph Co. on 4 Sep 1912. Advertisements often styled the company name and products as "U-S", a practice that helps to distinguish it from the earlier (unrelated) brown-wax-era firm, **U.S. Phonograph Co.** of Newark, New Jersey.

The Cleveland management (under president E. C. Beach) attracted the services of Chicago chemist Varian M. Harris, who had developed the processes that would be used in manufacturing **U-S Everlasting Records.** Harris felt that thinner celluloid would take a more faithful impression in the molding operation, but such thin material was not yet available in tubular form. Working in his home laboratory in Chicago in 1904, Harris rolled very thin sheet celluloid into tubes and bonded the edges together with a solvent. Granted U.S. patent #837927 for this technique on 11 Dec 1906, Harris assigned it (and at least one other) to the Cleveland Phonograph Record Co. on 20 Aug 1908.

In October 1909, Harris came to Cleveland to direct the setting up of the U-S record pressing plant at 1390 E. 30th St. After pressing the very first lot of records on 29 Oct 1909, he rejected, as unacceptable, 55 of the first 90 matrices that had been made from masters recorded in New York City by Isaac Norcross. Charles L. Hibbard (an engineer who left Edison to join U-S Phonograph) took over the New York recording operation and improved the quality of the masters.

Around November 1909, musician **Albert W. Benzler** became music director for U-S Phonograph. He had been in charge of the music room at the Edison Laboratory, but disagreed with Edison's methods for choosing the selections to be released. (Edison reportedly employed a "Jackass Committee" of factory employees to audition candidate recordings; Benzler thought this practice too vulgar. There may have also been a rivalry with Victor Herbert for the Edison post of music director.) It seems likely that all U-S masters were made in the New York City area; no recording facilities are known to have existed in Cleveland.

Meanwhile F. L. Fritchey, in the U-S machine shop at 1013 Oregon Ave., Cleveland, was preparing to build the first U-S phonograph. Cleveland inventor Harry B. McNulty had designed a unique dual-feedscrew machine with a pair of reproducers for playing either two- or four-minute cylinders by turning a single knob. Eventually, at least nine different models of U-S cylinder phonographs were offered, ranging in price from $24 to $200. U-S treasurer and general manager Thomas H. Towell took samples of the first U-S records to New York in November 1909 to show to R. D. Cortina; the **Cortina Academy of Languages** had already placed an order for 5,000 language records in August 1908.

U-S products were announced to the trade in May 1910. Two-minute and four-minute records and three models of machines were then available to dealers. By June 1910, U-S was in full production with a capacity of some 5,000 records per day. New U-S Everlasting records were released monthly through April 1913, with a few titles issued as late as October 1913.

Among the total of 1,100 selections were many well-recorded popular items, tunes from Broadway shows, foreign-language pieces, and operatic arias.

In addition to the U-S Everlasting brand of record, the firm manufactured Lakeside cylinders, a parallel series numbered identically with the Everlasting releases, for distribution by the Chicago mail-order house, Montgomery Ward and Co.; celluloid Cortina foreign-language instruction series; and the more obscure Medicophone series, for dissemination of medical information by the Medicophone Post-Graduate Co., also of New York City. All these label variants are identical in materials and construction.

Attacked in litigation by Edison's legal department, U-S Phonograph incurred heavy legal fees for several years, but Edison's attorneys never established any patent infringement or other offenses.

U-S Phonograph received continued support through an association with the Bishop-Babcock-Becker Co., under Kirk D. Bishop, who was USP president from 1910. But by spring of 1914, U-S Phonograph succumbed to market realities and ceased production.

Interestingly, some very late U-S recordings have been discovered on cylinders made by the **Indestructible Phonographic Record Co.** of Albany, New York. The Indestructible records numbered in the range from 3280 through 3316 were almost all made from U-S masters or matrices. The exact circumstances of this transfer remain to be understood.

While Edison's National Phonograph Co. was still producing only "wax' records, the U-S Phonograph Co. of Cleveland introduced the first truly high-quality unbreakable cylinders. The U-S Everlasting records delivered better sound quality with lower surface noise than the earlier **Lambert Co.** or Albany Indestructibles. Some collectors consider the U-S cylinders to have remained unsurpassed throughout the acoustic recording era.

Bill Klinger

VAGUET, ALBERT, 1865–? French tenor, one of the most prolific to record acoustic operatic discs, as well as French song records. He recorded for Pathé cylinders and discs from 1902 to 1919, and again in 1927–1928, creating over 300 recordings. While most of his output was from French composers, he also dealt with Italian opera and even some Wagner, but he sang everything in French.

VALESCA-BECKER, DORA. A violinist who made 16 cylinders for **Bettini** in 1898, beginning with a mazurka by Wieniawski. She was the first woman to record the violin.

VALIQUET, LOUIS P., 18?–1925. Inventor of several important audio components, holder of 33 U.S. patents filed from 1897 to 1909. His research formed the basis for products of the **Universal Talking Machine Co.** (for which he was factory superintendent) and the **National Gramophone Corp.** His patent # 651,904 (filed 21 Apr 1899; granted 19 June 1900) was for the machine that was marketed as the **Zonophone** by Frank Seaman from May 1900. He developed a horn-support device, needed in the days of large, heavy horns (U.S. patent #705,165; filed 19 Mar 1902; granted 22 July 1902). Another major invention was the disc turntable with a spring-loaded pin for securing the record (U.S. patent #780,246; filed 27 Mar 1902; granted 17 Jan 1905); it was used in 1900 models of the Zonophone even before the patent application had been filed. Other Valiquet patents were for a **coin-op**, a case, **soundboxes**, and a motor. [Koenigsberg 1990.]

VALLEE, RUDY, 1901–1986. American popular singer and orchestra leader, born Herbert Pryor Vallee on 28 July 1901 in Island Pond, Vermont. He attended Yale University, graduating in 1927; established and toured with his Yale Collegians band. He led groups in Boston and New York, with a repertoire of college songs and novelties. He became popular as Rudy Vallee and his Connecticut Yankees, and gained national attention on a weekly radio show from 1929. Vallee appeared on Broadway and in films. After service in World War II he gradually changed from music to comedy and serious acting. He died in New York City on 4 July 1986.

A number of well-received records were made for Victor between 1929 and 1936, among them the orchestra's theme song, "My Time is Your Time" (Victor #21924; 1929), "I'm Just a Vagabond Lover" (Victor # 20967; 1929), and "Betty Coed" (Victor # 22473; 1930). The Bluebird label carried a hit, "Whiffenpoof Song," with chorus by the Gentlemen Songsters (Bluebird #7135; 1937). LP reissues appeared from Victor, Capitol, Viva, and Unique labels. [Kiner 1985.]

VALLIN, NINON, 1886–1961. French soprano, born in Montalieu on 8 Sep 1886. She studied in Lyon, then sang in Paris and made her opera debut there at the Opéra-Comique, as Micaela, on 14 Oct 1912. She remained with the company to 1916, greatly popular as Manon and Mimi. Vallin was at La Scala in 1917, and performed throughout Europe and in Buenos Aires. Late in her career she appeared in

America—Chicago and Washington, but not at the Metropolitan Opera.

Vallin recorded extensively for Pathé (after two sides for HMV in 1913), covering the French repertoire and certain Italian arias. Her first Pathé records were duets from *Manon*. Her most renowned discs were the complete set of *Werther* with Georges Thill (Columbia #LFX 151/165; 1931), reissued on compact disc in 1990 and recognized by *Gramophone* as historical album of the year. She also did a *Louise* album for Columbia ca. 1935 (#RFX 47/54), and a *Tosca* set for Odeon (#123810/16) ca. 1932. [Barnes, H. 1953.]

VAN BRUNT, WALTER, 1892–1971. American tenor and comic singer, born in Brooklyn on 22 Apr 1892; widely known by the stage name Walter Scanlan. He played piano and sang in church, while collecting phonograph records and trying to sing like Billy Murray. In 1907 he began to record, for the Indestructible label, then went to Edison—where he became the inventor's favorite tenor, and maker of the most popular Edison Diamond Disc, "I'll Take You Home Again, Kathleen" (#80160; 1914). There were four Edison cylinders before 1912, and many more as an exclusive Edison artist in 1914–1918. He made 66 solo Edisons as Van Brunt, and 70 solos as Scanlan, plus 43 duet and ensemble records. During 1919–1920 he was with Emerson, then he returned to Edison. Before signing as exclusive with Edison, Van Brunt also recorded for Victor (from 1909), beginning with "Summer Reminds Me of You" (#16304). "When I Dream in the Gloaming with You" was his first Victor hit (#16363; 1909). There were 15 items in the Victor 1917 catalog. He made duets with Ada Jones, and substituted for Billy Murray when that worthy failed to appear at record sessions (for example, in the American Quartet). Finally he had Murray as his own duet partner, on eight Edison Diamond Discs (beginning with "My Blackbirds are Bluebirds Now" (#52422; 1928) and on the last Victors he made: "Oh Baby! What a Night" (#22040; 1929) and "In Old Tia Juana" (matrix #53510, not released).

One of Van Brunt's popular Irish numbers was "Wearin' o' the Green," made for Edison in 1923. He also did **tone tests**, in 1924. And he made Jewish dialect records. After the demise of Edison, Van Brunt recorded for Banner, Crown, Cameo, and other labels; and was a regular radio performer in the 1930s with Billy Murray, Marcella Shields, and others. He died in Ohio on 11 Apr 1971. [Corenthal 1984 lists dialect material; Walsh 1951/11–12; 1952/1–2.]

VAN DYKE, ERNEST, 1861–1923. Belgian tenor, born Ernest Van Dijck in Antwerp on 2 Apr 1861. After study in Louvain and Brussels, he made his opera debut in the French premiere of *Lohengrin* (Paris) on 3 May 1887, then went to the Vienna Opera from 1888 to 1898, also appearing in Bayreuth as Parsifal in 1888. From 1898 to 1902 he sang Wagner roles at the Metropolitan Opera, then returned to the European stage until 1906, when he retired and taught singing. Van Dyck died in Berlaer-lez-Lierre, Belgium on 31 Aug 1923.

He made **Bettini** cylinders in 1898, early Wagner vocal records; there were five items, including two songs and numbers from *Rheingold*, *Walküre*, and *Tannhäuser*. Van Dyck recorded later on Pathé cylinders in London, recording five songs and three arias, two from Wagner. In 1905 he made two sides for Fonotipia in Paris, then sang an aria from *Werther* for Homophone in 1906. IRCC reissued the *Walküre* "Spring Song" and "Stances d'ossian" from *Werther* (#5007). [Dennis 1950/2.]

VAN DYKE (label). An American record, one of the **Grey Gull** family, issued from 1929 to 1930. It was a low-cost ($.35) product, carrying dance music and popular vocals. Van Dyke was a successful record, even exported to Britain for sale in chain stores. [Rust 1978.]

VAN EPS, FRED. American banjoist; his name spelled at first Van Epps, then with one "p." He learned to play by listening to **Vess Ossman** on wax cylinders, and later had the satisfaction of remaking nearly all the Ossman records for Victor. He was a great success as soloist (George Gershwin was one of his accompanists), and with ensembles of his own devising, the Van Eps Trio (he and his brother William on banjos, with Felix Arndt at the piano—later replaced by Frank E. Banta; the second banjo later replaced by drummer Eddie King, who was in turn replaced by saxophonist Nathan Glantz) and the Van Eps Quartet (Joe Green, xylophonist, joining the trio).

Van Eps made his first Edison record in 1901: "Concert Waltz" (#7888). In 1910 he began with Victor ("The Burglar Buck") and with Columbia. He also did some work for Pathé, using the pseudonym Edward Boynton. Van Eps was with the Record Makers ensemble, and then with Eight Famous Victor Artists. His period of greatest success was 1913–1922 with the trio, performing dance and ragtime pieces for Victor, Edison, etc. He gave up recording for Victor in 1922; in that year he had 18 solo sides in the Victor catalog. The last of his dozen Edison Diamond discs was made in 1926: "Dinah" / "I'm Sitting on Top of the World" (#51703).

His son, also named Fred, was a guitarist with several leading bands in the 1930s. [Walsh 1956/1–4.]

VAN ROOY, ANTON, 1870–1932. Dutch bass-baritone, born in Rotterdam on 1 Jan 1870. He studied in Frankfurt, and after an audition with Cosima Wagner was engaged to sing Wotan at Bayreuth (1897). Subsequently he became one of the leading Wagnerian baritones, singing in leading houses of Europe, and at the Metropolitan Opera from 1898 to 1908. He then sang in Frankfurt until retirement in 1914. Van Rooy died in Monaco on 28 Nov 1932.

All but one of his few recordings were Wagnerian. For HMV in London, 1902, he sang "Wotan's Farewell" and four other Wagner airs. He made four Edison cylinders in 1906, the "Toreador" Song plus the "Evening Star" and "Oh kehr zurück" from *Tannhäuser*, and "Wie oft in Meeres tiefen Schlund" from *Fliegende Holländer*.

In 1906–1907 he was with Columbia in the U.S., for "Toreador Song" again, and five Wagner numbers. IRCC and Historic Record Society reissued three of his records on 78 rpm; and Top Artists Platters included one aria in their album of *Twenty Great Wagnerian Singers* (#T322).

VANCE, CLARICE, 1875–1961. American vaudeville artist, born in Louisville, Kentucky, on 14 May 1875. She specialized in Negro dialect numbers, becoming known as "The Southern Singer." Vance made two Edison cylinders in 1905: "Mariar" (#9051) and "Save Your Money, Cause de Winter Am Coming On" (#9214). Then she went to Victor in 1906, singing "If Anybody Wants to Meet a Jonah Shake Hands with Me" (#4931) and nine other sides by 1907. Her Victor hit was "I'm Wise" (#5253; 1907). Vance quit recording but remained on stage to ca. 1917. She died in Napa, California, on 24 Aug 1961. [Walsh 1963/4–5.]

VANITY RECORDS. A term taken from the book publishing field, where it refers to books produced and distributed at the expense of the author. Vanity records are made up for concerts, and sold to the audiences there; the idea seems limited to a pop/rock groups, and it is not widespread even among them. Some vanity records have been acquired and distributed by major labels.

VANNI, ROBERTO, 1861–1941. Italian tenor, born in Livorno on 21 Aug 1861. He was popular in many Italian cities, and sang in *Manon* and *Carmen* in Madrid. He performed opposite Adelina Patti in Buenos Aires and Chicago, and appeared in supporting roles at the Metropolitan Opera from 1894 to 1903; he also continued singing in South America and Europe. He retired to Italy in 1935, and died in Milan on 25 Sep 1941.

Vanni is of interest in recording history because he recorded four arias for **Bettini** in 1899, from *Otello, Trovatore, Lucia*, and *Martha*.

VARIETY (label). (I) An American record issued in 1927, having about 100 releases, all from **Cameo** matrices.

VARIETY (label). (II) A record produced by the publisher/agent Irving Mills in 1937. Good material was recorded, by Cab Calloway, Charlie Barnet, and other jazz groups. [Rust 1978.]

VARI-GROOVE RECORDING. The method of making a disc record which allows the lateral movement of the cutting stylus to determine the spacing between adjacent grooves. Thus the louder signals will have wider spaced grooves than the quieter signals. This practice permits a longer playing time for a given disc diameter. [Klinger*.]

VARSITY (label). A record issued by the United States Record Corp., New York, from 1939 to 1940; Eli Oberstein was the owner. Good jazz material was featured, including Harry James, Jack Teagarden, and Frank Trumbauer; Buddy Clark was one of the vocalists. It was a $.35 cent disc. When the label folded in 1940, the matrices went to Musicraft. In 1948 the label name was revived for LP issues by Varsity Records, 47 W. 63rd St., New York, again with Oberstein as president. Varsity seems to have been absorbed by the Record Corp. of America in 1953. [Rust 1978.]

VASSAR GIRLS QUARTET. A female singing group that appeared on Edison cylinder #9460 (1907) performing "Kentucky Babe." Members were Katherine Armstrong, Lovira Taft (or Tait), Florence Fiske, and E. Eleanor Patterson.

VAUGHAN, SARAH, 1924–1990. American popular singer, born in Newark, New Jersey, on 27 Mar 1924. As a teenager she won an amateur contest in New York's Apollo Theatre, and got a job with Earl Hines as singer/pianist. She later worked with Billy Eckstine and John Kirby, but essentially pursued a solo career. She and Ella Fitzgerald were probably the most influential and admired female vocalists of the 1940s and 1950s, regarded as successors to Billie Holiday. Her great popularity came in the mid-1950s, when she earned the nickname "Divine Sarah" and sold more than 3 million records in one six-month period. Among her 15 chart singles in 1955–1960, "Misty" (Mercury #71477; 1959) and "Eternally" (Mercury #71562; 1960) are the most memorable examples of her dulcet ballad style. Her 1982 CBS album, *Gershwin Live*, won a Grammy for best female jazz vocal.

V-DISCS. Records produced during and after World War II by the U.S. War Department for distribution to military personnel. The earliest issues appeared in October 1943, the final ones in May 1949. V-Discs were made of unbreakable vinyl, in 12-inch size; the pressing was done by Victor and CBS. By means of tight grooving (136 per inch) a playing time of up to 6 1/2 minutes was achieved, allowing more than one piece to appear on each side. Leading popular and classical artists donated their time for original recordings, and others were heard from contributed matrices. Often the performer would introduce a disc with some spoken lines, in the manner of the old **announcements** on acoustic discs and cylinders. It is interesting that many of the V-Discs were made during the recording ban ordered by the American Federation of Musicians, the only instrumental commercial records officially created during that period. More than 8 million V-Discs were distributed, and all the matrices were publicly destroyed when the project terminated. [Sears 1980.]

VEEJAY. A television or music video equivalent of the **disc jockey**: the person who announces the numbers. The first veejay was Cathy McGowan in U.K., who announced the ITV pop program *Ready! Steady! Go!* in the 1960s.

VELVET FACE EDISON BELL CELEBRITY RECORD (label). A British 10-inch and 12-inch record issued by **J.E. Hough, Ltd.**, from 1910 to 1915. The same firm had released its first Velvet Face Edison Bell disc in December 1910. [Andrews*.]

VELVET TONE (label). A Columbia low-cost disc issued from 1925 to 1932. About 1,500 releases were made, nearly all duplicated on the Harmony label, offering popular and dance material with some blues and race records. *See also* MARCONI VELVET TONE (label). [Rust 1978.]

VENETIAN INSTRUMENTAL TRIO. An ensemble that recorded two numbers for Edison cylinders in 1909. The members were Eugene

Jaudas, violin; Eugene C. Rose, flute; and Charles Schuetze, harp. The numbers offered by this combination of instruments were "Moszkowski's Serenade" (#10152) and "Song of the Mermaids" (#10027). In 1913 the group made an Edison Diamond Disc of "Dear Heart" (#50061; previously issued anonymously on #50005). It would seem that "Serenade" (#80006 and #80012; ca. 1913) was by the same artists. And they may have been three of the four members of an ensemble that made a dozen other Edison Diamond Discs in 1912–1913; that group was identified only as violin, flute, harp, and cello.

Vented baffle. *See* BASS REFLEX BAFFLE.

VENUTI, JOE, 1898–1978. Italian/American jazz violinist, born in Lecco on 4 Apr 1898. His family moved to Philadelphia, where he studied classical violin; then he turned to the popular styles, playing in a combo with guitarist Eddie Lang. They were successful in New York, and both were with Paul Whiteman in 1929–1930. Venuti freelanced in the 1930s, at times leading a Big Band, later smaller groups. In the 1940s he was in California, where "his great merit was to make the theretofore-suspect violin a respectable instrument among the plebs" (Slonimsky). He and Stéphane Grappelli are the only significant jazz violinists. He died in Seattle on 14 Aug 1978.

Venuti and Lang recorded first for Columbia in 1926, doing "Black and Blue Bottom" / "Stringing the Blues" (#914-D). They were joined by Adrian Rollini, bass saxophone, and pianist Arthur Schutt for four Okeh sides in 1927, and there were various other groups with them later. Jimmy Dorsey was one of Blue Four who recorded "Blue Room" for Okeh in 1928 (#41144). A group called the Blue Six—including Benny Goodman, Bud Freeman, and Rollini—did a sparkling "Sweet Lorraine" in 1933 (Columbia #CB-708). There were dozens of LP reissues.

VERTICAL CUT. The name given to a recording process (also known as hill and dale) that utilizes a vertical modulation or pattern made in the spiraling groove on a cylinder or disc. Vibrations are cut into the medium perpen-

dicularly to the surface. This was the method of the Thomas Edison phonographs. Both lateral-cut and vertical-cut recordings were made in the **Volta Laboratories** in the early 1880s. First used on commercial discs by Neophone Co., Ltd., in 1904, it was popularized by Pathé from 1906. Vertical cut was never as popular as the lateral-cut method, although Edison preferred it, making vertical-cut cylinders and Diamond Discs until 1929, at which time he also made some lateral records. *See also* LATERAL RECORDING.

VERVE (label). An American record issued by Norman Granz in Los Angeles from 1956 to 1960. The label was formed by Granz as a consolidation of his **Clef**, Down Home, and Norgran labels. Verve Records, 451 N. Canon Dr., Beverly Hills, was the main office address in 1956. Jazz, pop, folk, comedy, and gospel material was offered. Ella Fitzgerald was the first star performer, achieving great acclaim for her "songbooks" series. Ricky Nelson made his first records for Verve. Despite the success of Verve, Granz decided to sell in to MGM in December 1960. Creed Taylor was recording director from 1961 to 1967, and continued the popularity of the label with recordings by such luminaries as Count Basie, Duke Ellington, Bill Evans, Stan Getz, Johnny Hodges, Antonio Carlos Jobim, and Oscar Peterson.

On 5 May 1972, MGM sold all its record labels to Polydor, which concentrated on reissues in Europe and Japan. From 1980 the Verve catalog was given new importance by Polygram vice president Richard Seidel. [Ruppli 1986.]

VICTOR CAFE. A restaurant located in the Italian section of Philadelphia (1303 Dickinson St.), opened in 1933 by John Di Stefano, a former Victor record dealer. He played opera records during meals, attracting a distinguished clientele of recording artists from the Victor studios in neighboring Camden, New Jersey: Giovanni Martinelli, Giuseppe De Luca, Titta Ruffo, Beniamino Gigli, Ezio Pinza, and many others. Upon the death of Di Stefano in 1954, the business was continued by his son Henry (who died in 1986). Another son, Armand, also contributed an hour of weekly operatic records—from the family collection of 30,000 discs—to a Philadelphia radio station until his death in 1989. The custom of having waiters and waitresses sing operatic numbers created a delightful atmosphere in the establishment. Mario Lanza was one of those earnest vocalists. [A photo of the Cafe is in *TMR* #17 (August 1972).]

VICTOR LADIES QUARTET. A female vocal ensemble that recorded briefly for Victor ca. 1915, and was quickly set aside (no records in the 1917 catalog). Members were probably Elizabeth Wheeler, Olive Kline, Elsie Baker, and Marguerite Dunlap. [Walsh 1961/10.]

VICTOR LIGHT OPERA CO. An ensemble created ca. 1909 to record operettas and Broadway musicals. By the time of the 1917 catalog it was named the Victor Opera Co. A long list of excerpts appeared in that catalog, from nearly 80 stage works, some grand operas among them. Membership varied, but included at one time or another many of the leading Victor artists, for example, Reinald Werrenrath, S.H. Dudley, Elsie Baker, John Bieling, Steve Porter, Elise Stevenson, Harry Macdonough, Ada Jones, Billy Murray, Olive Kline, and William F. Hooley. Members of the Lyric and Orpheus Quartets, and of the Revelers, were often the basis for the company's recordings. The group was still in the catalog in 1940 (as the Victor Light Opera Co. again), but with a reduced list of discs.

Victor Male Quartet. *See* ORPHEUS QUARTET.

VICTOR MINSTRELS. A house group formed to make Victor records, known also as the Victor Minstrel Co. It was active from ca. 1903 to ca. 1909 (*see* MINSTREL RECORDINGS). Members included, at various times, Len Spencer and the Hayden Quartet. After a long hiatus, the group—or the concept—was restored with a disc by the Victor Minstrels in January 1929, named "Minstrel Show of 1929" (#35961). Singers included Billy Murray, Monroe Silver, and James Stanley. Frank Crumit joined in on the flip side. There were no further releases.

Victor Opera Co. *See* VICTOR LIGHT OPERA CO.

VICTOR OPERA SEXTET. A house group formed to make operatic ensemble discs for Victor in 1915. Members were Olive Kline, Marguerite Dunlap, Lambert Murphy, Harry Macdonough, and Reinald Werrenrath. They sang the *Lucia* Sextet on #70036; also available on a double-sided record with the *Rigoletto* Quartet on #55066 (a low-cost bargain, at $1.25 for the double, compared to the several $5 and $7 versions with Enrico Caruso et al).

VICTOR ORCHESTRA. A house ensemble formed in 1906 to record orchestral works for Victor. Walter B. Rogers conducted and played cornet. Other members were Charles D'Almaine, first violin; Louis Christie, clarinet; Darius Lyons, flute; Emil Keneke, cornet; Herman Conrad, bass; O. Edward Wardwell, trombone; Frank Reschke, violin and saxophone; Walter Pryor, cornet; A. Levy, clarinet; Arthur Trepte, oboe; Theodore Levy, violin; S.O. Pryor, percussion, and C.H.H. Booth, organ. They recorded movements from the Beethoven Fifth Symphony and the Dvorak New World Symphony (#35275), the *Egmont Overture* (#35493), and a few other symphonic masterworks; but most of their extensive list was made up of light classics and arrangements.

The Victor Concert Orchestra co-existed with this group, and was presumably similar in membership, as it was in repertoire. By the time of the 1927 catalog, the Victor Orchestra had been renamed the Victor Symphony Orchestra (the Concert Orchestra was connected to it by a "see also" reference), and there was also a Victor Salon Orchestra, with Nathaniel Shilkret directing. In the 1938 catalog Shilkret conducted the Victor Symphony Orchestra on both black label—where all the above ensembles had been kept—and on a Red Seal album of John Alden Carpenter's *Skyscrapers* (#M-130). Claude Lapham directed the Victor Symphony on a second Red Seal, doing a work of his own, *Mihara Yama* (#11895). In the 1940 catalog the Symphony Orchestra had three

Red Seal items; and the Victor Salon Group and Orchestra was well represented on Red Seal, directed by Shilkret, with various George Gershwin medley records, plus other Broadway musical "gems."

VICTOR RECORD SOCIETY. An organization established in 1937 by **Thomas F. Joyce**, as a promotion for Victor records. A small record player attachment for a radio was offered to members at $14.95, and the concept proved attractive enough to draw 150,000 members, who agreed to buy a specified number of discs. A boost to lagging sales resulted, especially in the popular record area.

Victor Salon Orchestra. *See* VICTOR ORCHESTRA.

Victor Symphony Orchestra. *See* VICTOR ORCHESTRA.

VICTOR TALKING MACHINE CO. This article has nine sections: 1. The first decade of Victor; 2. The 1910s; 3. The 1920s; 4. RCA and the 1930s; 5. The 1940s; 6. Engineering advances; 7. Studios; 8. Artists and repertoire; and 9. Victor officials. (Sections 1–3 were written by Edgar Hutto, Jr. Sections 4–9 were written by Warren Rex Isom.)

1. *The first decade of Victor.* The fledgling disc industry was in a state of confusion in 1900 (*see* DISC, 6). **Eldridge R. Johnson** was a machinist providing gramophones for **Emile Berliner**, the first producer of commercial disc records. Johnson began to make records himself in January 1900. He released his first commercial records a few months later, with gold print on black paper labels (Berliner discs had no labels), seven-inches in diameter. Those discs bore the label name Improved Gram-O-Phone Record. They sold for $.50. The first recording, listed as number A-1 in Johnson's matrix log, was a recitation by George Broderick of Eugene Field's poem "Departure.

In summer 1900 Johnson and **Leon F. Douglass** formed the **Consolidated Talking Machine Co.** to market Johnson's machines and records, and to utilize his improved recording process. There were daily recording sessions, and a few discs were pressed from material recorded in Europe by **Fred Gaisberg** and Belford Royal for the **Gramophone Co., Ltd.** In fall 1900 five models of disc players were advertised, not from Consolidated but from Eldridge R. Johnson: a Toy ($3), Type A ($12), Type B ($18), Type C ($25), and Type D ($6).

The company name was changed to "Eldridge Johnson, Manufacturing Machinist," to avoid a name conflict with Berliner's holding company, Consolidated Talking Machine Co. of America.

In January 1901 the first 10-inch discs were made. Johnson issued them at first (3–10 Jan) with the label name Victor Ten Inch Record; then as Victor Monarch Record. The cost was $1.

Following a court order of 1 Mar 1901, restraining Johnson from using the term Gramophone for his products, he changed the label name of the seven-inch disc to Improved Record. (That court ruling was reversed on appeal in June 1901, then restored on 22 July 1902. At that point Johnson chose to settle out of court with the instigator, **Frank Seaman**, rather than prolong the legal proceedings.) Yet another label name was introduced on 12 Mar 1901, as Johnson registered the trademark Victor Record for the seven-inch discs. A report of September 1901 showed that the previous 12 months had been successful for the Johnson firm, with a profit of $180,000.

Berliner and Johnson agreed to pool their patent, trademark and manufacturing interests, and incorporated the Victor Talking Machine Company on 3 Oct 1901. It was organized on 5 Oct 1901 with Eldridge Johnson, president; Leon F. Douglass, vice-president and general manager; Thomas S. Parvin, treasurer; A.C. Middleton, secretary; and Horace Pettit, general counsel. Berliner received 40 percent of Victor's stock but did not participate actively in the company. Terms of the incorporation included the issue of

20,000 shares of common, and 5,000 shares of 7 percent preferred [stock]. The Consolidated Talking Machine Company of America [Berliner's firm] received 8,000 shares of common for the Berliner patents, and paid $50,000 for 500 shares of preferred with a bonus of 1,000 additional shares of common. This provided the new company with much needed working capital. Mr. Johnson received 10,000 shares of common and 3,000 shares of preferred for his plant, his patents, and his going business. The remaining 1,000 shares of common and 1,500 shares of preferred went into the company's treasury.

A detailed contract was drawn up with the Gramophone Company which gave them an option on three times their purchases for the previous year up to 50 percent of the company's capacity. They agreed to contribute up to $10,000 a year to the expense of the company's experimental laboratories, to provide a 25 percent profit over costs, to protect the company's patents, trademark, etc., and to promote the sale of the product in Europe, in British colonies and possessions, and in Russia and Japan. (Aldridge 1964)

Thus the partnership between Victor and the Gramophone Co. was established, a relationship that was to continue until 1953.

When the Victor Talking Machine Co. was established, Johnson's records and instruments had already been accepted and sold by influential music stores, such as Wurlitzer, Lyon and Healy, and Sherman Clay. A large manufacturing complex was soon developed around Johnson's machine shop in Camden, New Jersey, across the Delaware River from Philadelphia. Executive offices were at 114 N. Front St.; instruments were assembled in a four-story factory at 120 N. Front St., using cabinets purchased from Sheip Manufacturing Co. Philadelphia was the site of the recording studio (10th and Lombard Streets), and a sales office (Girard Building, on 12th St.). Records were pressed by the **Duranoid Co.** until Victor's pressing facility was built at 23 Market Street, Camden, in 1902. (From 1907 all pressing was done in Camden.) One-half of Victor's instrument production was purchased by the Gramophone Co., Ltd., for sale in Europe and the British Empire (excepting Canada where Berliner Gramophone of Montreal had rights).

Nipper appeared for the first time on Victor record labels in January 1902. On 18 Jan 1902 Johnson and Douglass personally bought the **Globe Record Co.** from the Burt Co., and sold it on 15 Feb 1902 to the **American Graphophone Co.** These transactions formed part of a negotiation with the **Columbia** interests, ending patent litigations between the firms, and leading to a cross-licensing agreement that gave them control of the major industry patents. By the end of 1902, Victor had produced about 2 million records. Some 2,000 discs a day were coming from Camden, utilizing Johnson's new multiple stamper system. (*See* DISC, 3.)

In Europe the Gramophone Co. and others were releasing recordings of classical music by operatic artists such as Feodor Chaliapin and the new sensation, Enrico Caruso. The records had special red labels and sold at higher prices than non-classical records. In the U.S. most of the early recorded material consisted of popular songs, comic songs and recitations, and band music. Victor did have a little classical material in 1900, by George Broderick (opera arias in English), Rosalia Chalia, and Emilio de Gogorza. But the great advance came with first Red Seal records, announced in March 1903. That was the 5000 series, 25 imports (including Enrico Caruso's Milan recordings) from the Gramophone Co., selling for $2.50 each.

Victor made its own first Red Seal recording on 30 Apr 1903 in room 826 at Carnegie Hall with Australian mezzo-soprano Ada Crossley singing "Caro mio ben" on a 10-inch Monarch (#81001). Louise Homer, Johanna Gadski, and Antonio Scotti also recorded in room 826, as did Caruso on 1 Feb 1904, after he was signed to an exclusive contract by Victor. Other celebrities to sing on early Red Seals included Zélie de Lussan, Emma Eames, Marcel Journet, and Marcella Sembrich. Victor developed a strong hold on the operatic field that it never relinquished. Mauve-colored Victor "Melba" Records—a special label for the diva—were offered in March 1904, and Victor "Patti" Records (Red Seal) appeared in December 1905. Those were premium discs; the Patti items sold for $5.

One of Johnson's articles of faith was in the power of advertising. The F. Wallis Armstrong advertising agency handled Victor promotions to 1925, emphasizing the notions of product quality, the pleasure of gramophone ownership, and the greatness of Victor artists. In good times or hard times, Victor advertising was ubiquitous in newspapers and national magazines. Profits were substantial in the early years: 1902—$151,000; 1903—$495,000; 1904 (the year of a disruptive fire in the Camden complex)—$424,00; 1905—$607,000. More than 3.5 million records were sold by the end of 1905.

A permanent matrix numbering system was introduced in April 1903. In that year there was a new label line as well, the De Luxe series. On 11 March a 14-inch De Luxe, changed soon to the De Luxe Special Record, was announced; it ran 60 rpm, and sold for $2. A 12-inch De Luxe (black label) appeared in fall 1903 for $1.50, and a 12-inch De Luxe (Red Seal) for $3.

The first Red Seal duet was extremely popular: "Solenne in quest' ora" from *Forza del destino*, sung by Caruso and Antonio Scotti (#89001; March 1906). And the first recording of the *Rigoletto* Quartet was a great hit, selling for $4. It presented Caruso, Bessie Abott, Louise Homer, and Scotti (#96000; February 1907).

Eldridge Johnson continued to improve the instrument line. The tapered tone arm and goose neck were introduced in 1903. The recording laboratory was managed by **Calvin G. Child**. Harry O. Sooy was the chief recordist; he was later joined by his brothers Raymond A. and Charles E. Sooy. **Arthur Pryor** was the first musical director, succeeded shortly by **Walter Bowman Rogers**. As Douglass left his post of general manager because of illness, **Louis Geissler** succeeded him in 1906, remaining to 1918 (Geissler was then a director until 1921). A trade publication, *The Voice of the Victor*, was introduced for dealers in April 1906 to keep them informed about new records, sales methods, and artist tours. The Victor dealers formed the **National Association of Talking Machine Jobbers**.

In 1906 Victor introduced a new phonograph with the horn enclosed within its cabinet. It was the **Victrola**, styled at first the Victor-Victrola, priced at $200. It was a success in many console and table models, setting the industry standard. A less inspired invention

was also introduced in 1906, the **Auxetophone**. On 1 Sep 1906, Victor bought the 8,000 shares of its stock that Berliner's firm had acquired in the Victor incorporation.

Victor's Red Seal classical records were single-sided until 1923. But to match Columbia's double-sided discs (introduced in 1904) Victor began its 16000 popular series of double-sided records in September 1908. They sold for $.75 (10-inch) and $1.25 (12-inch), while single-faced records were selling for $.60 and $1.

At the end of its first decade, Victor was in an excellent position. More than 35 million records had been sold, and the phonographs (606,596 sold through 1910) had gained acceptance as the finest made.

2. *The 1910s*. The Camden complex continued to grow in response to the volume of sales. In 1911 124,000 phonographs were sold. External horn instruments accounted for 25 percent of sales, Victrola table models 42 percent and console Victrolas 33 percent of sales in 1911. In April 1911 an educational department was established, under the direction of Frances E. Clark, to develop an interest in music among school children.

Additions to Victor's artist roster from 1910 to 1913 included George M. Cohan, Al Jolson, John McCormack, Mischa Elman, Fritz Kreisler, Alma Gluck, Victor Herbert, Jan Paderewski, Jan Kubelik, Giovanni Martinelli, and the Flonzaley Quartet. Amelita Galli-Curci began recording for Victor in October 1916. There were around 600 titles in the Red Seal catalog in 1912. In 1916 Calvin Child became head of Victor's artist department and **Josef Pasternack** became musical director. In February 1917 Charles Sooy was able to successfully capture the Original Dixieland Jazz Band's new music on wax.

The *Victor Book of the Opera*, edited by **Samuel H. Rous**, appeared in the first of many editions in 1912, offering opera plots along with photos and promotions of Victor artists, for $.75. No fewer than six *Lucia* Mad Scenes were noted in the book.

Victor's instrument production was severely curtailed by the company's effort to supply material for World War I, as skilled workers of the cabinet factory made aircraft assemblies, rifle stock, and detonator cases. Recording artists appeared at war bond rallies, and their recordings helped boost morale. A new label design, the so-called Wing label, was introduced in 1914. During 1917–1934, the Victor name was replaced by Victrola on Red Seal issues.

There were 6,043 licensed Victor dealers in 1916, and 103 distributors. A "Tungstone Stylus" was marketed, as an alternative to steel needles. The Camden plant had its greatest period of investment from 1912 to 1917.

After satisfactory recordings were made by Pasternack and the 51 musicians of the Victor Symphony Orchestra, the Boston Symphony under Karl Muck and the Philadelphia Orchestra under Leopold Stokowski were brought to Camden to make their initial recordings. As the studio in Building 15 could not accommodate the large orchestras, the recordings were made in an auditorium in the new executive office building. The Trinity Baptist Church building located three blocks from the plant complex was purchased and used as a studio for the recording of large groups. Jascha Heifetz began recording for Victor in November 1917. Normal production in Camden after the war was reached in October 1919 and instrument sales reached 560,000 in 1920.

The Red Seal roster was the monumental achievement of the firm. In the 1917 catalog, celebrities not mentioned above included sopranos Lucrezia Bori, Emma Calvé, Emmy Destinn, Geraldine Farrar, Johanna Gadski, Maria Galvany, Alma Gluck, Frieda Hempel, and Alice Nielsen. Contraltos included Clara Butt, Julia Culp, Jeanne Gerville-Réache, Margarete Matzenauer, and Ernestine Schumann-Heink. Leading tenors were Fernando de Lucia, Francesco Marconi, Riccardo Martin, Giovanni Martinelli, Leo Slezak, Francesco Tamagno, and Evan Williams. Baritones included Mario Ancona, Mattia Battistini, Giuseppe de Luca, Maurice Renaud, Titta Ruffo, and Mario Sammarco. Pol Plançon was a leading bass. Instrumental stars included Jan Kubelik, Ignace Paderewski, and Efrem Zimbalist.

On black label records there were acclaimed artists as well, of which only a few will be mentioned: Henry Burr, Eddie Cantor, Billy Golden, Al Jolson, Harry Lauder, and Reinald Werrenrath.

More than 205 million Victor records had been sold by the end of 1919.

3. *The 1920s.* Sergei Rachmaninoff and Paul Whiteman became Victor artists in 1920. Caruso made his last recordings in Camden on 16 Sep 1920. His death in August 1921 ended the career of the single artist who contributed most to the success of Victor and the early phonograph industry. Victor's instrument sales dropped in 1921 as Brunswick and Sonora offered the flat-top cabinets that were preferred by the public. Phonograph sales were greatly eroded by the increasing popularity of radio as a form of home entertainment. By the fall of 1924 Victor halted instrument production and budgeted $5 million for a massive sales campaign. N. W. Ayer was engaged as advertising agent, replacing Armstrong.

The phonograph industry had been doing little to improve its product. James Owens and Albertis Hewitt had conducted electrical recording experiments at Victor as early as 1913, but their approach was strictly trial and error. Early in 1924 Victor had rejected an offer made by Bell Telephone Laboratories to witness a demonstration of a new electrical recording process and improved acoustical playback equipment. But by December 1924 Victor arranged to have a demonstration for its technical staff in Camden. Victor and Columbia obtained rights to use the new recording and reproduction systems. In March 1925 the studio in Camden began making electrical recordings for Victor's classical and popular catalogs. The New York studio made its first electrical recordings on 31 July 1925, in a process that Victor named "Orthophonic Recording." In a short time 10,000 Credenza **Orthophonic** Victrolas were built, hand-wound acoustic taking machines with re-entrant horns. The new products were introduced to the public on 2 Nov 1925, and by the end of 1926 there were 43 new Victrola models. Included in the new line were models with a radio chassis and electrical playback apparatus made by RCA. An "Electrola" line had electric amplification. The electrically recorded discs had a new scroll design on their labels. Public acceptance of the new records and instruments was satisfying, and by the end of 1926 the working loss of $6.5 million incurred in 1925 had been recovered. Great hit records emerged from the electrical process, including the J.S. Bach Toccata and Fugue in D Minor in a brilliant transcription for the Philadelphia Orchestra.

Eldridge Johnson sold his interest in Victor in December 1926 to bankers Speyer and Co. and J. & W. Seligman of New York, for an estimated $30 million. Johnson's inventiveness and business sense had developed the wheezy instrument and noisy discs of the 1890s into a product line that through 1929 resulted in the manufacture of nearly 8 million instruments and more than one-half billion records.

E.E. Shumaker, former purchasing agent and director of the company, became the new Victor president. Many new dance bands and popular groups were Victor artists during the late 1920s, including the Coon-Sanders Orchestra, Jan Garber, Ray Noble, Fred Waring, and Ted Weems. Jazz artists included Duke Ellington, Jean Goldkette, Jelly Roll Morton, Bennie Moten, Ben Pollack, and Fats Waller.

Nathaniel Shilkret was the principal conductor of the Victor Orchestra and accompanist of popular vocalists. Field recordings were made with portable electrical recording equipment during the summers of 1927 and 1928 in Virginia, Tennessee, North Carolina, and Georgia. Jimmie Rodgers and the Carter Family were among the artists discovered in these sessions.

New Red Seal performers of the 1920s included Marian Anderson, Pablo Casals, Richard Crooks, Vladimir Horowitz, Wanda Landowska, Lauritz Melchior, Yehudi Menuhin, Ezio Pinza, Rosa Ponselle, Sergei Rachmaninoff, Elisabeth Rethberg, Paul Robeson, Tito Schipa, and Lawrence Tibbett, Toscanini made records with the New York Philharmonic Symphony Orchestra, and Serge Koussevitzky recorded with the Boston Symphony Orchestra.

Another instrument advance came in March 1927, with the first record changer. The early version played either 10-inch or 12-inch records, while a later model (November 1928) could mix the two sizes.

In 1929 **RCA (Radio Corporation of America)** acquired Victor Talking Machine Co. Victor, in its 28-year existence, had made a major impact on home entertainment. It was an industry pioneer in the use of the advertising media. It provided jobs for 10,000 workers, and at least 30 investors in the company received investment returns of more than $1 million each. By the end of 1929, record sales had reached around 600 million. Some $700 million in total sales had been posted. About 8,130,000 instruments had been made.

4. *RCA and the 1930s.* When the Victor Talking Machine Co. was bought by RCA (Radio Corporation of America) on 4 Jan 1929, 60 percent of RCA was owned by the **General Electric Co.** (GE) and 40 percent by Westinghouse Electric and Manufacturing Co. (Westinghouse). Victor became the Victor Division, along with the Radiola Division, of the new Radio-Victor Co. (a sales organization). The Audio Vision Appliance Co. was the manufacturer for both divisions. This company was created by GE and Westinghouse to operate the large Victor plant in Camden, but beginning in 1931 all of these activities were brought together in the RCA Victor Co., Inc. That name appeared on record labels. Then, by a consent decree of 13 Nov 1932, RCA became independent of GE and Westinghouse. In 1935 RCA Victor and RCA Radiotron merged to form the RCA Manufacturing Co., Inc., and that name was given on record labels. In 1942, that company was merged with the parent corporation, RCA, and the responsibility for manufacturing given to its RCA Victor Division. In 1954, RCA Victor and the RCA Home Instruments Division were together in RCA Consumer Products. In 1969, RCA Victor became a part of the National Broadcasting Company (NBC).

This outline of the placement of RCA Victor in the hierarchy of RCA does not tell the whole story. RCA Victor had three units: Home Instruments, the Advanced Technology Laboratories, and the David Sarnoff Research Center (known as "The Labs") in Princeton, New Jersey. Home Instruments had the responsibility for the development, design, manufacture, and sales of the record players and radio-phonograph combinations. The role of what was first known as Advanced Development, then Applied Research, and finally as Advanced Technology Laboratories, was largely informal, voluntary, and self-directing. Since the beginning of RCA in 1919, this engineering adjunct was attached to one division and then to another. It was a place where first evaluations could be made of new technologies and proposed new products. "The Labs" supported RCA Victor with pure and practical research in all areas, particularly in the design of recording studios, acoustics, monitoring speakers, and sound compensation.

The acquisition of Victor cost RCA $150 million, but the value received was enormous. A prize item gained was the "His Master's Voice" (Nipper) trademark, with its heritage of customer loyalty and confidence. Another valuable item in the package was the extensive Victor phonographic and record business, which had earned more than 25 percent in average annual dividends for 20 years. There were more than 1,000 artists in the Victor catalog. And there was a sales and distribution network unequaled in the industry. A third significant item was the Camden manufacturing complex, one of the largest in the nation, with 16 buildings and more than 10,000 employees. Camden was immediately pressed into radio manufacture, to meet the ever increasing demand, while continuing to produce records. It had 160 swing leaf record presses on the fifth floor of Building 13. Those presses, dating from 1912, were used by RCA Victor until 1977 when they were replaced by 49 Alpha 12-inch automatics that provided somewhat more than the 75 million yearly production of the manual presses. The matrix department—with its plating tanks, inspection, packing, and shipping units—was in the same building.

Along with the Camden complex came full ownership of Victor of Canada, 67 percent of Victor of Japan, 50 percent interest in the Gramophone Co. Ltd., of Britain, and companies in Argentina, Brazil, and Chile.

The U.S. national economy was at its lowest point in 1931 and 1932, giving RCA its only deficit years. The radio business remained profitable, leading to demands within the firm that the phonographic products be eliminated. Yet radio stations and broadcast networks were dependent on records for program material. The technology developed for **Vitaphone** discs in the 1920s was applied to the transcription of continuing radio shows and commercials. These were "transcribed" on 16-inch plastic lacquers in studios in Chicago and New York. The lacquer was immediately heavily plated to produce a copper master that was used for pressing a few (never more than 50) approval copies. When approval was given, the lacquer was given normal matrix processing in the plant and pressings were made. These 33 1/3 rpm, narrow (2.5 mil) groove "Thesaurus" records on 16-inch plastic (Vitrolac) discs served the radio broadcast industry for more than 30 years.

Between radio applications and **juke box** sales, the record industry had enough business to survive the early years of the Depression. The 50,000 juke boxes in operation in 1930 accounted for about half of the 6 million records sold in that year. (*See* DISC, 6.) At the same time, Victor's recording facilities and manufacturing plant were held in readiness, and had some opportunities to bring some profits. In 1934 the Duo Jr. record player was sold for plug-in use with a radio; a second version had a lighter weight crystal pick-up, a smaller turntable, and a lower price. That was the machine used in 1937 to promote membership in the **Victor Record Society**.

During the 1930s popular records outsold Red Seals by a ratio of three to one. An advance for the Red Seals was made with the formation of the NBC Symphony Orchestra for Arturo Toscanini in 1937. Toscanini's weekly broadcasts created an audience for classical music and an increase in classical record sales. In the period 1932–1938, industry-wide record production increased by 661 percent; Victor's production increased 440 percent.

Artists who made their first Victor records in the 1930s included E. Power Biggs, Jussi Björling, the Boston Pops Orchestra, Budapest Quartet, Nelson Eddy, Kirsten Flagstad, José Iturbi, Helen Jepson, Lotte Lehmann, Lily Pons, Artur Rubinstein, Artur Schnabel, Rudolf Serkin, and John Charles Thomas.

5. *The 1940s.* During 1939–1945, RCA Victor was engaged in a variety of activities re-

lated to the war effort. At the same time research continued in phonographic products, among them the **vinyl** disc (introduced in 1945). And record sales climbed in both popular and classical categories. A large percentage of the internationally acclaimed classical soloists and orchestras were under contract. Alexander Kipnis, Andrés Segovia, and Helen Traubel made their first appearances on Victor. Red Seals were sold for $1, black label discs for $.75 and $.50, and **Bluebird** (a pop label introduced in 1933) records for $.35. Bluebird carried important material by Shep Fields, Earl Hines, Vincent Lopez, Freddy Martin, Glenn Miller, Artie Shaw, Fats Waller, and many others. Big Bands heard on regular Victor black label discs included Sammy Kaye, Wayne King, and Tommy Dorsey. Benny Goodman's Victor releases defined the swing era. Duke Ellington's Victors of 1940–1942 display his band at its creative peak.

In 1943 record labels showed a change from RCA Manufacturing Co., Inc., to RCA Victor Division of Radio Corporation of America. From January 1946 the label name was RCA Victor.

The seven-inch vinyl record, with a narrow groove for a light-weight crystal high fidelity pickup, was introduced in 1949 with a speedy record changer. Critical analysis had established that a record speed of 45 rpm was required for good performance of a seven-inch record. The next objective was to have the 33 1/3 rpm long-play RCA Victor record with a three-speed record changer available within one year. In the light of Columbia's acclaimed 33 1/3 microgroove LP disc (1948), the technical wisdom and the commercial expediency of the 45 was widely doubted, but by February of 1951 the small disc had found universal acceptance for popular music, and billions were sold in the next 30 years.

6. Engineering innovations. With the introduction of its 33 1/3 rpm LP in 1950, RCA Victor was able to compete effectively with other LP labels in the classical field. The next technical advance in the industry was **stereophonic recording**. In 1954, John F. Pfeiffer of RCA Victor's New York recording studio worked with Fritz Reiner and the Chicago Symphony Orchestra (in Orchestra Hall, Chi-

cago) to capture Strauss' Also *Sprach Zarathustra* and *Ein Heldenleben* in stereo. By today's standards, the setup in Orchestra Hall was primitive: 30 ips two-track tape, two Neumann M-50 omni microphones positioned 12 feet high and 24 feet apart with the orchestra between them. But the recordings are superb.

Stereo tape recordings spurred activity to develop stereo disc records. H. E. Roys, chief engineer of RCA Victor and chairman of the Electronic Industries Association (EIA) committee on the phonograph, was heavily involved in the establishment of worldwide industry standards for full stereo records before major producers placed them on sale in 1958. It took more than statesmanship to accomplish this. The "more" ingredient was the analytical skill that had established 45 rpm as the correct speed of a seven-inch record with five 1/2 minutes playing time and less than 10 percent tracing distortion. In 1957 Roys asked Murlan S. Corrington of the Advanced Development Section of Home Instruments to make a comparative analysis of the 45–45 degree and the vertical-lateral proposals for stereo discs.

Corrington reported on 27 Jan 1958 to the EIA committee on recording. His conclusions served as the basis for the choice of the 45–45 degree system and its standardization by the record industry.

In 1961 an electronic processor was sold that reproduced monaural records in stereo. The RCA New Orthacoustic Response Curve was adopted by the record and broadcast industries in June 1953. From 1953 to 1956, the Indianapolis plant installed 12 seven-inch automatic presses, adding an annual production potential of 32 million to the 18 million of the 46 seven-inch manual presses.

By 1977 the record plant in Indianapolis had reached a production capacity of 165 million discs a year, of which 90 million were 45s. There were three other U.S. plants, with a further capacity of 32 million discs. International plants, in Argentina, Australia, Brazil, Canada, Chile, Great Britain, Greece, Italy, Mexico, and Spain had about 200 presses and a 45-million production capacity, Thus the total RCA Victor capacity was 224 million records per annum. A fully automatic plant completely dedicated to tape duplication and cassette loading was opened in 1984 in Weaverville, North Carolina.

Abraham M. Max, manager of the chemical and physical laboratory, RCA Victor Records Engineering (1944–1972), and research director of the American Electroplating Society, applied and adapted state of the art processes to change the plating time of a record stamper, which had been as long as 60 hours, to one hour, and to increase the life of a Red Seal stamper from 100 to 2,500 records. For other pressings from unfilled compounds, 10,000 records per stamper was not uncommon.

RCA Victor sealed records in shrink-wrap beginning in 1964 and thereby participated in a bold change in product marketing. Other innovations did not fare so well, for example, four-channel sound. Near success was achieved even though the technology applied proved to be overextended. However, there was no great demand in the marketplace for something beyond stereo. The 1973 Dynaflex record was designed to have laminar flow of the compound in the press and to have a positive profile to achieve performance goals through the conformity of flexibility rather than the precision of rigidity. Record plant production facilities and personnel were not yet ready for this approach.

7. *Studios.* In the 1930s a converted livery stable with a colorful equestrian-motif entrance on 155 W. 24th Street in New York City became the flagship of RCA Victor recording studios. It housed studios A, B, and C. Studio C was in constant use as a storage room and after 1940 as a reverberation chamber. The first original cast recording of *Hello, Dolly* was one of many Broadway shows recorded in Studio A, which was used for recording Big Bands. Smaller ensembles, vocalists, and commercials were accommodated in Studio B. Victor had been scoring sound track movies and re-recording from film sound track to disc since doing the Paramount picture *Leatherneck* in 1929. RCA Photophone had a studio on Lexington Ave. where the first continuing radio shows were recorded on film phonographs. Then the "sound track" recording was taken to the 24th Street studios and there transcribed onto a lacquer. This operation gave origin to the name "transcriptions" for those recordings. At the

studios, the lacquer was processed for approval copies and passed onto the plant for the completion of matrixing and for final pressing as 16-inch 33 1/3 rpm "transcriptions" with the "Thesaurus" trademark. Radio shows were also transcribed in the Chicago studios. Although original recording on film persisted until the coming of stereo in 1958, a groove cut by a recording lathe was the predominant recording method until magnetic tape replaced it after World War II. The first tape machines used in the studios were the RT-11's of the RCA Broadcast Division. They were replaced by the Ampex two-track 201's and subsequently by multitrack models.

John E. Volkmann, head of the wartime government sound department at RCA, envisioned the recording studio as an integrated acoustical unit. After the war he set about translating his concept into RCA recording studios, large-scale auditoriums, and projection of sound for large gatherings of people. The 1962 grand opera RCA studio in Rome embodied the concept. That studio featured a built-in speaker system. The two 50-cubic-foot enclosures were protrusions from a brick wall. The speakers with 24-inch woofers and appropriate size mid-range units and tweeters were nearly transparent aurally inasmuch as there were hardly any of the usual speaker-induced artifacts.

In time the studio on 24th Street in New York, headed by Al Pulley, became overburdened and overcrowded with equipment. In 1969, RCA Victor launched the "Queen Mary" of studios at 1133 Avenue of the Americas, New York. Studio A, designed to be world class and number one, had size, variable ceiling height, variable acoustics, sonic insulation, and an integrated control room. The five other studios and supporting functional areas were similar in refinements. When Leonard Bernstein brought the company of *West Side Story* to Studio A for its first cast recording, John Volkmann and RCA Victor knew that their objective for Studio A had been achieved.

The Chicago studio had noteworthy accomplishments of its own. It was located during the 1930s in the Merchandise Mart—near NBC for "transcriptions." It moved to Lake Shore Drive in 1940 and handled a flow of recording engagements for such artists as Glenn Miller, Duke Ellington, and Tommy Dorsey. A new studio was opened on Wacker Drive, designed by Volkmann with the characteristics of New York's Studio A. The Hollywood studio moved in 1950 from above the record plant on Olive Ave. to a Volkmann-designed studio in the RCA building at 6363 Sunset Boulevard. It became the recording home for Henry Mancini, Hugo Montenegro, other Hollywood bands and motion picture stars, and any number of popular groups. Country and western recording, developed by A and R man Steve Sholes, outgrew the quonset hut studio in Nashville, and a new recording center was built. Managed by Chet Atkins, it became the home base for legendary artists.

Studio adequacy in the U.S. is augmented by the existence of concert halls, civic centers, and opera houses. Commercial recording takes place in such halls as the Academy of Music in Philadelphia, Orchestra Hall in Chicago, Carnegie Hall in New York, the Opera House in Pittsburgh, and many others. RCA Victor executed a landmark recording event on location on 13 Jan 1973. Studio Manager Larry Schnapf of New York headed a team that recorded Elvis Presley's *Aloha from Hawaii* live at the Honolulu International Center. Audio feed for satellite TV, four-channel sound records, stereo records, regular TV, radio, and for the public address system covering the live audience was carried out in an exemplary manner.

8. *Artists and repertoire.* Victor dominated the classical field, and from the 1940s it also held a high place in popular genres. It was the leading producer of country and western hits between 1944 and 1988, with 1,935 chart records. Million-selling albums included *The Sound of Music* (three years on the charts) and *Hello Dolly!* (on the charts longer than any other album). Perry Como, Tommy Dorsey, and Artie Shaw were among the stellar performers of the 1940s. John Denver and Elvis Presley were among the later pop artists. Henry Mancini received 20 Grammy awards. Between 1958 and 1978, 113 of the 134 Grammys received by the ten top winners went to RCA Victor artists. RCA Victor artists won a larger percent of awards and chart appearances than the RCA

Victor percentage of total record sales would indicate.

The Victor name, its trademark, its artists, its catalog, its studios, its RCA Music Services, its manufacturing business, and its heritage became a part of **Bertelsmann AG** on 15 Apr 1986.

9. *Victor officers. Presidents*: Eldridge R. Johnson, 1901–1925; Edward E. Shumaker, 1926–1928; Edward Wallenstein, 1932–1938; Frank B. White, 1938–1949; James Murray, 1949–1956; George Marek, 1956–1968; Norman Rascusin, 1968–1973; Kenneth Glancy, 1973–1975; Rocco Laginastra, 1975–1978; Robert Summer, 1978–1986.

Chief Engineers: Hill Reiskind, 1942–1956; H. E. Roys, 1956–1966; Warren Rex Isom, 1966–1976; James Frische, 1976–1980; Dave Mishra, 1980–1984.

Musical Directors: Arthur Pryor, Walter Rogers, Josef Pasternack, Rosario Bourdon, Nathaniel Shilkret, Edward King, Cliff Cairns, Roy Shields.

[Aldridge 1964; Baumbach 1981; Fagan 1983; Isom 1977; Rust 1970; Sherman 1987; Smart 1977. Several articles in *Hobbies* (by Stephen Fassett or Jim Walsh) are useful: a listing of the 5000 series, pressed in the U.S. from G & T masters in 1903, appeared in April, May and June 1947, and in March 1955. The first domestic Red Seals (2000 series) were listed in May 1942. The 76000 series of 12-inch singles-sided Red Seals appeared in April 1942. Black labels of the 5000 series were listed in July and December 1941, April 1942, July 1943, May 1945, and March 1946. The 10-inch 91000 series (G & T, 1902–1903) was listed in July 1941. The 12-inch 92000 series by G & T (1906–1908) was listed in November 1941. In December 1941 the G & T 94000 and 95000 series were listed (including the Melba, Tamagno, and Patti material). The Victor catalog of February 1901 was listed and discussed in January, February, and March 1968; the October 1901 catalog was listed in April 1968; the August 1902 catalog in May 1968. Notable releases from the catalogs of 1902–1905 were discussed in December 1949. Victor record sales of 1901–1942 were listed by year in June 1971 (the same data is in Sherman 1987). *Hobbies* of October, November, December 1968, and February, March, April 1969, explained "How to Tell When Victor Records Were Made."] *See also* articles about the recording artists mentioned, and entries beginning with "Victor."

Edgar Hutto, Jr. and Warren Rex Isom

VICTOR VAUDEVILLE CO. A group formed around 1908 to make comedy records for Victor. Members were Byron Harlan, Billy Murray, and Steve Porter. The 1917 catalog had one record by the group, identified as the Vaudeville Quartet: "Lucia Sextet Burlesque" (#17119). Record #35609 (1917) was listed in catalogs as a Victor Vaudeville Co. release, but it was in fact by the Peerless Quartet: "Court Scene in Carolina" / "Darktown Campmeetin' Experiences."

VICTORY (label). (I) A British record issued by Blum and Co., Ltd., from September 1912. They were actually re-labelled Stella records, identified first as Victory Gramophone Records, then as Victory Records. Material included military band numbers, popular material, and some items by Billy Williams. In June 1913 it was announced that Victory Records would henceforth be sold as **Diploma** Records. [Andrews 1988/10.]

VICTORY (label). (II) A seven-inch disc issued in Britain by **Crystalate Gramophone Record Manufacturing Co., Ltd.**, from 1928 to 1931. It was billed as a long-playing record, as it had approximately the playing time of a standard 10-inch disc.

VICTROLA. A trade name registered by the Victor Talking Machine Co., filed 1 Dec 1905 (registration #50,081/2), for a disc record player; it became the most popular and famous disc phonograph in the industry. Distinctive features of the instrument were the enclosure of all mechanical parts and the horn within a cabinet, a door on the front of the cabinet that could be opened or closed to control the volume, and storage space for records inside the cabinet. **Eldridge Johnson** held the patent covering these features, U.S. #856,704 (filed 8 Dec 1904; granted 11 June 1907), although in 1927

John Bailey Browning received credit for prior conception of the Victrola.

The Victrola (derivation of the name is uncertain) was announced to the trade on 7 Aug 1906. Advertising in 1906 identified the machine as a "Victor-Victrola," but the name was simplified to Victrola in 1907; it was also known as "Victrola the Sixteenth" or Model XVI. Table models were available from 1911, with sales rivalling those of the floor models. Either a spring motor or (from August 1913) AC (mains) electric power was offered.

Prices presented a wide range of choice. The open-top table models cost $15 (Victrola IV) and $25 (Victrola VI). Table models with lids cost $40 (Victrola VIII) or $50 (Victrola IX). Consoles varied greatly in size, record storage capacity, and finish. They cost from $75 (Victrola X) to $400 (the highest price for a Victrola XVIII).

By 1910 some 40,000 Victrola consoles had been sold. The table model quickly reached 50,000 sales in its first year, 1911. Thereafter the annual sales for each model were in six figures. In 1920 the console Victrola had its peak sales, 333,889; there were 212,363 table Victrolas sold that year. However the arrival of the radio brought about a slump from 1922. Production was halted in 1924, but resumed in the next year with the introduction of the Orthophonic Victrola.

Electrical recording created the need for an appropriate record player, since the new electric discs reproduced with excessive volume and stridency on the regular Victrolas. In June 1925 Victor announced its plan for a solution, a completely new machine (and set up a half-price sales campaign to move the older stock). On "Victor Day," 2 Nov 1925 there were nationwide demonstrations by dealers of the new Credenza model ($275.00–$405.00) of the **Orthophonic** Victrola—sales were strong from the outset: 42,446 before the end of 1925, and 260,436 in 1927.

Technically, the novelties in the Orthophonic were its pleated aluminum diaphragm (in place of the mica disc of the standard Victrola), a stylus assembly in ball bearings, and a folded exponential horn. Response was from about 100 Hz in the bass to about 5,000 Hz in the treble.

Varieties of the Orthophonic were numerous. The most expensive was the electric Borgia II model, at $1,000. It was housed in a double cabinet, with a radio in one of them (the Radiola 28); and the records could be played through the radio amplifier for complete volume control. There were spring motor machines also, and table models as well as elaborate consoles. Victor's all electric instrument was known as the Electrola-Victrola; it competed with the Brunswick **Panatrope**, made from the same RCA components. Victor's first record changer was introduced in 1927, the Automatic Orthophonic; it was the first changer to reach a mass market. Model 955, with a radio and record changer in its grand walnut cabinet, was "Victor's pride and joy in 1927, and is unquestionably the most impressive instrument they ever built" (Baumbach). It sold for $1550. With the creation of these combination radio-phonographs, run by electric power, and complete with disc changers, Victor established the format of the record player that was to remain the norm until the high fidelity era of the 1950s and the move toward separate components. [Baumbach 1981 describes and illustrates all models of the Victrola through 1929; Hoover 1971 has illustrations of table model IV (p. 50) and of the Automatic Orthophonic Victrola of 1927 (pp. 82–83).]

VIDEO RECORDING. The storage and reproduction of visual images, perfected by the Ampex Corp. in the U.S. in 1956, and offered commercially for professional studio use in 1957. The Ampex system was in tape format, using two-inch-wide tapes running at 15 inches per second. Video disc recording was first accomplished by Telefunken and Decca in 1966, using a microgroove record with 25 grooves in the space of a typical LP record groove. Signals were vertically inscribed and frequency modulated. The pickup sensed changes in pressure. In a demonstration at the AEG Telefunken building in Berlin, 24 June 1970, the discs were of thin flexible plastic foil, with a playing time of five minutes. They revolved at television picture frame rates: 1,500 rpm (in Europe; the American speed was 1,800 rpm). This was basically a mechanical system.

An optical video disc system was launched by Philips in 1978. In this process a laser beam traces a spiralling track of depressions or pits in a highly reflective aluminum layer on a vinyl disc. The spot of reflected light activates a photo-diode to produce the electric signal that is then processed to reproduce a color picture and audio signal in a conventional television set. From this technology the compact (audio) disc emerged.

Videotape research brought successful commercial applications in the 1980s. It appears that both laser disc and videotape will be acceptable media for carrying video-audio programming in the domestic markets.

VIENNA INSTRUMENTAL QUARTETTE. A piano and string ensemble, also known as the Vienna Quartette, that recorded for Edison cylinders in 1910–1911. Members were Jacques Grunberg, piano; Licco Liggy, violin; Otto Krist, cello; and Ludwig Schonberger, viola. Their numbers were "In Vienna—Serenade" (#10520) and "Tin Soldier" (#10304).

VIM (label). A Chicago record, issued by the Vim Co., with material of uncertain origin. Rust reports he has seen only one release, a banjo solo by Vess Ossman. The date is suggested as sometime in "the first decade of the century." [Rust 1978.]

VINYL. The compound used in making disc records, replacing **shellac** gradually in the 1940s and then totally with the advent of the LP record. Union Carbide developed a vinyl resin in the 1930s ("Vinylite") that was compatible with production equipment of the time, so that factories set up to make shellac records could make vinyl records as well, or change over completely. Western Electric used vinyl for radio transcriptions, and **Muzak** used it for its music services. RCA made vinyl ("Victrolac") radio transcriptions, and then the unbreakable **V-Discs** during the Second World War. In 1944 RCA issued a few Red Seal records on transparent cherry-red vinyl. Cosmo Records made the first major seller on vinyl, a children's item named "Tubby the Tuba." Red vinyl was also used for the RCA 45 rpm record, and for the Columbia microgroove LP of 1948.

The basic vinyl material is polyvinyl chloride (PVC). It is produced by cracking the hydrocarbons in petroleum products to derive vinyl monomer, which is the PVC raw material. Coal and agricultural products are alternative sources for the monomer. LP discs were compression molded of vinyl chloride vinyl acetate copolymer. Injection molding of seven-inch 45 rpm discs used modified polystyrenes.

Important factors in the vinyl disc manufacturing process include careful selection of the resins and stabilizers in the compound, use of carbon black with ideal particle size and distribution, selection of fillers, and blending of special additives. [Isom 1977; Khanna 1977.]

VIOLA (label). A rare American record issued by the Southern California Phonograph Co., Los Angeles, ca. 1921. Evidently the discs were distributed as incentives toward the purchase of the firm's Viola Phonograph. Matrices came from Olympic, Black Swan, and other labels. [Rust 1978.]

Violano. *See* MILLS NOVELTY CO.

VIOLIN RECORDINGS. The instrument, or its functional imitation, the **Stroh** violin, was heard on many early discs and cylinders. There were about 50 solo numbers in the Edison output by 1905, beginning with performances by **Fred Hager** in 1898 ("Annie Laurie" was his initial offering, on #6700). Two artists made **Bettini** cylinders in 1898: Henri Marteau (four numbers) and **Dora Valesca Becker**—the first female violinist on record (14 numbers). Another 1898 performer was T. Herbert Reed, on cylinders of **Reed, Dawson and Co.**, which claimed "the only successful violin records." Other very early violinists included **Charles D'Almaine**, on Columbia in 1899–1900, Edison in 1899, and Victor 1900–1907; and J. Scott Skinner, one of the persons recorded by Fred Gaisberg in his Glasgow expedition for the new Gramophone Co. in September 1899, later an Edison artist. Other Edison cylinder violinists were Eugene Jaudas, on Edison from 1905; Leopold Moeslein, on Edison from 1906; and William Craig, on Edison from 1910. Edison also recorded nine pieces for violin (Jaudas) and flute (Eugene C. Rose), during 1903–1905.

It was the Gramophone Co. that sought out the leading concert artists of Europe. Important violinists who recorded for HMV were, by year: *1901*—Paul Viardot; *1902*—**Jan Kubelik;** *1903*—Franz Drdla, Joseph Joachim, Ferenc von Vecsey; *1904*—Willy Burmeister, Pablo de Sarasate, Mary Hall, **Fritz Kreisler, Maud Powell;** *1905*—Jacques Thibaud; *1906*— Mischa Elman; *1908*—Joseph Szigeti.

An EMI LP of 1989 (#EX 761062-1) included material by these violinists, plus Eugène Ysaÿe, who recorded ca. 1912. Victor had about 200 titles listed in its 1917 catalog, including Gramophone Co. material. Most of those discs were arrangements, but Maud Powell did play a movement from the Mendelssohn Concerto (Victor #74026, from HMV # 85040). In the 1930s a more substantial repertoire was available. Fritz Kreisler recorded the Beethoven, Brahms, and Mendelssohn concertos. **Mischa Elman** and **Jascha Heifetz** performed major concertos, and Heifetz also did sonatas by Fauré, Mozart, and Richard Strauss. **Yehudi Menuhin** offered some uncommon material, such as the Elgar and Schumann concertos and the JS. Bach unaccompanied sonatas. **Albert Spalding**, who had recorded for Edison in 1909–1924, moved over to Victor in the 1930s and contributed some important repertoire by Tartini, Handel, Franck, and Brahms; he also made his acclaimed record of the Ludwig Spohr Concerto with Eugene Ormandy and the Philadelphia Orchestra.

As the LP era drew to a close in the late 1980s, the prominent violin artists were Zino Francescatti, Arthur Grumiaux, Leonid Kogan, Suzanne Lautenbacher, Yehudi Menuhin, Nathan Milstein, **David Oistrakh, Itzhak Perlman**, Ruggiero Ricci, Aaron Rosand, Alexander Schneider, **Isaac Stern**, Henryk Szeryng, and Pinchas Zukerman.

Among the outstanding violinists to emerge with the compact disc are Kyung-Wha Chung, Gidon Kremer, Midori, Schlomo Mintz, and Anne-Sophie Mutter.

The outstanding historical release of violin performers was issued by Pearl in 1991: *The Recorded Violin* on six compact discs, #BVA 1. It covered artists who recorded from the early acoustic days to the 1930s, presenting them in birth order: Joachim (born 1831) to Ida Haendel (born 1923).

VITAGRAPH CO.

A firm established in 1899 by James Stuart Blackton, Albert E. Smith, and W. T. Rock. Blackton bought an Edison Kinetoscope movie projector, and Smith adapted it to make films as well as show them. The firm made low-budget motion pictures in New York, and became an important part of the new industry. By 1913 it was making five-reel pictures with a variety of subjects. In 1914 it was located at E. 15th St. & Chestnut Ave., Brooklyn, New York, with branches in Chicago, London, Paris, and Berlin. There was also a New York office at 116 Nassau St. On 7 Feb 1914 the Vitagraph Theatre opened, with music by a **Wurlitzer** "orchestra."

Vitagraph was renamed VLSE in 1917, having bought out a consortium, and continued successfully until 1925; Warner Brothers acquired the firm at that time.

VITANOLA TALKING MACHINE CO.

A Chicago firm located in 1916 at 206 S. Wabash Ave. It marketed the Vitanola disc player, in eight models, selling for $25–$250. In 1919 the address in advertisements was 508 W. 35th St., an ominous change to a low rent district; and though advertising continued lavishly the firm announced bankruptcy in 1920. By 1922 it had reorganized and was back in business, moving in October to Saginaw, Michigan. Advertising continued to 1925.

VITAPHONE (label). (I)

A disc issued by the American Talking Machine Co., a licensee of American Graphophone Co., in 1898–1900. The records were of various colors, including red, green, and black. As the firm ceased operations in 1900, the Vitaphone label died with it. Later (ca. 1902–1903) there was a seven-inch issue named American Vitaphone Record.

VITAPHONE (label). (II)

An American record issued by the **Vitaphone Co.** of Plainfield, New Jersey, from ca. 1912–ca. 1917. The label was styled Music Master Vitaphone Record; it was purple, and pressed by American Graphophone Co.

VITAPHONE CO.

A New Jersey firm, incorporated 1 Mar 1907 in Plainfield. It produced the Vitaphone disc player in ca. 1912, capable of handling lateral-cut records (Victor and Columbia), Edison Diamond Discs, and Pathé vertical-cut records. It had a wooden tone arm, and a diaphragm located at the horn, activated by the vibrations sent along a cord from the tone arm. This novel approach was patented by Clinton B. Repp (U.S. #1,003, 655; filed 24 June 1909; granted 19 Sep 1911). Vitaphones were sold as external horn table models at $17.50, enclosed horn table models at $25, and console models up to $175 for the Vitaphone Grand. **Vitaphone** label records were also produced.

H.N. McMenimen was general manager from August 1912. *TMW* reported the firm was bankrupt in June 1917. [Fabrizio 1976.]

VITAPHONE CORP.

A New York firm, established 20 Apr 1926 as a joint venture of Warner Brothers and Western Electric. The purpose was to make disc records that would provide sound for motion pictures. This was one of the two active approaches to the making of talking pictures, the other being the optical **soundtrack.** While the soundtrack did become the norm eventually, in the late 1920s both systems were competing for attention in the film industry, which was of course dealing only with silents at the time. For a year the Vitaphone work was carried on in the Manhattan Opera House, then from 1927 in Hollywood.

Vitaphone is of special interest in the history of sound recording not so much for its technology, which soon took second place and was forgotten in a few years, but for the content of its productions, many of which were made by outstanding musical artists. The most famous of the 400+ Vitaphone short films was *The Jazz Singer* of 1927, with Al Jolson, the first commercial talking picture to achieve national success.

Discs used in the Vitaphone system were shellac, but with less of the usual abrasive filler, so that the surfaces were smoother and quieter. The disadvantage was rapid wear of the discs, which had to be replaced frequently in the projection room. Records played from inside to outside, probably to give the projectionist a better chance of seeing the needle come to the end of its playing surface, thus allowing a timely transfer to the next disc. Diameter was 16 inches, and speed was 33 1/3 rpm—the speed of the later commercial LP record. Synchronization between film and records was accomplished through manual placement of the needle at the starting point in the center of the disc when a cue flashed on the screen—although this seems a risky method, synchronization did not prove to be a problem in practice. Projection of the sound was from behind and below the theatre screen, using four long horns (12–14 feet).

Despite the success of the Vitaphone short subjects, Warner discontinued making them in 1930, as the advantages of soundtracks became more apparent. *See* MOTION PICTURE SOUND RECORDING for names of artists and for the ancestry of Vitaphone. [Taylor, G. 1985.]

VIVA-TONAL. The Columbia counterpart of the Victor **Orthophonic** record player, introduced in 1925. There was major advertising in 1927, which claimed a frequency range exceeding that of any "ordinary" player, but the instrument did not succeed in its competition with Victor.

VOCALION (label). (1) An American record marketed by the **Aeolian Co.**, New York, from May 1918 (as Aeolian-Vocalion). From 1921 to 1927 the name was simply Vocalion. They were vertical-cut discs (until 1920, then lateral), single- or double-sided at first, in 10- or 12-inch sizes. **Brunswick** acquired the label from Aeolian in 1924, retaining control until 1931, when **American Record Corp.** absorbed it. In 1938 CBS bought it from ARC.

A small but respectable roster of classical artists was assembled for the label, including John Charles Thomas, Marguerite d'Alvarez, and Florence Easton; but it was the jazz and popular realm that brought the label to great prominence.

The Original Dixieland Jazz Band recorded for Vocalion in 1917, not long after they made the first jazz recordings for Victor and Columbia. At one time or another, Vocalion recorded Bunny Berigan, Cab Calloway, the Dorsey Brothers Orchestra, Cliff Edwards, Erskine Hawkins, Fletcher Henderson, Earl Hines, Billie Holiday, the Louisiana Rhythm Kings, Wingy Manone, Jelly Roll Morton, King Oliver, Adrian Rollini, Joe Venuti, and Cootie Williams. **Jack Kapp** was responsible for much of the label's success; he became manager in February 1928. Columbia acquired the label in 1940, and changed the name to Okeh (reviving that label that had been silent for five years) in the same year.

An LP Vocalion was issued in 1949, with Decca as the parent label. The label name has continued into the CD era, a Decca subsidiary distributed by MCA.

VOCALION (label). (II) A British label issued from 1920 by the **Aeolian Co., Ltd.** In January 1925 the Aeolian Co., Ltd., sold its record business to a newly incorporated entity, the Vocalion Gramophone Co., Ltd. Vocalion records continued to appear from this source into 1927, then the label was terminated. In 1932 the **Crystalate Gramophone Record Manufacturing Co., Ltd.,** bought the business of the Vocalion Gramophone Record Co., Ltd., and proceeded to form a new Vocalion Gramophone Co., Ltd., the prior firm being in liquidation. Then in March 1937 **Decca Record Co., Ltd.,** acquired the record interests of Crystalate; and in 1951 the label was brought back once more. Like the American Vocalion label, the British record was distinguished for its jazz and popular artists, many taken from the U.S. masters. Vocalion remains an active label, distributed in the U.S. by MCA.

From 1963 to 1968 there was another Vocalion and a Vocalion Pop label, from Vogue Records, Ltd., in U.K.; those were 45s.

VOGUE (label). (I) An American record issued from the Vogue Recording Co., 4875 E. Eight Mile Rd., Detroit, from May 1946. Tom Saffady was president of the firm. Vogue was the most famous of the **picture discs**, pressed on vinyl surfaces over an aluminum core, with the illustration sealed inside the vinyl coating. Surfaces were quiet and durability was good. Among the artists signed by Vogue were Phil Spitalny and his "all-girl" orchestra; Art Kassel, Charlie Shavers, Shep Fields, Frankie Masters, Clyde

McCoy, and Joan Edwards. There are 98 records listed in Lindsay 1989.

Vogue discs sold for $1.05, while standard Victors and Deccas were selling for $.50. After an initial flurry of sales and several good critical reviews, business began to slip. By 1947 the firm was ready to quit new releases. Advertisements for liquidation of remaining stock appeared in July, and in August bankruptcy proceedings began.

The pictures were "multi-colored, almost cartoon-like representations of the song title"—"they were garish, obvious, and often downright silly" (Brooks). Despite the novelty of the illustrations, and the high quality of much recorded material, there was never a hit record on Vogue. It remains unique in recording history, the only label to have illustrated its entire output. [Brooks 1977; Curry 1990; Lindsay 1989 (a label list).]

VOGUE (label). (II) A record initiated in France in 1948, licensing jazz material from the U.S. A British subsidiary, Vogue Records, Ltd., was founded in 1951. Vogue discs included material by Sidney Bechet, Earl Hines, Thelonious Monk, Josh White, and Mahalia Jackson. Vogue came under control of Pye of Cambridge in 1965. Vogue-Coral discs were issued, via Coral of the U.S., which was Decca owned. Coral rights passed to British Decca in early 1956, and the Vogue label returned again—then changed to **Vocalion** in March 1963. Vocalion has remained a Decca subsidiary. [Andrews*.]

VOICEWRITER. The trade name of Edison dictating cylinder machines, made by the Voicewriter Division of **Thomas A. Edison, Inc.** It succeeded the Ediphone, which succeeded the original Edison Business Phonograph. When Edison ceased all other record production on 1 Nov 1929, dictation cylinders were continued. Production went on after a merger in 1956 with McGraw Electric Co.

VOLTA GRAPHOPHONE CO. An organization established in Washington, D.C., in January 1886 (incorporated on 3 Feb 1886) by Alexander Graham Bell, Chichester Bell, and Charles Sumner Tainter. It was a successor to the **Volta Laboratory Association**, established

by the same men in 1881. Acoustic and electrical research was the object of the Volta Laboratory, and the **graphophone** their principal product—which gave its name to the new company. Volta Graphophone Co. held the key Bell-Tainter patents, which it licensed to the new **American Graphophone Co.**, established 28 Mar 1887.

VOLTA LABORATORY ASSOCIATION. A group organized in Washington, D.C., on 8 Oct 1881, by **Alexander Graham Bell, Chichester Bell,** and **Charles Sumner Tainter**; location was first at 1325 L St., then 1221 Connecticut Ave. The purpose of the association was to carry on electrical and acoustic research. An early emphasis on the telephone was shifted to phonographic research, probably because of the interests of Tainter. Having developed and filed for a patent on the wax surface principle of the graphophone, the association endeavored in vain to bring Thomas Edison into the enterprise (Tainter spent two months in New York trying to stimulate the interest of Edison and Edward H. Johnson), then went ahead with the project independently. The **Volta Graphophone Co.** was established on 2 Feb 1886 to carry on with development. [Newville 1959; Wile 1990/2.]

VOLUME. The intensity of an audio signal, the function of the amplitude of the sound wave. It is expressed in **decibels** relative to a standard reference volume. *See also* AMPLITUDE; LEVEL.

VOLUME CONTROL. Early playback systems had no means of adjusting the intensity of the output signal, other than to change **needles**; there were needles that gave degrees of louder to softer output. In 1916 Pathé advertised an "exclusive on Pathéphone": a "tone control' knob on the side of the cabinet to adjust volume. Sonora had a comparable "tone modifier," and the Aeolian **graduola**, marketed in 1920, had the same function, although advertising copy clouded its purpose.

Von Karajan, Herbert. *See* KARAJAN, HERBERT VON, 1908–1989.

VORSETZER. The Welte-Mignon "push-up" attachment for the making of reproducing piano rolls.

VOX (label). (I) A German record issued by the Deutsche Schallplatten und Sprechmaschinen AG, Berlin, from 1921 to 1929. The disc, with a triangular label, enjoyed great success in the mid-1920s, and the firm opened an American office in New York, the Vox Corporation of America (1923). Gramophones were also manufactured. In the economic crisis of 1929, the firm collapsed. The Vox rights were taken over by the Kristall Schallplatten GmbH. [Sieben 1985.]

VOX (label). (II) An early American LP label, one of the eleven listed in the first edition of the Schwann catalog, October 1949. (It had begun with some 78 rpm issues in 1947.) The issues came from Vox Productions, Inc., 236 W. 55th St., New York. It was available in Britain from 1951. One of the interesting early issues was the Igor Stravinsky Concerto in D for Violin and Orchestra, with the composer conducting (#VLP-6340). A low-cost line of albums, "Vox Boxes," was popular in the late 1960s; the name has been carried over to compact discs, each "box" carrying two budget-priced CDs. The Moss Music Group is the present distributor of Vox/Turnabout, as it is now named, in the U.S.

VULCAN RECORD CO. A New York firm incorporated in June 1921, with an office at 15 E. 60th St. Fred Hedinger was general manager and secretary. Sets of three "indestructible" 10-inch discs in a Junior Operetta Series appeared from August 1923, packed in containers costing $2.50. The content was fairy tales set to music by **Charles A. Prince,** sung and played by well-known artists. Announcements continued through November 1923. [Andrews*.]

WAGNER, "HERR." A German tenor who sang five numbers for Edison cylinders, (#4401–#4405), all recorded before March 1888. Four were songs, and one was an aria: the *Tannhäuser* "Evening Star."

WAGONER, PORTER, 1930–. American country singer, songwriter, and record producer, born in West Plains, Missouri, on 12 Aug 1930. He began performing on radio in 1950, and then on television on Red Foley's *Ozark Jubilee* program. From 1955 he recorded for Victor, and had 52 solo chart songs by 1979. He also recorded successfully with Dolly Parton (22 chart records); he wrote many of her songs and also produced her recordings. Among Wagoner's most important discs were "Satisfied Mind" (Victor #6105; 1955) and "Cold Hard Facts of Life" (Victor #9067; 1967). The Parton duets included "Just Someone I Used to Know" (Victor #0267; 1969) and "Please Don't Stop Loving Me" (Victor #10010; 1974).

WALCHA, HELMUT, 1907–1991. German organist, born in Leipzig on 27 Oct 1907. He lost his eyesight at age 19, but persisted in his career as a church organist. He was assistant organist at the Thomaskirche in Leipzig, then organist in Frankfurt. Walcha became professor of music in the Leipzig Hochschule für Musik in 1938, and remained until his retirement in 1972. After World War II he recorded extensively for the Archiv label; his *Kunst der Fuge* of J.S. Bach was Archiv's first stereo offering (#2708002). He recorded the complete Bach organ works on 16 LPs (Archiv #413125-1).

WALLER, FATS, 1904–1943. American jazz pianist and organist, born Thomas Waller in New York on 21 May 1904. He studied violin and piano, but learned primarily from imitating piano rolls. At 14 he was organist for a Harlem theatre. He took lessons from James P. Johnson, and then from Leopold Godowsky. In 1929 he wrote a Broadway revue, *Hot Chocolates*, including the hit song "Ain't Misbehavin'." He also composed "Honeysuckle Rose." Waller had a brilliant stride piano style, mingled with his happy sense of humor, well suited to parody vocals on popular tunes. He toured widely in the 1930s, including Europe, made motion pictures in Hollywood, had a Big Band for a time. Organ playing was not neglected either: he had a radio program devoted to it, and he played organ at New York theatres in the 1920s. He died on a train arriving at Kansas City on 15 Dec 1943.

Waller recorded incessantly, from 1922 for Okeh, with "Muscle Shoals Blues" / "Birmingham Blues" (#4757); thereafter for Victor and Bluebird. He also made piano rolls for QRS, e.g., "I've Got to Cool My Doggies Now" (#2149; 1922). "Ain't Misbehavin'" was made in 1929, on Victor #22092, and "Honeysuckle Rose" in 1934 (Victor #24826). Later hits included "Fractious Fingering" (Victor #25652; 1936) and "Yacht Club Swing"—used as his theme song (Bluebird #10035; 1938). Waller's vocalization was exemplified in "A-Tisket, A-Tasket" (HMV #BD-5398; 1938) and "Sheik of Araby" (Victor #25847; 1938). "Your Feets Too Big" (Bluebird #10500; 1939) illustrated his comedic approach.

"Don't Try Your Jive on Me" had Waller at the organ and singing (HMV #BD-5415; 1938). The elaborated stride style is heard to advantage in several of his compositions recorded in 1929, such as "My Feelin's are Hurt" / "Smashing Thirds" (Victor #38613; 1929). There were numerous LP albums, originals and reissues. *The Complete Fats Waller* is a CD series from Bluebird. Biograph has issued the QRS roll material on compact discs. [Davies 1953.]

WALLERSTEIN, EDWARD, ca. 1892–1970. American record industry executive. He was with Brunswick from 1925, serving as eastern manager of the music division to 1930, then as sales manager. He left Brunswick in 1932 to head RCA-Victor Records. He addressed the economic problems of the times with a number of successful initiatives, including renewed publication of the Victor catalogs and promotion of a turntable that would play through a radio. The turntable, named Duo Junior, proved very popular, although it sold for $16.50, a stiff price during the Depression. Wallerstein left Victor in 1938 to become president of the newly organized **Columbia** Recording Co., just acquired by CBS from American Record Corp. Indeed it was Wallerstein who had recommended to William S. Paley, CBS president, the purchase and rehabilitation of the Columbia label. Wallerstein unveiled the new LP microgroove record at a press conference in 1948.

After 12 years at Columbia, during which the label prospered and he became chairman of the board as well as president, Wallerstein retired in 1951. He then served as a consultant to **Jack Kapp** and in 1959 was vice president of the Belock Instrument Corp., makers of Everest records. He died in Ft. Lauderdale, Florida, on 8 Sep 1970.

WALSH, ARTHUR, 1896–1947. American record industry executive, U.S. senator, and violinist, born in Newark, New Jersey, on 26 Feb 1896. He recorded for Edison from 1916, and participated in **tone tests**. From 1924 to 1931 he was an executive with Thomas A. Edison, Inc., rising to general manager of the phonograph division, and then executive vice-president of the company. He concluded his career with a successful run for the U.S. Senate,

where he served from 1943 to 1947. Walsh died in South Orange, New Jersey, on 13 Dec 1947.

WALSH, JIM, 1910–1990. Historian of the record industry, born Ulysses Walsh in Richmond, Virginia. He wrote a column in the monthly magazine *Hobbies*, "Favorite Pioneer Recording Artists," from January 1942 to May 1985. In his writings Walsh relied on an extensive personal communication with the artists and their families, producing accurate documentation that was infused with the human side of each performer. A chronological list of those articles to 1977 appeared in *NAG* #27 and *RR* #159–160, with an alphabetical index to the 1942–1982 articles in *NAG* #44.

Walsh wrote also for other journals, and contributed to *Edison Blue Amberol Recordings* by Ron Dethlefson (1981). His collection of records and materials was donated to the Library of Congress. He was posthumously honored with a Lifetime Achievement Award by the Association of Recorded Sound Collections in 1991.

WALTER, BRUNO, 1876–1962. German / American conductor, born Bruno Walter Schlesinger in Berlin, 15 Sep 1876. After study in Berlin, he went to Cologne at age 17 as opera coach. At 18 he was assistant conductor, under Gustav Mahler, at the Hamburg State Theater. He was then Mahler's assistant at the Vienna Opera, in 1901–1913. During the 1920s he became internationally famous, directing the Berlin Philharmonic Orchestra, the New York Philharmonic, and the Leipzig Gewandhaus. He was a guest conductor in Europe and the U.S. in the 1930s, then a resident in France during the Second World War. In the late 1940s he conducted at the Metropolitan Opera, and led the NBC Orchestra. He was appointed conductor of the New York Philharmonic in 1947, remaining to 1949. Walter retired to California in 1960, and died in Beverly Hills on 17 Feb 1962.

Known as a master of the Viennese school, and of Mahler, Walter inscribed some splendid recordings of those works. He directed the New York Philharmonic-Symphony Orchestra in major concertos: Beethoven's Violin Concerto with Joseph Szigeti (Columbia set #M-

177), the Beethoven Emperor Concerto with the Vienna Philharmonic Orchestra and Walter Gieseking (Columbia set #M-243) and also with the New York Philharmonic-Symphony Orchestra and Rudolf Serkin (Columbia #M-500). He recorded the Beethoven Eroica, Fifth, and Eighth Symphonies, also with the New York orchestra. In the album of the Fifth (#498) there is a side on which he is heard rehearsing the orchestra. Walter's recording of the Mahler *Lied von der Erde* brought attention of a wide audience to that work, and to its composer (Columbia #M-300; 1936); it was performed with the Vienna Philharmonic Orchestra, assisted by singers Charles Kullman and Kerstin Thorborg. Compact disc reissues of his Beethoven symphonies are available, and of the Mahler *Lied*, plus Walter's renditions of Mahler symphonies number 1, 2, 5 and 9; all from CBS.

WARING, FRED, 1900–1984. American orchestra leader, born Fred Malcolm Waring in Tyrone, Pennsylvania, on 9 June 1900. He learned the banjo and played in a four-man banjo "orchestra" in his teens, and continued music making while an engineering student at Pennsylvania State University. (Later his technical knowledge helped him to gain a lucrative patent, for the Waring Blender). He formed a larger orchestra and glee club—the Pennsylvanians—and gained engagements on college campuses. The group was a great success on a tour to France. The glee club was a hit everywhere, with its romantic arrangements and clear diction contrasted with hummed passages. In 1933 he was engaged for a radio program sponsored by Old Gold cigarettes (one of the group's favorite songs was "A Cigarette, Sweet Music, and You"). Other tunes associated with the ensemble included the their several theme songs, "Sleep," (Victor #19172; 1923) "I Hear Music," and "Breezin' along with the Breeze." "Dancing in the Dark" was a memorable arrangement (Victor # 22708; 1931).

The Waring orchestra and chorale appeared on numerous radio programs and toured widely, maintaining a high level of popularity, and had a television show in the early years of the medium. They made 145 Victor records, and worked also for Decca and

Reprise. Because they declined to make records at all for a nine-year period, 1923–1932, many of their popular renditions were not preserved. Waring died in Danville, Pennsylvania, on 29 July 1984. [Gottlieb 1972.]

WARNER BRUNSWICK, LTD. With Brunswick discs, of **British Brunswick, Ltd.,** demised in the U.K., the Hollywood film-maker Warner Brothers (which had purchased the Brunswick Radio Corp.) resuscitated the **Brunswick** label in Britain. Warner Brunswick, Ltd., was formed with £40,000 capital on 11 Oct 1930, with the registered trademark of Brunswick acquired for Britain. The new firm took over the **Panatrope** trademark as well, and serviced those machines. A factory was at Shepherds Bush, London. **Chappell Piano Co., Ltd.** of Bond Street was acquired to be the first distributors of Brunswick discs, all of them by American Brunswick artists but pressed in London. In December 1930 the first catalog of those discs appeared, offering 10-inch records at three shillings each.

In April 1931 Warner Brunswick, Ltd., introduced **Panachord** discs to the British market, with many masters from the U.S. **Melotone** label; the Panachord price was two shillings (reduced to 1s 6d in July). Chappell was the sole concessionaire. By September 1931 the business had achieved success, employing hundreds of British workmen at the factory, which covered hundreds of acres. There were studios in London, Milan, Buenos Aires, Sydney, Chicago, Los Angeles, and New York. Radios were also made at the London factory. All European business was transferred from London to the New York office.

Although British radio stations were not allowed to advertise, Warner Brunswick did broadcast commercials, beamed to Britain through Radio Paris. English recorded discs were introduced on the Brunswick and Panachord labels just before **Decca Record Co., Ltd.** purchased the business and share capital of Warner Brunswick, the parent company having already disposed of its end to the **American Record Corp.**, which then formed the **Brunswick Record Corp.** (The British **Crystalate Gramophone Record Manufacturing Co., Ltd.** had a third share in American

Record Corp.) The sale was reported in the first week of May 1932. Decca continued the record names, but added "Made by Decca" to the labels. Pressing was transferred to the Decca factory at New Malden. Warner Brunswick, Ltd., disappeared with the company's change of name to **Brunswick, Ltd.**, in July 1933. [Andrews*.]

Warner Communications, Inc. *See* WCI.

WARWICK, DIONNE, 1941– . American popular singer, born Dionne Warwicke in East Orange, New Jersey, on 12 Dec 1941. She began singing with her sister and a cousin, doing gospel songs, then worked in New York. She impressed composer Burt Bacharach and producer Hal David, and got a recording contract with Scepter, staying with the label from 1962 to 1971. Warwick became a sophisticated soul singer, thriving on songs written for her by Bacharach, such as "Walk on By" (Scepter # 1274; 1964) and "I'll Never Fall in Love Again" (Scepter #12273; 1969). She won a Grammy for the latter record, and another for "Do You Know the Way to San Jose?" (Scepter #12216; 1968). A great hit album, *Dionne* (Arista #AB4230; 1979), on the charts 40 weeks, included the popular singles "Deja Vu" (Arista #0459) and "I'll Never Love this Way Again" (Arista #0419). Her last chart album was *How Many Times Can We Say Goodbye?* (Arista #AL8 8104; 1983). Warwick had 44 chart singles and 33 chart albums.

WATERS, ETHEL, 1896–1977. American blues singer, born Ethel Howard in Chester, Pennsylvania, on 31 Oct 1896. She made an unfortunate marriage at age 13, then had to work as a laundress in Philadelphia, while breaking into vaudeville. She attracted attention and made some records in 1921. "New York Glide" / "At the New Jump Steady Ball" was on the Cardinal label (#2036), and "Oh Daddy" / "Down Home Blues" was on Black Swan (#2010). She was paid $100 for the Black Swan effort, which turned out to be a big enough hit to help save the new company from ruin. A few months later Waters had a Black Swan contract that made her "the highest paid colored recording star in the country" (Dixon) with the stipula-

tion that she would not marry again. She continued to work for the label until its demise in 1923, then went to Paramount, Vocalion, and Columbia. She gathered her own groups of sidemen, including distinguished artists like Tommy Dorsey, Jimmy Dorsey, Benny Goodman, Adrian Rollini, Eddie Lang, and Joe Venuti. "When Your Lover Has Gone" (Columbia #2409; 1931) had Tommy Dorsey, Goodman, Venuti, and Lang backing her up. Waters sang a fine "Stormy Weather" for Brunswick in 1933 (#6564).

She was in many Broadway musicals, most notably in *Cabin in the Sky*, with an all-Black cast (1940), and made a brilliant record of its hit song, "Taking a Chance on Love" (Liberty Music Shop #L-310; 1940). She became a serious stage actress, and then a partner to Billy Graham in his evangelistic travels. Waters died in New York on 1 Sep 1977.

WATERS, MUDDY, 1915–1983. American blues singer, born McKinley Morganfield in Rolling Fork, Mississippi, on 4 Apr 1915. He was reared on a plantation by his grandmother, learning to sing and play harmonica and guitar, and acquiring his nickname. Alan and John Lomax recorded him in 1941 for the Archive of Folk Song at the Library of Congress, doing "Country Blue" / "I Be's Troubled" (Archive of American Folk Song #18). He was successful thereafter in Chicago and nationally, singing blues in his own rough manner. He took up the electric guitar, requiring louder singing, and visited U.K. in 1958 with great effect. Mick Jagger was one of those impressed, sufficiently to name his rock group after one of the Waters songs, "Rolling Stone." A magazine took the same name, and Bob Dylan later composed a song in its honor, "Like a Rolling Stone." Waters' new approach distanced him from much of his earlier following. He was less active after an auto accident in 1970. Death came in Downers Grove, Illinois, on 30 Apr 1983.

In 1947 Waters made his earliest commercial discs, using his electric guitar. "Walkin' Blues" (Chess #1426; 1950) was a success, and "Louisiana Blues"—with harmonica player Little Walter—was another (Chess #1441; 1950). His more advanced and raucous manner was demonstrated in "Tiger in Your Tank" (Chess

#1765; 1960). Five of his records won Grammy awards. Only one LP album reached the charts, *Electric Mud* (Cadet Concept LPS #214; 1968).

WATERSON, HENRY, ca.1871–1933. American record industry executive, founder of the **Little Wonder** and **Cameo** labels. He was also a force in music publishing, as co-founder of the firm Waterson, Berlin and Snyder. He died in Saratoga, New York, on 10 Aug 1933. [Brooks*.]

WATSON, CAPRI, 1960– . American popular vocalist, born in Chicago on 23 Dec 1960. She was a rock singer, then developed a soft-soul style, heard to advantage on "You Made Me Love You" (Worth #7245).

WATT. The unit of electrical power measurement. In an audio system wattage is a consideration with regard to an **amplifier** (indicating the amount of work it can perform, primarily in the driving of loudspeakers) and to **loudspeakers** (referring to a speaker's efficiency in converting electrical power into acoustic power). [Klinger*.]

WAX. One of the earliest and most used materials for records, both cylinder and disc. Initially, waxes were carnauba (brittle yellow), from Brazilian palm leaves, or a mineral derived from brown coal. *See also* CYLINDER, 2; DISC, 3.

WCI (WARNER COMMUNICATIONS, INC.). A major record producer, and prototype of the multi-industry conglomerate. Beginning modestly as the music division of Warner Brothers (Hollywood film company), the label depended heavily on its comedian Bill Cosby for a market share. Then a significant merger created Warner/Reprise, bringing in **Middle of the Road (MOR)** repertoire. Valiant and **Atlantic** labels were acquired, and then **Elektra** and Nonesuch. These purchases brought in artists like the Grateful Dead, the Association, Led Zeppelin, the Bee Gees, Cream, and Eric Clapton. Nominal independence of operation was continued by the acquired labels. As other top names were signed up, the firm's roster featured Peter, Paul and Mary;

Joni Mitchell; Gordon Lightfoot; Jimi Hendrix; the Beach Boys; Paul Simon; Elton John; the Who; and Dionne Warwick. By 1983 WCI controlled one-fourth of the American record market. Other holdings of WCI include the original film studio, a publishing house, cable systems and networks. Addresses in 1992 were: Warner Brothers, 3300 Warner Blvd., Burbank California; and WEA International (Warner-Elektra-Atlantic), 75 Rockefeller Plaza, New York. WEA is the distribution agency for WCI products, whose sales approached $2 billion in 1988. WCI merged with Time, Inc. on 10 Jan 1990, creating **Time Warner, Inc.**

WEAVERS. American folk singing group, established in 1948 by **Pete Seeger**. The other members were Lee Hays, Ronnie Gilbert (the only female), and Fred Hellerman. Performing at the Village Vanguard in Greenwich Village from December 1949, they were soon successful in combining folk harmonies with current pop styles, and were an important influence in the folk song revival of the 1950s. Among their early recorded hits were "Goodnight Irene" (Decca #27077; 1950) "So Long" (Decca #27376; 1951), and "On Top of Old Smokey" (Decca #27515; 1951). The Weavers were world favorites in a few years, but suffered from Congressional investigations into alleged Communist sympathies and were blacklisted. Seeger departed in 1958, but wrote their last great hit song for them, "Kisses Sweeter than Wine." A grand farewell reunion appearance at Carnegie Hall in 1980 was presented on radio and television with the title *Wasn't That a Time*.

WEBB, CHICK, 1909–1939. American jazz drummer and Big Band leader, born William Webb in Baltimore on 10 Feb 1909. He taught himself drumming as a child, and went to New York in about 1925, setting up his own band. By 1928 he had found success, and was engaged at the Savoy Ballroom, where he remained through the 1930s. The band was one of the finest of the era, with strong arrangements by Edgar Sampson, and the imaginative driving performances of Webb, "the finest big-band drummer of his time" (Schuller). When 16-year old **Ella Fitzgerald** joined the ensemble in 1935, the style changed from hot to mild swing, with a novelty element, to a more commercially acceptable but much less interesting mode. Webb died in Baltimore on 16 June 1939.

Webb's early records, "Dog Bottom" and "Jungle Mama," made for Brunswick in 1929, already show his great abilities: and the 1931 "Heebie Jeebies," arranged by Benny Carter—who was with the band a short time—is a tour de force (Vocalion #1607). Other outstanding work included "Stompin' at the Savoy" in a potent Sampson arrangement (Columbia #2926D; 1934) and Sampson's "Let's Get Together (Columbia #CB-741; 1934).

After 1935 most of the records featured Ella Fitzgerald, but on the flip side of her great nonsense hit "A-Tisket, A-Tasket" (Decca # 1840; 1938) there was still a fine drumming display by Webb in "Liza." Fitzgerald herself developed gradually from an indifferent vocalist to an outstanding jazz stylist, but not until a decade after Webb's death.

WEBER, HENRI. A baritone who recorded extensively for Pathé cylinders in Paris, during 1897–1900. He made at least 42 records by 1900, and another nine in 1902. Columbia recorded him also, with 17 cylinders in 1902–1903, and Edison made three records in Paris in 1905. Weber was one of the very earliest to record operatic arias, offering first "De l'art splendeur" from *Benvenuto Cellini* by Diaz (#0020), followed by 14 other arias, mostly from French composers. He was apparently the first baritone to inscribe the "Toreador Song" (#0308).

In 1904 Weber began to record for G & T in Paris, with about 60 French songs and a few arias. His final effort was under the pseudonym D'Haller, in a chorale number made on 1 Sep 1911. His G & T work was not transferred to American Victor.

WEBSTER, BEN, 1909–1973. American jazz saxophonist, born in Kansas City, Missouri, on 27 Mar 1909. He studied violin and piano, and played during silent movies in Amarillo, Texas. Then he joined various groups, and learned tenor saxophone, which became his specialty. He had a distinctive human-like tone, particularly effective in ballads. In the 1930s he worked with Bennie Moten, Andy Kirk, Fletcher Henderson, Benny Carter, Cab Calloway, Roy

Eldridge, Duke Ellington, and Teddy Wilson; in 1940 he joined the Ellington band, staying to 1943, and returned to him in 1948–1949. Later he freelanced widely across the U.S. Webster settled in the Netherlands in 1964, then moved to Copenhagen, performing extensively in many European locales. He died in Amsterdam on 20 Sep 1973.

Webster was heard in solo work on Victor discs made in 1931 by Blanche Calloway and her Joy Boys, and later with many of the ensembles cited above. His first major solo in ballad tempo was "Dream Lullaby" with Benny Carter (Vocalion #2898; 1934). Webster's earliest solo on a Duke Ellington record was in "Truckin'" (Brunswick #7514; 1935). His later work with Ellington included outstanding presentations in "Mauve" (Standard Radio Transcription #P-132; 1941 [not issued on 78 rpm]), and "What Am I Here For?" (Victor #20-1598; 1942). Though slow numbers were best for Webster, he turned in some fine upbeat renditions, such as "This Can't Be Love" with the Oscar Peterson Trio. There were many LP albums on Verve, Impulse, and other labels. [Evensmo 1978.]

WEEMS, TED, 1901–1963. American Big Band leader, among the favorites of the late 1920s and 1930s. His recordings began with Victor in 1923, going to 1933; he also worked for Columbia in 1934 and for Decca in 1936–1940. His group performed in a swing/jazz style, marked by technical perfection and originality. Weems was fortunate in having a number of fine vocalists, including Dusty Rhoades, Parker Gibbs, Arthur Jarrett, Elmo Tanner—who was best known as a whistler—and Perry Como, in his first recordings (1936–1942). Among the fine Weems recordings were "Am I a Passing Fancy?" sung by Jarrett (Victor # 22038; 1929), "One of Us Was Wrong" sung by Tanner (Victor # 22877; 1931), and "T'ain't So" featuring Tanner. Tanner whistled while Como sang on several sides, including "Simple and Sweet" (Decca #2019; 1938), and Tanner whistled solo on "Heartaches" (Decca # 2020; 1938).

WEINRICH, CARL, 1904– . American organist, born in Paterson, New Jersey, on 2 July 1904. He studied at New York University and at the Curtis Institute in Philadelphia, and had instruction from Marcel Dupré and Lynwood Farnam. When the latter died suddenly, Weinrich succeeded him as organist at the Church of the Holy Communion, New York. He gave important recitals in New York and on tour, playing J. S. Bach. Weinrich taught at several universities, and directed music at Princeton's Chapel from 1943 to 1973.

The Weinrich recordings, made on the Praetorius organ of Westminster Choir College in Princeton, were landmarks in establishing the clean sound of the baroque organ in American consciousness. Well recorded by the new **Musicraft** label from 1937, Weinrich produced definitive versions of the Bach Trio Sonatas, earning great success (Musicraft #1040-1 and #1041-2). He then did the Bach Chorale Preludes in a five-disc album (Musicraft #MC-22), and the great Toccata and Fugue in D Minor (Musicraft #1116), plus other preludes and fugues. Unfortunately, none of the Weinrich-Bach records were available on CD in late 1991.

WEISSMANN, FRIEDER, 1895–1984. German conductor, born in Frankfurt am Main on 23 Jan 1895. One of the most prolific conductors on disc, he once estimated his output at around 1,500 records. He directed house orchestras for Odeon in the 1920s, and was the first conductor to inscribe all nine Beethoven symphonies. In the mid-1940s he conducted operas for Victor. A two-disc LP album of extracts from his 1926–1933 work was issued by Ritornello Records in 1983 (#R-1001-2).

WELK, LAWRENCE, 1903–1992. American dance band leader and accordionist, born in Strasburg, North Dakota, on 11 Mar 1903. He led local groups, performing polkas and other ethnic dance music, and had some radio time in the late 1920s in South Dakota. He enlarged the ensemble into a dance orchestra, achieving an airy sound referred to as "Champagne Music," and was successful in several midwest cities. His orchestra recorded for Gennett in 1928, and made three sides for Lyric in 1931, disguised as Paul's Novelty Orchestra. Welk settled in Chicago's Aragon and Trianon ballrooms in the late 1930s, and made records for

Vocalion. His great success came with television, on which he displayed a beguiling showmanship. His program was one of the most popular in the 1950s and 1960s, with music, comedy, and dancing. The polka remained his signature mode, heard on many of his best selling records: "Beer Barrel Polka" (Vocalion #4788; 1939), "Clarinet Polka" (Decca #3726; 1941), and "Pennsylvania Polka" (Decca #4309; 1942). Among his later chart singles were "Calcutta" (Dot #16161; 1960) and "Baby Elephant Walk" (Dot #16365; 1962)—both were also the titles of successful LP albums. There were 31 chart albums between 1955 and 1974, notably *Moon River* (Dot #DLP 3412; 1961) and *Wonderful, Wonderful* (Dot #DLP 3552; 1963). He died in Santa Monica, California, on 17 May 1992.

WELLS, JOHN BARNES, 1880–1935. American concert tenor, born in Ashley, Pennsylvania, on 17 Oct 1880. He was a church singer, then made his concert debut in New York in 1915. Before that event he was already recording for Edison, and had a popular Amberol of "Good Night, Dear" (#187; 1909). His first and most enduring disc for Victor was "Sweet Genevieve" with the Hayden Quartet, made in 1910. Another great success was the 1913 Victor of "The Rosary." Wells recorded also for U-S Everlasting cylinders. His last discs were for Aeolian-Vocalion in 1919, except for some special pressings by Columbia for Psi Upsilon fraternity, in which he was one of the quartet. He also sang for a time with the Stellar Quartet. Wells died in Roxbury, New York, on 8 Aug 1935.

WELLS, KITTY, 1919– . American country singer and songwriter, born Muriel Ellen Deason in Nashville on 30 Aug 1919. She sang on Nashville radio with her sister, and then teamed with (and married) singer Johnny Wright. Wells and Wright appeared on the *Louisiana Hayride* show from 1947 to 1952. Wells was heard on *Grand Ole Opry* from 1952. She recorded for Decca from 1952, and made 55 chart singles in the next 20 years. Among her great hits were "It Wasn't God Who Made Honky-tonk Angels" (Decca #28232; 1952), and "You Don't Hear" (Decca #31749; 1965). In

1976 Wells was elected to the Country Music Hall of Fame.

WERRENRATH, REINALD, 1883–1953.

American baritone, born in Brooklyn on 7 Aug 1883. He was highly versatile, singing in opera (Metropolitan Opera debut on 19 Feb 1919 as Silvio, with Enrico Caruso, remaining with the company through 1921), concert (more than 3,500 appearances), and the recording studio. His first recording was with the Criterion Quartet, for Edison in 1903, issued in 1905 on #8866: "Little Tommy Went A-Fishing." Werrenrath's first solo record was "My Dear" (Edison #9604; 1907). He began with Victor in 1909, singing "Danny Deever" (#31738), and was an immediate success. He was with the Victor Opera Co., the Orpheus Quartet, and the Lyric Quartet. He began on black label Victors (about 65 items in the 1917 catalog), then was heard on both black label and Red Seal. A fine version of the *Rigoletto* Quartet was made with John McCormack and Lucrezia Bori (#89080; 1914); it sold for $4 (later the price dropped to $2). Werrenrath's last concert was at Carnegie Hall on 23 Oct 1952. He died on 12 Sep 1953, in Plattsburg, New York. [Walsh 1948/8.]

WEST, DOTTIE, 1932–1991.

American country singer, born in McMinnville, Tennessee on 11 Oct 1932. She had a successful single in 1963, "Let Me Of at the Corner" (Victor #8225), then found sudden stardom in 1964, interpreting a song co-written with her husband Bill West: "Here Comes My Baby" (Victor #8374; it recieved a Grammy award, and remained 27 weeks on the charts). There was another hit single in 1964: "In Its Own Little Way" / "Didn't I?" (Victor #8467). Fifty chart singles followed by 1982, in addition to records made with Jimmy Dean, Don Gibson, Jim Reeves, and Kenny Rodgers. West died on 4 Sep 1991.

WEST COAST PHONOGRAPH CO.

One of the affiliates of the **North American Phonograph Co.**, established in Portland, Oregon, in 1890. **Louis Glass** was director.

WESTERN ELECTRIC CO.

A firm established in 1869 by Enos Barton and Elisha Gray, manufacturer of the equipment used by the Bell Telephone Co., and controlled by Bell after 1882. It has remained in the Bell family, currently as a subsidiary of American Telephone and Telegraph Co. (AT&T). In the 1920s at Western Electric, J. P. Maxfield and H. C. Harrison made important experiments in **electrical recording**, and developed the major system used by Victor and Columbia. A steel-tape magnetic recorder was developed by Western Electric in 1940.

WESTERN PENNSYLVANIA PHONOGRAPH CO.

A Pittsburgh firm, one of the affiliates of the **North American Phonograph Co.**, established 1900 at 146 Fifth Ave. George B. Motheral was president in 1892.

WESTERN PHONOGRAPH CO.

A Chicago firm, located at 163 LaSalle St. In 1896 it manufactured a **coin-op**, using the spring motor of **Edward Amet**, attached to an Edison top.

WESTMINSTER (label).

An American independent record, issued from 1949. James Grayson and two partners set it up, utilizing the new technology of recording on a magnetic tape and cutting LP masters from it. Many of the tapes were brought from Vienna. The high quality of the recordings and of the artists brought great success to Westminster, which had 500 items in the catalog by the end of 1954, and 1,000 items five years later. The first releases in Britain were in 1953, handled by Nixa. Hermann Scherchen, Paul Badura-Skoda, Jorg Demus, Fernando Valenti, and Antonio Janigro—fresh names on the American scene—dominated the lists. Baroque music was a specialty, as with most of the classical LP labels, but there were also important performances of Mahler, Gliere, and other (up to that time) neglected modern masters. The label survived into the mid-1970s, but has not reappeared in compact disc format.

WESTPORT (label).

A British record of 1922–1924, sold in the Curry's stores. It was produced by the **Edison Bell Consolidated Phonograph Co., Ltd.**, with some masters from Gennett. Artists were given pseudonyms. The label is also found as a pasteover on Imperial records of the Crystalate Gramophone Manufacturing Co., Ltd. [Andrews*; Rust 1978.]

WHEELER, ELIZABETH, AND WILLIAM WHEELER. An American singing duo, "the most successful husband and wife duet pair in the history of the phonograph" (Walsh). She was born Bess Nicholson in Kokomo, Indiana, on 20 July 1875; he was born in Shawano, Wisconsin, on 13 July 1879. They married in 1904, and performed widely, doing standard ballads, light opera, and hymns. Mrs. Wheeler made some solo cylinders for Leeds & Catlin, Edison, and others, and then the two began their duet recordings in 1910, for Victor. "Beautiful Isle of Somewhere" was an early hit (#16700; 1910), though it did not reach the 1917 Victor catalog, where there were 17 other titles by the pair. Their final Victor recording was the most popular one, "What a Friend We Have in Jesus" (#18287; 1917).

Mrs. Wheeler made many solo Victors, beginning in 1909; she sang ballads and children's songs, and also "Elizabeth's Prayer" from *Tannhäuser* (#35096). William Wheeler did some solo work for Pathé. They did not record after the acoustic period, and "What a Friend" was the only one of their titles to reach the 1927 Victor catalog. William Wheeler died in November 1916. [Walsh 1961/8–9.]

WHISTLING RECORDINGS. This was a popular type of record in the early days, both for bird imitations and for musical material. The Victor 1917 catalog had about 55 items, most of them by **Guido Gialdini**. **John Yorke AtLee** was apparently the earliest whistler to record, making Columbia cylinders from 1889 to 1897, and also Berliner discs. Another pioneer whistler on disc was Frank Lawton, who was heard on 11 seven-inch Berliner records of October/November 1898, commencing with "Il bacio" (#9261-X).

Edison cylinders presented 23 whistling numbers by 1912, including work by two of the most famous artists, AtLee and **Joe Belmont**, and a less familiar female whistler, Nina Angela. Other artists included Albert Whelan, "The Australian Entertainer," who often whistled his music hall signature tune ("The

Jolly Brothers Waltz") at the start and end of his records; Margaret McKee, on Victor; and Maude Dewey, "champion lady whistler of the world" according to advertising of Star cylinders (1904–1907).

The most famous whistling record was "Whistling Coon," written and performed by **George W. Johnson** in 1890–1891 for many cylinder labels. "Whistling Girl" was another Johnson number.

In the 1920s whistling records disappeared from the catalogs, except for occasional novelty numbers like "Whistler and His Dog" (done for Victor by Pryor's Band, #19869). Elmo Tanner revived interest in the art during the 1930s, performing with the Wayne King and Ted Weems orchestras. Hoagy Carmichael whistled and sang some of his own compositions for Decca, e.g., "Stardust" / "Hong Kong Blues" (#18395; 1942). Fred Lowery, "The Blind Whistler," made several Columbia discs with the Horace Heidt band in 1940–1941, including "Indian Love Call" (#36200) and "William Tell Overture" (#35234). Ronnie Ronalde performed for Columbia in U.K. after World War II. **Bing Crosby** sometimes whistled briefly on his records. *See also* ANIMAL IMITATIONS.

WHITE, EDNA, 1891– . American trumpeter, with a long career on stage and as a soloist with bands and orchestras. She had a vaudeville act with her second husband, and in the 1930s also sang in musicals. White was a prodigy, noticed by Frank Damrosch, who invited her to study at the Institute of Musical Arts (later the Juilliard School), whence she graduated at age 15; she then toured the U.S. with a female ensemble. The opening ceremony in March 1915 of the first transcontinental telephone transmission (Brooklyn to San Francisco) was enlivened by her performance of "Silver Threads among the Gold." In the 1930s she was on the radio, and on 9 Feb 1949 she gave a recital at Carnegie Hall. White retired in 1957; she was still alive in 1992. At age 97 she was interviewed by a Springfield, Massachusetts, newspaper.

White began to record with the Edna White Trumpet Quartet in 1918, for Columbia, doing first "Just a Baby's Prayer at Twilight" (#A-2538). She continued with Columbia to 1921. Her first Edison discs (15 Dec 1920) were "The

Debutante" (#80650) and "Recollections of 1861–1865" (#80613). She made eight more Edisons, the final one in September 1926: "Sweet Genevieve" (#52036). [Wile 1977.]

WHITE, JOE, 1891–1959. American tenor, born Joseph Malachy White in New York, on 14 Oct 1891. He was a boy soprano in church work, then served in World War I. He sang in minstrel troupes, and then 1925–1930 on radio. The novelty of wearing a mask while he performed brought him national attention, and the sobriquet of "silver-masked tenor." White recorded for Edison and Columbia, in 1917, and then for Victor in 1925–1929. Irish numbers were his specialty, for example, "Kathleen Mavourneen" /"The Harp that Once through Tara's Halls" (Victor #19916; 1925). White died in New York on 28 Feb 1959. [Walsh 1973/3.]

WHITE, JOSH, 1915–1969. American blues, folk, and gospel singer, and guitarist, born Joshua Daniel White in Greenville, South Carolina, on 11 Feb 1915. He was a street singer as a child, then teamed with Blind Joe Taggart at age 13. The two made a Paramount record, with White playing guitar and singing, "There's a Hand Writing on the Wall" (#12717; 1928). He recorded later for many labels, and by age 25 was nationally recognized. He formed a group, the Carolinians, for some records, and he used the nom du disque Pinewood Tom on others. On Vocalion he was Tippy Barton. He performed at the White House, and gradually moved to a more sophisticated style quite removed from his roots. White died in Manhasset, New York, on 5 Sep 1969.

"Crying Blues" was among White's most popular discs of the 1930s; it appeared as Melotone #12727, Perfect #0234, Romeo #5240, Oriole #8240, and Banner #32794. "Southern Exposure" (Keynote #514; 1941) exemplified his social protest songs of the 1940s. One of his last popular records was "House of the Rising Sun" (ABC #124; 1957).

White noise. *See* NOISE, III.

WHITEMAN, PAUL, 1890–1967. American violist and Big Band leader, born in Denver on 28 Mar 1890. He played viola in the symphony orchestras of Denver (1907–1913) and then San Francisco, and during World War I he directed a Navy band. After his military service he organized a dance band in San Francisco, and was in New York by 1920, making a sensational hit record of "Whispering" / "Japanese Sandman" (Victor #18690; 1920) that sold a million copies. A stream of Victor records followed, with many successes; the most popular was "Three O'Clock in the Morning" (Victor #18940; 1922).

In Whiteman's most famous concert, 12 Feb 1924 at Aeolian Hall, New York, the premiere of *Rhapsody in Blue* was performed, with George Gershwin at the piano. Whiteman and Gershwin recorded the work on 10 June (Victor #55225).

Whiteman, not a jazz musician, was nicknamed the King of Jazz. His orchestra was really a swinging dance band, but many notable jazz artists were featured at different times, including Matty Malneck, Tommy Dorsey, Jimmy Dorsey, Bix Beiderbecke, Frankie Trumbauer, Eddie Lang, Miff Mole, Red Nichols, Frankie Trumbauer, Bunny Berigan, Jack Teagarden, Joe Venuti, and Wingy Manone. Trumpeter Henry Busse and pianist Ferde Grofé started with Whiteman in 1919. Bing Crosby made early records with the orchestra, as one of the Rhythm Boys, including his first solo disc in 1927. Charles Harrison, Lewis James, Wilfred Glenn, Elliott Shaw, Mildred Bailey, Johnny Mercer, Paul Robeson, Joan Edwards, Lee Wiley, the Modernaires, and Red McKenzie were among the solo vocalists heard on Whiteman records. There were outstanding arrangers in Lennie Hayton, Grofé, and Bill Challis, who wrote complex scores for the 19 or 20 players who made up the typical forces. Altogether Whiteman recorded more than 600 sides, bringing jazz and swing together in a manner that was delightful to the public and that opened the door for the great hot bands of the 1930s.

There were radio shows and motion pictures through the 1940s, after which Whiteman was less active. He died in Doylestown, Pennsylvania, on 29 Dec 1967. [Rust*.]

WHITING, MARGARET, 1924– . American popular vocalist, born in Detroit on 22 July

1924. She sang on Hollywood radio with Johnny Mercer in 1941, and made appearances on *Your Hit Parade*. Her first hit record was "That Old Black Magic" (Capitol #126; 1943) with Freddie Slack, followed by a fine "Silver Wings in the Moonlight" (Capitol #146; 1944) also with Slack. "My Ideal" (Capitol #134; 1943) and "Moonlight in Vermont" (Capitol #182; 1944) both with Billy Butterfield, were much acclaimed. Whiting made popular recordings for Capitol of the great ballads of the 1940s. A particularly noteworthy side was "Baby, It's Cold Outside" with Johnny Mercer (Capitol #57-567; 1949). She brought out some fine LP albums, especially the *Jerome Kern Song Book* (Verve #V-3039), including the little known gem, "Let's Begin." In the 1950s she was less active.

WHITLOCK, BILLY, 1874–1951. British music hall artist, born Frederick Penna on 18 July 1874 in Cheltenham. He played xylophone and bells, and did comic numbers, being one of the earliest to do "laughing songs." He made thousands of records, for many U.K. labels, with numerous American reissues by Columbia and Vocalion. His recordings were issued also under many pseudonyms, both male and female, under English and foreign names, for example, Dudley Roy and Madame Paula. His first cylinders were for Edison Bell in 1904, starting with "The Laughing Friar" (#5740). He continued recording to 1926, then was inactive until the 1950s—his return occasioned by the 1949 Decca reissue disc (London label in the U.S.) of Whitlock's 1904 instrumental "Scotch Hot." Renamed "Hop Scotch Polka," it was re-recorded by Whitlock and became a best seller. Thus Whitlock, who had become an impoverished night watchman, had some brightness for his last years. He died in London on 26 Jan 1951. [Rust 1979; Walsh 1950/2.]

WHITNEY, EDWIN MORSE, 1877–1957. American actor and tenor, born in Parma Center, New York, on 17 Mar 1877. He sang in the Whitney Brothers Quartet (the other members were Alvin, William, and Yale Whitney), then became a radio actor; in 1928 he was program director for NBC. All his records were made in 1908–1910, for Victor. A hardy best seller was "Darky and the Boys" (Victor # 5636), his first

solo monolog. "Old Folks at Home" was the best of the quartet records (Victor #16454, released in 1912); it remained in the catalog, with another nine sides, to 1922, but all the Whitney discs were gone by 1927. Edwin Whitney died in New York on 5 June 1957.

WHITSIT, PERRY B. American record jobber, with an establishment at 213 S. High St., Columbus, Ohio, in 1913. He was active in the **National Association of Talking Machine Jobbers**, being its secretary in 1909 and 1913, and president in 1909.

WHO. British rock group ("The Who") formed in London in 1964. The original members were Peter Dennis Blandford Townshend (guitar and vocal), Roger Harry Daltrey (vocal), John Alec Entwistle (bass, French horn, vocal), and Keith Moon (drums). The foursome "showed up with blasts of power chords and shouts of adolescent rage, acting out teen aggression by smashing their instruments after concerts" (*Rolling Stone Encyclopedia*). They were stars in Britain within a year, and scored in America with "I Can't Explain" (Decca #31725; 1965). They placed 26 singles on the American charts by 1981, for Decca and MCA. Townshend's 1969 rock opera, *Tommy*, was an internationally acclaimed album in 1975 (MCA #Z-10005). *It's Hard* was the most successful Who album in the U.S., on the charts 32 weeks (Warner #9-23731; 1982. With the release of that album, the group made a farewell tour.

WIDMANN, EUGENE A., ca. 1877–1938. American record industry executive, born in New York. He was president of Pathé Frères Phonograph Co., the American branch of the firm, 1912–1923, and for a time also chairman of the board. Later he headed Widmann & Co., a firm of investment brokers. He died in Brooklyn on 3 Feb 1938.

WIEDOEFT, RUDY, 1893–1940. American saxophonist and clarinetist, born in Detroit on 3 Jan 1893. He was the first recognized saxophone virtuoso, concertizing and recording extensively in the 1920s. He added five keys to the saxophone to improve range and tone. Wiedoeft was heard on Edison Diamond Discs, beginning with "Valse Erica" (#50462; 1917) and "Saxophone Sobs" (#50454; 1917) and on Victor records, beginning with "Saxophobia" / "Valse Erica" (#18728; 1921). He had eight sides in the 1927 Victor catalog, and four remained in 1938, but they were deleted two years later. His Edison output included nine solos, two items with the Wiedoeft-Wadsworth Quartet (who were Wheeler Wadsworth, saxophone; J. Russell Robinson and Harry Akst, pianos; and Wiedoeft), four with Rudy Wiedoeft's Palace Trio, and three with Rudy Wiedoeft's Californians. The final Edison was made on 12 June 1922, with the Californians: "Rose of Bombay" (#51020). The Trio also recorded for Victor and Okeh in 1920–1921. The Californians appeared also on Vocalion. Wiedoeft died in Flushing, New York, on 18 Feb 1940.

WILDLIFE SOUNDS ON RECORDS. Ludwig Koch made the first wildlife recording in 1889, of an Indian thrush called a shama, and continued recording into the 1940s. Bird records were in demand in the early days of the recording industry; the Victor 1917 catalog had 40 titles with bird voices. The first commercial disc of wildlife sounds was issued by Beka (Berlin) ca. 1910, presenting material gathered by Koch. By 1968 there were 341 recordings tabulated by Jeffrey Boswall at the BBC, who estimated that he had found about 80% of the total issues. Records of captive birds were issued from 1910, the first being HMV #9439, a "unique bird record made by a captive nightingale." The proliferation of bird sound records was more or less summarized in a 1966 set of EMI seven-inch records, *Bird Recognition: An Aural Index*; the discs presented the complete vocabularies of selected species.

Apart from birds, which obviously have the most potential for interesting records, there have been extensive field expeditions to inscribe the voices of mammals and amphibians, and to catch the ambient sounds of natural settings.

When Koch fled Germany (leaving his large collection of records) to Britain in 1936, he was backed in the development of a new collection of sounds. Eventually he built up a substantial library, which was acquired by the BBC Sound Archives; holdings of the BBC were already inclusive of 3,000 species in 1972, on about 15,000 recordings. Britain remains the center of interest in wildlife recording. The Wildlife Sound Recording Society was established there in 1968 to foster recording and broadcasting, and to share information. Another active entity is the Swedish Broadcasting Corp.

The British Library of Wildlife Sounds was officially opened in London on 2 July 1969, as part of the British Institute of Recorded Sound (now the **National Sound Archive**). Within five years the sounds of some 700 species of animal had been collected.

In the U.S., the Laboratory of Ornithology at Cornell University, Ithaca, New York, is a major archive.

The current situation on compact discs displays a limited selection of wildlife material. The section "Nature Sounds" in the Summer 1991 Schwann *Spectrum* reveals a total of 17 titles. These include *Animals of Africa*, *Sounds of South American Rain Forest*, *Field Guide to Bird Songs*, *South Atlantic Islands*, and *Waldkonzert* [forest sounds]. A number of nature discs have no special focus on animals, but are intended to provide urbanites with peaceful background tapestries to relax by, like *The Surf*.

[Discographies of the British holdings cited above appeared in various issues of *Recorded Sound* magazine; several are listed in #85, p. 40. *Recorded Sound* #34 (April 1969) was devoted to articles on wildlife sounds and the collections of them. Books on the topic include Fisher 1977; Simms 1979; Bondesen 1977; Margoschis 1977; and Thielcke 1976.] *See also* ANIMAL IMITATIONS.

WILEY, LEE, 1915–1975. American popular vocalist, born on 9 Oct 1915 in Port Gibson, Oklahoma. After study in Tulsa, she moved to New York and sang in clubs and on radio. She was with the Leo Reisman band from 1931 to 1933; later she sang with Paul Whiteman, the Casa Loma Orchestra, and others. She married Jess Stacy and sang with his group in the mid-1940s. Wiley offered a loose swing style that was well suited to the ballads of the era. Among her fine records were the LP "song books" (reissues of 78s) she made of composers Vincent Youmans, Irving Berlin, Cole Porter, George

Gershwin, Harold Arlen, and Rodgers and Hart. An important early record was "A Hundred Years from Today" with the Casa Loma Orchestra (Brunswick #6775; 1934). One of her best singles was "It's Only a Paper Moon" with Stacy (Victor #20-1708; 1946).

WILLIAMS, ANDY, 1930– . American popular singer, born Andrew Williams in Wall Lake, Iowa, on 3 Dec 1930. He began singing on local radio as a child, then appeared with the Williams Brothers Quartet, gaining success in various American and European cities. Williams pursued a solo career from 1954, was acclaimed on television, and hosted *The Andy Williams Show* from 1959. His singing style was in the easy ballad manner. The earliest of his 46 chart singles was "Canadian Sunset" (Cadence #1297; 1956); the same title was used for a 1965 Columbia album (#CL 2324). Williams had two highly successful albums in 1962: *Moon River and Other Great Movie Themes* (Columbia #CL 1809), 107 weeks on the charts; and *Warm and Willing* (Columbia #CL 1879), 25 weeks. Other notable albums of the 1960s included *Days of Wine and Roses* (Columbia #CL 2015; 1963) and *Call Me Irresponsible and Other Academy Award Winners* (Columbia #CL 2171; 1964). There were 37 chart albums, the last in 1975.

WILLIAMS, BERT, ca. 1874–1922. Singer and comedian, born Egbert Austin Williams in the Bahamas on 12 Nov 1874. His family moved to California when he was a child, and he left home at 17 to join a traveling minstrel troupe, Seig's Mastodon Minstrels. They toured mining and lumber camps. He made his way to New York, and formed a successful vaudeville duo with George W. Walker. They appeared successfully in the operetta *Gold Bug,* and did blackface routines (though Williams was naturally Black) in many other shows. Walker retired, but Williams went on to the Ziegfeld Follies in 1910–1919, breaking the color barrier there. A sensation in Britain in *Dahomey* (1903), Williams gave a command performance for Edward VII at Buckingham Palace. He died in New York on 4 Mar 1922.

His first records were cylinders for the Universal Phonograph Co. of New York in 1897. He made discs for Victor in 1901, after which he made no records until 1906 when Columbia signed him exclusively. He stayed with Columbia, except for an Edison Diamond Disc, until his death. Williams and Walker made their first Victor on 11 Oct 1901, "I Don't Like That Face You Wear" (#V-987). "If You Love Your Baby" was Williams' first solo Victor. made on the same day; there were other duets and solos made then, too. Popular as they were, the duo did not last long in the Victor catalog, there being no listings for either of them in 1917.

The first Columbia was a 10-inch disc, "Nobody" (#3423; 1906). A great hit was "Let It Alone," made in 1906 and released on two sizes of cylinder and on disc. After dropping Williams from the catalog, Columbia brought him back in 1940 with some reissues of 1919 and 1920 songs.

Williams had a recitative style of singing, and a raspy voice well suited to his broad material. "One of the finest talking machine records ever made" (Walsh) was "You Can't Do Nothin' till Martin Gets Here" (Columbia #A-6216; 1913?). [Debus 1987; Walsh 1950/9–10–11.]

WILLIAMS, BILLY, 1854–1910. American vaudeville and minstrel artist; he should not be confused with Australian artist of the same name. He was performing from the 1860s, and made records as early as 1892, for the New Jersey Phonograph Co. He recorded with the **Spencer Trio** in 1894–1897.

WILLIAMS, BILLY, 1877–1915. Australian comedian and music hall artist, born in Melbourne; he should not be confused with American artist of the same name. He transferred to England in 1899, and quickly made his place on the stage, one of the star performers of his time, although his career was cut off by his untimely death on 9 Mar 1915. His first record was a great success, issued on more than 25 labels: "John, John, Go and Put Your Trousers On" (Edison two-minute cylinder #13539; 1906). John, it may be noted, was wearing kilts. There are 148 titles in the discography by Frank Andrews and Ernie Bayly, the last being made in May or June 1914: "There's Life in the Old Dog Yet" (Regal #G6783). Among his other hit records were "I Must Go Home Tonight" (Homophone Record #555; 1909) and "Where Does Daddy Go When He Goes Out?" (Columbia Rena Record #1978; 1912). [Andrews 1982 is a complete discography.]

WILLIAMS, COOTIE, 1910–1985. American jazz trumpeter, born Charles Melvin Williams in Mobile, Alabama, on 24 July 1910.

He was self taught on the trumpet, and at age 14 was touring with a band that included Lester Young. He went to New York in 1928, made recordings with James P. Johnson, and joined various bands. From 1929 to 1940 he was in the Duke Ellington band, and played solos in hundreds of compositions. He also had his own band, in 1941–1948, which had Charlie Parker and Bud Powell as members; then he led a small rhythm and blues group in the 1950s. In 1962 Williams returned to Duke Ellington, staying until the late 1970s. He died in New York on 15 Sep 1985.

Williams developed a swing style with remarkable shadings, and a way of handling all modes and situations. Among the sides with Ellington two stand out: "Echoes of the Jungle" (Victor #22743; 1931), and "Concerto for Cootie"—which Ellington wrote to observe the return of Williams to the flock in 1940—(Victor #26598; 1940). With words added, the Concerto became the great ballad "Do Nothing till You Hear From Me." "Harlem Air Shaft" was another outstanding record (Victor #26731; 1940). In the 1950s Williams released fine LP albums, especially *Porgy and Bess Revisited* (Warner #1260; 1958).

WILLIAMS, EVAN, 1867–1918. American tenor, born in Mineral Ridge, Ohio, on 7 Sep 1867. He sang in a church choir while working in a coal mine, studied in Cleveland and New York, and did church work in Brooklyn. He drew inspiration from a visit to Wales (he was of Welsh parentage), and became a leading concert singer after 1906, making many fine recordings. His earliest discs were made for G & T in 1906, the first being "Abide with Me" (#3-2485). Altogether he made 79 sides for HMV. Williams recorded six numbers for Pathé in London in 1911.

Williams was a Victor regular from 1906 to 1917, singing ballads, songs, and some oratorio and opera arias. He made 135 Victor sides, of which about 80 were in the Victor 1917 catalog, and his records were said to have sold more copies than any other singer except Enrico Caruso and John McCormack. "Sound an Alarm" from *Judas Maccabaeus* is one of the acoustic tenor discs most favored by collectors (Victor #74131, 6321). Other popular Victors were "Holy City" / "Face to Face" (#6312) and "Just A-wearyin' for You" / "Perfect Day" (#857); these were in the 1927 catalog, but were deleted in the 1930s. Williams died on 24 May 1918. [Lewis, G. 1978.]

WILLIAMS, HANK, 1923–1953. American country singer and guitarist, born Hiram Williams in Mount Olive, Alabama, on 17 Sep 1923. After local appearances in Alabama, he was on the *Louisiana Hayride* radio show in Shreveport, Louisiana in 1947–1949, and went on to Grand Ole Opry (1949–1952). He had a group called the Drifting Cowboys to back up his lugubrious style, a combination that led to a chain of popular records. "Lovesick Blues" (MGM #10352; 1949) was an early hit, "Cold, Cold Heart" (MGM #10904; 1951) was another. His manner of "moanin' the blues" was influential in shaping the primary country music style of the 1950s. He also recorded, as Luke the Drifter, a gospel repertoire.

He was elected to the Country Music Hall of Fame in 1961, eight years after his death on 1 Jan 1953, in Oak Hill, West Virginia, en route to a show. His son, **Hank Williams, Jr.,** is also a greatly successful country singer. The younger Williams sang his father's songs in the biographical film *Your Cheatin' Heart* (1964).

WILLIAMS, HANK, JR., 1949– . American country singer and guitarist, son of **Hank Williams,** who died when the boy was less than three years old. He was born Randall Hank Williams, in Shreveport, Louisiana, on 26 May 1949. He performed as a teen on his mother's radio program, and gained early renown in 1964 with two chart singles, "Long Gone Lonesome Blues" (MGM #13208) and "Endless Sleep" (MGM #13278). A great success followed in 1965, with his composition "Standing in the Shadows" (MGM #13504); the record was on the country charts 21 weeks and won an award from Broadcast Music, Inc. (BMI). Williams became a progressive country artist, influenced by rock. His group, the Bama Band, which included electric instruments, appealed to young listeners and was nationally prominent into the 1990s. Williams has had more than 50 chart singles and more than a dozen chart albums. His most successful album was *Hank Williams, Jr.'s Greatest Hits* (Elektra #9-60193-1; 1982).

WILLIAMS, MARY LOU, 1910–1981. American jazz pianist and arranger, born Mary Elfrieda Scruggs in Atlanta on 8 May 1910. She played piano as a child and joined various groups, one led by John Williams, who became her husband. They both joined the Andy Kirk band in 1929, where she did the arrangements, remaining to 1942. She then freelanced as a pianist and arranger, active into the 1970s, widely regarded as the leading female jazz artist. Williams taught at Duke University from 1977, and died in Durham, North Carolina, on 28 May 1981.

She composed *Zodiac Suite* and made a successful recording of it (Asch #620, 621; 1945); the work was performed in Carnegie Hall by the New York Philharmonic Orchestra. Another fine disc was her "Waltz Boogie" (Victor #20-2025; 1946). There were several popular LP albums, among them *From the Heart* (Chiaroscuro #103; 1970).

WILLS, BOB, 1905–1975. American country singer and fiddler, born near Kosse, Texas, on 6 Mar 1905. He played with several groups in the 1920s, then organized his Texas Playboys in 1934, gaining much attention regionally. The group relocated to California in 1942, and toured extensively. For a country group they were unusual in their instrumentation, which included drums and brass, and they played a wide non-country repertoire. Wills used to adlib, talking and shouting, while the soloists were performing. His style came to be known as Western Swing. Wills was elected to the Country Music Hall of Fame in 1968. He died in Fort Worth, Texas, on 13 May 1975.

Among his hit records, "Steel Guitar Rag" was an early standout (Okeh #03394; 1936), and "New San Antonio Rose" was the most popular of all (Okeh #05694; 1940). "Image of Me" was a later chart song (Liberty #55264; 1960).

WILLS, NAT, 1873–1917. American vaudeville artist, known as The Happy Tramp, born in Fredericksburg, Virginia, on 11 July 1873. He first performed at Ford's Theatre in Washington. He recorded for Victor and Columbia, making an early hit with "No News, or What Killed the Dog" (Victor #5612; Columbia #A1765); he had 12 items in the 1917 Victor catalog, and was listed until 1927. His first Edison record was "Down in Jungle Town" (#10178; 1909). The final record Wills made for Victor, in February 1917, was "Automobile Parody" (#35601), and ironically he died 10 months later of carbon monoxide fumes, on 9 Dec 1917. [Walsh 1951/6.]

WILSON, NANCY, 1937– . American popular singer, born in Chillicothe, Ohio, on 20 Feb 1937. She sang in clubs and on television in Columbus, Ohio, made a tour with Rusty Bryant's band, and went on to acclaimed performances in New York as a jazz and rhythm & blues singer. Her 1964 record, "How Glad I Am" (Capitol #5198) put her name on the charts for 14 weeks and won a Grammy. "Face It, Girl, It's Over" was another of her seven chart singles (Capitol #2136; 1968). Wilson made 22 solo chart albums, notably *Hollywood—My Way* (Capitol #T2712; 1963), 30 weeks on the charts, and *Yesterday's Love Songs—Today's Blues* (Capitol #T2012; 1964). She was a skilled ensemble vocalist as well as soloist, making notable albums with George Shearing in 1961 and with Cannonball Adderley in 1962. Her last hit album was *The Two of Us*, with Ramsey Lewis (Columbia #FC 39326; 1984).

WILSON, TEDDY, 1912–1986. American jazz pianist, born Theodore Shaw Wilson in Austin, Texas, on 24 Nov 1912. In college in Alabama he majored in music, then went to Detroit and Toledo, Ohio, where he worked with various groups. Moving to Chicago he performed with

Louis Armstrong, and Jimmie Noone; then he worked with Benny Carter in New York. Wilson accompanied Billy Holiday on records, and was with the Benny Goodman band from 1936 to 1939, when he formed his own band and later a sextet. After another period with Goodman he freelanced, toured in Europe, and taught at the Juilliard School.

Wilson's playing was often referred to as "impeccable," his contributions to any ensemble being invariably imaginative, tasteful, and supportive. He employed unusual chord formations and ingenious counterpoint, developing an airy relaxed texture. Among his finest recordings were "Don't Blame Me" (Brunswick #8025; 1937), "Smoke Gets in Your Eyes" (Columbia #36631; 1941), and "I Know that You Know" (Columbia #36633; 1941). In 1937 and 1938 Wilson won the *Down Beat* poll as favorite pianist, and in 1939 he won the *Metronome* poll.

WINNER (label). A British record from **J. E. Hough, Ltd.**, successor to the Edison Bell Co., issued from 1912 to 1933. The label name was variously Edison Bell Winner, Edison Bell Winner Record, Winner, and The Winner. The discs were nominally issued by the Winner Record Co., a syndicate controlled by Hough. A final series of Winner records was issued by the Decca Record Co., Ltd. [Andrews 1984/12.]

WISCONSIN PHONOGRAPH CO. An affiliated firm of the **North American Phonograph Co.**, located at 414 Broadway, Milwaukee, in 1890. W. S. Burnet was superintendent in 1890, and John H. Frank was president.

WISE (label). An American record of ca. 1926, issued by the Wise Co., New York. Masters came from Emerson and several of the Grey Gull labels. [Kendziora 1988/6.]

WOLVERINES. A jazz group of the 1920s, also known as the Wolverine Orchestra, featuring **Bix Beiderbecke**, cornet. They recorded for Gennett in 1924, making 18 sides. "Fidgety Feet" (#5408) was Beiderbecke's first recording. "Tiger Rag" and "Sensation" were among the other important numbers by the group.

WONDER, STEVIE, 1950– . American soul singer, instrumentalist, and composer, born Steveland Judkins or Steveland Morris on 13 May 1950 in Saginaw, Michigan. Blind from birth, he sang and played harmonica as a child. When Berry Gordy heard him perform, he gave the youngster a Motown contract and named him Little Stevie Wonder. In 1963 Wonder made a hit single, "Fingertips (Part 2)" (Tamla #54080). He remained with the Tamla label, developing a complex style that incorporated gospel, rock, jazz, African, and Latino idioms into songs of protest. By 1972, when he toured with the Rolling Stones, he was widely acclaimed by white audiences. He took over the production of his records, composed the songs, and played most of the instruments. *Talking Book* (Tamla #T319L) was a sensation in 1972, on the charts 57 weeks. In the next year he issued *Innerversions* (Tamla #T326L), 74 weeks on the charts. Wonder's most popular album was *Songs in the Key of Life* (Tamla #T13-340C2; 1976), which had 90 chart weeks. He had no albums after 1987, then achieved a new triumph in 1991 with the soundtrack to the film *Jungle Fever* (Motown #MOTD-6291). He was on the cover of *Down Beat* in September 1991.

WONDER (label). An American record issued by the Wonder Talking Machine Co., New York, known only from a printed catalog of ca. 1898. "The contents tally exactly with those of the Berliner catalog of the same presumed date" (Rust). It may be that the records were given to purchasers of the Wonder disc player, also produced by the firm. A player of that name was still being sold by a company of that name (located on 4th Ave.) according to a 1916 trade directory; there were five models, all under $20 in price. In March 1922 the Wonder Phonograph Co., incorporated in Delaware, succeeded the Wonder Talking Machine Co. [Paul 1991/1; Rust 1978.]

WOODWIND RECORDINGS. While never so prestigious as vocalists, violinists, or pianists, woodwind performers were still remarkably active in the earliest days of recorded sound. Commercial woodwind recordings of the acoustical era, though restricted in repertoire, document the outstanding artistry of notable virtuosi as well as the often unappreciated skills of many now long-forgotten flutists, clarinetists, oboists, and bassoonists. The electrical era brought a dramatic increase in the variety of recorded woodwind repertoire and the number of recorded virtuosi: by the mid-1920s contemporary composers were beginning to devote more attention to wind instruments, and through the recording of this new music important interpretations were preserved. Later the LP inspired an explosion of recordings by woodwind soloists and ensembles, presenting an array of works ranging from rediscovered renaissance dances to aggressive avant-garde experiments.

While the majority of today's classical woodwind artists are concert or orchestral performers, in the first two decades of this century many were members of professional bands that were already recording actively at the time. Musicians from the ensembles of **John Philip Sousa, Arthur Pryor, Patrick S. Gilmore**, and others recorded prolifically as soloists, with and without the accompaniment of the bands themselves, and often supplemented these activities by working as studio musicians. But apart from these featured band performers, woodwind soloists were something of a rarity in American concert life. Even principal players from the established orchestras seldom had the opportunity of being heard in solo concert performances, or of recording extensively. This situation changed slowly when major American orchestras began recruiting their principal woodwind players from France and Belgium, a procedure that brought musicians like Marcel Tabuteau, Georges Barrère, Gustave Langenus, and Georges Laurent to this country. The influence of these virtuosi on playing styles, repertoire, and public opinion would prove significant.

It is therefore disappointing that some of the most important of these woodwind virtuosi left a recorded legacy scarcely representative of their contemporary reputations, primarily because of restraints placed upon the recorded repertoire at the time. This was particularly true during the acoustical era. Music not usually associated with woodwinds was frequently arranged for their use, possibly in an effort to make these still-unusual instruments more accessible to the general public. Early recordings of woodwinds present a mixture of popular songs, well-known operatic arias, a few traditional instrumental showpieces, and familiar light classics. It was not until these instruments began to gain some individual stature that an indigenous woodwind repertoire began to appear extensively on record.

Popular songs, from familiar ballads and folk tunes to current stage successes, were especially common on pre-1900 woodwind recordings. Clarinet selections from the 1897 Columbia catalog, played by **William Tuson**, included "Comin' thro' the Rye," "Sally in Our Alley," and Foster's "Massa's in de Cold, Cold Ground." While there were many unadorned renditions of such songs, more often elaborate variations were added to enliven performances. A similar treatment befell operatic themes and medleys. Recordings by the British clarinetist Charles Draper, listed in the Edison Bell catalog for 1903, included selections from *Rigoletto* and *Fra Diavolo*, while a rare 1902 recording for G & T by the Spanish-born clarinetist Manuel Gomez offered a set of variations on "Caro nome."

Of a more purely instrumental nature were the many ostentatious works designed to display virtuosic agility. Julius Benedict's "Carnival of Venice," for example, was a favorite of virtually every instrumentalist in search of a reputation. While this type of music was frequently deplored, it was heavily recorded—often, ironically, by some of its principal critics. Closely related to these technical marvels were pieces which exploited particular instrumental eccentricities. Piccolos were thought to be especially well-suited to bird imitations, often in polka form. **George Schweinfest**, perhaps the earliest piccolist on record (for Edison cylinders in 1889), has 22 titles listed in Columbia's 1897 catalog, among which were nine "bird polkas." Much of this avian repertoire was composed by E. Damaré, a French piccolist who recorded twelve his own works for **Bettini**, listed in the latter's June 1901 catalog. The flute was assigned a similar pastoral role, albeit a slightly more dignified one, illustrated particularly well in the innumerable obbligati it provided for singers. Certain of those were recorded with pronounced frequency: "Charmant oiseaux" from David's *Perle du Brésil*, the Mad Scene from *Lucia di Lammermoor*, Henry Bishop's "Lo, Here the Gentle Lark," and several other titles featured not only famous sopranos, but some of the most noted flutists of the day.

Less fortunate in its extramusical associations was the bassoon, which was regarded almost wholly as a novelty in the acoustical era. It was usually relegated, often in combination with the piccolo, to descriptive works like "The Nightingale and the Frog," or "The Elephant and the Fly," or to purely comic orchestral effects.

A very large percentage of the woodwinds' early recorded repertoire was drawn from salon music, including minor works of well-known composers (two venerable examples are Mendelssohn's "Spring Song" and Beethoven's "Minuet in G"), and major works of forgotten composers: "Serenade" by Anton Titl (1809–1882), "The Herd Girl's Dream" by August Labitzky (1832–1903), and a long list of others, all ubiquitous fixtures in record catalogs between 1905 and 1935. Such works were particularly popular when arranged for small groups—flute and clarinet duets, or mixed trios of flute, violin, and harp, or flute, cello and harp. Every label seems to have had such an ensemble. Victor's Neapolitan Trio (flute, violin, and harp) began recording around 1911, reaching its peak in 1923 with 34 titles in print, and continued to record electrically. Columbia's house trio, usually composed of George Stehl [or Stell] (violin), Marshall Lufsky (flute), and Charles Schuetze (harp), pursued the same repertoire. That type of music lingered for many years before its eventual dismissal from the repertoire. As late as 1940 Victor's Red Seal catalog included "The Aeolians," a quartet of flute, violin, cello, and harp playing, among other things, MacDowell's "To a Wild Rose," and Rimsky-Korsakov's "Flight of the Bumblebee."

Serious music for woodwinds was slow to appear on record. German performers of the early electrical recording era did show a preference for baroque and classical music. The 1926–1927 Polydor catalog listed performances by the Leipzig Gewandhaus Quintet of works by Klughardt, Beethoven, Reicha, and Mozart. French performers had a predilection for the latest French compositions. Soloists and ensembles such as the Trio d'Anches, the Quintette Instrumentale (both of Paris), and the Société Taffanel commissioned and recorded modern works by many important 20th-century composers. In America, the growth of a distinctive, modern repertoire for woodwinds only began developing in the 1930s. Pioneering labels like **New Music Quarterly Recordings** featured such works, often performed by the composers or by the groups that had commissioned or premiered them. Concurrently, the major international labels began "modern music" series.

Flutists active at the turn of the century often recorded on the piccolo because of its piercing sound and its popularity as a band instrument. George Schweinfest has been mentioned. **Eugene Rose**, a flutist in Sousa's Band in 1900–1901, made cylinders for Edison in 1889, along with two other flutists, Carl Wehner and Gustav Gast. Many players recorded acoustically on both piccolo and flute—Frank Badollet (1870–?) of the **United States Marine Band**, and two members of Sousa's Band, Darius Lyons (1870–?) and Marshall Lufsky (1878–1948). Other flutists came to the recording studio from orchestral careers. Clement Barone (1876–1934) became a Victor studio flutist in 1910 after seven years with the Philadelphia Orchestra. His recordings include flute and piccolo solos, dozens of titles with the Neapolitan Trio and Florentine Quartet, and obbligati for numerous sopranos. Albert Fransella (1866–1934), a Belgian whose performing career was primarily in England, was at different times a member of the Scottish, Crystal Palace, Royal Philharmonic, and Queen's Hall orchestras. His earliest recordings were Berliners made in 1898 and 1899—flute and piccolo solos, and several selections by the "Fransella Flute Quartet." He later provided recorded obbligati for Nellie Melba and Ruth Vincent, and made several flute and piccolo recordings of popular material issued by English Columbia in 1911.

During the acoustical period, few flutists had performing careers completely independent of orchestras or bands. One or two did appear as concert artists, often in association with singers, particularly sopranos. John Lemmone (1862–1950), a self-taught Australian flutist who was for many years obbligatist and concert manager for Melba, recorded several colorful works with descriptive titles and picturesque musical effects for Victor. His 1910 recording of "By the Brook" (#70023) has a piano accompaniment by Melba herself. John Amadio of New Zealand (1884–1964), who also performed frequently as an obbligatist for numerous sopranos, possessed an amazing technical ability that was amply illustrated by his "Carnival of Venice," Paganini's "Witches' Dance," and other virtuosic works recorded for HMV.

Since the latter half of the 19th century, the influence of French flutists has been acknowledged throughout the world. It is significant that the first major reissues of historical flute recordings presented performances by six French flutists: Gaubert, Hennebains, Barrère, Laurent, Moyse, and Le Roy. It is unfortunate that of these six men, only the last two recorded extensively. Philippe Gaubert (1879–1941), also renowned as a composer and conductor, recorded two obbligati for Melba in 1904 and seven short selections, including two of his own works, for the French Gramophone Company in 1918–1920. Adolphe Hennebains (1862–1914), flutist at the Paris Opéra (1891–1914), recorded an assortment of short works by Chopin, Godard, Pessard, Massenet, and others in 1907 and 1908, also for the French Gramophone Co. Georges Barrère (1876–1944) and Georges Laurent (1886–1964) were influential concert and orchestral performers in America, but their recording careers were sporadic. Barrère's first American solo recordings, made for Columbia in 1913 and 1915, were of the light salon pieces so favored by the public. His later electrical recordings emphasized the baroque and contemporary literature that he himself preferred, but his discs were unfortunately few in number. Laurent, for many years principal flutist of the Boston Symphony, recorded only a handful of titles as a soloist— primarily the works of J. S. Bach and a few modern composers. such as Howard Hanson and Roy Harris.

Marcel Moyse (1889–1984) and René Le Roy (1898–1985), both of whom began recording in the early electrical period, are more fully represented on disc. Le Roy's first recordings were probably the J.S. Bach sonatas recorded by the National Gramophone Society in 1928. In the course of his career he recorded many of the works dedicated to him, such as Honegger's *Danse de la chèvre*. Moyse was probably the best-known flute virtuoso of the 78 era. A host of notable French flutists followed Moyse, the most prominent being **Jean-Pierre Rampal**.

Most of the American flutists who recorded electrically or on LP were students of these influential Frenchmen. **William Kincaid** (1895–1967), pupil of Barrère and for nearly 40 years the first flutist of the Philadelphia Orchestra, recorded as a soloist with that orchestra. John Wummer (1899–1977), another Barrère student, recorded extensively for Columbia, performing works by Debussy, Foote, Handel, Bach, and others. An Irish virtuoso, James Galway (b. 1939), is the most internationally famous flutist of recent times.

The clarinet ("clarionet" is some older record catalogs) was heard on Edison cylinders in 1889; Henry Giese was the artist. Like the piccolo, it was popular as a band instrument, and many of the clarinetists recording at the turn of the century were band players. William Tuson, of Sousa's and Gilmore's bands, had an active studio career for 10 years (*see* CLARINET RECORDINGS). Louis H. Christie, a Victor studio performer, made many early solo recordings for that company. In America, however, the major orchestral clarinetists were poorly represented on record until the electrical era. Gustave Langenus (1883–1957), an important performer and a principal of the New York Symphony and New York Philharmonic, appears to have made virtually no recordings outside of those made by the orchestras. He is said to have recorded at least one selection for his own Celesta label, established in 1926, but it is not known whether the recording was actually released.

Certain woodwind instruments have exhibited pronounced national ties. For many years, France had a monopoly on flutists, and was also considered by many to be the source of the best oboe and clarinet players. However, as French and French-trained musicians wandered about Europe in pursuit of performing opportunities, their influence began to spread. Britain, in particular, had a long succession of fine clarinetists. The Gomez brothers, Manuel (1859–1922) and Francisco (1866–1938), though born in Spain and educated in France, spent most of their lives in England where they were well-known performers. Both recorded: Francisco made at least one Berliner in 1899, and Manuel made a handful of G & Ts (later issued on Zonophone) in London in 1902. Charles Draper (1869–1952), a noted orchestral player and one of the co-founders of the New Symphony Orchestra of London, probably recorded first for the Gramophone Company in London in 1901. The Edison Bell catalog of 1903 also lists many recordings by him, including one of the earliest recorded performances of the Weber *Concertino* (an even earlier recording of this work played by Henri Paradis (1861–1940) appeared in the June 1901 Bettini catalog). Draper had a lengthy career, and later went on to record major works such as Brahms' Clarinet Quintet, released by Columbia in 1929.

Electrical recordings reflected the continuing French and British domination of the instrument. Frederick Thurston (1901–1953), particularly well known as a soloist with the BBC Symphony Orchestra (1930–1946) recorded primarily in the 1930s and 1940s, performing several of the British compositions he had premiered, such as the Bliss Clarinet Quintet in 1944. **Reginald Kell** (1906–1981), who is considered to have revolutionized clarinet playing, recorded extensively from both the standard and 20th-century repertoire. Kell's successors in Britain include Jack Brymer (b. 1915), Thea King (b. 1925), and Gervase de Peyer (b. 1926). In France, Gaston Hamelin (1884–1951) made the first recording of the Debussy *Première rapsodie* for clarinet in Paris in 1933. Louis Cahuzac (1880–1960), who had begun recording for Pathé in about 1904, continued to record into the 1950s. At age 78 he recorded Hindemith's Clarinet Concerto for Angel with the Philadelphia Orchestra, the composer conducting.

The discs of **Benny Goodman** are among the outstanding American recordings from the electrical period. Goodman and Josef Szigeti commissioned Béla Bartók's *Contrasts* and recorded the work for Columbia on 13 May 1940, with Bartók at the piano. Later releases by Goodman include other works written for him, such as Copland's Clarinet Concerto, and selections from the standard solo repertoire.

The double-reed instruments were never as well-represented on record as flute or clarinet in the acoustical era. The earliest oboe recordings were probably made in France, or at least by French oboists, who were considered the finest in the world at the time. The noted instructor at the Paris Conservatory, Georges Gillet (1854–1934) recorded in the first decade of this century for French Odeon. One of his pupils, Louis Gaudard, is said to have recorded prior to 1900, though none of these recordings have been documented. Gaudard did appear in the Edison Bell catalog for 1903, and by 1906 he had made several discs for the English Neophone Co., including the "Pastorale" from the overture to Rossini's *William Tell*. Other oboists appearing on record before 1910 were less well known, and may simply have been versatile reed players "doubling" on the instrument. B. Sylvester, who used the pseudonym "Orpheus" and recorded for Edison Bell in about 1903, performed a repertoire of Irish songs on both the oboe and the musette (bagpipe). Acoustical recordings of the English horn are even fewer, although some outstanding examples, usually solos from the operatic or orchestral literature, do exist—for example, the solo that precedes Gertrude Förstel's "Frau Holda kam" from *Tannhäuser*, recorded in Bayreuth in summer 1904 (G & T #43576).

Many European oboists moved to America. Marcel Tabuteau (1887–1966), a pupil of Gillet, came in 1905 to join the New York Symphony Orchestra under Damrosch. His subsequent career included 40 years as principal oboist of the Philadelphia Orchestra. While he is heard in many recordings by that orchestra, his solo recordings are fewer than his reputation should have demanded. They include Bach's *Brandenburg Concertos*, recorded for Victor, and major works by Handel and Mozart issued on Columbia LPs. Bruno Labate (1883–1943), soloist with the New York Philharmonic from 1919 to 1943, began recording acoustically for

Pathé, and continued recording throughout his career, performing works like Loeffler's *Two Rhapsodies* (Schirmer Set #10; 1941).

Leon Goossens was the first virtuoso oboist of international reputation. Many of his pupils, among them Evelyn Rothwell (b. 1911), have had active recording careers as well.

American oboists, many of them students of Tabuteau or Labate, began to assume equal stature with their European counterparts in the late 1940s and early 1950s. Among those whose recordings have been particularly outstanding are John de Lancie, Robert Bloom, Harold Gomberg (1916–1985) and Ralph Gomberg (b. 1921).

The bassoon was generally the most neglected of the woodwinds on early recordings, treated more as a sound effect than as a musical instrument. A mysterious "Mr. Cooper" who recorded for Berliner in London in 1898 may be the earliest bassoonist to have recorded solos—his selections included several popular songs and a theme with variations from *Don Pasquale*. Frederick James (1860–1920), who played in the Queen's Hall Orchestra, London Symphony Orchestra, and at Covent Garden, was also recording early in the century, with six titles in the Edison Bell catalog for 1903. But solo bassoon recordings were to remain few in number for many years. From 1915 to 1921, Victor offered only one solo bassoon recording, in addition to the brief examples of the instrument provided in their educational catalog. Several outstanding players did much to improve the bassoon's status on record in the electrical era. Archie Camden (1888–1979), a prominent English bassoonist, inscribed a diverse repertoire of solo and chamber music. His recording of the Mozart bassoon concerto, made for English Columbia in 1926, is the earliest made of that work. In France, bassoonist Fernand Oubradous (b. 1903) actively promoted chamber music through his recording and conducting activities. He began to record in the late 1920s, playing both the standard classical works and contemporary French material. Later European and British bassoonists include Maurice Allard (b. 1923), who recorded into the LP era, and Wilfred and Cecil James, son and grandson of Frederick James.

The growing importance of the bassoon in chamber music has contributed to its renaissance on LP. Many of the bassoonists in America have played with woodwind quintets while pursuing solo and orchestral careers. Leonard Sharrow (b. 1915), who has recorded works ranging from the Mozart Bassoon Concerto to the Hindemith Bassoon Sonata, was also a member of the American Woodwind Quintet. Arthur Weisberg (b. 1931) and Sol Schoenbach (b. 1915) are also chamber players.

Acoustical recordings of woodwind ensembles were even fewer than those of the individual instruments. In the acoustical period, duets were favored, using two matched instruments (piccolo duets were quite common) or two different ones. Flute and clarinet were frequently paired though more unusual combinations were heard, such as the flute and saxophone duets recorded for Victor in 1900 by Frank Badollet and Jean-Baptiste Moermans. American concert reviews reveal that even in the 1930s larger woodwind ensembles were regarded as oddities, or charming 18th-century anachronisms. While many ensembles were successful in concert, few recorded with any regularity. The Barrère Ensemble, Barrère Little Symphony, and Trio de Lutèce, all woodwind and mixed ensembles founded by flutist Georges Barrère, recorded for Columbia between 1915 and 1922, but played only arrangements of popular light pieces. In 1927, recordings by the London Flute Quartet included selections like "The Flight of the Bumblebee" and "Carnival of Venice."

Woodwind ensembles were heard to greater advantage in the electrical era. German quintets were especially active. The 1926–1927 Polydor catalog alone lists performances by the Berlin Opera Wind Sextet, the Dresden State Opera Orchestra Wind Quintet, and the Leipzig Gewandhaus Quintet. The Leipzig repertoire includes, along with classical serenades and divertimenti, Hindemith's *Kleine Kammermusik* op. 24, no. 2. The number of professional quintets and other small groups increased throughout the 1930s, with radio further encouraging the growth of chamber performance. In France, one of the most active woodwind groups was the Trio d'Anches de

Paris, founded in 1927 by the bassoonist Oubradous. It emphasized the modern French composers, such as Darius Milhaud, Jean Rivier, Georges Auric, and Henry Barraud. Other notable French ensembles included the Société des Instruments à Vent de Paris, and flutist René Le Roy's Quintette Instrumental de Paris (flute, strings, and harp), which was active from 1922 to 1939, and recorded for HMV in the mid-1930s.

In America, the formation of more or less permanent ensembles for the performance of woodwind music did not take place until the 1940s. The New York Woodwind Quintet was founded in 1949, the Boston Symphony Woodwind Quintet in 1954, and the Philadelphia Woodwind Quintet in 1950. These ensembles and others have made enormous contributions to the recorded repertoire, particularly in contemporary music. There are some striking parallels between the development of a discrete, sophisticated literature for woodwinds and the recorded history of the instruments themselves. The growth of woodwind music in the 20th century, achieved through the revival of older works and the creation of new ones, has been supported by the opportunities for presenting that literature through recordings. At the same time, the existence of a more suitable and varied repertoire has encouraged an increase in both live and recorded performing activity.

Two LP reissues by Pearl are of special importance: *The Great Flautists*, Vol. I (#GEMM 284; 1985) and Vol. 2 (#GEMM 302; 1986). [Dorgeuille 1986; Langwill 1965; Weston 1971; Weston 1977.]

Susan Nelson

WOOFER. A low-frequency, or bass, loudspeaker. Usually it is combined with a high-frequency **tweeter.**

WORLD BROADCASTING SYSTEM, INC. A New York firm, located at 711 Fifth Ave. It issued, for radio stations only, a series of "World Program Service" transcription discs, from 1933 to 1963. [Kressley 1968 is a label list and history.]

WORLD PHONOGRAPH CO. A Chicago firm, maker of the World record player in 1919–1920. It was bankrupt in October 1920.

WORLD RECORD CO., LTD. A British firm, active in 1922–1924, with showrooms in Piccadilly, London. The main product was a gramophone and a disc (World Record) designed to operate at a constant groove speed (outside RPM reduced, inside RPM increased). Use of this system, an invention of Pemberton Billing, provided three to five times the playing time per record of ordinary discs. The promise of this method was not fully exploited, however, as the firm sold its business to the Vocalion Gramophone Co., Ltd., in 1925, which company began issuing Vocalion Long Playing Records made under the Billing patents. Production ceased in late 1925. The World Record Co., Ltd., retained its corporate existence, but not with records or machines. [Andrews*; Frow 1970.]

WORLD'S COLUMBIAN EXPOSITION, CHICAGO, 1893. At this great world's fair there were important musical exhibits. Fifty-eight firms exhibited pianos and organs, but the only player piano seems to have been the Hupfeld Self Playing Piano, a "push-up" player attachment. Thomas Edison had an exhibit in the Electricity Building, including his Household Phonograph. [Musical 1895.]

World's fairs. *See* PANAMA PACIFIC EXPOSITION, SAN FRANCISCO, 1915; PARIS EXPOSITION, 1889; ST. LOUIS EXPOSITION, 1904; WORLD'S COLUMBIAN EXPOSITION, CHICAGO, 1893.

WORLD'S GREATEST MUSIC (label). Records issued in the U.S. in 1938–1940 by the Publishers Service Co., a subsidiary of the *New York Post*. The discs were pressed by RCA Victor, using Victor artists (not identified on the records), and sold at bargain prices to newspaper purchasers. Many of the performances were by members of the Philadelphia Orchestra, playing in the Academy of Music. [Gray 1975.] *See also* WORLD'S GREATEST OPERAS (label).

WORLD'S GREATEST OPERAS (label). Like the **World's Greatest Music** label, these records were distributed by the Publishers Service Co. Among the anonymous artists were Rose Bampton, Mack Harrell, Eleanor Steber, Norman Cordon, and Leonard Warren. Twelve operas were included, all released in 1940. [Gray 1975.]

WOW. A fluctuation in pitch (frequency) that results when a phonograph **turntable** does not rotate at constant speed, or when the disc is not fully stabilized on the turntable. In a tape player there is wow when the tape slips somewhere in the transport system, usually at the **capstan**. [Klinger*.]

WURLITZER (RUDOLPH) CO. A music instrument manufacturing firm, established in 1861 in Cincinnati, Ohio, by Rudolph Wurlitzer. At first it made drums and bugles for use in the Civil War, then other band instruments. It was soon the largest retailer of its kind. In 1890 the firm incorporated as the Rudolph Wurlitzer Co., Inc.

Wurlitzer made pianos, electric pianos, **coin-op** instruments, automatic piano roll changers, and other automatic musical devices. In 1913 the firm was located at 982 Fourth St., Cincinnati. It was active in furnishing theatre instruments. An advertisement in *Billboard*, September 1913, claimed that "thirty-three motion picture theatres in twenty-five cities installed Wurlitzer music during August alone." The reference was to the "One-Man Orchestra," a photoplayer (*see* MOTION PICTURE MUSIC). The company had 20 branches, including one at 115–119 W. 40th St., New York.

In the late 1920s there were also Wurlitzer coin-op phonographs, and then the fully developed **juke box** of the 1930s. About 750,000 juke boxes were made up to 1974, when production ceased. [Hoover 1971, cover, shows juke box model #1015, 1946.]

WYOMING PHONOGRAPH CO. A firm affiliated with the **North American Phonograph Co.**, established in 1893 in Cheyenne. E. L. Lindsay was manager in 1890.

XYLOPHONE. Charles P. Lowe appears to have been the earliest person to record the instrument, on cylinders that were in the 1893 catalog of the New Jersey Phonograph Co., and others for Columbia and Edison before 1900. In Europe, early recordings of the xylophone were made for the Gramophone Co. by M. Raphael (a polka, in July 1899) and Mlle. Borde (six sides in July 1900). Marches, polkas, and waltzes were the principal repertoire of the pioneer performers, but there was also a record about air travel, apparently the first song of that genre: "Come Take a Trip in My Airship," played by **Albert Benzler** (Edison #8931; 1905; sung a year earlier for Victor by Billy Murray.) The Edison artists—Lowe, Benzler, Charles Daab, and J. Frank Hopkins—compiled about 60 numbers before 1900. Victor had 37 xylo-phone items in its 1917 catalog, most by W. H. Reitz, who also played the bells. There were no xylophone records in the 1927 catalog, but four were listed in 1938.

As the xylophone declined in public interest during the 1920s, the vibraphone was introduced into jazz performance. While the instruments are similar, the xylophone has wooden bars while the vibraphone has metal bars; and the vibraphone has electric controls that allow it to produce vibrato. **Lionel Hampton** was the first jazzman to give identity to the vibraphone, with Benny Goodman's Quartet in 1936-1940. **Milt Jackson**'s vibes were highlights in the 1940s. In the 1950s George Shearing's Quintet featured a vibraphone, blending with the piano line.

Y

YALE COLLECTION OF HISTORICAL SOUND RECORDINGS. One of the principal archives of its kind, established as a department of the Yale University Libraries in 1961 with an initial deposit of about 20,000 recordings by Mrs. and Mrs. Laurence C. Witten II. Many other individuals and organizations have since contributed records and documentation to the collection, which numbered 140,000 recordings in 1989. Composer recordings are a major concentration; another focus is on early singers. Jazz collecting has been emphasized in recent years. There are important holdings also in musical theatre, poetry, and drama. [Berger, K. 1974; Blair 1989; Moore 1964.]

YAW, ELLEN BEACH, 1868–1947. American soprano, born in Boston on 14 Sep 1868. She made her opera debut in London in 1895, and sang at Carnegie Hall in 1896, acclaimed for her remarkable range, from G below middle C to the highest F on the piano. Yaw sang Lucia in Rome in 1907 and at the Metropolitan Opera in the 1907–1908 season. Her first records were made in 1900 for the Gramophone Co.: the Queen of the Night aria (#3095) and seven others. She recorded four published sides for Victor (1907) and made one Edison Diamond Disc, "Annie Laurie" (#82049; 1913). Yaw also worked for Keen-O-Phone, whose 1914 catalog included her *Mignon* Polonaise (#50001), "Annie Laurie" (#50003) and a song of her own, "Skylark" (#50002). The "Annie Laurie" also appeared as Rex #1054, and on the Rishell label. In the Victor 1917 catalog, Yaw was represented on Red Seal by two of the 1907 recordings: the Bell Song from *Lakme* (#74090) and the

"Nightingale's Song" from *Noces de Jeannette* (#74092). She was not in the 1927 catalog. She made some private recordings in 1937 for HMV and in 1941 for Co-Art. IRCC #3082 has "Skylark" and the *Mignon* aria from the Keen-O-Phone material. Yaw died in West Covina, California, on 9 Sep 1947. [Altamirano 1955.]

YERKES DANCE RECORDS (label). An American record issued briefly in 1924 by the Yerkes Recording Laboratories, 102 W. 38th St., of New York. The founder was Harry A. Yerkes, a successful dance band leader, most prominently as director of the S. S. Flotilla Orchestra. [Kendziora 1982/10; Rust 1978.]

YOUNG, LESTER, 1909–1959. American saxophonist, born in Woodville, Mississippi, on 27 Aug 1909. His family settled in New Orleans, where his father taught him several instruments. He played drums in a touring band, then teamed with Art Bronson's Bostonians, taking up the tenor saxophone. Young gained recognition in Minneapolis clubs (the city was his family home from 1919), and in 1933 with Bennie Moten's band in Kansas City. He left Kansas City in 1934 with Count Basie, then shifted to Fletcher Henderson—replacing Coleman Hawkins—and rejoined Basie in 1936. He made an important series of appearances with Billie Holiday, led his own band, saw military service, and became famous after World War II in the Jazz at the Philharmonic events staged by Norman Granz. He was a freelancer, struggling with poor health the rest of his life, gradually gaining the status of prime performer on his instrument, "the most influential artist after Armstrong and before Charlie Parker" (Schuller). His last major engagements were in Paris, and he died shortly after, on 15 Mar 1959 in New York.

Young was heard on eight sides of the Kansas City Six, notably on his cheap metal clarinet in "I Want a Little Girl" (Commodore #509), illustrating a tender lyrical style, contrasting with the percussive tendency of Hawkins. In a 1939 session for Columbia, with Glenn Hardman and His Hammond Five, Young was featured on sax and clarinet. "Lester Leaps In" was done in 1939 (Vocalion #5118) with the Kansas City Seven for the Keynote label, offering a loose and biting line. Young

was with King Cole in 1942, recording a remarkable "Body and Soul" (Philo #1000) and an inspired "These Foolish Things" (Philo/Aladdin #142) that kept the spirit of the melody without sounding it. Records made immediately after Young's military service show signs of decline in his powers, but in 1950–1951 he was superbly supported by pianist John Lewis in some sides of great brilliance, for example, "Let's Fall in Love"; and there was another resurgence with the Oscar Peterson Trio in 1952, notably in "I Can't Get Started"—all these on the Verve label, and reissued on CD. Young is well represented on compact discs, with a dozen titles in the 1991 catalog.

Z

ZARVAH ART (label). An American record of 1922, the name derived from the names of its founders, Zarh Myron Bickford and Vahdah Olcott-Bickford, its home being in the Zarvah Art Record Co., 616 W. 116th St, New York. The two Bickfords played a guitar-mandolin duet on one of the few sides issued. [Rust 1978.]

ZENATELLO, GIOVANNI, 1876–1949. Italian tenor, born in Verona on 22 Feb 1876. He began as a baritone, singing Silvio in his 1898 debut. After further study he made a second debut, also in *Pagliacci*, this time as Canio (Naples, 1901). He created the role of Pinkerton at La Scala on 17 Feb 1904, and sang Enzo in *Gioconda* for his American debut in New York, 1907. Zenatello did not appear with the Metropolitan Opera, but sang with the Boston Opera in 1909–1914, with the Chicago Opera, and then on extended world tours. He retired in 1928, and settled with his wife, soprano Maria Gay, to teach in New York, where he died on 11 Feb 1949.

Zenatello was a prolific maker of phonograph discs, commencing with nine G & T sides in Milan in 1903, including the "Improvviso" from *Andrea Chenier* (#52702), "Salve dimora" ("Salut demeure") from *Faust* (#52703), and "Donna non vidi mai" from *Manon Lescaut* (#52721). He went to the Fonotipia label from 1905 to 1911, and turned out about 100 records from the Italian/French repertoire; among them were two sides from *Madama Butterfly*, some seven years after the premiere. An outstanding disc from this series was "Sulla tomba," the *Lucia* duet, with Maria Barrientos (#39825).

In the U.S. Zenatello worked with Columbia from 1912, and made Edison Diamond Discs from 1921 to 1922, starting with the tomb duet from *Aida*, with Maria Rappold (#83035). Then he recorded in Europe again, for HMV, doing one of his famous roles, Otello. His last discs were for Victor in 1928–1930. Zenatello was one of the few opera singers who recorded a duet with his wife (Maria Gay): "Ai nostri monti" (Columbia #A5370). LP reissues were extensive, from IRCC, Rococo, Eterna, and Belcanto Disc. [Hutchinson 1962.]

ZIMBALIST, EFREM, 1889–1985. Russian/American violinist, born in Rostov-on-the-Don, 21 Apr 1889. He took a gold medal at the St. Petersburg Conservatory, as a student of Leopold Auer. After European concertizing in his teens, he emigrated to the U.S. in 1911. He performed with the Boston Symphony Orchestra on 27 Oct 1911, and then with many orchestras and in recital. His second wife was Mary Louise Curtis Bok, founder of the Curtis Institute of Music in Philadelphia, which Zimbalist directed from 1941 to 1968. He retired to Nevada, and died on 22 Feb 1985. His son, Efrem Zimbalist, Jr., became a noted film actor.

Zimbalist recorded prolifically. There were 20 solos in the Victor 1917 catalog, and duets with Alma Gluck (his first wife) and Fritz Kreisler. The Kreisler duet was the first recording of J.S. Bach's Concerto for Two Violins (Victor #76028/29). In his records Zimbalist did not exploit the great repertoire of the instrument, but focussed on arrangements, such as "Old Black Joe" (Victor #64640) and César Cui's "Orientale." His recordings were deleted from the catalog after the 1920s. He did not have an LP revival, and has so far (1991) not been brought back on compact discs. [Lewis, J. 1986.]

ZITHER RECORDINGS. This instrument was heard on very early records: there were 14 cylinders by **Bettini** in 1898, all by a Prof. D. Wormser. The same artist made six records for Edison in 1899–1902, and about 20 Columbia cylinders ca. 1899. Sometime after 1908 he began to work for Victor; there were eight records in the 1917 Victor catalog. Zither music was made up of arrangements, with much of the Wormser repertoire drawn from German folksongs. The zither category was dropped from Victor catalogs in the 1920s. A revival of interest in the instrument occurred after its featured appearance in the motion picture *Third Man* (1949), with Anton Karas performing "The Harry Lime Theme" and other numbers; Decca recorded two LP albums by Karas (#LF 1053 and #LF 1145).

ZIV (FREDERIC W.) CO. An American firm, located in Cincinnati, producer or syndicator of about 7,050 radio programs plus many television programs. Transcriptions of certain series are of interest to collectors, e.g., those that covered Wayne King, Guy Lombardo, and Freddy Martin. Extensive lists of the titles were compiled by David Kressley. [Kressley 1983.]

ZONOPHONE. A disc record player made by the **Universal Talking Machine Co.** and marketed for $25 by the **National Gramophone Co.** from October 1898; **Frank Seaman** being associated with the former company and the founder of the latter. The machine was merely a Berliner gramophone, and indeed the first advertising referred to it as the "Improved Gramophone (Zon-O-Phone)." Eldridge Johnson had been the developer of the **Improved Gramophone**, based on the original machines of Emile Berliner, and Seaman had been a successful authorized promoter of it for **Berliner Gramophone Co.** But the new name for the product brought conflicts between Seaman and Berliner (and Johnson). In June 1900 Berliner stopped doing business with Seaman, but Seaman obtained a court injunction that

actually prevented Berliner from selling Berliner products—as Seaman had the exclusive sales contract for all the U.S. except the Washington, D.C. area. This dispute was complicated by an earlier action (October 1898) brought against Seaman by the Columbia (Graphophone) interests for infringement of their patents. During the ensuing litigation, the Universal Company was tooling up to manufacture genuine Zonophone machines, and the National Gramophone Co. business in Berliner products was acquired by a new firm, the **National Gramophone Corp.**, established March 1889, with Seaman as treasurer. Modifications were introduced, so that differences could be noted between the Zonophone and its parent Gramophone; for example the winding crank was moved to rotate parallel to the side of the machine, instead of parallel to the surface. Nevertheless the court order did materialize, and both Seaman and the National Gramophone Corp. were enjoined in May 1900 from producing or selling any more talking machines, under any name whatsoever. A consent agreement between National Gramophone Corp. / Universal Talking Machine Co. and Columbia Phonograph Co., General, gave Columbia an entry into the disc and disc player market by use of the Zonophone line.

When the National Gramophone Corp. failed in 1901, a new manufacturer of the Zonophones was established by the name of Universal Talking Machine Manufacturing Co., the original Universal firm becoming the temporary sales outlet. Zonophones were exported to Europe, and the **International Zonophone Co.** was founded in New York and Berlin in spring 1901 to control the business. In June 1903, the Gramophone & Typewriter, Ltd. purchased the two Universal companies and the majority of stock shares in International Zonophone. In Europe, Zonophone machines remained on the market. They continued to be available in the U.S. as well, but from September 1903 under the Victor Talking Machine Co.—which was sold the American end of the Zonophone business by G & T. Because the Universal Talking Machine Manufacturing Co. had not been licensed by Columbia, that firm brought a successful action against it for patent infringement, and the Zonophone business in

America was terminated by court order in 1912. The European Zonophone business continued. [Andrews*.]

ZONOPHONE (label). (Also written Zon-O-Phone; later styled Zonophone Record.) An American record produced by the **Universal Talking Machine Co.** (established 10 Feb 1898). It was marketed by the **National Gramophone Corp.**, in which Frank Seaman had a strong commitment, once Seaman had ceased ordering gramophones from the Berliner Gramophone Co. Berliner retaliated by refusing to deliver discs to Seaman's agency. The earliest discs suitable for the new Zonophone machines were modified "Berliners" which were either copied or had a hole drilled through near their centers to locate on the peg in the first Zonophone turntables, as an anti-skid device.

Actual manufacture of the discs may have been done at the Yonkers, New York, factory of the Universal Talking Machine Co., with materials provided by the Burt Co. or the Auburn Button Works. Records with the Zonophone name went on sale in spring 1900, in seven-inch size, single-faced, through the National Gramophone Corp. But on 5 May 1900 the company was enjoined by a U.S. court, following an action brought by the Columbia interests, its machines and discs deemed in infringement of Columbia patents. However, two weeks later both National Gramophone Corp. and the manufacturing arm, Universal Talking Machine Co., were licensed by the Columbia interests to make and sell the Zonophone products.

One year later, a nine-inch diameter "Superba" disc was introduced—later described as the "Concert" size record. The seven-inch disc, designated the "Parlour" size, was also marketed. Selections from both sizes were exported to Europe for inclusion in the catalogs of the **International Zonophone Co.** and its agencies. But in the very month that International Zonophone issued its first lists, September 1901, National Gramophone Corp. went into liquidation. There was a reorganization of the Zonophone business in New York, after which the discs underwent a change. They were then made of a brown material, with paper labels (following the example of the International Zonophone discs), and were styled Universal Zonophone Record. Further changes ensued after Victor acquired the American end of the Zonophone businesses from their new (June 1903) owners: The Gramophone & Typewriter, Ltd. The seven- and nine-inch discs were terminated and in September 1903 new sizes appeared: 10-inch, 11-inch, and 12-inch. The new discs were of black material with labels printed gold on green or gold on black, and became double-sided before Universal Talking Machine Manufacturing Co. was court-ordered out of business in 1912. That action followed from the claim of patent infringement by the Columbia interests.

In European countries, from September 1901, Zonophone Records—and labels with local translations of the name—began coming from the Berlin presses. Agents were appointed in many countries, who arranged the contracting of artists and then for advertising and sales in their respective territories. Where no agencies were contracted, International Zonophone dealt with dealers directly and arranged for its own recordings through representatives.

Zonophone Records had different price categories in the seven-inch and 10-inch sizes. Label colors were black, orange, or blue, according to celebrity status of the artists. In Italy there was a dark blue Disco Reale, but it is uncertain whether that line was out before or after Gramophone & Typewriter took control of International Zonophone (June 1903). In 1902 double-sided Zonophone discs were produced for Casa Edison, a South American agency—they were the first double-sided discs to be marketed.

Under Gramophone & Typewriter, International Zonophone was used to produce cheaper records than the regular G & T lines. Green labels were substituted for black, and the higher-priced labels were gradually phased out. Double-sided Zonophone Records were sold on the continent before they were sold in Britain, where Zonophone remained single-faced until May 1911. At that time the Zonophone catalog was merged with that of the Twin Record Co., Ltd. (a Gramophone Co. subsidiary) and nearly all Zonophones became coupled as "Zonophone Record—The Twin." Exceptions were the Zonophone Grand Opera

Records, which remained single until 1913. Zonophone Records persisted in Britain (the name simplified to Zonophone in 1926) until December 1932, when the catalog was merged with **Regal** to become "Regal-Zonophone." Regal-Zonophone continued to 1949.

Two price wars in Europe brought the introduction of the brown-label Zonophone Record (September 1909) and the cheap lilac label (September 1913). In many countries Zonophone Records were converted into green-label HMV discs from ca. 1911. Zonophones had separate catalogs in various parts of the British Empire.

In America, Zonophone's early repertoire was simply taken over from Berliner discs. Later material was comparable to other cheaper American labels, mostly dance and popular vocals. Material on the British Zonophone records came from Victor masters (including jazz and dance music, plus country music) and from recording in Europe. The most famous Zonophone records were made by the Italian branch, in 1903: 10 numbers by the young Enrico Caruso. [Andrews*; Andrews 1989.]

Zonophone Quartet. *See* RAMBLER MINSTREL CO.

Bibliography and Key to Citations

The works cited at the ends of articles are here arranged in alphabetical order by author or main entry, and chronologically under each author. In some instances the sequence under an author is only approximately chronological. Entries in bold face type are those that have been used often, although not always specifically cited.

Certain citations found at the ends of articles are to series of writings, usually named features in periodicals, by one author. Such citations identify the year and month of the feature, but do not name the feature each time. For example the series "Disco-ing In," by George Blacker, was a monthly feature in *Record Research* from 1955 to 1990. The citation "Blacker 1970/5" refers to that column in the May 1970 issue. Another example is the feature "Favorite Pioneer Recording Artists" by Jim Walsh, which appeared in *Hobbies* magazine from 1942 to 1985.

The entry style for journal articles gives the journal name (some abbreviated), volume number and issue number connected with a hyphen, date in parenthesis, and pagination. These periodical titles are abbreviated as shown: *Antique Phonograph Monthly (APM), Association for Recorded Sound Collections Journal (ARSCJ); Hillandale News (HN); New Amberola Graphic (NAG); Record Collector (RC); Record Research (RR); Talking Machine Review International (TMR).*

Because relevant periodical titles are entered in the article "Sound Recording Periodicals" they are not repeated as entries in the Bibliography.

It should be emphasized that the Bibliography is basically a list of the writings cited in the text, and not an inventory of writings about recorded sound.

[Abell 1969] "Richard Tauber" / G. O. Abell, L. E. Abell, and James F. E. Dennis. — RC 18–8/12 (Oct.-Dec. 1969): 171–272; 19–3/4 (June 1970): 81–86.

[Adamson 1973] "Berliner Labels" / P. G. Adamson. — TMR 24 (Oct. 1973): 247–254.

[Adamson 1983] "Berliner and 7–inch G & T Records" — / P. G. Adamson. — TMR 65/66 (1983): 1,793–1,794. A commentary on Rust 1981.

[Adrian 1989] *Edison Bell Winner Records* / Karlo Adrian and Arthur Badrock. — Rev. ed.— Bournemouth, England: Talking Machine Review, 1989. 9 parts in 1 vol.; unpaged. (1st ed. 1974.)

[Aeppli 1985] *Heart of Stone; The Definitive Rolling Stones Discography, 1962–1983* / Felix Aeppli. — Ann Arbor, Mich.: Pierian Press, 1985. 575 p.

[Aldridge 1964] *The Victor Talking Machine Company* / Benjamin L. Aldridge. — Camden, N.J.: RCA Sales Corp., 1964. 120 p. Reprinted in Fagan 1983.

[Allen 1955] *King Joe Oliver* / Walter C. Allen.— Stanhope, N.J.: Author, 1955; London: Sidgwick & Jackson, 1959. 224 p.

[Allen 1971] *Studies in Jazz Discography. I. Proceedings of the First and Second Annual Conferences on Discographical Research, 1968–1969, and of the Conference on the Preservation and Extension of the Jazz Heritage, 1969* / Edited by Walter C. Allen. — New Brunswick, N.J.: Rutgers University, Institute of Jazz Studies, 1971. 112 p.

[Allen 1973] *Hendersonia: The Music of Fletcher Henderson and His Musicians; A Bio-discography /*

Walter C. Allen. — Highland Park, N.J.: Author, 1973. 651 p.

[Altamirano 1955] "Ellen Beach Yaw" / Antonio Altamirano. — RC 10–7 (Dec. 1955): 149–161.

[American 1982] *American Music Recordings: A Discography of 20th-century U.S. Composers* / Edited by Carol J. Oja. — Brooklyn: Institute for the Study of American Music, 1982. 368 p.

[Andrews 1971/1] "The 'Jumbo' Story As I See It" / Frank Andrews. — HN 61 (June 1971): 21–22.

[Andrews 1971/2] "Toward the Complete Documentation of All So-called 78 RPM Records" / Frank Andrews. —TMR 12 (Oct. 1971): 108–110.

[Andrews 1972] "Record Research No. 5" / Frank Andrews. — TMR 16 (June 1972): 108–210.

[Andrews 1974/4] "Lambert in Britain" / Frank Andrews. — TMR 27 (Apr. 1974): 70–91; 29 (Aug. 1974): 152.

[Andrews 1974/5] "Guiniphones" / Frank Andrews. — HN 80 (Oct. 1974): 233–235.

[Andrews 1974/10] "The International Indestructible Cylinder Records" / Frank Andrews. — TMR 30 (Oct. 1974): 190–196.

[Andrews 1976/2] "The North American Phonograph Company" / Frank Andrews. — TMR 38 (Feb. 1976): 571–582.

[Andrews 1976/5] "A Fonotipia Fragmentia" / Frank Andrews. — TMR 40/41/42/44/45/48/49b (1976–1977). Serialized in seven parts.

[Andrews 1976/6] "Some Errors in the Society's Cylinder Catalogues" / Frank Andrews. — HN 90 (June 1976): 508–509.

[Andrews 1976/10] "The Columbia Bubble Books" / Frank Andrews. — HN 92 (Oct. 1976): 46–49.

[Andrews 1977/1] "Minstrels, Minstrel Shows, and Early Recordings" / Frank Andrews. — TMR 47 (1977): 1,063–1,066, 1,071–1,076.

[Andrews 1977/10] "The Recordings of 1907 in Britain" / Frank Andrews. — HN 98 (Oct. 1977): 239–241.

[Andrews 1978/3] "Neophone" / Frank Andrews. — TMR 51 (Apr. 1978): 1,304–1,313; 52/53 (June–Aug. 1978): 1,333–1,339; 54/55 (Oct.–Dec. 1978): 1,397–1,400.

[Andrews 1978/4] "Edisonia—Edison Bell" / Frank Andrews. — TMR 51 (Apr. 1978): 1,301–1,302.

[Andrews 1979/10] "Star Records" / Frank Andrews. — TMR 60/61 (Oct.–Dec. 1979): 1,617–1,622; 68 (June 1984): 1,873–1,874.

[Andrews 1980/2] "A Further Look at the International Zonophone Company, May 1901 to June 1903" / Frank Andrews. — TMR 62 (1980); 1,691–1,696; 63/64 (1981): 1,717–1,725; 65/66 (Feb. 1983): 1,811–1,818.

[Andrews 1980/10] "From Orchestrelle to Vocalion; An Account of the Aeolian Companies and Their Involvement with Talking Machines" / Frank Andrews. — HN 116 (Oct. 1980): 99–106; 117 (Nov. 1980): 120–155.

[Andrews 1981/1] "British Brunswick; The History of Brunswick Cliftophone, Brunswick Cliftophone Ltd., and Brunswick in the 1920s" / Frank Andrews. — HN 122 (Oct. 1981): 265–273.

[Andrews 1982] *Billy Williams Records; A Study in Discography* / Frank Andrews and Ernie Bayly. — Bournemouth, England : Talking Machine Review, 1982. 72 p.

[Andrews 1982/12] "Broadcast; The Story of A Record" / Frank Andrews. — HN 129 (Dec. 1982): 126–131; 130 (Feb. 1983): 148–149.

[Andrews 1983/10] "The History of the Crystalate Companies in the Recording Industry, 1901–1937" / Frank Andrews.—HN 134 (Oct. 1983): 259–290; 135 (Dec. 1983): 291–297; 136 (Feb. 1984): 317–324.

[Andrews 1984/4] "Duo-Trac" / Frank Andrews. — HN 137 (Apr. 1984): 16–23.

[Andrews 1984/12] "Genuine Edison Bell Records" / Frank Andrews. — HN 141 (Dec. 1984): 125–130; 142 (Mar. 1985): 159–164; 143 (Apr. 1985): 179–184; 145 (Aug. 1985): 233–242.

[Andrews 1984/13] "Imperial Records" / Frank Andrews. — TMR 69 (Dec. 1984): 1,908–1,912.

[Andrews 1985/1] *Columbia Ten-inch Records Issued 1904 to 1930* / Frank Andrews. — London: City of London Phonograph and Gramophone Society, 1985. Unpaged. Lists U.K. issues of the various Columbia labels.

[Andrews 1985/6] "The Birth of Electrical Recording" / Frank Andrews. — HN 144 (1985): 199–202.

[Andrews 1985/12] "Homophone in Britain" / Frank Andrews. — HN 147 (Dec. 1985): 284–290; 148

(Dec. 1986): 312–317; 149 (Apr. 1986): 5–8; 150 (June 1986): 32–35.

[Andrews 1986] *The Edison Phonograph; The British Connection* / Frank Andrews. — Rugby, England: City of London Phonograph and Gramophone Society, 1986. 140 p.

[Andrews 1987/4] "The Coming and Demise of the Marathon Records and Machines" / Frank Andrews. — *TMR* 72 (Apr. 1987): 2,081–2,105.

[Andrews 1987/10] "The His Master's Voice Record Catalogues" / Frank Andrews. — *HN* 158 (Oct. 1987): 255–261; 159 (Dec. 1987): 284–291; 160 (Feb. 1988): 320–329.

[Andrews 1988/2] "John Bull Records and Ercophone Gramophones" / Frank Andrews. — *TMR* 73 (Feb. 1988): 2,139–2,150.

[Andrews 1988/4] "The Under-twenty-fives; A History of British Disc Records of Less than 25 cm (10 Inch) Diameter" / Frank Andrews. — *HN* 161 (Apr. 1988): 6–11; 162 (June 1988): 40–46.

[Andrews 1988/10] "Joseph Leonard Blum and His Gramophone Records" / Frank Andrews. — *TMR* 75 (Autumn 1988): 2,182–2,196.

[Andrews 1989] "The Zonophone Record and Its Associated Labels in Britain" / Frank Andrews. — *HN* 166 (Feb. 1989): 150–156; 167; 168 (June 1989): 206–211. Corrections by Andrews in *HN* 170 (Oct. 1989): 276.

[Andrews 1990] "Nipper's Uncle; William Barraud and His Disc Records" / Frank Andrews. — *HN* 174 (June 1990): 37–42; 175 (Aug. 1990): 67–72; 176 (Oct. 1990): 112–116; 177 (Dec. 1990): 134–138.

[Andrews 1991] "Records in Store" / Frank Andrews. — *HN* 181 (Aug. 1991): 268–276.

[Annand 1966] *The Complete Catalogue of the United States Everlasting Indestructible Cylinders, 1905–1913* / H. H. Annand. — London: City of London Phonograph and Gramophone Society, 1966. 38 p.

[Annand 1973] *The Catalogue of the United States Everlasting Indestructible Cylinders, 1980–1913* / H. H. Annand. — 2nd ed. — Bournemouth, England: Talking Machine Review International, 1973. 36 p.

[Annand 1970] *Block Catalogue of the Cylinder Records Issued by the U.S. Phonograph Company, 1890–1896* / H. H. Annand. — Hillingdon, Middlesex, England, 1970.

[Ardoin 1991] The Callas Legacy: The Complete Guide to Her Recordings / John Ardoin. — New York: Scribner, 1991. xvii, 236 p.

[Arfanis 1990] *The Complete Discography of Dimitri Mitropoulos* / Stathis A. Arfanis; research associate Nick Nickson. — Athens: IRINNA, 1990. 111 p.

[Association 1967] *Preliminary Directory of Sound Recordings Collections in the United States and Canada* / Association for Recorded Sound Collections. — New York: New York Public Library, 1967. 157 p.

[Association 1988] *Audio Preservation: A Planning Study; Final Performance Report* / Elwood A. McKee. — Rockville, Md.: Association for Recorded Sound Collections, Associated Audio Archives Committee, 1988. 2 vols., looseleaf.

[Atchison 1984] "The Musical Theatre in Canada—on Stage and on Record" / Glenn Atchison. — In Hummel 1984, xxxiv–xl.

[Audio C 1977] *Audio Cyclopedia* / Edited by Howard M. Tremaine.— 3rd ed. — Indianapolis: Sams, 1977. 1,757 p. (1st ed. 1959.)

[Ault 1986] "CBS and the Columbia Phonograph Company" / Bob Ault. — *Antiques and Collecting Hobbies*, Nov. 1986: 53–56.

[Ault 1987] "A Few Observations on the Art of Playing Old Records" / Bob Ault. — *Antiques and Collecting Hobbies*, Feb. 1987: 48–50.

[Australian 1987] *The Australian Music Industry; An Economic Evaluation* / Music Board of the Australian Council. — Sidney: The Board, 1987.

[Bachman 1962] "Disk Recording and Reproduction" / W. S. Bachman, B. B. Bauer, and P. C. Goldmark. — *IRE Proceedings* 50 (May 1962): 738–744. Reprinted in Roys 1978.

[Backensto 1969] "Red Nichols Memorial Issue" / Woody Backensto. — *RR* 96/97 (Apr. 1969): 2–18.

[Backus 1969] *The Acoustical Foundations of Music* / John Backus. — New York: Norton, 1969. 312 p.

[Badmaieff 1966] *How to Build Speaker Enclosures* / Alexis Badmaieff and Don Davis. — Indianapolis: Sams, 1966. 144 p.

[Badrock 1965] "Aco" / Arthur Badrock and Derek Spruce. — *R.S.V.P.* 2 (June 1965) to 15 (Aug. 1966); 17 (Oct. 1966) to 25 (June 1967); 27 (Aug. 1967) to 31 (Dec. 1967); 34 (Mar. 1968); 35 (Apr. 1968), 40

(Sep. 1968) to 42 (Nov. 1968). Additions and corrections in 43 (Dec. 1968), 47 (Apr. 1969), 52 (Jan.–Feb. 1970).

[Badrock 1976] *Dominion Records: A Catalogue and History* / Arthur Badrock. — Bournemouth, England: Talking Machine Review, 1976. 31 p.

[Badrock 1988] "Unravelling Ariel" / Arthur Badrock. — *TMR* 75 (Autumn 1988): 2,197–2,199.

[Badrock 1991] *The Complete Regal Catalogue* / Arthur Badrock and Frank Andrews. — Malvern, England: City of London Phonograph and Gramophone Society, 1991. 358 p.

[Bahr 1988] *Trombone / Euphonium Discography* / Edward Bahr. —Stevens Point, Wisc.: Index House, 1988. 502 p.

[Bailey 1965] "A Non-resonant Loudspeaker Enclosure" / A. R. Bailey. — *Wireless World*, Oct. 1965: 483–486.

[Baker 1990] *The Sir Harry Lauder Discography* / Darrell Baker and Larry F. Kiner. — Metuchen, N.J.: Scarecrow Press, 1990. 198 p.

[Barnes, H. 1951] "Conchita Supervia" / Harold M. Barnes and Victor Girard. — *RC* 6–3 (Mar. 1951): 51, 54–71; 8–2 (Feb. 1953): 41–44.

[Barnes, H. 1953] "Ninon Vallin" / Harold M. Barnes. — *RC* 8–3 (Mar. 1953): 52–65.

[Barnes, K. 1974] "Record Cleaning" / Ken Barnes. — *APM* 2–10 (Dec. 1974): 3, 8; 3–1 (Jan. 1975): 5–7.

[Barnes, K. 1975] "The Bristophone: An 'L' of a Reproducer" / Ken Barnes. — *APM* 3–3 (Mar. 1975): 3–5.

[Barr 1982] "Gull(s) of My Dreams" / Stephen C. Barr. — *NAG* 39 (Winter 1982): 3–12.

[Barr 1983] "Ring Out Wild Bells! A Study of Bell Records" / Steven C. Barr. — *NAG* 46 (Autumn 1983): 3–7.

[Basart 1985] *The Sound of the Fortepiano; A Discography of Recordings on Early Pianos* / Ann P. Basart. — Berkeley, Calif.: Fallen Leaf Press, 1985. 472 p.

[Batten 1956] *Joe Batten's Book; The Story of Sound Recording* / Joseph Batten; foreword by Compton Mackenzie. — London: Rockliff, 1956. 201 p.

[Bauer, B. 1945] "Tracking Angle in Phonograph Pickups" / Benjamin B. Bauer. — *Electronics* 18 (Mar. 1945): 110–115. Reprinted in Roys 1978.

[Bauer, B. 1963] "Vertical Tracking Improvements in Stereo Recording" / Benjamin B. Bauer. — *Audio*, Feb. 1963: 19–22. Reprinted in Roys 1978.

[Bauer, B. 1971] "A Compatible Stereo-quadraphonic (SQ) Record System" / Benjamin B. Bauer, Daniel W. Gravereaux, and Arthur J. Gust. — *Journal of the Audio Engineering Society* 19–8 (1971): 638–646. Reprinted in Roys 1978.

[Bauer, R. 1947] *The New Catalogue of Historical Records, 1898–1908/09* / Robert Bauer. — 2nd ed. — London: Sidgwick and Jackson, 1947. Foreword signed by Roberto Bauer. (1st ed. 1937.) Reprinted by Sidgwick and Jackson 1970.

[Baumbach 1981] *Look for the Dog; An Illustrated Guide to Victor Talking Machines, 1901–1929* / Robert W. Baumbach. —Woodland Hills, Calif.: Stationery X-Press, 1981. 326 p.

[Bayly 1974/2] "The Decca Portable" / Ernie Bayly. —*TMR* 26 (Feb. 1974): 596–597.

[Bayly 1974/6] "Small Records" / Ernie Bayly. — *TMR* 28 (June 1974): 116–119.

[Bayly 1976] "Double Sided Records" / Ernie Bayly. — *TMR* 38 (Feb. 1976): 596–597.

[Bayly 1976/12] "Zonophone Pseudonyms" / Ernie Bayly. — *TMR* 43 (Dec. 1976): 857–858.

[Bayly 1985] "DeWolf Hopper" / Ernie Bayly. — *TMR* 70 (Dec. 1985): 1,966, 1,979.

[Bayly 1988] "5–inch Berliner" / Ernie Bayly. — *HN* 163 (Aug. 1988): 71.

[Bebb 1972] "The Actor Then and Now" / Richard Bebb. — *Recorded Sound* 47 (July 1972): 85–93; 48 (Oct. 1972): 115–124.

[Bennett, B. 1981] "Capitol, 1942 to 1949 and Beyond" / Bill Bennett. — *RR* 183/184 (July 1981) 11; 185/186 (Oct. 1981): 12; 187/188 (Dec. 1981): 12; 189/190 (Mar.–Apr. 1982): 11; 191/192 (July 1982): 12, 14; 193/194 (Oct. 1982): 10; 197/198 (Mar.–Apr. 1983): 11; 199/200 (June 1983): 13.

[Bennett, B. 1987] "Capitol 15000 Series 78 RPM, Oct. 1947 to Mar. 1949" / Bill Bennett. — *RR* 227/228 (Mar. 1987): 1–2; 229/230 (June 1987): 10; 231/232 (Oct. 1987): 10; 233/234 (Feb. 1988): 9; 239/240 (Apr. 1989): 8; 241/242 (Sep.-Oct. 1989): 24; 243/244 (May–June 1990): 23; 245/246 (Jan. 1991): 23.

[Bennett, J. 1954] "Fonotipia Catalogue" / John R. Bennett. — *Hobbies*, Feb. 1954: 25–27.

[Bennett, J. 1981] *Melodiya; A Soviet Russian L.P. Discography* / John R. Bennett. — Westport, Conn.: Greenwood Press, 1981. 832 p.

[Benson 1987] *Uncle Joe's Record Guide: The Rolling Stones* / Joe Benson. — Glendale, Calif.: J. Benson Unlimited, 1987. 124 p.

[Berger, K. 1974] "The Yale Collection of Historical Sound Recordings" / Karol Berger. — *ARSCJ* 6–1 (1974): 13–25.

[Berger, M. 1982] *Benny Carter; A Life in American Music* / Monroe Berger, Edward Berger, and James Patrick. — Metuchen, N.J.: Scarecrow Press, 1982. 877 p.

[Berliner 1977] "Wags and Tales That Started a Revolution" / Oliver Berliner. *Audio*, Dec. 1977: 36–40.

[Bettini 1898] *Bettini Catalog for June 1898; Bettini Catalog for April 1900; Bettini Catalog for June 1901.* — Stanford, Calif.: Stanford University Archive of Recorded Sound, 1965. (Reprint Series, 1.)

[Betz 1976] "Uncle Josh before Cal Stewart" / Peter Betz. — *TMR* 41 (Aug. 1976): 726–728.

[Betz 1990] "John Kreusi [sic]—The Man Who 'Made This' " / Peter Betz. — *HN* 177 (Dec. 1990): 131–133.

[Bianco 1988] *Heat Wave: The Motown Fact Book* / David Bianco. — Ann Arbor, Mich.: Pierian Press, 1988. 524 p.

[Biel 1982/1] "For the Record" / Michael Biel. — *ARSCJ* 14–1 (1982): 97–113.

[Biel 1982/2] "For the Record" / Michael Biel. — *ARSCJ* 14–3 (1982): 101–111.

[Blacker] Columns entitled "Disco-ing In" by George Blacker in *RR* are usually cited only by year and month.

[Blacker 1973] "How to Play Old Records on New Equipment" / George Blacker. — *High Fidelity*, Apr. 1973: 48–57.

[Blacker 1975] "The Pennsylvania Vertical Group—Preliminary Report" / George Blacker. — *RR* 131 (Jan. 1975): 1, 6; 132 (Apr. 1975): 5–6; 133 (June 1975): 5–6. Considers relationships among vertical-cut labels Domestic, Keen-O-Phone, McKinley, Phono-Cut, Rex, and Rishell.

[Blacker 1975//8] "Playing Oldies the New Way" / George Blacker. — *APM* 3–7 (Aug.-Sep. 1975): 3–6.

[Blacker 1976/5] "The Data Sheet—Again!" / George Blacker. — *RR* 139/140 (May–June 1976): 12.

[Blacker 1978] "Some Pointed Remarks about Styli" / George Blacker. — *RR* 159/160 (Dec. 1978): 2.

[Blacker 1980/1] "Parade of Champions, 1925 to 1930, 1500 to 16133" / George Blacker. — *RR* 169/170 (Jan. 1980): 2–16; 171/172 (Mar. 1980): 6–6; 173/174 (June 1980): 8, 24; 175/176 (Sep. 1980): 12; 179/190 (Feb. 1981): 11.

[Blacker 1980/9] "Further Remarks on Electronic Cylinder Playback" / George Blacker. — *RR* 175/176 (Sep. 1980): 2.

[Blacker 1981] "Some Comments on the Edison Kinetophone Cylinders of 1912" / George Blacker. — *APM* 6–10 (1981): 3–7.

[Blacker 1981/2] "Cylindrography or Cylindrographically Yours" / George Blacker. — *RR* 179/180 (Feb. 1981): 2, 23.

[Blacker 1983] "Little Wonder Records" / George Blacker. — *RR* 197/198 (Mar.–Apr. 1983): 1–2; 199/200 (June 1983): 8; 201/202 (Sep. 1983): 12; 203/204 (Dec. 1983): 7; 205/206 (Mar. 1984): 10–11; 207/208 (June 1984): 10; 209/210 (Oct. 1984): 11; 211/212 (Feb. 1985): 10; 213/214 (May 1985):12; 215/216 (July 1985):10; 217/218 (Oct. 1985): 11; 219/220 (Jan. 1986): 14; 221/222 (Apr. 1986): 12.

[Blacker 1984] "The English Singers and Roycroft Revisited" / George Blacker. — *RR* 209/210 (Oct. 1984): 3–4; 211/212 (Feb. 1985): 4–5, 11.

[Blacker 1989] "Beginning of the Emerson Dynasty" / George Blacker. — *RR* 239/240 (Apr. 1989): 1–2; 241/242 (Oct.–Nov. 1989): 2; 243/244 (May–June 1990): 5; 245/246 (Jan. 1991): 6; 247/248 (Sep. 1991): 6.

[Blacker 1990] "Talk-O-Photo" / George Blacker. — *RR* 243/244 (May–June 1990): 4; 247/248 (Sep. 1991): 5.

[Blackmer 1972] "A Wide Dynamic Range Noise Reduction System" / David E. Blackmer. — *db*, Aug.-Sep. 1972: 54–56.

[Blair 1989] "The Yale Collection of Historical Sound Recordings" / Linda W. Blair. — *ARSCJ* 20–2 (Feb. 1989): 167–176.

[Bloesch 1986] "Artur Schnabel: A Discography" / David Bloesch. — *ARSCJ* 18–1/3 (1986): 33–143.

[Blyth 1979] *Opera on Record* / Alan Blyth. — London: Hutchinson, 1979, 1984. 2 vols.

[Blyth 1986] *Song on Record* / Alan Blyth. — New York: Cambridge University Press, 1986, 1988. 2 vols.

[Bolig 1973] *The Recordings of Enrico Caruso* / John Bolig. — Dover, Delaware: Delaware State Museum, 1973. 88 p.

[Bond 1978] *The Recordings of Jimmie Rodgers; An Annotated Discography* / Johnny Bond. — Los Angeles: John Edwards Memorial Foundation, University of California, 1978. 76 p. (JEMF Special Series, 11.)

[Bondesen 1977] *North American Bird Songs—A World of Music* / Poul Bondesen. — Klampenborg, Denmark: Scandinavian Science Press, 1977. 254 p.

[Boots 1981] *Military Music Holdings at the United States Army Military History Institute* / Robert C. Boots. — Carlisle Barracks, Penn.: U.S. Army Military History Institute, Audio Visual Archives, 1981. 391 p.

[Bordman 1978] *American Musical Theatre* / Gerald Bordman. — New York: Oxford University Press, 1978. 749 p.

[Borwick 1975] "The Diamond Stylus Company" / John Borwick. — *Gramophone*, July 1975: 258.

[Borwick 1976] "Dual Gebrüder Steidinger" / John Borwick. — *Gramophone*, Apr. 1976: 1,693.

[Borwick 1982] *The Gramophone Guide to Hi-Fi* / John Borwick. — London: David & Charles, 1982. 256 p.

[Borwick 1987/1] *Sound Recording Practice* / John Borwick. — 3rd ed. — New York: Oxford University Press, 1987. 557 p. (1st ed. 1976.)

[Borwick 1987/3] "A Music-lover's Guide to CD and Hi-Fi" / John Borwick. — *Gramophone*, Mar.–Aug. 1987. A series of six articles.

[Borwick 1988] *Loudspeaker and Headphone Handbook* / John Borwick. — London: Butterworths, 1988. 573 p.

[Borwick 1989/7.] "The British Library National Sound Archive" / John Borwick. — *Gramophone*, July 1989: 251–252.

[Borwick 1989/10] "JVC, Japan" / John Borwick. — *Gramophone*, Oct. 1989: 787–788.

[Borwick 1990] "Microphone Balance" / John Borwick. — *Gramophone*, May 1990: 2,094.

[Bott 1980] "Riccardo Martin" / Michael F. Bott. — *RC* 26–1/2 (May 1980): 5–42.

[Bridges 1968] *Pioneers in Brass* / Glenn Bridges. — Detroit: Sherwood, 1968. 129 p.

[Brooks, E. 1982] *The Bessie Smith Companion; A Critical and Detailed Appreciation of the Recordings* / Edward Brooks. — New York: Da Capo Press, 1982. 229 p.

[Brooks 1975] "Columbia Acoustic Matrix Series; Preliminary Research" / Tim Brooks. — *RR* 133 (June 1975): 1–8; 134 (Aug. 1975): 3–4; 135/136 (Nov.–Dec. 1975): 8–12.

[Brooks 1977] "Vogue, the Picture Record" / Tim Brooks. — *RR* 148 (July 1977): 1–8; 151/152 (Jan. 1978): 4–10; 153/154 (Apr. 1978): 10; 159/160 (Dec. 1978): 10; 161/162 (Feb.–Mar. 1979): 3.

[Brooks 1978] "Columbia Records in the 1890s: Founding the Record Industry" / Tim Brooks. — *ARSCJ* 10–1 (1978): 5–36.

[Brooks 1979] "A Directory to Columbia Recording Artists of the 1890s" / Tim Brooks. — *ARSCJ* 11–2/3 (1979): 102–138.

[Brooks 1979/1] "Current Bibliography" / Tim Brooks. — *ARSCJ* 10–2/3 (1979)- . Continuing series.

[Brooks 1979/2] "The Artifacts of Recording History: Creators, Users, Losers, Keepers" / Tim Brooks. — *ARSCJ* 11–1 (1979): 18–28.

[Brooks 1983] "ARSC; Association for Recorded Sound Collections—An Unusual Organization" / Tim Brooks. — *Goldmine*, Feb. 1983: 22–23.

[Brooks 1984] "A Survey of Record Collectors' Societies" / Tim Brooks. — *ARSCJ* 16–3 (1984): 17–36.

[Brooks 1990] "One-hit Wonders of the Acoustic Era (... And a Few Beyond)" / Tim Brooks. — *APM* 9–2 (1990): 8–11.

[Brown, A. 1976] "The Kinetophonograph" / Alan Brown. — *TMR* 40 (June 1976): 716–719.

[Brown, D. 1991] *Sarah Vaughan; A Discography* / Denis Brown. — Westport, Conn.: Greenwood Press, 1991. 192 p.

[Brown, S. 1986] *The Life and Music of James P. Johnson* / Scott Brown and Robert Hilbert. — Metuchen, N.J.: Scarecrow Press, 1986. 503 p.

[Brownstein 1990] "One Disc at a Time: Moldy Discs" / Mark Brownstein. — *CD-ROM Enduser*, Feb. 1990: 29.

[Bruun 1962] "A Bibliography of Discographies" / C. L. Bruun and J. Gray. — *Recorded Sound* 1–7 (1962): 206–213.

[Bruyninckx 1980] *60 Years of Recorded Jazz* / Walter Bruyninckx. — Mechelen, Belgium: Author, 1980. 36 vols.

[Bryan 1975] *Oxford and Silvertone Records, 1911–1918* / Martin F. Bryan and William R. Bryant. — St. Johnsbury, Vermont: New Amberola Phonograph Co., 1975. 56 p.

[Bryan 1982] "Columbia BC Half-foot-long Records" / Martin F. Bryan. — *NAG* 41 (Summer 1982): 3–9.

[Bryan 1990] "Orlando R. Marsh, Forgotten Pioneer" / Martin F. Bryan. — *NAG* 71 (Jan. 1990): 3–14. Supplemented in *NAG* 72 (Spring 1990): 3–5.

[Bryant 1962] *Collecting Gramophone Records* / E. T. Bryant. — New York: Focal Press, 1962. Reprint—Westport, Conn.: Greenwood Press, 1978. 153 p.

[Bryant 1985] *Music Librarianship: A Practical Guide* / E. T. Bryant; with the assistance of Guy A. Marco. — 2nd ed. — Metuchen, N.J.: Scarecrow Press, 1985. 449 p. (1st ed. 1959.)

[Bullard 1977] "Lawrence Tibbett" / Thomas R. Bullard and William R. Moran. — *RC* 23–11/12 (Aug. 1977): 242–287; 24–1/2 (Jan. 1978): 36–46.

[Bullock 1986] "A Transmission Line Woofer Model" / Robert M. Bullock, III, and Peter E. Hillman. — Paper read at the 81st Conference of the Audio Engineering Society, Nov. 1986.

[Bunnett 1984] "The British Musical" / Rexton S. Bunnett. — In Hummel 1984, xix-xxvi.

[Burlingame 1944] "Emile Berliner" / Roger Burlingame. —*Dictionary of American Biography*, Supplement 1, 1944, pp. 75–76.

[Burros 1946] "Frida Leider" / Harold Burros. — *RC* 1–5 (Sep. 1946): 50–53. Burros also wrote the discography in *Playing My Part*, by Frida Leider (New York: Da Capo Press, 1978).

[Burt 1977] "Chemical Technology in the Edison Recording Industry" / Leah Burt. — *Journal of the Audio Engineering Society* 25–10/11 (Sep.-Oct. 1977): 712–717.

[Buth 1975] "Scores and Recordings" / Olga Buth. — *Library Trends* 23 (Jan. 1975): 427–450.

[Capes 1956] "Early Pianoforte Records" / S. J. Capes. — *British Institute of Recorded Sound. Bulletin* 3 (Winter 1956): 13–19.

[Carolan 1987] *A Short Discography of Irish Folk Music* / Nicholas Carolan. — Dublin: Folk Music Society of Ireland, 1987. 40 p.

[Carreck 1960] "Early Organ Recordings" / J. N. Carreck. — *HN* 1 (Oct. 1960): 4, 8.

[Carreck 1974] "Obituary: Dr. Ludwig Koch, Sound Recording Pioneer, 1881–1974" / J. N. Carreck. — *HN* 79 (Aug. 1974): 223–224.

[Carter 1965] *Edison Two-minute Cylinder Records: The Complete Catalogue of the Edison Gold Moulded Two-minute Cylinder Records, 1901–12* / Sydney H. Carter. — Abbots Close, Worthing, England: Author, [1965?]. 156 p.

[Carter 1965/1] *Edison Amberol Cylinder Records . . . Foreign Issues, 1908–12* / Sydney H. Carter. — Abbots Close, Worthing, England: Author, [1965?]. 39 p.

[Carter 1975] *Sterling* / Sydney H. Carter, Frank Andrews, and Leonard L. Watts. — Bournemouth, England: Talking Machine Review, 1975. 108 p. Contents: "A Catalogue of Sterling Cylinder Records," by Sydney H. Carter; "A History of Their Manufacture," by Frank Andrews; "Sterling Cylinders on Pathé Discs," by Len Watts.

[Carter 1977] *A Catalogue of Clarion and Ebonoid Records* / Sydney H. Carter. — Bournemouth, England: Talking Machine Review, 1977. 70, 27 p.

[Carter 1977/12] "Air-pressure Operated Amplifying Gramophone" / Sydney H. Carter. — *HN* 94 (Dec. 1977): 98–101.

[Carter 1978] *Blue Amberol Cylinders: A Catalogue* / Sydney H. Carter. — Bournemouth, England: Talking Machine Review, 1978. 130 p.

[Caruso 1990] *Enrico Caruso: My Father and My Family* / Enrico Caruso, Jr., and Andrew Farkas. — Amadeus, Oregon: Amadeus Press, 1990. 850 p. Includes a discography by William R. Moran.

[Castleman 1976] *All Together Now. The First Complete Beatles Discography, 1961–1975* / Harry Castleman and Walter Podrazik. — Ann Arbor, Mich.: Pierian Press, 1976. 387 p. Two supplementary volumes were issued by the same authors and publisher: *The Beatles Again* (1977; 280 p.) and *The End of the Beatles?* (1985; 553 p.).

[Catalogue 1904] *Catalogue of Twelve-inch Monarch Records in March 1904* — London: Gramophone & Typewriter, Ltd., 1904. Reprint—Bournemouth, England: E. Bayly, 1972. 35 p.

[Catalogue 1971] *Catalogue of Nicole Records, Season 1905–1906.*—London: Nicole, 1905. Reprint—Bournemouth, England: Talking Machine Review, 1971. 25 p.

[Celletti 1964] *Le grandi voci* / Rodolfo Celletti. — Rome: Istituto per la Collaborazione Culturale, 1964. 1,044 columns.

[Chambers 1985] *Urban Rhythms: Pop Music and Popular Culture* / Iain Chambers. — London: Macmillan, 1985. 272 p.

[Charters 1960] "Sears Roebuck Sells the Country Blues" / Samuel B. Charters. — *RR* 27 (Mar.–Apr. 1960): 3, 20.

[Chew 1981] *Talking Machines* / V. K. Chew. — 2nd ed. — London: Her Majesty's Stationery Office, 1981. 80 p. (1st ed. 1967.)

[Chew 1982] "Disc Tinfoil Phonograph" / V. K. Chew. — *HN* 124 (Feb. 1982): 328–329.

[Clough 1952] *The World's Encyclopedia of Recorded Music* / Francis F. Clough and G. J. Cuming. — London: Sidgwick & Jackson, 1952. 890 p. First Supplement (Apr. 1950–May/June 1951) bound in. Second Supplement (1951–1952), 1952. 262 p. Third Supplement (1953–1955), 1957. 564 p. Reprint—Westport, Conn. : Greenwood Press, 1970. 3 vols. Usually cited as WERM.

[Clough 1964] "Discography" / Francis F. Clough and G. J. Cuming. — In *Minor Recollections*, by Otto Klemperer, translated from the German by J. Maxwell Brownjohn (London: Dobson, 1964; 124 p.), pp. 103–117.

[Clough 1966] "Myra Hess Discography" / Francis F. Clough and G. J. Cuming. — *Recorded Sound* 24 (Oct. 1966): 104–106.

[Cohen 1968] *Hi-Fi Loudspeakers and Enclosures* / Abraham B. Cohen.— 2nd ed. — Rochelle Park, N.J.: Hayden Book Co., 1968. 438 p.

[Cole 1970] "The Aeolian Company" / Roger Cole. — *HN* 57 (Oct. 1970): 161–165.

[Collier 1983] *Louis Armstrong, An American Genius* / James Lincoln Collier. — New York: Oxford University Press, 1983. 383 p.

[Collins 1979] "Giovanni Martinelli" / William J. Collins and James F. E. Dennis. — *RC* 25–7/8/9 (Oct. 1979): 149–215; 25–10/11/12 (Feb. 1980): 221–255; 26–9/10 (May 1981): 237–239.

[Connor 1988] *Benny Goodman: Listen to His Legacy* / D. Russell Connor. — Metuchen, N.J.: Scarecrow Press, 1988. 409 p.

[Cooper, D. 1975] *International Bibliography of Discographies: Classical Music, and Jazz and Blues, 1962–1972* / David E. Cooper. — Littleton, Colo.: Libraries Unlimited, 1975. 272 p.

[Cooper, R. 1980] "Independent Record Companies" / Reg Cooper. — *TMR* 62 (1980): 1,669–1,671.

[Copeland, G. 1990] "Understanding the Edison Reproducer" / George A. Copeland. — *NAG* 73 (July 1990): 10–14.

[Copeland, P. 1990] "Playback" / Peter C. Copeland.—*HN* 172 (Feb. 1990): 336. Comments on this article were made in a letter to *HN* 174 (June 1990): 52.

[Corenthal 1984] *Cohen on the Telephone; A History of Jewish Recorded Humor and Popular Music, 1892–1942* / Michael G. Corenthal. — Milwaukee, Wisc.: Yesterday's Memories, 1984. 108 p.

[Corenthal 1986] *Iconography of Recorded Sound, 1886–1986* / Michael G. Corenthal. — Milwaukee, Wisc.: Yesterday's Memories, 1986. 243 p.

[Cott 1984] *Conversations with Glenn Gould* / Jonathan Cott. — Boston: Little, Brown, 1984. Discography pp. 139–150.

[Cotter 1972] "Flexo, San Francisco's Obscure Record Company" / Dave Cotter. — *RR* 118 (Oct. 1972): 1, 4–7.

[Cotter 1975] "National Music Lovers" / Dave Cotter. — *NAG* 1–25 (Fall 1975–Apr. 1988). Series of brief articles.

[Creighton 1974] *Discopaedia of the Violin, 1889–1971* / James Creighton. — Toronto: University of Toronto Press, 1974. 987 p.

[Cros 1877] "Comptes rendus des séances de l'Académie des Sciences . . . 3 decembre 1877" / Charles Cros.—Paper deposited with the Académie on 30 Apr. 1877.

[Croucher 1981] *Early Music Discography: From Plainsong to the Sons of Bach* / Trevor Croucher — Phoenix, Ariz.: Oryx, 1981. 2 vols.

[Crowhurst 1960] *The Stereo High Fidelity Handbook* / Norman Crowhurst. — New York: Crown, 1960. 183 p.

[Crutchfield 1986] "Brahms by Those Who Knew Him" / Will Crutchfield. — *Opus* 2–5 (Aug. 1956): 12–21, 60.

[Culshaw 1967] *Ring Resounding; The Recording in Stereo of Der Ring des Nibelungen* / John Culshaw. — London: Secker & Warburg, 1967. 284 p.

[Culshaw 1976] *Reflections on Wagner's Ring* / John Culshaw. — London: Secker & Warburg, 1976. 105 p.

[Culshaw 1981] *Putting the Record Straight* / John Culshaw. — New York: Viking, 1981. 362 p.

[Curry 1990] *Vogue: The Picture Record* / Edgar L. Curry. — Everett, Wash.: Author, 1990. 92 p.

[Cuscuna 1988] *The Blue Note Label: A Discography* / Michael Cuscuna and Michel Ruppli. — Westport, Conn.: Greenwood Press, 1988. 544 p.

[Czada 1983] "Tefifon" / Peter Czada and Frans Jansen. — *HN* 130 (Feb. 1983): 169–171.

[Dales 1980] "Edison Dictation Cylinders" / J. S. Dales. — *TMR* 62 (1980): 1,675.

[Danca 1978] *Bunny Berigan: A Bio-discography* / Vince Danca. — Rockford, Ill. : Author, 1978. 66 p.

[D'Andrea 1981] *Tito Schipa nella vita, nell'arte, nel suo tempo* / Renzo D'Andrea. — Fasano di Puglia, Italy: Schena, 1981. 246 p. Discography by Daniele Rubboli, pp. 225–240.

[Dangarfield 1991] "Nina Koshetz" / Jim Dangarfield. — *Sound Record* 7–4 (June 1991): 154–155.

[Daniels 1985] *The American 45 and 78 RPM Record Dating Guide, 1940–1959* / William R. Daniels. — Westport, Conn.: Greenwood Press, 1985. 157 p.

[Dannen 1990] *Hit Men: Power Brokers and Fast Money inside the Music Business* / Frederick Dannen. — New York: Times Books, 1990. 387 p.

[Darrell 1936] *The Gramophone Shop Encyclopedia of Recorded Music* / Ed. Robert H. Reid. — New York: Crown, 1948. —3rd ed. — 639 p. Reprint— Westport, Conn.: Greenwood Press, 1970. (1st ed., compiled by R. D. Darrell, New York: Gramophone Shop, 1936.) 574 p.

[Davies 1953] *The Music of Fats Waller* / John R. T. Davies and Roy Cooke. — 2nd ed. — London: Century Press, 1953. 40 p. (1st ed. 1950.)

[Davies 1968] *Morton's Music* / John R. T. Davies and Laurie Wright. — 2nd ed. — Chigwell, Essex, England: Storyville Publications, 1968. 40 p.

[Davis 1958] "The Westrex Stereo Disk System" / C. C. Davis and J. G. Frayne. — *IRE Proceedings* 46 (1958): 1,685–1,693. Reprinted in Roys 1978.

[Davis, C. K. 1960] "Record Collections, 1960; LJ's Survey of Fact and Opinion" / Chester K. Davis. — *Library Journal* 85 (1 Oct. 1960): 3,375–3,380.

[Davis, L. 1983] *A Paul Robeson Research Guide; A Selected, Annotated Bibliography* / Lenwood G. Davis. — Westport, Conn.: Greenwood Press, 1983. 879 p. Discography, pp. 771–795.

[Day 1989] "Where's the Rot?" / Rebecca Day. — *Stereo Review* 54–4 (Apr. 1989): 23–24.

[Deakins 1960] *Comprehensive Cylinder Record Index* / Duane D. Deakins. — Stockton, Calif. [varies]: Author, 1956–1961. Five parts in one volume. Contents in Rust 1980, p. 92.

[Dearling 1984] *The Guinness Book of Recorded Sound* / Robert Dearling and Celia Dearling; with assistance of Brian Rust. — Enfield, Middlesex, England: Guinness Books, 1984. 225 p.

[Debenham 1988] *Laughter on Record: A Comedy Discography* / Warren Debenham. — Metuchen, N.J.: Scarecrow Press, 1988. 387 p.

[Debus 1987] "Bert Williams on Record" / Allen Debus. — *HN* 154 (Feb. 1987): 154–157.

[De Cock 1957] "Maurice Renaud" / Alfred De Cock. — *RC* 11–4/5 (Apr.–May 1957): 74–119; 11–7 (July 1957): 166–167; 12–1/2 (Jan.–Feb. 1958): 37.

[Delalande 1984] "The Busch Brothers—A Discography" / Jacques Delalande and Tully Potter. — *Recorded Sound* 86 (1984): 29–90.

[Delaunay 1936] *New Hot Discography* / Charles Delaunay and George Avakian. — 4th ed. — New York: Criterion Books, 1948. 608 p. (1st ed., *Hot Discography*, Paris: Hot Club de France, 1936.)

[De Lerma 1969] "Philosophy and Practice of Phonorecord Classification at Indiana University" / Dominique René De Lerma. — *Library Resources and Technical Services* 13 (Winter 1969): 86–98.

[Denisoff 1975] *Solid Gold; The Popular Record Industry* / R. Serge Denisoff. — New Brunswick, N.J.: Transaction Books, 1975. 504 p.

[Denisoff 1986] *Tarnished Gold; The Record Industry Revisited* / R. Serge Denisoff. — New Brunswick, N.J.: Transaction Books, 1986. 487 p.

[Dennis 1946] "Dating by Labels" / James F. E. Dennis. — *RC* 1 (Aug. 1946): 22–23.

[Dennis 1950/1] "Jean De Reszke" / James F. E. Dennis. — *RC* 5–1 (Jan. 1950): 3, 6–11.

[Dennis 1950/2] "Ernest Van Dyck" / James F. E. Dennis. — *RC* 5–2 (Feb. 1950): 27–32.

Dennis 1950/10] "Sigrid Onegin" / James F. E. Dennis. — *RC* 5–10 (Oct. 1950): 223–231; 5–12 (Dec. 1950): 280–281; 12–8/9 (Nov. 1959): 200.

[Dennis 1951/5] "Edouard De Reszke" / James F. E. Dennis. — *RC* 6–5 (May 1951): 99–106.

[Dennis 1951/9] "Lillian Nordica" / James F. E. Dennis. — *RC* 6–9 (Sep. 1951): 195–206.

[Dennis 1952] "Kirsten Flagstad" / James F. E. Dennis. — *RC* 7–8 (Aug. 1952): 172–190.

[Dennis 1953/11] "Mattia Battistini" / James F. E. Dennis. — *RC* 8–11/12 (Nov.–Dec. 1953): 244–265.

[Dennis 1971] "Friedrich Schorr" / James F. E. Dennis, Alfred Frankenstein, and Boris Semeonoff. — *RC* 19–11/12 (Apr. 1971): 243–284; 20–3 (Oct. 1971): 71.

[Dennis 1976] "Helge Rosvaenge" / James F. E. Dennis. — *RC* 23–5/6 (Sep. 1976): 99, 140; 25–5/6 (Aug. 1979): 120–122.

[Dennis 1981/2] "Lili Lehmann" / James F. E. Dennis and John Stratton. — *RC* 26–7/8 (Feb. 1981): 150–190; 26–9/10 (May 1981): 199–214.

[Dennis, P. 1981] "Jacques Urlus" / Pamela Dennis and James F. E. Dennis. — *RC* 26–11/12 (Sep. 1981).

[Dethlefson 1980] *Edison Blue Amberol Recordings* / Ronald Dethlefson. — Brooklyn: APM Press, 1980–1981. 2 vols.

[Dethlefson 1983] "Dubbing De-Mystified" / Ronald Dethlefson. — *APM* 7–2 (1983): 3–5.

[Dethlefson 1985] *Edison Disc Artists and Records, 1910–1929* / Ronald Dethlefson and Raymond R. Wile. — Brooklyn: APM Press, 1985. 177 p. Revised edition entered at Wile 1990/4.

[De Veaux 1988] "Bebop and the Recording Industry: The 1942 AFM Recording Ban Reconsidered" / Scott De Veaux. — *Journal of the American Musicological Society* 51–1 (Spring 1988): 126–165.

[Dezettel 1968] *Record Changers: How They Work* / Louis M. Dezettel. — Indianapolis: Sams, 1968. 144 p.

[Di Cave 1973] "Lina Pagliughi" / Luciano Di Cave. — *RC* 21–5/6 (Oct. 1973): 99–125.

[Dickason 1987] *The Loudspeaker Design Cookbook.* / Vance Dickason — 3rd ed. — Marshall Jones Co., 1987. 75 p.

[Directory 1982] *Directory of Member Archives* / Compiled by Grace Koch. — 2nd ed. — Milton Keynes, England: International Association of Sound Archives, 1982. 174 p. (1st ed. 1978.)

[Directory 1985] *Directory of Australian Music Organizations* / Compiled by Bill Flemming. — Rev. ed. — Sydney: Australia Music Center, 1985. 67p. (1st ed. 1978.)

[Directory 1989] *Directory of Recorded Sound Resources in the United Kingdom* / Compiled and edited by Lali Weerasinghe. — London: British Library, 1989. 173 p.

[Dixon 1970] *Recording the Blues* / Robert M. W. Dixon and John Godrich. — London: Studio Vista, 1970. 85 p.

[Docks 1980] *American Premium Record Guide* / L. R. Docks. — Florence, Ala.: Books Americana, 1980. 737 p. Includes 500 label illustrations.

[Doran 1985] *Erroll Garner: The Most Happy Piano* / James M. Doran. — Metuchen, N.J.: Scarecrow Press, 1985. 500 p.

[Dorgeuille 1986] *The French Flute School, 1860–1950* / Claude Dorgeuille. — 2nd ed. — London: Tony Bingham, 1986. 138 p.

[Drummond 1969] "The Seven Zonophone Records" / H. J. Drummond. — *Gramophone*, Sep. 1969: 140–143.

[Dubal 1989] *The Art of the Piano* / David Dubal. — New York: Summit Books, 1989. 476 p.

[Duckenfield 1990] "Sir Landon Ronald and the Gramophone" / Bridget Duckenfield. — *HN* 177 (Dec. 1990): 139–142.

[Duckles 1955] "Musical Scores and Recordings" / Vincent Duckles. — *Library Trends* 4 (1955/1956): 164–173.

[Dyment 1977] "The Recordings of Karl Muck; Some Unresolved Problems" / Christopher Dyment. — *ARSCJ* 9–1 (1977): 66–68. Followed by a discography by Dyment and Jim Cartwright, pp. 69–77.

[Dyment 1986] "Misunderstanding Toscanini" / Christopher Dyment. — *ARSCJ* 18–1/3 (1986): 144–171a.

[Eargle 1977] "Loudspeakers" / John E. Eargle. — *Journal of the Audio Engineering Society* 10–11 (1977): 685–688.

[Edison 1893] *Edison Phonograph.* — New York: North American Phonograph Co., 1893. Unpaged. Reprint—Brooklyn: Allen Koenigsberg, 1974.

[Edison 1906] *Edison Coin-slot Phonographs.* — Orange, N.J.: National Phonograph Co., 1906. 20 p. Reprint—Brooklyn: Allen Koenigsberg, 1974.

[Edison 1987] *Edison, Musicians, and the Phonograph* / Ed. and with an introduction by John Harvith and Susan Edwards Harvith. — Westport, Conn.: Greenwood Press, 1987. 478 p.

[Edwards 1965] *Big Bands Discography* / Ernie Edwards, George Hall, and Bill Korst. — Whittier, Calif.: Erngeobil, 1965–1969. 7 vols. Contents in Cooper 1975.

[Einstein 1968] "Zinka Milanov: A Complete Discography" / Edwin K. Einstein, Jr. — *Le grand baton,* May 1968: 7–16.

[Eke 1946] "Alma Gluck" / Bernard T. Eke. — *RC* 1–8 (Dec. 1946): 81–88; 6–2 (Feb. 1951): 27, 33–45; 6–3 (Mar. 1951): 53.

[Elste 1977] "100 Jahre Schallaufzeichnung; eine Chronologie" / Martin R. O. Elste. — *Fonoforum* 5 (May 1977): 434–447.

[Enderman 1989] "Original Dixieland Jazz Band and Its Recreations" / Hans Enderman. — *Micrography* 77 (May 1989): 4–10.

[Englund 1967] *Durium / Hit of the Week* / Björn Englund. — Stockholm: Nationalfonotekets, 1967. 14 p.

[Englund 1970] "Scandinavian Record Labels, No. 2: Grand" / Björn Englund. — *TMR* 4 (June 1970): 101.

[Englund 1971] "Sixty-five Years of Deutsche Grammophon Gesellschaft, 1898–1963" / Björn Englund. — *HN* 63 (Oct. 1971): 49–59. Condensed translation of a booklet issued by DGG in 1963.

[Evans 1989] "A Hot Performer" / H. Evans. — *HN* 168 (June 1989): 214–215. Describes the hot air motor of 1910.

[Evans, R. 1979] "More for Less" / Roy Evans. — *RR* 165/166 (Aug. 1979): 14; 167/168 (Oct. 1979): 14.

[Evensmo 1976] *The Guitars of Charlie Christian, Robert Normann, Oscar Aleman* / Jan Evensmo. — Hosle, Norway: Author, [1976]. [52 p.]

[Evensmo 1978] *The Tenor Saxophone of Ben Webster, 1931–1943* / Jan Evensmo. — Hosle, Norway: Author, 1978. 50 p.

[Fabrizio 1973] "Disc Records of the Talking Machine Companies of Chicago" / T. C. Fabrizio. — *TMR* 20/21 (Feb.–Apr. 1973): 118–120.

[Fabrizio 1976] "Survey of American Talking Machines Employing Unusual Methods of Reproduction" / T. C. Fabrizio. — *TMR* 42 (Oct. 1976): 787–791.

[Fabrizio 1977] "The Chicago Companies" / T. C. Fabrizio. — *TMR* 48 (1977): 1,085–1,089.

[Fabrizio 1979] "The Twilight of the O'Neill-James and Aretino Companies of Chicago, 1910–1914" / T. C. Fabrizio. — *TMR* 56/57 (Feb.–Apr. 1979): 1,480–1,481.

[Fabrizio 1980] "The Disc Records of Turn-of-the-century Chicago and the Companies Which Sold Them" / T. C. Fabrizio. — *ARSCJ* 12–1/2 (1980): 18–25.

[Fagan 1981] "Pre-LP Recordings of RCA at 33 1/3 RPM 1931 to 1934" / Ted Fagan. — *ARSCJ* 13–1 (1981): 20–42; 14–3 (1982): 41–61; 15–1 (1983): 25–68.

[Fagan 1983] *The Encyclopedic Discography of Victor Recordings* / Ted Fagan and William R. Moran. — Westport, Conn.: Greenwood Press, 1983, 1986. 2 vols. Vol. 1 includes a reprint of Aldridge 1964.

[Farkas 1985] *Opera and Concert Singers: An Annotated International Bibliography of Books and Pamphlets* / Andrew Farkas. — New York: Garland, 1985. 363 p. Includes comments by William R. Moran on the discographical components of many biographies.

[Farmer 1967] "The Reproducing Piano" / John Farmer. — *Recorded Sound* 25 (Jan. 1967): 131–134; 26 (Apr. 1967): 172–180; 28 (Oct. 1967): 249–254.

[Favia-Artsay 1949] "Amelita Galli-Curci" / Aida Favia-Artsay and Gordon Whelan. — *RC* 4–10 (Oct. 1949): 162–179.

[Favia-Artsay 1951] "Frances Alda" / Aida Favia-Artsay. — *RC* 6–10 (Oct. 1951): 219–233.

[Favia-Artsay 1952] "Francesco Tamagno" / Aida Favia-Artsay and John Freestone. — *RC* 7–2 (Feb. 1952): 26, 29–39.

[Favia-Artsay 1955/2] "The Speeds of DeLuca's Acoustical Victors" / Aida Favia-Artsay.—*Hobbies*, Feb. 1955: 24–25.

[Favia-Artsay 1955/12] "Bettini Catalogs" / Aida Favia-Artsay. —*Hobbies*, Dec. 1955: 26–27; Feb. 1956: 28–31; Mar. 1956: 26–29, 35. Contents of Bettini catalogs of May 1897, June 1898, and 1899.

[Favia-Artsay 1965] *Caruso on Records: Pitch, Speed, and Comments* / Aida Favia-Artsay. — Valhalla, N.Y.: The Historic Record, 1965. 218 p.

[Federal 1984] *Federal Cylinder Project* / U. S. Library of Congress. — Washington: Government Printing Office, 1984. Vols. 1–3, 5, 8. Vol. 8 includes a list of 101 cylinders made at the World's Columbian Exposition, Chicago, 1893.

[Feinstein 1985] "Caruso and Bettini: The Eternal Youths" / Robert Feinstein — *APM* 8–2 (1985): 5.

[Fellers 1978] *Discographies of Commercial Recordings of the Cleveland Orchestra (1924–1977) and the Cincinnati Symphony Orchestra (1917–1977)* / Frederick P. Fellers and Betty Meyers. — Westport, Conn.: Greenwood Press, 1978. 224 p.

[Fellers 1984] *The Metropolitan Opera on Record: A Discography of the Commercial Recordings* / Frederick P. Fellers. — Westport, Conn.: Greenwood Press, 1984. 101 p.

[Fenton 1971] "Where Have All the Big Bands Gone?" / Alasdair Fenton. — *TMR* 11 (Aug. 1971): 67–70.

[Ferrara 1975] "The Legacy of Early Recordings by Pupils of Liszt" / D. E. Ferrara. — *Piano Quarterly* 23 (1975): 42–44.

[Ferrara 1988/1] "Virginia Rea (A.K.A. Olive Palmer)" / D. E. Ferrara. — *NAG* 63 (Jan. 1988): 10–11.

[Ferrara 1988/7] "A Spalding Centenary" / D. E. Ferrara. — *NAG* 65 (July 1988): 12–15.

[Ferrara 1991/7] "Charles W. Harrison; An Edison Retrospect" / Dennis E. Ferrara. — *NAG* 77 (July 1991): 4–6.

[Fewkes 1890/1] "A Contribution to Passamaquoddy Folk-lore" / Jesse W. Fewkes. — *Journal of American Folklore* 3 (1890): 257–280.

[Fewkes 1890/2] "On the Use of the Phonograph among Zuni Indians" / Jesse W. Fewkes. — *American Naturalist* 24 (1890): 687–691.

[Field 1988] "The Bell-Tainter Graphophone" / Mike Field. — *HN* 161 (Apr. 1988): 12–15.

[Fitterling 1987] *Thelonious Monk: sein Leben, seine Musik, seine Schallplatten* / Thomas Fitterling. — Waakirchen, Germany: OREOS, 1987. 175 p.

[Flower 1972] *Moonlight Serenade: A Bio-discography of the Glenn Miller Civilian Band* / John Flower. — New Rochelle, N.Y.: Arlington House, 1972. 554 p.

[Foerster 1987] *Elvis Just for You: A Special Goldmine Anthology* / Edited by Try Foerster.—Iola, Wisc.: Krause Publications, 1987.

[Foote 1970] "The Labels of the U.S. Black and Silver Columbia Records of 1902–1908" / Robert Foote. — *TMR* 4 (June 1970): 97–99.

[Ford 1962] "History of Sound Recording" / Peter Ford. —*Recorded Sound* 1–7 (Summer 1962): 221–229, "The Age of Empiricism"; 1–8 (Autumn 1962): 266–276, "The Evolution of the Microphone, and Electrical Disc Recording"; 1–10/11 (Apr.–July 1963): 115–223, "The Evolution of Magnetic Recording"; 1–12 (Oct. 1963): 146–154, "Motion Picture and Television Sound Recording"; 2–1 (Jan. 1964): 181–188, "Evolution of Stereophonic Sound Techniques."

[Foreman 1974] *Systematic Discography* / Lewis Foreman. — Hamden, Conn.: Linnet Books, 1974. 144 p.

[Francis 1989] "The Gilbert & Sullivan Operettas on 78s" / John W. N. Francis. — *ARSCJ* 20–1 (Spring 1989): 24–81.

[Frankenstein 1972] "Maria Ivoguen" / Alfred Frankenstein, D. Brew, Tom Kaufman, and James F. E. Dennis. — *RC* 20–5 (Jan. 1972): 98–119; 20–12 (Dec. 1972): 283–284.

[Frankenstein 1974] "Alexander Kipnis" / Alfred Frankenstein and James F. E. Dennis. — *RC* 22–3/4 (July 1974): 51–79; 23–7/8 (Dec. 1976): 166–171.

[Frankenstein 1978] "Kerstin Thorberg" / Alfred Frankenstein and Carl Bruun. — *RC* 24–9/10 (Oct. 1978): 196–215.

[Frankenstein 1979] "Jarmila Novotna" / Alfred Frankenstein and James F. E. Dennis. — *RC* 25–5/6 (Aug. 1979): 101–140.

[Frederick 1932] "Recent Fundamental Advances in Mechanical Records on 'Wax'" / H. A. Frederick. — *Society of Motion Picture Engineers Journal* 18 (Feb. 1932): 141–152. Reprinted in Roys 1978.

[Frow 1970] "Some Notes on the World Record, and Its Inventor Noel Pemberton Billing" / George Frow. — *HN* 54 (Apr. 1970): 69–71.

[Frow 1978] *Edison Cylinder Phonographs, 1877–1929* / George L. Frow and Al Sefl. — West Orange, N.J.: Edison National Historical Site, 1978. 207 p.

[Frow 1982] *The Edison Disc Phonographs and the Diamond Discs: A History with Illustrations* / George L. Frow. — Sevenoaks, England: Author, 1982. 286 p.

[Gaeddert 1977] *The Classification and Cataloging of Sound Recordings: An Annotated Bibliography* / Barbara Knisely Gaeddert. — Ann Arbor, Mich.: Music Library Association, 1977. 32 p.

[Gaisberg 1943] *The Music Goes Round* / Frederick W. Gaisberg. — New York: Macmillan, 1943. 273 p. British edition titled *Music on Record*.

[Galo 1982] "Transmission Line Loudspeakers. Part I: Theory" / Gary Galo. — *Speaker Builder*, Feb. 1982: 7–9.

[Galo 1984] "Caruso: The 'Unpublished' Recordings of ARM4–0302 and the Question of Authenticity" / Gary Galo. — *APM* 7–9 (1984): 6–8.

[Galo 1990] Review of "The Bayer Complete Caruso" [sound recording] / Gary Galo. — *ARSCJ* 21–2 (1990): 283–289.

[Galo 1991] Review of *The Complete Caruso* and *The Caruso Edition, I, II*" [sound recordings] / Gary Galo. — *ARSCJ* 22–1 (Spring 1991): 118–125.

[Gambaccini 1976] *Paul McCartney in His Own Words* / Paul Gambaccini. — New York: Flash Books, 1976. 111 p.

[Garlick 1977] "The Graphic Arts and the Record Industry" / Lewis Garlick. — *Journal of the Audio Engineering Society* 25–10/11 (Sep.-Oct. 1977): 779–784.

[Garrod 1984] *Charlie Barnet and His Orchestra* / Charles Garrod and Bill Korst. — Zephyrhills, Fla.: Joyce Record Club, 1984. 79 p.

[Garrod 1984/1] *Larry Clinton and His Orchestra* / Charles Garrod. — Zephyrhills, Fla.: Joyce Record Club, 1984. 30 p.

[Garrod 1984/2] *Stan Kenton and His Orchestra (1940–1951)* / Charles Garrod. — Zephyrhills, Fla.: Joyce Record Club, 1984. 64 p.

[Garrod 1984/3] *Stan Kenton and His Orchestra (1952–1959)* / Charles Garrod. — Zephyrhills, Fla.: Joyce Record Club, 1984. 64 p.

[Garrod 1984/4] *Gene Krupa and His Orchestra (1935–1946)* / Charles Garrod and Bill Korst. — Zephyrhills, Fla.: Joyce Record Club, 1984. 51 p.

[Garrod 1984/5] *Gene Krupa and His Orchestra (1947–1973)* / Charles Garrod and Bill Korst. — Zephyrhills, Fla.: Joyce Record Club, 1984. 63 p.

[Garrod 1985] *Claude Thornhill and His Orchestra* / Charles Garrod. — Zephyrhills, Fla.: Joyce Record Club, 1985. 35 p.

[Garrod 1985/1] *Woody Herman, Vol. 1 (1936–1947)* / Charles Garrod. — Zephyrhills, Fla.: Joyce Record Club, 1985. 60 p.

[Garrod 1985/2] *Harry James and His Orchestra (1937–1945)* / Charles Garrod. — Zephyrhills, Fla.: Joyce Record Club, 1985. 66 p.

[Garrod 1985/3] *Harry James and His Orchestra (1946–1954)* / Charles Garrod. — Zephyrhills, Fla.: Joyce Record Club, 1985. 70 p.

[Garrod 1985/4] *Harry James and His Orchestra (1955–1982)* / Charles Garrod. — Zephyrhills, Fla.: Joyce Record Club, 1985. 65 p.

[Garrod 1986] *Woody Herman, Vol. 2 (1948–1957)* / Charles Garrod. — Zephyrhills, Fla.: Joyce Record Club, 1986. 64 p.

[Garrod 1986/2] *Kay Kyser and His Orchestra* / Charles Garrod and Bill Korst. — Zephyrhills, Fla.: Joyce Record Club, 1986. 51 p.

[Garrod 1986/3] *Artie Shaw and His Orchestra* / Charles Garrod and Bill Korst. — Zephyrhills, Fla.: Joyce Record Club, 1986. 64 p.

[Garrod 1986/4] *Charlie Spivak and His Orchestra* / Charles Garrod. — Zephyrhills, Fla.: Joyce Record Club, 1986. 38 p.

[Garrod 1987] *Nat King Cole: His Voice and Piano* / Charles Garrod and Bill Korst. —Zephyrhills, Fla.: Joyce Record Club, 1987. 70 p.

[Garrod 1987/1] *Bob Crosby and His Orchestra* / Charles Garrod and Bill Korst. — Zephyrhills, Fla.: Joyce Record Club, 1987. 59 p.

[Garrod 1987/2] *Glen Gray and the Casa Loma Orchestra* / Charles Garrod and Bill Korst. — Zephyrhills, Fla.: Joyce Record Club, 1987. 45 p.

[Garrod 1988] *Jimmy Dorsey and His Orchestra* / Charles Garrod. — Rev. ed. — Zephyrhills, Fla.: Joyce Record Club, 1988. 65 p.

[Garrod 1988/1] *Tommy Dorsey and His Orchestra (1928–1945)* / Charles Garrod. — Rev. ed. — Zephyrhills, Fla.: Joyce Record Club, 1988. 93 p.

[Garrod 1988/3] *Tommy Dorsey and His Orchestra (1946–1956)* / Charles Garrod. — Rev. ed. — Zephyrhills, Fla.: Joyce Record Club, 1988. 80 p.

[Garrod 1988/4] *Woody Herman, Vol. 3 (1958–1987)* / Charles Garrod. — Zephyrhills, Fla.: Joyce Record Club, 1988. 57 p.

[Garrod 1988/5] *Dick Jurgens and His Orchestra* / Charles Garrod. —Zephyrhills, Fla.: Joyce Record Club, 1988. 35 p.

[Garrod 1988/6] *Sammy Kaye and His Orchestra* / Charles Garrod. —Zephyrhills, Fla.: Joyce Record Club, 1988. 71 p.

[Garrod 1989] *Eddy Duchin and His Orchestra* / Charles Garrod. — Zephyrhills, Fla.: Joyce Record Club, 1989. 28 p.

[Garrod 1989/1] *Shep Fields and His Orchestra* / Charles Garrod. — Zephyrhills, Fla.: Joyce Record Club, 1989. 36 p.

[Garrod 1989/2] *Spike Jones and the City Slickers* / Charles Garrod. —Zephyrhills, Fla.: Joyce Record Club, 1989. 39 p.

[**Gart 1989**] *ARLD; The American Record Label Directory and Dating Guide, 1940–1959* / Galen Gart. — Milford, N.H.: Big Nickel Publications, 1989. 259 p.

[Geduld 1975] *The Birth of the Talkies: From Edison to Jolson* / Harry M. Geduld. —Bloomington, Ind.: Indiana University Press, 1975. 337 p.

[**Gelatt 1977**] *The Fabulous Phonograph, 1877–1977* / Roland Gelatt. —2nd rev. ed. [i.e. 3rd ed.] — New York: Macmillan, 1977. 349 p. (1st ed. 1955.)

[Geller 1983] *Care and Handling of Computer Magnetic Storage Media* / Sidney B. Geller. —Washington: National Bureau of Standards, 1983. 128 p. — (NBS Special Publication, 500–101; SuDoc #C 13.10:500–101).

[Gibson 1991] "Preservation and Conservation of Sound Recordings" / by Gerald Gibson. — In *Conserving and Preserving Library Materials in Nonbook Formats*, edited by Kathryn Luther Henderson and William T. Henderson (Urbana, Ill.: University of Illinois, Graduate School of Library and Information Science, 1991), pp. 27–44. (Allerton Park Institute, 30.)

[Giese 1990] *Art Blakey: sein Leben, seine Musik, seine Schallplatten* / Hannes Giese. — Schaftlach, Germany: OREOS, 1990. 217 p.

[Ginell 1989] *The Decca Hillbilly Discography, 1927–1945* / Gary Ginell. —Westport, Conn.: Greenwood Press, 1989. 402 p.

[**Girard 1964**] *Vertical Cut Cylinders and Discs: A Catalogue of All "Hill-and-dale" Recordings of Serious Worth Made and Issued between 1887–1932 Circa* / Victor Girard and Harold M. Barnes. — London: British Institute of Recorded Sound, 1964. 196 p.

[Goddard 1989] "The Beatles Sessions, CDs, VHS and FDS" / Steve Goddard. — *Discoveries* 2–3 (Mar. 1989): 34–35.

[Godrich 1969] *Blues and Gospel Records, 1902–1942* / John Godrich and Robert M. W. Dixon. — Rev. ed. — London: Storyville Publications, 1969. 912 p. Additions and corrections by Carl Kendziora appeared in issues of *RR* from 86 (Sep. 1967).

[Goldmark 1949] "The Columbia Long-playing Microgroove Recording System" / Peter C. Goldmark, Rene Snepvangers, and William S. Bachman. — *IRE Proceedings* 37–8 (1949): 923–927. Reprinted in Roys 1978.

[Goslin 1983] "Revolving Thoughts" / John G. Goslin. — *TMR* 65–2 (1983): 1,778.

[Gottlieb 1972] "Waring's Pennsylvanians" / R. E. M. Gottlieb. —*RR* 116 (May 1972): 3–8; 119/120 (Dec. 1972–Jan. 1973): 8–9; 121 (Mar. 1973): 8–9; 122 (June 1973): 4–5.

[Grable 1979] "Mr. Edison's Right Hand Man: Ernest L. Stevens" / Ronald J. Grable. —*RR* 161/162 (Feb.–Mar. 1979): 4–5; 163/164 (May–June 1979): 10–11.

[Grainger 1908] "Collecting with the Phonograph" / Percy Grainger. — *Journal of the Folk-song Society* 12 (May 1908): 147–169.

[Gray 1973] "The Arturo Toscanini Society" / Michael H. Gray. — *ARSCJ* 5–1 (1973): 26–29.

[Gray 1975] "The 'World's Greatest Music' and 'World's Greatest Opera' Records: A Discography" / Michael H. Gray. — *ARSCJ* 7–1/2 (1975): 33–55.

[Gray 1977] *Bibliography of Discographies. Vol. 1: Classical Music, 1925–1975* / Michael H. Gray and Gerald D. Gibson. — New York: Bowker, 1977. 164 p. Continued by Gray 1989.

[Gray 1979] *Beecham: A Centenary Discography* / Michael H. Gray. — New York: Holmes & Meier, 1979. 129 p.

[Gray 1983] *Popular Music* / Michael H. Gray. — New York: Bowker, 1983. 205 p. (Bibliography of Discographies, 3.)

[Gray 1986] "The Birth of Decca Stereo" / Michael H. Gray. — *ARSCJ* 18–1/3 (1986): 4–19.

[Gray 1989] *Classical Music Discographies, 1976–1988* / Michael H. Gray. — New York: Greenwood, 1989. 334 p. Continues Gray 1977.

[Green 1976] *Encyclopedia of the Musical Theatre* / Stanley Green. — New York: Dodd, Mead, 1976. 492 p. Reprint—New York: Da Capo Press, 1980.

[Green 1985] *Broadway Musicals, Show by Show* / Stanley Green. — London: Faber, 1987. 361 p. (Originally published: Milwuakee, Wisc.: H. Leonard Books, 1985.)

[Greenfield 1982] *Dinah Shore; An Exploratory Discography* / Mark Greenfield and Tony Middleton. — London: Authors, 1982. 24 p.

[Greenfield 1989] *The New Penguin Guide to Compact Discs and Cassettes* / Edward Greenfield, Robert Layton, and Ivan March.—Harmondsworth, England: Penguin Books, 1989. 1,366 p.

[Griffin 1985] "Preservation of Rare and Unique Materials at the Institute of Jazz Studies" / Marie P. Griffin. — *ARSCJ* 17–1/3 (1985): 11–17.

[Griffiths 1976] "Composers' Recordings of Their Own Music" / Peter H. Griffiths. — *Audiovisual Librarian* 3–2 (Autumn 1976): 48–55.

[Gronow 1969] "American Columbia Finnish Language 3000 Series" / Pekka Gronow. — *RR* 101 (Oct. 1969): 8–9; 102 (Nov. 1969): 10.

[Gronow 1974] *American Columbia Scandinavian E and F Series* / Pekka Gronow. — Helsinki: Finnish Institute of Recorded Sound, 1974. 113 p.

[Gronow 1979] *The Columbia 33000–F Irish Series; A Numerical Listing* / Pekka Gronow. — Los Angeles: John Edwards Memorial Foundation, University of California at Los Angeles, 1979. 78 p. (JEMF Special Series, 10.)

[Gronow 1982] "Sources for the History of the Record Industry" / Pekka Gronow. — *Phonographic Bulletin* 34 (Nov. 1982): 50–54.

[Gronow 1983] "Early Gramophone Periodicals in Russia" / Pekka Gronow.—*TMR* 65/66 (Feb. 1983): 1,784–1,785.

[Guy 1964] *Disc Recording and Reproduction* / P. J. Guy. — New York and London: Focal Press, 1964. 232 p. (Encyclopedia of High Fidelity, 3.)

[Haggin 1938] *Music on Records* / B. H. Haggin — 4th ed. —New York: Oxford University Press, 1946. 279 p. (1st ed. 1938.)

[Haines 1973] "The British 'Toy' Gramophone Records of the 1920s" / D. E. Haines. — *TMR* 20/21 (Feb.–Apr. 1973): 111–118.

[Halban 1960] "Selma Kurz" / Desi Halban and Arthur E. Knight. — *RC* 13–3 (May 1960): 51–56; 17–1/3 (Oct. 1968): 46.

[Hall 1940] *The Record Book* / David Hall. — New York: Smith and Durrell, 1940. 771 p. Subsequent editions: *The Record Book, International Edition,* by David Hall (New York: Smith and Durrell, 1948), 1,394 p.; *Records: 1950 Edition,* by David Hall (New York: Knopf, 1950), 524 + 20 p. ; *The Disc Book,* by David Hall and Abner Levin (New York: Long Player Publications, 1955), 471 p. + unpaged addenda and index.

[Hall 1974] "The Rodgers and Hammerstein Archives of Recorded Sound—History and Current Operation" / David Hall. — *ARSCJ* 6–2 (1974): 17–31.

[Hall 1980] "An Era's End" / David Hall. — *ARSCJ* 12–1/2 (1980): 2–5.

[Hall 1981] "The Mapleson Cylinder Project" / David Hall. — *ARSCJ* 13–3 (1981): 5–20.

[Hall 1981/2] "A Provisional Mapleson Cylinder Chronology" / David Hall.—*ARSCJ* 13–3 (1981): 14.20.

[Hall 1982/1] "A Mapleson Afterword" / David Hall. — *ARSCJ* 14–1 (1982): 5–10.

[Hall 1982/7] "The Mapleson Cylinder Project" / David Hall. — *Recorded Sound* 82 (July 1982): 39–60; 83 (Jan. 1983): 21–56.

[Hall 1984/1] "New Music Quarterly Recordings—A Discography" / David Hall. — *ARSCJ* 16–1/2 (1984): 10–27.

[Hall 1984/10] "Recordings: Live at the Met, 1901–1903" / David Hall. — *Ovation*, Oct. 1984: 26–33; Nov. 1984: 19–21, 34.

[Hall 1989] "Discography: A Chronological Survey" / David Hall. — In *Modern* 1989, pp. 173–184.

[Hall, G. 1985] *Jan Savitt and His Orchestra* / George Hall, — Zephyrhills, Fla.: Joyce Record Club, 1985. 32 p.

[Hamilton, C. 1986] "Hines—Not 57 Varieties" / Chris Hamilton. — *HN* 150 (June 1986): 46–49.

[Hamilton, D. 1982] *Listener's Guide to the Great Instrumentalists* / David Hamilton. — New York: Facts on File, 1982. 137 p.

[Hamilton, D. 1984] Review of *The Metropolitan Opera on Record* by Frederick P. Fellers / David Hamilton. — *ARSCJ* 16–3 (1984): 57–62.

[Hammond 1977] *John Hammond on Record: An Autobiography* / John Hammond; with Irving Townsend. — New York: Ridge Press; 1977. 416 p.

[Hanna 1990] "The Gramophone Company, 1898–1925" / John Hanna. — *Journal of the Phonograph Society of New South Wales* 6–4 (July 1990): 6–11. Continues in the *Sound Record* (new name of the *Journal*), 7–1 (Sep. 1990): 16–19 (covering 1925–1952).

[Hansen 1972] *Lauritz Melchior: A Discography* / Hans Hansen. — Rev. ed. — Copenhagen: Nationaldiskoteket, 1972. 40 p. (1st ed. 1965.)

[Harman 1974] "Composers Recordings, Inc." / Carter Harman. — *ARSCJ* 6–1 (1974): 26–29.

[Harris 1987] *Jazz on Compact Disc: A Critical Guide to the Best Recordings* / Steve Harris. — New York: Harmony Books, 1987. 176 p.

[Harrison 1975] *Modern Jazz: The Essential Records* / Max Harrison, et al. — London: Aquarius Books, 1975. 131 p.

[Harrison 1984] *The Essential Jazz Records. Vol. 1: Ragtime to Swing* / Max Harrison, Charles Fox, and Eric Thacker. — Westport, Conn.: Greenwood Press, 1984. 595 p.

[Hart, M. 1989] *The Blues: A Bibliographical Guide* / Mary L. Hart, Brenda M. Eagles, and Lisa N. Woworth. — New York: Garland, 1989. 636 p.

[Hart, P. 1987] "Towards a Reiner Discography" / Philip Hart. — *ARSCJ* 19–1 (1987): 63–70.

[Hartel 1980] "The H3 Chrono-matrix File" / Harold H. Hartel. — *RR* 175/176 (Sept. 1980): 5–10–. A series that had reached 36 parts, with 247/248 (Sep. 1991). It is a chronological list of the jazz, blues, and gospel recordings that appeared in Rust 1961 (1969 ed.) and Godrich 1969. Artist, matrix, label number, title, and references are given for each disc. The time period covered is Feb. 1922 to Aug. 1933 (as of *RR* 247/248).

[Harvey 1949] "Nellie Melba" / H. Hugh Harvey. — *RC* 4–12 (Dec. 1949): 202–215.

[Hasse 1985] *Ragtime: Its History, Composers, and Music* / John Edward Hasse. — New York: Schirmer Books, 1985. 460 p.

[Hayes, C. 1988] "Imperial Matrix Listing (IM 1 to IM 2000)" / Cedric J. Hayes. — *RR* 235/236 (June 1988): 8; 237/238 (Nov. 1988): 8; 239/240 (Apr. 1989): 8; 241/242 (Oct.–Nov. 1989): 9; 243/244 (May–June 1990): 9; 245/246 (Jan. 1991): 9; 247/248 (Sep. 1991): 10. A continuing series that extends Rotante 1985.

[Hayes, J. 1971] "Sherlock Holmes? No, It's 'Shellac Hayes'" / Jim Hayes. — *TMR* 10 (June 1971): 42, 44–45.

[Hayes, J. 1974] *Panachord and Rex* / Jim G. Hayes. — Liverpool: Author, 1974. 23 p.

[Hayes, R. 1977] *Kate Smith Discography* / Richard K. Hayes. — Cranston, R.I.: Author, 1977.

[Hazelcorn 1976] *A Collector's Guide to the Columbia Spring-wound Cylinder Graphophone* / Howard Hazelcorn. — Brooklyn: Antique Phonograph Monthly, 1976. 36 p. (APM Monographs, 2.)

[Hedberg 1978] "Rescuing the Voices of the Dead—A Laser-read Sound Reproducing System" / Tom Hedberg. — *APM* 5–8 (1978): 7–8.

[Heintze 1985] *Scholars Guide to Washington, D.C., for Audio Resources* / James R. Heintze. — Washington: Smithsonian Institution Press, 1985. 395 p.

[Helmbrecht 1978] *Fritz Reiner: The Comprehensive Discography of His Recordings* / Arthur J.

Helmbrecht, Jr. — Novelty, Ohio: Fritz Reiner Society, 1978. 79 p. Supplement, Apr. 1981, 9 p.; and Addenda, Apr. 1991, 4 p. (Madison, N.J.: Author, 1981).

[Helmholtz 1877] *On the Sensations of Tone as a Physiological Basis for the Theory of Music* / Hermann L. Helmholtz. — Reprint of the 2nd English ed., trans. and rev. by Alexander J. Ellis, based on the 4th German ed. (1887); with a new introduction by Henry Margenau. — New York: Dover, 1954. 576 p.

[Hemphill 1970] *The Nashville Sound* / Paul H. Hemphill. — New York: Simon & Schuster, 1970. 289 p.

[Henriksen 1968] "Gennett Research" / Henry Henriksen. — RR 94 (Dec. 1968): 3–5.

[Henriksen 1975] "Herschel Gold Seal" / Henry Henriksen. — RR 131 (Jan. 1975): 1, 5.

[Henriksen 1978] "Autograph" / Henry Henriksen. — RR 153/154 (Apr. 1978): 4–7.

[Henriksen 1979] "Black Patti" / Henry Henriksen. — RR 165/166 (Aug. 1979): 4–8; 167/168 (Oct. 1979): 4–8; 171/172 (Mar. 1980): 4–5, 24; 173/174 (June 1980): 9; 177/178 (Nov. 1980): 8; 181/182 (Apr. 1981): 10; 183/184 (July 1981): 9; 185/186 (Oct. 1981): 8; 187/188 (Dec 1981): 8. At this point a label list begins: 189/190 (Mar,-Apr. 1982): 8; 191/192 (July 1982): 8; 193/194 (Oct. 1982): 9; 195/196 (Jan. 1983): 13; 197/198 (Mar.–Apr. 1983): 9.

[Henrysson 1984] *A Jussi Björling Phonography* / Harald Henrysson and Jack W. Porter. — Stockholm: Svenskt Musikhistoriskt Arkiv, 1984. 269 p.

[Henstock 1991] *Fernando De Lucia* / Michael Henstock. — London: Duckworth, 1991. 505 p. Discography, pp. 437–482.

[Hernon 1986] *French Horn Discography* / Michael Hernon. — Westport, Conn.: Greenwood Press, 1986. 292 p.

[Hervingham-Root 1953] "Pol Plançon" / Laurie Hervingham-Root and James F. E. Dennis. — RC 8-7/8 (July–Aug. 1953): 148–191; 8–10 (Oct. 1953): 236–237; 10–12 (Nov. 1956): 277; 12–7 (Oct. 1959): 165.

[Hervingham-Root 1970] "David Bispham—Quaker Baritone" / Laurie Hervingham-Root. — TMR 7 (Dec. 1970): 197–199. Continued in TMR 8, 9, 10, 12, 13, and 14.

[Heyworth 1983] *Otto Klemperer: His Life and Times* / Peter Heyworth. — Cambridge, England: Cambridge University Press, 1983. Discography by Michael H. Gray, pp. 444–452.

[Hillman 1989] "Symmetrical Speaker System with Dual Transmission Lines" / Peter E. Hillman. — *Speaker Builder*, Sep. 1989: 10–27

[Hinze 1977] "Medallion Revisited" / Michael Hinze. — RR 144/145 (Mar. 1977): 12–13.

[Hirsch 1988] "Feelin' Groovy; Head to Head Lab and Listening Tests of Five Leading Phono Cartridges" / Julian Hirsch. — *Stereo Review*, Jan. 1988: 74–79.

[Hoffmann 1979] *The Development of Library Collections of Sound Recordings* / Frank W. Hoffmann. — New York: Dekker, 1979. 169 p.

[Hoffmann 1981] *The Literature of Rock, 1954–1978* / Frank Hoffmann. — Metuchen, N.J.: Scarecrow Press, 1981. 349 p. Continued by Hoffmann 1986/2.

[Hoffmann 1983] *The Cash Box Singles Charts, 1950–1981* / Frank Hoffmann; with the assistance of Lee Ann Hoffmann. — Metuchen, N.J.: Scarecrow Press, 1983. 876 p.

[Hoffmann 1984] *The Cash Box Country Singles Charts, 1958–1982* / George Albert and Frank Hoffmann. — Metuchen, N.J.: Scarecrow Press, 1984. 605 p.

[Hoffmann 1986/1] *The Cash Box Black Contemporary Singles Charts, 1960–1984* / Frank Hoffmann and George Albert; with the assistance of Lee Ann Hoffmann. — Metuchen, N.J.: Scarecrow Press, 1986. 704 p.

[Hoffmann 1986/2] *The Literature of Rock II* / Frank Hoffmann and B. Lee Cooper; with assistance by Lee Ann Hoffmann. — Metuchen, N.J.: Scarecrow Press, 1986. 2 vols. Continues Hoffmann 1981.

[Hoffmann 1987] *The Cash Box Album Charts, 1975–1985* / Frank Hoffmann and George Albert; with the assistance of Lee Ann Hoffmann. — Metuchen, N.J.: Scarecrow Press, 1987. 556 p.

[Hoffmann 1988] *The Cash Box Album Charts, 1955–1974* / Frank Hoffmann and George Albert; with the assistance of Lee Ann Hoffmann. — Metuchen, N.J.: Scarecrow Press, 1988. 528 p.

[Hoffmann 1989/1] *The Cash Box Black Contemporary Album Charts, 1975–1987* / Frank Hoffmann and George Albert. — Metuchen, N.J.: Scarecrow Press, 1989. 249 p.

[Hoffmann 1989/2] *The Cash Box Country Album Charts, 1964–1988* / Frank Hoffmann and George Albert. — Metuchen, N.J.: Scarecrow Press, 1989. 300 p.

[Hogarth 1982] "Nellie Melba" / Will H. Hogarth. — *RC* 27–3/4 (Mar. 1982): 72–87.

[Hogarth 1987] "Marjorie Lawrence Discography" / Will Hogarth and R. T. See. — *RC* 32–1/2 (Jan. 1987): 7–18; 33–11/12 (Nov. 1988): 300–303.

[Hoggard 1978] *Bob Dylan: An Illustrated Discography* / Stuart Hoggard. — Oxford, England: Transmedia Express, 1978. 108, 23 p.

[Holcman 1960] "The Honor Roll of Recorded Chopin, 1906–1960" / Jan Holcman. — *Saturday Review*, 27 Feb. 1960: 44–45, 61–62.

[Holcman 1961/11] "Liszt: Piano Recordings" / Jan Holcman. — *Music Magazine*, Nov. 1961: 14–16, 48.

[Holcman 1961/12] "Liszt in the Records of His Pupils" / Jan Holcman. — *Saturday Review*, 23 Dec. 1961: 45–46, 57.

[Holcman 1961/13] "Liszt Records: Part Two" / Jan Holcman. — *Music Magazine*, Dec. 1961: 24–25, 60.

[Holcman 1962] "Debussy on Disc: 1912–1962" / Jan Holcman. — *Saturday Review*, 25 Aug. 1962: 34–35.

[Holdridge 1975] "Charles Hackett" / Lawrence F. Holdridge. — *RC* 22–8/9 (Feb. 1975): 171–214; 22–10/11 (Apr. 1975): 257.

[Holmes 1982] *Conductors on Record* / John L. Holmes. — London: Gollancz; Westport, Conn.: Greenwood Press, 1982. 734 p.

[Hoover 1971] *Music Machines—American Style; A Catalog of the Exhibition* / Cynthia A. Hoover. — Washington: Smithsonian Institution Press, 1971. 140, 15 p.

[Horn 1988] "Geoffrey Horn Visits Celestion" / Geoffrey Horn. — *Gramophone*, Nov. 1988: 66, 896–898.

[Hounsome 1981] *Rock Record* / Terry Hounsome and Tim Chambre. — 3rd ed. — New York: Facts on File, 1981. 526 p. (Published in Britain as *New Rock Record*, 1981. 1st ed. titled *Rockmaster*, 1978; revised as *Rock Record*, 1979.)

[Hume 1982] *You're So Cold I'm Turnin' Blue* / Martha Hume. — New York: Viking, 1982. 202 p.

[Hummel 1984] *Collector's Guide to the American Musical Theatre* / David Hummel. — Metuchen, N.J.: Scarecrow Press, 1984. 2 vols.

[Humphreys 1990] "ARCAM" / Ivor Humphreys. — *Gramophone*, Oct. 1990: 857–862.

[Hunt 1985] *The Furtwängler Sound* / John Hunt. — 2nd ed. — London: Furtwängler Society, 1985. Apparently superseded by a later edition, cited in *Gramophone* May 1990, p. 1,935.

[Hunt 1987] *From Adam to Webern: The Recordings of Von Karajan* / John Hunt. — London: Author, 1987. 130 p. (Bound with *Philharmonia Orchestra: Complete Discography 1945–1987*, by Stephen J. Pettitt.)

[Hurd 1990] "35 Shades of Black: The Johnny Cash Story" / Daniel Hurd. — *Discoveries*, Aug. 1990: 94–97. Includes a discography of LPs.

[Hurst 1963] *The Golden Age Recorded* / P. G. Hurst. — 2nd ed. — Lingfield, Surrey, England: Oakwood, 1963. 187 p. (1st ed. 1947.)

[Hutchinson 1957] "Alessandro Bonci" / Tom Hutchinson. — *RC* 11–7 (July 1957): 148–162; 11–9/10 (Sep.-Oct. 1957): 234–235; 12–4/5 (Feb.–Mar. 1959): 108, 116; 18–1/2 (Oct. 1968): 47.

[Hutchinson 1962] "Giovanni Zenatello" / Tom Hutchinson and Clifford Williams. — *RC* 14–5/6 (1962?): 100–143; 14–7/8 (1962?): 170–171. Copies seen did not have dates.

[Hutchinson 1960] "Tito Schipa" / Tom Hutchinson. — *RC* 13–4/5 (June–July 1960): 75–109.

[International 1983] *Catalog of the Reproducing Piano Roll Collection* / International Piano Archives at Maryland. — College Park, Md.: 1983. 281 p.

[Isom 1972] "How to Prevent and Cure Record Warping" / Warren Rex Isom. — *High Fidelity* 22 (Sep. 1972): 50–53.

[Isom 1977] "Evolution of the Disc Talking Machine" / Warren Rex Isom. — *Journal of the Audio Engineering Society* 25–10/11 (Sep.-Oct. 1977): 718–723.

[Jackson 1975] *Collectors' Contact Guide* / Paul T. Jackson. — Rev. ed. — Springfield, Ill.: Recorded Sound Research, 1975. 58 p. (1st ed. 1973.)

[Jansen 1983] "Non-magnetic Sound Recording on Tape" / F. A. Jansen. — *HN* 133 (Aug. 1983): 239–241.

[Jasen 1971] "Zez Confrey, Creator of the Novelty Rag: Preparatory Research" / David A. Jasen. — *RR* 111 (July 1971): 5, 10.

[Jasen 1973] *Recorded Ragtime, 1897–1958* / David Jasen. —Hamden, Conn.: Archon Books, 1973. 155 p.

[Jefferson 1988] *Lotte Lehmann, 1888–1976* / Alan Jefferson — London: Julia MacRae Books, 1988. 333 p. Discography, pp. 243–322.

[Jepsen 1962] *A Discography of Stan Kenton* / Jorgen Grunnet Jepsen. — Brande, Denmark: Debut Records, 1962. 2 vols.

[Jepsen 1963] *Jazz Records 1942–1962* / Jorgen Grunnet Jepsen. —Holte, Denmark: Knudsen, 1963–1969. 12 vols.

[Jepsen 1969] *A Discography of Dizzy Gillespie, 1937–1952* / Jorgen Grunnet Jepsen. —Copenhagen: Karl Knudsen, 1969. 39 p.

[Jepsen 1969/1] *A Discography of Dizzy Gillespie, 1953–1968* Jorgen Grunnet Jepsen. — Copenhagen: Karl Knudsen, 1969. 30 p.

[Jepsen 1969/3] *A Discography of John Coltrane* / Jorgen Grunnet Jepsen. —Rev. ed. —Copenhangen: Karl Knudsen, 1969. 35 p.

[Jewell 1977] *Veteran Talking Machines* / Brian Jewell. — Tunbridge Wells, England: Midas, 1977. 128 p.

[Johnson, C. 1983] "The Oldest Person to Record?" / Colin Johnson. —*HN* 130 (Feb. 1983): 167.

[Johnston 1988] *Count John McCormack* / Brian Fawcett Johnston. — Bournemouth, England: Talking Machine Review, 1988. 57 p. Errata noted in *HN* 165 (Dec. 1988): 126–127.

[Jorgensen 1988] *The Complete Handbook of Magnetic Recording* / Finn Jorgensen. — 3rd ed. — Blue Ridge Summit, Penn.: Tab Books, 1988. 740 p.

[Kallman 1981] *Encyclopedia of Music in Canada* / Edited by Helmut Kallman, Gilles Potvin, and Kenneth Winters. — Toronto: University of Toronto Press, 1981. 1,108 p.

[Kastlemusick 1981] *Kastlemusick Directory for Collectors of Recordings.* — 1981–1982 ed. — Wilmington, Delaware: Kastlemusick, 1981. 84 p. (1st ed. 1977.)

[Kaufman 1964] "Leo Slezak" / Tom Kaufman and James F. E. Dennis. — *RC* 15–9/10 (1964): 195–235.

[Kay 1953] "Those Fabulous Gennetts" / George W. Kay. —*Record Changer* 12 (June 1953): 4–13.

[Kay 1961] "The Superior Catalog" / George W. Kay — *RR* 37 (Aug. 1961): 1–4; 38 (Oct. 1961): 10–11; 41 (Feb. 1962): 11; 42 (Mar.–Apr. 1962): 11.

[Kelly 1979] "Selma Kurz: A Discography" / Alan Kelly, John F. Perkins, and John Ward. — *Recorded Sound* 73 (Jan. 1979): 2–5.

[Kelly 1988] *His Master's Voice—La voce del padrone: The Italian Catalogue . . . 1898 to 1929* / Alan Kelly. — Westport, Conn.: Greenwood Press, 1988. 462 p.

[Kelly 1988/1] "Discography" / Alan Kelly and Vladimir Gurvich. — In *Chaliapin: A Critical Biography,* by Victor Borovsky (New York: Knopf, 1988), pp. 541–587.

[Kelly 1990] *His Master's Voice—La voix de son maitre: The French Catalogue. . . 1898–1929* / Alan Kelly. — Westport, Conn.: Greenwood Press, 1990. 679 p.

[Kendziora] Carl Kendziora's columns, "Behind the Cobwebs," published in *RR* 1949–1986, are cited by date only.

[Kendziora 1971] "Problems of Dating Recorded Performances" / Carl Kendziora. — In Allen 1971, pp. 8–18.

[Kennedy 1973] *Barbirolli, Conductor Laureate* / Michael Kennedy. —London: Hart-Davis, 1973. 416 p. Reprint—New York: Da Capo Press, 1982. Discography, pp. 341–402.

[Kenyon 1973] "Pasquale Amato" / Percy Kenyon, Clifford Williams, and William R. Moran. — *RC* 21–1/2 (Mar. 1973): 3–47; 21–5/6 (Oct. 1973): 128–132.

[Khanna 1977] "Vinyl Compound for the Phonographic Industry" / S. K. Khanna. — *Journal of the Audio Engineering Society* 25–10/11 (Sep.-Oct. 1977): 724–728.

[Kiner 1983] *The Al Jolson Discography* / Larry F. Kiner. — Westport, Conn.: Greenwood Press, 1983. 194 p.

[Kiner 1985] *The Rudy Vallee Discography* / Larry F. Kiner. — Westport, Conn.: Greenwood Press, 1985. 190 p.

[Kiner 1987] *The Cliff Edwards Discography* / Larry F. Kiner. — Westport, Conn.: Greenwood Press, 1987. 260 p.

[Kinkle 1974] *The Complete Encyclopedia of Popular Music and Jazz, 1900–1950* / Roger D. Kinkle. — New Rochelle, N.Y.: Arlington House, 1974. 4 vols.

[Kirvine 1977] *Jukebox Saturday Night* / John Kirvine. — London: New English Library, Times-Mirror, 1977. 160 p.

[Klee 1981] "From the Golden Age of Opera Recordings" / Joe Klee. — APM 7–1 (1981): 8–9.

[Klee 1983] "From the Golden Age: Caruso Reissues" / Joe Klee. — APM 7–6 (1983): 6–7.

[Klee 1987] "From the Golden Age...Caruso on Compact Disc" / Joe Klee. — APM 8–6 (1987): 15–16.

[Klee 1990/3] "In the Beginning . . . From Berliner to World War I" / Joe Klee. — APM 9–3 (1990): 13–15.

[Klein 1983] "A History of the Starr Piano Factory" / Andrew Klein. — TMR 65/66 (Feb. 1983): 1,787–1.789, 1.818.

[Klein, L. 1989] "Amplifier Damping Factor: How Important Is It?" / Larry Klein. — *Radio Electronics* 60–1 (Jan. 1989): 78–79.

[Kline 1989] "The Capitol Years" / Pete Kline. — *Discoveries* 2–7 (July 1989): 18–21. Discography of Frank Sinatra's Capitol records, 1953–1962.

[Klinger 1991] "The Short-lived Harris Everlasting Record" / Bill Klinger. — APM 10–1 (1991): 3–4.

[Knight, A. 1955] "Roland Hayes" / Arthur E. Knight. — RC 10–2 (July 1955): 27–45; 12–3/4 (Feb.-Mar. 1959): 116; 12–8/9 (Nov.-Dec. 1959): 215.

[Knight, G. 1977] "Factors Relating to the Long Term Storage of Magnetic Tape" / G. A. Knight. — *Phonographic Bulletin* 18 (July 1977): 16–35.

[Koeningsberg 1980] "In the Pink: A Lambert Discography" / Allen Koenigsberg. — APM 6–8 (1980): 4–10; 6–9 (1980): 8–9.

[Koenigsberg 1987] *Edison Cylinder Records, 1889–1912, With an Illustrated History of the Phonograph* / Allen Koenigsberg. — 2nd ed. — Brooklyn: APM Press, 1987. 42 + 172 p. (1st ed. 1969.)

[Koenigsberg 1990] *The Patent History of the Phonograph, 1877–1912* / Allen Koenigsberg. Brooklyn: APM Press, 1990. 72 + 87 p.

[Kogen 1968] "Gramophone Record Reproduction: Development, Performance and Potential of the Stereo Pickup" / James H. Kogen. — *Proceedings of the IEE*, Aug. 1968: 116–118.

[Kogen 1977] "Record Changers, Turntables, and Tone Arms — A Brief Technical History" / James H. Kogen. — *Journal of the Audio Engineering Society* 25–10/11 (Sep.-Oct. 1977): 749–758.

[Korenhof 1977] "Maria Callas discographie" / Paul Korenhof. — *Luister* 302 (Nov. 1977): 197–122.

[Koster 1974] *Charlie Parker Discography* / Piet Koster and Dick M. Bakker. — Amsterdam: Micrography, 1974–1976. 4 vols. Covers 1940–1955.

[Koster 1985] *Dizzy Gillespie, Volume I, 1937–1953* / Piet Koster and Chris Sellers. — Amsterdam: Micrography, 1985. 68 p.

[Kressley 1968] "Catalog of World Transcriptions (1933–1963)" / David Kressley. — RR 89 (Mar. 1968): 1–8; 90 (May 1968): 6–7; 91 (July 1968): 5; 92 (Sep. 1968): 5; 93 (Nov. 1968): 8–10; 94 (Dec. 1968): 7; 98 (May 1969): 7–9.

[Kressley 1983] "The Frederic W. Ziv Company" / Dave Kressley. — RR 201/202 (Sep. 1983): 4–6 [on Wayne King]; 203/204 (Dec. 1983): 1–2; 205/206 (Mar. 1984): 8; 207/208 (June 1984): 8; 209/210 (Oct. 1984): 9; 211/212 (Feb. 1985): 11.

[Kunstadt 1962] "The Lucille Hegamin Story" Len Kunstadt. — RR 40 (Jan. 1962): 3, 19.

[Kunstadt 1987] "The Labels behind Black Swan" / Len Kunstadt. — RR 229/230 (June 1987): 1, 4–5. Continues a compilation that began in RR 221/222 under Carl Kendziora's name. The Kendziora articles were reprinted from *Record Changer*, but the Kunstadt continuation is new material.

[Kunstadt 1988] "Unmasking the Associateds" / Len Kunstadt. — RR 235/236 (June 1988): 1, 4; 237/238 (Nov. 1988): 1, 4; 239/240 (Apr. 1989): 5–9; 241/242 (Oct.-Nov. 1989): 6.

[Kweskin 1979] "Woody Guthrie" / Jim Kweskin. — RR 161/162 (Feb.-Mar. 1979): 13; 163/164 (May-June 1979): 13.

[Lambert, M. 1983] "Decca Records, 1929–1980" / M. J. Lambert. — HN 130 (Feb. 1983): 156–161; 131 (Apr. 1983): 176–181.

[Lambert, R. 1985] "Needle Tins" / Ruth L. Lambert. — TMR 70 (Dec. 1985): 1,945–1,947; 1,997–1,999.

[Lane 1982] "Equalization and Equalizers" / Michael R. Lane. — ARSCJ 14–2 (1982): 29–36.

[Lane 1984] "On 'Fifty Questions on Audio Restoration and Transfer Technology'" / Michael R. Lane and Richard C. Burns. — ARSCJ 16–3 (1984): 5–

11. A response to Owen 1983. Owen replied; then Lane and Owen had further comments in *ARSCJ* 17 (1985): 1–3.

[Lane 1991] "Sonic Restoration of Historical Recordings" / Michael R. Lane. — *Audio*, June 1991: 35–44; July 1991: 26–37.

[Langwill 1965] *The Bassoon and Contrabassoon* / Lyndesay Langwill. — New York: Norton, 1965. 269 p. Discography, pp. 223–258.

[Laubich 1982] *Art Tatum: A Guide to His Recorded Music* / Arnold Laubich and Ray Spencer. — Metuchen, N.J.: Scarecrow Press, 1982. 359 p.

[Lawrence 1962] "Emma Eames" / A. F. R. Lawrence and Steve Smolian. — *American Record Guide* 29 (1962): 210.

[Leder 1985] *Women in Jazz: A Discography of Instrumentalists, 1913–1968* / Jan Leder. — Westport, Conn.: Greenwood Press, 1985. 310 p.

[Lee 1979] *Native North American Music and Oral Data: A Catalogue of Sound Recordings, 1893–1976* / Dorothy Sara Lee. — Bloomington, Ind.: Indiana University Press, 1979. 479 p.

[Lenoir 1877] "Procédé d'enregistrement et de reproduction des phénomènes perçus par l'ouïe" / Abbe Lenoir. — *Semaine du clergé*, 10 Oct. 1877.

[Léon 1960] "Bidú Sayão" / J. A. Léon and Alusio R. Guimaraes. — *RC* 13–6 (Aug. 1960): 123–133; 16–2 (Sep. 1964): 46–47.

[Leonard 1986] *Masquerade in Black* / William Torbert Leonard. — Metuchen, N.J.: Scarecrow Press, 1986. 431 p.

[Levarie 1977] "Noise" / Siegmund Levarie. — *Critical Inquiry* 4–1 (Autumn 1977): 21–31.

[Levarie 1980] *Tone: A Study in Musical Acoustics* / Siegmund Levarie and Ernst Levy. — 2nd ed. — Kent, Ohio: Kent State University Press, 1980. 248 p. Reprint—Westport, Conn.: Greenwood Press, 1981. (1st ed. 1968.)

[Levarie 1983] *Musical Morphology: A Discourse and a Dictionary* / Siegmund Levarie and Ernst Levy. — Kent, Ohio: Kent State University Press, 1983. 344 p.

[Lewine 1984] *Songs of the Theater* / Richard Lewine and Alfred Simon. — New York: H. W. Wilson, 1984. 897 p. Replaces their *Songs of the American Theater* and *Encyclopedia of Theater Music*.

[Lewis, G. 1978] "Evan Williams" / Gareth H. Lewis. — *RC* 24–11/12 (Dec. 1978): 242–277.

[Lewis, J. 1976] "Fritz Kreisler: The First Hundred Years (1987–1975)" / John Sam Lewis. — *RR* 139/140 (May–June 1976): 8–10.

[Lewis, J. 1977] "Stokowski: The Centenary" / John Sam Lewis.— *RR* 149/150 (Oct. 1977): 4–5, 12.

[Lewis, J. 1979] "Early Violinists" / John Sam Lewis. — *RR* 167/168 (Oct. 1979): 12.

[Lewis, J. 1979] "First Lady of the Keyboard: Wanda Landowska" / John Sam Lewis. — *RR* 163/164 (May 1979): 9; 165/166 (Aug. 1979): 13.

[Lewis, J. 1980] "The Beecham Celebration" / John Sam Lewis.— *RR* 171/172 (Mar. 1980): 12; 173/174 (June 1980): 12; 175/176 (Sep. 1980): 11.

[Lewis, J. 1981] "Jan Kubelik and Jacques Thibaud" / John Sam Lewis. — *RR* 179/180 (Feb. 1981): 9, 23 [about Kubelik]; *RR* 181/182 (Apr. 1981): 11, 24 [about Thibaud].

[Lewis, J. 1985] "The Violinists: Samuel Gardner" / John Sam Lewis. — *RR* 213/214 (May 1985): 11–12.

[Lewis, J. 1986] "Efrem Zimbalist (1889–1985)" / John Sam Lewis. — *RR* 221/222 (Apr. 1986): 8–9; 223/224 (Aug. 1986): 9; 225/226 (Nov. 1986): 2.

[Lewis, J. 1988] "The Pupils of Franz Liszt" / John Sam Lewis. — *RR* 235/236 (June 1988): 5; 237/238 (Nov. 1988): 5; 239/240 (Apr. 1989): 7; 241/242 (Oct.–Nov.1989): 8.

[Lewis, T. 1964] "Our Society" / Ted Lewis. — *HN* 18 (Apr. 1964): 24–25. About the City of London Phonograph and Gramophone Society.

[Lieb 1983] *Mother of the Blues: A Study of Ma Rainey* / Sandra R. Lieb. — Amherst, Mass.: University of Massachusetts Press, 1983. 226 p.

[Liliedahl 1971] "Swedish Record Labels: Dacapo" / Karleric Liliedahl. — *TMR* 10 (June 1971): 35–36.

[Liliedahl 1973] *Dixi-Silverton* / Karleric Liliedahl. — Trelleborg, Sweden: Author, 1973. 93 p.

[Liliedahl 1987] *Comprehensive Discography of Swedish Acoustic Recordings, 1903–1928* / Karleric Liliedahl. — Stockholm: Arkivet för Ljud och Bild, 1987. 800 p. Lists 10,000 titles on 52 labels; excluding Gramophone Co.

[Lindsay 1989] "Vogue, the Original Picture Disc Label" / Joe Lindsay. — *Discoveries* 2–3 (Mar. 1989): 24–27.

[Lindsay 1990] *Picture Discs of the World: Price Guide and International Reference Book* / Joe Lindsay, Peter Bukoski, and Marc Grobman. — Scottsdale, Ariz. : Biodisc, 1990. 205 p.

[Linkwitz 1976] "Active Crossover Networks for Noncoincident Drivers" / Siegfried H. Linkwitz. — *Journal of the Audio Engineering Society* 1–2 (1976).

[Litchfield 1982] *Canadian Jazz Discography: 1916–1980* / Jack Litchfield. — Toronto: University of Toronto Press, 1982. 945 p.

[Little 1977] "Discography of Tuba Solo Literature" / Donald C. Little. — *NACWPI Journal* 26 (Winter 1977–1978): 43–44.

[Long 1986] "SME V Tonearm and Talisman Virtuoso DTi Cartridge" / Edward M. Long. — *Audio*, June 1986: 88–96.

[Long 1988] "Mats & Clamps by the Numbers" / Edward M. Long. — *Audio*, Apr. 1988: 45–52. Discusses mats for turntables.

[Lonstein 1979] *The Revised Compleat [sic] Sinatra* / Albert L. Lonstein. — Ellenville, N.Y.: S. M. Lonstein, 1979. 702 p.

[Lorcey 1983] *Maria Callas: d'art et d'amour* / Jacques Lorcey. — Rev. ed. — Paris: Editions PAC, 1983. 615p. Discography, pp. 537–585; 609–612. (1st ed. 1977.)

[Lorenz 1981] *Two-minute Brown Wax and XP Cylinder Records of the Columbia Phonograph Company; Numerical Catalog, August 1896–ca. March 1909* / Kenneth M. Lorenz. — Wilmington, Delaware: Kastlemusick, 1981. 75 p.

[Lowery 1990] *Lowery's International Trumpet Discography* / Alvin L. Lowery. — Baltimore: Camden House, 1990. 2 vols.

[Lumpe 1990] "Pseudonymous Performers on Early LP Records: Rumors, Facts, and Finds" / Ernst A. Lumpe. — *ARSCJ* 21–2 (Fall 1990): 226–231.

[Lustig 1987] "Giuseppe Anselmi" / Larry Lustig and Clifford Williams. — *RC* 32–3/4/5 (Apr. 1987): 51–85.

[Lyle 1934] "Phonograph Collection in Antioch College Library" / G. R. Lyle and Rose Krauskopf. — *Library Journal* 59 (15 Mar. 1934): 266–267.

[Lynch 1987] *Broadway on Record: A Directory of New York Cast Recordings of Musical Shows, 1931–1986* / Richard Chigley Lynch. — Westport, Conn.: Greenwood Press, 1987. 357 p.

[MacDonald 1982] *Don't Touch That Dial: Radio Programming in American Life, 1920–1960* / J. Fred MacDonald. — Chicago: Nelson-Hall, 1982. 412 p.

[MacKenzie 1963] "The Broadway Race Series" / John R. MacKenzie and John Godrich. — *Matrix* 48 (Aug. 1963): 3–13.

[Magnetic 1982] *Magnetic Tape Recording for the Eighties* / Edited by Ford Kalil. — Washington: National Aeronautics and Space Administration, 1982. 170 p. — (NASA Reference Publications, 1075.)

[Magnusson 1983] "The Gene Austin Recordings" / Tor Magnusson. — *Skivsamlaren* 15 (Feb. 1983): 1–82.

[Malone 1968] *Country Music U.S.A.: A Fifty-year History* / Bill C. Malone. — Rev. ed. — Austin, Tex.: University of Texas Press, 1985. 562 p. (1st ed. 1968.)

[Manildi 1983] "The Rubinstein Discography" / Donald Manildi. — *Le grand baton* 20–56 (Dec. 1983): 56–100.

[Manzo 1980] "A Lambert Sampler" / J. R. Manzo. — *NAG* 32 (Spring 1980): 4–7.

[Marco 1989] "Bibliographic Control of Sound Recordings: An International View" / Guy A. Marco. — *Audiovisual Librarian* 15 (Feb. 1989): 19–24.

[Margoschis 1977] *Recording Natural History Sounds* / Richard M. Margoschis. — Barnet, England: Print & Press Services, 1977. 110 p.

[Marsh 1984] "Solti in Chicago: A Critical Discography" / Robert C. Marsh. — *Harmonie-panorama-musique*, new series 20–46 (Oct. 1984): 26–29, 35.

[Martel 1988] "Roger Harding—A Forgotten Recording Pioneer" / Joseph Martel. — *NAG* 65 (July 1988): 3–8.

[Martland 1988] "Colonel Gouraud's Present" / Peter Martland. — *HN* 162 (June 1988): 30–32.

[Martland 1989] "Theodore Birnbaum" / Peter Martland. — *HN* 168 (June 1989): 225.

[Marty 1979] *Illustrated History of Talking Machines* / Daniel Marty. — New York: Dorset Press, 1979. 193 p. Originally in French: *Histoire illustrée du phonographe* (Lausanne: Edita-Vilo, 1979).

[Mason 1984] "Aviation on Records" / David Mason. — *TMR* 68 (June 1984): 1,843–1,848.

[Masters 1990] "The Demon Room" / Ian Masters. — *Stereo Review*, Apr. 1990: 23–25.

[Masters 1990/1] "The Basics" / Ian Masters. — *Stereo Review*, Jan. 1990 to Feb. 1991. A series covering various components of the home audio system.

[Mathews 1986] *John McCormack: Centenary Discography, 1904–1942* / Emrys G. Mathews. — Llandeilo, Wales: Author, 1986. 72 p.

[Matthews 1977] "Cadenzas in Piano Concertos" / Denis Matthews. — *Recorded Sound* 68 (Oct. 1977): 723–727.

[Mauerer 1970] "Sidney Bechet Discography" / Hans J. Mauerer. — Rev. ed. — Copenhagen: Knudsen, 1970. 86 p.

[Mawhinney 1983] *MusicMaster, The 45 RPM Record Directory: 35 Years of Recorded Music, 1947 to 1982* / Paul C. Mawhinney. — Allison Park, Penn.: Record-Rama, 1983. 2 vols.

[McCarthy 1964] "Discography" / Albert J. McCarthy. — In *Big Bill Blues,* by William Broonzy; as told to Yannick Bruynoghe (New York: Oak Publications, 1964; 176 p.), pp. 153–173.

[McCormick 1989] "The Toscanini Legacy" / Don McCormick and Seth Winner. — *ARSCJ* 20–2 (1989): 182–190.

[McCoy 1990] *Every Little Thing: The Definitive Guide to Beatles Recording Variations, Rare Mixes & Other Musical Oddities, 1958–1986* / William McCoy and Mitchell McGeary. — Ann Arbor, Mich.: Popular Culture, 1990. 368 p.

[McCulloh 1982] *Ethnic Recordings in America— A Neglected Heritage* / Judith McCulloh. — Washington: Library of Congress, 1982. 269 p.

[McKee 1989/1] "ARSC/AAA: Fifteen Years of Cooperative Research" / Elwood McKee. — *ARSCJ* 20–1 (Spring 1989): 3–13.

[McPherson 1967] "Ernestine Schumann-Heink" / J. McPherson and William R. Moran. — *RC* 17–5/6 (June 1967): 98–144; 17–7 (Aug. 1967): 154–159; 20–6/7 (May 1972): 165; 25–3/4 (June 1979): 75–77.

[McPherson 1973] "Jeanne Gerville-Réache" / J. McPherson and William R. Moran. — *RC* 21–3/4 (July 1973): 51–79; 21–7/8 (Dec. 1973): 190–191.

[McWilliams, A. 1964] *Tape Recording and Reproduction* / A. A. McWilliams. — New York and London: Focal Press, 1964. 287 p. — (Encyclopedia of High Fidelity, 4).

[McWilliams, J. 1979] *The Preservation and Restoration of Sound Recordings* / Jerry McWilliams. — Nashville, Tenn.: American Association for State and Local History, 1979. 138 p.

[McWilliams, J. 1983] "Sound Recordings" / Jerry McWilliams. — In *Conservation in the Library,* edited by Susan G. Swartzburg (Westport, Conn.: Greenwood Press, 1983), pp. 163–184.

[Melville-Mason 1977] "Re-scoring for Recording" / Graham Melville-Mason. — In *Phonographs and Gramophones* (Edinburgh: Royal Scottish Museum, 1977), pp. 95–96.

[Merriman 1976] "Sound Recording by Electricity, 1919–1924" / H. O. Merriman. — *TMR* 40 (June 1976): 666–681.

[Methuen-Campbell 1981] *Chopin Playing: From the Composer to the Present Day* / James Methuen-Campbell. — New York: Taplinger, 1981. 289 p.

[Methuen-Campbell 1983] "Early Soviet Pianists and Their Recordings" / James Methuen-Campbell. — *Recorded Sound* 83 (Jan. 1983): 1–16.

[Methuen-Campbell 1984] *Catalogue of Recordings by Classical Pianists. Vol. 1. Pianists Born before 1872.* / James Methuen-Campbell. — Chipping Norton, England: Disco Epsom, 1984. 66 p.

[Migliorini 1952] "Olive Fremstad" / Louis Migliorini and James F. E. Dennis. — *RC* 7–3 (Mar. 1952): 51–65.

[Migliorini 1953] "Emma Eames" / Louis Migliorini and James F. E. Dennis. — *RC* 8–4 (Apr. 1953): 74–96.

[Migliorini 1957] "Johanna Gadski" / Louis Migliorini and Nicholas Ridley. — *RC* 11–9/10 (Sep.-Oct. 1957): 196–231; 11–11/12 (Nov.–Dec. 1957): 257–281, 281–285; 12–1/2 (Jan.–Feb. 1958): 36.

[Miller, P. 1972] "In Memory of the Carnegie Set" / Philip L. Miller. — *ARSCJ* 4 (1972): 21–28.

[Miller, P. 1976] "Margarete Matzenauer" / Philip L. Miller. — *RC* 23–1/2 (Jan. 1976): 3–47.

[Mitchell, P. 1982] "Which Tracks Best, a Pivoted or a Radial Tonearm?" / Peter W. Mitchell. — *Audio,* June 1982: 25–29.

[Mitchell, R. 1966] "Panachord Label" / Ray Mitchell. — *Matrix* 68 (Dec. 1966) through 91 (Feb. 1971). A series listing issues of 1931–1939.

[Modern 1989] *Modern Music Librarianship: Essays in Honor of Ruth Watanabe* . Edited by Alfred Mann. — Stuyvesant, N.Y.: Pendragron Press, 1989. 252 p. — (Festschrift Series, 8.)

[Montgomery 1975] "Piano Rollography of Adrian Rollini" / Michael Montgomery. — *RR* 135/136 (Nov.–Dec. 1975): 5–7.

[Montgomery 1978] "Eubie Blake Piano Rollography" / Michael Montgomery. — *RR* 159/160 (Dec. 1978): 4–5.

[Moogk 1975] *Roll Back the Years* / Edward B. Moogk. — Ottawa: National Library of Canada, 1975. 443 p.; phonodisc in pocket. Parker 1988 is a title index to Canadian works cited.

[Moon 1990] *Full Frequency Stereophonic Sound. A Discography and History of Early London/Decca Stereo Classical Instrumental and Chamber Music Recordings (1956–1963) on Records and Compact Discs* / Robert Moon and Michael Gray. — San Francisco: Robert Moon, 1990. 83 p.

[Moore 1964] "Yale University Historical Sound Recordings Program: Its Purpose and Scope" / Jerrold N. Moore. — *Recorded Sound* 16 (Oct. 1964): 270–279.

[Moore 1976] *A Voice in Time: The Gramophone of Fred Gaisberg, 1873–1951* / Jerrold N. Moore. — London: Hamilton, 1976. 248 p.

[Moran 1960] "Geraldine Farrar" / William R. Moran.— *RC* 13–9/10 (1960–1961): 194–240; 13–11/12 (Apr. 1961): 279–280; 14–7/8 (1961): 172–174; 20–6/7 (May 1972): 163–164.

[Moran 1963] "Discography" / William R. Moran. — In *Yankee Diva; Lillian Nordica and the Golden Days of Opera*, by Ira Glackens (New York: Coleridge Press, 1963; 366 p.), pp. 285–300.

[Moran 1965/1] "Mario Ancona" / William R. Moran. — *RC* 16–5/6 (Apr. 1965): 100–139; 16–7/8 (Sep. 1965): 188; 20–6/7 (May 1972): 164.

[Moran 1965/2] "Bettini Cylinders" / William R. Moran. — *RC* 16–7/8 (Sep. 1965): 148–185.

[Moran 1977] "Discography" / William R. Moran.— In *Forty Years of Song*, by Emma Albani (New York: Arno Press, 1977), pp. i–v.

[Moran 1977/1] "The Recordings of Emma Calvé" / William R. Moran.— In *My Life*, by Emma Calvé (New York: Arno Press, 1977), pp. i–viii.

[Moran 1977/2] "The Recordings of Emma Eames" / William R. Moran. — In *Some Memories and Reflections*, by Emma Eames (New York: Arno Press, 1977), pp. 313–320.

[Moran 1977/3] "The Recordings of Olive Fremstad" / William R. Moran. — In *The Rainbow Bridge*, by Mary Watkins Cushing (New York: Arno Press, 1977), pp. i–iv.

[Moran 1977/4] "The Recordings of Sir Charles Santley" / William R. Moran. — In *Reminiscences of My Life*, by Charles Santley (New York: Arno Press, 1977), pp. i–ii.

[Moran 1977/5] "The Recordings of Ernestine Schumann-Heink" / William R. Moran. — In *Schumann-Heink, the Last of the Titans*, by Mary Lawton (New York: Arno, 1977), pp. 339–428.

[Moran 1977/6] "The Recordings of Francesco Tamagno" / William R. Moran. — In *Tamagno*, by Mario Corsi (New York: Arno Press, 1977), pp. 215–218.

[Moran 1977/7] "Discography" / William R. Moran. — In *Mattia Battistini: il re dei baritoni*, by Francesco Palmegiani (New York: Arno Press, 1977), unpaged.

[Moran 1977/8] "Discography" / William R. Moran. — In *The Glory Road*, by Lawrence Tibbett (New York: Arno Press, 1977), pp. i–xxii.

[Moran 1984/1] "Discography" / William R. Moran. — In *Nellie Melba, a Contemporary Review* (Westport, Conn.: Greenwood Press, 1984), pp. 447–472.

[Moran 1984/2] "Discography" / William R. Moran. — In *Titta Ruffo: An Anthology* (Westport, Conn.: Greenwood Press, 1984), pp. 251–269.

[Morby 1952] "Aureliano Pertile" / P. Morby. — *RC* 7–11 (Nov. 1952): 244–260; 7–12 (Dec. 1952): 267–277; 8–1 (Jan. 1953): 37–41; 10–12 (Nov. 1956): 277.

[Morgan 1979] "John Charles Thomas" / Charles I. Morgan. — *RC* 25–1/2 (Mar. 1979): 5–31.

[Morin 1982] *Conversations avec Pablo Casals* / Philippe Morin. — Paris: A. Michel, 1982. Discography, pp. 417–444.

[Morritt 1979] "Carson J. Robison" / Robert D. Morritt. — *NAG* 29 (Summer 1979): 4–8.

[Moses 1949] *Collector/s Guide to American Recordings, 1895–1925* / Julian Morton Moses. — New York: American Record Collectors Exchange, 1949. 200 p. Reprint—New York: Dover, 1977.

[Mulholland 1980] *The Music Recording Industry in Australia* / Pauline Mulholland. — Fitzroy, Victoria, Australia: Victorian Commercial Teachers Association and Victoria Education Department, 1989.

[Music Recording 1978] "The Music Recording Industry in Australia" / Industries Assistance Commission. — Canberra: The Commission, 1978.

[Musical 1895] *Musical Instruments at the World's Columbian Exposition.* — Chicago: Presto Co., 1895. 328 p.

[Myers 1978] *Index to Record Reviews: Based on Material Originally Published in Notes, the Quarterly Journal of the Music Library Association, between 1949 and 1977* / Compiled and edited by Kurtz Myers. — Boston: G. K. Hall, 1978–1980. 5 vols. Supplements 1985, 1989. Supersedes *Record Ratings* (New York: Crown, 1956).

[New Grove 1986] *New Grove Dictionary of American Music* / Edited by H. Wiley Hitchcock and Stanley Sadie. — London: Macmillan, 1986. 4 vols.

[Newsom 1985] *Wonderful Inventions: Motion Pictures, Broadcasting, and Recorded Sound at the Library of Congress* / Edited by Iris Newsom; with an introduction by Erik Barnouw. — Washington: Library of Congress, 1985. 384 p.; two 12–inch LP records included.

[Newville 1959] "Development of the Phonograph at Alexander Graham Bell's Volta Laboratory" / Leslie J. Newville. — In *Contributions from the Museum of History and Technology* 5(Washington: Smithsonian Institution, 1959), pp. 69–79.

[Nolden 1990] *Count Basie; sein Leben, seine Musik, seine Schallplatten* / Rainer Nolden. — Schaftlach, Germany: OREOS, 1990. 184 p.

[Novitsky 1988] "The Mercury 5000 Series" / Ed Novitsky. — *RR* 233/234 (Feb. 1988): 4–5; 235/236 (June 1988): 9; 237/238 (Nov. 1988): 9; 239/240 (Apr. 1989): 9; 241/241 (Oct.–Nov. 1989): 9; 243/244 (May–June 1990): 9; 245/246 (Jan. 1991): 9; 247/248 (Sep. 1991): 9. The 5000 series appeared in 1946–1952.

[O'Brien 1992] *Sinatra: The Man and His Music . . .* / Ed O'Brien and Scott P. Sayers. — Austin, Tex.: TSD Press, 1992. 303 p.

[Odell 1974] "The Edison Diamond Disc Phonograph—Perfect Fidelity 60 Years Ago!" / L. Brevoort Odell. — *ARSCJ* 6 (1974): 3–12.

[Olson, H. 1947] *Elements of Acoustical Engineering* / Harry F. Olson. — 2nd ed. — New York: Van Nostrand, 1947. 539 p.

[Olson, H. 1954] "Recent Developments in Direct-radiator High-fidelity Loudspeakers" / Harry F. Olson, John Preston, and Everett G. May. — *Journal of the Audio Engineering Society* 2 (October 1954): 219–227.

[Olson, H. 1964] "The RCA Victor Dynagroove System" / Harry F. Olson. — *Journal of the Audio Engineering Society* 12–2 (1964): 98–114. Reprinted in Roys 1978.

[Olson, H. 1977] "Microphones for Recording" / Harry F. Olson. — *Journal of the Audio Engineering Society* 25–10/11 (Oct.–Nov. 1977): 676–684.

[Olson, R. 1986] "The Grey Gull 4000 Series" / Robert C. Olson. — *NAG* 56 (Spring 1986): 3–10.

[Oprisko 1990] "Frank Sinatra 7–inch Collectibles" / Peter Paul Oprisko. — *Discoveries*, Sep. 1990: 24–32.

[Ord-Hume 1984] *Pianola: The History of the Self-playing Piano* / Arthur W. J. G. Ord-Hume. — London: Allen & Unwin, 1984. 394 p.

[Owen, H. 1952] "Elisabeth Schumann" / H. G. Owen. — *RC* 7–10 (Oct. 1952): 220–239.

[Owen, H. 1969] "Marcella Sembrich" / H. G. Owen and William R. Moran. — *RC* 18–5/6 (May 1969): 99–138; 20–6/7 (May 1972): 165.

[Owen, T. 1982] "Electrical Reproduction of Acoustically Recorded Discs and Cylinders" / Tom Owen. — *ARSCJ* 14–1 (1982): 11–18.

[Owen, T. 1983] "Fifty Questions on Audio Restoration and Transfer Technology" / Tom Owen. — *ARSCJ* 15–2/3 (1983): 38–45. Comments noted at Lane 1984.

[Palmer 1983] *The Rolling Stones* / Robert Palmer and Mary Shanahan. — Garden City, N.Y.: Rolling Stones Press, Doubleday, 1983. 253 p.

[Palmieri 1985] *Sergei Vasil'evich Rachmaninoff: A Guide to Research* / Robert Palmieri. — New York:

Garland, 1985. 335 p. —(Garland Composer Resource Manuals, 3.) Discography, pp. 93–118.

[Park 1960] "Lily Pons" / Bill Park. — RC 13–11/12 (Apr. 1960): 243–271, 283.

[Park 1982] "Discography" / Bill Park. — In *Ponselle, a Singer's Life,* by Rosa Ponselle and James A. Drake (Garden City, N.Y.: Doubleday, 1982), pp. 248–307.

[Parker 1988] "Title Index to Canadian Works Listed in Edward B. Moogk's *Roll Back the Years. . .*" / C. P. Gerald Parker and David Emerson. — Ottawa: Canadian Association of Music Libraries, 1988. 13 p.

[Paul 1984] "The Kalamazoo Duplex" / George Paul. — NAG 48 (Spring 1984): 6–7.

[Paul 1985] "The Metaphone / Echophone" / George Paul. — NAG 51 (Winter 1985): 4.

[Paul 1988] "Phonograph Forum" / George Paul. — NAG 66 (Oct. 1988): 6–6.

[Paul 1991/1] "Step on It! Dance on It! A Wonder Record Surfaces" / George Paul. — APM 10–1 (1991): 5.

[Paul 1991/2] "The First Spring-Motor Gram-O-Phone" / George Paul. — NAG 77 (July 1991): 3.

[Pavarotti 1981] *Pavarotti: My Own Story* / Luciano Pavarotti. — Garden City, N.Y.: Doubleday, 1981. 316 p. Discography, pp. 291–308.

[Pearmain 1964] "Miliza Korjus" / M. D. J. Pearmain and R. P. Seemungal. — RC 16–2 (Sep. 1964): 28–45; 16–7/8 (Sep. 1965): 188–189.

[Peel 1985] "Riccardo Stracciari" / Tom Peel and Cliff Williams. — RC 30–1/2 (Feb. 1985): 39–53; 31–8/10 (Sep. 1986): 239.

[Peel 1990] "Beniamino Gigli" / Tom Peel and John Holohan. — RC 35–8/9/10 (Aug.-Sep.-Oct. 1990): 191–240.

[Perkins 1981] "The Gramophone & Typewriter Ltd. Records of Camille Saint-Saëns (1835–1921)" / John F. Perkins and Alan Kelly. — *Recorded Sound* 79 (Jan. 1981): 25–27.

[Petersen 1973] "The Origin of the I.C.S. Language Cylinders" / Phillip Petersen. — APM 1–4 (Apr. 1973): 3–4.

[Petersen 1975] "Amberol: A Word Study" / Phillip Petersen. — TMR 33 (Apr. 1975): 316–322.

[Petts 1973] "A Host of Angels" / Leonard Petts. — TMR 23 (Aug. 1973): 210–211. Descriptions and illustrations of labels with the Angel trademark.

[Petts 1983] *The Story of "Nipper" and the "His Master's Voice" Picture Painted by Francis Barraud* / Leonard Petts; with an introduction by Frank Andrews. — 2nd ed. — Bournemouth, England: Talking Machine Review, 1983. 68 p.

[Petts 1988] "Berliner's Compact Disc" / Leonard Petts. — HN 165 (Dec. 1988): 114–119.

[Petty 1976] "A Look at a Phenomenal Recording Schedule: Cal Stewart's 1919 Columbia Matrices" / John A. Petty. — NAG 16 (Winter 1976): 3–5.

[Petty 1984] "Kalamazoo Discs" / John A. Petty. — NAG 48 (Spring 1984): 10–11.

[Petty 1988] "Busy Bee Labels" / John A. Petty. — HN 163 (Aug. 1988): 68–70.

[Phillips 1947] "Mattia Battistini" / Ronald Phillips. — RC 2–9 (Sep. 1947): 129–133; 3 (May 1948): 73.

[Phonograph 1972] *The Phonograph and Sound Recording after One Hundred Years* / Edited by Warren Rex Isom. — *Journal of the Audio Engineering Society* 25 (Oct.–Nov. 1977). Centennial issue of the *Journal.* Individual articles cited separately in this Bibliography are Burt 1977, Isom 1977, Khanna 1977, Kogen 1977, and Olson 1977.

[Phonographs 1909] "Phonographs in Libraries." — *Library Journal* 34 (July 1909): 324.

[Pickett 1959] *Preservation and Storage of Sound Recordings* / A. G. Pickett and M. M. Lemcoe. — Washington: Library of Congress, 1959. 74 p.

[Pinne 1984] "Australian Theatre on Disc" / Peter Pinne. — In Hummel 1984, pp. xxvii-xxxiii.

[Pinta 1987] *A Chronologic Jan Peerce Discography, 1932–1980* / Emil R. Pinta. — Worthington, Ohio: Author, 1987. 29 p.

[Pitts 1986] *Radio Soundtracks: A Reference Guide* / Michael R. Pitts. — 2nd ed. — Metuchen, N.J.: Scarecrow Press, 1986. 349 p.

[Pitts 1988] *Kate Smith, a Bio-bibliography* / Michael R. Pitts. — Westport, Conn. : Greenwood Press, 1988. 320 p.

[Pohlmann 1989] *The Compact Disc: A Handbook of Theory and Use* / Ken C. Pohlmann. — Madison, Wis. : A-R Editions, 1989. 288 p.

[Polic 1989] *The Glenn Miller Army Air Force Band* / Edward F. Polic. — Metuchen, N.J.: Scarecrow Press, 1989. 2 vols.

[Poole 1947] "Louise Homer" / Louis Poole. — RC 2–7 (July 1947): 96–98.

[Popa 1987] *Cab Calloway and His Orchestra, 1925–1958* / Jay Popa; revised by Charles Garrod. — Zephyrhills, Fla.: Joyce Record Club, 1987. 38 p. (1st published 1976.)

[Porter 1977] "National Records" / Bob Porter. — RR 149/150 (Oct. 1977): 8–9; 151/152 (Jan. 1978): 15; 153/154 (Apr. 1978): 11–12; 155/156 (July 1978): 13, 16.

[Porter 1978] "Majestic Masters Listing" / Bob Porter. — RR 157/158 (Sep. 1978): 8–9; 159/160 (Dec. 1978): 12; 161/162 (Feb.–Mar. 1979): 12; 163/164 (May–June 1979): 12; 165/166 (Aug. 1979): 12; 167/168 (Oct. 1979): 9.

[Porter 1980] "List of Signature Masters" / Bob Porter. — RR 171/172 (Mar. 1980): 11; 173/174 (June 1980): 11; 177/178 (Nov. 1980): 14; 179/180 (Feb. 1981): 12; 181/182 (Apr. 1981): 9.

[Potter 1985] *Adolf Busch: The Life of an Honest Man* / Tully Potter. — Billericay, Essex, England: Author, 1985. Vol. 1– . Discography, pp. 59–135.

[Potterton 1967] "Zélie de Lussan" / Robert Potterton and James F. E. Dennis. — RC 17–8 (Dec. 1967): 171–182.

[Powell 1989] "Audiophile's Guide to Phonorecord Playback Equalizer Settings" / James R. Powell, Jr. — ARSCJ 20–1 (Spring 1989): 14–23.

[Proceedings 1974} *Proceedings of the 1890 Convention of Local Phonograph Companies* / Introduction by Raymond R. Wile. — Reprint ed. — Nashville, Tenn.: Country Music Foundation Press, 1974. 210 p.

[Proudfoot 1980] *Collecting Phonographs and Gramophones* / Christopher Proudfoot. — New York: Mayflower Books; London: Studio Vista, 1980. 119 p.

[Randel 1986] *The New Harvard Dictionary of Music* / Edited by Don Michael Randel. — Cambridge, Mass.: Harvard University Press, 1986. 942 p.

[Raymond 1981] "A Numerical Listing of Liberty Music Shop Records" / Jack Raymond. — RR 181/182 (Apr. 1981): 8; continued by Len Kunstadt: 185/186 (Oct. 1981): 9; 187/188 (Dec. 1981): 9; 189/190 (Mar.–Apr. 1982): 10; 191/192 (July 1982): 10; 195/196 (Jan. 1983): 12; 197/198 (Mar.–Apr. 1983): 8; 201/202 (Sep. 1983): 11; 203–204 (Dec. 1983): 9; 205/206 (Mar. 1984): 12; 207/208 (June 1984): 11; 209/210 (Oct. 1984): 12; 215/216 (July 1985): 11; 217/218 (Oct. 1985): 2; 219/220 (Jan. 1986): 5; 221/222 (Apr. 1986): 4; 227/228 (Mar. 1987): 10; 229/230 (June 1987): 14; 231/232 (Oct. 1987): 12; 233/234 (Feb. 1988): 6.

[Raymond 1982] *Show Music on Record from the 1890s to the 1980s* / Jack Raymond. — New York: Ungar, 1982. 253 p.

[Read 1976] *From Tin Foil to Stereo: Evolution of the Phonograph* / Oliver Read and Walter L. Welch. — 2nd ed. — Indianapolis, H. W. Sams, 1976. 550 p. (1st ed. 1959.)

[Record/Tape 1978] *Record/Tape Collector's Directory*. — 2nd ed. — Santa Monica, Calif.: Rare Record/Tape Collector's Directory, 1978. 47 p. (1st ed. 1976.)

[Reed 1955] "Frieda Hempel" / Peter Hugh Reed. — RC 10–3 (Aug. 1955): 51–71.

[Reid 1990] "CEDAR" / Gordon Reid. — HN 172 (Feb. 1990): 314–319.

[Reinhard 1961] "The Berlin Phonogramm-Archiv" / Kurt Reinhard. — *Recorded Sound* 1–2 (June 1961): 44–45.

[Reiss 1986] *The Compleat Talking Machine: A Guide to the Restoration of Antique Phonographs* / Eric Reiss. — Vestal, N.Y.: Vestal Press, 1986. 184 p.

[Rektorys 1971] "Emmy Destinn" / Artus Rektorys and James F. E. Dennis. — RC 20–1/2 (July 1971): 3–47; 20–4 (Dec. 1971): 93–94.

[Renton 1949] "Toti dal Monte" / Arthur Renton. — RC 4–9 (Sep. 1949): 142, 147–150.

[Richards 1948/2] "Elisabeth Rethberg" / John B. Richards. — RC 3–2 (Feb. 1948): 26–30; 3–4 (Apr. 1948): 51–56; 4–11 (Nov. 1949): 192–196; 5–1 (Jan. 1950): 11–16; 8–1 (Jan. 1953): 4–19.

[Richards 1948/10] "Lucrezia Bori" / John B. Richards. — RC 3–10 (Oct. 1948): 161–166; 4–1 (Jan. 1949): 2–12; 4–5 (May 1949): 98–99; 9–5 (1954): 104–123; 21–7/8 (Dec. 1973): 147–168.

[Richards 1949] "Luisa Tetrazzini" / John B. Richards and Phillip Wade. — RC 4–8 (Aug. 1949): 122–139.

[Richards 1950] "Elisabeth Rethberg" / John B. Richards. — *Hobbies*, Mar. 1950: 18–19; Apr. 1950: 18; May 1950: 18–19.

[Richards 1957] "Eva Turner" / John B. Richards. — RC 11–2/3 (Feb.–Mar. 1957): 28–57, 71; 11–8 (Aug. 1957): 183–184; 11–9/10 (Sep.-Oct. 1957): 231–233.

[Richards 1964] "Hipolito Lazaro" / John B. Richards. — RC 16–3/4 (Nov.–Dec. 1964): 52–94; 16–9/10 (Jan. 1966): 226–228; 18–11/12 (Dec. 1969): 280–281.

[Richards 1966] "Gemma Bellincioni" / John B. Richards. — RC 16–9/10 (Jan. 1966): 196–219; 18–5/6 (May 1969): 139–140.

[Richards 1968] "Claudia Muzio" / John B. Richards. — RC 17–9/10 (Feb. 1968): 197–237; 17–11 (Apr. 1968): 256–263; 28–5/6 (Oct. 1983): 120–128.

[Richards 1973] "Lucrezia Bori" / John B. Richards. — RC 21–7/8 (Dec. 1973): 147–168.

[Richards 1980] "Ezio Pinza" / John B. Richards and J. P. Kenyon. — RC 26–3/4 (Aug. 1980): 51–95; 26–5/6 (Dec. 1980): 101–137.

[Ridley 1959] "Emma Albani" / Nicholas A. Ridley. — RC 12–4/5 (Feb.–Mar. 1959): 76–101; 12–8/9 (Nov.–Dec. 1959): 197–198; 14–9/10 (1961): 236.

[Riemens 1947] "Julia Culp" / Leo Riemens. — RC 2–7 (July 1947): 100–104.

[Riemens 1951] "Irene Abendroth" / Leo Riemens. — RC 6–4 (Apr. 1951): 75–85.

[Riggs 1970] "The Revelers" / Quentin Riggs. — TMR 6 (Oct. 1970): 158–163.

[Roach 1988] "Two Women of Caedmon" / Helen Roach. — ARSCJ 19–1 (May 1988): 21–24.

[Robertson, A. 1983] "Canadian Gennett and Starr-Gennett 9000 Numerical" / Alex Robertson. — RR 195/196 (Jan. 1983): 1–7; 197/198 (Mar.–Apr. 1983): 7; 199/200 (June 1983): 10–11; 201/202 (Sep. 1983): 10; 203/204 (Dec. 1983): 4.

[Robertson, A. 1986] "The Rare Canadian Aurora Label from Victor Masters" / Alex Robertson. — RR 219/220 (Jan. 1986): 1, 3–8.

[Robertson, J. 1978] "Leonid Sobinoff" / John Robertson and James F. E. Dennis. — RC 24–7/8 (Sep. 1978): 147–190.

[Rolling 1979] Rolling Stone Record Guide / Edited by Dave Marsh and John Swenson. — New York: Random House, 1979. 631 p.

[Rose 1979] Eubie Blake / Al Rose. — New York: Schirmer, 1979. 214 p. Discography, pp. 174–188.

[Rosenberg 1983] Dictionary of Library and Educational Technology / Kenyon C. Rosenberg and Paul T. Feinstein. — 2nd ed. — Littleton, Colo.: Libraries Unlimited, 1983. 185 p. (1st ed. 1976: Media Equipment: A Guide and Dictionary, by Kenyon C. Rosenberg and John S. Deskey.)

[Rosenberg 1987] A Basic Classical and Operatic Recordings Collection for Libraries / Kenyon C. Rosenberg. — Metuchen, N.J.: Scarecrow Press, 1987. 255 p.

[Rosenberg 1990] A Basic Classical and Operatic Recordings Collection on Compact Discs for Libraries / Kenyon C. Rosenberg. — Metuchen, N.J.: Scarecrow Press, 1990. 395 p.

[Rosenberg, N. 1974] Bill Monroe and His Blue Grass Boys: An Illustrated Discography / Neil V. Rosenberg. — Nashville, Tenn.: Country Music Foundation Press, 1974. 120 p.

[Rotante 1959] "The 'King' of R & B Labels" / Anthony Rotante. — RR 22 (Apr.–May 1959), 24, 25, 27, 29, 30, 87, 90, 91, 92, 93, 94, and 98 (1969). A serial label list, with background on the firm in issue 87. Title varies.

[Rotante 1966] "Bluesville" / Anthony Rotante. — RR 73 (Jan. 1966): 5.

[Rotante 1971] "Federal; The Federal 12000 Series" / Anthony Rotante. — RR 111 (July 1971), 113/114, 115, 116, 117, 119/120, 121, 122 (June 1973).

[Rotante 1973] "De Luxe 6000 Series" / Anthony Rotante. — RR 124 (Nov. 1973): 10; 125/126 (Feb. 1974): 14.

[Rotante 1975] "Maurice Chevalier on Pathé/Salabert Labels" / Anthony Rotante. — RR 135/136 (Nov.–Dec. 1975): 4.

[Rotante 1983] "Edith Piaf—the Early Years, Polydor Records 1936–1944" / Anthony Rotante. — RR 199/200 (June 1983): 4; 201/202 (Sep. 1983): 10; 203/204 (Dec. 1983): 8.

[Rotante 1985] "Imperial" / Anthony Rotante. — RR 215/216 (July 1985): 1, 3–4; 217/218 (Oct. 1985): 6–7; 219/220 (Jan. 1986): 12; 221/222 (Apr. 1986): 10–11; 223/224 (Aug. 1986): 12; 225/226 (Nov. 1986): 10; 227/228 (Mar. 1987): 8; 229/230 (June 1987): 11; 231/232 (Oct. 1987): 8–9; 233/234 (Feb. 1988): 10–11. Continues as Hayes, C. 1988.

[Royal 1977] Phonograph and Gramophone Symposium, 2 July 1977 / Royal Scottish Museum. — Edinburgh: The Museum, 1977. 142 p.

[Roys 1978] Disc Recording and Reproduction / Ed. Henry Edward Roys. — Stroudsburg, Penn.:

Dowden, Hutchenson and Ross, 1978. 394 p. Consists of 42 papers, reprinted from technical journals.

[Rules 1978] *Rules for Archival Cataloging of Sound Recordings* / Association for Recorded Sound Collections, Associated Audio Archives Committee.— Silver Spring, Md.: The Association, 1978. 72 p.

[Ruppli 1979] *Atlantic Records: A Discography* / Michel Ruppli. — Westport, Conn.: Greenwood Press, 1979. 4 vols.

[Ruppli 1980] *The Prestige Label: A Discography* / Michel Ruppli; with assistance from Bob Porter. — Westport, Conn.: Greenwood Press, 1980. 378 p.

[Ruppli 1980/1] *The Savoy Label: A Discography* / Michel Ruppli; with assistance from Bob Porter. — Westport, Conn.: Greenwood Press, 1980. 443 p.

[Ruppli 1981] *Charles Mingus Discography* / Michel Ruppli.— Frankfurt: Norbert Ruecker, 1981. 47 p. — (Jazz Index Reference Series, 1.).

[Ruppli 1983] *The Chess Labels: A Discography* / Michel Ruppli. — Westport, Conn.: Greenwood Press, 1983. 2 vols.

[Ruppli 1986] *The Clef/Verve Labels: A Discography* / Michel Ruppli. — Westport, Conn.: Greenwood Press, 1986. 2 vols.

[Rust 1970] *The Victor Master Book, II (1925–1936)* / Brian Rust. — Stanhope, N.J.: Allen, 1970. 776 p. Covers Victor black label issues and Bluebird issues of 1933–1936. Vol. 1 has not been published.

[Rust 1973] *The Complete Entertainment Discography, 1897–1942* / Brian Rust. — 2nd ed. — New York: Da Capo Press, 1989. 794 p. An "updated and expanded" reprint of the 1st ed. (New Rochelle, N.Y.: Arlington House, 1973).

[Rust 1975] *The American Dance Band Discography, 1917–1942* / Brian Rust. — New Rochelle, N.Y.: Arlington House, 1975. 2 vols. A series of additions and corrections has been appearing in issues of *RR* since 157/158 (Sep. 1978).

[Rust 1977] *London Musical Shows on Record, 1897–1976* / Brian Rust and Rex Bunnett. — Rev. ed. — London: British Institute of Recorded Sound, 1977. 672 p. (1st ed. 1958, with Supplement 1959.) A revised edition is Seeley 1989.

[Rust 1978] *The American Record Label Book* / Brian Rust.— New Rochelle, N.Y.: Arlington House, 1978. 336 p.

[Rust 1979/1] *Discography of Historical Records on Cylinders and 78s* / Brian Rust. — Westport, Conn.: Greenwood Press, 1979. 327 p.

[Rust 1979/2] *British Music Hall on Record* / Brian Rust. — Harrow, England: General Gramophone Publications, 1979. 301 p.

[Rust 1980] *Brian Rust's Guide to Discography* / Brian Rust. — Westport, Conn.: Greenwood Press, 1980. 133 p.

[Rust 1981] "(British) Berliner, G & T and Zonophone 7–inch Records" / Brian Rust. — *TMR* 63/64 (Autumn 1981): 1,726–1,758. Adamson 1983 has useful comments on this list.

[Rust 1982] *Jazz Records, 1897–1942* / Brian Rust. — 5th ed. — Chigwell, England: Storyville, 1982. 2 vols. (1st ed. 1961.)

[Rust 1989] *British Dance Bands on Record, 1911 to 1945, and Supplement* / Brian Rust and Sandy Forbes. — Harrow, England: General Gramophone Publications, 1989. 1,496 p. A reprint of the original (1986) edition, with a 72 p. supplement.

[Salewicz 1986] *McCartney* / Chris Salewicz. — New York: St. Martin's, 1986. 263 p.

[Samuels 1980] "A Complete Discography of the Recordings of Emanuel Feuermann" / Jon Samuels. — *ARSCJ* 12–1/2 (1980): 33–77.

[Samuels 1987] "A Complete Discography of the Recordings of the Flonzaley Quartet" / Jon Samuels. — *ARSCJ* 19–1 (1987): 25–62.

[Sanders 1981] *Sir Adrian Boult: A Discography* / Alan Sanders. — Harrow, England: General Gramophone Publications, 1981. 37 p.

[Sanders 1984] *Walter Legge: A Discography* / Alan Sanders.— Westport, Conn.: Greenwood Press, 1984. 452 p.

[Sarnoff 1948] *Edison (1847–1931)* / David Sarnoff. — New York: Newcomen Society, 1948. 24 p.

[Schuller 1968] *Early Jazz: Its Roots and Musical Development* / Gunther Schuller. — New York: Oxford University Press, 1968. 401 p. — (History of Jazz, 1.).

[Schuller 1989] *The Swing Era: The Development of Jazz, 1930–1945* / Gunther Schuller. — New York: Oxford University Press, 1989. 919 p. — (History of Jazz, 2.).

[Schwartz 1984] "The Coon-Sanders Orchestra" / Leonard Schwartz. — *TMR* 69 (Dec.1984): 1,898–1,902.

[Schwarzkopf 1982] *On and Off the Record: A Memoir of Walter Legge* / Elisabeth Schwarzkopf. — New York: Scribner's Sons, 1982. 292 p.

[Scott 1977] *The Record of Singing to 1914* / Michael Scott. — London: Duckworth, 1978. 243 p. Issued with the EMI record series, *The Record of Singing* (EMI #RLS 724). Continued by Scott 1979.

[Scott 1979] *The Record of Singing: Volume Two, 1914–1925* / Michael Scott. — London: Duckworth; New York: Holmes & Meier, 1979. 262 p. Continues Scott 1977.

[Scott 1988] *The Great Caruso* / Michael Scott. — New York: Knopf, 1988. 322 p. "A Chronology of Caruso's Appearances," by Thomas G. Kaufman, pp. 201–264; "A Caruso Discography," by John R. Bolig, pp. 265–293.

[Sears 1980] *V-Discs: A History and Discography* / Richard S. Sears. — Westport, Conn.: Greenwood Press, 1980. 1,166 p. —(ARSC Reference Series.). 1st Supplement, 1986 (272 p.).

[Seeliger 1963] "Tiana Lemnitz" / Ronald Seeliger and Bill Park. — *RC* 15–2 (1963): 28–43.

[Seeger 1987] *Early Field Recordings: A Catalogue of Cylinder Collections at the Indiana University Archives of Traditional Music* / Anthony Seeger and Louise S. Spear. — Bloomington, Ind.: Indiana University Press, 1987. 198 p.

[Seeley 1989] *London Musical Shows on Record, 1889–1989* / Robert Seeley and Rex Bunnett. — Harrow, England: General Gramophone Publications, 1989. 457 p. A revision of Rust 1977.

[Segond 1981] *Renata Tebaldi* / André Segond. — Lyon, France: Laffont, 1981. 260 p. Discography, pp. 237–253.

[Semeonoff 1974] "New Complete Discography of Feodor Chaliapin" / Boris Semeonoff and Alan Kelly. — *RC* 20–8/9/10 (Aug. 1972): 171–230.

[Seymour 1918] *The Reproduction of Sound* / Henry Seymour. — London: W. B. Tattersall, 1918. 324 p.

[Shaman 1991] "The Operatic Vitaphone Shorts" / William Shaman. — *ARSCJ* 22–1 (Spring 1991): 35–94.

[Shaw 1974] *The Rockin' 50s* / Arnold Shaw. — New York: Hawthorne, 1974. 296 p. Reprint—New York: Da Capo Press, 1987.

[Shawe-Taylor 1961] "Arthur Nikisch" / Desmond Shawe-Taylor and E. Hughes. — *Recorded Sound* 4 (Oct. 1961): 114–115.

[Sheridan 1986] *Count Basie: A Bio-discography* / Chris Sheridan. — Westport, Conn.: Greenwood Press, 1986. 1,350 p.

[Sherman 1987] *The Paper Dog: An Illustrated Guide to 78 RPM Victor Record Labels, 1900–1958* / Michael W. Sherman. — Brooklyn: APM Press, 1987. 43 p.

[Sherman 1990] "The First Commercial Berliner Records Made in America" / Michael Sherman. — *APM* 9–3 (1990): 3–7.

[Shipway 1983] "Getting the Best Results from 78 RPM Records in 1984 [*sic*]" / E. L. M. Shipway. — *TMR* 65/66 (Feb. 1983): 1,888–1,889.

[Sieben 1985] "Vox and Successor" / Hansfried Sieben. — *TMR* 70 (Dec. 1985): 2,000–2,001.

[Simms 1979] *Wildlife Sounds and Their Recording* / Eric Simms. — London: Elek, 1979. 144 p.

[Simon 1974] *The Big Bands* / George T. Simon. — Rev. ed. — New York: Macmillan, 1974. 584 p. (1st ed. 1967.)

[Sitsky 1985] *Busoni and the Piano* / Larry Sitsky. — Westport, Conn.: Greenwood Press, 1985. 409 p. Discography, pp. 326–333.

[Sitsky 1990] *The Classical Reproducing Roll: A Catalogue-index* / Larry Sitsky. — Westport, Conn.: Greenwood Press, 1990. 2 vols.

[Slide 1982] *Great Radio Personalities in Historic Photographs* / Anthony Slide. — New York: Dover, 1982. 117 p.

[Slonimsky 1984] *Baker's Biographical Dictionary of Musicians* / Nicholas Slonimsky. — 7th ed. — New York: Schirmer, 1984. 2,577 p.

[Small 1972] "Closed-box Loudspeaker Systems" / Richard H. Small. — *Journal of the Audio Engineering Society*, Dec. 1972: 798–808; Jan.–Feb. 1973: 11–17.

[Smart 1970] *The Sousa Band: A Discography* / James R. Smart. — Washington: Library of Congress, 1970. 123 p.

[Smart 1977] "*A Wonderful Invention*"; *A Brief History of the Phonograph from Tinfoil to the LP* / James

R. Smart and Jon W. Newsom. — Washington: Library of Congress, 1977. 40 p.

[Smart 1982] *Radio Broadcasts in the Library of Congress, 1924–1941: A Catalog of Recordings* / James R. Smart. — Washington: Library of Congress, 1982. 149 + xiv p.

[Smart 1983] "Carl Engel and the Library of Congress's First Acquisitions of Recordings" / James R. Smart. — *ARSCJ* 15–2/3 (1983): 6–18.

[Smiraglia 1989] *Music Cataloging* / Richard P. Smiraglia. — Englewood, Colo.: Libraries Unlimited, 1989. 222 p.

[Smith 1985] *The Johnny Cash Discography* / John L. Smith. — Westport, Conn.: Greenwood Press, 1985. 203 p.

[Smithson 1990] *The Recordings of Edwin Fischer* / Roger Smithson. — Rev. ed. — London: Author, 1990. 25 p. (1st ed. 1983.)

[Smolian 1970] *Handbook of Film, Theatre and Television Music on Records, 1948–1969* / Steven Smolian. — New York: Record Undertaker, 1970. 2 vols. in 1; 64 p. + 64 p.

[Smolian 1970/1] "Four Decades of the Budapest Quartet" / Steven Smolian. — *American Record Guide* 37 (Dec. 1970): 220–224+.

[Smolian 1976] "Standards for the Review of Discographic Works" / Steve Smolian. — *ARSCJ* 7–3 (1976): 47–55.

[Smolian 1987] "Preservation, Deterioration and Restoration of Recording Tape" / Steve Smolian. — *ARSCJ* 19–2/3 (1987): 37–53.

[Southall 1982] *Abbey Road: The Story of the World's Most Famous Recording Studios* / Brian Southall. — Cambridge, England: Patrick Stephens, 1982. 217 p.

[Special 1980] *Special Collections in the Library of Congress; A Selective Guide.* — Washington: Library of Congress, 1980. 464 p.

[Spottswood 1991] *Ethnic Music on Records: A Discography of Ethnic Recordings Produced in the United States, 1893–1942* / Richard K. Spottswood. — Urbana, Ill.: University of Illinois Press, 1991. 7 vols.

[Stambler 1983] *Encyclopedia of Folk, Country and Western Music* / Irwin Stambler and Grelun Landon. — 2nd ed. — New York: St. Martin's, 1983. 396 p. (1st ed. 1969.)

[Stambler 1989] *Encyclopedia of Pop, Rock and Soul* / Irwin Stambler. — 2nd ed. — New York: St. Martin's, 1989. 881 p. (1st ed. 1974.)

[Stark 1990] "Dolby S; A New Standard for Cassette Recording?" / Craig Stark. — *Stereo Review*, May 1990: 78–79.

[Steane 1974] *The Grand Tradition: Seventy Years of Singing on Record* / J. B. Steane. — London: Duckworth, 1974. 628 p.

[Steane 1979] "Discography" / John Steane. — In *My Life*, by Tito Gobbi (London: Macdonald and James, 1979), pp. 201–210.

[Stephenson 1983] "The Impressive Dominion Autophone" / Tom Stephenson. — *HN* 135 (Dec. 1983): 288–289.

[Sterling 1978] *Stay Tuned: A Concise History of American Broadcasting* / Christopher H. Sterling and John M. Kittross. — Belmont, Calif.: Wadsworth, 1978. 562 p.

[Stevens 1965] *Sound and Hearing* / S. S. Stevens and Fred Warshofsky. — 2nd ed. — New York: Time-Life Books, 1969. 200 p.

[Stevenson 1972] "Discography: Scientific, Analytical, Historical and Systematic" / Gordon Stevenson. — *Library Trends* 21–1 (July 1972): 101–135.

[Stover 1990] "The 'Fair Use' of Sound Recordings: A Summary of Existing Practices and Concerns" / Suzanne Stover. — *ARSCJ* 21–2 (1990): 232–240.

[Stratton 1967] "The Recordings of Jean de Reszke" / John Stratton. — *Recorded Sound* 27 (July 1967): 209–213.

[Stratton 1973] "Dmitri Smirnov" / John Stratton. — *RC* 14–11/12 (July 1973): 244–247.

[Stratton 1974] "Florence Eaton" / John Stratton. — *RC* 21–9/10 (Jan 1974): 195–239; 21–11/12 (Mar. 1974): 256.

[Stroff 1988/5] "Django's Dream; The Life of Django Reinhardt" / Stephen Stroff. — *Antiques and Collecting Hobbies*, May 1988: 70–71; June 1988: 57–59.

[Stroff 1988/10] "Young Jussi Björling" / Stephen Stroff. — *Antiques and Collecting Hobbies*, Oct. 1988: 59–64.

[Stroff 1989] "Gennett Records; the Label that Changed History" / Stephen Stroff. — *Antiques and Collecting Hobbies*, June 1989.

[Summers 1958] *A Thirty-year History of Programs Carried on National Radio Networks in the United States, 1926–1956* / Harrison B. Summers. — Columbus, Ohio: Department of Speech, The Ohio State University, 1958. 228 p. Reprints—New York: Arno Press, 1971; Salem, N.H.: Ayer, 1986.

[Sunier 1986] "A History of Binaural Sound" / John Sunier. — *Audio*, Mar. 1986: 36–44.

[Sutton 1991] *A.K.A.: Pseudonyms on American Records, 1900–1932* / Allan Sutton. — Baltimore: Author, 1991. 16 p.

[Swartz 1992] *Handbook of Old-time Radio: A Comprehensive Guide to Golden Age Radio Listening and Collecting* / Jon D. Swartz and Robert C. Reinehr. — Metuchen, N.J.: Scarecrow Press, 1992. (In press.)

[Swartzburg 1980] *Preserving Library Materials* / Susan G. Swartzburg. — Metuchen, N.J.: Scarecrow Press, 1980. 282 p. (2nd ed. in press, 1992).

[Taylor, G. 1983] "Dating Gramophone Co. London Recordings, 1908–1925" / George Taylor. — *HN* 132 (June 1983): 204–206.

[Taylor, G. 1985] "Vitaphone" / George W. Taylor. — *HN* 144 (June 1985): 218–222; 146 (Oct. 1985): 257–260; 149 (Apr. 1986): 19–22.

[Taylor, G. 1987/4] "Opera on Bettini" / George Taylor. — *HN* 155 (Apr. 1987): 174–185.

[Taylor, G. 1987/8] "The Mapleson Cylinders" / George W. Taylor. — *HN* 157 (Aug. 1987): 228–236.

[Taylor, G. 1988] "The Recorded Legacy of Jean de Reszke" / George W. Taylor. — *RC* 33–1/2 (Jan. 1988): 22–25.

[Taylor, G. 1990] "Berliner at the Opera" / George Taylor. — *HN* 173 (Apr. 1990): 2–4. Comments by P. G. Adamson in *HN* 174 (June 1990): 36.

[Tesoriero 1990] "Beniamino Gigli—the One and Only" / Michael Tesoriero. — *Journal of the Phonograph Society of New South Wales* 6–3 (Apr. 1990): 20–26; 6–4 (July 1990): 21–29.

[Thielcke 1976] *Bird Sounds* / Gerhard Thielcke. — Ann Arbor, Mich.: University of Michigan Press, 1976. 190 p.

[Thiele 1971] "Loudspeakers in Vented Boxes" / A. N. Thiele. — *Journal of the Audio Engineering Society*, May 1971: 382–391; June 1971: 471–483.

[Thorgerson 1977] *Album Cover Album* / Storm Thorgerson and Roger Dean. — New York: A & W Visual Library, 1977. 160 p.

[Thorgerson 1982] *Album Cover Album: The Second Volume* / Storm Thorgerson, Roger Dean, and David Howells. — New York: A & W Visual Library, 1982. 159 p.

[Thorin 1984] *The Acquisition and Cataloging of Music and Sound Recordings: A Glossary* / Suzanne E. Thorin and Carole Vidali Franklin. — Washington: Music Library Association, 1984. 40 p. — (Technical Reports, 11.)

[Timner 1988] *Ellingtonia: The Recorded Music of Duke Ellington and His Sidemen* / W. E. Timner. — 3rd ed. — Metuchen, N.J.: Scarecrow Press, 1988. 554 p.

[Toborg 1970] "Tex Ritter Collection" / D. Toborg. — *RR* 108 (Dec. 1970)-139/140 (May–June 1976). A series of label lists that appeared in most issues of *RR* in the period shown.

[Toborg 1979] "Tex Ritter: The Complete Capitol Discography" / D. Toborg. — *RR* 163/164 (May–June 1979)-217/218 (Oct. 1985). A series of listings that appeared in most issues of *RR* in the period shown.

[Treichel 1978] *Woody Herman's Second Herd, 1947–1949* / James Treichel. — Zephyrhills, Fla.: Joyce Record Club, 1978. 56 p.

[Tron 1954] "Maggie Teyte" / David Tron and James F. E. Dennis. — *RC* 9–6 (Nov. 1954): 128–138; 9–11/12 (Apr.–May 1955): 270–271.

[Tron 1977] "Recordings of Maggie Teyte" / David Tron. — In *Star on the Door*, by Maggie Teyte (New York: Arno Press, 1977), pp. 188–192.

[Tuddenham 1988] "Record Processing for Improved Sound" / Adrian Tuddenham and Peter Copeland. — *HN* 162 (June 1988): 34–39; 163 (Aug. 1988): 72–77; 164 (Oct. 1988): 89–97.

[Tudor 1983] *Popular Music: An Annotated Guide to Recordings* / Dean Tudor. — Littleton, Colo.: Libraries Unlimited, 1983. 647 p. Supersedes Tudor's 1979 books *Jazz*, *Black Music*, *Grass Roots Music*, and *Contemporary Pop Music*.

[Turner, P. 1990] *Dictionary of Afro-American Performers* / Patricia Turner. — New York: Garland, 1990. 433 p.

[Turner, R. 1988] *The Illustrated Dictionary of Electronics* / Rufus P. Turner and Stan Gibilisco. — 4th ed. — Blue Ridge Summit, Penn.: Tab Books, 1988. 648 p. (1st ed. 1985.)

[Usill 1980] "A History of Argo" / Harley Usill. — *Recorded Sound* 78 (July 1980): 31–44.

[Vaché 1987] *This Horn for Hire: The Life and Career of Pee Wee Erwin* / Warren W. Vaché. — Metuchen, N.J.: Scarecrow Press, 1987. 441 p.

[Variety 1989] *Variety's Directory of Major Show Business Awards* / Edited by Mike Kaplan. — 2nd ed. — New York: Bowker, 1989. 750 p. (1st ed. 1985.)

[Villchur 1965] *The Reproduction of Sound in High Fidelity and Stereo Phonographs* / Edgar M. Villchur. — New York: Dover, 1965. 92 p.

[Villetard 1984] "Coleman Hawkins, 1922–1944" / Jean François Villetard. — Amsterdam: Micrography, 1984. 80 p. Continued by "Coleman Hawkins, 1945–1957" (1985; 80 p.) and "Coleman Hawkins, 1958–1969" (1987; 80 p.).

[Vincent 1975] *Dictionary Catalog of the G. Robert Vincent Voice Library at Michigan State University* / Edited by Leonard E. Cluley and Pamela N. Engelbrecht. — Boston: G. K. Hall, 1975. 677 p.

[Voices 1955] *Voices of the Past* / John R. Bennett et al. — Lingfield, Surrey, England: Oakwood Press, 1955–1970. Facsimile typescript listings of vocal records on labels issued by the Gramophone Co. and affiliates. Coverage by volume (full titles of the volumes are in Rust 1980):

1. HMV English catalogues, 1898–1925 (1955);
2. HMV Italian catalogues, 1898–1925 (1958);
3. Dischi Fonotipia (1964?);
4, 6. International red label catalogues (1961, 1963);
5. HMV black label catalogues, D and E series (1960);
7. German catalogues (1967);
8. Columbia catalogue of English celebrity issues (1972);
9. French catalogues (1971?);
10. Plum label C series;
11. Russian catalogues, 1899–1915 (1977);
12. (Vol. LP1) Columbia blue and green labels, 1952–1962 (1975);
13. (Vol. LP2) HMV red label, 1952–1962 (1975);
14. (Vol. LP3) HMV plum label, 1952–1962 (1975).

[Von Békésy 1960] *Experiments in Hearing* / Georg Von Békésy. — New York: McGraw-Hill, 1960. 745 p. Reprint—Huntington, N.Y.: Robert E. Krieger, 1980.

[Vreede 1971] *Paramount 12000–13000* / Max E. Vreede. — London: Storyville Publications, 1971. Unpaged.

[Wachhorst 1981] *Thomas Alva Edison: An American Myth* / Wyn Wachhorst. — Boston: Massachusetts Institute of Technology Press, 1981. 328 p.

[Wade 1983] *Segovia, a Celebration of the Man and His Music* / Graham Wade. — London: Allison & Busby; New York: Schocken Books, 1983. 153 p. Discography, pp. 121–132.

[Wallman 1989] "The Berne Convention and Recent Changes in U.S. Copyright Law" / James Wallman. — *Cum notis variorum* 132 (May 1989): 8–10.

[Waltrip 1990] "Function and Restoration of Edison Rice Paper Diaphragms" Bob Waltrip. — *NAG* 73 (July 1990): 9–10.

[Want 1976] "The Great Beka Expedition, 1905–06" / John Want. — *TMR* 41 (Aug. 1976): 729–733.

[Ward 1990] *A Manual of Sound Archive Administration* / Alan Ward. — Aldershot, England; Brookfield, Vermont: Gower, 1990. 288 p.

[Warner 1984] "Researching the Pre-LP Original Cast Recording" / Larry Warner. — In Hummel 1984, pp. xli-xliv.

[Warren 1979] "A Preliminary Bibliography of Published Basic Source Materials and Guides to Dates of Recording for Pre-LP Classical Music and Spoken Word Sound Recordings" / Richard Warren, Jr. — *ARSCJ* 10–2/3 (1979): 163–166.

[Waters 1960] "The Hit-of-the-Week Record; A History and Discography" / Howard J. Waters. — *RR* 26 (Jan. Feb. 1960): 2–18.

[Watts 1979] "The Vertical-cut Disc Record" / Len Watts and Frank Andrews. — *HN* 108 (June 1979): 249–255.

[Watts 1989] "Pathé Records in Britain" / Len Watts and Frank Andrews. — *HN* 170 (Oct. 1989): 258–263; 171 (Dec. 1989): 289–295; 172 (Feb. 1990): 320–325; 173 (Apr. 1990): 8–11.

[Welch 1972] *Charles Batchelor: Edison's Chief Partner* / Walter L. Welch. — Syracuse, N.Y.: Syracuse University Press, 1972. 128 p.

[Weston 1971] *Clarinet Virtuosi of the Past* / Pamela Weston. — London: Hale, 1971. 292 p.

[Weston 1977] *More Clarinet Virtuosi of the Past* / Pamel Weston. — London: Author, 1977. 392 p.

[Whisler 1981] *Elvis Presley: Reference Guide and Discography* / John A. Whisler. — Metuchen, N.J.: Scarecrow Press, 1981. 265 p.

[Whitaker 1966] "Brass Recordings" / Donald W. Whitaker. — *Instrumentalist* 20 (June 1966): 73–78.

[White, D. 1962] "Florence Austral" / Don White and William Hogarth. — *RC* 14–1/2 (1962): 4–29; 14–7/8 (1962): 168–169.

[White, G. 1987] *The Audio Dictionary* / Glenn D. White. — Seattle: University of Washington Press, 1987. 291 p.

[Whittington 1981] *Literary Recordings: A Checklist of the Archive of Recorded Poetry and Literature in the Library of Congress* / Jennifer Whittington. — Rev. ed. — Washington: Library of Congress, 1981. 299 p. (1st ed. 1966.)

[Whyte 1986/4] "Shure Things" / Bert Whyte. — *Audio*, Apr. 1986: 26–27.

[Whyte 1986/8] "Fingering Prints" / Bert Whyte. — *Audio*, Aug. 1986: 16–18.

[Whyte 1989] "Put on Your Happy Feet" / Bert Whyte. — *Audio*, July 1989: 36–40. Discusses tweaking.

[Wile 1967] "The First Electrics" / Ray Wile. — *RR* 85 (Aug. 1967): 5.

[Wile 1968] "The Edison Long-playing Record: Complete List of Issued and Unissued Masters" / Ray Wile. — *RR* 88 (Jan. 1968): 8; 90 (May 1968): 9.

[Wile 1971/1] "How Well Did Edison Records Sell?" / Ray Wile. — *ARSCJ* 3–2/3 (1971): 59–78.

[Wile 1971/2] "The First Martinelli Recordings" / Raymond R. Wile. — *ARSCJ* 3–2/3 (Fall 1971): 25–45.

[Wile 1971/3] "The Edison Discs of Frieda Hempel" / Raymond R. Wile. — *ARSCJ* 3–2/3 (Fall 1971): 47–51.

[Wile 1972] "Edisonia—Local Phonograph Companies (1890–1893)" / Raymond R. Wile. — *RR* 115 (Feb. 1972): 8; 116 (May 1972): 9; 117 (Aug 1972): 10.

[Wile 1976] "The Edison Recordings of Gladys Rice" / Ray Wile. — *RR* 143 (Dec. 1976): 5–7.

[Wile 1976] "The Rise and Fall of the Edison Speaking Phonograph Company, 1877–1880" / Raymond R. Wile. — *ARSCJ* 7–3 (1976): 4–31, with 9 plates.

[Wile 1977] "The Edison Recordings of Edna White, Trumpet" / Raymond R. Wile. — *RR* 144/145 (Mar. 1977): 5.

[Wile 1978] *Edison Disc Recordings* / Raymond R. Wile. — Philadelphia: Eastern National Park and Monument Association, 1978. 427 p.

[Wile 1979/1] "The Edison Recordings of Anna Case" / Raymond R. Wile. — *ARSCJ* 10–2/3 (1979): 167–184.

[Wile 1979/2] "Berliner Sales Figures" / Raymond R. Wile. — *ARSCJ* 11–2/3 (1979): 139–143.

[Wile 1982] "The Edison Invention of the Phonograph" / Raymond R. Wile. — *ARSCJ* 14–2 (1982): 5–28.

[Wile 1985] "Record Piracy" / Raymond R. Wile. — *ARSCJ* 17–1/3 (1985): 18–40.

[Wile 1985/2] "The Last Years of Edison Recording Activities Day by Day, January 1928 to October 1929" / Raymond R. Wile. — *RR* 213/214 (May 1985): 1, 3–10; 215/216 (July 1985): 8–9; 217/218 (Oct. 1985): 1, 12–13; 219/220 (Jan. 1986): 13; 223/224 (Aug. 1986): 10–11.

[Wile 1987] "Jack Fell Down and Broke His Crown: The Fate of the Edison Phonograph Toy Manufacturing Company" / Raymond R. Wile. — *ARSCJ* 19–2/3 (FEb. 1989): 5–36.

[Wile 1990/1] "Etching the Human Voice: The Berliner Invention of the Gramophone" / Raymond R. Wile. — *ARSCJ* 21–1 (Spring 1990): 2–22.

[Wile 1990/2] "The Development of Sound Recording at the Volta Laboratory" / Raymond R. Wile. — *ARSCJ* 21–2 (Fall 1990): 208–225.

[Wile 1990/3] "From the Edison Vault: Edison Blue Amberol 28100 Series" / Raymond R. Wile.— *NAG* 74 (Oct. 1990): 3–13. Lists 189 records in the "Concert" or "Grand Opera" series.

[Wile 1990/4] *Edison Disc Artists and Records, 1910–1929* / Compiled by Raymond R. Wile; edited by Ronald Dethlefson. — 2nd ed. — Brooklyn: APM Press, 1990. 187 p. (1st ed. entered at Dethlefson 1985.)

[Wile 1991] "Edison and Growing Hostilities" / Raymond R. Wile. — *ARSCJ* 22–1 (Spring 1991): 8–34.

[Williams, C. 1956] "Adelina Patti" / Clifford Williams and William R. Moran. — *RC* 10–8/9 (July–Aug. 1956): 168–196.

[Williams, C. 1957] "Giuseppe De Luca" / Clifford Williams and Edward Hain. — *RC* 11–6 (June 1957): 124–140; 11–7 (July 1957): 184–185; 12–8/9 (Nov.–Dec. 1959): 199.

[Williams, C. 1957/11] "Giacomo Lauri-Volpi" / Clifford Williams and T. Hutchinson. — *RC* 11–11/12 (Nov.–Dec. 1957): 233–272; 12–1/2 (Jan.–Feb. 1958): 34–35; 12–3 (Mar. 1958): 66–67; 12–4/5 (Feb.–Mar. 1959): 108; 20–8/10 (Aug. 1972): 239.

[Williams, C. 1958] "Celestina Boninsegna" / Clifford Williams and John B. Richards. — *RC* 12–1/2 (Jan.–Feb. 1958): 4–33; 12–8/9 (Nov.–Dec. 1959): 200 (by Rodolfo Celletti); 12–10/11 (Dec. 1959): 257–258 (by C. de Villiers); 12–12 (Feb. 1958): 267–283 (by William R. Moran).

[Williams, F. 1972] "The Times as Reflected in the Victor Black Label Military Band Recordings from 1900 to 1927" / Frederick P. Williams. — *ARSCJ* 4–1/2/3 (1972): 33–46; 8–1 (1976): 4–14; 13–3 (1981): 21–59.

[Williams, F. 1985] "Eugene Ormandy Meets the Dorsey Brothers" / Frederick P. Williams. — *NAG* 52 (Spring 1985): 4–6.

[Williamson 1971] "Electrical Reproduction of Acoustical Records" / B. A. Williamson. — *TMR* 10 (June 1971): 45, 48.

[Wilson 1957] *The Gramophone Handbook* / Percy Wilson. — London: Methuen, 1957. 227 p.

[Wodehouse 1977] "Early Recorded Pianists: A Bibliography" / Artis Stiffey Wodehouse. — Ph.D. dissertation, Stanford University, 1977. 221 leaves.

[Wolf 1971] "Mengelberg Recordings: A Discography" / Robert Wolf. — *Le grand baton*, Aug.–Nov. 1971: 40–54.

[Wölfer 1987] *Dizzy Gillespie: sein Leben, seine Musik, seine Schallplatten* / Jürgen Wölfer. — Waakirchen, Germany: OREOS, 1987. 195 p.

[Wonderful 1985] *Wonderful Inventions* / Edited by Iris Newsom — Washington: Library of Congress, 1985. 384 p. A collection of articles, including three of interest to sound recording: "A Sound Idea: Music for Animated Films," by Jon Newsom; "Emile Berliner and Nineteenth-century Disc Recording," by James R. Smart; and "Cartoons for the Record: The Jack Kapp Collection," by Samuel Brylawski.

[Woods 1970] "Report on National Program Archives" / Robin Woods, — *ARSCJ* 2–2/3 (Spring-Summer 1970): 3–21.

[World 1970] *World Wide Record Collectors' Directory*. — Los Angeles: Hollywood Premium Record Guide, 1970. 46 p. (May be a revision of *World Wide Collectors' Directory*, by Will Roy Hearne, 1957.)

[Worth 1986] *John McCormack: A Comprehensive Discography* / Paul W. Worth and Jim Cartwright. — Westport, Conn.: Greenwood Press, 1986. 185 p.

[Yankovsky 1990] "Nikolai Figner" / M. O. Yankovsky; translated by John W. Robertson; revised and edited by Boris Semeonoff. — *RC* 35–1/2 (Jan.–Feb. 1990): 3–21.

[Young, E. 1990] "Serge Koussevitzky: A Complete Discography" / Edward D. Young. — *ARSCJ* 21–1 (Spring 1990): 45–129; 21–2 (Fall 1990): 241–265.

[Young, J. 1984] *Spike Jones and His City Slickers* / Jordan R. Young. — Beverly Hills, Calif.: Moonstone Press, 1984. 192 p. Includes a 35–page discography.

Checklist of Joint Authors and Editors

For the convenience of readers who wish to identify the authors and editors (and others with some responsibility in the publication) whose names do not appear as main entries above, those subordinate names are listed below.

Albert, George — *see* Hoffmann (several titles).

Andrews, Frank — Badrock 1991.

Andrews, Frank — Carter 1975.

Andrews, Frank — Petts 1983.

Andrews, Frank — Watts 1979.

Andrews, Frank — Watts 1989.

Avakian, George — Delaunay 1936.

Bachman, William S. — Goldmark 1949.

Badrock, Arthur —Adrian 1989.

Barnes, Harold M. — Girard 1964.

Barnouw, Erik — Newsom 1985.

Bauer, B. B. — Bachman 1962.

Bayly, Ernie — Andrews 1982.

Bennett, John R. — Voices 1955.

Bolig, John R. — Scott 1988.

Brew, D. — Frankenstein 1972.

Bruun, Carl — Frankenstein 1978.

Bryant, William R. — Bryan 1975.

Brylawski, Samuel — Wonderful 1985.

Bukoski, Peter — Lindsay 1990.

Bunnett, Rex — Rust 1977.

Bunnett, Rex — Seeley 1989.

Burns, Richard C. — Lane 1984.

Cartwright, Jim — Dyment 1977.

Cartwright, Jim — Worth 1986.

Celletti, Rodolfo — Williams, C. 1958.

Chambre, Tim — Hounsome 1981.

Cluley, Leonard E. — Vincent 1975.

Cooke, Roy — Davies 1953.

Copeland, Peter — Tuddenham 1988.

Cuming, G. J. — Clough 1952.

Cuming, G. J. — Clough 1964.

Cuming, G. J. — Clough 1966.

Davis, Don — Badmaieff 1966.

De Villiers, C. — Williams, C. 1958.

Dean, Roger — Thorgerson 1982.

Dean, Roger — Thorgerson 1977.

Dennis, James F. E. — Collins 1979.

Dennis, James F. E. — Frankenstein 1972.

Dennis, James F. E. — Frankenstein 1974.

Dennis, James F. E. — Frankenstein 1979.

Dennis, James F. E. — Hervingham-Root 1953.

Dennis, James F. E. — Kaufman 1964.

Dennis, James F. E. — Migliorini 1952.

Dennis, James F. E. — Migliorini 1953.

Dennis, James F. E. — Potterton 1967.

Dennis, James F. E. — Rektorys 1971.

Dennis, James F. E. — Robertson, J. 1978.

Dennis, James F. E. — Tron 1954.

Deskey, John S. — Rosenberg 1983.

Dethlefson, Ronald — Wile 1990/4.

Dixon, Robert M. W. — Godrich 1969.

Eagles, Brenda M. — Hart, M. 1989.

Ellis, Alexander J. — Helmholtz 19877.

Emerson, David — Parker 1988.

Engelbrecht, Pamela N. — Vincent 1975.

Farkas, Andrew — Caruso 1990.

Feinstein, Paul T. — Rosenberg 1983.

Flemming, Bill — Directory 1985.

Forbes, Sandy — Rust 1989.

Fox, Charles — Harrison 1984.

Frankenstein, Alfred — Dennis 1971.

Franklin, Carole Vidali — Thorin 1984.

Frayne, J. G. — Davis 1958.

Freestone, John — Favia-Artsay 1952.

Garrod, Charles — Popa 1987.

Gibilisco, Stan — Turner, R. 1988.

Gibson, Gerald D. — Gray 1977.

Girard, Victor — Barnes, H. 1951.

Godrich, John — Dixon 1970.

Godrich, John — MacKenzie 1963.

Goldmark, P. C. — Bachman 1962.

Gravereaux, Daniel W. — Bauer, B. 1971.

Gray, J. — Bruun 1962.

Gray, Michael — Moon 1990.

Grobman, Marc — Lindsay 1990.

Guimaraes, Alusio R. — Léon 1960.

Gurvich, Vladimir — Kelly 1988/1.

Gust, Arthur J. — Bauer, B. 1971.

Hain, Edward — Williams, C. 1957.

Hall, George — Edwards 1965.

Harvith, John — Edison 1987.

Harvith, Susan Edwards — Edison 1987.

Hearne, Will Roy — World 1970.

Hilbert, Robert — Brown, S. 1986.

Hillman, Peter E. — Bullock 1986.

Hitchcock, H. Wiley — New Grove 1986.

Holohan, John — Peel 1990.

Howells, David — Thorgerson 1982.

Hughes, E. — Shawe-Taylor 1961.

Hutchinson, T. — Williams, C. 1057/11.

Isom, Warren Rex — Phonograph 1972.

Jansen, Frans — Czada 1983.

Kalil, Ford — Magnetic 1982.

Kaplan, Mike — Variety 1989.

Kaufman, Tom — Frankenstein 1972.

Kaufman, Tom — Scott 1988.

Kelly, Alan — Perkins 1981.

Kelly, Alan — Semeonoff 1974.

Kenyon, J. P. — Richards 1980.

Kiner, Larry F. — Baker 1990.

Kittross, John M. — Sterling 1978.

Knight, Arthur E. — Halban 1960.

Koch, Grace — Directory 1982.

Korst, Bill — *see* Garrod (several titles)

Korst, Bill — Edwards 1965.

Krauskopf, Rose — Lyle 1934.

Kunstadt, Len — Raymond 1981.

Landon, Grelun — Stambler 1983.

Layton, Robert — Greenfield 1989.

Lemcoe, M. M. — Pickett 1959.

Levin, Abner — Hall 1940.

Levy, Ernst — Levarie 1980.

Levy, Ernst — Levarie 1983.

Mackenzie, Compton — Batten 1956.

Mann, Alfred — Modern 1989.

March, Ivan — Greenfield 1989.

Marco, Guy A. — Bryant 1985.

Margenau, Henry — Helmholtz 1877.

Marsh, Dave — Rolling 1979.

May, Everett G. — Olson, H. 1954.

McGeary, Mitchell — McCoy 1990.

McKee, Elwood A. — Association 1988.

Meyers, Betty — Fellers 1978.

Middleton, Tony — Greenfield 1982.

Moran, William R. — Bullard 1977.

Moran, William R. — Fagan 1983.

Moran, William R. — Farkas 1985.

Moran, William R. — Kenyon 1973.

Moran, William R. — McPherson 1967.

Moran, William R. — McPherson 1973.

Moran, William R. — Owen, H. 1969.

Moran, William R. — Williams, C. 1956.

Moran, William R. — Williams, C. 1958.

Newsom, Iris — Wonderful 1985.

Newsom, Jon W. — Smart 1977.

Newsom, Jon W. — Wonderful 1985.

Oja, Carol J. — American 1982.

Park, Bill — Seeliger 1963.

Patrick, James — Berger, M. 1982.

Podrazik, Walter — Castleman 1976.

Porter, Bob — Ruppli 1980.

Porter, Bob — Ruppli 1980/1.

Porter, Jack W. — Henrysson 1984.

Potter, Tully — Delalande 1984.

Potvin, Gilles — Kallman 1981.

Preston, John — Olson, H. 1954.

Reid, Robert H. — Darrell 1936.

Reinehr, Robert C. — Swartz 1992.

Richards, John B. — Williams, C. 1958.

Ridley, Nicholas — Migliorini 1957.

Robertson, John W. — Yankovsky 1990.

Rubboli, Daniele — D'Andrea 1981.

Ruppli, Michel — Cuscuna 1988.

Rust, Brian — Dearling 1984.

Sadie, Stanley — New Grove 1986.

Sayers, Scott P. — O'Brien, 1992.

See, R. T. — Hogarth 1987.

Seemungal, R. P. — Pearmain 1964.

Sefl, Al — Frow 1978.

Sellers, Chris — Koster 1985.

Semeonoff, Boris — Dennis 1971.

Semeonoff, Boris — Yankovsky 1990.

Shanahan, Mary — Palmer 1983.

Simon, Alfred — Lewine 1984.

Smart, James R. — Wonderful 1985.

Smolian, Steven — Lawrence 1962.

Snepvangers, Rene — Goldmark 1949.

Speer, Louise S. — Seeger 1987.

Spencer, Ray — Laubich 1982.

Spruce, Derek — Badrock 1965.

Stratton, John — Dennis 1981/2.

Swenson, John — Rolling 1979.

Thacker, Eric — Harrison 1984.

Townsend, Irving — Hammond 1977.

Tremaine, Howard M. — Audio C 1977.

Wade, Phillip — Richards 1949.

Warshofsky, Fred — Stevens 1965.

Watts, Leonard L. — Carter 1975.

Weerasinghe, Lali — Directory 1989.

Welch, Walter L. — Read 1976.

Whelan, Gordon — Favia-Artsay 1949.

Wile, Raymond R. — Dethlefson 1985.

Wile, Raymond R. — Proceedings 1974.

Williams, Clifford — Hutchinson 1962.

Williams, Clifford — Kenyon 1973.

Williams, Clifford — Lustig 1987.

Williams, Clifford — Peel 1985.

Winters, Kenneth — Kallman 1981.

Woworth, Lisa — Hart, M. 1989.

Wright, Laurie — Davies 1968.

Index

The index includes entries for all individuals named in the text as well as all firms and performing organizations. Major topics are also entered. Reference lists of persons and groups in various categories are interspersed, e.g., Cornetists, Orchestras.

To make the index practical and uncluttered, uninformative citations are omitted. This means that passing references to a person or group, where no facts are given that do not appear in main articles, are not indexed.

Categories not indexed include radio and television show titles, motion picture titles, song titles, and titles of publications. Exceptions are made when such items are the topic of discussion.

Certain alphabetical listings in the text are not duplicated in the index, e.g., Edison record players, Pseudonyms, Sound recording periodicals. There are advisory notes in the index at appropriate places to inform the user about such conventions.

An italicized page number refers to a principal source of information, usually a full article about the person or topic.

Inclusive pagination is given for extended articles. However, only the initial page number is given for shorter articles that conclude on a following page.

Arrangement of the entries is word-by-word alphabetical order, the sequence found in most U.S. library catalogs and databases:

New Zealand
Newark Tinware and Metal Works
Newbury, Mickey

In sorting entries that begin with the same word, the sequence is personal name first, then record labels, followed by other entries in alphabetical order with all words considered:

Edison, Thomas Alva
Edison (label)
Edison Bell (label)
Edison Bell Consolidated Phonograph Co., Ltd.
Edison Reproducers
Edisonia Co.

Numerals are filed ahead of letters, in number order.

Hyphenated words and names with prefixes are filed as though they were one word:

Delay System
De Leath, Vaughn
De-Lite (label)
Delius Society recordings

Entries in upper-case refer to full articles on the topic of the entry.

AGC. *See* AUTOMATIC GAIN CONTROL.

Aiken, Edward L. (inventor). 512.

Ainley, Henry (actor). 393.

Air Arts, Inc. 711.

Air checks. 534.

Air shots. 534.

Air suspension. *See* ACOUSTICAL SUSPENSION.

Airline (disc record player). 340.

Airplane records. *See* AVIATION RECORDS.

AJAX (label). *9*, 561.

Ajax horn. 465.

Akst, Harry (pianist). 766.

ALABAMA (country group). *9*, 152.

ALABAMA PHONOGRAPH CO. 9.

ALBANESE, LICIA (soprano). 9.

ALBANI, EMMA, *Dame* (soprano). 10.

Albers, Henri (baritone). 488.

Albion Record Co., Ltd. 354.

ALBUM. 10.

ALBUM COVER. 10.

ALBUM NUMBER. 11.

ALBUM ORIENTED ROCK (AOR). 11.

ALC. *See* AUTOMATIC LEVEL CONTROL.

ALDA, FRANCES (soprano). 11.

ALDRIDGE, SALMON & CO., LTD. *10*, 44, 729.

ALEXANDER, GEORGE (baritone). 11.

Alexandra, Queen of England. 361.

Alice Nielsen Quartet (vocal group). 469.

ALIGNMENT. 12.

ALL-AMERICAN MOHAWK CORP. 12.

Allard, Joseph (fiddler). 91.

Allard, Maurice (bassoonist). 775.

Allegro (label). 337.

Allegro/Elite (label). 572.

Allegro/Royale (label). 572.

Allen, Thomas (baritone). 487.

ALLEN, WALTER C. (discographer). 12.

ALLGEMEINE ELEKTRIZITÄTS GESELLSCHAFT (AEG). 12.

Alligator (label). 269.

Allman Brothers Band (rock group). 594.

Almanac Singers (folk group). 266.

Almeida, Laurindo (guitarist). 285.

Alouette (label). 92.

ALTHOUSE, PAUL (tenor). 12.

Alto Brake (automatic stop). 12.

ALTO SALES CO. 12.

Altobrake (automatic stop). 35.

Altschuler, Modest (conductor). 495.

Alvarez, Albert (tenor). 417.

Am-Par Record Co. 3.

Amadio, John (flutist). 773.

AMATO, PASQUALE (baritone). 12.

AMBASSADORS (dance band). 13.

AMBEROL. 13.

Amberola. *See* EDISON RECORD PLAYERS—AMBEROLA.

AMBIANCE. 13.

Ambient noise. 471.

AMBIENT SOUNDS. 13.

AMBISONICS. 13.

AMCO (label). 13.

American (label). 478.

American Band. 439.

American Brass Quintet. 75.

American Broadcasting Co. 3.

American Engineering Standards Committee. *See* AMERICAN NATIONAL STANDARDS INSTITUTE (ANSI).

AMERICAN FEDERATION OF MUSICIANS OF THE UNITED STATES AND CANADA. 13.

AMERICAN FOLKLIFE CENTER. 14.

AMERICAN GRAMOPHONE CO. 14.

AMERICAN GRAPHOPHONE CO. (AGC). 14–15.

AMERICAN HOME RECORDER CO. 15.

American Indian (disc record player). 16.

American Multinola Co. 450. *See also* MULTINOLA.

American Music Lover (periodical). 579.

AMERICAN NATIONAL STANDARDS INSTITUTE (ANSI). 15.

AMERICAN ODEON CORP. *15*, 478.

American Odeon Phonograph Corp. 479.

American Odeon Record (label). 15, 479.

American Odeon Record Corp. 479.

AMERICAN PHONOGRAPH CO. 15.

AMERICAN PHONOGRAPH CO. (Detroit). 15.

AMERICAN PHONOGRAPH CO. (New York City). 15.

AMERICAN PHONOGRAPH RECORD CO. 15.

American Photoplayer Co. 446.

AMERICAN PIANO CO. 15.

American Quartet. *See* PREMIER QUARTETTE.

AMERICAN RECORD CO. 16.

AMERICAN RECORD CORP. (ARC). *16*, 562, 600.

American Record Guide (periodical). 578.

American Record Manufacturing Co. 720.

AMERICAN RECORDING LABORATORIES. 17.

AMERICAN RECORDING STUDIOS. 17.

AMERICAN SINGERS (male quartet). 17.

AMERICAN SOCIETY OF COMPOSERS, AUTHORS AND PUBLISHERS (ASCAP). 17.

American Standards Association. *See* AMERICAN NATIONAL STANDARDS INSTITUTE.

American String Quartette. 695.

AMERICAN TALKING MACHINE CO. *17*, 751.

AUTOGRAPH (label). 34.
AUTO-LOCATE. 34.
Automatic double tracking
    (ADT). *See* DOUBLE
    TRACKING.
Automatic Entertainer. *See*
    JOHN GABEL'S AUTO-
    MATIC ENTERTAINER.
AUTOMATIC LEVEL CON-
    TROL (ALC). 34.
AUTOMATIC MACHINE
    AND TOOL CO. 34.
Automatic Music Co. 447.
AUTOMATIC MUSICAL CO.
    34.
AUTOMATIC MUSICAL
    INSTRUMENT CO. 35.
Automatic Orthophonic (record
    changer). 749.
AUTOMATIC PHONOGRAPH
    EXHIBITION CO. 35.
Automatic record changer. *See*
    RECORD CHANGER.
Automatic Reginaphone (disc
    record player). 580.
Automatic Reginaphone. *See*
    also REGINA MUSIC BOX
    CO.
AUTOMATIC REPLAY. 35.
AUTOMATIC REVERSE. 35.
AUTOMATIC SEARCH. 35.
Automatic sequence. *See*
    MANUAL SEQUENCE.
AUTOMATIC SHUTOFF. 35.
Automatic Speaker (Edison
    reproducer). 239.
AUTOMATIC STOP. 35.
Automatic turntable. *See*
    TURNTABLE.
AUTOMOBILE SOUND
    SYSTEMS. 36.
AUTOPHONE (cylinder
    phonograph). 36.
AUTOPIANO CO. 36.
Autostop. *See* AUTOMATIC
    STOP; CONDON-
    AUTOSTOP CO.
AUTRY, GENE (country artist).
    36. 148.
AUXETOPHONE (disc record
    player). 37.
AUXILIARY INPUT. 37.
Avalon, Frankie (rock per-
    former). 593.

Avco (label). 588.
Avery, Charles (pianist). 71.
AVIATION RECORDINGS. 37.
AVON COMEDY FOUR. 38.
Ayer, N. W. (advertising agent).
    742.
AYLSWORTH, JONAS
    WALTER (inventor). 38.
AZIMUTH. 38.

—B—

B & H FIBRE MANUFACTUR-
    ING CO. 39.
B SIDE. 39.
Babbitt, Harry (popular singer).
    378.
Babin, Victor (pianist). 529.
Babson, H. B. (executive). 112.
BABY (label). 39.
Baby (cylinder phonograph). 8.
BABY GRAND
    GRAPHOPHONE. 39.
BABY ODEON (label). 39.
BABY TOURNAPHONE (disc
    record player). 39, 718.
Baby-Platten (label). 39.
BACCALONI, SALVATORE
    (bass). 39.
Bacharach, Burt (composer).
    758.
Bachman, W. S. (inventor). 515.
BACK COATING. 40.
BACK CUEING. 40.
BACK TRACKING. 40.
Background noise. 11.
BACKHAUS, WILHELM
    (pianist). 40, 493.
Backing. *See* BASE.
Bacon, F. J. (banjoist). 42.
Badgerow, Harve J. (executive).
    419.
Badini, Ernesto (baritone). 487.
Badische Anilin und Soda
    Fabrik. *See* BASF AG.
Badollet, Frank (flutist). 772,
    775.
Badrock, Arthur (discogra-
    pher). 212.
Badura-Skoda, Paul (pianist).
    762.
Baerwald, H. G. (engineer). 714.
BAEZ, JOAN (popular singer).
    40.
BAFFLE (loudspeaker). 40, 399.

BAGSHAW (W. H.) CO. 40,
    463.
BAILEY, MILDRED (popular
    singer). 40, 472, 475.
Bakelite (plastic). 140.
Baker, Chet (trumpeter). 721.
BAKER, ELSIE (contralto). 41.
    738.
BAKER, GEORGE (baritone).
    41. 287.
Baker, Ginger (drummer). 153.
Baker, LaVern (blues singer).
    587, 589.
Bakersfield sound. 150, 308.
BALANCE. 41.
BALANCE CONTROL. 41.
Baldwin, Dwight Hamilton
    (executive). 41.
BALDWIN (label). 41.
BALDWIN PIANO CO. 41, 426.
Balfa Brothers (folk artists). 268.
Balin, Marty (guitarist). 353.
Ballard, Florence (soul singer).
    697.
BALLARD, GEORGE WILTON
    (tenor). 42, 446.
Balleran, J. (executive). 709.
BALLEW, SMITH (popular
    singer). 42, 367, 538.
Balm, Edmund A. (executive).
    337.
Baltsa, Agnes (mezzo-soprano).
    487.
Bama Band (country group).
    769.
Bamberger & Co. (department
    stores). 521.
Bamboo needle. 39. 308.
Bampton, Rose (soprano). 433,
    776.
BAND 42.
Band Music. *See* BIG BANDS;
    MILITARY BAND
    RECORDINGS.
Band of H. M. Grenadier
    Guards. 439.
BAND OF THE COLDSTREAM
    GUARDS. 42, 439.
Banda di Policia (Mexico). 205.
BANDA ROSSA. 42.
Bandrowski, Alexander von
    (tenor). 417.
BANDWIDTH. 42.
Banjo Kings. 43.

BANJO RECORDINGS. 42.
Banjoists. See in this index:
Aron, M; Bacon, F. J; Berger, Karl; Bland, Jack; Brooks, Ruby; Cammeyer, Alfred; Flatt, Lester Raymond; Grimshaw, Emile; Grinsted, W. S; Hermann, Sammy; Hunter, Parke; Lyle, Will; Maphis, Joe; Miller, Polk; Morley, Joe; Oakley, Olly; Ossman, Vess; Paul, Jad; Peabody, Eddie; Pidoux, John; Rogers, Charlie; Scruggs, Earl; Sealy, Helen; Skinner, Bessie; Skinner, Rose; Spaulding, Shirley; Taylor, Henry L.; Van Eps, Fred; Van Eps, William; Weaver, Richard L.
Bank, Harry W. (executive). 146.
BANNER (label). *43*, 561.
"Banner" discs (Columbia). 509.
BANTA, FRANK E. (pianist). *43*, 527, 586, 734.
BANTA, FRANK P. (pianist). *43*, 527.
Baquet, Achille (clarinetist). 501.
BAR AUTOMATICO (phonograph parlor). 43.
Barbaini, Augusto (tenor). 487.
Barber, John (executive). 124.
BARBIROLLI, JOHN, *Sir* (conductor). *43*, 604.
Barbour, Inez (singer). 159.
BARDINI (disc record player). *43*, 644.
BARENBOIM, DANIEL (conductor). 44.
Barn dance programs. 148.
Barnes, Harold M. (discographer). 167.
BARNET, CHARLIE (saxophonist). 44.
Barnett Samuel. *See* SAMUEL (BARNETT) AND SONS, LTD.
Barone, Clement (flutist). 772.
Barr, Max (violist). 363.
BARRAUD, FRANCIS (painter). 44.

BARRAUD, WILLIAM ANDREW (executive). 45.
Barraud (W. A.), Ltd. 45.
Barrère, Georges (flutist). 720, 773.
Barrère Ensemble. 775.
Barrère Little Symphony. 775.
Barretto, Ray (rock and salsa performer). 594.
BARRIENTOS, MARIA (soprano). 45, 783.
Barry, Phillips (ethnologist). 265.
Barry, Walter FitzHugh (executive). 342.
Barrymore, John (actor). 393.
Barth, Hans (pianist). 529, 583.
Bartlett, Ethel (pianist). 529.
BARTÓK, BÉLA (composer, folklorist). 45, 584.
Barton, Alfred J. (executive). 344.
Bartow, W. (cornetist). 145.
Barzin, Leon E. (violist). 524.
BASE. 45.
BASEBALL RECORDINGS. 45.
BASF AG. 46.
Basic amplifier. *See* POWER AMPLIFIER.
BASIE, COUNT (Big Band leader). 46, 294, 351.
Basket (loudspeaker). 399.
BASS. 46.
Bass reflex (loudspeaker). 401.
BASS REFLEX BAFFLE. 46.
Bass singers. See in this index:
Baccaloni, Salvatore; Baughman, Stanley; Blass, Robert; Broderick, George; Brondi, Alfredo; Chaliapin, Feodor; Cherry, Jim; Christoff, Boris; Cordon, Norman; Cornwall, A. Duncan; Croxton, Frank; Donaghy, Harry; Ghiaurov, Nicolai; Girardi, Vittorio; Glenn, Wilfred; Gresse, André; Joseph, Robert; Journet, Marcel; Kipnis, Alexander; Knupfer, Paul; List, Emanuel; Meyer, John H.; Moll, Kurt; Parmet, Leon; Plançon, Pol; Rains, Leon;

Robeson, Paul; Salminen, Matti; Snow, Walter; Stamper, James L.; Stanley, Frank C.; Stanley, James; Talvela, Martti.
BASS TRAP. 46.
Basses. *See* Bass singers.
Bassists (string bass). See in this index:
Brown, Ray; Bruce, Jack; Conrad, Herman; Gottlieb, Lou; Heath, Percy; Jones, Orville; Marshall, Wendell; Mingus, Charles; Page, Walter; Safranski, Eddie; Stewart, Slam; Vola, Louis; Wright, Eugene.
BASTIANINI, ETTORE (baritone). 46.
BATCHELOR, CHARLES (inventor). 46, 512.
Bates, Charles H. (tenor). 373.
Bates, Will (cornetist). 205.
BATTELLE MEMORIAL INSTITUTE. 47.
BATTEN, JOE (executive). 47.
BATTISTINI, MATTIA (baritone). 47.
Battle, Kathleen (soprano). 487.
Bauer, B. B. (engineer). 714.
Bauer, Harold (pianist). 528, 583, 584.
Bauer, Robert (discographer). 211.
Baughman, Stanley (bass). 521.
Baum, A. J. (executive). 509.
BAUR, FRANKLIN (tenor). *48*, 538, 586, 621.
Bavarian Radio Symphony Orchestra. 377.
Bay, Emanuel (pianist). 318.
Bay, Harry C. (executive). 48.
BAY (H. C.) CO. 48.
Bayreuth Festival. 450.
BBC *See* BRITISH BROADCASTING CORP. (BBC).
BBC Sound Archives. 766.
BBC Symphony Orchestra. 73.
BEACH BOYS (rock group). *48*, 594.
Beach, E. C. (executive). 730.
Beacon (label). 646.
Beacon Street Union (rock group). 594.

Beans, Hal T. (inventor). 221.
Beat Era (in rock). 594.
BEATLES (rock group). 49, 294.
Beaver (Canadian firm). 92.
Bébé Jumeau (talking doll). 391.
BEBOP. 49.
BECHET, SIDNEY (clarinetist). 49.
Beckwith, Martha (ethnologist). 265.
Bee Gees (rock group). 594.
BEECHAM, THOMAS, *Sir* (conductor). *50*, 412, 489, 491, 631, 716.
Beerbohm-Tree, Herbert (actor). 393.
Begg (Charles) and Co., Ltd. 467.
BÉGUÉ, BERNARD (tenor). 51.
Behrens, Hildegard (soprano). 433, 487.
BEIDERBECKE, BIX (cornetist). *51, 770.*
Beka Meister Records (label). 510.
BEKA RECORD GmbH. 51.
Beka Records. 438.
BEL CANTO (label). 52.
Bel Canto Record GmbH. 52.
BELAFONTE, HARRY (popular singer). 52.
Belfer Audio Library and Archive. 591, 699.
Belhomme, Hippolyte (conductor). 488.
BELL, ALEXANDER GRAHAM (inventor). *52*, 435.
BELL, CHICHESTER A. (inventor). 52.
Bell, Raymond T. (executive). 414.
Bell, William (tuba player). 75.
Bell and Tainter patents. 14, 53.
BELL (label). 53.
Bell Laboratories. *See* BELL TELEPHONE LABORATORIES.
Bell Record Corp. 53.
BELL RECORDING LABORATORIES. 53.
BELL TALKING MACHINE CO. 53.
Bell Telephone Co. 52.
BELL TELEPHONE LABORATORIES. *54*, 448, 514.

BELLINCIONI, GEMMA (soprano). *54*, 718.
Belling, Charles (tenor). 315.
Bellson, Louis (drummer). 521.
BELMONT, JOE (whistler). 403.
Belock Instrument Corp. 756.
BELTONA (label). 403.
Beltona (needle). 462.
Beneke, Tex (popular singer, Big Band leader). 440.
Benjamin Lincoln Jazz Collection. 684.
Bennet, Bert (singer). 272.
BENNETT, CHARLES K. (executive). *55*, 458.
Bennett, John R. (discographer). 212.
Bennett, Lee (popular singer). 280.
BENNETT, TONY (popular singer). 55.
Benny Goodman Sextet. 291, 607.
BENOIST, ANDRÉ (pianist). *55*, 527.
BENSON, ERASTUS A. (executive). *55*, 462.
Benson, P. D. (executive). 248.
Benton, Brook (blues singer). 589.
Benzell, Mimi (mezzo-soprano). 433.
BENZLER, ALBERT (xylophonist). *55*, 499, 527, 731, 779.
Berge, William E. (pianist). 707.
BERGER, ERNA (soprano). 55.
Berger, Karl (banjoist). 406.
Bergh, Arthur (executive). 249.
Bergmann, S. (tinfoil phonograph manufacturer). 240.
Bergonzi, Carlo (tenor). 486.
BERIGAN, BUNNY (trumpeter). 55.
Berlin Museum for Folk Culture. 56.
Berlin Opera Wind Sextet. 775.
BERLIN PHILHARMONIC ORCHESTRA. *56*, 377, 469, 493.
BERLIN PHONOGRAMM-ARCHIV. 56.
Berlin State Opera. 371–372.
Berlin University Psychological Institute. 56.

BERLINER, EMILÉ (inventor). 56.
Berliner, Herbert Samuel (executive). 91.
BERLINER, JOSEPH (executive). 57.
Berliner, Oliver. 114.
BERLINER (label). 57.
Berliner (E.), Montreal (firm). 59, 91.
BERLINER GRAMOPHONE CO. 58.
Berliner Gramophone Co. of Canada. 90.
Berliner (J.) Telephon-Fabrik. 57.
Berman, Shelley (comedian). 136.
Bern Convention, 1886 (copyright agreement). 144.
BERNARD, AL (popular singer). *59*, 571.
Bernard, Mike (singer). 568.
BERNHARDT, SARAH (actress). *59*, 395, 509.
BERNSTEIN, LEONARD (conductor). *59*, 294.
BEROLINA SCHALLPLATTEN GmbH. 59.
BERRY, CHUCK (popular singer). 60.
Berry, J. (executive). 337.
Bertelsmann, Carl (executive). 60.
BERTELSMANN AG. 60.
Berthon, Mirielle (soprano). 490.
Bessinger, Frank (singer). 563.
Best, Peter (drummer). 49.
Bethel Jubilee Quartet. 60.
BETHEL QUARTET (male vocal group). 60.
Betti, Adolfo (violinist). 263.
BETTINI, GIANNI (inventor). 60.
Bettini Phonograph Co. 61.
Bettini Phonograph Laboratory. 60.
Biagini, Henry (Big Band leader). 102.
BIAMPING. 61.
BIANCHI, "PROFESSOR" (conductor). 61.
BIAS. 61.

BIAS TRAP. 61.

Biasing. *See* BIAS.

Bickford, Zarh Myron (executive). 783.

Bidirectional microphone. 435.

Biele, Andreas (executive). 376.

BIELEFELDER KATALOG. 61.

BIELING, JOHN (tenor). 61.

BIG BAND. 62.

Big Brother and the Holding Company (rock group). 359.

Big Maybelle (blues singer). 587.

BIGARD, BARNEY (clarinetist). 62.

BIGGS, E. POWER (organist). *63*, 500.

Biggs, Richard K. (organist). 499.

BIKEL, THEODORE (folk artist). 63.

BILL, EDWARD LYMAN (journalist). 63.

Bill, Raymond (journalist). 63.

Billboard (periodical). 136, 574.

Billing, Pemberton (inventor). 776.

Billy Heins Ancient City Quartet (minstrel group). 443.

BINAURAL SOUND. 63.

BINDER. 64.

Bing Corp. 64.

BINGHAM, RALPH (comedian). 64.

Binghampton Automatic Music Co. 390.

BINGOLA (label). 64.

Biophone (cylinder and disc player). 186.

Bioscope (film apparatus). 281.

Bird sounds. *See* ANIMAL IMITATIONS; WHISTLING RECORDINGS.

Birdsong, Cindy (soul singer). 697.

BIRNBAUM, THEODORE B. (executive). 64.

Bisbee, Sherwin N. (executive). 484.

BISCUIT. 65.

Bishop, Kirk D. (executive). 731.

Bishop-Babcock-Becker Co. 731.

Bismarck, Otto von (German chancellor). 373.

BISPHAM, DAVID SCULL (baritone). 65.

Bizeray School of Languages. 382.

BJÖRLING, JUSSI (tenor). 65.

Black and White Minstrel Show. 443.

Black Bottom Stompers (jazz group). 214.

Black contemporary music. 590.

Black Diamonds Minstrels. 442.

Black, Frank (pianist; conductor). 586.

BLACK PATTI (label). *65*, 561.

Black Sabbath (rock group). 595.

BLACK SWAN (label). *65*, 561.

Black Swan Phonograph Co. 65.

BLACKER, GEORGE (discographer). *66*, 167.

BLACKMAN, J. NEWCOMB (executive). *66*, 458.

Blackman Distributing Co. 66.

BLACKMAN TALKING MACHINE CO. 66.

Blackmer, David E. (inventor). 175.

Blackton, James Stuart (executive). 750.

BLAKE, EUBIE (pianist). *66*, 584.

Blake transmitter microphone. 435.

BLAKEY, ART (drummer). 66.

Bland, Jack (banjoist). 425.

Blanker. 505.

Blass, Robert (bass). 417.

Blasting. 638.

Blattner, Ludwig (inventor). *66*, 411.

BLATTNERPHONE. 67.

BLAUVELT, LILLIAN (soprano). 67.

Blech, Leo (conductor). 490, 584.

BLEND CONTROL. 67.

Bloch, Ray (conductor). 624.

Blood, Sweat & Tears (rock group). 595.

BLOOD TONE ARM. *67*, 354.

Bloom, Robert (oboist). 775.

Bloomfield-Zeisler, Fanny (pianist). 584.

BLU-DISC (label). 67.

Blu-Disc Record Co. 67.

BLUE AMBEROL. 67–68.

Blue Grass Boys (country group). 445.

BLUE NOTE (label). 68.

Bluebird (disc record player). 461.

BLUEBIRD (label). *68*, 562.

BLUEBIRD TALKING MACHINE CO. 68.

Bluegrass music. 151.

BLUES RECORDINGS. 68.

Blues singers (including rhythm & blues). See in this index: Baker, LaVern; Benton, Brook; Big Maybelle; Booker T and the M.G.'s; Bradshaw, Tiny; Broonzy, Big Bill; Brown, Charles; Brown, Roy; Brown, Ruth; Cardinals; Carr, Leroy; Charles, Ray; Clovers; Cooke, Sam; Crows; Cymone, Andre; Darin, Bobby; Dibango, Manu; Dixie Hummingbirds; Domino, Fats; Drifters; Dyke & the Blazers; Enchanters; Estes, Sleepy John; Famous Garland Jubilee Singers; Flamingos; Floyd, Eddie; Gant, Cecil; Harptones; Harris, Marion; Harris, Wynonie; Harrison, Wilbert; Hegamin, Lucille; Henderson, Rosa; Hooker, John Lee; Howard, Rosetta; Howlin' Wolf; Hunter, Alberta; Hunter, Ivory Joe; Jackson, Charlie; James, Elmore; Jefferson, Blind Lemon; Jordan, Louis; King, B. B.; Leadbelly; Longhair, Professor; Lymon, Frankie; Mar-Keys; McPhatter, Clyde; Milbern, Amos; Millinder, Lucky; Milton, Roy; Mimms, Garnett; Miracles; Mississippi Delta; Moonglows; Orioles; Patton, Charley; Penguins; Pickett, Wilson; Platters; Pullem, Joe; Rainey, Ma; Rushing, Jimmy; Sam and Dave; Sheila E; Shepard, Ollie; Sly & the Family Stone; Smith, Bessie; Smith,

Mamie; Smith, Trixie;
Spaniels; Spivey, Victoria;
Taggart, Blind Joe; Tampa
Red; Taylor, Johnnie;
Teenagers; Temple,
Johnnie; Tharpe, Rosetta;
Thomas, Carla; Thomas,
Rufus; Time; Turner, Ike;
Turner, Joe; Vanity;
Walker, T-Bone; Wash-
board Sam; Waters, Ethel;
Waters, Muddy;
Wheatstraw, Peetie; White,
Josh; Williams, Big Joe;
Willis, Chuck; Wilson,
Jackie.
BLUESVILLE (label). 69.
Blum, Joseph Leonard (execu-
tive). 70.
BLUM & CO., LTD. 70, 363.
BLUMLEIN, ALAN DOWER
(inventor). 70, 514.
BMG Classics (label). See
BERTELSMANN AG.
Bobo, Roger (tuba player). 75,
722.
BOB-O-LINK TALKING
BOOK. 70.
Boegli, C. P. (engineer). 406.
Boggs, Dock (folk artist). 268.
Bogue, Merwyn (popular
singer). 378.
Boguslawski, Moissaye
(pianist). 34.
BÖHM, KARL (conductor). 70.
Bohnke, Emil (violist). 84.
Boite à Musique (label). 569.
Bolcom, William (composer).
568.
BOLET, JORGE (pianist). 70.
Bolis, Luigi (tenor). 489.
BONCI, ALESSANDRO (tenor).
71.
Bondam, Karee (pianist). 527.
Bone, Red (arranger). 216.
BONINSEGNA, CELESTINA
(soprano). 71.
BOOGIE WOOGIE. 71.
Bookcassettes. 702.
Booker T and the M.G.'s (blues
singers). 589, 594.
Book-of-the-Month Club. 433.
Books on Tape (firm). 395, 702.
Bookshelf (loudspeaker). 401.
Boone, Steve (bass guitarist).
406.

Booth, Christopher H. H.
(pianist). 528. 568, 738.
Booth, Edwin (actor). 392.
Bootleg. See PIRATED
RECORDS.
Borde, Mlle. (xylophonist). 779.
Borge, Victor (pianist; come-
dian). 136.
BORI, LUCREZIA (soprano).
71, 612.
Borwell, Montague (baritone).
485.
Bos, Conrad (pianist). 329.
Bose, Amar (engineer). 72.
BOSE CORP. 72.
BOSS RADIO. 72.
Boston Pops Orchestra. 72.
BOSTON SYMPHONY
ORCHESTRA. 72, 294.
Boston Symphony Trombone
Quartet. 75.
Boston Symphony Woodwind
Quintet. 776.
BOSTON TALKING MA-
CHINE CO. 72.
Boswell, Connie (Connee)
(popular singer). 72.
Boswell, Helvetia (Vet) (popu-
lar singer). 72.
Boswell, Martha (popular
singer). 72.
BOSWELL SISTERS (popular
vocal trio). 72.
Boswell (D. E.) Co. 678.
Bott, Thomas (baritone). 485.
BOTTOM. 73.
Bottom radius. See GROOVE.
BOULEZ, PIERRE (conductor).
73, 294.
BOULT, ADRIAN, Sir (conduc-
tor). 73.
Bourdon, Rosario (conductor;
cellist). 106, 747.
Bourne, Una (pianist). 583.
Bowen, C. C. (executive). 434.
Bowen, Jean (librarian). 598.
BOWERS, JAMES F. (execu-
tive). 73, 458.
Bowie, David (rock performer).
620.
BOWLLY, AL (popular singer).
73.
Bowman, Brian (euphonium
player). 75.
BOXING RECORDINGS. 73.

BOYD, BILL (country singer).
74.
Boyer, Alexis (conductor). 488.
Boyer, Anita (popular singer).
582.
Boyer, Charles (actor). 394.
Boyer, Eugene (inventor). 472.
Bracewell, Robert Miles
(executive). 249.
Brackenbush, A. C. (executive).
344.
Bradley, W. P. (executive). 343.
Bradley, Will (trombonist). 624,
721.
Bradshaw, Tiny (blues singer).
587.
Brady, Pat (comedian). 126.
Braff, Ruby (trumpeter). 541.
Bragg, Billy (rock singer). 269.
Bragg, Thomas Frederick.
(executive). 11, 729.
Brahms, Johannes (composer).
140, 527.
BRAIN, DENNIS (hornist). 74.
Brand, Oscar (folk artist). 267.
Branigan, Laura (rock per-
former). 595.
BRASS INSTRUMENT RE-
CORDINGS. 74. See also
CORNET RECORDINGS;
TROMBONE RECORD-
INGS; TRUMPET RE-
CORDINGS; TUBA
RECORDINGS.
Braun, Jules (executive). 181.
Brazos Valley Boys (country
group). 711.
BRC Productions. 567.
Bream, Julian (guitarist). 304.
Breeskin, Elias (violinist). 248.
Brenard Manufacturing Co.
117.
Brenmer Brothers (tinfoil
phonograph manufac-
turer). 241.
Brenston, Jackie (rock per-
former). 593.
Bréval, Lucienne (soprano). 417.
Bridge, Professor (organist).
499.
BRIDGEPORT DIE AND
MACHINE CO. 76, 329,
421, 443, 457, 521, 557, 585,
601.
BRIDGING. 75.

Brightston, S. E. (executive). 644.

Brilliance Corp. 702.

BRILLIANT QUARTETTE (male vocal group). 76.

BRILLIANTONE STEEL NEEDLE CO. 76.

Bristol Co. 76.

BRISTOPHONE (cartridge). 76.

British Blattnerphone Co. 67, 411.

BRITISH BROADCASTING CORP. (BBC). 76.

BRITISH BRUNSWICK, LTD. 76.

BRITISH COPYRIGHT PRO-TECTION ASSOCIATION. 77.

British Grenadiers Band. 439.

BRITISH HOMOPHONE CO., LTD. 77.

British Institute of Recorded Sound. See NATIONAL SOUND ARCHIVE.

British Invasion. 594.

British Library of Wildlife Sounds. 766. See also NATIONAL SOUND ARCHIVE.

BRITISH OZAPHANE, LTD. 77.

BRITISH PHONOGRAPH INDUSTRIES, LTD. 77.

BRITISH SONOGRAM CO., LTD. 77.

British Talking Picture Corp. 448.

British Thomson Houston Co., Ltd. 76.

BRITISH ZONOPHONE CO. 78.

BRITT, ELTON (country artist). 78, 148.

Broad, John (executive). 249.

BROADCAST (label). 33.

Broadcast Junior (label). 718.

BROADCAST MUSIC, INC. (BMI). 78.

BROADWAY (label). 78.

BROADWAY QUARTET. 79, 154.

BROCKMAN, JAMES (tenor). 79.

Broderick, George (bass). 486, 739.

Brogan, Joseph F. (executive). 299, 710.

Brondi, Alfredo (bass). 487.

Brooks, Mel (comedian). 136.

Brooks, Ruby (banjoist). 42.

Brooks, Stanley (saxophonist). 445.

Brooks, Tim (discographer). 212.

Brooks (disc record player). 79.

BROOKS MANUFACTURING CO. 79.

BROONZY, BIG BILL (blues singer). 79, 562.

Brothers Four (folk group). 268.

Brown, Alec (saxophonist). 626.

Brown, Bert (cornetist). 75.

Brown, Charles (blues singer). 587.

Brown, Fred (saxophonist). 626.

Brown, G. G. (firm). 274.

Brown, George W. (inventor). 448.

BROWN, JAMES (soul singer). 79, 590.

Brown, Joseph N. (inventor). 728.

Brown, Les (Big Band leader). 175.

Brown, Milton (country artist). 152.

Brown, Ray (bassist). 523.

Brown, Roy (blues singer). 587.

Brown, Ruth (blues singer). 587, 589.

Brown, Tom (saxophonist). 626.

Brown, Vern (saxophonist). 626.

Brown, William (saxophonist). 626.

Browning, John Bailey (inventor). 81, 512, 513.

Browning, Robert (poet). 293.

BROWNLEE, JOHN (baritone). 80.

Brox Sisters (popular singers). 626.

BRUBECK, DAVE (pianist). 80.

Bruce, Jack (bassist). 153.

Bruce, Lenny (comedian). 136.

Bruch, Max (composer). 584.

BRUCKNER (FRANZ) MANU-FACTURING CO. 80.

Brunis, Georg (trombonist). 465.

BRUNSWICK (label). 80, 353.

Brunswick Corp. 81.

Brunswick Male Quartet. 81.

BRUNSWICK QUARTET (male vocal group). 81.

Brunswick Radio Corp. 80.

BRUNSWICK-BALKE-COLLENDER CO. 80.

Brush, Charles (executive). 81.

BRUSH DEVELOPMENT CORP. 81.

Bruun, C. L. (discographer). 212.

Bryan, A. G. (executive). 244.

Bryan, William Jennings (statesman). 85.

BRYANT, ERIC THOMAS (librarian). 82.

BRYANT, LILLIAN (pianist). 82, 528.

Bryant, Rose (singer). 253.

Bryce, Tom (singer). 205, 485.

Brymer, Jack (clarinetist). 774.

BUBBLE BOOKS. 82.

Bucktown Five (jazz group). 679.

BUDAPEST QUARTET (string quartet). 82.

BUDDY (label). 82.

BUEHN, LOUIS (executive). 82, 458.

Buehn (Louis), Inc. 82.

Buehn Phonograph Co. 82.

Buffalo Springfield (rock group). 269.

Buffett, Jimmie (folk artist). 269.

BULK ERASER. 82.

Bullis, Henry C. (inventor). 411.

Bumb, Heinrich (executive). 51.

Bumb and König's Institute for Modern Inventions. 51.

BUMP. 83.

BUREAU INTERNATIONAL DE L'ÉDITION MÉCANIQUE (BIEM). 83.

Burgstaller, Alois (tenor). 417.

BURKE AND ROUS PHONO-GRAPH RECORDS. 83.

Burleigh, Lewis A. (executive). 337.

Burmeister, Willy (violinist). 750.

Burnette, Johnny (country artist). 152.

Burnishing facet. See STYLUS.

Burns, Richard C. (engineer). 642.

BURR, HENRY (tenor). *83*, 432, 521, 691.

BURROWS AND CO. 83.

BURT, GEORGE HENRY (executive). 83.

Burt (George) Co. 83.

BUSCH, ADOLF (violinist). *83*, 620.

BUSCH, FRITZ (conductor). *84*, 490, 631.

Busch, Hermann (cellist). 84.

Busch Chamber Players. 84.

BUSCH QUARTET (string quartet). 84.

BUSH & LANE PIANO CO. 84.

BUSONI, FERRUCCIO (pianist). *84*, 531, 584.

BUSSE, HENRY (trumpeter). 84.

Busser, Henri (conductor). 490.

BUSY BEE (label). 85.

Butler, Jerry (soul singer). 594.

Butler, Joe. (drummer) 406.

Butler, Nicholas Murray (executive). 465.

Butler, Robert E. (executive). 111.

BUTT, CLARA, *Dame* (contralto). 85.

Butterfield, Billy (trumpeter). 765.

Butterfly (label). 646.

BUTTERFLY HEAD. 85.

BUTTERFLY RECORDS. 85.

BWP Radio (firm). 567.

Byard, Jaki (pianist). 442.

Byas, Don (saxophonist). 611.

Byers, Hale (saxophonist). 611.

Byrds (folk rock group). 269, 594.

Bytown Troubadours (vocal group). 91.

—C—

C & S Phonograph Co. 109.

C/S. 87.

Caballé, Montserrat (soprano). 486.

Cabaret Voltaire (rock group). 595.

Cabinet and Accessories Co. 447.

Cactus needles. 462.

Cadena, Ozzier (executive). 610.

Cadet (label). 110.

CADILLAC (label). 87.

Cadman, Charles Wakefield (pianist) composer. 584.

CAEDMON (label). *87*, 267.

Cahuzac, Louis (clarinetist). 774.

CAILLE BROTHERS (firm). 87.

Cailophone (picturized phonograph). 87.

Cairns, Cliff (conductor). 747.

Cajun music. 151, 269.

Cali, John. 25, 43.

CALIFORNIA RAMBLERS (dance band). 87.

Californians (instrumental group). 766.

CALLAS, MARIA (soprano). *88*, 496, 535, 701, 722.

CALLOWAY, CAB (Big Band leader). 88.

CALORIC SALES CO. 88.

CALVÉ, EMMA (mezzo-soprano). 88.

CALYPSO (label). 88.

Camden, Archie (bassoonist). 775.

CAMDEN (label). 89.

Cameo (label). 89.

CAMEO RECORD CORP. 88.

Cameo-Kid (label). 88.

CAMERAPHONE (disc record player). 89.

Cameraphone (sound and film synchronizer). 448.

Cammeyer, Alfred (banjoist). 42.

Camp, Walter (football player), exercise records. 315.

Campanari, Giuseppe (baritone). 485.

CAMPBELL, ALBERT (tenor). *89*, 521, 691, 711.

Campbell, G. A. (engineer). 405.

CAMPBELL, GLEN (country artist). 90.

Campus Glee Club. 621.

CAMRAS, MARVIN (engineer). *90*, 411, 515.

CANADA. 90–97.

Note: Names of Canadian labels, production companies, and distributors are not entered individually in this index. There is a separate checklist of those names on pp. 94–96.

Canadian Academy of Recording Arts and Sciences (CARAS). 93.

Canadian Brass. 75.

CANADIAN BROADCASTING CORP. 97.

Canadian Independent Record Production Association (CIPRA). 94.

Canadian Music Hall of Fame. 93.

Canadian Music Industry Awards. 93.

Canadian Music Publishers Association (CMPA). 94.

Canadian Music Sales (firm). 92.

Canadian Phonograph Supply Co. 92.

Canadian Record Catalogue. 93.

Canadian Vitaphone (firm). 91.

CANS. 97.

CANTILEVER. 97.

Cantor, Eddie (comedian; singer). 248.

Cantrill, S. W. (executive). 124.

CAPACITANCE. 97.

CAPACITOR. 97.

Capacitor microphone. 435.

CAPEHART, HOMER EARL (executive). 97.

Capehart Automatic Phonograph Co. 98.

CAPEHART CO. 98.

CAPITOL (label). 98.

Capitol Industries-EMI, Inc. 98.

Capitol Records, Inc. 98.

Capitol Records of Canada, Ltd. 92.

Capitol Roll and Record Co. 484.

Capitol Theater Orchestra. 502.

CAPPS, FRANK L. (inventor). *98*, 409, 465.

CAPRICCIO (label). 98.

CAPSTAN. 98.

Carawan, Guy (folk artist). 256.

Carbon microphone. 435.

Carbona (disc cleaner). 98.

CARBONA CO. 99.

CARDINAL (label). 99.

Cardinal Phonograph Co. 99.
Cardinals (blues singers). 587.
Cardioid microphone. 435–436.
Carle, Frankie (pianist). 317
CARLOS, WALTER (organist). 99.
Carlos, Wendy (organist). 99.
Carlson, W. L. (inventor). 411, 515.
Carmichael, Hoagy (composer). 102, 529, 763.
Carneal, Robert (engineer). 257.
Carnegie Corp. 99.
CARNEGIE MUSIC SET. 99.
CARNIVAL (label). 99.
Carolinians (folk group). 764.
Carpenter, G. W. (inventor). 411.
Carpenter, James (ethnologist). 265.
Carpenter, Mary Chapin (country artist). 269.
Carr, Joe "Fingers" (pianist). 568.
Carr, Leroy (blues singer). 69, 562.
Carreño, Teresa (pianist). 584.
Carron, Arthur (tenor). 433.
CARRYOLA COMPANY OF AMERICA. 99.
Carson, Fiddlin' John (country artist). 148, 265.
CARSON, MARY (soprano). 99.
Carter, Alvin Pleasant (country artist). 100.
CARTER, BENNY (saxophonist). 100, 760.
Carter, June (country artist). 104.
Carter, Maybelle (country artist). 100.
Carter, Sara (country artist). 100.
Carter, Sydney H. (discographer). 167.
Carter, Wilf ("Montana Slim") (country artist). 91.
CARTER FAMILY (country group). 100, 148.
CARTRIDGE. 100.
CARUSO, ENRICO (tenor). 101, 678.
CARVER CORP. 102.
Cary, H. E. (executive). 462.
Casa Edison (Brazil). 371.

CASA LOMA ORCHESTRA. 102, 766.
Casablanca (label). 538.
Casadesus, Robert (pianist). 700.
Casady, Jack (guitarist). 353.
CASALS, PABLO (cellist). 102, 631, 710.
Cascode; cascoding. 34.
CASE, ANNA (soprano). 103, 715.
Case, Theodore W. (inventor). 448.
Casella, Alfredo (pianist) composer. 584, 584.
CASH, JOHNNY (country artist). 103, 149.
Cash, Roseanne (country artist). 269.
Cash Box (periodical). 574.
CASSETTE. 104.
Cassette book. See TALKING BOOK.
CASSETTE DECK. 105.
CASSETTE NUMBER. 105.
Cassi, Emil (trumpeter). 721.
CASWELL, JOHN WALLACE (executive). 105.
CASWELL MANUFACTURING CO. 105.
Catalina (label). 336.
Catalog number (disc number). 209.
Cataloging and Classification. See SOUND RECORDINGS AND THE LIBRARY.
Catalogs. See DISCOGRAPHY.
Cathedral Quartet (male vocal group). 586, 621.
Catlett, Sid (drummer). 356.
Cawley, Joe (pianist). 406.
Caypless, Edgar (collector). 122.
CBS Records Canada, Ltd. 91.
CBS. See COLUMBIA BROADCASTING SYSTEM (CBS).
CD See COMPACT DISC.
CD DIRECT. 106.
CEDAR (reprocessor). 106, 637.
CELESTION INTERNATIONAL, LTD. 106.
Celletti, Rodolfo (discographer). 211.
Cellists. See in this index: Barbirolli, John; Bourdon, Rosario; Busch, Hermann;

Casals, Pablo; D'Archambeau, Iwan; Droge, Max; Du Pré, Jacqueline.; Feuermann, Emanuel; Fournier, Pierre; Grümmer, Paul; Herbert, Victor; Hollman, Josef; Janigro, Antonio; Kefer, Paul; Kindler, Hans; Krist, Otto; Kronold, Hans; Mazzucchi, Oswaldo; Penha, Michael; Piatigorsky, Gregor; Rose, Leonard; Rostropovich, Mstislav; Schneider, Mischa; Son, Harry; Squire, William Henry; Starker, Janos; Taylor, Albert W.; Tortelier, Paul; Van Vliet, Cornelius; Willeke, Willem.
CELLO RECORDINGS. 106.
CELLOPHONE. 106.
Celluloid, cylinder material. 118.
Censorship and related issues. 330.
CENTER CHANNEL. 107.
CENTRAL NEBRASKA PHONOGRAPH CO. 107.
CENTRAL STATES TALKING MACHINE JOBBERS ASSOCIATION. 107.
Ceramic cartridge (pickup). 100.
Ceramic microphone. 434.
CETRA (label). 107.
Cetra-Soria (label). 645.
Chad Mitchell Trio (folk group). 268.
Chadbourne, C. H. (executive). 442.
Chailly, Riccardo (conductor). 602.
Chalfont, Mr. (whistler). 681.
CHALIA, ROSALIA (soprano). 107, 485.
CHALIAPIN, FEODOR (bass). 107.
CHALLENGE (label). 108.
Challis, Bill (arranger). 764.
Chalmers, Donald (singer). 715.
CHALMERS, THOMAS (bass-baritone). 108, 433, 446, 542, 715.
Chaloff, Serge (bass saxophonist). 319.

CHAMBERS, W. PARIS
(cornetist). *109*, 145.
Chaminade, Cécile (composer).
528, 583, 584.
CHAMPION (label). *109*, 646.
Champion Gamgage Record
(label). 279.
CHANDOS (label). 109.
CHANNEL. 109.
CHANNEL BALANCE. 109.
CHANNEL REVERSAL. 109.
CHANNEL SEPARATION.
109.
Channing, Carol (popular
singer). 722.
Chapman, Edith (singer). 429.
Chapman, Tracy (rock per-
former). 269.
Chapman, Walter (pianist). 527.
CHAPPELL PIANO CO., LTD.
109.
Chappelle, Thomas (vaudeville
artist). 109.
CHAPPELLE AND
STINNETTE (label). 109.
Chaput, Roger (guitarist). 560.
Charles, Milton (organist). 499.
CHARLES, RAY (popular
singer). *109*, 294, 589.
Charles Williams Stores. 585.
Chase, W. W. (executive). 518.
CHASSIS. 110.
CHECKER, CHUBBY (rock
performer). *110*, 594.
Checker (label). 110.
CHEEVER, CHARLES A.
(executive). *110*, 433, 464.
Chelotti, Teresa (soprano). 487.
Cheney, George K. (inventor).
512.
CHENEY TALKING MA-
CHINE CO. 110.
Chenier, Clifton (zydeco
singer). 269, 594.
Cherkassky, Shura (pianist).
528.
CHEROKEE RANCH (record-
ing studio). 110.
Cherry, Jim (bass). 415.
Chess, Leonard (executive). 110.
Chess, Marshall (executive).
599.
Chess, Philip (executive). 110.
CHESS (label). *110*, 423.
Chestang, Norman (tenor). 60.

CHEVALIER, MAURICE
(singer). 111.
Chicago (rock group). 595.
CHICAGO CENTRAL PHO-
NOGRAPH CO. 111.
CHICAGO PUBLIC LIBRARY.
111.
CHICAGO RECORD CO. 111.
Chicago style jazz. 273, 350.
CHICAGO SYMPHONY
ORCHESTRA. *111*, 294,
387, 430, 745.
CHICAGO TALKING MA-
CHINE CO. *112*, 538.
Chickering & Sons. 30.
Chiffons (rock group). 594.
CHILD, CALVIN G. (execu-
tive). *112*, 741.
Children's Record Co. 718.
CHILDREN'S RECORDS. 112.
Chilton, Carrol Brent (inven-
tor). 31.
Chilton Piano Co. 8.
Chip. *See* SWARF.
Chipmunks (rock group). 594.
Chocolate City (label). 538.
CHR. *See* CONTEMPORARY
HITS RADIO.
CHRISTIAN, CHARLIE
(guitarist). 112.
Christian, Frank (cornetist). 501.
Christie, Louis H. (clarinetist).
738, 773.
CHRISTMAS RECORDS. 113.
CHRISTOFF, BORIS (bass). 113.
Christy, Edwin Pearce (minstrel
show promoter). 442.
Christy, June (popular singer).
367.
Christy's Minstrels. 442.
Chronophone (sound and film
synchronizer). 448.
Chung, Kyung-Wha (violinist).
750.
Cigada, Francesco (baritone).
487.
Cigna, Gina (soprano). 491.
Cimera, Jaroslav (trombonist).
75.
CINCH (disc record player).
113.
Cincinnati Pops Orchestra. 113.
CINCINNATI SYMPHONY
ORCHESTRA. *113*, 580,
693.

Cinemascope. 448, 689.
Cinephone (sound and film
synchronizer). 448.
CIRCUIT. 114.
Cirelligraph (disc record
player). 114.
CIRELLIGRAPH CO., INC. 114.
CITY OF LONDON PHONO-
GRAPH &
GRAMOPHONE SOCI-
ETY. 114.
City Slickers (novelty group).
358.
Claffey, A. E. (executive). 248.
Clair, Herbert (pianist). 501.
CLANCY, A. W. (executive).
114, 443, 460.
Clancy, James A. (executive).
511.
Clancy Brothers (folk artists).
267.
Clapp, Sunny (saxophonist).
627.
Clapton, Eric (guitarist). 153.
CLARANCE, EDWARD
(singer). 114.
Clarence, Edward (singer). *See*
Clarance, Edward.
CLARINET RECORDINGS.
114. *See also* Clarinetists.
Clarinetists. See in this index:
Baquet, Achille; Bechet, Sidney;
Bigard, Barney; Brymer,
Jack; Cahuzac, Louis;
Christie, Louis H.; De
Franco, Buddy; De Peyer,
Gervase; Dodds, Johnny;
Dolphy, Eric; Draper,
Charles; Drucker, Stanley;
Fazola, Irving; Fountain,
Pete; Giese, Henry; Giuffre,
Jimmy; Gomez, Francisco;
Gomez, Manuel;
Goodman, Benny;
Hamelin, Gaston;
Hamilton, Jimmy; Herman,
Woody; Kell, Reginald;
King, Thea; Kirk, Roland;
Langenus, Gustave; Levy,
A.; Lytell, Jimmy; Matlock,
Matty; Medaer, Leo;
Noone, Jimmie; Nunez,
Alcide; Paradis, Henri;
Roppolo, Leon; Rostaing,
Hubert; Rubel, George;

Harmony label, 129; Homophon GmbH acquired, 129; Indestructible cylinder, 127; long-playing record, 130; Nipponophone acquired, 129; Okeh records acquired, 129; orchestral recordings, 128; Pathé (France) acquired, 129; record players, 130; Red label series, 127; Sony Corp. acquisition of U.S. Columbia, 130; Tisch (Laurence A.) chief executive, 130; Velvet Tone record, 127; Viva-Tonal record player, 129; Wallerstein (Edward) general manager, 129; war of the speeds, with Victor, 129.

Columbia (label). 508.

COLUMBIA BAND. 130, 438.

COLUMBIA BROADCASTING SYSTEM (CBS). *125*, 508.

COLUMBIA DOUBLE QUARTET (vocal group). 130.

Columbia Gold Moulded cylinder records. 541.

Columbia Graphophone Co. 125.

Columbia Graphophone Co., Ltd. 125.

Columbia Graphophone Manufacturing Co. 125.

Columbia Indestructible Records. *See* INDESTRUCTIBLE PHONOGRAPHIC RECORD CO. (III).

Columbia (International) Ltd. 125.

COLUMBIA LADIES QUARTET. 131.

COLUMBIA MALE QUARTET. 131.

COLUMBIA MANTEL CO. 131.

COLUMBIA MIXED QUARTET. 131.

Columbia Octette. *See* COLUMBIA DOUBLE QUARTET.

COLUMBIA ORCHESTRA. *131*, 549.

Columbia Phonograph Broadcasting System. 508.

Columbia Phonograph Co. 125, 607.

Columbia Phonograph Co., Inc. 125.

Columbia Phonograph Co., General. 125.

Columbia Phonograph Co., General—London Branch. 125.

Columbia Quartet (male vocal group). 521.

Columbia Record Club. 389.

Columbia record players. 131–135, Models are not listed individually in this index. An alphabetical list of models is on page 134.

Columbia Recording Co. 125.

Columbia Records, Inc. 125.

COLUMBIA SEXTET (mixed vocal group). 135.

COLUMBIA STELLAR QUARTETTE (male vocal group). 135.

Columbia-Rena (label). *See* RENA (label).

COLUMBO, RUSS (popular singer). 135.

COMBINATION PHONOGRAPH. 135.

Comedians. See in this index: Avon Comedy Four; Berman, Shelley; Bingham, Ralph; Borge, Victor; Brady, Pat; Brooks, Mel; Bruce, Lenny; Cantor, Eddie; Cohen, Myron; Collins, Arthur; Cook, Ben R.; Cosby, Bill; Diamond Comedy Four; Duprez, Fred; Edwards, Jonathan (Paul Weston); Elliott, Bob; Fields, Gracie; Flanders and Swann; Forde, Florrie; Foxx, Red; Freberg, Stan; Gallagher and Shean; Girard, Gilbert; Golden, Billy; Goulding, Ray; Gregory, Dick; Halley, William J.; Happiness Boys; Hare, Ernest; Harlan, Byron; Harris, Marion; Hill, Murry K.; Hoffnung Music Festival; Hope, Bob; Hunting, Russell; Irwin, Mary; Johnson, George W.;

Jones, Ada; Jones, Billy; Jones, Spike; Kaye, Danny; Keillor, Garrison; Lauder, Harry; Leachman, Silas F.; Lehrer, Tom; May, Elaine; Meader, Vaughn; Meeker, Edward; Miller, Eddie; Morton, Eddie; Murphy, Eddie; Murray, Billy; Natus, Joe; Nevsky, Peter; Newhart, Bob; Nichols, Mike; Paul, Darlene (Jo Stafford); Pryor, Richard; Quinn, Dan W.; Reiner, Carl; Roberts, Robert; Russell, Anna; Sadler, Josie; Sahl, Mort; Shepard, Burt; Sherman, Allan; Silver, Monroe; Spencer, Len; Stewart, Cal; Williams, Bert; Williams, Billy (American).; Williams, Billy (Australian).; Wills, Nat.

COMEDY RECORDINGS. 135.

COMMODORE (label). 137.

COMMODORE MUSIC SHOP. *137*, 579.

COMO, PERRY (popular singer). *137*, 760.

COMPACT DISC. *137*, 505, 545.

Compact disc clubs. 139.

COMPAGNIE AMERICAINE DU PHONOGRAPH EDISON. 139.

Compagnie du Phonograph Edison. 139.

COMPAGNIE FRANÇAISE DU GRAMOPHONE. 139.

Compagnie Général d'Electricité. 28.

Compagnie Général des Cinématographes, Phonographes et Pellicules. 515.

Compagnie Général des Machines Parlantes. 518.

COMPAGNIE GÉNÉRALE DES PHONOGRAPHES. *139*, 515.

Compagnie Microphonographes Bettini. 61.

COMPANDING. 139.

COMPATIBLE. 139.

Conrad, Herman (bassist). 738.
Consolidated Film Industries. 562.
CONSOLIDATED RECORD CORP. 140.
CONSOLIDATED RECORDS, INC. 140.
CONSOLIDATED TALKING MACHINE CO. 141–142.
CONSTANT AMPLITUDE.
Constant angular velocity. 679.
Constant linear velocity. 680.
CONSTANT VELOCITY. 142.
Constellation (coin-operated disc record player). 441.
Contact microphone. 435.
Contemporary (label). 547.
CONTEMPORARY HITS RADIO (CHR). 142.
CONTEMPORARY RECORDS (label). 142.
Content announcements. See ANNOUNCEMENTS.
Contino, Dick (accordionist). 5.
Continuous loop cartridge. 100.
Continuous noise suppressor. 505.
CONTOUR PULSE. 142.
Contraltos. See in this index: Anderson, Marian; Baker, Elsie; Butt, Clara; Desvignes, Carlotta; Gerville-Réache, Jeanne; Jordan, Mary; Kelso, May; Minghini-Cattaneo, Irene; Morgan, Corinne; Olszewka, Maria; Onegin, Sigrid; Reuss-Belce, Luise; Schumann-Heink, Ernestine; Swarthout, Gladys; Thorborg, Kerstin; Van der Veer, Nevada. *See also* Mezzo-sopranos.
Control amplifier. See PREAMPLIFIER.
CONTROL UNIT. 142.
CONTROLS. 142.
Cook, Ben R. (comedian). 136.
Cook, J. Lawrence (executive). 559.
Cook, Stu (bass guitarist). 153.
Cook's Athletic Co. 335.
Cooke, Sam (blues singer). 589.
Cool, Harry (popular singer). 361, 624.

COOL JAZZ. 143.
Cooley, Spade (country artist). 152.
Coolidge, Rita (country artist). 376.
COOMBS, FRANK (countertenor). 143.
Coon, Carlton A. (Big Band leader). 143.
COON SONGS. 143.
COON-SANDERS ORCHESTRA. 143.
Coontown Minstrels. 443.
Cooper, Alice (rock performer). 595.
Cooper, David (discographer). 212.
Cooper Brothers, Ltd. 624.
Cooper, Mr. (bassoonist). 775.
Copland, Aaron (composer). 584.
COPY MASTER. 144.
COPYCODE. 144.
COPYRIGHT. 144.
CORAL (label). 145.
Corbett, Frank (vaudeville artist). 38.
Cordon, Norman (bass). 776.
Corelli, Franco (tenor). 486.
Corey, James Albert (executive). 460.
CORNER HORN (loudspeaker). *145*, 404.
CORNET RECORDINGS. 145.
See also Cornetists; Trumpet recordings.
Cornetists. See in this index: Armstrong, Louis; Bartow, W.; Bates, Will; Beiderbecke, Bix; Brown, Bert; Chambers, W. Paris; Christian, Frank; Clark, Tom; Clarke, Herbert L.; Dana, D. B.; Dann, M. Felice; Hackett, Bobby; Hazel, John; Henke, "Mr."; Hoch, Theodore; Jaeger, Alvin; Keneke, Emil; Kryl, Bohumir; La Rocca, Nick; Levy, Jules; Martin, Frank; McPartland, Jimmy; Mittauer, John; Oliver, King; Rogers, Walter Bowman; Schlossberg, M.; Schmitt, J.; Sonty, Frederico; Spanier, Muggsy; Stewart, Rex.

See also Trumpeters.
Cornwall, A. Duncan (bass). 81.
Corrington, Murian S. (engineer). 745.
CORT (label). 145.
Cortina, Rafael Diaz de la (language teacher). 145.
CORTINA ACADEMY OF LANGUAGES. 146.
CORTOT, ALFRED (pianist). *146*, 528, 710, 583.
Coryell, Larry (guitarist). 304.
Cosby, Bill (comedian). 136, 759.
Cosentino, Orazio (tenor). 487.
COSMO (label). 146.
Cosmo Records (label). 749.
Cosmopolitan Records, Inc. 146.
Cotton, Larry (popular singer). 317.
Counterpoint (label). 689.
COUNTRY AND WESTERN MUSIC RECORDINGS. 146–153. Bakersfield sound, 150; barn dance programs, 148; *Billboard,* 149; bluegrass music, 148, 150; cajun, 151; conjunto, 151; country blues, 151; country rock, 149, 151; crossover recordings, 148; drums added, 149; electric guitar added, 148; first recordings, 148; folk music revival, 149; gospel, 151; Grammy awards, 149; Grand Ole Opry, 148, 149, 150; hard country, 151; high lonesome sound, 150; honky tonk, 148, 151; juke boxes, effect on country performers, 148; Midwestern Hayride, 149; Nashville sound, 150, 151; Nashville studios and recordings, 149; National Barn Dance, 148; old time, 151; outlaw music, 150; progressive, 152; redneck rock, 152; rockabilly, 149, 152; sales of recordings, 152, 153; singing cowboy style, 152; televised country programs, 148, 149, 150; Tex-Mex country, 152; Texas

DESTINN, EMMY (soprano). *183*, 487.

Desvignes, Carlotta (contralto). 485.

De Sylva, Buddy (executive). 98.

Dethlefson, Ron (discographer). 167.

Detroit Brass and Iron Works Co. 183.

Detroit Symphony Orchestra. 430.

DETROIT TALKING MACHINE (disc record player). 183.

Dett, Nathaniel (pianist; composer). 584.

DEUTSCHE GRAMMOPHON GESELLSCHAFT (DGG). *183*, 530.

Deutsche Schallplatten und Sprechmaschinen AG. 754.

Deutscher Industrie Normenausschus (DIN). *See* DIN DEUTSCHES INSTITUT FÜR NORMUNG.

DEUXPHONE (cylinder or disc record player). 185.

Deuxphone Manufacturing Co., Ltd. 186.

DEVINE, ANDREW (executive). 186.

Devineau, Louis (executive). 186.

DEVINEAU BIOPHONE CO. 186.

DeVry Corp. 559.

Dewey, Maude (whistler). 686, 763.

DF. *See* DAMPING FACTOR.

DGG. *See* DEUTSCHE GRAMMOPHON GESELLSCHAFT (DGG).

Dial (label). 396.

Diameter equalization. 642.

Diameter equalization. *See also* EQUALIZATION; GRAPHIC EQUALIZER.

Diamond, George (tenor). 126.

DIAMOND (label). 186.

DIAMOND COMEDY FOUR. 186.

Diamond Record Co. 186.

DIAMOND STYLUS CO., LTD. 186.

Diamond Universal Gramophone Records, Ltd. 186.

Diamonds (rock group). 594.

DIAPASON CATALOGUE. 186.

DIAPHRAGM. 187.

Dibango, Manu (blues singer). 590.

Dickens, Little Jimmy (country artist). 149.

Dickinson, Charles (executive). 112.

DICKSON, WILLIAM KENNEDY (inventor). 187.

DICTATING MACHINES. 187.

DIDDLEY, BO (popular singer). 187.

Diémer, Louis (pianist). 528, 530, 584.

Dietrich, Marie (conductor). 487.

DIFFERENTIAL AMPLIFIER. 188.

DIFFRACTION. 188.

DIFFUSOR (diaphragm). 188.

DIGITAL COUNTER. 188.

Digital microphone. 437.

DIGITAL RECORDING. 188.

Digital to analog converter. *See* DAC.

Dilworth, George (pianist). 501.

Di Modrone, Duke Uberto Visconti (executive). 270.

DIN DEUTSCHES INSTITUT FÜR NORMUNG. 188.

Diode. 263.

DIPLOMA (label). 188.

DIPPEL, ANDREAS (tenor). 188.

Direct cut. *See* DIRECT TO DISC.

Direct disc recording. *See* DIRECT TO DISC.

DIRECT INJECTION. 189.

Direct recording. 189.

DIRECT TO DISC. 189.

Direct-to-stereo. 575.

DISC. 189–208. Grooves, 193; history of the format, 190; industry. 195–205; lacquer-coated discs, 191; lamination, 192; manufacturing, 191; materials, 191; repertoire, 205; shellac, 192; sizes, 191; speeds, 191;

terminology, 189; vinyl, 193; wax introduced, 191.

DISC JOCKEY. 208.

Disc jockeys. See in this index: Clark, Dick; DiStefano, Armand; Drake, Bill; Freed, Alan; Haley, Bill; Harrison, Mike; Hirsch, David; Jacobs, Ron; Jarvis, Al; Miller, Larry; Stone, Christopher; Syracuse, Russ "The Moose."

DISC NUMBER. 209.

Disc Record Co., Ltd. 468, 586, 678.

Dischi Fonotipia. *See* FONOTIPIA, LTD.; SOCIETÀ ITALIANA DI FONOTIPIA.

DISCO. 209.

Discographers (and writers about sound recording). See in this index: Allen, Walter C.; Andrews, Frank; Annand, H. H.; Badrock, Arthur; Barnes, Harold M.; Bauer, Robert; Bennett, John R.; Bill, Edward Lyman; Bill, Raymond; Blacker, George; Brooks, Tim; Bruun, C. L.; Bryant, Eric Thomas; Carter, Sydney H.; Celletti, Rodolfo; Cooper, David; Darrell, Robert Donalon; Deakins, Duane; Delaunay, Charles; Dennis, James F. E.; Dethlefson, Ron; Fagan, Ted; Favia-Artsay, Aida; Foreman, Louis; Frankenstein, Alfred; Frow, George; Gibson, Gerald; Girard, Victor; Gray, J.; Gray, Michael; Hall, David; Harmon, Jim; Hickerson, Jay; Hill, Richard S.; Keepers, Walter M.; Kendziora, Carl; Koeningsberg, Allen; Moogk, Edward B.; Moran, William R.; Myers, Kurtz; Oja, Carol J.; Reed, Peter Hugh; Richards, John B.; Riemens, Leo; Rosenberg, Kenyon; Rust, Brian; Salomonson, Terry;

Schwann, William; Siegel, David S.; Smolian, Steven; Stanich, Raymond; Stearns, Marshall; Stevenson, Gordon; Stratton, John; Walsh, Jim; Weber, J. F.; Whitburn, Joel; Witten, Laurence C.

DISCOGRAPHY. 209–213. Descriptive, 209; enumerative, 210; historical, 212; methodology, 212; monographic publications, 212; national discographies, 210; periodicals, 211–212; standards, 212.

Discophone. See PICTURIZED PHONOGRAPHS.

Discos Castello (record shop). 573.

DISCOTECA DI STATO (Italian national sound archive). 213.

Discotheque. See DISCO (I).

Discrete circuit. See INTEGRATED CIRCUIT.

Discwasher Compact Disc Cleaner. 117.

DISKO CO. 213.

DISPERSION. 213.

Disque Aspire (label). 28.

Disques (periodical). 629.

Di Stefano, Armand (disc jockey). 737.

DI STEFANO, GIUSEPPE (tenor). 213.

Di Stefano, John (executive; cafe owner). 737.

DISTORTION. 213.

Distronics (firm). 33.

Ditcham, William (organist). 499.

DIVA (label). 214.

Dividing network. 158.

DIXI (label). 214.

Dixie Hummingbirds (gospel group). 588.

DIXIELAND JAZZ. 214.

Dockstader, Ray (librarian). 13.

DODDS, JOHNNY (clarinetist). 214.

DODGE, PHILIP T. (executive). 214.

Doherty, Dennis (rock performer). 414.

Dohnányi, Christoph von (conductor). 118.

Dohnányi, Ernö von (composer). 584.

Doktor, Karl (violinist). 84.

Dolby, Raymond M. (inventor). 214.

DOLBY NOISE REDUCTION SYSTEM. 214.

Dolphy, Eric (saxophonist; clarinetist; flutist). 442.

DOMAINS. 215.

Dome tweeter (loudspeaker). 405.

Domestic (disc record player). 215.

DOMESTIC TALKING MACHINE CORP. 215.

DOMINGO, PLACIDO (tenor). 215.

Dominion (label). 92, 215.

Dominion Autophone Co. 36.

DOMINION GRAMOPHONE RECORD CO., LTD. 215.

DOMINO, FATS (pianist). *216*, 587, 594.

DOMINO (label). 216.

Domino Phonograph Co. 216.

Domino Record Co. 216.

Donaghy, Harry (bass). 311, 460.

Donaldson, Bobby (drummer). 541.

Donaldson, Will (singer). 428.

Donner, W. A. (executive). 467.

Doors (rock group). 595, 620.

DORATI, ANTAL (conductor). 216.

DORFMANN, ANIA (pianist). 216.

DORIAN (label). 216.

Dorian Recordings (firm). 216.

DORSEY, JIMMY (Big Band leader). *216*, 578.

Dorsey, Lee (rock performer). 594.

DORSEY, TOMMY (Big Band leader). *216*, 483, 625.

Dorsey Brothers Orchestra. 216, 502.

Dory, Craig (executive). 216.

Dot (label). 423.

DOUBLE TRACKING. 217.

Douglas Phonograph Co. 241.

DOUGLASS, LEON F. (executive; inventor). *217*, 462, 745.

Douste, Irene (pianist). 529, 626.

Douste, Jeanne (pianist). 529, 626.

Down Home (label). 118.

Dr. Feelgood (rock performer). 595.

Drake, Bill (disc jockey). 72.

Drama recordings. See LITERARY RECORDINGS.

Draper, Charles (clarinetist). 771, 774.

Drasein, Alexander (violinist). 707.

Drdla, Franz (violinist). 750.

Dresden Piano Co. 467.

Dresden State Opera Orchestra Wind Quintet. 775.

Drifters (blues singers). 587, 589, 594.

Drivers (loudspeakers). 399.

Droge, Max (cellist). 363.

DROP-IN. 217.

DROPOUT. 217.

Dropout count. 217.

Drucker, Stanley (clarinetist). 115.

DRUG LYRICS. 217.

DRUGOLA. 218.

Drummers. See in this index: Baker, Ginger; Bellson, Louis; Best, Peter; Blakey, Art; Butler, Joe; Catlett, Sid; Clarke, Kenny; Clifford, Doug; Donaldson, Bobby; Dryden, Spencer; Greer, Sonny; Johnson, Osie; Jones, Jo; Kay, Connie; King, Eddie; Krupa, Gene; Lada, Anton; Lent, James L.; Love, Mike; Loyacano, Arnold; Manne, Shelly; McKinley, Ray; Moon, Keith; Morello, Joe; Pelequin, Jerry; Pollack, Ben; Pryor, S. O.; Rich, Buddy; Richmond, Danny; Roth, Jack; St-Cyr, Johnny; Sbarbaro, Tony; Singleton, Zutty; Starr, Ringo; Thigpen, Ed; Tough, Dave; Watts, Charlie; Webb, Chick; Wettling, George; Wilson, Dennis.

Dryden, Spencer (drummer). 353.

Du Pré, Jacqueline (cellist). 106.

DUAL GEBRÜDER STEIDINGER. 217.

Dual track. *See* TRACK.

DUBBING. 218.

Dubrico, Ltd. 221.

DUCHIN, EDDY (pianist). 218.

DUCKING. 218.

DUCRETET ET CIE (firm). *218,* 536.

DUCRETET-THOMSON (label). 218.

Dudley, Audley (mandolinist). 503.

Dudley, George F. (guitarist, harpist). 503.

DUDLEY, S. H. (singer; executive). 218.

Duey, Phil (baritone) 428, 586.

Duffy and Imgrund's Fifth Regiment Band. 438.

Dulcephone. *See* APOLLO (I).

Dulcephone Decca (disc record player). 608.

DUMMY HEAD STEREO. 218.

DUMPING. 219.

Duncan, Rosetta (singer). 219.

DUNCAN, TODD (baritone). 219.

Duncan, Vivian (singer). 219.

Duncan Automatic Stop. 35.

DUNCAN SISTERS. 219.

Dunham, Frank J. (executive). 459.

Dunlap, Marguerite (singer). 738.

Dunn, Johnny (trumpeter). 629.

Dunton, John C. (inventor). 450.

Duo Junior (turntable). 756.

DUO-ART (reproducing piano). 219.

Duophone (label). 219.

DUOPHONE (disc record player). 219.

DUO-TRAC (recording on film). 220.

Duo-Vox (disc record player). 84.

DUPLEX (Pathé disc record player). 220.

DUPLEX (soundbox). 220.

Duplex Pathéphone (disc record player). 523.

DUPLEX PHONOGRAPH CO. 220.

Duplexophone (disc record player). 220, 363.

DUPLEXTONE NEEDLE. 220.

DUPRÉ, MARCEL (organist). 220, 500.

DUPREZ, FRED (comedian). 220.

Duran Duran (rock group). 595.

DURANOID CO. 221.

Durante, Jimmy (pianist). 481, 501.

DURA-TONE RECORD (label). 221.

Dura-Tone Record Co. 221.

Durham, Eddie (trombonist). 363.

DURIUM (label). 221.

Durium Products (G.B.), Ltd. 221.

DURIUM PRODUCTS CORP. 221.

Dyer, Frank B. (engineer). 244.

DYER, FRANK LEWIS (executive; inventor). 222.

Dyer, Louise (executive). 480.

DYER-BENNET, RICHARD (folk artist). 222.

Dyke & the Blazers (blues singers). 590.

DYLAN, BOB (folk and country artist; popular singer). 149, 222.

DYNAGROOVE (RCA microgroove record). 222.

DYNAMIC. 222.

Dynamic (loudspeaker). 399.

Dynamic cartridge. 100.

Dynamic headroom. 35.

Dynamic microphone. 434, 435, 437.

DYNAMIC RANGE. 223.

DYNE. 223.

—E—

E. M. G. HANDMADE GRAMOPHONES, LTD. 225.

E.U. (rock group). 595.

EAGLE (cylinder phonograph). 225.

EAMES, EMMA (soprano). 225.

Ear (organ of hearing). 315.

Early Music Consort. 324.

Earphone. 315.

Earth Opera (rock group). 594.

Earth, Wind, and Fire (rock group). 595.

East Liverpool China Co. 684.

EASTERN PENNSYLVANIA PHONOGRAPH CO. 225.

EASTERN TALKING MACHINE CO. 226.

EASTERN TALKING MACHINE JOBBERS ASSOCIATION. 226.

Eastman-Rochester Symphony Orchestra. 430.

Eastman Wind Ensemble. 430.

EASTON, EDWARD DENISON (executive). 226, 460.

Easton, Eric (executive). 599.

EASTON, FLORENCE (soprano). 226.

EBERLE, RAY (popular singer). 226.

EBERLY, BOB (popular singer). *226,* 578.

EBONOID (label). 227.

ECHO. 227.

ECHO CHAMBER. 227.

ECHOPHONE (cylinder phonograph). 227.

Eckersley, Peter B. (BBC engineer). 76.

Eckert, Walter L. (executive). 518.

ECLIPSE (label). 227.

Eclipse Musical Co. 403.

Eddy, Duane (rock performer). 594.

EDDY, NELSON (baritone). 227.

Edgerton, E. D. (executive). 445.

EDIBEL SOUND FILM APPARATUS, LTD. 226.

Ediphone Standard Practice Records. *See* EDISON SCHOOL RECORDS.

EDISON, CHARLES A. (executive). 226.

EDISON, THOMAS ALVA (inventor). 226–230, 540. Automatic repeating telegraph, 1872–1877, 229; Blue Amberol cylinder, 228; childhood, 229; City of London Phonograph & Gramophone Society

(patron), 114; dictation records, 239; Edison Diamond Disc, 228, 231; Edison disc phonographs, 238; Edison Effect, 229; Edison National Historic Site, 229, 232; Edison Phonograph Co., 228, 233; Edison Phonograph Toy Manufacturing Co., 233; Edison Phonograph Works, 228, 233; Edison phonographs, 233–238; electric power system, 229; electrical recording (1927), 229; horns, 232; Improved Phonograph (1887), 228; incandescent lamp (1879), 229; long-playing record (1926), 229; Menlo Park laboratory, 228; marriages, 229; motion pictures (1889-1915), 229; musical knowledge and taste, 229; National Phonograph Co., 228; New Phonograph (1887), 228; North American Phonograph Co., 227; Perfected Phonograph (1888), 228; Quadraplex telegraph (1874), 229; school records, 239; spring motor, 228; stock market printer (1870), 229; telephone transmitter (1877), 229; telegraph relay experiments, 228; Thomas A. Edison, Inc., 228; tinfoil phonograph (1877), 228; tone tests, 228; voice on records, 230; vote recorder (1869), 229; wartime research, 229.
EDISON (label). 230.
EDISON BELL (label). 230.
EDISON BELL CONSOLI-DATED PHONOGRAPH CO., LTD. 231.
EDISON BELL ELECTRON (label). 231.
EDISON BELL INTERNA-TIONAL, LTD. 232.
EDISON BELL PHONO-GRAPH CORP., LTD. 232.

Edison Bell Radio (label). See EDISON BELL (label).
Edison Bell Winner (label). 770. See also EDISON BELL (label).
Edison Bell Winner Record (label). 770.
Edison Brass Quartette. 75.
Edison Concert Band. 438.
EDISON DIAMOND DISC. 231.
Edison dictation records. See EDISON SCHOOL RECORDS.
Edison Effect. 263.
Edison General Electric Co. 283.
EDISON HORNS. 232.
Edison Male Quartet. 315.
Edison Minstrels. 443.
EDISON NATIONAL HIS-TORIC SITE. 232, 484.
Edison Phonograph Agency. 314, 542.
EDISON PHONOGRAPH CO. 233.
EDISON PHONOGRAPH CO. (OHIO). 233.
EDISON PHONOGRAPH TOY MANUFACTURING CO. 233.
EDISON PHONOGRAPH WORKS. 233.
EDISON RECORD PLAYERS. 233–238. Cylinder and disc phonographs marketed by Edison are listed on pp. 233–238. They are not entered individually in this index.
EDISON REPEATING AT-TACHMENTS. 239.
EDISON REPRODUCERS. 239.
EDISON SCHOOL RECORDS. 239.
EDISON SHAVERS. 240.
EDISON SPEAKING PHONO-GRAPH CO. 240.
EDISON (THOMAS A.), INC. 230.
EDISON UNITED PHONO-GRAPH CO. 241, 577.
EDISON VENETIAN TRIO (instrumental group). 241.
EDISONIA CO. 241.
EDISONIA, LTD. 241.

Edlin, Louis (violinist). 467.
EDMUNDS, HENRY (execu-tive). 242, 603.
Edna White Trumpet Quartet. 764.
Educational Record Co. 272.
EDUCATIONAL RECORD-INGS. 239.
Edward Tarr Brass Ensemble. 75.
Edward VII, King of England. 373, 603, 708.
EDWARDS, CLIFF (popular singer; ukulele player). 242.
Edwards, Eddie (trombonist). 500, 721.
EDWARDS, JOAN (popular singer). 242, 752.
EDWARDS, JOHN (collector). 242.
Edwards, Jonathan (Paul Weston; comedian). 136.
Edwards, Webley (Hawaiian artist). 313.
EFFICIENCY. 242.
EIA. See ELECTRONIC INDUSTRIES ASSOCIA-TION (EIA).
Eibenschütz, Ilona (pianist). 528.
Eichhorn, Charles (executive). 264.
Eiffel, Gustave (engineer). 510.
EIGENTON. 243.
EIGHT FAMOUS VICTOR ARTISTS. 243.
Eight Popular Victor Artists. 243.
Eight-track cartridge. 705, 718.
Eight-track tape. See TAPE.
ELBOW. 243.
ELCASET (modified cassette). 243.
Eldred, George (singer). 373.
ELDRIDGE, ROY (trumpeter). 243, 478.
Eldridge Johnson, Manufactur-ing Machinist (firm). 739.
ELECTRADISK (label). 244.
Electret microphone. 435, 437.
ELECTRIC (label). 244.
Electric Lady (recording studio). 319.
Electric Light Orchestra (rock group). 595.

Thiele, Bob; Tisch, Laurence A.; Tomlinson, John C.; Towell, Thomas H.; Tremaine, William B.; Trostler, Arthur A.; Tyler, W. H.; Urles, William T.; Villchur, Edgar; Vogt, Albert; Volkmann, John E.; Waldman, Phillip; Walker, Jimmy; Wallace, E. P.; Wallerstein, Edward; Wallichs, Glenn; Walsh, Arthur.; Wangemann, Adelbert Theo; Waterson, Henry; Watters, James; Weinstock, Bob; Wexler, Jerry; Wheelan, Pat; White, Frank B.; White, John H; Whitsit, Perry B.; Widmann, Eugene A.; Williams, Edmund Trevor Lloyd; Williams, J. Mayo; Willson, H. L.; Wilson, C. H.; Wilson, J. W.; Wilson, J. W.; Winkelman, H. A.; Winterhalter, Hugo; Wiswell, Lester C.; Wohlgemuth, F.; Wolfe, Frank; Wood, J. C.; Woollacott, Arthur; Wright, Barclay; Wulsin, Lucien; Wurlitzer, Rudolph; Wychoff, Richard D.; Yerkes, Hulbert A.; Young, J. L.; Young, Louis. (See also inventors and engineers.)

EXHIBITION SOUNDBOX. 8, 253.

Exponential horn. *See* HORN.

Exposition Universelle, Paris. 509.

EXTENDED PLAY DISCS. *See* LONG PLAYING RECORDS.

EXTERNAL PROCESSOR LOOP. 253.

—F—

Fabian (rock performer). 593.

Fagan, Ted (discographer). 685.

Fair use principle (copyright law). 145.

Fairbanks, I. L. (executive). 337.

Fairchild, Edgar (pianist). 501.

FAITH, PERCY (conductor). 255.

Falcon, Joe (cajun singer). 265.

Falla, Manuel de (pianist) composer. 584.

Fame (label). 588.

FAMOUS (label). 255.

Famous Garland Jubilee Singers. 561.

FAMOUS SINGERS RECORDS, INC. 255.

Fanciulli, Francesco (bandmaster). 728.

Fancourt, Darrell (singer). 287.

FANTASIA (motion picture). 255.

FANZINE. 256.

Farber Sisters (popular singers). 626.

Farina, Mimi (folk artist). 268.

Farkas, Philip (hornist). 75.

Farkoa, Maurice (singer). 452, 453.

Farnon, Christine M. (executive). 458.

Farnsworth Television and Radio Corp. 97.

Farr, Hugh (country fiddler). 644.

Farr, Karl (country artist). 644.

FARRAR, GERALDINE (soprano). 256.

FARRELL, EILEEN (soprano). 256.

FARRELL, MARGUERITE E. (soprano). 256.

Farwell, Granger (executive). 687.

Fauré, Gabriel (composer). 584.

Favero, Mafalda (conductor). 489.

Favia-Artsay, Aida (discographer). 123.

FAVOR, EDWARD M.(tenor). *256, 452, 453.*

FAVORITA (cylinder phonograph). 256.

FAVORITE (label). 256.

Favorite (disc record player). 257.

Favorite Schallplatten Fabrik. 335, 478.

FAVORITE TALKING MACHINE CO. 257.

Fay, Hugh Patrick (inventor; executive). 257.

FAY HOME RECORDERS, LTD. 257.

Fazola, Irving (clarinetist). 115.

FCC. *See* FEDERAL COMMUNICATIONS COMMISSION (FCC).

Federal (cylinder label). 257.

FEDERAL (disc label). 257.

FEDERAL COMMUNICATIONS COMMISSION (FCC). 257.

FEDERAL CYLINDER PROJECT. 257.

FEDERAL PHONOGRAPH CO. 257.

Federal Radio Corp. 644.

FEEDBACK. 257.

FEEDFORWARD. 248.

Fender, Freddy (country artist). 152.

Fender Co. 304.

Fennell, Frederick (conductor). 430.

Feraldy, Germaine (soprano). 490.

Ferguson, Arthur C. (inventor). 389.

Ferguson, Maynard (trumpeter). 367.

Ferrara, Frank (Hawaiian artist). 313.

Ferras, Christian (violinist). 716.

Ferrer, Jose (actor). 394.

Ferrier, Kathleen (mezzosoprano). 73.

Festival du Disque. 93.

Festival Records. 33.

FEUERMANN, EMANUEL (cellist). *248,* 318.

FEWKES, JESSE WALTER (ethnologist). 248.

ffrr. *See* FULL FREQUENCY RANGE RECORDING (ffrr).

Fiber needles. 462.

FIEDLER, ARTHUR (conductor). 248.

FIELD RECORDINGS. 258.

FIELDS, ARTHUR, (baritone). 27, 38, *258,* 712, 725.

FIELDS, GRACIE (comedienne). *259.*

FIELDS, SHEP (Big Band leader). 259.

Fields (Arthur) Record Co. 27.
FIFTH AVENUE PRESBYTE-
RIAN CHOIR. 259.
Fifth Dimension (rock group).
595.
Fifty-Second Street Stompers
(jazz group). 692.
FIGNER, FREDERICO (execu-
tive). 260.
Figner, Medea Mey (soprano).
260.
FIGNER, NIKOLAI (tenor). 260.
Figure eight microphone. 435.
Fikes, Betty Mae (folk artist).
269.
Film music. See MOTION
PICTURE MUSIC.
Film, recording medium. 106.
FILM SPEED. 260.
FILMOPHONE (label). 260.
Filmophone Flexible Records,
Ltd. 260.
FILTER. 260.
Fina, Jack (pianist). 419.
Finberg, William S. (executive).
433.
Finck, Herman (conductor). 10,
493.
Fine, Robert (recording
engineer). 430.
Finishing groove. 140.
Finkelstein, Harry (saxophon-
ist). 626.
FIO RITO, TED (Big Band
leader). 260.
Firestone Tire and Rubber Co.
524.
First Drama Quartette. 394.
Firsts in recording history:
Actress (famous) to make
commercial recordings,
409; Advertisement
recording, 89; Album cover
exhibition, 10; Album set,
10; Amberol record, 13;
Artist discography, 123;
Asian music recorded, 258;
Banjo recording, 42;
Baseball player to record,
390; Baseball recording,
390; Berliner artist, 290; Big
Band on commercial radio,
143; Binaural recordings.
63; Bird song recordings,
373; Black artist to have a

sponsored radio show, 121;
Black artist to be widely
known on recordings, 355;
Black country artist on a
major label, 548; Black firm
to issue records, 73; Black
group to record, 683; Black
jazz recordings, 350; Black
record distributor, 385;
Blues instrumental
recording, 68; Blues vocal
recording, 59, 68, 313;
Canadian recordings 90;
Canadian recordings,
commercial, 91; Choral
hymn recording, 332;
Christmas record, 113;
Coin-operated phonograph
on location, 505; Columbia
artist identified by name,
348; Columbia attempt at
serious classical music, 549;
Complete symphony
recording (almost) by a
major orchestra, 469;
Composer (famous) to
record, 140; Composer to
record, 323; Country artist
to record, 265; Country
artist to host a television
program, 27; Country
record 148, 265; Country
record to sell a million
copies, 78; Crossover
conductor, 502; Cylinder
phonograph, operating,
511; Deluxe movie house in
U.S., 525; Digital recordings, 188; Disc record
player, 406; Disc record-
ings, commercial, 406; Disc,
wax, 406; Discography,
extensive, 179; Documen-
tary on-site recording, 278;
Double-sided disc records
marketed in Europe, 478;
Double-sided disc records,
to be marketed, 343; Drum
solo recording, 521;
Dynamic loudspeaker for
domestic use, 509; Edison
jazz record, 275; Eldridge
Johnson commercial
recording, 739; Electric
guitar (featured) recording,

363; Electrical recording,
Columbia, 245; Electrical
recording, Gramophone
Co., 245; Electrical recording laboratory, 419;
Electrical recording, U.S.,
419; Electrical recording,
U.S., commercial 34, 245;
Electrical recording, Victor,
243, 245; Entertainment
records, 702; Exclusive
artist contract, 355; Field
recordings, 258; Field
recordings in Europe, 45,
258; Flutist with a chart
album, 569; Gold discs,
290; His Master's Voice
trademark use, 44; Home
disc recorder, 325; Home
disc recorder, United
States, 15; Hymn disc
recording, 332; Indepen-
dent jazz label, successful,
137; Internal horn record
player, 61, 333; Jazz ("true
jazz") recordings, 349; Jazz
record on Edison, 275; jazz
recording by a Black
group, 473; Jazz recordings
by Black artists, 350; jewel
needle, permanent, 522;
Knighthood to a recording
industry figure, 690;
Language instruction
records, 146; Lateral
recording, 406; Library
(academic) in U.S. with
sound recordings, 674;
Library in U.S. to have any
sound recordings, 674;
Magnetic recorder (func-
tional), 411; *Messiah*
complete recording, 397;
Million selling classical
record, 119; Motion picture
(feature length) with
talking, 357; Motion
picture with talking, 59;
Motion picture with sound,
187, 369; Musician (recognized performer) to record,
323; Nashville, commercial
recordings, 121; National
convention of the phono-
graph industry, 226;

FITZGERALD, ELLA (popular singer). 262, 760.

Fitzwilson, George H. (executive). 473.

FLAGSTAD, KIRSTEN (soprano). 262.

FLAMEPHONE (disc record player). 263.

Flamingos (blues singers). 587.

Flanagan, Ralph (Big Band leader). 440.

Flanagan, Tommy (pianist). 605.

Flanders and Swann (comedians). 136.

FLANGING. 263.

Flapper (label). 520.

Flash Cadillac & the Continental Kids (rock group). 595.

FLAT RESPONSE. 263.

FLATT, LESTER RAYMOND (banjoist). 150, 263.

FLEMING, AMBROSE, Sir (inventor). 263.

FLEMISH-LYNN PHONOGRAPH CO. 263.

Fletcher, John (executive). 65, 483, 491.

Fletcher, John (tuba player). 722.

FLETCHER RECORD CO., INC. 263, 483.

Fletcher Record Co. 582.

FLETCHER-MUNSON EFFECT. 263.

FLEXO (label). 263.

FLONZALEY QUARTET. 264.

Florentine Quartet (instrumental group). 772.

FLORIDA PHONOGRAPH CO. 263.

FLOWER HORN. 263.

Floyd, Eddie (blues singer). 589.

Floyd, Pink (rock performer). 595.

Floyd, Troy (dance band leader). 611.

Flutists. See in this index:

Amadio, John; Badollet, Frank; Barone, Clement; Barrère, Georges; Dolphy, Eric; Fransella, Albert; Galway, James; Gast, Gustav; Gaubert, Philippe; Hennebains, Adolphe;

Jaeger, Henry; Kincaid, William; Laurent, Georges; Lemmone, John; LeRoy, René; Lufsky, Marshall; Lyons, Darius; Mann, Herbie; Mazziotta, Frank; Moyse, Marcel; Rampal, Jean-Pierre; Rose, Eugene; Schweinfest, George; Wehner, Carl; Wummer, John.

FLUTTER. 263.

FLUTTER ECHO. 263.

Flybush, F. (executive). 68.

Flying Burrito Brothers (rock group). 595.

Flying Fish (label). 267.

FM. See FREQUENCY MODULATION.

Foa, Dino (executive). 631.

Fogerty, John (rock singer). 153.

Fogerty, Tom (guitarist). 153.

Foggy Mountain Boys (country group). 263.

FOLDED HORN. 263.

FOLEY, RED (country artist). 148, 149, 264, 722.

Folk artists (singers and instrumentalists). See in this index:

Almanac Singers; Anderson, Eric; Ashley, Clarence; Balfa Brothers; Bikel, Theodore; Boggs, Dock; Brand, Oscar; Brothers Four; Buffalo Springfield; Buffett, Jimmie; Byrds; Carawan, Guy; Carolinians; Carpenter, Mary Chapin; Cash, Roseanne; Chad Mitchell Trio; Chenier, Clifton; Clancy Bros; Clayton, Paul; Cohen, John; Country Gentlemen; Crowell, Rodney; Dyer-Bennet, Richard; Falcon, Joe; Farina, Mimi; Fikes, Betty Mae; Freedom Singers; Gateway Singers; Gauthier, Conrad; Gibson, Bob; Gilbert, Ronnie; Goodman, Steve; Greenbriar Boys; Greenway, John; Griffith, Nanci; Guard, David;

Guthrie, Arlo; Guthrie, Woody; Harris, Rutha; Hassilev, Alex; Hays, Lee; Hellerman, Fred; Herald, John; Hester, Carolyn; Highwaymen; Holcomb, Roscoe; Hopkins, Sam "Lightnin'"; House, Son; Hurt, John; Hurt, Mississippi John; Ian and Sylvia; Ian, Janice; Ives, Burl; Johnson, Bernice; Keillor, Garrison; Kennedy, Peter; Kossov Sisters; Lightfoot, Gordon; Limelighters; MacColl, Ewan; McCurdy, Ed; McDowell, Fred; McGee, Dennis; Mitchell, Joni; Moffatt, Hugh; Neblett, Charles; Neil, Fred; New Christy Minstrels; New Lost City Ramblers; Newbury, Mickey; Niles, John Jacob; Ochs, Phil; Odetta; Okun, Milt; Paley, Tom; Paxton, Tom; Peter, Paul, and Mary; Prine, John; Reagon, Cordell; Reed, Susan; Reynolds, Nick; Rinzler, Ralph; Rooftop Singers; Rush, Tom; Safka, Melanie; Ste.-Marie, Buffy; Schlamme, Martha; Seeger, Mike; Seeger, Peggy; Seeger, Pete; Serendipity Singers; Shane, Bob; Simon, Carly; Sparks, Randy; Stevens, Cat; Stewart, John; Taylor, James; Wakefield, Frank; Watson, Arthel "Doc"; Weavers.; White, Josh; Yellin, Bob.

See also Country and western artists.

FOLK MUSIC RECORDINGS. 265–269. *See also* COUNTRY AND WESTERN MUSIC RECORDINGS.

Folk music revival. 149.

Folk singers. *See* Folk artists.

Folklyric (label). 270.

FOLKWAYS RECORDS (label). 270.

FONOTIPIA (label). 45. *See also*
FONOTIPIA, LTD;
SOCIETÀ ITALIANA DI
FONOTIPIA.
FONOTIPIA, LTD. 270.
FOONG, YUEN SING (Victor
agent in China). 271.
Foot treadle graphophone. 702.
Forbes Library. 673.
Forbes-Robertson, Johnston
(actor). 393.
Ford, Mary (popular singer).
520.
FORD, TENNESSEE ERNIE
(country artist). 271.
Ford, Tom (baritone). 571.
Ford (disc record player). 249.
FORDE, FLORRIE (comedi-
enne). 271.
Foreman, Louis (discographer).
212.
FORESMAN EDUCATIONAL
MUSIC RECORDS (label).
272.
Forgflo Corp. 82.
Formichi, Cesare (baritone).
488.
FORREST, HELEN (popular
singer). 272, 621.
Foster, Charles (singer). 205.
Foster, George G. (executive)
30.
Foster-Armstrong (firm). 30.
Foundation to Assist Canadian
Talent on Records (FAC-
TOR). 94.
FOUNTAIN, PETE (clarinetist).
272.
FOUR ARISTOCRATS (male
quartet). 272.
Four channel stereo. *See*
QUADRAPHONIC
SOUND.
FOUR-IN-ONE (label). 272.
Fournier, Pierre (cellist). 106,
710.
Foxx, Red (comedian). 136.
Fraad (label). 272.
Fraad Jr. (disc record player).
272.
FRAAD TALKING MACHINE
CO. 272.
Francescatti, Zino (violinist).
750.

Franceschetti, Aristide (bari-
tone). 332.
Franchini, Anthony (Hawaiian
artist). 313.
FRANCIS, CONNIE (popular
singer). 750.
Francisco, Signor. *See* DE
GOGORZA, EMILIO.
Frank, John H. (executive). 770.
Frankenstein, Alfred (discogra-
pher). 123.
FRANKLIN, ARETHA (soul
and gospel singer). 272,
590.
Franklin, C. L. (preacher). 110.
Franklin Institute. 406, 428.
Franklin, Melvin (popular
singer). 709.
Franko, Nahan (conductor).
432, 492.
Fransella, Albert (flutist; piccolo
player). 532, 772.
Franz Joseph, Emperor of
Austria-Hungary. 603, 708.
Freberg, Stan (comedian). 136.
Free University, Berlin. 405.
FREED, ALAN (disc jockey).
273.
Freedom Singers (folk group).
268.
FREE-FORM PROGRAM-
MING. 273.
FREEMAN, BUD (saxophonist).
273.
FREEMANTLE, FREDERIC C.
(tenor). 273.
Freie Universität Berlin. 405.
Frelinghuysen, George (execu-
tive). 465.
FREMSTAD, OLIVE (soprano).
273.
Freni, Mirella (soprano). 486.
FRENOPHONE (radio). 274.
FREQUENCY. 274.
Frequency distortion. *See*
DISTORTION, II.
FREQUENCY MODULATION
(FM). 274.
FREQUENCY RESPONSE. 274.
Friar's Society Orchestra. 465.
Friberg, Oscar W. (pianist). 707.
Fried, Oskar (conductor). 495.
Friedheim, Arthur (pianist) 531,
584.

FRIEDMAN, IGNAZ (pianist).
274, 528, 531, 584.
Friml, Rudolf (composer). 584.
Frische, James (engineer). 747.
Frisco Jazz Band. 349.
Fritchey, F. L. (engineer). 731.
FROLICKERS (male trio). 274.
FROSINI, PIETRO (accordion-
ist). 274.
Frow, George (discographer).
114.
Fugs (rock group). 620.
FULL FREQUENCY RANGE
RECORDINGS (ffrr). 274,
514.
Full Moon (label). 246.
Fuller, Earl (jazz group leader).
275.
Fuller, R. A. (executive). 703.
Fuller, Verdi B. (executive). 715.
FULLER'S FAMOUS JAZZ
BAND. 275.
FUNDAMENTAL FRE-
QUENCY. 275.
Funk. 590.
Fuqua, Charles (tenor). 339.
FURTWÄNGLER, WILHELM
(conductor). 275.
Fusion (jazz style). 173, 352.
FUZZ. 275.
FWR (label). 535.

—G—

Gabel, John (inventor). 34. 597.
Gabel Entertainer. *See* JOHN
GABEL'S AUTOMATIC
ENTERTAINER.
Gabelola (disc record changer).
34.
Gabler, Julius (retailer). 137.
Gabler, Milt (executive). 136,
145.
Gabrilowitsch, Ossip (pianist).
528, 584, 584.
GADSKI, JOHANNA (so-
prano). 277.
GAELIC PHONOGRAPH CO.
277.
Gage, Henry (executive). 301.
Gaillard, Slim (guitarist). 693.
Gain riding. 638.
Gain. *See* AMPLIFICATION.
GAISBERG, FREDERICK
WILLIAM (executive).
277–278, 527.

GAISBERG, WILLIAM (executive). 278, *278*.

Gala Nursery Records (label). 718.

Galeffi, Carlo (baritone). 489.

Gall, Yvonne (soprano). 488. 699.

Galla-Rini, Anthony (accordionist). 5.

Gallagher, Ed (vaudeville artist). 278.

GALLAGHER AND SHEAN (vaudeville team). 278.

GALLI-CURCI, AMELITA (soprano). *278*, 612.

GALVANY, MARIA (soprano). 279.

Galway, James (flutist). 773.

GAMAGE (label). 279.

Gamage (A. W.), Ltd. 279.

Gant, Cecil (blues singer). 587.

Ganz, Rudolf (pianist). 584, 529.

GAP. 279.

GAP ALIGNMENT. 279.

GARBER, JAN (Big Band leader). 279.

GARDE RÉPUBLICAINE BAND. *280*, 439.

GARDEN, MARY (soprano). 280.

GARDNER, SAMUEL (violinist). 280.

Garfunkel, Art (popular singer). 625.

GARLAND, JUDY (popular singer). 280.

GARNER, ERROLL (pianist). 281.

Garrard (record changer). 571, 714.

GASKIN, GEORGE J. (tenor). 281.

Gast, Gustav (flutist). 772.

Gates, J. M., Reverend. 561.

Gateway Singers (folk group). 268.

Gaubert, Philippe (flutist). 773.

Gaudard, Louis (oboist). 774.

GAUMONT, LÉON (inventor). 281.

Gaumont Co. 448.

Gauthier, Conrad (folk artist). 91.

GAY, MARIA (mezzo-soprano). *281*, 783.

GAYE, MARVIN (popular singer). 281.

Gebrüder Stollwerk AG. 694.

GEDDA, NICOLAI (tenor). 282.

GEISSLER, H. D. (executive). *282*, 467.

GEISSLER, LOUIS FREDERICK (executive). 282.

GELATT, ROLAND (critic and writer). 282.

GEM (label). 283.

GENERAL (label). 283.

GENERAL ELECTRIC CO. 283, 470.

General Electric Co., Ltd. 76, 283.

GENERAL PHONOGRAPH CO. 283.

GENERAL PHONOGRAPH CO., LTD. *283*, 464.

General Phonograph Corp. of Canada, Ltd. 481.

General Phonograph Manufacturing Co. 283.

General Wireless Co. 283.

Gennett, Clarence (executive). 687.

Gennett, Henry (executive). 687.

GENNETT (label). *283–284*, 561.

Gentlemen Songsters. 733.

George Shearing Quintet (jazz instrumental group). 622.

George V, King of England. 603.

Georgia Jazz Band. 569.

GEORGIA PHONOGRAPH CO. 284.

Gerhardt, Elena (mezzo-soprano). 308.

Gerhäuser, Emil (tenor). 417.

Gershwin, George (composer). 584.

GERVILLE-RÉACHE, JEANNE (contralto). 284.

GESELLSCHAFT FÜR MUSIKALISCHE AUFFÜHRUNGS- UND MECHANISCHE VERVIELFÄLTIGUNGS-RECHTE (GEMA). 285.

Ghiaurov, Nicolai (bass). 486.

GIALDINI, GUIDO (whistler). *285*, 763.

Giandolfi, Professor (mandolinist). 414.

GIANNINI, FERRUCCIO (tenor). *285*, 485.

Gibbs, Parker (popular singer). 760.

Gibson, Bob (folk artist). 267.

Gibson, Corley (executive). 36.

GIBSON, DON (country artist). 286.

Gibson, Gerald D. (discographer; librarian). 342.

Gibson Patent Tapering Sound Arm. 714.

Gibson, Robert L. (inventor). 513.

Gielen, Michael (conductor). 113.

Gielgud, John (actor). 393.

Giese, Henry (clarinetist). 115, 773.

GIESEKING, WALTER (pianist). *286*, 584, 757.

Gifford, Gene (arranger). 103.

GIGLI, BENIAMINO (tenor). *286*, 491.

Gigout, Eugène (organist). 499.

Gilbert, Charles (baritone). 417.

Gilbert, Paul J. (singer). 341.

Gilbert, Ronnie (folk artist). 759.

GILBERT AND SULLIVAN OPERAS. 287.

Gilbert, Kimpton and Co. 335.

Gilberto, Joao (guitarist). 285.

GILLESPIE, DIZZY (trumpeter). *287*, 693.

Gillet, Georges (oboist). 774.

Gilley, Mickey (country artist). 150.

GILLHAM, ART (pianist). 287.

GILLILAND, EZRA TORRANCE (inventor). 287.

Gilliland, Henry (country artist). 150.

Gilliland (Edison) Sales Co. 287.

Gillingham, L. E. (executive). 568.

Gilman, B. I. (ethnologist). 258.

GILMORE, PATRICK S. (bandmaster). 288.

Gilmore's Band. 287, 438.

Gimell (label). 337.

Ginn, E. M. (executive). 225.

Giorni, Aurelio (pianist). 247.

GIRARD, GILBERT (comedian). 288.

Girard, Victor (discographer). 167.

GIRARDI, VITTORIO (bass). 288.

Giuffre, Jimmy (clarinetist). 115.

GIULINI, CARLO MARIA (conductor). 288.

Gladstone, William (statesman). 293.

Glancy, Kenneth (executive). 747.

Glantz, Nathan (saxophonist). 610, 735.

Glaser, Tompall (country artist). 150, 151.

GLASS, LOUIS (executive). *289*, 682, 762.

Glaue, Henry (executive). 695.

Glazunov, Alexander (composer). 584.

Gleason, Edward D. (inventor). 512.

GLENN, WILFRED (bass). 253, *289*, 621, 586.

Global Village (label). 270.

GLOBE (label). 289.

Globe Distributing Co. 289.

Globe Phonograph Record Co. 454.

GLOBE RECORD CO., LTD. 289.

GLOBE RECORD CO. 289.

GLOBE RECORD DISTRIBUTING CORP. 289.

Globe Style (label). 270.

GLORY (label). 289.

GLUCK, ALMA (soprano). *289*, 783.

Glyndebourne Festival. 80, 84, 490, 631.

GOBBI, TITO (baritone). 290.

Gobel, George (country artist). 148.

Godfrey, Dan (conductor). 496.

Godfrey, Isidore (conductor). 287.

GODOWSKY, LEOPOLD (pianist). *290*, 528, 584.

GOLD DISCS. 290.

Gold molded cylinder. 38.

Gold Mountain (label). 423.

Goldberg, Reiner (tenor). 433.

GOLDEN, BILLY (comedian). *290*, 681.

Golden Earring (rock group). 595.

GOLDEN (label). 290.

Golden Gate Quartet (male vocal group). 413.

Golden Record Co. 290.

Goldman Band. 439.

GOLDMARK, PETER CARL (inventor). 290.

GOLDRING MANUFACTURING CO., LTD. 291.

Goldsmith, Oliver (executive). 447.

Goldstein, Kenneth (ethnologist). 267.

Goldwax (label). 588.

Golterman, Guy (executive). 462.

Gomberg, George W. (inventor). 513.

Gomberg, Harold (oboist). 775.

Gomberg, Ralph (oboist). 775.

Gomez, Francisco (clarinetist). 773.

Gomez, Manuel (clarinetist). 771, 773.

GOODMAN, BENNY (clarinetist; Big Band leader). *291*, 351, 683, 700, 774.

Goodman, Steve (folk artist). 269.

GOODSON (label). 292.

Goodson Record Co., Ltd. 292.

Goodwin, Harry (vaudeville artist). 38.

Goodwin, Henry D. (executive). 461.

Goossens, Eugene (conductor). 113, 489, 584.

GOOSSENS, LEON (oboist). *292*, 775.

Gordon, Dexter (saxophonist). 611.

Gordon, Robert Winslow (ethnologist). 265.

Gordon Highlanders Regimental Band. 91.

GORDY, BERRY, JR. (executive). 292.

Gordy (label). 709.

Gorman, Ross (saxophonist). 611.

Gospel music. 151.

Gottlieb, Lou (bassist). 389.

Gottschalk, Felix (executive). 35, 433.

GOULD, GLENN (pianist). 292.

Gould, Morton (composer). 584.

Goulding, Ray (comedian). 136.

GOULET, ROBERT (baritone). 292.

Gounod Quartet (male vocal group). 586.

GOURAUD, GEORGE E., *Colonel* (executive). 293.

Gouraudophone (compressed air amplifier). 37.

GRADUOLA (disc record player). 293.

GRAFTON HIGH GRADE RECORD (label). 293.

Graham, Billy (evangelist). 758.

GRAINGER, PERCY ALDRIDGE (pianist; ethnologist). *293*, 521, 528, 531, 584.

Gramavision (label). 538.

Gramercy Five (jazz group). 621.

Grammavox (label). 646.

GRAMMY. *293*, 747.

GRAMOPHONE. 294.

Gramophone (label). 572.

Gramophone (periodical). 123, *294*,

Gramophone & Typewriter, Ltd. 295.

GRAMOPHONE CO. 295-299. Gramophone Co.. record players are listed on pp. 297-299. The names of those players are not entered individually in this index.

Gramophone Exchange (British firm). 271.

GRAMOPHONE QUARTET (male vocal group). 299.

GRAMOPHONE RECORD. 299.

GRAMOPHONE RECORDS, LTD. 299.

GRAMOPHONE SHOP. *299*, 573.

GRAMOPHONE SOCIETIES. 299.

Granados, Enrique (composer). 584.

GRAND (label). 300.

Grand Concert Band. 438.

Grand Funk Railroad (rock group). 595.

Grand Master Flash (rap group). 595.

GRAND OLE OPRY. 148, 149, 150, *300*.

GRAND RAPIDS PHONO-GRAPH CO. 300.

Granforte, Apollo (tenor). 489.

Grant, Amy (rock performer). 595.

Grant, George W. (executive). 367.

Grant (W. T.) stores. 401.

Granz, Norman (executive). 28, 118, 737.

GRAPHIC EQUALIZER. 300.

GRAPHOPHONE. 300.

GRAPPELLI, STÉPHANE (violinist). 300.

Grateful Dead (rock group). 594.

Graves, Randall (singer). 440.

Graves (J. G.), Ltd. 25.

Gray, Glen. *See* CASA LOMA ORCHESTRA.

Gray, J. (discographer). 212.

Gray, Jerry (arranger). 621.

Gray, Michael (discographer). 212.

Grayson, George B. (country artist). 265.

GRAYSON, JAMES (executive). *301*, 762.

GREAT NORTHERN MANU-FACTURING CO. 301.

Great Scott (label). 695.

Great White Way (male vocal quartet). 311.

GREATER NEW YORK QUARTETTE. 301.

GREATER NEW YORK PHONOGRAPH CO. 301.

Green, Joe (xylophonist). 735.

Green, Martyn (baritone). 287.

GREEN, THOMAS H. (executive). *301*, 458.

Green Linnet (label). 269.

GREENBERG, NOAH (conductor). 301.

Greenbriar Boys (bluegrass group). 267.

Greene, Charlie (trombonist). 629.

Greene, Freddy (guitarist). 363.

GREENE, GENE (popular singer). 301.

GREENE, JACK (country artist). 302.

Greenfield, Edward (writer). 154.

Greenfield, Elizabeth Taylor (soprano). 65.

GREENHILL, J. E. (inventor). 302, 682.

Greenhill Mechanical Phono-graph Motor Co. 302.

Greenus, Irene (Hawaiian artist). 313.

Greenway, John (folk artist). 267.

GREER, SONNY (drummer). 302.

Greet, Ben (actor). 393.

GREGORIAN CHANT. 302.

Gregory, Dick (comedian). 136.

GRENADIER GUARDS BAND. 302.

Gresse, André (bass). 488.

Gressing, O. A. (executive). 607.

Greville, Ursula (executive; recording expert). 699.

GREY GULL (label). 302.

Grieg, Edvard (composer). 528.

Griffes, Charles Tomlinson (composer). 584.

Griffin, Merv (popular singer). 420.

Griffith, Nanci (country artist). 269.

Grigsby, B. J. (executive). 303.

GRIGSBY-GRUNOW, INC. 303.

Grimes (David) Radio and Cameo Record Corp. 89.

Grimes, Tiny (guitarist). 706.

Grimshaw, Emile (banjoist). 42.

GRINDERINO, SIGNOR (organ grinder). 303.

Grinsted, W. S. (banjoist). 42.

Grofé, Ferde (arranger; composer). 584, 764.

GROOVE. 303.

GROOVE SPEED. 303.

Gross, P. P. (pianist). 528.

Grosses Odeon-Streichorchester. 493.

Grossi, Edward J. (executive). 353.

Grossman, Joseph F. (executive). 414.

Gruberova, Edita (soprano). 487.

Grumiaux, Arthur (violinist). 750.

Grümmer, Paul (cellist). 84.

Grunberg, Jacques (pianist). 749.

GRUNDIG, MAX (executive). 303.

Grünfeld, Alfred (pianist). 528, 528, 584.

Grunow, William C. (executive). 303.

Grunt (label). 353.

Guard, David (folk artist). 370.

GUARDBAND. 303.

GUARDSMAN (label). 303.

Guess Who (rock group). 594.

Guest, Edgar A. (poet). 394.

GUEST, LIONEL (inventor). *304*, 514.

Guidi, Scipione (violinist). 524.

Guild (label). 396.

Guillou, Jean (organist). 216.

Guinea Gramophone Co. 304.

GUINIPHONE (portable disc record player). 304.

GUITAR RECORDINGS. 304–304.

Guitarists. See in this index: Almeida, Laurindo; Balin, Marty; Boone, Steve; Bream, Julian; Casady, Jack; Chaput, Roger; Christian, Charlie; Clapton, Eric; Cook, Stu; Coryell, Larry; Dudley, George F.; Ellis, Herb; Fogerty, John; Fogerty, Tom; Gaillard, Slim; Gilberto, Joao; Greene, Freddy; Grimes, Tiny; Harrison, George; Harvey, Bob; Hendrix, Jimi; Jardine, Alan; Jobim, Antonio Carlos; Kantner, Paul; Kaukonen, Jorma; Kress, Carl; Laine, Dennis; Lang, Eddie; Lennon, John; McCartney, Paul; McLaughlin, John; Methany, Pat; Montgom-ery, Wes; Musical Avolos; Parkening, Christopher; Paul, Les; Reinhardt, Django; Reinhardt, Joseph; Rey, Alvino; Romero, Pepe; Romeros; Sebastian, John;

Segovia, Andres; Van Eps, Fred, Jr; Watanabe, Kazumi; Williams, John; Wilson, Brian; Wilson, Carl; Wolf, M. L.; Yanovsky, Zalman; Yarbrough, Glenn.
GUN MICROPHONE. 304.
GUTHRIE, ARLO (folk artist). 304.
GUTHRIE, WOODY (folk artist). 304.
Guttinuer, Mr. (pianist). 527.
Gwirtz, I. R. (executive). 186.

—H—

H. Royer Smith. Co. 573.
H.I.T.S. (label). 728.
Hackel, Alexander (violinist). 707.
Hackett, Aubrey (tenor). 81.
Hackett, Bobby (cornetist). 317.
HACKETT, CHARLES (tenor). 307.
Haddock, John W. 35.
HADDY, ARTHUR CHARLES (inventor). 307.
Haendel, Ida (violinist). 750.
Hagen, Uta (actress). 394.
HAGER, FRED (violinist). 307, 365, 586.
HAGGARD, MERLE (country artist). 150, *256.*
Haggin, B. H. (writer on recordings). 154.
Hahn, Reynaldo (pianist) composer. 584.
Haile, Luther T. (inventor). 513.
Hain, Stephan (executive). 371.
Haines, Connie (popular singer). 216.
Haines, John P. (executive). 465.
Haines, Julia (accordionist). 5.
HAITINK, BERNARD (conductor). 308.
HALE, E. F. G. (executive). 308.
HALEY, BILL (rock performer, disc jockey). *308,* 594.
HALF-SPEED MASTERING. 308.
Hall & Oates (soul singers). 595.
HALL, ARTHUR (tenor). *308,* 460.
Hall, David (discographer; librarian). 154, 417, 430, 598.

HALL, FREDERICK DURIVE (inventor; executive). 309.
Hall, Mary (violinist). 750.
HALL, WENDELL (singer; ukulele player). 309, 593.
Hall acoustics. *See* ROOM ACOUSTICS.
Hall Manufacturing Co. 308.
Halle Orchestra. 609.
HALLEY, WILLIAM J. (comedian; popular singer). 309.
Halo (label). 572.
Hambourg, Mark (pianist). 206, 584.
Hamelin, Gaston (clarinetist). 774.
Hamill, Ernest A. (executive). 111.
Hamilton, David (producer). 417.
Hamilton, George (country artist). 150.
Hamilton, Jimmy (clarinetist). 115.
Hammer, M. C. (rap singer). 595.
Hammond Five (jazz group). 781.
HAMMOND, JOHN HENRY, JR. (critic; executive). *309,* 430.
HAMPTON, LIONEL (vibraphonist). *309,* 779.
Han (B. H.) (firm). 374.
Hand, Arthur (dance band leader). 87.
Handel Festival, Crystal Palace, London, 1888. 10.
Handleman, David (rack jobber). 562.
Handy, W. C. (composer). 65.
Hanson, Howard (composer). 430.
HAPPINESS BOYS (male duo). 310.
Happy Time Records (label). 718.
Hard country music. 151.
Hardin, Lil (pianist). 25, 350.
Harding, Muriel (singer). 287.
HARDING, ROGER (tenor; executive). 253, *310,* 681, 681.
Hardwick, Otto (saxophonist). 611.

Hardwicke, Cecil (actor). 394.
Hardy, E. (tinfoil phonograph manufacturer). 241.
HARE, ERNEST (singing comedian). 13, *310,* 432.
Hargrave, Mr. (singer). 301.
HARLAN, BYRON G.(tenor; comedian). *310,* 521, 569, 715.
HARMOGRAPH (label). 311.
Harmograph Record Co. 310.
Harmograph Talking Machine Co. 310.
Harmon, Jim (discographer). 567.
HARMON-KARDON, INC. 311.
HARMONIA MUNDI (label). 311.
HARMONIC. 311.
Harmonic distortion. *See* DISTORTION, VI.
Harmonicists. See in this index: Adler, Larry; Howlin' Wolf; Lacroix, Henri; Little Walter; Sebastian, John.
HARMONIZERS QUARTET (male vocal group). 311.
Harmonola (disc record player). 311.
HARMONOLA CO. 311.
HARMONY. 312.
HARMONY (label). 312.
HARMONY FOUR (mixed vocal group). 312.
Harmony Records (firm). 312.
HARNONCOURT, NIKOLAUS (conductor). 312.
Harper, Alfred C. (executive). 110.
Harpists. See in this index: Dudley, George F.; Salzedo, Carlos; Scheutze, Charles.
Harptones (blues singers). 587, 588.
HARPVOLA TALKING MACHINE CO. 312.
Harrell, Mack (baritone). 776.
Harris, Bill (trombonist). 721.
Harris, David (publisher). 256.
HARRIS, GWIN (engineer). 312.
Harris, Herbert (executive). 267.
HARRIS, MARION (comedienne; blues singer). 312.

JONES, ADA (soprano). *357,* 681.

Jones, Arthur S. (executive). 221.

Jones, Bartlett (inventor). 219.

JONES, BILLY (tenor; comedian). *357,* 586.

Jones, Brian (rock performer). 599.

Jones, Earle W. (engineer). 88.

JONES, GEORGE (country artist). 149.

Jones, Grandpa (country artist). 43, 148.

JONES, ISHAM (Big Band leader). 357.

JONES, JO (drummer). 348, *358,* 363.

JONES, JONAH (trumpeter). 358.

JONES, JOSEPH W. (inventor). 358.

Jones, Orville "Hoppy" (bassist). 339.

JONES, QUINCY DELIGHT, JR. (conductor; composer). 358.

Jones, Ramona (country artist). 148.

JONES, SISSIERETTA JOYNER (soprano). 359.

JONES, SPIKE (Big Band leader). 359.

Jones, W. Bartlett (inventor). 688.

Jones, Will C. (singer). 186.

JOPLIN, JANIS (rock singer). 359.

JOPLIN, SCOTT (composer). *359,* 568, 584.

Jordan, Clifford (saxophonist). 442.

Jordan, Louis (blues singer). 69, 587.

JORDAN, MARY (contralto). 359.

JOSE, RICHARD JAMES (ballad singer). 360.

Joseph, Robert (bass). 60.

JOURNET, MARCEL (bass). 360, 490.

JOYCE, THOMAS F. (executive). 360.

JUKE BOX. 148, *360.*

JUMBO RECORD (label). 361.

Jumbola (label). 361.

Jump. *See* BUMP.

June Appal (label). 269.

Juno (cylinder phonograph). 361.

Juno Awards. 93.

JUNO PHONOGRAPH MANUFACTURING CO. 361.

JURGENS, DICK (Big Band leader). 361.

JURINAC, SENA (soprano). 362.

JVC. *See* JAPANESE VICTOR CO. (JVC).

—K—

Kaempfert, Bert (executive). 395.

Kaili, Pale (Hawaiian artist). 313.

Kaiser, John (executive). 473.

KALAMAZOO NOVELTY CO. 363.

Kallen, Kitty (popular singer). 348.

Kalliope, Ltd. 363.

Kalliope, Menzenhauer & Schmidt (firm). 363.

KALLIOPE MUSIKWERKE AG. 363.

Kaltenborn, Frank (violinist). 363.

KALTENBORN STRING QUARTET. 363.

Kämmer und Reinhardt (firm). 406.

Kamplain, Frank (yodeler). 571.

Kanarak, Rudolph (executive). 249.

Kansas City Five (jazz group). 364.

Kansas City jazz style. 350,447.

Kansas City Seven (jazz group). 782.

KANSAS CITY SIX (jazz group). *363,* 782.

KANSAS PHONOGRAPH CO. 364.

Kantner, Paul (guitarist). 353.

Kanui and Lula (Hawaiian artists). 511.

KAPP, JACK (executive). *364,* 562.

KARAJAN, HERBERT VON (conductor). 364.

Karas, Anton (zither player). 784.

KARLE, THEO (tenor). 364.

KASSEL, ART (Big Band leader). 364.

Katzman, Louis (dance band leader). 13.

KAUFMAN, IRVING (vaudeville artist). 13, *365,* 712, 725.

Kaufman, Jack (singer). 712, 725,

KAUFMAN, LOUIS (violinist). 365.

Kaukonen, Jorma (guitarist). 353.

Kay, Connie (drummer). 443.

Kaye, Danny (comedian). 722.

KAYE, SAMMY (Big Band leader). 365.

Kazakov, Yuri (accordionist). 5.

Kazee, Buell (country artist). 265.

KC & the Sunshine Band (rock group). 594.

Keating Talking Machine (label). 381.

Keeler, C. M. (singer). 341.

Keen, Morris (executive). 72.

KEEN-O-PHONE (label). *365,* 779.

Keen-O-Phone Co. 365.

Keepers, Walter M. (collector). 567.

Kefer, Paul (cellist). 714.

Keillor, Garrison (singer; comedian). 269.

Keith Monks Record Cleaning Machine. 117.

KEITH PROWSE (label). 366.

KELL, REGINALD (clarinetist). *366,* 774.

KELLER, ARTHUR CHARLES (engineer and inventor). 366.

Keller, Richard (engineer). 12.

Kellogg, Clara Louise (soprano). 694.

Kellogg, E. W. (actor). 399.

KELLY, DAN (vaudeville artist). 366.

Kelly, Gene (dancer). 281.

KELSO, MAY (contralto). 366.

LeRoy, René (flutist). 773.

Les Phonographes Pathé (firm). 515.

Leschetizky, Theodor (pianist). 584.

Letorey, Omar (organist). 499.

LEVAPHONE (label). 387.

Levarie, Siegmund (musicologist). 316.

LEVEL. 387.

LEVINE, JAMES (conductor). 387, 433.

Levitzki, Mischa (pianist). 529, 583.

Levy, A. (clarinetist). 738.

LEVY, JULES (cornetist). 145, 387.

Levy, Theodore (violinist). 738.

LEVY'S (record shop). 387.

Levy's Public Phono & Cycle Stores. 501.

Levy's Sound Studios, Ltd. 501.

Lewis, Ed (singer). 272.

LEWIS, EDWARD ROBERT, Sir (executive). 388.

Lewis, Jerry Lee (rock performer). 152, 593.

Lewis, John (pianist). 443, 782.

Lewis, Ramsey (pianist). 769.

Lewis, Ted (Big Band leader). 723.

LHÉVINNE, JOSEF (pianist). 388, 584.

Lhotak, Frank (trombonist). 501.

Liapunov, Sergei (composer). 584.

Liberty (label). 98.

LIBERTY MUSIC SHOP. 388, 573.

LIBERTY PHONOGRAPH CO. 388.

Liberty Quartet (male vocal group). 621.

Liberty Record (label). 388.

Librarians and archivists. See in this index:

Bowen, Jean; Bryant, Eric Thomas; Dockstader, Ray; Engel, Carl; Gibson, Gerald D.; Hall, David; Hill, Richard S.; Jabbour, Alan; Koprowski, Richard; Mapleson, Lionel S.; McCormick, Donald;

Moogk, Edward B.; Myers, Kurtz; Schwegel, Richard; Seeger, Anthony; Woods, Robin.

Libraries and archives. See in this index:

American Folklife Center; Antioch College; Archive of Maori and Pacific Music; Archives of Traditional Music; Baseball Hall of Fame, Cooperstown, New York; BBC Sound Archives; Belfer Audio Library and Archive; Berlin Phonogramm-Archiv; British Library of Wildlife Sounds; Budapest Ethnographic Museum; Canadian Broadcasting Corp.; Chicago Public Library; Country Music Foundation; Discoteca di Stato (Italy); Evanston Public Library; Forbes Library; Hocken Library; Laboratory of Ornithology; Library of Congress; Michigan State University; Middle Tennessee State University. John Edwards Archive; Musée de la Voix, Paris Opéra; National Library of Australia; National Library of Canada; National Library of New Zealand; National Museum of American History; National Sound Archive; National Voice Library; New York Public Library; Queens College, New York; Radio New Zealand Sound Archive; Rodgers and Hammerstein Archives of Recorded Sound; Saint Paul Public Library; Stanford Archive of Recorded Sound; Syracuse Audio Archives; University of Toronto; University of Wisconsin; Vienna Phonogramm-Archiv; White House Music Library; Yale

Collection of Historical Sound Recordings.

LIBRARY OF CONGRESS. 388, 591, 702.

Licette, Miriam (soprano). 489.

Lichstein, Arthur (violinist). 524.

Lido (label). 289.

Lieban, Julius (conductor). 487.

LIEBERSON, GODDARD (executive). 389.

Liggy, Licco (violinist). 749.

Lightfoot, Gordon (folk artist). 268.

LIGHTOPHONE (photographic sound reproducer). 389.

LIMELIGHTERS (folk group). 389.

LIMITER. 389.

LIN-O-TONE (horn). 390.

LINCOLN (label). 389.

Lincoln Record Corp. 389.

Lindsay, E. L. (executive). 777.

Lindström (Carl) AG. 390, 478, 510.

LINDSTRÖM (CARL), GmbH. 390.

Lindström (Carl) London), Ltd. 390, 438.

LINEAR PREDICTOR. 390.

Linear tracking. 720.

Linear tracking arm. 704.

Link, Edwin A. (executive) 390.

LINK PIANO CO. 390.

Linkwitz, Siegried (engineer). 405.

LINOPHONE (dictation device). 390.

Lion, Alfred (executive). 68.

LIORET, HENRI JULES (inventor). 390, 510, 512.

Lioretograph (cylinder phonograph). 391.

LIPPINCOTT, JESSE H. (executive). 391, 464.

Liquid Archival Sound Treatment (record cleaner). 117.

"Lisbon Traviata." 535.

List, Emanuel (bass). 490.

Listening booths. 573.

Listening stations. 573.

LITERARY RECORDINGS. 392–395.

LITTLE CHAMPION (label). 395.

—M—

MacColl, Ewan (ethnologist; folk artist). 267.

MacCormack, Franklyn (poet). 369.

Macdonald, Jeanette (soprano). 227.

Macdonald, John S. (executive). 129.

MACDONALD, THOMAS HOOD (inventor). 409.

MACDONOUGH, HARRY (tenor). *409*, 502, 613, 738.

MacDowell Sisters (popular singers). 626.

Mackenzie, Compton (editor). 294,

MacMahon, Louise (singer). 130.

MacNeil, Cornell (baritone). 486.

Macon, Uncle Dave (country artist). 43, 148, 265.

MacPherson, James E. (executive). 89, 519.

MacRae, Gordon (popular singer). 317.

Macy's (department store). 457.

MADISON (label). 410.

Madison Record Co. 410.

Madness (rock group). 595.

Madonna (rock performer). 621.

Maestrola (disc record player). 678.

Mag-Ni-Phone (disc record player). 623.

Magic-Glo (juke box). 597.

Magid, Lee (executive). 610.

Magliuolo, Elvira (soprano). 487.

Magnante, Charles (accordionist). 5.

MAGNAVOX CONSUMER ELECTRONICS CO. 410.

Magnavox Corp. 410.

Magnetic Recording Industry Association. 246.

MAGNETIC RECORDING. 410–412.

MAGNETOPHON. 412.

Magnola (disc record player). 412.

MAGNOLA TALKING MACHINE CO. 412.

Mahavishnu Orchestra (rock group). 595.

Mahler, Gustav (composer). 584.

Maier, Guy (pianist). 529, 584.

Main amplifier. *See* POWER AMPLIFIER.

Mainguard (firm). 33.

Mairs, George A. (executive). 458.

Maison de Soul (label). 269.

Maison Jumeau (doll making firm). 702.

Majestic (disc record player). 413.

MAJESTIC (label). 412, 413.

MAJESTIC PHONOGRAPH CO. 412, 413.

Majestic Radio and Television Co. 413.

Majestic Record Corp. 412.

Majestic Records, Inc. 413.

MALE QUARTETS. 413.

MALNECK, MATTY (violinist). 414.

MAMAS AND THE PAPAS (rock group). *414*, 595.

Mancinelli, Luigi (conductor). 417.

MANCINI, HENRY (composer). 414.

Mandel, Louis (executive). 414.

MANDEL (label). 414.

MANDEL MANUFACTURING CO. 414.

Mandel Phono Parts Co. 414.

Mandolin Orchestra of Paris. 415.

MANDOLIN RECORDINGS. 414.

Mandolinists. See in this index: Dudley, Audley; Giandolfi, Professor; Pallavicini, Professor; Penney, Clarence; Place, William, Jr.; Siegel, Samuel S.; Townsend, W. C.; Volpe, Guido.

Mandrell Sisters (country artists). 150.

MANHASSET (MANHANSETT) QUARTETTE (male vocal group). 415.

Manhattan (juke box). 505.

Manhattan (label). 33.

MANHATTAN LADIES QUARTET (vocal group). 415.

MANHATTAN QUARTET (male vocal group). 415.

Manhattan Trio (mixed vocal trio). 432.

MANILOW, BARRY (popular singer). *415*, 438.

Manley, W. P. (executive). 344.

MANN, ESTELLA LOUISE (soprano). 415.

MANN, HERBIE (flutist). 415.

Manne, Frank (Big Band leader). 625.

MANNE, SHELLY (drummer). 416.

Manning, Henry Edward, *Cardinal*. 293.

MANOIL (JAMES) CO., INC. 416.

MANONE, WINGY (trumpeter). 416.

Manophone (disc record player). 416.

Mantell, Marianne (executive). 87.

MANTELLI, EUGENIA (soprano). *416*, 511.

Mantia, Simone (euphonium player). 75.

MANTOVANI, ANNUNZIO PAOLO (conductor). 417.

MANUAL SEQUENCE. 417.

Manualo reproducing piano. 41.

Maphis, Joe (banjoist). 43.

Maple City Four (male vocal quartet). 413.

Mapleson, Lionel S. (librarian). 417.

MAPLESON CYLINDERS. 417.

Mar-Keys (blues singers). 589.

MARATHON (label). 418.

MARATHON RECORD (label). 418.

MARC format for cataloging. 676.

Marco Polo (label). 462.

MARCONI, FRANCESCO (tenor). 418.

Marconi, Guglielmo (inventor), 263, 418, 515.

MARCONI VELVET TONE (label). 418.

MC PARTLAND, JIMMY (cornetist). 425.

MC PARTLAND, MARIAN (pianist). 426.

Mc Phatter, Clyde (blues singer). 589, 594.

Mc Shann, Jay (Big Band leader). 510.

Mc Sweeney, Henry (executive). 337.

Meader, Vaughn (comedian). 136.

MECHANICAL ELECTRICAL ANALOGIES. 426.

Mechanical Orguinette Co. 8.

Mechanical recording. *See* ACOUSTIC RECORDING.

Mechau, Emil (engineer). 12.

Medaer, Leo (clarinetist). 115.

MEDALLION (label). 426.

Medicophone (label). 731.

Medtner, Nicolai (composer). 584.

MEEKER, EDWARD WARREN (comedian). 426.

MEEKLENS, BESSIE (saxophonist). 426.

Mega horn. 613.

MEHTA, ZUBIN (conductor). 426.

MEISSELBACH (A. F.) AND BRO., INC. 426.

Meister Orchester. 399.

Meisterschaft (language teaching system). 382.

MELBA, NELLIE, *Dame* (soprano). *426*, 608, 772.

MELCHIOR, LAURITZ (tenor). *427*, 490, 613, 719.

Melodee (piano roll label). 8.

MELODISC RECORDS (label). 428.

MELODIYA (label). 427.

Melodograph (label). 428.

MELODOGRAPH CORP. 428.

MELODY (label). 428.

MELODY THREE. 428.

MELOGRAPH (label). 428.

Melograph Disc Record Co., Ltd. 428.

Melograph Record GmbH. 428.

Melophone (coin-operated disc record player). 618.

MELOPHONE TALKING MACHINE CO. 428.

MELOTO (label). 428.

Meloto Co., Ltd. 428.

MELOTONE (label). 33, *428*.

MELTON, JAMES (tenor). *428*, 586, 621.

MELVA (label). 429.

Melva Record Co. 429.

Memories of Radio (firm). 567.

Memphis Jug Band. 69.

Memphis sound. 32.

Men About Town (male vocal trio). 428.

Mendelssohn, Fred (executive). 610.

MENDELSSOHN MIXED QUARTETTE. 429.

MENGELBERG, WILLEM (conductor). *429*, 494.

Menon, Bhaskar (executive). 249.

Menter, Sophie (pianist). 584.

MENUHIN, YEHUDI, *Sir* (violinist). *429*, 750.

Mercer, Johnny (composer; executive). 98, 765.

MERCURY (label). 430–431.

Mercury Radio and Television Corp. 430.

Mercury Theatre. 393.

Mering, Constance (pianist). 527.

MERITT (label). 431.

MERLI, FRANCESCO (tenor). 379, *431*.

Merö, Yolanda (pianist). 583.

Merrill, Robert (baritone). 486.

MERRIMAN, HORACE OWEN (engineer). *431*, 514.

Merrymakers (male vocal group). 586.

Messer, William F. (inventor; executive). 337, 381, 512.

Messter, Oskar (inventor). 447.

Metal master. 421.

Metaphone. *See* ECHOPHONE.

Metcalf, P. H. (singer). 341.

METEOR (label). 431.

Methany, Pat (guitarist). 304.

METRO (label). 432.

METRO-GOLDWYN-MAYER (label). 432.

Metro-Phone (disc record player). 80.

METROPOLE (label). 432.

Metropole Gramophone Co., Ltd. 70, *432*, 532.

Metropole Industries, Ltd. 432.

METROPOLITAN BAND. 432.

METROPOLITAN ENTERTAINERS. 432.

METROPOLITAN MIXED TRIO. 432.

Metropolitan Opera Annals. 619.

METROPOLITAN OPERA COMPANY. 417, *432–433*.

Metropolitan Opera House String Orchestra. 432, 492.

Metropolitan Opera Record Club. 433.

METROPOLITAN PHONOGRAPH CO. 433.

METROPOLITAN QUARTETTE (mixed vocal group). 433.

Metropolitan Record Co. 432.

Metropolitan Vickers Electrical Co., Ltd. 76.

Metzger, C. G. (executive). 703.

Meyer, Augie (country artist). 151.

Meyer, Erwin (engineer). 12.

MEYER, JOHN H. (bass). *434*, 521, 691.

Mezzo-sopranos. See in this index:

Anitua, Fanny; Baltsa, Agnes; Benzell, Mimi; Calvé, Emma; Colombati, Virginia; Ferrier, Kathleen; Gay, Maria; Gerhardt, Elena; Homer, Louise; Horne, Marilyn; Ludwig, Christa; Obraztsova, Elena; Simionato, Giulietta; Spencer, Elizabeth; Stevens, Rise; Strakosch, Madame; Verrett, Shirley. *See also* Contraltos.

MGM (label). 434.

Michaelis, Alfred (executive). 270.

Michaelis, William (executive). 464.

Michaelis, Foa and Co. 631.

Michalowski, Alexander (pianist). 528, 531.

MICHIGAN PHONOGRAPH CO. 434.

Michigan State University Library. 462.

MICKEL, GEORGE E.(executive). *434*, 462.

MURPHY, LAMBERT (tenor). *451*, 502, 738.

MURRAY, BILLY (comedian). *451*, 521, 542, 569, 591, 628, 686, 734.

Murray, Charles J. (saxophonist). 691.

Murray, James (executive). 747.

Murray, Michael (organist). 500.

Murray's Trio (male vocal group). 451.

MUSE (label). 451.

Muse Records. 610.

Musée de la Voix, Paris Opéra. 115.

Museum für Völkerkunde, Berlin. 405.

Music Corporation of America. *See* MCA, INC.

Music Discount Centre (record shops). 573.

Music Library Association. 675, 676.

Music Master horn. 232.

Music Master Vitaphone Reocrd (label). 751.

Music Minus One (label). 7.

Music Salon (Edinburgh). 271.

Musical Avolos (guitar and mandolin players). 568.

MUSICAL HERITAGE SOCIETY. 451.

MUSICAL THEATRE RECORDINGS. 452 -454.

MUSICASSETTE. 453.

MusicBank (compact disc system). 457.

Musicmaster horn. 622.

Musicmasters (label). 451.

MUSICRAFT (label). 453.

Musicraft Corp. 453.

Musola (label). 499.

Musy, Louis (baritone). 490.

MUTE. 454.

MUTE (label). 454.

MUTI, RICCARDO (conductor). 454.

MUTING CIRCUIT. 454.

Mutoscope. 187.

Mutter, Anne-Sophie (violinist). 750.

MUTUAL TALKING MACHINE CO. 454.

MUZAK CORP. 454.

MUZIO, CLAUDIA (soprano). 454.

Myer, Fred (executive). 687.

Myers, Frederick (inventor). 513.

Myers, James A. (singer). 261.

MYERS, JOHN W. (baritone). 455.

Myers, Kurtz (discographer; librarian). 154, 321.

Mylar tape base. 704.

—N—

NADSCO (label). 457.

Naida, Michael (executive). 301.

NAKAMICHI. 457.

NANES ART FURNITURE CO. 457.

NAP Consumer Electronics Corp. 410.

NAPOLEON, PHIL (trumpeter). 457, 501.

Napoleon's Emperors (jazz group). 457.

NARELLE, MARIE (soprano). 457.

Nash, Heddle (tenor). 489.

Nashville (label). 713.

Nashville Grass (bluegrass band). 263.

Nashville sound. 29, 150, 151.

Nashville studios and recordings. 149.

Nassau (disc record player). 457.

NASSAU (label). 457.

Nast, Minnie (soprano). 487.

Nathan, Sidney (executive). 370.

NATION'S FORUM (label). 457.

NATIONAL (label). 457.

NATIONAL ACADEMY OF RECORDING ARTS AND SCIENCES (NARAS). 458.

National Association of Broadcasters. 251, 264.

NATIONAL ASSOCIATION OF TALKING MACHINE JOBBERS. 458.

NATIONAL AUTOMATIC MUSIC CO. 35, 459.

NATIONAL BARN DANCE. 148, 459.

National Certificate Co. 457.

National Disc Sales, Inc. 458.

National Federation of Gramophone Societies. 299.

NATIONAL GRAMOPHONE CO. 459.

National Gramophone Co. (1913), Ltd. 417, 459.

NATIONAL GRAMOPHONE CO., LTD. 459.

NATIONAL GRAMOPHONE CORP. 459.

National Institute for the Blind. 702.

National Library of Australia. 33.

National Library of Canada. 446.

National Library of New Zealand. 468.

NATIONAL MALE QUARTET. 460.

National Metals Depositing Corp. 402.

National Museum of American History. 630.

National Music Appreciation Committee. 433.

NATIONAL MUSIC LOVERS, INC. (label). 460.

National Phonogram Co. 38.

NATIONAL PHONOGRAPH ASSOCIATION. 460.

NATIONAL PHONOGRAPH CO. 461.

NATIONAL PHONOGRAPH CO. LTD. 461.

National Piano Manufacturing Co. 35.

National Promenade Band. 438.

National Record Co. 457.

National Record Exchange Co. 457.

NATIONAL SOUND ARCHIVE (NSA). 461.

NATIONAL TALKING MACHINE CO. 462.

NATIONAL VOICE LIBRARY. 462.

NATUS, JOE (comedian). 462.

NAXOS (label). 462.

NBC Studio 8H. 716.

NBC Symphony Orchestra. 716, 744.

Neapolitan Trio (instrumental group). 772.

ORCHESTRELLE CO., LTD. 499.
Orchestrola (disc record player). 711.
ORCHESTROPE (coin-operated disc player). 499.
ORGAN RECORDINGS. 499–500.
ORIGINAL DIXIELAND JAZZ BAND. 349, *500*.
Original Lyric Trio. *See* LYRIC TRIO.
ORIGINAL MEMPHIS FIVE. 349, *501*.
ORIGINAL NEW ORLEANS JAZZ BAND. 501.
ORIGINAL PIANO TRIO. 501.
Original Wolverines. *See* WOLVERINES.

ORIOLE (label). *501*, 561.
Oriole Records, Ltd. 718.
Orioles (blues singers). 587.
ORMANDY, EUGENE (conductor). 480, *501–502*, 562, 620, 679, 750.
Oro-Tone Co. 563.
ORPHEUS QUARTET (male vocal group). 502.
Orpheus Quartette (male vocal group). 532.
ORTHOPHONIC. 532.
ORTOFON (firm). 502.
ORY, KID (trumpeter). *502*, 697.
Oscar (binaurally equipped dummy). 63.
Oscar Peterson Trio (jazz instrumental group). 522, 760, 782.
OSSMAN, VESS (banjoist). 503.
Ossman-Dudley Trio. 503.
Otala, Matti (engineer). 35.
Ott, John F. (inventor). 513.
Ott, S. S. (executive). 364.
Oubradous, Fernand (bassoonist). 775.
OUT OF PHASE. 503.
OUT-TAKE. 503, 702.
Outlaw music (country style). 152.
OUTPUT. 503.
Output switch. 143.
Overdubbing. 576, 577.
Overload. *See* DISTORTION, III, VI.
OVERSAMPLING. 503.
Owen, Tom (engineer). 417.
OWEN, WILLIAM BARRY (executive). 503.
Owens, Buck (country artist). 150.
Owens, James (engineer). 742.
OXFORD (label). 503.
OZAWA, SEIJI (conductor). 504.

—P—

P CHANNEL. 505.
Pace, Harry (executive). 65, 483.
Pace Phonograph Co. 483.
Pace Phonograph Record Corp. 483.
Pacific Coast Record Corp. 263.
PACIFIC PHONOGRAPH CO. 505.

Radial tone arm. 714.

RADIEX (label). 563.

Radio Communication Co., Ltd. 76.

RADIO FRANKS (male vocal trio). 563.

Radio Memories (firm). 568.

Radio microphone. 435.

Radio New Zealand Sound Archive. 467.

RADIO PHONOGRAPHS. 563.

RADIO PROGRAM RECORD-INGS. 563–567. Adventures, 564; children's programs, 566; collectors and collections, 567; comedies, 564; detective stories, 564; dramas, 565; first transcription broadcast, 563; musical shows, 565; mysteries, 564; producers and distributors, 567; quiz shows, 566; science fiction, 566; soap operas, 565; variety shows, 565; westerns, 566. (The names of radio programs mentioned in the article are not entered individually in this index.)

Radio-Victor Co. 743.

Radiogram. See RADIO PHONOGRAPHS.

Radiola. See RADIO PHONO-GRAPHS.

Rafuse, Irad S. (engineer). 366.

Ragas, Henry (pianist). 500.

RAGTIME RECORDINGS. 568.

RAINBOW (label). 568.

Rainbow Music Shop. 23.

RAINEY, MA (blues singer). 509, 569.

Rainey, Robert R. (singer). 154.

Rains, Leon (bass). 488.

RAISA, ROSA (soprano). 569.

Ralf, Torsten (tenor). 719.

RAMBLER MINSTREL CO. (male quartet). 569.

Rambler Minstrels. 443.

Ramey, Samuel (baritone). 487.

Ramones (rock group). 595.

RAMPAL, JEAN-PIERRE (flutist). 569, 773.

Randall, Charles Adams (inventor). 121.

Rank, Bill (trombonist). 721.

Rap music recordings. 595, 620, 645.

Raphael, M. (xylophonist). 779.

RAPKE (VICTOR H.) CO. 569.

RAPPOLD, MARIE (soprano). 569, 715, 783.

RARITIES. 570.

Rascals (soul singers). 595.

Rascusin, Norman (executive). 747.

Raspberries (rock group). 595.

Raucheisen, Michael (pianist). 329.

Rauth, E. C. (executive). 458.

Rawles, Walter Hansen (executive). 460.

RAY, JOHNNY (popular singer). 570.

Rayleigh, Lord (engineer). 688.

Raymond, Charles L. (executive). 111.

RCA (label). 570.

RCA (RADIO CORPORATION OF AMERICA). 570.

RCA Consumer Products. 743.

RCA Home Instruments Division. 743.

RCA Manufacturing Co., Inc. 743.

RCA Model 77 microphone. 436.

RCA Radiotron. 743.

RCA VICTOR (label). 570.

RCA Victor Co., Inc. 743.

REA, VIRGINIA (popular singer). 570.

Read, T. Herbert (violinist). 579.

Reagon, Cordell (folk artist). 268.

REAL TIME SPECTRUM ANALYZER. 571.

RECEIVER. 571.

Rechanneled stereo. See REPROCESSED STEREO.

Record balance arm. 571.

RECORD BOYS (male trio). 571.

Record brush. 65.

RECORD CATALOGS. 571.

RECORD CHANGER. 356, 571, 714.

RECORD CLUBS. 571.

Record collecting. See COL-LECTING AND COLLEC-TORS.

Record collector societies. See GRAMOPHONE SOCIET-IES.

RECORD CONDITION. 572.

RECORD CORPORATION OF AMERICA. 572, 603, 736.

Record label. See LABEL.

Record leveler arm. 571.

Record Maker Troupe (Eight Famous Victor Artists). 243.

Record Makers. 734.

RECORD OUT SWITCH. 572.

RECORD PLAYER. 572.

RECORD REPEATER CO. 572.

RECORD SALES AGENCY. 572.

RECORD SHOPS. 572–573.

Record support arm. 571.

Record World (periodical). 574.

RECORDER (soundbox and stylus). 573.

Recording ban, United States (1942). 13.

Recording characteristic. See RECORDING CURVE.

RECORDING CURVE. 573.

RECORDING HEAD. 573.

RECORDING INDUSTRY. 573.

RECORDING INDUSTRY ASSOCIATION OF AMERICA (RIAA). 573.

RECORDING INDUSTRY CHARTS. 573–575.

Recording industry executives. See Executives and other officials.

RECORDING PRACTICE. 575–577.

RECORDING STUDIOS. 577. Canadian studios. 92. See in this index: Abbey Road; Cherokee Ranch; Electric Lady; NBC Studio 8H; New York Phonograph Co.; Wangemann, A. T. T.

Recordion (disc record player). 131.

Recordite (record cleaner). 577.

RECORDITE CO. 577.

Recordol (record cleaner). 578.

RECORDOL CO. 578.

Recoton needles. 463.

Red and Miff's Stompers (jazz group). 467.

Rishell (label). 592.

RISHELL PHONOGRAPH CO. 592.

Risler, Edouard (pianist). 529, 583.

RITTER, TEX (country artist). 147, 509, *592*.

Riva (label). 538.

RIVERSIDE (label). 592.

RMS (root-mean-square power). 35.

Robert Shaw Chorale. 621, 716.

Roberts, Henry T. Cramer (executive). 342.

ROBERTS, ROBERT (baritone; comedian). 592.

Robertson, Dick (popular singer). 582.

Robertson, Rae (pianist). 529.

Robertson, Uncle Eck (country artist). 147, 265.

ROBESON, PAUL (bass). 393, *592*.

Robinson, J. Russell (pianist). 508, 766.

Robinson, John (executive). 474.

Robinson, Prince (saxophonist). 611.

Robinson, Smokey (soul singer). 645.

ROBISON, CARSON J. (country artist). 586, *593*.

ROBYN, WILLIAM (tenor). 593.

Rochester Philharmonic Orchestra. 386.

Rock groups. *See* Rock performers.

ROCK MUSIC RECORDINGS. 593–597.

Rock performers. See in this index:

Abba-Focus; Aerosmith; Allman Brothers Band; Anderson, Laurie; Avalon, Frankie; Barretto, Ray; Beach Boys; Beacon Street Union; Beatles; Bee Gees; Berry, Chuck; Big Brother and the Holding Co.; Black Sabbath; Blood, Sweat & Tears; Bowie, David; Bragg, Billy; Branigan, Laura; Brenston, Jackie; Buffalo Springfield; Byrds; Cabaret Voltaire;

Chapman, Tracy; Checker, Chubby; Chicago; Chiffons; Chipmunks; Coasters; Cocker, Joe; Cockney Rejects; Cooper, Alice; Cream; Creedence Clearwater Revival; Crickets; Crystals; Daltrey, Roger Harry; Danny and the Juniors; Dave Clark Five; Dee, Joey; Diamonds; Doherty, Dennis; Doors; Dorsey, Lee; Dr. Feelgood; Duran Duran; E.U.; Earth Opera; Earth, Wind and Fire; Eddy, Duane; Electric Light Orchestra; Elliott, Cass; Entwistle, John Alec; Everly Brothers; Everly, Don; Everly, Phil; Fabian; Fifth Dimension; Flash Cadillac & the Continental Kids; Floyd, Pink; Flying Burrito Brothers; Fogerty, John; Fugs; Golden Earring; Grand Funk Railroad; Grant, Amy; Grateful Dead; Guess Who; Haley, Bill; Hendrix, Jimi; Holly, Buddy; Human League; Iron Butterfly; J. Geils Band; Jackson, Michael; Jagger, Mick; James, Rick; James, Tommy; Jan & Dean; Jefferson Airplane; Jefferson Starship; John, Elton; Jones, Brian; Joplin, Janis; KC & the Sunshine Band; Kraftwerk; Led Zeppelin; Lennon, John; Lynurd Skynyrd; Madonna; Mamas and the Papas; McCartney, Linda; McCartney, Paul; Morrison, Jim; Nelson, Rick; Newton-John, Olivia; Ochs, Phil; Ohio Player; Orbison, Roy; Parker, Graham; Penguins; Phillips, John; Phillips, Michelle Gilliam; Presley, Elvis; Prince; Quatro, Suzy; Ramones; Raspberries; Reddy, Helen; Richards,

Keith; Richie, Lionel; Righteous Brothers; Rip Chords; Rolling Stones; Ronettes; Ronnie & the Daytonas; Rydell, Bobby; Ryder, Mitch; Santana; Scott, Jack; Seeds; Sex Pistols; Sha Na Na; Shirelles; Shocked, Michelle; Slick, Grace; Smith, Huey; Specials; Springsteen; Standells; Stevens, Ray; Stray Cats; Taylor, James; Taylor, Mick; Thompson Twins; Three O'Clock; Throbbing Gristle; Time Zone; Townshend, Dennis Blandford; Traffic; Trammps; Trouble Funk; Turtles; Valens, Richie; Vandross, Luther; Vega, Suzanne; Ventures; Vincent, Gene; Weather Report; White, Barry; Who; Williams, Lucinda; Wilson, Brian; Wings; Wood, Ron; Wyman, Bill.

Rock singers. *See* Rock performers.

Rock, W. T. (executive). 751.

Rockabilly. 149, 152.

ROCKOLA, DAVID C. (executive). 597.

Rock-Ola Manufacturing Co. 597.

ROCOCO (label). 597.

Rodeheaver, Homer (executive). 568.

Rodeheaver Record Co. 356, 568.

RODGERS, JIMMIE (country artist). 148, 149, *597*.

RODGERS AND HAMMERSTEIN ARCHIVES OF RECORDED SOUND. 591, *597–598*.

Rodkinson, N. M. (executive). 184, 689.

Rodzinski, Artur (conductor). 111, 490.

Roever, Julius (inventor). 36.

Roger-Miclos, Maria (pianist). 528, 530, 584.

Rogers, Charlie (banjoist). 42.

Wesley; Wright, Frank; Yanovsky, Zalman; Young, John.

See also Baritones; Basses; Blues singers; Contraltos; Countertenors; Folk artists; Mezzo-sopranos; Popular singers; Rock performers; Sopranos; Soul singers; Tenors; Vocal groups; Vocal-instrumental groups.

Singing cowboy (country music style). 152.

Singing Sophomores (male vocal group). 586.

SINGLETON, ZUTTY (drummer). 604, *626*.

SIR HENRI (label). 626.

SISTER TEAMS. 626.

Sistine Chapel Choir. 302, 332.

Sittard, Alfred (organist). 500.

SIX BROWN BROTHERS (saxophone group). 626.

SIZES (of records). 627.

SKATING FORCE. 627.

Skelly, Thomas V. (inventor), 627.

SKELLY MANUFACTURING CO. 627.

Skinner, Bessie (banjoist). 42.

Skinner, Cornelia Otis (actress). 393.

Skinner, J. Scott (violinist). 750.

Skinner, Otis (actor). 393.

Skinner, Rose (banjoist). 42.

Slack, Freddie (Big Band leader). 765.

Sledge, Percy (soul singer). 594.

SLEEVE. 627.

Sleeves (disc envelopes). 543.

Slevin, Dick (kazoo player). 425.

SLEZAK, LEO (tenor). 627.

Slick, Grace (rock singer). 353.

Sliding bias circuit. 34.

Slim and Slam (novelty/jazz duo). 693.

Slokar, Branimir (trombonist). 75.

Sly & the Family Stone (blues singers). 590.

SMALL RECORDS. 628.

SMALLE, ED (popular singer). 25, 586, 621, *628*.

SMIRNOV, DMITRI (tenor). 628.

Smith, Albert E. (executive). 751.

Smith, Arthur (executive). 481.

SMITH, ARTHUR (fiddler). 628.

SMITH, BESSIE (blues singer). 561, *628*.

Smith, Edward J. (bootlegger). 535.

Smith, Fay (country artist). 148.

SMITH, H. ROYER (executive). 629.

Smith, Huey (rock performer). 594.

Smith, Joe (vaudeville artist). 38.

SMITH, KATE (popular singer). 629.

SMITH, MAMIE (blues singer). 629.

Smith, Oberlin (inventor). 411.

SMITH, PINE TOP (pianist). 629.

Smith, R. B. (inventor). 630.

Smith, Trixie (blues singer). 69.

SMITH, WILLIE (pianist). 630.

SMITH, WILLIE (saxophonist). 611, 630.

SMITH REPEATOSTOP CO. 630.

SMITHSONIAN INSTITUTION. 630–631.

Smithsonian/Folkways (label). 270.

Smolian, Steven (discographer). 212.

Snow, Hank (country artist). 91.

Snow, Walter (bass). 415.

Snowden, George (executive). 337.

Snowden, James H. (executive). 337.

Snowden, P. M. (executive). 337.

SOBINOV, LEONID (tenor). 631.

SOCIETÀ ITALIANA DI FONOTIPIA. 631.

Società Italiana di Fonotipia. Società Anonima. 270.

Société des Auteurs, Compositeurs et Editeurs de Musique. 522.

Société des Instruments à Vent de Paris. 775.

Société des Microphonographes Bettini. 61.

Société Pathé Marconi. 517.

SOCIETY RECORDS. 631.

SODERO, CESARE (conductor). 632.

Sokoloff, Nikolai (conductor). 118.

Solesmes Abbey, Monks Choir. 302.

SOLEX (label). 632.

SOLID STATE. 632.

Solo (anti-copying system). 144.

SOLO ART (label). 632.

Solo Art Recordings (firm). 632.

Solo Plus (anti-copying system). 144.

Solophone (disc record player). 632.

SOLOPHONE CO. 632.

SOLTI, GEORG, *Sir* (conductor). *632*, 707.

Son, Harry (cellist). 82.

SONIC RESTORATION OF HISTORICAL RECORDINGS. 632–644. Acoustic Dimension Synthesizer, 642; ambience, 641; blasting, 638; cartridges and styli, 634. 635; CEDAR, 637; compression, 642; de-essing, 642; diameter equalization, 642; Dynafex Audio Noise Reduction System, 637, 640; dynamic expansion, 640; editing, 642; equalization 635; equalization curves, 635; equalization settings (table), 638–639; gain riding, 638; high and low frequency enhancement, 641; hum, 634; limiting, 642; multi-graphic equalizer, 636; noise, 637; non-linearity and selective gain riding, 637; NoNoise, 637; notch filter, 636; parametric, 635; phase effects, 640; pitch, 634; processing sequence, 643; quasi-stereo, 643; Re-Equalizer, 636; re-pressing, 633; record condition 633; reissues, 633; resonance and

parametrics, 637; rever-
beration, 641; Soundstream
restorations, 637; spectrum
analyzers, 641; time delay,
641; tone arm, 635;
tracking, 635; turntable
speed and pitch 634.
Sonola (disc record player). 582.
SONORA (label). 643.
Sonora Chime Co. 644.
SONORA PHONOGRAPH CO.
31, *644*.
Sonora Record Co. 644.
Sonora Record Corp. 644.
SONS OF THE PIONEERS
(country group). 147, *644*.
Sonty, Frederico (cornetist).
145.
Sony Classical (label). 645.
SONY CORPORATION. 644–
645.
Sooy, Charles E. (executive).
741.
Sooy, Harry O. (executive). 741.
Sooy, Raymond A. (executive).
741.
Sopranos. See in this index:
Abendroth, Irene; Abott, Bessie;
Ackté, Aino; Adami, Bice;
Adams, Suzanne;
Albanese, Licia; Albani,
Emma; Alda, Frances;
Arangi-Lombardi,
Giannina; Arral, Blanche;
Austral, Florence;
Bampton, Rose; Barrientos,
Maria; Battle, Kathleen;
Behrens, Hildegard;
Bellincioni, Gemma;
Berger, Erna; Berthon,
Mirielle; Blauvelt, Lillian;
Boninsegna, Celestina;
Bori, Lucrezia; Bréval,
Lucienne; Caballé,
Montserrat; Callas, Maria;
Carson, Mary; Case, Anna;
Chalia, Rosalia; Chelotti,
Teresa; Cigna, Gina;
Connor, Nadine; Crossley,
Ada Jessica; Culp, Julia;
Cummings, Irene; Dalla
Rizza, Gilda; Dal Monte,
Toti; Davis, Jessie Bartlett;
De Los Angeles, Victoria;
De Lussan, Zélie; Destinn,

Emmy; Eames, Emma;
Easton, Florence; Engle,
Marie; Farrar, Geraldine;
Farrell, Eileen; Farrell,
Marguerite E.;
Feraldy, Germaine; Figner,
Medea Mey; Flagstad,
Kirsten; Fremstad, Olive;
Freni, Mirella; Gadski,
Johanna; Gall, Yvonne;
Galli-Curci, Amelita;
Galvany, Maria; Garden,
Mary; Gluck, Alma;
Greenfield, Elizabeth
Taylor; Gruberova, Edita;
Heldy, Fanny; Hempel,
Frieda; Herzog, Emilie;
Huguet, Josefina; Ivogün,
Maria; Jepson, Helen;
Jones, Ada; Jones,
Sissieretta Joyner; Jurinac,
Sena; Kellogg, Clara
Louise; Kerns, Grace;
Korjus, Milizia; Koshetz,
Nina; Krull, Amy; Kurz,
Selma; Labia, Maria;
Larsen-Todsen, Nanny;
Lawrence, Marjorie;
Lehmann, Lilli; Lehmann,
Lotte; Leider, Frida;
Lemnitz, Tiana; Licette,
Miriam; Macdonald,
Jeanette; Magliuolo, Elvira;
Mann, Estella Louise;
Mantelli, Eugenia; Martón,
Eva; Matzenauer,
Margarete; Melba, Nellie;
Milanov, Zinka; Moffo,
Anna; Morris, Elida;
Muzio, Claudia; Narelle,
Marie; Nast, Minnie;
Nielsen, Alice; Nilsson,
Christine; Nordica, Lillian;
Norman, Jessye; Novotna,
Jarmila; Pagliughi, Lina;
Patti, Adelina; Pons, Lily;
Ponselle, Rosa; Popp,
Lucia; Price, Leontyne;
Raisa, Rosa; Rappold,
Marie; Rethberg, Elisabeth;
Ricciarelli, Katia; Rice,
Gladys; Romaine, Marie;
Sanderson, Julia; Saville,
Frances; Sayao, Bidu;
Scheff, Fritzi; Schumann,

Elisabeth; Schwarzkopf,
Elisabeth; Scotto, Renata;
Sembrich, Marcella; Sills,
Beverly; Sinclair, Elsa;
Spencer, Grace; Steber,
Eleanor; Stevenson, Elise;
Supervia, Conchita;
Sutherland, Joan; Sylva,
Gertrude; Te Kanawa, Kiri;
Tebaldi, Renata; Ternina,
Milka; Tetrazzini, Luisa;
Teyte, Maggie; Torriani,
Madame; Tourel, Jennie;
Traubel, Helen; Turner,
Eva; Vallin, Ninon; Verlet,
Alice; Von Stade,
Frederica; Weiman, Henry;
Welch, Elizabeth; Welitsch,
Lluba; Wheeler, Elizabeth;
Yaw, Ellen Beach; Young,
Beulah Gaylord.
SORIA, DARIO (executive).
645.
Sothern, E. H. (actor) 393.
SOUL MUSIC RECORDINGS.
645.
Soul singers. See in this index:
Ballard, Florence; Birdsong,
Cindy; Booker T & the
M.G.'s; Brown, James;
Butler, Jerry; Hall & Oates;
Impressions; Jackson,
Mahalia; O'Jays; Rascals;
Robinson, Smokey; Ross,
Diana; Sam & Dave;
Sledge, Percy; Stylistics;
Supremes; Temptations;
Wonder, Stevie.
SOUND EFFECTS RECORD-
INGS. 645.
SOUND RECORDING. 646.
SOUND RECORDING CO.,
LTD. 336, 395, 483, *646*.
SOUND RECORDING PERI-
ODICALS. 646–673. An
alphabetical list of the
periodicals mentioned in
the article is given on
pages 666–673. The titles
are not entered individu-
ally in this index.
SOUND RECORDINGS AND
THE LIBRARY. 673–678.
Cataloging, 675; classifica-
tion, 676; collection

development, 675, 678; early library collections, 673; equipment, 677; ISBD(NBM), 676; MARC format, 676.

SOUND REPRODUCTION CO. 678.

Sound Solutions (firm). 637.

SOUNDBOX. 678.

Sounds Australia. 34.

SOUNDSTREAM. 637, *678*.

Soundtrack. 448.

SOUSA, JOHN PHILIP (bandmaster). 678.

Sousa's Band. 439, 549.

SOUTH DAKOTA PHONO-GRAPH CO. 678.

South East Record Co., Ltd. 250.

Southern California Phonograph Co. 750.

Southern Four. *See* FISK JUBILLE QUARTET.

Southern States Phonograph Co. 447.

SOVEREIGN (label). 678.

SPALDING, ALBERT (violinist). *678–679*, 715.

Spaniels (blues singers). 587.

SPANIER, MUGGSY (cornetist). 679.

Sparks, Randy (folk artist). 464.

Sparks-Worthington (firm). 91.

Sparton of Canada, Ltd. 91, 92.

Spaulding, Shirley (banjoist). 42.

Speak-O-Phone Co. 339.

SPECIAL RECORD (label). 679.

Specials (rock group). 595.

SPECTACLE (recorder-reproducer). 679.

Spectrum (periodical). 614.

SPEEDS. 679–680.

Spencer, Charles Baldwin (ethnologist). 32, 258.

SPENCER, ELIZABETH (mezzo-soprano). 325, 432, 433. *680*, 715.

SPENCER, GRACE (soprano). 680.

Spencer, Henry C. 32.

SPENCER, LEN (baritone). 681.

Spencer, Tim (country artist). 644.

SPENCER TRIO (male vocal group). 681.

Speyer and Co. (bankers). 743.

Spider (loudspeaker). 399.

Spider (stylus-diaphragm connector). 61.

Spiel Mit (label). 7.

SPINDLE. *681*, 723.

Spitalny, Phil (Big Band leader; executive). 222, 752.

SPIVAK, CHARLIE (trumpeter). 681.

Spivey, Victoria (blues singer). 69.

SPLICING TAPE. 682.

SPLITDORF RADIO CORP. 682.

SPOKANE PHONOGRAPH CO. 682.

Spoken Arts (label). 394.

Spoken word recordings. *See* LITERARY RECORDINGS.

Sportsmen (male vocal quartet). 413.

SPRING MOTOR RECORD PLAYERS. 682.

Springfield Accordion Orchestra. 5.

SPRINGSTEEN, BRUCE (rock performer). 682.

Spross, Charles Gilbert (pianist). 528, 584.

Squire, William Henry (cellist). 106.

Squires Gate (record shop). 573.

St. and Ste. Names beginning with St. and Ste. are filed as though spelled out: Saint, Sainte.

STACY, JESS (pianist). 683.

STAFFORD, JO (popular singer). 683.

Stamper, James L. (bass). 440.

STAMPER. 683.

Standard (disc record player). 684.

STANDARD (label). 646, *683*, 684.

Standard discs. 1.

STANDARD GRAMOPHONE APPLIANCE CO. 683.

STANDARD METAL MANU-FACTURING CO. 683.

Standard Music Roll Co. 27, 401.

STANDARD PLAY. 683.

STANDARD PNEUMATIC ACTION CO. 683.

STANDARD QUARTETTE (male vocal group). 683.

Standard sequence. *See* MANUAL SEQUENCE.

STANDARD TALKING MACHINE CO. 683–684.

Standards and standardization. 15.

Standells (rock group). 594.

STANDING WAVES. 601, *684*.

STANFORD ARCHIVE OF RECORDED SOUND (StARS). 591, *684–686*.

Stanich, Raymond (discographer). 572.

STANLEY, AILEEN (vaudeville artist). 686.

STANLEY, FRANK C. (bass). 429, 432, 446, 485, 521, 613, *686*, 692.

Stanley, Henry M. (explorer). 356, 392.

Stanley, James (bass). 521.

Stanley Brothers (country artists). 150.

Stanton, Frank (executive). 508.

STAR (label). 686, 687.

Star Talking Machine (disc record player). 622.

STARCK (label). 687.

Starker, Janos (cellist). 106.

Starr, Kay (popular singer). 44.

Starr, Ringo. (drummer). 395.

STARR (label). 687.

Starr Co. of Canada. 92, 687.

STARR. PIANO CO. 520, 686, *687*, 711.

STATE PHONOGRAPH CO. OF ILLINOIS. 687.

State Street Pathéphone Co. 484, 518.

Statler Brothers (country artists). 152.

Status (label). 69.

Stavenhagen, Bernhard (pianist). 529, 584.

Stavophone (label). 646.

Stax (label). 645.

Stax/Volt/Enterprise (label). 588.

Stearns, Marshall (discographer). 340.

Steber, Eleanor (soprano). 433, 776.

Stech (George) and Co. 8.

Trombonists. See in this index:
Boston Symphony Trombone Quartet; Bradley, Will; Brunis, Georg; Cimera, Jaroslav; Coniff, Ray; Dorsey, Tommy; Durham, Eddie; Edwards, Eddie; Greene, Charlie; Harris, Bill; Higginbotham, J. C.; Hunt, Pee Wee; Johnson, J. J.; Kleinhammer, Edward; Lhotak, Frank; Miller, Glenn; Mole, Miff; Morton, Benny; Panelli, Charlie; Pryor, Arthur; Rank, Bill; Sauer, Ralph; Scholl, Nicholas; Slokar, Branimir; Teagarden, Jack; Teschmacher, Frank; Wardwell, O. Edward; Wick, Dennis; Winding, Kai; Zimmerman, Leo A.

Trostler, Arthur A. (executive). 458.

Trotter, John Scott (pianist; arranger). 367.

Trouble Funk (rock group). 595.

TRUETONE NEEDLES. 721.

Truetone process (electrical recording system). 481.

TRUMBAUER, FRANKIE (saxophonist). 721.

TRUMPET RECORDINGS. 721. *See also* CORNET RECORDINGS; TRUMPETERS.

Trumpeters. See in this index:
André, Maurice; Armstrong, Louis; Baker, Chet; Berigan, Bunny; Braff, Ruby; Butterfield, Billy; Cassi, Emil; Clayton, Buck; Coles, Johnny; Coniff, Ray; Davis, Miles; Dunn, Johnny; Edna White Trumpet Quartet; Eldridge, Roy; Elman, Ziggy; Erwin, Pee Wee; Ferguson, Maynard; Gillespie, Dizzy; Hirt, Al; James, Harry; Jones, Jonah; Klein, Manny; Manone, Wingy; Mares, Paul; Marsalis, Wynton; McCoy, Clyde; Napoleon, Phil; Nichols, Red; Oliver,

Sy.; Ory, Kid; Page, Hot Lips; Page, Walter; Prince, Gene; Quealey, Chelsea; Sauter, Eddie; Schwarz, Gerard; Shavers, Charlie; Spivak, Charlie; Stevens, Thomas; Tarr, Edward; Thomas, Joe; Voisin, Roger; White, Edna; Williams, Cootie. *See also* Cornetists.

Tuba players. See in this index:
Bobo, Roger; Fletcher, John; Jacobs, Arnold; Phillips, Harvey.

TUBA RECORDINGS. 722.

TUBB, ERNEST (country artist). 148, 149, 722.

TUCKER, RICHARD (tenor). 433, 722.

TUCKER, SOPHIE (popular singer). 722.

Tuckwell, Barry (hornist). 75.

Tufts, Ben Q. (singer). 336.

TUNER. 723.

Tungstone Stylus. 742.

TUNING BAND. 723.

TURNER, ALAN (baritone). 723.

TURNER, EVA (soprano). 723.

Turner, Ike (blues singer). 587.

Turner, Joe (blues singer). 587, 589.

Turnover (crossover point). 158, 252.

TURNTABLE. 1, 723–724.

Turpin, Tom (pianist). 568.

Turtles (rock group). 594.

Tuson, William (clarinetist). 115.

TWEAKING. 724.

TWEETER. 724.

TWENTIETH CENTURY GRAPHOPHONE. 724.

Twenty-third Regiment Band. 438.

TWIN DOUBLE SIDED DISC RECORD (label). 724.

Twin Record Co. 724.

Twin Record Co., Ltd. 786.

Twist (dance). 109.

TWITTY, CONWAY (country artist). 724.

TWO KAUFIELDS (male vocal duo). 725.

Tyler, W. H. (executive). 299.

—U—

U.S. Everlasting Record. *See* U-S EVERLASTING RECORD (U-S entries are at the end of the U items).

U.S. PHONOGRAPH CO. 727.

U.S. Phonograph Co. (Cleveland). *See* U-S PHONOGRAPH CO.

U.S. Record Manufacturing Corp. 591.

ULTONA. 727.

Ultraphon (label). 708.

Ultrasound microphone. 437.

Uncle Josh. 692.

Union Carbide Corp. 749.

Unisette (modified cassette). 243.

UNITED (label). 727.

United Hebrew Disk and Cylinder Co. 727.

UNITED HEBREW DISK RECORDS. 727.

UNITED HOT CLUBS OF AMERICA (UHCA). 727.

United Record Distributorship. 385.

United States. Copyright Act, 1976. 145.

UNITED STATES GRAMOPHONE CO. 728.

UNITED STATES MARINE BAND. 438, 728.

United States of America Standards Institute. 15.

United States Phonograph Co. *See* U-S PHONOGRAPH CO.

UNITED STATES RECORD MANUFACTURING CO. 728.

United States Record Co. 477.

United States Record Corp. 603.

UNITED STATES TALKING MACHINE CO. 728.

UNITED TALKING MACHINE CO. 728.

Universal Copyright Convention, 1955. 144.

UNIVERSAL PHONOGRAPH CO. 728.

UNIVERSAL QUARTET. 731.

Universal Shaving Machine. 621.

Voss' First Regiment Band. 438, 486.

Votey Organ Co. 8.

VOX (label). 753, 754.

Vox Boxes. 754.

Vox Corp. of America. 754.

Vox Productions, Inc. 754.

Vox/Turnabout (label). 754.

Vronsky, Vitya (pianist). 529.

VULCAN RECORD CO. 754.

—W—

Wadsworth, F. Wheeler (saxophonist). 610, 766.

WAGNER, "HERR" (tenor). 755.

WAGONER, PORTER (country artist). 755.

Wain, Bea (popular singer). 120.

Wakefield, Frank (country artist). 268.

WALCHA, HELMUT (organist). 755.

Waldman, Phillip (executive). 519.

Walker, George W. (vaudeville artist). 767.

Walker, Jimmy (executive). 413.

Walker, T-Bone (blues singer). 587.

Walkman (portable cassette player). 540, 645.

Wallace, E. P. (executive). 225.

Wallace Institute. 315.

Wallace Reducing Method records. 116, 315.

WALLER, FATS (pianist). 529, 755.

WALLERSTEIN, EDWARD (executive). 756.

Wallichs, Glenn (executive). 98.

WALSH, ARTHUR (executive). 756.

WALSH, JIM (discographer). 756.

Walt, Hartwick W. (executive). 31.

WALTER, BRUNO (conductor). 490, 700, 756.

Walter, Gustave (tenor). 482.

Wangemann, A. T. T. (recording studio). 577.

Wangemann, Adelbert Theo (executive; inventor). 513.

Wardwell, O. Edward (trombonist). 738.

WARING, FRED (orchestra and chorus leader). 757.

Waring, Richard (actor). 394.

Warner, Frank (ethnologist). 267.

Warner Brothers (firm). 81, 713, 751, 759.

Warner Brothers Records (label). 713.

WARNER BRUNSWICK, LTD. 508, 757.

Warner Communications Inc. See WCI.

Warner Record Co. (Kansas City). 465.

Warner/Reprise (label). 759.

Warren, Fran (popular singer). 712.

Warren, Leonard (baritone). 776.

Wartime documentary recordings. 278, 331.

WARWICK, DIONNE (popular singer). 438, 758.

Washboard Sam (blues singer). 69, 562.

Washburn, William A. (singer). 154.

Washington Military Concert Band. 438.

Wassenich, Joseph (inventor). 513.

Watanabe, Kazumi (guitarist). 304.

Waterfield, Clifford and Co. 540.

WATERS, ETHEL (blues singer). 561, 758.

WATERS, MUDDY (blues singer). 395, 587, 758.

WATERSON, HENRY (executive). 88, 759.

Watson, Arthel "Doc" (folk artist). 268.

Watson, Fanny (popular singer). 626.

Watson, Ivory (baritone). 339.

Watson, Johnny (popular singer). 610.

Watson, Kitty (popular singer). 626.

WATT. 759.

Watters, James (executive). 518.

Watts, Charlie (drummer). 599.

WAX. 759.

WCI (WARNER COMMUNICATIONS, INC.) 759.

Weather Report (rock group). 595.

Weaver, Richard L. (banjoist). 568.

WEAVERS (folk group). 759.

WEBB, CHICK (drummer). 509, 759.

Webb, Clifton (popular singer; actor). 582.

Weber, Fred (singer). 272.

WEBER, HENRI (baritone). 485, 760.

Weber, J. F. (discographer). 212.

Weber, Kay (popular singer). 216.

Weber, Peter (inventor). 512.

Weber Piano Co. 8.

Weber pianola. 532.

Webster, Arthur G. (inventor). 404.

WEBSTER, BEN (saxophonist). 760.

WEEMS, TED (Big Band leader). 509, 760.

Wehner, Carl (flutist). 772.

Weil, M. (inventor). 404.

Weill, Hermann (baritone). 488.

Weiman, Henry (singer). 415.

Weingartner, Felix (conductor). 495, 584.

WEINRICH, CARL (organist). 500, 760.

Weinstock, Bob (executive). 547.

Weisberg, Arthur (bassoonist). 775.

WEISSMANN, FRIEDER (conductor). 495, 761.

Welch, Elizabeth (soprano). 592.

Welitsch, Lluba (soprano). 487, 580.

WELK, LAWRENCE (dance band leader). 761.

Welles, Orson (actor). 393.

WELLS, JOHN BARNES (tenor). 761.

WELLS, KITTY (country artist). 761.

Welsh Bethesda Choir. 686.

Welte, Edwin (inventor). 583.

Welte-Mignon (reproducing piano). 583.

Wenrich, Percy (composer; popular singer). 140.